# Great Places™
# COLORADO

*A Recreational Guide to Colorado's Public Lands and Historic Places for Birding, Hiking, Photography, Fishing, Hunting, and Camping*

## Titles Available from Wilderness Adventures Press, Inc.™

### Flyfishers Guide to™

Flyfisher's Guide to Alaska
Flyfisher's Guide to Arizona
Flyfisher's Guide to Chesapeake Bay
Flyfisher's Guide to Colorado
Flyfisher's Guide to the Florida Keys
Flyfisher's Guide to Freshwater Florida
Flyfisher's Guide to Idaho
Flyfisher's Guide to Montana
Flyfisher's Guide to Michigan
Flyfisher's Guide to Minnesota
Flyfisher's Guide to Missouri & Arkansas
Flyfisher's Guide to Nevada
Flyfisher's Guide to New York
Flyfisher's Guide to the New England Coast
Flyfisher's Guide to New Mexico
Flyfisher's Guide to the Northeast Coast
Flyfisher's Guide to Northern California
Flyfisher's Guide to Northern New England
Flyfisher's Guide to Oregon
Flyfisher's Guide to Pennsylvania
Flyfisher's Guide to Saltwater Florida
Flyfisher's Guide to Texas
Flyfisher's Guide to the Texas Gulf Coast
Flyfisher's Guide to Utah
Flyfisher's Guide to Virginia
Flyfisher's Guide to Washington
Flyfisher's Guide to Wisconsin & Iowa
Flyfisher's Guide to Wyoming
Flyfisher's Guide to Yellowstone National Park

### Best Fishing Waters™

California's Best Fishing Waters
Colorado's Best Fishing Waters
Idaho's Best Fishing Waters
Montana's Best Fishing Waters
Oregon's Best Fishing Waters
Washington's Best Fishing Waters

### Anglers Guide to™

Complete Anglers Guide to Oregon
Saltwater Angler's Guide to the Southeast
Saltwater Angler's Guide to Southern California

### On the Fly Guide to™

On the Fly Guide to the Northwest
On the Fly Guide to the Northern Rockies

### Field Guide to™

Field Guide to Fishing Knots
Field Guide to Retriever Drills
Field Guide to Dog First Aid

### Fly Tying

Go-To Flies™

### Great Places™

Great Places Montana
Great Places Washington
Great Places Colorado

# Great Places™
# COLORADO

A Recreational Guide to Colorado's Public Lands and Historic Places for Birding, Hiking, Photography, Fishing, Hunting, and Camping

**Marty Bartholomew**

*To Brad,*
*Colorado, where the spirit of the prairie meet the Peaks @ the edge of the heavens!!*

Great Places™ Series

Wilderness Adventures Press, Inc.™

Belgrade, Montana

*Marty Bartholomew*

© 2010 Marty Bartholomew

Cover photographs: © 2010 Marty Bartholomew
    Author photo by Cole Bartholomew
Photographs contained herein © 2010 Marty Bartholomew or otherwise noted.
    Photo on page 144 provided by Dan Will
    Photo on page 200 by Dick Williams
    Photo on page 413 provided by the U.S. Forest Service

Maps, cover and book design, © 2010 Wilderness Adventures Press, Inc.™
Great Places™

Great Places™ Series

    Published by Wilderness Adventures Press, Inc.™
    45 Buckskin Road
    Belgrade, MT 59714
    866-400-2012
    Website: www.wildadvpress.com
    email: books@wildadvpress.com

    First Edition

All rights reserved, including the right to reproduce this book or portions thereof in any form or by any means, electronic or mechanical, including photocopying, recording, or by any information storage and retrieval system, without permission in writing from the publisher. All inquiries should be addressed to: Wilderness Adventures Press™ Inc., 45 Buckskin Rd., Belgrade, MT 59714

Printed in South Korea.

ISBN: 978-1-932098-68-6 (8-09206-98682-4)

# Dedication

*To Carol and Dwight who put my fascination with the outdoors in first gear; to Joe who motivated the fascination into overdrive; and of course my wife, Ann, who continually lets me out the front door to pursue my passion.*

# Acknowledgements

*Thanks to the Colorado Division of Wildlife and all the officers and employees out there that put me on prairie chicken leks, led me down a special back road that led to a rare photo, and answered my tedious phone calls. I thoroughly appreciate the hospitality of Carl and Cherry and their help facilitating short-grass prairie for my encounter with the rare mountain plover. They are magnificent ambassadors for the mountain plover and all wildlife in the Karval area, for that matter. One should take advantage of their work by visiting the Mountain Plover Festival in the spring. Thanks to my son, Cole, who rode shotgun on many a trip, spotted a mountain goat for me, and patiently waited for the sun to come up or go down so I could get a few photos. And the sleepless night when a pair of porcupines was chewing the undercoating off the wheel wells! A special thanks to Chuck and Blanche Johnson for the opportunity to work with Wilderness Adventures Press on another book project – hope this one is as successful as my first. And last but not least, I want to thank the idiots that raised the price of gasoline to $3.85 a gallon while I was doing the bulk of my traveling and research for this book?!?*

# Table of Contents

Dedication . . . . . . . . . . . . . . . . . . . . . . . . . . . . . . . . . . . . . . . . . . . . . . . . . . . . . . . . . . . . . . . . v
Acknowledgements . . . . . . . . . . . . . . . . . . . . . . . . . . . . . . . . . . . . . . . . . . . . . . . . . . . . . v
Introduction. . . . . . . . . . . . . . . . . . . . . . . . . . . . . . . . . . . . . . . . . . . . . . . . . . . . . . . . . . . . 1
For Your Information . . . . . . . . . . . . . . . . . . . . . . . . . . . . . . . . . . . . . . . . . . . . . . . . . . . 7
**FRONT RANGE**. . . . . . . . . . . . . . . . . . . . . . . . . . . . . . . . . . . . . . . . . . . . . . . . . . . . . . **11**
    Butterfly Pavilion . . . . . . . . . . . . . . . . . . . . . . . . . . . . . . . . . . . . . . . . . . . . . . . . . . 13
    Garden of the Gods . . . . . . . . . . . . . . . . . . . . . . . . . . . . . . . . . . . . . . . . . . . . . . . 19
    High Creek Fen Preserve . . . . . . . . . . . . . . . . . . . . . . . . . . . . . . . . . . . . . . . . . . . 27
    Mount Evans (Colorado Scenic Byway) . . . . . . . . . . . . . . . . . . . . . . . . . . . . . . 31
        Bristlecone Pines . . . . . . . . . . . . . . . . . . . . . . . . . . . . . . . . . . . . . . . . . . . . . 33
    National Parks and Monuments . . . . . . . . . . . . . . . . . . . . . . . . . . . . . . . . . . . . . 39
        Rocky Mountain National Park (RMNP) . . . . . . . . . . . . . . . . . . . . . . . . . . . 39
            Trail Ridge Road . . . . . . . . . . . . . . . . . . . . . . . . . . . . . . . . . . . . . . . . . . . 42
            Endovalley . . . . . . . . . . . . . . . . . . . . . . . . . . . . . . . . . . . . . . . . . . . . . . . . 46
            Moraine Park . . . . . . . . . . . . . . . . . . . . . . . . . . . . . . . . . . . . . . . . . . . . . . 48
            Wild Basin . . . . . . . . . . . . . . . . . . . . . . . . . . . . . . . . . . . . . . . . . . . . . . . . 48
            Bear Lake Road . . . . . . . . . . . . . . . . . . . . . . . . . . . . . . . . . . . . . . . . . . . . 50
            Lumpy Ridge & Cow Creek Entrances . . . . . . . . . . . . . . . . . . . . . . . . . . 51
    Scenic Byways . . . . . . . . . . . . . . . . . . . . . . . . . . . . . . . . . . . . . . . . . . . . . . . . . . . . 60
        Guanella Pass . . . . . . . . . . . . . . . . . . . . . . . . . . . . . . . . . . . . . . . . . . . . . . . . 60
        Lariat Loop . . . . . . . . . . . . . . . . . . . . . . . . . . . . . . . . . . . . . . . . . . . . . . . . . . 62
        Mount Evans Scenic Byway . . . . . . . . . . . . . . . . . . . . . . . . . . . . . . . . . . . . . 66
        Peak to Peak Scenic Byway . . . . . . . . . . . . . . . . . . . . . . . . . . . . . . . . . . . . . . 67
        Top of the Rockies National Scenic & Historic Byway . . . . . . . . . . . . . . . . 71
            Trail Ridge Road . . . . . . . . . . . . . . . . . . . . . . . . . . . . . . . . . . . . . . . . . . . 72
    Wildlife Refuges . . . . . . . . . . . . . . . . . . . . . . . . . . . . . . . . . . . . . . . . . . . . . . . . . 74
        Two Ponds National Wildlife Refuge . . . . . . . . . . . . . . . . . . . . . . . . . . . . . . 74
**SOUTHERN FRONT RANGE**. . . . . . . . . . . . . . . . . . . . . . . . . . . . . . . . . . . . . . . . . . **77**
    Aiken Canyon Preserve . . . . . . . . . . . . . . . . . . . . . . . . . . . . . . . . . . . . . . . . . . . 79
    Blanca Wetlands (owned by BLM) . . . . . . . . . . . . . . . . . . . . . . . . . . . . . . . . . . 83

    Lake Pueblo State Park and State Wildlife Area.................................87
    Pikes Peak Highway............................................................91
    Royal Gorge Bridge and Park....................................................97
National Parks and Monuments.......................................................101
    Florissant Fossil Beds National Monument.......................................101
    Great Sand Dunes National Park and Preserve....................................107
Scenic Byways.....................................................................120
    Frontier Pathways Scenic Byway.................................................120
    Gold Belt Tour.................................................................123
        Mueller State Park.........................................................127
        Dome Rock State Wildlife Area..............................................127
    Highway of Legends.............................................................128
        Trinidad Lake State Park...................................................130
        Lathrop State Park.........................................................131
    Los Caminos Antiguos Scenic Byway..............................................134
        San Luis State Park........................................................136
Wildlife Refuges..................................................................139
    Alamosa National Wildlife Refuge...............................................139
    Baca National Wildlife Refuge..................................................143
        The San Luis Valley........................................................148
    Monte Vista National Wildlife Refuge...........................................157
    Russell Lakes State Wildlife Area..............................................165

## **SOUTHWESTERN COLORADO..................................................169**

    Curecanti National Recreation Area.............................................171
    The Maroon Bells (mountain)....................................................181
National Parks and Monuments......................................................189
    Black Canyon of the Gunnison National Park.....................................189
    Colorado National Monument.....................................................211
    Hovenweep National Monument....................................................225
    Mesa Verde National Park.......................................................231
    Yucca House National Monument..................................................241
Scenic Byways.....................................................................244
    The Alpine Loop................................................................244
    Grand Mesa Scenic Byway........................................................247
        Plateau Creek Valley.......................................................247
        Vega State Park............................................................247
        Mesa Lakes Area............................................................248
        Land O' Lakes Area.........................................................249
    Silver Thread Scenic Byway.....................................................250
        Wheeler Geological Area....................................................251
        Lake San Cristobal.........................................................253
        Ryan Ranch – Nature Conservancy Preserve..................................255

San Juan Skyway..................................................256
   San Miguel River South Fork Preserve .......................257
   San Miguel River Canyon Preserve ..........................258
Trail of the Ancients Scenic Byway.................................262
Uncompahgre-Tabeguache Scenic and Historic Byway............264
   Tabeguache Creek Preserve ................................266
West Elk Loop ..................................................269
   Paonia State Park ........................................270
   Crawford State Park .....................................271
   Glenwood Hot Springs ....................................274

## NORTHWESTERN REGION .....................................277

Yampa River State Park..........................................279
   Yampa River Preserve ....................................284
   Sharp-tailed Grouse Viewing ..............................284
National Parks and Monuments...................................289
   Dinosaur National Monument .............................289
Scenic Byways..................................................300
   Cache la Poudre/North Park Scenic Byway ..................300
     Lory State Park .......................................300
     Phantom Canyon Preserve (Nature Conservancy) .........302
     Joe Wright Reservoir ..................................304
     Long Draw Reservoir..................................305
   Colorado River Headwaters Scenic Byway....................306
     Lake Granby .........................................307
     Windy Gap Reservoir..................................308
     Willow Creek Reservoir................................309
     Williams Fork Reservoir................................309
     Wolford Mountain Reservoir............................310
     Radium State Wildlife Area .............................310
   Dinosaur Diamond Scenic Byway ..........................312
   Flat Tops Trail Scenic Byway ..............................316
     Stagecoach State Park.................................318
     Trappers Lake .......................................320
Wildlife Refuges ................................................323
   Arapaho National Wildlife Refuge ..........................323
   Browns Park National Wildlife Refuge.......................337

## NORTHEASTERN GREAT PLAINS ..............................353

Fox Ranch.....................................................355
Greater Prairie Chicken Viewing Tours.............................361
Pawnee National Grasslands.....................................365
Scenic Byways..................................................372
   Pawnee Pioneer Trails Scenic Byway........................372
     Jackson Lake State Park ...............................375

South Platte River Trail Scenic Byway......376
Barr Lake State Park and Wildlife Refuge......381
Rocky Mountain Arsenal National Wildlife Refuge......393
The Wild Animal Sanctuary......399

**SOUTHEASTERN GREAT PLAINS......409**
    Comanche National Grasslands......411
    Mountain Plover Festival......427
Scenic Byways......432
    Santa Fe Trail Scenic Byway......432
        Sand Creek Massacre National Historic Site......433
        John Martin Reservoir State Park......434
        Bent's Old Fort National Historic Site......437
    Wildlife Refuge System......439
    Audubon Society for Colorado......440
    National Parks Passes......441
    State Parks Passes......443
    Official Checklist of Colorado Birds......445
    Index......465

*Putting one in the bag*

# Introduction

As I started writing this reference, I was shocked at how many times I looked for synonyms to help me replace descriptions like beautiful, gorgeous, stunning, unbelievable, and astonishing to describe the wonders of the state of Colorado. It may be a predisposition though; I am one of the remaining natives living in Colorado. Born and raised here, cut my teeth as they say, discovering what a beautiful, gorgeous, stunning, unbelievable, and astonishing place this actually is.

This book, *Great Places Colorado*, is based on the idea that someone out there likes the outdoors and likes to spend time in "great places". Colorado has many. There are four national parks, five national monuments, dozens of state parks, and two immense national grasslands. These places are visually stunning, but have the added benefit of being "great places" to view wildlife and spend time birding. Add to that, six national wildlife refuges and several Nature Conservancy preserves, and Colorado happens to turn into a major destination for wildlife and birding enthusiasts. I would also suggest taking some time walking your local open-space areas and don't forget your own backyard. I had put in a bunch of time trying to get a photo of a kestrel and ended up getting said photo with the bird sitting in a tree just on the other side of my back fence. I have had as many as five blue jays, eight dark-eyed juncos, and two flickers in my backyard at the same time. Much effort was put into this book to point out and put one in the right place to observe Colorado's diverse wildlife inhabitants.

Colorado has an extensive system of roadways designated as Colorado Scenic Byways. They are a windshield's view into the breathtaking "great places" in Colorado. If the byways themselves can be overlooked as a great place, they definitely lead you to the vast list of great places in Colorado. One person's "great place" is not the same as another's, so I hope you find your "great place" even if it is not listed in this book. Our byway system provides that potential.

I have had the gratification of traveling most, if not all, of the 25 byways. At minimum, I have made partial trips up and down, going to and from other points of interest. Over the years, a large number of miles have been put on my tires along these byways.

As would be expected, 22 of the 25 scenic byways are west of Interstate 25, which includes the mountainous portion of our colorful state. I grew up east of the mountains, even though I could wake up every morning and see them, and I acquired a special place in my heart for the short-grass prairie and the wildlife that thrives there. The western edge of the Great Plains is often overlooked for its natural beauty.

I have also flavored the book with bits and pieces of Colorado's history, if for no other reason than it might win you a prize in a trivia contest.

I guess I would have to consider myself a lifelong outdoorsman (at least as long as I can remember) and have thoroughly enjoyed my quest. My dad wasn't much of an outdoorsman, so my inspiration came from the likes of Grizzly Adams and Jeremiah Johnson. I just thought it would be cool to live in the woods and survive off the land. I guess every kid is a dreamer to some extent! I ended up settling for a couple camping trips every summer with Carol and Dwight, my sister and brother-in-law. I eventually became very adept with a pellet gun, learned how to sharpen a knife, and cast a cheap spin fishing outfit with a Mepp's spinner. I was eating rabbit and brook trout, and I was on my way to being a true outdoorsman.

My high school buddy and neighbor, Joe, was also a die-hard outdoorsman. Joe mentored me in the art of spotting wildlife. He had (and still has) an uncanny ability to see the unobvious and taught me how to connect the pieces of this elusive puzzle. There were several years in there that we were pretty much inseparable, when it came to spending time outdoors. To this day, I think the time spent in the field with Joe turned out to be the most valuable. Here it is some 35 years later and we still hook up on occasion to see what we can see. He came along on one of my trips this year to the San Luis Valley so I could photograph the sandhill cranes.

Backpacking, a bow and arrow, and a driver's license opened up a whole new set of doors into the maturity of a pilgrim. I plotted my way though the next stage of my internship with blisters, speeding tickets, bald tires, and venison on the dinner table so I felt something was going right. It wasn't a dream anymore; I actually did love the outdoors. However, life shook me until I awoke from the dream and found that it took money to spend all this time afield, so I settled into life's agenda of work and family.

Even my stint with the golf clubs wetted my appetite for the outdoors. That indisputable aroma of fresh cut grass first thing in the morning, the geese dodging an unintended shank, the silence broken only by the breeze rustling the leaves in the trees and energetic birds chirping, and of course the occasional "FORE". It seemed to fill in the time between my regular routine of spring fishing and fall hunting.

The next major turn in my adventure as an outdoorsman came in the mid-1980s. A fly rod was placed in my hands and my dream took me on a path that I look back on now with total astonishment. I have to pinch myself every so often just to make sure it is real. I traveled the state of Colorado extensively, dropping a fly on just about any moving water my friend Gus and I could find on a map. Again, fortune looked my way and put a master of the sport in my midst. Gus and I work for the same company, so we would see each other often and always planned another trip. I latched on to Gus' back pocket and learned the art of the long stick. Fifteen years, thousands of miles, too many beers to count, and who knows how many bags of soft batch cookies later I was offered a book contract to write the *Flyfisher's Guide to Colorado* (published by Wilderness Adventures Press). I settled into this new life as an outdoorsman; it just meant I had a different style hat to wear.

So here I am today, putting the final touches on my third book, *Great Places Colorado*. When my publisher approached me to do this book, I had my apprehensions. I know from past experience that putting a book together is a bundle of work; however it does have its rewards. So, it was just a matter of weighing the work against the rewards. The work is a given, the rewards unknown. Looking back, I think there were two or three reasons I decided to take on this project.

Number one: When the publisher told me it would be a full-color book with a couple hundred photos, the thought of spending the next year or so photographing wildlife – well – the challenge was irresistible. I was already accomplished with the camera, not a pro by any means, but what better reason to improve that skill than to have my work displayed for all to see. I mean what true outdoorsman wouldn't want to spend his time photographing the very thing that makes him happy.

Number two: I have the experience and the success of writing under my belt, so why squander that talent? Just between you and me, it has tested my patience (if pressed, I think all authors would admit to that), it HAS been a lot of work, and I cannot wait to put this project to press.

Number three: I am a Colorado native. I have been there and done that, several times in some cases. In the time it took me to become an expert at flyfishing Colorado,

*Broad-tailed hummingbird*

I became an expert at traveling Colorado. I love Colorado and have no intention of leaving. Making the decision to take this book on was built on that foundation. Why would anyone want to buy a book on Colorado if the author was a transplant from Wisconsin? I am not picking on Wisconsin mind you, but some state had to be the brunt of my joke. I have met many wonderful people from Wisconsin and I am sure they will take the ribbing in stride. I guess I could have said Canada.

My last thought was, "Am I qualified to write this book? I hope so!"

Besides the hours I depleted on the road, 75 percent of my time was spent with the camera and tripod resting on my shoulders hiking to and from locations. There were a couple years in there that I carried the camera everywhere I went. I was amazed at the number of bird and wildlife images I have that came right from the driver's seat of the vehicle. I acquired a window clamp with a ball-pod so I wouldn't have to open the door and leave the vehicle. This proved to be a very useful tool as some wildlife seems to be used to vehicles, but as soon as your feet hit the dirt, they bolt. For clean, well focused images, I cannot express the importance of a tripod enough.

Even with a telephoto lens equal to 600 mm (or about 720 mm with the digital conversions), the need to be as close to an animal or bird for photographic detail is of utmost importance. After seeing a subject, whether I was on foot or in the vehicle, I always tried to get at least one photo from a distance. I would then approach slowly, close the distance by 10 to 20 feet and set up and take another photo. If the bird or animal would show signs of being nervous, I would stop and set up again, however this time I would wait much longer. One of two things would happen at this point. They would move away or they got used to my presence. There were several times when I would get set and be very still, and the subject would approach me. A friend that I was with one time asked me how I got a sandpiper to come into the camera. I don't really know, but often times I just talk softly to them or try to imitate them with a whistle.

One of my most interesting stalks was approaching a pair of American dippers feeding their chicks. The nest was on a cliff across the river from where I was fly-fishing. I put down the rod and waded slowly toward the nest. I set up the tripod and waited. Sure enough the adults would come in with insects and feed them quickly and off they would go to catch more food. I would move a little closer, set up and they would come back. I repeated this action a few more times until I had a great angle to the opening of the nest and when all the chicks would have their mouths open; I would start firing the shutter.

I am not claiming to be a bird whisperer or anything like that, but I have been able to get up close and personal with numbers of birds and animals without the use of a blind.

Since I mentioned the blind, I have to admit that I have one and have used it many times. It especially came in handy while photographing the greater prairie chickens and sharp-tailed grouse. However, if I found a place where either a bird or animal was returning to on a regular basis, I would set it up for a couple days and get in before sun-up or late in the afternoon before sundown and see what opportunities it presented.

Now, let me discuss a few ideas about the images of wildlife themselves. When I started photographing wildlife on a regular basis, I was just happy to get a clean, focused image. After a little practice and staring at hundreds of my photos on the computer, I would see a great photo and several so-so photos. So, what were the makings of a great photo? The great images either had outstanding lighting or showed a distinct personality of the subject.

Lighting can be set up in some cases, while in others you take what you can get. It is not like landscape photography where you can choose the time of day and angles that produce the images you want. When photographing wildlife, you usually get only one opportunity.

I do like an image of an animal that is back lit. What I mean by that is, the source of light is behind the subject which causes a rim-lighting effect. The body of the subject or the antlers on a deer has a white "rim" around them.

Capturing the personality of an animal is quite different and takes an enormous amount of patience and a lot of luck. The first aspect that I always try to define is the eyes. Have you noticed what the first thing you notice when looking at an image of wildlife? When photographing wildlife, focus on the eyes. Then look for a tilt of the head, a position of an ear, or any gesture you are fortunate enough to open the shutter on that gives the subject a distinctive look. How about a pinyon jay with a piñon nut in its beak?

I truly hope you enjoy this reference and the content and tips puts you in a "great place" at a great time. I anticipate your experience will be memorable. This is not a book that you would read cover to cover; although I do have a sense of optimism that as you thumb through the pages it will help you dream of a place not explored and light a fire in your belly to go and meet that place head on. It may a bird that you have not scribed to your list, it may be a mountain that you have not climbed, it may be a photograph that you do not have. Just make sure *Great Places Colorado* is in your travel bag to help guide you along your way.

Writing this book has rewarded me; rewarded me with the sense of accomplishment that only hard work and perseverance can do. It wasn't all hard work; after all, I just completed a whirlwind tour of a state that has more to offer than I will ever have time to witness.

*Mule deer buck in velvet.*

However, I do have memories; memories of the sun coming up in Monte Vista Wildlife Refuge with hundreds of sandhill cranes waking up with mist coming off the wetlands. It was one of the most amazing settings I have ever witnessed. Or, recalling the time my son and I were hiking the Maroon Bells area. We were headed back to the car and Cole looked back and spotted a mountain goat on the rock face to the north. He spotted an animal before the old man! He was pumped and I felt like I had just passed on the torch.

It has inspired me; inspired me to continue that childhood dream planted by mountain men, fact or fiction, to stay outdoors and pursue that sense of independence that only the wide open spaces can produce. There are still images I would like to capture, creatures I have yet to see, and solace I have up until now, not experienced. My pace has slowed, but I am sure my vision is intact to continue on my journey. And I am afforded the privilege of wearing yet another new hat.

*Pinyon jay with piñon nut*

# For Your Information

| | |
|---|---|
| **Nickname** | Colorado has been nicknamed the "Centennial State". It became the 38th state in 1876 – 100 years after the Declaration of Independence was signed. Colorado's most popular nickname is "Colorful Colorado" which could only be because of its impressive panorama of mountains, colorful river canyons, and rolling plains. |
| **State Animal** | Bighorn sheep |
| **State Bird** | Lark bunting |
| **State Dance** | Square dance |
| **State Fish** | Greenback cutthroat trout |
| **State Flower** | Rocky Mountain columbine (lavender & white) |
| **State Fossi** | Stegosaurus |
| **State Gemstones** | Aquamarine |
| **State Grass** | Blue grama grass |
| **State Tree** | Colorado blue spruce |
| **State Butterfly** | Colorado hairstreak butterfly |
| **State Songs** | #1 – *Where the Columbines Grow* #2 – *Rocky Mountain High* by John Denver |
| **State Soil** | Seitz |
| **Admitted to the Union** | August 1, 1876 – the 38th state |
| **Population** | 4,301,261; the 24th most populous state with 41 persons per square mile |
| **Capital & Largest City** | Denver – population 598,707 |
| **State Name** | "Colorado" is from the Spanish language for "Colored Red" from the muddy Colorado River |
| **Size** | 104,100 square miles – eighth largest state in the union |

| | |
|---|---|
| **Greatest Distance from East to West** | 387 miles |
| **Greatest Distance from North to South** | 276 miles |
| **Number of Counties** | 64 |
| **Highest Point** | 14,433 feet (4,399 meters) above sea level at the summit of Mount Elbert in the Sawatch Mountains in Lake County, 12 miles southwest of Leadville. |
| **Number of Peaks exceeding 14,000 feet** | 54 |
| **Lowest Point** | 3,315 feet in Yuma County on the Arikaree River |
| **Time Zone** | Mountain |
| **Area Code** | 303, 970, 719 |
| **Postal Abbreviation** | CO |
| **Resident** | Coloradan |
| **State Motto** | "Nil sine Numine" – Nothing Without Providence |

*Fairy trumpets*

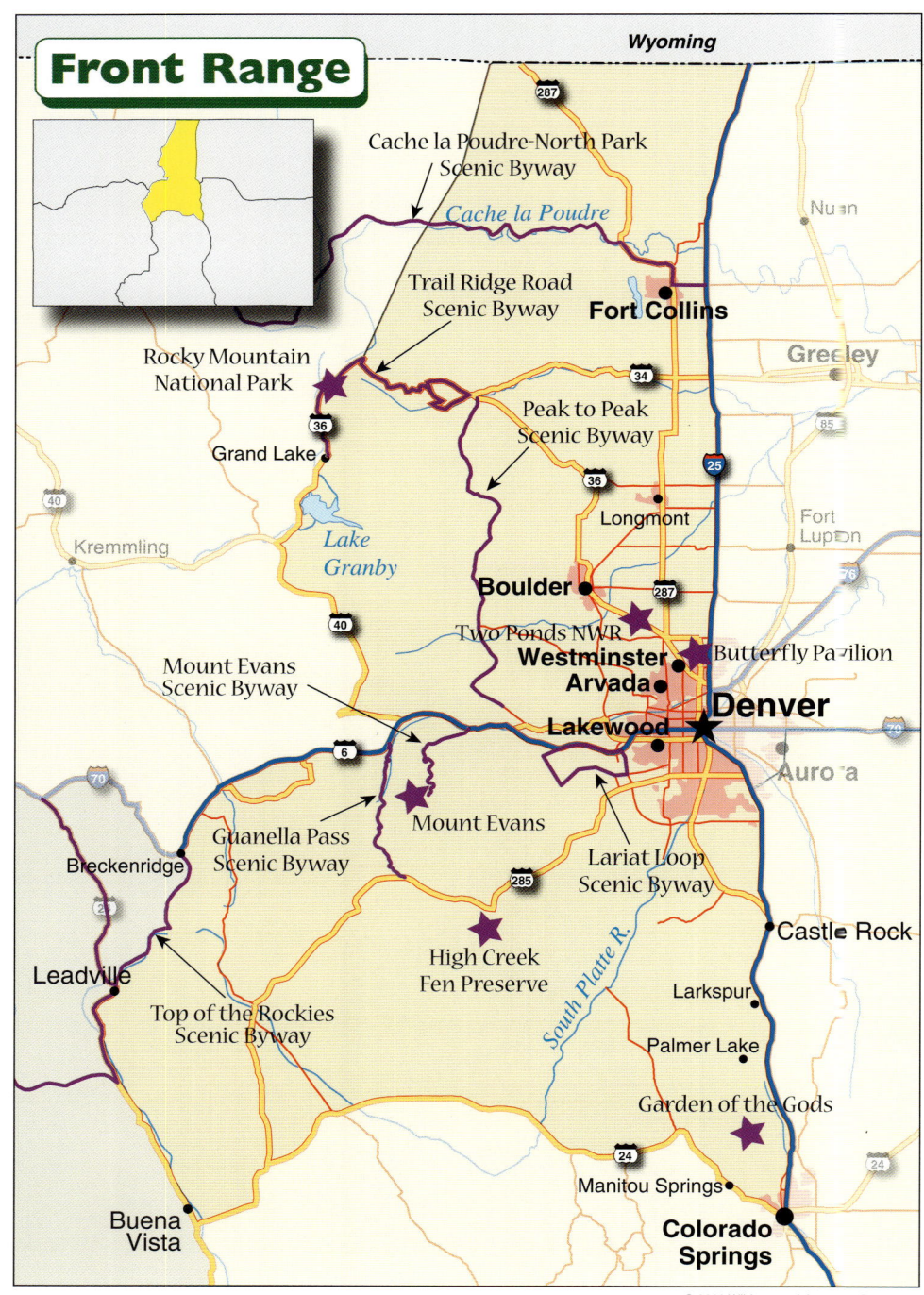

# Front Range

# Butterfly Pavilion

### 8,000 square foot observatory; located in Westminster

## History

The Butterfly Pavilion was created by the Rocky Mountain Butterfly Consortium, a Colorado non-profit organization founded in 1990. The pavilion opened its doors in July of 1995. In the ensuing years, it has hosted over 3,000,000 visitors and provided education to 420,000 school children. The Butterfly Pavilion was the first freestanding butterfly house and invertebrate zoo in the United States. Since its inception in 1995, the pavilion has served an average of 250,000 visitors each year. The *Rocky Mountain News* recently ranked the pavilion fourth in Denver metro attractions in paid attendance.

## Points if Interest

The Butterfly Pavilion, which is situated on an 11-acre campus and includes an 8,000-square-foot structure, is an educational institution whose mission is to foster an appreciation of insects and other invertebrates. They particularly want to educate the public about the importance of preserving threatened habitats around the world. There are few places in the world, and only one in Colorado that allow people to share a living, tropical eco-system with invertebrates from around the world. The pavilion directly supports sustainable business practices internationally by purchasing quantities of butterfly chrysalides, thus helping to give indigenous people an economic reason to protect the tropical forests.

The pavilion has a tropical conservatory, numerous classrooms, several butterfly/habitat gardens, and a one-half mile nature interpretation trail. In addition, the Butterfly Pavilion recently dedicated its Discovery Garden. The purpose and function of the garden is to serve as a link between our classroom education and the nature trail. The garden consists of an educational amphitheatre, habitat, sensory and xeriscape gardens (a landscaping method that utilizes drought-resistant plants and materials so as to conserve water in dry climates), a gazebo that acts as an outdoor classroom space, and a water feature with natural filtration.

The pavilion's education department now serves the curricular needs of over 45,000 students a year through an array of on-site classes, workshops, camps, and outreach programs. Their goal as an education organization is to instill knowledge and understanding of our natural world, thereby developing an appreciation for invertebrate creatures and their habitats. Education programs at the Butterfly Pavilion are predicated upon full-immersion, experiential technique that permits visitors close-up, hands-on animal encounters. Their curriculum is created by professional educators and in collaboration with a Scientific Advisory Board, which is comprised of entomologists and horticulturists at Ph. D or postdoctoral levels.

I actually had the Butterfly Pavilion listed on my outline for this book, but was not sure if it would fit in with our theme of wildlife and bird viewing. However, after meeting up with my old fishing buddy and educational director for the pavilion, Patrick Tennyson, I was convinced it would fit right in with Colorado's other great places.

The wildlife, although exclusively invertebrates, plays a big part in our overall existence as humans. Then to go in and see for myself what a diverse collection of species the pavilion has on hand, surely locked up the arrangement.

In the Crawl-a-See-Em area, visitors can get "up-close and personal" with arthropods native to Colorado, as well as exotic species from around the world. A touching area, called the Critter Cabana, affords the opportunity to touch, hold or photograph a friendly tarantula, hissing cockroach, stick insects, or a giant mealworm.

The Water's Edge area, a comparative invertebrate exhibit, is home to a multitude of marine invertebrates from the Atlantic and Pacific tide-pool habitats.

*Common morpho butterfly*

*Postman butterfly*

    A Chrysalis Viewing Area allows visitors to witness the magic of the last stages of metamorphosis, as adult butterflies emerge from their gem-like chrysalides. The pavilion receives regular chrysalis shipments from butterfly farmers throughout the world's tropical regions to maintain the butterfly population. This sustainable agricultural approach helps create successful economic reasons to preserve and not destroy vital rainforest habitat around the world.

    The most fun for me was the Wings of the Tropics conservatory. It houses over 1,200 individual butterflies, representing over 215 different tropical species basking in an average climate of 80 degrees with 70-percent humidity. I spent a couple hours with my camera and tripod shooting a number of species. However, if you do get a chance to photograph in the "Tropics", bring a lens cloth to wipe the fog off your lens. The humidity will immediately make the lens useless. It takes about 15 minutes for your equipment to adapt to the humid environment; even then, a cloth will come in handy. Along with the butterflies, the habitat includes over 100 tropical and sub-tropical plants providing continuous exotic blooms and a nectar source for the colorful free-flying butterflies. The conservatory also features a waterfall with a winding stream, flowing into a pond with tropical water lilies, fish, and an occasional turtle.

    I was very impressed with the classes provided for children of all ages. They are offered on a continuous basis to stimulate the excitement of learning about invertebrates and their habitats. Group tours can be arranged to include a personalized presentation on a variety of "bug talks". The SHRUNK area is a hands-on, larger than life insect exploration exhibit that provides answers to frequently asked questions like "how do insects eat?" or "how do they fly?" through fun, interactive activities, and hands-on manipulative displays.

The Dee Lidvall Discovery Garden provides visitors an outdoor exploration that leads to an interesting half-mile outdoor interpretive nature trail. Seasonal butterfly habitat gardens and the nature trail give visitors an opportunity to view native butterflies and other insects. The Discovery Garden provides an extensive sensory garden, an outdoor educational amphitheater, as well as a series of demonstration gardens for sharing local gardening techniques like Drought-Tolerant Gardening and Integrated Pest Management. Visitors can even pick up a guide to learn how to create their own butterfly habitat havens in their backyards. As a bonus, local birds have taken to the environs of the Discovery Garden. Mourning doves, western kingbirds, house finches, robins, and red-winged blackbirds are common. Watch the undergrowth for cottontail rabbits and red fox squirrels clamoring in the branches of the many trees on the campus.

*White admiral butterfly*

The Butterfly Pavilion's objectives are as follows:

> *To provide quality invertebrate education programs that meet standardized, age-appropriate content requirements for visitors. Success will impart awareness and a commitment to the natural world around them. Basically, the Pavilion wants to be the premier invertebrate education center in the nation.*
>
> *To provide children of all ethnic and financial backgrounds an opportunity to explore the natural world through invertebrate conservation education.*
>
> *To support ethics-based global conservation efforts that sustain living systems while developing collective support and awareness to local and regional conservation efforts that empower society to embrace our vanishing natural heritage.*

## Location

The Butterfly Pavilion is located at 6252 West 104th Avenue in Westminster. From the intersection of Interstate 70 and Interstate 25 in Denver, take Interstate 25 north to the Boulder Turnpike. Go west on Highway 36 towards Boulder. Go north on 104th Avenue about two blocks and the pavilion will be on the left.

## Contact

**The Butterfly Pavilion & Insect Center**
  6252 West 104th Avenue, Westminster, CO  80020
  303-469-5441
  Admission fees: $7.95 Adult, $5.95 Seniors (62 and over), $4.95 Child (4 to 12)
  Website: www.butterflies.org
  Open daily, year round from 9:00am-5:00pm (closed Thanksgiving and Christmas)

# Garden of the Gods

### 1,320 Acres; just west of Colorado Springs

## History

The Garden of the Gods is a public park best known for its colorful sedimentary rock formations. It was named by a couple of its first explorers. Surveyor and founder of Colorado City, Melancthon S. Beach, and his partner Rufus Cable, while exploring the area, came upon these massive red stones jutting from the ground. Beach thought the sandstone formations would be a "capital place for a beer garden". Cable, a younger and more lyrical chap suggested a more spiritual idea, "Beer Garden! Why it is a fit place for the Gods to assemble. We will call it the Garden of the Gods." The name stuck and has been known as such since that memorable day in August of 1859.

The township of Colorado Springs with its impressive view of Pikes Peak was founded by a railroad man, General William Jackson Palmer, in 1871. In 1879, Palmer advised his friend, Burlington Railroad mogul Charles Elliott Perkins, to build his railroad from Chicago to Colorado Springs. Even though the railroad did not make it to Colorado Springs directly, in 1879 Perkins did purchase land in the Garden of the Gods for a summer home. He expanded his real estate holdings in the garden but never built on it. He decided to leave this beautiful spot in its natural state and even opened it up to the public for their viewing pleasure. Perkins died in 1907; however his children made arrangements for the land to become a park. In 1909, knowing their father's passion for the Garden of the Gods, Perkins' children passed on his 480 acres to the city of Colorado Springs. It would be known forever as the Garden of the Gods "where it shall remain free to the public, where no intoxicating liquors shall be manufactured, sold, or dispensed, where no building or structure shall be erected except those necessary to properly care for, protect, and maintain the area as a public park." The Garden of the Gods is now a registered National Natural Landmark in Colorado Springs.

The Garden of the Gods also has a defined archaeological past. Remnants of animal bones and stone tools were found in the area. Inhabitants from as far back as 3,000 years could have used the nearby rock spires for shelter from summer sun or winter winds.

Ancient fire rings of stones were found by an archaeologist. A layman could have found these sites if only they knew what to look for. Erosion had rendered them in plain view looking much like the normal landscape, but no one had realized the importance of the stones or the charcoal coloring of the ground. Some of these fire rings are pretty recent, but charcoal from one fire ring was carbon-dated to 3,300 years ago.

Most recent visitors, before the white man appeared, were probably Ute Indians. Before them, a nomadic people who hunted on foot with spear-throwers lived there. They probably hunted buffalo, antelope, elk, and deer. Small groups who lived on the High Plains and in the foothills shared elements of culture including the use of plants for food and basket-making.

An ancient piece of pottery was also found in the Garden of the Gods. It was revealed that it was probably from a shallow bowl or large vessel, in a style similar to that made in Mesa Verde from A.D. 575 to 900. This artifact could reflect how widely people traveled on foot, as this was long before horses were brought to America. Not only did it require miles of travel by foot to get the pottery to the area, it may have been traded for buffalo meat and skins from the people of the plains to the east. Could the

*A look through the Siamese Twins*

Garden of the Gods have been a sacred meeting place for sociable tribes to exchange supplies for corn, pottery, cotton, and blankets from the southwest?

There is all the information dating back to the Paleocene era some 60 to 70 million years ago when the Front Range was uplifted and sedimentary formations of the Garden of the Gods were tilted up, which I am not fool enough to try and explain, but there is a distinctive historical point that I found very interesting. Apparently a dinosaur skull was found in the late 1870s by Colorado College professor James H. Kerr, who wrote to associates back east of his discovery. This caught the interest of O.C. Marsh, a famous dinosaur paleontologist from Yale University. In 1886, Marsh came to Colorado Springs and obtained the fossil skull, identified it as a Camptosaurus dinosaur, and shipped it to the Peabody Museum in New Haven, Connecticut.

Dr. Kerr's dinosaur fossil was forgotten until 1994, when the new visitor center for the Garden of the Gods was being built. Exhibits for the center were discussed and a dinosaur display was decided on. Information on Kerr's finding came to the forefront by Dr. Ken Carpenter. He remembered seeing in his files "something about a dinosaur fossil found in the Garden of the Gods". It was found and a replica was cast and put on display in 1997. For more than ten years, the dinosaur known as "Campi" had been part of the Jurassic exhibit. After a bit of research, Carpenter had his doubts about this dinosaur's true identity. In 2006, Dr. Carpenter along with his associate, Kathleen Brill, published a paper – A Description of a New Ornithopod from the Lytle Member of the Purgatoire Formation (Lower Cretaceous) and a Reassessment of the Skull of Camptosaurus. Apparently with all the new technology, irregularities were found in the shape of the skull and the position of nasal and eye-socket openings. Adding these issues with the soils originally embedded around the fossil, resulted in the designation of the first and only *Theiophytalia kerri*.

On May 24, 2008, Garden of the Gods Visitor & Nature Center announced the world's only known fossil of an entirely new dinosaur species, *Theiophytalia kerri*. Theios is of Greek origin, meaning "belonging to the gods" and phytalia means "garden". *Kerri* honors the name of the scientist who first discovered this 125-million-year-old skull in Garden of the Gods Park.

## Wildlife

Over the years, I have hiked around the Garden of the Gods several times and driven by even more. I have always been amazed at the number of birds that exist here and it never fails that I see a mule deer. The diverse landscape is a melting pot of feathered species and wildlife types. Within the 1,320-acre park, the large red rock spires steal the show visually, and they create superb habitat for bats and several birds including tree swallows, white-throated swifts, rock doves (pigeons), and falcons. The gaps and fractures in the rock features offer roosting and nesting areas in these natural dwellings.

The Garden is a unique area of connectivity between many ecosystems in a very small area. There is a small plains zone (that includes short-grass prairie) and a cottonwood-willow area. This locale supports small game such as bunnies and ground squirrels. Snakes and lizards can be found crawling about and mourning doves, house finches, meadow larks, horned larks, common grackles, and house sparrows flying above. You should always have a camera while at the Garden because there is an infinite number of photo ops – landscape and wildlife alike.

The foothills-transition zone, which covers the largest percentage of the Garden of the Gods extends from 6,000 to 8,000 feet and merges the Great Plains to the Rocky Mountains.

A stand of healthy pinyon-juniper flourishes in the Garden, which is within the northernmost reaches of its range. You can find big game like mule deer, elk, and an occasional bighorn sheep grazing this zone. Mule deer are by far the most populous and I would be surprised if you did not spot one sometime during the day. Mornings and evenings are definitely the best times. Bighorns from the Pikes Peak herd are seen on the hillside just north of the main parking lot by the Kissing Camels rock structure. The junipers vary from common juniper shrubs to the twisted, one-seed junipers to the proportioned Rocky Mountain juniper. These habitats support mountain bluebirds, gray jays, Steller's jay, common magpies, black-headed grosbeak, and the spotted towhee. Intermingled with the junipers are common plant species like Gambel oak, mountain mahogany, and skunkbrush. Coyotes, gray fox, and bobcats hunt the area for bunnies, squirrels, and chipmunks. There have been several sightings of mountain lions in surrounding areas – in fact, one of the more

*Deer can be seen along most trails at the Garden of the Gods*

popular areas to hunt mountain lions is just to the west on Rampart Range. The large population of deer in the area must have something to do with the number of big cats.

## Activities

The Garden of the Gods is loaded with trails; both easily traveled concrete and moderately steep dirt trails, accessing all areas of the park. There are about 5 miles of trails for hiking and mountain biking. In fact, the paved roads in the park have bike lanes.

There are daily walks led by city of Colorado Springs interpreters at 10:00am and 2:00pm These outings are free and participants are presented with stories about wildflowers, rattlesnakes, gold-seekers, and many other topics. Special programs may be arranged for school and scout groups to include a Junior Ranger Program. Nature presentations also take place on a daily basis at the Garden of the Gods Visitor Center. They are also free, last about 20 minutes, and explore a wide variety of topics, including the geology, ecology, wildlife, and the cultural history of the park. For additional information, call 719-219-0108.

Rock climbers must first register at the Garden of the Gods Visitor and Nature Center. Technical climbing is permitted on established routes, in groups of two or more. Proper climbing equipment is mandatory, and the use of Eco Chalk is recommended. All other climbing or rock scrambling is illegal.

You can even get married here. Weddings in Garden of the Gods are free, however you must fill out a "Minor Event" form to reserve the area and obtain the permit. Call 719-385-5940 for more information.

A multi-media presentation is offered daily in the center's theater. "How Did Those Red Rocks Get There?" is shown every 20 minutes during the summer and every 30 minutes in winter months. Admission is $2 for adults, $1 for children 5 to 12 years old, with special group rates available.

School programs (Outdoor Educational Programs) help students focus on ecosystems or geology in two educational programs – "Meet the Park" and "Geology" offered for grades K-3 and 3-6 respectively. These two-hour programs begin with a slide presentation or the multi-media theater program, followed by a participatory activity. Small group guided walks conclude the program. The fee is $2 per student, payable the day of the program.

In 1994, the Garden of the Gods Foundation was created to preserve and maintain the Garden of the Gods Park. Contributions are accepted from the public and a volunteer board annually approves projects and materials to improve the Garden. In the first ten years, the Foundation made contributions of more than a million dollars to the park.

The Foundation is a tax deductible 501 (c) (3) organization with an all-volunteer staff.

For more information about the Garden of the Gods Foundation, please visit www.gardenofthegodsfoundation.com.

## Location

The Garden of the Gods is on the west side of Colorado Springs just north of Manitou Springs. The visitor center is located at 1805 North 30th Street, is open daily from 9:00am to 5:00pm in the winter months and 8:00am to 8:00pm Memorial Day weekend through Labor Day weekend.

Both the park and visitor center are free and open to the public.

*Rappelling the face of the Kissing Camels (for experts only)*

## Contact

**Garden of the Gods**
1805 N. 30th Street, Colorado Springs, CO  80904
719-634-6666
719-219-0108
www.gardenofgods.com

## Fast Facts

**Getting There:** From Interstate 25 in Colorado Springs, take Exit 146 west on West Garden of the Gods Road. Continue west about 2 miles to North 30th Street. Turn left (south) a little over a mile to the Garden of the Gods Visitor & Nature Center on the left. From Manitou Springs take Highway 24 east to North 31st Street. Turn left and continue north to West Fontanero Street. Turn right (east) for a block and turn left on North 31st Street. Continue north for about a mile to the Garden of the Gods Visitor & Nature Center on the right.
**Activities:** Birding, wildlife viewing, hiking, biking, and nature presentations.
**Principal Mammals:** Mule deer, bighorn sheep, coyote, raccoon, gray fox, and number of smaller game such as, cottontail rabbits, squirrels, bats and field mice.
**Mammals of Special Interest:** Mule deer.
**Principal Birdlife:** Tree swallows, white-throated swifts, rock doves (pigeons), falcons, mountain bluebirds, gray jays, Steller's jay, common magpies, black-headed grosbeak, and the spotted towhee.
**Birds of Special Interest:** White-throated swift and prairie falcons.
**Habitat Overview:** Transitional foothills juniper and shrub.
**Flora of Special Interest:** Mountain mahogany.
**Best Wildlife Viewing Ops:** Early morning and late evening when they are on the move. Wildlife can be seen from any road or trail.
**Best Birding Ops:** Winter is especially good for raptors. Spring, summer, and fall for just about all others.
**Best Photo Ops:** Early mornings and late evening for both landscape and wildlife.
**Hunting Ops:** None
**Fishing Ops:** None
**Camping Ops:** None
**Boating Ops:** None
**Hiking Trails**: Several throughout the park.
**Motor Trails:** A main paved road circling the area between entrances.

# High Creek Fen Preserve

## 1,200 acres; located in South Park near Fairplay

## History

Positioned at just under 10,000 feet, the High Creek Fen is the most ecologically diverse, plant-rich fen known to exist in the southern Rocky Mountains. It contains more rare plant species than any other wetland known in Colorado. A fen is basically a type of marsh that is covered by spring water that is constantly flowing to the surface, similar to a bog. Fens usually have alkaline-rich, spongy soil.

The first recordable visitors and settlers of the South Park area were the Ute Indians. They lived off the abundant wild game and edible plants in the area. Several other bands of Native Americans visited the South Park area; proof lies at several archeological sites between Fairplay and Antero Reservoir. In 1804, Europeans started trapping beaver in the area while other important visitors to the region include Zebulon Pike, John Fremont, and Kit Carson. Cattle ranching commenced in the 1860s and is still the principal way of life in South Park today.

The Nature Conservancy (TNC) selected this site for protection in the late 1980s, partly due to a report by Dr. David Cooper. He identified High Creek Fen as the best example of an "extreme rich fen" wetland in Colorado. (Only two or three other fens with this classification exist in the entire United States.) They began acquiring acreage in 1991 with the help of the Helen K. & Arthur E. Johnson Foundation. More donors pitched in with financial needs including the "Fen Kids". As a school project to help the youngsters at Deer Creek Elementary in Bailey understand the meaning of a million, a group of fifth and sixth graders collected 1,000,000 pennies. They hauled the pennies, by armored car no less, to the bank and presented a check for $10,000 to TNC to acquire additional land at the fen. The Nature Conservancy continues working to keep the fen intact and protect the extraordinary diversity of plants and animals that it supports.

## Wildlife

On my visit to the fen, I was no more than a half mile east on the gravel road heading to the parking area when I noticed a small herd of pronghorn antelope just east of the parking area. They seemed uninterested until I got out of the truck in preparation for my hike into the fen. They slowly moved to the north, but not before I was able to pop a few long distance images.

There are no established trails in the fen and much of the area is very boggy and hard to maneuver. Although the terrain is somewhat level, passing through the fen can be hazardous. Rubber boots or a pair of old shoes that you're willing to throw away afterwards is highly recommended. It is quite easy to get stuck in the saturated peat, so proceed with care. On top of these inconveniences, during the summer months deer flies are a nuisance and I had several welts to prove it. I was within 50 yards of the green belt of the fen when I was inundated by the pests. I recommend a long sleeved shirt, regular pants, even a light pair of gloves, and insect repellent.

Elk and mule deer are abundant in the area. They are best seen early in the morning and late in the evening just before dark. Most years, during the summer months, the elk will be in the higher, more wooded areas on either side of South Park. Black bear are in the area, but rarely seen in the prairie. Coyotes run freely in South Park and an occasional bobcat may be seen. Wyoming ground squirrels, jack rabbits, beaver, porcupines, ermine, and the mountain cottontail round out the small game in the area.

The unique wetlands provide outstanding habitat for a great mix of birds in the fen and surrounding area. The marshlands in the fen can hold several species of shorebirds and waterfowl including the Wilson's phalarope, common snipe, and spotted sandpiper. Mallards and American coot stop and may nest at the fen. The rare mountain plover can be found nesting in the short-grass prairie surrounding the fen. The plover is a very unique bird to Colorado, most often found in prairies of eastern Colorado. South Park is the only mountain area in the state where they can be found. Large counts of raptors rule the sky of South Park. Swainson's hawks,

*A lesser yellowlegs fluffing its feathers*

red-tailed hawks, an occasional golden eagle, and prairie falcons regularly work the High Creek Fen. I wouldn't be surprised to see great-horned owls or burrowing owls in the vicinity.

## Activities

A visit during the month of July would be the best time to enjoy wildflowers in bloom. You can see Indian paintbrush, bluebell, day lily, wood lily, and shrubby cinquefoil. High Creek Fen supports two globally rare plant communities. There are two sedge species recorded in Colorado only a few times and twelve plant species of special concern as listed by the Colorado Natural Heritage Program. Most of the fen's 14 state-rare plant species which include autumn willow, bladderwort, green sedge, sedge, Greenland primrose, hoary willow, little bulrush, moss, myrtle-leaf willow, pale blue-eyed grass, Porter feathergrass, and ragwort are isolated populations of arctic and northern Rocky Mountain species. These isolated populations survived here after the glaciers receded. The Colorado blue spruce is also a standout here at the fen, as it is atypical to the South Park area. Make sure to visit the stand of bristlecone pines at Bristlecone Pine Scenic Area on Windy Ridge located near Alma. See the chapter on Mount Evans for directions.

South Park is an outdoorsman's paradise. Some of the state's best elk and deer hunting is available as well as prime trout fishing. Backpacking, four-wheeling, and snowmobiling are popular pastime activities. You can camp at the U.S. Forest Service's Buffalo Springs Campground, located 5 miles south of the preserve on U.S. Route 285.

Pike National Forest and Buffalo Peaks Wilderness Area provide excellent back country action for the outdoor activist and hunter. The Middle Fork of the South Platte and the South Fork of the South Platte River drain right through the middle of South Park and provide many access points for the flyfisher. Throw Antero Reservoir, Spinney Mountain Reservoir, Eleven Mile Reservoir, and Tarryall Reservoir into the mix and there is no end to fishing opportunities in the area. Camping is also available at these reservoirs.

The High Creek Fen is open year round, dawn to dusk. Please leave pets at home while enjoying your visit to the High Creek Fen. Be prepared for afternoon thunder showers. Not only can the rains be unpredictable and sometimes very heavy, lightning is a real threat.

## Location

From the intersection of I-25 and C-470 in Denver, take C-470 west to Highway 285. Take Highway 285 south to Fairplay. The High Creek Fen Preserve is on the left (east) about 8.5 miles south of Fairplay. Turn east on a private gravel road that is 0.2 miles south of milepost 175. The milepost is on the west side of the road; the gravel road is on the east. The entrance is pretty non-descript, but it is marked with a small Nature Conservancy sign. Cross the cattle guard, then drive about a mile to a small parking area and visitor kiosk.

# Mount Evans (Colorado Scenic Byway)

### 70,000 Acres; 30 miles west of Denver on Interstate 70

This stretch of road from Interstate 70 to the top of Mount Evans is one of Colorado's Scenic Byways. When you get on it, you will see why. It presents a variety of the most stunning vistas in Colorado. As the road climbs toward 14,130 feet, views of high mountain lakes, wildflowers, startling rocky peaks, and outlooks back to the east of the foothills and downtown Denver will astonish you. Three miles past the entrance to Mount Evans Road is a nature area where a visitor can witness some of the oldest living entities on earth, the bristlecone pine trees. Some of the trees in this modest forest are over 1,600 years old. This area is the northernmost range of this tree. They do not exist north of Interstate 70 in Colorado. Apparently the oldest bristlecone pines are in the White Mountain Range in California. Located at an elevation very close to the trees found in Colorado (over 11,000 feet) the oldest living tree in the world, the Methuselah as it is named, is over 4,700 years old.

## Wildlife

The trip to the top of Mount Evans is absolutely the best place in the state of Colorado to see Rocky Mountain goats. I have not been able to get an actual count for the entire Mount Evans herd, but I have seen them every time I have taken the trip. On a recent trip, I was the first to see a herd of about 25 topping a rock outcropping as they fed towards the road. I was able to get my camera and tripod into position for this wildlife spectacle before the crowds showed up. You see, the most common way of spotting the goats is to come across a line of cars parked on the side of the very narrow road. Visitors then line up with cameras and binoculars for a closer look. In this particular bunch, there were several kids from this year's crop bouncing along the rocks, stopping to playfully butt heads with their sister or brother, maybe their cousin. Nannies paid little attention to the youngsters, as they continued to chow on the tundra's succulents. As the folks started to line up, the goats veered away from the road showing little concern for the number of eyes watching them.

On another trip, folks were already gathered on the side of the road by the time my family and I showed up. Even though the regulations suggest that you do not approach or feed the wildlife, there were dozens of onlookers walking right out

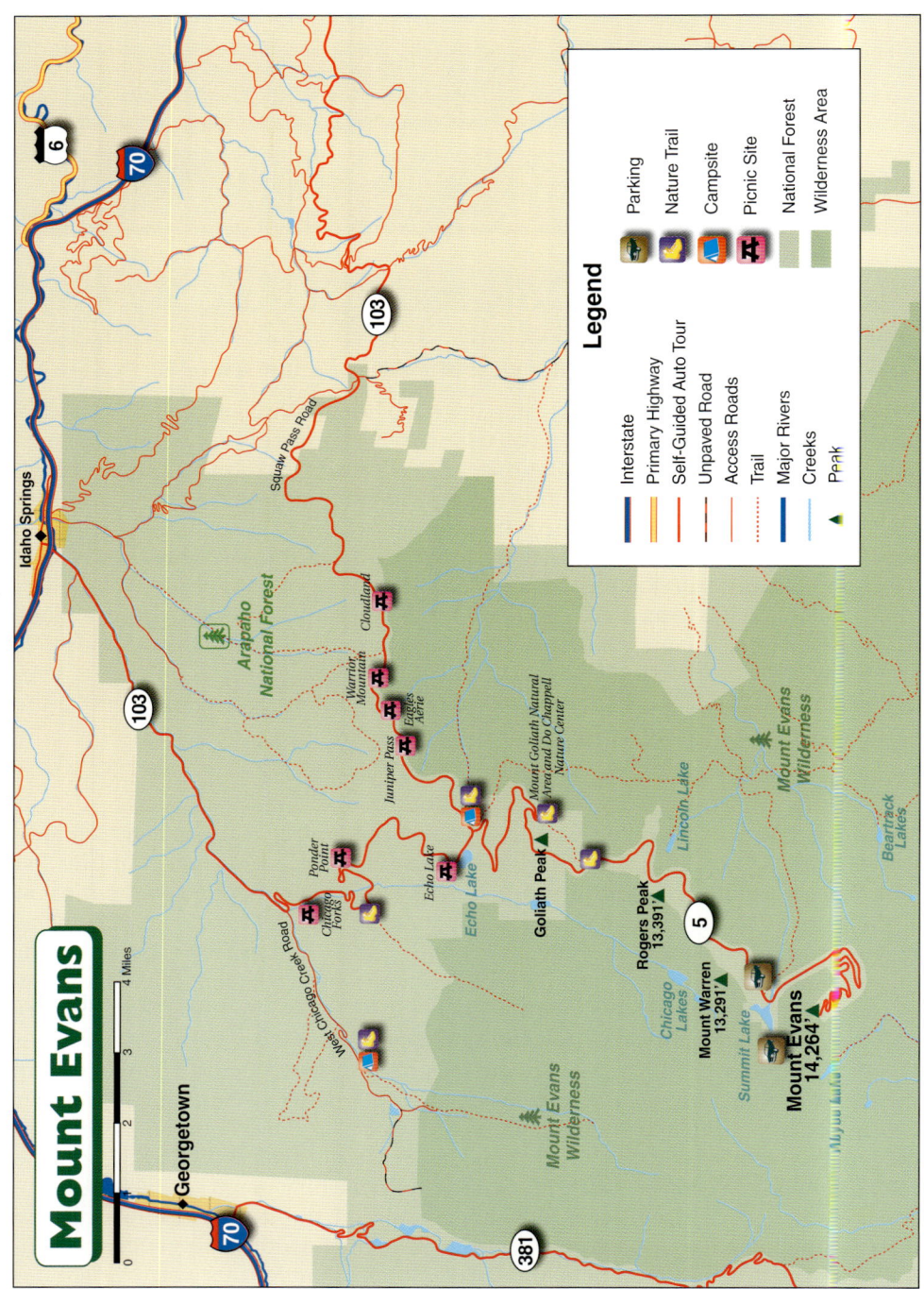

amongst the goats. Again, the goats paid little attention as they filled their bellies. They must be used to the smell of humans and have learned they are not a real threat. I found a spot at a reasonable distance and got some great images of the animals interacting. Even though the situation appeared very unnatural, the goats presented in a stress-free attitude and intermingled very naturally.

I enjoy images of wildlife when they look calm, having their true expressions show through. So that is what I try to accomplish when I am behind the lens.

Bighorn sheep are the next big game animal to watch for. They are also very abundant in the area and easy to spot. Again, roadside viewing is most popular and the sheep, especially the ewes, seem oblivious to humans. I had four ewes walk within 10 feet of me. So close, I had to switch to a wide angle lens just to get their heads in the viewfinder. These gals were looking a little ratty as they were shedding last winter's coat, none the less, having them walk in close enough to hear them breath was quite a treat.

Deer and elk can be seen at lower elevations, often along the foot trails in the area. The elk in the area are referred to as the Mount Evans herd and can often be seen grazing above timberline during the summer months. This herd ranges as far north as Interstate 70 at Idaho Springs, south to Highway 285, east to the Evergreen, Conifer (both towns) area and who knows how far west.

Coyotes, red fox, bunnies, pine squirrels, fox squirrels are common, as are the marmots and pika when above timberline.

Eagles can be seen gliding with the thermals above; crows and ravens are common throughout the Mount Evans Wilderness. American pipits, Steller's jays, northern flickers, Clark's nutcrackers, mountain chickadees, pine siskins, and nuthatches can be seen on a regular basis. The evening grosbeak, ptarmigan, and the white-crowned sparrow would be exceptional finds.

## Bristlecone Pines

The bristlecone pine forest located along Mount Evans Road can be found at the Mount Goliath Natural Area, 3 miles up from the pay station at the entrance. The nature area provides exhibits inside the center and a couple short trails that loop through the bristlecone trees. A longer hike along M. Walter Pesman Trail provides more access to this great stand of ancient trees. Abundant with birds and small game, this trail of about 3 miles round trip also takes a visitor above the timberline for outstanding panoramic views and plentiful wildflowers.

The unique bristlecone pine is an unusually small tree for its age. It is celebrated for growing to a very old age on rocky soil in harsh conditions. It can grow in cold climates that lack water, where it grows so slowly that the growth rings are microscopic. It is normally found from 7,000 feet above sea level to the timberline.

The dark green needles grow in bundles of five, usually to about an inch and a half. Some needles will be speckled with sticky whitish drops of resin. The needles are close together and persist on the branches for many years, 12 to 14 years or even more, making the branches look like a long brush.

The cones are dark brown, and some actually look purple to me. They're normally about 3 inches in length. Some cone scales have sticky resin drops on the tips; sometimes the resin will coat the entire cone.

The bark on young trees is thin, fairly smooth, and white to gray in color. You may see a dash of red or purple. On older trees, the bark becomes thick and brown or gray. In windy locations the bark may be non-existent on the upwind side of the tree.

The bristlecones are an unnatural contradiction to the wild. It seems that the harsher the conditions, the longer they live. Bristlecones with the riches of good soil and adequate water grow too fast and often die young. The trees that are constantly stressed grow slow but hard, actually just a few millimeters a year. The trip up Mount Evans Road is a very unique and educational experience for anyone old enough to walk. I highly recommend the adventure.

Here is a sad story I found about the oldest bristlecone pine found to date

Apparently a young geographer was in the Southwest searching for evidence of Ice Age glaciers. The Wheeler Peak glacier in central California caught his attention and he came to the area. The geographer and his associate came upon a stand of bristlecone pines right at timberline. After taking core samples from several trees, they discovered one to be over 4,000 years old! After their only coring tool broke, they moved on for the season. They asked for and, unbelievably, they were granted

*Sap-laden bristlecone pinecones*

permission by the U.S. Forest Service to cut the tree, known as "Prometheus", down. After cutting the trunk at a convenient level, which happened to be more than 8 feet above the original base, 4,844 rings were counted. This geographer had just killed the oldest living thing on earth! Eventually, it was determined the tree was 4,862 years of age.

There are a few more locations in Colorado to find the bristlecone pines:

Bristlecone Pine Scenic Area is located on Windy Ridge at the eastern foot of Mount Bross, the 22nd highest peak in the state at 14,172 feet in elevation. The winds, from which the ridge gets its name, have caused the trees to take on a tilted appearance. The Windy Ridge bristlecones are incredibly hardy. They endure summer drought, poor rocky soil, thin air and harsh sunlight, hurricane-force winds, and bitter winter cold. They are twisted and gnarled; yet keep growing about a hundredth of an inch each year. Most of their energy goes into survival and seed production. Good views of South Park are also available from this ridge. A visitor also has a chance to estimate the age of these trees. There are several stumps left behind from the mining days where the rings of those trees are visible. Artists and photographers from around the world find the Bristlecone Pine Scenic Area an excellent place for images.

To find the Bristlecone Pine Scenic Area, go to the junction of Colorado 9 and US 285 in Fairplay. Follow Colorado 9 north to the Alma city limit. Turn left at Park County Road 8, an intersection with a side road on the left in the middle of town across from a gas station. Continue straight and you will pass a blue sign (Park County Road 8) on the right side of this good dirt road. Continue on this road and turn right onto Forest Development Road (FDR) #415 at the intersection marked by a sign as access to Mineral Park. I would recommend a 4-wheel drive vehicle from this point as it becomes a rough, steeper grade and has standing water (seasonally) in several places.

Continue on this dirt road past Sawmill Creek to a point where the road seems to empty into a mining area. Bear left and wind uphill through the remains of this Mineral Park Mine area. As the road curves to the right, ignore a side road on the left marked as FDR #857. Immediately thereafter, ford a small stream and continue up the hill on a slightly steeper portion. The road then curves to the left around some concrete foundations and then to the right as it climbs to the rim of Windy Ridge. A small parking area is provided on the right side. From the parking lot you can wander out onto the ridge and enjoy viewing the bristlecone pines. It takes about an hour to reach this point and you are now at 11,714 feet. Mid- to late summer would be the best time to visit. Bristlecone pines near South Park are the oldest trees in Colorado. The oldest bristlecone pine in Colorado is at least 2,436 years old, and grows in Park County near Guffey. However, that area is closed to the public.

Bristlecone pine is also found on Highway 40 south of Berthoud Pass and James Peak in Colorado. They are never found north of the 40th parallel. Groves of bristlecone pine are found above Manitou Springs on Pikes Peak. Larger groves can be found in the San Juan Forest of southwest Colorado. Bristlecone pine is not a common tree in Colorado, or anywhere in its range, which extends on mountains west to California and south into New Mexico.

## Activities

The 74,401-acre Mount Evans Wilderness Area harbors a plethora of outdoor activities. The drive up Mount Evans Road (Highway 5) is a given, but care should be taken. The road is narrow, and unimproved or damaged stretches should be driven with caution. Watch your speed, pay attention to the engine gauges, and use a low gear going back down instead of riding the brakes. However, at the top of the road at 14,130 feet, a quarter-mile steep trail leading to the top is well within most visitor's reach. The air is thin and often very cool at the top, but the view is amazing and well worth the walk. Restrooms are available at the parking lot.

*A lone billy shedding its winter coat*

Summit Lake is located at 12,800 feet and is a must-stop along the way. A wonderful view of the lake is available at the parking lot and foot trails do take visitors right to the shore. The encompassing rock slides can be a great place to view wildlife such as mountain goats, bighorn sheep, and marmots.

Many bicycling enthusiasts find the 14-mile trip to the top "the ultimate ride". I photographed a lady along the way, both going up and coming back down. When I met up with her at the intersection of Highway 5 and Highway 103 to thank her for the photos, she took off her head gear and I found out she was well into her 60s. She rode like a 20-year-old. She was in awesome physical shape, hardly breathing above normal.

Trailheads leading into the wilderness area include Resthouse Meadows Trail, Captain Mountain Trail, and the well-used Chicago Lakes Trail, which leads to a pair of alpine lakes with eager cutthroat trout. They are a destination for many anglers looking for a remote location off the main road.

## Location

From Denver, take Interstate 70 west to Idaho Springs. Take Exit 240 and follow Highway 103 south 14 miles to Mount Evans Highway (Highway 5). Turn right and continue another 14 miles to the top of Mount Evans.

## Contacts

Clear Creek Ranger Station: 303-567-3000
www.mountevans.com

## Access Fees

| | |
|---|---|
| 1-12 passengers per vehicle | $10 |
| 13-40 passengers per vehicle | $25 |
| 40+ passengers per vehicle | $40 |
| Annual Pass | $25 |
| Motorcycles, bicycles, hikers | $ 3 |
| Travel non-stop on the road | No Charge |
| Senior or Volunteer Pass | No Charge |

Full access is available to holders of valid Golden Eagle, Golden Age, Golden Access Passport and National Parks Pass with hologram upgrade or holders of valid Interagency America the Beautiful Pass.

# National Parks and Monuments
## Rocky Mountain National Park (RMNP)

400 Square miles; Front Range of the Rocky Mountains 50 miles northwest of Denver just west of Estes Park

## Introduction

Even though Rocky Mountain National Park is all mountainous in nature, it has three very distinct life zones. As you enter the park on the east side at about 7,500 feet, Trail Ridge Road, which usually opens on Memorial Day, courses through a montane zone. Ponderosa pines and open meadows dominate the landscape. Aspen groves will intermingle above the meadows. Wildlife and birds are diverse. Expect to see elk, bighorn sheep, deer, and any number of small game animals. Raptors, blue jays, woodpeckers, and the occasional blue grouse can be seen. At about 9,000 feet, the subalpine zone is ruled by Douglas firs and spruce forests. Aspen groves persist in the subalpine zone. Elk and deer are still present along with bighorn sheep. Blue grouse continue to thrive at this elevation as do raptors, owls, hummingbirds, and many sparrows. At or near 11,400 feet elevation, the timberline is the mark of the alpine zone. Tundra and small wildflowers take over the countryside. **Brown-capped rosy finch** and white-tailed ptarmigan are found above timberline. Often considered a prairie bird, the horned lark is also found in the tundra. Yellow-bellied marmot and pika are numerous up here. The elevation at the top of Trail Ridge Road is 12,183 feet.

Passing through all three zones can take less than an hour, so I would suggest a mint gum to chew to help your ears pop as the air pressure changes. Be prepared for what is known as high-altitude sickness. A throbbing headache and nausea are the main symptoms, which can make you pretty miserable for a few hours. There are medications for high-altitude sickness, but staying hydrated and taking a bit of time as altitude is gained are the best known prevention.

Encompassing more than 400 square miles, Rocky Mountain National Park consists of meadows, wetlands, coniferous forest, and tundra, all lying on both sides of the Continental Divide. RMNP is a scientist's sandbox. Everyone from ornithologists, preschoolers, biologists, teachers, and archeologists can enjoy their favorite natural sciences while taking pleasure in the breathtaking beauty of this park. Over 150 lakes and 450 miles of streams are the foundation of the riparian environment in the park. Flourishing plant life and abundant wildlife are the trademarks of these areas. The wetlands dot the park and help separate the other ecosystems. The forest provides shelter to any number of mammals and birds, while the tundra is a very distinct environment, for use by only the most unique of plants and animals. The high elevation and extremely jagged terrain are habitat for one of the highest concentration of glaciers in the lower 48 states. Glaciers can be accessed by foot trails throughout the park. Most trails are fairly lengthy, but the views are astounding.

There are several areas to access in RMNP. There are two main entrances on the east side of the park and one on the west side. From the east side of the park, Horseshoe Park, Endovalley, Moraine Park, Glacier Basin, and the Bear Lake area are accessible. From the extremities of the park along Highway 7 south of Estes Park, Longs Peak and Wild Basin are accessed, while Lumpy Ridge Trailhead and Cow Creek Trailhead can be accessed from Devils Gulch Road north of Estes Park. From the west side at Grand Lake, Kawuneeche Visitor Center, the headwaters of the Colorado River, and several other trailheads can be found. The west side of the park is well known for the opportunity to see the Shiras moose. For those who enjoy getting off the beaten path, access to hiking trails and backpacking is almost limitless. A permit is required for backcountry camping.

## History

Rocky Mountain National Park was inhabited by Native Americans since at least 12,000 years ago. The major inhabitants of the park area in historic times were the Ute and Arapaho tribes. The Apache tribe may have been in the park for several hundred years based on the existence of their pottery. There are accounts of a skirmish with the Arapaho in the 1830s in Upper Beaver Meadow. The Arapaho migrated from Minnesota into Colorado in the 1790s.

Due to the high elevation and brutal winters, the time spent by these tribes was probably confined to the warmer months, primarily in the fall when elk were more available. Elk were driven from the higher elevation into crudely assembled traps and killed for meat, clothing, and tools. Driving animals is one of the oldest and most successful hunting strategies known to man. It has been used worldwide for thousands of years. The basic idea is to drive as many animals as possible into a trap of some sort where they can be eradicated. There are remains of eight known drives in the park. All of the drives were made of lines of rock, hides propped up on sticks, and even the Native Americans themselves that formed a conduit, with pits dug at the constricted end of the conduit. All are found in the tundra. The drives were done in the tundra because that is where large numbers of elk lived in the early fall before making their annual migration down to the valleys to mate. Game drives were used to obtain as much meat in the shortest period of time. The meat was dried, ground, and mixed with berries, roots, and fat to make pemmican. Pemmican is a very nutritious food, equivalent to the modern energy bar and used for winter consumption.

FRONT RANGE: ROCKY MOUNTAIN NATIONAL PARK — 41

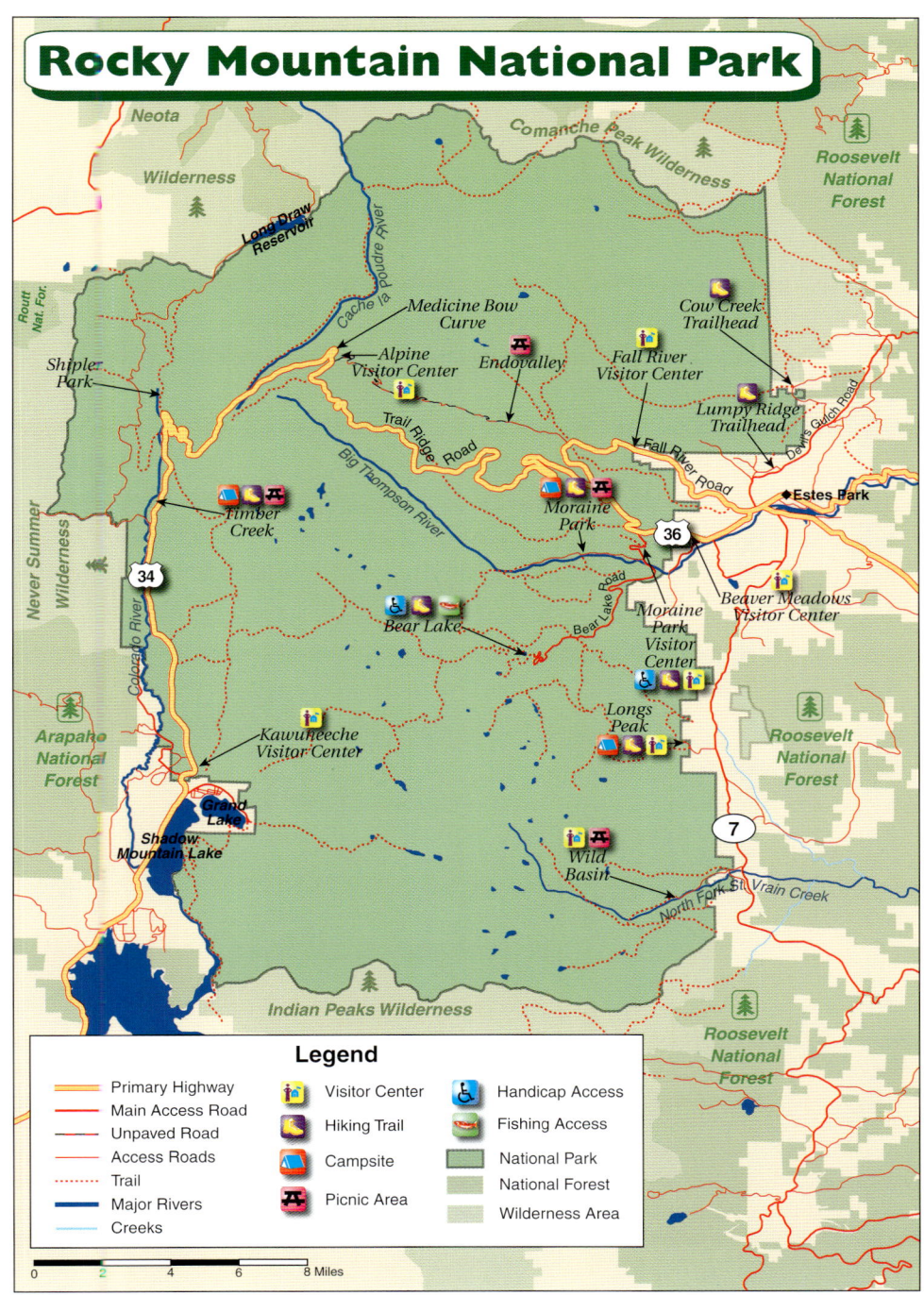

Congress created Rocky Mountain National Park in 1915, as the nation's tenth national park. Congress created the National Park Service a year later. During a recent five-year survey of the park by the University of Northern Colorado, the assemblage found 400 prehistoric and 600 historic archeological sites.

## TRAIL RIDGE ROAD

### Location

Trail Ridge Road can be accessed from either the east or west entrance to the park. Basically this is the continuation of Highway 34 from either direction. It is one of Colorado's Scenic Byways and the highest, continuously paved road in the United States. If you were to visit Rocky Mountain National Park for no other reason than to drive Trail Ridge Road, your time and money would be well spent. The views are breathtaking; expansive valley floors, dense forest, unique wind damaged trees, stark tundra, and jagged peaks are all within an hour's drive.

### Wildlife

The wildlife viewing from Trail Ridge Road ranges from the smallest of game to the large-framed Shiras moose. I have seen hundreds of stately elk from the east entrance

*Wildflowers at sunset*

to the west entrance in just one passing. Our family had a French exchange student for a couple weeks a few years ago so we made the trip to RMNP to show him what Colorado was really all about. After the usual stops at the many turn outs to take in the view and photograph the memories and marmots, we finally reached the timberline. In the open tundra countryside, over 50 elk were grazing and bedded down right off the side of the road. Massive bulls in the 6- to 7-point range were oblivious of the traffic jam and the clicking cameras in their backyard. In fact, I could swear one of them turned his head giving full view of his impressive antlers and smiled like a model as if it were just another day at the office.

The boisterous yellow-bellied marmots holed up in the rock gardens at the timberline are easy subjects for photos. They bark just enough to let you know they are not exactly happy about your presence, but sit still long enough for a photo encounter. Pika, on the other hand, are more elusive; but if time and a slow approach are taken once one is seen, you can be rewarded with an intimate photo. Colorado and least chipmunks are also abundant.

The prairie falcon is the most common raptor of the tundra, but watch for the larger red-tailed hawk. The most rewarding find in the tundra is the white-tailed ptarmigan. They can be found throughout the park in alpine meadows and rocky areas at or above the tree line; however one of the best opportunities would be at the Medicine Bow Overlook located just west of the Visitor Center at the top of Trail Ridge Road. They are hard to find though. Not that they are scarce or elusive, they

*A pair of young bull elk above timberline*

are just hard to see because of their elegant camouflage. They blend in perfectly with splotchy-colored rocks. A sharp pair of binoculars and a patient eye looking for the slightest movement is the best way to spot one. They are not a "flight to safety" type of bird. They sit tight amongst the lichen-covered rocks and tundra grasses, totally expecting not to be seen.

The white-tailed ptarmigan is a small, pear-shaped grouse. It is 12 to 14 inches in length, is the smallest of the ptarmigans (grouse family) and the only ptarmigan with a totally white, short tail. Its scientific name, *Lagopus leucura*, is a Latinized version of the Greek leukos (white) and oura (tail). It is a gorgeous bird that sports a mottled gray and brown coat in the summer and is entirely white in winter. The white-tailed ptarmigan's defensive coloration keeps it hidden from predators which, in RMNP, are mainly prairie falcons and red-tailed hawks. It has white wings and feathered legs and feet which act as snowshoes, so the bird can walk on top of the snow. It has a small black beak and black eyes. Males and females look alike in winter. A large part of the white-tailed ptarmigan's diet is made up of the buds and leaves of willows. It also eats berries, insects, leaves, and flowers. It also eats grit to help digest its food.

In breeding season, the male has a red comb over his eyes and makes soft, low hoots and low clucking noises. Much like other birds in the grouse family, the male white-tailed ptarmigan fans out his tail and struts to attract a female. He aggressively protects his territory by running low to the ground, flaring out his eye combs and calling out with a harsh cackle. The female lays two to eight eggs in roughly designed scrapes on the ground. The eggs incubate for 20 to 24 days and the chicks leave the nest a few hours after hatching and can feed themselves right away.

Early morning (before the wind starts to blow and the people begin to show) is the best time to start looking for the ptarmigan. Oftentimes they can be heard before they are seen. The weather is unpredictable and more than likely it will be just above freezing, even in July. Dress accordingly; warm jacket and pants, gloves and earmuffs are desirable attire. As the sun climbs higher in the sky, the wind will likely pick up and the chill will continue.

The brown-capped rosy finch is the next high-elevation bird to watch for. It is usually restricted to the highest elevations except in the dead of winter. They love the snow and frigid temperatures of the highest elevations. Besides the ptarmigan, no other North American bird species breeds at this high of an elevation and stays in this blustery area even in the winter. This bird is found almost exclusively in the high peaks of Colorado, but it does range from southern Wyoming to northern New Mexico. It does not migrate; instead, it moves to lower elevations when food sources are covered by snow. Males are cinnamon-brown with rosy-tipped feathers in the breast, rump, tail, and at the bend of wing. The female is very similar to the male, but is of a much lighter shade. They have black beaks in summer and yellow with a black tip in winter. In their swift bouncy flight, the underwings look silver. Audubon Colorado has identified Rocky Mountain National Park as an Important Bird Area that is thought to support a breeding population of 1,000 to 2,000 brown-capped rosy finches.

They nest in cliff-like rock structures in crevices, where they stay entirely in the shade. This pretty little finch lines its nest with grass, feathers, and rootlets. It has been witnessed using cotton, pieces of cloth, bits of burlap, and basically any soft fiber, including paper. After hatching, chicks stay in the nest for a couple weeks and can feed themselves within 14 to 20 days after they fledge. As a rule, only one clutch is produced in a season, but substitute clutches are occasionally laid when a brood does not make it. They feed on seeds and insects on and near the snowfields, so the tundra is ideal habitat for the brown-capped rosy finch. Here is an unusual piece of trivia: a group of rosy-finches is known as a bouquet.

Also watch for the lively little American pipit in the rocky tundra. Its back is light brown in color; buff-colored breast plumage with black legs about the same size as a common sparrow make them very hard to see. They are fairly easy to spot after they are heard. A pleasant, medium-pitched chirp will give their position away.

Continuing west on Trail Ridge Road, just before you get to Milner Pass, the headwaters of Cache la Poudre River are flowing out of Poudre Lake to the northeast. This is a good place to stop and snoop around. The willows surrounding the lake often hold several types of sparrows, which may actually nest here. There is a delightful little trail that follows the river that may be worth a short hike. Definitely watch for moose as this area has a good population. I have fished several lakes and streams, particularly Long Draw Reservoir just over the mountains to the north and seen as many as thirteen moose in one day. My son and I had a bull, cow, and calf standing on the dam as we kicked by in float tubes on another nearby lake. I am still kicking myself for not having the camera with me that day. We were within 20 or 30 feet of this trio. They enjoy this wet, marshy type of habitat. However, if you do see a moose, keep your distance. I have had several close encounters without incident, but a moose is a large unpredictable animal capable of putting a good stomping on you. That is always at the back of my mind when I see one.

As Milner Pass is breached, you will cross the Continental Divide be on the west side of the park. A few miles down the road a fun stretch of hairpin turns will grab your attention as you descend into the Colorado River valley. Passengers should continue to look for elk. The headwaters to the mighty Colorado River (it doesn't look all that mighty yet) start just north of here. There is a trailhead to follow taking you through Shipler Park and on toward the many branches that form the main channel. All types of birds and wildlife can be viewed here. Gray jays, pine grosbeaks, and red crossbills can be seen in the forested areas, while Wilson's warblers and Lincoln's sparrows adore the willow riparian zone. Many types of squirrels, beaver, muskrat, and larger game such as deer can be viewed along the river. The highway is now going directly south towards Grand Lake. Four more pull-offs and parking areas gain more access to the river bottom and hours of prolonged exploring. Red-winged blackbirds are plentiful along the river and the potential to see a great blue heron exists.

Outside of the park, Grand Lake and Shadow Mountain Reservoir hold great prospect for waterfowl birding. Bald eagles and osprey are often seen perched around these lakes.

# Endovalley

## Location

Endovalley is a very diverse area of RMNP and probably one of the better birding areas. To find Endovalley, enter the park via the Fall River Road entrance. Continue west for about 2 miles and take a right on the road marked Endovalley.

## Wildlife

The large meadow about a half mile into the park from the Fall River entrance is called Horseshoe Park. It is very well known as a bighorn sheep viewing area and is worth a stop to view the area with binoculars. Don't be surprised if an elk or a mule deer is feeding in the area early and late in the day. Coyotes, ermine, and bunnies are common especially in the early hours of the day while red fox, Albert's squirrels and Colorado chipmunks are spotted throughout the day. Sheep Lakes at the west end of Horseshoe Park is a good spot for viewing waterfowl. Mallards, Canada geese, and blue-winged teal are common; this would also be a splendid spot to see a spotted sandpiper. Check the sky above for a prairie falcon, golden eagle, or red-tailed hawk.

Endovalley itself is a mix of ponderosa pines with spruce, firs, and aspens set on the hillsides above wetlands. Many slopes covered with rock outcroppings make up habitat that is second to none for just about every bird found in RMNP. Fall River courses through Endovalley on the south, eventually flowing into and out of Fan Lake. While the most common viewing time is summer, Endovalley is near the entrance to the park (near the lowest elevations), so access is pretty much year round. There are several pull-offs and parking areas along Endovalley Road and they are all first rate for wildlife and bird viewing.

One of the first parking areas as you enter Endovalley is a trailhead leading to Lawn Lake. Most of the trail follows the Roaring River, a smallish tumbling stream with a good number of greenback cutthroat trout available to all anglers. The trail continues on to the lake.

Further along Endovalley Road, there are several more parking areas with shorter trails gaining access through the trees for viewing. It is possible to see nesting three-toed woodpeckers in the larger aspen trees. More nesters include red-naped sapsuckers, violet-green swallows, mountain bluebirds, house wrens, and northern flickers. The willows along Fall River hold Wilson's warblers, nuthatches, and western tanagers. Another highlight along the road is the bridge where the Roaring River heads towards it confluence with Fall River. The alluvial fans north of the road and on both sides of the stream are wonderful areas for birding. Cassin's finch, MacGillivary's warbler, ruby-crowned kinglet, white-crowned sparrow, swallows, and blue grouse can be seen along with the American dipper near the stream itself. Small game is abundant in the area and you can expect to see a mule deer doe with fawns and an occasional elk. Muskrat and beaver might be taking residence in the stream bottom meadow.

Just west of the alluvial fans, notice all of the aspen trees that have been scarred by bull elk rubbing their antlers in preparation for breeding season. It looks like the bottom 5 or 6 feet of every tree is dark gray with rub marks.

At the end of Endovalley Road, the Old Fall River Road begins. It is a gravel road – passable by most vehicles – which continues on to the Alpine Visitor Center near the top of Trail Ridge Road. There are fewer vehicles traveling this road: it is subject to weather conditions; it is slower going; and it can be rough in some places. But, it gives you a backside view of the park few take the time to see. Later in the season, it is only open depending on snowpack. Check with the park staff for availability.

*Downy woodpecker*

## Moraine Park

### Location

Enter the park from Estes Park at the Beaver Meadows entrance, and turn south toward Bear Lake. At Moraine Park Road, turn right. Continue west and the Big Thompson River will soon be on the south side of the road. Access to Cub Lake and Fern Lake trails is near the west end of the park.

### Wildlife

Take a walk through the soggy riparian area of the Big Thompson River and up the valley. This is one of the best areas in the park to look for the northern pygmy owl. They are rarely seen, however other birds in the area may give away the owl's location. Listen for the erratic notes of songbirds ganging up on an owl they've spotted in daylight. Moraine Park is another excellent spot in RMNP for a wide array of common and sometimes uncommon birds, including Steller's jay, black-billed magpie, black-capped and mountain chickadees, broad-tailed hummingbird, black-headed grosbeak, Williamson's sapsucker, northern flicker, violet-green swallow, pygmy nuthatch, western wood-pewee, plumbeous vireo, Townsend's solitaire, MacGillivray's and Wilson's warblers, and western tanager. Blue grouse are seen along the road between Cub Lake trailhead and Fern Lake trailhead. Sharp-shinned hawks, red-tailed hawks, and golden eagles can be seen riding the air currents above.

I think I have seen mule deer every trip I have taken through Moraine Park. Sightings of elk, black bear, coyotes, gray fox, porcupine, and beaver are always a possibility. There are always small game such as muskrat, red fox and Albert's squirrels, rabbits, and ermine in the area.

Fern Lake Trail is one of my favorites for a day of fly fishing. Fern Lake is one of the better success stories for the recovering greenback cutthroat trout. The trout is reproducing and doing well in this remote lake. It is a solid 5 miles in – watch for Fern Falls and Marguerite Falls.

## Wild Basin

### Location

From Estes Park, take Highway 7 south about 20 miles to the Wild Basin entrance (it is well marked). Along the way, notice access to Lily Lake which is a great waterfowl birding spot during the spring and fall migrations. The fishing can be good at times, but the greenback cutthroats here can turn very selective due to the fishing pressure, because of its close proximity to the highway. There is another access to the park via the Long's Peak Trailhead. It is one of the well-used routes to the tallest peak in RMNP at 14,259 feet.

## Wildlife

One of the first things you will notice about the Wild Basin entrance is the North Fork of the St. Vrain River. It is a reasonably good-sized park, willow choked at the stream bottom, creating an excellent riparian habitat. I wish I could tell you how many wild trout have put a bend in my fly rod here, but there are too many to remember. A solid mix of brown, rainbow, brook, and cutthroat trout inhabit this meandering stream. Again, due to the fairly easy access, the trout can become elusive and bolt at the slightest misstep.

There is a convenient picnicking area on the west side of Copeland Lake, not only for a quick bite to eat but for birding itself. Look for Steller's jays, chickadees, white-breasted nuthatches, northern flickers, green-tailed towhees, and red-naped sapsuckers. There has been a dusty flycatcher nest right in the picnic area. There should be a number of crumb-grabbing chipmunks moving about the picnic area; remember though, feeding the wildlife is not allowed.

Across the road from the picnic area and to the west, a visible trail can be followed along the edge of the willows. This is one of the most dependable places in RMNP to see black swifts. There can be a number of swallows in the area also. The trail leads you by several small gravel ponds where a number of ducks may be seen. Watch for spotted sandpipers and other birds stopping in for a splash of water. Mountain chickadees, western tanagers, yellow-rumped warblers and MacGillivray's warblers are a few to be found here. Always keep an eye open for dark-eyed juncos, Lincoln's sparrows and Wilson's warblers flitting in and out of the willows. American dippers frequent the stream and red-tailed hawks hunt this area from above.

Beavers and muskrat den up in the stream bottom, especially in the short oxbow on the north side of the main channel a few hundred yards from the picnic area. You should see remnants of beaver activity all along the streams riparian boundaries. Most wildlife will be hard to notice because of the dense growth in the area, however they are there. Don't be surprised if a deer, raccoon, porcupine, ermine, or bunny bolts right under your feet. As my daughter and I were leaving the area after an afternoon of hiking and photography, we were delighted to see a wild turkey pecking the road side for newly sprouted grasses. The Merriam's turkey is a very spooky bird and our attempts for a photo only produced a faintly recognizable blurry image. Along the foot trail to Cascade Falls on Cony Creek, we encountered six doe mule deer, and got some great close ups of them browsing the hillside.

Another main attraction to the Wild Basin area is the abundance of trailheads. These trailheads lead you into the heart of a truly wild basin. Close up views of Ouzel Peak, Isolation Peak, and Tanima Peak are available. Finch Lake Trail heads to said lake, Bluebird Lake Trail takes you by Ouzel Falls as it heads to Ouzel Lake and Bluebird Lake, which sits at the base of Ouzel Peak. Thunder Lake Trail continues along the North Fork of the St. Vrain on its way to Thunder Lake at the base of Tanima Peak. All of these trails are vigorous hikes, gaining a couple thousand feet in elevation, and require thoughtful planning. Water, snacks, rain gear, and a solid, comfortable pair of boots will make the journey more enjoyable.

# Bear Lake Road

## Location

From the Beaver Meadows Entrance (south entrance), continue west about a mile to the Bear Lake Road. Turn left and carry on for about 10 miles to Bear Lake. Along the way, accesses to Hollowell Park, Glacier Basin, and Sprague Lake are available. Trailheads into the backcountry include Mill Creek Basin, Storm Pass, Bierstadt Lake, and Glacier Gorge. This area of RMNP has to be the most overcrowded with visitors. Parking areas are usually full by 9:00am and there is a shuttle bus that runs from the parking area at Glacier Basin to Bear Lake.

## Wildlife

There is always a possibility to see wildlife anywhere in Rocky Mountain National Park, but Bear Lake Road isn't one of the best. In my opinion, this is because it is so extensively used and the animals and birds are pushed back from easy viewing. The trails in and out of the backcountry should be two lanes to accommodate foot travel. The picnic areas do attract the occasional camp robber (gray jay), pine grosbeak, and mountain chickadee. Many of the park's special birds, such as northern goshawk, blue grouse, northern pygmy owl, Williamson's sapsucker, three-toed woodpecker, and red crossbill are present. Stay on the constant lookout to see any of these birds. Also keep an eye out for the cute little fur bearers. Colorado chipmunks, Albert's squirrels, snowshoe hares, and rock squirrel can be seen, but remember it is illegal to feed the animals and birds in RMNP. All bodies of water will have a few common waterfowl

*The boisterous pika*

birds and riparian areas should hold Wilson's warblers and Lincoln's sparrows. Glacier Creek can be accessed at several spots along the road and it provides good dry-fly fishing for rainbow, brown, cutthroat, and brook trout.

## Scenic Views

There are more scenic opportunities along Bear Lake Road and its trailheads than most places in the park. Excellent views of the mountain range to the west and the north face of Long's Peak can be had from the road and at the Bear Lake parking area. If a day hike in the backcountry is in order, I would suggest Glacier Gorge trailhead located at Bear Lake. A little over a half mile will get you to Alberta Falls on Glacier Creek. Another half mile or so up, the trail forks to either North Long's Peak Trail to the left or Glacier Gorge to the right. Both are challenging trails but the rewarding views of what most would call God's Country are worth it.

There is another trailhead at Bear Lake that takes route to Haiyaha Lake. This is a favorite of mine, not only for the jagged skyline of Hallett and Otis Peaks, but for the greenback cutthroat trout that swim the crystal-clear waters. I always take a fly rod when I head to Haiyaha. Large rocks are strewn about and it is very challenging to get to the lake and fish, but it is always worth it.

# Lumpy Ridge & Cow Creek Entrances

## Location

These are the last two entrances to RMNP on the east side. They are basically just foot trails into the park which are often overlooked by the auto traveling visitors. Locals, especially birders, that want to enter the park use these entrances often. From Estes Park at the intersection of Highway 34 and Highway 36, take the 34 Bypass about a half mile to MacGregor Avenue and turn right. You will pass the historic Stanley Hotel just before you reach MacGregor Avenue (the 1980 movie, *The Shining*, was filmed at the Stanley Hotel, and starred Jack Nicholson and Shelley Duvall). Follow MacGregor Avenue another mile and a half to the Lumpy Ridge Trailhead parking area. To reach Cow Creek Trailhead, continue on MacGregor Avenue (which is now called Devil's Gulch Road) another 2 miles to a dirt road called McGraw Ranch Road and turn left. The parking area for Cow Creek is about 3 miles at the end of this dirt road.

## Wildlife

Both of these areas are mule deer country. They love the steep rocky hillsides and the heavy cover of the ponderosa and spruce forests (as do mountain lions, bobcats, coyotes, and black bear). This area will hold a number of small game animals such as bunnies, mice, chipmunks and blue grouse – all table fare for the predators. Speaking of predators, the granite ridge is a great nesting area for raptors. Sharp-shinned hawks, red-tailed hawks, golden eagles, and prairie and peregrine falcons hunt this area, so keep an eye out for these great birds.

The birding can be extraordinary in both of these areas. The diversity of terrain gives way to a number of species. Riparian bottoms should hold red-winged blackbirds, common snipe, yellow-rumped warblers, Wilson's warblers, and song sparrows. Mountain chickadees, mountain bluebirds, red-breasted nuthatches, western tanagers, and olive-sided flycatchers can be found in the woods along with three-toed woodpeckers, hairy woodpeckers, red-naped sapsuckers and northern flickers, specific to the aspen groves. Cow Creek area can be one of the better places in the park to see the northern pygmy owl. Watch and listen for them early in the morning and late in the afternoon when they are more active. In the rock structures high on the ridge expect to see white-throated swifts, violet-green swallows, barn swallows, and common ravens. Again raptors abound in this area.

## Scenic Views

Lumpy Ridge is actually a huge granite ridge which could be considered the northern boundary of Estes Valley. The trail follows the southern side of the ridge giving way to spectacular views of the ridge. The Twin Owls are a rock formation near the east end of the ridge just as you start up the trail. They can be seen from the parking area also. There is also a chance to see rock climbers on the ridge, as it is very popular with that recreation group.

The highlight of the Cow Creek Trail is Bridal Veil Falls on Cow Creek. It is a little over 3 miles to the falls. I wouldn't walk into the falls with blinders on though, as the walk in is also appealing to the eye. There are a few open meadows giving to long range views of the mountain sides, both north and south. Starting at just under 8,000 feet, ponderosa pine, spruce, aspen groves, and riparian habitat rule this lower elevation of the park.

## Activities

In early October, the city of Estes Park puts together a weekend called Elk Fest. They have activities including seminars on the elk breeding season (the rut), elk management and biology, how to safely observe wildlife, and raptor information. There are elk-viewing tours departing every hour. For more information, contact the Events Office at 970-586-6104.

## Contact

**Rocky Mountain National Park**
1000 Highway 36, Estes Park, Colorado 80517
970-586-1206
www.nps.gov/romo/
**U.S. Fish and Wildlife Service**
www.fws.gov

## Fast Facts

**Getting There:** From Interstate 25, turn west on state Highway 34 to Estes Park. In Estes Park, stay on Highway 34 via the Highway 34 bypass and continue west to the Fall River Entrance. This is the main entrance to Trail Ridge Road. The Beaver Meadows Entrance and Rocky Mountain National Park headquarters and Visitor Center is found by taking a left on Moraine Avenue (also recognized as Highway 36) from Highway 34 in Estes Park. This is the best way to reach Moraine Park (upper Big Thompson River) and Bear Lake Road. Trail Ridge Road can also be reached by veering right before taking the left turn to Moraine Park.

**Activities:** Scenic drives, bird and wildlife viewing.

**Principal Mammals:** Elk, moose, mule deer, bighorn sheep, coyote, black bear, raccoon, porcupine, skunk, marmot, pika, beaver, cottontail rabbits, squirrels, ermine, muskrat, mink, and number of smaller game such as voles, and field mice.

**Mammals of Special Interest:** Elk, moose, bighorn sheep, and mule deer.

**Principal Birdlife:** Common waterfowl, woodpeckers, prairie and peregrine falcon, and golden eagle.

**Birds of Special Interest:** White-tailed ptarmigan, brown-capped rosy finch.

**Habitat Overview:** Riparian, aspen groves, spruce and ponderosa forest, and open tundra.

**Flora of Special Interest:** Columbine.

**Best Wildlife Viewing Ops:** Early morning and late evening when they are on the move from bedding to feeding areas. Wildlife can be seen from most public roads and foot trails.

**Best Birding Ops:** Winter is especially good for raptors; March and April begin the lower elevation migration of song and shorebirds; summer and fall for just about all others at all elevations.

**Best Photo Ops:** Early and late light for landscape and much of the day can be good for wildlife and birds. The fall colors are spectacular.

**Hunting Ops:** None.

**Fishing Ops:** Nearly all water is open except as posted. Greenback cutthroat is catch and release only.

**Camping Ops:** Five drive-in campgrounds; two campgrounds – Moraine Park and Glacier Basin – are on the reservation system. Aspenglen, Longs Peak, and Timber Creek campgrounds are on a first-come first-served basis. Backpackers may choose from over 200 backcountry campsites when they apply for their backcountry camping permits.

**Boating Ops:** None.

**Hiking Trails:** Over 350 miles of trails throughout the park.

**Motor Trails:** Main roads only.

## Bird List

### LOONS, GREBES

Arctic loon
Common loon
Pied-billed grebe
Horned grebe
Red-necked grebe
Eared grebe
Western grebe

### PELICANS, HERONS, ALLIES

American white pelican
American bittern
Least bittern
Great blue heron
Snowy egret
Green-backed heron (green heron)
Black-crowned night heron
White-faced ibis

### SWANS, GEESE, DUCKS

Tundra swan (whistling swan)
Greater white-fronted goose
Snow goose
Canada goose
Wood duck
Green-winged teal
Mallard
Northern pintail
Blue-winged teal
Cinnamon teal
Northern shoveler
Gadwall
American wigeon
Canvasback
Redhead
Ring-necked duck
Lesser scaup
Oldsquaw
White-winged scoter
Common goldeneye
Barrow's goldeneye
Bufflehead
Hooded merganser
Common merganser
Red-breasted merganser
Ruddy duck

### VULTURES, HAWKS, EAGLES

Turkey vulture
Osprey
Bald eagle
Northern harrier (marsh hawk)
Sharp-shinned hawk
Cooper's hawk
Northern goshawk
Swainson's hawk
Red-tailed hawk
Ferruginous hawk
Rough-legged hawk
Golden eagle
American kestrel (sparrow hawk)
Merlin (pigeon hawk)
Peregrine falcon (duck hawk)
Prairie falcon

### GROUSE, PTARMIGAN

Chukar
Ring-necked pheasant
Blue grouse
White-tailed ptarmigan
Sage grouse
Wild turkey
Northern bobwhite

### RAILS, COOTS, CRANES

Virginia rail
Sora
Common moorhen (common gallinule)
American coot
Sandhill crane

## SHOREBIRDS

Semipalmated plover
Killdeer
American avocet
Greater yellowlegs
Lesser yellowlegs
Solitary sandpiper
Willet
Spotted sandpiper
Long-billed curlew
Marbled godwit
Western sandpiper
Least sandpiper
Baird's sandpiper
Common snipe
Wilson's phalarope
Red-necked phalarope (northern phalarope)
Pomarine jaeger
Franklin's gull
Bonaparte's gull
Ring-billed gull
California gull
Herring gull
Forster's tern
Black tern

## DOVES, PIGEONS, CUCKOOS

Rock dove (common pigeon)
Band-tailed pigeon
Mourning dove
Yellow-billed cuckoo

## OWLS

Flammulated owl
Eastern screech-owl
Great horned owl
Northern pygmy
Long-eared owl
Boreal owl
Northern saw-whet owl

## NIGHTHAWKS, SWIFTS

Common nighthawk
Common poorwill
Black swift
Chimney swift
White-throated swift

## HUMMINGBIRDS, KINGFISHER

Magnificent hummingbird (Rivoli's hummingbird)
Calliope hummingbird
Broad-tailed hummingbird
Rufous hummingbird
Belted kingfisher

## WOODPECKERS

Lewis' woodpecker
Red-headed woodpecker
Yellow-bellied sapsucker
Williamson's sapsucker
Downy woodpecker
Hairy woodpecker
Three-toed woodpecker
Northern flicker

## FLYCATCHERS

Olive-sided flycatcher
Western wood-pewee
Willow flycatcher
Least flycatcher
Hammond's flycatcher
Dusky flycatcher
Western flycatcher
Say's phoebe
Ash-throated flycatcher
Cassin's kingbird
Western kingbird
Eastern kingbird

## LARKS

Horned lark
Purple martin
Tree swallow
Violet-green swallow
Northern rough-winged swallow
Cliff swallow
Barn swallow

### JAYS, CROWS, MAGPIES

Gray jay
Steller's jay
Blue jay
Scrub jay
Pinyon jay
Clark's nutcracker
Black-billed magpie
American crow
Common raven

### CHICKADEES, NUTHATCHES, CREEPER

Black-capped chickadee
Mountain chickadee
Red-breasted nuthatch
White-breasted nuthatch
Pygmy nuthatch
Brown creeper

### WRENS, DIPPER

Rock wren
Canyon wren
Bewick's wren
House wren
Winter wren
Dipper

### KINGLETS, GNATCATCHERS

Golden-crowned kinglet
Ruby-crowned kinglet
Blue-gray gnatcatcher

### BLUEBIRDS, THRUSHES, THRASHERS

Eastern bluebird
Western bluebird
Mountain bluebird
Townsend's solitaire
Veery (willow thrush)
Swainson's thrush (olive-backed thrush)
Hermit thrush
American robin
Varied thrush
Gray catbird
Northern mockingbird
Sage thrasher
Brown thrasher

### PIPITS, WAXWINGS, SHRIKES

Water pipit
Sprague's pipit
Bohemian waxwing
Cedar waxwing
Northern shrike
Loggerhead shrike

### STARLINGS, VIREOS

European starling
Solitary vireo
Warbling vireo
Red-eyed vireo

### WOOD WARBLERS

Tennessee warbler
Orange-crowned warbler
Nashville warbler
Virginia's warbler
Northern parula
Yellow warbler
Chestnut-sided warbler
Magnolia warbler
Black-throated blue warbler
Yellow-rumped warbler (Audubon's warbler)
Black-throated gray warbler
Townsend's warbler
Black-throated green warbler
Grace's warbler
Palm warbler
Bay-breasted warbler
Black-and-white warbler
American redstart
Worm-eating warbler
Ovenbird
Northern waterthrush

Connecticut warbler
MacGillivray's warbler
Common yellowthroat
Hooded warbler
Wilson's warbler (pileolated warbler)
Yellow-breasted chat

## TANAGERS

Hepatic tanager
Scarlet tanager
Western tanager

## GROSBEAKS, BUNTINGS, SPARROWS

Rose-breasted grosbeak
Black-headed grosbeak
Lazuli bunting
Green-tailed towhee
Rufous-sided towhee
American tree sparrow
Chipping sparrow
Clay-colored sparrow
Brewer's sparrow
Vesper sparrow
Lark sparrow
Sage sparrow
Lark bunting
Savannah sparrow
Fox sparrow
Song sparrow
Lincoln's sparrow
White-throated sparrow
White-crowned sparrow
Harris' sparrow
Dark-eyed junco

## BLACKBIRDS, MEADOWLARKS, ORIOLES

Bobolink
Red-winged blackbird
Western meadowlark
Yellow-headed blackbird
Rusty blackbird
Brewer's blackbird
Common grackle
Brown-headed cowbird
Northern oriole (Bullock's oriole)

## FRINGILLID FINCHES

Rosy finch (brown-capped rosy finch)
Pine grosbeak
Cassin's finch
House finch
Red crossbill
White-winged crossbill
Common redpoll
Pine siskin
Lesser goldfinch
American goldfinch
Evening grosbeak

## OLD WORLD SPARROWS

House sparrow (English sparrow)
(Bird list courtesy U.S. Department of the Interior / U.S. Geological Survey)

## Mammal List:

Pronghorn antelope
Bison
Bighorn sheep
Coyote
Gray wolf (transplanted)
Gray fox
Red fox
Beaver
Moose
Elk
Mule deer
White-tailed deer
Southern red-backed vole
Sagebrush vole
Long-tailed vole
Montane vole
Bushy-tailed woodrat
Mexican woodrat
Muskrat
Rock mouse

Deer mouse
Heather vole
Porcupine
Mountain lion
Lynx (transplanted)
Bobcat
Northern pocket gopher
Snowshoe hare
White-tailed jackrabbit
Nuttall's cottontail
Wolverine
River otter
Marten
Striped skunk
Ermine
Long-tailed weasel
Mink
Western spotted skunk
Badger
Pika
Raccoon
Yellow-bellied marmot
Abert's squirrel
Wyoming ground squirrel

Golden-mantled ground squirrel
Rock squirrel
Least chipmunk
Colorado chipmunk
Uinta chipmunk
Chickaree
Masked shrew
Pygmy shrew
Merriam's shrew
Montane shrew
Dwarf shrew
Water shrew
Black bear
Western jumping mouse
Big brown bat
Silver-haired bat
Hoary bat
Long-eared myotis
Small-footed myotis
Little brown bat
Long-legged myotis
Townsend's big-eared bat

## Accommodations

### Columbine Inn
1540 Big Thompson Avenue, Estes Park, CO 80517
970-586-4533
www.estescolumbineinn.com

### Boulder Brook on Fall River
1900 Fall River Road, Estes Park, CO 80517
970-586-0910 or 800-238-0910
www.boulderbrook.com

### Rapids Lodge & Restaurant
209 Rapids Lane, Grand Lake, CO 80447
970-627-3707

*Common wildflowers of the Rocky Mountains*

# Scenic Byways

## Guanella Pass

The Guanella Pass Scenic Byway is a 22-mile byway from Georgetown to Grant. It is an impressive hour drive that tops out at 11,669 feet on Guanella Pass. It is passable most of the year and could only get better in years to come as paving work repairs the road. From Denver, take Interstate 70 to Georgetown. From Georgetown, take County Road 381 to begin the byway.

Again, I would think a drive in mid-September would be best because of the colorful aspen trees. The road follows the South Fork of Clear Creek up the north face and Duck Creek, which in turn flows into Guanella Creek on the south face. At the top – well above the timberline – this old logging road has extraordinary views of Mount Bierstadt and Mount Evans (both over 14,000 feet) to the east and Argentine Peak and Mount Wilcox to the west.

This drive demonstrates a prime example of the Rocky Mountain environment. The byway passes through a succession of diverse ecosystems. The lower elevations are lush with thick stands of spruce, fir, and aspen growing along the tumbling creeks. Nearer the top, the landscape opens into expansive meadows where beavers start to do their work. This is great riparian habitat for nesting birds and the livelihood of many animals. At the top, the fragile tundra exists almost unscathed. This is a barren wonderland (I often wonder how anything lives here) that bears a minutia of succulent grasses and flowers that doggedly renew every spring.

Watch for our state animal, the bighorn sheep, near the top during the summer months. Bighorns are often seen right along Interstate 70 between Idaho Springs and Georgetown year round. Mountain bluebirds, American pipits, and the common crow are seen above timberline, while the elusive ptarmigan remains a ghost, even though it is one of the best areas in the state to see them. Lower elevations will generate sightings of mountain chickadees, downy woodpeckers, Steller's jays, and grosbeaks. I have also spotted several dark-eyed juncos in the pines. There are many small lakes along the byway that draw in waterfowl. Deer, elk, snowshoe hare, coyotes, and squirrels are common sightings.

As mentioned previously, this byway is a blueprint of the typical settings found throughout the Rocky Mountains in Colorado. And it is not uncommon to see the differences on relatively short drives because of the abrupt elevation changes.

This old mining area boasts two of the state's best-preserved Victorian towns – Georgetown and Silver Plume – where many abandoned mines and structures can be viewed.

## Contact

**Clear Creek County Chamber & Tourism Bureau**
P.O. Box 100, Idaho Springs, CO  80476
303-567-4660
www.clearcreekcounty.org

*Evening grosbeak*

# Lariat Loop

The Lariat Loop Scenic Byway runs 40 miles and is Colorado's only byway that travels through an urban environment. The byway starts at the intersection of US Highway 6 and 68 Road in Golden. Take 68 Road, also known as Lookout Mountain Road, southwest over Lookout Mountain to US Highway 40. Go west on Highway 40 to Interstate 70 at Genesee. Take westbound I-70 to Exit 252 (the Evergreen exit) and connect with CO Highway 74 to the town of Evergreen. Continue the loop on Highway 74 beside Bear Creek to Morrison. Take Highway 26 north from Morrison back to Highway 6. Plan about two hours drive time as the byway is filled with winding roads and speed limits are in the 30s and 40s.

The Lariat Loop is a combination of two historic routes: the Lariat Trail Scenic Mountain Drive ascending Lookout Mountain and the Bear Creek Canyon Scenic Mountain Drive. In combination, these routes were part of several of the "scenic circles" developed and promoted by officials from Denver from 1915 to the 1920s to help Coloradans experience the mountains in proximity to the Denver metropolitan area. These roadways were designated to the National Register of Historic Places in 1976. In August 2002, the Lariat Loop route achieved formal status as Colorado's 24th Scenic & Historic Byway.

The start of this byway is an amazing drive up Lookout Mountain Road, which follows the historic Lariat Trail. The original trail, which zigzags for 4.6 road miles, was built by the tenacious "Cement Bill" Williams. It rises 2,000 feet to the Buffalo Bill Museum and Grave, and is quite the engineering feat. Cement Bill moved to Golden from Deadwood, South Dakota in 1901 and became a successful cement contractor of bridges, sidewalks, and reservoirs.

Using his own savings, Bill surveyed Lookout Mountain in 1910 and completed a 2-foot-wide switchback trail up to Windy Point in 1911. His stamina and perseverance must have been impressive, because Adolph Coors contributed $1,000 and Charles Boettcher donated materials from his Portland Cement Company. Other firms donated tools, a ditcher, and pipeline. His gritty fortitude paid off when he completed the Lariat Trail in 1914. Denver placed the road on the National Register of Historic Places as part of their Mountain Park System developed from 1912 to the 1930s.

The Buffalo Bill Museum and Grave is the final resting place of William F. "Buffalo Bill" Cody. By his request, Buffalo Bill was buried on Lookout Mountain in 1917,

*The gateway to the Lariat Loop Scenic Byway*

overlooking the Great Plains and the Rockies. The museum includes exhibits about Buffalo Bill's life and the Wild West shows, Indian artifacts, Western art and firearms. Also check out the Lookout Mountain Nature Center and the Boettcher Mansion. Lookout Mountain Nature Center is far more than a building; it is a 110-acre park with trails winding through towering ponderosa pines and open meadows. It is also wildlife habitat where the Abert's squirrel, deer, songbirds, and more can be seen.

The byway continues down to Highway 40 and then onto I-70. Chief Hosa Lodge and Campground can be found at Exit 253. The south campground opened in 1913 as "America's first motor camping area". Historic Chief Hosa Lodge was built in 1918 and has the distinction of being Colorado's oldest standing stagecoach stop, built in 1857. The nearby Genesee Mountain Park has access to pastureland with buffalo and elk herds. There are many shaded, wooded sites, some with privacy. Address: 27661 Genesee Drive, Golden, CO, 80401

Continuing on, Exit 252 connects with Highway 74. In Bergen Park, turn right on Soda Creek Road to find the Humphrey Memorial Park and Museum. It is located on 43 unspoiled acres of mountain and meadows, offering a soothing setting for visitors. Outdoor summer events include the popular "Summer under the Stars" series which includes plays, concerts, dance recitals, poetry readings, a writer's festival and more. Our natural amphitheatres and English gardens create the ideal venue for summer cultural events.

Inside the museum, the Humphrey family's treasures are viewed just as they lived with them in this historic homestead. Each item that belonged to the family is still housed here nearly exactly as the last resident, Hazel Lou Humphrey, left them.

Continue south to the town of Evergreen. Look for the Hiwan Homestead Museum, historic downtown Evergreen, and Evergreen Lake and Nature Center. The 17-room Hiwan Homestead Museum is a log lodge which was placed on the National Register of Historic Places because of its unique construction. Hiwan's restored 1890- to 1930-era rooms illustrate a comfortable style of early mountain summer home living. Downtown Evergreen, at an elevation of 7,200 feet is surrounded by blue spruce and pine forests with a moderate climate offering relief from the hot summer days in the city below. Well established as one of Colorado's hidden treasures and a popular day escape, the Evergreen community offers an array of parks, art galleries, theatre, restaurants, entertainment, and more. Evergreen Lake is a beautiful setting fed by tributaries (primarily Bear Creek) from Mount Evans and is known for its all-season recreational activities such as boating, fishing, birding, iceskating, and concerts. It is bordered by mountain parks with miles of trails for hiking, biking, snowshoeing, and horseback riding. The Evergreen Nature Center is a project of the Evergreen Audubon Society.

The byway from this point follows Bear Creek to Morrison. Red Rocks Park and Amphitheatre is the next area worth visiting. Well known for its summer outdoor music concerts, it has welcomed the likes of U2, Bonnie Raitt, John Denver, Grateful Dead, Dave Matthews Band, R.E.M., Neil Young, Stevie Nicks, Steve Martin, and Jimi

*A common sighting at Red Rocks Park*

Hendrix. It is also a great place to visit if wildlife viewing, birding, and hiking are of interest. The Trading Post Loop hiking trail is 1.4 miles in length, and goes through the spectacular red rock formations. Some of the terrain is rough, so hiking boots are recommended. Red Rocks is also home to a number of wildlife species. Herds of mule deer are common and often visit Red Rocks in winter. An occasional mountain lion from the surrounding areas is seen in the park searching for deer and other smaller animals. Early mornings and at dusk, it is not unusual to spot a fox, raccoon, skunk, chipmunk, or squirrel (especially after a concert munching on the gourmet buffet of leftovers). A potentially dangerous inhabitant of the park is the rattlesnake. Though they are seen more frequently in the summer months, rattlesnakes do take advantage of the rocks for sun bathing in the early spring and late fall. Rattlesnakes are naturally shy, though they may become aggressive if they feel threatened. These snakes usually flee when they sense danger, however they are venomous and Red Rocks visitors are urged to use caution when hiking off the trails. Red Rocks, with its towering spires, is also home to a number of birds such as house finches, scrub jays, robins, and mountain bluebirds. The mountain bluebird can be identified by its slender beak, stout abdomen, and two-pronged tail. Males are sky blue and females are silvery-gray. In the winter, golden crowned sparrows and rosy finches are the main attraction. The American kestrel can be seen hovering over the park. This rust-and-gray-colored bird is in the falcon family and feeds on large insects, birds, reptiles, amphibians, and small rodents. Larger raptors are seen seasonally.

The byway turns north on Highway 26 and it would be well worth the stop at Dinosaur Ridge at the intersection with Alameda Parkway. The Dinosaur Ridge Trail is about 1.5 miles along Alameda Parkway and has hundreds of dinosaur tracks, a quarry of dinosaur bones, and interesting geologic features. To hike the ridge will take between one and two hours.

Continuing north towards the end of the byway, you will notice the entrance to Heritage Square. Heritage Square is a unique mock-up of a Western village with Victorian architecture and provides an affordable, fun experience for the whole family. There is an array of shops, Colorado's best alpine slide, go-cart rides, old-time photos, miniature golf, narrow gauge train, and a varied selection of food vendors. Rides operate weekends in the spring and fall, and daily from Memorial Day to Labor Day. The Heritage Square Music Hall features a fun evening with a family-style dinner followed by a theater act in audience-participation melodrama style. It is great fun.

The Lariat Loop is sure to please. Enjoy the legacy of the Old West cultural and historic landmarks. There are several open space parks to take pleasure in wildlife viewing and hiking our Front Range forests.

## Contact

**Lariat Loop Heritage Alliance**
P.O. Box 356, Golden, CO  80402
720-971-9649
www.lariatloop.org

*A nice bighorn sheep ram*

## Mount Evans Scenic Byway

The Mount Evans Scenic Byway is 49 miles total and climbs more than 7,000 feet in just 28 miles, reaching an elevation of 14,130 feet. At the summit, a view of the entire Front Range, especially Denver, is presented. From Denver, take Interstate 70 to Idaho Springs and take Clear Creek CR 103 south to the interchange with Mount Evans Road, also known as CR 5. Turn right and check in at the toll station to continue to the top of Mount Evans. (See Mount Evans chapter for more information.) A new extension was recently added to the byway from Echo Lake to Bergen Park via CR 103 and Jefferson County Road 66. Make sure to check out the bristle cone pine forest at Mount Goliath Natural Area. The weather is volatile so be prepared for wind, rain, lightning, snow, and hail any day of the year.

### Contact

**Clear Creek County Chamber & Tourism Bureau**
 P.O. Box 100, Idaho Springs CO  80452
 303-567-4660
 www.clearcreekcounty.org

## Peak to Peak Scenic Byway

The Peak to Peak Byway is a 55-mile tour showcasing the Front Range Mountains of the Colorado Rockies. Established in 1918 this is Colorado's first and oldest scenic byway. This is a fairly short tour and could easily take less than two hours to complete. It would be wise to plan more time to take in the many possibilities to enjoy the scenery, recreation, and history of this area. For this illustration, the Peak to Peak Byway starts at the interchange of US Highway 6 and Colorado Highway 119 just east of Idaho Springs. It follows Highway 119 to the town of Nederland and then continues north on Highway 72. It follows Highway 72 to Highway 7 near the town of Raymond. Veer left on Highway 7 until the byway ends at the town of Estes Park.

The first stretch of the Peak to Peak Byway along Highway 119 follows the North Fork of Clear Creek on its way to one of the limited-stakes gambling centers of Colorado at Blackhawk and Central City. These historic gold rush towns have been renovated into small casinos and hotels. The twin towns of Central City and Blackhawk in Clear Creek Canyon west of Denver are so close, it's hard sometimes to tell where one begins and the other ends. At 8,496 feet, Central City nearly became the state capitol during Colorado's Gold Rush, which started here in 1859. Because of its newfound riches, it had more culture than Denver, and all that gold didn't hurt. The opera houses here sprung up by the early 1860s and the most enduring, the Central City Opera House still holds performances today, including a summer opera festival. Black Hawk has more gambling casinos than Central City, and many of the historic buildings are really historic storefronts attached to modernized structures.

*A storm a brewing over Longs Peak*

Continuing on Highway 119 about 10 miles, a right turn on Highway 46 sidetracks the byway and takes a visitor to Golden Gate Canyon State Park. With more than 12,000 acres, the park has miles of backpacking, biking, and horseback trails awaiting the recreation enthusiast. Streams and ponds will keep an angler busy. The dense forest and aspen-rimmed meadows host a number of wildlife and bird species. Golden Gate Canyon State Park offers two campgrounds with electrical hook-ups and tent sites. There are picnic sites and check out Panorama Point Scenic Overlook, where visitors can see 100 miles of rocky peaks along the Continental Divide.

Back on Highway 119, we'll continue north to the town of Nederland. This stretch of the drive is filled with wonderful views of the Continental Divide and a number of side roads heading west, leading to 4-wheel-drive and backpacking trails right under the Divide. High-mountain lakes and small streams abound. Barker Reservoir and the spillway to Boulder Creek are just east of Nederland and Eldora, a small ski resort, is just west of Nederland on 130 RD.

Now take Highway 72 north. There are a couple forest roads that head west, giving access to the Indian Peaks Wilderness Area. This is a no-motor area with access by foot or horse only. Trails are numerous as are high mountain lakes for destinations. This area is the part of the headwaters for Boulder Creek and the St. Vrain River. From the town of Ward, take 102 RD west to the Brainard Lake Recreation Area. The South Fork of the St. Vrain flows out of Brainard Lake and there are trails to Long Lake and Lake Isabelle above the timberline. There is good fishing here, both in the lakes and in the stream. Expect to start seeing elk and deer, marmots, and snowshoe hares. Mountain bluebirds, mountain chickadees, Steller's jays, gray jays, and hummingbirds are a joy to observe. There is a campground at Brainard Lake.

*Evening grosbeak, what a gorgeous bird*

About 7 or 8 miles north on Highway 72 is an area called Peaceful Valley and the Middle Fork of the St. Vrain River. There are two campgrounds and access to the Indian Peaks Wilderness Area. The forest is very dense here and provides a nice quiet spot on the road to stop.

Another 5 miles down the road is the intersection with Highway 7. Take a left and soon you will reach the small burg of Allenspark and your first clean view of the infamous Longs Peak. The 14,255-foot peak is the most notable on the Front Range north of Denver. The first entrance into Rocky Mountain National Park is at the Wild Basin pull-out just north of Allenspark. A major trailhead into the park follows the third fork of the St. Vrain. The North Fork of the St. Vrain River is an important drainage for the snowpack in RMNP (see Rocky Mountain National Park for more information). Down the highway a bit further, the East Longs Peak Trail can be found; a very popular trailhead for the hiker looking to put another "fourteener" under their belt.

Finally the byway ends at Estes Park. Estes Park is a fashionable mountain town with many outdoor activities, shopping, and the renowned Stanley Hotel. The main entrance into Rocky Mountain National Park can be found heading west on Highway 34.

## Contact

**Boulder Convention & Visitors Bureau**
2440 Pearl Street, Boulder CO  80302
303-442-2911

## Accommodations

**Arapaho Ranch Cabins**
1250 Eldora Road
Nederland, CO  80466
303-258-3405
www.vrbo.com/20685

**Silver Moon Inn**
175 Spruce Drive
PO Box 1879
Estes Park, CO 80517
800-818-6006

## Community Resources:

**Black Hawk/Central City Visitors and Convention Bureau**
303-282-8800 / 877-282-8804
www.visitbhcc.com

# Top of the Rockies National Scenic & Historic Byway

The Top of the Rockies National Scenic & Historic Byway is 82 miles in length and gives a visitor a look at the tallest mountain in Colorado: Mount Elbert. The second tallest mountain, Mount Massive, sits just to the north of Mount Elbert for a one-two wallop. At 14,433 feet and 14,421 feet respectively, it is worth the time and effort to come and see these behemoths. They are to the south and west of Leadville along Highway 24. At 10,200 feet, Leadville is the highest incorporated municipality in the United States. Due to its astonishing scenic beauty and importance in history, this route was designated in 1999 as one of only 53 roads in the United States as a national scenic byway.

The byway starts 6 miles west of Frisco at the intersection with Interstate 70 and Highway 91. Take Highway 91 south towards Fremont Pass. At the town of Leadville, take Highway 24 south to the end of this leg of the byway at the town of Granite. The northern leg of the Top of the Rockies National Scenic & Historic Byway starts in Leadville by taking Highway 24 north over Tennessee Pass towards the town of Minturn. This leg ends at the intersection of Highway 24 and Interstate 70.

The first leg of the byway on Highway 91 follows Ten Mile Creek, and the rocky peaks of the Ten Mile Range do not disappoint. One of my favorite views of the Rocky Mountains is along this highway at Clinton Gulch Reservoir. It is on the left hand side of the road with the 14,265-foot Quandary Peak set as a backdrop. Totally awesome!

After topping the 11,318-foot Fremont Pass, look directly to the east and check out the cluster of four 14,000-foot peaks. Mount Lincoln, Mount Cameron, Mount Democrat, and Mount Bross sit just inside the Continental Divide. Add to these peaks Mount Tweto and Mount Arkansas, where the headwaters of the lengthy Arkansas River are created. It doesn't look like much at this point, but the Arkansas River travels 1,450 miles across four states and becomes a major tributary to the Mississippi River.

The next point of interest along the byway is the historic mining town of Leadville. The National Mining Hall of Fame and Museum is located here, as are the Healy House and Dexter Cabin. These structures were a couple of the first buildings in town owned by mining and silver tycoons.

Head south on Highway 24 to continue along the byway. The landscape opens up into a wide river valley bordered to the west by the tallest mountains in Colorado. The impressive Mount Massive (the northernmost peak) and Mount Elbert (the southernmost peak) capture your attention immediately.

Side trips around the base of these peaks are plentiful. Check out Turquoise Lake, the National Fish Hatchery, and Twin Lakes Reservoir. Highway 82 heads west from the Twin Lakes area and heads toward the famous mountain town of Aspen. This is a breathtaking drive that takes you over the 12,095-foot Independence Pass. This is a narrow road towards the top and can easily give you a queasy stomach. This leg of the byway ends just south of the intersection with Highway 82 at the town of Granite.

The northern leg of the byway follows Highway 24 north from Leadville. After a short drive through Tennessee Park, the ascent over the 10,424-foot Tennessee Pass begins. You once again cross the Continental Divide at the top of the pass and drop into the Eagle River drainage, which is a tributary to the Colorado River. When the road levels out after the descent, draw your attention to the right-hand side of the road to Camp Hale. This area was used for training by the 10th Mountain Division during World War II. At the present time, it provides a very good stretch for trout fishing on the Eagle River. Two miles down from Camp Hale is FR 703, which heads up the Homestake Creek drainage to Homestake Reservoir. Again, fishing and camping are the main pastimes. More fishing access to the Eagle River can be found at the town of Minturn and at the intersection with Interstate 70 where Gore Creek flows into the Eagle. The byway ends here.

If these scenic mountains were not enough, your chance to see wildlife in this high country is very good. Much of this byway is above 9,000 feet, so opportunities to see bighorn sheep and mountain goat are above average. Mule deer, elk, and pronghorn antelope are common and if you are lucky, a red fox, coyote, marmot, or pica may cross your path. Bald eagles are seen during the winter and early spring.

One thing to remember about Colorado's 14,000-foot peaks – there is a trail to the top of each one of them. It is all-the-rage to be a member of the "fourteener club". Hiking and backpacking into the high country of this region starts in late June to mid-July.

## Contact

**Greater Leadville Area Chamber of Commerce**
 P.O. Box 861, Leadville, CO  80461
 719-486-3900 / 800-933-3901

**Top of the Rockies National Scenic Byway Committee**
 PO Box 603, Leadville, CO  80461
 www.topoftherockiesbyway.org/map.htm

# Trail Ridge Road

The Trail Ridge Road Scenic Byway is a 48-mile trip right through the heart of Rocky Mountain National Park. This byway is normally open from Memorial Day through October and takes about two to three hours. If you drove it straight through, it would take a little more than an hour but it is hard to take this drive without stopping for a photo or two. Cars slowing down along the roadway to view wildlife – primarily elk – also backs up the traffic. The byway starts at Estes Park on Highway 34 and ends at Grand Lake. It takes about 42 days most years to plow Trail Ridge Road, at a cost of more than $30,000.

Soaring to an elevation of 12,183 feet, Trail Ridge Road – originally built in 1938 – is the highest paved through-road in the country today. You will not find a road like this one anywhere outside of Colorado. Trail Ridge Road was designated by the U.S. Secretary of Transportation as an All-American Road – the highest level of designation – in 1996. It is one of ten America's Byways designated in Colorado.

There is an impressive 11 miles of road above 11,000 feet with views of several distant peaks and high mountain lakes in the background. At the 10,758-foot Milner Pass, the road tops the Continental Divide. Two of Colorado's major rivers – the Colorado and Cache la Poudre – start on either side of Milner where streamflows are separated Atlantic from Pacific. Visitors can take the short Tundra World Nature Trail from the Rock Cut parking area to get a closer look at the alpine plant life. At night, sky gazing is a popular past time on Trail Ridge Road, as there are no city lights to compete with the stars (see the Rocky Mountain National Park chapter for more in-depth information on activities, history, and wildlife.)

## Contact

**Rocky Mountain National Park**
  1000 Highway 36
  Estes Park, CO  80517
  970-536-1206

*The view above the timberline*

# Wildlife Refuges

## Two Ponds National Wildlife Refuge

The 72-acre Two Ponds National Wildlife Refuge is the smallest urban entity in the national wildlife refuge system. It is located in the city limits of Arvada.

Sitting in the middle of prime residential real estate, it took a huge effort from local citizens to save this unique site from development and urbanization. Their efforts contributed to the establishment of Two Ponds NWR in 1992. To follow suit with all national wildlife refuges, the goal for administrators of the site is to protect and

*A male goldfinch filling up on seeds*

enhance wildlife and habitat and provide opportunities for environmental education. Two Pond NWR is committed to providing a sanctuary of wildlife for all to enjoy. The Two Ponds Preservation Foundation and its volunteers continually improve and enhance the site to preserve the landscape and the habitat. The area is protected for migrant and resident wildlife alike. The interpretative facilities help visitors with wildlife viewing opportunities, photography, and environmental education.

There are several trails intertwined through the refuge to access much of the site. There are two main habitats within the refuge to explore. Basic grassland (short-grass prairie) with brome grass, thread grass, yucca, prickly pear cactus, and rabbitbrush dominates the landscape. Riparian habitat includes three ponds surrounded by cattails, rushes, and willows. Adding to the background is a substantial stand of cottonwood trees.

These short trails are easy to navigate and provide an opportunity to encounter 120 bird species, of which 22 species nest here. Each year Two Ponds NWR provides valuable environment and resting points along flyways for native and non-native birds. It is common to spot song sparrows, white-crowned sparrows, dark-eyed juncos, and red-winged blackbirds. Watch for young kestrels practice their flying skills. Bullock's orioles can be seen gathering grasses to make their unusual hanging nests high in the trees. Belted kingfishers, downy woodpeckers, northern flickers, blue jays, and the common goldfinch may be seen darting about. The ponds attract mallards, wigeon, Canada geese, swallows, great blue herons, and double-crested cormorants.

Watch the shoreline for bullfrogs and painted turtles.

Mammals are pretty much restricted to small game, but the occasional deer does pass through. Coyote, red fox, muskrat, raccoons, beaver, and bunnies find protection from the urban surroundings.

## Location

From Interstate 70 take Wadsworth Boulevard (Exit 269) north to West 80th Avenue. Turn left (west) and go about 3 miles to the east entrance. To gain access to the west entrance, continue west on West 80th Avenue to Kipling Street. Turn left (south) and go about a mile to the entrance. The entrance is available from the medical center parking lot. The east entrance is open from May through September. The west entrance is open year round, dawn to dusk. Call for information 303-289-0867.

## Contact

**Two Ponds National Wildlife Refuge**
  9210 W. 80th Avenue, Arvada, Colorado
  303-289-0867

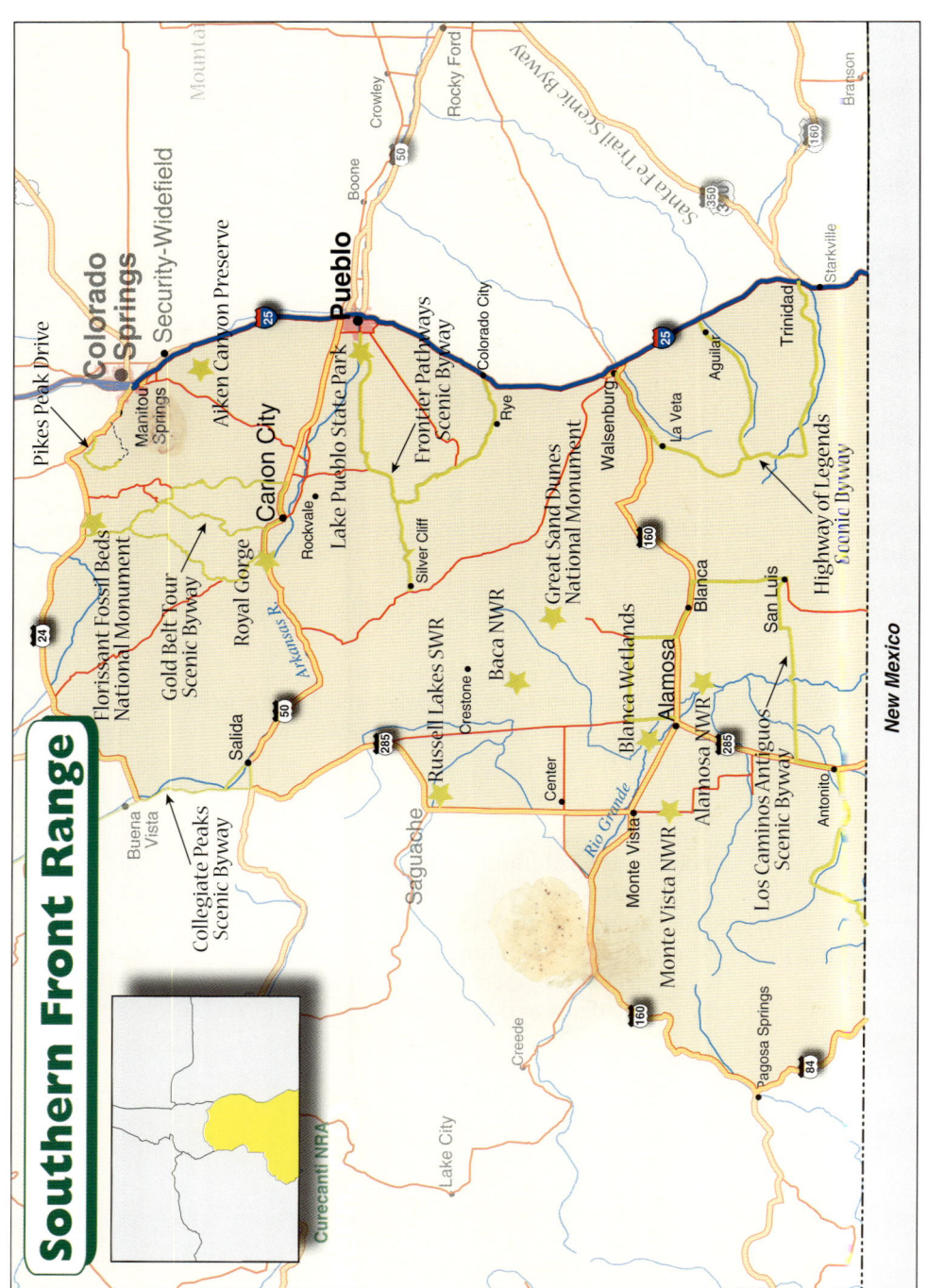

# Southern Front Range

# Aiken Canyon Preserve

**1,621 Acres; Front Range south of Colorado Springs on Highway 115**

## History

In 1991, the Nature Conservancy pursued the acquisition of Aiken Canyon as one of the last high-quality examples of the southern Rocky Mountain Front Range foothills ecosystem. They signed a 99-year lease, giving it exclusive rights to manage the conservation of 1,080 state land acres. The Nature Conservancy then acquired another 541 acres, bringing the entire Aiken Canyon Preserve to 1,621 acres. The preserve is a striking area of transition between the high plains and the gradual climb into the dense mountain vegetation. The conservation efforts include maintaining the canyon systems, foothills riparian systems, lower montane shrublands, local birds, and the tall grass prairie butterfly community.

The field station located at the entrance doubles as an educational facility for visitors and students. Given the relative proximity to Colorado Springs, the preserve is in a prime location for engaging the public. The Nature Conservancy recently revised the management plan. The Conservancy's mission to actively engage their neighbors and key public partners in conservation action in the landscape is key to their goal. However, they can always use more volunteers and researchers to assist with interacting with visitors when the field station is open, inventory and weed management efforts, leading field trips, maintaining trails and facilities, ongoing bird monitoring, and teaching school programs.

## Wildlife

This canyon area was named after Colorado's pioneer ornithologist Charles Aiken. Aiken first surveyed this region in the 1870s and homesteaded in 1871 in the area off Highway 115 now named for him. The first year he was here, Aiken collected 115 species of birds in the canyon. He was employed as a U.S. surveyor and enjoyed taxidermy and collecting information on wildlife and plant species. Today there are still over 100 species of birds seen in the area, making it a great destination for birders.

This was one of my most enjoyable hikes while collecting photography and information for this book. I wish I would have gotten there earlier in the morning, but

I was still blessed with the constant music of birds singing and squirrels barking. By the end of the 4-mile trail, I had seen several species of birds, including wild turkey, one hen of which I was able to get an awesome close-up as she moseyed by my concealed position.

There are two globally rare plant communities that provide shelter and concealment for all animals in the area. I found this out as I tried to photograph a number of birds including Western bluebirds, pigmy nuthatch, white-breasted nuthatch, Cordilleran flycatcher, and the mountain chickadee. The tight growth of pinyon pine, one-seeded juniper, and Scribner needle grass woodland proved challenging, as did the Gambel oak and mountain mahogany shrubland. You will also encounter rocky areas along the trail with yucca plants and cactus, so a good pair of boots is a must. This is also excellent rattlesnake habitat so watch your step.

The observant birder and wildlife enthusiast in this transition zone will also have a chance to see Cooper's hawks, golden eagles, northern harriers, sharp-shinned hawks, prairie falcons, northern flicker, and hairy and downy woodpeckers. When the wildflowers are in bloom, expect any number of hummingbirds to include black-chinned, broad-tailed, and rufous. Mammals could include black bear, gray fox, mountain lion, mule deer, elk, coyote, cottontail rabbit, spruce squirrels, and tuft-eared squirrels. Snakes and lizards are common.

*Pine squirrel*

*Cordilleran flycatcher with lunch for chicks.*

The Nature Conservancy has incorporated the use of interpretive signs along the trail to highlight important features and plant life. At just about the 2-mile point of the trail, an additional 3/4 mile path branches off and makes its way farther up the canyon for added exploration. The conservancy also requests visitors to leave pets at home while they enjoy the hike at Aiken Canyon.

## Location

It is located about 16 miles south of Colorado Springs on Highway 115. From Denver, take Interstate 25 south to Colorado Springs. Take Exit 135 (Academy Boulevard) west to State Highway 115. Continue south on Highway 115 about 12 miles to Turkey Canyon Ranch Road. It is located 0.1 mile south of milepost 32. Turn right (west) and drive 200 yards to the preserve parking area. The preserve is open year round, dawn to dusk, on Saturdays, Sundays, and Mondays. There is a Field Station/Visitor Center at the entrance to the preserve and it is open Memorial Day to Labor Day on Saturdays, Sundays, and Mondays from 10:00am to 3:00pm. During the rest of the year, it's open on Sunday only, from 10:00am to 3:00pm.

# Blanca Wetlands (owned by BLM)

### 10,000 acres; about 15 miles northeast of Alamosa

## History

These wetlands, that many locals still call "Dry Lakes", were not the thriving ecologically significant wetland complex they are now. The lowlands, marshes, and once-thriving ponds became dry due to water diversions and well pumping within the San Luis Valley. The heavy use of water for agriculture altered the delivery of water to the area and eventually, the former lake became a series of dry basins. These dry basins became part of a restoration effort by the Bureau of Land Management (BLM). Efforts began in the 1960s to rewet the 200 basins BLM identified as a priority within this massive 10,000-acre plot. Water was pumped in and artesian wells were drilled to replace the natural water source that was once there. As the area continued to flood with well water, the salt levels increased in the ponds, which in turn allowed incredibly high numbers of desirable insects, such as fairy and brine shrimp to thrive within the basins. These new food sources became the groceries for the hundreds of birds and amphibians. Currently, 13 threatened, endangered, and sensitive species have found refuge here. Globally, it hosts the only known population in the world of a distinct fairy shrimp.

    This restoration effort would not have been possible without the BLM's many partners including Ducks Unlimited, the Colorado Division of Wildlife, the National Fish and Wildlife Foundation, the Nature Conservancy, Trout Unlimited, Great Outdoors Colorado, the U.S. Fish and Wildlife Service, Intermountain West Joint Venture, Alamosa County, the Bureau of Reclamation, San Luis Valley Rural Electric Cooperative, Rio Grande Water Conservation District, and the Rocky Mountain Elk Foundation.

## Wildlife

Blanca Wetlands are most peculiar, when compared to the other wetlands I have been to. The shallow lakes are surrounded by whitish, alkali salt flats setting just west of Mount Blanca. At your first glimpse, the salty, almost-desert environment would not impress; however, the more diligent onlooker will soon see the plethora of birds, amphibians, mammals, fish, and yes, insects. Positioned between the Great Sand Dunes National Park and Preserve and the town of Alamosa, this complex is surrounded by sagebrush and jackrabbits. Not the usual locale for vibrant living wetlands. The area has the status as an Important Bird Area in Colorado and is a nationally significant area for shorebird migration.

The first item on the agenda to consider before heading to Blanca Wetlands: the area is closed for the protection of nesting birds from February 15 to July 15. However, when it is open it has to be one of the best birding spots in the county. Numerous ponds, both shallow and deep support essentially all the breeding and migratory water birds of the area. That is a long list. The highlights of the list that are present here are sandhill cranes, Wilson's phalarope, Clark's grebe and western grebe, redhead, American avocet, and white ibis. The marshes are loaded with thousands of sandpipers (significant numbers of Baird's sandpipers), hundreds of gulls, and dozens of pelicans. They find refuge at these wetlands along with the other 158 bird species found here.

The real ornithological jewel here is a breeding population (more than 20 pairs) of snowy plover, but a visitor will be lucky to find this elusive bird. Not only is this site one of the few remaining breeding areas for snowy plovers in Colorado, but the wetlands are closed while this bird is mating. They are about 6 inches overall in length and have nearly the same makings as a piping plover (which is very rare), but have black legs. They enjoy the barren sandy beaches of these wetlands.

Other species a birdwatcher may see here include the yellow-headed blackbird, song sparrow, marsh wren, mourning dove, belted kingfisher, swallows, and loggerhead shrike. Peregrine falcons frequent the area because this habitat supports such a massive number of nesting waterfowl and water birds. It is common to see a couple dozen hawks in a day and very likely a golden eagle will come over to case the joint.

Mule deer are very common to the area. Coyotes and fox run the area in search of bird eggs or an unwary rabbit. Jackrabbits thrive in the sagebrush surrounding the wetlands.

This amazing marshland hosts a number of reptiles and amphibians. Tiger salamander, Woodhouse's toad, northern leopard frog, a scary-looking snapping turtle, bull snake, milk snake, and maybe an eastern fence lizard are crawling under your feet. Locally, it is a key area for amphibian production. The deeper, more vegetated lakes are stocked with warmwater fish.

Before birding here, you might want to stop at one of the BLM offices to pick up a map of the area.

## Location

Take State Hwy. 150 south from the park to Road 4S at mile marker 3 (3 miles north of US Hwy. 160). Turn right (west), and take this dirt road exactly 8 miles to Baca Lane (Road 116S). Turn right (north) and go 2 miles to the entrance on the right (Road 2S).

The wetlands begin about a mile east down this road. Stop and pick up a wetlands map at the kiosk.

## Contact

**La Jara Field Office (BLM/USFS)**
15571 County Road T.5, La Jara, Colorado 81140
719-274-8971

**Del Norte Field Office (BLM/USFS)**
13308 W. Hwy. 160, Del Norte, Colorado 81132
719-657-3321

**San Luis Valley Public Lands Center (BLM/USFS)**
1803 West Hwy 160, Monte Vista, CO 81144
719-852-5941

*One of many ponds at Blanca Wetlands*

# Lake Pueblo State Park and State Wildlife Area

17,000 Acres; located immediately west of the city of Pueblo on the Arkansas River

## Wildlife

The western end of Pueblo Reservoir is a designated wildlife area managed by the Colorado Division of Wildlife. The area can be reached by taking the gravel road just before entering the state park's west entrance. Turn south to reach accesses on the north shore of the lake. Boats launched in the state park can enter the wildlife area, however, once inside the wildlife area it is regulated as a no-wake zone. The north bank is mostly short grass prairie in nature with narrow bays of water supporting riparian habitat with spots of pinyon, juniper, and greasewood shrub communities. Four rare plant species grow within the area: showy prairie gentian, round-leaved four-o'clock, Arkansas River feverfew, and Pueblo oonopsis.

Although best known for two heronries, the wildlife area supports a diverse mammal population of mule deer, white-tailed deer, bobcats, coyotes, badgers, raccoons, beavers, cottontail rabbits, jackrabbits, and prairie dogs. Reptiles like the rattlesnake, sagebrush lizard, and turtles love the warm climate of southern Colorado.

Upwards of 100 mating pairs of great blue herons can be found in the wildlife area. The double-crested cormorant uses the same areas as the herons to nest. There are literally thousands of these pesky fish eaters. American white pelicans are commonly seen in the open water as are western grebes, eared grebes, and gulls. The reservoir lays within the central waterfowl flyway, so any number of ducks and geese stop here yearly.

Raptors also frequent this area in great numbers. Bald eagles winter here as do golden eagles and osprey. A couple pair of ospreys have been nesting here since the early 1990s and their population is increasing. The rare ferruginous hawk winters here as do mountain bluebirds. Swainson's hawks, red-tailed hawks, prairie falcons, and American kestrel are seen quite often. Some raptors nest in the limestone bluffs around the lake as do thousands of cliff swallows. White-throated swifts and barn owls also call the cliffs home. I spotted and photographed my first canyon towhee in the brambles right along the north shore. There could very well be 100 to 200 mating pairs of this unadorned little songbird. Watch for yellow warblers, Bullock's oriole, rock wren, red-winged blackbirds, and sage thrasher, curved-billed thrasher, shrike, and juniper titmouse in the sparse woodlands around the lake. The short grass prairie holds a good population of scaled quail, and food plots of sunflower and millet are planted for wild turkey and mourning dove.

*Canyon towhee*

Flood regimes of the Arkansas River have been disrupted or altered by dams and dewatering. This has led to a lack of cottonwood regeneration in riparian habitats and invasions of tamarisk. Colorado State University is conducting a study in the area below the dam on a species of beetle that may be used for controlling tamarisk.

## Activities

As with most bodies of water in Colorado, the 4,500-acre Pueblo Reservoir is primarily used as a supply for agricultural use and city water, but this state park is one of the most heavily used recreational areas in the state. More than 1.5 million people visit here each year. With three large campgrounds (Arkansas Point Campground on the south side of the lake, Northern Plains Campground and Juniper Breaks Campground on the north side of the lake) totaling 401 campsites, this state park can accommodate recreational vehicles, trailers, and tents. Each site has a picnic table and fire ring. As mentioned, this can be a busy place so campground reservations can be made by calling 800-678-2267 or 303-470-1144.

Boating is very popular on Pueblo Reservoir. Two six-lane boat ramps are located at the Northshore Marina and Southshore Marina. Sail boating and sail boarding are accepted, while the warm waters of the lake make jet skiing and water skiing all the rage.

Fishing is also a great past time for visitors to the park. Pueblo Reservoir is an excellent fishery for walleye, wiper, and bass (both largemouth and smallmouth). A nice population of channel catfish, crappie, and a few species of sunfish, brown trout, and rainbow trout should keep any angler busy throughout the year.

Hunting is allowed in designated areas only during seasons set aside by regulators. Waterfowl are the primary species hunted.

## Location

Lake Pueblo State Park & State Wildlife Area is located west of the city of Pueblo on the Arkansas River and continues west for 11 miles. From Interstate 25 at Pueblo, take Highway 50 west a little over 7 miles to West McCulloch Boulevard. Turn left and go about 2 miles to South Nichols Road. Turn left and continue to the west entrance to the state park. The wildlife area can be accessed by turning right on a gravel road just before the west entrance.

## Contact

**Park Office**
 640 Pueblo Reservoir Road, Pueblo, CO  81005
 719-561-9320
 Office Hours: 8:00am-4:00pm, Monday-Friday
 Park Hours: 24 Hrs/day
 Boat Ramp Hours: 5:00am-11:00pm

# Pikes Peak Highway

### 10 Miles west of Colorado Springs

Pikes Peak is the most famous peak in Colorado; in fact, it is the second most visited mountain in the world. Only Mount Fuji in Japan is visited more often. Pikes Peak is basically the first visible mountain if one is traveling from the east. It was an especially well-known landmark from the popular southern routes across the Great Plains used in the early explorations of the west. It juts up from the plains, giving first view of the formidable Rocky Mountains.

Pikes Peak was surveyed in the early 1800s by Zebulon Montgomery Pike. President Jefferson dispatched Pike to determine the newly acquired Louisiana Purchase's southwestern borders. Contrary to popular belief, Pike did set out to climb the peak in November of 1806, but was forced back due to a blizzard (he should have known better than to try something like that in November.) The actual first recorded ascent of the mountain was by Dr. Edwin James. James, a doctor, botanist, and historian was led on the expedition by Major Stephen H. Long. They made it to the top in July of 1820. Major Long named the mountain after Dr. James, but the name did not stick. Pikes Peak soon became the official name, as shown by military maps of 1835.

However, the mountain did gain notoriety and was made famous during the 1859 Gold Rush. Covered wagons crossing the Great Plains filled with pioneers seeking riches were laden with the catchphrase "Pikes Peak or Bust".

Thankfully, today we are able to access the summit of the 14,110-foot Pikes Peak via the Pikes Peak Highway. This 19-mile road curls up the northwest face of the mountain, presenting a visitor with outstanding views and ample photographic opportunities. Only the last couple miles are unpaved. One travels through the thick forest of the montane zone up to about mile marker 10. At mile 13, visitors enter the treeless landscape of the alpine zone. The highest reaches of the peak are what most visitors come here to see. Over a half million people travel to the summit of Pikes Peak every year. Nearly 15,000 of those climb the mountain on foot via Barr Trail. This 13-mile hiking trail begins at the base of the mountain in Manitou Springs. Then there is the physically elite group that runs in the grueling Pikes Peak Marathon every August. It is a 26-mile round trip foot race up Barr Trail and then back down that draws thousands of runners from all over the world.

Another viable way to reach the top – and a one of its kind experience – is by train. The Manitou & Pike's Peak Railway (also called Pike's Peak Cog Railway) provides a 9-mile trip from about 6,600 feet in elevation to the summit of Pikes Peak. This train uses a cog or rack railroad, which uses a gear called a "cog wheel" that meshes into a special rack rail mounted in the middle between the outer rails. This unusual setup is needed to climb the steep grades (up to a 25-percent grade) to reach its destination at the top. Conventional trains can only climb grades of 4 to 6 percent. The main disadvantage of a rack railroad is its speed. They cannot go much faster than 25 miles per hour or they run the risk of derailment. Manitou & Pike's Peak Railway's top speed is about 9 miles per hour. This distinctive little railroad has been in business since 1889.

I find the top of this mountain quite unique. Unlike the succulent tundra scenery of Mount Evans and the trip over Trail Ridge Road in Rocky Mountain National Park, the top of this peak has a lunar look to it. Now I have not been to the moon, but I have been over most mountain passes in Colorado and the rocky, creviced landscape of Pikes Peak definitely has a look of its own. Not only is landscape unique, but since it one of the easternmost peaks in Colorado, the views of the city of Colorado Springs and the Great Plains below are nothing short of phenomenal.

## Wildlife

The trip along Pikes Peak Highway offers many opportunities for wildlife viewing and birding. The main attraction has to be the bighorn sheep, Colorado's state animal. The Pikes Peak sheep herd numbers are near the 300 mark. They are often seen from the road but do spend most of their time resting on inaccessible cliffs. Have a good pair of binoculars handy for distant viewing. After the fall rutting season, most of the herd will linger at or above timberline for the remainder of the year; however, the pregnant ewes will head for the lower elevation of the Dome Rock State Wildlife Area to drop their lambs in the spring.

Another high-elevation occupant of Pikes Peak is the yellow-bellied marmot. They are the largest of the ground squirrel family and are closely related to the woodchuck. You will recognize them by their distinct whistle, even if you do not see them. The whistle is an alarm call to warn the others in their social network of danger, so they have probably seen you. Marmots live in small colonies consisting of a male and several females. They hibernate in deep burrows much like the black bear; however, unlike the bear who mates in the summer, the marmot waits until the spring when a good food source starts to bloom.

Black bears are common to the area, but their nocturnal nature limits most sightings. Mule deer can be seen anywhere below timberline. There is a strong population of mule deer in the area due to the lack of hunting as well as excellent food sources. With the strong population of deer, the chance for its main predator, the mountain lion, to exist in the area is also possible. Good friends of mine live in Manitou Springs and have seen mountain lions on the trails they use for walking their dogs. The number of lion sightings on the Front Range has gone up considerably in the last ten years.

Birders will enjoy the possibilities on Pikes Peak as well. There always seems to be an extraordinary number of crows near the top of the Pikes Peak Highway. Also look for American pipits and mountain bluebirds.

This is not all that enjoyable, but it is a funny story. I was coming down Pikes Peak Highway and was required to stop at the Glen Cove parking area because my brakes were too hot. I would have kept going, but there is a ranger that requires everyone to stop and have the temperature of their brakes checked with some new fangled temperature gun. This stopping point is just below the last of the steepest, windiest stretch of the descent, so of course your brakes will be warm. There is a gift shop and food store, so economics may have something to do with the inconvenience. I complied and got out to stretch my legs. I noticed a couple of gray jays landing behind a rock, picking something up and flying to a nearby tree and finishing their meal. It looked like a photo op to me, so I got the tripod and camera set up and stalked my way in for a closer view. Sure enough the birds pretty much ignored me and continued with their routine. I got some nice photos and moved in closer to see what they were chowing on. Apparently someone couldn't handle the elevation change or the zigzagging road, because I almost stepped in their lunch that didn't make it through the entire digestive system (I told you it wasn't pretty!). I did spot a pair of Steller's jays, mountain chickadees, a batch of juncos, and a northern flicker while I was stopped.

*A pair of Rio Grande turkeys*

There is a self-guided nature trail at Crystal Reservoir that should provide ample opportunities to see waterfowl and shore birds.

I was also fortunate enough to spot a group of wild turkeys on my way down. I got a photo of a pair in a backlit situation. The caruncles under their chin are brightly colored by the blood-engorged skin.

Needless to say, the camera and the binoculars will get a nice workout on a drive up Pikes Peak. When stopping for photos, please use turnouts provided. It is also recommended to leave a note on your windshield if you plan to be away from your vehipcle for an extended period of time. Plan at least two hours for the round trip and make sure to check times when the gates close at the end of the day. During the summer months, the downhill gate is usually closed by 8:00pm.

## Activities

Besides the popular Barr Trail, the Elk Park Trail is another great spot for photography and wildlife viewing. This is a moderate-to-difficult 5.5-mile hiking trail starting at mile marker 14 on the Pikes Peak Highway. It skirts along timberline at 11,800 feet elevation, eventually connecting with Barr Trail at 10,200 feet. The trail is also used by mountain bikers and horseback riders.

There are three main fishing prospects along the highway: Crystal Creek Reservoir, South Catamount Reservoir and North Catamount Reservoir. Colorado fishing regulations apply; however, the 210-acre North Catamount is restricted to flies

*A rugged look on the road to Pikes Peak*

and lures only. Boating is by float tubes or craft propelled by oars or electric motors. Trailers are not allowed on Pikes Peak Highway, so boats must be brought in on top of your vehicle or in the back of a pickup truck.

Mountain bikers can enjoy using trails in the area of the reservoirs. Trailheads are available at the parking lots for the reservoirs.

## Contact

**Pikes Peak – America's Mountain**
P.O. Box 1575 MC 060, Colorado Springs, CO 80901
719-385-PEAK (7325)
800-318-9505

**Manitou & Pike's Peak Railway Co.**
PO Box 351, Manitou Springs, CO 80829
719-685-5401 or 719-685-9033
800-745-3773

## Directions to the Pikes Peak Cog Railway:

**Cog Railway Depot**
515 Ruxton Ave., Manitou Springs, CO 80829
From Interstate 25 in Colorado Springs, take Exit 141 (which is Highway 24) and go west 4 miles to Manitou Avenue in Manitou Springs. Go west on Manitou Avenue about 1.5 miles to Ruxton Avenue. Turn left and go to the top of Ruxton Avenue, about 0.75 mile, to the Depot.

## Accommodations

**Rocky Mountain Lodge and Cabins**
4680 Hagerman Avenue, Cascade, CO 80809
719-684-2521 / 888-298-0348

**The Inn at Cascade**
4675 Hagerman Avenue, Cascade, CO 80809
719-684-2194 / 800-507-4030

**Best Western Skyway Inn and Suites**
311 Manitou Avenue, Manitou Springs, CO 80829
719-685-5991 / 800-938-5991

# Royal Gorge Bridge and Park

## Introduction

The Royal Gorge Bridge, which is listed on the National Historic Register, was built in 1929 for an amazing $350,000. The bridge hangs 1,053 feet over the Arkansas River and is recognized as the highest suspension bridge in the world. This remarkable engineering feat is 1,270 feet across with a walkway made of 1,270 planks of decking wood. Nearly a quarter of those planks are replaced every year. The views and photo opportunities of the Royal Gorge and the Arkansas River from the bridge are incredible.

There is also a full-fledged train ride through the Royal Gorge Route Railroad. The welcome center is at 330 Royal Gorge Boulevard in Cañon City (888-724-5748). There are package deals that include the train ride into the Royal Gorge and entrance into the park, or the train ride and a rafting trip down the mighty Arkansas. There is even an upgrade train ride with a wine-tasting package.

## Activities

The aerial tram at the Royal Gorge – at 2,200 feet – is the world's longest single-span aerial tram. It starts about 1,100 feet above the Arkansas River and the ride will give you a full view of the Royal Gorge and a glimpse of the Sangre de Cristo Mountains.

The incline railway is a quick ride down the south-facing wall of the gorge. Going down over 1,500 feet at a 45-degree angle, the ride ends right at river level. The views are just as stunning looking up at the bridge as they are looking down into the canyon. Built in 1931, it is still recognized as one of the most complicated structures ever built.

The Royal Gorge Silver Rock Railway is a scale-model of "Old 424", an original 1893 locomotive. It is a mile-long ride through the park in open-air cars and is a great experience for children and parents alike.

The Royal Rush Skycoaster is one of the most unique rides in the state of Colorado. It is one of those "strap you in and start screaming" sort of rides, only this one drops you at 50 miles per hour and stops to let you hang momentarily over 1,200 feet above the Arkansas River. This skycoaster is one of only 87 in the world.

Burro rides are available for the kids. They are gentle and tame and would make for a memorable experience for the young ones.

The Arkansas River is a world class trout fishery and is praised by all flyfishers.

## Wildlife

Mule deer inhabit the pinyon/juniper habitat around the Royal Gorge Bridge, as do wild turkey. Pinyon jays, mountain bluebirds, flycatchers, goldfinches, ravens, and evening grosbeaks are commonly spotted in the park and surrounding area. While traveling the area it would not be unusual to see bighorn sheep, elk, and bald eagles. While spending time along the river, it is possible to spot great blue herons, ducks and their ducklings, and canyon towhees.

## Location

From Denver, take Interstate 25 about 70 miles south to Colorado Springs. Take Highway 115 about 30 miles southwest to Penrose and then take Highway 50 west. Continue west 17 miles though Cañon City to County Road 3A. Turn left and follow the signs to the bridge.

## Contact

**Royal Gorge Bridge and Park**
 4218 County Road 3A, Cañon City, CO 81215
 719-275-7507 / 888-333-5597
 There are several unimproved campsites in the area and lodging can be had in Cañon City.

**Comfort Inn**
 311 Royal Gorge Blvd, Canon City, CO
 877-477-8004

**Holiday Inn Express**
 110 Latigo Lane, Canon City, CO
 800-315-2621

**Hampton Inn**
 102 McCormick Parkway, Canon City, CO
 719-269-1112
 Guided fly fishing trips and general information:

**Royal Gorge Anglers**
 1210 Royal Gorge Boulevard, Cañon City, CO 81212
 888-994-6743

*An uncommon view of the Arkansas River*

100 — Great Places - Colorado

# National Parks and Monuments
## Florissant Fossil Beds National Monument

**5,992 acres; 35 miles west of Colorado Springs**

## Introduction

Even though much of the treasures this site clings to are still hidden beneath the surface, I found Florissant Fossil Beds National Monument very fascinating and thought provoking. This monument was set aside in 1969 to protect a world-class paleontological resource (fossils). The Florissant formation is dated at over 34 million years old and represents the latest Eocene epoch of earth history. This is approximately 30 million years after the age of dinosaurs and at least 33 million years before humans appeared. It is still one of the richest fossil deposits in the world.

How these fossils came to be is a prehistoric tale of life and oh, so sudden death. Around 35 million years ago, Lake Florissant stretched 15 miles through an ancient forested valley. Dominating the scene were towering redwoods, cedars, pines, and a colorful mix of hardwood trees like maples, hickories, and oaks. Lush ferns and shrubs thrived under this canopy. In this warm, humid climate, thousands upon thousands of insects existed. Numerous species of fish and mollusks inhabited the lake, and numbers of birds and mammals lived on its shores. Then a nearby volcano erupted. The explosion sent a devastating shower of ash, dust, and pumice across the countryside. Millions of tons of this debris cloud blanketed the forest and buried Lake Florissant with widespread death and destruction. Anything caught in this deadly cloud – insects, leaves, and fish that could not escape – died. Many fell to the lake bottom where they are buried today. It is believed that eruptions occurred again and again for perhaps as long as 700,000 years. Each time, fragments of life were trapped in a layer of volcanic sediments at the bottom of the lake. Eventually these sediments became finely layered shale and transform the buried plant and animal life into fossils.

The rich deposits discovered at Florissant Fossil Beds give us an unusually detailed look at life in ancient North America. Up to 1,700 different kinds of fossil insects have been found here, making it one of the most diverse insect fossil sites in the world. These fossilized impressions of prehistoric plants and animals are relatively young in geologic terms. Paleontologists have collected more than 60,000 specimens

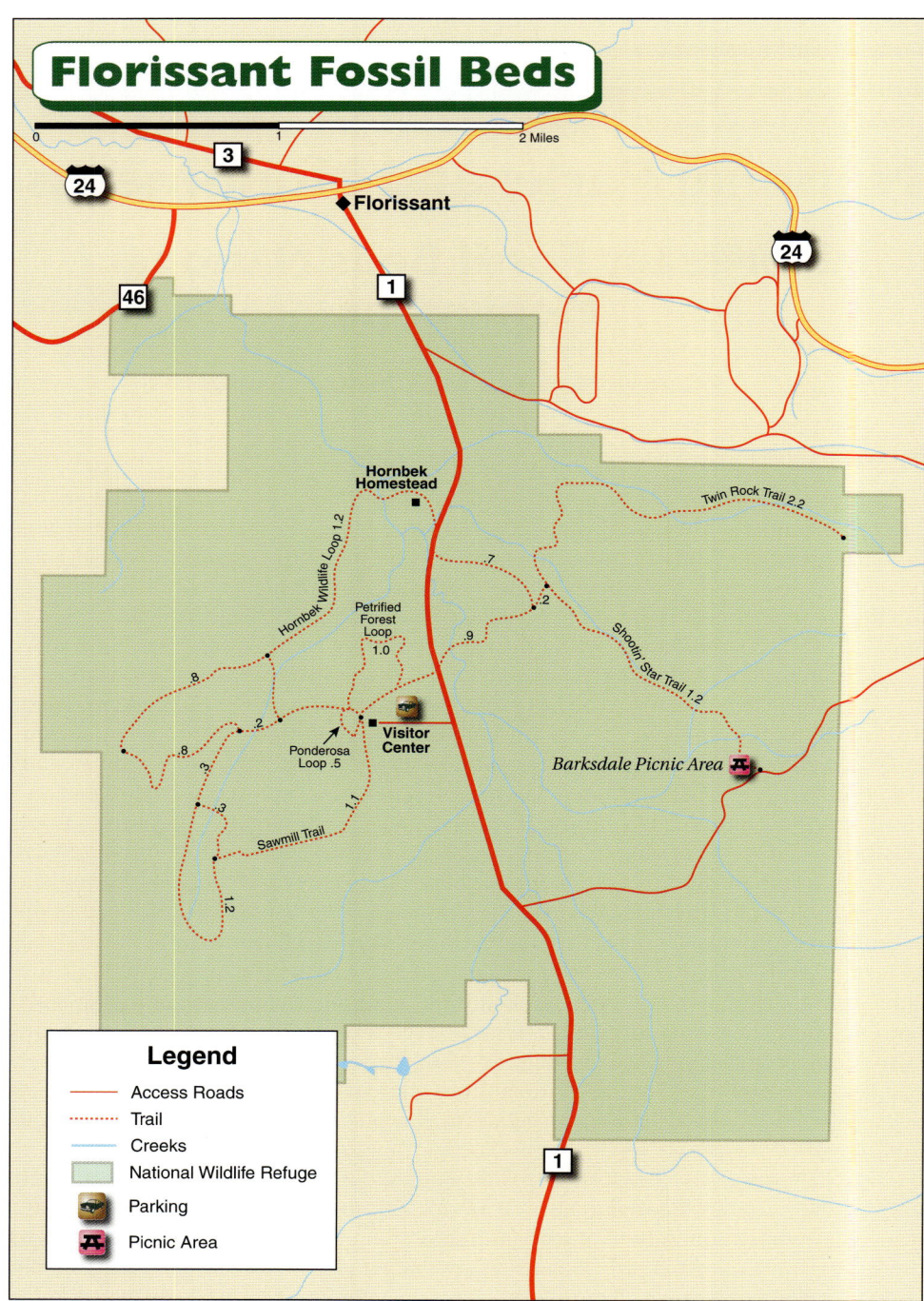

for museums and universities around the world. The fossils reveal, in significant detail, what life was like so long ago. Ever so fragile and tiny, it is amazing a creature like a butterfly can be preserved as a fossil that clearly shows its antennae, legs, hairs, and the pattern of its wings.

The massive petrified sequoia stumps are evidence that ancient life, at that point, had its giants also. They stand today where they were buried by volcanic activity millions of years ago. The stumps turned to stone as minerals seeped into the wood and gradually crystallized within the living tissue. The tops of these colossal trees (long since eroded away) were not protected by the layer of ash that preserved the rest of this site. Make sure to check out the petrified stump that has a pine tree growing out of it. The stumps have been reinforced with banding material to help keep them intact.

There are a couple trails that should be on your must-do list. A Walk through Time Trail is a half-mile loop trail where you can see the fossil-bearing shale and petrified stumps. The mile-long Petrified Forest Loop Trail leads to several petrified stumps, including Big Stump, the remains of a giant sequoia 74 feet in circumference. Both trails are wheelchair accessible.

More than 100 species of trees and other plants have been discovered at Florissant. The most common fossils found are leaves, but an incredibly diverse mix of fossil twigs, seeds, cones, flowers, and pollen grains also occur. Like the insect fossils, plant fragments have usually been preserved as life-size, color-enhanced impressions. The fossil record suggests that the ancient forest was not like any now in Colorado. In it grew many trees and shrubs whose closest living relatives are now found in widely scattered places such as the southeastern United States, Mexico, China, and South America.

Fossil bones, teeth, shells, and feather impressions reveal the existence of mollusks, fish, birds, opossums, mesohippus (an ancestor of the modern horse), and oreodonts (extinct pig-like animals). Future scientific explorations promise to unearth more of Florissant's "buried treasures."

Today, most of Florissant's fossils are exhibited and studied at various museums and universities. A small number are displayed in the park visitor center. Surface exposures of the paper-thin, light-gray fossil-bearing shale – which erodes easily – are limited and occur in only a few places. Fortunately many more fossils in yet undisturbed portions of the fossil beds are now sheltered by its federally protected status.

## Wildlife

At 8,400 feet, Florissant Fossil Beds National Monument falls into the montane life zone. The zone is dominated by ponderosa pine trees with some stands of spruce, fir, and aspen which provide superb habitat for large and small mammals alike. It is perfect cover for the elusive mule deer and elk, while providing food sources for the Abert's squirrels, porcupines, and pine squirrels, and birds like the Steller's jay and the diminutive mountain chickadee. Mountain lions are known to roam the area, as well as black bear, coyote, and bobcat; and pronghorn antelope are seen on occasion. The monument is rounded out with some riparian habitats and open mountain meadows. Everything from tiger salamanders to golden eagles hunting Richardson's ground squirrels and bunnies could be seen. The monument has more than 10 miles of trails to access not only the many fossil sites, but also leads to many encounters with wildlife.

The day I entered the monument, I was met by several Steller's jays and a handful of pine siskins. I immediately got the camera ready, chatted with the park ranger about the access trails, and was off with an itchy shutter finger. I am still not quite sure why, but I had a challenging time photographing the Steller's jay, not only here, but throughout my travels working on this book. Not to say I didn't have the opportunities, but this species of jay seemed to have hot feet and would not sit still long enough for me to get a focused image. The pine siskins on the other hand were a delight to work with. I also had an Abert's squirrel within range, barking and carrying on about something. He seemed oblivious to my movement, but when I would get set up, he would move and I had to reposition. This went on for some time, until he was so high in the ponderosa pine, there was no opening for a picture. I have been photographing wildlife for quite some time and you just never know how an animal or bird will react.

I was fishing with a friend of mine from Utah and we had this spotted sandpiper buzzing by us several times and finally landed in a rock pile next to the river. I popped

the camera out and got to a comfortable distance and sat down. In the next 10 minutes or so, this piper got closer and closer as I took image after image. It finally backed off and I went back to fishing. My buddy came up to me and said, "How did you get that thing to come so close?" I just shook my head and said, "Wildlife can be so unpredictable".

However, if viewing with a pair of binoculars is more important than photographing, this national monument is tailor made for you. The trails are easy to moderate in length and difficulty, and they progress through all habitats, giving generous opportunities for birding and wildlife viewing. Expect to see (in addition to previously mentioned) evening grosbeaks, spotted towhees, mountain bluebirds, northern flickers, downy and hairy woodpeckers, dark-eyed juncos, and cordilleran flycatchers. Red-tailed hawks also prey on the small game here. Ask for a trail brochure at the visitor center.

## Activities

Located within the boundaries of Florissant Fossil Beds National Monument is the Hornbek Homestead. The Hornbek Homestead was built in 1878 and owned by Adeline Hornbek, a rancher and single mother of four teen-aged children. The 1878 homestead recalls the life of early pioneers. Many were drawn to the region by gold, but Hornbek and her children, like many others, came to farm and ranch. The historic site includes the original cabin and a reconstructed barn, carriage shed, and root cellar.

Picnicking and horseback riding are enjoyed year round. Horseback riders must pay the daily entrance fee at the visitor center or possess an annual pass. Horseback riders must park their horse trailers at the designated pull-off, which is located on Lower Twin Rock Road. Pets are prohibited.

When there is enough snow, Florissant Fossil Beds' gentle meadows, hills, and trails can be a great place to snowshoe or cross-country ski. During the winter, there may be an opportunity to go on a ranger-guided snowshoe hike. Please call for more details or for current conditions, call the monument at 719-748-3253.

Florissant is a French word meaning "flowering". Throughout the summer, meadows in the area are filled with wildflowers and offer an excellent opportunity for photography.

Mueller State Park, Dome Rock State Wildlife Area, and Garden of the Gods are nearby sites that are worth checking out. A drive up Pikes Peak or a few hours of small stakes gambling at Cripple Creek are also within an hour's drive. Heading south on Teller County Road 1 from the intersection with Highway 24 is the start of the Colorado Scenic Byway, the Goldbelt Tour.

West of Florissant on Highway 24, anglers can find access to Elevenmile Reservoir, Spinney Mountain Reservoir, and the tailwaters of the South Platte River below the dams. These waters represent some of the finest fishing in Colorado. Catamount Reservoirs on Pikes Peak and Rampart Reservoir near Woodland Park are also good coldwater fisheries.

## Location

From Denver, take Interstate 25 south to Colorado Springs. Take Highway 24 (Exit 141) west 35 miles to town of Florissant. Turn left (south) on CR 1 and follow signs about 2 miles and look for the entrance to the visitor center on the right.

## Contact

**Florissant Fossil Beds National Monument**
P.O. Box 185, Florissant, CO  80816-0185
719-748-3253
www.nps.gov/flfo
The visitor center and museum is filled with informative literature and fossil exhibits are on display. Schedules of talks and other special activities are posted. Park programs and your own imagination will help you discover the present and bring the past to life. A picnic area is nearby. The park also offers environmental education programs for school groups. Call for details. The center is open daily 9:00am to 5:30pm in the summer and 9:00am to 5:00pm in winter. It is closed Thanksgiving, Christmas Day, and New Years Day.

## Entrance Fees

Individuals, 16 years and older is $3 and is good for 7 days. Anyone under the age of 16 years is free.

A local passport is available for an annual fee of $15 and is good for the cardholder and immediate family for entrance to Florissant Fossil Beds National Monument.

Federal passes such as the Golden Age, Golden Access, Golden Eagle, and National Park Passes are accepted at the visitor center until they expire. Please show them to the ranger at the visitor center desk. PLEASE NOTE: The above mentioned passes can no longer be purchased, as they have been replaced by the America the Beautiful passes.

Nearby Services: Lodging, restaurants, gasoline, and groceries are available in the town of Florissant, 2 miles north. Colorado Springs, with the range of facilities of a modern metropolitan area, is 30 miles east and easily reached on U.S. 24. Public and private campgrounds are nearby.

# Great Sand Dunes National Park and Preserve

### 150,000 Acres; South-central Colorado 34 miles northeast of Alamosa on Highway 150

Have the camera loaded and batteries charged because there are countless landscape photo ops at Great Sand Dunes National Park and Preserve. Over half of the expanded park is now grasslands, shrublands, and wetlands surrounding the main dune field on three sides. Geologically, this area is a critical part of the sand system. These areas of the park are currently seldom visited, so there are outstanding opportunities for solitude, wildlife watching, and the enjoyment of open space.

## History

As early as the 1920s, San Luis Valley citizens saw the need to protect and preserve the great sand dunes, so the works started to do just that. The government took notice and President Hoover declared them a national monument in 1932. Boundaries of the monument continued to expand in the 1940s, 1950s, and the 1970s. Then a huge chronological move came on November 22, 2000 when the national monument was officially upgraded to a national park. With the purchase of adjoining ranchland – adding 110,000 acres – it is now known as the Great Sand Dunes National Park and Preserve. At the same time, the government announced the creation of the new Baca National Wildlife Refuge adjacent to the Great Sand Dunes National Park and Preserve, which now occupies another large undeveloped area of the valley.

Both actions were made possible when the Department of the Interior reached agreement on acquisition and management of the 97,000-acre Baca Ranch. Some 31,000 acres of the Baca Ranch are part of the new Great Sand Dunes National Park and Preserve. With the addition of another 14,000 acres from the U.S. Forest Service, this once small national monument has expanded its boundaries to exceed 150,000 acres. The Nature Conservancy played a big part initially in the acquisition of the Baca Ranch before turning over the land to the National Parks Service.

A significant aspect of the creation of this new national park is its capacity to protect the overall ecosystem, including groundwater. The whole San Luis Valley profits from groundwater that is so close to the surface. Many have wanted this water, and the Baca Ranch became a focal point of this controversy. The citizens of San Luis Valley united in opposition to efforts to send Baca Ranch water out of the valley to neighboring states and Mexico. Water is such a complex issue in Colorado; it seems there is always a statute or law that needs to be examined. Through court fights and other efforts, the citizens of San Luis Valley successfully protected, for the short-term, the water beneath the dunes that protects the livelihoods of those in the valley. Valley citizens had also looked for a way to permanently protect the dunes and wetlands. This led to the enactment of the Great Sand Dunes National Park and Preserve Act. That law expanded the park boundaries and transferred land from the U.S. Forest Service to the National Park Service. It authorized the government to purchase lands and land rights within the monument. It required the federal government to follow state procedures in establishing water rights.

In layman's terms, the dunes were formed by the prevailing westerly winds blowing over the Rocky Mountains. The dunes probably started to form about 12,000 years ago, when the swollen Rio Grande spread sand across the San Luis Valley. The wind picked up the sand particles and then deposited those particles at the east edge of the valley as the wind rises to cross the Sangre de Cristo Mountains. For thousands of years, Mother Nature has been moving sand in the valley and the process continues today. The dunes are gradually enlarged by the wind and moving sand, which also changes the shape and sand patterns of the dunes daily. This is one place where footprints are definitely not a problem, unlike many desert parks of the Southwest where the delicate sandy soil is easily damaged by visitors.

## Wildlife

In such close proximity to the Sangre de Cristo Mountains, the land included in the Great Sand Dunes National Park and Preserve is home to many wildlife species. Opportunities for wildlife photography are abundant here. Elk frequent the park especially in the winter and early spring as they move from the cover of the foothills to the valley floor for water and food. Deer and pronghorn antelope can be seen every day along the roads in the park. Expect to see bison, coyote, porcupine, thirteen-lined ground squirrel, a jackrabbit or two, cottontail rabbit, an occasional bighorn sheep, red or gray fox, black bear, and beaver, and raccoon will show up when you least expect it. And if you are really lucky, a mountain lion or bobcat might expose its presence. In summer, look closely for miniature short-horned lizards among the grasses. Their camouflage resembles the sandy soil, so you may not see one until it moves. Please do not try to pick up this protected species. Migratory fowl in the park are sandhill crane, Canada goose, gadwall, American wigeon, mallard, blue-winged teal, cinnamon teal, northern shoveler, northern pintail, and green-winged teal. Raptors in the park include osprey, bald eagle, northern harrier, Swainson's hawk, American kestrel, and prairie falcon. There are number of blue grouse, white-tailed ptarmigan, and wild turkey. With smaller water and song birds calling the park home, the music of the wild abounds here.

The dunes themselves are not a haven for tons of flora or fauna, but you will find some 20 species of plants, pinyon pine and juniper forests. The geography of the preserve ranges from mountain tundra and pine forest to wetlands and desert, sheltering many endemic species.

Here is a little entomology:

The Great Sand Dunes tiger beetle, the best known of these endemics, is one of at least seven insect species endemic only to the Great Sand Dunes. The circus beetle is also endemic to the sand dunes. Its specific name, *hirtipennis*, means "hairy wings". If there is 'fuzz' on its back, you're observing one of these endemic circus beetles. Werner's antlike flower beetle is a very tiny, light yellowish-brown beetle. When I say tiny, I mean tiny. It is not much larger than the period at the end of this sentence. Antlike flower beetles apparently feed on dead-insect parts which have been blown into small depressions in the sand. The beetle allows itself to be blown into the depressions and actively forages on the debris. Triplehorn's antlike flower beetle is also a tiny beetle which looks similar to the Werner's, but is slightly larger. It prefers only the most barren dunes. It is easily observed on the bare dune ridges as one approaches the high dunes. The Hister beetle is tiny, shiny black, and globe shaped. Hister beetles are found in the grassy margins of the sand dunes. The adults are scavengers, while the larvae (caterpillars) are predatory, probably preying on weevils. The noctuid moth is pale yellow, and its wingspan is about 1.5 inches. Adults can be found in the scantly vegetated areas during the day, and are attracted to light. Not much more is known about this particular moth. The robber fly has been found in the Great Sand Dunes and surrounding habitat. It is one of the largest insects documented at almost a full inch. Robber flies do not seem to have

*American bison*

a preference for a particular type of sandy habitat; they have been encountered in sand-grass, sand-shrub, and even bare sand environments. Robber flies are often observed foraging on other flying insects (wasps, bees, and flies) during the heat of the day; after all crawling insects have taken cover from the extreme heat of the sand. The giant sand treader camel cricket is perhaps Great Sand Dunes' best-known insect. The giant sand treader camel cricket is not endemic to the dunes, although it was originally thought to be. The sand treader camel cricket was originally described from the Great Sand Dunes in 1962, but recently was found to inhabit other sandy ecosystems in other states. It is about 1.5 inches long and is omnivorous.

## Activities

Just past the visitor center on Highway 150, turn left to the designated parking area and main access point to the sand dunes. There are no roads or official trails into the dunes, so exploration is limited to hiking. It is acceptable to walk anywhere in the dune field and one popular target is the top of the High Dune (a 650-footer), which is only half of a mile from the parking area. Medano Creek runs at the base of the sand dunes and must be crossed to enter the dunes. It may or may not be running, so be prepared for your feet to get wet. Still, the journey takes up to one hour if you're in shape and somewhat longer if you take your time and rest every so often. The soft, ever-shifting sand, presents a case of one step up, half a step sliding back down. The view from the top is spectacular though, once it is reached. It looks like the tallest dune until you get to the top, then directly to the west Star Dune (a 750-footer) stands out as the tallest dune in North America. However, once on top it is easier to walk along sand ridges, rather than up the side of the dunes. Carry water and snacks, take rain gear, and watch out for lightning in the summer.

The dunes are a great place for children. I watched several youngsters with tubes and disks, normally used in the snow, sliding down the sand having a great time. Parents beware – the kids were having a tough go of it getting their rides back to the top of the dunes, so be ready to help out. The park can get very crowded in summer but a more tranquil, almost eerily quiet experience awaits those willing to walk a little farther into the sandy setting. The surface temperature of the sand can rise to over 140 degrees Fahrenheit, much too hot for barefoot walking. A comfortable, at least ankle high boot is recommended. Low-top tennis shoes are comfortable but they will fill with sand and comfort becomes suspect. There are open air showers to rinse the sand off upon returning to the parking/picnic area.

Medano Creek is another amazing feature of the Great Sand Dunes. It is a small stream fed by melting snow that only flows during spring and early summer. Its headwaters are in the Sangre de Cristo Mountains and it flows the length of the east edge of the dunes. For several hundred yards, the creek flows across a flat sandy area many meters wide. The clear, warm water constantly changes course and intensity, and moves in babbling wave-like ripples across the sand. One can be standing in a fast-moving current over a foot deep and then suddenly the water will stop and flow instead several meters away. What makes this stream unique is that it is only 10 miles long when it disappears below ground in the valley.

*Crestone Peak north of the Sand Dunes on a cloudless day*

Next to the dunes lay thousands of acres of spacious grasslands and shrublands, which are the national park's least visited area. Access to some western areas of the park is currently limited. Please read the access information for each area carefully. It is your responsibility to use a good map and know where you are. Areas that are open to the public are sometimes next to areas that have no access, or are open to private tours only. They contain diverse wildlife, migrating dunes, panoramic mountain views, wildflower blooms, and intricate beauty. Insect repellent is recommended for the wetlands and some of the grasslands that may have biting gnats or mosquitoes in summer months. Check with a ranger if you are uncertain of the locations of open areas.

Ute, Apache, and other tribes peeled bark from pine trees for food and medicine. Over 100 of these culturally peeled trees are still living in Great Sand Dunes National Park and Preserve.

Bison tours are offered throughout the year, weather permitting, on Nature Conservancy lands. Via hayride, horseback ride, or four-wheel-drive-vehicle tour, bison managers take you to parts of the park that few visitors get to see. Trail rides or four-wheel-drive-vehicle tours are offered anytime as staffing permits, and as long as there is a minimum of two people. Hayrides are normally offered on summer Saturday mornings, or by reservation for groups of six or more. Please call ahead to confirm available dates and times and to reserve a tour. Some of the wetlands within Great Sand Dunes National Park, including Cotton Lake, Dollar Lake, Twin Lakes, Indian Spring, and Little Spring, are currently managed by the Nature Conservancy, and are open to the public only on bison tours or Conservancy education programs. For more information on dates, times, and prices, please call 719-378-2356, ext. 110.

In 1807, explorer Zebulon Pike, for whom Pikes Peak in the front range is named, recorded the earliest known description of the Great Sand Dunes as a "sea in a storm, except as to color, not the least sign of vegetation existing".

## Location

Along with the tallest sand dunes in North America with awe-inspiring views, uncommon plant and animal life, and rich geological and cultural history, the new park is located in the northeastern corner of the San Luis Valley. The view of the dunes is dramatically back-dropped with the likes of Cleveland Peak, Music Mountain, Crestone Peak, Mable Mountain, Mount Herard, and Blueberry Peak – all part of the Sangre de Cristo Mountains. The park is about 14 miles east of Alamosa, San Luis Valley's largest city, on Highway 160 and 20 miles north on Highway 150.

## Lodging

Pinyon Flats Campground (National Park Service)
719-378-6399 first-come, first-served
Fills Thursdays, Fridays, and Saturdays during warmer months.
Great Sand Dunes Lodge is a modern motel lodging located just outside the park
    entrance on Highway 150. 719-378-2900. Open generally April through October.

In Blanca and Fort Garland, Colorado (25 and 28 miles southeast of park entrance):
Blanca RV Park: 719-379-3201
Fort Garland Motor Inn: 719-379-2993
The Lodge Motel: 719-379-3434
Ute Creek RV Park: 719-379-3238
In Alamosa, Colorado (38 miles southwest):
Best Western Alamosa Inn: 719-589-2567
Comfort Inn of Alamosa: 719-587-9000
Cottonwood Inn B&B: 719-589-3882
Days Inn: 719-589-9037
Holiday Inn: 719-589-5833
KOA Campground: 719-589-9757
Lamplighter Motel: 719-589-6636
Rio Grande Motel: 719-589-9095
Skyvue Motel: 719-589-4945
Super 8 Motel: 719-589-6447
Navajo Trail Campground: 719-589-9460

## Contact

**Great Sand Dunes National Park and Preserve**
11999 Highway 150
Mosca, Colorado 81146-9798
www.nps.gov/grsa/index.htm

*Broad-tailed hummingbird*

## Fast Facts

**General Info:** 719-378-6300; visitor center: 719-378-6399

**Getting There:** From Highway 160 in Alamosa, head east 14 miles to Highway 150. (Look for the sign). Turn north on Highway 150 and go about 20 miles to the entrance to the park.

**Activities:** Hiking, bird and wildlife viewing.

**Principal Mammals:** Elk, mule deer, pronghorn antelope, coyote, black bear, raccoon, porcupine, beaver, cottontail rabbit, squirrel.

**Mammals of Special Interest:** Elk and mule deer

**Principal Birdlife:** Waterfowl to include many duck, geese, and teal species, sandhill crane, heron, whooping crane, and any number of small non-game wetland birds.

**Birds of Special Interest:** Bald eagle, prairie falcon, and green-tailed towhee.

**Habitat Overview:** Sand dunes, grasslands, shrublands, and some wetlands valley rimmed by the Sangre de Cristo Mountains.

**Flora of Special Interest:** Slender spider flower.

**Best Wildlife Viewing Ops:** Early morning and late evening when they are on the move from bedding to feeding areas. Wildlife can be seen from most public roads.

**Best Birding Ops:** Winter is especially good for raptors; songbirds most any time in the summer.

**Best Photo Ops:** Early morning and evening for big game.

**Hunting Ops:** None

**Fishing Ops:** Surrounding mountains

**Camping Ops:** Pinyon Flats (within the park) campground is open year round, and has 88 campsites available on a first-come, first-served basis. Fire grates, picnic tables, flush toilets, and drinking water available.

**Boating Ops:** None

**Hiking Trails:** Unrestricted hiking on the sand dunes themselves. From the northern park boundary, you may hike on the historic Liberty Stage Road, or cross-country away from trails. You may also backpack into this area from the Liberty Gate or via the Sand Ramp Trail; ask at the visitor center for a free permit and details.

You may explore on foot for many miles into the park's grasslands and shrublands from the park entrance road, between the park entrance sign and the Visitor Center. Park at designated pull-outs on the west side of the road. Fences indicate Nature Conservancy boundaries; do not cross any fences without permission.

**Motor Trails:** Just into the park. Medano Pass Primitive Road Tours in an open-air vehicle are offered in warmer months by the Oasis store, near the main entrance of the park. The tours start at the store, following a sandy road along the eastern edge of the dunes. Adults $21, $12 for children 12 to 18, $5 for children under 12. Tours take place at 11:00am and 2:00pm in summer months or in shoulder seasons as long as there is a minimum of 6 people. Call 719-378-2222 for reservations and information.

## Bird List

### LOONS, GREBES
Pied-billed grebe
Red-necked grebe
Eared grebe
Western grebe
Clark's grebe

### PELICANS, HERONS, ALLIES
American white pelican
Double-crested cormorant
American bittern
Great blue heron
Great egret
Snowy egret
Cattle egret
Black-crowned night-heron
White-faced ibis

### VULTURES
Black vulture
Turkey vulture

### SWANS, GEESE, DUCKS
Snow goose
Ross' goose
Canada goose
Gadwall
American wigeon
Mallard
Blue-winged teal
Cinnamon teal
Northern shoveler
Northern pintail
Green-winged teal
Canvasback
Redhead
Ring-necked duck
Lesser scaup
Bufflehead
Common goldeneye
Hooded merganser
Common merganser
Ruddy duck

### HAWKS, EAGLES
Osprey
Bald eagle
Northern harrier
Sharp-shinned hawk
Cooper's hawk
Northern goshawk
Swainson's hawk
Red-tailed hawk
Ferruginous hawk
Rough-legged hawk
Golden eagle
American kestrel
Merlin
Peregrine falcon
Prairie falcon

### GROUSE, PTARMIGAN
Blue grouse
White-tailed ptarmigan
Wild turkey

### RAILS, COOTS, CRANES
Virginia rail
Sora
American coot
Sandhill crane

### SHOREBIRDS
Snowy plover
Killdeer
Mountain plover
American avocet
Greater yellowlegs
Lesser yellowlegs
Solitary sandpiper
Willet

Spotted sandpiper
Long-billed curlew
Marbled godwit
Western sandpiper
Least sandpiper
Baird's sandpiper
Long-billed dowitcher
Wilson's snipe
Wilson's phalarope
Red-necked phalarope
Franklin's gull
Ring-billed gull
California gull
Forster's tern
Black tern

### DOVES, PIGEONS

Rock dove
Band-tailed pigeon
Mourning dove

### OWLS

Flammulated owl
Western screech-owl
Great horned owl
Northern pygmy owl
Burrowing owl
Long-eared owl
Short-eared owl
Northern saw-whet owl

### NIGHTHAWKS

Common nighthawk
Common poorwill

### SWIFTS

Black swift
White-throated swift

### HUMMINGBIRDS

Black-chinned hummingbird
Calliope hummingbird
Broad-tailed hummingbird
Rufous hummingbird

### KINGFISHER

Belted kingfisher

### WOODPECKERS

Lewis' woodpecker
Williamson's sapsucker
Yellow-bellied sapsucker
Red-naped sapsucker
Downy woodpecker
Hairy woodpecker
American three-toed woodpecker
Northern flicker

### FLYCATCHERS

Olive-sided flycatcher
Western wood-pewee
Willow flycatcher
Hammond's flycatcher
Dusky flycatcher
Gray flycatcher
Cordilleran flycatcher
Say's phoebe
Vermilion flycatcher
Ash-throated flycatcher
Cassin's kingbird
Western kingbird

### SHRIKES

Northern shrike
Loggerhead shrike

### VIREOS

Plumbeous vireo
Warbling vireo

### JAYS, CROWS, MAGPIES

Gray jay
Steller's jay
Western scrub-jay
Pinyon jay
Clark's nutcracker
Black-billed magpie
American crow
Common raven

## LARKS

Horned lark

## Purple martin

Tree swallow
Violet-green swallow
Northern rough-winged swallow
Bank swallow
Cliff swallow
Barn swallow

## CHICKADEES, NUTHATCHES, CREEPERS

Black-capped chickadee
Mountain chickadee
Juniper titmouse
Bushtit
Red-breasted nuthatch
White-breasted nuthatch
Pygmy nuthatch
Brown creeper

## WRENS, DIPPERS

Rock wren
Canyon wren
House wren
Marsh wren
American dipper

## KINGLETS, GNATCATCHERS

Golden-crowned kinglet
Ruby-crowned kinglet
Blue-gray gnatcatcher

## BLUEBIRDS, THRUSHES, THRASHERS

Western bluebird
Mountain bluebird
Townsend's solitaire
Veery
Swainson's thrush
Hermit thrush
American robin
Gray catbird

Northern mockingbird
Sage thrasher
Brown thrasher

## PIPITS, WAXWINGS, STARLINGS

American pipit
Bohemian waxwing
Cedar waxwing
European starling

## WOOD WARBLERS

Orange-crowned warbler
Virginia's warbler
Yellow warbler
Yellow-rumped warbler (Myrtle)
Yellow-rumped warbler (Audubon's)
Black-throated gray warbler
Townsend's warbler
Grace's warbler
Black-and-white warbler
Ovenbird
MacGillivray's warbler
Common yellowthroat
Hooded warbler
Wilson's warbler

## TANAGERS

Western tanager

## GROSBEAKS, BUNTINGS, SPARROWS

Green-tailed towhee
Spotted towhee
Canyon towhee
American tree sparrow
Chipping sparrow
Brewer's sparrow
Vesper sparrow
Lark sparrow
Sage sparrow
Lark bunting
Savannah sparrow
Fox sparrow
Song sparrow

Lincoln's sparrow
White-throated sparrow
Harris' sparrow
White-crowned sparrow (Gambel's)
White-crowned sparrow (mountain)
Dark-eyed junco (slate-colored)
Dark-eyed junco (Oregon)
Dark-eyed junco (pink-sided)
Dark-eyed junco (white-winged)
Dark-eyed junco (gray-headed)
Northern cardinal
Rose-breasted grosbeak
Black-headed grosbeak
Blue grosbeak
Lazuli bunting
Indigo bunting
Dickcissel

**BLACKBIRDS, MEADOWLARKS, ORIOLES**

Red-winged blackbird
Western meadowlark
Yellow-headed blackbird
Brewer's blackbird
Common grackle
Brown-headed cowbird
Bullock's oriole

**FRINGILLID FINCHES**

Gray-crowned rosy finch
Black rosy finch
Brown-capped rosy finch
Pine grosbeak
Cassin's finch
House finch
Red crossbill
Common redpoll
Pine siskin
Lesser goldfinch
American goldfinch
Evening grosbeak

**OLD WORLD SPARROWS**

House sparrow

# Mammal List

Pronghorn
Bighorn sheep
Bison
Coyote
Gray fox
Red fox
Beaver
Elk
Mule deer
Gapper's red-backed vole
Long-tailed vole
Meadow vole
Bushy-tailed woodrat
Muskrat
Northern grasshopper mouse
Apache pocket mouse
Silky pocket mouse
Deer mouse
Rock mouse
Heather vole
Western harvest mouse
Western jumping mouse
Porcupine
Mountain lion
Bobcat
Northern pocket gopher
Ord's kangaroo rat
Snowshoe hare
Black-tailed jack rabbit
White-tailed jack rabbit
Desert cottontail
Nuttall's cottontail
Marten
Striped skunk
Spotted skunk
Short-tailed ermine
Long-tailed weasel
Badger

Wolverine
Pika
Raccoon
Golden-mantled ground squirrel
Gunnison's prairie dog
Least chipmunk
Colorado chipmunk
Yellow-bellied marmot
Abert squirrel
Thirteen-lined ground squirrel
Rock squirrel
Chickaree/pine squirrel
Masked shrew
Water shrew
Vagrant or wandering shrew
Black bear
Long-eared myotis
Small-footed myotis
Little brown bat
Long-legged myotis
Western big-eared bat
Big brown bat

## REPTILES AND AMPHIBIANS

Bull snake
Smooth green snake
Western terrestrial garter snake
Short-horned lizard
Plateau lizard
Many-lined skink
Painted turtle
Tiger salamander
Great Plains toad
Woodhouse's toad
Striped chorus frog
Northern leopard frog
Plains spadefoot toad

## FISH

Rio Grande cutthroat trout
Rio Grande sucker
Rainbow trout
Brook trout
Rio Grande chub

*Doe mule deer in early-morning light*

# Scenic Byways

## Frontier Pathways Scenic Byway

The Frontier Pathways Scenic Byway is 103 miles long and follows a much-traveled corridor of early Colorado history. The Ute Indians left their footsteps and then came the Spanish and American explorers. What must have taken days in wagons and horseback, can now be covered in three to four hours. The byway follows the southern side of the Arkansas River Valley where Native American, Spanish, French, and American territories intersected. Traders, fur trappers, homesteaders, ranchers, and gold prospectors viewed the same snow-capped mountains, jagged canyons, carpeted meadows, and aspen-covered hillsides that we marvel at today.

Frontier Pathways Scenic Byway was designated by the U.S. Secretary of Transportation as a National Scenic Byway in 1998. It is one of ten America's Byways designated in Colorado.

The byway starts west of Pueblo at the intersection of Highway 45 and Highway 96. Take Highway 96 west about 40 miles to the little burg of McKenzie Junction. At McKenzie Junction, Highway 165 heads south as a spur to the Frontier Pathways Scenic Byway. Continuing west on Highway 96 another 20 miles will land you in Silver Cliff. Just a mile farther west to the end of this leg of the byway is Westcliffe. Back at McKenzie Junction, take Highway 165 south through the Wet Mountains and enjoy the picturesque San Isabel National

*Wild rose*

Forest. Continue on Highway 165 as it drops down into the foothills and eventually ends at Interstate 25 in the town of Colorado City.

The first point of interest on the Frontier Pathways Scenic Byway is Lake Pueblo State Park. Pueblo Reservoir and the surrounding state wildlife area is one of the most popular recreational facilities in Colorado. The central location and easy access from Interstate 25 make it a favorite destination (see the Lake Pueblo State Park chapter for more detailed information).

About 30 miles west of Pueblo on Highway 96 you come to the town of Wetmore. This stretch of the byway takes you out of the high plains climate zone and into the low montane zone. The increase in precipitation of the montane zone is evident as the grasses and cacti give way to the junipers and pinyon pines of the foothills. The byway crosses over Hardscrabble Creek at Wetmore and veers south to follow the Hardscrabble drainage. At the town of Greenwood a few miles down the road, the climb into the San Isabel National Forest begins. The route travels up Hardscrabble Canyon to McKenzie Junction. The canyon tightens and large granite outcroppings take over the rugged landscape. This is especially awesome during the month of June, when run-off is in full swing. I couldn't image a trip to Colorado without a drive and a few stops along this beautiful and historic stretch of road.

*The view from Mueller State Park*

Continuing west out of McKenzie Junction, one starts the descent into the Wet Mountain Valley and the Grape Creek drainage. This particular valley in the Colorado Rocky Mountains is famous for its unparalleled views and endless miles of thriving wilderness trails and mountain meadows bursting with wildflowers, including the state flower, the Rocky Mountain columbine (lavender & white). Westcliffe and the historic mining town of Silver Cliff sit at approximately 8,000 feet elevation and are surrounded by the grandiose Sangre de Cristo mountain range (ascending to 14,000 feet) to the west and the Wet Mountains to the east. The Collegiate Mountains can be viewed to the north, and the Spanish Peaks can be viewed to the south. The end of this stretch of the Frontier Pathways Scenic Byway is at the town of Westcliffe. Water from Grape Creek is held in De Weese Reservoir just north of Westcliffe on RD 241. De Weese Reservoir State Wildlife Area sits at 7,800 feet elevation and provides access to fishing for cutthroat, rainbow, brown, brook trout, and smallmouth bass. Expect to see a host of waterfowl, mourning dove, dark-eyed junco, and evening grosbeak. Mule deer, antelope, coyote, bobcat, and bunnies can be seen.

Let's go back to McKenzie Junction and head south on Highway 165. Lake Isabel is about 25 miles from McKenzie Junction and would be a nice little spot to spend a little time fishing or even set up camp for the night. One of my earliest remembrances of camping and fishing took place here. My older sister and brother-in-law brought me and my younger brother for a weekend. The only thing I remember about the trip though was my sister getting hooked in the behind with a treble hook. I can still see her standing on a rock jumping around and screaming for somebody to help her. What a sight!

Continuing just a short distance from Lake Isabel on Highway 165, the descent down through the foothills begins. The road veers due east and ends up in Colorado City where this leg of the byway ends at Interstate 25.

## Contact

**El Pueblo Museum**
   301 North Union Avenue, Pueblo, CO 81003
   719-583-8631
   www.frontierpathways.org

**San Isabel National Forest**
   2840 Kachina Drive, Pueblo, CO 81008
   719-553-1400

# Gold Belt Tour

The Gold Belt Tour Scenic Byway is a total of 131 miles traveling over three different roads. If all three sections of the byway are driven, it would take about 5 or 6 hours. The byway starts west of Colorado Springs at the intersection of Highway 24 and CR 1 (also known as Cripple Creek-Florissant Road) at the town of Florissant. Go south on CR 1 to Road S. This is the first of three options for the byway.

**Option 1:** Veer right on Road S and continue to the tee at High Park Road. Turn left on High Park Road and continue southwest to Highway 9. Turn left on Highway 9 and continue to Highway 50. To complete this section of the byway, take Highway 50 east to Cañon City.

**Option 2:** Going back to the intersection of CR 1 and Road S, the second option for this byway continues on CR 1 to the town of Cripple Creek. County Road 1 now turns into Highway 67. Follow Highway 67 to the south end of town. Here the byway splits again. To continue on with option 2, veer right on CR 881 (also known as Shelf Road). Stay on Shelf Road all the way to the town of Cañon City. Take Highway 50 east to the town of Florence. We will call this the end of leg two of the byway.

**Option 3:** Going back to the town of Cripple Creek, take Highway 67 through the town of Victor. The road now turns to CR 67 and veers south out of town. This stretch continues south through Phantom Canyon and is also nicknamed Phantom Canyon Road. Stay on this road all the way to Florence at Highway 50. To avoid confusion, I took option 3 back to Cripple Creek, when in reality the second and third sections form a loop and the end of option 2 could have been the start of the Phantom Canyon section.

Combined, this byway travels along everything from four-lane highway to narrow one-lane gravel road. The section that follows High Park Road is a two-lane paved road the entire length. The Shelf Road section is unpaved and narrow. It is actually recommended that a high clearance, four-wheel-drive vehicle be used. Vehicles over 25 feet are not suggested because of the winding road with steep drop-offs. The Phantom Canyon Road is also improved gravel road most of the way. It is also narrow with several sections of road where only one vehicle could pass, including two narrow tunnels. The speed limit is 20 miles per hour most of the way. Vehicles over 25 feet are

not permitted. There are sections of road that are pretty rough, but a passenger car can make the trip.

The going could be tough if the weather is dire and the roads are wet. The roads are not maintained in the winter, so traveling the back roads this time of year would be spotty at best.

The Gold Belt Tour is a beautiful drive in the fall as the aspens, willows, and ivies are in full dress colors. It was designated by the U.S. Secretary of Transportation as a national scenic byway in 2000. It is one of ten America's Byways designated in Colorado.

The Gold Belt Tour starts by passing through the Florissant Fossil Beds National Monument, however the majority of this byway follows the back-country roads once used by miners as they picked gold from the depths of the earth. In the early 1890s, the historic town of Cripple Creek was the center of the greatest gold boom the state has ever known. It is still turning out riches for the state (in the form of tax revenues) as a small-stakes gambling town. Victor, a small burg 6 miles east of Cripple Creek was also an important part of history at the time. There are still remains of former gold camps along these narrow back roads.

The byway remains as a historic marker of times past, but it's the present-day splendor of the countryside west of the infamous Pikes Peak that most come to see today. After all, it is a "scenic" byway. The tight inclusion of the Phantom Canyon Road is nothing short of spectacular. The views of Cripple Creek Canyon from Shelf Road are wonderful. Watching the change in landscape from the montane zone to desert shrub country of the Arkansas River valley along the High Park Road will "shock and awe".

There are a number of places to check out while taking in this drive. The chance to explore Pikes Peak, the unspoiled Beaver Creek Wilderness Study Area, Mueller State Park, the bighorn sheep breeding grounds of Dome Rock State Wildlife Area, the impressive Royal Gorge, and the Garden Park Dinosaur Fossil Area are either along the byway or just a few miles away. (See the Florissant Fossil Beds National Monument chapter for more information on this area).

This byway presents a host of different landscapes and, in turn, provides the chance to see birds and wildlife in good numbers and variety. Starting in the lower elevations near Florence and Cañon City, the semi-arid grasslands and shrubs are habitat for scaled quail, western meadowlarks, horned larks, and mountain bluebirds. Prairie dog towns are abundant and if watched closely with binoculars, the ground nesting burrowing owl can be seen. Black-tailed jackrabbits and kangaroo rats may be seen. It seems that every time I am down there along Highway 50, I see a coyote. The popular Swainson's hawk, red-tailed hawk, and golden eagle might be seen hunting the prairie dog towns. Although pretty rare this far north, roadrunners have also been seen here.

As the countryside changes to undulating hills and secluded canyons, willows and cottonwoods show up and then the ever-present pinyon pine and juniper woodland habitat appears. This is perfect country to support an abundance of mule deer. Although you're not likely to see a mountain lion, this is also prime habitat for them.

At higher elevations, the pines and firs start to take over the landscape. Look for golden eagles, prairie falcons, and red-tailed hawks riding the air currents above the rugged cliffs along Shelf and Phantom Canyon Roads. These cliffs are also home to Rocky Mountain bighorn sheep. Blue grouse and wild turkey are often found in the aspen groves feeding on new growth. Elk, black bears, and marmots are found here, along with the broadtail hummingbird, white-breasted nuthatch, and evening grosbeak. The riparian areas along the creek bottoms provide a valuable combination of food, water, and shelter for wildlife. It is well known that a large percentage of wildlife depend on riparian areas.

To optimize your wildlife viewing and birding, be patient, avoid making sound, and avoid sudden movements. Binoculars are important for viewing and a lens of 300mm or greater is best for photographing wildlife. Early morning and evening are the best times to observe wildlife.

*This youngster was right along the highway (see the white line).*

## Mueller State Park

Mueller State Park is 5,000 acres of open space filled with outdoor activities. The park has 50 miles of trails used by hikers and mountain bikers. Nineteen miles of Mueller's trails are designated for mountain biking. Bikers must stay on designated trails and expect moderate to steep gravel terrain – sorry, no easy trails here. There are 41 picnic sites for visitors who just want to spend the day with the kids and have a basket lunch. Each site includes a table and raised grill. All picnic tables are on a first-come, first-served basis.

Mueller has always been known as a wonderful wildlife-viewing area and, being so close to Colorado Springs, it does get plenty of traffic. However, my experience did require me to mingle with numbers of people, but it seemed there was plenty of room and no one was stepping on each other's feet. I was able to see and photograph several birds, bunnies, and squirrels. The northern section of the park was closed so the elk could calve in peace, but I did see two cows from one of the many vantage points that the trails provide.

Mueller State Park is also a popular winter destination. The cross-country skiing, snowshoeing, and sledding draw winter lovers from neighboring communities. It is also a great place for winter camping. Revenuer's Ridge Campground is open in the winter from approximately October 15 until May 15 on a first-come, first-served basis.

There is one large camping area with 123 sites broken down into 7 sub-campgrounds. Peak View Campground, Revenuer's Ridge Campground, Pisgah Point Campground, Conifer Ridge Campground, and Grouse Mountain Campground all have electrical hook-ups. Prospector Ridge Campground and Turkey Meadow Campground are walk-in tent sites. There are also three rental cabins available.

## Dome Rock State Wildlife Area

The adjacent Dome Rock State Wildlife Area adds almost another 7,000 acres to the wildlife viewing opportunities provided by Mueller State Park. Expect to see deer, elk, cottontail rabbit, and dusky (blue) grouse. One of the many trails in the area follows Fourmile Creek and provides coldwater, small stream fishing for brown and brook trout.

Public access is restricted to foot or horseback only from designated parking lots and connecting trails from Mueller State Park. One of the most unique things about Dome Rock: it is a prime calving ground for Rocky Mountain bighorn sheep. Migrants from the Pikes Peak herd move into Dome Rock State Wildlife Area in the late winter and spring to bear their young. Expect seasonal closures during the spring.

## Contact

**Gold Belt Tour Scenic and Historic Byway**
  6778 County Road 102, Guffey, CO  80820
  719-689-2461
  www.goldbeltbyway.com

# Highway of Legends

The Highway of Legends Scenic Byway is an 82-mile trip over the dramatic settings of the Park Plateau, San Isabel National Forest, and Spanish Peaks Wilderness Area. This passage – which inspired tall tales among Native American nomads, Spanish explorers, and Anglo and Hispanic settlers – starts in Trinidad on CO Highway 12. It heads west following the Picketwire Valley of the Purgatoire River. After topping the 9,941-foot Cucharas Pass the byway tracks the headwaters of the Cucharas River and gives way to an awesome look at the 13,626-foot West Spanish Peak and the 12,683-foot East Spanish Peak. This stretch of the byway ends just past the town of La Veta at US Highway 160. Take Highway 160 east to the town of Walsenburg to finish

the tour. A 35-mile spur of the byway starts at the top of Cucharas Pass at FR 415. This is an improved gravel road that tops the 11,743-foot Cordova Pass within the first 10 miles. The road changes to 46.0 Road and continues along the Apishapa River to the little burg of Gulnare. The road again changes to 43.7 Road and the spur ends at the town of Aguilar on Interstate 25. This stunning drive will take nearly two hours, or quite a bit longer if you include the spur to Aguilar.

West of Trinidad Lake State Park on Highway 12, the byway weaves its way along the headwaters of the Purgatoire River through Picketwire Valley. It is a small stream twisting its way through open meadows and willow bottoms. It's a great place for viewing all types of wildlife and birds.

Check out the Wall of Legends Guest Ranch and RV Park in the town of

Stonewall. Private pond and stream fishing is available right outside your cozy cabin. Contact them at 719-868-2285 or 719 868-3049.

About 30 miles from Trinidad Lake, you will come to Monument Lake and then North Lake a few miles farther. Both are nestled in the foothills above the Picketwire Valley and provide seclusion from the day-to-day bustle. The drive from here, over Cucharas Pass, to the town of Cuchara could be rated the best drive in the state for viewing the fall aspen colors. The aspen groves are thick and lush along this stretch. From Cuchara to the town of La Veta, the tour affords amazing views of the Spanish Peaks and the Sangre de Cristos Mountain Range. Views of the threatening red rock abutments of the Dakota Wall and the Great Dikes (also known as Devil's Stairsteps) near La Veta are remarkable geological formations.

I was coming down Highway 12 from Cuchara one evening and was just amazed at the wildlife. I spotted two red fox on the outer boundary of the golf course hunting mice. They were little red statues staring into the grass and then making a quick leap forward, snout first, nipping at their next meal. Finally one came up with a mouthful of grey fur. I had already seen several mule deer along the road, but was totally blown away when I got into town. The number of deer in the streets and people's yards was astonishing. There could have easily been 30 to 40 meandering through town feeding on flower beds and shrubs. I crossed over the Cuchara River as I was heading out of town and noticed another 20 deer along the river bottom. I have been back to La Veta a few times and have seen deer again, just not as many as I did that one evening.

*The Devil's Stairsteps (West Spanish Peak in background)*

## Trinidad Lake State Park

Just west of Trinidad on Highway 12 is Trinidad Lake State Park. Fishing is one of the primary activities at Trinidad Lake, with a wide variety of warm- and coldwater species. There is an amazing 50,000-trout stock here every year. Add this to a good population of largemouth bass, wipers, walleye, several species of panfish, as well as the tasty channel catfish and every type of fisherman will be satisfied. Working structure and weed beds with a boat is a popular tactic, but shore fishing can be just as rewarding. All boats are inspected before launch and when coming off the lake. Colored seals are attached to inspected boats leaving the lake. This should simplify the inspection process upon return. A normal boat inspection should take around five minutes. These inspections are the result of zebra mussels being discovered at Lake Pueblo. Vigorous inspection programs have been implemented at many Colorado state parks to help eliminate the spread of this non-native evasive pest. Trinidad Lake is also an important winter destination for ice fishing.

When snow is available, cross-country skiing and snowshoeing are popular pastimes. On the reverse side of the spectrum, the warm climate of southern Colorado makes the 800-acre Trinidad Lake a popular summer destination for water sports like jet skiing and water skiing. There are over 9 miles of trails and access roads in the park for mountain biking and hiking. Enjoy the exercise and wonderful views of lake, mountains, and the open vistas.

The pinyon-juniper woodland and mixed grass prairies that occupy the park uplands provide mixed habitat for big and small game alike. Mule deer take to the

*Bull snake*

pinyon-juniper woodlands that occur on rocky outcrops and slopes over one-third of the west side of the park. The scrubland species such as Gambel oak, mountain mahogany, and serviceberry dominate the browse for the deer. Cottontail rabbits, collared lizards, bull snakes, and field mice are abundant. A watchable wildlife area has been established in Long's Canyon, located in the southwest corner of the park. This site features a 0.75-mile self-guided nature trail with two wildlife observation blinds overlooking a pond and wetland area. Great blue herons, snowy egrets, white pelicans, and several species of ducks can be viewed. Look for canyon towhees, evening grosbeaks, spotted towhees, and broad-tailed hummingbirds in the shrubland surrounding the lake. This is a popular area for mule deer. Long's Canyon also contains a unique geological feature called the KT boundary; interpretive signing explains its significance. This site is accessible via Highway 12 at the Madrid Bridge on the west side of the lake.

Two campgrounds are available at Trinidad Lake with a total of 73 sites. The South Shore Campground has ten non-electric sites close to the lake. Cross the dam to the south side of the lake to find these RV-friendly sites. You will enjoy panoramic views of the lake and neighboring mountains. The Carpios Ridge Campground is located 150 feet above the lake, up on a ridge on the north side of the lake. With 63 improved campsites accommodating RVs, trailers, or tents, this campground has a spot for everyone. Restroom facilities, fresh water, coin-operated laundry, showers, and flush toilets are on hand. All sites have electrical service. Make sure to spend a few hours lounging outside watching the stars and listening to the coyotes howl.

## Contact

**Park Office**
 32610 Highway 12, Trinidad, CO 81082
 Office Hours: 8:00am-4:00pm, Monday through Friday
 Park Hours: 24 Hours a day, self-serve
 719-846-6951
 http://parks.state.co.us/parks/trinidadlake/

## LATHROP STATE PARK

Moving along the byway, take Highway 160 east towards Walsenburg. The last point of interest on this stretch is Lathrop State Park, Colorado's first state park. Lathrop State Park is made up of two lakes, several ponds and bird watching wetlands, a wildlife management area, golf course, two campgrounds, and several picnic areas. This superbly laid out 1,594 acres is a recreationalist's wonderland.

Martin Lake is stocked with rainbow trout, channel catfish, bass, walleye, blue gill, crappie, and wipers. Martin Lake is especially known for the toothy northern pike and saugeye. Horseshoe Lakes has much of the same, but is the only body of water with the notorious tiger muskie. Both lakes are open and fishing can be very good for trout and northern pike.

There are two very nice trails for hiking and biking at Lathrop. The Hogback Nature Trail is a foot trail only, winding through sandstone formations, making a climb up the rocky Hogback Ridge which forms the park's northern boundary. As the trail follows the top of the ridge, spectacular views of the Spanish Peaks and Sangre de Cristo Mountain Range can be enjoyed. The 2-mile trail is a self-guided hike with signage containing information about the area's plant and animal life as well as its history. The Cuerno Verde Trail is a 3-mile closed loop trail that is handicap accessible and very popular with the bicyclists. This asphalt trail encircles Martin Lake and is within walking distance from both campgrounds. The views are exceptional and even have restrooms along the way.

The warm ambiance of southern Colorado encourages water sports such as jet skiing, water skiing, and swimming here at Lathrop. Let's not forget the golf course. It's the nine-hole Walsenburg Golf Course at Lathrop State Park. The golf course offers nine-hole, eighteen-hole, or all-day rates.

Lathrop State Park is a fantastic place for birding and wildlife viewing. Many migratory and resident birds can be seen from the bird watching area south of Horseshoe Lake. It's great for both sora and Virginia rails, and rare sightings of tundra swans and Pacific loons have been seen. One summer, a brown pelican graced the lakes for several days. Northern water thrushes and the rare alder flycatcher have been seen in this area, as well as summer tanagers, American redstarts, and black & white warblers. Expect to see several species of raptors, pinyon and scrub jays, western meadowlarks, and canyon towhees. The lakes and wetland habitats attract a variety of waterfowl and shorebirds. Osprey are commonly seen in summer, and bald eagles have become familiar winter residents. Many visitors have reported seeing roadrunners in the campground.

Mule deer can be spotted just about anywhere in the park. Coyotes, bobcats, and fox make occasional appearances. The mountains just west of Lathrop support a very good population of black bears and do come into the park regularly. Take care with your food and do not leave your vehicle open. More commonly seen small game are cottontail rabbits, black-tailed jackrabbits, raccoons, and thirteen-lined ground squirrels.

There are two campgrounds at the Lathrop State Park. Yucca and Pinon Campgrounds have 103 campsites combined. Yucca Campground has 21 basic campsites that accommodate tents and small camping units such as pop-up campers, camper vans, pickup trucks with camper tops, and small RVs. Vault toilets, water hydrants, and a dump station are provided. Each site has a picnic table and a fire pit. Trash receptacles are provided at the campground entrance. Pinon Campground has 82 campsites and features electrical hookups, fire pits, and picnic tables. It also has new restrooms, pay showers, and water hydrants that are located throughout the campground. A dump station is available and trash receptacles are located at the entrance to each of the campground's four loops. Handicap sites are also available. Children will enjoy the centrally located playground.

## Contact

**Park Office**
70 County Road 502, Walsenburg, CO 81089
Office Hours: 8:00am-4:00pm Tuesday-Saturday, 9:00am-3:00pm Sunday, Closed Monday.
Park Hours: 5:00am-10:00pm, fishing from shoreline 24 hours
719-738-2376

**Trinidad Welcome Center**
309 Nevada Avenue, Trinidad, CO 81082
719-742-3822
www.sangres.com/shol/index.htm

*White-faced ibis*

## Los Caminos Antiguos Scenic Byway

The Los Caminos Antiguos Scenic Byway is 129 miles in length and bestows a great overview of the expansive San Juan Valley. Based on mileage alone, it should take somewhere in the two- to three-hour range to complete the drive, but I would allow 4 or 5 hours to take in the sights. Some of Colorado's earliest settlements were constructed in the valley, primarily by Spanish explorers coming from the south along the Rio Grande River.

The best place to start the tour of the Los Caminos Antiguos is in Alamosa on Highway 160. Take Highway 17 north about 13 miles to just past the town of Mosca and turn right (east) on 6N. Continue east about 16 miles to Highway 150. Turn right

(south) on Highway 150 and travel about 14 miles to Highway 160. Turn left (east) on Highway 160 and go about 10 miles to the town of Fort Garland. Turn right (south) on Highway 159 and drive about 15 miles to San Luis. San Luis was the first township in Colorado, founded June 21, 1851. This area reeks of history, so make sure to stop and take in the culture. The heart of the town lies at the Sangre de Christo Church. From San Luis, take Highway 142 west about 8 miles to the little town of San Acacio. Continuing on Highway 142, the road veers to the south about 2 miles and then turns back to the west. Travel another 24 miles to the intersection with Highway 285 at the town of Romeo. Turn left (south) on Highway 285 and go 7 miles to Antonito. Take a right (west) on Highway 17. About 10 miles down the road, the byway changes its look and treks out of the San Luis Valley into the foothills. The road now follows the Conejos River for several miles and then veers away south to the high country, climbing La Manga Pass at 10,230 feet. The 11,766-foot Jarosa Peak can be seen to the west. No sooner do you coast down the back side of La Manga Pass, you get a double whammy by climbing Cumbres Pass at 10,022 feet. The Los Caminos Antiguos Scenic Byway ends just a few more miles at the New Mexico border.

Before starting the tour of the San Luis Valley, which is infamous for wetlands and migratory bird populations, I should mention a few points of interest in the vicinity of Alamosa. The Monte Vista National Wildlife Refuge is west on Highway 160 about 20 miles (see the Monte Vista NWR chapter for more detailed information). Just east and south of Alamosa is the Alamosa National Wildlife Refuge (see the Alamosa NWR chapter). North and west of town is Russell Lakes State Wildlife Area. Russell Lakes State Wildlife Area is located in the northern part of the San Luis Valley, 10 miles south of the town of Saguache on Highway 285. At 4,000 acres, it is the largest contiguous wetland area managed by the Colorado Division of Wildlife (see Russell Lakes SWA chapter). Also just northeast of town about 15 miles is the Blanca Wetlands (see the Blanca Wetlands chapter). Another unique (especially for Colorado) wildlife opportunity in the area is Colorado Gators. The alligator farm and reptile park is located 17 miles north of Alamosa on Highway 17 at CR 9.

## Contact

**Colorado Gators**
9162 CR 9 North
Mosca, CO 81146
719-378-2612

Continuing east of San Luis State Park on 6N about 9 miles is the intersection with Highway 150 and the entrance to the Great Sand Dunes National Park and Preserve. The Great Sand Dunes are one of nature's most interesting formations. Hundreds of feet high and more than a thousand miles from the nearest ocean beach, these drifting dunes accumulated over the eons as winds swept sand against the west face of the Sangre de Cristo Range (see the Great Sand Dunes National Park chapter for more detailed information).

The byway heads south from here and you are treated with a spectacular view of Blanca Peak at 14,345 feet. It is the southernmost peak in this section of the Sangre de Cristos. At Highway 160, take a left and continue to Fort Garland. Fort Garland was one of Colorado's first military posts. Built in 1858, the fort was designed to protect settlers in the San Luis Valley. Smith Reservoir State Wildlife Area and Mountain Home Reservoir State Wildlife Area are within a few miles of Fort Garland. Smith Reservoir can be an outstanding fishery, quite windy at times, but all in all a good lake. It is also quite the bird sanctuary. Mountain Home Reservoir is also a great wildlife viewing and birding opportunity.

Take Highway 159 south from here to the town of San Luis. San Luis, as mentioned earlier, is the oldest established town in Colorado. South of San Luis is Sanchez

Reservoir State Wildlife Area. It sits back in a secluded corner east of the San Pedro Mesa and boasts a good population of northern pike and carp.

From San Luis, drive west on Highway 142 to Highway 285. This is a 40-mile stretch of open country at the southern end of the San Luis Valley. Small drainages including Culebra Creek are the norm and a stretch of Bureau of Land Management land (public access) through the San Luis Hills dominates the landscape. At Highway 285, turn south towards Antonito. Just north of Antonito the oldest church in Colorado, Our Lady of Guadalupe, can be found in Conejos.

The remainder of the Los Caminos Antiguos Scenic Byway is a genuine treat. I find this stretch of road to be one of my favorites in Colorado. I think it goes back to my first trip to flyfish the Conejos River. I remember the miraculous transition of the barren valley floor to the rise of the pine forest in the matter of just a few miles. It seemed so dramatic to me at the time.

As mentioned, the Conejos River is the center of attraction for the first 20 miles or so until the highway veers south away from the river. However, if you continue north on FR 250, it follows the river all the way to Platoro Reservoir. This is a gorgeous drive and I am dumbfounded that this section of road was not included in the scenic byway. There are a number of fishing accesses and unimproved campgrounds along the way. I like to take FR 724 and fish the South Fork of the Conejos River. There are backpacking trails galore that lead to a number of high mountain lakes. Many of these lakes have populations of Rio Grande cutthroat (a native fish to Colorado). Mule deer and elk can be seen on a regular basis. It is customary for bald eagles to roost in this remote canyon. Coyotes, black bear, red fox, and porcupines are sighted quite often. Mountain bluebirds, Steller's Jays, crows, and mountain chickadees are common to the area.

The continuation of the byway on Highway 17 is no less spectacular. The drive takes the traveler over La Manga and Cumbres Passes, both over 10,000 feet.

## Contact

**Los Caminos Antiguos**
P.O. Box 86, Fort Garland, CO 81133
719-379-3500
www.loscaminos.com

# San Luis State Park

San Luis State Park is located on 6N about 7 miles east of Highway 17. This 2,054-acre park is an important wetlands environment for migratory waterfowl and shorebirds. It is actually the largest body of water in the valley. The unique combination of wetlands, lakes, and saltbrush/sage valley floor environments provide a fantastic habitat for all sorts of wildlife. San Luis Lake has become a premier wildlife-viewing and recreation area because of it. I got some of my best images of an American avocet from one of the shoreline picnic locations.

Migratory waterfowl and other birds are frequent visitors to these tranquil waters. Northern pintails, Clark's grebes, white pelicans, blue-winged teal, and the common coot can be seen on the lake while great blue herons, avocets, snowy egrets, lesser yellowlegs, and black-necked stilts might hang in the wetlands. Coyotes, kangaroo rats, and rabbits are often seen in the surrounding flats. Elk use much of the surrounding lands for calving, mule deer abound, sage thrasher and Brewer's sparrow breed throughout the brush lands, raptors are everywhere, and reptiles and amphibians all find refuge in this unlikely riparian oasis hidden in the San Luis Valley.

The lake is a popular boating and fishing destination. I have spent a few hours over the years casting flies to the numerous carp in the lake. They are not necessarily easy to hook up with and you can wear your arm out throwing flies at them. Trout are stocked annually and panfish are always a possibility.

There are numerous foot trails in the wildlife area and wetlands north of the state park.

The Mosca Campground is located on the west side of San Luis Lake, just north of the entrance. There are 51 campsites with a clear view of the lake, the Sangre de Cristo Mountains, the valley floor, and the Great Sand Dunes. All sites have electrical hookups, sheltered tables, and fire grills. Drinking water and a dump station are also available on site. A bathhouse with modern restrooms, hot showers, and laundry facilities is located in the campground.

## Contact

**Park Office**
  P O Box 150, Mosca, CO 81146
  Park Hours: 5:00am-10:00pm
  719-378-2020

*American avocet*

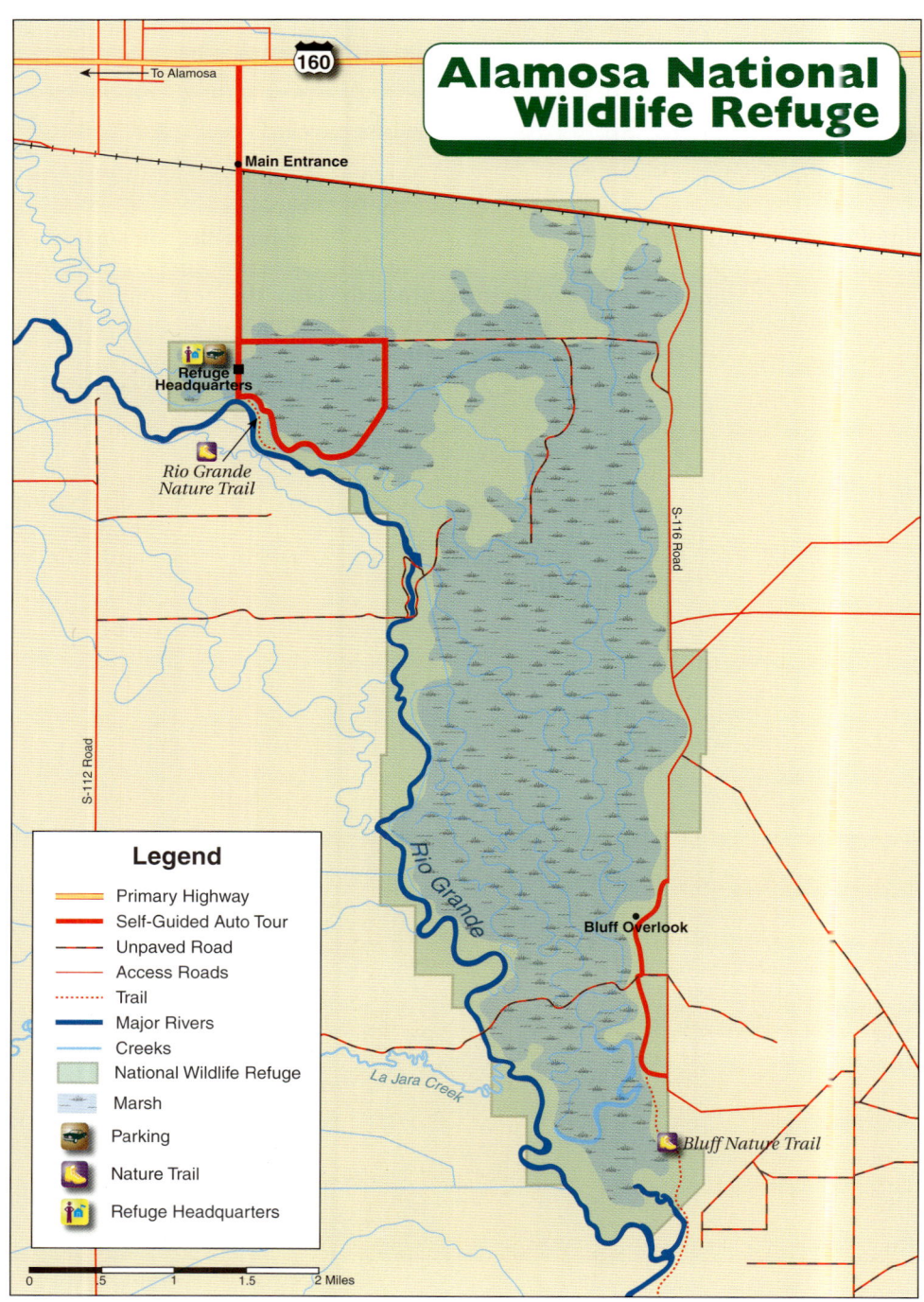

# Wildlife Refuges

## Alamosa National Wildlife Refuge

11,169 Acres; South-central Colorado 6 miles southeast of Alamosa off of Highway 160

## History

Alamosa National Wildlife Refuge is primarily set aside for migratory birds and other wildlife. It was established in 1962 and encompasses 11,169 acres of wetlands inside the Rio Grande River flood plain. The Rio Grande River, one of the five largest drainages in Colorado, traces much of the western boundary of the refuge. The river is of utmost importance to the San Luis Valley, not only for the wildlife, but for farming and public use as well. The spillover as the river oxbows through the valley creates natural wet meadows and wooded bands of cover. It supports a great variety of wildlife including deer, pronghorn antelope, an assortment of raptors, water birds and songbirds, beaver, and coyotes.

## Wildlife

A nature trail following the Rio Grande River begins at the Visitor's Center. The 2-mile hike provides the opportunity to photograph birds, waterfowl, and small game in fairly close proximity. I wasn't 100 yards down the trail when I saw a porcupine meandering in the wild grass next to the trail. It didn't seem to matter how nicely I talked to it, coaxing it to stop in just the right light for a picture of its face, it just would not listen. I could have gotten a nice shot of its quill-covered tail as it slipped into a burrow, but I couldn't convince myself to push the shutter. Photographing wildlife is a challenging endeavor!

There is a 3.5-mile auto tour that starts at the visitor's center also. It circles a section of the lower wetlands providing ample opportunities to photograph waterfowl, songbirds, and some interesting fauna and water compositions. Watch for many different species of hawks, owls, and eagles.

As I toured the Alamosa NWR, I noticed it has a much different character than Monte Vista NWR. There were raptors at Monte Vista, but the numbers at Alamosa were astounding. From a distance, I watched an adult golden eagle perched atop a dead cottonwood take flight and circle above the river, several harrier and/or Swainson's hawks, and what must have been the smaller American kestrel. On the east side of the auto tour, I spotted another young eagle in a barren cottonwood. From the driver's seat, I quickly tried to get a few shots, however the handheld long lens produced less than adequate focus. It did take flight shortly after my attempts.

There is an area of dry land increasing in elevation leading to a bluff, which is the southeastern boundary at the corner of the refuge. It is covered with wild grasses, greasewood, saltbush, and an occasional cottonwood tree. This environment supports smaller animals, food sources for predators, and browse for the big game. While driving along the bluff on the east side of the refuge, more hawks were hovering in the air currents above and a lone bald eagle was spotted about a quarter mile away sitting on an ice shelf on one of the lower ponds. The refuge is less intensively managed than Monte Vista NWR, but the river is supplemented by local artesian wells and water pumped from the Closed Basin Project (a system of recovering water that would otherwise be lost to evaporation). Controlled burns and grazing are also used to round out the management to improve the quality of the landscape and start new growth. The Bluff Overlook on the southeastern side of the refuge can be reached by car and provides a fifteen-mile auto tour. It gives the viewer a topside look at the incredible and assorted wetlands. Another nature trail takes you along the eastern edge for a closer look at the bottom of the wetlands. Photo ops abound.

*Alamosa NWR still frozen in early March*

*Bank swallow*

Side note:
    The Closed Basin Project, a politically and legally charged mission, was created to help supply the states of New Mexico and Texas as well as Mexico with water. Near the end of the 19th century (a series of dry years), the valley-wide canal system our industrious pioneers built in San Luis Valley detached so much of the historical water flows from the Rio Grande that Mexico sued Colorado for more water. Reservoirs were built along the river to catch water, but the legal wrangling continued between our neighboring states well into the 1960s. In 1972, laws were passed which gave the Secretary of the Interior permission to construct and operate the Closed Basin Project. Basically a series of constructed salvage wells constitute the core of the project. The unconfined salvaged water is delivered through a 42-mile channel to the Rio Grande River and then on to the south. The project also provides for the delivery of water to the Alamosa NWR and the Blanca Wildlife Habitat Area, stabilization of San Luis Lake, recreational facilities at San Luis Lake, and fish and wildlife enhancement.

## Location

The main headquarters and visitor center for the Alamosa, Monte Vista, and Baca National Wildlife Refuge Complex is located on Alamosa NWR. From Alamosa, go east on Highway 160 4 miles to El Rancho Lane. Turn south and continue 2 miles until you reach the headquarters. Information on the refuges and exhibits can be found there. Providing a dramatic backdrop for this refuge, Mount Blanca towers at 14,345 feet and is the first peak at the southern end of the Sangre de Cristo Mountains.

## Contact

**Alamosa/Monte Vista National Wildlife Refuges**
9383 El Rancho Lane, Alamosa, CO 81101
719-589-4021
http://alamosa.fws.gov

**U.S. Fish and Wildlife Service**
www.fws.gov
For refuge information
800-344-WILD

## Fast Facts

**Getting There:** From Alamosa, go east on Highway 160 for 4 miles to El Rancho Lane. Turn south and continue 2 miles until you reach the headquarters. Information on the refuges and exhibits can be found there.
**Activities:** Bird and wildlife viewing, hiking
**Principal Mammals:** Elk, mule deer, pronghorn antelope, coyote, black bear, raccoon, porcupine, skunk, red fox, beaver, cottontail rabbit, squirrel, ermine, muskrat, mink, and number of smaller game such as, voles, field mice, and Ord's kangaroo rat
**Mammals of Special Interest:** Elk and mule deer
**Principal Birdlife:** Waterfowl to include many duck, geese, and teal species, sandhill crane, heron, whooping crane, and any number of small non-game wetland birds
**Birds of Special Interest:** Bald eagle and red-tailed hawk
**Habitat Overview:** Wetlands valley, farmlands rimmed by the Sangre de Cristo and San Juan Mountains
**Flora of Special Interest:** Slender spider flower
**Best Wildlife Viewing Ops:** Early morning and late evening when they are on the move from bedding to feeding areas. Wildlife can be seen from most public roads
**Best Birding Ops:** Winter is especially good for raptors; March for the sandhill cranes and then again in October; spring, summer, and fall for just about all others
**Best Photo Ops:** Early mornings for the sandhill cranes
**Hunting Ops:** Yes
**Fishing Ops:** None
**Camping Ops:** None
**Boating Ops:** None
**Hiking Trails:** Rio Grande River Nature Trail at the refuge headquarters and the Bluff Nature Trail at the Bluff Overlook
**Motor Trails:** A 15-mile ride from the headquarters via east on CR-8 and then south on CR-116 take you to the Bluff Overlook

# Baca National Wildlife Refuge

**53,000 Acres; South-central CO 20 miles north of Alamosa on Highway 17**

## History

Congress authorized the establishment of the Baca National Wildlife Refuge in November of 2000. The newest addition to the national wildlife refuge list in the San Luis Valley was authorized for establishment in Public Law 106-530 under Section 6 of the Act entitled, *The Great Sand Dunes National Park and Preserve Act of 2000*. In addition to the Baca NWR, the act authorized the federal acquisition of lands adjacent to the Great Sand Dunes National Monument for the Great Sand Dunes National Park and Preserve. Total acreage of lands included for the Baca NWR and the Great Sand Dunes is approximately 110,000 acres.

In approving *The Great Sand Dunes National Park and Preserve Act of 2000*, Congress determined that the lands acquired under the act offered distinctive hydrological, educational, wildlife, recreational, and other diverse resources deserving preservation for the enjoyment of future generations. The refuge boundary abuts lands owned and/or controlled by other conservation entities including The Nature Conservancy, the National Park Service, the U.S. Forest Service, and the Colorado Land Board of Commissioners. The lands including these neighboring landowners will represent the largest and most diverse collection of wetlands in the state of Colorado.

The 53,000 acres of Baca NWR includes over 4,000 acres of wetlands registered in the National Wetlands Inventory. The cool, clear waters of five major streams – San Luis Creek, Crestone Creek, Willow Creek, Cottonwood Creek, and Deadman Creek – flow out of the Sangre de Cristo Mountains to the northwest into the flatlands of the upper San Luis Valley and into the Baca NWR. These wetlands are considered to be among the most unspoiled and biologically diverse wetlands in the state, and maybe the entire southwestern United States.

Along with these important points, an abundant history of the valley lies buried under very old layers of sand. Hundreds of ancient Native American artifacts and world-class archeological sites dating back some 11,500 years have been found nearby.

*A rare view of a mountain lion (photo provided by Dan Will).*

With all the good news, there is inevitably going to be bad news. There is a huge controversy over proposed oil and natural gas drilling at Baca NWR. The refuge was created from a 100,000-acre purchase of the Baca Ranch, but apparently the mineral rights on the ranch land are owned by Toronto-based Lexam Energy Exploration and Conoco Phillips. The U.S. Fish and Wildlife Service couldn't reach a deal with the oil giants to sell these rights. United States taxpayers paid over $30 million to purchase the Baca NWR in perpetuity for the American people. Then Lexam Explorations notified the refuge of its intention to explore for natural gas. Without a leg to stand on, the US Fish and Wildlife Service (USFWS) announced that it would not attempt to stop their right to explore on Baca NWR. Due to something called split-estate – basically dual ownership – the USFWS said it did not have authority to stop Lexam under the National Environmental Protection Act (NEPA). Allowing Lexam Explorations to exercise its mineral rights on public land is in direct contradiction to the purpose for which the refuge was established. According to the USFWS *Conceptual Management Plan*, the Baca NWR was created with the purpose of:

> *"Restoring, enhancing and maintaining wetland, upland, riparian and other habitats for wildlife, plants and fish species that are native to the San Luis Valley, Colorado. Management of the refuge will emphasize migratory bird conservation and will consider the refuge's role in broader landscape conservation efforts."*

So the lawyers stepped in for a group called the Luis Valley Ecosystem Council and filed suit against the USFWS in April of 2007. As a result of the lawsuit, USFWS abruptly reversed its position and is currently preparing environmental assessment documents as required under NEPA. To date, over 48,000 public comments were submitted to USFWS during the 30-day assessment process, virtually all in favor of protecting the Baca NWR from gas and oil development. Clearly, the American people have had enough of seeing their most precious and irreplaceable public lands destroyed for fossil fuel energy development. In December of 2007, a federal district court ruled in favor of Luis Valley Ecosystem Council including issuing an order to the USFWS to, "…prohibit all ground disturbing activities related to the exploration and development of the mineral estate underlying the Baca NWR during the National Environmental Policy Act process".

Politics, I hate it! The timing on the purchase of the Baca Ranch seems suspect to me. The purchase of the ranch and establishment of the Baca NWR and the Great Sand Dunes National Park and Preserve happened in 2000. Guess what year Lexam and Conoco Phillips acquired the mineral rights to the ranch – 2000. Sounds like some of the under the table dealings came to the surface just in time. Let's hope the pursuit of the truth will help the longevity of the refuge. So for now, I guess only time will tell. As Dennis Miller would say after he went on a rant, "That's my opinion and I may be wrong".

## Wildlife

Thousands of migrating birds visit the refuge each spring and fall. The refuge provides habitat for numerous waterfowl, primarily mallards, blue-winged and cinnamon teal, American coot, and Canada geese. Numerous shore bird and wading bird species breed here: the common American avocets, killdeer, common snipe, phalaropes, black-crowned night herons, and snowy egrets to name a few. Raptors such as marsh hawk and Swainson's hawk breed here, while the rough-legged hawk, golden eagle, and bald eagle winter here. The rare Brazilian free-tailed bat, mountain plover, northern goshawk, Wilson's phalarope, and a locally unique subspecies of the globally vulnerable northern pocket gopher also inhabit Baca NWR. A recent assessment of the refuge's biomass was conducted by the prominent Colorado Natural Heritage Program (CNHP). The CNHP study indicates that the refuge supports at least 28 rare, threatened, or endangered species, including the federally endangered southwestern willow flycatcher and one of the largest known populations of the globally imperiled slender spider flower. Colorado Division of Wildlife (CDW) biologists recently discovered a genetically unique population of the endangered Rio Grande sucker (fish) in the refuge. This strong population is considered by CDW to be significant to the recovery of the species throughout the Rio Grande watershed. The CNHP study also identified healthy instances of the narrow leaf cottonwood tree (actually in the willow family) and Rocky Mountain juniper woodland along the transitional stretches of Cottonwood Creek, South Crestone Creek, Spanish Creek, and Willow Creek riparian corridors.

## Location

Baca NWR is located north of Alamosa about 20 miles on Highway 17. The wetland and riparian areas located here are vitally important, not only providing maintenance for regional aquifers, but because they support some of the richest plant and animal communities in the world. The refuge supports important calving grounds for deer and elk. It also provides innate sanctuary for imperiled wildlife, including the ferruginous hawk, the threatened burrowing owl, the greater and lesser sandhill crane, and the Rio Grande sucker, an endangered fish. As many as 4,000 elk from the Sangre de Cristo Mountains depend on the area for important winter habitat and calving grounds to protect newborns.

## Contact

**Alamosa/Monte Vista National Wildlife Refuges**
9383 El Rancho Lane Alamosa, CO 81101
719-589-4021
http://alamosa.fws.gov

**U.S. Fish and Wildlife Service**
www.fws.gov
**For Refuge Information**
800-344-WILD

## Fast Facts

**Getting There:** To reach the refuge from Highway 160, turn north (at the east of Alamosa) on Highway 17. Continue a little over 20 miles to the refuge.
**Activities:** Bird and wildlife viewing
**Principal Mammals:** Elk, mule deer, coyote, black bear, raccoon, porcupine, skunk, red fox, beaver, cottontail rabbit, squirrel, ermine, muskrat, mink, and number of smaller game such as voles, and the northern pocket gopher
**Mammals of Special Interest:** Elk and mule deer
**Principal Birdlife:** Waterfowl to include many duck, geese, and teal species, sandhill crane, heron, whooping crane, and any number of small non-game wetland birds
**Birds of Special Interest:** Greater sandhill crane and Wilson's phalarope
**Habitat Overview:** Wetlands valley, farmlands rimmed by the Sangre de Cristo and San Juan Mountains
**Flora of Special Interest:** Slender spider flower
**Best Wildlife Viewing Ops:** Early morning and late evening when they are on the move from bedding to feeding areas. Wildlife can be seen from most public roads
**Best Birding Ops:** Winter is especially good for raptors; March for the sandhill cranes and then again in October; spring, summer, and fall for just about all others
**Best Photo Ops:** Early mornings for the sandhill cranes
**Hunting Ops:** None
**Fishing Ops:** None
**Camping Ops:** None
**Boating Ops:** None
**Hiking Trails:** None as of yet
**Motor Trails:** None as of yet

# The San Luis Valley

The San Luis Valley is the largest alpine valley in Colorado's mountainous regions. In fact, it is the largest in the world by some accounts. Spanning 8,000 square miles at an average elevation of 7,500 feet, the valley is surrounded by two of Colorado's impressive mountain ranges. It separates the Sangre de Cristo and San Juan Mountain ranges in south-central Colorado. The Rio Grande River and many of its tributaries drain the snowpack from these mountains to supply the precious lifeblood to the valley. Over the course of a year, it provides crucial resting, feeding, and breeding habitat for hundreds of bird species and a wide variety of other wildlife.

The valley sits on top of a geological formation called the Rio Grande Rift; basically it is a large split in the earth's crust where the sides are pulling away from each other. Mind you, this is happening ever so slowly. The mountains surrounding the valley have been eroding for millions of years, in turn filling the crack with the crumbling earth. Bedrock can be found about 30,000 feet below the valley floor, a little over 4 miles below sea level! Another thing I found very interesting is the number of streams that actually flow into the valley, only to disappear into the earth before reaching any definitive destination. The Rio Grande River is the only water to leave the valley as it follows this enormous gouge. Some of this water does leach to the surface to form the wetlands for which the valley is famous. The aquifer under the valley is huge, which accounts for a number of artesian wells as well.

A continuation of the rift can be found at the dramatic Rio Grande Gorge, farther south in New Mexico.

One important landmark in the valley is the Great Sand Dunes National Park and Preserve. It is also home to three vital national wildlife refuges: Alamosa, Monte Vista, and Baca. In the spring, large numbers of migrating birds stop in the valley to replenish their energy while journeying to northern breeding grounds. Monte Vista National Wildlife Refuge is well known for the flocks of sandhill cranes that stop there. As these migratory birds return to southern wintering grounds in the fall, they stop again at the refuges to reenergize. Local grain fields and privately owned croplands provide essential feeding habitat in close proximity to safe roosting areas found on these refuges.

Early summer also brings nesting shorebirds and water birds to all three refuges. Throughout the summer, the riparian passageway along the Rio Grande in the San Luis Valley offers habitat for many species of songbirds, including the rare southwestern willow flycatcher. This could be the northernmost habitat for the southwestern willow flycatcher (it is primarily found in Arizona). When winter hits the valley, some waterfowl may be found, but raptors will dominate the landscape. Short-eared owls winter and breed on the refuges, while bald eagles can be seen fishing and roosting along the Rio Grande at Alamosa NWR.

Elk, deer, antelope, beaver, coyote, and porcupine are some of the wildlife you may see while visiting the valley. Deer, elk, and pronghorn antelope reside on the refuges year round and many herds from higher elevations are seen in the fall and winter, moving to the valley bottom for food and refuge from hunting pressure.

The first people to hunt these elk and deer were the Ute Indians, also known as the "Blue Sky People". Comanche Indians did raid the valley, harassing the Ute for their fine elk meat and abundant waterfowl and small game. During this era, the Ute dominated the mountains and Comanche ruled the plains in southern Colorado. Europeans made it into the valley in 1694 led by Don Diego de Vargas. The Spaniards butted heads with the Comanche for nearly 100 years until a treaty was finally signed in the 1780s. The treaty was only achieved after several major battles in which the muskets of the Spaniards finally overwhelmed the feisty Comanche. Juan Bautista de Anza established a lasting peace with the Comanche in 1773, which led to the Arapaho and Cheyenne Indians moving into the valley. They developed a long-term, peaceful trading arrangement with the Spaniards as they rode from Santa Fe and Taos.

The first actual American to see the San Luis Valley was Zebulon Pike. Following him were trappers and fur traders. The valley became American territory at the conclusion of the Mexican-American War in 1848 and then on to statehood in 1876.

The San Luis Valley is rich in history and now, in the present day, the riches of the valley continue to provide for man and beast. Hunting, fishing, backpacking, and tourism dominate the outdoor activities in the valley. Waterfowl and small game hunting are allowed in the Alamosa NWR during their respective seasons. Check with state regulations for time and access. The national forests and BLM land provide access to big game hunting. The Rio Grande River is a very popular trout fishing destination, especially farther west from Creede to Del Norte (Wilderness Adventures Press makes a wonderful flyfishing map of two sections of this river). Northern pike are the predominant fish in the river near Alamosa. Smith Reservoir east of Alamosa is good for trout, while Sanchez Reservoir is a popular pike and carp fishery. San Luis State Park and the body of water named after it is good for several species. A number of my friends love the carp fishing there with their fly rods. Backpacking trails abound in the mountains surrounding the valley, following small streams or heading directly to high mountain lakes. The higher elevations are a great place to find brook trout and cutthroats.

Expect exhilarating hikes in the clean mountain air; however always be aware of the weather. Rain and lightning are common happenstances in the high country of Colorado.

*White-faced ibis*

## Bird List (Courtesy U.S. Fish and Wildlife Service)

### LOONS, GREBES

Pacific loon
Common loon
Pied-billed grebe
Eared grebe
Western grebe
Clark's grebe

### PELICANS

American white pelican

### CORMORANTS

Double-crested cormorant

### BITTERNS, HERONS, AND EGRETS

American bittern
Least bittern
Great blue heron
Great egret
Snowy egret
Little blue heron
Cattle egret
Green heron
Black-crowned night heron

### IBISES AND SPOONBILLS

White-faced ibis

### SWANS, GEESE, AND DUCKS

Greater white-fronted goose
Snow goose
Ross' goose
Canada goose
Tundra swan
Wood duck
Gadwall
American wigeon
Mallard
Blue-winged teal
Cinnamon teal
Northern shoveler
Northern pintail
Green-winged teal
Canvasback
Redhead
Ring-necked duck
Greater scaup
Lesser scaup
Bufflehead
Common goldeneye
Hooded merganser
Common merganser
Red-breasted merganser
Ruddy duck

### OSPREY, KITES, HAWKS, AND EAGLES

Osprey
Bald eagle
Northern harrier
Sharp-shinned hawk
Cooper's hawk
Northern goshawk
Swainson's hawk
Red-tailed hawk
Ferruginous hawk
Rough-legged hawk
Golden eagle

### FALCONS AND CARACARAS

American kestrel
Merlin
Peregrine falcon
Prairie falcon

### GALLINACEOUS BIRDS

Ring-necked pheasant

## RAILS

Virginia rail
Sora
Purple gallinule
Common moorhen
American coot

## CRANES

Sandhill crane
Whooping crane

## PLOVERS

Black-bellied plover
Semipalmated plover
Killdeer
Mountain plover

## STILTS AND AVOCETS

Black-necked stilt
American avocet

## SANDPIPERS AND PHALAROPES

Greater yellowlegs
Lesser yellowlegs
Solitary sandpiper
Willet
Spotted sandpiper
Whimbrel
Long-billed curlew
Marbled godwit
Sanderling
Western sandpiper
Least sandpiper
Baird's sandpiper
Pectoral sandpiper
Stilt sandpiper
Long-billed dowitcher
Common snipe
Wilson's phalarope

## SKUAS, JAEGERS, GULLS, AND TERNS

Franklin's gull
Bonaparte's gull
Ring-billed gull
Caspian tern
Common tern
Forster's tern
Least tern
Black tern

## PIGEONS AND DOVES

Rock dove
Band-tailed pigeon
Mourning dove

## BARN OWLS

Barn owl

## TYPICAL OWLS

Great horned owl
Burrowing owl
Long-eared owl
Short-eared owl

## NIGHTJARS

Common nighthawk
Common poorwill

## SWIFTS

White-throated swift

## HUMMINGBIRDS

Black-chinned hummingbird
Broad-tailed hummingbird
Rufous hummingbird

## KINGFISHERS

Belted kingfisher

## WOODPECKERS

Lewis' woodpecker
Red-headed woodpecker
Williamson's sapsucker
Red-naped sapsucker
Downy woodpecker

Hairy woodpecker
Northern flicker

**TYRANT FLYCATCHERS**

Olive-sided flycatcher
Western wood-pewee
Willow flycatcher
Say's phoebe
Vermilion flycatcher
Cassin's kingbird
Western kingbird
Eastern kingbird

**SHRIKES**

Loggerhead shrike
Northern shrike

**VIREOS**

Warbling vireo

**CROWS, JAYS, AND MAGPIES**

Black-billed magpie
American crow
Common raven

**LARKS**

Horned lark

**SWALLOWS**

Purple martin
Tree swallow
Violet-green swallow
Northern Rough-winged swallow
Bank swallow
Cliff swallow
Barn swallow

**TITMICE AND CHICKADEES**

Black-capped chickadee
Mountain chickadee

**NUTHATCHES**

White-breasted nuthatch

**WRENS**

Rock wren
House wren
Marsh wren

**KINGLETS**

Ruby-crowned kinglet

**THRUSHES**

Western bluebird
Mountain bluebird
Swainson's thrush
American robin

**MIMIC THRUSHES**

Northern mockingbird
Sage thrasher

**STARLINGS**

European starling
Wagtails and pipits
American (water) pipit

**WOOD WARBLERS**

Orange-crowned warbler
Yellow warbler
Yellow-rumped warbler
Townsend's warbler
Black-and-white warbler
Prothonotary warbler
Northern waterthrush
MacGillivray's warbler
Common yellowthroat
Hooded warbler
Wilson's warbler

**TANAGERS**

Western tanager

**SPARROWS AND TOWHEES**

Green-tailed towhee
Spotted towhee

Cassin's sparrow
American tree sparrow
Chipping sparrow
Brewer's sparrow
Vesper sparrow
Lark sparrow
Black-throated sparrow
Sage sparrow
Lark bunting
Savannah sparrow
Grasshopper sparrow
Song sparrow
Swamp sparrow
White-crowned sparrow
Dark-eyed junco
Lapland longspur

### CARDINALS, GROSBEAKS, AND ALLIES

Black-headed grosbeak
Blue grosbeak
Indigo bunting

## MAMMALS

Cinereus or masked shrew
Dusky or montane shrew
Common water shrew
Western small-footed myotis
Long-eared myotis
Little brown myotis
Yuma myotis
Hoary bat
Silver-haired bat
Big brown bat
Townsend's big-eared bat
Brazilian free-tailed bat
Desert cottontail
Mountain cottontail
White-tailed jackrabbit
Least chipmunk
Yellow-bellied marmot
Thirteen-lined ground squirrel
Gunnison's prairie-dog

### BLACKBIRDS AND ORIOLES

Bobolink
Red-winged blackbird
Western meadowlark
Yellow-headed blackbird
Brewer's blackbird
Great-tailed grackle
Brown-headed cowbird
Bullock's oriole

### FINCHES

Gray-crowned rosy finch
Cassin's finch
House finch
Pine siskin
Lesser goldfinch
American goldfinch

### OLD WORLD SPARROWS

House sparrow

Botta's pocket gopher
Northern pocket gopher
Plains pocket mouse
Silky pocket mouse
Ord's kangaroo rat
American beaver
Western harvest mouse
Deer mouse
Northern grasshopper mouse
House mouse
Long-tailed vole
Montane vole
Meadow vole
Western jumping mouse
Porcupine
Coyote
Red fox
Common gray fox
Black bear

Raccoon
Ermine
Long-tailed weasel
American mink
American badger
Western spotted skunk
Striped skunk
Mountain lion
Bobcat
Wapiti or elk
Mule deer
White-tailed deer
Pronghorn antelope

**AMPHIBIANS**

Tiger salamander
Plains spadefoot
Western frog
Great Plains toad
Woodhouse's toad
Striped chorus frog
Bullfrog
Northern leopard frog

**REPTILES**

Snapping turtle
Short-horned lizard
Eastern fence lizard
Many-lined skink
Milk snake
Bull snake
Western terrestrial garter snake
Western rattlesnake

*Yellow-bellied marmot*

# Monte Vista National Wildlife Refuge

14,804 Acres; South-central Colorado 6 miles south of Monte Vista on Highway 160

## History

Monte Vista National Wildlife Refuge is one of the three national wildlife refuges in the San Luis Valley. It was established in 1953. The Migratory Bird Conservation Commission helped set aside 14,804 acres to provide important habitat for wildlife, predominantly waterfowl.

As an artificially created wetland, water is rigorously managed on Monte Vista NWR. There are numerous dikes and water control structures creating a collage of diverse wetland habitats. Artesian wells, pumped wells, and irrigation canals supply water to shallow wet meadows and many deeper ponds. Some of these structures date back to the 1880s, an era referred to as the "ditch boom". Managing the refuge is diversified, and concerns other than water must be taken into account. Some areas are mown, others are grazed. Farming is important to ensure that refuge lands continue to provide food; there is habitat for waterfowl and many other birds, and believe it or not, prescribed burns are performed to renew the landscape.

## Wildlife

Canada geese, mallards, many species of teal, and pintails are familiar waterfowl found here. Other very common water birds include American avocets, killdeer, egrets, herons, and white-faced ibis. However, the Monte Vista NWR stands out from the others in the San Luis Valley because it is an important stopover for large numbers of migrating greater sandhill cranes. While on their northward journey from wintering areas around Bosque del Apache NWR in New Mexico, they stop in the valley to rest and feed on the abundant food sources before taking flight to breeding grounds in the northern United States and southern Canada. Between 23,000 and 27,000 cranes, nearly 95 percent of the Rocky Mountain population, passes through in the spring and then again in the fall to take advantage of the wetlands. Apparently they have been doing this for quite some time. There were fossils matching the sandhill crane found in Nebraska that date back 6 million years. This would give the sandhill crane the distinction of being the world's oldest still-living bird species.

Several species of waterfowl take up residence on the refuge through the summer to mate and rear young. Monte Vista NWR is recognized as one of the most productive duck breeding wetlands in North America.

I made a trip to Monte Vista NWR in mid-March to take advantage of the photo opportunities the sandhill cranes offered. I was not disappointed. I made it to the refuge late in the afternoon, just in time to catch the low waning light.

I drove through several times viewing a number of mallards, American coots, northern pintails, and teal. I noticed a pair of cranes on the first pass through but was unable to get an image. Western meadow larks and red-winged blackbirds were perched on the fences, raggedy cattails, and barren tree limbs, while mountain bluebirds picked up seeds and pesky magpies were unhappy about the intrusions from both the other birds and this strange four-wheeled predator. I was able to get several images from the driver's seat with a nifty window clamp and ball-head. A small grazing pronghorn antelope buck stood still long enough for a soft backlit shot and then a doe looked up and posed for me in the shrubbery. But where are the sandhill cranes?

On my last pass around the ponds I notice several flights of large birds farther to the south. However, they were not making it all the way to these ponds. Another mile or so south on Highway 15 is a paved pullout – a useful pullout with a high-powered monocular for viewing the thousands of cranes that were coming in to roost for the night. With the last of the sun at my back and Mount Blanca as a backdrop, I set up the tripod and clicked away at these remarkably boisterous birds. They make numerous different calls, much different from anything I have ever heard from other birds. It is very much like a bugle, but not quite. I stayed until after dark watching in amazement as thousands of these tall, gray feathered, long-necked birds landed in the shallow marsh. Males and females are comparable in appearance by means of a red crown, with males slightly larger. Adults can stand up to 5 feet tall and have a wingspan of around 6 or 7 feet. I would say that most of the cranes I was viewing were in the 3- to 4-foot-tall range. They like to roost in shallow water, maybe 4 to 6 inches deep, for protection from predators, primarily coyotes. I guess coyotes don't like to get their feet wet.

I was up early the next morning to begin where I left off the night before. Since it was 30 to 45 minutes before light would be available, I decided to take a quick trip to the southernmost part of the refuge at CR 8S and headed east. There is another pullout and viewing area on the left about a half mile east of Highway 15. I did not stop, as I was just trying to get the lay of the land. I talked with a photographer that had spent the previous evening at this viewing area and got some great images of the cranes as they were flying into the refuge. Continuing east a few miles confirmed the side roads into the refuge that I noticed on a map. As I turned around, there was just enough light to see the outline of 20 to 25 elk browsing just inside the refuge.

I put on my insulated coveralls, hooded jacket, and gloves to ward off the freezing temperature and waited for the sun to come up. Two other photographers and I were treated to a stunning sunrise. As the light started to paint our backdrop, steam was rising in the midst of the cranes and the only sounds to be heard were the snap of

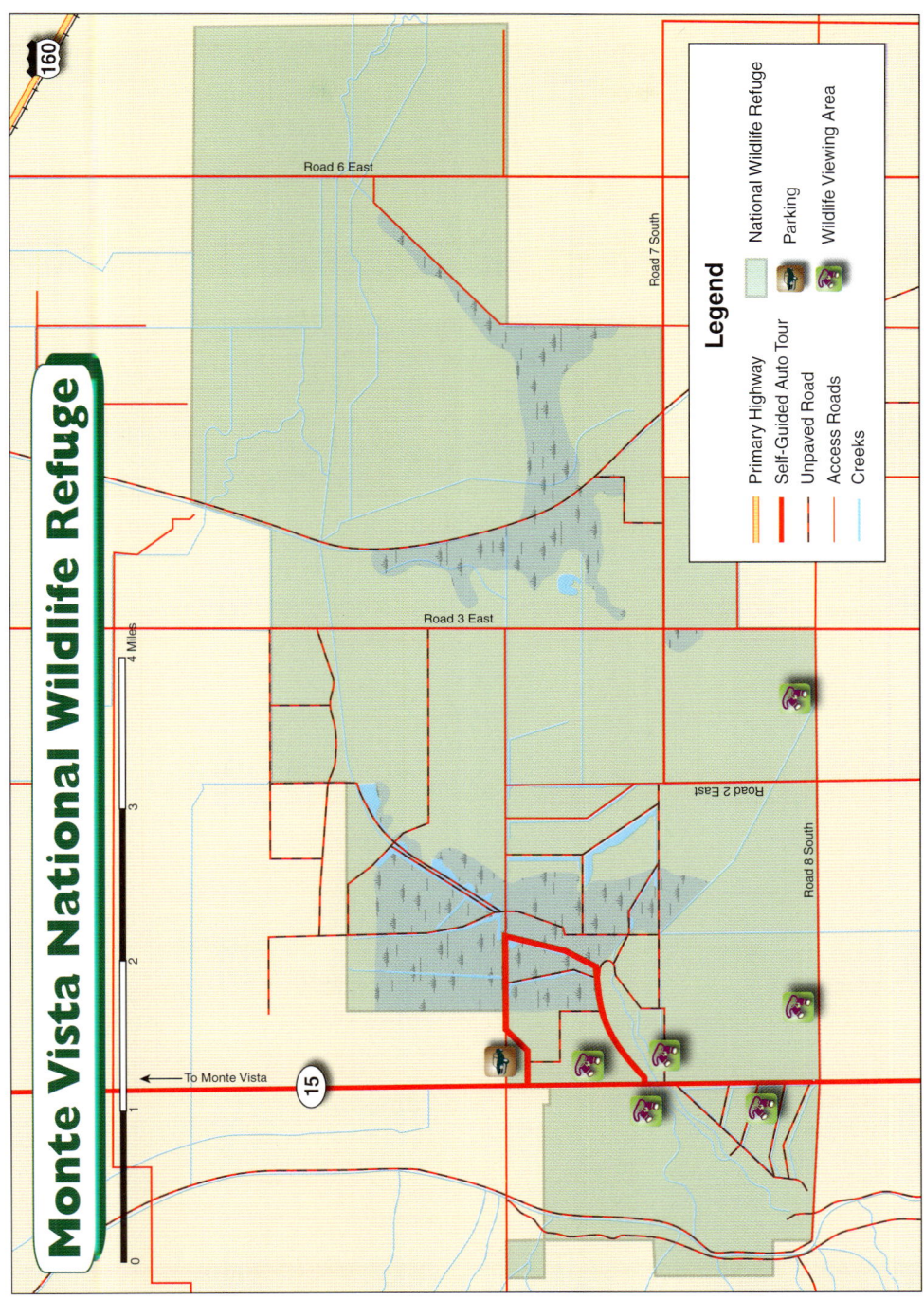

three camera shutters and the muffled calls of the cranes as they woke up. One of the photographers stopped composing long enough to say, "Looks like someone turned on the special effects for us this morning." I replied, "Cranes in the mist!"

As the sun advanced into the sky, the cranes were taking flight regularly for their daily treat in the grain fields around the Monte Vista area. It is very interesting to see them prepare for takeoff. It reminded me of an airport. A dozen or so birds would line up at the south end of the area we were watching, stretch out their necks, run a few steps and off they would go. Some banking into the sun and heading north toward town, some continuing south, and still others would head back to the west in search of food. Before they were out of sight, the next group would be in the air. Try some shots with a high powered zoom to tighten in on just one or two birds, then a medium wide angle to catch the whole group taking flight, and then try a wide angle to get the big picture. Shooting towards the east required the use of a lens hood to eliminate glare. It is also a good idea to bracket the exposure when your subject is backlit as was the case this morning. This once in a lifetime event went on for a couple hours and I enjoyed every finger numbing, nose dripping minute of it.

A relevant compositional tip was given to me and I feel obligated to pass it along to you. When you see a group of cranes moving in the direction the previous birds were taking off (for example to the right) and leaning forward with necks straightened, this is the sign they are ready to take flight. Position the cranes in the lower left of your viewfinder and focus on the closest bird so when they take off you can start

*Red-winged blackbird*

releasing the shutter as the birds are centered in your viewfinder. Make sure to loosen the tripod head's tilt and pan adjustments so several progressive images can be taken while panning with the group going away. If your camera has continuous advance feature, use it. You never know which image will be the finest when the camera is moving.

*Mallard at sunset*

The refuge is occupied by several hundred elk later in the fall and through the winter in quest of winter food and sanctuary from hunting pressure on nearby public lands. With the trees void of leaves in early spring, it was very nice to see the plentiful number of raptor nests. Most of the wildlife on the refuge could be seen along a 4-mile auto tour and from county roads which are kept open year round.

The San Luis Valley is a unique environment. It only receives about 7 to 10 inches of rain a year, so it can be as dry as a desert just across the road from the wetlands. Monte Vista NWR makes certain all types of wildlife will continue to have a place to feel secure.

## Annual Monte Vista Crane Festival

Late in February, sandhill cranes, the San Luis Valley's oldest visitors, begin their annual trek from south to north, stopping off near the Monte Vista National Wildlife Refuge to load up on fuel. For millions of years, the sandhills have been spending their "Spring Break" in Colorado's Valley of the Cranes. Early March is when crane watchers come from far and wide to join this celebration at the Monte Vista Crane Festival. While the festival offers outstanding opportunities for viewing and understanding cranes and other wildlife, the 20,000 or so greater sandhill cranes are the show stoppers.

The festival hosts wildlife experts, local naturalists and biologists who present educational workshops at the Monte Vista Middle School, while flocks of dancing sandhills assemble in the neighboring farm fields, just east of town. Bus tours to the nearby refuge and adjacent farmlands provide visitors with the opportunity to view this spectacle up close and personal, with a knowledgeable local guide. Special tours feature raptor identification, sunset trips to view cranes, and visits to closed areas of the refuge for Crane Fest participants.

A dinner with live entertainment, a pancake breakfast, and local restaurants and concessions provide sustenance for happy crane watchers from as far away as Japan. Motels and B&Bs fill up weeks in advance, and the population of Monte Vista nearly doubles during the weekend of Crane Fest. Come visit the Valley of the Cranes and enjoy their annual spring return to one of Colorado's most spectacularly scenic places.

## Location

Six miles south of Monte Vista on Highway 15, there is an entrance into the refuge on the left. An information station and a short auto tour are found here.

## Contact

**Monte Vista Crane Festival**
 P.O. Box 585, Monte Vista Colorado 81144
 719-852-3552
 www.cranefest.com

**Alamosa/Monte Vista National Wildlife Refuges**
9383 El Rancho Lane Alamosa, CO 81101
719-589-4021
http://alamosa.fws.gov

**For Refuge Information**
800-344-WILD

**International Crane Foundation**, www.savingcranes.org

## Fast Facts

**Getting There:** From Highway 160 in Monte Vista, turn south on Highway 15. Go 6 miles and the refuge will be on the left. County Road 8 South is the southernmost boundary with dirt road access into the refuge on CR 2E and CR 3E.
**Activities:** Bird and wildlife viewing.
**Principal Mammals:** Elk, mule deer, pronghorn antelope, coyote, black bear, raccoon, porcupine, skunk, red fox, beaver, cottontail rabbit, squirrel, ermine, muskrat, mink and number of smaller game such as, voles, field mice, and Ord's kangaroo rat
**Mammals of Special Interest:** Elk and mule deer
**Principal Birdlife:** Waterfowl to include many duck, geese, and teal species, sandhill crane, heron, whooping crane, and any number of small non-game wetland birds
**Birds of Special Interest:** Greater sandhill crane and whooping crane
**Habitat Overview:** Wetlands valley, farmlands, rimmed by the Sangre de Cristo and San Juan Mountains
**Best Wildlife Viewing Ops:** Early morning and late evening when they are on the move from bedding to feeding areas. Wildlife can be seen from most public roads
**Best Birding Ops:** Winter is especially good for raptors; March for the sandhill cranes and then again in October; spring, summer and fall for just about all others
**Best Photo Ops:** Early mornings for the sandhill cranes
**Hunting Ops:** None
**Fishing Ops:** None
**Camping Ops:** None
**Boating Ops:** None
**Hiking Trails:** A short walk is available at the northern entrance to tour the open ponds, however you are encouraged to stay in your vehicle to prevent interaction with the wildlife.
**Motor Trails:** A short ride at the northern entrance to tour the open ponds. County roads that border the refuge such as CR 8S, CR 2E, CR 3E, CR 7S, and CR 6E.

# Russell Lakes State Wildlife Area

### 3,000 acres; 20 miles north of Alamosa

## Wildlife

At 3,000 acres, Russell Lakes State Wildlife Area has one of the nicest collections of wetlands in Colorado and it just so happens to be the largest adjoining wetland area managed by the Colorado Division of Wildlife. Most of it is off-limits to the public, but many seasonal ponds can be scanned from roads in the area, and the Johnson Lake Nature Trail at the west entrance to the wetlands provides year-round access to ponds and marshes.

The overall area is fantastic habitat for breeding waterfowl and shore birds including cinnamon teal, western grebes and Clark's grebes, American bittern, sora, Virginia rail, black-necked stilt, white-faced ibis, marsh wren, common yellowthroat, and Savannah sparrow. Audubon Colorado has found that species like the snowy egret has as many as 20 breeding pairs in the area; the white-faced ibis could have 50 breeding pairs; and the thick-necked black-crowned night heron has 20 pairs.

White pelican, American avocet, and great-tailed grackle are seen on a regular basis. Several of the ponds hold warmwater fish, which fetch in such bird species as osprey, mergansers, double-crested cormorants, and a number of gulls.

The mix of cottonwood trees at the parking area can hold a number of bird species because of the close proximity to the water. Look for migrant warblers, sparrows, and flycatchers. One of my favorite birds, the Bullock's oriole, can be seen as well as the yellow warbler, mourning dove, and house wren. Great horned owls have been found roosting here. In the saltbush and sage surrounding the ponds, sage thrasher and Brewer's sparrow thrive.

Through my research of the San Luis Valley, I had found out that the national wildlife refuges in the area, particularly Baca, are important calving areas for elk. Wouldn't you know it, I was heading east late in the afternoon on R Road to access the north end of Russell Lakes SWA and off to the north (on private property) was a herd of cows and calves. There must have been 50 to 60 animals. Well off the road and too far for a photo, I just stopped and glassed them with my binoculars. Some were bedded down, a few of the young were rough-housing a bit, and the constant "bleeb-bleeb" of the cows talking was mesmerizing. It pays to make inquiries before you go into an area, just to be better prepared. Now I may or may not have seen the elk since they were so far off the road, but I was looking because of what I had read on the area. The other big game animal that turned up on a regular basis is the trusty mule deer. They are thick in the valley and I jumped a couple does and a fawn as I entered Russell Lakes from the north side. I parked and hiked out to Island Lake. Camera and tripod over the shoulder, it did not take long to connect with a couple nice images of black-necked stilts. There were four that I was able to crawl up on, but two of them seemed to be working together to catch an early evening snack. I was able to see some nice interaction between the two and locked it on the memory card. I backed off and just about stepped on a Woodhouse's toad. I was able to zoom in and bring home a close-up of it.

I hope you are catching onto the point I am trying to get across. Wildlife is everywhere in the San Luis Valley. To close this section, I would be lax in my information if I didn't pass along this last tidbit. I was seeing Swainson's hawks on a very regular basis driving to Russell Lakes. There may have been another species in there somewhere, maybe a red-tailed or even a prairie falcon (I am not that good at recognizing raptor species yet), but driving back to Alamosa that evening was unbelievable. I was seeing so many that I decided to start counting. I counted 38 raptors and at least 30 of them were sitting on utility poles. I would pull up under them, pop the camera on the window clamp and let the shutter take over. Counting the birds I had observed earlier in the day, I must have seen a total of four dozen

*Woodhouse toad*

*This great-horned owl nest is right in the parking lot.*

raptors. That is a huge number in my books. The only time I had seen more than that was when I was in high school driving a tractor for a farmer in town. I was kicking up mice and these hawks were swooping in, one right after the other, grabbing up hundreds of mice throughout the day.

Enjoy your time here; it is a fantastic outing for the whole family!

## Location

Russell Lakes State Wildlife Area is located in the northern part of the San Luis Valley, 10 miles south of the town of Saguache on Highway 285. There are actually two entrances into the area. The main entrance is just south of R Road on Highway 185, turn east into the parking area and trailhead access. The secondary entrance is a couple miles east on R Road from Highway 285, turn south to access parking and trailheads.

As with many wetlands in the San Luis Valley, much of Russell Lakes SWA is closed to the public February 15 to July 15 to protect nesting birds from disturbance. However, the Johnson Lake Trail is open year round.

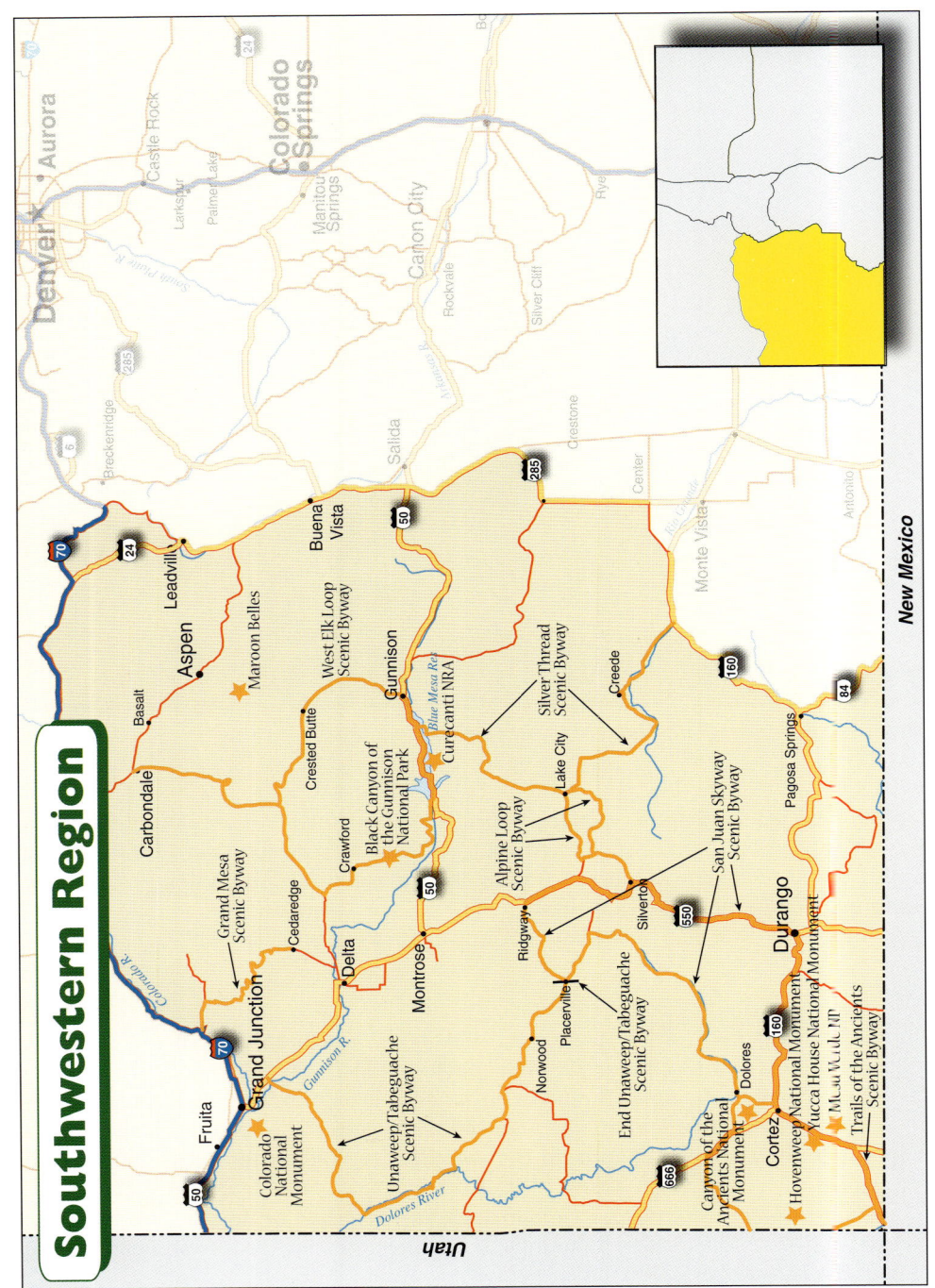

# Southwestern Colorado

# Curecanti National Recreation Area

**Southwest Colorado, includes about 40 miles of the Gunnison River basin east of Montrose**

## Introduction

Starting with the Blue Mesa Dam, the Gunnison River is backed up forming the largest body of water in Colorado, the Blue Mesa Reservoir. Three historic Colorado towns – Iola, Cebolla, and Sapinero – were abandoned and flooded when Blue Mesa Reservoir was created. To its credit, Blue Mesa Reservoir is the largest kokanee salmon fishery in the United States and produced the state-record mackinaw (lake trout) in 2007 that measured 44.5 inches and tipped the scales at just over 50 pounds. Every year in late August and September, a marathon run of spawning kokanee swim upstream through the town of Gunnison to the East River and the Roaring Judy fish hatchery. Hundreds of anglers pursue this run for the chance to fill a shelf in the freezer with this tasty fare.

The next dam and reservoir downstream is Morrow Point. A unique opportunity to view the upper end of Black Canyon by boat exists at Curecanti. A pontoon boat carrying 42 passengers leaves the dock twice a day from Memorial Day weekend through Labor Day weekend. The Morrow Point Boat Tour runs twice a day at 10:00am and 12:30pm every day except Tuesday. For an hour and a half, passengers ride through the canyon accompanied by a national park ranger or volunteer to tell the story behind the scenery. Morrow Point Reservoir popped the state record rainbow trout in 2003. It weighed in at 19 pounds, 11 ounces. Reservations are required and walk-ons will not be permitted. Call 970-641-2337, ext. 205 or stop by the Elk Creek Visitor Center (15 miles west of Gunnison off of Highway 50) to make reservations. Special tours for educational groups are available upon request. Reservations for the season begin on May 1. As of this printing, fees are $16 for adults, $8 for all children 12 and under, and $8 for adults with an Interagency Senior/Access Pass.

Note: The tour begins at the Pine Creek boat dock. The 1.5-mile round-trip hike along the Pine Creek Trail to the dock includes a stairway of 232 steps. The trailhead is located just off U.S. Highway 50 at mile marker 130, which is a mile west of the junction with Colorado Highway 92. Allow one hour to hike from the trailhead to the boat dock. Be prepared for a hike and a half-day outing. Be sure to bring drinking water and a

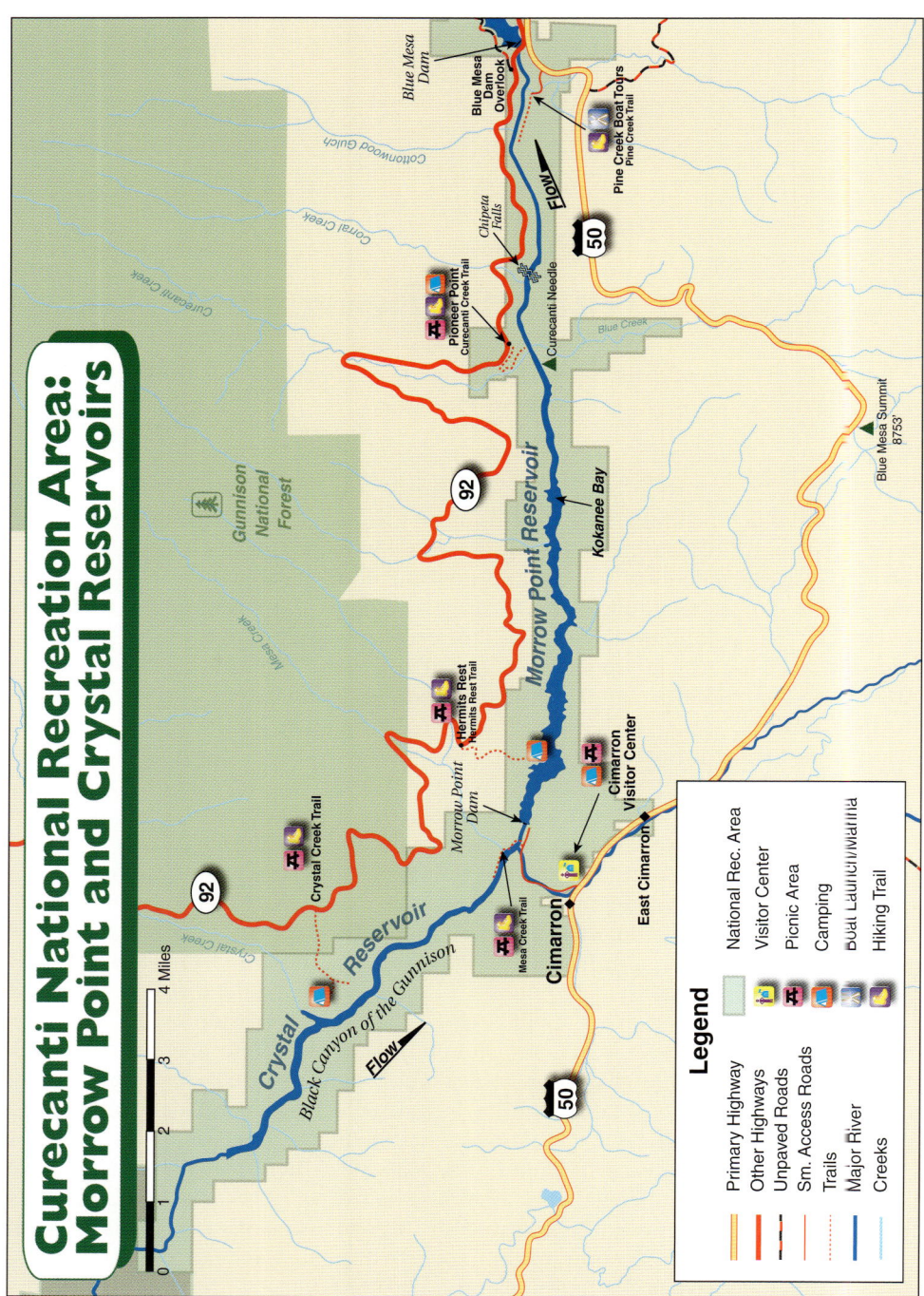

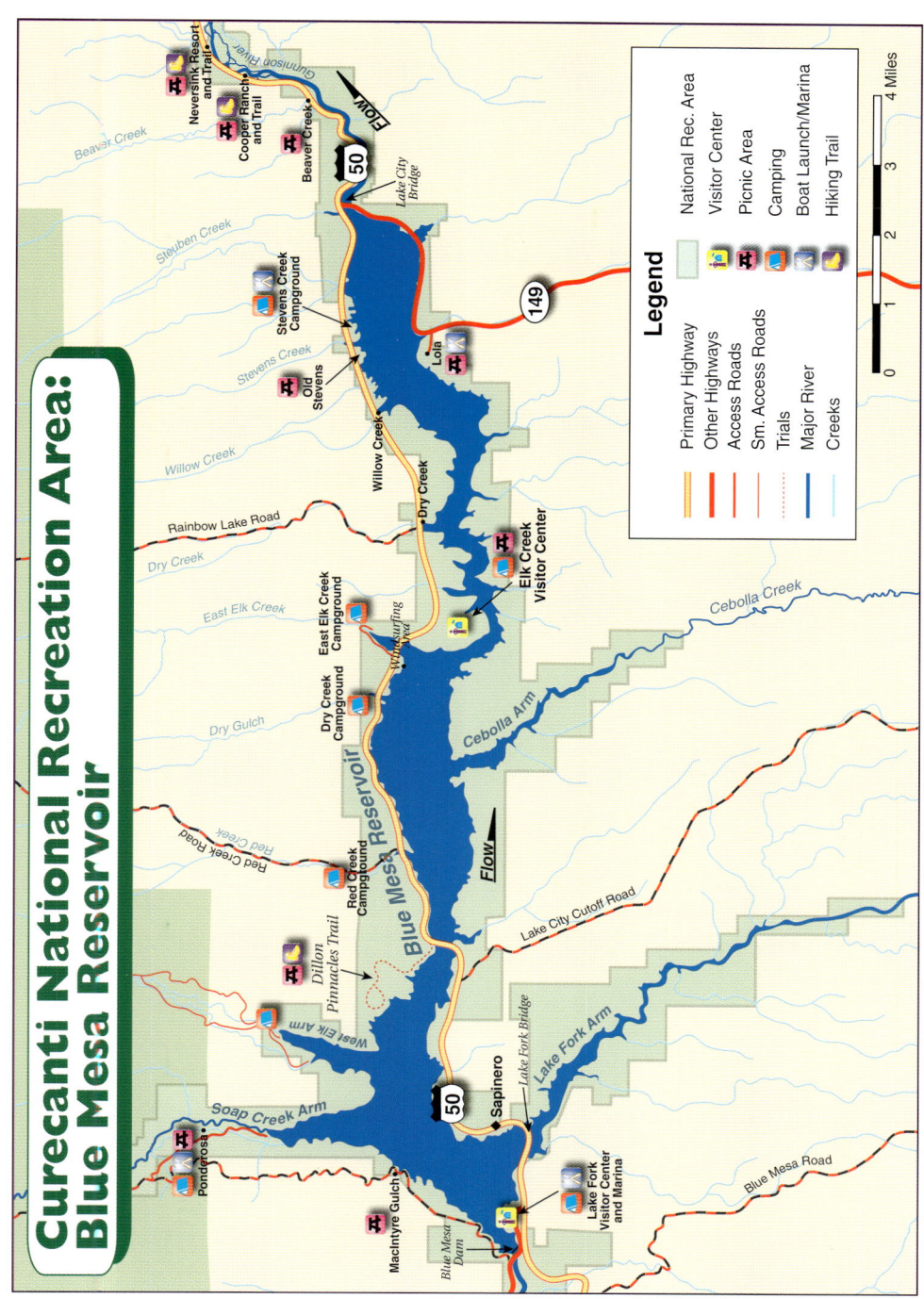

jacket. Mountain weather can be very unpredictable. A sunny morning can suddenly become a stormy afternoon. Expect the air temperature to be significantly cooler on the water. Feel free to bring your lunch, as picnic tables are provided along the trail and at the boat dock. Sorry, no pets, smoking, or alcoholic beverages are allowed on the boat. Don't forget the camera!

Crystal Dam is the third structure in line controlling the flow of the Gunnison River. Crystal Reservoir is a long narrow reservoir with limited access. From the south side, a road from the East Portal Campground follows the river bottom up to the dam and a road from the town of Cimarron drops down to a picnic area at the top of the reservoir. From the north side, take Highway 92 to Crystal trailhead and walk down to a picnic area on the north shore.

## Wildlife

The mesa country of southwestern Colorado has always been a point of interest for wildlife viewing and birders. The rich sagebrush country and juniper forests with the addition of all the water in the Gunnison Valley can only mean a diverse and abundant wildlife population. Elk, deer, coyote, black bear, mountain lion, badger, and bighorn sheep all live in the Curecanti area. Elk are seasonal; black bear, bighorn

*House finch*

sheep, and mountain lions are elusive and very rarely seen. Mule deer are by far the most visible big game in the area. In the spring, when the snows begin to melt on the mesas, the deer move up from the area surrounding Blue Mesa Reservoir. They have spent the winter in lower, more protected areas and now move into Curecanti to take advantage of new food sources such as wildflowers and flowering shrubs and trees. They spend the summer raising young, avoiding predators, and fattening up for the upcoming mating season. I have grown up with mule deer and still, to this day, find them as fascinating as I did in my early years when I hunted them with a bow and arrow. It is so hard to get in their "zone" undetected. They have a keen sense of smell (and apparently loathe the smell of humans) and have great hearing. The mule deer is named for its large mule-like ears, which act like satellite dishes to collect the smallest of noises and alert the deer of possible danger. I now pursue them with a camera and long lens; even as non-threatening as I am, they are very difficult to get close to. I have taken a number of very nice images of muleys the past couple years and cherish every hour spent in that quest.

With the amazing amount of habitat in the area, birders need to stay alert to many possibilities. The wooded area along the river is prime habitat for song birds, owls, and woodpeckers. The sharp buzz of hummingbirds poking around the wildflowers is common and you can also expect to hear the cooing of mourning doves. Warblers, flycatchers, blackbirds, and the common robin are popular. From the many overlooks into the canyon itself, a bird watcher can find the brisk, irregular flight of swifts and swallows as they dive for insects along the canyon wall. Expect to see turkey vultures riding the thermals above the canyon rim. Black-billed magpies, red-tailed hawks, western bluebirds, and the diving peregrine falcons can also be seen from these viewpoints. The majestic bald eagle winters at Curecanti, feeding on trout and salmon until the water becomes iced over.

The water habitat will not disappoint. Great blue herons can be found feeding on morsels along the shore and western grebes will be diving just out of reach in slightly deeper water. Sandpipers and scavenging gulls are common also. There are a few boisterous sandhill cranes that pass through in the spring.

The sagebrush country surrounding the canyon is important habitat for the struggling Gunnison sage grouse. The grouse in the Gunnison Basin, including those in and around Curecanti National Recreation Area, account for the majority of the population of these beautiful birds. Counts of the birds indicate a decline in the species within the Gunnison Basin of more than 60 percent since the 1950s. There are areas of the Curecanti that are closed off during the mating season to help avoid contact with people. Please respect these closures as to help with the conservation efforts. If you do spot the Gunnison sage grouse, please view them in silence from your car and keep pets on a leash.

## Fishing

With a full gamut of trout species, the Gunnison River and its many tributaries offer up some of the best fly fishing in the state. From the massive trout in the Taylor River below Taylor Park Reservoir to the tiny brook trout in the small creeks that find their way to the Gunnison, variety abounds in the Gunnison Valley. Try the Gunnison River just above Blue Mesa Reservoir at the Neversink access or at the East Portal, the Lake Fork of the Gunnison near Gateway, or the East River above Almont. There are great summer hatches of caddis, green drakes, and stoneflies throughout the drainage.

Blue Mesa Reservoir is best fished from a boat. Mackinaw (lake trout) are the most popular species amongst anglers and best fished through the deep subsurface canyons of the reservoir. The deep, cold water provides excellent habitat for the predatory lakers. Kokanee salmon run a close second in popularity. The salmon are stocked from the Roaring Judy Fish Hatchery north of Gunnison. When they are ready to spawn at the end of their third or fourth summer, they travel upriver to return to the hatchery. At this time, they no longer feed, and after they reproduce, they die. Rainbow trout and yellow perch provide excellent game also. All boaters on Blue Mesa Reservoir should be aware that strong afternoon winds, sometimes accompanied by violent storms, can cause hazardous conditions. Be diligent and watch for the buildup of threatening clouds. As soon as strong winds begin to blow, head for shore.

Please check fishing regulations for the area before taking to any water in Colorado.

*Hen mallard*

## Camping

There are ten campgrounds within or very close to the Curecanti National Recreation Area. They vary in size and amenities. The Curecanti NRA is very close to and is an excellent area in which to stay when visiting the Black Canyon of the Gunnison National Park. Amenities such as water, flush toilets, dump stations, and electrical hookups are available during the summer months (mid-May to mid-September). Many of these campgrounds can be booked online at: www.nps.gov/cure/planyourvisit/camping.htm.

Here is a list of the campgrounds:

### Elk Creek

This campground is located 16 miles west of Gunnison on U.S. Highway 50 on the north shore of Blue Mesa Reservoir in treeless, sagebrush country. It has 160 sites with all the amenities including a boat ramp for Blue Mesa Reservoir and is open year round with limited services. At this printing most sites are $12. With electric hook up, they are $18.

### Lake Fork

This campground is located 27 miles west of Gunnison on U.S. Highway 50 on the south shore of Blue Mesa Reservoir near Blue Mesa Dam. The campground is paved except for walk-in sites and it has 90 sites open during the summer months with all the amenities, except electric. It includes a boat ramp for Blue Mesa Reservoir. At this printing, most sites are $12.

### Stevens Creek

This campground is located 12 miles west of Gunnison on U.S. Highway 50 on the north shore of Blue Mesa Reservoir in open sagebrush country. It has 53 sites open during the summer months with water during the summer months, vault toilets, tables and fire grates, and a boat ramp for Blue Mesa Reservoir's Iola Basin. At this printing, most sites are $12.

### Cimarron

This campground is located 20 miles east of Montrose on U.S. Highway 50, located in the vicinity of the historic narrow gauge railroad town from which it is named, Denver and Rio Grande Western Railroad exhibits, and access to Crystal Reservoir near Morrow Point Dam. It has 21 sites with water, flush toilets, dump station, and visitor center during the summer months. At this printing most sites are $12.

### East Portal

This campground is located 2 miles downstream of Crystal Dam at the top of Black Canyon. Take CO Highway 347 for 6 miles to the north from the junction of 347 and U.S. Highway 50 to entrance of Black Canyon of the Gunnison National Park. Turn right just past the entrance station, and follow East Portal Road 5 miles down to the campground. Note: Vehicles exceeding 22 feet in length (including trailer) are not permitted on the East Portal Road because of the steep 16-percent grade and sharp, narrow curves. Black Canyon of the Gunnison National Park entrance fee applies to those accessing East Portal.

The campground is shaded by box elder trees and is near the historic Gunnison River Diversion Tunnel. It is due east of the Black Canyon of the Gunnison National Park boundary. It only has 15 sites with water, vault toilets, tables and fire grates and is open during the summer months. At this printing, most sites are $12.

## Dry Gulch

This campground is located just north of U.S. Highway 50, 17 miles west of Gunnison. The campground is shaded by large cottonwood trees. It only has nine sites open during the summer months with water, vault toilets, tables and fire grates. This campground does have a horse corral. At this printing, most sites are $12.

## Ponderosa

This campground is located at the northwest end of the Soap Creek Arm of Blue Mesa Reservoir. From U.S. Highway 50, follow CO Highway 92 a half mile past Blue Mesa Dam to Soap Creek Road. Proceed 7 miles north on the gravel Soap Creek Road. It has 28 sites and is open during the summer months with water, vault toilets, tables and fire grates. This campground does have a horse corral. At this printing most sites are $12. Note: During dry conditions, the first 7 miles of Soap Creek Road are passable to trailers and motor homes. Rain can make the Soap Creek Road hazardous or impassable.

## Gateview

This campground is located in a deep, narrow canyon at the extreme south end of the Lake Fork Arm of Blue Mesa Reservoir. Take CO Highway 149 to 7 miles west of Powderhorn, then 6 miles north on the gravel Blue Mesa Cutoff Road. It only has six sites and is open during the summer months with water, vault toilets, tables and fire grates. At this printing most sites are $12.

## Red Creek (Individual and Group Campground)

This campground is located 19 miles west of Gunnison just north of U.S. Highway 50. The two individual sites and one group site are located among large cottonwood trees. The group site can accommodate 20 people. It is open during the summer months and has water, vault toilets, tables and fire grates. At this printing the individual sites are $12 and the group site is $28.

## East Elk Creek (Group Campground)

This campground is located 16.5 miles west of Gunnison just north of U.S. Highway 50. The site is located among large cottonwood trees and accommodates a total of 50 people. It is open during the summer months and has water, vault toilets, tables and fire grates. There is a picnic shelter and the site goes for $53 per night.

## Location

Curecanti National Recreation Area consists of a series of three dams and reservoirs on the Gunnison River located between Montrose and Gunnison along Highway 50. It is approximately 200 miles southwest of Denver via Interstate 70 and Highway 50. The recreation area is also accessed from the south via Highway 149 and by the north via Highway 92.

## Contact

**National Park Service**
 102 Elk Creek
 Gunnison, Colorado 81230
 Park Headquarters: 970-641-2337

**Elk Creek Visitor Center**
 Open all year.
 Hours: Fall, Winter: 8:30am-4:00pm Monday through Friday, closed on federal holidays.
 Spring: 8:30am-4:00pm every day, closed on federal holidays.
 Summer: 8:00am-6:00pm every day.
 970-641-2337 extension 205
 Location: 16 miles west of Gunnison Highway 50.

**Cimarron Visitor Center**
 Open intermittently mid-May through the end of September.
 Hours: 9:00am-4:00pm
 970-249-4074
 Location: The town of Cimarron 35 miles west of Gunnison on Highway 50
 Commercial airline service is available to Gunnison, Montrose, and Grand Junction.

Please refer to this website if you would like a preferred outfitter to help with a visit to Curecanti and surrounding areas: www.nps.gov/cure/planyourvisit/outfitters.htm

# The Maroon Bells (mountain)

181,117 Acres; Eastern entrance to the Maroon Bells-Snowmass Wilderness Area, southwest of Aspen

## Introduction

The splendid view of the 14,156-foot South Maroon Bell and 14,014-foot North Maroon Bell at Maroon Lake is the most photographed of mountains in Colorado, if not North America. These photos grace the covers of books and magazines whenever Colorado is in the subject line. Actually it doesn't have to involve Colorado. These photographs are used in advertisements covering everything from nature to beer. The Maroon Bells truly exemplifies Colorado's nickname of "Colorful Colorado". The jagged red stone, reflections from Maroon Lake, the aspen trees both in the summer and fall, and the fir forest produce an array of color and texture, hence the enormous popularity of the area. The famous photographer Ansel Adams was able to compose stunning black and white images of this amazing place.

Maroon Lake has limited accessibility by car during the restricted hours of the summer season. Due to the popularity of this wilderness area, there are shuttle buses from Aspen Highlands Ski Area that take visitors to Maroon Lake. This is from about mid-June through Labor Day, plus weekends in September. While the shuttle buses are running, Maroon Creek Road is closed from 8:30am to 5:00pm. Visitors need to take the bus which leaves from Aspen Highlands Ski Area. Ask forest service visitor information personnel for bus schedule info or call 970-925-3445. Early birds may drive in before the 8:30am deadline; however the parking area will fill quickly. There is a $10 fee to enter the area if you do not have an America the Beautiful Interagency Annual Pass. If you visit federal lands frequently such as national parks, national forests, Bureau of Land Management lands, or US Fish and Wildlife Service lands, look into purchasing an America the Beautiful Interagency Pass. Just a few visits to federal lands could easily pay for the annual pass.

## History

The Maroon Bells are part of a formation developed from ancient sea-bed deposits, more than 290 million years old, which were compressed under enormous pressure.

The rock that makes up the Maroon Bells is soft red shale and a paler siltstone (called the Maroon Formation) that lifted up along with the rest of the Rockies. The Bells are named for their "bell" shape. The reddish color comes from tiny iron particles that have been oxidized over the years. When the light is right, usually just as the sun bathes them in the early morning, they take on a beautiful maroon color.

The Maroon Bells area and the valley below were formed by glaciers and the stream erosion that followed. Avalanches and landslides leave their fingerprint on the area also. Evidence of erosion is noticeable throughout the valley. Treeless avalanche chutes and loose rocky slopes are seen everywhere. A glacial leftover called the "hanging valley" is located about 4 miles down from Maroon Lake on the west side. In fact, Maroon Lake was formed by mud and debris slides from Sievers Mountains located on the west side of the valley. This immense earth slide dammed West Maroon Creek, in turn forming the lake. Debris slides still occur in the upper valley during any prolonged period of moisture. The most recent slide in 1989 destroyed two campsites in the old Maroon Lake Campground near Maroon Lake. During an early June trip to the Bells, my son and I noticed the remains of a 2007-2008 winter avalanche. It was an extremely heavy snow fall year and trees were laid down like toothpicks in a hundred yard wide swath.

Few areas compare with the Elk Mountains and Maroon Bells-Snowmass Wilderness Area when it comes to sheer mountain grandeur. Congress recognized Maroon Bells-Snowmass Wilderness Area as one of the five original Colorado wilderness areas designated by the 1964 Wilderness Act. The initial designation comprised only the most rugged interior of the range. Through the concerted efforts of conservationists, the area was enlarged in 1980 with the help of Colorado wilderness legislation. The added extras include familiar sights such as the 12,953-foot Mount Sopris to the northwest; Castle Peak at 14,265 feet is the tallest peak in the area; and the Conundrum Creek valley. Maroon Bells-Snowmass Wilderness Area is Colorado's fourth largest designated wilderness.

## Wildlife

If you can take your eyes off the spectacular views of the Maroon Bells long enough, you cannot help but notice the plethora of wildlife in the area. Birds, waterfowl, small game and big game abound in here, and mountain song birds are very popular. My son and I encountered mountain chickadees, American robins, black-throated sparrow, western tanager, and goldfinch the first week of June. I was pleasantly surprised to see the gorgeous little yellow-rumped warbler, but unhappy that it eluded my attempts at a focused picture. We were entertained by an American dipper bobbing up and down in a slow bend on Maroon Creek. I am sure a much more varied list of birds would be available as the season warms.

A pair of Canada geese was parked on the bank of Maroon Lake and let us approach very close. We did not see a nest and they were not in a protective mode, so I was able to get a couple of close-up images. A couple drake mallards intermingled with the geese to add to our enjoyment.

As we were getting back to the car our first evening there, my son noticed a white spot on the south facing slope of the Sievers Mountains to the north of Maroon Lake. Sure enough the white spot was moving and we saw our first billy goat of the trip. Another scan of an adjoining mountain side produced two more Rocky Mountain goats, a nanny and kid. We hiked back with camera in tow for a closer look. The light was getting low and even with a high ISO setting the long lens created only a couple marginal images. We spotted four goats the next morning with sun on the mountain side and got a usable image, again at long range.

Our night in the campground was very interesting also. As we settled into a mild slumber, we heard a scratching or clawing on the underside of the car. We turned on the lights and saw two porcupines scurrying away. No sooner had we shut the lights off when the scraping started up again – a third porky we did not spook with the first lights. Finally we got him out from under the car and we were off to sleep again. To make a long story (night) short, we moved the car twice and within a short amount of time, they were back at it again. They were actually chewing the undercoating off the wheel well and frame. After talking to a few people about this, I found out this is pretty common. A porcupine will in fact chew the hoses off the radiator if given a chance. They like the soft "barky" feel of the rubber. Many overnight backpackers have come back to their car with several points of damage caused by porcupines. Not sure what to tell you to do to avoid this problem, but at least you are aware of it.

We encountered bunnies, chipmunks, and marmots. I attained an unusual photo of a road sign saying "Marmot Crossing" with a marmot sitting underneath it.

## Recreation

During the summer months, I would say that hiking is the most popular pastime in the Maroon Bells-Snowmass Wilderness. With over a hundred miles of trails leading

*American robin*

over nine mountain passes over 12,000 feet, thousands of hikers and backpackers make excellent use of the area. Most of the trails lead to high alpine lakes for the recreationist interesting in fishing. Maroon Lake is stocked by the Colorado Division of Wildlife.

A list of four popular trails near Maroon Bells are West Maroon Creek/Pass (trail #1970), Carter Lake (trail #1975), Conundrum Creek (trail #1981), and East Maroon Creek (trail #1983). There are several more trails to explore, some well over 10 miles, some very difficult, but this short list will get you into some marvelous country.

In order to provide quality recreation experiences and to protect the wilderness lands, the forest service must gather data regarding visitor use and travel patterns. Each party staying overnight in the Maroon Bells-Snowmass Wilderness is required to self-register at the trailhead and to carry a copy of the registration with them during their visit. There is no fee charged and no limit to the number of permits issued.

There are a few regulations that must be followed within the Maroon Bells-Snowmass Wilderness:
1. Dogs must be leashed out of consideration for both other people and wildlife.
2. Limit group sizes to 10 people and 15 stock/pack animals.
3. Bury human waste 100 feet from water and 6 inches in the soil.
4. Lightweight camp stoves are recommended and required above the timberline.
5. Building, maintaining, attending, or using any campfire within 100 feet of any lake, stream, or national forest system trail or within 0.25 mile of the treeline, above the treeline, is prohibited. This includes the entire Bear Creek drainage, or within 0.25 mile of Crater Lake, Conundrum Hot Springs, Copper Lake, Geneva Lake, Capital Lake, Snowmass Lake or Cathedral Lake.

After going around Maroon Lake on the short scenic trail, Carter Lake Trail begins. Follow the signs. At 1.8 miles, this is the first leg into the Maroon Bells country. Carter Lake basically sits at the base of Maroon Bells and gives up a tremendous new view of the peaks – a photographer's dream. This is a heavily used trail of moderate difficulty. Veer right as soon as you get to the lake and the trail continues another 3 miles to the west, towards Buckskin Pass. About a mile from Carter Lake, a steep climb brings you to Minnehaha Gulch where campsites can be found. Your site must be 100 feet from the trail or stream. A rigorous hike continues northwest that tops at Buckskin Pass (12,462 feet) on a well-used, difficult trail. Again views are top notch, but the oxygen is thin. This is a very popular day hike and is often used as a starting spot for comprehensive backpacking trips deeper into the wilderness. Depending on snow pack, this trail should not be attempted until late June or early July. Keep your eyes open for elk, deer, mountain goats, and bighorn sheep. Marmots love this high country and several bird species can be seen. Following trail #1975 another 4 miles will take you to Snowmass Lake.

West Maroon Pass trail (#1970) starts at Carter Lake at an elevation of 10,076 feet. This trail follows the base of the Maroon Bells as it heads southwest. Again, this will give you an amazing up-close and personal view of these popular peaks. The trail is about 4 miles in length and takes you over West Maroon Pass at 12,500 feet. The 2,000-foot ascent is the most well-used trail in the Aspen area, but difficult in nature. This could be one of the best trails in the Maroon Wilderness for wildflower viewing.

Conundrum Creek Trail can be found south of Aspen on the Castle Creek Road (FR 128). From the roundabout in Aspen, take Castle Creek Road (FR 102) south for 5 miles and turn right on Conundrum Creek Road. The trailhead starts at the parking lot, 1.1 miles from the turn. The highlight of this trail is the Conundrum Hot Springs located near the top of the trail. Needless to say, this is a heavily-used trail, but it is 8.5 miles in length. It is considered moderate in difficulty with about a 2,500-foot gain in elevation. Some would consider it difficult because of its length; however it is an easy walk through the woods and meadows with bridged crossings of Conundrum Creek. An overnight backpacking trip may be the way to go. Wildlife and wildflowers abound.

East Maroon Creek trail (#1983) takes you on a 10.5-mile jaunt around the base of Pyramid Peak (14,018ft) – the third fourteener in the Maroon-Snowmass Wilderness – and on to East Maroon Pass (11,800ft). From the roundabout on Highway 82 in Aspen, turn right on Maroon Creek Road. Drive 6.4 miles on Maroon Creek Road to East Maroon Portal and turn left into the parking lot. If you get an early start just stop at the forest service entrance station to pick up a pass for overnight use at the East Maroon lot. If the lot is full, you will need to return to Aspen Highlands and enter by bus. Backpackers may enter Maroon Creek Road at any time. The trail begins here at the parking lot. This is a tough trail with a gain of 3,000 feet over its length. Heavily used by horseback riders, destinations vary, but Copper Lake could be used as an ending point. At about 6 miles, a huge avalanche area can be seen and the first of two stream crossings is in store. If the stream flows are high, crossing on foot is not advised. Hiking boots should be removed and sandals used to cross. Again horses have the best chance with high flows. This is just a great hike or ride into the heart of the Maroon Bells-Snowmass Wilderness Area.

Mountain biking, horseback riding, and mountaineering are also popular during the summer. Cross-country skiing, snowshoeing, and snowmobiling fill the needs of winter enthusiasts.

There are several mountains in the area that offer the challenging sport of mountaineering, most notably the Maroon Bells themselves. Climbers come in droves, even though these peaks are among the most difficult to scale in the state. The Maroon Bells consist of precariously layered rock and are extraordinarily misleading. The rock is down-sloping, rotten, loose, and unstable. The Maroon Bells have claimed many lives in the past years. They are not extremely technical climbs, but do require the knowledge of correct routes and proper use of climbing equipment. A rope and a hard hat are needed for personal safety. Remember to check in with someone so they know where you will be, just in case. It is the individual's responsibility to know the hazards and how to handle situations like changing weather and trail conditions. Caution and skill are advised, but the prize can be breathtaking.

Pack it in – pack it out. Leave no trace!

How about that for a photo?

## Location

The Maroon Bells are located in the Gunnison and White River National Forests; specifically known as the Maroon Bells-Snowmass Wilderness Area. The area was established with the help of the 1964 Wilderness Act and covers approximately 181,117 acres. From Interstate 70 at Glenwood Springs take Highway 82 south a little over 40 miles to Aspen. At the roundabout on the northwest edge of town, take Maroon Creek Road (FR 125) west about 11 miles to Maroon Lake. Trailheads and viewing start here.

## Contact

**Aspen Ranger District**
806 West Hallam, Aspen, CO 81611
970-925-3445
www.fs.fed.us/r2/whiteriver/recreation/wilderness/maroonbells/index.shtml

## Fast Facts

**Getting There:** From Interstate 70 at Glenwood Springs, take Highway 82 south a little over 40 miles to Aspen. At the roundabout on the northwest edge of town, take Maroon Creek Road (FR 125) west about 11 miles to Maroon Lake. Trailheads and viewing start here.

**Activities:** Bird and wildlife viewing, hiking.

**Principal Mammals:** Elk, mule deer, mountain goat, bighorn sheep, coyote, black bear, raccoon, porcupine, marmot, beaver, cottontail rabbit, squirrel, ermine, muskrat, mink.

**Mammals of Special Interest:** Elk and mountain goats.

**Principal Birdlife:** Canada geese, mallard ducks, American dipper, western tanager, yellow-rumped warbler

**Birds of Special Interest:** Mountain chickadee

**Habitat Overview:** Jagged mountains, glacial valley, aspen groves, and fir forest

**Flora of Special Interest:** Aspen groves in the fall. Any number of wildflowers in mid-summer.

**Best Wildlife Viewing Ops:** Early morning and late evening when they are on the move from bedding to feeding areas. Wildlife can be seen from most public roads.

**Best Birding Ops:** As soon as the road opens.

**Best Photo Ops:** Early mornings and evenings.

**Hunting Ops:** Yes

**Fishing Ops:** Yes

**Camping Ops:** Yes. Silver Bar Campground, Silver Bell Campground, and Silver Queen Campground. Fees required.

**Boating Ops:** None

**Hiking Trails:** Many trails into the wilderness.

**Motor Trails:** Maroon Creek Road (FR 125) is the main road into the wilderness.

# National Parks and Monuments
## Black Canyon of the Gunnison National Park

About 47 Square Miles; Southwest Colorado, 15 miles east of Montrose

### Introduction

The Black Canyon of the Gunnison National Park (BCNP) was originally set aside as a U.S. national monument on March 2, 1933. It was finally established as a national park on October 21, 1999. The park service commemorated the event by adding 10,000 acres of wilderness to help protect the striking beauty and wildlife habitat of this river corridor. Aptly named "Black Canyon", the depth and sheerness of the canyon walls combined with the narrow gorge, create an uninterrupted gloom that, in some areas, sees sunlight for only a few hours a year. Yes I said "year". That amazes me. This is one of the most unique canyons in the world. Not as dramatic as the Grand Canyon, but in just 48 miles, the river drops more in elevation than the mighty Mississippi does in its full 2,500-mile length. The Black Canyon contains some of the oldest exposed rock on earth. Precambrian, or "basement" rock, is nearly 2 billion years old. The far west end of the South Rim Road, at Warner Point, the gorge is 2,772 feet deep. Located on the north wall, but viewable from the South Rim Road, the Painted Wall is the highest cliff in Colorado. From river to rim it stands 2,250 feet. To give a bit of perspective, it is 1,000 feet taller than the Empire State Building.

Before the creation of three dams upstream of Black Canyon of the Gunnison National Park, the Gunnison River was as much as five times more powerful than it is today. When the river was free of these dams and during spring run-off, the flows could be as high as 12,000 cubic feet per second. This much force could be equal to 2,750,000 horsepower. Year after year of this amazing power scoured and eroded the canyon into the spectacle it is today.

The Black Canyon does not get the traffic that the Grand Canyon and Yosemite get, but is well worth the visit. It does not have the fancy restaurants, lodges, and facilities that the big national parks have, but there are two campgrounds, one situated on the South Rim and one on the North Rim. The South Rim Campground has 88 sites in an oak-brush habitat with vault toilets, tables, and grills. The North Rim Campground has 13 sites and is surrounded by a pinyon-juniper forest, also with vault toilets, tables, and grills. A third campground very close to the BCNP is the East

Portal Campground. It is located 2 miles downstream of Crystal Dam at the top of the Black Canyon. Take CO Highway 347 for 6 miles north from the junction of 347 and U.S. Highway 50 to entrance of Black Canyon of the Gunnison National Park. Turn right just past the entrance station, and follow East Portal Road 5 miles down to the campground. It has the same facilities as the campgrounds in the park.

## History

By all accounts, the canyon had been thoroughly explored by the late 1800s and into the early 1900s. One of the first recorded visitors to the Black Canyon was John Williams Gunnison in 1853. Born in Goshen, New Hampshire, Gunnison graduated from West Point Military Academy in 1837. After a short stint serving in the military in the east, the adventurer in him showed through as he made his first trip west to Utah Territory in 1849 with Captain Stansbury. Lieutenant Gunnison returned east and was soon promoted to captain. He was selected to lead the search for a railroad route to the Pacific via the Kansas-Nebraska border. He crossed the Rocky Mountain at a point which brought him to the Gunnison River Valley where the town of Gunnison is today. The captain's first look at the Black Canyon was on September 7, 1853. Just a short month and a half later, John W. Gunnison, whose name was given to the river and the early settlement in the valley, was killed in the early morning hours on the banks of the Sevier River in Utah by a band of Paiute Indians. Apparently the attack was in retribution for the death of a Paiute leader killed by emigrants heading west.

The history-making expedition of Abraham Lincoln Fellows and Will Torrence took place in 1901. They set out to float and explore the river in the Black Canyon to see if an irrigation tunnel to water the Uncompahgre Valley was feasible. Instead of trying to float the river in boats, they used an inflatable rubber air mattress. The 33-mile trip battered the gentlemen and tested their fortitude, but after the nine-day journey, they returned with a report that the proposed tunnel was a realistic undertaking. Construction of the nearly 6-mile Gunnison Diversion Tunnel began in 1905 and was dedicated in 1909. This tunnel continues to milk water from the mighty Gunnison River for irrigation.

Citizens in the area started lobbying the national park service in the 1930s to include it in the park system.

## Wildlife

Wildlife is abundant in the Black Canyon of the Gunnison National Park, especially birds. The cliff walls make perfect, undisturbed nesting sites for white-throated swifts, black crows, ravens, and peregrine falcons. Peregrine falcons are the fastest birds in the world and would be a fine sighting here in the Black Canyon. Peregrines have been clocked at speeds over 200 miles per hour in an aerial dive. *Falco peregrinus anatum*, described by American Ornithologists' Union, is known as the American peregrine falcon, or "duck hawk". There are 19 accepted subspecies listed in the *Handbook of the Birds of the World* but this subspecies is found primarily in the Rocky Mountains. It was formerly common throughout North America between the tundra and northern

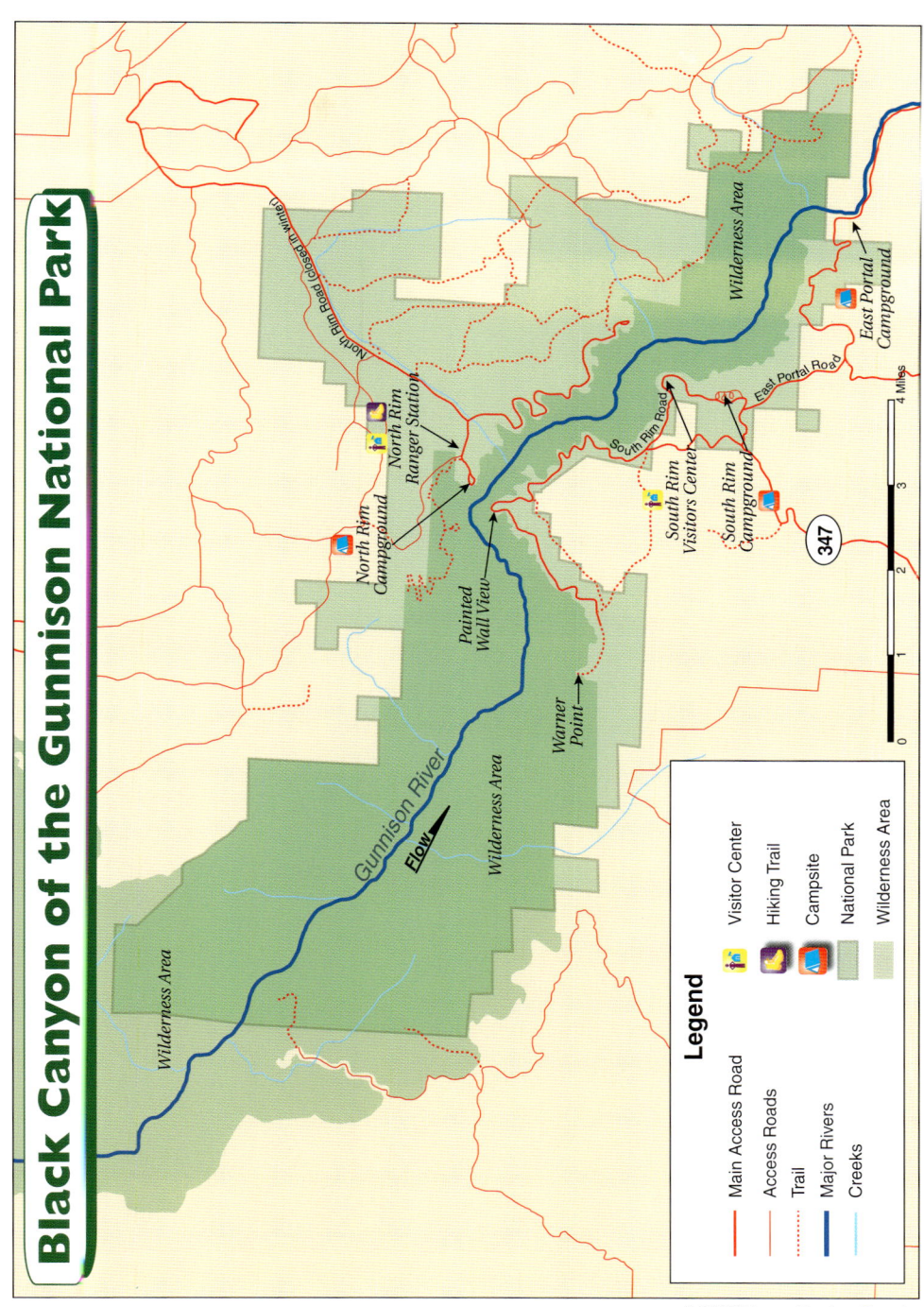

Mexico, until pesticides such as DDT were used for pest control in agriculture. Today there are many reintroduction efforts seeking to restore the population. The peregrine falcons can be found in the park year round since they normally winter in their breeding range.

The peregrine falcon has a body length of 13 to 23 inches and a wingspan of around 31 to 47 inches. This is about the size of a common crow. The male and female have similar markings and plumage, but the female measures up to 30 percent larger than the male. In flight, the best way to recognize a falcon is by its long pointed, black wing tips. The belly is normally whitish to rusty in color with black and brown barring. The tail is long and narrow, rounded at the end with black tips and a white band. A gorgeous bird of prey, to say the least!

Their main food sources are other small to medium-sized birds, which can be seen throughout the park.

The juniper and Gambel's oak forests and western chokecherry along with the sagebrush and rabbitbrush flats provide excellent habitat for mountain bluebirds, Steller's and pinyon jays, canyon wrens, mountain chickadees, mourning doves, and barn swallows. Add to this list, the Townsend's warbler, evening grosbeak, white-crowned sparrow, and dark-eyed junco, all of which keep the falcon and the bird enthusiast busy.

*You can see why they are called "mule" deer*

*Sage brush lizard*

Keep an eye out for the Gunnison grouse and the more common blue grouse. I spotted a grouse about 20 feet inside the Gambel's oak as my son and I were traveling the south rim and I quickly tried to find a wide spot in the road to pull over. However, someone else had spotted the grouse before I did and was on hands and knees in pursuit of a photo, so I did not interrupt their stalk.

I am not sure what kind of grouse it was, but after a bit of research I found out some interesting details about the Gunnison sage grouse. I contacted Dr. Patrick Magee of Western State College of Colorado in Gunnison. I tossed a few questions about population and conservation his way and he replied, "There are approximately 6,000 Gunnison sage grouse in southwestern Colorado and eastern Utah. This species is smaller than the greater sage grouse of northwestern Colorado with slightly different tail markings, and was given its own designation in 2000." And to my question on conservation, "This question requires a longer answer, but I will simply say that there are a couple different conservation plans in place and they are being implemented more aggressively now than they were about five years ago. The birds are highly vulnerable to extinction based on their small population and unless the numbers increase and the small populations increase, the long-term sustainability is fairly low. A large drought, increased impacts of global climate change, a disease such as West Nile Virus, and genetic depression are all forces that act on small populations and can suck these species toward extinction in one quick event. If we can manage the habitat and restore much of the sagebrush ecosystem, we have the best chance of seeing increased populations that may eventually rise above the threshold for low sustainability. But the landscape has been highly modified and the progress toward restoration is slow at best."

We cannot forget about the numerous mammals in BCNP. Mule deer are very noticeable and quite abundant. The day I was there was cloudy with spotty rain throughout the day and the muleys were out and about much of the day. Normally the early morning and early evening hours are best for spotting big game. Pronghorn antelope are present at the edges of the park and elk can be seen during spring and fall migration periods. Numbers of bunnies, snowshoe hares, chipmunks, deer mice, and rock squirrels keep predators like the coyote, red fox, and bobcat fed. Sightings of black bear, mountain lion, bighorn sheep, and American badger are uncommon to say the least, but possible.

## Activities

There are students at Western State College in Gunnison who coordinate the access to a Gunnison sage grouse viewing trailer. The lek (breeding grounds) that the trailer overlooks is usually active from April through May.

There is a $100 fee for reserving the trailer and you also need to have a Colorado Division of Wildlife Habitat Stamp, which, at this printing, is $10.

## Kayaking

Expert kayakers find the Gunnison River through the national park an arduous challenge. This stretch of the Gunnison is for only the most experienced and well-equipped kayakers. The rapids within the national park are considered Class V and some sections are not runnable. This is a very technical paddle and includes numerous long, difficult and dangerous portages. Poison ivy is nearly impossible to avoid, and can be found growing 5 feet tall along the river. The Gunnison River through Black Canyon of the Gunnison National Park drops at an average of 95 feet per mile. By comparison, the Colorado River through Grand Canyon National Park drops an average of 7.5 feet per mile.

Important note: Kayakers run the river at their own risk. The Gunnison River through the park has claimed the lives of even the most experienced, respected kayakers. The river's hydraulics can make self-rescue or rescue by others impossible.

Here is a list of general water flow ratings:

750-950 cfs – minimal hydraulics

1200-1500 cfs – River is "pushy" with major hydraulics

1500-3000 cfs – River is very "pushy" with extreme hydraulics

3000 or greater cfs – Kayaking should not be attempted even by experts, portages disappear, death is probable

These are general water-flow guidelines. Local kayak experts suggest the unique hydraulics of the Gunnison River through Black Canyon of the Gunnison National Park make kayaking even more difficult than the above ratings.

Water temperatures are cold year round, usually around 50 degrees Fahrenheit or less. Swimming or wading is not recommended. A free permit is required for all backcountry and wilderness use (both day use and overnight) including hiking the inner canyon or off established trails, rock climbing, and all river use. Permits are available at the South Rim Visitor Center, North Rim Ranger Station, and East Portal registration board (located west of the campground). Permits are available on a first-come, first-served basis. If these facilities are closed, there are self registration stations with instructions at each location.

## Hiking the Inner Canyon

Hiking the inner canyon – although the ultimate in beauty – is a very dangerous and strenuous endeavor. Only the most physically fit should attempt this activity. The trails are not maintained and often very hard to follow. Preparing for the hike into and out of the canyon should be done well in advance. Bring high energy foods and at least 4 quarts of water per person per day. Giardia is in all water sources, including the river; therefore all water must be purified. Sturdy hiking boots are an absolute must, due to the unstable terrain covered in loose talus and scree. Always pack in rain gear, afternoon thunderstorms are common. Please pack out what you pack in. Once a hiker gets to the river, fishing is available. A valid Colorado fishing license is required, and Gold Medal Water regulations apply. As of this writing, special regulations include: artificial lures only; the possession limit for brown trout is four, of which only one fish may equal or exceed 16 inches in length; all fish between 12 and 16 inches must be released. Rainbows are catch and release only. Check current regulations before fishing anywhere in Colorado, as they change frequently.

**Guide Services:**

Scenic River Tours
  703 W Tomichi Avenue, Gunnison
  970-641-3131
Dragonfly Anglers (Fishing)
  307 Elk Avenue, Crested Butte
  970-349-1228
Gene Taylor's Sporting Goods
  201 W Tomichi Avenue, Gunnison
  970-641-1532
Gunnison Valley Adventure Guides
  Gunnison
  970-641-5541

## Location

The Black Canyon of the Gunnison National Park is located approximately 250 miles southwest of Denver via westbound Interstate 70 and southbound Colorado Highway 50.

To access the south rim, take US Highway 50 west from Montrose about 8 miles, turn left (north) on CO Highway 347. Travel another 7 miles to the park entrance. To access the north rim from Delta, take CO Highway 92 east 21 miles to Hotchkiss. Stay on CO Highway 92 as it veers to the south and travel another 3 miles to Black Canyon Road. Turn right (west) and follow Black Canyon Road about 5 miles. Just past CR 7750 and turn left (south) to stay on Black Canyon Road. Travel another 6 miles to North Rim Road. There is no bridge between the north and south rims of the canyon. Allow two to three hours to drive from one side to the other. Commercial airline service is available to Montrose, Gunnison, and Grand Junction.

## Accommodations

Lathrop House Bed & Breakfast
  718 East Main Street
Black Canyon of the Gunnison National Park
  970-240-6075
Holiday Inn Express
  1391 South Townsend Avenue, Montrose, CO  81401
  970-240-1800
Black Canyon Motel
  1605 East Main Street
Black Canyon of the Gunnison National Park
  970-249-3495

*A blooming cactus*

## Contact

**National Park Service**
102 Elk Creek
Gunnison, CO  81230
970-641-2337
www.nps.gov/blca/index.htm

## Fast Facts

- **Entrance Fee:** The entrance fee is $15 per vehicle at the South Rim entrance station and the North Rim ranger station of Black Canyon. It covers all persons in a single, private, noncommercial vehicle and is valid for seven calendar days. The entry fee for pedestrians, bicyclists, motorcycles, motor scooters, or mopeds is $7 per person, not to exceed $14 per vehicle. There is no fee charged for persons 16 years of age or younger.
- **Black canyon annual pass:** An annual pass to Black Canyon of the Gunnison National Park is available at the entrance station for $30. This pass admits the permit holder and all accompanying passengers in a single, private, noncommercial vehicle to the park. It is valid for 12 months from date of purchase and covers entry fees only.
- **Commercial bus tour fees:**
  Bus with 26 or more passenger seating capacity: $100
  Bus with 7-25 passenger seating capacity: $40
  Bus with 6 or less passenger seating capacity: $25 plus $4 per person
- **Park Hours:**
  South Rim – open every day. The South Rim Road is open to vehicles from early April to mid-November. In winter, the South Rim Road is open to Gunnison Point. The remainder of the road is closed to vehicles, but open to cross-country skiing and snowshoeing.
  North Rim – North Rim Road and ranger station are closed in winter. The road typically closes late November and reopens mid-April. North Rim Ranger Station is open intermittently during the summer and closed in winter. The road typically closes late November and reopens mid-April.
- **South Rim Visitor Center:** open all year; Hours: Fall, winter, spring: 8:30am-4:00pm; Summer: 8:00am-6:00pm; Closed Thanksgiving, Christmas, New Years Day
- **Phone:** 970-249-1914, extension 423
- **Location:** Two miles from the south rim entrance station on the South Rim Road.
- **Getting There:** The Black Canyon of the Gunnison National Park is located approximately 250 miles southwest of Denver via westbound Interstate 70 and southbound Colorado Highway 50. To access the south rim, take US Highway 50 west from Montrose about 8 miles, turn left (north) on CO Highway 347. Travel another 7 miles to the park entrance. To access the north rim from Delta, take CO Highway 92 east 21 miles to Hotchkiss. Stay on Colorado Highway 92 as it

diverts to the south and travel another 3 miles to Black Canyon Road and turn right (west). Follow Black Canyon Road about 5 miles, just past CR 7750 and turn left (south) to stay on Black Canyon Road. Travel another 6 miles to North Rim Road. There is no bridge between the north and south rims of the canyon. Allow two to three hours to drive from one side to the other.

**Activities:** Scenic drives, hiking, bird and wildlife viewing, rock climbing, and kayaking

**Principal Mammals:** Mule deer, elk, occasional bighorn sheep, coyote, black bear, mountain lion, porcupine, skunk, red fox, cottontail rabbit, rock squirrel, Colorado chipmunk, and long-tailed weasel.

**Mammals of Special Interest:** Mule deer, yellow-bellied marmot, and elk.

**Principal Birdlife:** Several species of hawks, golden eagle, blue grouse, Steller's Jay, white-throated swift.

**Birds of Special Interest:** Peregrine falcon, Gunnison sage grouse and canyon wren.

**Habitat Overview:** Wetlands valley, farmlands, rimmed by the Sangre de Cristo and San Juan Mountains

**Best Wildlife Viewing Ops:** Early morning and late evening when they are on the move from bedding to feeding areas. Wildlife can be seen from most access roads.

**Best Birding Ops:** Most anytime is good for raptors. All the hiking trails and main roads will present exceptional birding.

**Best Photo Ops:** Early mornings for the north rim and late evenings for the south rim present the best lighting situations.

**Hunting Ops:** None

**Fishing Ops:** The river within Black Canyon of the Gunnison National Park is designated as Gold Medal Water and Wild Trout Water. Hiking to bottom is tough work.

**Camping Ops:** South Rim Campground, North Rim Campground and East Portal Campground.

**Boating Ops:** Kayaking

**Hiking Trails:** Four main trails on the south rim and three trails on the north rim.

**Motor Trails:** The main scenic drives along both rims.

## Bird List

American dipper
American goldfinch
American kestral
American robin
Ash-throated flycatcher
Bald eagle
Band-tailed pigeon
Barn swallow
Belted kingfisher
Black swift
Black-billed magpie
Black-capped chickadee
Black-chinned hummingbird
Black-headed grosbeak
Black-throated gray warbler
Black-throated sparrow
Blue grouse
Blue-gray gnatcatcher
Brewer's blackbird
Brewer's sparrow
Broad-tailed hummingbird
Brown creeper
Brown-headed cowbird
Bushtit
California condor
Canada goose
Canyon wren
Cassin's finch
Chipping sparrow
Chukar
Clark's nutcracker
Common merganser
Common nighthawk
Common poorwill
Common raven
Cooper's hawk accipiter
Downy woodpecker
Dusky flycatcher
European starling
Evening grosbeak
Golden eagle
Golden-crowned kinglet
Gray catbird
Gray flycatcher
Gray jay
Gray vireo
Gray-headed junco (dark-eyed)
Great blue heron
Great horned owl
Green-tailed towhee
Hairy woodpecker
Hammond's flycatcher
Hermit thrush
House finch
House wren
House wren
Killdeer
Lark sparrow
Lazuli bunting
Lewis woodpecker
Loggerhead shrike
Long-eared owl
MacGillivray's warbler
Mallard
Mountain bluebird
Mountain chickadee
Mourning dove
Northern flicker
Northern goshawk
Northern harrier
Northern mockingbird
Northern oriole
Olive-sided flycatcher
Orange-crowned warbler
Peregrine falcon
Pine grosbeak
Pine siskin
Pinyon jay
Plain titmouse
Prairie falcon
Red crossbill
Red-breasted nuthatch

Red-tailed hawk
Red-winged blackbird
Ring-necked pheasant
Rock dove
Rock wren
Ruby-crowned kinglet
Rufous hummingbird
Rufous-sided towhee
Sage grouse
Sage thrasher
Sage thrasher
Saw whet owl
Say's phoebe
Scrub jay
Sharp-shinned hawk
Solitary vireo
Song sparrow
Spotted sandpiper
Steller's jay
Tennessee warbler
Townsend's solitare
Townsend's warbler
Tree swallow
Turkey
Turkey vulture
Vesper sparrow
Violet-green swallow
Virginia's warbler
Warbling vireo
Western flycatcher
Western kingbird
Western meadowlark
Western tanager
Western wood-peewee
White-breasted nuthatch
White-crowned sparrow
White-throated swift
Williamson's sapsucker
Wilson's warbler
Yellow warbler
Yellow-bellied (red-naped) sapsucker
Yellow-rumped warbler

*Above: The Gunnison sage grouse (Photo by Dick Williams). Right: The Gunnison River*

# Canyons of the Ancients National Monument

### 164,000 acres; Southwestern Colorado west of Cortez

## Introduction

The Canyons of the Ancients National Monument contains the highest known archaeological site density in the United States, with rich, well-preserved evidence of native cultures. It was designated as a national monument by President Clinton in June of 2000. The Canyons of the Ancients National Monument is 164,000 acres of federal land administered by the Bureau of Land Management (BLM). There are an estimated 20,000 to 30,000 individual sites with more than 6,000 recorded sites reflecting all the physical components of past human life. These include full-fledged villages, field houses, check dams, reservoirs, great kivas, cliff dwellings, shrines, sacred springs, agricultural fields, petroglyphs, and sweat lodges. Some areas have more than 100 sites per square mile.

There are five major sites that are accessed by vehicle and several by foot. To start with, I would suggest a visit to the Anasazi Heritage Center in Delores. The center is 10 miles north of Cortez and 3 miles west of Dolores on Highway 184. The on-site museum features permanent exhibits on archaeology, local history, and Native American cultures, two 12th-century archaeological sites, special exhibits and events, traveling exhibits available for loan, educational resources for teachers, a research library of archaeology and anthropology resources, and a research collection of over three million artifacts and records. There is also a picnic area and half-mile nature trail. All museum facilities are wheelchair accessible. A small village called Escalante Pueblo is on the Anasazi Heritage Center grounds at the end of a half-mile-long, wheelchair-accessible trail overlooking the Dolores River. The pueblo is a rectangular block with as many as 28 rooms surrounding a central kiva. Kivas are found in just about all pueblo sites and were probably for ceremonial purposes. These rooms are larger than those typical of the region, and their walls were enclosed with a rubble-filled core – both features are typical of Chacoan construction. Chacoan construction is a sophisticated design, usually multistoried structures, used by the ancient Puebloans throughout the San Juan River Basin in Colorado and New Mexico. The architecture and masonry indicate that Escalante Pueblo was one of the northernmost settlements influenced by the culture of Chaco Canyon in New Mexico, about 100 miles to the south. There is evidence that the shapes of the structures correspond with the solar and lunar cycles. There is another small structure, the Dominguez Pueblo, at the Anasazi Heritage Center which sits at the base of a hill below the much larger Escalante Pueblo. It was probably home to a family of four to six people. The Dominguez site has four rooms marked by low stone walls — all that remains of a roofed structure built (around the year 1120) with poles, brush, and earth. The easternmost room appears to have been added after the first three were built. Just south of this room block is a dirt-walled kiva that is 11 feet in diameter. It was not possible to stabilize the kiva, so it was reburied to keep it intact. With its blocky stonework and separate kiva, Dominguez Pueblo is a good architectural example of the local Northern San Juan branch of the ancestral Pueblo culture.

The next location to visit is the Lowry Pueblo. It was constructed in about 1060 on top of abandoned pit houses from an earlier period of occupation. It is a self-guided interpretive tour of one of the largest and best preserved elements of Canyons of the Ancients National Monument. This archaeological site was named after early homesteader George Lowry. Lowry was home to about 100 people who were more than likely farmers who also hunted small game, made elaborately decorated pottery, and wove cotton they obtained by trade. There is evidence that many rooms were probably plastered inside and painted with bold geometric designs. There is also a great kiva located just east of the Lowry Pueblo. Initial excavations in the 1930s revealed the kiva had a well-preserved decorative mural on the inside walls. The kiva was backfilled to preserve it. After re-excavation in 1974, the mural began to discolor and peel away due to exposure to light and air. None of it survives today, except for a salvaged fragment at the Anasazi Heritage Center. The pueblo was declared a national historic landmark in 1967. There are picnicking sites and trails for hiking.

Painted Hand Pueblo is the next site on the list. It was a small village covered in petroglyphs with a striking tower perched on a boulder. The site has never been excavated, but stone rubble shows where rooms were built against the cliff face and on boulders. The site gets its name from pictographs of hands painted on a boulder (please don't touch these fragile paintings). The oil and dirt from hands can eventually destroy these remnants of past inhabitants. Painted Hand is a backcountry site, so you should get a good map from the Heritage Center and use a vehicle with good clearance.

The Sand Canyon Pueblo is a large prehistoric settlement within the Canyon of the Ancients. Sand Canyon Pueblo has 420 rooms, 100 kivas, and 14 towers; but today it has no exposed walls. There are well-marked trails and interpretive signage providing insights and archaeological perspectives on how the site was laid out and show what it might have looked like in the mid-1200s. Partial excavations from 1983 to 1993 were backfilled to protect intact features and preserve the site. There is very little of the site that is actually exposed, but it does give a visitor an idea of how the people lived. Again, there is a live spring at the top of this canyon as a source of water. The Sand Canyon Pueblo is adjacent to the upper (north) trailhead for Sand Canyon.

There is a small parking area but no water, toilet, phone, or wheelchair access.

The Sand Canyon Trail is the next opportunity to view many ancestral Puebloan archaeological sites. The popular Sand Canyon Trail is 6.5 miles (one way) from Sand Canyon Pueblo down to the lower trailhead in McElmo Canyon. The trail is open to hiking, horseback riding, and mountain biking, but the upper section is steep and rugged – not recommended for bicycles. Part of the single-track dirt trail crosses slick rock marked with rock cairns. A vehicle shuttle is a good idea if you are going to hike the entire trail: leave one vehicle at Sand Canyon Pueblo, and leave a second vehicle at the bottom (south) end of the trail in McElmo Canyon. I hiked in from the lower end about 2 miles just to check out the trail. I was by myself and did not have a shuttle, so I had no plans to hike the entire canyon. The first part of the trail is a maze of broken trails, but finally turns into a single trail. About a mile and half in, you climb about 680 feet in elevation in a half mile. Lots of switchbacks and loose gravel make for a tough hike. Good boots, plenty of water, and a camera are must-haves if you make this trip.

## Wildlife

The desert environment of this area is home to many unique animals. One of its inhabitants is the Mesa Verde nightsnake, whose survival totally depends upon this locale. Other inhabitants of the area are long-nosed leopard lizards, twin-spotted spiny lizards, bull snakes, and the poisonous rattlesnake. Important raptors to the area are golden eagles and red tailed hawks. Mule deer, elk, mountain lion, coyote, fox, wild turkey, bunnies, mountain bluebirds, the gorgeous western bluebird, and mourning doves are found here. Peregrine falcons and bald eagles hunt in the area from November to May. I was surprised to see the number of mule deer I did because most of my time in the area was right in the middle of the day. There is very good habitat with juniper forest and canyons everywhere. I actually got a couple very unique images of deer here. I spotted a doe in a field where the wheat was so tall; all I could see was her head poking out of the golden spikes. Another was inside a thicket and she was sure I could not see her, so she just sat tight while I set up the camera. It is one of those images that you have to stare at for a few seconds to actually see what you are looking at. The mountain bluebirds and mourning doves were thick and I did spot a pair of wild turkeys. When you get off the main roads in this locale, the wildlife is amazingly abundant.

## History

The pre-Puebloan people called Basketmakers migrated into the area about 1500 B.C. They were primarily hunter-gatherers but, unlike earlier inhabitants, they are associated with the earliest traces of corn agriculture. They excelled at basketry, and interacted with a wider cultural region including Mesa Verde and beyond.

By about A.D. 750, their architecture had developed from pit-house clusters into square-roomed pueblo-style villages. They developed excellent pottery and farmed extensively.

Factors including population growth, soil exhaustion, and changing rain/snow patterns began to reduce the natural resources of the area. By about A.D 1300, the Ancestral Puebloans had migrated south, east, and west to where their descendants live today as the modern Pueblo Indians of New Mexico and Arizona.

Soon afterwards, nomadic Ute and Navajo bands began to frequent the monument's mesas and canyons. Forked-stick hogans and brush shelters remain as evidence of these later occupants.

European settlers followed and established farms and ranches. Many of the settlers' descendants still live in or near their ancestors' homesteads.

Historic uses of the monument include recreation, hunting, livestock grazing, and energy development.

The planning process now underway will determine how to protect objects of scientific and historic interest that have been identified.

## Activities

Except for the Delores River and McPhee Reservoir, fishing in the area is very limited. McElmo Creek looked like it might be fishable, but access looked very limited. Sightseeing, exploring, birding, and photography would be high on a list of things to do here. Hiking and mountain biking would be next on the list. Horseback riding is very popular in the backcountry. There are a few improved campgrounds outside of the monument, but inside the monument "roughing it" is the name of the game.

## Location

The monument is located in the Four Corners region of southwestern Colorado, about 50 miles west of Durango, 10 miles west of Cortez and 12 miles west of Mesa Verde National Park.

The Anasazi Heritage Center is 10 miles north of Cortez and 3 miles west of Dolores on Highway 184.

The Lowry Pueblo can be found from Cortez by traveling about 18 miles north on U.S. Highway 491 to the "Pleasant View and Lowry" sign at County Road CC. Turn west (left) and follow the signs for about 9 miles.

The Painted Hand Pueblo can be found by driving north from Cortez on Highway 491 (formerly 666). Turn west (left) from the highway on County Road BB and travel 6 miles to the intersection with County Road 10. Turn south (left) and travel 11.3 miles. Turn left onto a rocky, high-clearance dirt road (#4531). Go about a mile and turn left into the small parking area.

To reach the Sand Canyon Pueblo take Highway 491 north from Cortez 3.5 miles. Turn west (left) on Road P. the road curves north a bit and the road turns into Road P.3, which immediately comes to a tee at Road 18. Turn south (left) on Road 18 and it veers to the west (right) turning into Road P again. The pavement ends about here and you need to turn south (left) on Road 17. Go a mile or two and turn west (right) on Road N. Follow N to the site. The road signs are pretty small so pay close attention.

To reach the lower Sand Canyon trailhead, head south of Cortez on Highway 491 about 3 miles. Turn west (right) on Road G at the signs for the airport. Go 12 miles on this paved road. Trailhead parking is an unimproved slick rock surface on the north (right) side of the road.

## Contact

**The Anasazi Heritage Center**
27501 Highway 184
Dolores, Colorado 81323
970-882-5600

## Fast Facts

**Entrance Fee:** $3 adults March-October; free November-February 17 & under free. School groups free.
Federal Recreational Lands Passes are honored.
**Hours:** 9:00am-5:00pm March-October; 10:00am-4:00pm November-February
**Location:** The monument is located in the Four Corners region of southwestern Colorado, about 50 miles west of Durango, 10 miles west of Cortez and 12 miles west of Mesa Verde National Park.

The Anasazi Heritage Center is 10 miles north of Cortez and 3 miles west of Dolores on Highway 184.

The Lowry Pueblo can be found from Cortez by traveling about 18 miles north on U.S. Highway 491 to the "Pleasant View and Lowry" sign at County Road CC. Turn west (left) and follow the signs for about 9 miles.

The Painted Hand Pueblo can be found by driving north from Cortez on Highway 491 (formerly 666). Turn west (left) from the highway on County Road BB and travel 6 miles to the intersection with County Road 10. Turn south (left) and travel 11.3 miles. Turn left onto a rocky, high-clearance dirt road #4531. Go about 1 mile and turn left into the small parking area.

To reach the Sand Canyon Pueblo take Highway 491 north from Cortez 3.5 miles. Turn west (left) on Road P. the road curves north a bit and the road turns into Road P.3, which immediately comes to a tee at Road 18. Turn south (left) on Road 18 and it veers to the west (right) turning into Road P again. The pavement ends here somewhere and you need to turn south (left) on Road 17. Go a mile or 2 and turn west (right) on Road N. Follow N to the site. The road signs are pretty small so pay close attention.

To reach the lower Sand Canyon trailhead, head south of Cortez on Highway 491 about 3 miles. Turn west (right) on Road G at the signs for the airport. Go 12 miles on this paved road. Trailhead parking is an unimproved slick rock surface on the north (right) side of the road.
**Getting There:** The Canyons of the Ancients National Monument is located approximately 430 miles southwest of Denver via southbound Interstate 25

and westbound Colorado Highway 160, or 400 miles via southbound CO Highway 285 and westbound Colorado Highway 160. Even though the route is longer via I-25, the time it takes is marginal because of speed limits and fewer mountainous roads. From Denver (via I-25), travel 160 miles south on Interstate 25 to Walsenburg. Follow signage through town to access CO Highway 160. Take CO Highway 160 west 220 miles to Durango. Follow signage through town and continue on CO Highway 160 another 50 miles to the monument.

From Denver (via CO Highway 285), travel 220 miles south on CO Highway 285 to Monte Vista. Take CO Highway 160 west 130 miles to Durango. Follow signage through town and continue on CO Highway 160 another 50 miles to the monument. Allow 6.5 to 7 hours from Denver.

**Activities:** Scenic drives, hiking, bird and wildlife viewing, and photography

**Principal Mammals:** Mule deer, coyote, mountain lion, wild turkey

**Mammals of Special Interest:** Mule deer, wild turkey

**Principal Birdlife:** Several species of hawks, golden eagle, turkey vultures, kestrel, mountain bluebird, mourning dove

**Birds of Special Interest:** Peregrine falcon, bald eagle

**Habitat Overview:** Desert environs, canyon lands. The lower elevation is dominated by big sagebrush, rabbitbrush, and several herbaceous species. The pinyon-juniper woodland is dominated by Utah juniper.

**Best Wildlife Viewing Ops:** Early morning and late evening when they are on the move from bedding to feeding areas. Wildlife can be seen from most trails and the main roads.

**Best Birding Ops:** Most anytime is good for raptors. All the hiking trails and main roads will present exceptional birding.

**Best Photo Ops:** Early mornings and late evenings present the best lighting situations. However, good photos can be had anytime of the day.

**Hunting Ops:** Yes

**Fishing Ops:** Delores River, McPhee Reservoir

**Camping Ops:** Backcountry, unimproved.

**Boating Ops:** McPhee Reservoir

**Hiking Trails:** Throughout the monument.

**Motor Trails:** The main scenic drive through the monument.

# Colorado National Monument

**32 Square Miles; Located in western Colorado just west of Grand Junction and south of Fruita**

## History

The Colorado National Monument safeguards one of the most majestic backdrops in Colorado. In 1907, John Otto wrote, "I came here last year and found these canyons, and they feel like the heart of the world to me. I'm going to stay and build trails and promote this place, because it should be a national park." Stay he did; he lived in a tent in what is now known as Monument Canyon, off and on for nearly 30 years. As the trailblazer and promoter of the monument, Otto gathered support from surrounding communities to petition Washington D.C. to establish these sheer-walled canyons and immense monoliths as a national park. It was preserved as a national monument in 1911 largely through his efforts. Otto's wishes finally came true.

The visitor's center at the west entrance is a superb place to start your exploration. A narrated video program orients the visitor to the monument, and maps, informational brochures and books, and restrooms are found here.

The real history of the Colorado National Monument lies in the geological structure of this remarkable landscape. It lies within a large expanse of land called the Colorado Plateau. This 150,000-square-mile area includes much of western Colorado, almost the entire eastern and southwestern parts of Utah, northern Arizona, and a good deal of western New Mexico. It embraces nearly 30 national parks and national monuments including the famous Grand Canyon National Park in Arizona, Arches National Park in Utah, and Aztec National Monument in New Mexico.

Over the last 10 million years, cracks and fault lines in the earth's crust have risen thousands of feet, creating the plateau. Through history much of this area was under water at times, so most of the surface is compressed sandstone. The Colorado Plateau is dissected by the Colorado River and many of its major tributaries, in turn creating some of the most dramatic scenery in the United States. The rivers eroded the relatively soft stone, exposing these magnificent red rock canyons we see today.

Much of the plateau is considered a semi-arid desert with elevations ranging from 4,000-foot intersperses with volcanic peaks, to mountains as high as 12,000 feet. Annual precipitation averages less than 12 inches, with much of the moisture coming in August through October. The Colorado Plateau is sparsely populated. Many believe that, in some areas, there were greater populations of ancients Indian civilizations than there are modern societies today. Temperatures are highly variable with summer highs ranging into the low 100s on the valley floor and, in some cases, 110-plus degrees inside the canyon country. However, these red rock badlands are home to a diverse and abundant populace of plant life and unique wildlife.

The Colorado National Monument can be viewed primarily from Rim Rock Drive. It is a 23-mile scenic drive that leads visitors along the rim of a colorful vista of cavernous, sheer-sided canyons, and high rock spires. Pullouts along the way provide information about the natural and human history of the park. Foot trails provide a closer look at the many geological features of the monument. Allow 45 minutes of driving time, plus extra time for walking and photography.

One of the most popular spires in the monument is the Independence Monument. It is all that remains of a continuous ridge that once formed a wall between Monument and Wedding Canyons. A cap of durable Kayenta formation rock has protected this picturesque 450-foot-high monolith from the relentless erosion that carried away the surrounding rock.

## Wildlife

Colorado National Monument is representative of semi-desert and upland climates and holds a variety of animal species that thrive in this environment. The most famous would be the desert bighorn sheep. Mule deer, pronghorns, black bear, coyotes, mountain lions, bobcats, badgers, red and kit fox, porcupines, desert cottontails, Hopi chipmunks, rock squirrels, a number of smaller mice, and several species of bats inhabit the sandstone cliffs. The desert climate is especially pleasing for reptiles including the midget faded rattlesnake, a subspecies of the western rattlesnake. It is the only poisonous snake found in the monument. Also found here are the Great Plains rat snake, striped whipsnake, plateau lizard, sagebrush lizard, collared lizard and the side-blotched lizard.

Desert bighorn sheep, also known as Nelson's bighorn sheep, are one of the most fascinating mammals of canyon country. They are considered by most biologists to be a unique subspecies. Unlike the Rocky Mountain bighorn, the desert bighorn have adapted to hot, dry climates. They have much smaller bodies with a lighter coat and longer legs.

Bighorn sheep are common in petroglyphs, an indication of their existence and importance in early American cultures. There are accounts dating back to the late 1600s that estimate a population of desert bighorn in excess of two million animals. However, by the late 1800s, bighorn sheep had disappeared in many areas and declined in others. They are vulnerable to diseases brought in from European livestock, especially the domestic sheep. Herds of wild sheep were decimated by pathogens like scabies (an ear mite) and anthrax introduced by domestic sheep. These beautiful and unique animals were also killed by early explorers and trophy hunters.

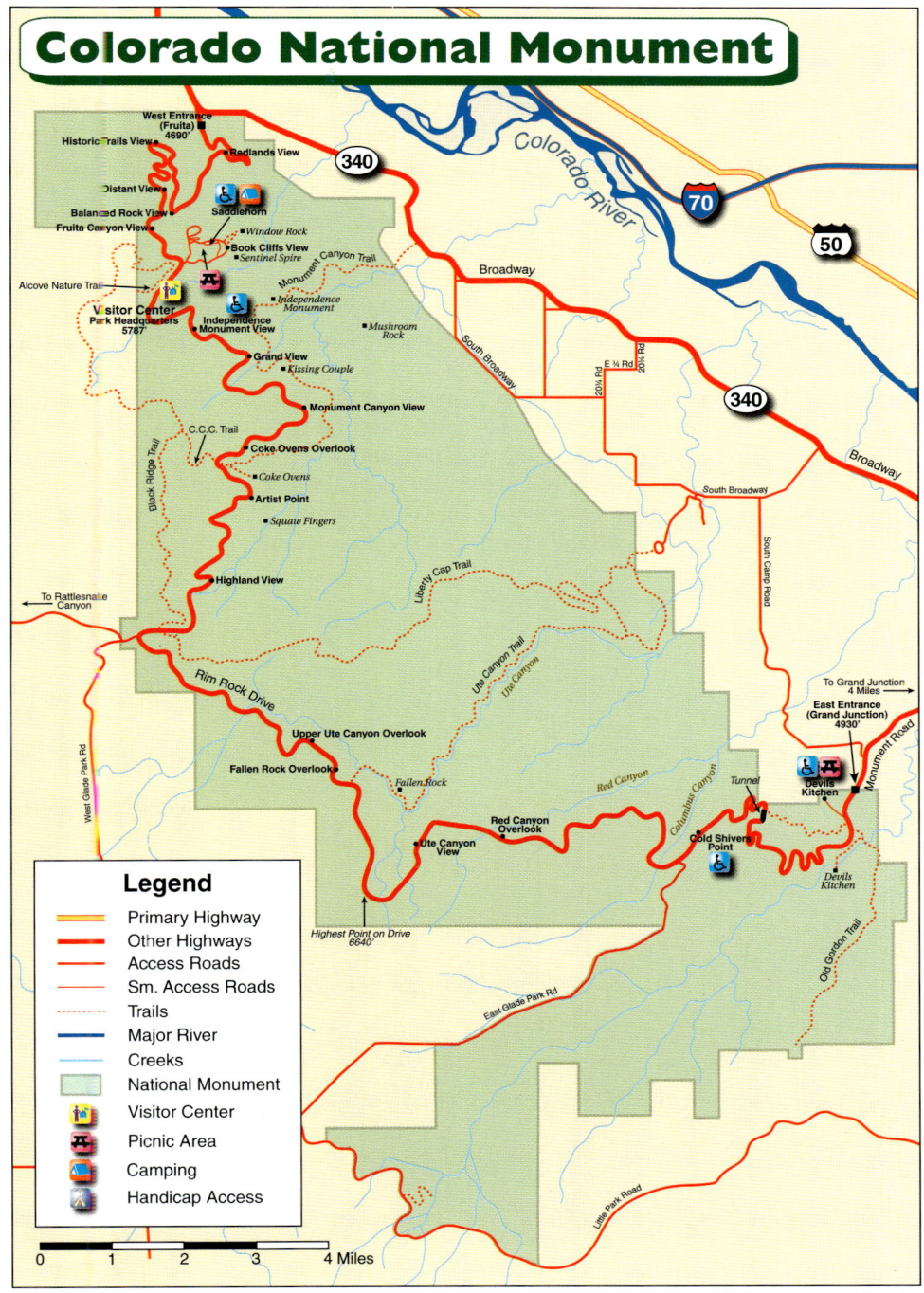

They have developed a keen sense of human encroachment and blend so well into the territory they inhabit that sightings are an extraordinary event. Once in danger of extinction, the desert bighorn are making a tentative comeback in southeast Utah due to a comprehensive reintroduction effort by the National Park Service. With one of the few remaining native herds, Colorado National Monument has been a critical area for restoration efforts. I searched far and wide for the sheep and was not able to spot one.

Reptiles are among the most noticeable animals found in the monument. They can be seen from March through late October; however activity is highest in May and June. The collared lizard is one of the boldest lizards in the monument. Their survival depends on their ability to escape predators. Collared lizards can run upright and have been clocked at 16 to 17 miles per hour, ranking them as one of the world's fastest reptiles. Most reptiles, especially lizards, are most active on warm, sunny days. They are frequently seen sunbathing on rocks throughout the park. In colder temperatures they hibernate, relying on food stored as fat in their tails for nutrition. Snakes on the other hand are rarely seen because they are most active at night.

A wide variety of birds are found within the monument's boundaries. In fact, the Colorado National Monument was designated as an important bird area (IBA) by the National Audubon Society and the American Bird Conservatory on May 10, 2000. The

*First light on the monument*

most visible are raptors. Red-tailed hawks, golden eagles, and an occasional peregrine falcon can be seen soaring within the canyon walls and in the upper level air currents above the monument. Turkey vultures are common as are crows. Wild turkey and Gamble's quail can be seen at any time crossing the road or feeding along any of the foot trails. Over 50 breeding songbird species have been identified in the monument and several other species pass through during migration in the spring and fall.

Watch and listen for the pinyon jay, Steller's jay, western bluebird, canyon wren, spotted towhee, MacGillivray's warbler, dark-eyed junco, black-capped chickadee, and many more. Unless you are a seasoned birder, a book to help identify the species would be invaluable.

As I stood on the edge of Book Cliffs Overlook late one evening, I was bombarded by tree swallows and white-throated swifts. It was an amazing aerial display as they buzzed by me within just a few feet. The sandstone walls of the monument are perfect habitat for these birds. I was also delighted to watch a pair of white-throated swifts enter a nest in a crack of a rock wall near the Serpent's Trailhead, apparently feeding a young one. What I found most amazing was the number of different bird songs I heard – especially the Say's phoebe – but was unable to see the composer. The thick pinyon and juniper trees aided by the undergrowth of mountain mahogany and Gambel's oak hid the birds well.

## Activities

Hiking and bicycling are very popular in the Colorado National Monument. There are a variety of hiking trails in the monument, short and long, easy to difficult, that meet the needs of just about everyone. Bicycling along Rim Rock Drive is popular and very challenging. Camping is available at Saddlehorn Campground year round near the west entrance. It is first-come, first served, however there is a fee. Tables, charcoal grills, drinking water, and restrooms are available.

There is an event every November where runners come to Colorado National Monument to compete in the 23-mile Rim Rock Run. The race covers the entire length of the Rim Rock Road. It is one of the longest through any National Park Service site.

Each Independence Day, local climbers scale the iconic Independence Monument and raise an American flag on top. This tradition dates back to early park advocate and caretaker, John Otto. Climbers still take the same route Otto used to get up Independence Monument.

Book Cliffs Overlook is a unique shelter and is on the National Register of Historic Places. It provides a wonderful view of Wedding Canyon and the Grand Valley. Weddings have been held here for generations.

I would be remiss if I didn't mention photography as an activity. A photo from anywhere in the monument has the potential of making a magazine or book cover. The early morning as the sun is coming up presents an amazing warm light that bathes the red sandstone walls and monoliths within the monument. Don't forget about the wildlife and birds that also pose as photo ops. There are literally photo opportunities around every corner, so have the camera and tripod ready.

The biggest percentage of the shorter hiking trails take a visitor to the varied overlooks in the monument. Window Rock Trail is a half-mile round trip walk with views of the northern end of the monument. Canyon Rim Trail, located at the visitor's center, is about a mile round trip with a great view of Wedding Canyon. Adjacent to Canyon Rim Trail is Alcove Nature Trail, a self-guided trail into an ancient sand dune. Otto's Trail, named after John Otto, is a 1-mile round trip taking you to an excellent overlook of the most popular spires. Coke Ovens Trail, also a mile round trip, descends to an overlook of the Coke Ovens. The Devil's Kitchen Trail and Serpent's Trail are near the east entrance and measure 1.5 miles and 3.5 miles roundtrip, respectively. The Serpent's Trail was built in the early 1900s and was once known as the "Crookedest Road in the World".

The longer backcountry trails in the monument, ranging from 6.5 to 17 miles roundtrip, take a visitor right down into the heart of the monument. A 12-miler called the Monument Canyon Trail descends 600 vertical feet from the eastern plateau off of Highway 340 down into Monument Canyon. Close-up views of the monument's major rock formations like Independence Monument, Kissing Couple, and Coke Ovens are nothing short of spectacular. Also entered from the eastern side of the monument from Highway 340 is Corkscrew Trail. This trail interconnects with Liberty Cap Trail and Ute Canyon Trail. Both of these trails span the monument and end at Rim Rock Drive at the far west part of the monument. Unless you have arranged a pick-up at Rim Rock Drive, it is another 7 miles back to the east side for each trail. Liberty Cap Trail traverses a pinyon and juniper woodland with some sagebrush flats. A close-up

*Bicycling is very common in the Colorado Monument*

view of Liberty Cap, an ancient rock structure, will fascinate the hiker. Ute Canyon Trail drops into the steep Ute Canyon via a well-maintained trail. The streambed at the bottom is loaded with cottonwood trees and willows. Be prepared for water flowing early in the season or after major rainfalls. Wildlife can be abundant and birds will surely be going about their daily activities. Peregrine falcons are often seen in Ute Canyon. Near the west end of Ute Trail watch for the Fallen Rock, a massive slab of sandstone that broke away from the canyon wall several thousand years ago. Old Gordon Trail is found near the east entrance; this 8-mile round trip hike follows an old cattle drive road. The trail is renowned for its geologic story of the monument. Views of the sediment layers along the trail are very distinctive.

I spent most of my time exploring in the Colorado Monument early in the morning and late in the evening. It was cooler and the natural light was at its best for photography. This was also when I needed to be extra alert for bicyclists as I drove from overlook to overlook. Bicycling activity was at its greatest in the morning. It seemed to me that most bicycling enthusiasts used the east entrance as a starting point for their early morning excursions. The beginning of this grueling ride starts at 4,930 feet and climbs to 6,198 feet in just the first 4 miles. There was some huffing and puffing going on as they passed by me at Serpent's Trailhead, which is about the 3-mile mark. I chatted with a gentleman who lives near the east entrance of the monument. I met up with him at the pull-out for Ute Canyon overlook, which is just short of the highest point of 6,640 feet along Rim Rock Drive. I would say that it is about 8 miles of the 23-mile trip. This is the point where he turns around and heads back. However, I watched people throughout the day making the full trip across the monument. Returning to a starting point via public roads outside the park, either at the west or east entrance is about 33 miles. From either entrance, the entire trip will gain about 2,000 vertical feet. They say to allow three hours, but my tired old bones would probably take four to five hours. Whether you decide to ride the entire circuit or only a part of it will depend on how much time you have and how fit you are.

To insure your bicycling safety, please share the road with automobiles and follow these park regulations:

- Bicyclists are required to obey all traffic laws including speed limits, passing zones, and stop signs.
- Bicyclists are required to ride single file at all times within the monument.
- Always ride as far to the right as is safely possible.
- Please allow vehicles to pass you.
- Do not pass vehicles in the tunnels.
- Bicycles or riders must be equipped with reflectors or lights visible from the front and rear for safe passage through the tunnels.
- Bicyclists are required to stop at stop signs during periods when entrance stations are staffed.
- Bicyclists are required to pay entrance fees.
- Use of bicycles is allowed only on park roads. There is no off-road usage allowed.

Even though off-road biking is not permitted in the monument, there are surrounding areas that are ideal for it. Watch out for large trucks on the east side of the monument. There are roadways that access the community of Glade Park.

The average annual high temperature is 61 degrees Fahrenheit, but expect temperatures well into the 90s and even 100s during the summer months. Total rainfall for the year is just over 11 inches, most of which comes in August through October. The average low temperature is 39 degrees Fahrenheit with lows occasionally dipping below zero during the winter. Annual snowfall averages approximately 38 inches, with the heaviest accumulations usually occuring during January and February.

## Contact

Colorado National Monument is open 24 hours a day, seven days a week.

**Visitor center:** Memorial Day to Labor Day: Operating hours are from 8:00am until 6:00pm. The bookstore is operated here by the Colorado National Monument Association.

**Labor Day to Memorial Day:** Operating hours are from 9:00am until 5:00pm. The visitor center is closed on Christmas.

**Colorado National Monument**
Fruita, CO 81521-0001
Visitor Information 970-858-3617
www.nps.gov/colm

**Colorado Welcome Center**
340 Highway 340. Fruita, CO 81521
970-858-9335
www.fruita.org

**Grand Junction Visitor Center**
740 Horizon Dr., Grand Junction, CO 81506
1-800-962-2547
www.grandjunction.net

## Fast Facts

**Getting There:** From Interstate 70 at Grand Junction, go west 11 miles to Fruita (Exit 19). Go south on Highway 340 to the west entrance, which is approximately 3 miles from Fruita. The visitor center and campground are 4 miles up from the west entrance. The east entrance can be reached from Grand Junction proper via Grand Ave. Go west and Grand Avenue merges into Broadway (Highway 340). Continue a couple miles to Monument Road and turn left (south) for 5 miles to the east entrance.

**Activities:** Bird and wildlife viewing, bicycling, photography, and history.

**Principal Mammals:** Desert bighorn sheep, mule deer, pronghorn antelope, coyote, black bear, mountain lion, raccoon, porcupine, skunk, red fox, desert cottontail rabbit, squirrel, piñon mouse, and Ord's kangaroo rat.

**Mammals of Special Interest:** Desert bighorn sheep and mule deer.
**Principal Birdlife:** Raptors, canyon wren, jays.
**Birds of Special Interest:** Peregrine falcon.
**Habitat Overview:** Pinyon and juniper woodlands, red sandstone canyons.
**Flora of Special Interest:** Cliff rose and cliff prickly pear cactus.
**Best Wildlife Viewing Ops:** Early morning and late evening when they are on the move from bedding to feeding areas. Wildlife can be seen from Rim Rock Drive and any number of foot trails.
**Best Birding Ops:** Winter is especially good for raptors, Songbirds and jays during the summer and fall.
**Best Photo Ops:** Early morning is the best light for landscape photography. Wildlife is good in the mornings and late afternoon.
**Hunting Ops:** None
**Fishing Ops:** None
**Camping Ops:** Saddlehorn Campground is open all year.
**Boating Ops:** None
**Hiking Trails:** Opportunities abound throughout the monument.
**Motor Trails:** Rim Rock Drive.

*Side-blotched lizard*

## Mammal List

American badger
American bison
American black bear
Big brown bat
Big free-tailed bat
Bighorn sheep
Black-tailed jackrabbit
Bobcat
Botta's pocket gopher
Brazilian free-tailed bat
Brush mouse
Bushy-tailed woodrat
California myotis
Canyon mouse
Coyote
Crawford's desert shrew
Deer mouse
Desert cottontail
Elk
Fringed myotis
Golden-mantled ground squirrel
Gray fox
Hoary bat
Hopi chipmunk
House mouse
Kit fox
Least chipmunk
Little Brown myotis
Long-eared myotis
Long-legged myotis
Long-tailed vole
Long-tailed weasel
Mexican woodrat
Mountain lion
Mule deer
North American porcupine
Northern grasshopper mouse
Northern raccoon
Ord's kangaroo rat
Pallid bat
Pinon mouse
Plains pocket mouse
Pronghorn
Red fox
Ringtail
Rock squirrel
Silver-haired bat
Spotted bat
Striped skunk
Townsend's big-eared bat
Western harvest mouse
Western pipistrelle
Western small-footed bat
Western spotted skunk
White-tailed antelope squirrel
White-tailed jackrabbit
White-tailed prairie dog
Yellow-bellied marmot
Yuma myotis

## Bird List

American crow
American goldfinch
American kestrel
American pipit
American robin
American tree sparrow
Ash-throated flycatcher
Bald eagle
Band-tailed pigeon
Bank swallow
Barn owl
Barn swallow
Belted kingfisher
Bewick's wren
Black rosy finch
Black-and-white warbler
Black-billed magpie
Black-capped chickadee
Black-chinned hummingbird
Black-headed grosbeak
Black-throated gray warbler
Black-throated sparrow

Blue grosbeak
Blue grouse
Blue-gray gnatcatcher
Bohemian waxwing
Brewer's blackbird
Brewer's sparrow
Broad-tailed hummingbird
Brown creeper
Brown-capped rosy finch
Brown-headed cowbird
Bullock's oriole
Burrowing owl
Bushtit
Canyon wren
Cassin's finch
Cassin's vireo
Cedar waxwing
Chipping sparrow
Chukar partridge
Clark's nutcracker
Cliff swallow
Common nighthawk
Common poorwill
Common raven
Common yellowthroat
Cooper's hawk
Cordilleran flycatcher
Dark-eyed junco (gray-headed)
Dark-eyed junco (Oregon)
Dark-eyed junco (pink-sided)
Dark-eyed junco (slate-colored)
Downy woodpecker
Dusky flycatcher
Eastern bluebird
Eastern kingbird
European starling
Evening grosbeak
Ferruginous hawk
Gambel's quail
Golden eagle
Golden-crowned kinglet
Gray catbird
Gray flycatcher
Gray vireo
Gray-crowned rosy finch

Great blue heron
Great horned owl
Green-tailed Towhee
Gunnison sage grouse
Hairy woodpecker
Hammond's flycatcher
Hermit thrush
Horned lark
House finch
House sparrow
House wren
Juniper titmouse
Killdeer
Lark sparrow
Lazuli bunting
Lesser goldfinch
Lewis' woodpecker
Lincoln's sparrow
Loggerhead shrike
Long-eared owl
MacGillivray's warbler
Magnificent hummingbird
Mallard
Merlin
Mountain bluebird
Mountain chickadee
Mourning dove
Northern flicker
Northern goshawk
Northern harrier
Northern mockingbird
Northern pygmy owl
Northern rough-winged swallow
Northern saw-whet owl
Northern shrike
Olive-sided flycatcher
Orange-crowned warbler
Osprey
Peregrine falcon
Pine grosbeak
Pine siskin
Pinyon jay
Plumbeous vireo
Prairie falcon
Red crossbill

Red-breasted nuthatch
Red-naped sapsucker
Red-tailed hawk
Red-winged blackbird
Ring-necked pheasant
Rock dove
Rock wren
Rose-breasted grosbeak
Rough-legged hawk
Ruby-crowned kinglet
Rufous hummingbird
Sage sparrow
Sage thrasher
Savannah sparrow
Say's phoebe
Scott's oriole
Sharp-shinned hawk
Song sparrow
Spotted towhee
Steller's jay
Swainson's hawk
Townsend's solitaire
Townsend's warbler
Tree swallow
Turkey vulture
Vaux's swift
Vermilion flycatcher
Vesper sparrow
Violet-green swallow
Virginia's warbler
Warbling vireo
Western bluebird
Western kingbird
Western meadowlark
Western screech-owl
Western scrub-Jay
Western tanager
Western wood-pewee
White-breasted nuthatch
White-crowned sparrow
White-throated swift
Wild turkey
Williamson's sapsucker
Willow flycatcher
Wilson's warbler
Yellow warbler
Yellow-breasted chat
Yellow-rumped warbler
Zone-tailed hawk

## Reptile List

Common sagebrush lizard
Eastern collared lizard
Eastern racer
Gophersnake
Great Plains rat snake
Greater short-horned lizard
Long-nosed leopard lizard
Midget faded rattlesnake
Milk snake
Night snake
Plateau lizard
Plateau striped whiptail
Side-blotched lizard
Smith's black-headed snake
Striped whipsnake
Terrestrial garter snake
Tree lizard
Western whiptail

## Amphibian List

Canyon treefrog
Great Basin spadefoot
Northern leopard frog
Red-spotted toad
Tiger salamander
Woodhouse's toad

*Independence Monument*

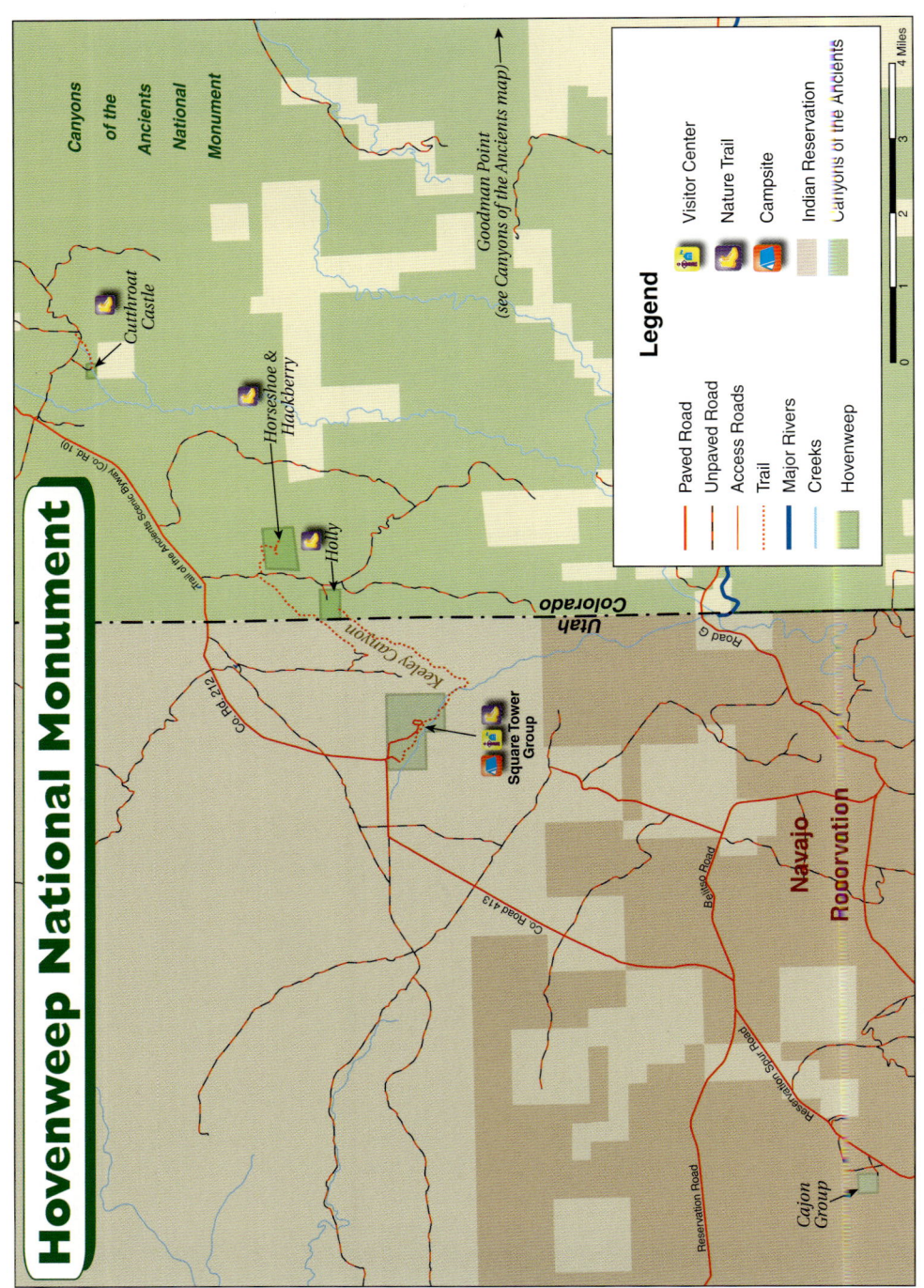

# Hovenweep National Monument

### 784 acres; 35 miles west of Cortez

## Introduction

Hovenweep National Monument was established in 1923 and consists of six sites of ruins spread over a 20-mile expanse of mesa tops and canyons located on a total of 784 acres. The sites are spread over the Colorado-Utah border. The Goodman Point, Cutthroat Castle, Holly, and Horseshoe & Hackberry are in Colorado, the Square Tower located at the visitor center is in Utah, and Cajon is about 8 miles south of the Square Tower site. The uniqueness of these prehistoric sites is in relation to the architecture. They are all multi-storied towers perched on canyon rims and balanced on boulders. They leave visitors in awe at the skillfulness of their builders over 700 years ago.

Goodman Point is the easternmost unit located in Montezuma County, Colorado and contains ruins that were the first archeological resources to be set aside for protection by the federal government. The unit now contains one of the best-preserved clusters of sites in the Four Corners region. Goodman Point Pueblo is the largest site in the unit and contains the collapsed remains of an extensive village complex, complete with public architecture such as a great kiva, plazas, at least one compact, multi-storied "tower" and other features. The National Park Service has recently entered into a cooperative agreement with Crow Canyon Archaeological Center out of Cortez to begin a multi-year testing project at Goodman Point Pueblo in order to better understand the nature of the site and its relationship with surrounding prehistoric communities. Crow Canyon is a non-profit organization that provides experiential and educational opportunities to the public related to archeology, a mission that dove-tails with that of the National Park Service. I did not visit, nor could I find a map to the Goodman Point Pueblo. The National Park Service suggests that if you would like to visit Goodman Point Unit and view the ongoing archeological efforts, contact the Hovenweep National Monument Visitor Center at Square Tower Unit (970-562-4282) for directions and to obtain additional information about the project.

The first record of the Cutthroat Castle dates back to 1929, when it was documented by archeologist Paul Martin. The site was added to the Hovenweep National Monument in 1956. The reason this site may have had its late discovery is its unusual location. The structures at Cutthroat Castle are not located immediately at the head of a canyon, but farther downstream. The site also appears to have a large number of kivas relative to other building types. Puebloan kivas are usually built into the earth, and are typically round. An exception is the kiva incorporated into Cutthroat Castle, which rests on top of a boulder. In Puebloan religion, the kiva is a ceremonial structure that connects with different worlds. The floor is related to the world below, and is usually built below ground level. The entrance to a typical kiva is through the roof, which relates to the world above. Cutthroat Castle Kiva is surrounded by another structure or room. Access into this structure appears to have been from below the boulder on which the kiva is built. There was a convenient split in the boulder through which the people entered. The geology of the surrounding landscape produces springs and seeps. In these canyons, permeable Dakota sandstone rests on top of impermeable Burro Canyon shale. Water from rain and snow soaks through the sandstone, but is forced to flow outward when it meets the shale. When this water reaches the wall of a canyon it forms a spring. For the Puebloans, these canyons with seeps and springs were the ideal place to locate a village. The Cutthroat Castle can be accessed from 10 Road on the Colorado side. It is a rough road marked with a sign.

The Holly Pueblo site includes the Tilted Tower and Boulder House. They are located at the head of Keeley Canyon about 2 miles off of 10 Road on the Colorado side. Access to the structures is by an ambler trail. The base of a tower structure can be seen along the canyon rim. This multi-story pueblo called Tilted Tower was built atop a large sandstone boulder. Sometime after the canyon was abandoned, the boulder shifted, causing the upper stories of the tower to tumble into the canyon while the footing remained attached in a somewhat tilted position. The Boulder House is a large multi-story tower located inside Keeley Canyon just below the Tilted Tower. It is also built atop a large sandstone boulder, but on the canyon bottom. Boulder House is detached from the canyon rim, and like many of the towers at Hovenweep National Monument, it is located adjacent to a water seep. The rock it sits upon is such that the structure had to be built from the inside. There are visible hand and foot holds notched into the rock that had to be climbed to enter the Boulder House.

The Horseshoe Group and Hackberry group is on the same high-clearance road that the Holly site is located. A small parking area and a walking trail to Hackberry Canyon start your investigation. The mile-long round-trip Canyon Rim Trail accesses both the Horseshoe and Hackberry sites. Structures at these sites were built approximately 800 years ago by the ancestors of today's Puebloan people. Horseshoe Tower is built on a point that marks the start of the Horseshoe Site. From this tower, the ancients could see clearly into Horseshoe Canyon. Farther along the Canyon Rim Trail is Horseshoe House, which is composed of four masonry structures that together form a horseshoe shape. From the trail it is easy to see the precisely cut stone-masonry that forms the outside wall of Horseshoe House. Each stone was shaped for a precise fit before being set into place. Clay, sand, and ash, mixed with water from seeps in the canyon below, made the mortar that still holds these walls together. About 500 yards east of the Horseshoe structures is the Hackberry Site. Archeologists speculate that Hackberry Canyon may have had one of the largest populations of all the Hovenweep elements because of the constant seepage of water in the canyon. As many as 250 to 350 people may have lived here. The concentrations of structures at both Horseshoe and Hackberry demonstrate the importance of water to the people who lived here. Large multi-story pueblos and towers, located at canyon heads with seeps and springs, are the defining characteristics of the late Pueblo III time period. In this climate, precipitation came in the form of winter snows, spring rains, and isolated summer thunderstorms. The intermittent rains of summer were crucial to the survival of crops. The Puebloans responded by constructing water control features. In washes on the mesa tops, small stone dams were built so that sediment could accumulate and water could soak into the ground and flow slowly into nearby garden plots. A 23-year-long drought beginning in 1276 possibly combined with warfare, overpopulation, and limited resources, forced the ancestors of today's Pueblo people to leave Hovenweep. These Puebloan communities across southeast Utah and southwest Colorado migrated south, joining the pueblos of the Rio Grande River Valley in New Mexico and the Hopi in Arizona.

The Square Tower Group is the only site in the monument that is accessible by a paved road and is located near the visitor center. A somewhat strenuous trail follows the canyon rim and offers excellent views of every structure. It would be very easy to spend a couple hours exploring the area. The trail between the visitor center and the first overlook is paved and can be traversed by visitors in wheelchairs with assistance. The Square Tower trail consists of three loops totaling 2 miles. This primitive trail, which takes approximately two hours to walk, is marked with rock cairns. A trail guide can be purchased at the ranger station for $0.35. Please remember to always carry water. The Square Tower, for which this site is named, is a three-story tower built on a boulder at the head of Little Ruin Canyon. The proximity of a nearby spring makes for a classic location, which would have been an important resource for the people of Hovenweep.

There is also evidence of a check-dam these clever people built above the spring to increase water storage during storm runoff. The unique location and appearance of Square Tower fuels speculation that it was a ceremonial structure.

The Square Tower Group contains the largest collection of Ancestral Puebloan structures at Hovenweep National Monument. The remains of nearly 30 kivas have been discovered on the slopes of Little Ruin Canyon and a variety of other structures are perched on the canyon rims. Many are balanced on boulders and tucked under ledges. It's possible that as many as 500 people occupied the Square Tower while the area was active.

There is a 31-site campground at the visitor center that has restrooms and drinking water. Each site has a table and fire grate. Fires are allowed in the grates only. Wood gathering is not permitted. While most sites can accommodate small trailers, there are no hookups. Camping is on a first-come, first-served basis, with no reservations taken. The camping fee of $10 per night, per site is collected from about April to October.

The Cajon Group (pronounced ca-hone) can be accessed by heading west at the junction of Belitso Road and Reservation Road. Continue west on Reservation Road about 0.5 mile and turn left on 471 Road (also known as Reservation Spur). Go 2 miles to the site. This site consists of a small village constructed in the same configuration as Hackberry, Horseshoe, and Holly. The surviving structures are situated at the head of a small canyon and evidence indicates that 80 to 100 people may have lived here. Under a ledge are several small structures as well as pictographs painted in the Mesa Verde pottery style. In the canyon below, the remains of an earthen dam built to store water can still be seen today. On the western slope of the canyon stand the remains of a remarkable circular tower that conforms perfectly to the shape of three large, irregular boulders. This round structure on a completely uneven surface demonstrates the skill and determination of the ancestral Puebloans that lived at Hovenweep.

## Wildlife and Environment

The climate in this high desert environment is dry with an average of 12 inches of precipitation per year. Winter low temperatures average from -10 to 10 degrees Fahrenheit; however daytime temperatures can be quite pleasant. Summer highs average 90 to 100 degrees and can be unbearable at times. Spring and fall are generally mild, ranging up to 80 degrees.

Wildlife consists primarily of reptiles, birds, and small game. The mule deer is basically the only large mammal in the area with a few straggler elk in the winter. Reptiles include bull snakes, rattlesnakes, desert striped whipsnake, northern plateau lizard, and yellow-headed collared lizard. The colorful collared lizard is one of the most frequently seen animals at Hovenweep. When not chasing flies or basking in the sun, they are often seen doing what appears to be push-ups. Scientists believe this and other behaviors signal dominance and facilitate courtship. Birds include the ever-present raven and crow, Swainson's hawk, and golden eagle. A variety of smaller species include western scrub-jay, pinyon jay, and black-billed magpie. Common desert mammals include coyotes, bobcats, mountain lions, fox, bunnies, and bats. Snake food consists of the canyon mouse, deer mouse, and pinyon mouse. During the late spring and early summer, biting gnats are plentiful.

## Activities

General sight seeing and photography are going to be the core of outdoor activities in southwest Colorado. Hiking and mountain biking could put a visitor into "great places" for these primary activities.

There are places in close proximity for fishing, but the area of Hovenweep National Monument is pretty much void of any water sources that hold fish. The Delores River below McPhee Reservoir and the Animas River in Durango are good trout fisheries. Warmwater lakes for walleye, crappie, largemouth bass, and catfish can be found at Totten Reservoir near Cortez, Narraguinnep Reservoir near Delores, and Summit Reservoir north of Mancos. These reservoirs are all located on state wildlife areas. Mancos State Park is north of Mancos and has camping, boating, and fishing. Mesa Verde National Park is located 75 miles east of the monument. This world heritage site contains a large number of ancestral Puebloan cliff dwellings and other interesting archeological sites. A world renowned archeological museum is also located at Mesa Verde National Park.

Durango-Silverton Narrow Gauge Railroad is located in the historic railroad town of Durango. It is located 90 miles east of Hovenweep. One of its main attractions is a historic steam-powered railroad, which offers visitors a high mountain rail trip to the historic mining town of Silverton.

## Location

There are basically two ways to get to the Hovenweep National Monument:

From Cortez, take 491 south about 3 miles to Road G. Turn west (right) on Road G at the signs for the airport. Go about 25 miles on this paved road into Utah and turn right on Belitso Road. Travel about 5 miles to Reservation Road and turn right. Continue another 6 to 7 miles to the monument.

From the Anasazi Heritage Center near Delores, take Highway 184 west to Highway 491 and turn right (north). Travel 7 to 8 miles to BB Road and turn left (west). Go another 6 miles to 10 Road and turn left (south). Stay on 10 Road for about 20 miles, again just into Utah to the monument.

The Cutthroat Castle can be accessed from 10 Road on the Colorado side. It is a rough road marked with a sign.

## Contact

**Hovenweep National Monument**
 McElmo Route, Cortez, CO  81321-8901
 970-562-4282
 www.nps.gov/hove
 Hovenweep is open year-round and there is no entrance fee.
 The visitor center is open daily from 8:00am-6:00pm April through September, 8:00am-5:00pm the rest of the year.
 The visitor center is closed winter holidays.
 Hiking trails are open during daylight hours.
 Pets must be kept on leash at all times.
 Firearms are prohibited.
 There are very few services available in this uninhabited area. Gasoline and general supplies can be found in Colorado at the Ismay Trading Post, which is 14 miles from the visitor center. In Utah, the Hatch Trading Post is 16 miles. Larger towns like Cortez in Colorado and Blanding in Utah are between 40 and 50 miles away.
 Lodging can be found in Cortez, Colorado, Bluff, Utah or Blending, Utah. All are less than 50 miles away.

# Mesa Verde National Park

## 52,122 Acres; Southwestern Colorado 36 miles west of Durango

## Introduction

President Theodore Roosevelt established Mesa Verde National Park (MVNP) in June of 1906. It was the first park of its variety, recognized as a "preserve for the works of man". The preservation of the cultural and natural resources of this area remains the focus of the management's staff. With more than 4,000 known archeological sites dating back to A.D. 550-1300, the most impressive are the cliff dwellings.

Mesa Verde, Spanish for "Green Table", includes nearly 600 cliff dwellings, only a very small percentage can be explored and many cannot even be seen. They are some of the most extraordinary and best preserved sites in the United States. It is an amazing look into the lives of an ancient people and their offspring who inhabited this location for more than 700 years. Local cowboys first described finding the dwelling and pit houses in the early 1880s.

The Mesa Verde National Park is divided into two separate mesas; the Chaplin Mesa and the Wetherill Mesa. They both start at the Far View Visitor Center. The Chaplin Mesa Drive is divided into two loops, the Mesa Top Loop and the Cliff Palace Loop where the Cliff Palace, Balcony House, and Chaplin Mesa Museum are found; while the Step House, Long House, and Badger House Community are found on the Wetherill Mesa Drive. A minimum of four hours should be set aside to view MVNP, as it takes nearly two hours just to drive from one end of the park to the other. A full day would be a better plan, to take in all the sights and when the day is finished, it would not surprise me if a visitor would plan more time to view what could not be fit in the single day.

Time should be spent viewing and exploring these impressive dwellings (tour times and reservations are available at the Far View Visitor Center). The largest of the cliff dwellings is the Cliff Palace. It has as many as 150 rooms with an additional 75 open areas. Twenty-one of the rooms are ceremonial rooms called kivas, and another 30 rooms resemble structures where people would have lived. The number of Ancestral Puebloans living in the Cliff Palace at any one time was 100 to 120. The smallest of the cliff dwellings are of the one room variety.

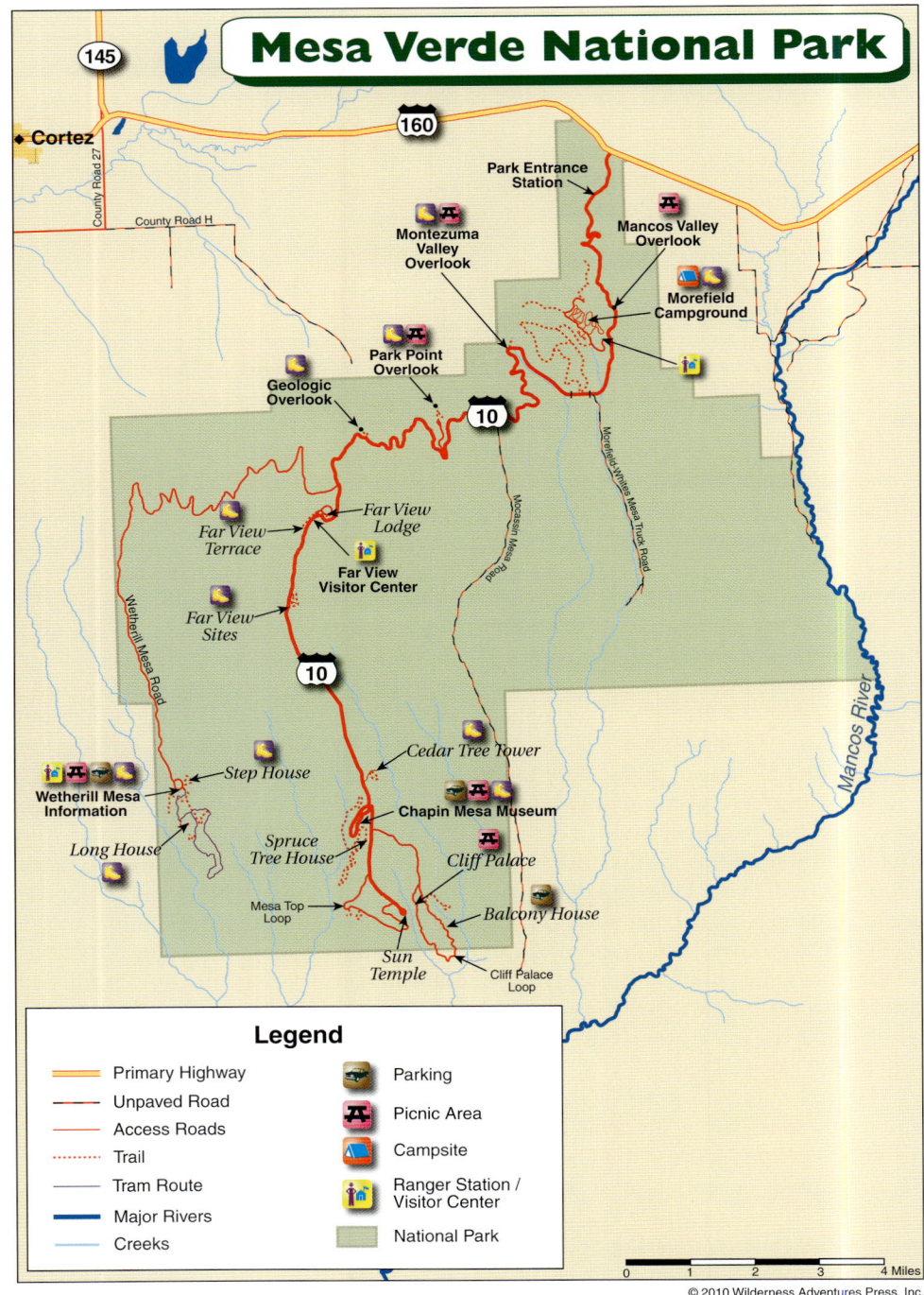

Early archeologists referred to these early people as Anasazi, from a Navajo word translated as "the ancient foreigners"; however, today they are called Ancestral Puebloans, reflecting their modern descendants.

The true story of these ancients may never be known. They left no written record of their existence and even after decades of careful excavation and analysis, their history remains vague. Things that are known tell a story of a resilient people who had the ingenuity to build structures, farm, hunt, use bones for tools, weave baskets, and eventually made pottery. Many new sites have been recently discovered by the numerous fires that have scorched the area.

## History

Mesa Verde is rich in history; however most of it is by and large speculative. It is known that the Ancestral Puebloans inhabited Mesa Verde for more than 700 years (A.D. 550 to A.D. 1300). For the first six centuries, they primarily lived in pit houses and pueblos on the mesa tops and it was not until the final 100 years or so that they constructed and lived in the cliff dwellings. Why they moved to the cliffs is unknown and can only be hypothesized: For defense from encroaching societies? For better shelter from weather conditions? Maybe even religious or psychological reasons?

The cliff dwellings have no architectural consistency and they seem to be built into the space available. Even the masonry work is inconsistent within the same dwelling. The structures in Mesa Verde are, however, evidence of an accomplished and energetic people bound by community. Their skills and traditions should be ranked among the best expressions of human culture in North America. The best preserved mesa top sites are the Badger House Community, the Sun Temple, the Far View Sites Complex, and the Cedar Tree Tower. I found the Sun Temple especially interesting and the structure is extraordinary. It is presumed to be a ceremonial structure as no pottery, tools, or wood beams were exhumed from the site. Even though the top of the walls are covered with concrete to prevent deterioration, the overall size and the meticulous nature of this fine construction point to the amount of ingenuity and exertion put into it.

Many other pit houses and ancient farming villages with informative placards illustrating their presumed way of life can be found along the Mesa Top Loop.

As with many early civilizations, gathering food was their most important and time consuming labor. Even though skilled in farming corn, beans and squash, they still gathered wild plants and hunted small game and killed the occasional deer. There may be evidence that they domesticated the turkey.

A burgeoning population and the numerous skills of the Ancestral Puebloans could have led to a surplus of their hand-made items. This could have led to trade and bartering amongst themselves and with other tribes. Items such as seashells from the Pacific coast, turquoise and cotton from the south, and pottery made their way to Mesa Verde, which could have been traded for baskets, tools, sandals, and arrow points. The true start of the American economy?

The preservation of the Mesa Verde National Park is of utmost importance. At this writing, a large percentage of the dwellings have been left unexposed and are not open to the public due to the Antiquities Act of 1906 and, more recently, the Archeological Resources Protection Act of 1979. The acts prohibit the excavation, injury, or destruction of any archeological site on federal land. The defacing or removal of any antiquity in the park is punishable with fines up to $100,000 and imprisonment for up to 20 years. Think twice before you scratch your initials in a dwelling wall. In 1996, the Condition Assessment Project began at MVNP. Under this program, standing walls in the dwellings are assessed for damage from the elements, fire, and structural instability. To date, 230 cliff dwellings have been assessed and recommendations have been made to help decrease or annul the undesirable outcome.

## Wildlife

Much like the other national parks in Colorado, Mesa Verde has a diverse and hefty number of wildlife species. With an impressive bird list of over 200 species, 74 mammals, and over 20 different reptiles and amphibians, Mesa Verde is a wildlife viewer and birder's nirvana. The mesa country of western Colorado has always been known as prime habitat for mule deer, wild turkey, coyote, mountain lion, and raptors.

The Audubon Society has named MVNP an "Important Bird Area" – a very distinct honor. They have helped set up two Protected Activity Centers and three breeding areas, totaling over 5,000 acres, for the threatened Mexican spotted owl. The

*Cliff Palace*

Colorado Natural Heritage Program and the Nature Conservancy have classified the entire park within their Network of Conservation Areas because of the extraordinary amount of rare plants and animal species.

    I observed many birds during my trip there, however was not quite rewarded with the photography that I had hoped. Visitors (photographers) must stay on marked paths, so with the number of people I had walking the paths with me, the birds were a bit skittish. There are a number of burned areas that provide an excellent environment for woodpeckers. You may see a few flutters now and then as you drive along the main roads, but it is definitely best to stop and look over these areas with binoculars. The black bark of the junipers and new birth of undergrowth is a stark contrast, but great habitat for the northern flicker and the hairy woodpecker. Add the mourning dove, western bluebird, mountain chickadee, vesper sparrow, the noisy black-billed magpie and the elusive wild turkey to the mix, and you will surely have a pleasurable day of birding. I was fortunate enough to watch several turkey vultures come to roost near the Spruce Tree House cliff dwelling. The appearance of a vulture, at least from a profiled blood-red-colored head view, is less than desirable, but I have always enjoyed watching them soar in the air currents. This more than makes up for their dreadful looks. They have that very distinctive half-silver underside of the wings and their flight looks so effortless.

    The trails around the Chaplin Mesa Museum, including Spruce Canyon Trail and Petroglyph Trail are very good for warbler species, pinyon jays, juniper titmouse,

Clark's nutcrackers and out along the edge of the canyon, the turkey vultures and red-tailed hawks may be seen. Before leaving the park, the Knife Edge Trail that heads west out of Morefield Campground is a great hike to overlook the Montezuma Valley. This is a wonderful place to watch the sunset and may be one of the better places to spot a peregrine falcon. The wild turkeys also like to hang out around the campground area.

The usual small game such as the Colorado chipmunk, bunnies and jack rabbits, rock squirrels, and Gunnison's prairie dog can be seen on a regular basis. The Abert's squirrel with its pointy ears and silvery white tail would be an exceptional sighting.

Spotting the mule deer is definitely an early morning or late in the evening opportunity. Visitors can run into them just about anywhere in the park, however, I spotted them near the park entrance/exit late in the day as I was leaving. Healthy full-bodied animals with shiny coats were the norm. The park asks that you fill out a wildlife sighting card to record your special sighting if you are fortunate enough to spot a rarely seen animal, such as a mountain lion or bear.

## Contact

**Mesa Verde National Park**
PO Box 8, Mesa Verde, CO  81330-0008
970-529-4465
www.nps.gov/meve/index.htm

**Entrance Fee:** The entrance fee from January 1-May 23 and September 8-December 31 is $10 per vehicle. From May 24–September 7 it is $15. It covers all persons in a single, private, noncommercial vehicle and is valid for seven calendar days. The entry fee for pedestrians, bicyclists, motorcycles, motor scooters, or mopeds from January 1-May 23 and September 8 - December 31 is $5 per individual. From May 24–September 7 it is $8. There is no fee charged for persons 16 years of age or younger.

**Mesa Verde Annual Pass:** An annual pass to Mesa Verde National Park is available at the entrance station for $30. This pass admits the permit holder and all accompanying passengers in a single, private, noncommercial vehicle to the park. It is valid for 12 months from date of purchase and covers entry fees only.

**Park Hours:** Open daily, year round. 8:00am to 6:30pm are the basic hours for the summer months. The park closes at 5:00pm during the winter months. Check with the park information for cliff dwelling closures after the summer season.

The visitor center is open April-October.

**Hours:** Fall and Spring: 8:00am-5:00pm
**Summer:** 8:00am-7:00pm
970-529-4465

**Location:** Fifteen miles from the main entrance. The Far View Lodge, restaurant, gift shop, and tour tickets are available.

## Fast Facts

**Getting There:** The Mesa Verde National Park is located approximately 420 miles southwest of Denver via southbound Interstate 25 and westbound Colorado Highway 160, or 391 miles via southbound CO Highway 285 and westbound Colorado Highway 160. Even though the route is longer via I-25, the time it takes is marginal because of speed limits and fewer mountainous roads. From Denver (via I-25), travel 160 miles south on Interstate 25 to Walsenburg. Follow signage through town to access CO Highway 160. Take CO Highway 160 west 220 miles to Durango. Follow signage through town and continue on CO Highway 160 another 40 miles to the park entrance.

From Denver (via CO Highway 285), travel 220 miles south on CO Highway 285 to Monte Vista. Take CO Highway 160 west 130 miles to Durango. Follow signage through town and continue on CO Highway 160 another 40 miles to the park entrance.

**Activities:** Scenic drives, cliff dwelling tours, hiking, bird and wildlife viewing, and photography. Park Point, the highest elevation in the park (8,427ft) has a 360-degree panoramic view of the surrounding area that must be considered one of the most magnificent in the state.

**Principal Mammals:** Mule deer, coyote, black bear, mountain lion, porcupine, western spotted skunk, red fox, cottontail rabbits, rock squirrels, Colorado chipmunk, long-tailed weasel, and ermine.

**Mammals of Special Interest:** Mule deer, piñon mouse, and big free-tailed bat.

**Principal Birdlife:** Several species of hawks, golden eagle, turkey vulture, warblers, flycatchers, woodpeckers, jays, and chickadees.

**Birds of Special Interest:** Peregrine falcon, golden eagle, and Mexican spotted owl.

**Habitat Overview:** The lower elevation is dominated by big sagebrush, rabbitbrush, and several herbaceous species. The pinyon-juniper woodland is dominated by Utah juniper and Colorado pinyon pine. It covers the mesa tops and upper canyon slopes lying at or below 7,800 feet in elevation.

**Best Wildlife Viewing Ops:** Early morning and late evening when they are on the move from bedding to feeding areas. Wildlife can be seen from most trails and the main roads.

**Best Birding Ops:** Most anytime is good for raptors. All the hiking trails and main roads will present exceptional birding.

**Best Photo Ops:** Early morning and late evening present the best lighting situations.

**Hunting Ops:** None

**Fishing Ops:** None

**Camping Ops:** Morefield Campground

**Boating Ops:** None

**Hiking Trails:** Nine main trails

**Motor Trails:** The main scenic drive through the park.

## Bird List

**NEW WORLD VULTURES**

Turkey vulture

**KITES, HAWKS, EAGLES**

Golden eagle
Sharp-shinned hawk
Cooper's hawk
Red-tailed hawk

**FALCONS AND CARACARAS**

American kestrel
Grouse (*phasianidae*)
Wild turkey

**PIGEONS AND DOVES**

Mourning dove

**TYPICAL OWLS**

Long-eared owl
Great horned owl
Northern pygmy owl
Northern saw-whet owl

**NIGHTJARS**

Common poorwill

**SWIFTS**

White-throated swift

**HUMMINGBIRDS**

Black-chinned hummingbird
Broad-tailed hummingbird
Rufous hummingbird

**WOODPECKERS**

Northern flicker
Hairy woodpecker

**TYRANT FLYCATCHERS**

Western kingbird
Ash-throated flycatcher
Western wood-pewee
Say's phoebe
Gray flycatcher
Dusky flycatcher

**SWALLOWS**

Violet-green swallow

**JAY'S, CROWS, MAGPIES**

Western scrub-Jay
Pinyon jay
Steller's jay
Clark's nutcracker
Black-billed magpie

**COMMON RAVEN CHICKADEES AND TITMICE**

Mountain chickadee
Juniper titmouse

**BUSHTITS**

Bushtit

**NUTHATCHES**

White-breasted nuthatch

**WRENS**

House wren
Bewick's wren
Canyon wren
Rock wren

**THRUSHES**

Ruby-crowned kinglet
Blue-gray gnatcatcher
Western bluebird
Townsend's solitaire
American robin

**VIREOS**

Plumbeous vireo

### WOOD-WARBLERS

Virginia's warbler
Yellow-rumped warbler
Black-throated gray warbler

### TANAGERS

Western tanager

### NEW WORLD SPARROWS

Green-tailed towhee
Spotted towhee
Vesper sparrow
Chipping sparrow
Dark-eyed junco

### CARDINALS

Black-headed grosbeak
Lazuli bunting

### FINCHES

Pine siskin
Lesser goldfinch
House finch

## Mammal List

### SHREW FAMILY

Merriam's shrew
Masked (*Cinereus*) shrew
Montane shrew
Dwarf shrew
Gray shrew

### BAT FAMILY

California myotis
Long-eared myotis
Western small-footed bat
Fringed myotis
Long-legged myotis
Occult myotis
Yuma myotis
Big brown bat
Mule-eared bat (Townsend's big-eared bat)
Silver-haired bat
Hoary bat
Western pipistrelle
Spotted bat
Allen's big-eared bat
Pallid bat
Brazilian free-tailed bat
Big free-tailed bat

### HARE AND RABBIT FAMILY

Black-tailed jackrabbit
Desert cottontail
Nuttall's cottontail

### SQUIRREL FAMILY

Abert's squirrel
Red squirrel
Golden-mantled ground squirrel
Rock squirrel
White-tailed antelope squirrel
Yellow-bellied marmot
Gunnison's prairie dog
Least chipmunk
Colorado chipmunk

### POCKET GOPHER FAMILY

Botta's pocket gopher
Apache (Plains) pocket mouse

### BEAVER FAMILY

American beaver

### MOUSE AND RAT FAMILY

Western harvest mouse

Brush mouse
Canyon mouse
Deer mouse
Piñon mouse
Bushy-tailed woodrat
White-throated woodrat
Mexican woodrat
Long-tailed vole
Mexican vole
Montane vole muskrat

**NEW WORLD PORCUPINE FAMILY**

Porcupine

**DOG FAMILY**

Coyote

**COMMON GRAY FOX**

Red fox

**BEAR FAMILY**

American black bear

**RACCOON FAMILY**

Raccoon (not native)
Ringtail

**WEASEL FAMILY**

Long-tailed weasel
Ermine (short-tailed weasel)
American mink
Western spotted skunk
Striped skunk
American badger

**CAT FAMILY**

Mountain lion
Bobcat

**DEER FAMILY**

Mule deer
Rocky Mountain elk

## Reptile List

Yellow-headed collared lizard
Speckled earless lizard
Great Basin sagebrush lizard
Northern plateau lizard
Northern tree lizard
Northern side-blotched lizard
Mountain short-horned lizard
Plateau whiptail lizard
Two-lined skink

Wandering garter snake
Desert striped whip snake
Western smooth green snake
Great Basin gopher snake
New Mexico milk snake
Mesa Verde night snake
Prairie (western) rattlesnake (possibly other subspecies as well)

# Yucca House National Monument

### 34 acres; Southwest Colorado 10 miles south of Cortez

## Introduction

The Yucca House is one of the largest archeological sites in southwest Colorado. President Woodrow Wilson proclaimed the site a national monument on December 19, 1919. To this day, the site is mostly unexcavated and is much like it was found a century and a half ago. The location is actually managed by Mesa Verde National Park.

A private landowner donated 9.5 acres of land to the federal government in July of 1919 to accommodate this new designation. It was one of many research national monuments designated during that era to preserve them for future investigation, and not necessarily as sites expected to be significant public attractions. As a National Park Service historic area, the park was listed on the National Register of Historic Places on October 15, 1966. It is expected that by 2016, research on the site will be further advanced, and public visitation will be actively encouraged. However, these advancements are totally dependent on available government funds, so this date is only an estimate. Currently there are no facilities or fees at Yucca House.

The site has two distinctive structural areas: the Lower House and West Complex. The Lower House has some of the only visible standing stonework. It is a smallish pueblo with at least eight rooms and a central kiva. The West Complex was a much larger pueblo with an estimated 600 rooms and at least 100 kivas. There are trails and interpretive signage with information about what you are seeing. Even though the site is not much more than a couple piles of stone rubble, I am sure it was an impressive structure for the era it existed. Another important aspect of the site is the live spring. It was very common for the Ancestral Puebloans to build their villages around natural water sources. The water was used for drinking, making mud mortar, and irrigating crops.

The Yucca House was first written about by Professor William H. Holmes in 1878. While on an expedition for the United States Geological Survey Service, Holmes discovered this vast dwelling and described a prolific spring surrounded by rubble on three sides. He drew the first map of the site, sketching the fallen walls and piles of stone. At the time of his visit, archeologists believed these ancient sites were built by the Aztec people of Mexico. To follow with those thoughts, Holmes named the site "Aztec Springs". The site was renamed for its location at the base of Sleeping Ute Mountain to clarify that it was not built by the Aztecs and to avoid confusion with nearby Aztec Ruins National Monument. Sleeping Ute Mountain is known to the Ute Indians and other tribes as the "mountain with lots of yucca growing on it." Thus, "Aztec Springs" became "Yucca House." Interestingly, there is no yucca growing in the monument today.

The Yucca House was an important community center for the Ancestral Puebloan people from about 1150 to 1300. It is an excellent example of what these people called home. The site has remained well protected with the assistance of Hallie Ismay, until her death in 2002. In fact, Hallie was honored by the U.S. Department of the Interior for 62 years of service as the unofficial custodian of Yucca House National Monument.

Yucca House National Monument is a great example of public/private stewardship of our cultural resources and hopefully will remain protected well into the future. The long-term preservation of Yucca House ensures that archeologists will be able to continue studying Ancestral Puebloan society and what caused them to migrate from this region in the late 1200s. As I walked around the site and drove through the area, I couldn't help but imagine how it might have been when this was a pulsating pueblo, full of people and surrounded by crudely plowed farmland. There could have been families tending their fields with hand-made tools. Maybe a dance and song urging a rain shower to quench the dry soil and cool the hot summer afternoon. The smell of a smoky fire grilling a rabbit or some tasty bird. It makes one appreciate the comforts of home.

## Wildlife

Today, the Yucca House is surrounded by productive agricultural lands and has beautiful views across the Montezuma Valley. This rich land and the water available from springs much like the one at this site provide important resources for the wildlife living in the area today. Mule deer, coyotes, bobcats, bunnies, lizards, and rattlesnakes all live in and around Yucca House National Monument. Mountain bluebirds, mourning doves, Townsend's solitaire, loggerhead shrike, yellow-rumped warblers, and yellow-breasted chat could all be seen in the area. I spent some time driving the local vicinity and noticed a number of kestrels. There seemed to be a pair hanging around every tree-lined side road.

The monument preserves and protects the local vegetation. The monument also protects one of the largest claret cup cacti in the area. The desert shrub environment within the monument which includes sagebrush, four-winged saltbush, cacti, and a number of grasses, is very good habitat for smaller rodents. There were a number of bull snakes here and I am sure they were well fed.

## Regulations

The Federal Antiquities Act of 1906 and the Archeological Resources Protection Act of 1979 prohibit the removal of any object of antiquity or the destruction of any architectural site on federal land. Report any damaging behavior immediately to a park ranger at Mesa Verde.

Be respectful of the wildlife and plants in the monument.

## Location

From Cortez, take Highway 491 south to Road B. Take a right on Road B, which is a dirt road and drive 0.8 mile, crossing a paved road and take a right on Road 20.5, the next dirt road. Follow this road north and west for 1.4 miles, head towards the white ranch house with the red roof on the western horizon. Please be courteous toward the private landowners and close all gates behind you as you enter to prevent livestock from escaping. Once at the ranch house, Yucca House National Monument is on the left side of the driveway. The road is not marked very well at all, but if you follow these instructions it will lead to the Yucca House. Once at the parking area, enter the small corral through the gate, and use the stile over the far corral fence to enter the monument.

## Contact

**Mesa Verde National Park**
Yucca House National Monument
PO Box 8, Mesa Verde NP, CO 81330
970-529-4465
www.nps.gov/yuho/

*Southwest Colorado*

# Scenic Byways

## The Alpine Loop

The Alpine Loop is one of the few byways that take to gravel roads, often times needing four-wheel drive to pass. This 63-mile byway is best driven from July through September and takes between four and six hours.

Starting at Silverton on Highway 550, take Road 110 east out of town, which eventually turns into 2 Road. This follows the Animas River to its headwaters, which in turn leads into the most rugged and spectacular portion of the San Juan Mountains. Travelers will pass through the ghost towns of Howardsville and Middleton, strewn with old buildings and mining structures. This was once a rich mining area. Turn right on 5 Road along Cinnamon Creek. At this point you will experience a road that is demanding and rough in places, heading up and over the 12,680-foot Cinnamon Pass. A high-clearance four-wheel-drive vehicle is recommended, but this will be a rewarding journey. These unsound roads were first used by 19th-century miners, who carted their ore off to Silverton, Ouray, and Lake City in mule-drawn wagons. Hook up on 4 Road and follow it for about 10 miles to the old ghost town of Sherman. Not much left there but a few original cabins; however, along the way you will notice the 14,048-foot Handies Peak on the right and 14,034-foot Redcloud and 14,001-foot Sunshine Peak on the left. The gravel road improves greatly as it turns into 30 Road. This road follows the headwaters of the Lake Fork of the Gunnison. The road is paved the last 4 miles heading into Lake City. This completes the first leg of the drive.

Take a left on Highway 149 into Lake City and then turn west (left) on 20 Road, following Henson Creek. Henson Creek is a great little stream for the flyfisher and I shot the image that graced the first edition of my first book, *Flyfisher's Guide to Colorado* along this section of road. Capital City, an abandoned ghost town founded in 1877 and thrived into the 1890s, is the first main stop in the road. A number of structures still stand here, making it worth a look around. Continue on 20 Road over the 12,805-foot Engineer Pass. Shortly after coming down from the pass, veer left onto 2 Road, which will take you back to Silverton.

There is an amazing amount of history enduring in these mountains. Spend a day exploring the abandoned town sites and structures, and a few of the ex-mining haunts. Once a visitor travels these high mountain roads, it will become obvious the hardships our early mining communities endured for a few bags of precious ore.

There are numerous camping opportunities; expect ample solitude and pristine mountain views. Photography is a given and for the fit-minded crew, there are numerous trails for hiking and mountain biking.

This is one of the best areas in the state for elk, but also expect to see plenty of mule deer, an occasional bighorn sheep, and maybe even a moose. There is plenty of small game and look for mountain bluebirds, grosbeaks, and water birds along the route.

## Contact

**BLM-Gunnison Resource Area**
216 North Colorado, Gunnison, CO 81230
970-641-0471
www.lakecity.com/outdoorrecreation.html

*Colorado chipmunk*

# Grand Mesa Scenic Byway

The Grand Mesa Scenic Byway starts at Exit 49 on Interstate 70 at the intersection with Highway 65, about 10 miles east of Grand Junction. It follows Highway 65 about 65 miles to the town of Cedaredge. This two-hour tour begins in the Plateau Creek Valley, travels through the Mesa Lakes Area, and finishes up exploring the Land O' Lakes area. About 30 miles into the byway, turn right on FR 100. This is a 20-mile spur that takes you along FR 100, also known as Lands End Road, to the western edge of the mesa. This switchback road provides incredible views of the Colorado River Valley below. You can also see the Colorado National Monument west of Grand Junction (see the Colorado National Monument chapter for more detailed information).

## Plateau Creek Valley

The Plateau Creek Valley area follows Plateau Creek, a small tributary to the Colorado River. It is a high desert canyon of sandstone cliffs and rock formations. Before starting the climb into the Grand Mesa, enjoy this picturesque little canyon and its wildlife and birding possibilities. Expect to see mule deer in the evening and early morning. Coyotes are common, and wild turkey and raptors can be seen from the road.

## Vega State Park

About 10 miles from Interstate 70 on Highway 65, turn left on Highway 330 and follow it about 30 miles to Vega State Park. Vega Reservoir is the largest body of water in the Grand Mesa area and is a popular location for boating and fishing. Rainbow trout are by far the most populous species, but browns, brookies, and cutthroats are also caught here. Winter activities are enjoyed here as well. Ice fishing, ice skating, sledding, snowmobiling, and winter camping are all important activities.

Many birders and wildlife photographers are attracted to Vega's outstanding bird habitat. Migratory and resident birds alike inhabit the park. Watch for blue heron, and a few rarities like red-throated loon, American golden plover, and red phalarope. More popular species include wild turkey, blue grouse, common raven, scrub jay, and red-tailed hawks. Mule deer and elk are a common sight, as are marmot, cottontail rabbit, least chipmunk, beaver, coyote, and ground squirrel.

The park is surrounded by a diverse ecosystem dominated by aspen forest and Gambel's oak. Colorado blue spruce, Rocky Mountain maple, and red-osier dogwood are also part of this diversity. The mountain shrubland include serviceberry, chokecherry, and snowberry. Add to this the meadows and assorted wetland and riparian plant communities that have established around the reservoir, and wildlife and birds cannot resist the temptation.

There are four campgrounds: Early Settlers Campground, Aspen Grove Campground, Oak Point Campground, and Pioneer Campground totaling 109 campsites. Early Settlers Campground has electric and water hook-ups, flush toilets, and coin-operated showers. The remainder of the campgrounds has water and vault toilets.

## Contact

**Vega State Park**
P.O. Box 186, Collbran, CO 81624
970-487-3407
Office Hours: 8:00am-4:00pm Thursday through Monday.
Park Hours: Vega State Park is open year round.

# Mesa Lakes Area

Continuing on Highway 65 into the Grand Mesa, the next area you come to is the Mesa Lakes Area. This gorgeous section of the northern slope of Grand Mesa surrounds the visitor in spectacular stands of aspen and evergreen. Mesa Lake is the largest of the lakes in the area and can be accessed right off of Highway 65. There are a couple small forest service campgrounds, picnic areas, and trails leading to many more lakes. You can even launch a boat on Sunset Lake. Trail 709, found just west of Mesa Lake, leads to the Grand Mesa Rim at 10,400 feet in elevation for a view of the valley below.

## Lands End Area

From Highway 65 just south of Mesa Lake, take a right on FR 100 (Lands End Road). Follow it to the Lands End Visitor Center. This section of the Grand Mesa Scenic Byway may just be the most scenic of all the roads in the Grand Mesa. There are views of five different mountain ranges, three rivers, and two canyons. A visitor can see from Utah to central Colorado without turning the head. Five thousand feet below, the Gunnison River Canyon cuts through the Colorado Plateau, a backdrop that has supported man for thousands of years. At the end of the spur is the historic Land's End Ranger Observatory. There was an archeological excavation in 1999 that revealed 8,000 years of human occupation. This overlook is absolutely spectacular.

## Land O' Lakes Area

The first major lake you come to in the Land O' Lakes Area is Island Lake, probably the best known lake on the Grand Mesa. I would suggest taking FR 123 east from Island Lake and hooking up with FR 121 to get an overall picture of the amazing amount of water on this south slope of the Grand Mesa. There are literally hundreds of lakes to see from the road and access from the generous number of trails on the mesa. In a stretch of about 15 miles from Island Lake east along FR 121 there are 13 forest service campgrounds. They are basic campgrounds with tables and fire pits, some with vault toilets.

Needless to say, fishing is a favorite pastime on the mesa. More than 300 stream-fed lakes provide a bevy of rainbow, brown, cutthroat, and brook trout. The many trails draw hikers and mountain bikers. Shimmering blankets of snow cover the Grand Mesa in the winter for snowshoeing, skiing, and snowmobiling.

This beautiful environment supports a host of wildlife and bird species. Winter is also a fine time to find the American three-toed woodpecker and white-winged crossbill. Spring is a good time to see dusky grouse (formerly blue grouse), and from March through May, boreal owls are frequently found. I have seen porcupines just about every time I have visited the Grand Mesa. Elk and deer thrive here, as do coyotes and red fox. Since 2005, the Colorado Division of Wildlife has been undertaking a multi-year moose reintroduction project on the Grand Mesa. The project began with three Shiras moose (two young bulls and one adult cow) that were captured near Creede and released approximately a couple miles east of Vega Reservoir in Mesa County. Since then, transplants of 20 to 30 moose a year have been brought in from various locations. During their habitat analysis, wildlife biologists conservatively estimated the Grand Mesa could sustain as many as 1,912 moose in the summer, and a high of 464 in winter, providing the moose use winter habitat down to an elevation of 7,000 feet. Generally, moose do not migrate long distances like deer and elk because they are tall enough to weather snow drifts as high as five feet. The moose in Colorado are a major success story since their reintroduction in 1978, so I would say the success here should follow suit.

## Contact

**Grand Mesa Byway Association**
  P.O. Box 122, Cedaredge, CO 81413
  800-436-3041 / 970-856-7554
  www.grandmesabyway.org

**Grand Mesa Lodge**
  2825 Highway 65, PO Box 49, Cedaredge, CO 81413
  800-551-6372 / 970-856-3250

**Thunder Mountain Lodge**
  PO Box 726, 20658 Baron Lake Drive, Cedaredge CO 81413
  877-470-6548 / 970-856-6240

# Silver Thread Scenic Byway

The Silver Thread Scenic Byway is a 117-mile drive through the historic mining country between the Rio Grande River drainage and the Gunnison River drainage. In the three hours it takes to complete the drive, a visitor can see the remains of abandoned mining structures, most of them accessible via rugged backcountry roads. This byway includes the entire stretch of Highway 149 from the intersection of Highway 160 at the town of South Fork all the way to the intersection with Highway 50 at Blue Mesa Reservoir. The first portion of the byway was designated in 1990. It included the highway from South Fork to Lake City. In 2005, the byway was extended on the north end from Lake City to Blue Mesa Reservoir. This new section provides access to a variety of indispensable scenic areas, historical landmarks, and wide-ranging recreational opportunities for hiking, camping, and fishing.

Starting at South Fork, the Silver Thread Scenic Byway enters the Rio Grande National Forest and follows the Rio Grande River. The first stop along the way might be Coller State Wildlife Area. Here, you can gain access to the river for a stint of wade fishing for brown trout. Browns are the primary trout in the Rio Grande with a few rainbows mixed in. Much of the water in the area is designated Gold Medal Water. Contact Mike at Wolf Creek Anglers for more information.

*Cow Moose*

## Contact

**Wolf Creek Anglers, LLC**
001 Brown Drive
P.O. Box 263, South Fork, CO 81154
719-873-1414

This is a beautiful stretch of river bottom with ample opportunities for birding and wildlife viewing. This is probably one of the best places in the area to search for migrant land birds. A fishing access road parallels the riverside willows, but the best habitat is around the bridge at the second Coller State Wildlife Area sign. Cottonwoods and willows are the main habitat and a fine spot to see house wren, Cordilleran flycatcher, green-tailed towhee, warbling vireo, yellow warbler, and song sparrow. Canada geese and mallards nest in the area; and watch for American dippers as they nest in nearby structures along the river. Beavers and muskrat might be seen nosing up in the river for a breath of air, mule deer are abundant, and there is always a chance to view elk along the road, especially early and late in the day.

A few miles down the byway you will find Palisades Campground which overlooks a remarkable rock structure called the Palisades. The town of Wagon Wheel Gap is a couple miles beyond. Built in 1870, this was the first stage stop between South Fork and Lake City. The town's railroad station is listed on the National Register of Historical Places.

## WHEELER GEOLOGICAL AREA

About 3 to 4 miles northwest on Highway 149, find the access to FR 600. Take a right on FR 600 (also called Pool Table Road) to access the trailhead to Wheeler Geological Area. Wheeler Geological Area is a jumbled mass of pinnacles and domes hidden deep within the La Garita Mountains. Wheeler is 640 acres of haunting landscape, also referred to as the Sandstones, the City of Gnomes, White-Shrouded Ghosts, Dante's Lost Souls, and Phantom Ships. To reach the trailhead, rumble about 10 miles on FR 600 to Hanson's Mill. The two-wheel drive road ends here. The trail heads north for 8 miles, starting about 10,800 feet and rising to almost 12,000 to the formations. It is said four-wheel-drive vehicles can continue, but the road is so tough that it might be faster to walk. Make sure to take TR 790 to hike into the area. This is one spot in Colorado I have not been to, but is definitely in my plans. The photographic possibilities look unbelievable. One is bound to see numbers of bird species and the sky is the ceiling as to the numbers of wildlife species to see. The trail traverses excellent spruce-fir habitat, with specialty birds like crossbills, Steller's jays, and boreal owls as possible sightings.

Continuing on the Silver Thread Scenic Byway northwest about 6 miles for Wagon Wheel Gap is the town of Creede. The historic buildings of the quaint seven-block downtown section of Creede, is a vision of the famous silver-mining era. The magnificent Pillars of Hercules, a cluster of volcanic cliffs rising nearly 1,000 feet at the edge of town is a stunning backdrop for this mountain town. Simply viewing the old downtown area against this magnificent canyon vista makes a visit to Creede worthwhile in any season. Our family used to make a trip down here every year in the late 1970s and early 1980s. My older sister and brother-in-law were coming down here with friends and it soon became a family affair. We stayed in cabins outside of Creede somewhere (I don't remember the name of them) and used them as a base camp to play around the area and fish the Rio Grande Reservoir. On one particular trip I had just learned about a new bait using marshmallows, dipped in food dye, garlic, and parmesan cheese (it must have been one of the first experiments with power bait). Everyone was making fun of me and complaining about how bad it smelled. It wasn't so funny the next day at the reservoir. Dwight, my brother-in-law was a die-hard salmon-egg man, so he and his oldest son used that set up. His youngest son and I used the marshmallows and we were hooking up 10- to 14-inch trout almost immediately. We were whooping and hollering, having a great old time. Dwight and crew were stubbornly sticking to their guns until I was helping my nephew unhook a fish and my pole was being dragged into the water. After splashing around, grabbing the pole, and gaining control of the fish, they came over with their tails between their legs begging for the secret bait. Needless to say, we all ended up having a great time and ate very well that night. Unfortunately, Rio Grande Reservoir is a shadow of what it once was. Water fluctuations and demand have taken a toll on the quality of fishing at the reservoir.

*Bull elk on siesta*

Highway 149 veers back to the south and west following the river. There are a couple more unimproved campgrounds along this stretch and the sights continue to impress. This area is the main collection point for the headwaters of the Rio Grande River. Collecting water from many rivulets and smaller streams, the Rio Grande is the third longest river in the United States. Even though it begins its 1,800-mile journey here, it is best known as the international border between Texas and Mexico, eventually dumping into the Gulf of Mexico.

The byway turns back to the northwest and leaves the Rio Grande River drainage as it continues west towards Rio Grande Reservoir on FR 520. The next point of interest is Santa Maria Reservoir. At the intersection with FR 510, take a right turn and follow the road about 2 miles to FR 509. Turn right on FR 509 and follow it to the reservoir. There are campgrounds at the intersections of Highway 149 and FR 510 and at FR 510 and FR 509. If one continues north on FR 510, there is a pull out and overlook for North Clear Creek Falls. It is one of the most photographed waterfalls in Colorado. A scenic overlook and rest area is easily accessible from Highway 149 and FR 510. Another interesting point about this location, it was the second area where moose were reintroduced into the state. Moose populations have made steady growth since that day in 1978. Also, in 1999 the Division of Wildlife began the first reintroduction of lynx back into the Colorado wild in the San Juan Mountains near here. The last recorded capture or sighting of the animal was in 1973. The lynx was a native species to many parts of Colorado but hunting and development eventually reduced their numbers. Since 1999 there have been several other lynx releases in other parts of the Colorado mountains. More commonly viewed wildlife in the area are bighorn sheep, mule deer, elk, red fox, coyote, weasel, ermine, and gray squirrels, and if luck is on your side, a black bear or mountain lion might be seen. Mallards and Canada geese are common at any water source. Broad-tailed hummingbirds, red-tailed hawks, golden and bald eagles are known to frequent the region.

Back on Highway 149, continue north a couple miles from the FR 510 intersection to FR 515. Another forest campground and access to Brown Lakes State Wildlife Area is presented. Brown Lakes SWA is very good for waterfowl viewing. The next 8 miles of the Silver Thread Scenic Byway starts the ascent to the summit of Spring Creek Pass at 10,901 feet and Slumgullion Pass at 11,361 feet. Just on the other side of Slumgullion Pass is the Slumgullion Earth Flow.

## Lake San Cristobal

This rare natural disaster blocked the Lake Fork of the Gunnison River and formed Lake San Cristobal. It sits at an elevation of 9,000 feet and at 350 surface acres is the second largest natural lake in Colorado. It holds a variety of trout in its cold waters, including rainbows, brookies, and cutthroats. You can fish from any of the public access areas of the shore, including those near the lake outlet and those located on the east side of the lake along County Road 33 at Wupperman Campground. Canoeing and kayaking are well-liked pastimes. Camping is available at Wupperman Campground. It is located on the east side of Lake San Cristobal on FR 7. It is a county-owned public campground featuring 31 sites with excellent views of the lake. Various sites will accommodate RVs and/or tents. Fresh water is available, as are vault toilets, picnic tables, grills and fire grates. There is no electricity but there is trash removal and a dump station.

Migratory birds, including geese and a variety of ducks, can be seen at the marshy, south end of the lake. Goldfinch, mountain bluebirds, nuthatches, and jays can also be seen. Visitors will likely see beavers, mule deer, elk, and maybe a moose.

Near the turn-off to the lake on Highway 149 is the Alfred Packer Memorial, marking the gruesome place where Alfred Packer supposedly cannibalized his companions on a fateful winter journey into the San Juan Mountains. Packer was guiding five men through the mountains of central Colorado in 1874 when they ran out of food and energy in shoulder-deep snows. At his trial in 1883, the court held that Packer killed four of the men in their sleep and killed the fifth after a struggle. He then ate parts of the remains until he was able to walk 50 miles to an Indian agency in the Cochetopa Hills and then walk another 50 miles over the Continental Divide to Saguache. He was arrested in 1883 in Wyoming and brought back for trial. Sentenced to 40 years, he was released from prison in 1901 and died in 1907.

The byway continues north about 4 miles to the town of Lake City. Lake City is one of the most popular tourist mountain towns in southern Colorado. It is centrally located for all kinds of recreational activities. The Lake Fork of the Gunnison River is a real hit with flyfishers. An important note for all you anglers: there is approximately 250 miles of fishable water within 50 miles of Lake City. Camping, hiking, mountain biking, and backpacking are great pastimes. Horseback riding ranks up there also.

*Old wily coyote*

The byway carries on to the north following the Lake Fork towards Blue Mesa Reservoir (see the Curecanti National Recreation Area chapter for more detailed information).

## Ryan Ranch – Nature Conservancy Preserve

Ryan Ranch on the Lake Fork of the Gunnison River is a cooperative effort with the Bureau of Land Management (BLM) to acquire and protect this 829-acre site near Lake City.

From Lake City, travel north on Highway 149 for about 7 miles. Turn right (east) on a gravel road at the BLM sign. Drive a short distance to the river and park on the left (west) side of the road. The property extends downstream for about a mile on the east bank of the river.

The site harbors an excellent example of the globally rare narrowleaf cottonwood, beautiful Colorado blue spruce, and thinleaf alder plant community. The land also provides important public access to the BLM's Powderhorn Wilderness Study Area.

For more information, call 303-444-2950.

## Accommodations

**Inn at the Lake**
  600 County Road 33, Lake City, CO  81235
  970-944-2032 or cell 936-499-1323

**Pleasant View Resort**
  549 South Gunnison Avenue, Lake City, CO  81235
  970-944-2262

**Lake City/Hinsdale County Chamber of Commerce**
  P.O. Box 430, Lake City, CO  81235
  800-569-1874 or 970-944-2527

## Contact

**Creede Chamber of Commerce**
  P.O. Box 580, Creede, CO  81130
  719-658-2374
  www.creede.com

**South Fork Visitors Center**
  800-571-0881 or 719-873-5512

**Del Norte Ranger Station**
  13308 West Hwy. 160, Del Norte, CO 81132
  719-657-3321

# San Juan Skyway

At 236 miles, the San Juan Skyway is the second longest byway in Colorado, only bested by the 486-mile Dinosaur Diamond in northwestern Colorado (which includes a number of miles in Utah). This byway was designated by the U.S. Secretary of Transportation as an All-American Road – the highest level of designation – in 1996. It is one of ten America's Byways designated in Colorado. There are a couple of places where the San Juan Skyway overlaps the Trails of the Ancients Byway near the town of Cortez. The byway encompasses 5 million acres of mostly undisturbed national forest, impressive canyons, and river valleys. The skyway itself snakes through the woods in the shadow of impressive 14,000-foot peaks and a variety of 10,000-foot-plus mountain passes. I would suggest it's best driven from May through October and can easily take between six and eight hours, if you include time to stop and take in the scenery.

Let's start on Highway 160 at the town of Durango. Heading west on Highway 160, the byway heads to Cortez. This is a straight forward beginning to the byway. The ponderosa pines turn to firs over a short trip up an easy pass. It drops down into the Mancos River valley where farmland, willows, and cottonwoods are the predominant landscape. This area is loaded with mule deer. About 10 miles west of the town of Mancos, you will find the entrance to Mesa Verde National Park. Mesa Verde National Park is home to one of the densest collections of prehistoric ruins in the United States (see the Mesa Verde National Park chapter for more information). You should find this first leg quite a gorgeous beginning to your trip

From Cortez, take Highway 145 north to Delores. Continue on Highway 145 north and east to the picturesque town of Telluride. This section of the byway follows the upper Delores River to its headwaters near Lizard Head Pass at 10,222 feet. I would also recommend a jaunt up Highway 535 for a little fly fishing on the West Fork of the Delores River. This is a very appealing drive with a great view of the Black Mesa to the north. There are a few campgrounds along the way if you are planning to stay in the area overnight. Back on Highway 145, passing the little burg of Rico, the climb to Lizard Head Pass begins. Make sure to stop at a few of the pull offs along the way to take in great views of the San Juan Mountains. This is by far one of the ultimate views of the Rocky Mountains. The views of Grizzly Peak, Sheep Mountain, Vermillion Peak, Mount Wilson, and Lizard Head Peak make the trip around the San Juan Skyway worth the time and effort. There are a couple small campgrounds along the way with limited services.

## SAN MIGUEL RIVER SOUTH FORK PRESERVE

Make sure to stop by the South Fork Preserve, a Nature Conservancy preserve midway down the north side of Lizard Head Pass on the South Fork of the San Miguel River. Turn left on FR 625 near the town of Ames to find the preserve.

*One of my all time favorite photos - American dippers*

This preserve is the smallest of the three Nature Conservancy properties along the San Miguel River at 67 acres, but it is also the most prominent. Lying below the towering 14,246 feet Wilson Peak, the natural flood cycles and a history of minimum development have kept many parts of this river in pristine condition, and this is one of them. The rare narrowleaf cottonwood and black twinberry habitat, trimmed with Colorado blue spruce drew the interest of the Nature Conservancy.

Except for the 180-foot handicap-accessible boardwalk and viewing platform with interpretive signage, much of what you see here would be just as it was before the state was settled. This site is especially good for birding and has been designated as an Important Bird Area (IBA) by the Audubon Society. Look for the interesting black phoebe, Say's phoebe, belted kingfisher, pine grosbeak, white-crowned sparrow, spotted sandpiper, and Steller's jay.

Beaver activity is present and visitors should look closely for river otters. Mule deer and black bear claim the area as home; and watch for a peregrine falcon near Ames Wall, which is composed of stratified granite, sandstone, and shale. To the east of the preserve is the unusual backdrop of the Ophir Needles, a designated national natural landmark.

A day could easily be spent roaming the streets of Telluride. Planning a trip to Telluride for its world-class skiing and film, jazz, and bluegrass festivals should be in order at some point in time.

A nearby point of interest is Bridal Veil Falls. Head east of Telluride about 3 miles to the falls overlook. Good birding can be found by hiking the trails or roads along the east side of Telluride. According to Colorado County Birding, the cliff face at this large waterfall is the home of a large nesting colony of black swift. The thick willow habitat along Ingram and Bridal Veil Creeks has Swainson's thrush, Wilson's warbler, and Lincoln sparrow at hand.

Another great side trip from this byway is the Woods Lake State Wildlife Area. Take Highway 145 about 12 miles northwest to CR 57P. Take a left (south) and travel 5 miles where this road becomes FR 618. Continue another 5 miles on this switchbacked gravel road to the campground and lake. This high mountain area lies in the shadow of Mount Wilson and Dolores Peak. This is mainly spruce and fir habitat; however a hike up Trail 406 towards Mount Wilson gives way to subalpine meadow and alpine tundra. Numbers of birds species associated with those habitats are present.

Back on Highway 145, continue northwest alongside the San Miguel River to Placerville. To start the next leg of this byway, turn right on Highway 62 to Ridgeway.

## SAN MIGUEL RIVER CANYON PRESERVE

There is another Nature Conservancy preserve if you continue on Highway 145 instead of taking Highway 62. The San Miguel River Canyon Preserve is just 4 miles north from the intersection. The preserve covers about 2 miles of river bottom and about 280 acres of surrounding area, so look for pull-outs along the road for access. The Nature Conservancy acquired this stretch of the San Miguel in 1989 because it supports one of the best known examples of the globally rare narrowleaf cottonwood, as well as the Colorado blue spruce and thinleaf alder riparian plant community. More than 80 percent of Colorado's wildlife depends on rivers and riverside habitat for survival, so keep the binoculars handy for fur and feather sightings. This habitat along the San Miguel River can produce raccoons, long-tailed weasels, mule deer, American dippers, belted kingfishers, and numerous songbirds.

There are no established trails in this preserve, but foot traffic is allowed. From my own experience, I will tell you the habitat is thick so the going can be rough. Even if you had waders and/or a good pair of wading boots and got in the river, it is still not easy going. The river is swift in the course of this area and the boulders create some very deep pockets to maneuver through. What bush-whacking you do can be rewarding. I was able to photograph a nest of American dippers as the adult birds fed their chicks.

The San Miguel River and its tributaries are fine trout streams. I have spent plenty of time on them with a fly rod and it can be sneaky good. There can be good dry-fly fishing, but expect to spend the majority of time nymphing.

*Steller's jay*

The home stretch of the San Juan Skyway follows Highway 550 from Ridgeway south to Durango. However, just north of Ridgeway is Ridgeway State Park and Reservoir. Camping, boating, and fishing are available. The Uncompahgre River, a tailwater below the reservoir went through a major redesign in 1992. The state parks put in a recreational area with a campground and looked to the Division of Wildlife to see if the river could sustain a population of trout. After monitoring the stream habitat and stocking the river, the conclusion was made: There was no habitat. The river was too swift and trout could not maintain a reasonable number. With the concerted efforts of the Division of Wildlife, State Parks & Recreation, and the Bureau of Reclamation, $200,000 was raised for stream habitat improvements. Two miles of river were improved below the dam. With simple calculations, that's $100,000 per mile just for a home for trout. Truck loads of large boulders were strategically placed in the stream to form weirs and pools. They produced the all important living quarters that trout need to sustain life.

It is like fishing in a well-groomed park. Sidewalks follow the river; the pools are one right after the other and loaded with hefty, willing trout. Get this - there is a gazebo nearby that serves as a great place to spread out a lunch. Another point of interest would be the Billy Creek State Wildlife Area on the east side of Highway 550 and just a mile north of the state park.

The trip south from Ridgeway is a beautiful one, following the Uncompahgre River valley. You are headed into some of the oldest gold and silver mining country in the state. The first Victorian jewel presented along the way is Ouray. Check out the hot springs and Box Canyon Falls before continuing south to Silverton. About half way between Ouray and Silverton, prepare for the exciting drive over Red Mountain Pass, the highest paved pass in the San Juan Mountains at 11,018 feet. If one has a weak stomach, keep your eyes closed as this is one of the most breathtaking passes in Colorado. In places there is only a guard rail between you and a thousand-foot drop. I remember driving over this pass at night during a snowstorm. I had to pry my fingers off the steering wheel when we got to the bottom. This segment of Highway 550 from Ouray to Silverton is called the "Million Dollar Highway". But you can't put a price tag on this experience. Get off the highway and check out the historic district in Silverton. It is an amazing old mountain town. Traveling south from Silverton, a driver will get the feeling of being on top of the world as you crest two 10,000-foot passes back to back. Molas Pass and Coal Bank Pass give way to dramatic alpine scenery of the West Needle Mountains to the east in the Weminuche Wilderness Area. The Colorado Trail, which connects Durango to Denver, crosses the highway near the top of Molas Pass.

Durango is an old west town founded in 1880 as a bustling railhead to serve the booming mining industry. It has many restored historical landmarks lining the downtown streets. A visitor should check out the historic Durango & Silverton Narrow Gauge Train. The three-and-a-half hour rail trip departs daily from Durango and ends in Silverton. There is usually a couple hour layover and then heads back to Durango. There is an option to stay in Silverton overnight and use the return ticket the next day.

Contact: 888-872-4607 / www.durangotrain.com

There are plenty of outdoor activities to be had in the Durango area. Rafting the upper Animas River affords the adventurer with continuous Class III rapids and very nasty Class IV and V while the lower Animas can be enjoyed by all. Mountain biking and four-wheeling are popular activities in this area. Make sure to have the camera and binoculars handy. At any moment, wildlife including deer, elk, black bear, beaver, mink, porcupine, eagle, or a Peregrine falcon may appear before your eyes. There are backpacking trails galore attracting the hiker into high mountain streams and lakes. Make sure the fishing gear is stowed away while traveling this scenic byway.

## Contacts

**San Juan National Forest**
15 Burnett Court, Durango, CO 81301
970-247-4874
www.sanjuanskyway.com

**Adventures Beyond/Over the Hill Outfitters**
4140 County Road 234, Durango, CO 81301
970-385-7656
Provides a variety of outfitting trips including hunting, fishing, horseback rides, and hiking trips.

**Colorado Mountain Expeditions**
3636 County Road 301, Durango, CO 81301
970-375-1250 / 877-600-COLO
Licensed fishing outfitters providing multi-day fishing adventure packages by hiking or horseback riding to backcountry streams.

**Duranglers Flies and Supplies**
923 Main Avenue, Durango, CO 81301
970-385-4081 / 888-347-4346
www.duranglers.com
The Four Corners area's premier fly fishing outfitter provides information, equipment, and custom-guided fly fishing trips.

**Mild to Wild Rafting and Jeep Trail Tours**
50 Animas View Drive, Durango, CO 81301
970-247-4789 / 800-567-6745
Mild to Wild Rafting & Jeep Trail Tours, Inc. offers 27 whitewater rafting and jeep trail tour trips in southwest Colorado, eastern Utah, and central Arizona. Rafting tours take place on such rivers as the Colorado, Verde, and the Upper Salt River Canyon.

# Trail of the Ancients Scenic Byway

The Trail of the Ancients is a 116-mile byway that covers the southwestern-most corner of the state. Also recognized as the "Four Corners Area", it includes Mesa Verde National Park, Hovenweep National Monument, and a host of ancient cliff dwellings and historical sites of the Anasazi Indians. Trail of the Ancients is a fairly new byway, designated by the U.S. Secretary of Transportation as a national scenic byway in 2005. It is one of ten America's Byways designated in Colorado. This trip can be enjoyed throughout the year; however, weather can be an issue anytime from November through February. The entire drive can be covered in three to five hours, but I would suggest at least a couple days to see the national park and investigate the many remains in the Canyons of the Ancients National Monument.

*Bull Snake*

Starting in the town of Cortez, the byway takes a route south on Highway 160 to the Utah border and a short stint north on Highway 41, also to the Utah border. This branch of the byway connects with Utah's Trail of the Ancients byway. The area is basically an extension of the Colorado Plateau, but does include bottom land with a ranching atmosphere. Many fields of alfalfa can be seen from the road, as well as river bottom with dense growth of cottonwood trees, and land so desolate that you wonder how anything could live there. This is the Ute Mountain Ute Indian Reservation, a broken and arid terrain. Sleeping Ute Mountain – at only 9,978 feet – dominates the western skyline, as it is the only "high rise" to the west. To the east on Highway 160, it goes as far as the entrance to Mesa Verde National Park. Mesa Verde National Park is a "must-see" affair when in the extreme southwest of Colorado (see the Mesa Verde National Park chapter for more information).

The Trail of the Ancients Byway continues north out of Cortez on Highway 145 to the town of Delores. Turn left on Highway 184 and continue a couple miles to the Anasazi Heritage Center. The center is a museum setting full of artifacts, interpretive information, and a mock pueblo that the Anasazi could have lived in years ago. It is a very informative stop and the attendants are more than helpful, leading you to the best sites in the Canyons of the Ancients National Monument (see the Canyons of the Ancients National Monument chapter for more information). McPhee Reservoir is a large body of water just north of Delores that is a playground of numerous water sports. Continue west on Highway 184 and turn right on Highway 491. Finally, take CC Road west which takes visitors into the heart of the Canyons of the Ancients National Monument. Make a left turn on 10 Road to complete the trip at Hovenweep National Monument.

The Anasazi "Ancient Ones" dominated the Colorado Plateau for hundreds of years, yet basic questions about them like who they were, how they lived, and what they believed remain unresolved. Canyons of the Ancients National Monument, Hovenweep National Monument, and Mesa Verde National Park contain dense clusters of Anasazi remains, including cliff dwellings, rock art, and pottery shards.

Sightseeing and photography will occupy most of your time. There are numerous hiking trails in the area; in fact, many of the ancient sites are only accessible by foot. However, touring the area on a bike would not be out the question.

Wildlife and birds are plentiful. Snakes and lizards are definitely high on the list of possible sightings. Mule deer can be seen in the canyon lands and feeding in the farmland on top. Mountain bluebirds, mourning doves, ravens, and any number of raptors are in the area. I saw a number of kestrels while touring the area.

## Contact

**Anasazi Heritage Center**
  27501 Highway 184
  Dolores CO  81323
  970-882-4811
  Also check out this website: www.colorado.explorefourcorners.com/dolores.html

# Unaweep-Tabeguache Scenic and Historic Byway

The Unaweep-Tabeguache Scenic and Historic Byway is a 133-mile journey through history, geology, and nature alongside the Umcompahgre Plateau. I believe the correct pronunciation for Tabeguache is "tah-bay-WAH-chay". This byway is best driven from April through October and takes about three to four hours. The byway starts at Whitewater on Highway 141 just south of Grand Junction on Highway 50 and ends at Placerville on Highway 145. The spectacular scenery along this byway will keep you on the edge of your seat the entire trip.

Heading west on Highway 141 from Whitewater, one immediately enters the Unaweep Canyon. It is a very enjoyable drive, especially early in the morning when the sun is just coming up. The first point of interest is the historic Driggs Mansion. Even when it was newly built, it would be hard pressed to be called a mansion by today's perception, but in the day and the area it was built made it a prized possession. It did have six rooms which included two bedrooms, a kitchen, a large commons area, and a utility room. Lawrence LaTourette Driggs acquired the 320 acres of land that the mansion was built on through the Desert Entry Act with the intention of developing and cultivating the desert environment. A petition with the General Land Office (better known as the Bureau of Land Management) helped establish water rights for irrigation. Nearby is an interesting geological rock formation called Thimble Rock which is worth a photo or two.

Travel west another 30 miles or to the town of Gateway. It may be a good time to take on fuel and enjoy a bite to eat because there is little civilization for the next part of the journey. The landscape changes dramatically from here, as the route veers south through the Delores River Canyon. The word tabeguache is a Ute Indian word meaning "place where snow first melts". This section runs south from Gateway to the communities of Nucla and Naturita. The river slices through this ageless desert region with red cliffs that tower 1,000 feet overhead, adding to this sheer scenic wonder. The river and its small tributaries eroded the rock away, exposing hundreds of millions of years of geologic record (including fossils of dinosaurs and early amphibians). If you are lucky enough to encounter any of these artifacts, please do not take them. It is a crime to alter, deface, or take these artifacts. Other secrets of the earth were searched out by miners with picks and shovels. The canyon witnessed a copper boom in the early 1900s. Decades later, the U.S. Army processed ore from nearby Uravan to produce the uranium used in the first atomic bombs. About 30 miles south of Gateway on the west side of the road is a dome-shaped coke oven built in the 1880s. Coal was heated in the oven to produce coke. Coke is a combustible material that burns especially hot and almost smoke free. The coke was believed to be used by blacksmiths during the erection of the Hanging Flume. Drive 2 more miles south on Highway 141 and you can view the leftover structure of the Hanging Flume. It was fixed to the walls of the Wingate Sandstone cliffs along the river. It delivered upwards of 23 million gallons of water per day from the San Miguel River to drive the mining equipment.

*Phenomenal scenery along the Delores River*

Near Uravan, the San Miguel River flows into the Delores River and the highway now follows the San Miguel River. The canyon eventually drops into a meandering stream bottom with thick cottonwood, willow trees, and rich farmland.

## Tabeguache Creek Preserve

The Nature Conservancy has a preserve along the San Miguel called Tabeguache Creek Preserve. This 7-mile stretch of the San Miguel River was established to help preserve riparian habitat, especially the globally rare Rio Grande cottonwood/skunkbrush sumac and Rio Grande cottonwood/coyote willow plant communities. The San Miguel is one of just a few naturally functioning rivers in the West (river without a dam) and this 610-acre preserve supports a very nice streamside habitat. The water conditions of this broad floodplain are mostly docile and serene, unlike most of the fast-dropping gradient of the canyon above here. A raft or canoe would be a great way to see the preserve from a different point of view. There are no put-ins or take-outs on the preserve, but these smaller vessels should be easy to manage. There are legitimate put-ins or take-outs found upstream and downstream from the preserve.

The fall would be a great time to visit as the summer heat subsides and the seasonal colors start to display. There is a visitor's area with picnic tables, a marked trail along the river, and an informational kiosk.

With the natural habitat comes wildlife. This is black bear and mountain lion country, so be aware of these species. Mule deer, beaver, and river otter thrive here. Expect to see a great blue heron; peregrine falcon are in the area; and a common winter resident is our nation's bird, the bald eagle. Many song birds nest and breed here. Much work has been done to eliminate the invasive and water siphoning tamarisk, also known as salt cedar.

Unaweep-Tabeguache Scenic and Historic Byway and the entire surrounding area are home to a fine cross section of wildlife. The most unique of which is the desert bighorn sheep. Factions of this heat-tolerant subspecies of the bighorn sheep can be found along the rocky terrain of the canyons here. The characteristics and behavior of desert bighorn sheep generally follow those of other bighorn sheep, except for their adaptation to the lack of water. In these desert conditions, this species of bighorn sheep can go for extended periods of time without drinking water. Some bighorns may go without drinking water for weeks or even months. They sustain their body fluids from eating grasses, sedges, and forbs and sipping rainwater collected in temporary rock pools. They have the ability to lose up to 30 percent of their body weight and still survive. After drinking water, they quickly recover from their dehydrated condition. Desert bighorn are stocky, heavy-bodied animals, with unique padded hooves. They are able climb the steep, rocky terrain of the desert mountains swiftly and with ease. Bighorns rely on their keen eyesight to detect potential predators such as mountain lions, coyotes, and bobcats, and they use their climbing ability to escape. They are

*The Delores River*

similar in size to a mule deer – mature rams range from 125 to 200 pounds while ewes are somewhat smaller. Expect to see golden eagles, bald eagles, peregrine falcons, and turkey vultures suspended above the river and canyon walls. If there were ever a place for mountain lions to flourish, it would be here in the Umcompahgre Plateau. Coyotes, bobcats, rattlesnakes, bull snakes, and many species of lizards are also adept at surviving these harsh conditions. Mule deer, fox, and bunnies endure here as do black bear and migrating elk. Best viewing always takes place early in the morning and in the evening. The riparian habitat along the rivers and streams provides homes for important species like great blue herons and river otters. Beaver, muskrat, and mink can also be found. The upper streams and rivers are home to rainbow and brown trout and countless aquatic insects.

The Unaweep-Tabeguache Scenic and Historic Byway will fill a camera's memory card in short order. There are many photo opportunities along this byway, so be prepared with an extra battery and card. Even though computer rendering can be done at a later time, I found the use of a polarizing filter a great addition to my pocket. It really brought out the contrasts of the red rocks and the cloudless blue skies I encountered the day I traveled this route. A good wide-angle lens to 18mm for the many landscape shots and a full blown telephoto for wildlife close-ups are recommended. Mountain biking is a huge outdoor activity in western Colorado, including the Umcompahgre Plateau and Colorado Plateau. See www.copmoba.org and www.backcountrybiker.com for more information.

Backpacking, fishing, hunting, camping, rafting, and kayaking are also available outlets in this area. Unaweep Canyon is well known in bouldering and rock climbing circles. Because of the unique nature of the canyon, there are virtually endless possibilities. The boulder fields within the first 5 miles of the canyon are on BLM land and easily accessible. Use every precaution when attempting this activity. Only the experienced should take a shot at this opportunity.

## Contact

### The Synergist Group
836 East Pabor, Fruita, CO 81521
970-270-8394
www.utbw.org

### Gateway Canyons Resort
43200 Hwy 141
PO Box 339, Gateway, CO 81522
970-931-2458

### Norwood Inn
PO Box 179, Norwood, CO 81423
970 327-4982 / 888 272-6715

# West Elk Loop

The West Elk Loop is a 205-mile byway cutting right through the heart of Colorado. It is passable year round but if I had my druthers, I would make the trip in mid-September when the aspen trees are in their peak color. This is a lengthy byway and could easily take between six and eight hours to complete. The West Elk Loop starts in Carbondale by heading west on Highway 133. Carbondale is 20 miles south of Interstate 70 at Glenwood Springs on Highway 82. The initial part of the tour is actually a spur on Highway 133 that tops the 8,755-foot McClure Pass and drops down to the town of Hotchkiss. From Hotchkiss, take Highway 92 to start the loop and begin the second leg of the ride. Follow Highway 92 to the interchange with Highway 50 at Blue Mesa Dam. Take Highway 50 east to Gunnison and then Highway 135 to Crested Butte. From Crested Butte, take 12 Road over the 9,980-foot Kebler Pass back to Highway 133 just below Paonia Reservoir to complete the loop. There are a vast number of things to see on this trip, so let's get started.

    As you start in Carbondale, your attention will automatically turn to the impressive twin summits of the 12,953-foot Mount Sopris. There is a campground – Crystal River Resort – on Highway 133 at the base of the mountain where I have pitched a tent many times. There is a grand view of the mountain from there. Continuing west, the road follows the Crystal River to near its headwaters at McClure Pass. Just before the pass, I would suggest a quick jaunt on FR 314 to the historic town of Marble. The town is the location of the historic Yule Marble Quarry that began operations in the 1890s and is the source of the town's name. The marble of the quarry is considered to be of exceptional quality and has been used for the Tomb of the Unknowns, as well as for parts of the Lincoln Memorial. If it is September, then you are enjoying the splendor of the aspens in their fall colors and almost certainly cannot get the camera out of your hands.

## Paonia State Park

As McClure Pass is breached, you enter into the North Fork of the Gunnison River drainage. The stream is actually called Muddy Creek at this point, but is renamed as it exits the dam at Paonia Reservoir. Paonia State Park is located here and its natural beauty and abundance of wildflowers make it a "must-see" for photographers and nature lovers. Many migratory and resident birds like raptors, waterfowl, and shorebirds are attracted to the upland and reservoir habitats. Mule deer and elk are a common sight, because the park lies in big game winter range. Black bear may occasionally be observed foraging for wild fruits. Other common mammals include cottontail rabbit, marmot, raccoon, skunk, coyote, and ground squirrel.

Anglers should have ample opportunity for coldwater fishing with fluctuating populations of northern pike and brown trout. Snow melt and fluctuations of water demand have caused silting over the years, so fish populations are spotty at best.

*Mountain chickadee*

## Contact

**Paonia State Park**
 P O Box 147, Crawford, CO  81415
 Park Hours: 24 hours a day
 970-921-5721

Below the reservoir is a stunning river drainage and as the landscape flattens into a mesa near Paonia and Hotchkiss, fruit orchards and wineries come into view. Colorado is quickly gaining a reputation for wine production, and this area is becoming a major player.

From Hotchkiss, take Highway 92 south. We now begin the stretch on the north rim of the Black Canyon of the Gunnison River. The canyon is not visible from this stretch of road, but the entrance into the national park is along here (see the Black Canyon of the Gunnison National Park and Curecanti National Recreation Area chapter for more information).

# Crawford State Park

The next point of interest is Crawford State Park and Reservoir. With the Black Canyon of the Gunnison so close, it is easy to envision the stimulating scenery found here. Crawford State Park embraces many water sports for boaters, jet skiing, and water skiing. Anglers, hikers, bird watchers, and photographers enjoy this quiet little hideaway on the western slope.

There are two campgrounds – Iron Creek Campground and Clear Fork Campground. Iron Creek has 45 sites with electric and water hookups, hot showers, and flush toilets. There is a boat ramp close by and an informative wildlife viewing kiosk. Clear Fork Campground has 21 sites without hookups, five of which are set up as tent sites. There is potable water located throughout the campground, as well as showers, flush toilets, and vault toilets.

## Contact

**Crawford State Park**
 PO Box 147
 40468 Hwy 92
 Crawford, CO  81415
 970-921-5721
 Office Hours: 8:00am-4:00pm as staffing permits
 Park Hours: 24 hours a day

Finally, Highway 92 nears the canyon above the Curecanti National Recreational Area. A glimpse or two into the Black Canyon is available here. The Curecanti Needle can be seen just a few miles before the Highway 50 interchange. Take Highway 50 east into Gunnison.

From Gunnison, take Highway 135 along the Gunnison River toward Crested Butte. The river and riparian habitat next to the river dominate the landscape all the way to the town of Almont. This is where the Taylor River and the East River merge to form the Gunnison River. Veer left to stay on Highway 135 and follow the East River. Within a few miles, the Roaring Judy State Fish Hatchery will come into view. This is a great place to stop and see if a tour of the facility is possible and do a little birding.

Farther north is Crested Butte, which is a very popular winter destination in Colorado, well known for its skiing and snowboarding. Basically anything that you can do on snow, a visitor can do here. There are many trails for the cross-country skier. If skiing is not your thing, sleigh rides, ice skating, and snowshoeing are enjoyable winter pursuits.

The last leg of the loop begins by heading west on 12 Road. The road does turn into well-maintained gravel; maybe not a great passageway in the winter, but it is just fine in the summer and fall. Topping Kebler pass at 9,980 feet presents you with the headwaters of Anthracite Creek. There are a few pull-outs along the way that, with a short hike to the stream, put an angler on some of the best small-stream brock trout fishing available. The trout rise well to dry flies, which makes it all the more fun. There are only about 3 miles of stream here that follow the road and then the creek drops into a canyon. An angler can still hike to the stream and fish down from here, but I guarantee the hike back up will seem twice as long. However, there is another access to Anthracite near the bottom of the canyon. There is a pull-out and an unimproved campground just as you cross the creek, about 25 miles down from Kebler Pass. Park and look for the trailhead marked Dark Canyon. Not quite the stature of the Black Canyon, but impressive none the less. And again the fishing can be pretty good with rainbow and brown trout entering into the picture. The picturesque canyon is also enjoyed by photographers and hikers. The loop ends in about 7 miles at the intersection with Highway 133 just below Paonia Reservoir.

Before leaving the area, there are a couple places to check out: Glenwood Canyon on Interstate 70 and the Glenwood Hot Springs in Glenwood Springs. Glenwood Canyon is on Interstate 70 about 140 miles west of Denver and 90 miles east of Grand Junction. The 16-mile-long canyon was cut by the Colorado River between the towns of Gypsum and Glenwood Springs. Glenwood Springs is also on Interstate 70 about 160 miles from Denver.

Starting in the 1980s, a huge challenge was undertaken to complete one of the last stretches of the Interstate Highway System championed by President Eisenhower in 1956. Today there are almost 47,000 miles of interstate highways in the United States. The main reason it was the last stretch of highway to be built was the daunting Glenwood Canyon. Engineers were tasked to design a freeway snaking through the length of the canyon using bridges, tunnels, and retaining walls to create a highway that did not spoil the canyon's appearance. Soon after construction started, there were of course a few naysayers that fought the project for a number of reasons, but a federal judge rejected the ideas and construction continued. However, contractors

were required to enter into environmental mitigation so that as little of the canyon was disturbed as possible. In some cases, individual trees were tagged as fineable if the work disturbed them. The completion and opening of the Glenwood Canyon stretch of highway was in 1992. There are rest areas and a trail to Hanging Lake that takes you up the side of the canyon. Overall it is really one of the great engineering achievements in the United States, and definitely worth the drive.

## GLENWOOD HOT SPRINGS

The Glenwood Hot Springs – "The Grand Spring" as it was known – is a timeless natural wonder discovered by the Ute Indians. For thousands of years this mineral-rich water has created legends of healing, mountain adventure, and relaxation. Captain Richard Sopris led a surveying and prospecting expedition to the area in 1860; and in 1879, Fort Defiance was established at the junction of the Colorado and Roaring Fork Rivers. In 1883, the thriving population had the establishment renamed to Glenwood Springs because the name Defiance did not sit well. The infamous Doc Holliday spent his last years here before succumbing to tuberculosis. From Interstate 70, take Exit 116 toward the traffic light. Turn on North River Street and look for signage and parking for the Hot Springs Pool on your left.

*Prickly pear cactus bloom*

Glenwood Hot Springs is one of the most popular vacation destinations in the Rocky Mountains. On the grounds is the World's Largest Hot Springs Pool with water slides, a 107-room lodge, mini-golf, a premier athletic club, and the spectacular new Spa of the Rockies. In the tradition of the West, the complete renovation of the historic sandstone bathhouse is a tribute to the spiritual beauty of this majestic landscape. There is much history in the area and a great place to tour.

## Glenwood Hot Springs Lodge

415 East 6th Street
Glenwood Springs, CO  81601
www.hotspringspool.com

**Lodge Reservations:** 1-800-537-SWIM (7946)
**Pool Desk:** 970-947-2955
**Athletic Club Desk:** 970-947-2953
**Spa of the Rockies:** 970-947-3331
**The Grill:** 970-947-2959
**Sport Shop:** 970-947-2940
**Business Offices:** 970-947-2954
**Central Operator (24 Hours):** 970-945-6571

## Other Accommodations

**Hotel Colorado**
526 Pine St., Glenwood Springs, CO  81601
800-544-3998

**The Inn at Crested Butte**
P.O. Box 4234510
Whiterock Avenue, Crested Butte, CO  81224
877-343-2111

**Purple Mountain Bed and Breakfast**
714 Gothic Ave
P.O. Box 1879, Crested Butte, CO  81224
www.purplemountainlodge.com
877-349 5888

## Contact

**U.S. Forest Service**
P.O. Box 309, Carbondale CO  81623
970-963-2266

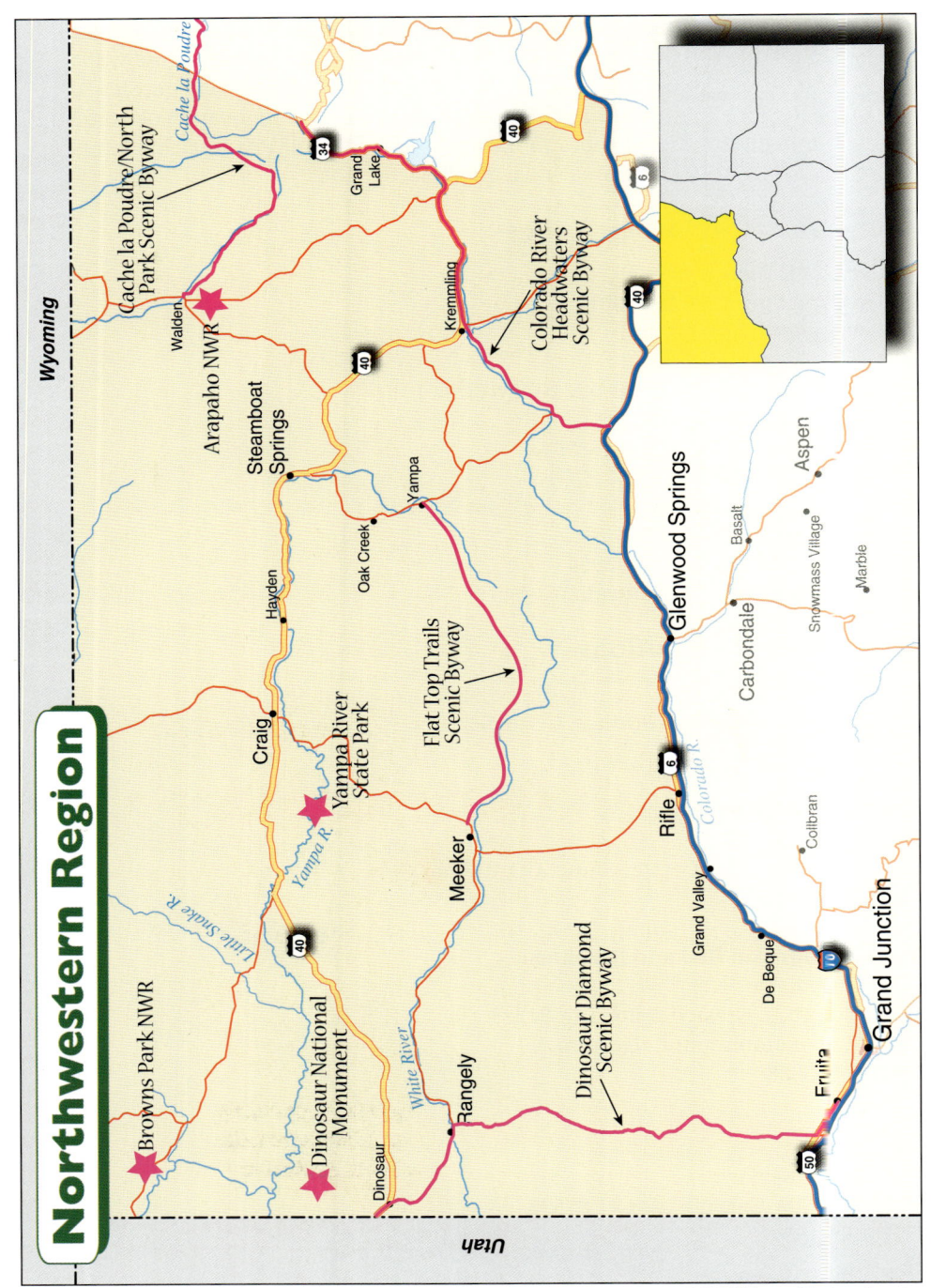

# Northwestern Region

# Yampa River State Park

The Yampa River State Park is a unique state park when compared to other parks in Colorado. It has multiple access points along a 134-mile stretch of the unspoiled Yampa River. The Yampa River is the largest drainage in northwestern Colorado and has largely been passed up as a recreational destination. More than likely, its remoteness from the more populous areas of Colorado has played a big part in that lack of interest. None the less, the river has a very diverse list of activities for the outdoor enthusiast.

Northwestern Colorado has always been a haven for wildlife with large herds of elk, mule deer, and pronghorn antelope. Coyotes, bunnies, snowshoe hares, raptors, and waterfowl follow suit. However, the river is often overlooked as a fantastic fishery, rafting and kayaking destination, and camping opportunity. I would hope you take the time to investigate this secluded river valley and enjoy the treasures within.

## Accesses within the Yampa River State Park

### Pump Station

Starting about 5 miles east of Hayden on Highway 40, the first access is Pump Station. It is located on the north side of the highway. This site has a developed boat ramp and toilet facilities, but it is a small area and not recommended for large vehicles. No camping is allowed here. Access to public lands is very limited downstream, so boaters need to be aware of private property. Also be aware of the Public Service Company's intake structure property and please do not trespass. This site does access some very good bird nesting habitat, so be very conscious of nesting birds and do not disturb them. This is a very unique stretch of river with a diversity of raptors and water birds as well as other wildlife. A state park pass is required.

### Double Bridges

The next park access is known as Double Bridges. It is located about 1.5 miles west of Hayden on the south side of Highway 40. This site offers boat access to the river and has limited parking with a tight turning radius. Large vehicles are not recommended. There are picnic sites here, but overnight camping is not allowed. The site has restrooms and trash receptacles. Visitors should watch for owls, bald eagles, and many different hawks perched in the riverside cottonwood trees. The next stretch of river offers good wildlife viewing and fishing for smallmouth bass and northern pike, as well as great flat-water boating. The south side of the river for approximately 7 miles is private land, so respect private property. A state park pass is required.

**Yampa River Visitor Center & Campground**

The visitor center is located at the Headquarters Campground 2 miles west of Hayden on the south side of Highway 40. The visitor center provides visitor and traveler information as well as maps and other printed resources. It has a conference room for rent to the public for social events or business meetings and is in close proximity to a group picnic shelter for outdoor occasions. There are trails along the river including observation decks and a group picnic area.

**Headquarters Campground**

The Headquarters Campground has 50 campsites of which 35 have electrical access. There are ten basic tent-only sites, one teepee for rent, and five group tent-only campsites. There is a building with showers and laundry facilities.

**State Wildlife Area**

The fourth access is the Yampa River State Wildlife Area, located about 6 miles west of Hayden. Again, the access is on the south side of Highway 40 near a small metal

*Colorado can spoil you!*

railroad building called Dorsey. At 6,200 feet in elevation, these 860 acres of river bottom provide homes for hundreds of species of wildlife. This area is especially well suited for wildlife photography. Expect to see bald eagles (which roost here in winter), great blue herons, sandhill cranes, Canada geese, teal, mallards, wigeons, and sandpipers. It can be a good area to spot deer; and fishing in the Yampa River for northern pike, smallmouth bass, and rainbow trout can be very good. The Colorado Division of Wildlife manages the site. There are no improvements and no overnight camping is allowed. Passes are not required.

## Yampa Valley Golf Course

Another unique aspect of this state park is the addition of a golf course. The Yampa Valley Golf Course is located south of Craig off Highway 394 near the airport. No overnight camping is allowed. Passes are not required. The city of Craig and Moffat County own the site.

## Loudy Simpson Park

Loudy Simpson Park is located off Highway 394 south of Craig at the developed ball field complex. This site has a boat launch and parking area on the river. Moffat County manages and owns the land. A pass is not required. Overnight camping is available by permission only (ask a county park manager).

## South Beach

The next access to the Yampa River is South Beach, also known as the Yampa Project Pump Station. It is located approximately 3 miles south of Craig on the west side of Highway 13. This site houses the water intake for Tri-State and Trapper Mining, so there are some parking and access restrictions. This site has good access to the river with limited primitive camping available. The camping is limited to a maximum two-night stay; camping permits are required. This area has restroom facilities, a boat ramp, day-use picnic sites, and trash receptacles. River users should park in the large gravel parking lot on the west side of the pump station. To protect natural resources, the wooded area northeast of the pump station is open to foot traffic only. Overnight camping is available. State park passes are required. This access site opens up a rare opportunity to float into "Little Yampa Canyon" and a stretch of river that is 32 miles to the next take-out. The downstream access is by boat only, so any vehicle use is extremely limited to access from private property or a few roads across BLM. Because of the remoteness of this area, trash and wastes must be packed out.

## Duffy Mountain

The next access to the Yampa River State Park is Duffy Mountain. It is located 32 miles downstream from South Beach and about 30 miles southwest of Craig. Take Highway 40 west out of Craig about 19 miles to Moffat CR 17. Turn left (south) and drive about 7 miles to Government Bridge. Continue on CR 17 for another 4 miles to Bureau of Land Management Road 1593 and turn left immediately before the cattle guard.

The river access site is a mile farther on the left. Improvements at the site include a vault toilet and picnic sites. Five primitive sites are available for overnight camping. This area below the Little Yampa Canyon is great for wildlife viewing. Mule deer are abundant all year and elk winter here for access to food and water. Look for soaring golden and bald eagles. State park passes are required.

NOTE: For legal and safety reasons, parking at Government Bridge is not recommended.

**Juniper Canyon**

To access Juniper Canyon, which is located 12 miles downriver from Duffy Mountain, take Highway 40 west out of Craig for about 22 miles to Moffat CR 53. Turn left (south) and go about 4 miles to Moffat CR 74 and turn right (west) for just under a mile. The improved site has a vault toilet, picnic sites, parking, and boat ramp. A dozen primitive overnight camping sites are available. Mountain bikers and hikers will enjoy the great access to surrounding BLM public lands. This area offers excellent wildlife viewing and fishing for smallmouth bass. Elk, pronghorn antelope, and mule deer roam the area. Coyotes, bunnies, and more small game can also be seen here. State Park passes are required.

CAUTION: Because of Class III rapids, open canoeists should not travel over the diversion dam that is downstream in Juniper Canyon. Canoeists and inexperienced boaters should portage on the right or left side of the river.

*They don't have to be big to be pretty*

### Maybell Bridge

The next take out for river runners is Maybell Bridge. It is located 28 miles west of Craig on Highway 40. The access site is located south of the highway and east of the Yampa River. The improved site has a vault toilet, parking, a boat ramp, and trash receptacles. Primitive camping and picnic areas are along the river. There is limited foot access to the river. This area offers great wildlife viewing. Deer and antelope are abundant throughout the year, and elk wander the area in the winter. I have seen golden eagles near Maybell several times. State park passes are required. The town of Maybell is 3 miles farther west on Highway 40.

### Sunbeam

The next access point is Sunbeam. It is located approximately 7 miles northwest of Maybell. Take Highway 40 west out of Maybell less than a mile to Highway 318. Turn right and go about 6 miles to Moffat CR 23. Turn left and follow CR 23 a short distance to the access site. There are minimal improvements and facilities. No overnight camping is allowed. A state park pass is required.

### East Cross Mountain

East Cross Mountain is located approximately 18 miles southwest of Maybell. Take Highway 40 west out of Maybell about 14 miles to Moffat CR 85. Turn right (north) and follow CR 85 to the Bureau of Land Management Road 1551 and go about 2 miles. At the fork of the road, turn left and follow the road about a mile to the river access site. The improved site has a vault toilet, parking, and boat ramp. Picnic sites with tables and fire rings are provided and camping is permitted. State Park passes are required.

### West Cross Mountain & Deerlodge Park

West Cross Mountain & Deerlodge Park are located between Cross Mountain Canyon and Dinosaur National Monument. Both access sites are in the care of the National Park Service. Boaters at Deerlodge Park must have a permit to float on the Yampa River through Dinosaur National Monument.

## Contact

**Yampa River Legacy Project/State Parks Headquarters**
 P.O. Box 759, Hayden, CO 81639
 970-276-2061

**Park Office**
 6185 W. US Hwy. 40, Hayden, CO 81639
 Office Hours: 8:00am-4:30pm Mon-Fri, weekends as staff allows
 Park Hours: 8:00am-4:30pm

## Yampa River Preserve

From Steamboat Springs, take Highway 40 west about 17 miles. After crossing the railroad and going over the 5-mile Bridge over the Yampa River, make an immediate left into the parking area. The preserve includes about 3 miles of river frontage.

The Nature Conservancy selected this site to help preserve 6,000 acres of extensive riparian ecosystem along a 10-mile stretch of the Yampa River. This includes a 265-acre broad floodplain called the Morgan Bottoms. Its natural flooding processes are relatively intact since the only dam on the drainage is higher up at Stagecoach Reservoir. When the river floods and subsequently recedes, it usually flows through a new channel, creating fresh, new habitat. This section of river also hosts one of the largest remaining examples of a rare riparian forest dominated by narrowleaf cottonwood, box elder, and red-osier dogwood.

The 2-mile round trip trail within the preserve is an excellent site for birding and viewing wildlife. One might see beaver, mink, and river otters. Mule deer and elk frequent the area for an early evening drink of water. It is a popular area for bald eagles, especially in the winter. A couple of unusual finds might be the Swainson's thrush and the grey cat bird.

### Contact

**Yampa River Project/Carpenter Ranch**
  P.O. Box 955
  13250 U.S. Highway 40 West, Hayden, CO  81639
  970-276-4626

## Sharp-tailed Grouse Viewing

The grouse species in Colorado have definitely raised my interest level to new heights. I have had more fun over the last couple years sitting on the breeding leks and photographing these birds than anything else I have done working on this book. They have just been a hoot!

Colorado has another grouse species to introduce to you. The Columbian sharp-tailed grouse, also known as mountain sharp-tailed grouse, has raised my curiosity even further. They follow in the same habits as the other grouse mentioned in this book, however they have their own special habitat. Sharp-tailed grouse leks are typically located on knolls or ridge-tops. An average of 14 birds display and breed on an area about 100 feet in diameter. Males begin displaying in late March or April and continue through mid-May.

The sharp-tailed grouse are located in the hill country along the Yampa River, primarily in the vicinity of Hayden. Hayden is located in northwest Colorado on Highway 40 between Steamboat Springs and Craig.

They are a unique bird with distinct black v-shaped marks on the breast feathers, giving them a frosty gray appearance. Feathering continues to the base of the toes.

Both sexes have inconspicuous crests, and the head and upper body parts are extensively patterned with barring and spotting of white, tawny brown, and black.

Sharp-tailed grouse weigh in at around 1.5 pounds and go through the customary mating ritual much like other grouse species from April through mid-May.

Much like the other species of grouse, the males have a beautiful mating display. Underneath the male's mottled exterior are splendid purple neck sacs that emerge only during their courtship dances. Some say that true beauty is found beneath the surface, and nowhere is this truer than with the sharp-tailed grouse. They really are a gorgeous bird.

My experience with the sharp-tailed grouse was much like my time spent with the greater prairie chicken. Getting up before light, dressing in warm camouflage, walking to the blind in the dark (flashlight, camera, and tripod in tow) and setting up to wait for enough light to start shooting. The sharptails are more than likely already there and talking to each other. There is a great thing about this species – if they are spooked off the lek, they will return within minutes and get right back to their business.

Once it is light enough and you can see what they are doing, I guarantee you will be chuckling. The males do this little face off – wings spread like airplane wings, squatting low to the ground "dancing" by stomping their feet and running in a circle,

*Sharp-tails in their battle stance*

beak to beak staring at each other, accompanied by this threatening bird talk. Then all of a sudden one of them will lunge forward, feet first, attacking the other to show dominance and attract females. The dominant grouse wins the best spot in the lek, giving him a better chance of mating with a female. It is serious business, but I can't help but laugh. If you are a birder or interested in the wild outdoors, this is a must-see event.

After breeding, females build a ground nest in a grassy area or near the protection of shrubs. A typical clutch is 10 to 12 eggs which the hen incubates for approximately 23 days. After hatching, the chicks are tended by the female and are largely dependent for 6 to 8 weeks. In late fall and winter, the birds form small flocks and are dependent on shrubs for food and cover. As is common with other grouse species, snow roosting is an important means of thermoregulation during the winter months. In spring, the males head toward the leks and the cycle begins again.

Sharp-tailed grouse are doing well in Colorado as compared to other portions of their range. This can be attributed somewhat to mine reclamation efforts (re-vegetation using up to 20 different seeds of grasses, forbs, and shrubs) and the presence of the Conservation Reserve Program (CRP) fields within their range. This species uses the high mountain shrub and grassland communities and associated edges. They are commonly found in high elevation grassland areas interspersed with serviceberry, chokecherry, oak brush, sagebrush, snowberry, and aspen. Shrubs and small trees play an important role in sharp-tailed grouse survival, especially in winter when they provide both food and cover. They are even known to feed on cultivated crops like wheat and alfalfa in spring and summer. Unlike sage or dusky grouse, sharptails may utilize agricultural fields and feed on waste grain and associated insects.

## Contact

The Colorado Division of Wildlife offers limited guided tours to view sharp-tailed grouse near Hayden. Tours are provided by the Division of Wildlife's local district wildlife manager or by private land owners. Participants must arrange for meals and accommodations on their own. For more information on viewing opportunities in the Yampa Valley area, contact the Division of Wildlife office in Steamboat Springs, 970-870-2197.

*It is imperative to use a blind to capture a photo like this.*

# National Parks and Monuments
## Dinosaur National Monument

### 211,000 acres; Northwest Colorado

## Introduction

The Dinosaur National Monument was designated in 1915. This designation came after the discovery of the site by paleontologist Earl Douglass in 1909. He first came to Utah looking for mammal fossils when he came across this massive deposit of dinosaur bones. Today, there is a quarry that has excavated numerous dinosaur fossils. The main visitor center was built in 1957 over the top of the quarry. The sandstone the center was built on ended up being an unstable foundation. The building developed structural problems and a formal monitoring program began in May 2006. A detailed inspection of the building recognized some previously unknown conditions that presented serious life, safety, and health hazards. Because of those concerns, park management made the complicated decision; the prudent course of action would be to close the building. The family and I did visit the monument in the summer of 1996, so we were able to see the working quarry. We watched the quarry paleontologists as they exposed the fossils along one of the walls. This wall of fossil-bearing sandstone forms one of the inner walls of the Dinosaur Quarry building. Here, the prehistoric bones are still exposed in, but not removed from, the face of the wall. It is quite a unique exhibit of the bones in their natural setting. Hopefully someday soon the funds will become available to reinforce or rebuild this unique site.

    The Temporary Visitor Center is located at the visitor parking lot. Many of the replica fossils have been moved to this "Outdoor Visitor Center" so that people can view and touch them. There is a makeshift auditorium set up with an informative video illustrating the fossil wall and paleontologists at work. The Junior Ranger and Junior Paleontologist programs are still available at the Outdoor Visitor Center. Rangers are available at the Outdoor Visitor Center to answer questions and present programs.

    The canyon lands of the Green and Yampa Rivers were added to the original area in 1938 which brought in much of the land that is now in Colorado. The addition more than doubled the size of the monument. The canyon country is pretty much isolated from any main traveled routes and is perhaps overshadowed by the distinctiveness of the dinosaur quarry. This wilderness country has remained relatively unexplored. The Harper's Corner Auto Tour starting at the Canyon Area Visitor Center is the only paved road that offers a glimpse into this strikingly colorful landscape.

There are two scenic drives available inside the Dinosaur National Monument, the Tour of Tilted Rocks starting near the Temporary Visitor Center and the Harper's Corner Scenic Drive starting at the Canyon Area Visitor Center.

The Tour of the Tilted Rocks is an 11-mile (one-way) auto tour route along Cub Creek Road that ends at Josie Basset Morris Cabin. Features along the route include petroglyph and pictograph panels, excellent views of geologic features and formations, views of and access to the Green River, and the Josie Basset Morris Cabin, a log cabin built in 1913. Note: A little known fact about a petroglyph and a pictograph is that petroglyphs are images pecked into rock while pictographs are painted images. Dinosaur National Monument preserves both forms of Native American rock art. The last 2 miles of the route are unpaved but well maintained. The last 3 to 4 miles are unplowed in the winter and are generally not passable by car.

The Harpers Corner Scenic Drive is a 31-mile (one-way) auto tour route from the Canyon Area Visitor Center to Harpers Corner. Dinosaur fossils are not located in this section of the park, but the views and overlooks are well worth the trip. The route goes by colorful Plug Hat Butte, which contains a wheelchair-accessible trail and a picnic area. As the road continues to gain elevation, the scenery reflects the changing ecosystems. The last 12 miles include several striking viewpoints and overlooks, some as high as 2,500 feet above the Green and Yampa Rivers. Steamboat Rock hides the confluence of the two rivers from view at the Echo Park overlook. A 1-mile (one-way) trail at the end of the route leads to a vista with nearly 300-degree views into Whirlpool, Lodore, and Yampa Canyons.

I believe the best way, and really the only way, to get a close up view of the monument is by foot. Hiking in Dinosaur is an excellent way to appreciate the park's scenery and rugged landscape. The most popular trails begin near the visitor centers, while other trails begin at more remote locations. Remember that this is high desert country and considerations should be taken before heading out on any of these trails. Plenty of water, a hat, sunscreen, and good hiking boots should be on your must-have list.

## Trails near the main Visitor Center

The Fossil Discovery trailhead is located at the Temporary Visitor Center. It is 1.5 miles in length and is easy to moderate in difficulty. A few large dinosaur fossil bones, including a good section of vertebrae, are exposed in the cliff along the trail. The Morrison Formation stop features an outcropping of several small pieces and a few large pieces of dinosaur bones.

The Desert Voices Trail trailhead is located about 4 miles east of the Temporary Visitor Center at the Split Mountain Boat Ramp. This moderately difficult trail is a 1.5-mile loop. The trail offers excellent views of Split Mountain and several adjacent rock layers. Geology is the outstanding feature on this trail. Many of the signs on the

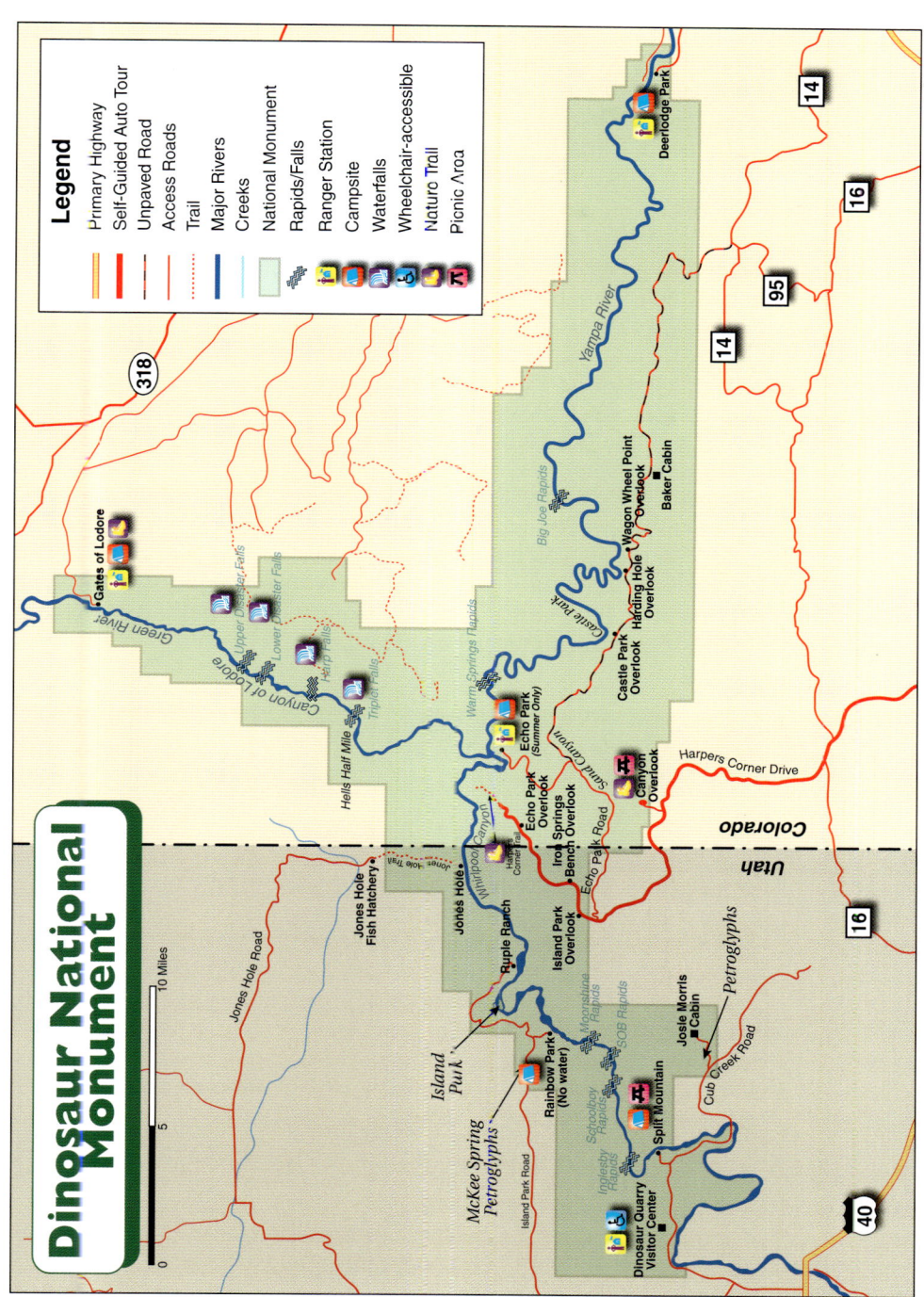

trail were written and drawn by children for children. There is no shade. This trail ties to the Sound of Silence Trail via a quarter-mile connector trail.

The Sound of Silence trailhead is located about 2 miles east of the Temporary Visitor Center at the Tour of the Tilted Rocks auto tour road. This moderate to difficult trail is a 3-mile loop. This is a hike through several of Dinosaur's most interesting rock layers. It provides excellent geologic diversity with some steep sections on slickrock. Be sure to use the trail guide, even if you plan to return it at the end of your hike, since portions of the trail can be confusing. There is no shade. This trail ties in with Desert Voices Trail via a quarter-mile connector trail. A trail brochure is available at trailhead and at visitor centers.

The River Trail trailhead is located at the north end of Green River Campground or south end of Split Mountain Campground. This is a pretty easy mile-long trip that connects Green River campground with Split Mountain Campground. It follows the Green River, affording great views of Split Mountain.

The Hog Canyon Trail trailhead is located at Josie's Cabin on the auto tour road 12 miles east of the Temporary Visitor Center. This is an excellent trail for small children. This easy 1.5-mile walk goes through a scenic box canyon. There are live springs, which mean there are trees that provide shade along the trail.

The Box Canyon trailhead is located at Josie's Cabin, on the Tour of the Tilted Rocks auto tour road 12 miles east of the Temporary Visitor Center. This half-mile walk, which leads into a shady box canyon, is excellent for small children. It provides nice exposures of the craggy sandstone of Split Mountain.

*A dinosaur fossil*

## Trails near the Canyon Area Visitor Center

The Cold Desert Trail trailhead is located at the Canyon Area Visitor Center. This easy half-mile loop opens your eyes to the diversity of the desert shrub community found around Dinosaur.

The Plug Hat Trail trailhead is located about 5 miles north of Canyon Area Visitor Center on Harpers Corner Auto Tour Road. This trail is paved and wheelchair accessible. It is only 0.25 mile in length and skirts along the top of a butte. It affords an excellent view of the surrounding landscape and provides an introduction to the pinyon pine-juniper community. There is informative signage along the trail. A level wheelchair-accessible picnic area is across the road from the trailhead.

The Ruple Point trailhead is located 27 miles north of the Canyon Area Visitor Center at the Island Park Overlook on the Harpers Corner Auto Tour road. It is a moderate to difficult 8-mile round trip. Most of the trail follows rolling terrain of sagebrush and juniper. The descent at the end brings you to a breathtaking view of Split Mountain Canyon. The trail is hard to follow as you descend at the end.

The Harper's Corner trailhead is located 32 miles from the Canyon Area Visitor Center at the end of the Harpers Corner Auto Tour road. It is an easy to moderate 2-mile round trip with an outstanding overlook into three river canyons at the end of the trail. There are a few steep drop-offs, so keep close tabs on small children.

## Wildlife

When looking at the entire 211,000 acres of the Dinosaur National Monument, it becomes quickly apparent that wildlife habitat ranges from the stark barrenness of deserts to the lush greenness of dense forests. The canyon-carving rivers provide riparian environment and the canyons provide cliff and ledge habitat. So it is only fitting that the wildlife inhabitants will be as diverse.

The rocky desert floor and the slow rise to a desert shrub environment in the area have a unique list of reptiles, birds, and small rodents. Most desert wildlife are nocturnal to avoid the intense heat during the day, but do show themselves on occasion. Dinosaurs became extinct 65 million years ago, but lizards are still a common sight at Dinosaur National Monument. The small, inquisitive reptiles have endured on earth for more than 300 million years, far outlasting their giant cousins. There is always a chance to catch a glimpse of collared lizards, plateau-striped lizards, western whiptails, bull snakes, and the startling rattlesnake. Birds in the area include the horned lark, turkey vulture, and burrowing owls. The desert shrub brings desert cottontails, black-tailed jackrabbits, badgers, prairie dogs, coyotes, and pronghorn antelope into play. The river beds can be a birding wonderland. Waterfowl of all sorts, spotted sandpipers, American avocets, white-faces ibis, and belted kingfishers can be seen. I viewed at least a thousand Canada geese on the banks of the river. As I was hiking one of the trails near the visitor center, I heard the distinct call of sandhill cranes. Upon further investigation with my binoculars, I spotted about 50 birds in a

*A good-sized bull snake*

grain field just south of the Green River. The playful river otter, beaver, muskrat, and the Yuma myotis bat make their homes along the rivers and streams. The canyon walls are home to canyon wrens, bighorn sheep, mountain lion, and a population of peregrine falcons has been established at Dinosaur National Monument. The park's rugged canyons make ideal habitat for the once-endangered raptor, and bighorn sheep like to use the steep ledges for lambing to avoid predators. In the eastern portion of the monument, especially in Colorado, the landscape changes to a mountain shrub and pinyon-juniper habitat. This is where the mule deer thrive, coyotes carry over, porcupines are established, and elk may be seen migrating from the higher country as the snow starts to fly. The gorgeous lazuli bunting and the greater sage grouse breed in this environment. Clark's nutcrackers and pinyon jays enjoy the food that these trees provide. Finally the elevation tops into the moisture rich montane zone. Elk, black bear, mule deer, wild turkey, mountain bluebirds, chickadees, hermit thrushes, and warblers can be found.

All in all, the assortment of wildlife and birds found here will keep any nature lover busy for days.

## Activities

Along with the previously mentioned scenic drives and hiking trails, opportunities for photography, river rafting, bicycling, fishing, and backcountry camping are possible for the adventurous.

Whitewater rafting is a popular way to experience the remote canyon areas at Dinosaur National Monument. By far, the most popular raft trip in Dinosaur is the Green River float from the Gates of Lodore to the Split Mountain takeout. This trip should never be mistaken for a simple little raft trip. Even today, many a boat ends up pinned on rocks and many a boater bruised and battered. Gates of Lodore contains multiple challenging Class III and Class IV rapids.

The Yampa River sports many Class III rapids and one Class IV known as Warm Springs Rapid, which has a hydraulic named Maytag that has the tendency to flip boats. Rafting permits may be needed.

Bicycling is a popular pastime at the monument and is permitted anywhere in the area. The main scenic drives are well-liked by cyclists, but a couple of the more remote roads can be a real treat. Rainbow Park to Island Park is a challenging ride with views of the Green River and colorful geologic features. The Yampa Bench Road is a colorful ride along the Yampa River, with changing views of the river and its canyons.

Fishing is allowed in Dinosaur National Monument, subject to the regulations of the state in which you are fishing. A valid state fishing license is required for fishing even though the monument is federal land. I don't think anyone would consider the waters in Dinosaur world-class fisheries, but if you are a fisherman, you fish. Anglers should be informed that there are four endangered species of fish found in rivers in the monument: Colorado pikeminnow, razorback sucker, humpback chub, and bonytail. These fish should be immediately released with as little harm as possible if caught.

Backcountry camping permits are required for overnight stays outside established campgrounds. There is no cost for the permit. I would consider any backpacking trip in the backcountry of the Dinosaur National Monument, and extreme camping should be considered by experienced backpackers only. The beauty and solitude are inspiring. But the terrain is isolated and rugged, and it is very difficult to find water in the backcountry.

There is one designated backcountry location in the monument. It is at the confluence of Jones Hole Creek and Ely Creek, along the Jones Hole Trail. Reservations are required to use this location (call 435-781-7700 for reservations). There are two sites at this location and there are a few regulations.

- Maximum group size is eight at each site.
- Treat water in creek before drinking.
- Vault toilet available.
- Pack out all trash.
- No fires.
- No bicycles.
- No pets.
- No soap discharge in creek.

Other than designated sites, you can basically camp anywhere, provided you are:

- At least 1 mile from developed areas, like the Dinosaur Quarry and boat ramps.
- At least 0.25 mile from roads.
- At least 0.25 mile from hiking trails.
- At least 300 feet from water.
- At least 0.25 mile from cultural sites.
- At least 0.125 mile from the Green or Yampa Rivers. River campsites are closed to backpackers during the "high-use river-running season", which is the second Monday in May until the second Friday in September.

With proper planning, a backcountry trip at Dinosaur can be a wonderful experience of solitude and serenity.

## Camping

Camping fees are charged at most developed campgrounds in the park. Reservations are only taken for group campsites. Backcountry camping is free but a free permit is required.

Green River Campground is 5 miles east of the Temporary Visitor Center, accessible via the park tour road. It has 80 sites which are suitable for tents or RVs. Each site has a picnic table and fire pit. Drinking water and plumbed toilets are available. There are no showers, and there are no electrical hook-ups for RVs. Firewood is available for sale. The fee is $12 per night, per site.

There are no reservations. Generally, the campground does not fill up, except on major holiday weekends such as Memorial Day and 4th of July. Green River Campground is open from mid-April to mid-October. Nearby Split Mountain Campground is open the rest of the year for general camping.

Deerlodge Park Campground is located 53 miles east of the Canyon Area Visitor Center. It is located on the Yampa River by the boat ramp at the head of Yampa Canyon. It has seven shady sites suitable for tents. The sites have tables and fire pits. There are running water and vault toilets, but no showers. The fee is $8 per site, per night. The water is turned off from October to mid-April, and there is no camping fee at that time. Deerlodge Campground is open year round, but winter access can be very difficult due to snow.

Rainbow Park Campground is 26 miles from the Temporary Visitor Center. It is located on a dirt road that is impassable when wet. The campground is on the Green River by the boat ramp at the head of Split Mountain Canyon. This campground has three shady sites with limited facilities. There is no running water. It has a vault toilet. There are tables and fire pits, and it's suitable for tent camping only. There is no fee. Rainbow Park Campground is open year round, but there is no winter maintenance on the dirt road leading to the campground.

Split Mountain Campground is 4 miles east of the Temporary Visitor Center by the Split Mountain boat ramp. It functions as a group campground during the high-visitation season. It serves as a general purpose campground in the off-season. There are four group sites. Each site is shaded and can handle up to 20 people and six vehicles. Each site has a picnic table and fire pit. Plumbed restrooms and drinking water are available. There are no showers. Cost is $25 per night, with a non-refundable reservation fee of $10.00 per site. Please call 435-781-7759 to have a form mailed to you for reservations. Fill out and return the group reservation form.

During the off-season (mid-October to mid-April), Split Mountain Campground serves as a general campground. There is no water, but a vault toilet is available. There are no reservations at Split Mountain during the off-season and no fees are charged.

Echo Park Campground is located 38 miles north of the Canyon Area Visitor Center. It is located near the confluence of the Green and Yampa Rivers. Access to the campground requires high-clearance vehicles. RVs and trailers are strongly discouraged due to sharp turns, steep grades, and rough roads. Echo Park Campground has 22 sites, including one handicapped-accessible site and four walk-in sites. There is one group site. Call 435-781-7759 to have a reservation form mailed to you for group site reservations. There is some shade. Suitable for tent camping, there is running water and vault toilets but no showers. Check with a ranger for current fire-use policy. The fee is $8 per site, per night. There are no reservations, but the campground rarely fills. The water is turned off from September to mid-April, and there is no camping fee at that time.

Echo Park Campground is open year round, but access is dependent on weather. The last 13 miles of dirt road are impassable when wet. Winter access is often impossible due to snow.

Gates of Lodore Campground is located 106 miles north of the Canyon Area Visitor Center. It is located on the Green River by the boat ramp at the head of Lodore Canyon. There are 17 sites, some with shade. The sites have tables and fire pits. There are running water and vault toilets, but no showers. The campground handles tents and RVs (but there are no hook-ups). Camping fee is $8 per site, per night. The water is turned off from mid-September to mid-April, and there is no camping fee at that time. Gates of Lodore Campground is open year round, but winter access can be difficult due to snow.

## Location

To the Temporary Visitor Center from Denver, take Interstate 70 west to Rifle. Take the exit for Highway 13, and follow Highway 13 north toward Meeker. Turn left on Highway 64, about 40 miles north of Rifle. Follow Highway 64 west about 80 miles to the town of Dinosaur. Turn west onto Highway 40 toward Jensen, Utah. Turn north (right) on Utah 149 in Jensen and follow the signs for the visitor center. Driving time from Denver is about 5.5 hours.

To Canyon Area Visitor Center from Denver, take Interstate 70 west to Rifle. Take the exit for Highway 13, and follow Highway 13 north towards Meeker. Turn left on Highway 64, about 40 miles north of Rifle. Follow Highway 64 west about 80 miles to

Dinosaur. Turn east on Highway 40 for 2 miles. Turn north (left) on Harpers Corner Road at the signs and make the first right into the parking lot. Driving time from Denver is about 5 hours.

## Contact

**Dinosaur National Monument**
4545 East Highway 40, Dinosaur, CO 81610
970-374-3000
Temporary Visitor Center: 435-374-3000
www.nps.gov/dino

Temporary Visitor Center (near Jensen, Utah) is open 8:30am-4:30pm daily. (Closed Thanksgiving, Christmas, December 26, and New Years Day)
Ranger-led programs are scheduled throughout the day during summer.
Canyon Area Visitor Center (near Dinosaur, Colorado) is open:
May 20 through September 6, 8:30am-4:30pm
September 7 through October 31, 8:30am-4:30pm Wednesday-Sunday (closed Mondays and Tuesdays)
November 1, closed for the winter season.
Entrance fees are charged from Memorial Day Weekend through Labor Day on the Utah side of the monument.
Private, non-commercial vehicle: $10 – valid for 7 consecutive days.
Motorcycle: $5 for single rider, $10 for double rider – valid for 7 consecutive days.
Individual (Hiker, bicyclist): $5 – valid for 7 consecutive days.
Dinosaur National Monument Pass: $20 – Allows unlimited entry to Dinosaur for the pass holder and his or her passengers in a single, private, non-commercial vehicle for 12 months from the date of purchase.
America the Beautiful Pass – National Parks and Federal Recreational Lands Pass Program.
Commercial tour fees based on the seating capacity of the vehicle:
Motor coach (capable of carrying 26 or more passengers): $150
Minibus (capable of carrying 16-25 passengers): $60
Van (capable of carrying 7-15 passengers): $50
Sedan (1-6 passengers): $25 plus $5 per person

# Scenic Byways

## Cache la Poudre/North Park Scenic Byway

The Cache la Poudre/North Park Scenic Byway is a 101-mile journey through one of Colorado's most magnificent river canyons. In fact, the Cache la Poudre River is Colorado's only federally designated National Wild and Scenic River. At only 101 miles, you would think you could breeze over it in a couple of hours. The truth is that it will take more like three or four. Highway 14 is a very good road, but it winds through this canyon, climbs the 10,276-foot Cameron Pass, and has too many sights to see in just two hours.

The Cache la Poudre/North Park Scenic Byway starts at the intersection of Interstate 25 and Highway 14. Head west on Highway 14 through the college town of Fort Collins. It is a little tricky getting through town, but just follow the signage closely and there should be no problem. You eventually are heading north out of town on Highway 287 which is also Highway 14. At the corner called "Ted's Place" turn left (west) on Highway 14. Continue on Highway 14 all the way to Walden in North Park where the byway ends.

### Lory State Park

The first point of interest just west of Fort Collins is Lory State Park. From Highway 287 north of Fort Collins, take CR 54G west through the town of Laporte. Take a left on CR 52E and continue about a mile. Take another left on CR 23 and continue about 2 miles to CR 25G. Take a right on CR 25G to the park entrance. Lory State Park is also an entrance to Horsetooth Reservoir.

This state park offers a number of hiking and biking trails ranging from easy to difficult through a variety of foothill-type habitat. They are anywhere from just under a mile to 3.5 miles in length and are especially popular with mountain bikers. They offer great views of Horsetooth Reservoir, wildflowers, and an assortment of wildlife.

There have been almost 200 species of migratory and resident birds sighted in this area. Grassland species like the lark bunting, horned lark, and western meadowlark are common. Watch for Swainson's hawks, red-tailed hawks, and prairie falcons. Golden eagles can be seen and bald eagles are popular during the winter. Waterfowl and shorebirds are attracted to the open water of Horsetooth Reservoir, the park wetland, and riparian habitats. Smaller birds like the canyon wren, yellow-breasted chat, western tanager, and broad-tailed hummingbird love the variety of habitat. Big game includes mule deer, white-tailed deer, elk, black bear, and mountain lion. Predators like the wily coyote, red fox, and bobcat are spotted occasionally, while raccoon, striped skunk, Abert's squirrel, cottontail rabbit, and porcupine are common sightings.

Horsetooth Reservoir to the east of Lory State Park is operated by the Larimer County Department of Natural Resources. On the west side of the reservoir from the park itself, access is by foot only. There are several coves on the west side that offers smallmouth bass, trout, and walleye fishing. All Colorado Division of Wildlife fishing regulations apply.

*Cow moose*

Camping at Lory State Park is in the backcountry only. There are no campgrounds, car camping, or RV camping available. Primitive sites can be accessed by at least a 2-mile, one-way hike. The backcountry sites are a good training ground for Boy Scouts and other groups who want to train for longer backpacking and camping trips. There is no water, restrooms, or tent pads at these sites, and fires are prohibited.

## Contact
**Park Office**
708 N CR 25G, Bellvue, CO  80512
970-493-1623
Office Hours: Mon-Sun 9:00am-3:00pm
Park Hours: 6:00am-6:00pm

# Phantom Canyon Preserve (Nature Conservancy)

The next point of interest as you start up the Cache la Poudre River canyon is the Phantom Canyon Preserve. I found a quote from the journal of an early American explorer and military officer:

> *"It was a mountain valley of the narrowest kind - almost a chasm; and the scenery very wild and beautiful. ... Below, the green river bottom was a wilderness of flowers, their tall spikes sometimes rising above our heads as we rode among them."*
> ~John Charles Fremont, July 29, 1843

*Those wings are fast!*

So many years ago, this remote canyon was found and documented; today it remains a protected location owned by the Nature Conservancy. The Conservancy acquired this land in 1987. The only way to gain access is through a guided field trip or by participating in a volunteer workday. The Nature Conservancy selected this site because this broad foothills ecosystem supports the Larimer aletes, a rare member of the parsley family. The plant's distribution is limited to only two counties in Colorado: Larimer and Boulder. Most occurrences are right here on this 1,700-acre preserve. This preserve features a stunning roadless canyon and 6 miles of the North Fork of the Cache la Poudre River. It may be one of the last great undeveloped landscapes along the Front Range, maybe even the entire state.

The preserve is accessed by two well-maintained trails. Visitors start out on the Rim Trail, which is an easy half-mile loop through prairie habitat interspersed with shrublands above the canyon. The views of the canyon and distant mountains are nothing short of spectacular. The Canyon Trail winds 500 feet in elevation down to the canyon floor, where one can inspect the banks of the Cache La Poudre River. There are beats set up for anglers that want to spend some time casting to happy brown trout. There are plenty of rocky areas with low brush and cactus, so do not be surprised if a rattlesnake appears out of nowhere! Just joking, I know you will be surprised. Wear appropriate footwear.

Besides the frisky little prairie rattlers, more than 100 bird species have been spotted in this foothills ecosystem. The prairie habitat will boast the popular meadow lark, horned lark, and loggerhead shrike. Lazuli buntings, black-headed grosbeaks, American dippers, and western tanagers are often found nesting in the riparian canyon environment; and golden eagles, red-tailed hawks, prairie falcons, and white-throated swifts find refuge in the cliffs of the canyon walls. Bald eagles are often seen here in the winter months.

The preserve and surrounding area is good habitat for the mule deer, cottontail rabbits, and badgers. This habitat supports black bear, mountain lion, and bobcat. The possibilities of seeing any of these secretive animals are short, but all three can be found on the Colorado species of special concern list.

Late spring and early summer is a great time to visit and experience the astoundingly colorful display of native wildflowers. Try to find the one-sided penstemon.

The Conservancy staff and volunteers are always working to protect and enhance the preserve by managing invasive weed growth, reintroducing the natural ecological processes of grazing and fire, and creating partnerships and relationships within the local community to promote conservation through conservation easements and best management practices.

## Contact

**Laramie Foothills/Phantom Canyon Preserve**
  P.O. Box 270, Livermore, CO  80536
  970-631-7645

Continuing west on the byway is a pleasure for the eyes. Views of the Cache la Poudre River and its crystal clear waters come one right after another, one bend after another. The popularity of this canyon shows with the number of pull-out picnic areas, forest service campgrounds, and fishing accesses. In fact, there are five campgrounds in a 10-mile stretch of highway about 20 miles west of Ted's Corner. This stretch of river is used heavily by rafters and kayakers. Highway 14 weaves along the river, so expect slower speeds and pay attention to staying in your lane.

There are also several side roads that take you into the high country on either side of the river. These side roads lead to trailheads for backpackers and day hikers. They take adventure seekers into the depths of the Roosevelt National Forest. One side road in particular is CR 63E which follows the South Fork of the Cache la Poudre to its headwaters in Comanche Peak Wilderness. This area is on the northern border of Rocky Mountain National Park, so one can only imagine how beautiful it is. Again, pack trails are abundant. This is deer and elk country and any number of small game species may be seen. Mountain birds are plentiful so expect to see grosbeaks, jays, bluebirds, and hummingbirds.

The town of Rustic is one of the more popular stops along the way. There are several places for RV camping, cabin rentals, and tent camping.

**Glen Echo Resort**
970-881-2208

**Archer's Poudre River Resort**
Cabins, Camping & Store
888-822-0588

**Bighorn Cabins**
970-881-2142

Just a few miles west of Rustic is an interesting rock formation called Profile Rock, which is well worth a photo or two. This is a good area to watch for bighorn sheep. The aspens will be in full color starting in mid-September.

## Joe Wright Reservoir

I make an annual outing to the area and meet up with my old friend Jerry and his friend, Uncle Jerry (that's how I tell them apart) to fish a few lakes in the area. Jerry has a cabin in Rustic, so we have a great central location to work from and a comfy place to stay. Every August, we fish Joe Wright Reservoir for grayling. It is one of just a few places in Colorado to find this arctic native. Joe Wright is about 30 miles west of Rustic. I have tried to take my son up there as often as possible, as it is a wonderful place for young anglers to get hooked up with a fish. On one trip, Cole and I were casting from our float tubes along the dam and right above us on top of the dam, a bull moose, a cow and calf appeared. What a sight; they were not 20 yards away from us! Float tubing or pontoons are the norm, dry flies are well-liked, and afternoon rain showers are possible.

## Long Draw Reservoir

For the last few years, we have been going up to Long Draw Reservoir. The reservoir is about 10 miles south on FR 156, also known as Long Draw Road. The fishing can be very good for cutthroats, but the unique thing about this little 10-mile drive is that we have seen moose on EVERY trip. Last year, since I was working on this book, I left the fly rod in the truck and spent the whole day with my camera and tripod in the front seat with me. I was able to pop several good images. I was so close to a cow at one time that I could hear her crunching the willow twigs between her teeth. It was a little unnerving, but very cool at the same time. Do use caution around these animals, they are the largest of the deer family and have a very unpredictable disposition.

Continuing along the byway you begin the ascent of the 10,276-foot Cameron Pass. As you top the pass, the highway intercepts Colorado State Forest, a 70,000-acre preserve of glaciated mountains and evergreen thickets. There are amazing views from up here. This is also the headwaters of the Michigan River which flows down to North Park. The river gains size at the town of Gould and creates some of the finest riparian habitat you will see anywhere in the state. Most of the land here is private, so access is very limited until you get to Walden. Walden is the major stopping point for North Park and its many outdoor activities. Enthusiasts will enjoy Walden Reservoir, Delaney Butte Lakes State Wildlife Area, Lake John, and Cowdrey Lake State Wildlife Area. North Park is loaded with mule deer, antelope, elk, moose, beaver, and coyotes, as well as thousands of migrating waterfowl flock to the Arapaho National Wildlife Refuge (see the Arapaho National Wildlife Refuge chapter for more detailed information).

## Contact

**Canyon Lakes Ranger District**
 2150 Centre Avenue Building E
 Fort Collins, CO  80526
 970-295-6700
 www.fs.fed.us/r2/arnf/recreation/scenic-drives/index

# Colorado River Headwaters Scenic Byway

The Colorado River Headwaters Scenic Byway is an 80-mile tour of the upper Colorado River as it comes out of Rocky Mountain National Park and starts its journey west to the Pacific Ocean. This two- to three-hour drive is dotted with reservoirs storing water from the river itself and its many tributaries. Even though the Colorado River is best known for its powerful rapids in the Grand Canyon, irrigating thousands of acres of farmland, and providing power to most of the southwestern United States, the beginning of this byway proves large things can come in small packages. Here, at its source, it is no different from dozens of other Rocky Mountain waterways, a clear little stream tumbling across green meadows and picking up steam down narrow red-rock gorges.

The Colorado River Headwaters was designated by the U.S. Secretary of Transportation as a National Scenic Byway in 2005. It is one of ten America's Byways designated in Colorado.

Starting in the quaint mountain village of Grand Lake, take Highway 34 south about 15 miles to the intersection with Highway 40. Turn right (west) on Highway 40 about 30 miles to the town of Kremmling. Take Highway 9 south about 2 miles out of town and turn right on CR 1. This gravel road veers to the southwest and reengages the river at Pump House. Pump House is a boat ramp to put in boats and rafts for a float downstream to Radium or State Bridge. It is also a trail head to walk up into the Gore Canyon of the Colorado River. Continue on CR 1 for about 25 miles to the end of the byway at State Bridge.

The Grand Lake region offers a host of year-round recreation for the whole family. It is the western entrance to Rocky Mountain National Park (see the Rocky

Mountain National Park chapter for more details). Flyfishing is very popular on the upper Colorado River in the park, on the small streams in the area, and below Shadow Mountain Reservoir. There are nesting bald eagles and osprey, waterfowl galore, and the river basin is one of the best places in the state to see the Shiras moose. With three bodies of water in the vicinity, boating, sailing, and water skiing are all the rage. Grand Lake itself is a beautiful, naturally occurring lake. At 600 acres, it is the largest and deepest natural lake in Colorado. Cultural events, wine tastings, festivals and fairs are held throughout the year, including the acclaimed Rocky Mountain Repertory Theatre, which offers a stimulating summer season of musical theatre. Mountain biking, horseback riding, camping, hiking, and backpacking are also great pastimes. When the snow flies, this area becomes a Mecca of outdoor activities with snowmobiling ranking number one. Grand Lake is known nationwide for its 300 miles of snowmobile trails, suitable for beginner, intermediate, and advanced riders. Grand Lake consistently ranks in the top ten for snowmobile destinations in the United States. Toss in cross-country skiing, snowshoeing, ice skating, sledding, and tubing to fill in the gaps.

This region has a diverse habitat and with it comes a diverse list of wildlife and birding opportunities. The lakes and reservoirs speak for themselves; however the streams with thick willow habitat and grassy mountain meadows expand the possibilities immensely. Shadow Mountain Reservoir and Grand Lake are very good for waterfowl, particularly the Barrow's goldeneye, which holds over for the winter from about mid-October to late April. They are often seen in large numbers. Great blue herons, Canada geese, and mallards are seen in decent numbers. Watch for shorebirds like spotted sandpiper, lesser yellowlegs, and American avocet. We must not forget the ponderosa and lodgepole forests where downy woodpeckers, evening grosbeaks, dark-eyed junco, and broad-tailed hummingbirds thrive. Mule deer and elk are also seen along the outskirts of Rocky Mountain National Park.

## Lake Granby

Lake Granby is about 6 miles south of Grand Lake on Highway 34. Lake Granby, second only to Blue Mesa Reservoir in size, is routinely stocked with rainbow trout, brown trout, and kokanee salmon. However, Lake Granby is best known for its lake trout (mackinaw) fishing. Again, this lake is also home to the bald eagle and the osprey.

The dam at Lake Granby was built in the 1940s to store water for the Front Range, mainly the high agricultural area surrounding Greeley. Lake Granby has the capacity to be well over 7,000 surface acres, can get up to 221 feet deep, and has 40 miles of shoreline.

There are three campgrounds at Lake Granby: Arapaho Bay Campground, Stillwater Campground, and Cutthroat Bay Campground. There are 250 campsites in all and three boat ramps. Most campsites include flush toilets, drinking water, picnic tables, and fire pits. Groceries are available at several marinas and a number of cafes are located off Highway 34 on the lake's western shore.

## Contact

**U.S. Forest Service**
62429 Highway 40, P.O. Box 10, Granby, CO 80446
970-887-4100

# Windy Gap Reservoir

Continue south on Highway 34 about 5 miles to the intersection with Highway 40. Turn right and just a couple miles west of the intersection is Windy Gap Reservoir. This reservoir is built at the confluence of the Fraser River and the North Fork of the Colorado River. It is a very small reservoir and very little water is actually held here, however during the peak of runoff every spring, water is pumped back up to Lake Granby. Amazingly, water from Lake Granby is then pumped up to Grand Lake and rushes at 400 cubic feet per second through a long tunnel under the Continental Divide to the Front Range.

After all this finagling with water, Windy Gap Reservoir is a phenomenal place to view waterfowl and shorebirds. There are accessible viewing blinds, a half-mile trail, and information kiosks. A variety of birds and animals can be spotted here. Mallards, wigeon, and geese are the main stay and it is an excellent spot for Barrow's goldeneye in the colder months. Keep an eye out for terns, small gulls, western grebes, herons, and sandpipers. The roadside pull-off offers restrooms and covered picnic tables.

*Cow moose*

## Willow Creek Reservoir

The Willow Creek Reservoir is just north of Windy Gap Reservoir about 4 miles on Highway 125. It is designated as an Arapaho National Forest Recreational Area. Camping and fishing are the norm. I have fly fished Willow Creek above the reservoir several times and have had moose in sight about half the time. The first reintroduction of the Shiras moose into Colorado in 1978 happened in the Illinois and Willow Creek drainages around Rand. Rand is about 30 miles north on Highway 125. The moose have done very well and have expanded their range to include the Colorado River drainage.

I was fishing with a couple people there years ago and one of them starting whoopin' and hollerin'. I caught up to them and they had just had a black bear in the creek with them. I didn't see it, which is par for the course for me. I have tromped, fished, and driven thousands of miles in this state and have yet to see a black bear in the wild.

Following the byway west on Highway 40, the river bottom is in view, but is mostly private until you get to the town of Hot Sulfur Springs. There is fishing access and ample opportunity to bird watch as well as view mule deer. Just below Hot Sulfur Springs, the river drops into Byers Canyon. At the bottom of the canyon is the Hot Sulfur Springs State Wildlife Area. Again, access to the river and riparian habitat provides excellent cover for wildlife.

## Williams Fork Reservoir

The town of Parshell is just west of the SWA and is the entrance to Williams Fork Reservoir. Take a right on RD 3 and follow signage to the reservoir. Williams Fork Reservoir is best known for its northern pike fishing – in fact this reservoir held the state record for a short period of time. As the lake starts to warm up in June, the pike fishing comes in to full swing. Pike move into the shallows where the water is the warmest, so casting from the banks of Williams Fork can provide a memorable day for any fishing enthusiast. Flyfishers find this lake especially suitable to their needs. Wade fishing the shallows trying to spot pike is the norm, but some anglers have incorporated the use of drift boats to cover more water and gain a height advantage in order to see the fish lurking on the bottom. For a change of pace, the Williams Fork River running from the reservoir to the Colorado River provides great stream fishing for brown and rainbow trout. It is good most of the year, but spring and fall seem to be the most crowded.

The facilities are not as plush as you might find at a state park, but camping is available all around the lake. The more developed campgrounds are located near the southern shores. There are a few restrooms, but no fresh water.

### Contact

**Cutthroat Anglers**
 400 Blue River Parkway, Silverthorne, CO 80498
 970-262-2878

## Wolford Mountain Reservoir

Continue west on Highway 40 to the town of Kremmling, which has long been a stop off point for fishermen and hunters for as long as I can remember. Hotels and cafes are extremely busy during the fall hunting season with moderate travel during the spring and summer. However, it has become much more popular since the building of Wolford Mountain Reservoir. The $42 million construction of Wolford Mountain Dam started in 1992 and the reservoir began filling in 1995. Kremmling and surrounding communities have benefited from enhanced tourism from the added camping, fishing, and boating opportunities in this beautiful Rocky Mountain setting. Wolford Mountain Reservoir is located off of Highway 40 north of Kremmling about 4 miles.

The reservoir and dam backs up 1,550 surface acres of the Muddy Creek drainage, providing much-needed water storage for the Colorado River Basin. The future economic health of towns, cities, recreation, industry, and agriculture all depend on a secure source of water. Wolford Mountain Reservoir provides this source.

As with most Colorado reservoirs, recreation plays a big part in the overall plans. Wolford is no different. Wolford Mountain Reservoir can be enjoyed by all outdoor recreationalists. Anglers and boaters will find the facilities very accommodating. Boat ramps are very good and there is a state-of-the-art fish cleaning station. The fishing below the dam on Muddy Creek can be very good also. There are several picnic areas with tables and grills. Trails for hiking and mountain biking are available.

Wildlife viewing is very good because of habitat improvements on Wolford Mountain's east side. It has helped reduce big game movement across Highway 40 and the reservoir. Elk and deer can be seen grazing in the areas adjacent to Muddy Creek and below the dam through much of the winter. Visitors can expect to see numbers of waterfowl species hold up in the many secluded bays around the entire lake.

There are 48 overnight camping spots with RV hookups. Electrical hook-ups are available, but sanitary hook-ups are not. Facilities for the physically challenged are also available.

## Radium State Wildlife Area

To continue the Colorado River Headwaters Scenic Byway go south on Highway 9 from Kremmling. About 1 mile from Kremmling, turn right on CR 1 (Trough Road). This next stretch of the Colorado River from just below Kremmling to State Bridge offers first-class fishing, canoeing, and rafting along with plenty of quiet spaces where you can check out the wildlife and add a bird or two to your checklist.

From the start of CR 1, it is just over 10 miles southwest to CR 106 which leads to the Pumphouse Recreation Area. There is a boat ramp for rafts and a trailhead into the Gore Canyon of the Colorado River. The canyon is BLM land so you can walk in as far as you like. This is a beautiful hiking trail along the Colorado River with good riparian shrub. There is very good habitat for many species of birds, and mule deer are very common. Much of this immediate area is either BLM land or part of the Radium State

Wildlife Area. There is private land so be aware of your surroundings.

County Road 11 is about 15 miles from Highway 9 and leads to the small burg of Radium. Radium itself is 17 miles from Highway 9. This access provides some great pinyon/juniper habitat and terrific riparian areas. This area can be very productive for pinyon jay, juniper titmouse, blue-gray gnatcatcher, rock wren, and black-throated gray warbler. This corner of the Radium State Wildlife Area is probably the best area to search for lower-elevation species like common poorwill, Lewis' woodpecker, and lesser goldfinch.

The byway ends at State Bridge about 15 miles from Radium. There is a big sweeping corner in the river here that is one of my favorite places to fly fish. Big rainbows and browns lurk in this deep hole along with the tasty mountain whitefish. October and November is a great time to catch the whitefish and load up the smoker for a scrumptious feast.

## Contact

**Granby Chamber of Commerce**
  P.O. Box 35, Granby, CO  80446
  970-837-2311

*Spotted sandpiper (this one walked right towards me)*

# Dinosaur Diamond Scenic Byway

The Dinosaur Diamond Scenic Byway is a 486-mile trip through northwest Colorado and east-central Utah. The most famous landmark and where this byway gets its name is the Dinosaur National Monument. This byway starts in Grand Junction on Interstate 70. Travel west through Fruita to Exit 15 and take Colorado Highway 139 north to Rangely. From Rangely, take Highway 64 northwest to the town of Dinosaur. Now take Highway 40 west to the state border. From here the remainder of the loop continues into Utah as it circles back to Grand Junction. Allow ten hours for the entire drive, but it would be impossible to cover the overall package of things to see and do in less than two or three days. Dinosaur Diamond was designated by the U.S. Secretary of Transportation as a National Scenic Byway in 2002. It is one of ten America's Byways designated in Colorado.

Starting in Grand Junction, the byway heads west on Interstate 70 to the town of Fruita. Fruita is the northern entrance to the Colorado National Monument and the Dinosaur Journey Museum (see the Colorado National Monument chapter for more information).

Some of the world's most significant dinosaur fossil quarries and museums are clustered along this route and they start right here in Fruita. The Dinosaur Journey Museum exhibits real fossils, cast skeletons, and robotic reconstructions of dinosaurs, along with a historic tale of life in western Colorado. Real bones of dinosaurs such as apatosaurus, stegosaurus, and allosaurus, along with robotic reconstructions of triceratops and tyrannosaurus will hold your interest. There are full-size cast skeletal mounts of several other dinosaur species including the allosaurus. Historic photos of dinosaur digs in the area dating from as far back as 1900 can also be viewed. There is an exhibit that compares the size of a tiny jurassic lizard pelvis to the pelvis of an apatosaurus, a dinosaur that could have been a million times heavier than the tiny lizard. My family enjoyed the visit and had fun with the hands-on interactions.

*Dinosaur National Monument*

**Dinosaur Journey Museum**
550 Jurassic Court, Fruita, CO 81521
970-858-7282
Hours: Monday-Saturday, 10:00am to 4:00pm; Sunday, Noon to 4:00pm

Just west of Fruita is an immense area of BLM land called the McInnis Canyons National Conservation Area. It is basically an extension of the Colorado National Monument without all the amenities. This is an untamed area with little access except rugged foot trails. However, if you travel west on Interstate 70 to Exit 2, there are trailheads that lead to overlooks of the Colorado River as it leaves the state. This could be a great spot to see the desert bighorn sheep.

Heading north on Highway 139, you traverse some of the most rugged, but stunningly beautiful plateau landscapes on the west slope of the Rocky Mountains. The landscape looks fractured and broken, stained with every color imaginable. Juniper and shrub country giving way to acres of sagebrush is the norm. This deserted landscape holds numbers of mule deer and has a population of some of the largest bull elk in Colorado. There is a hunting unit here that is envied by all elk hunters, and it takes a number of points to even get in the drawing. I have heard it said that it has an 80:20 ratio of bulls to cows. This undisturbed country holds a plethora of wildlife and birds. I wouldn't expect to see one, but mountain lion love this big, game-rich region. Gray and red fox, black bear, coyotes, bobcats, porcupines, badgers, bunnies, and raccoons find the remoteness appealing. Highway 139 follows West Douglas Creek all the way to its confluence with the White River in Rangely, so it could be possible to see beavers, muskrats, mink, and ermine right along the road. Once you get to the bigger water of the White River, it might be possible to see a river otter. Mountain bluebirds, western bluebirds, blue grosbeak, dark-eyed junco, lazuli buntings, yellow-breasted chat, and goldfinch take to this habitat quite nicely. Any of the water habitats may produce sightings of mallards, wood ducks, gadwall, merganser, common goldeneye, Canada geese, and great blue herons.

From Rangely, the Dinosaur Diamond Scenic Byway veers northwest on Highway 64 to the small burg of Dinosaur. The east entrance into Dinosaur National Monument is located here (see the Dinosaur National Monument chapter for more information).

Connect with Highway 40 west into Utah to continue the tour of the byway.

## Contact

**Bureau of Land Management**
2815 H Road, Grand Junction, Colorado 81506
970-244-3000
www.dinosaurdiamond.org

*Floating the Green River through Dinosaur National Monument.*

# Flat Tops Trail Scenic Byway

The Flat Tops Trail Scenic Byway is a remote combination of forest roads connecting the towns of Yampa and Meeker. This 82-mile byway cuts through the heart of the original White River Plateau Timberland Reserve. It was set aside in the late 19th Century as the second component of what eventually became the national forest system, aptly named the White River National Forest. The backdrop of this byway is called the Flat Tops Wilderness Area. The scenery is superlative and the wildlife viewing is incredible. The Flat Tops Wilderness Area is the northwestern most section of the 2 million acre White River National Forest and eastern Routt National Forest. This area is now protected by the Wilderness Act of 1964.

It states:

> "In order to assure that an increasing population, accompanied by expanding settlement and growing mechanization, does not occupy and modify all areas within the United States... leaving no lands designated for preservation and protection in their natural condition, it is hereby declared to be the policy of the Congress to secure for the American people of present and future generations the benefits of an enduring resource of wilderness."

The act defines wilderness in this way:

> "Wilderness is hereby recognized as an area where the earth and its community of life are untrammeled by man, where man himself is a visitor who does not remain."

The White River National Forest was made famous by President Theodore Roosevelt. He spent many a hunting trip in Colorado's Flat Top region. Deep Lake Campground, which is in the southeastern part of the Flat Tops, has a particularly interesting claim. It was here that Teddy Roosevelt often made camp while hunting elk. The campground still exists, but it is in a very remote, hard to get to, spot.

The drive time for this byway could easily exceed two hours because of the "backcountry roads". The byway is a mixture of two-lane paved roads and improved gravel that weave through the most pristine countryside in Colorado.

Starting in the town of Yampa on Highway 131, take 17 Road north out of town about 5 miles and turn left on FR 16. Follow FR 16 about 25 to 30 miles along this switchback mountainous road to the intersection with FR 8, also known as Flat Top Road. Turn right and stay on this road following the North Fork of the White River to the town of Meeker.

Unlike the descriptions I have done for the other scenic byways in this book, I am going to leave it to the reader to be the spectator on this tour. For one reason, my words would not give this unspoiled wilderness justice. I do not want to hype it up or play it down; you need to see it for yourself. It is just too hard to describe this remote wonderland and I don't want to give you any preconceived ideas of what you might witness. However, I will describe a few points of interest that are definitely worth checking out.

## Contact:

**USFS-Yampa Ranger District**
P.O. Box 7
300 Roselawn, Yampa, CO 80483
970-638-4516

*This homestead has seen better days.*

## STAGECOACH STATE PARK

Before we start the byway, a point of interest needs to be mentioned. Stagecoach State Park is not directly on the byway route, but it is an important recreational area in this neck of the woods. The way in to the park is 8 miles north of Yampa on Highway 131 at 14 Road. Follow 14 Road for 4 miles to the park entrance and reservoir. Stagecoach Reservoir is the main attraction to the park and the fishing is world class. A state record northern pike that weighed over 30 pounds was caught here in 2006. The cold waters also hold rainbow, brook, German brown and cutthroat trout. Stagecoach State Park encourages the practice of selective harvest. This is simply the act of keeping some average-sized fish to eat while returning the larger and smaller fish to the lake to continue to grow. We must return some of the fish to the lake to help maintain a good mix of size classes. It is literally impossible for any lake to withstand modern fishing methods and still produce trophy-quality fishing without some individual intervention. Selective harvest is not catching and releasing all fish; just some.

The tailwater below the Stagecoach Dam is designated as catch and release only and surely fits in the top ten fisheries in the state. This area is touted by many experts

*Dave Hilton lands a trout on the Yampa River. Nice Job, Dave.*

as "Colorado's best rainbow trout fishery" and has received several accolades from *Fly Fisherman* magazine. It also has a good population of brown trout with a few brook trout and cutthroats mixed in. Mountain whitefish can also be found a little farther down from the dam.

There is a good mix of foot trails in Stagecoach State Park. Lakeview Trail and Overlook Trail are both easy-to-moderate trails on the north side of the reservoir. They are both about a mile in length. Mountain biking is also allowed. Elk Run Trail is a 5-miler that traverses the entire southern shore of the reservoir. It cuts in and out of coves, making it ideal for mountain biking, running, hiking, and equestrian uses. Enjoy the cliffs of Blacktail Mountain and the outstanding views of Stagecoach Reservoir. This side of the park also borders the Blacktail Mountain Wildlife Area. It is an important elk calving ground in the late winter and early spring.

The Wetlands Trail is my favorite. It is an easy gravel pathway west of the reservoir following the Yampa River. The trail is constructed on top of the wetlands via a system of boardwalks; it boasts two waterfowl viewing blinds and access to two fishing areas. The riparian wetlands provide wildlife with rich food and habitat resources, providing the park with its highest concentration of wildlife.

Stagecoach State Park offers excellent opportunities for bird watching. I was amazed at the number of birds finding refuge here. Birds frequenting the park and the wetlands include Eurasian coots, white-faced ibis, American white pelicans, great blue herons, belted kingfishers, wigeon, and western grebes. Blue grouse, sharp-tailed grouse, and a wide variety of songbirds can be found in the adjacent brushland habitat. Watch for the common raven, mountain bluebird, Cordilleran flycatcher, and tree swallow. I am sure you will see hawks and prairie falcons sitting on the utility poles and fancy lodgepole entrances to local homes and ranches.

Water sports like boating, jet skiing, sail boarding, water skiing, and swimming are allowed. Winter activities are also available.

There are four campgrounds totaling 92 sites. Junction City Campground has two loops with electricity at each of the 27 sites. Pinnacle Campground is located next to the marina and has electricity available at each of the 38 sites. Harding Spur Campground borders the reservoir and has 17 sites. There is no electricity, but it does have flush toilets. McKindley Campground overlooks the park with 10 sites and vault toilets only.

## Contact

**Stagecoach State Park**
 P O Box 98
 25500 Routt County Road 14 , Oak Creek, CO  80467
 Office Hours: 8:00am-4:30pm seven days a week or as staffing permits.
 Park Hours: 6:00am-10:00pm
 970-736-2436

## Trappers Lake

Located at the end of FR 205, Trappers Lake is best known for the Colorado River cutthroat trout fishing. It has the largest population of this native species in the state, if not the world. From the intersection of FR 16 and FR 8 on the scenic byway, head southeast on FR 205 about 6 miles to the lake.

At 320 acres, Trappers Lake is the third largest natural lake in Colorado. Belly boating and canoeing are popular means for fishing and these eager cutthroats will willingly come to the surface for a dry fly. There are a number of hiking trails in the area leading to small higher elevation lakes, small stream fishing, and a number of small campgrounds. Campgrounds are along FR 205 and at the lake itself.

Some of the largest elk herds in the state are located here and in the surrounding areas; so sightings of this majestic animal are common, especially in the early morning and just as the sun is going down. Mule deer are also abundant. Snowshoe hares, porcupines, and grey squirrels also frequent the area.

Mallards with ducklings can be seen throughout the summer and grey jays, mountain bluebirds, and mountain chickadees are common.

*American wigeon*

## Contact

**Trappers Lake Lodge & Resort**
7700 Trappers Lake Road, Meeker, CO 81641
970-878-3336

**Marvine Ranch (Guest Ranch)**
4378 County Road 12, Meeker, CO 81641
970-878-3595

The upper White River all the way down to Buford is one of my favorite stretches of water to fly fish in the state. I don't get over there as often as I would like because of the distance and drive time, but I thoroughly enjoy myself every time I do. The aspen groves along this stretch of the byway are phenomenal and there is no better time than September to come and observe the changing of the seasons. The South Fork of the White River at Buford is also very good. You do need to follow the South Fork along FR 10 about 10 miles to the campground to get access. It is all private ranchland from Buford to the campground. It is small stream fishing at its finest. Lake Avery is just outside of Buford in the Oak Ridge State Wildlife Area. The 8,000-acre wildlife area is just over 6,000 feet in elevation and boasts an enormity of recreational possibilities. Lake Avery can be very good fishing for rainbow trout, and a chance to tangle up with a brook or cutthroat trout. Wildlife viewing for waterfowl, deer, elk, black bear, blue grouse, cottontail rabbit, dove, and band-tailed pigeon is a popular pastime. Excellent hunting for big game in the late fall is available.

**Adams Lodge Outfitters**
200 County Road 43, Meeker, CO 81641
970-878-4312

**Cherry Ranch Outfitters**
PO Box 1107, 2053 County Road 15, Meeker, CO 81641
970-878-4544

**River Camp**
38723 Highway 13, PO Box 540, Meeker, CO 81641
970-878-5677

**The Historic Brickhouse Bed & Gourmet Breakfast**
687 Garfield Street, PO Box 717, Meeker, CO 81641
970-878-5055

# Wildlife Refuges
## Arapaho National Wildlife Refuge

**24,804 acres; 4 miles south of Walden**

### History

It seems that I have started many sections of this book with "before the white man, Native Americans roamed this area". How was it that the Native Americans knew about all these "great places" in Colorado? Native Americans traveled through, lived in, or scouted their sphere of influence for one reason and one reason only: to fill their grocery bags. In other words, there needed to be wildlife and plenty of it. The nomadic Ute Indians were no different and more than likely were the first visitors to the area. They referred to North Park as Cow Lodge and Bull Pen, maybe for their summer hunting expeditions for bison. They would only take up residence in the valley long enough to fill their stores and move back down to lower elevations before the long, snowy, and exceptionally frigid winters would take over the landscape.

North Park itself is an ancient intermountain glacial basin. The basin is approximately 35 miles wide and 45 miles long. It is the northernmost of four such "parks" in Colorado from which it gets its name "North Park". North Park opens north into Wyoming and is rimmed on the west by the Park Range, on the south by the Rabbit Ears Mountains, on the southeast by the Never-Summer Range, and on the east and northeast by the Medicine Bow Range. Numerous slow, meandering streams like Grizzly Creek and Roaring Fork are interspersed on the basin floor and eventually come together to form the headwaters of the North Platte River. The Illinois River runs into the Michigan River and then along with the North Fork and the Canadian River pours into the North Platte River forming a very substantial waterway by the time it enters Wyoming to the north.

The first record of eastern explorers belongs to Jacques Bijeau in the year 1820. Like many of his French countrymen Bijeau was lured by the promise of profit in trapping beaver. In 1844, Lieutenant John F. Fremont traversed the park from Northgate to Willow Creek Pass and recorded the following in his journal:

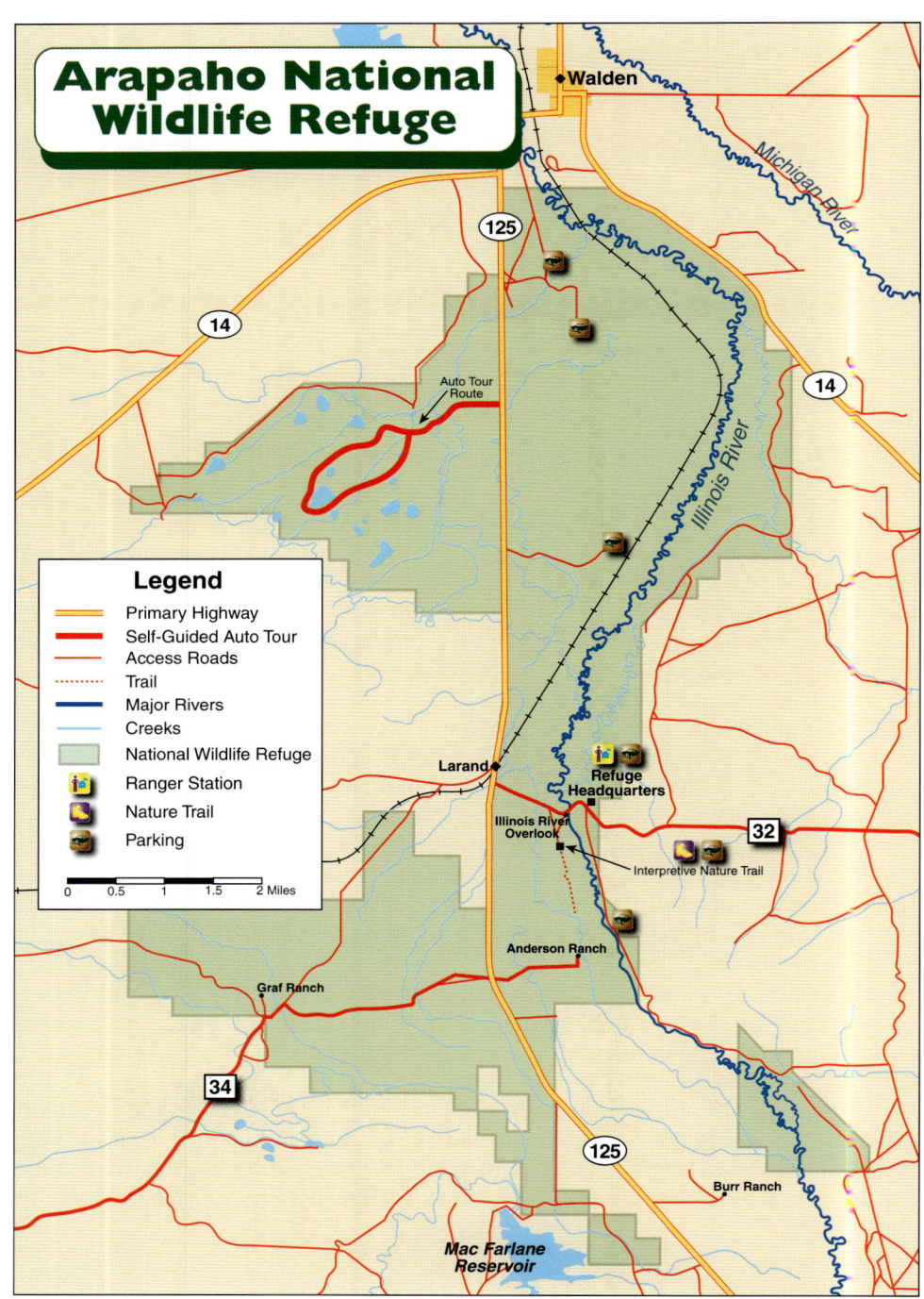

> "The valley narrowed as we ascended and presently divided into a gorge, through which the river passed as through a gate – a beautiful circular valley of 30 miles in diameter, walled in all around with snowy mountains, rich with water and grass, fringed with pine on the mountain sides below the snow, and a paradise to all grazing animals."

Then along came the miners. James O. Pinkham came to make the most of the mineral riches, which was not much. The first residents to brave the cold were Jacob Fordyce and his family. They stayed the winter of 1878, two years after Colorado became a state and a full 50 years after the first explorers entered the valley. That is a testament to just how harsh the winters can be.

Today, the flood plain along the streams of North Park is utilized to irrigate the meadows for raising hay and alfalfa. In turn, cattle ranching has become the greatest source of local income in the Walden area. The higher ground adjacent to the flood plain can be characterized as sagebrush grasslands and is ideal for grazing cattle.

## Wildlife

The Arapaho National Wildlife Refuge's 24,804 acres support an array of wildlife habitats, including sagebrush-grassland uplands, grassland meadows, willow riparian areas, and wetlands. The refuge was established in 1967 to furnish waterfowl with a suitable place to nest and rear their young. Primary nesting species include the mallard, pintail, gadwall, and American wigeon. Several diving ducks, including the lesser scaup and redhead, nest on the larger ponds and adjacent wet meadows. All in all about 200 species occur here with 82 species breeding regularly. Most species may be observed during the entire summer season.

The story of lost habitat applies to the Arapaho NWR, this time to the wildlife's benefit. The rolling prairies to the northeast in the Dakotas and Minnesota, where thousands of waterfowl-producing wetlands have been and continue to be destroyed by man's need for growth needed to be replaced. Arapaho NWR was created to offset, in part, losses of nesting habitat in the wet and region of the Midwest due to farming operations, road construction, and housing developments. To assure availability of water in such a dry climate, water is diverted from the Illinois River and directed through a complex system of ditches to irrigate meadows and fill waterfowl brood ponds.

Periodic burning, irrigation, and various grazing systems are management tools used on the refuge meadows to maintain vegetative vigor for nesting purposes. Manipulation of water levels in the shallow ponds assures adequate aquatic vegetation for food and escape cover. The ponds also produce many insects and other invertebrates (protein) needed by most female waterfowl for successful egg laying. These insects also serve as an essential food item for the growth of ducklings and goslings during the summer months.

The first waterfowl arrive at Arapaho NWR when the ice vanishes in late March to mid-April. Peak migration occurs in late May when 5,000 or more ducks can be present. Canada geese, once scarce in the North Park area, have been reestablished and begin nesting on the refuge during April. Ducks will start nesting in early June and reach their peak by the end of the month. The refuge produces an estimated 8,000 to 9,000 ducklings and 300 to 400 goslings each year.

*A rare purple felwort*

This provides a great opportunity for refuge visitors to view and photograph the waterfowl in the area. Possible species of waterfowl and birds in the refuge at this time could be Wilson's phalarope, American avocet, willet, sandpipers, yellowlegs, and dowitchers. Other species of wildlife include sage grouse, golden eagles, and northern harrier hawks.

Visitors may be lucky enough to see sage grouse in the refuge. The upland hills harbor sage grouse year round with a winter population of more than 200 birds. They can be spotted on occasion from any of the roads in North Park, but the absolute best time to see them is during the spring mating ritual. The birds assemble on "leks" (seasonal breeding grounds) to find mates. The male birds display and "boom" (a call the birds make) to attract a female. This is an amazing way to spend a couple hours watching the sun come up and listening to the "Cock of the Plains". Expect to be up well before the sun and bring coveralls, winter jacket, gloves, and ear warmers, but watching these birds go through their mating ritual is one of the greatest wildlife experiences you will ever see. A thermos of your favorite hot beverage will also be in order. There is a public viewing area at Delaney Buttes Lakes west of Walden. Another great way to sit on a lek and watch the ritual of the largest grouse species in North America is through the North Park Chamber of Commerce. You can find out more information and dates the viewings are held by contacting:

**North Park Chamber of Commerce**
416 4th Street
P.O. Box 68, Walden, CO 80480
970-723-4600

Fall migration reaches its height in late September or early October when 8,000 to 10,000 waterfowl may be on the refuge. Refuge wetlands also attract numerous marsh, shore, and water birds. Sora and Virginia rails are numerous, but these shy, secretive birds are seldom seen. When they are present, Wilson's phalarope, American avocet, willet, sandpipers, yellowlegs, and dowitchers will be easy to observe. Less common species that might be seen include the great blue heron, black-crowned night heron, American bittern, and eared grebe and pied-billed grebe. The American bittern are pretty tough to spot and get close to, as they like to sneak into the tall cattails and wait for the coast to clear. I did spot one from a distance and was able to put a sneak on it and produced a few good images. This was the first one (in about six tries) I was able to put the long lens on and actually get to press the shutter.

The real treats at the refuge are the two auto tours. They offer you such great access to refuge and present exceptional opportunities for viewing and photography. Additionally, the road tours let you see the various habitats up close.

The tour on the west side of Highway 125 is a splendid example of the wetlands and surrounding low-lying grasslands. I would say mallards dominate in numbers; however, you should see numbers of young coots, Canada geese, white pelicans, lesser scaup, Forster's terns, black terns, and eared grebes in the marshes and yellow-headed blackbirds and Brewer's blackbirds in the cattails. My son and I must have driven around the eight-mile loop five or six times and witnessed something new each time around. The shorebirds and waterfowl were a given, but what about all the jackrabbits and prairie dogs? The next go around we had an ermine show itself on the side of the road and meadow larks were on display.

The raptors were also thick as thieves. We were coming up to one of the cattle guards and saw a northern harrier swoop down and try to pick something up. At first glance we did see a rabbit along the road, but that wasn't its target. As we got closer, we saw something kicking up dust – there was a badger giving that hawk the business. The hawk bailed on us and when the badger saw the vehicle, he headed for cover also. Later, a pair of buck pronghorn antelope was feeding along the side of the road and presented several good photos. What a great experience!

The east road starts at the very south end of the refuge at the visitor center and headquarters. This road, a bit rougher than the road around the wetlands, follows the Illinois River riparian habitat. Follow the road from the refuge headquarters north back to Highway 14. There are a couple of low-lying ponds with pelicans and geese, but the main attraction for visitors is the thick willow cover and the possibility to see willow flycatchers, mountain bluebirds, tree swallows, and yellow warblers. I was able to capture a vesper sparrow on film (memory card), another new bird species for me to check off and another to add to my images of nearly 120 bird species. I knew it was a different sparrow, but was not sure until I got the book out. The white ring around its eye was the key to identifying this one. The sage flats along this road are particularly

*Arapahoe National Wildlife Refuge in North Park*

good for sage thrasher, Brewer's sparrows, and Savannah sparrows. Walk around a little and you could find sage grouse, as well. Early and late in the day could very well produce a coyote sighting.

This drive would be one of the best opportunities to see the prized sighting of the refuge, a Shiras moose. The soggy river bottom and the tasty willow browse attract this famous big game. Since their reintroduction to the state in 1978, the Arapaho NWR has been a key area of support for the moose. Spotting antelope and deer are also strong possibilities. As many as 400 mule deer winter here and up to 200 elk are frequently seen on the valley floor during the winter months.

Arapaho NWR is a vibrant wildlife sanctuary in the midst of one of the most beautiful locales in Colorado. It is a "great place" to view and photograph wildlife and birds or to just sit and listen to the babble of the streams and contemplate life. Aldo Leopold, a thoughtful and sensitive conservationist of a generation ago wrote:

> "When we see land as a community to which we belong, we may begin to use it with love and respect."

Public fishing is permitted on the Illinois River except in those areas posted as **"CLOSED"**. Fishing is challenging because of dense willow growth along the river banks. These willows are essential to the fish, keeping water temperatures low. Expect to catch mostly brown trout with an occasional rainbow or brook trout.

IMPORTANT: The refuge is closed to fishing from June 1 through July 31 each year to minimize disturbance to nesting waterfowl.

Portions of the refuge are open to public hunting of some game species during appropriate state seasons. Consult the refuge manager for more information concerning seasons and regulations.

Arapaho NWR is open to day use only. Fires are not allowed on refuge lands. Designated refuge roads are open to the public for wildlife viewing and hunting access. These roads are closed during the winter months due to cold temperatures and drifting snow. If you plan a trip to Arapaho during these months (December through April) it is best to call ahead to find out about road conditions and closures. The road leading to refuge headquarters is open year round.

Arapaho NWR and the visiting public owe Wild Lands Restoration Volunteers recognition and thanks. Due to their efforts, a nature trail along the Illinois River is now partially open. You may enjoy this boardwalk from the parking area over the new bridge the group installed to cross the Illinois River. More volunteer effort will continue to improve this walking trail for visitors' enjoyment.

## Activities

Check out Walden Reservoir on the western edge of Walden for water birds and migrant shorebirds. California gulls nest here.

Lake John SWA, Cowdrey Lake SWA, and Delaney Butte Lake SWA are all in North Park close to Walden. They are great fishing destinations, and boating and camping are available. The North Platte River (especially the North Gate access), Michigan River, and North Fork are excellent fly fishing prospects.

Elk, deer, moose, and antelope hunting are top notch in the surrounding areas (check state hunting regulations for dates).

Winter sports such as snowmobiling and ice fishing are also popular.

## Contact

**Refuge Manager Arapaho National Wildlife Refuge**
953 JC Road #32, Walden, CO 80480
970-723-8202
www.fws.gov/arapaho/index.html

## Fast Facts

**Getting There:** From Interstate 25 at Fort Collins, go west on Highway 14 over Cameron Pass Walden. Take Highway 125 south to the refuge. The refuge visitor center and headquarters is 8 miles south of Walden on Highway 125, turn east County Road 32 and travel 1 mile. The auto tour route is 4 miles south of Walden on Highway 125. Turn west to begin the tour. From Interstate 70, take Highway 40 north to Granby and then take Highway 125 north to Walden.

**Activities:** Bird and wildlife viewing

**Principal Mammals:** Moose, elk, mule deer, pronghorn antelope, coyote, badger, raccoon, porcupine, skunk, red fox, beaver, cottontail rabbits, squirrels, ermine, muskrat, and mink

**Mammals of Special Interest:** Moose

Principal Birdlife: Waterfowl to include many duck, geese, and teal species, herons, and any number of small non-game wetland birds

**Birds of Special Interest:** Northern pintail and sage grouse

**Habitat Overview:** Wetlands valley, upland sage/grasslands, rimmed by several mountain ranges

**Flora of Special Interest:** Sagebrush

**Best Wildlife Viewing Ops:** Early morning and late evening when they are on the move from bedding to feeding areas. Wildlife can be seen from most public roads.

**Best Birding Ops:** Winter is especially good for raptors; May and June for migrating ducks and geese, then again in October.

**Best Photo Ops:** Early mornings for best light

**Hunting Ops:** Yes

**Fishing Ops:** Yes

**Camping Ops:** Yes

**Boating Ops:** Yes

**Hiking Trails:** In the surrounding national forests

**Motor Trails:** Self-guide auto tours of the refuge

## Bird List

**GREBES**

Pied-billed grebe
Eared grebe
Western grebe

**PELICANS**

American white pelican

**CORMORANTS**

Double-crested cormorant

**BITTERNS, HERONS, AND EGRETS**

American bittern
Great blue heron
Snowy egret
Cattle egret
Green heron
Black-crowned night-heron
Yellow-crowned night-heron

**IBISES AND SPOONBILLS**

White-faced ibis

**NEW WORLD VULTURES**

Turkey vulture

**SWANS, GEESE, AND DUCKS**

Snow goose
Canada goose
Trumpeter swan
Tundra swan
Wood duck
Gadwall
American wigeon
Mallard
Blue-winged teal
Cinnamon teal
Northern shoveler
Northern pintail
Green-winged teal
Canvasback
Redhead
Ring-necked duck
Lesser scaup
Bufflehead
Common goldeneye
Hooded merganser
Common merganser
Ruddy duck

**OSPREY, KITES, HAWKS, AND EAGLES**

Osprey
Bald eagle
Northern harrier
Sharp-shinned hawk
Cooper's hawk
Northern goshawk
Swainson's hawk
Red-tailed hawk
Ferruginous hawk
Rough-legged hawk
Golden eagle

**FALCONS AND CARACARAS**

American kestrel
Merlin
Peregrine falcon
Prairie falcon

**GALLINACEOUS BIRDS**

Sage grouse

**RAILS**

Virginia rail
Sora
American coot

**CRANES**

Sandhill crane

### PLOVERS
Black-bellied plover
Killdeer

### STILTS AND AVOCETS
Black-necked stilt
American avocet

### SANDPIPERS AND PHALAROPES
Greater yellowlegs
Lesser yellowlegs
Solitary sandpiper
Willet
Spotted sandpiper
Upland sandpiper
Long-billed curlew
Marbled godwit
Western sandpiper
Least sandpiper
Baird's sandpiper
Long-billed dowitcher
Common snipe
Wilson's phalarope
Red-necked phalarope

### SKUAS, JAEGERS, GULLS, AND TERNS
Franklin's gull
Bonaparte's gull
Ring-billed gull
California gull
Forster's tern
Black tern

### PIGEONS AND DOVES
Mourning dove

### CUCKOOS AND ANIS
Yellow-billed cuckoo

### OWLS
Barn owl

### TYPICAL OWLS
Great Horned owl
Burrowing owl
Long-eared owl
Short-eared owl
Northern saw-whet owl

### NIGHTJARS
Common nighthawk

### HUMMINGBIRDS
Calliope hummingbird
Broad-tailed hummingbird
Rufous hummingbird

### KINGFISHERS
Belted kingfisher

### WOODPECKERS
Lewis' woodpecker
Yellow-bellied sapsucker
Red-naped sapsucker
Downy woodpecker
Hairy woodpecker
Northern flicker

### TYRANT FLYCATCHERS
Olive-sided flycatcher
Western wood-pewee
Willow flycatcher
Hammond's flycatcher
Dusky flycatcher
Cordilleran flycatcher
Say's phoebe
Western kingbird
Eastern kingbird

### SHRIKES
Loggerhead shrike
Northern shrike

### VIREOS
Warbling vireo

## CROWS, JAYS, AND MAGPIES

Steller's jay
Pinyon jay
Clark's nutcracker
Black-billed magpie
American crow
Common raven

## LARKS

Horned lark

## SWALLOWS

Tree swallow
Violet-green swallow
Northern rough-winged swallow
Bank swallow
Cliff swallow
Barn swallow

## TITMICE AND CHICKADEES

Black-capped chickadee
Mountain chickadee

## NUTHATCHES

Red-breasted nuthatch

## WRENS

Rock wren
House wren
Sedge wren
Marsh wren

## DIPPERS

American dipper

## KINGLETS

Ruby-crowned kinglet

## THRUSHES

Eastern bluebird
Western bluebird
Mountain bluebird
Swainson's thrush
Hermit thrush
American robin

## MIMIC THRUSHES

Gray catbird
Northern mockingbird
Sage thrasher
Brown thrasher

## STARLINGS

European starling

## WAGTAILS AND PIPITS

American (Water) pipit

## WAXWINGS

Bohemian waxwing
Cedar waxwing

## WOOD WARBLERS

Orange-crowned warbler
Nashville warbler
Virginia's warbler
Yellow warbler
Chestnut-sided warbler
Magnolia warbler
Yellow-rumped warbler
Townsend's warbler
American redstart
Northern waterthrush
MacGillivray's warbler
Common yellowthroat
Wilson's warbler

## TANAGERS

Western tanager

## SPARROWS AND TOWHEES

Green-tailed towhee
Spotted towhee
Eastern towhee
American tree sparrow
Chipping sparrow
Brewer's sparrow

Vesper sparrow
Lark sparrow
Sage sparrow
Lark bunting
Savannah sparrow
Fox sparrow
Song sparrow
Lincoln's sparrow
Harris' sparrow
White-crowned sparrow
Dark-eyed junco
McCown's longspur
Lapland longspur
Chestnut-collared longspur
Snow bunting

## GROSBEAKS AND ALLIES

Rose-breasted grosbeak
Black-headed grosbeak
Blue grosbeak
Lazuli bunting
Indigo bunting
Dickcissel

## BLACKBIRDS AND ORIOLES

Bobolink
Red-winged blackbird
Western meadowlark
Yellow-headed blackbird
Brewer's blackbird
Common grackle
Brown-headed cowbird
Bullock's oriole

## FINCHES

Gray-crowned rosy finch
Black rosy finch
Brown-capped rosy finch

*Greater sage grouse*

House finch
Pine siskin
Lesser goldfinch
American goldfinch
Evening grosbeak

**OLD WORLD SPARROWS**

House sparrow

## Mammal List

Shrews
Masked shrew
Nuttall's cottontail
White-tailed jackrabbit
Least chipmunk
Yellow-bellied marmot
Wyoming ground squirrel
Thirteen-lined ground squirrel
Golden-mantled ground squirrel
White-tailed prairie dog
Beaver
Deer mouse
Northern grasshopper mouse
Montane vole
Muskrat
House mouse
Western jumping mouse
Porcupine
Coyote
Red fox
Black bear
Raccoon
Ermine
Long-tailed weasel
Mink
River otter
Badger
Striped skunk
Bobcat
Elk
Mule deer
White-tailed deer
Moose
Pronghorn

**FISH**

Rainbow trout
Brown trout
Brook trout
Northern redbelly dace
Fathead minnow
Creek chub
Johnny darter
Long-nosed sucker
White sucker

**AMPHIBIAN & REPTILES**

Barred tiger salamander
Western toad
Wood frog
Northern leopard frog
Striped chorus frog
Wandering garter snake

# Browns Park National Wildlife Refuge

## 13,455 acres; Northwestern Colorado

## History

Browns Park National Wildlife Refuge was established in 1963 by Public Land Order 4973 under the Migratory Bird Conservation Act and the Refuge Recreation Act. The Browns Park NWR exists to provide sanctuary for migratory birds, protect natural resources, conserve endangered and threatened species, and offer fish and wildlife-dependent recreational opportunities. The remoteness of this national treasure's sheltered valley remains a place for wildlife, solitude, scenic beauty, and cultural history.

## Introduction

The Green River is the main attraction to Browns Park NWR. The natural flow and the annual flooding of the river originally created excellent waterfowl nesting, feeding, and resting marshes and backwater sloughs in the old streambed. However, that all changed when the Flaming Gorge Dam was constructed in 1962. The dam stopped the flooding, eliminating much of this waterfowl habitat. Low and behold, someone promptly noticed the situation and Browns Park NWR was established in 1963 by Public Land Order 4973.

Water is now pumped from the Green River and small tributaries and diverted to maintain nine marshland units embracing roughly 1,430 acres. Well-vegetated grasslands interspersed with cottonwoods, willows, salt cedar, greasewood, and sage cover another 5,000 acres. Alluvial bench lands and steep rocky mountain slopes cover another 6,000 acres of the refuge with elevations varying from 5,355 to 6,200 feet above sea level. The river bottom itself takes up about 1,000 acres of the refuge.

In the early days, Comanche, Shoshoni, and Ute tribal groups occupied the Browns Park area. Several other Native Americans including the Blackfeet, Sioux, Cheyenne, Arapaho, and Navaho people also visited or used the area. Fort Davy Crockett was built in 1837 on what is now refuge property. It was primarily set up as a trading post but also protected settlers and trappers from the aggressive Blackfoot Indians. The fort was abandoned in the 1840s as trapping declined, and white residents left.

Browns Park became a major hideout for horse thieves and cattle rustlers along the Outlaw Trail. Not as famous as the "Hole-in-the-Wall" north in Wyoming and "Robbers Roost" just west in Utah, Browns Park was none the less an important area for villains to hole up. Law officers were often frustrated as their quarry could easily cross state lines from Browns Park and be out of their jurisdiction. In fact, Butch Cassidy was often seen in the Browns Park area.

By the 1860s, Browns Park was used as wintering range by cattlemen. By 1873, settlement of the Browns Park area began. Today, evidence of the early settlers and Native Americans can be found throughout the refuge. Three historical sites at the south end of the refuge are the Two Bar Ranch headquarters, Fort Davy Crockett, and Lodore Hall, which still serves as a community center. Several old abandoned cabins and homesteads give testament to the rich history of the area.

## Wildlife

I had a wonderful time exploring Browns Park NWR; however, my enjoyment really started the night before while traveling to the refuge. This was my last major trip of the year doing research for this book. It was a late September whirlwind tour of the northwest part of the state to include Browns Park NWR, Dinosaur National Monument, Carpenter Ranch, fall color photography, and a couple days of fishing the Yampa River with a friend from Utah. Trying to cover as many places as possible during the day required me to do much of my traveling at night. So, on the way to the refuge from Maybell, let's say about 9:00pm, a cow elk crossed the road in front of me (surely just sent there to make certain I was still awake). Then it dawned on me that September plus elk equal bugling bulls. I immediately pulled over to the side of the road and rolled my window down and shut off the truck. The night was especially dark without a moon and the elk did not disappoint. A bull, surely within a couple hundred yards, crooned me (I know he had other things on his mind and could care less about me) with the wildest of all outdoor sounds. He bugled for about 35 minutes and I stayed for the whole composition. Another 10 miles down the road and one more elk, this time a large six-point bull, crossed in front of me. I stopped again and waited for the "wapiti melody", which did not transpire this time. This was my first day of travel and it was off to a great start.

This being my first time to the refuge and road signs not producing the best information left me at a bit of a loss. I found a turn into the refuge and knew immediately I wasn't going to find the campgrounds. I turned onto a double rutted path, found a wide spot, and pulled over for the night. I reclined my seat and slept like a rock. I woke up at first light, readied my camera, and set out to find a good early-morning image.

Wildlife abounds at the Browns Park NWR. The diversity of the landscape and the remote location has much to do with the amount of wildlife. The thick riparian habitat along the Green River, the seven wetland areas, the abundant grasslands, and the uplands habitat provide needed food, cover, and breeding locales for a wide variety of wildlife and birds. Current management methods, along with the excellent

# NORTHWESTERN: BROWNS PARK NWR — 339

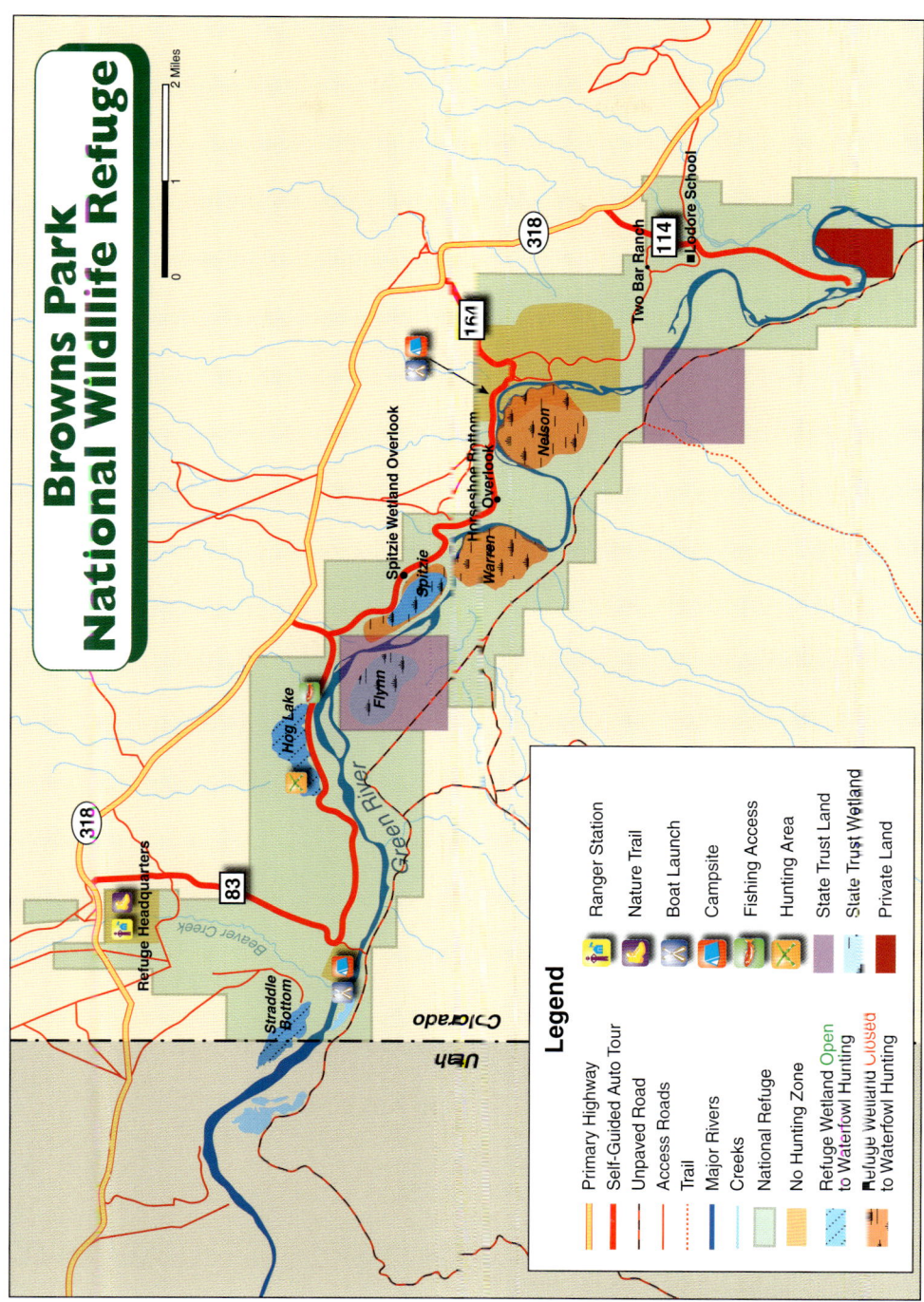

refuge habitats, have helped support no less than 68 mammal species, 15 species of reptiles and amphibians, and at least 223 species of birds. Historically, waterfowl were given management precedence with the redevelopment of the wetlands, but today's team is focused on the big picture. Emphasis is still on migratory birds, but the reserve maintains a variety of native habitats with special interests leaning towards threatened and endangered species, and species of special concern.

Access to view the entire habitat in Browns Park NWR is by the 8-mile River's Edge Wildlife Drive, which is an improved dirt road, easily accessible by car. Much of the riparian habitat along the Green River and at Browns Park NWR is made up of cottonwoods, buffalo berry, and willows. Likewise, many species of wildlife depend on riparian plants to fulfill their life needs. Big game such as the Shiras moose and the delightful river otter raise their young in the riparian area. Beaver, mink, and muskrat construct their living quarters here. Coyotes and raccoons use the area as their lunchbox. Although I was not able to get a usable image of the lively Lazuli bunting, I did see several of these birds for the first time. I was very disappointed to come away without a photo of this gorgeous little bird. Come to find out, thousands of the Lazuli buntings migrate through here every year. More songbirds like the Wilson's warbler, yellow warbler, MacGillivray's warbler, and spotted towhee rely on riparian habitat for refueling when traveling farther north to their breeding grounds. Other songbirds such as the black-chinned hummingbird, western tanager, and Bullock's oriole stop

*A very nice mule deer buck (what's that you say?)*

*Muskrat*

to nest. This is also very important habitat for the great blue heron. The cottonwoods are used by the great-horned owl for nests. Bald eagles, Swainson's hawks, red-tailed hawks, and rough-legged hawks are dependent on the water here for their survival.

Water development has definitely changed the riparian habitat over time. The biggest change was right after the Flaming Gorge Dam was finished in 1962. Water used to fill the dam reduced the flows downstream, and natural spring flooding as we know it is history. Natural marshlands bordering the river filled with spring flooding and became the primary source of water, not only for waterfowl, but the plant life itself. Over time, all of these changes to the natural scheme of things resulted in the gradual deepening of the river channel; also reducing the likelihood of flooding, making it difficult for cottonwood and willow roots to reach water. Now the germination of new seedlings is inhibited. Field research has confirmed that cottonwood forests are aging and not being replaced. Instead, nonnative species such as perennial pepper weed and the water guzzling tamarisk are overtaking this habitat. Research is ongoing to help determine how to increase the production of new cottonwoods and willows in the riparian areas.

Beaver Creek, although affected by water use upstream, still remains a prime example of an undisturbed riparian habitat in this beautiful high desert region. This tributary is located at the north end of the refuge and can be accessed from the Swinging Bridge Campground.

The seven wetlands at Browns Park NWR provide essential foraging and resting grounds for migratory waterfowl during their spring and fall migrations. Species dependent upon the wetlands include the American bittern, pied-billed grebe, and white-faced ibis. The refuge and the adjacent State of Utah's waterfowl management area contain the only significant wetland habitat for miles around, so migrating birds are attracted to these marshlands. As mentioned, the refuge management siphons water from the Green River and diverts water from Beaver Creek and Vermillion Creek, onto the seven wetland units. Expect to see mallards, American wigeon, blue-winged teal, redhead duck, ring-necked duck, and common merganser. Flocks of snow geese move through the area during the fall.

The grassland areas of the refuge are covered with plants such as the alkali sacaton, inland saltgrass, western wheatgrass, and Great Basin wild rye. The refuge grasslands are primarily found in the low-lying areas along Beaver Creek and the Green River. This habitat provides nesting cover for some species of waterfowl and songbirds such as the savannah sparrow. The northern harrier is especially at home here. The combination of grasslands and wetlands provide nesting and abundant food sources such as mice and frogs. The grasslands also provide cover for small mammals like the montane vole, and crucial winter range for elk and deer. From time to time, the refuge management must use controlled burns to eliminate the matted vegetation that becomes so heavy the nesting habitat is lost. More birds that can be found living in the grasslands include the horned lark, bank swallow, marsh wren, western bluebird, lark bunting, and western meadowlark.

The upland habitat in Browns Park NWR should be considered semi-desert dominated by tall shrubbery. More than half of the refuge is covered by big sagebrush, greasewood, Indian ricegrass, and the non-native, invasive cheatgrass.

This mix of plant species are relied upon for breeding by sage grouse, Brewer's sparrow, loggerhead shrike, Ord's kangaroo rat, and sagebrush vole. The shrubland also provides excellent winter browse for mule deer and a few pronghorn antelope. After a quick round trip tour of the refuge to get my bearings, I returned to the point where I had slept for the night. It was actually near Hog Lake which is one of the wetlands. However, less than 200 yards in either direction, the tall sagebrush took over the landscape. My first morning produced several very nice images of three mule deer bucks. I could just see the tops of their backs as they moseyed along in the thick sage. They stopped and watched me as I attached my long lens to my window clamp.

There is also a good mix of pinyon-juniper trees along the southern boundary of the refuge. Many varieties of wildlife depend on this dry environment away from the river including the gray flycatcher, black-throated gray warbler, pinyon jay, and several species of bat. This is also prime country for the western rattlesnake.

## Refuge Regulations

Special regulations are necessary to protect wildlife and habitat. Please familiarize yourself with the refuge regulations and respect the rights of other visitors. Your understanding of regulations will make your visit a safe and enjoyable one.

**Hours:** The refuge is open daily from sunrise to sunset. After sunset, public activity is limited to the Swinging Bridge and Crook Campgrounds. The office and visitor center are open from 7:30am to 4:00pm Monday through Friday, and are closed for federal holidays.

**Access:** To protect wildlife from disturbance and minimize habitat damage, vehicles and bicycles must stay on developed roads. The speed limit on all refuge roads is 25mph unless posted otherwise. Horseback riding is permitted only on developed roads. Use of certified weed-free hay is required to minimize further introduction of invasive plants. Horses are not permitted in campgrounds.

**Parking:** Vehicles must park in pullouts or within 10 feet of the road. Overnight parking is not permitted unless camping in the designated campgrounds.

**Firearms, Explosives, and Other Weapons:** Carrying, possessing, or discharging firearms, including archery equipment, on the refuge is prohibited except when using legal firearms during hunting seasons, as prescribed and approved by the state of Colorado. Firearms must be unloaded (no ammunition in either the chamber or the magazine) and cased when transported in a vehicle. Carrying, possessing, or discharging explosives, including fireworks, is strictly prohibited. Target shooting is also prohibited.

**Animal and Plant Life:** Collecting, possessing, or destroying any plant or animal or part thereof (alive or dead) is prohibited (except legally taken game). Plants and animals, or their parts, may not be introduced or placed on the refuge.

**Historical Artifacts and Other Valued Objects:** Searching for, removing, or damaging historic items, Native American artifacts, or fossils is prohibited. No person shall search for or remove rocks, stones, or mineral specimens. Possession and use of metal detectors are prohibited.

**Pets:** Pets are permitted only if they are confined or leashed (except hunting dogs when participating in a legal hunt).

**Disposal of Waste:** Dumping of litter, sewage, liquid wastes, or any other material on the refuge is prohibited.

## Contact

**Browns Park NWR**
1318 Hwy 318
Maybell, CO  81640
970-365-3613
The refuge is open daily from sunrise to sunset. After sunset, public activity is limited to the Swinging Bridge and Crook Campgrounds. The office and visitor center are open from 7:30am to 4:00pm, Monday through Friday, and are closed for Federal holidays.

## Fast Facts

**Getting There:** From Highway 40 in Maybell, take Highway 318 north about 55 miles. The refuge is on the left (west) and there are two main entrances. County Road 164 is the first entrance into Browns Park National Wildlife Refuge (NWR) on the southern end. To reach the refuge office and visitor center at the north end of the refuge, turn left on County Road 83 and follow the signs.

**Activities:** Bird and wildlife viewing. Waterfowl hunting and fishing during appropriate seasons.

**Principal Mammals:** Elk, mule deer, moose, pronghorn antelope, coyote, raccoon, porcupine, skunk, badger, beaver, cottontail rabbit, river otter, ermine, muskrat, mink and number of smaller game such as, field mice and montane vole

**Mammals of Special Interest:** Moose and river otter

**Principal Birdlife:** Waterfowl to include many duck, geese, and teal species, herons, pied-billed grebes, American bittern, and white-faced ibis. Lazuli bunting and several species of warblers.

**Birds of Special Interest:** American bittern, pied-billed grebes, and Lazuli bunting

**Habitat Overview:** A combination of riparian, wetlands, marshlands, grasslands, and upland sage and cliff country

**Best Wildlife Viewing Ops:** Early morning and late evening when they are on the move from bedding to feeding areas. Wildlife can be seen from the 8-mile River's Edge Wildlife Drive.

**Best Birding Ops:** The spring and late fall waterfowl migration. Winter is especially good for raptors and owls; and summer for all songbirds.

**Best Photo Ops:** Early morning for most wildlife activity and good lighting.

**Hunting Ops:** Yes, during waterfowl season. An accessible waterfowl hunting blind and fishing pier is located near Hog Lake.

**Fishing Ops:** Yes

**Camping Ops:** Yes, camping is permitted only in designated campgrounds – Swinging Bridge Campground at the north end of the refuge and Crook Campground to the south – and is limited to 14 days. To protect the solitude of the refuge, the use of generators is prohibited. Please pack out all your trash to keep the refuge beautiful. Developed Bureau of Land Management campgrounds are available nearby at Irish Canyon, Indian Crossing, and Taylor Flats.

**Boating Ops:** The Green River can be floated

**Hiking Trails:** There are short trails and viewing areas throughout the refuge

**Motor Trails:** The 8-mile River's Edge Wildlife Drive and a four-wheel-drive-only road on the west side of the refuge across the Swinging Bridge

*Browns Park National Wildlife Refuge*

## Bird List

### LOONS
Common loon

### GREBES
Pied-billed grebe
Horned grebe
Eared grebe
Western grebe
Clark's grebe

### PELICANS
American white pelican

### CORMORANTS
Double-crested cormorant

### BITTERNS, HERONS, AND EGRETS
American bittern
Great blue heron
Snowy egret
Cattle egret
Green heron
Black-crowned night-heron

### IBISES AND SPOONBILLS
White-faced ibis

### NEW WORLD VULTURES
Turkey vulture

### SWANS, GEESE, AND DUCKS
Snow goose
Canada goose
Trumpeter swan
Tundra swan
Wood duck
Gadwall
American wigeon
Mallard
Blue-winged teal
Cinnamon teal
Northern shoveler
Northern pintail
Green-winged teal
Canvasback
Redhead
Ring-necked duck
Lesser scaup
Surf scoter
Bufflehead
Common goldeneye
Barrow's goldeneye
Hooded merganser
Common merganser
Red-breasted merganser
Ruddy duck

### OSPREY, KITES, HAWKS, AND EAGLES
Osprey
Bald eagle
Northern harrier
Sharp-shinned hawk
Cooper's hawk
Northern goshawk
Swainson's hawk
Red-tailed hawk
Ferruginous hawk
Rough-legged hawk
Golden eagle
Falcons and caracaras
American kestrel
Merlin
Peregrine falcon
Prairie falcon

### GALLINACEOUS BIRDS
Chukar (introduced)
Greater sage grouse
Rails
Virginia rail

Sora
American coot

### CRANES

Sandhill Crane

### PLOVERS

Black-bellied plover
Semipalmated plover
Killdeer
Mountain plover

### STILTS AND AVOCETS

Black-necked stilt
American avocet

### SANDPIPERS AND PHALAROPES

Greater yellowlegs
Lesser yellowlegs
Solitary sandpiper
Willet
Spotted sandpiper
Long-billed curlew
Marbled godwit
Western sandpiper
Least sandpiper
Baird's sandpiper
Wilson's phalarope
Red-necked phalarope

### SKUAS, JAEGERS, GULLS, AND TERNS

Franklin's gull
Bonaparte's gull
Ring-billed gull
California gull
Forster's tern
Black tern

### PIGEONS AND DOVES

Rock dove (introduced)
Mourning dove
Ground-dove

### CUCKOOS AND ANIS

Yellow-billed cuckoo

### BARN OWLS

Barn owl

### TYPICAL OWLS

Western screech-owl
Great horned owl
Burrowing owl
Long-eared owl
Short-eared owl
Northern saw-whet owl

### NIGHTJARS

Common nighthawk
Common poorwill

### SWIFTS

White-throated swift

### HUMMINGBIRDS

Black-chinned hummingbird
Calliope hummingbird
Broad-tailed hummingbird
Rufous hummingbird

### KINGFISHERS

Belted kingfisher

### WOODPECKERS

Lewis' woodpecker
Red-naped sapsucker
Downy woodpecker
Hairy woodpecker
Northern flicker

### TYRANT FLYCATCHERS

Olive-sided flycatcher
Western wood-pewee
Willow flycatcher
Least flycatcher
Hammond's flycatcher

Gray flycatcher
Dusky flycatcher
Cordilleran flycatcher
Say's phoebe
Ash-throated flycatcher
Western kingbird
Eastern kingbird
Shrikes
Loggerhead shrike
Northern shrike

## VIREOS

Gray vireo
Blue-headed vireo
Warbling vireo

## CROWS, JAYS, AND MAGPIES

Western scrub-Jay
Pinyon jay
Clark's nutcracker
Black-billed magpie
American crow
Common raven

## LARKS

Horned lark

## SWALLOWS

Tree swallow
Violet-green swallow
Northern rough-winged swallow
Bank swallow
Cliff swallow
Barn swallow

## TITMICE AND CHICKADEES

Black-capped chickadee
Mountain chickadee
Juniper titmouse

## BUSHTIT

Bushtit

## NUTHATCHES

Red-breasted nuthatch
White-breasted nuthatch

## CREEPERS

Brown creeper

## WRENS

Rock wren
Canyon wren
Bewick's wren
House wren
Marsh wren

## DIPPERS

American dipper

## KINGLETS

Golden-crowned kinglet
Ruby-crowned kinglet

## OLD WORLD WARBLERS

Blue-gray gnatcatcher

## THRUSHES

Western bluebird
Mountain bluebird
Townsend's solitaire
Swainson's thrush
Hermit thrush
American robin
Mimic thrush
Gray catbird
Northern mockingbird
Sage thrasher
Brown thrasher

## STARLINGS

European starling

## WAGTAILS AND PIPITS

American (Water) pipit

## WAXWINGS

Bohemian waxwing
Cedar waxwing

## WOOD WARBLERS

Orange-crowned warbler
Virginia's warbler
Yellow warbler
Yellow-rumped warbler
Black-throated gray warbler
Townsend's warbler
American redstart
Northern waterthrush
MacGillivray's warbler
Common yellowthroat
Wilson's warbler
Yellow-breasted chat

## TANAGERS

Scarlet tanager
Western tanager

## SPARROWS AND TOWHEES

Green-tailed towhee
Spotted towhee
American tree sparrow
Chipping sparrow
Brewer's sparrow
Vesper sparrow
Lark sparrow
Black-throated sparrow
Sage sparrow
Lark bunting
Savannah sparrow

Song sparrow
Lincoln's sparrow
White-throated sparrow
Harris' sparrow
White-crowned sparrow
Dark-eyed junco
Lapland longspur

## CARDINALS, GROSBEAKS, AND ALLIES

Black-headed grosbeak
Blue grosbeak
Lazuli bunting

## BLACKBIRDS AND ORIOLES

Red-winged blackbird
Western meadowlark
Yellow-headed blackbird
Brewer's blackbird
Common grackle
Brown-headed cowbird
Bullock's oriole
Baltimore oriole
Scott's oriole
Finches
Brown-capped rosy finch
Cassin's finch
House finch
Red crossbill
Common redpoll
Pine siskin
Lesser goldfinch
American goldfinch
Evening grosbeak

# Mammals List

Merriam's shrew
Montane shrew
California myotis
Western small-footed myotis
Long-eared myotis
Little brown myotis

Fringed myotis
Long-legged myotis
Yuma myotis
Hoary bat
Silver-haired bat
Western pipistrelle

Big brown bat
Spotted bat
Townsend's big-eared bat
Pallid bat
Desert cottontail
Mountain cottontail
Black-tailed jackrabbit
White-tailed jackrabbit
Cliff chipmunk
Least chipmunk
Hopi chipmunk
Yellow-bellied marmot
Wyoming ground squirrel
Golden-mantled ground squirrel
Thirteen-lined ground squirrel
White-tailed prairie dog
Northern pocket gopher
Olive-backed pocket mouse
Great basin pocket mouse
Ord's kangaroo rat
American beaver
Western harvest mouse
Canyon mouse
Deer mouse
Pinyon mouse
Northern grasshopper mouse
Bushy-tailed woodrat
Long-tailed vole
Montane vole
Sagebrush vole
Common muskrat
Common porcupine
Coyote
Red fox
Gray fox
Black bear
Ringtail
Raccoon
Long-tailed weasel
Mink
American badger
Western spotted skunk
Striped skunk
Northern river otter
Mountain lion
Bobcat
American elk
Mule deer
White-tailed deer
Moose
Pronghorn
Bighorn sheep

## REPTILES

Short-horned lizard
Sagebrush lizard
Eastern fence lizard
Tree lizard
Side-blotched lizard
Western whiptail
Racer
Striped whipsnake
Great Basin gopher snake
Western terrestrial garter snake
Western rattlesnake
Bull snake

## AMPHIBIANS

Tiger salamander
Great Basin spadefoot
Woodhouse's toad
Northern leopard frog

*A typical setting in Colorado.*

# Northeastern Great Plains

# Fox Ranch

**14,700 Acres; Located in eastern Colorado southwest of Wray**

**NOTE:** Because this is an operating cattle ranch, it is not open for public visitation. However, arrangement can be made to visit the ranch through the Nature Conservancy.

## History

As a flyfisherman of nearly 25 years, I have always known that water is big business in Colorado. It is regulated, patrolled, and distributed based on rights and availability. What I didn't realize, was just how precious it is in eastern Colorado. The only major water sources that actually make it out of state in a free flowing nature are the South Platte River to the north and the Arkansas River to the south. Most years Nebraskans and Kansans complain they do not get their fair share. Here on Fox Ranch, the smallish Arickaree River is the only surface water to be found for miles. In some wet years, it may actually reach the Kansas border. What makes this ranch so special is the water only shows up after pushing to the surface from the great aquifer of eastern Colorado, west-central Nebraska, and west-central Kansas. It may be the shortest distance for the water to travel because the lowest point in the state is just a few miles away at 3,315 feet. Without getting into the legal wrangling of water rights, it is important to know that they are there and they influence the way the United States' grain farmers and cattle ranchers do business. They also influence the way city governments run day-to-day operations. This area of eastern Colorado is coupled with the Republican Basin at the eastern edge of the great Ogallala Aquifer. These great grain-producing states rely on this groundwater, and concern from overuse is at its highest. There has been a large drawdown of the aquifer, dating back to the droughts of the 1930s. The aquifer naturally replenishes itself through rain and snow pack from the mountains, but not at the rate it is being guzzled up by huge numbers of irrigation water pivots and increased population. Community and national leaders are concerned on a number of levels. Should we consume the water resource today or conserve it for the future? Will the predicted climate changes make it more favorable for use when the weather in the region may not be as favorable as it is today? Rising grain prices put pressure on the water as farmers try to cash in on favorable profit potential, while high fuel costs diminish those profits. Nevertheless, the issues of intergenerational impartiality should be addressed now when there is less weight to decide one way or another. Let's hope they don't put it off as long as they have with our country's energy needs. Conservation measures are being used to avoid reverting back to dryland farming practices, but are they enough? The Nature Conservancy is involved in this process at Fox Ranch, not only for the benefit of the ranch, but for the preservation of the riparian habitat itself. They have gone so far as to negotiate with landowners upstream of the ranch to slant towards conservation of water to help the Arickaree River maintain its flow. I think everyone in the vicinity knows what a treasure they have in their hands and will work toward protecting it.

Wildlife: This oasis in the eastern plains of Colorado, called the Arickaree River, with its towering old cottonwoods and willow undergrowth is a gathering place for many species of birds from across the United States. Many are at the farthest extent of their ranges. Special birds found here are the Bell's vireo, ferruginous hawk, upland sandpiper, and the lark bunting (Colorado's state bird). More common birds include lark sparrows, fox sparrows, mourning doves, blackbirds, and yellow-headed blackbirds. Raptors and owls like the Swainson's hawk, red-tailed hawk, kestrel, burrowing owl, and great horned owl call the ranch home. Also watch for a turkey vulture soaring above. Throw in a nice mix of upland game birds like quail, pheasant, and wild Rio Grande turkeys and you have a diverse, abundant blend of birds. While in eastern Colorado, I would suggest trying to get a morning on a greater prairie chicken lek. A lek is a site historically used by prairie chickens for their seasonal mating ritual. The timing for this ritual is early spring, normally mid-March to mid-April.

Rare fish to the area include the orange-throated darter, plains minnow (historic presence), river shiner (historic presence), and brassy minnow, which are present in the river and adjoining water holes. Rare amphibians like the plains leopard frog and northern cricket frog are also present.

My early spring excursion was well before the trees and willows were fully leafed and before the majority of birds had migrated north. However, as I walked the river bottom, I was pleasantly surprised by the assortment of wildlife on the ranch. I really should have known better, but trying to cover as much of the ranch as I could in as short a period as I could, I blundered by spooking my first flock of turkeys. The sight of red heads and thick feathered bodies moving out of the bottom to the adjacent prairie was all I got. I slowed down, moved more deliberately, and searched with the binoculars. I was treated to five white-tailed deer bedded down well over 100 yards away. They love the heavily treed river bottoms of eastern Colorado for cover and food. Come to find out, there is a herd of elk that move through the area on occasion.

The Nature Conservancy selected the Fox Ranch as a preserve to protect because it is home to high-quality examples of native prairie and riparian plant communities. Such good habitat also supports a diverse range of animals. The 14,700-acre ranch was acquired in 1998. They choose to manage the ranch for both conservation and agricultural values. They maintain cattle grazing leases and use grazing management plans compatible with their conservation goals. The Nature Conservancy conservation plans include maintaining the many native grasses thriving here These include big bluestem Indian grass (a wet, tall prairie grass), the blue grama grass

*Yellow-headed blackbirds*

(a short prairie grass), little bluestem side-oats grama of the Great Plains, needle-and-thread mixed prairie grass, and northern sandhill prairie grass. To do this, managing invasive noxious weeds is of utmost importance. The Conservancy wants to create relationships and partnerships within the community to ensure long-term research and protection within this region. This will include educational programs on native and non-native animals and outreach activities focused on riparian habitat and the role groundwater plays on the Arickaree River.

At one point, I spotted a coyote paralleling the river bottom, out of range for the camera. He finally topped the horizon and was out of sight. I caught a glimpse of a great blue heron and three mallards just before the heron took flight – I am sure it was annoyed by my presence. While I was headed back to the truck after my first walk, I spotted what looked like a raptor nest, however it turned out to be a porcupine. I am sure it was sound asleep as it did not move or acknowledge my being there. I was able to get an image and went along my way. Right after that I came across a herd (not sure what else to call them) of turtles, must have been eight of them sunning on the bank of a slough. As soon as I tried to set up for a photo, they bolted for the deep water (don't believe it when someone tells you turtles are slow). I came across four more groups of turkeys and four more blue herons before the end of the day and was able to get a few photos; however when I got them on the computer I found the focus was not quite there on 90 percent of the shots of turkeys. A new lens, crawling around on hands and knees and a heavy shutter finger may have been the culprits. I stayed until after sunset and whitetails were getting active. I just sat and watched.

*Whitetail buck*

Don't let the thought of the desolate prairie detour you from visiting the Fox Ranch or any other place in eastern Colorado. It has a beauty of its own; you just need to look a little harder than you would at 10,000 feet going over Vail Pass. This is truly a "great place" that needs to be protected and studied. Contact TNC for an opportunity to visit the ranch.

## Location

The 14 700-acre Fox Ranch is located north of Colorado Highway 36 on County Road U. Because this is an operating cattle ranch, it is not open for public visitation. However, arrangement can be made to visit the ranch through the Nature Conservancy.

## Contact

**The Nature Conservancy**
 2424 Spruce Street, Boulder, CO  80302
 303-444-2950

**Arickaree River Platform Project**
 2424 Spruce Street, Boulder, CO  80302
 720-974-7022

## Fast Facts

**Getting There:** From Denver, take Interstate 70 east to Byers. Take Highway 36 east about 140 miles to County Road U. Turn left (north) and continue about 12 miles to the ranch on the right.
**Activities:** Bird and wildlife viewing
**Principal Mammals:** White-tailed deer, pronghorn antelope, coyote, raccoon, porcupine, skunk, red fox, beaver, cottontail rabbit, squirrels, ermine, muskrat
**Mammals of Special Interest:** White-tailed deer
**Principal Birdlife:** Waterfowl to include many duck and teal species, great blue herons. Wild turkey, quail, mourning dove, lark bunting, blackbirds
**Birds of Special Interest:** Wild turkey
**Habitat Overview:** Riparian and short-grass prairie
**Flora of Special Interest:** Prairie grasses
**Best Wildlife Viewing Ops:** Early morning and late evening when they are on the move from bedding to feeding areas. Wildlife can be seen from most public roads.
**Best Birding Ops:** Spring, summer and fall – early morning and late evening
**Best Photo Ops:** Early morning
**Hunting Ops:** None
**Fishing Ops:** None
**Camping Ops:** None
**Boating Ops:** None
**Hiking Trails:** Visible trail along the river bottom

# Greater Prairie Chicken Viewing Tours

## The town of Wray, eastern plains on Highway 34.

The Wray Museum in Wray, Colorado sponsors viewing tours of the greater prairie chicken mating ritual. Every year, starting in late March and continuing to late April they schedule two trips every weekend. See these remarkable birds at their best. Watch them do their longstanding mating ritual and hear them "boom" in an effort to find a mate.

## Viewing

There are a couple different packages to choose from. A basic tour and a special tour are available depending on which day is chosen. Only 24 seats per tour are available and reservations must be made. The basic tour starts on Friday evening with check in and an orientation program at the Wray Museum. Everyone meets Saturday morning, bright and early, for breakfast and transportation to the prairie chicken lek. The special package starts Saturday afternoon at the Wray Museum with registration and transportation to a steak dinner, orientation and entertainment. You will then be returned to your vehicles at the museum. Everyone meets Sunday morning, bright and early, for breakfast and transportation to the prairie chicken lek. Both packages include hotel, meals, and transportation to and from the lek.

    Registrations are accepted on a prepaid, first-come, first-served basis. Payment must be received to reserve a viewing seat. Prices are available for those with RVs. However, you are responsible for being at the motel on time to leave for the prairie chicken viewing.

    Departure times may vary. Most tours leave Wray between 4:00am and 5:00am. Exact departure time is announced during the orientation program. The viewing is done from a trailer, but dress for intense cold. Tours are on schedule, no matter the weather. There are no heaters or bathrooms at the lek, so be prepared – the last opportunity for a bathroom will be at the breakfast site. Approximate time in the viewing trailer is 1.5 hours. Cameras are allowed.

    For questions and additional information, contact the Wray Chamber of Commerce at 970-332-3484. Or send email to wraychambercomm@centurytel.net.

My schedule didn't work out to make the tours put on by the Wray Museum, so I scrambled around on the Division of Wildlife website and contacted one of their officers in the area. I am sure they do not do this on a regular basis, but after I explained the book project I was working on, Jack Wieland informed me that he could show me a lek they have monitored for years to help with their total count of prairie chickens. After contacting the land owner, he took me to the lek at mid-afternoon. I brought along a small hunting blind and we discussed the best place to set it up for the next morning's ritual. The lek is a barren saddle top (the grass has been beaten down) covered with droppings and beautifully mottled feathers from chicken encounters. A scattering of yucca plants sets the stage for a show of dominance that is so common in the wildlife world. We decided on the northeast corner about 25 yards off of the lek. This spot insured that the sun would be at my back the next morning and give the blind a buffer zone from the birds.

I secured a reservation with the landowner to park on his land near the chicken lek. The front windows were down just a bit as I rolled into the sleeping bag so I could listen to the night. I wasn't disappointed; the coyotes talked most of the night and the cool breeze was refreshing.

*Displaying his orange throat sack*

Before I knew it, the clock had ticked its way to 4:30am and I was up in my insulated coveralls and headed to my blind. A small flashlight in hand, camera and tripod slung over my shoulder, I was sitting on my padded 5-gallon buckle within ten minutes.

Came to find out, there is an incredibly motivating success story involving the greater prairie chicken. Records of estimated counts in 1953 indicated about 2,500 birds in Colorado. Just ten years later in 1963, only 700 prairie chickens could be counted. The decline continued to 600 birds in 1973. The greater prairie chicken was listed as an endangered species and cooperative projects with eastern Colorado landowners were taken on to improve habitat. The chickens prefer the sand-sage grasslands of northeastern Colorado's and southwestern Nebraska's sandhills. Throw in a few cornfields and you have a perfect habitat for the greater prairie chicken. Improvements were made and in 1993 the birds were considered threatened and then delisted to special concern/non-game status in 1998. As of this writing in 2008 an estimated 10,000 to 12,000 birds now reside in Colorado, which supports a limited harvest. Bravo!

The slightest morning light was peeking over the eastern horizon when the chickens started booming and drumming their wings. I may have seen or heard this on television somewhere along the line but it did not prepare me for an up close and personal view of this aged ritual. The booming is almost mournful, with what sounded like 10 to 15 male birds trying to win over a mate. It was nearly 45 minutes before I could see a thing, but I could feel the urgency. I wish I had brought a tape recorder to the blind with me because this is so hard to describe to someone. Finally, I could see a couple of birds drumming their wings, bouncing up and down a couple feet in the air. Orange throat sacs were bright as the sun came up. The camera got a workout in the two and a half hours I sat in the blind.

Coyotes were calling in the distance and one barking at close range. I did notice a couple of lucky males and a hen take flight to the west, apparently off to take care of business. The experience ended almost as fast as it started when the whole flock busted to the surrounding sandhills. I think that coyote may have gotten too close or it may have just been time to leave. I would have liked to have moved the blind to a different position a couple times. My camera was set up close to ground level and another foot or two of elevation would have eliminated some of the grass that obscured my view. I was reasonably happy with the resulting images, but totally blown away with the experience.

## Location

All tours originate in Wray. From Denver, take Interstate 76 north to Brush. Take Highway 34 east to Wray. Depending on where you start, it is at least a two-hour drive.

# Pawnee National Grasslands

193,060 acres; Northeastern Colorado, 40 miles east of Fort Collins

## Introduction

The Pawnee Grasslands are divided into two parcels totaling 193,060 acres in the remote regions of northern Colorado between Highway 14 and the Wyoming border. It is overseen by the Arapaho-Roosevelt National Forest from the U.S. Forest Service office in Fort Collins and a sub-office in Greeley. The Pawnee National Grasslands were made famous by James Michener when he wrote the novel *Centennial* (later expanded into a television miniseries) which takes place in this area. These grasslands are the westernmost reaches of the Great Plains within sight of the Rocky Mountains to the west. Besides the windmill generators, there are few houses, cars, telephone wires, or any similar offensiveness to pollute the view. Visiting the Pawnee Grasslands can be an exceptional and dramatic experience. Take time to observe the landscape and the broad variety of wildlife – especially birds. The wide expanses of grassland are very scenic, especially at dusk and dawn. With few exceptions, once off of Highway 14, the roads are primarily maintained gravel roads. Care must be taken during any type of wet weather as many of these roads become susceptible to runoff and become pretty greasy.

    I have one more warning: the weather. As you drive through the area, you will notice a hefty number of wind generators, and for good reason. The wind can be intense in these grasslands; some say, "There is nothing to get in the way except a few old broken-down barbed-wire fences!" There can be steady winds of 35 miles per hour just about any time of year and when it really gets riled up, gusts of 50 to 70 mph are not uncommon. Care should also be taken when thunderstorms and lightning are predicted. The lack of weather in July and August indicate high temperatures; close to and often breaking 100 degrees Fahrenheit. When hiking the grasslands at this time of year, make sure you have plenty of water. The grasslands are open year round and this brings in another set of concerns. Although the winter can be a wonderful time to view the Pawnee Grasslands, winter on the prairie can be dangerous. If a traveler becomes stranded in a snowstorm without proper equipment, the consequences can be dire. Back in the 1970s, I had a friend that got out of his vehicle during a blizzard

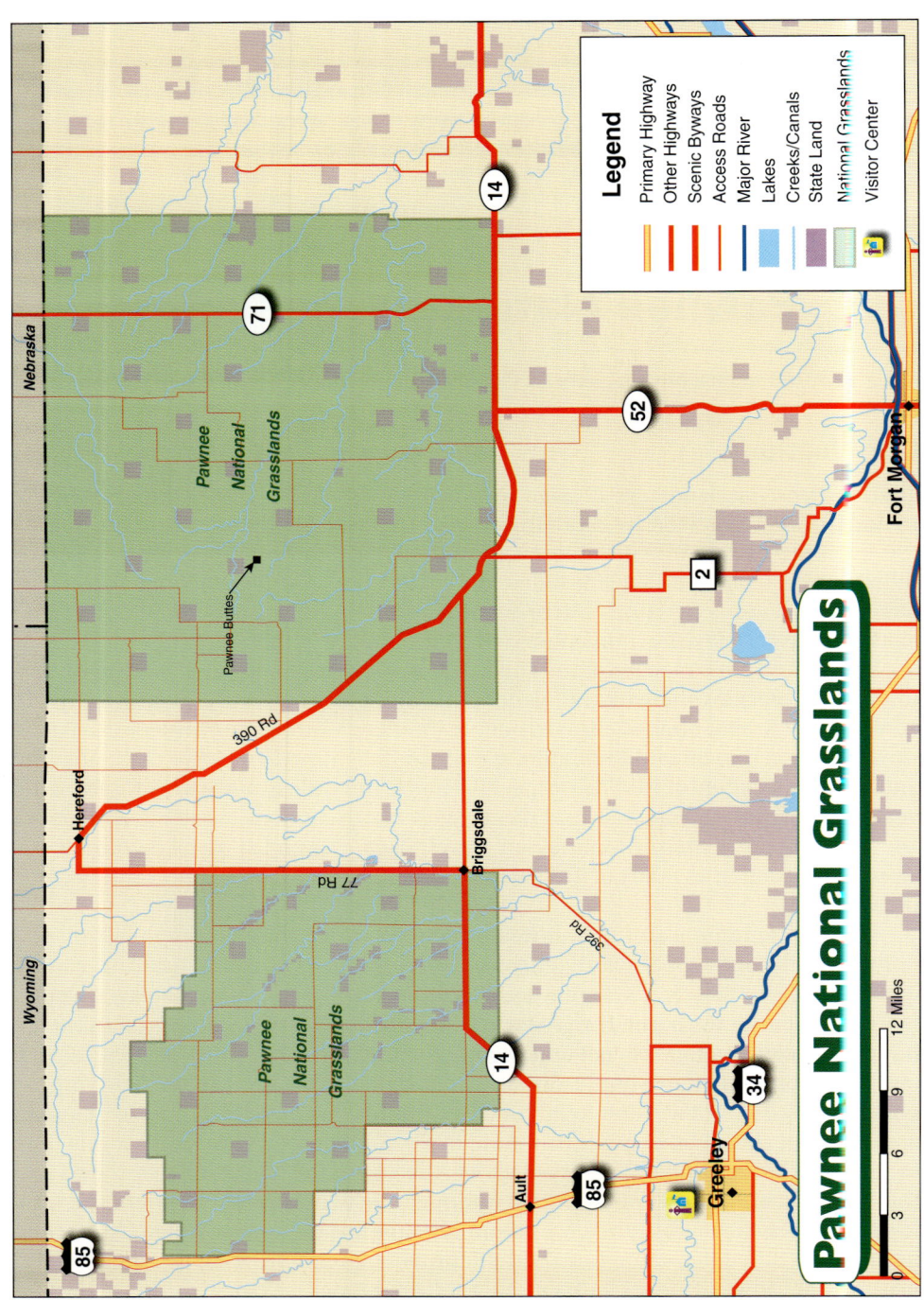

and was found expired just 100 yards from his vehicle in a snow bank. Before starting an excursion in the winter, make sure to check the weather reports. Take extra clothing, blankets, tire chains, a shovel and sand, and some non-perishable food in the event you become stuck or stranded. Tell a friend or neighbor where you are going and the time you should return home.

A great place to start viewing the Pawnee National Grasslands is at the Crow Valley Recreation Area. This is a unique facility on the open prairie, nestled within a grove of elm and cottonwood trees. There is a group camping area, a picnic area, a ball diamond, and the Steward J. Adams Education Site. The Birdwalk Trail, an easy trail starting at the campground, is a perfect prelude for birding. I would suggest a spring, early summer, or fall visit. The springtime on the grasslands is mild and is the best time for birding. Winter weather could still be an issue the first part of April, but May through mid-June is the perfect time of year to witness the beauty of the Great Plains. Wildflowers are at their peak and it is breeding season for most birds.

There are motor vehicle bird tours that leave the Crow Valley Recreation Area. The Auto Bird Tour takes birders through the west side of the Pawnee Grasslands. The passageway is around 36 miles long, includes 13 stops, and takes about four hours to complete. Most of the tour follows deeply rutted dirt roads, which slows the trip incalculably. The use of mountain bicycles on the grassland is increasing and the Auto Bird Tour route is suggested for these enthusiasts also. Using CR 96 for the return trip to the Crow Valley Recreation Area will avoid traffic on Colorado Highway 14. Information and maps are available at Crow Valley and the forest service offices.

This is the only developed facility on the grassland and is a wonderful site for bird watching, team sports and games, camping, picnicking, or just relaxing. The fee for the family campground at this writing is $10 per unit per night for a single, or $14 per unit per night for a double. Facilities include tables, fire rings, drinking water, and toilets. Parties interested in reserving the group picnic area or education site should contact the Greeley office:

**Pawnee National Grasslands**
660 O Street, Greeley, CO 80631
970-353-5004

A must-see for anyone visiting the Pawnee Grasslands are the Pawnee Buttes. The buttes are the most notable geologic feature of the grasslands and are about 45 minutes northeast of Crow Valley Recreational Area. Access is primarily by gravel road. The roads are maintained, but if the weather is wet, the roads can be difficult to pass. The road ends at a developed parking area situated on top of a bluff overlook. The parking area has ample room for several vehicles and is the trailhead for the Pawnee Buttes Trail. The Pawnee Buttes Trail is the best way to view the buttes up close. It is an easy 1.5-mile trail that takes the hiker near the bottom of the buttes. The trail immediately drops down the face of the Lips Bluff heading east towards the buttes. Once near the bottom, take a gander off to the left and view the impressive face of Lips Bluff. These bluffs are important breeding habitat for raptors.

According to the U.S. Forest Service, the site of the Pawnee Buttes was a vast sea between 70 and 90 million years ago. Eventually, as the earth's surface began to move, the sea drained, and streams crossing the area deposited sediments which hardened into sandstones and siltstones. About 5 million years ago, the entire region was uplifted thousands of feet and powerful streams caused tremendous erosion. The tops of the buttes represent the pre-erosion ground surface, approximately 300 feet above the surrounding prairie.

They are very susceptible to erosion, so climbing them is prohibited. Early morning and late evening lighting provide excellent exposures for landscape photography of this striking backdrop.

Signage at the parking area will inform visitors that the trail along the bluff is closed from March 1 to June 30 to protect nesting hawks and falcons. Please do not disturb these wonderful birds. The adults have been known to desert their eggs or young birds when threatened, especially during the important period from March through June.

Because the trail is closed during the earlier part of the year, mid-summer is the predominant time to visit. Temperatures over 100 degrees can be encountered in July and August. Use a wide-brimmed hat, sunscreen lotion, and make sure you carry plenty of water. Gloves help protect your hands when crossing fences or opening gates, and a waterproof windbreaker helps protect against the unexpected cold wind and rain. I would also suggest long pants or trousers and sturdy boots for better protection from insect bites, cactus spines, sharp-pointed yucca leaves, and sudden drops in temperature. Mosquitoes and gnats can become a real nuisance during the summer, especially when the wind dies down.

See the Pawnee Pioneer Trail Scenic Byway for access to more regions of the Grasslands.

## Wildlife

The Pawnee Grasslands are in an especially depopulated area of the Great Plains, which creates excellent prospects for wildlife and birds to live unabated. The landscape is primarily short-grass prairie with the usual contours and gullies cut by time to allow natural runoff. The eastern unit is drained by Pawnee Creek to the east and eventually runs into the South Platte River. The western unit is largely drained by Crow Creek also a tributary to the South Platte River.

Most of these creek bottoms are dry except during the spring snow melt or after a raging thunderstorm, but they do provide cover and habitat for a wide range of wildlife. American badgers, black-tailed jackrabbits, and skunks dwell in the high-sided banks; short-horned lizards, rattlesnakes, and bull snakes find refuge, while coyotes and swift fox use the rolling landscape for hunting. Pronghorn antelope dot the countryside and prairie dog towns and burrowing owls thrive in this unforgiving environment. Mule deer may be seen early and late in the day.

The Pawnee Grasslands is a very well-known birding area and is mentioned in the top ten list for Colorado by the Audubon Society. It supports many bird species, well over 200, especially during migration. It is one of the best places in the state to view the lark bunting, recognized as the Colorado state bird. They are abundant on the grassland in spring and summer. The grasslands also have many unique high plains bird species such as the mountain plover. The mountain plover is a possible threatened or endangered species and must not be disturbed when nesting. Breeding mountain plovers are relatively inconspicuous and easily overlooked, however, when you do spot them, use binoculars and telephoto lens to observe this species. After one has spotted a mountain plover and can recognize what they look like afield, the next spotting will be much easier. They are actually a fairly large bird, but their light brown color and slight markings are perfect camouflage for the open grasslands they inhabit. In breeding plumage, this species has a dark cap and a black line from the base of the bill to the eye. Research indicates human activity closer than 200 meters may disturb the birds. Disturbances from people wanting to get closer can drive an adult off the nest, and this may result in a destroyed generation due to sunlight heating the eggs. This species has fairly specific habitat requirements, preferring level areas with very short grass and scattered cactus. Intensive grazing is beneficial for mountain plovers, and they also regularly occupy prairie dog towns. Much is being done to improve plover habitat in the Pawnee Grasslands The very short grass they require to scrape out their nests can be enhanced by prescribed burns. Burns take place irregularly, but do take the prairie back to nothing but root balls to enhance habitat for the coming years flock.

*The western prairie rattler*

The grasslands is filled with a diverse specie list of birds, including mourning doves, lark sparrows, horned larks, western kingbirds, American crows, and black-billed magpies, while red-headed woodpeckers, blue jays, gray catbirds, and vesper sparrows may be seen around areas of trees and shrubs. In particular, the horned larks are everywhere and are quite fun to observe. Grasshopper sparrows, red-breasted nuthatch, McCown's larkspurs, and chestnut-collared longspurs also take to the sky here.

The Pawnee National Grassland is known internationally as a place to see birds of prey. As mentioned previously, the Lips Bluff is prime hawk, eagle, and falcon resting habitat. As the sun climbs, it draws red-tailed hawks, Swainson's hawks, and the occasional ferruginous hawk aloft to start their daily pursuit for food. Golden eagles and prairie falcons round out the big birds, while a chance to see the magnificent northern harrier gliding a few feet above the ground in search of mice is possible. In the evening, nighthawks may be seen taking to the sky, great-horned owls venture out, and the frantic wail of coyotes mark the end of the day as the sun sets behind the mountains.

## Activities

Photography is very popular and it is not unusual to see folks like me carrying a tripod and a long lens looking for that perfect image. Mountain biking is becoming very popular and the myriad back roads in the area supply miles of physical activity for these devotees.

*Blue jay*

There are several lakes in the surrounding areas to fish, mostly for warmwater species such as bass, walleye, perch, and wipers. Hunting coyotes is very popular because of the overall numbers of the varmint. Horseback riding is still admired out here in the West.

The Pawnee Buttes are considered one of the finest sites for vertebrate fossils in the world. Over 100 species have been recovered. In 1870, O.C. Marsh of Yale's Peabody Museum led the first scientific expedition to the buttes to collect fossils. Finds included several species of horse (including three-toed and dwarf versions), rhinoceros, ancient swine and camel, a hippopotamus-like animal, turtle, large vulture and cormorant. Artifacts over 50 years old are protected by law and must stay put.

## Location

From Denver, take Interstate 25 north about 60 miles to Fort Collins. Take CO Highway 14 east about 40 miles to Briggsdale. The Crow Valley Recreation Area is 0.25 mile north of Colorado Highway 14 on Weld County Road 77 (also referred to as CR 392) just west of Briggsdale.

To find the Pawnee Buttes, continue east on Highway 14 another 10 miles to CR 105. Turn north (left) on CR 105 and go 3.5 miles to the intersection with CR 390. Turn left and travel about a mile and turn right on CR 105 again. Go past the town of Keota about 3 miles to CR 104. Turn right and travel 3 miles and turn left on CR 111. Continue another 4 miles to the parking area and Pawnee Buttes Trailhead. The view of Lips Bluff and the Pawnee Buttes from here is spectacular.

## Contact

### Pawnee National Grasslands
660 O Street, Greeley, CO 80631
970-353-5004

### Arapaho and Roosevelt National Forests and Pawnee National Grasslands Visitor Center
2150 Centre Avenue
Building E, Fort Collins, CO 80526
970-295-6600
The Pawnee Grasslands are one of 20 national grasslands administered by the U.S. Forest Service and Department of Agriculture. This is public land and it is yours to use, to enjoy, and to protect.
www.fs.fed.us/r2/arnf/recreation/arpvisitorguidefinalweb.pdf

# Scenic Byways

## Pawnee Pioneer Trails Scenic Byway

The Pawnee Pioneer Trails Scenic Byway is a 128-mile byway introducing the visitor to the remote grasslands of northeastern Colorado. The three-hour drive navigates the harsh Colorado Piedmont, a wide-open expanse anchored by the towering Pawnee Buttes. From Denver, take Interstate 25 north to Fort Collins. Take Highway 14 east to the town of Ault. The byway starts here and continues east on Highway 14 about 40 miles to Briggsdale. Turn north on CR 77 and continue 15 miles to CR 120. Go east on CR 120 for 5 miles to the town of Grover. Take a right turn onto CR 390 and continue southeast to CR 112. Turn left on CR 112 and continue east about 8 miles to CR 111. At this point, you are at the parking area and trailhead for the Pawnee Buttes. From here,

take CR 111 south a short distance to CR 110 and turn left. Road conditions are a bit sub-par in this stretch of the byway. Even though a normal two-wheel-drive vehicle can make it, be extra careful. Continue east on CR 110 about 8 miles (the road takes a couple jogs, but eventually ends up back on CR 110) to CR 127. Turn right on CR 127 and head south about 12 miles to the town of Raymer. At this point, the byway is back on Highway 14. Turn left on Highway 14 and head east another 35 miles to the end of the Pawnee Pioneer Trails Byway at the town of Sterling. There is a spur to the byway at the town of Raymer that heads south 24 miles to the town of Fort Morgan

### Introduction

This byway gives the visitor a birds-eye view of the Pawnee National Grasslands. For most people, Colorado is a state that invokes an image of stunning mountain vistas, forested hills speckled with golden aspens, and streams teeming with beautiful trout. Few notice the other "colorful Colorado". The difference between the viewing experience on the prairie and the Rocky Mountains is simply a mind set. You can drive through the mountains and say "Gee, that is beautiful" to anything you see, where the prairie requires the mind to be engaged to be grateful for its beauty. Anyone can gaze at a rocky mountain goat posing on a crag and appreciate the beauty of the situation; however to engulf your senses on the bloom of a purple penstemon takes more focus and wonder as to how that plant came to be there in the first place. The beauty of the prairie requires close-focus; the groves of golden aspen don't.

One can only imagine how the short-grass prairie appeared to Native Americans centuries ago, and to the cattle ranchers and homesteaders who followed trying to scrape out a living. Settlers endured many hardships including wind, drought, and the isolation of such a remote existence. The small communities that remain are as tough and resilient as the land they occupy; hardy symbols of America's pioneering spirit. The climate here is dry with high winds being commonplace and recurring cycles of drought. The annual average rainfall is little more than a dozen inches per year.

The landscape looks much like it did 100 years ago; a few old abandoned homesteads, classic western windmills pumping cool water into oblong tanks for cattle, broken-down windmills that have seen better days, and nothing but the wide open country of the short-grass prairie. It is the natural refuge for coyotes, prairie dogs, rattlesnakes, and pronghorn antelope. Vast numbers of bird species are hidden from the untrained eye. After spending as much time as I have exploring the prairie, it has become obvious to me that a large number of species have adapted to the conditions

*An early 1900s homestead*

of this short-grass habitat. One of the more important species is the mountain plover. Practically half of the remaining breeding population is found here in Weld County and in Phillips County, Montana. With very local distribution elsewhere in its range, it relies on the undisturbed short grass of northern Colorado.

To achieve a flavor for the area, I would suggest a stop in Briggsdale to begin your tour. The Briggsdale Heritage House is in an old school house and has many photo albums as well as other written history pertaining to the area. The hours are flexible, just call to make arrangements for a visit by calling 970-656-3612.

To the north in the town of Grover is the Grover Grassland Museum. It is in the old railroad depot; call 970-895-2349 for information.

There are opportunities for the public to explore old homesteads and gain an appreciation of history. However, on national forests and grasslands, collecting artifacts, arrowheads, vertebrate fossils or barn wood is prohibited. All these things would be best studied by a trained archaeologist to gain knowledge of past inhabitants. If you take artifacts home, the knowledge is lost forever. Contact the district office if you find arrowheads or other important artifacts. The vast network of side roads and numbered county roads can take you within easy walking distance of almost all parts of the grassland.

Southeast of Grover are the stunning Pawnee Buttes. According to the U.S. Forest Service, the site of the Pawnee Buttes was a vast sea between 70 and 90 million years ago. Eventually, as the earth's surface began to move, the sea drained, and streams crossing the area deposited sediments which hardened into sandstones and siltstones. About 5 million years ago, the entire region was uplifted thousands of feet and powerful streams caused tremendous erosion. The tops of the buttes represent the pre-erosion ground surface.

(See the Pawnee National Grasslands chapter for more information.)

The remainder of the byway provides a unique opportunity for solitude and quiet to enjoy the prairie and all this open space. Turn off the radio, shut off the cell phone (there is probably no signal anyway) and take the time to enjoy a soaring hawk or a gentle breeze passing over the carpet of flowers and grasses. One of the main recreation uses is bird watching. The area is known internationally as an area to see birds of prey, and has good breeding populations of unique high plains species such as the previously mentioned mountain plover, McCowan's longspur, and the chestnut-collared longspur. A visitor may not see the wildlife at first, but this area is teeming with life. There are immense fields of yellow three-toothed ragwort. On the drier and higher ridges, massive patches of reddish winged dock (sometimes called wild begonia) can be seen breaking through the chalky, sandy soil. With the backdrop of grasses – the blue grama, side oats grama, and buffalo grass – look for white primrose or the orange flowers of the scarlet globemallow. Another unique plant of the short-grass prairie is the unusual 6-inch domes of green here and there called sandwort.

You may have the opportunity to observe the power of a thunderstorm and enjoy the freshness and earthy perfume after it passes.

The end of the byway is at the town of Sterling. It is a small college town and farming community. The Overland Trail Museum is a popular attraction and Sterling Reservoir provides 3,000 acres of aquatic recreation fed by the South Platte River. The warmwater impoundment is great for water skiing, sailing, and swimming. There are plenty of facilities for camping and if fishing is your pastime, try for the bass, bluegill, catfish, crappie, perch, tiger muskie, walleye, and wipers that inhabit the lake.

Highway 52, the spur that heads south to Fort Morgan, is a nice paved road and brings one closer to the South Platte River valley. The river valley is another great opportunity to get in a little time birding and an excellent chance to see a white-tailed deer.

## Jackson Lake State Park

Jackson Lake State Park is a dozen miles west of Fort Morgan on Highway 144. Jackson Lake, also known as the "Oasis in the Plains", is another popular boating and fishing destination. It has a significant population of carp for those of you interested in that immensely fun activity. It is rated as one of the "Top 15 Park Beaches" by Reserve America, which means that swimming and waterskiing rank right up there in importance. The park is located in the Central Flyway for migratory birds, making it an excellent birding destination. Pelicans, great blue herons, Canada geese, gulls, pipers, and several species of duck can be found here. Bald eagles, great horned owls, and the gorgeous cedar waxwing can also be seen here.

This state park has 260 campsites, including a group campground with 18 sites. There is an area set aside as a state wildlife area for hunting during the appropriate season.

Prewitt Reservoir State Wildlife Area is northeast of Fort Morgan about 25 miles on Interstate 76. Take Exit 102 and follow the signs to the area. This is an irrigation lake, so levels can fluctuate quite a bit, but it can also be a great birding and wildlife-viewing opportunity.

## Contact

**Pawnee National Grasslands**
  660 O Street, Greeley, CO  80631
  970-353-5004

**Jackson Lake State Park**
  26353 County Road 3, Orchard CO  80649
  970-645-2551

# South Platte River Trail Scenic Byway

The South Platte River Trail Scenic Byway is a short 19-mile loop at an elevation of 3,477 feet, in the northeastern corner of Colorado. From Interstate 76, take Exit 180 north on US Highway 385. To start the byway, turn left (west) on 28 Road. This road follows the tree-lined South Platte River. Turning right on 29 Road, cross the river and then you will come to the little town of Ovid. Turn right on CO Highway 138 and follow the north side of the river. Turn right on Highway 385, cross the river and the byway ends at the intersection with 28 Road. It is a 30-minute drive with interpretive signage at the original Julesburg town site and the location of Colorado's only Pony Express home station.

This short byway is on the main route that thousands of gold seekers took west during the 1859 gold rush. This highway was known as the Lincoln Highway. Later, it became the first automobile highway to go across the country.

Points of interest along the South Platte River Trail start at the Colorado Welcome Center. It boasts numerous picnic areas and displays of historical interest related to the byway. Continuing west on 28 Road, the next spot is called the Devil's Dive. It is a point on the river where horse-drawn wagons used to cross. It was a steep drop-off and posed danger to horses, wagons, and human life. Many found other passages. There are the remains of an old homestead at this site. The next point of interest along the route is the site where Julesburg No. 2 was built. It was the start of a new Julesburg, after the original town was burned during the great Indian raids of 1865. The original town was the battleground where Cheyenne, Sioux, and Arapahoe warriors attacked a United States cavalry unit to avenge those who were killed in the Sand Creek Massacre. Not much remains today except a couple of scars in the earth. A bit farther west is an opportunity to photograph an old windmill. A good source of water was imperative on the historic prairies of the Great Plains.

The next site you come to is where Fort Sedgwick was established. At its peak, nearly 1,000 soldiers were stationed here. The saga of Fort Sedgwick is of fraud and corruption, triumph and tragedy, all at a post where the accommodations were considered unlivable, the food was horrific, and the nearest bath was the South Platte River.

After crossing the river, the town of Ovid comes to view. Check out the old steam-powered locomotive displayed in the town's park. It was used at the sugar beet processing plant here. The old sugar-refining town was actually the site of a World War II prisoner-of-war camp. An Ovid native, Thad Sowder, performed with Buffalo Bill's Wild West Show. This is also the site called the Upper California Crossing. Used by the early-day pioneers, it is where Lodgepole Creek and the South Platte come together.

Julesburg #3 was the next attempt to restore a populace that had been battered and burned. The Transcontinental Railroad reached Colorado in 1867 and this site sprang up and became one of the largest towns in the state. The boom ended just a few short months later, when the Union Pacific moved its hub to Cheyenne, Wyoming. While this settlement was active, it had numbers of saloons, whore houses, and gambling halls, which led to the violence associated with these activities. This crime wave moved to Cheyenne with the railroad and the town shriveled up and died, again. Finally, the town of Julesburg came to be just to the east of the last site. Mr. Jules Beni, after whom the town was named, finally got his dream. The end of the South Platte River Trail Scenic Byway is at the present day junction of Interstate 76 and Interstate 80. After all these years, it is still located on the main thoroughfare across the United States.

Wildlife abounds along the river and surrounding prairie. Large animals including white-tailed deer and pronghorn antelope and the occasional bald eagle can be seen here. The large numbers and diversity of birdlife is northeastern Colorado's claim to fame, and many birds can be seen when traveling the byway. Mallards, wood ducks, and wigeons may nest in the area and it is not uncommon to see a great blue heron or a snowy egret. There are bird houses set up along the byway to accommodate swallows, bluebirds, and orioles. The greater prairie chicken, ring-necked pheasant, lark bunting, horned lark, and meadowlark find home and shelter in the short-grass prairie and farmland in the area. Wild turkeys also live along the river bottom.

Additional outdoor activities such as birding, fishing, and hunting can be found at the Sedgwick Bar State Wildlife Area, Julesburg State Wildlife Area, Jumbo Lake, and Red Lion State Wildlife Area.

## Contact

**The South Platte River Trail**
114 E. 1st, Julesburg, CO  80737

**Sedgwick County Economic Development**
114 East First Street, Julesburg, CO 80737
970-474-3504
www.rivertrailonline.org

**Budget Host Platte Valley Inn**
15225 U.S. Hwy 385, Julesburg, CO  80737
1-800-283-4678

*Above: Doe whitetail deer. Right: The famous South Platte River*

# Barr Lake State Park and Wildlife Refuge

2,715 Acres, 1,900 Acre Reservoir; 20 miles Northeast of Denver on Interstate 76

## History

As with most bodies of water in Colorado, the lake water is used for either city water supply or irrigation for farmland. Barr Lake is primarily used for irrigation, owned and operated by the Farmer's Reservoir & Irrigation Company. The Denver-Hudson Canal that runs along the eastern edge of the lake is owned and operated by the Henrylyn Irrigation District.

Once no more than a shallow basin in the countryside that collected water, the Barr Lake area was seasonally inundated by hundreds of thousands of American bison. Native Americans such as the Arapahoe and Cheyenne would gather here to hunt the bison along with great numbers of pronghorn antelope and deer. As settlers from the East came to the area, the landscape was changed forever. In 1876, when Colorado was granted statehood, the situation for the great herds of bison became dire. Their migration routes were bisected by railroads, fences, and homesteads. Bison were slaughtered to make way for longhorn cattle. The cattle were driven from Texas along the Goodnight-Loving Trail to the bison wallow, and then shipped via newly constructed railroads to the burgeoning East Coast population. By the early 1890s, water from the South Platte River was diverted to the wallow to form Oasis Reservoir. More farmers pounced on the new water source and the development of large communities was in the making.

The new lake and growth of cottonwood trees did catch the attention of hundreds of birds. In turn, the birds attracted hunters. In 1896, a group of well-to-do citizens of Denver formed the Oasis Hunting Club to take advantage of the new recreational opportunities.

By the early 1900s, demand for water was greater than Oasis Reservoir could supply so Farmer's Reservoir & Irrigation Company tied the neighboring Burlington Reservoir together and poured in more water from the South Platte River, creating Barr Lake. It was touted that the new, larger lake could irrigate 25,000 acres of farmland annually.

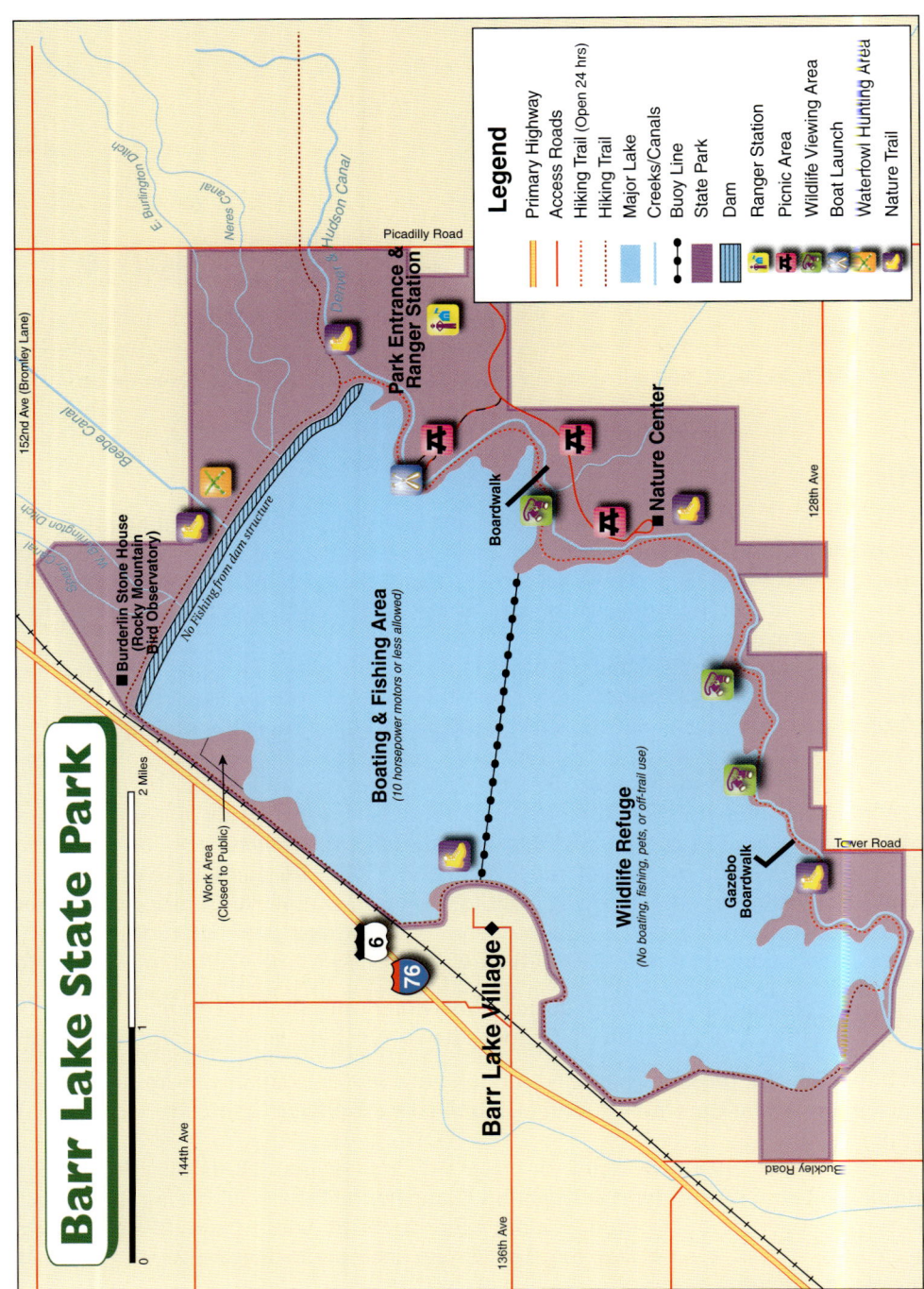

After many trials and tribulations from overuse and pollution, this unique body of water was finally established as Barr Lake State Park in 1977. It is preserved as "an island of habitat in the sea of urban development" and is known today as one of Colorado's top birding destinations. Colorado State Parks manage the recreational aspects of the park through uninterrupted easements with Farmer's Reservoir & Irrigation Company and Henrylyn Irrigation District.

## Wildlife

One of the most significant points of Barr Lake State Park is the wildlife refuge at the southern half of the lake and surrounding lands. The refuge area of the lake is off limits to boating, hunting, and fishing. Visitors must stay on trails around the lake and pets are prohibited. This sanctuary in the prairie is home to several nesting birds including the bald eagle. Deer, pheasants, squirrels, prairie dogs, and bunnies take up residence in the prairie surrounding the lake.

A pair of bald eagles has been observed in the refuge every year since 1985. The first young eagle to make it past fledging was in 1989. Since then, as many as 29 new eagles have survived their first year. The protection of the refuge and the important habitat is vital to the success of this eight-month rearing process. In late February, the eagles start their courtship rituals and egg laying follows shortly thereafter. The new quarter-pound eaglets will hatch from late March to early April and start a feeding regimen that includes prairie dogs and fish. At only two weeks old, they can weigh in at as much as 2 pounds. Eight to ten weeks later, a new set of dark brown feathers have replaced their thick woolly down and they are ready to leave the nest. Learning the arduous process of feeding themselves follows. By the time the young eagles actually fledge, they are the same size as their parents. The mottled dark brown feathers remain for as many as four to six years, when the distinctive white feathers develop on the head and tail. The eagle is now sexually mature. If you are interested in becoming an eagle watcher, contact the Colorado Bird Observatory by calling the education line at 303-637-9220.

Besides the bald eagle, there are many more raptors that call Barr Lake home. Swainson's hawks are most prevalent, along with the red-tailed hawk and northern harrier. The American kestrel is often seen hunting from the cover of the huge cottonwoods surrounding the lake and can be seen year round. Ferruginous and rough-legged hawks show up during the winter months. Uncommon migrants include the sharp-shinned hawk, Cooper's hawk, northern goshawk, and the golden eagle.

A nature center is located on the east side of Barr Lake near the northeastern corner of the wildlife refuge. Raptor displays and general information on the refuge are located inside. The folks inside are very helpful and will answer questions you might have. This is also a good parking area and starting point for trails around the lake and into the surrounding prairie.

Birds I have seen on a regular basis around the lake include many waterfowl species Mallards, American wigeon, blue-winged and cinnamon teal, northern shoveler, and redhead can be seen quite often as well as the Canada goose and great blue heron. American coot, greater yellowlegs, western sandpiper, and Baird's sandpiper are commonly seen along the shoreline and in the canals. As you are walking the trail around the lake, watch for mourning dove, northern flicker, downy woodpecker, western and eastern kingbird, black-capped chickadee, and the house wren. Several observation stations are set up along the way for viewing, and at the southwest end of the lake is a new path called Rookery View Trail. A gazebo is set up with great views of the rookery, various raptor nests, and the lake in general. Spotting deer, squirrels, bunnies, and snakes is common. Binoculars and spotting scopes are recommended for closer views of the birds and animals.

The Prairie Welcome Trail is a short loop (about a mile in length) that takes the visitor on a self-guided tour into the short-grass prairie. Again, deer, ring-necked pheasants, and coyotes roam this area frequently. All in all, Barr Lake's wildlife refuge provides a well-rounded experience and fascinating look at a unique habitat very close to a highly populated urban environment.

## Activities

The northern end of Barr Lake is open to more diverse recreation that includes boating, fishing, picnicking, and waterfowl hunting. Needless to say, viewing and photographing wildlife and birds is hugely popular, as is studying nature through interpretive programs and guided walks.

*Bullock's oriole*

The park is also the headquarters for the Rocky Mountain Bird Observatory (RMBO). The old stone house, built in the 1880s and 1890s located at the northwestern end of the park is used by the RMBO to run their conservation efforts and offer public programs. They can be contacted at 303-659-4348 or on their web site at www.rmbo.org.

A ramp on the east side of the lake allows boats with 10-horsepower motors or less. Sailboats, hand-propelled crafts, and boats with electric motors are also allowed; however no boats are allowed past the buoy markers into the south end of the lake (wildlife refuge). The Colorado Division of Wildlife continues to stock Barr Lake with catchable-sized rainbow trout, wiper, tiger muskie, walleye, smallmouth bass, and largemouth bass. Channel catfish are also common fare. Three picnic areas are available and all are supplied with tables and grills. Waterfowl hunting is permitted on the northern end of the lake during regular waterfowl seasons. However, hunting is only allowed on Wednesdays and Saturdays.

## Location

From Denver, take Interstate 76 northeast and take Exit 23 onto Bromley Lane. Go east about a mile to Piccadilly Road, turn right, and continue about 2 miles to the park entrance on the right.

From E-470, take Exit 34 onto 120th Avenue. Go east about a mile to Tower Road. Turn left onto Tower Road and follow the pavement to Piccadilly Road. Make a left (north) at Piccadilly and continue about a mile to the park entrance on the left.

## Contact

**Barr Lake State Park**

13401 Piccadilly Road
Brighton, CO 80603
http://parks.state.co.us/parks/barrlake

**Office Hours**
9:00am-4:00pm Mon-Fri / 9:00am-5:00pm Sat-Sun
**Park Hours**
5:00am-10:00pm
**Phone**
303-659-6005
303-655-1495
**Access Fees**
Daily Pass: $6
Annual Pass $60

## Bird List

Birders have been flocking to Barr Lake since the reservoir was created in the 1880s. Field records of bird sightings date back to this time. Several prominent ornithologists explored the area, seeking to document the rich variety of birdlife. Please help protect this valuable habitat!

### LOONS

Pacific loon
Common loon

### GREBES

Pied-billed grebe
Horned grebe
Red-necked grebe
Eared grebe
Western grebe
Clark's grebe

### PELICANS

American white pelican

### CORMORANTS

Double-crested cormorant
Neotropic cormorant

### WADING BIRDS

American bittern
Least bittern
Great blue heron
Great egret
Snowy egret
Little blue heron
Tri-colored heron
Cattle egret
Green heron
Black-crowned night-heron
Yellow-crowned night-heron
White-faced ibis

### WATERFOWL

Tundra swan
Trumpeter swan
Greater white-fronted goose
Snow goose
Ross' goose
Brant
Canada goose
Wood duck
Green-winged teal
American black duck
Mallard
Northern pintail
Blue-winged teal
Cinnamon teal
Northern shoveler
Gadwall
Eurasian wigeon
American wigeon
Canvasback
Redhead
Ring-necked duck
Greater scaup
Lesser scaup
Harlequin duck
Oldsquaw
Black scoter
Surf scoter
White-winged scoter
Common goldeneye
Barrow's goldeneye
Bufflehead
Hooded merganser
Common merganser
Red-breasted merganser
Ruddy duck

### RAPTORS

Turkey vulture
Osprey
Bald eagle

Northern harrier
Sharp-shinned hawk
Cooper's hawk
Northern goshawk
Red-shouldered hawk
Broad-winged hawk
Swainson's hawk
Red-tailed hawk
Ferruginous hawk
Rough-legged hawk
Golden eagle
American kestrel
Merlin
Prairie falcon
Peregrine falcon
Gyrfalcon

## GROUSE, QUAIL

Chukar partridge
Ring-necked pheasant

## RAILS & COOTS

Yellow rail
Virginia rail
Sora
American coot

## CRANES

Sandhill crane
Whooping crane

## PLOVERS

Black-bellied plover
American golden-plover
Snowy plover
Semipalmated plover
Piping plover
Killdeer
Mountain plover

## STILTS & AVOCETS

Black-necked stilt
American avocet

## SANDPIPERS

Greater yellowlegs
Lesser yellowlegs
Solitary sandpiper
Willet
Spotted sandpiper
Upland sandpiper
Whimbrel
Long-billed curlew
Hudsonian godwit
Marbled godwit
Ruddy turnstone
Red knot
Sanderling
Semipalmated sandpiper
Western sandpiper
Least sandpiper
White-rumped sandpiper
Baird's sandpiper
Pectoral sandpiper
Dunlin
Stilt sandpiper
Buff-breasted sandpiper
Ruff
Short-billed dowitcher
Long-billed dowitcher
Common snipe
Wilson's phalarope
Red-necked phalarope
Red phalarope

## JAEGERS, GULLS & TERNS

Pomarine jaeger
Parasitic jaeger
Long-tailed jaeger
Franklin's gull
Little gull
Bonaparte's gull
Ring-Billed gull
California gull
Herring gull
Thayer's gull
Glaucous gull

Black-legged kittiwake
Sabine's gull
Caspian tern
Common tern
Forster's tern
Least tern
Black tern

## PIGEONS & DOVES

Rock dove
Band-tailed pigeon
Mourning dove

## CUCKOOS

Black-billed cuckoo
Yellow-billed cuckoo

## OWLS

Barn owl
Eastern screech-owl
Great horned owl
Snowy owl
Burrowing owl
Spotted owl
Long-eared owl
Short-eared owl
Northern saw-whet owl

## NIGHTJARS

Common nighthawk
Common poorwill

## SWIFTS

Black swift
Chimney swift

## HUMMINGBIRDS

Calliope hummingbird
Broad-tailed hummingbird
Rufous hummingbird

## KINGFISHERS

Belted kingfisher

## WOODPECKERS

Lewis' woodpecker
Red-headed woodpecker
Yellow-bellied sapsucker
Red-naped sapsucker
Williamson's sapsucker
Downy woodpecker
Hairy woodpecker
Northern flicker

## FLYCATCHERS

Olive-sided flycatcher
Western wood-pewee
Alder flycatcher
Willow flycatcher
Gray flycatcher
Least flycatcher
Hammond's flycatcher
Dusky flycatcher
Cordilleran flycatcher
Eastern phoebe
Say's phoebe
Vermilion flycatcher
Ash-throated flycatcher
Great crested flycatcher
Cassin's kingbird
Western kingbird
Eastern kingbird
Scissor-tailed flycatcher

## LARKS

Horned lark

## SWALLOWS

Purple martin
Tree swallow
Violet-green swallow
Northern rough-winged swallow
Bank swallow
Cliff swallow
Barn swallow

### JAYS, MAGPIES & CROWS

Steller's jay
Blue jay
Scrub jay
Pinyon jay
Clark's nutcracker
Black-billed magpie
American crow
Common raven

### CHICKADEES

Black-capped chickadee
Mountain chickadee

### NUTHATCHES

Red-breasted nuthatch
White-breasted nuthatch
Pygmy nuthatch

### CREEPERS

Brown creeper

### WRENS

Rock wren
Canyon wren
Carolina wren
Bewick's wren
House wren
Winter wren
Marsh wren

### KINGLETS & GNATCATCHERS

Golden-crowned kinglet
Ruby-crowned kinglet
Blue-gray gnatcatcher

### THRUSHES

Eastern bluebirds
Western bluebird
Mountain bluebird
Townsend's solitaire
Veery
Gray-cheeked thrush
Swainson's thrush
Hermit thrush
Wood thrush
American robin
Varied thrush

### MOCKINGBIRDS & THRASHERS

Gray catbird
Northern mockingbird
Sage thrasher
Brown thrasher
Long-billed thrasher
Curve-billed thrasher

### PIPITS

American pipit

### WAXWINGS

Bohemian waxwing
Cedar waxwing

### SHRIKES

Northern shrike
Loggerhead shrike

### STARLINGS

European starling

### VIREOS

White-eyed vireo
Bell's vireo
Solitary vireo
Yellow-throated vireo
Warbling vireo
Philadelphia vireo
Red-eyed vireo

### WARBLERS

Blue-winged warbler
Golden-winged warbler
Tennessee warbler
Orange-crowned warbler
Nashville warbler

Virginia's warbler
Northern parula
Yellow warbler
Chestnut-sided warbler
Magnolia warbler
Black-throated blue warbler
Yellow-rumped warbler
Black-throated gray warbler
Townsend's warbler
Black-throated green warbler
Blackburnian warbler
Yellow-throated warbler
Pine warbler
Palm warbler
Bay-breasted warbler
Blackpoll warbler
Black and white warbler
American redstart
Worm-eating warbler
Ovenbird
Northern waterthrush
Kentucky warbler
Connecticut warbler
Macgillivray's warbler
Common yellowthroat
Hooded warbler
Wilson's warbler
Yellow-breasted chat

## TANAGERS

Summer tanager
Scarlet tanager
Western tanager

## CARDINALS, GROSBEAKS & BUNTINGS

Northern cardinal
Rose-breasted grosbeak
Black-headed grosbeak
Blue grosbeak
Lazuli bunting

Indigo bunting
Dickcissel

## TOWHEES, SPARROWS & LONGSPURS

Green-tailed towhee
Rufous-sided towhee
Spotted towhee
Cassin's sparrow
American Tree sparrow
Chipping sparrow
Clay-colored sparrow
Brewer's sparrow
Field sparrow
Vesper sparrow
Lark sparrow
Black-throated sparrow
Lark bunting
Savannah sparrow
Grasshopper sparrow
Fox sparrow
Song sparrow
Lincoln's sparrow
Swamp sparrow
White-throated sparrow
White-crowned sparrow
Harris' sparrow
Dark-eyed junco
Mccown's longspur
Lapland longspur
Chestnut-collared longspur
Snow bunting

## BLACKBIRDS & ORIOLES

Bobolink
Red-winged blackbird
Western meadowlark
Yellow-headed blackbird
Rusty blackbird
Brewer's blackbird
Brown-headed cowbird
Great-tailed grackle
Common grackle

Orchard oriole
Baltimore oriole
Bullock's oriole

**FINCHES**

Gray-crowned rosy finch
Purple finch
Cassin's finch
House finch

Red crossbill
Common redpoll
Pine siskin
Lesser goldfinch
American goldfinch
Evening grosbeak

**WEAVERS**

House sparrow

*An oriole nest*

# Rocky Mountain Arsenal National Wildlife Refuge

### 17,000 acres; 11 miles northeast of downtown Denver

The Rocky Mountain Arsenal National Wildlife Refuge is one of a few urban national wildlife refuges in the United States. The refuge is the largest contiguous open space in the Denver metropolitan area. The refuge's close proximity to the Denver metro area makes it a noteworthy site for understanding and edification of wildlife in an urban setting. In 1992, Congress passed the Rocky Mountain Arsenal National Wildlife Refuge Act, designating the site as a wildlife refuge.

The refuge is an old U.S. Army facility used to produce chemical weapons. In 1942, this farmland and short-grass prairie was bought by the U.S. Army. Thirty square miles was established as the Rocky Mountain Arsenal. Weapons produced here during World War II were used to dissuade the use of chemical weapons by our enemies and helped achieve victory over Germany and Japan. After the war, the army leased land to private companies that produced commercial pesticides. During the Cold War of the 1950s the Army again stepped in to produce chemical weapons to counter the Soviet threat. Since there were few environmental laws before the 1960s, one can only imagine the contamination of the soil and groundwater at the site. Today, the entire site is currently a Superfund site controlled by the U.S. Army.

Visitors can observe wildlife, industrial components left behind that altered the natural environment, and learn from the environmental cleanup activities. The refuge is a unique site that can serve to educate future generations about their natural and cultural heritage.

## Wildlife

Once a native short-grass prairie of the western Great Plains, it was inhabited by bison, gray wolf, black-tailed prairie dog and the black-footed ferret that were pushed out by settlement and farming. The grazing and burrowing activity of those species created habitat for many other types associated with the prairie. Today, the refuge's grasslands, water impoundments, and woodlands provide a variety of habitats for a wide range of wildlife species. Over 300 species of wildlife can be found here, including 227 birds, 32 mammals, and 18 reptiles and amphibians. The predominant big game species in this ecosystem in years past was the bison. It was reintroduced to the refuge in March of 2006.

While the environmental clean-up progressed, the importance of this area as a wildlife sanctuary was discovered. Biologists determined the arsenal was home to a large population of wintering bald eagles. The discovery of the eagles was a major wake-up call and made everyone involved take note of the broad and healthy wildlife populations within the area. Even though the industrial core of the site was contaminated, mule deer, white-tailed deer, prairie dogs, coyotes, many species of hawks, owls and other birds thrived in the abandoned fields and large cottonwood trees. Low and behold, all of this unused grassland and wood lots that had been protected from 40 years of urban sprawl and development has now been secretly taken over by the natural scheme of things.

*Juvenile bald eagle*

It is amazing how, when left alone, wildlife can actually manage itself pretty well. Since hunting has never been allowed on the Rocky Mountain Arsenal NWR and the decades prior to its designation left the animals pretty much undisturbed, the wildlife has done very well on its own. The mule deer have naturally balanced the sex ratio of their population and there are many older, mature bucks inhabiting the refuge. There will always be concerns about big game in an urban setting, so biologists are stepping in to study the deer and their survival rate in, what most would consider, tight quarters. The limited area these deer have to travel, the limited amount of food sources, and their breeding success are taken into account.

How about the burrowing owl? The burrowing owl is a small, ground-dwelling raptor of arid, open habitats. Though adaptable to some landscape change, the burrowing owl is declining in many parts of its range in western North America due to habitat loss and control of burrowing mammals. It is a species of management concern in much of the western United States and is listed as threatened in Colorado. The refuge however, is very important to the burrowing owl – dozens of pairs of burrowing owls raise their young each year in its prairie dog towns. Burrowing owl populations are depressed across North America, but this vast urban prairie supports the largest remaining breeding population along the Colorado Front Range. There are other studies taking place concerning the burrowing owl that may answer questions about their migration habits, nest observations to estimate the number of young fledged at each nest, and the potential long-term impacts of West Nile Virus (WNV) on wild raptor populations along the Colorado Front Range.

Many species of waterfowl use the refuge's lakes, and because prairie dogs provide a food source, many species of hawks and owls are seen. Western hognose snake, eastern yellow-bellied racer, western bullsnake, western terrestrial garter snake, plains garter snake, common garter snake, and prairie rattlesnake also take advantage of the prairie dogs for food and shelter in abandoned burrows. Snakes are also a food source for birds of prey.

The introduction of water and the creation of lakes and wetlands has provided habitat for snapping turtles, western painted turtles, and tiger salamanders. You may also spot or at least hear the common bullfrog or the northern leopard frog.

Many small birds like the grasshopper sparrow and lark bunting, that cannot adapt to live in agricultural or suburban settings, find good native habitats on the refuge.

Changes in small game abundance and species diversity are also being monitored. With all of the activities taking place during the restoration, habitat is rearranged and food sources are replanted for smaller mammals. Small game must adapt to new habitat and survive the rigors of weather trends. If that isn't enough, the small game population is also preyed upon by coyotes, eagles, owls, and the common Swainson's hawks.

At the Rocky Mountain Arsenal NWR, the coyote is a primary predator and scavenger and has a potentially important influence on other wildlife such as deer and small game. Only limited coyote population information exists, so they are also being studied. The number of dens is counted and litter sizes are checked to indicate reproductive success. I know they are abundant because every trip I have made to the refuge has presented at least one sighting, in fact one day I spotted four coyotes in just a few hours.

As one can see from this limited information, the Rocky Mountain Arsenal NWR is a work in progress, but once you visit the locale you will be amazed at the numbers of wildlife species present. Visitors may come across plains pocket gopher or the eastern fox squirrel, which builds a nest of sticks and leaves in trees during the summer and spends the winter in a tree-hole nest. The riparian habitat may produce muskrat or a rare sighting of a mink. Raccoons, striped skunks, and porcupines may be seen in the wooded areas, as will cottontail rabbits. The common deer mouse, jackrabbit, and badger live in dry, open country. A red fox may be seen anywhere, but coyotes outcompete fox and frequently kill them (or at minimum, push them out of the area).

In the future, following the cleanup of past pollution and upon completion of the restoration project, several species will hopefully be reintroduced. Pronghorn antelope and sharp-tailed grouse are on the list of potential candidates.

The overall ecosystem of the Rocky Mountain Arsenal NWR has been improving year over year and the future looks bright.

## Activities

The refuge has four main trails totaling approximately 9 miles of wildlife observation and photographic opportunities. These trails range from flat lakeside strolls to sloping prairie hills. The staff at the visitor center can provide advice on trails, however my findings are that the trails are easy to moderate in difficulty and the length of the trails are doable for most fitness levels. Trail maps are available upon check-in.

The Prairie Trail takes a hiker through the short-grass prairie for a chance to see prairie dogs, meadowlarks, and lark buntings.

The Woodland Trail provides a great opportunity to spot mule deer, white-tailed deer, geese, ducks, wading birds like the American avocet, and a number of song birds. About 2 miles into the trail, visitors will find the newly created wetland viewing blind. The Rod and Gun Club Viewing Blind provides a wonderful opportunity to learn about the importance of wetland habitat. The well-done interpretative displays are rich with information about the area and the wildlife and well worth the hike.

The Havana Ponds Trail and the North Landora Trail skirt the north side of Lake Mary and Landora Lake. Views of the riparian habitat and the cottonwoods to the east side of Landora Lake can be enjoyed. One late fall evening while hiking this trail, I had over 5,000 Canada geese fly overhead and land on Landora Lake. What a sight!

The Lake Mary Trail is right at the visitor center and this unique floating boardwalk takes you around the lake. It is common to see mallards, coots, and blue-winged teal.

There are two-hour wildlife viewing tours available every Wednesday, Saturday, and Sunday except holidays, departing at 10:00am. Wildlife you may see on the tour includes bison, coyotes, raptors, mule and white-tailed deer, and many song birds.

Reservations are required and can be made by calling 303-289-0930.

Fishing is available on Lake Mary and Landora Lake. The season normally opens mid-April and goes through mid-October. Gamefish in Lake Mary include largemouth bass, northern pike, channel catfish, white and black crappie, bluegill, and yellow perch. Grass carp are present in Lake Mary to control vegetation growth and common carp are present in both lakes. Pike are often pursued by flyfishers.

## Location

Rocky Mountain Arsenal NWR is located in Adams County just northeast of Denver. From Interstate 70, take the Havana Street exit (Exit 280) north about 3 miles to the entrance of the Refuge at 56th Avenue.

## Contact

**US Fish & Wildlife Service**
 Rocky Mountain Arsenal NWR
 5650 Havana Street Bldg 121, Commerce City, CO 80022
 303-289-0232
 **Refuge hours:** Open year round on Tuesday, Wednesday, Thursday, Saturday and Sunday. Hours vary with the season.
 **Access**: All visitors must enter through the south gate, which is located at 56th Avenue and Havana Street in Commerce City.
 **Nature Programs and Tours:** For information about specific nature programs and tours, please call the visitors center at 303-289-0930.

*Coyote scanning the prairie*

# The Wild Animal Sanctuary

240 Acres; Eastern plains 30 miles northeast of Denver at Keenesburg

## History

One of the oldest and largest of only 15 or so nonprofit sanctuaries in North America for exotic and endangered great cats, bears, and wolves, the 240-acre Wild Animal Sanctuary is also the leader in providing large acreage habitats for its rescued animals. Situated on the high plains 30 miles northeast of Denver, the sanctuary's 160-plus rescued lions, tigers, bears, leopards, mountain lions, wolves, servals, and bobcats come from private homes where they were kept as "pets", surpluss from zoos, breeding compounds, exotic animal auctions, from the entertainment industry, from traveling shows, from other facilities that were shut down due to neglect and abuse, and from other terrible situations.

Established by Executive Director Pat Craig in 1980, the Wild Animal Sanctuary is a state and federally licensed zoological facility and a 501(c)(3) nonprofit organization. For the past 28 years, the Wild Animal Sanctuary has responded to more than 800 requests from private citizens and government agencies to rescue animals. These requests have come from across the United States (42 states, so far), and also Mexico. The Wild Animal Sanctuary's mission is to rescue captive exotic and endangered great cats, bears, and wolves, then provide them a wonderful home for as long as they live, and educate visitors about the tragic plight faced by tens of thousands of these animals in North America.

A true sanctuary for unfortunate victims of America's "Captive Wildlife Crisis" (which includes some 30,000 exotic and endangered large carnivores) the Wild Animal Sanctuary is a refuge like no other. The rescued animals live out their days in a comfortable safe haven, with plenty of space, exceptional diets, and joyful enrichment, living at peace with others of their own kind.

The sanctuary does not breed, sell, train, or take the animals on road shows, nor are they commercially exploited. Visitors can view the refuge on ramps and observation decks high above the animals, so that they may observe the animals enjoying a peaceful life.

## Going Green

The Wild Animal Sanctuary's small staff and volunteer crew have constructed ten habitats of up to 25 acres, underground dens, the Visitor Welcome Center/Gift Shop and the Visitor Education Center, as well as viewing ramps and observation decks, using mostly recycled materials. These construction materials include in-kind donations of miles of chain link fence from Colorado's Rocky Flats National Wildlife Refuge, gates, telephone poles, gas pipes, fire hoses, highway construction panels, landscape materials, trees, and more.

## Wildlife

In addition to seeing more than 160 tigers, black and grizzly bears, African lions, black and spotted leopards, mountain lions, wolves and other rescued species, the Wild Animal Sanctuary also offers the occasional chance to see many species native to Colorado as well as migratory birds. This includes golden and bald eagles, red-tailed and Swainson's hawks, great horned owls, barred owls, coyotes, deer, fox, rabbits and jackrabbits, ground squirrels, geese, ducks, and ring-necked pheasant. More common bird species include red-winged blackbirds, meadow larks, finches, starlings, and boat-tailed and common grackle. There are also non-native species of birds present, including sea gulls. This area is one of the migratory waterfowl flyways, so expect to see Canada geese, pelicans, many species of ducks, and great blue herons fly by.

*There is very good habitat for lions at the Wild Animal Sanctuary.*

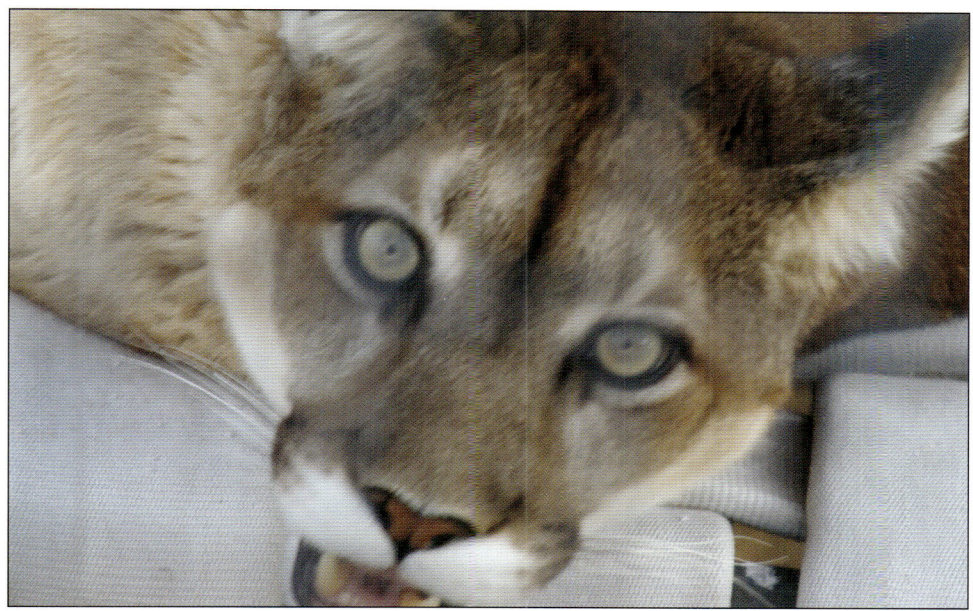

*Meet Romeo, a mountain lion at the sanctuary.*

    I have always been apprehensive about so-called animal sanctuaries. They always seem to give me the impression of a zoo, which I have always had a somewhat mixed feeling about. I know they are there for educational purposes, help support endangered species, and for human enjoyment and interaction, but I seem to have a problem with zebras and polar bears locked up in such a small, restricted area. These feelings come from a life spent outdoors hunting and fishing with a camera in tow, seeing wildlife in their natural setting. So, as I drove into the Wild Animal Sanctuary, I had to release old thoughts and open my mind to a new experience. I must tell you, I was not disappointed. Not only does the sanctuary serve an honorable purpose, they do it with the animal's needs, and (as corny as it sounds) feelings in mind. The staff here has taken on an unbelievably difficult job and every one of them loves what they do.

    The day before I made my visit, the sanctuary had just rescued 15 black bears from Idaho. They were in an enclosure next to the road on the way to the entrance to the Welcome Center. Notice that I referred to an enclosure instead of a cage. The double, 10- to 12-foot-high fence is there as a necessity for our protection and theirs, but it did not give me the impression of a cage. The bears had acres of open area to roam. After just a day together, they seemed calm and were mutually interacting with the customary bumping and pushing. I was equally impressed as I toured more species from the observation decks above the animals. Again, I had to mentally get by the fencing, which I was glad was there, because I was talking to a black leopard not 15 to 20 feet away. Further along the deck, I met Romeo, a 170-pound mountain lion. "Hi Romeo," I said softly. His eyes trained directly to my voice, he returned my gesture with a polite growl-purr combination. He seemed cheerful as we exchanged pleasantries, however there was a bit of tension in the air as the female in the next enclosure was crying and pacing anxiously. She was in heat. This was great; I had gotten there late in the afternoon just as the animals were getting active as the day cooled off.

Make sure to bring a camera. At the west end of the observation deck, you have a full view of several large enclosures for tigers and lions. I would also suggest a powerful lens for your camera for some first-rate close up shots. There are so many tigers that they are rotated from smaller enclosures to a larger enclosure with a swimming pool. The tigers love frolicking in the water. Over the years, the sanctuary has established a group of tigers that have actually learned to get along so well together they have an exceptionally large enclosure with several acres of roaming space to themselves. There are dens built into the side of a hill with lush, deep grass to rest in, and wooden structures for climbing and playing. This group of cats will live out their days together.

The tigers love playing with big, heavy duty beach balls. Visitors can purchase these balls and donate them back to the cats. This is one of the many ways folks can help the sanctuary's $1.2-million annual budget. They spend $400,000 a year just on meat for these great beasts.

The timing of my visit couldn't have been any better. As I was viewing and photographing the lions waking up from their afternoon siesta, a bald eagle landed in the lion's enclosure. It was far enough away that my long lens (750mm) was still not long enough for a good image. It was eating something, not sure exactly what but it spent a good 15 minutes before it took flight back to the west. At this point I noticed several cottontail rabbits in with the lions. I think this is what the eagle may have been eating.

I loaded up the camera and headed to the east end of the deck where the grizzly bears, black bears, and wolves can be seen. Oh yeah, along with another couple of tigers. The wolves were also up and actively moving about. A wolf howling from inside 200 yards is the embodiment of the definition of "wild". I couldn't imagine an outdoorsman hearing this without a chill going down his back. It brought back a fond memory of my past. I was very fortunate to see a pair of wolves in Colorado in the late 1970s. I was bow hunting for elk and mule deer in the Sawatch Range west of Buena Vista, skirting timberline, when my hunting partner and I crossed over a saddle overlooking a deep valley. We heard the howl and at the far end of the valley, well over 1,000 yards away, a black wolf sat on its haunches, nose in the air. It got up and trotted into the scrub oak and came out with a cohort and topped over the next saddle, out of sight. What an experience!

I think anyone interested in viewing wild animals should put the Wild Animal Sanctuary on their list of "must dos". To have a place in the middle of Colorado to view the big cats, grizzly bears, and wolves is pretty amazing in itself. It is a "great place". The sanctuary is open daily from 9:00am to 4:00pm, except during holidays and bad weather. During summer months (June through September), it stays open until sunset. Visitors are given an orientation about the sanctuary, and are provided with guide books to take with them. The guide books indicate which habitats the animals live in, and tell their histories before they were rescued. There is a large Welcome Center with a gift shop, an informative Education Center, picnic areas on observation decks, restrooms, and drink and snack machines. Ramps are wheel-chair accessible. Group tours are available, and reservations must be made in advance. The Wild Animal Sanctuary is strictly a non-smoking facility; all smoking materials must be extinguished before driving on to the property. Dogs are not allowed. A map and directions are on the web site, at www.wildanimalsanctuary.org.

*A bengal tiger living the life of luxury beside the pool.*

Here are just a few stories about the animals that live at the Wild Animal Sanctuary. As you will read, most are animals that were simply discarded or abused. However, the black bears, Daisy and Dusty, were brought here because of state laws in Michigan that made it illegal to have them as pets. All of the animals at the sanctuary have names and it seemed to me they knew when their name was spoken to them.

- **Eddy:** Born to USDA-confiscated animals — Born to Sam and Gina, Eddy is a black leopard that will never have to know the dreadful life his parents, Sam and Gina, endured, along with hundreds of other exotic animals at Colton, California's infamous "Tiger Rescue" facility. When Gina arrived at the sanctuary, she was already pregnant and soon came Eddy. Eddy leads a charmed life. He has lots of love from the humans and dogs he has grown up with, was the star of Animal Planet's "Growing Up Black Leopard", and plays with the other leopards in their specially designed enclosure.
- **Jules:** Private surrender — Jules is a male African serval that was someone's "pet" in California. But like so many other servals, he started to become temperamental with his owners, and began marking his territory, profusely. His owner relinquished him to a sanctuary in Arizona but they were unable to keep him, and so the Wild Animal Sanctuary gladly took him in.
- **Beatty and Tigger II:** USDA confiscation — Beatty and Tigger II came from the "Tiger Ranch" facility in Texas, where their owner walked off and abandoned 23 animals after realizing the expense and difficulty involved in caring for these animals. Siberian tiger, Tigger II, weighs 750 pounds and his roommate, Beatty, a Bengal tiger, weighs 425 pounds. A little observation leaves no doubt as to who's in charge in their dwelling!

*Timber wolf*

**Halloween and Pumpkin:** Houston SPCA and USDA confiscation — As a result of new laws against owning tigers as "pets", Texas breeders began to abandon their animals because they could no longer make money from them. Siberian tigers Halloween and Pumpkin were rescued from that dismal existence of living in concrete and steel cages. Both are very friendly and very sweet now, and Halloween takes the prize of being the sanctuary's largest cat at 850 pounds.

**Romeo:** Montana Fish & Game confiscation — Chained by the neck in a Montana man's backyard, Romeo was confiscated and came to the Wild Animal Sanctuary at just a year old. He is the sanctuary's biggest mountain lion, weighing 170 pounds, and has a wonderfully friendly disposition, thus his name, Romeo. He chirps and whistles (a mountain lion's way of displaying affection) whenever spoken to.

**Masai:** California Fish & Game confiscation — For every animal actor who works successfully with people, 20 to 30 animals are bred that don't make it. Masai was one of those, coming from a business in California that uses animals for films until they won't work anymore, and then forgets them as if they never existed. Masai now rules over his own pride.

**Kelty:** US Fish & Wildlife confiscation — Kelty the grizzly bear was shipped to the sanctuary from a California facility. The stress he suffered at this facility (due to a poor environment) was so great that he would pound his head against his cage wall until he bled. With plenty of space, he is having the time of his life. Kelty takes the prize of being the sanctuary's largest animal at 1,100 pounds.

**Daisy and Dusty:** Private forfeiture — A Michigan couple owned Daisy and Dusty, but when a state law was passed making it illegal for them to be owned as pets, they were brought to the sanctuary. The Michigan couple continues to visit their bear "kids" often.

**Hondo:** Private forfeiture — Hondo is a timber wolf that was being kept as a pet in an apartment. When Hondo's owner became engaged to be married he decided not to keep Hondo and relinquished him to the sanctuary. No longer in an apartment, Hondo has plenty of room to play.

## Location

The Wild Animal Sanctuary is located 30 miles northeast of Denver, and 40 miles directly east of Boulder. From Denver, take Interstate 76 north to Exit 31, the Hudson exit. Take Highway 52 east 4 miles to Weld County Road 53 (CR 53). Turn right/south and travel on the gravel road for 3 miles to the Wild Animal Sanctuary's entrance on the left.

From Boulder, go east on Colorado Highway 52, past I-25, past Dacono, past Fort Lupton, and past Hudson; continue as above.

A square 4x4 directional sign, featuring "Masai", the king of the sanctuary's lion pride, is in the field just before the right turn to the sanctuary on CR 53.

## Fast Facts

**The Wild Animal Sanctuary**
1946 WCR 53, Keensburg, CO  80643
303-536-0118
www.wildanimalsanctuary.org

## Contact

- **Activities:** Viewing of rescued exotic and endangered captive great cats, bears, wolves, and other species. Occasional spotting of native species of birds and other mammals.
- **Principal Mammals:** More than 160 animals, including Bengal and Siberian tigers (75 of them), black and grizzly bears, African lions, spotted and black leopards, mountain lions, arctic and timber wolves, servals, bobcats and coati mundi.
- **Habitat Overview:** The 240-acre Wild Animal Sanctuary is comprised of ten large species-specific habitats (5 to 25 acres) which surround a main animal complex and Visitor Welcome and Education Centers. Each habitat contains large temperature-controlled dens, built from gigantic concrete culverts. The dens are underground, and stay a mellow 60 degrees year round, providing shelter for the animals in extreme cold or hot weather. Animals in the central animal complex have heating of various types, including solar panels, electric, or propane. All species are provided with a variety of enrichment toys and activities, including special play structures, and swimming pools and tanks for tigers and bears (species who love to play in water). There are seasonal lakes for the tigers and bears as well.
- **Best Viewing Ops:** In spring, summer, and fall, early morning and evening hours (until sunset from June through September) are best. Animals are fed on a random schedule, just like they'd eat in the wild, and they are more active on the mornings of feeding days (usually Tuesday, Thursday, and Saturday). Summer evening hours often elicit impromptu wolf and lion concerts (humans are welcome to join in), and the bears are typically in playful form. In winter, the animals (except for the hibernating bears) are more active in the middle of the day, when temperatures are warmest.
- **Hunting, Fishing, Camping & Boating Ops:** None. However, Barr Lake State Park is within about 15 miles, where fishing, birding, and wildlife viewing is available.
- **Hiking Trails:** None. However, Banner Lakes State Wildlife Area, just 4 miles north of the sanctuary at Colorado Highway 52 and Weld County Road 53, offers hiking, nature trails, birding, and wildlife viewing.

*Grizzly bear*

# Southeastern Great Plains

# Comanche National Grasslands

**443,764 acres; Southeastern corner of Colorado**

## Introduction

The Comanche Grasslands are in the remote regions of the southeast part of the state ranging from about 4,300 feet to 4,700 feet in elevation. There are two units within the grasslands – the Timpas Unit and the Carrizo Unit – with four separate areas to explore. Picket Wire Canyon and Vogel Canyon are in the Timpas Unit, while Carrizo Canyon and Picture Canyon are in the Carrizo Unit. Directions to each are listed below under "Location". The towns where these directions will start are La Junta and Springfield.

The first point of interest in the Timpas Unit is Picket Wire Canyonlands. It became part of the Comanche National Grasslands in December 3, 1991. The U.S. Army transferred more than 16,000 acres of land to the U.S. Forest Service via congressional legislation. In turn, the U.S. Forest Service is mandated by law to protect and conserve the cultural, paleontological, wildlife, vegetative, aquatic, and other natural resources in Picket Wire Canyonlands. Public access into this canyon is by the Withers Canyon trailhead. No motorized vehicles are allowed, so hiking, mountain biking, and horseback riding are the best choices. This secluded canyon is the home of the largest documented "Dinosaur Tracksite" in North America. It covers about 0.25 mile of river bank, and contains over 1,300 visible tracks. About 150 million years ago, two types of dinosaurs – the upright meat-eating allosaurus and giant plant eating brontosaurs – left their footprints in the mud and they hardened in place, leaving behind a unique piece of history. Investigating the dinosaur tracks is an excellent reason to make the 10-mile round trip hike into the canyon, but the sites along the way easily draw attention to the unassuming beauty of the landscape. The hike starts at the east end of the parking area and, to get things interesting right away, you drop down 250 feet in elevation in the first half mile into the bottom of Withers Canyon. Follow the two-track dirt road (east) into Picket Wire Canyon. Once in Picket Wire Canyon, the trail turns south-southwest and heads up canyon. Trail markers are placed approximately every 1.5 miles. Please leave gates as you find them and do not disturb livestock.

Along the way, you can find ancient rock art made by early peoples. Images are carved or painted onto rock surfaces of the canyon walls. Archaeologists think a nomadic, hunter-gatherer people, who may have visited the area for short periods of time as they followed migrating game, left the art. Some of the rock art in this area may be 375 to 4,500 years old. Please do not touch or disturb these sites in any way.

At about 4 miles into the hike, the Delores Mission and Cemetery can be found. It was built sometime between 1871 and 1889 when Mexican pioneers first settled in the valley. Partial remains of the mission and cemetery are still visible.

When I made the hike, I did not go too far in because I was by myself and it was 102 degrees in the middle of the afternoon. I bring this up for a few points on safety. If you cannot resist and go in alone, always notify someone of your expected route, departure and return times. The heat is intense here and there is no drinking water. Plan for several hours of drinking water, wear light clothing and sunscreen to cover your skin, use sunglasses, and wear a hat. In the spring, use a layering technique to adjust to cool mornings, warm afternoons, and possible weather changes. A couple more safety tips would be to try and be in good physical condition. This is a very remote area so know your limits and the limits of the weakest member of your group. And last but not least, I would recommend high-top hiking boots that are broken in before your hike. Blisters are painful and could render you disabled. Carry moleskin or molefoam and use it as soon as you feel a "hot spot", do not wait until the blister has formed. Tennis shoes are not recommended because they offer little protection from prickly pear and cholla cactus that are abundant throughout the canyon.

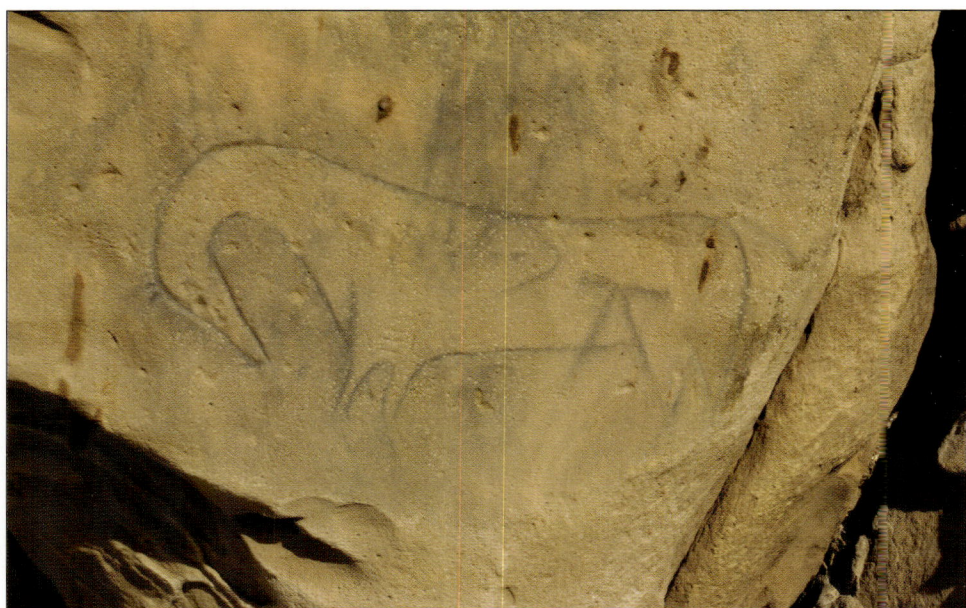

*Pictograph in Picture Canyon*

*Dinosaur tracks in Picketwire Canyon (photo provided by U.S. Forest Service)*

A small first-aid kit is strongly recommended as prairie rattlesnakes and scorpions are common. A badger would be another species of wildlife that should be avoided. Avoid tall grass, and watch where you place your hands and feet. Generally, these animals are as afraid of you as you are of them, but they could react unfavorably. In case of emergency, call the Otero County Sheriff Office at 719-384-5941 or 911. You are only allowed in the canyonlands area from dawn to dusk, so plan your hike carefully. Overnight camping is not allowed in Picket Wire Canyonlands.

I would encourage you to stop by or call the Comanche National Grasslands Office in La Junta for current weather and road information on Canyonlands, at 719-384-2181.

The second site in the Timpas Unit is Vogel Canyon. There are two live springs in the area which help support an assortment of wildlife and birds. This drainage is a tributary of the Purgatoire River and supported a population of the American Indians some 300 to 800 years ago. They left behind a bevy of rock art on the canyon walls for viewing. There is also a spur of the Santa Fe Trail that runs through the area. The ruts from the stage coach road and ruins of an old station can be seen. More recent, remains of the Westbrook homestead from the 1930s can be seen.

The parking area has three covered picnic tables with grills (only charcoal fires are allowed). A vault toilet, room for horse-trailer parking, and rails for hitching horses are also available.

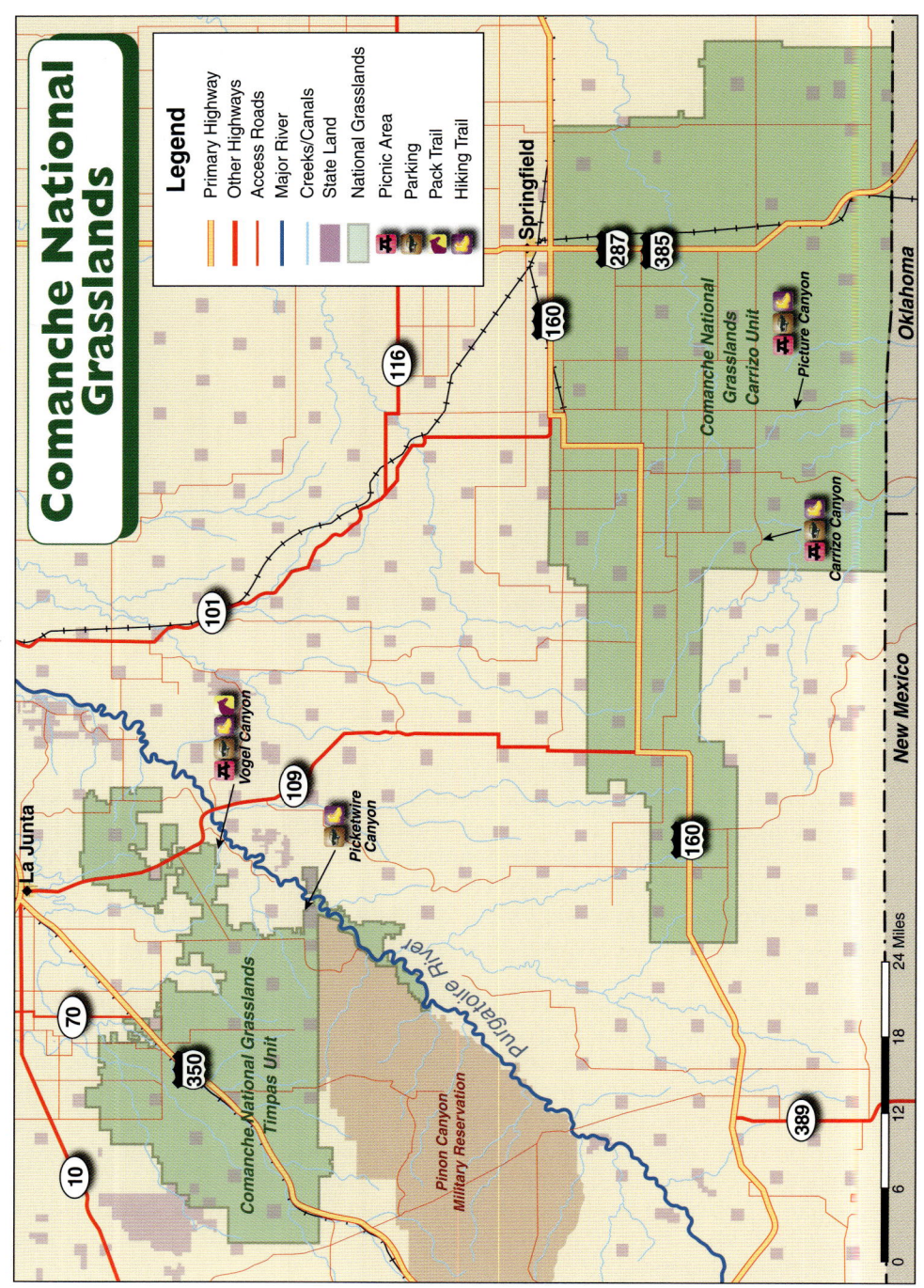

The best way to view this canyon is by hiking or horse backing the four well-marked trails:

- The Canyon Trail, which is 1.75 miles in round-trip length, starts at the parking area and takes the visitor into the canyon bottom where access to the rock art is best. Ruins of the old homestead can also be seen. Near the end of this easy trail is one of the active springs. This is a good area to view birds and other wildlife coming in to drink. The end of this trail is also the start of the Prairie Trail and intersects with the Overlook Trail.
- The Overlook Trail also starts at the parking area. It is a mile in length round trip. It is an easy trail that offers great views of this scenic geological site.
- The Mesa Trail is a spur of the Overlook Trail. Starting at the parking area, take the Overlook Trail for about 0.5 mile and take a left (west) onto the Mesa Trail. This 2.25-mile hike begins with short-grass prairie and eventually takes you through some juniper woods. This moderately difficult trail shows the diversity of this amazing landscape.
- The Prairie Trail is the longest of the trails at about 3 miles. It is moderate in difficulty and starts about 0.5 mile before you get to the parking area on RD 505A. There is a small pull out at the trailhead. The trail actually starts in the short-grass prairie along the old Barlow & Sanderson Stage Road. This is the spur of the Santa Fe Trail previously mentioned. Remains of the stage tracks can be seen. A little over a mile into the hike the trail veers left (south) into the juniper forest and intersects the Mesa Trail. It eventually drops down into the western end of Vogel Canyon. Another spring and homestead ruins can be seen. Continue following the trail through the canyon and it eventually turns into the Canyon Trail and back to the parking area.

The Carrizo Unit south of Springfield consists of two viewable areas: Picture Canyon and Carrizo Canyon.

Picture Canyon is a beautiful, lively area with large trees and abundant plant life due to the live springs in the area. Wildlife finds the area pleasing also. However the most interesting feature of Picture Canyon is the near-perpendicular rock wall winding around the bottom of the canyon with numerous fragments of rock art (pictures) left behind by the American Indians, for which the canyon is named. Petroglyphs as well as pictographs can be found along the canyon walls. Some petroglyphs may have actually had astronomical significance. From what most people have told me, plan to visit Picture Canyon during the spring or fall equinox when the forest service leads a free tour into Crack Cave, where many etchings in the rock walls can be found. At sunrise on these two days, the sun's rays appear over the east canyon rim to penetrate the cave entrance, illuminating specific marks on the north cave wall. These petroglyphs are brilliantly lit for 10 to 12 minutes soon after sunrise, only to fade away until the next equinox. Reservations are required. To reserve your spot on the tour and get more details on meeting locations, please call the Comanche National Grassland District Office in Springfield at 719-523-6591.

I was there in the middle of the summer, but I had a great time exploring the area anyway. It was very interesting to me to see the simplicity in the drawings and how the natives of our country sought out and inhabited such unique spots in the landscape. It was a bit disturbing to see the canyon walls were defaced in spots. There was one signature, I don't recall the woman's name or the exact year, but it was scribed something like "Maria 1938". That one I can understand because in that time of history, folks didn't know any better, but the so-in-so hearts so-in-so is totally uncalled for. However, who knows, someone viewing the area in 2095 might find this form of communication very unusual!

You must remember for the time being, these sites are on public lands and are protected under federal law. Please report any acts of vandalism, defacement, or theft to the U.S. Forest Service Office in La Junta at 719-384-2181 or Springfield at 719-523-6591.

There are 8 miles of trails through Picture Canyon and surrounding areas for self exploration, three covered picnic tables, and a vault toilet at the parking area. There is no electricity, drinking water, or garbage cans so bring in what you need and take out what is left over.

Carrizo Canyon is the second point of interest in the Carrizo Unit. It is located near the western edge of the unit and I didn't have enough time to get in there and see the area. However, with Carrizo Creek running through the canyon, it is surely a lush little area with cottonwood and juniper trees. It should be a great area for birding, and camping is available in the parking area. Remember, there is no electricity or drinking water. Please pack out all trash.

The Santa Fe Trail passes through portions of the Timpas Unit in the Comanche Grasslands (see the Santa Fe Trail Scenic Byway chapter for more information).

## Wildlife

The grasslands are amazingly diverse in birds and wildlife, but are often very secretive in letting you know that. Over 235 bird species are present on the Comanche Grassland and provide excellent bird-watching opportunities.

With so little cover, the wildlife and birds remain hidden with remarkable ease, especially when the sun is high and the temperature is up. I did find areas where they could be found, especially birds. Wherever there is water, there are birds. Windmills are a favorite hideout. The structures usually supply the much needed water, but what I found to be more important during the heat of the day was that they provided shade from the sun. Lark buntings, meadowlarks, loggerhead shrikes, and western and eastern kingbirds would take refuge in any piece of shade they could find. They sulked in the shade with wings spread slightly to allow the insignificant breeze to help cool their bodies.

As I was driving out of the Picket Wire Canyon area, I spotted a bird on the branch of a juniper tree. I stopped and got out the binoculars for a closer look. It was a female grackle, however she was not alone. There were at least 25 birds in that one tree, all on the north side away from the sun. I could identify kingbirds, lark buntings, lark sparrows, and mourning doves. This same afternoon, the clouds started to roll in and a rain shower or two started to pelt the dry prairie. Birds were everywhere! Literally hundreds of lark buntings, in their family groups of 10 to 15 birds, were flitting from seed pod to seed pod. It was as if they were in total ecstasy, happy and full of life; quite the reversal of what I had witnessed a couple hours earlier. A covey of the very common scaled quail showed themselves near a water hole. While exploring areas with water and trees, a birder may encounter the Say's phoebe, Bullock's orioles, wild turkey and, along the cliffs, a rock wren may be flitting about. Without doubt, bird watchers should see many birds of prey. Swainson's hawks, red-tailed hawks, northern harrier, burrowing owl, and the smaller American kestrel are regularly seen cruising above. There are a few threatened ferruginous hawks that have been banded and kept under a watchful eye by people from the Tri-National Migration Study. Also, the grasslands are in the migratory route for the threatened bald eagle and endangered whooping crane. The Comanche National Grasslands is currently monitoring population trends of these species. A sharp eye may spot the occasional greater roadrunner or snowy plover, which are known to breed in the Comanche Grasslands. Another great find is the long-billed curlew, also a spring breeder.

In Colorado, the lesser prairie chicken is restricted to the far southeastern corner of the state in fragmented pockets of the Comanche Grasslands. This species prefers sand, sagebrush-bluestem, and shinnery oak-bluestem grasslands found on sandy soils of the southern Great Plains. They are now considered a threatened species and unfortunately all viewing leks are closed until further notice. I have become totally fascinated with all of the Colorado grouse species and I have yet to see one

*A respectable pronghorn buck*

of the lesser species. After sitting on greater prairie chicken, greater sage grouse, and sharp-tailed grouse breeding leks, I am looking forward to a chance to see the lessers in action. There are opportunities in the Cimarron National Grasslands across the border in Kansas to view the lesser prairie chicken, so I may have to pursue that option.

The short-grass prairie is home for many ground dwellers, including rattlesnakes, badgers, black-tailed jack rabbits, cottontail rabbits, field mice, skunks, and many species of lizards as well as the plains leopard frog. No ecosystem would be viable without predators. Coyotes, swift fox, the elusive bobcat, and the abovementioned birds of prey are common. Mountain lions live in the canyonlands and black bear have been seen in the Purgatoire River drainage. Both mule deer and white-tailed deer can be seen in the river bottoms and juniper woods. Large numbers of pronghorn antelope take up residence in the short grass of Comanche Grasslands.

## Location

To get to La Junta from Denver, take Interstate 25 south about 100 miles to Pueblo. Take Highway 50 east about 65 miles to La Junta. Highway 50 is a stretch of road that runs alongside the Arkansas River and can be a very nice drive.

To get to Springfield from Denver, take Interstate 70 east about 80 miles to Limon. Take Highway 287 east about 60 miles to Kit Carson. Continue on Highway 287 as it veers to the south. Follow the signage about 50 miles to Lamar. In Lamar, there is a short jaunt east on Highway 50 and then take Highway 287 south again for another 50 miles to Springfield.

**Picket Wire Canyonlands:** From La Junta, take Highway 109 south for 13 miles; turn right (west) on CR 802, also known as David Canyon Road. Continue west and travel for 8 miles. Turn left (south) on CR 25 and go 6 miles. Turn left (east) at Picket Wire Corrals onto Forest Service Road 500A. Travel along FR 500A for 3 miles, following the signs to Withers Canyon Trailhead.

From Springfield, take Highway 160 west 48 miles. Turn right (north) on Highway 109 for 43 miles and then turn left (west) on CR 802, also known as David Canyon Road. Continue west for 8 miles. Turn left (south) on CR 25 and go 6 miles. Turn left (east) at Picket Wire Corrals onto Forest Service Road 500A. Travel along FR 500A for 3 miles, following the signs to Withers Canyon Trailhead. Park at Withers Canyon Trailhead parking loop.

**Vogel Canyon:** From La Junta, take Highway 109 south for 13 miles. Turn right (west) on CR 802 also known as David Canyon Road. Continue west for 1.5 miles. Turn left (south) on Forest Service Road 505A for 1.5 miles to the Vogel Canyon parking lot.

From Springfield, take Highway 160 west 48 miles. Turn right (north) on Highway 109 for 43 miles and then turn left (west) on CR 802, also known as David Canyon Road. Continue west for 1.5 miles. Turn left (south) on Forest Service Road 505A for 1.5 miles to the Vogel Canyon parking lot.

**Carrizo Canyon:** From La Junta, take Highway 109 south for 58 miles. Turn left (east) on Highway 160 and go 25 miles. Turn right (south) on CR 10 for 9 miles. Turn right (west) on CR M for 5.5 miles and then turn left (south) on Forest Service Road 539 for 1.9 miles to the parking area.

From Springfield, take Highway 287 south for 17 miles. Turn right (west) on CR M for 22 miles and then turn left (south) on Forest Service Road 539 for 1.9 miles to the parking area.

**Picture Canyon:** From La Junta, take Highway 109 south for 58 miles. Turn left (east) at Highway 160 for 25 miles. Turn right (south) at CR 10 for 9 miles. Turn left (east) on CR M for 8 miles. Turn right (south) on CR 18 for 8 miles. Turn right (south) at the Picture Canyon road sign, Forest Service Road 533 and continue 1 mile to the parking area.

From Springfield, Take Highway 287 south for 17 miles. Turn right (west) on CR M for 8 miles. Turn left (south) on CR 18 for 8 miles. Turn right (south) at the Picture Canyon road sign, Forest Service Road 533 and continue 1 mile to the parking area.

## Contact

**USDA Forest Service:** Rocky Mountain Region

**Cimarron & Comanche National Grasslands**
2840 Kachina Drive, Pueblo, CO 81008

**Carrizo Unit**
P.O. Box 127
27204 Highway 287, Springfield, CO 81073
719-523-6591

**Timpas Unit**
1420 East 3rd Street, La Junta, CO 81050
719-384-2181
Office hours are from 8:00am to 12:00pm and 1:00pm to 5:00pm, Monday through Friday.
www.fs.fed.us/r2/psicc/coma/

## Bird List

Many of the birds listed are shown as migrants and usually cannot be seen except during the spring and fall migrations.

### LOONS

Common loon

### GREBES

Pied-billed grebe
Horned grebe
Eared grebe
Western grebe

### PELICANS

American white pelican

### CORMORANTS

Double-crested cormorant

### BITTERNS AND HERONS

American bittern
Great blue heron
Great egret
Snowy egret
Cattle egret
Green heron
Black-crowned night-heron

### IBISES AND SPOONBILLS

White-faced ibis

### SWANS, GEESE, AND DUCKS

Greater white-fronted goose
Snow goose
Ross' goose
Canada goose
Wood duck
Green-winged teal
Mallard
Northern pintail
Blue-winged teal
Cinnamon teal
Northern shoveler
Gadwall
American wigeon
Canvasback
Redhead
Ring-necked duck
Lesser scaup
Common goldeneye
Bufflehead
Hooded merganser
Common merganser
Red-breasted merganser
Ruddy duck

### AMERICAN VULTURES

Turkey vulture

### KITE, EAGLES, HAWKS, AND ALLIES

Osprey
Mississippi kite
Bald eagle
Northern harrier
Sharp-shinned hawk
Cooper's hawk
Northern goshawk
Swainson's hawk
Red-tailed hawk
Ferruginous hawk
Rough-legged hawk
Broad-winged hawk
Golden eagle

### CARACARAS AND FALCONS

American kestrel
Merlin
Peregrine falcon
Prairie falcon

## PARTRIDGES, GROUSE, TURKEYS, AND QUAIL

Ring-necked pheasant
Lesser prairie chicken
Wild turkey
Northern bobwhite
Scaled quail

## RAILS, GALLINULES, AND COOTS

Virginia rail
Sora
American coot

## CRANES

Sandhill crane

## PLOVERS AND LAPWINGS

Black-bellied plover
American golden plover
Snowy plover
Semipalmated plover
Piping plover
Killdeer
Mountain plover

## STILTS AND AVOCETS

Black-necked stilt
American avocet

## SANDPIPERS AND PHALAROPES

Greater yellowlegs
Lesser yellowlegs
Solitary sandpiper
Willet
Spotted sandpiper
Upland sandpiper
Long-billed curlew
Marbled godwit
Sanderling
Semipalmated sandpiper
Western sandpiper
Least sandpiper
White-rumped sandpiper
Baird's sandpiper
Pectoral sandpiper
Stilt sandpiper
Long-billed dowitcher
Common snipe
Wilson's phalarope
Red-necked phalarope

## SKUAS, GULLS, TERNS AND SKIMMERS

Franklin's gull
Ring-billed gull
Herring gull
Common tern
Forster's tern
Least tern
Black tern

## PIGEONS AND DOVES

Rock dove
Mourning dove

## CUCKOOS AND ROADRUNNERS

Black-billed cuckoo
Yellow-billed cuckoo
Greater roadrunner

## OWLS

Barn owl
Eastern screech owl
Western screech owl
Great horned owl
Burrowing owl
Long-eared owl
Short-eared owl
Northern saw-whet owl

## GOATSUCKERS

Common nighthawk
Common poorwill

## SWIFTS

Chimney swift
White-throated swift

## HUMMINGBIRDS

Ruby-throated hummingbird
Black-chinned hummingbird
Rufous hummingbird

## KINGFISHERS

Belted kingfisher

## WOODPECKERS

Red-headed woodpecker
Red-bellied woodpecker
Ladder-backed woodpecker
Downy woodpecker
Hairy woodpecker
Lewis' woodpecker
Northern flicker

## TYRANT FLYCATCHERS

Olive-sided flycatcher
Least flycatcher
Western wood-pewee
Willow flycatcher
Eastern phoebe
Say's phoebe
Vermilion flycatcher
Ash-throated flycatcher
Great-crested flycatcher
Cassin's kingbird
Western kingbird
Eastern kingbird
Scissor-tailed flycatcher

## LARKS

Horned lark

## SWALLOWS

Purple martin
Tree swallow
Northern rough-winged swallow
Bank swallow
Cliff swallow
Barn swallow

## JAYS AND CROWS

Blue jay
Pinyon jay
Western scrub jay
Black-billed magpie
American crow
Chihuahuan raven
Common raven

## CHICKADEES

Black-capped chickadee
Bushtit

## NUTHATCHES

Red-breasted nuthatch
White-breasted nuthatch

## CREEPERS

Brown creeper

## WRENS

Rock wren
Canyon wren
Bewick's wren
House wren
Marsh wren

## KINGLETS

Golden-crowned kinglet
Ruby-crowned kinglet
Blue-gray gnatcatcher

## THRUSHES

Eastern bluebird
Mountain bluebird
Townsend's solitaire
Gray-cheeked thrush
Swainson's thrush
Hermit thrush
American robin
Veery

### MOCKINGBIRDS AND THRASHERS

Gray catbird
Northern mockingbird
Brown thrasher
Curved-billed thrasher

### PIPITS

Sprague's pipit
American pipit
Water pipit

### WAXWINGS

Cedar waxwing

### SHRIKES

Northern shrike
Loggerhead shrike

### STARLINGS

European starling
Starlings

### VIREOS

Bell's vireo
Plumbeous vireo
Cassin's vireo
Blue-headed vireo
Warbling vireo
Red-eyed vireo

### WOOD-WARBLERS

Tennessee warbler
Orange-crowned warbler
Yellow warbler
Yellow-rumped warbler
Black-throated gray warbler
Black-throated green warbler
Black-and-white warbler
American redstart
Ovenbird
Northern waterthrush
Mourning warbler
MacGillivray's warbler
Virginia's warbler
Common yellowthroat
Yellow-breasted chat

### TANAGERS

Western tanager

### GROSBEAKS AND BUNTINGS

Northern cardinal
Rose-breasted grosbeak
Black-headed grosbeak
Blue grosbeak
Lazuli bunting
Lark bunting
Indigo bunting
Dickcissel

### EMBERIZINES

Green-tailed towhee
Spotted towhee
Cassin's sparrow
Rufous-crowned sparrow
American tree sparrow
Clay-colored sparrow
Brewer's sparrow
Field sparrow
Vesper sparrow
Lark sparrow
Savannah sparrow
Grasshopper sparrow
Fox sparrow
Song sparrow
Lincoln's sparrow
Swamp sparrow
White-throated sparrow
White-crowned sparrow
Harris' sparrow
Black-throated sparrow
Chipping sparrow
Dark-eyed junco
McCown's longspur
Lapland longspur
Chestnut-collared longspur

## BLACKBIRDS AND ALLIES

Bobolink
Red-winged blackbird
Western meadowlark
Yellow-headed blackbird
Rusty blackbird
Brewer's blackbird
Great-tailed grackle
Common grackle
Brown-headed cowbird
Orchard oriole
Baltimore oriole
Bullock's oriole

## FINCHES AND ALLIES

Purple finch
House finch
Red crossbill
Pine siskin
Lesser goldfinch
American goldfinch

## OLD WORLD SPARROWS

House sparrow

*Fog has set in for the morning.*

# Mountain Plover Festival

**The town of Karval on the eastern plains south of Interstate 70**

## Introduction

The unassuming town of Karval is the home of the Mountain Plover Festival, a homespun event started and run by the Karval Community Alliance. The residents and ranchers of Karval have coexisted with the mountain plover for years, not realizing the significance of the bird. The festival is put on with cooperation of local ranchers, so access to private land can be gained to mountain plover habitat and breeding grounds for visitors of the festival. The festival is done just one weekend a year and is normally the latter part of April. The weekend's participants meet on Friday night to open the event. This takes care of registration and is topped off with an ice cream social. The Early Riser Tour normally heads to the field Saturday morning about 6:00am, right after breakfast. Make sure to bring scopes, and/or binoculars, and a camera. The tour is reminiscent of a hay ride in search of birds instead of Christmas caroling. The tour returns to Karval for lunch about noon. Evening tours begin at 3:30pm and is followed by a hearty "chuck wagon dinner" and western entertainment. Sunday starts bright and early with a Last Chance Early Riser's Tour, again at 6:00am. A Sunday brunch is at 11:00am and participants are turned loose to explore designated properties. There are packages to accommodate the whole weekend, Saturday only, or Sunday only.

## Contact

**Karval Community Alliance**
P.O. Box 37, Karval, CO 80823
719-446-5354

## Wildlife

The mountain plover is the most popular bird in the area, definitely not the most common though. It is 8 to 9 inches long and weighs just less than 4 ounces. In appearance, it is characteristic of plovers, except that it has no black band across the breast. The upper parts are sandy brown with a white belly, and brown-white breast and face. There are black feathers on the front portion of the crown and a black stripe from each eye to the bill. Otherwise the plumage is a natural color and blends in with the prairie very well. The mountain plover is quieter than its more well-known relative, the killdeer. Its calls are often low-pitched, babbling whistles. In mating season it makes a call much like the mooing of a cow. Most of the plovers I saw in the two days I spent there were paired up and I was able to get pretty close with the vehicle and I didn't hear them say a thing. I stepped out of the truck to try and get a better angle for a photo and the plovers high tailed it well out of range for my long lens. Mind you, they did not fly, just walked/ran away. The window clamp and tripod proved useful again for nice close-up images.

Besides the mountain plover, a number of other bird and animal species can be found in this area. The black-tailed prairie dog, the burrowing owl (that lives in the prairie dog towns), the horned lark (Colorado's most abundant bird), and the lark sparrow are popular residents. Add the pronghorn antelope, mule deer, swift fox, jack rabbit, thirteen-striped ground squirrel, scaled quail, ferruginous hawk, meadowlark, red-tailed hawk, loggerhead shrike, and the common mourning dove to keep the binoculars focused can easily fill the weekend. I was able to spot and photograph a golden eagle, long-billed curlew, and a Swainson's thrush.

*The rare mountain plover*

The Rocky Mountain Bird Observatory recognizes the Karval area as a stop on the Colorado Birding Trail.

There are thousands of prairie dog towns in the area and the swift fox has thrived here. They dig out and take over many of the holes left by the prairie dogs and then go about thinning the population of the surrounding dog colonies. In fact, they are so popular here that a ranch in South Dakota wanted to transplant some north. After all the negotiations with the Colorado Division of Wildlife and landowners, a team set up to trap 30 foxes for transport. The team had made arrangements to stay for 30 days with the anticipation of capturing 1 or 2 per night. Thirty-five live box traps were set, traps were baited with a cut of meat, and GPS coordinates were recorded for each trap. The first morning count produced 18 healthy swift foxes. Blood samples were taken and sent overnight to Colorado State University in Fort Collins. Out of the 45 foxes captured in three nights, only one older female had any kind of blood problem. The leftover foxes were taken back to the exact coordinates of capture and released. The team canceled reservations, loaded up their swift fox, and headed to South Dakota.

I sneaked around from sunup to sundown on three different ranches for two days watching known swift fox dens, and did not spot a fox. Just wasn't my time. However, it is truly amazing how much wildlife, large and small, lives in such a sparse environment. This is definitely rattlesnake country so take precautions when you are here.

I would like to thank Carl and Cherry Stogsdill for their hospitality and help accessing the local ranches on my expedition to find the mountain plover. They were a source of unending information. They not only helped me, but it appears they have been very active in helping the Colorado Division of Wildlife with wildlife studies and negotiating with other landowners in the area to help with these studies. In 2005, they were awarded the *Wildlife Landowner of the Year* by the Division of Wildlife. I asked Carl and Cherry about my assistant high school football coach who was from Karval, and they said, "Yes, he still lives here". I walked up to his door and even after 35 years, he recognized me immediately. I also appreciate his time showing me around his property and the time we had to catch up.

## Karval Reservoir State Wildlife Area

While in the area, it would be well worth your time to visit Karval Reservoir. This little oasis in the prairie is east of town 2 miles on CR S and a mile south on CR 31. Four mule deer were bedded on the hillside just inside the gate when I made my first visit. Stocked rainbow trout were rising in the glassy surface of the west cove and mallards were diving in the cattail reeds.

There are several picnicking sites where a number of birds were taking advantage of the brush line reservoir. Of course red-winged blackbirds were flitting about as were Cassin's sparrows and common yellowthroat. I am sure this spot will attract many more birds later in the year as the migration north continues.

## History

In 1999, the mountain plover was proposed for listing as a threatened species. However, as early as 2003, the U.S. Fish and Wildlife Service listing was withdrawn because new information indicated that the threats to the species were not as significant as earlier believed.

Much of the information acquired over the last few years relating to the mountain plover can be directly related to the private landowner. This is a controversial issue when it comes to landowners. Whenever an agency wants to question or access private land with the intention to study a supposed endangered species, they often times run into a less-than-cooperative landowner. Frequently, this can lead to restrictions on how the landowners can manage their land and conduct business. This is their livelihood, their land, and they do not like to be told what they can and cannot do with it.

In this case though, the previous studies and bird counts for the mountain plover were done primarily on public land, which only accounts for about 20 percent of all short-grass prairies. Breeding mountain plovers are well camouflaged and easily unnoticed. They tend to be poorly sampled by roadside surveys and trend guesstimates should be viewed with considerable caution. Most data for this species are obtained on fewer than five routes that have been consistently surveyed since the 1960s. This data may not be representative of trends throughout their range. The survey-wide indices are variable but with a declining tendency. By accessing private land, researchers were able to get a much broader view of the habitat and more practical time in the field found a viable and steady population of the mountain plover. The North American population is estimated at between 8,000 and 11,000. This indicates that the population is larger than had been thought and was no longer declining. In addition, a variety of conservation efforts initiated for mountain plovers and other species of the high plains in several western states have benefited the mountain plover. These landowners have taken great pride in their involvement towards the species conservation and the biodiversity of their land.

A very unique situation exists in the Karval area. Historically, the mountain plover bred and summered on the short-grass prairie intensively grazed by bison. This habitat is duplicated here by the widespread grazing of black-tailed prairie dog colonies and cattle. Everyone in the area recognized the plover and knew it by name, but was unaware that they were right in the middle of prime habitat for this unique bird. The plover has co-existed unimpeded in prairie dog towns, grazing cattle, and the ranchers for years.

The plover's primary diet consists of insects, which means the prairie dogs and cattle pastures are ideal breeding grounds for a number of six-legged creatures. Prairie dog dung produces dung beetles and cow manure breeds any number of fly larvae that are dined on by the mountain plover.

## Location

From Denver, take Interstate 70 east a little over 75 miles to Limon. Take Highway 71 south about 36 miles to County Road T. Turn east (left) and continue to County Road 23, veer right for another mile and veer left on County Road S. Karval is another 5 miles east on CR S.

*A ground squirrel with a snack.*

# Scenic Byways
## Santa Fe Trail Scenic Byway

The Santa Fe Trail Scenic Byway is a 188-mile trip following the footsteps and wagon wheel ruts of some of the first explorers to our state. This part of the Santa Fe Trail is often referred to as the Mountain Route. This journey through southeastern Colorado starts in the town of Holly on US Highway 50 and tracks a major stretch of the Arkansas River. At the town of La Junta, the trail veers southwest following CO Highway 350 to Trinidad. The drive takes about four to five hours and would be a great trip to catch up on the history of the old west. The Santa Fe Trail was designated by the U.S. Secretary of Transportation as a National Scenic Byway in 1998. It is one of ten America's Byways designated in Colorado.

The Santa Fe Trail served as a conduit from the east to the west from about 1821 to 1846. One of the southernmost routes across the Great Plains, the trail basically follows the lowlands of the Arkansas River and then veers south along the Purgatoire River. It provided passageway for explorers such as Buffalo Bill Cody and supplied a route for the exchange of goods for a number of new settlements. This stretch of the Santa Fe Trail was one of the last strongholds of the nomadic Plains Indians and one of the first toeholds of Anglo-American pioneers, who began homesteading along the Arkansas River in the 1860s.

Bent's Old Fort near La Junta, now a National Historic Site, was a major meeting place for traders, trappers, and explorers, a virtual cultural melting pot. In peaceful times, American travelers, the U.S. Army, Spaniards, and Native Americans all spent time here to barter their possessions.

From the town of Holly near the Colorado-Kansas border, one is treated to a phenomenal view of the Arkansas River valley and the rich farmlands the short-grass prairie supports. This is the home of the elusive white-tailed deer, ring-necked pheasant, and the lark bunting (Colorado's state bird). The river bottom is a birdwatcher's paradise with a whole list of waterfowl, herons, and rails. Expect to see western sandpiper, barn swallows, and Bullock's orioles.

## Sand Creek Massacre National Historic Site

One of the first points of interest along the Santa Fe Trail that I would direct you to is the site of the Sand Creek Massacre. It is located in Kiowa County northeast of Lamar. To visit the site from Highway 50, take Highway 385 north about 30 miles to Highway 96. Turn west (left) and travel 6 miles to the town of Brandon. Turn north (right) onto CR 59 and go 7 miles to CR W. Turn west (left) and the park entrance is along CR W a few miles west. If coming from Lamar on Highway 50, take Highway 287 north about 25 miles to Highway 96. Turn east (right) and travel about 12 miles to Chivington. Turn north (left) onto CR 54 for about 7 miles to CR W. Turn east (right) and the park entrance is just west of the turn. The county roads are gravel and can be influenced greatly by weather. Vehicles towing a trailer or a motorcycle may have a rough go of it.

On November 29, 1864, this National Historic Site was the location of one of the most brutal attacks on Native Americans in all of Colorado history. An army of Colorado volunteer soldiers attacked a camp of Cheyenne and Arapaho along Sand Creek. Over 150 Indians were killed in the attack, many of whom were women and

*Hawks are plentiful along the Santa Fe Trail.*

children. Finally in the late 1990s (with a sense of political correctness I'm sure) the National Park Service was directed to identify the location of the massacre and create a suitable place of remembrance and make it part of the national park system. Sand Creek Massacre National Historic Site was established in 2007. The site was created to preserve and protect the cultural landscape of the massacre and enhance public understanding.

Protecting the native biological resource, including animals, is essential to safeguarding the cultural landscape. Sand Creek Massacre NHS is principally made up of short-grass prairie and sage shrubland. Sand Creek, a sporadic flowing stream, which has a small number of cottonwood trees, is included in the site. There is also a small pond on site that attracts a number of wildlife species, many on the federally protected or species of special interest list. The burrowing owl, mountain plover, black-tailed prairie dog, northern harrier, and northern leopard frog have been seen on site. The lesser prairie chickens historically occupied this area but more than likely have been pushed farther south into the Comanche Grasslands and east into Kansas. Adding jackrabbits, cottontails, a number of smaller burrowing animals, rattlesnakes, Swainson's hawk, scaled quail, loggerhead shrike, red-headed woodpecker, lark bunting, and the white-faced ibis, the location presents a well-rounded list of fur and feather.

## Contact

**Sand Creek Massacre NHS**
910 Wansted, POB 249, Eads, CO 81036
or
35110 Highway 194 East, La Junta, CO 81050
719-438-5916 / 719-383-5051 / 719-729-3003

The Sand Creek Massacre National Historic Site is open 9:00am-4:00pm daily. The site is normally closed for the season from December 1-March 31.

To schedule a visit between December 1 and March 31 please call or write the park at least two weeks in advance. Access may be available depending on availability of staff and weather conditions.

## JOHN MARTIN RESERVOIR STATE PARK

Following the byway west on Highway 50 one will find John Martin Reservoir State Park. It is located 16 miles west of Lamar with access south of the town of Hasty. This remote state park is an outdoor recreationist's dream.

Of course boating and fishing are high on the list of things to do, while excellent facilities provide sanctuary at the end of a long day on the water. Two campgrounds – Lake Hasty Campground and Point Campground – have 213 campsites with great views of the reservoir. Group sites can be found at the Caddoa Shelter. Lake Hasty Campground has all the amenities: electrical hookups, water, laundry room, flush toilets, and a coin-operated shower. The Lake Hasty Campground is a preferred winter roosting spot for magnificent bald eagles. They can be seen soaring above the reservoir and sitting on the ice. Point Campground is more rustic with picnic tables, fire grill, tent pads, and vault toilets.

John Martin Reservoir supports a host of warmwater fishing. Spring is very good for crappie and saugeye fishing. Anglers will find exceptional bass and wiper fishing in early to mid-summer. Late-night anglers should find the channel catfish and walleye fishing to be good all summer long. Bluegill and perch are active in the spring during their pre-spawn but can be found throughout all the seasons. The cooling waters of the fall usually fire up the crappie and wiper again.

Jet skiing, sailboarding, swimming, and water skiing are favored activities, as are hiking, biking, and horseback riding. The John Martin State Wildlife Area is just five minutes south of the reservoir and is open to hunting during regular seasons.

Wildlife viewing and birding are exceptional at John Martin. White-tailed and mule deer are seen regularly in the mornings and evenings as are coyotes and fox. Raccoons love the proximity of the water, squirrels take up residence in the trees and prairie dogs can be found throughout the grasslands of the park.

John Martin Reservoir State Park is a very important bird sanctuary for waterfowl, shorebirds, raptors, and game birds. In fact, the least tern and the piping plover two federally protected shorebirds, nest here in the spring. Gadwall ducks and American wigeon are common during both the spring and fall migration, as are redheads and pintails. Western grebe, double-crested cormorant and white pelicans can be seen fishing on the reservoir most of the summer. Great blue herons nest here and sandhill cranes pass through here during spring and fall migrations.

At the northwest end of the reservoir, you can find more birding sites. Van's Grove is part of the John Martin State Wildlife Area and can be found on CR JJ about a mile west of CR 18. It is a grove of elm trees at an abandoned homestead. Yellow warblers and blue-winged warblers (a rare eastern warbler) have been sighted here. Wood Thrush Grove, also part of the John Martin State Wildlife Area, is a small cluster of tall trees and thick undergrowth at the corner of CR16 and CR JJ. This might be a good place to see a western wood-pewee, mourning dove, or vesper sparrow. Fort Lyon State Wildlife Easement is accessed from CR 16 and CR HH. This is a fairly large grove of drought stricken elms that is good for viewing red-headed woodpeckers, downy woodpeckers, and northern flickers. Please do not disturb the nesting great blue herons. The Fort Lyon Marshes, also at CR 16 and CR HH present good habitat for American bitterns and Virginia rails. It is best to park on the road at night and listen to these species. The Green Heron Slough is also on CR HH opposite the Fort Lyon State Wildlife Easement. It is beautiful habitat for migrating and resident birds alike. The cattail marsh hides American coots, American bitterns, snowy egret, house wren, and white-crowned sparrow.

To the north about 12 miles on CR 10 is Adobe Creek Reservoir State Wildlife Area. This is another outstanding birding location.

## Contact

**Park Office**
30703 County Road 24, Hasty, CO 81044
Office Hours: 8:00am-4:00pm daily; extended hours weekends
Park Hours: 24 hours a day
719-829-1801

The next major township just west of John Martin Reservoir on Highway 50 is Las Animas. Much of this area is very well known for its melon harvest in the late summer and fall. Some of the tastiest cantaloupe and watermelons you will ever eat are available at roadside stands and farmer's markets.

The Kit Carson Museum is located in Las Animas and is of historical interest. The old adobe building itself was used to house German prisoners captured during World War II and then later for migrant workers that helped with the agricultural business in the area. The museum consists of artifacts from the days of Kit Carson through World War II.

Christopher "Kit" Carson, born in Kentucky in 1809, was an important figure to the area along the Santa Fe Trail. He was a translator and dealt with the American Indians remarkably, served as an Indian Agent in the late 1850s, was an accomplished trapper and hunter, and eventually became a Brigadier General for his meritorious accomplishments. An important individual to the exploration of the west, John C. Fremont appreciated Kit Carson's experience in the backwoods and brought Carson along as guide in several explorations. Carson died at Fort Lynn, Colorado in 1868. Kit Carson Museum is located at Bent Ave. and 9th St, PO Box 68, Las Animas (719-456-2507). The museum is open year round by appointment. From Memorial Day to Labor Day, the museum is open from 1:00pm-5:00pm, 7 days a week and is run by local volunteers.

*Bent's Old Fort National Historic Site*

## BENT'S OLD FORT NATIONAL HISTORIC SITE

Continuing west along the Santa Fe Trail Scenic Byway, one will find the town of La Junta. La Junta is the home of Bent's Old Fort National Historic Site. The site is a reconstruction of the old fort that burned in 1849. To reach the site from Highway 50 at La Junta, take Highway 109 north 1 mile to Highway 194. Turn right (east) on Highway 194 and travel about 6 miles to the fort.

The original fort was built on this site in 1833 by William Bent and his brother Charles, along with Ceran St. Vrain. For much of its 16-year history, the fort was the only major permanent white settlement on the Santa Fe Trail between Missouri and the Mexican settlements. It was not a military post as one might believe because of the old classic westerns at the movie theater, but was constructed to trade with plains Indians and trappers. The primary trade was with the Southern Cheyenne and Arapaho Indians for buffalo robes. However, with time, the trade room at Bent's Fort was stocked with items from around the world. There were glass beads from Italy, trade guns from England and Belgium, blankets and fabric from England, brass hawk bells from France, silver jewelry from Germany, and vermillion from China.

Although the Army did acquire supplies here and use the fort as a staging point during the war with Mexico in 1846, the fort primarily provided explorers and adventurers with a stopping point for wagon repairs, good food, fresh water, rest, and protection. Unfortunately, several untimely events and disease caused the fort's abandonment in 1849. Bent's Old Fort was reconstructed in 1976 based on archeological excavations, original sketches, paintings, and diaries found in the fort.

Today, visitors can tour inside the fort and gain knowledge and a feeling of how the Old West really was. Inside, you can view a 20-minute documentary film, "Traders, Tribes and Travelers". Self-guided tours, documentation, exhibits and fort personnel can help visitors with questions about the history of this national historic site. Interpreters provide guided tours and demonstrations June 1 through September 1.

When I pulled into the location for the first time, I was amazed to find a huge pond and wetlands to the east of the fort's position. In fact, hidden out of site was another smaller pond and wetlands nearer the Arkansas River. There are nearly 150 acres in total.

For such a small area, there is a remarkable number of wildlife species that take refuge here. Nearly 100 species of birds frequent or migrate through this area. Great horned owls, wild turkeys, northern bobwhite, and red-headed woodpeckers are commonly seen or heard south of the fort along the river in the cottonwoods. Mallards, wigeon, snow geese, and Canada geese can be found in the large wetlands and the beautiful white-faced ibis migrate through the site in the spring. In the winter, northern harrier and red-tailed hawks prey on the black-tailed prairie dogs and small rodents in the trees along the river. There are even a couple of resident peacocks that live in and around the fort.

Spiny softshell turtles can also be seen in the large wetland and along the Arkansas River.

The most commonly seen animals at Bent's Old Fort are white-tailed deer, mule deer, and coyotes. Desert cottontail, red fox squirrel, skunks, raccoons, yellow-bellied racer, bullsnake, plains garter snake, and western rattlesnake follow a close second.

## Contact

**Bent's Old Fort**
35110 Highway 194 East, La Junta, CO 81050-9523
719-383-5010
Summer hours (June 1 through August 31): 8:00am-5:30pm; Winter hours (September 1 through May 31): 9:00am-4:00pm The park is open every day except Thanksgiving, Christmas, and New Year's Day.

From La Junta, the byway heads southwest on Highway 350. The first 30 miles or so traverse the scenic Comanche National Grasslands (see the Comanche National Grasslands chapter for more information). To the west, you may notice the Spanish Peaks. These peaks, along with Pikes Peak to the north, were used as landmarks as explorers journeyed west. The elevation rises slightly as the Great Plains give way to the transitions of foothills and eventually the Rocky Mountains. Many would call this country "desolate", but I would say diverse (I would, however, suggest filling up the gas tank in La Junta before taking out on this last leg of the byway). It is a magnificent drive, especially if you live in the city, that gives you a novel look at a country of juniper-covered ridges, the overlooked exquisiteness of the short-grass prairie, and sunrises and sunsets that rival any on earth. Take the time to stop and take in the fleet-footed pronghorn antelope snacking on forbs and sagebrush. Watch for red-tailed hawks and coyotes hunting a fence line, take a picture of a blooming yucca plant, or just get out and take a deep breath of the wide open spaces. It is exhilarating!

Even though the byway ends at the state line with New Mexico on Interstate 25, Trinidad will more than likely be the end of the tour. The Trinidad History Museum is a complex that includes the Baca House, Bloom Mansion, and Santa Fe Trail Museum and heritage gardens. The Baca House was bought by Felipe and Dolores Baca in 1973 for 22,000 pounds of wool. The two-story adobe house is worth a visit. The Bloom Mansion, constructed in 1882 by cattle baron and financier Frank Bloom, is an impressive Victorian home that depicts the lifestyle of an influential family. The Santa Fe Trail Museum has photographs, heirlooms, and a buckskin coat worn by Kit Carson on display.

## Contact

**Santa Fe Trail Scenic & Historic Byway**
PO Box 377
312 East Main Street, Trinidad, CO 81082
719-846-7217
www.santafetrailscenicandhistoricbyway.org

# Wildlife Refuge System

Colorado has six national wildlife refuges that offer opportunities for hunting, fishing, wildlife viewing, photography, and more (although certain refuges are closed to certain activities – be sure to check before you go). All of the refuges listed in this guide, except Baca NWR which is closed, offer free public access.

According to the Rocky Mountain Arsenal website:

"The National Wildlife Refuge System is:

> *The only system of federal lands dedicated specifically to wildlife conservation*
>
> *The largest and most complete collection of habitats managed by any resource agency in the world*
>
> *Five hundred and forty units including nearly 95 million acres. The National Wildlife Refuge System stretches from the caribou-tracked tundra of Alaska to the rain forests of Puerto Rico*
>
> *The waterfowl nesting grounds in the prairie potholes of North Dakota to the teeming coastal marshes of Louisiana*
>
> *The puffin colonies on the rocky coast of Maine to the turtle nesting beaches on Rose Atoll in the South Pacific"*

Wildlife Comes First! Refuges provide essential habitat for hundreds of threatened and endangered species and many more thousands of species of migratory birds, mammals, reptiles, amphibians, fish, invertebrates, and plants.

The refuge system was born at a tiny 3-acre island off the east coast of Florida in 1903. As the 20th Century dawned, the feathers of pelicans, egrets, and other wading birds were in high demand to adorn women's hats, and 'plume hunters' had ravaged the great rookeries of the southeast. On March 14, 1903 the great conservationist President Theodore Roosevelt set aside Pelican Island as a bird sanctuary – the first national wildlife refuge.

# Audubon Society for Colorado

## State Office

**Audubon Colorado**
1966 13th Street, Suite 230, Boulder, CO 80302
303-415-0130

## Local Chapters

**Aiken Audubon Society**
6660 Delmonico Drive D-195, Colorado Springs, CO 80919

**Arkansas Valley Audubon Society**
PO Box 11187, Pueblo, CO 81001
719-547-2245

**Audubon Society of Greater Denver**
9803 S. Wadsworth Blvd., Littleton, CO 80128
303-973-9530

**Black Canyon Audubon Society**
PO Box 387, Delta, CO 81416

**Boulder County Audubon Society**
P.O. Box 2081, Boulder, CO 80306

**Evergreen Naturalists Audubon Society**
PO Box 523, Evergreen, CO 80437

**Fort Collins Audubon Society**
PO Box 271968, Fort Collins, CO 80527-1968

**Grand Valley Audubon Society**
P.O. Box 1211, Grand Junction, Colorado 81502
970-241-4670

**Platte & Prairie Audubon Society**
30 South Freemont Avenue, Johnstown, CO 80534
970-587-2844

**Roaring Fork Audubon Society**
P.O. Box 1192, Carbondale, CO 81623

**Weminuche Audubon Society**
PO Box 4060, Pagosa Springs, CO 81157
970-883-3066

# National Parks Passes

At this printing, the federal government has set up several new passes that can save a visitor several dollars over a year's time if planning to visit a number of our national parks and monuments. Children under 16 are admitted free. Passes can be obtained in person at the park, by calling 1-888-ASK-USGS Ext. 1, or via the internet at http://store.usgs.gov/pass.

## America the Beautiful – National Parks and Federal Recreational Lands Pass

**Annual Pass:** Cost $80. This pass is available to the general public and provides access to, and use of, federal recreation sites that charge an entrance or standard amenity fee for a year, beginning from the date of sale. The pass admits the pass holder/s and passengers in a non-commercial vehicle at per-vehicle fee areas and pass holder plus 3 adults, not to exceed 4 adults, at per-person fee areas.

**Senior Pass:** Cost $10. This is a lifetime pass for U.S. citizens or permanent residents age 62 or over. The pass provides access to, and use of, federal recreation sites that charge an entrance or standard amenity. The pass admits the pass holder and passengers in a non-commercial vehicle at per-vehicle fee areas and pass holder plus 3 adults, not to exceed 4 adults, at per-person fee areas. The pass can only be obtained in person at the park. The Senior Pass provides a 50-percent discount on some expanded amenity fees charged for facilities and services such as camping, swimming, boat launch, and specialized interpretive services. In some cases where expanded amenity fees are charged, only the pass holder will be given the 50-percent price reduction. The pass is non-transferable and generally does not cover or reduce special recreation permit fees or fees charged by concessionaires.

**Access Pass:** Free. This is a lifetime pass for U.S. citizens or permanent residents with permanent disabilities. Documentation is required to obtain the pass. Acceptable documentation includes: statement by a licensed physician; document issued by federal agency such as the Veteran's Administration, Social Security Disability Income or Supplemental Security Income; or document issued by a state agency such as a vocational rehabilitation agency. The pass provides access to, and use of, federal recreation sites that charge an entrance or standard amenity fee. The pass admits the pass holder and passengers in a non-commercial vehicle at per-vehicle fee areas and pass holder plus 3 adults, not to exceed 4 adults, at per-person fee areas. The pass can only be obtained in person at the park. The Access Pass provides a 50-percent discount on some expanded amenity fees charged for facilities and services such as camping, swimming, boat launching, and specialized interpretive services. In some cases where expanded amenity fees are charged, only the pass holder will be given the 50-percent price reduction. The pass is non-transferable and generally does not cover or reduce special recreation permit fees or fees charged by concessionaires.

**Volunteer Pass:** Free. This pass is for volunteers acquiring 500 service hours on a cumulative basis. It provides access to, and use of, federal recreation sites that charge an entrance or standard amenity fee for a year, beginning from the date of award. The pass admits the pass holder and passengers in a non-commercial vehicle at per-vehicle fee areas and pass holder plus 3 adults, not to exceed 4 adults, at per-person fee areas. Contact the park VIP coordinator at any national park or monument to learn about volunteer opportunities in the park.

**Fee Waivers:** Groups may be eligible to apply for a fee waiver. To meet these requirements your group must be a tax-exempt group that is coming to the monument for educational or scientific purposes. Educational institutions must be accredited or otherwise recognized as a bona fide educational institution. The visit must support specific, for-credit curriculum as its purpose. The park resources and facilities must be related to the educational purpose of the visit.

# State Parks Passes

**Annual Parks Pass:** $60 per vehicle. Annual passes provide unlimited access to all Colorado State Parks for a 12-month period. Passes are available for purchase: Online, at any state park or region office, or at select retail outlets.

**Annual Multiple Pass:** $25 for each additional vehicle pass. To purchase a Multiple Pass for additional vehicles registered in the same name, please provide: proof of Colorado registration on all vehicles under the same name and address, and proof of first Annual Pass purchased or receipt of original. Multiple passes are not available online, but can be purchased at any state park or parks office.

**Annual Replacement Pass:** $5. If your pass is lost or damaged, replacement passes are available. Customer is required to show receipt/pass cover from the original Annual Pass. Replacement passes are not available online, but can be purchased at any state park or parks office.

**Aspen Leaf Pass:** $30 per vehicle. Aspen Leaf Passes are for Colorado residents 64 years or older and allow unlimited access to all Colorado state parks. This pass has the added bonus of 50-percent off camping, Sunday through Thursday, excluding holidays. Beginning in 2009, the Aspen Leaf Pass is available for purchase at any time of year and is valid for 12 months from date of purchase. To purchase, please provide proof of age and a current Colorado vehicle registration. The Aspen Leaf pass may be purchased only at a state park or state park office (not available online).

**Aspen Leaf Multiple Pass:** $15 for each additional vehicle. To purchase an Aspen Leaf Multiple Pass for additional vehicles in the same name, provide proof of Colorado registration on all vehicles under the same name and proof of purchase for original Aspen Leaf Pass.

**Aspen Leaf Free Pass:** No cost. This pass is for Colorado residents born in 1922 or prior. It allows unlimited access to all Colorado state parks. The Aspen Leaf Free Pass may be acquired only at a state park or state park office. Camping discounts also apply. To obtain a free Aspen Leaf Pass, provide proof of age, a signed affidavit of eligibility and proof of vehicle registration.

**Columbine Pass:** $12.50. The Columbine Pass is for disabled Colorado residents and is transferable between vehicles. It is available by application only with proof of eligibility, and will allow other vehicle occupants park entrance. The pass holder must be present for the pass to be valid. For eligibility requirements and application information, visit http://parks.state.co.us.

**Colorado Disabled Veterans Pass:** No Cost. Colorado residents with current Disabled Veterans license plates may access Colorado state parks for free without a pass on the windshield. These plates are obtained through the Division of Motor Vehicles. The law for individuals with Disabled Veterans license plates provides free entrance to state parks and does not provide special camping rates. The veteran must be present in the vehicle. Disabled veterans who are 64 years of age or older and a Colorado resident may opt to purchase the reduced-fee Aspen Leaf Pass (with special camping benefits) or apply for the Columbine Pass.

**Centennial Pass:** $12.50. The Centennial Pass is for income-eligible Colorado residents. Applicants must be Colorado residents, at least 18 years of age, and have a gross federal income for the previous calendar year below a specific income level, depending on family size. The Centennial Pass may be purchased at the three regional offices of Colorado State Parks and the Division headquarters in Denver – not at the individual parks or through any pass concessionaires. In order to purchase the Centennial Pass, the applicant must show a photo identification card and provide documentation, in the form of the previous year's federal income tax return that the federal gross annual income of the individual was at or below a determined amount. The only tax documents that can be used to determine eligibility for the Centennial Pass are U.S. federal tax forms 1040, 1040-A, and 1040-EZ. Call 303-866-3437 to have an application sent to you.

# Official Checklist of Colorado Birds
Courtesy of the Colorado Birding Society

## SWANS, GEESE & DUCKS

| | |
|---|---|
| Black-bellied Whistling Duck | *Dendrocygna autumnalis* |
| Fulvous Whistling Duck | *Dendrocygna bicolor* |
| Greater White-fronted Goose | *Anser albifrons* |
| Snow Goose | *Chen caerulescens* |
| Ross' Goose | *Chen rossii* |
| Canada Goose | *Branta canadensis* |
| Cackling Goose | *Branta hutchinsii* |
| Brant | *Branta bernicla* |
| Trumpeter Swan | *Cygnus buccinator* |
| Tundra Swan | *Cygnus columbianus* |
| Wood Duck | *Aix sponsa* |
| Gadwall | *Anas strepera* |
| Eurasian Wigeon | *Anas penelope* |
| American Wigeon | *Anas americana* |
| American Black Duck | *Anas rubripes* |
| Mallard | *Anas platyrhynchos* |
| Blue-winged Teal | *Anas discors* |
| Cinnamon Teal | *Anas cyanoptera* |
| Northern Shoveler | *Anas clypeata* |
| Northern Pintail | *Anas acuta* |
| Garganey | *Anas querquedula* |
| Green-winged Teal | *Anas crecca* |
| Canvasback | *Aythya valisineria* |

| | |
|---|---|
| Redhead | *Aythya americana* |
| Ring-necked Duck | *Aythya collaris* |
| Tufted Duck | *Aythya fuligula* |
| Greater Scaup | *Aythya marila* |
| Lesser Scaup | *Aythya affinis* |
| Harlequin Duck | *Histronicus histronicus* |
| Surf Scoter | *Melanitta perspicillata* |
| White-winged Scoter | *Melanitta fusca* |
| Black Scoter | *Melanitta nigra* |
| Long-tailed Duck | *Clangula hyemalis* |
| Bufflehead | *Bucephala albeola* |
| Common Goldeneye | *Bucephala clangula* |
| Barrow's Goldeneye | *Bucephala islandica* |
| Hooded Merganser | *Lophodytes cucullatus* |
| Common Merganser | *Mergus merganser* |
| Red-breasted Merganser | *Mergus serrator* |
| Ruddy Duck | *Oxyura jamaicensis* |

## QUAIL, GROUSE & TURKEY

| | |
|---|---|
| Chukar | *Alectoris chukar* |
| Ring-necked Pheasant | *Phasianus colchicus* |
| Ruffed Grouse | *Bonasa umbellus* |
| Greater Sage Grouse | *Centrocercus urophasianus* |
| Gunnison Sage Grouse | *Centrocercus minimus* |
| White-tailed Ptarmigan | *Lagopus leucurus* |
| Dusky Grouse | *Dendragapus obscurus* |
| Sharp-tailed Grouse | *Tympanuchus phasianellus* |
| Greater Prairie Chicken | *Tympanuchus cupido* |
| Lesser Prairie Chicken | *Tympanuchus pallidicinctus* |
| Wild Turkey | *Meleagris gallopavo* |
| Scaled Quail | *Callipepla squamata* |
| Gambel's Quail | *Callipepla gambelii* |
| Northern Bobwhite | *Colinus virginianus* |

## LOONS

| | |
|---|---|
| Red-throated Loon | *Gavia stellata* |
| Arctic Loon | *Gavia arctica* |
| Pacific Loon | *Gavia pacifica* |
| Common Loon | *Gavia immer* |
| Yellow-billed Loon | *Gavia adamsii* |

## GREBES

| | |
|---|---|
| Pied-billed Grebe | *Podilymbus podiceps* |
| Horned Grebe | *Podiceps auritus* |
| Red-necked Grebe | *Podiceps grisegena* |
| Eared Grebe | *Podiceps nigricollis* |
| Western Grebe | *Aechmophorus occidentalis* |
| Clark's Grebe | *Aechmophorus clarkii* |

*Ring-necked pheasant*

## PELICANS

| | |
|---|---|
| American White Pelican | *Pelecanus erythrorhynchos* |
| Brown Pelican | *Pelecanus occidentalis* |

## CORMORANTS

| | |
|---|---|
| Neotropic Cormorant | *Phalacrocorax brasiliana* |
| Double-crested Cormorant | *Phalacrocorax auritus* |

## ANHINGAS

| | |
|---|---|
| Anhinga | *Anhinga anhinga* |

## FRIGATEBIRDS

| | |
|---|---|
| Magnificent Frigatebird | *Fregata magnificens* |

## BITTERNS & HERONS

| | |
|---|---|
| American Bittern | *Botaurus lentiginosus* |
| Least Bittern | *Ixobrychus exilis* |
| Great Blue Heron | *Ardea herodias* |
| Great Egret | *Ardea alba* |
| Snowy Egret | *Egretta thula* |
| Little Blue Heron | *Egretta caerulea* |
| Tricolored Heron | *Egretta tricolor* |
| Reddish Egret | *Egretta rufescens* |
| Cattle Egret | *Bubulcus ibis* |
| Green Heron | *Butorides virescens* |
| Black-crowned Night Heron | *Nycticorax nycticorax* |
| Yellow-crowned Night Heron | *Nyctanassa violacea* |

## IBISES & SPOONBILLS

| | |
|---|---|
| White Ibis | *Eudocimus albus* |
| Glossy Ibis | *Plegadis falcinellus* |
| White-faced Ibis | *Plegadis chihi* |
| Roseate Spoonbill | *Platalea ajaja* |

## STORKS

| | |
|---|---|
| Wood Stork | *Mycteria americana* |

## AMERICAN VULTURES

| | |
|---|---|
| Black Vulture | *Coragyps atratus* |
| Turkey Vulture | *Cathartes aura* |

## KITES, HAWKS, EAGLES, HARRIERS

| | |
|---|---|
| Osprey | *Pandion haliaetus* |
| Swallow-tailed Kite | *Elanoides forficatus* |
| Mississippi Kite | *Ictinia misisippiensis* |
| Bald Eagle | *Haliaeetus leucocephalus* |
| Northern Harrier | *Circus cyaneus* |
| Sharp-shinned Hawk | *Accipiter striatus* |
| Cooper's Hawk | *Accipiter cooperii* |
| Northern Goshawk | *Accipiter gentilis* |
| Common Black-Hawk | *Buteogallus anthracinus* |
| Harris' Hawk | *Parabuteo unicinctus* |
| Red-shouldered Hawk | *Buteo lineatus* |
| Broad-winged Hawk | *Buteo platypterus* |
| Swainson's Hawk | *Buteo swainsoni* |
| Zone-tailed Hawk | *Buteo albonotatus* |
| Red-tailed Hawk | *Buteo jamaicensis* |
| Ferruginous Hawk | *Buteo regalis* |
| Rough-legged Hawk | *Buteo lagopus* |
| Golden Eagle | *Aquila chrysaetos* |

## CARACARAS & FALCONS

| | |
|---|---|
| Crested Caracara | *Caracara cheriway* |
| American Kestrel | *Falco sparverius* |
| Merlin | *Falco columbarius* |
| Gyrfalcon | *Falco rusticolus* |
| Peregrine Falcon | *Falco peregrinus* |
| Prairie Falcon | *Falco mexicanus* |

## RAILS, GALLINULES, & COOTS

| | |
|---|---|
| Yellow Rail | *Coturnicops noveboracensis* |
| Black Rail | *Laterallus jamaicensis* |
| King Rail | *Rallus elegans* |
| Virginia Rail | *Rallus limicola* |
| Sora | *Porzana carolina* |
| Purple Gallinule | *Porphyrio martinica* |
| Common Moorhen | *Gallinula chloropus* |
| American Coot | *Fulica americana* |

## CRANES

| | |
|---|---|
| Sandhill Crane | *Grus canadensis* |
| Whooping Crane | *Grus americana* |

## PLOVERS & LAPWINGS

| | |
|---|---|
| Black-bellied Plover | *Pluvialis Squatarola* |
| American Golden Plover | *Pluvialis dominica* |
| Snowy Plover | *Charadrius alexandrinus* |
| Semipalmated Plover | *Charadrius semipalmatus* |
| Piping Plover | *Charadrius melodus* |
| Killdeer | *Charadrius vociferus* |
| Mountain Plover | *Charadrius montanus* |

## STILTS & AVOCETS

| | |
|---|---|
| Black-necked Stilt | *Himantopus mexicanus* |
| American Avocet | *Recurvirostra americana* |

## SANDPIPERS & PHALAROPES

| | |
|---|---|
| Spotted Sandpiper | *Actitis macularia* |
| Solitary Sandpiper | *Tringa solitaria* |
| Greater Yellowlegs | *Tringa melanoleuca* |
| Willet | *Catoptrophorus semipalmatus* |
| Lesser Yellowlegs | *Tringa flavipes* |

| | |
|---|---|
| Upland Sandpiper | *Bartramia longicauda* |
| Eskimo Curlew | *Numenius borealis* |
| Whimbrel | *Numenius phaeopus* |
| Long-billed Curlew | *Numenius americanus* |
| Hudsonian Godwit | *Limosa haemastica* |
| Marbled Godwit | *Limosa fedoa* |
| Ruddy Turnstone | *Arenaria interpres* |
| Red Knot | *Calidris canutus* |
| Sanderling | *Calidris alba* |
| Semipalmated Sandpiper | *Calidris pusilla* |
| Western Sandpiper | *Calidris mauri* |
| Least Sandpiper | *Calidris minutilla* |
| White-rumped Sandpiper | *Calidris fuscicollis* |
| Baird's Sandpiper | *Calidris bairdii* |
| Pectoral Sandpiper | *Calidris melanotos* |
| Sharp-tailed Sandpiper | *Calidris acuminata* |
| Dunlin | *Calidris alpina* |
| Curlew Sandpiper | *Calidris ferruginea* |
| Stilt Sandpiper | *Calisdris himantopus* |
| Buff-breasted Sandpiper | *Tryngites subruficollis* |
| Ruff | *Philomachus pugnax* |
| Short-billed Dowitcher | *Limnodromus griseus* |
| Long-billed Dowitcher | *Limnodromus scolopaceus* |
| Wilson's Snipe | *Gallinago delicata* |
| American Woodcock | *Scolopax minor* |
| Wilson's Phalarope | *Phalaropus tricolor* |
| Red-necked Phalarope | *Phalaropus lobatus* |
| Red Phalarope | *Phalaropus fulicarius* |

## GULLS, TERNS, & SKIMMERS

| | |
|---|---|
| Laughing Gull | *Larus atricilla* |
| Franklin's Gull | *Larus pipixcan* |
| Little Gull | *Larus minutus* |

| | |
|---|---|
| Black-headed Gull | *Larus ridibundus* |
| Bonaparte's Gull | *Larus philadelphia* |
| Mew Gull | *Larus canus* |
| Ring-billed Gull | *Larus delawarensis* |
| California Gull | *Larus californicus* |
| Herring Gull | *Larus argentatus* |
| Thayer's Gull | *Larus thayeri* |
| Iceland Gull | *Larus glaucoides* |
| Lesser Black-backed Gull | *Larus fuscus* |
| Slaty-backed Gull | *Larus schistisagus* |
| Glaucous-winged Gull | *Larus glaucescens* |
| Glaucous Gull | *Larus hyperboreus* |
| Great Black-backed Gull | *Larus marinus* |
| Kelp Gull | *Larus dominicanus* |
| Sabine's Gull | *Xema sabini* |
| Black-legged Kittiwake | *Rissa tridactyla* |
| Ross's Gull | *Rhodostethia rosea* |
| Ivory Gull | *Pagophila eburnea* |
| Least Tern | *Sterna antillarum* |
| Caspian Tern | *Sterna caspia* |
| Black Tern | *Chilidonias niger* |
| Common Tern | *Sterna hirundo* |
| Arctic Tern | *Sterna paradisaea* |
| Forster's Tern | *Sterna forsteri* |
| Royal Tern | *Sterna maxima* |
| Black Skimmer | *Rynchops niger* |
| Pomarine Jaeger | *Stercorarius pomarinus* |
| Parasitic Jaeger | *Stercorarius parasiticus* |
| Long-tailed Jaeger | *Stercorarius longicaudus* |

## AUKS, MURRES, & PUFFINS

| | |
|---|---|
| Long-billed Murrelet | *Brachyramphus perdix* |
| Ancient Murrelet | *Synthliboarmphus antiquus* |

## PIGEONS & DOVES

| | |
|---|---|
| Rock Pigeon | *Columba livia* |
| Band-tailed Pigeon | *Patagioenas fasciata* |
| Eurasian Collared Dove | *Streptopelia decaocto* |
| White-winged Dove | *Zenaida asiatica* |
| Mourning Dove | *Zenaidura macroura* |
| Inca Dove | *Columbina inca* |
| Common Ground-Dove | *Columbina passerina* |

## CUCKOOS, ROADRUNNERS & ANIS

| | |
|---|---|
| Yellow-billed Cuckoo | *Coccyzus americanus* |
| Black-billed Cuckoo | *Coccyzus erythrophthalmus* |
| Greater Roadrunner | *Geococcyx californianus* |
| Groove-billed Ani | *Crotophaga sulcirostris* |

## BARN OWLS

| | |
|---|---|
| Barn Owl | *Tyto alba* |

## TYPICAL OWLS

| | |
|---|---|
| Flammulated Owl | *Otus flammeolus* |
| Western Screech Owl | *Megascops kennicottii* |
| Eastern Screech Owl | *Megascops asio* |
| Great Horned Owl | *Bubo virginianus* |
| Snowy Owl | *Bubo scandiacus* |
| Northern Pygmy Owl | *Glaucidium gnoma* |
| Burrowing Owl | *Athene cunicularia* |
| Spotted Owl | *Strix occidentalis* |
| Barred Owl | *Strix varia* |
| Long-eared Owl | *Asio otus* |
| Short-eared Owl | *Asio flammeus* |
| Boreal Owl | *Aegolius funereus* |
| Northern Saw-whet Owl | *Aegolius acadicus* |

## GOATSUCKERS

| | |
|---|---|
| Lesser Nighthawk | *Chordeiles acutipennis* |
| Common Nighthawk | *Chordeiles minor* |
| Common Poorwill | *Phalaenoptilus nuttalii* |
| Whip-poor-will | *Caprimulgus vociferus* |

## SWIFTS

| | |
|---|---|
| Black Swift | *Cypseloides niger* |
| Chimney Swift | *Chaetura pelagica* |
| White-throated Swift | *Aeronautes saxatalis* |

## HUMMINGBIRDS

| | |
|---|---|
| Green Violet-ear Hummingbird | *Colibri thalassinus* |
| Broad-billed Hummingbird | *Cynanthus latirostris* |
| White-eared Hummingbird | *Hylocharis leucotis* |
| Blue-throated Hummingbird | *Lampornis clemenciae* |
| Magnificent Hummingbird | *Eugenes fulgens* |
| Ruby-throated Hummingbird | *Archilochus colubris* |
| Black-chinned Hummingbird | *Archilochus alexandri* |
| Anna's Hummingbird | *Calypte anna* |
| Costa's Hummingbird | *Calypte costae* |
| Calliope Hummingbird | *Stellula calliope* |
| Broad-tailed Hummingbird | *Selasphorus platycercus* |
| Rufous Hummingbird | *Selasphorus rufus* |

## KINGFISHERS

| | |
|---|---|
| Belted Kingfisher | *Ceryle alcyon* |

## WOODPECKERS

| | |
|---|---|
| Lewis' Woodpecker | *Melanerpes lewis* |
| Red-headed Woodpecker | *Melanerpes erythrocephalus* |
| Acorn Woodpecker | *Melanerpes formicivorus* |
| Red-bellied Woodpecker | *Melanerpes carolinus* |

| | |
|---|---|
| Williamson's Sapsucker | *Sphyrapicus thyroideus* |
| Yellow-bellied Sapsucker | *Sphyrapicus varius* |
| Red-naped Sapsucker | *Sphyrapicus nuchalis* |
| Ladder-backed Woodpecker | *Picoides scalaris* |
| Downy Woodpecker | *Picoides pubescens* |
| Hairy Woodpecker | *Picoides villosus* |
| American Three-toed Woodpecker | *Picoides dorsalis* |
| Northern Flicker | *Colaptes auratus* |

## TYRANT FLYCATCHERS

| | |
|---|---|
| Olive-sided Flycatcher | *Contopus cooperii* |
| Western Wood-Pewee | *Contopus sordidulus* |
| Eastern Wood-Pewee | *Contopus virens* |
| Alder Flycatcher | *Empidonax alnorum* |
| Willow Flycatcher | *Empidonax traillii* |
| Least Flycatcher | *Empidonax minimus* |
| Hammond's Flycatcher | *Empidonax hammondii* |
| Gray Flycatcher | *Empidonax wrightii* |
| Dusky Flycatcher | *Empidonax oberholseri* |
| Cordilleran Flycatcher | *Empidonax occidentalis* |
| Yellow-bellied Flycatcher | *Empidonax flaviventris* |
| Buff-breasted Flycatcher | *Empidonax fulvifrons* |
| Brown-crested Flycatcher | *Myiarchus tyrannulus* |
| Black Phoebe | *Sayornis nigricans* |
| Eastern Phoebe | *Sayornis phoebe* |
| Say's Phoebe | *Sayornis saya* |
| Vermilion Flycatcher | *Pyrocephalus rubinus* |
| Dusky-capped Flycatcher | *Myiarchus tuberculifer* |
| Ash-throated Flycatcher | *Myiarchus cinerascens* |
| Great Crested Flycatcher | *Myiarchus crinitus* |
| Brown-crested Flycatcher | *Myiarchus tyrannulus* |
| Sulphur-bellied Flycatcher | *Myiodynastes luteiventris* |
| Cassin's Kingbird | *Tyrannus vociferans* |

| | |
|---|---|
| Thick-billed Kingbird | *Tyrannus crassirostris* |
| Western Kingbird | *Tyrannus verticalis* |
| Eastern Kingbird | *Tyrannus tyrannus* |
| Scissor-tailed Flycatcher | *Tyrannus forticatus* |

## SHRIKES

| | |
|---|---|
| Loggerhead Shrike | *Lanius ludovicianus* |
| Northern Shrike | *Lanius excubitor* |

## VIREOS

| | |
|---|---|
| White-eyed Vireo | *Vireo griseus* |
| Bell's Vireo | *Vireo bellii* |
| Gray Vireo | *Vireo vicinior* |
| Yellow-throated Vireo | *Vireo flavifrons* |
| Plumbeous Vireo | *Vireo plumbeus* |
| Cassin's Vireo | *Vireo cassinii* |
| Blue-headed Vireo | *Vireo solitarius* |
| Warbling Vireo | *Vireo gilvus* |
| Philadelphia Vireo | *Vireo philadelphicus* |
| Red-eyed Vireo | *Vireo olivaceus* |

## JAYS, MAGPIES, & CROWS

| | |
|---|---|
| Gray Jay | *Perisoreus canadensis* |
| Steller's Jay | *Cyanocitta stellerii* |
| Blue Jay | *Cyanocitta cristata* |
| Western Scrub-Jay | *Aphelocoma californica* |
| Pinyon Jay | *Gymnorhinus cyanocephalus* |
| Clark's Nutcracker | *Nucifraga columbiana* |
| Black-billed Magpie | *Pica hodsonia* |
| American Crow | *Corvus brachyrhynchos* |
| Chihuahuan Raven | *Corvus cryptoleucus* |
| Common Raven | *Corvus corax* |

## LARKS

| Horned Lark | *Eremophila alpestris* |

## SWALLOWS

| Purple Martin | *Progne subis* |
| Tree Swallow | *Tachycineta bicolor* |
| Violet-green Swallow | *Tachycineta thalassina* |
| Northern Rough-winged Swallow | *Stelgidopteryx serripennis* |
| Bank Swallow | *Riparia riparia* |
| Cliff Swallow | *Petrochelidon pyrrhonota* |
| Barn Swallow | *Hirundo rustica* |

## CHICKADEES & TITMICE

| Black-capped Chickadee | *Poecile atricapilla* |
| Mountain Chickadee | *Poecile gambeli* |
| Juniper Titmouse | *Baeolophus ridgwayi* |
| Tufted Titmouse | *Baeolophus bicolor* |

## BUSHTITS

| Bushtit | *Psaltriparus minimus* |

## NUTHATCHES

| Red-breasted Nuthatch | *Sitta canadensis* |
| White-breasted Nuthatch | *Sitta carolinensis* |
| Pygmy Nuthatch | *Sitta pygmaea* |

## CREEPERS

| Brown Creeper | *Certhia americana* |

## WRENS

| Rock Wren | *Salpinctes obsoletus* |
| Canyon Wren | *Catherpes mexicanus* |

| | |
|---|---|
| Carolina Wren | *Thyrothorus ludovicianus* |
| Bewick's Wren | *Thyromanes bewickii* |
| House Wren | *Troglodytes aedon* |
| Winter Wren | *Troglodytes troglodytes* |
| Sedge Wren | *Cistothorus platensis* |
| Marsh Wren | *Cistothorus palustris* |

## DIPPERS

| | |
|---|---|
| American Dipper | *Cinclus mexicanus* |

## OLD WORLD WARBERS, OLD WORLD FLYCATCHERS & THRUSHES

| | |
|---|---|
| Golden-crowned Kinglet | *Regulus satrapa* |
| Ruby-crowned Kinglet | *Regulus calendula* |
| Blue-gray Gnatcatcher | *Polioptila caerulea* |
| Eastern Bluebird | *Sialia sialis* |
| Western Bluebird | *Sialia mexicana* |
| Mountain Bluebird | *Sialia currucoides* |
| Townsend's Solitaire | *Myadestes townsendi* |
| Veery | *Catharus fuscescens* |
| Gray-cheeked Thrush | *Catharus minimus* |
| Swainson's Thrush | *Catharus ustulatus* |
| Hermit Thrush | *Catharus guttatus* |
| Wood Thrush | *Hylocichla mustelina* |
| American Robin | *Turdus migratorius* |
| Varied Thrush | *Ixoreus naevius* |

## MOCKINGBIRDS & THRASHERS

| | |
|---|---|
| Gray Catbird | *Dumetella carolinensis* |
| Northern Mockingbird | *Mimus polyglottos* |
| Sage Thrasher | *Oreoscoptes montanus* |
| Brown Thrasher | *Toxostoma rufum* |
| Long-billed Thrasher | *Toxostoma longirostre* |

| | |
|---|---|
| Bendire's Thrasher | *Toxostoma bendirei* |
| Curve-billed Thrasher | *Toxostoma curvirostre* |

## STARLINGS

| | |
|---|---|
| European Starling | *Sturnus vulgaris* |

## PIPITS

| | |
|---|---|
| American Pipit | *Anthus rubescens* |
| Sprague's Pipit | *Anthus spragueii* |

## WAXWINGS

| | |
|---|---|
| Bohemian Waxwing | *Bombycilla garralus* |
| Cedar Waxwing | *Bombycilla cedrorum* |

## SILKY-FLYCATCHERS

| | |
|---|---|
| Phainopepla | *Phainopepla nitens* |

## WOOD-WARBLERS, TANAGERS

| | |
|---|---|
| Blue-winged Warbler | *Vermivora pinus* |
| Golden-winged Warbler | *Vermivora chrysoptera* |
| Tennessee Warbler | *Vermivora peregrina* |
| Orange-crowned Warbler | *Vermivora celata* |
| Nashville Warbler | *Vermivora ruficapilla* |
| Virginia's Warbler | *Vermivora virginiae* |
| Lucy's Warbler | *Vermivora luciae* |
| Northern Parula | *Parula americana* |
| Tropical Parula | *Parula pitiayumi* |
| Yellow Warbler | *Dendroica petechia* |
| Chestnut-sided Warbler | *Dendroica pensylvanica* |
| Magnolia Warbler | *Dendroica magnolia* |
| Cape May Warbler | *Dendroica tigrina* |
| Black-throated Blue Warbler | *Dendroica caerulescens* |
| Yellow-rumped Warbler | *Dendroica coronata* |

| | |
|---|---|
| Black-throated Gray Warbler | *Dendroica nigrescens* |
| Black-throated Green Warbler | *Dendroica virens* |
| Townsend's Warbler | *Dendroica townsendi* |
| Hermit Warbler | *Dendroica occidentalis* |
| Blackburnian Warbler | *Dendroica fusca* |
| Yellow-throated Warbler | *Dendroica dominica* |
| Grace's Warbler | *Dendroica graciae* |
| Pine Warbler | *Dendroica pinus* |
| Prairie Warbler | *Dendroica discolor* |
| Palm Warbler | *Dendroica palmarum* |
| Bay-breasted Warbler | *Dendroica castanea* |
| Blackpoll Warbler | *Dendroica striata* |
| Cerulean Warbler | *Dendroica cerulea* |
| Black-and-White Warbler | *Mniotilta varia* |
| American Redstart | *Setophaga ruticilla* |
| Prothonotary Warbler | *Protonotaria citrea* |
| Worm-eating Warbler | *Helmitheros vermivorus* |
| Swainson's Warbler | *Limnothylpis swainsonii* |
| Ovenbird | *Seiurus aurocapillus* |
| Northern Waterthrush | *Seiurus noveboracensis* |
| Louisiana Waterthrush | *Seiurus motacilla* |
| Kentucky Warbler | *Oporornis formosus* |
| Connecticut Warbler | *Oporornis agilis* |
| Mourning Warbler | *Oporornis philadelphia* |
| MacGillivray's Warbler | *Oporornis tolmiei* |
| Common Yellowthroat | *Geothlypis trichas* |
| Hooded Warbler | *Wilsonia citrina* |
| Wilson's Warbler | *Wilsonia pusilla* |
| Canada Warbler | *Wilsonia canadensis* |
| Red-faced Warbler | *Cardellina rubrifrons* |
| Painted Redstart | *Myioborus pictus* |
| Yellow-breasted Chat | *Icteria virens* |
| Hepatic Tanager | *Piranga flava* |
| Summer Tanager | *Piranga rubra* |

| | |
|---|---|
| Scarlet Tanager | *Piranga olivacea* |
| Western Tanager | *Piranga ludoviciana* |

## SPARROWS & BLACKBIRDS

| | |
|---|---|
| Green-tailed Towhee | *Pipilo chlorurus* |
| Spotted Towhee | *Pipilo maculatus* |
| Eastern Towhee | *Pipilo erythrophthalmus* |
| Canyon Towhee | *Pipilo fuscus* |
| Cassin's Sparrow | *Aimophila cassini* |
| Rufous-crowned Sparrow | *Aimophila ruficeps* |
| American Tree Sparrow | *Spizella arborea* |
| Chipping Sparrow | *Spizella passerina* |
| Clay-colored Sparrow | *Spizella pallida* |
| Brewer's Sparrow | *Spizella breweri* |
| Field Sparrow | *Spizella pusilla* |
| Black-chinned Sparrow | *Amphispiza bilineata* |
| Vesper Sparrow | *Pooecetes gramineus* |
| Lark Sparrow | *Chondestes grammacus* |
| Black-throated Sparrow | *Amphispiza bilineata* |
| Sage Sparrow | *Amphispiza belli* |
| Lark Bunting | *Calamospiza melanocorys* |
| Savannah Sparrow | *Passerculus sandwichensis* |
| Grasshopper Sparrow | *Ammodramus savannarum* |
| Baird's Sparrow | *Ammodramus bairdii* |
| Henslow's Sparrow | *Ammodramus henslowii* |
| LeConte's Sparrow | *Ammodramus leconteii* |
| Nelson's Sharp-tailed Sparrow | *Ammodramus nelsoni* |
| Fox Sparrow | *Passerella iliaca* |
| Song Sparrow | *Melospiza melodia* |
| Lincoln's Sparrow | *Melospiza lincolnii* |
| Swamp Sparrow | *Melospiza georgiana* |
| White-throated Sparrow | *Zonotrichia albicollis* |
| Harris' Sparrow | *Zonotrichia querula* |

| | |
|---|---|
| White-crowned Sparrow | *Zonotrichia leucophrys* |
| Golden-crowned Sparrow | *Zonotrichia atricapilla* |
| Dark-eyed Junco | *Junco hyemalis* |
| McCown's Longspur | *Calcarius mccownii* |
| Lapland Longspur | *Calcarius lapponicus* |
| Smith's Longspur | *Calcarius pictus* |
| Chestnut-collared Longspur | *Calcarius ornatus* |
| Snow Bunting | *Plectrophenax nivalis* |
| Northern Cardinal | *Cardinalis cardinalis* |
| Pyrrhuloxia | *Cardinalis sinuatus* |
| Rose-breasted Grosbeak | *Pheucticus ludovicianus* |
| Black-headed Grosbeak | *Pheucticus melanocephalus* |
| Blue Grosbeak | *Passerina caerulea* |
| Lazuli Bunting | *Passerina amoena* |
| Indigo Bunting | *Passerina cyanea* |
| Painted Bunting | *Passerina ciris* |
| Dickcissel | *Spiza americana* |
| Bobolink | *Dolichonyx oryzivorus* |
| Red-winged Blackbird | *Agelaius phoeniceus* |
| Eastern Meadowlark | *Sturnella magna* |
| Western Meadowlark | *Sturnella neglecta* |
| Yellow-headed Blackbird | *Xanthocephalus xanthocephalus* |
| Rusty Blackbird | *Euphagus carolinus* |
| Brewer's Blackbird | *Euphagus cyanocephalus* |
| Common Grackle | *Quiscalus quiscula* |
| Great-tailed Grackle | *Quiscalus mexicanus* |
| Bronzed Cowbird | *Molothrus aeneus* |
| Brown-headed Cowbird | *Molothrus ater* |
| Orchard Oriole | *Icterus spurius* |
| Hooded Oriole | *Icterus cucullatus* |
| Streaked-backed Oriole | *Icterus pustulatus* |
| Bullock's Oriole | *Icterus bullockii* |
| Baltimore Oriole | *Icterus galbula* |
| Scott's Oriole | *Icterus parisorum* |

## NORTHERN FINCHES

| Brambling | *Fringilla montifringilla* |
| Gray-crowned Rosy Finch | *Leucosticte tephrocotia* |
| Black Rosy Finch | *Leucosticte atrata* |
| Brown-capped Rosy Finch | *Leucosticte australis* |
| Pine Grosbeak | *Pinicola enucleator* |
| Purple Finch | *Carpodacus purpureus* |
| Cassin's Finch | *Carpodacus cassinii* |
| House Finch | *Carpodacus mexicanus* |
| Red Crossbill | *Loxia curvirostra* |
| White-winged Crossbill | *Loxia leucoptera* |
| Common Redpoll | *Carduelis flammea* |
| Pine Siskin | *Carduelis pinus* |
| Lesser Goldfinch | *Carduelis psaltria* |
| American Goldfinch | *Carduelis tristis* |
| Evening Grosbeak | *Coccothraustes vespertinus* |

## OLD WORLD SPARROWS

| House Sparrow | *Passer domesticus* |

*Ruby-throated hummingbird*

# Index

## A

Aiken Canyon Preserve  78-81
Alamosa National Wildlife Refuge  138-142
Arapaho National Wildlife Refuge  322-335
  Bird List  331-334
  Mammal List  335
  Map  324
Audubon Society for Colorado  440

## B

Baca National Wildlife Refuge  143-155
  Bird List  151-155
Barr Lake State Park and Wildlife Refuge  380-391
  Bird List  386-391
  Map  382
Bear Lake Road  50-51
Bent's Old Fort  437-438
Black Canyon of the Gunnison National Park  188-201
  Map  191
Blanca Wetlands  82-85
Bristlecone Pines  33-35
Browns Park National Wildlife Refuge  336-351
  Bird List  346-349
  Mammals List  350
  Map  339

Butterfly Pavilion  12-17

## C

Cache la Poudre/North Park Scenic Byway  300-305
  Joe Wright Reservoir  304-305
  Long Draw Reservoir  305
Canyons of the Ancients National Monument  202-209
  Map  205
Colorado National Monument  210-223
  Bird List  220-222
  Mammal List  220
  Map  213
  Reptile List  222
Colorado River Headwaters Scenic Byway  306-311
  Lake Granby  307
  Radium State Wildlife Area  310-311
  Williams Fork Reservoir  309
  Willow Creek Reservoir  309
  Windy Gap Reservoir  308
  Wolford Mountain Reservoir  310
Comanche National Grasslands  410-425
  Bird List  420-424
  Map  414
Cow Creek  51-52
Crawford State Park  271-274

Curecanti National Recreation Area 170–179
   Map 172–173

## D

Deerlodge Park 283
Dinosaur Diamond Scenic Byway 312–315
Dinosaur National Monument 288–299
   Map 291
Dome Rock State Wildlife Area 127
Double Bridges 279
Duffy Mountain 281

## E

East Cross Mountain 283
Endovalley 46–47

## F

Flat Tops Trail Scenic Byway 316–321
   Stagecoach State Park 318–319
   Trappers Lake 320–321
Florissant Fossil Beds National Monument 100–106
For Your Information 7–9
   Map 8
Fox Ranch 354–359
Frontiers Pathways Scenic Byway 120–122
Front Range 10–76
   Butterfly Pavilion 12–17
   Garden of the Gods 18–25
   High Creek Fen Preserve 26–29
   Map 10
   Mount Evans 30–35
     Bristlecone Pines 33–35
     Map 32
   National Parks and Monuments 38–59
     Rocky Mountain National Park 38–59
       Accommodations 58
       Bear Lake Road 50
       Bird List 54–58
       Cow Creek 51
       Endovalley 46
       Lumpy Ridge 51–52
       Mammal List 57–58
       Map 41
       Moraine Park 48
       Trail Ridge Road 42
       Wild Basin 48
   Scenic Byways 60–73
     Guanella Pass 60–61
     Lariat Loop 62–65
     Mount Evans Scenic Byway 66
     Peak to Peak Scenic Byway 67–69
     Top of the Rockies National Scenic & Historic Byway 70–73
     Trail Ridge Road 72–73
   Wildlife Refuges 74–75
     Two Ponds National Wildlife Refuge 74–75

## G

Garden of the Gods 18–25
Glenwood Hot Springs 274–275
Gold Belt Tour 123–127
Grand Mesa Scenic Byway 246–249
   Land O' Lakes Area 249
   Mesa Lakes Area 248
   Plateau Creek Valley 247
   Vega State Park 247
Greater Prairie Chicken Viewing Tours 360–363
Great Sand Dunes National Park and Preserve 107–119
Guanella Pass 60–61

## H

Headquarters Campground 280
High Creek Fen Preserve 26–29
Highway of Legends 128–133
   Lathrop State Park 131–133
   Trinidad Lake State Park 130–131
Hovenweep National Monument 224–229

The Maroon Bells 180–187
The San Luis Valley 148–150
The Wild Animal Sanctuary 398–407
Top of the Rockies National Scenic & Historic Byway 70–73
Trail of the Ancients Scenic Byway 262–263
Trail Ridge Road 42–45, 72–73
Trappers Lake 320–321
Trinidad Lake State Park 130–131
Two Ponds National Wildlife Refuge 74–75

## U

Unaweep-Tabeguache Scenic and Historic Byway 264–268

## V

Vega State Park 247

## W

West Cross Mountain 283
West Elk Loop 269–275
   Crawford State Park 271–274
   Glenwood Hot Springs 274–275
   Paonia State Park 270–271
Wheeler Geological Area 251–253
Wild Basin 48–49

Wildlife Refuges 74–75, 138–167, 322–351
   Alamosa National Wildlife Refuge 138–142
   Arapaho National Wildlife Refuge 322–335
   Baca National Wildlife Refuge 143–155
      The San Luis Valley 148–150
   Browns Park National Wildlife Refuge 336–351
   Monte Vista National Wildlife Refuge 156–163
      Map 159
   Russell Lakes State Wildlife Area 164–167
Wildlife Refuge System 439
Williams Fork Reservoir 309
Willow Creek Reservoir 309
Windy Gap Reservoir 308
Wolford Mountain Reservoir 310

## Y

Yampa River Preserve 284
Yampa River State Park 278–287
Yampa Valley Golf Course 281
Yucca House National Monument 241–243

# Methods of Experimental Physics

VOLUME 24

GEOPHYSICS

PART A

Laboratory Measurements

# METHODS OF EXPERIMENTAL PHYSICS

Robert Celotta and Judah Levine, *Editors-in-Chief*

*Founding Editors*

L. MARTON
C. MARTON

Volume 24

# Geophysics

PART A
Laboratory Measurements

*Edited by*

## Charles G. Sammis

*Department of Geological Sciences
University of Southern California
Los Angeles, California*

## Thomas L. Henyey

*Department of Geological Sciences
University of Southern California
Los Angeles, California*

1987

## ACADEMIC PRESS, INC.
Harcourt Brace Jovanovich, Publishers

Orlando  San Diego  New York  Austin
Boston  London  Sydney  Tokyo  Toronto

COPYRIGHT © 1987 BY ACADEMIC PRESS, INC.
ALL RIGHTS RESERVED.
NO PART OF THIS PUBLICATION MAY BE REPRODUCED OR
TRANSMITTED IN ANY FORM OR BY ANY MEANS, ELECTRONIC
OR MECHANICAL, INCLUDING PHOTOCOPY, RECORDING, OR
ANY INFORMATION STORAGE AND RETRIEVAL SYSTEM, WITHOUT
PERMISSION IN WRITING FROM THE PUBLISHER.

ACADEMIC PRESS, INC.
Orlando, Florida 32887

*United Kingdom Edition published by*
ACADEMIC PRESS INC. (LONDON) LTD.
24–28 Oval Road, London NW1 7DX

Library of Congress Cataloging in Publication Data

Geophysics.

(Methods of experimental physics; v. 24)
Includes index.
Contents: pt. A. Laboratory measurements.
1. Geophysics.　I. Sammis, Charles G.　II. Henyey,
Thomas L. (Thomas Louis), Date　.　III. Series.
QE501.G48　1987　　551　　86-17439
ISBN 0–12–475966–1 (v. A : alk. paper)

PRINTED IN THE UNITED STATES OF AMERICA

87 88 89 90    9 8 7 6 5 4 3 2 1

# CONTENTS

PREFACE . . . . . . . . . . . . . . . . . . . . . . . . ix

## 1. Elastic Properties of Rocks and Minerals
DONALD J. WEIDNER

1. Introduction . . . . . . . . . . . . . . . . . . . . 1
2. Ultrasonic Techniques . . . . . . . . . . . . . . . 2
3. Brillouin Spectroscopy . . . . . . . . . . . . . . . 13
4. Thermal Diffuse Scattering . . . . . . . . . . . . . 23
   References . . . . . . . . . . . . . . . . . . . . 28

## 2. Laboratory Measurement of Internal Friction in Rocks and Minerals at Seismic Frequencies
LOUIS PESELNICK AND HSI-PING LIU

1. Introduction . . . . . . . . . . . . . . . . . . . . 31
2. Characterization of Nonelastic Behavior of Solids . . . . . . 33
3. Experimental Methods and Associated Problems . . . . . . . 38
4. Conclusions . . . . . . . . . . . . . . . . . . . . 52
   References . . . . . . . . . . . . . . . . . . . . 53

## 3. Measurement of Rock Deformation at High Temperatures
D. L. KOHLSTEDT AND P. N. CHOPRA

1. Introduction . . . . . . . . . . . . . . . . . . . . 57
2. Deformation Apparatus . . . . . . . . . . . . . . . 58
   References . . . . . . . . . . . . . . . . . . . . 86

## 4. Diffusion Measurements: Experimental Methods
F. J. RYERSON

1. Introduction . . . . . . . . . . . . . . . . . . . . 89
2. Theory . . . . . . . . . . . . . . . . . . . . . . 91

##### CONTENTS

3. Solutions to Fick's Second Law . . . . . . . . . . . . . 92
4. Experimental Methods . . . . . . . . . . . . . . . . . 94
5. Analytical Methods. . . . . . . . . . . . . . . . . . . 106
6. Summary . . . . . . . . . . . . . . . . . . . . . . . 124
   References . . . . . . . . . . . . . . . . . . . . . . 127

### 5. Rock Fracture and Frictional Sliding
HARTMUT SPETZLER

1. Introduction . . . . . . . . . . . . . . . . . . . . . . 132
2. Single-Crack Propagation . . . . . . . . . . . . . . . 132
3. Double Torsion Technique . . . . . . . . . . . . . . . 134
4. Double Cantilever Beam Technique . . . . . . . . . . 138
5. Notched Bending Beam Technique . . . . . . . . . . . 142
6. *In Situ* Measurements . . . . . . . . . . . . . . . . . 146
7. Acoustic Emissions . . . . . . . . . . . . . . . . . . 153
8. Frictional Sliding . . . . . . . . . . . . . . . . . . . 170
9. Permeability . . . . . . . . . . . . . . . . . . . . . 173
   References . . . . . . . . . . . . . . . . . . . . . . 181

### 6. Shock Wave Techniques for Geophysics and Planetary Physics
THOMAS J. AHRENS

1. Introduction . . . . . . . . . . . . . . . . . . . . . . 185
2. Impedance Match Solutions . . . . . . . . . . . . . . 193
3. Shock-Induced Dynamic Yielding
   and Phase Transitions . . . . . . . . . . . . . . . . . 200
4. Shock Wave Velocity Measurements . . . . . . . . . . 203
5. Release Isentrope Experiments . . . . . . . . . . . . . 209
6. Measurement of Sound Speed behind
   the Shock Front . . . . . . . . . . . . . . . . . . . . 222
7. Shock and Postshock Temperatures . . . . . . . . . . 228
   References . . . . . . . . . . . . . . . . . . . . . . 233

### 7. The Multianvil Press
E. K. GRAHAM

1. Introduction . . . . . . . . . . . . . . . . . . . . . . 237
2. Design and Construction of Multianvil Presses . . . . . 238

CONTENTS vii

    3. Pressure Cell–Sample Assemblies . . . . . . . . . . . . 249
    4. Pressure Calibration and Accuracy. . . . . . . . . . . . 259
    5. Conclusions: Experiments with Multianvil Systems . . . . . 266
        References . . . . . . . . . . . . . . . . . . . . . 267

## 8. Thermal Conductivity of Rocks and Minerals
K. HORAI AND T. SHANKLAND

    1. Thermal Conductivity. . . . . . . . . . . . . . . . . 271
    2. Radiative Thermal Conductivity. . . . . . . . . . . . . 292
        References . . . . . . . . . . . . . . . . . . . . . 301

## 9. Experimental Methods in Rock Magnetism and Paleomagnetism
M. FULLER

    1. Introduction . . . . . . . . . . . . . . . . . . . . 303
    2. Fundamental Concepts in Rock Magnetism
       and Paleomagnetism . . . . . . . . . . . . . . . . 305
    3. Experimental Methods of Paleomagnetism . . . . . . . . 331
    4. Rock Magnetism. . . . . . . . . . . . . . . . . . . 418
    5. Concluding Comments . . . . . . . . . . . . . . . . 465
        References . . . . . . . . . . . . . . . . . . . . . 466

INDEX . . . . . . . . . . . . . . . . . . . . . . . . . 473

CONTENTS OF VOLUME 24, PART B . . . . . . . . . . . . . 477

# PREFACE

Geophysics uses many of the methods and techniques of physics to study the solid earth and planets. Experimental techniques in modern geophysics naturally fall into two categories: field and laboratory. Field experiments are designed to collect basic data on the structure of earth and planetary interiors, the dynamic processes by which these bodies evolve, and the nature and source of any planetary field. Laboratory experiments are designed to aid the interpretation of the basic field data, and to make inferences when no primary data are available. We have followed this division in organizing the two volumes in this set. Volume 24, Part A discusses the laboratory techniques, and Volume 24, Part B discusses the field techniques used in geophysics.

The basic data set used to infer the structure of the earth and planetary interiors is provided by seismological investigation. The travel time, amplitude, and waveform of elastic waves are used together with the total mass, moment of inertia, and periods of free oscillations to construct seismological "earth models." Such models specify the density, elastic constants, and anelastic parameters within the planet to varying degrees of spatial resolution. Interpretation of these elastic and anelastic parameters in terms of temperature, pressure, composition, and crystal structure has motivated much of the work in experimental geophysics. Chapter 1, by D. J. Weidner, reviews techniques by which the elastic properties are measured to high pressures and temperatures. Chapter 2, by L. Peselnick and H. P. Liu, reviews techniques used to determine anelastic parameters of materials likely to make up planetary interiors.

The most significant development in the earth sciences over the past 20 years has been the development of the plate tectonics model for the evolution of earth's surface. Earthquakes, volcanoes, and mountains are now understood in terms of the relative motions between the boundaries of rigid plates, which are themselves the cool boundary layer of internal convection cells in the hot silicate mantle. The need to understand the nature of such convection has motivated laboratory studies of the flow properties of silicates at the high pressures and temperatures that characterize the mantle. Experimental techniques by which this has been accomplished are reviewed in Chapter 3 by D. L. Kohlstedt and P. N. Chopra. The closely related studies in diffusion transport are reviewed in Chapter 4 by F. J. Ryerson; measurements of the thermal conductivity of rocks and minerals under mantle conditions are reviewed in Chapter 8 by K. Horai and T. Shankland.

At shallow depths in the crust, rock deformation is brittle. The desire to understand the basic nature of the instability that produces earthquakes has motivated experimental work in the fracture and frictional sliding of rock. Experimental techniques in this area are reviewed in Chapter 5 by H. Spetzler.

Special techniques are required to simulate the extremes of pressure and temperature found deep within planetary interiors. These techniques include diamond anvils with laser heating, multianvil presses, and exploitation of the high pressures and temperatures that propagate as shock waves. Shock wave techniques are reviewed in Chapter 6 by T. J. Ahrens; the multianvil press is reviewed in Chapter 7 by E. K. Graham. We have not included an article on the diamond anvil press, but a description of this technique can be found in Jeanloz and Heinz (1984).

Early studies of the earth's magnetic field were motivated by the desire to improve navigation during the age of exploration. However, the recent discovery that the earth's magnetic field is recorded by the ferromagnetic minerals in rocks as they cool through their Curie temperatures has provided a method by which historical variations in the field can be determined. Such paleomagnetic studies have provided much of the key evidence in support of the plate tectonics model. Experimental techniques in rock magnetism and paleomagnetism are reviewed by M. Fuller in Chapter 9.

The breadth of methods in experimental geophysics makes it difficult to present the topic completely. We have tried to cover many of the key areas, but there will naturally be some omissions. Those areas treated in this volume, however, should give the nonspecialist a useful and broad-based introduction to the motivations and methods of modern experimental geophysics.

CHARLES G. SAMMIS<br>
THOMAS L. HENYEY

## Reference

Jeanloz, R., and D. L. Heinz (1984). Experiments at high pressure and temperature: Laser heating through the diamond cell. *J. Phys.* **45** 83–92.

# 1. ELASTIC PROPERTIES OF ROCKS AND MINERALS

## Donald J. Weidner

Department of Earth and Space Sciences
State University of New York
Stony Brook, New York 11794

## 1. Introduction

Progress in our understanding of the earth and earth processes comes through an integrated approach involving field observations, theories, and laboratory experimental studies. The most accurate and best resolved property of the earth at almost every depth is the acoustic velocity determined from seismology. Since acoustic velocity is a reflection of the elastic properties of the constitutive material, laboratory studies of elasticity of earth materials take a very important place in earth science research.

The development and utilization of experimental techniques have followed a path that is defined by the specific nature of the earth science problem. The type of problem is manifest in terms of the type of samples that are the object of the elasticity studies. These sample types are generally represented by two extremes. On the one side are polycrystalline samples, which can be single- or multiphase, often with a fluid phase present. These samples are either synthetic or natural models of rocks. Sample size is generally not limited. The physical properties of such samples often reflect the state of aggregation and the properties of the pore fluids. Typically the samples significantly attenuate acoustic energy. Elastic properties are desired as a function of several parameters including pressure, temperature, pore fluid pressure, nonhydrostatic stress, and failure history. Acoustic velocities are generally measured for these samples by ultrasonic transmission techniques. Often the experiments are defined to determine both the acoustic velocities and acoustic attenuation.

At the other extreme of samples are single crystals. Data from single crystals are useful for comparison with acoustic velocities for the bulk of the earth, where the state of aggregation is not a dominant parameter. Within the earth, pressures reach several million atmospheres and a few thousand degrees centigrade of temperature. The materials undergo several phase transformations as a result of the pressures and temperatures encountered. Thus, elasticity data are required as a function of phase, composition, pressure, and temperature for the ranges of these variables which are possible within the earth. The major experimental restriction is imposed by the availability of suitable samples. Only a few relevant minerals occur naturally as large single crystals (1 cm or larger). Other materials must be synthesized, some at extremes in pressure and temperature capabilities. Often the sample volume of the high-pressure equipment is less than 1 mm$^3$. The resulting single crystals of successful experiments have dimensions of tens to hundreds of micrometres. Two types of experimental responses have been made to these extremes in sample availability. One has been to sinter many crystallites to form a polycrystalline sample. Then ultrasonic transmission measurements are made on the aggregate. The second approach has been to develop single-crystal methods that require smaller samples than were needed previously. To this end, ultrasonic transmission and resonance techniques have been used for samples of millimeter dimensions, and Brillouin spectroscopy has proved useful for elasticity characterizations for samples with dimensions of tens of micrometers.

In this chapter I will discuss all of these experimental techniques with particular emphasis on their utility in addressing earth science problems. Each of the subjects has, at one time or another, been the focus of broad and careful reviews. My aim is to give enough details to demonstrate the important considerations in each of the experimental approaches.

## 2. Ultrasonic Techniques

Ultrasonic wave transmission techniques have defined the standard for elasticity characterizations for the past three decades. When these measurements are tractable, they provide the most accurate results of all experimental techniques. Both the sample size and experimental conditions limit the applicability of ultrasonic techniques. Many of the advances in ultrasonic experimental techniques have come in the areas of adapting standard techniques to extreme conditions. In this section I will review the principles of several of the currently used techniques and discuss the specific requirements for addressing earth science needs.

### 2.1. Pulse Transmission

The simplest and most direct method of obtaining the acoustic velocity in a material is to measure the time required for an acoustic wave to travel through a sample of known length. This is the basis of the pulse transmission method. This type of measurement has been in wide use since 1961, when Birch[1] measured compressional wave velocities in a suite of rock samples to

# 1. ELASTIC PROPERTIES OF ROCKS AND MINERALS

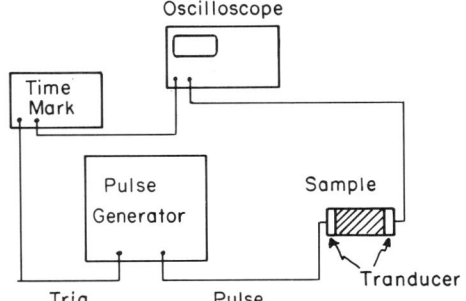

FIG. 1. Pulse transmission ultrasonic system.

pressures of 10 kbar, and 1964, when Simmons[2] completed similar measurements for the shear wave velocities.

A typical experimental configuration is illustrated in Fig. 1. The essential elements include a pulse generator, an oscilloscope, a time base, and transducers. The transducers are made of piezoelectric materials and serve to convert the electrical signal to an acoustic pulse at one end of the sample and the acoustic pulse to an electrical signal at the other end. The time of flight is then measured as the time delay between the introduction and the reception of the signal. The resonance frequencies of the transducers tend to range from a few kilohertz to a few megahertz.

The pulse transmission technique yields the least precise results of all the wave transmission methods. It is generally used in attenuating samples, where high-quality, high-frequency reflections cannot be observed. The precision is limited by the attenuation of the high frequencies, which yields an emergent arrival of the transmitted pulse. The result is that the time of the arrival is uncertain.

Modifications and improvements in the basic technique have been made to meet a variety of experimental requirements and to reflect the advances in technology since the method was originally developed. Winkler and Plona[3] describe such a modification which allows measurement of acoustic phase velocity and attenuation as a function of frequency. In their experiment, only one transducer is used for both sending and receiving. The transducer is attached to a buffer rod, which in turn is attached to the sample. The opposite end of the sample is attached to a backing buffer rod. The transducer is designed to be highly damped and broadband. A broadband signal is introduced into the transducer and reflections from the buffer rod–sample interface and the sample–backing buffer interface are digitally recorded. Then by comparing the phase and amplitude of these signals as a function of frequency, it is possible to extract the frequency dependence of the phase velocity and attenuation.

The modest advances in the pulse transmission technique in three decades do not serve to illustrate the utility of this technique for providing insight into a variety of phenomena; rather, they demonstrate that the tool, as it was initially developed, was both simple and eloquent. The pulse transmission technique has been used primarily for characterizations of rock or synthetic polycrystalline samples. Single crystals generally are much less attenuating and are amenable to the more precise techniques discussed later.

Acoustic properties of rock samples provide two types of information. On the one hand, the acoustic velocities are directly related to the acoustic velocities measured in the field with seismic experiments. On the other hand, the acoustic properties reflect the mechanical state of the rock. The presence and state of voids within the sample dictate several physical properties. Acoustic velocities provide an experimentally convenient tool for characterizing these samples. The role of the voids in the natural environment is extremely diverse, dramatically influencing our understanding of such broad problems as petroleum exploration and recovery, earthquake prediction, lunar vs. earth seismic signals, induced seismicity, and the composition of the crust, to mention a few.

Several studies have measured acoustic velocities in rocks to define the variations due to mineralogical variations.[4,5] For the acoustic velocities to reflect the properties of the minerals, the samples must be dry and the measurements must be accomplished on jacketed samples at pressures high enough to close most of the voids—typically a few kilobars. Such experimental conditions have become standard since the early work of Birch[1] and Simmons.[2] Often, 10 kbar has been the upper bound for these measurements. However, in some cases, such as the work of Christensen,[6] the measurements have been accomplished at hydrostatic pressures as high as 30 kbar. The extended pressure range may permit determination of the pressure derivative of the elastic properties of the constituent minerals and not just define the effects of void closures.

In many cases the minerals are not elastically isotropic. If they are not randomly oriented in rocks, then the composite will not be isotropic. Christensen and Ramananantoandro[7] and Babuska[8] made detailed studies of the anisotropy of a few rock types. They concluded that the observed anisotropy can be related to the anistropy of the minerals and a description of the preferred orientations of the individual grains.

It is much more difficult to measure the acoustic velocities under conditions of simultaneously elevated temperature and pressure than under elevated pressure alone. The first consideration is the pressure-transmitting medium. Liquids which are adequate for high-pressure work are generally not useful at high temperatures. Thus, a gas such as argon is the most common hydrostatic pressure-transmitting medium. These systems are quite dangerous as the energy stored at high pressure is much greater than that in a liquid medium. Furthermore, the pressurizing equipment must be capable of accommodating large volume changes of the pressure medium during compression. Higher pressures and fewer dangers result when hydrostatic conditions are not required and solid pressure media are used. A second consideration concerns the transducer material and sample–transducer configuration. All transducers lose their piezoelectric properties at elevated temperature. High-temperature measurements thus require choosing a transducer material which is useful in the requisite temperature range and perhaps using a buffer rod to remove the transducer from the high-temperature portion of the sample assembly. Several investigators have successfully solved these problems and obtained acoustic data at high temperature and pressure.[9-16]

Pore fluids have profound effects on the elastic properties of rocks. The effects of a saturating fluid on acoustic velocities were demonstrated by Nur and Simmons.[17,18] Subsequent studies have explored these effects as a function of pressure, temperature, and pore pressure.[19,20] One of the main effects of pore fluids is to attenuate the acoustic wave. The attenuation measurements are beyond the scope of this review; a comprehensive compilation of papers has been assembled by Toksoz and Johnston.[21]

In the early 1970s field observations led to a model of earthquake prediction known as the dilatancy diffusion model.[22,23] The model explained an apparent change in the ratio of the compressional wave velocity to the shear wave velocity prior to an earthquake. The change in acoustic velocity was related to voids formed prior to failure and the interaction of these voids with the regional ground water. The model stimulated laboratory studies of the elastic properties of rocks as a function of nonhydrostatic stress to the point of failure.[24-26]

The pulse transmission method has proved invaluable in providing properties of monomineralic samples. The acoustic properties of the earth's mantle are governed by the properties of minerals, which are not stable at ambient conditions. Large single crystals of these materials cannot be synthesized, which restricts the utility of single-crystal ultrasonic techniques. In contrast, it is often possible to synthesize low-porosity polycrystalline aggregates of such materials.[27] These samples can be characterized by using the pulse transmission method.[28-30] However, Spetzler[31] recommended caution in deriving the mineral properties from such measurements. Ambiguities in the internal strains and the state of aggregation can detract from the accuracy of this method.

Acoustic velocities obtained with the pulse transmission technique have thus provided a wide range of data important for problems in the earth sciences. The discussion above is not complete; rather it illustrates the breadth of problems addressed with this method. Other applications of the method include determining the acoustic velocities as a material undergoes a phase transformation.[32, 33]

## 2.2. Echo Methods

For high-quality samples with dimensions of roughly 1 cm or larger, there are a number of very precise ultrasonic techniques for determining acoustic velocities. Here I will emphasize experimental techniques which measure the time between successive echoes. This measurement along with the sample length is sufficient to define the acoustic velocity. Three such methods include pulse–echo overlap, pulse superposition, and phase comparison. These techniques simply measure the phase delay between two echoes of a monochromatic tone burst. They differ in the manner in which this measurement is accomplished.

The phase within the $n$th echo $\Phi_n$, is given by

$$\Phi_n(t) = (t - t'_n)2\pi f + \phi_n + 2\pi k_n \tag{1}$$

where $t'_n$ is the actual transit time of a peak in the acoustic wave which travels $n$ round trips, $f$ the frequency of the monochromatic wave train, $\phi_n$ the accumulated phase shifts due to the reflections of the acoustic signal from both ends of the sample, and $k_n$ an integer specifying a peak within a wave train. The identification of $k_n$ must be verified in general. The usage of these terms is illustrated in Fig. 2. All the techniques discussed here require matching the phase in one echo with that in another echo which has been time delayed. The phase of the signal in the $n$th echo evaluated at a time $t - t_0$ is thus given as

$$\Phi_n(t - t_0) = (t - t_0 - t'_n)2\pi f + \phi_n + 2\pi k_n \tag{2}$$

The three methods differ either in the manner of verifying the phase matching condition or in the method of measuring the time delay $t_0$.

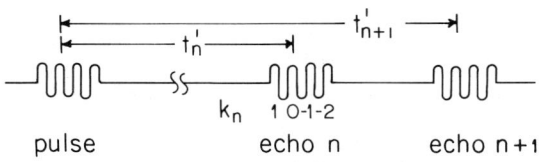

FIG. 2. Echo time trace. The original pulse and two echoes are illustrated as a function of time, defining the time $t'_n$ and the integer $k_n$, under the condition that $\phi_n = 0$.

In the pulse–echo overlap method,[34] echoes are viewed on an oscilloscope which is triggered to present two echoes on different channels of the oscilloscope. By applying a synchronous voltage to the $z$ axis of the oscilloscope, all but two of the echoes can be eliminated from the visual display. By varying the triggering rate of the oscilloscope, the relative phase of the two echoes is altered. In this case, the $n$th echo is delayed by $t_0 = 1/F$, where $F$ is the triggering frequency of the oscilloscope. Then the phase difference between echo $n$ and echo $n - 1$ is given by

$$\Phi_n(t) - \Phi_{n-1}(t - 1/F) = (1/F + t'_{n-1} - t'_n)2\pi f + \phi_n - \phi_{n-1}$$
$$+ 2\pi(k_n - k_{n-1}) \qquad (3)$$

When the oscilloscope is triggered at a frequency $F_0$ such that the peaks in the wave trains coincide, the wave trains are in phase and the above quantity is equal to zero. The quantity $t'_n - t'_{n-1}$ is just the round trip travel time $t_{RT}$ and is given by

$$t_{RT} = 1/F_0 + \phi 2\pi f + (k_n - k_{n-1})/f \qquad (4)$$

where $\phi$ is the total phase shift due to reflections in one round trip. The integer phase shift $k_n - k_{n-1}$ can be determined by repeating the measurements at slightly different frequencies $f$ as long as the reflection phase shift $\phi$ is reasonably independent of frequency.

Both the pulse superposition and the phase comparison techniques involve mechanically superposing two or more echoes by introducing additional tone bursts into the sample before the echo train has decayed.[35-38] In fact, the additional tone bursts are injected into the sample synchronous with an echo. The relative phases of echo $n$ from the first pulse and echo $n - j$ from the second can be determined from Eq. (3) to be

$$\Phi_n(t) - \Phi_{n-j}(t - 1/F) = (1/F + t'_{n-j} - t'_n)2\pi f + j\phi$$
$$+ 2\pi(k_n - k_{n-j}) \qquad (5)$$

In this case $F$ is the frequency of tone bursts. When $F$ is adjusted to produce a maximum in the amplitude of the superposed echoes (frequency $F_0$) the echoes are in phase. The round trip travel time $t_{RT} = (t_n - t_{n-j})/j$ is given by a relation similar to Eq. (4). The value of the integer can be defined in the same fashion as before.

The phase comparison technique differs from the pulse superposition method[31, 39, 40] in that the phases in each tone burst are coherent. In this case, the time delay $t_0$ of Eq. (2) is just $mf$, where $m$ is an integer. The phase delay between two echoes is varied by changing the frequency $f$. Again, the in-phase condition is defined by a maximum in the superposed echo amplitude.

At that condition with $f = f_0$, we find

$$(t'_{n-j} - t'_n)2\pi f_0 + 2\pi(m + k_n - k_{n-j}) + j\phi = 0 \tag{6}$$

This equation also involves an integer that must be defined. A common approach is to measure frequencies corresponding to two successive in-phase conditions $f_0$ and $f_1$. Then the integer difference $m$ for these two measurements is 1. Equation (6) then yields

$$t'_n - t'_{n-j} = 1/(f_1 - f_0) + [\phi(f_1) - \phi(f_0)]j/(f_1 - f_0) \tag{7}$$

This equation has the appearance of the derivative of Eq. (4). In practice both Eq. (6) and Eq. (7) have been used to define the acoustic velocity (compare references 39 and 40).

The three techniques are thus very similar in philosophy and yield results with comparable precision. The pulse–echo overlap method has a slight advantage in that the echoes can be individually inspected without interference from the second pulse; the phase comparison technique is probably the easiest to automate under computer control.

## 2.3. Transducer-Bond Phase Shifts

Davies and O'Connell[39] demonstrate that while the echo methods have the capability of accuracies of 0.05%, the variation in reported elastic moduli ranges from 0.2 to 1.0%. Pressure and temperature derivatives of the moduli have discrepancies of the order of 10%. They attribute these variations to uncertainties in the phase shift $\phi$. All three echo techniques will be similarly affected by uncertainties in the phase shift associated with reflection, $\phi$. If the phase comparison approach utilizes the results of Eq. (7) instead of Eq. (6), this method will be sensitive to the frequency derivative of the phase shift rather than the absolute value.

The uncertainty in the phase shift occurs primarily at the end of the sample bonded to the transducer. The phase shift results since both the transducer and the bonding material interact with the acoustic wave. The size of this effect can be quite large. A transducer with a 10-MHz resonance frequency has a 0.1 $\mu$s round trip acoustic wave travel time. If this transducer is attached to a sample in such a manner that an echo is not created at the sample–transducer interface, but only at the free surface of the transducer, then the total round trip travel time is that of the sample plus the 0.1 $\mu$s of the transducer. This is to be compared with a 2-10-$\mu$s sample time delay. If the transducer is excited at its reasonance frequency, then this situation corresponds to changing the integer phase shift of Eq. (4) by one. In a more realistic case, there are reflections from the sample–bond interface, from the bond–transducer interface, and from the transducer free surface. In addition, energy is lost from the acoustic wave in differing proportions in the three media. The final acoustic wave is a composite resulting from all of these processes.

It is often convenient to represent this process by a complex reflection coefficient[39]

$$\mathbf{R} = Re^{i\phi} \tag{8}$$

where

$$\phi = 2\phi_{tb} - \pi \tag{9}$$

In the simplest case, with infinitely thin bonding material and ignoring piezoelectric interactions and loss of wave energy due to attenuation, the phase shift of the transducer reduces to

$$\tan \phi_{tb} = (Z_t/Z_s) \tan(2\pi df/v) \tag{10}$$

where $Z$ is the acoustic impedance (density times velocity) of sample or transducer (subscript s or t), $d$ the transducer thickness, $f$ the frequency, and $v$ the acoustic velocity of the transducer. This relation yields a zero phase shift for frequencies which are multiples of the resonance frequency, that is, for $f = n(v/2d)$. When all terms are included, the frequency for zero phase shift is much more complex. The number of added unknowns (such as thickness of the bond) requires that the phase shift be measured rather than calculated. Jackson et al.[40] directly measured the transducer-bond phase shift by measuring the phase difference between a sample with one transducer mounted on one end and a free surface at the other and a sample with transducers mounted on both ends. The phase measurement for both cases was accomplished in the same manner. Similar phase comparisons were made on samples of different lengths. Then the phase delay of the samples could be accurately determined and the transducer-bond phase shift deduced. They found that the transducer-bond phase shift was quite reproducible from one mounting to another for transducers of the same material and characteristics. Figure 3 shows their results for 20-MHz LiNbO$_3$ transducers on a fused silica sample obtained by both the phase comparison (PC) and echo overlap (EO) techniques. A value of 1 for the phase shift would correspond to changing the integer of Eq. (4) by one. The phase shift, in this example, is not zero at the resonance frequency of the transducer. Had the measurement been conducted at the resonance frequency with no correction for transducer-bond phase shift, the round trip travel times would be in error by 0.01 and 0.02 $\mu$s for longitudinal and shear waves, respectively. Using the phase comparison method through Eq. (7) does not gain an advantage as the frequency derivative of the phase shift represents the effect of the transducer-bond phase shift. As indicated in Fig. 3, if this is evaluated at the frequency corresponding to zero phase shift, an error of 0.1 $\mu$s is obtained for both longitudinal and shear waves.

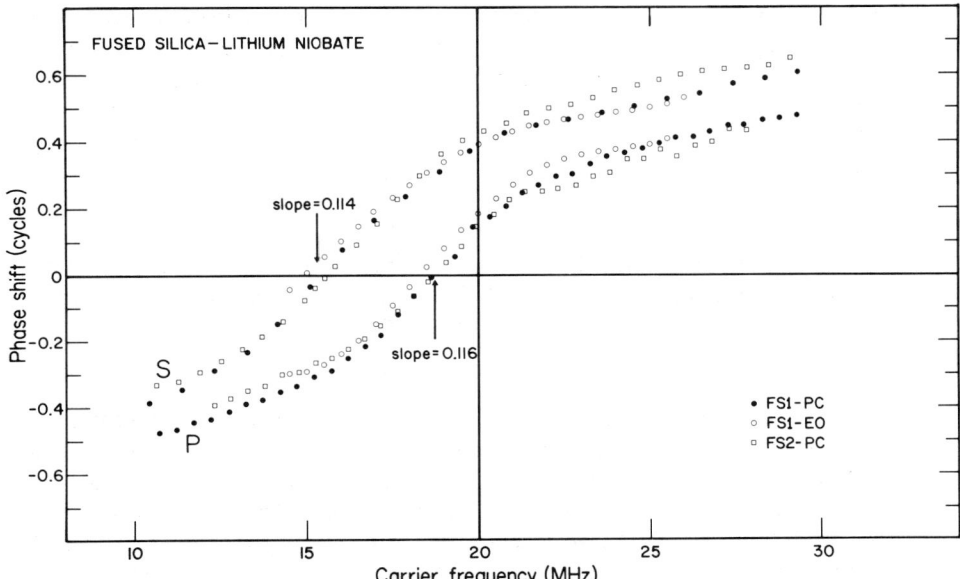

Fig. 3. Measured transducer–bond phase shifts as a function of frequency. The 20-MHz LiNbO$_3$ transducers are mounted on fused silica samples. Phase shifts are from phase comparison (PC) and echo overlap (EO) techniques. The slope given is in microseconds. (After Jackson et al.[40] Copyright 1981 by the American Geophysical Union.)

The transducer–bond phase shift also may affect pressure derivatives of elastic moduli. Characteristics of the bond may change with pressure, as will the resonant frequency of the transducer. In addition, the properties of the pressurizing medium will change with pressure, thus altering the mechanism of acoustic energy loss from the sample assembly. Thus, there can be a significant pressure derivative of the transducer–bond phase shift.

A final effect of the transducer–bond phase shift results from its frequency dependence together with the bandwidth of the acoustic signal. A tone burst, such as that illustrated in Fig. 2, is not monochromatic but has a frequency bandwidth due to the turning on and off. Consequently, the transducer–bond phase shift which affects the signal is not limited to a simple single value. The manifestation of this effect is the introduction of transient phase shifts associated with the beginning and the end of the tone burst. Figure 4 illustrates the overlap of the first and second echoes on a fused quartz sample with an LiNbO$_3$ 20-MHz transducer (carrier frequency 18 MHz). While the central peaks are in phase, several peaks at the beginning and the end are clearly not in phase. As the width of the tone burst is increased, thus

# 1. ELASTIC PROPERTIES OF ROCKS AND MINERALS

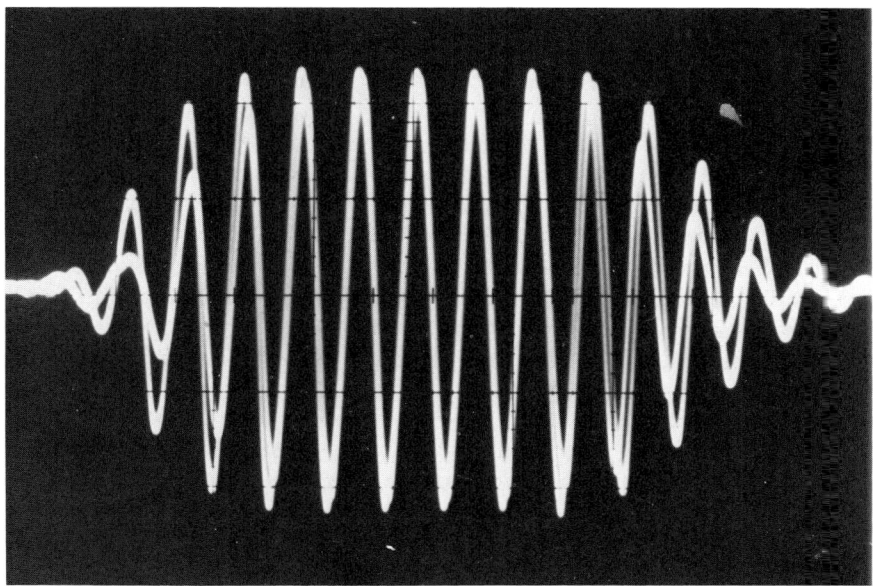

FIG. 4. Overlap of first and second echoes. The 20-MHz LiNbO$_3$ transducer is mounted on a fused silica sample. The transient phase shifts appear at both ends of the wave train. (After Jackson et al.[40] Copyright 1981 by the American Geophysical Union.)

increasing the number of cycles, the central area will eventually all have the same phase, indicating that the transducer–bond effects have reached steady state. These transient phase shifts should be carefully evaluated because they can easily introduce undetected errors, particularly with methods such as pulse superposition, where the echo is not directly observed. Also, if the width of the tone burst is too narrow, the phase match may be dominated by the transient phase shifts.

The difficulty of accounting for the transducer–bond phase shift has been approached in several ways, reflecting the variety in experimental limitations. Jackson and Niesler[41] directly evaluated the phase shift as discussed above. This was necessary because of the limited sample size which could be used in these experiments. Peselnick[42] eliminated the transducer–bond phase shift by comparing signals which were simultaneously introduced into samples of different lengths. The samples could be separate or prepared by making a step on one sample. The result is that the transducer–bond effect is eliminated. Many of the problems resulting from the transducer–bond effect can be avoided if a buffer rod is inserted between the transducer and the sample.[31, 35, 36, 39] However, experimental conditions often preclude this solution.

## 2.4. Free Vibrations

The elastic properties of an object along with the boundary conditions dictate the resonance frequencies of the object. Acoustic resonance techniques capitalize on this relationship by extracting the elastic properties from observations of the free-vibration frequencies. In comparison to wave transmission methods, resonance measurements utilize longer wavelengths in relation to the sample dimensions. This can be important if the grain size or inhomogeneities of a polycrystalline sample are significant compared to the transmission wavelength. Furthermore, smaller single-crystal samples can be elastically characterized for a fixed frequency range by resonance techniques. This approach has been used fruitfully during the past decade to provide a broad range of single-crystal elasticity data with an emphasis on the temperature dependence.

Both the elastic symmetry and the shape of the sample define the limitations of resonance techniques for determining the elastic properties. The mathematical relationships between these properties and some of the resonance frequencies for spherical isotropic samples have been defined since the work of Lamb.[43] Fraser and LeCraw[44] demonstrated the utility of this approach and provided results for spherical samples with dimensions of a few millimeters. Spinner and Tefft[45] detail an approach to determining elastic moduli for an isotropic sample which is applicable to sample shapes of either rectangular or cylindrical bars. Schreiber et al.[46] review the experimental techniques for characterizing isotropic samples. The utility of resonance techniques for single-crystal elasticity measurements was greatly increased by work of Demarest,[47] who derived the necessary relationships for free vibrations of a cubic sample with cubic elastic symmetry. This analysis was extended by Ohno[48] to include samples with rectangular parallelepiped shapes and orthorhombic crystallographic symmetry.

The experimental considerations for all shapes and symmetries have several similarities. A monochromatic acoustic signal is introduced into the sample, and the amplitude of the resulting vibrations is monitored as the frequency is varied. The elastic properties are related to the frequencies of the resonance peaks while the quality factor $Q$ is related to the frequency width of the resonance peaks.

The most difficult, yet most important, task in the data analysis is the proper identification of each resonant mode. An incorrect identification will result in an incorrect assignment of elastic moduli. The number of resonance peaks increases both as the symmetry of the crystal is lowered and the symmetry of the shape is lowered. Rectangular parallelepipeds of orthorhombic symmetry, therefore, present a great deal of complexity in the peak identification. Ohno[48] describes a methodology to aid in proper peak identification. First, it is very useful to have an accurate estimate of the unknown elastic moduli. Next, the dependence of each peak on the experimental conditions helps to confirm the tentative identification. In this regard, some modes are not sharp while others are sensitive to the force applied to couple the transducer to the specimen. Finally, the resonance frequencies have individual dependences on the sample dimensions. Thus, by changing the lengths of the dimensions and monitoring the frequency changes, it is often possible to identify specific modes.

A second complexity results from the influence of the measuring equipment on the measured quantity. The resonance equations are valid for a body with stress-free boundary conditions. Yet some contact with the sample is necessary both to introduce vibrations and to measure the resulting amplitudes. This problem has been addressed by trying to minimize the contact area and force across this area. Birch[49] mounted magnets on some samples and excited the vibration with electromagnets. Other modes were excited with transducers. The system $Q$, which is a measure of the influence of the experimental system, was reported to be about 6000. Sumino et al.,[50] in using the rectangular parallelepiped method, mount the specimen so that only opposite corners contact the two transducers. They then measure the resonance frequency as the force holding the sample between the transducers is reduced. The deduced resonance frequency is obtained as this force is extrapolated to zero.

Resonance techniques have been used for characterizing isotropic samples as reported by Soga and Anderson[51] and Birch.[49] Soga and Anderson used the resonance technique in order to use small (millimeter-size) samples, while Birch was concerned with having the wavelengths large compared to the inhomogeneities of the rock samples. The single-crystal method has been used to define the elastic properties of several materials at ambient conditions and as a function of temperature.[52-58] The maximum temperature that has been used with this technique is approximately 1000°C.

## 3. Brillouin Spectroscopy

During the past decade, Brillouin spectroscopy has been the most productive experimental technique for measuring elastic properties of earth materials at ambient conditions. The utility of this technique for defining the effect of pressure on the elastic properties has also been demonstrated. These measurements have been facilitated principally by the sample requirements of the technique. While ultrasonic methods require samples with centimeter (wave transmission) or millimeter (resonance) dimensions, Brillouin spectroscopy requires samples with dimensions of approximately 100 $\mu$m. This distinction increases the numbers of accessible natural and synthetic samples of interest in the earth sciences by orders of magnitude.

Brillouin scattering can provide the acoustic velocity as a function of direction in single crystals. Thus, the data base is similar to that of ultrasonics[59] but with different limitations. All signal generation and reception is optical. Thus, mechanical coupling with the sample is not necessary. However, the optical properties of the sample become very important. Weidner et al.[60] demonstrate the utility of this method for defining elastic properties of small single crystals. Because of the optical character of the measurement, sample size becomes limited by the diffraction limits of optics and by the need to isolate and mount the sample. X-ray studies have developed techniques for handling 100-$\mu$m single crystals. Use of these techniques makes a comparable sample size available for elasticity studies. Other type of studies have made use of the distinguishing features of Brillouin spectroscopy. Gornall and Stoicheff[61] utilized the features of Brillouin scattering to determine the elastic properties of rare gas solids. They could characterize a sample without removing it from the low-temperature growing environment.

Brillouin scattering is a phenomenon involving the interaction between acoustic energy and light energy. The acoustic velocity becomes encoded in the frequency of the scattered light. The governing principles of Brillouin scattering can be obtained from the conservation laws for the interactions of photons and phonons. When a photon is scattered by a phonon, conservation of wave momentum requires that

$$\mathbf{q} = \pm(\mathbf{k}_i - \mathbf{k}_s) \tag{11}$$

where $\mathbf{q}$ is the wave vector of the phonon, $\mathbf{k}$ is the wave vector of the photon, and the subscripts s and i indicate scattered and incident. In a similar fashion, conservation of energy requires

$$\Omega = \pm(\omega_i - \omega_s) \tag{12}$$

where $\Omega$ is the phonon frequency and $\omega$ the photon frequency. The phonon phase velocity is then just

$$v = \Omega/q \tag{13}$$

where $q$ is $|\mathbf{q}|$. The direction of the phonon wave normal is parallel to $\mathbf{q}$. When considering the absolute values, Eq. (11) reduces to

$$q = (\omega_i/c)(n_i^2 + n_s^2 - 2n_i n_s \cos\theta)^{1/2} \tag{14}$$

where $n$ is the refractive index of the incident or scattered wave, $c$ the speed of light in a vacuum, and $\theta$ the scattering angle as illustrated in Fig. 5. Thus, the acoustic velocity is given by

$$v = c(\omega_i - \omega_s)/\omega_i(n_i^2 + n_s^2 - 2n_i n_s \cos\theta)^{1/2} \tag{15}$$

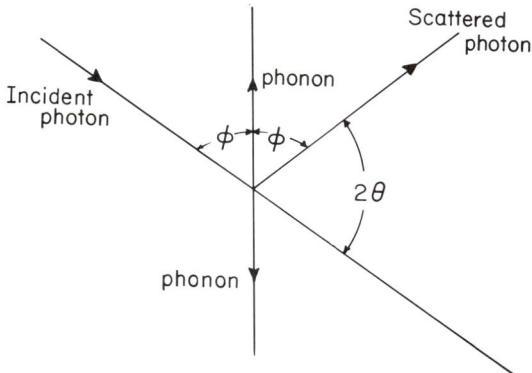

FIG. 5. Scattering geometry for Brillouin spectra. The angle $\theta$ is defined and the phonon direction bisects the angle between the incident and scattered photons.

Thus, if the light frequency, sample refractive index, and scattering geometry are known, the acoustic velocity requires measurement of the frequency shift of the scattered light. This acoustic velocity is appropriate for the phonon direction defined by Eq. (11).

### 3.1. Experimental System

A Brillouin spectrometer used for microcrystal studies is illustrated in Fig. 6. The light source is typically an argon ion laser. This laser is operated in a single-mode configuration, thereby providing a single monochromatic signal. Argon lasers can easily be operated at both 514.5 and 488.0 nm wavelengths. Often this flexibility is very useful as it can remove ambiguities of the order number of the Brillouin signal. Argon lasers rated at 2 W in multimode operation can provide a few hundred milliwatts in the single-mode configuration. This level of power is usually sufficient and does not heat transparent samples. Helium–neon lasers have also been used for Brillouin scattering experiments. The power is usually less (50 mW) and the red light is less efficiently scattered.

### 3.2. Fabry–Pérot Interferometer

The principles of Brillouin scattering require measurement of the spectra of the scattered light. The frequency shifts are typically a few tens of gigahertz and of quite low amplitude compared with light that has been scattered with no frequency shift. The spectrometer should have both high contrast and good frequency resolution. A Fabry–Pérot interferometer and associated photon counting equipment constitute the standard detection

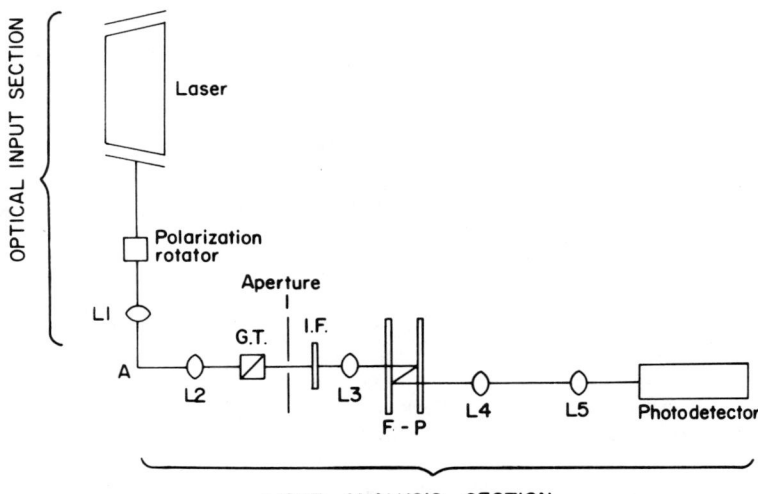

FIG. 6. Brillouin spectrometer. L1–L5, Lenses; G.T., polarization analyzer; I.F., interference filter; F–P, Fabry–Pérot interferometer. The sample is located at position A. (After Weidner et al.[66])

equipment for Brillouin spectrometry. The Fabry–Pérot interferometer operates as a tuned optical cavity. The two surfaces are mirrors with high reflectivities (90–99%). A parallel-focused light wave whose wavelength is such that an integer number of half-wavelengths exactly fit between the mirrors will constructively interfere. Some of this light will pass through the mirrors and can be detected by the photon counting system. All other wavelengths will destructively interfere and will not pass through the second mirror.

The frequency dependence of the light amplitude is determined by changing the optical length between the two mirrors. This can be accomplished by either changing the refractive index of the material between the two mirrors or changing the spacing of the mirrors. The first of these is achieved by changing the pressure of the gas between the mirrors. In the second case, one mirror is mounted on a piezoelectric stack which changes the mirror separation as a voltage is externally applied. While the pressure-scanned system is inherently more stable, the piezoelectrically scanned system can sweep faster and, if the mirror is mounted on three piezoelectric stacks which are independently driven, can be servo-controlled to maintain mirror alignment. Thus, the gain in control in the second system can more than compensate for the loss in stability. For the remainder of this discussion, I will focus on the piezoelectrically scanned interferometer.

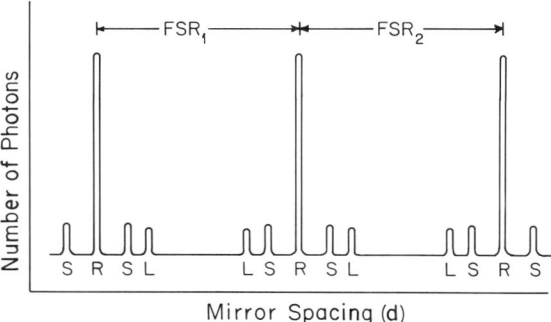

FIG. 7. Schematic of raw Brillouin data. The peaks R represent Rayleigh scattering and are at the laser frequency; L and S indicate scattering from longitudinal and shear waves; FSR is the free spectral range.

The light that comes through the Fabry–Pérot interferometer is detected by a photomultiplier tube and the number of detected photons is recorded as a function of the mirror spacing by a multichannel analyzer or the equivalent. The driving voltage ramp and the multichannel analyzer should thus be synchronized. Figure 7 schematically illustrates data which would be obtained for a ramp amplitude of about 1.3 wavelengths. As the mirror spacing changes by one half-wavelength (i.e., one order) the same interference condition is defined for the interferometer. The large peaks represent light scattered at the laser frequency (Rayleigh scattering), while the symmetrically displayed smaller peaks represent light scattered from interactions with phonons. The free spectral range (FSR) corresponds to the frequency shift which would be required to displace a peak by an amount equivalent to one order. It is dependent on the plate spacing and is given by

$$FSR = c/2d \qquad (16)$$

Thus the display as given in Fig. 7 is calibrated in frequency if the spacing between the plates is known. Furthermore, the frequency range of the interferometer can be adjusted by changing the plate spacing.

There are several methods for measuring the plate spacing. Direct length measurements are possible, but they may not be accurate because of the inaccessibility of the plates. A second method is to measure the Brillouin spectra of a standard for which the acoustic velocities are accurately known. A third method is to measure spectra with a well-determined structure. The best procedure is first to measure a spectrum where the structure is within half of the free spectral range. This yields a good first-order estimate of the plate spacing. The hyperfine structure of the Hg 546.1-nm line has proved useful in my laboratory. Then examination of structures which span more than one free spectral range can be used to more accurately define the plate spacing. Examples are the Na 589.6/589.0-nm doublet, the Hg 579/577-nm doublet, and the individual Ar laser lines. The accuracy of the estimate will improve as the structure spans a greater frequency range, with the ultimate accuracy dependent on the accuracy of the frequency shifts within the structures.

Piezoelectric stacks often display a displacement which has some nonlinear dependence on the applied voltage. As a result, the free spectral range $FSR_1$ of Fig. 7 will be of a different length than $FSR_2$ if the horizontal axis is proportional to applied voltage. Our observations suggest that this nonlinearity is mostly controlled by the time from the beginning of the ramp rather than the absolute voltage. In particular, the nonlinearity depends on the sweep rate, yet is reasonably independent of the amplitude of a dc voltage bias added to the stack voltage. Several commercially available ramp generators have the capability of adding a quadratic term to the time dependence of the ramp voltage in order to compensate for the piezoelectric stack response. However, it is quite simple to remove the nonlinearity numerically if the data are recorded in a computer. Our approach is to define a new frequency axis $z$ which is a polynomial of the original frequency variable $y$. Then

$$z = a_1 y + a_2 y^2 + a_3 y^3 + \cdots \qquad (17)$$

To define the unknown coefficients, we rescale the distance between Rayleigh peaks to an arbitrary value, say 1.0. Then

$$z(R_2) - z(R_1) = a_1[y(R_2) - y(R_1)] + a_2[y^2(R_2) - y^2(R_1)]$$
$$+ a_3\{y^3(R_2) - y^3(R_1)\} + \cdots$$
$$= 1.0 \qquad (18)$$

Several spectra can be generated with different locations of the Rayleigh peaks by changing the dc bias on the ramp voltage. Then a linear regression can be used to define the nonlinear coefficients for as many terms as desired.

The response of the interferometer to a monochromatic light source is described by the finesse $F$, the contrast $C$, and the transmission $T$.[62] These quantities depend primarily on the reflectivity of the mirrors $R$ and the surface flatness as defined by the surface finesse, $F_s = m/2$, where the surface of the mirror is flat to $\lambda/m$. The system finesse is defined as the ratio of peak separation (FSR) to peak width at half-height. The system finesse depends on the flatness finesse and the reflectivity finesse $F_R$, defined by

$$F_R = \pi R^{1/2}/(1 - R) \qquad (19)$$

The system finesse is less than either $F_s$ or $F_R$. The transmission $T$ is given by

$$T = K \frac{1}{1 + (4F^2/\pi^2)\sin^2(2\pi d/\lambda)} \quad (20)$$

where $K$ is a constant depending on the reflectivity and absorptivity of the mirrors, $d$ the plate spacing, and $\lambda$ the wavelength. The constrast $C$ is the ratio of maximum transmission to minimum transmission. This indicates the amount of light that passes through the interferometer even though it is tuned to a different frequency and is given by

$$C = 1 + 4F^2/\pi^2 \quad (21)$$

In the study of microcrystals, the light scattered from the surfaces of the sample as well as the interior is difficult to remove. Thus, often a weak Brillouin signal must be extracted from a bright signal at the laser frequency. The optimal spectrometer will have a very high contrast, a high finesse, and a high value for transmission. These tend to be mutually exclusive demands. However, a contrast of $10^4$ is possible without a major sacrifice in transmission. The contrast can be further increased by passing the light through the interferometer several times. Each time the contrast is multiplied, yielding a net contrast of $C^n$, where $n$ is the number of passes. The contrast can be increased without significantly altering the transmission or finesse if mirrors with lower reflectivity are used in the multipass configuration.

An interferometer in a multipass configuration requires extra efforts to maintain mechanical stability. Each pass of the light through the mirrors must experience mirrors which are spaced by the same amount. Deviation by as much as 1.0 nm will significantly deteriorate the signal. Each pass may be physically separated by 3 cm. Thus, the mirrors must be very parallel and remain parallel during the data gathering period, which typically is at least a few tens of minutes. Now most systems that operate in a multipass configuration utilize three separate piezoelectric stacks to drive the one mirror and a servo control which changes the dc bias on each stack to maintain finesse. Such systems are now commercially available.

3.3. Sample

In order to determine the single-crystal elastic moduli of the sample, it is necessary to measure the acoustic velocities as a function of crystallographic direction. This can be done by placing an oriented sample in the spectrometer of Fig. 6. Then, through Eq. (11) the phonon direction can be determined from the relationship between the crystallographic axes and the spectrometer coordinate system. Propagation directions are varied by rotating the sample

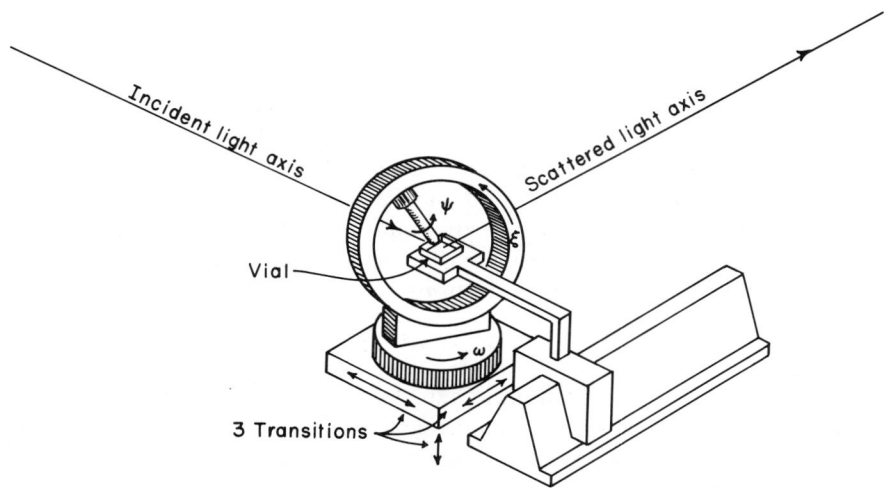

FIG. 8. Schematic diagram of three-circle goniometer used for mounting sample. Such a system provides three rotational axes for orientation and three translational positioners. (After Weidner et al.[66])

with respect to the spectrometer. Figure 8 illustrates a three-circle goniometer which can be used to vary the orientation of the sample. Such goniometers are standard in x-ray laboratories.

It is often very difficult to prepare optical flats on microcrystals. Yet the wave vectors of Eq. (11) and the scattering angle $\theta$ of Eq. (15) depend on the optical geometry inside the sample. This geometry will differ from that in the laboratory if the light is refracted either in entering or in leaving the sample. Refraction will occur if the refractive index of the sample is different from that of the surrounding medium and the light is not passing through a surface which is normal to its propagation direction. This problem is reduced if the sample is placed in a vial of fluid whose refractive index matches those of the crystal, as illustrated in Fig. 8. In the case of an exact match, there is no refraction at the crystal surface regardless of the orientation of the surface. If the refractive indices do not match but the orientation of the crystal surfaces is known, the effects of refraction can be completely compensated in the data reduction as outlined by Vaughan and Bass.[63] The most difficult case occurs when the crystal does not have natural growth faces and is too small to polish. Weidner and Vaughan[64] showed that if the entrance and exit faces were normal to each other but not normal to the optical paths, the deduced velocity was correct but the phonon direction was in error by

$$\xi = (n_f/n_s - 1)\eta \qquad (22)$$

where the subscript $f$ represents fluid, s solid, and $\eta$ is the angle between the face normal and the light direction. If the faces are not orthogonal but at an angle $\pi/2 + \beta$ ($\beta$ given in radians), then the error in velocity is approximately

$$\Delta v/v = \tfrac{1}{2}(1 - n_f/n_s)\beta \tag{23}$$

Thus, if the fluid and crystal differ in refractive index by 10%, $\beta = 25°$ would yield a 2% error in velocity. We have found adequate fluids with refractive indices as great as 1.63. Accurate results for samples with significantly higher indices can be obtained only with good control on the orientation of the crystal surfaces.

### 3.4. Intensities and Polarizations

Fabelinski[65] demonstrated that the intensity of the Brillouin spectra is given as

$$I = K(B_{ij}\alpha_i\beta_j)^2/\lambda^4 \tag{24}$$

where $K$ is proportional to the absolute temperature, $B_{ij}$ is the perturbation in the dielectric impermeability resulting from the phonon, $\alpha_i$ the vector component of the polarization of the incident photon, $\beta_j$ the same quantity for the scattered photon, and $\lambda$ the optical wavelength. The repeated indices imply summation. The matrix $B_{ij}$ is related to the photoelastic tensor $P_{ijkl}$ and the displacement vector $u_l$ and wave normal $n_k$ of the acoustic wave by

$$B_{ij} = P_{ijkl}n_k u_l \tag{25}$$

Thus, the Brillouin signal amplitude is proportional to the square of the photoelastic constants and inversely proportional to the fourth power of the wavelength.

Ultrasonic wave transmission techniques are capable of obtaining acoustic velocities with known displacement vectors, particularly in instances of pure longitudinal or shear modes. Brillouin spectroscopy has a similar capability. Weidner *et al.*[66] use Eq. (24) and (25) to demonstrate the possibility of defining the phonon polarization by controlling the photon polarization for orthorhombic crystals. Vacher and Boyer[67] provide extensive tables for many crystal symmetries which are useful for isolating the phonon polarizations. The results rest on the crystal symmetry as expressed in the photoelastic tensor of Eq. (25). Defining the scattering plane as the plane containing the incident and scattered photons as well as the phonons, we describe a polarization orthogonal to this plane as vertical and a polarization within the plane as horizontal. We can define a few rules which are usually applicable to 90°

scattering but whose validity should be confirmed by analysis of the specific crystal symmetry and sample geometry. They are as follows:

1. A pure shear acoustic mode whose polarization is vertical will be the only Brillouin signal observed when the incident photon is vertical and the scattered photon is horizontal (optical polarization VH) or when the incident is horizontal and the scattered photon vertical (HV).

2. A pure longitudinal acoustic mode will be the only Brillouin signal recorded under (HH) or (VV) conditions.

3. A pure shear mode whose polarization is horizontal will not contribute any Brillouin signal regardless of optical polarization conditions.

The conditions allow the isolation of pure mode acoustic waves and hence provide a data base equivalent to that of ultrasonic measurements.

Brillouin spectroscopy has been used to define the elastic properties of several minerals measured at ambient conditions.[66-70] Because of the broader sample availability for Brillouin spectroscopy measurements, several studies have been made to define elastic properties of different polymorphs of the same compositions.[63, 71-73] As the elevated pressure and temperature within the earth induce polymorphism, it is important to study the elastic properties of the high-pressure phases of candidate compositions. With the great advances in large-volume high-pressure technology of recent years, it has become possible to synthesize single crystals of several such phases which are adequate for Brillouin spectroscopy measurements. Elastic properties of the high-pressure phases of silica were reported by Weidner and Carleton[74] and Weidner et al.[75] Elastic properties of the high-pressure phases of forsterite have been obtained and reported by Weidner et al.[76] and Sawamoto et al.[77]

Whitfield et al.[78] describe an experimental system for Brillouin spectroscopy of samples in a diamond anvil high-pressure apparatus capable of 10 GPa hydrostatic pressure. Such measurements can provide the important pressure derivatives of elastic moduli, which are necessary for extrapolating the laboratory data to conditions of the earth's interior. The effects of refraction and of the sample's refractive index cancel when the incident and scattered photons traverse parallel sample surfaces. Thus, as long as all surfaces are planar and parallel, these effects do not have to be considered explicitly. Bassett and Brody[79] demonstrate the error introduced by nonparallel diamond faces. The utility of the experiment for defining the pressure derivatives of the relatively hard minerals was demonstrated by Bassett et al.[80] for forsterite. While many of the pressure derivatives determined from Brillouin spectroscopy measurements agreed well with those obtained from ultrasonics, some differed by as much as 20%. The disagreement could be due to nonlinearities in the modulus vs. pressure relation (as argued by the authors) or inaccuracies in the measurements.

## 3.5 Acousto-Optical Measurements

Brillouin spectroscopy is one method which utilizes the interaction between light and sound to define acoustic velocities. It is also possible to use optical methods to measure velocities of ultrasonic acoustic waves that are introduced into the sample with transducers. In these experiments a monochromatic ultrasonic continuous wave provides a diffraction grating for scattering light. The frequency is accurately measured ultrasonically and the angle of light scattering depends on the wavelength of the ultrasonic wave by a relation similar to Eq. (11). With Eq. (13) the acoustic velocity can be calculated.

The sample requirements for these measurements combine those of ultrasonics (in terms of size) and Brillouin spectroscopy (in terms of optical properties). These measurements do afford some advantages over ultrasonic wave transmission. First, problems with transducer-bond phase shifts are less severe. Thus, accurate velocities and their derivatives can be determined. Liu et al.[81] used this method to define the temperature derivatives of single-crystal spinel. A second advantage is the ease of separating the contributions of the three modes for low-symmetry crystals. The echo techniques of ultrasonics require that only one acoustic mode be excited in a single experiment; otherwise interference between modes would obscure the individual echoes. Low symmetry crystals have fewer directions where pure modes exist and at the same time require more measurements to constrain the elastic properties. Thus, triclinic crystals are virtually impossible to characterize with the echo techniques. Kuppers and Siegert[82] employed acousto-optic techniques to define the elastic properties of triclinic crystals. Since each mode is characterized by a distinctive velocity, each mode gave rise to a different diffraction angle of the light. As a result, all three acoustic velocities could be determined for an arbitrary direction.

# 4. Thermal Diffuse Scattering

The most precise information that is known concerning the material which constitutes the earth's mantle is its acoustic velocity. These velocities, which are determined as a function of depth from seismology, demonstrate at least two discontinuities in properties in the depth range 400 to 700 km. These discontinuities can be associated with phase transformations in the olivine and pyroxene components of the mantle to phases involving $\gamma$-spine, $\beta$-spinel, stishovite, and a complex garnet. These phases in turn are expected to transform to a perovskite and magnesiowustite assemblage at greater depth. The final test of these phase transformation models and the refinement of compositional models for this region require laboratory measurements of acoustic velocities of the phases for different compositions under the pressure and temperature regime found in the earth. In the previous sections I have outlined the techniques and limitations of experiments which have begun to address these questions. Brillouin spetroscopy has demonstrated its potential for yielding acoustic velocities for samples synthesized at very high pressures and temperatures. The potential for defining the pressure derivatives of these properties has also been established. In this section I wish to suggest an alternative method for determining the elastic properties of these small synthetic samples at elevated pressures and temperatures. This method is based on using thermal diffuse scattering of x rays in conjunction with diamond anvil pressure cells. The potential of this approach depends on the utilization of synchrotron x-ray sources, which can provide high-intensity, monochromatic, well-collimated x rays.

X rays interact with thermal phonons in much the same way as visible light in the Brillouin scattering phenomenon. The manifestation of phonon interaction with x rays is a diffuse scattering centered about a Bragg reflection. The shape and distribution of the diffuse scattering depend on the elastic moduli of the solid. It is thus possible to recover the elastic moduli from the measurement of x-ray scattering in the vicinity of the Bragg reflection. The advantages of using x-ray diffuse scattering to determine elastic properties include:

1. X rays are not refracted by the crystal or by the diamonds in the case of high-pressure experiments.
2. Small single crystals (100 μm) can be measured.
3. Opaque minerals can be measured (which cannot be done with Brillouin scattering).

The disadvantages of determining elastic properties from the thermal diffuse scattering of x rays include:

1. The intensities are low.
2. The x-ray source must be very monochromatic (or the energy distribution must be well known).
3. The x-ray beam must have very small divergence.
4. Photon intensity (as opposed to energy) is measured.

These factors have limited the use of thermal diffuse scattering with conventional x-ray sources in defining elastic properties. Some of these difficulties may be surmountable by using a synchrotron as the x-ray source with appropriate monochromators. The source is of high intensity and can be extremely well collimated.

The theory of thermal diffuse scattering of x rays is not new and is outlined by Ramachandran and Wooster[83] and in great detail by Wooster.[84] They demonstrate that the intensity of the thermal diffuse scattering is given by

$$I = (kT/\tau)|F_T|^2 I_0 (R/q)^2 \sum_{i=1}^{3} \cos^2(\mathbf{R}, \mathbf{d}_i)/(\rho v_i^2) \qquad (26)$$

where $k$ is Boltzmann's constant, $T$ is temperature (kelvins), $\tau$ is the unit cell volume, $F_T$ the structure factor of the Bragg reflection at temperature $T$, $I_0$ the intensity of the incident x-ray beam, $\mathbf{R}$ the reciprocal-lattice vector of the Bragg reflection of length $R$, $\mathbf{q}$ the vector in reciprocal space from the Bragg reflection to the point of measurement of length $q$, $\mathbf{d}_i$ the displacement vector of the $i$th phonon mode corresponding to a phonon with wave vector $\mathbf{q}$, $\rho$ the density, $v_i$ the phase velocity of the phonon with wave vector $\mathbf{q}$ and displacement vector $\mathbf{d}_i$, and $(\mathbf{R}, \mathbf{d}_i)$ the angle between the two vectors.

This relationship is most applicable to the region close to the Bragg reflection, because the classical equipartitioning of energy into the phonon frequencies is most appropriate in this region (through the term $kT$). In this region the nondispersive portion of the acoustic branch will dominate the contributions to the diffuse scattering. Thus, the deduced phase velocities will reflect static elastic properties insofar as the crystal exhibits no dissipative mechanisms at lower frequencies.

The dependence of the distribution of diffuse scattering about a Bragg reflection on the acoustic velocity can be deduced from Eq. (26). An acoustic wave is completely defined by its propagation direction (or wave normal) and its particle displacement vector. The wave normal of the acoustic waves contributing to the diffuse scattering is parallel to $\mathbf{q}$. The intensity of the diffuse scattering depends on a particular acoustic mode as the square of the cosine of the angle between the reciprocal-lattice vector $\mathbf{R}$ and the particle displacement vector $\mathbf{d}$. Thus, when a displacement vector is parallel to the reciprocal-lattice vector, only that acoustic wave contributes to the diffuse scattering. As a result, by examining the diffuse scattering in specific directions about judiciously chosen Bragg reflection, various modes of acoustic velocities can be isolated and measured.

Equation (26) expresses the intensity due to single interactions between an x-ray photon and a lattice phonon. Higher-order scattering will also contribute to the observed diffuse scattering. Second-order contributions include scattering involving two photon–phonon interactions. The higher-order terms become progressively weaker as their probability of occurrence quickly diminishes. Lucas[85] demonstrates that it is possible to explicitly correct for the effect of second-order scattering since it is also dependent on the elastic properties of the material. While the first-order scattering decays as $1/q^2$, the second-order scattering decays as $1/q$. Thus, the second order will become relatively more significant farther from the Bragg position.

Equation (26) can be exploited to determine the acoustic velocities from the dependence of the intensity as a function of distance from the Bragg reflection. The intensity decays as $1/q^2$. The coefficient of this term is proportional to $1/v^2$. However, the constant of proportionality contains variables that are not always easily deduced. In particular, the product of structure factor and absolute amplitude of the incident x-ray beam is the most difficult to measure accurately. This is particularly true for samples which are smaller than the x-ray beam. However, ratios of the coefficients for different directions from a Bragg reflection will reflect ratios of acoustic velocities. Thus, the relative values of the acoustic velocities will be the most accurately determined. Alternatively, the shapes of equal-intensity contours about the Bragg position reflect the ratios of the acoustic velocities for the different modes. In addition, changes in the acoustic velocities with pressure or temperature should be more easily determined than the absolute values. Careful measurement of the incident x-ray intensity or of one elastic modulus

TABLE I. Comparison of Properties Measured Ultrasonically (Ac) and with Thermal Diffuse Scattering of X Rays (TDS)[a,b]

| | | PART A. | Elastic Moduli | | |
|---|---|---|---|---|---|
| | | | | Reference[b] | |
| | $ij$ | $C_{ij}^{TDS}$ (Mbar) | $C_{ij}^{Ac}$ (Mbar) | TDS | Ac |
| FeS$_2$ | 11 | 3.77 | 3.79 | 1 | 2 |
| | 12 | 0.32 | 0.31 | | |
| | 44 | 1.09 | 1.09 | | |
| Pb | 11 | 0.50 | 0.50 | 3 | 4 |
| | 12 | 0.39 | 0.42 | | |
| | 44 | 0.14 | 0.15 | | |
| Ge | 11 | 1.33 | 1.29 | 5 | 6 |
| | 12 | 0.51 | 0.48 | | |
| | 44 | 0.70 | 0.67 | | |
| Sn | 11 | 0.86 | 0.75 | 7 | 8 |
| | 33 | 1.33 | 0.96 | | |
| | 44 | 0.49 | 0.22 | | |
| | 66 | 0.53 | 0.23 | | |
| | 12 | 0.35 | 0.62 | | |
| | 13 | 0.30 | 0.44 | | |
| KCl | 11 | 0.439 | 0.41 | 9 | 10 |
| | 12 | 0.055 | 0.07 | | |
| | 44 | 0.080 | 0.06 | | |

TABLE I—continued

PART B. Acoustic Velocities

| | Direction | Mode | $V^{\text{TDS}}$ (km/s) | $V^{\text{Ac}}$ (km/s) | Reference[b] TDS | Ac |
|---|---|---|---|---|---|---|
| NaF | 111 | T | 3.63 | 3.46 | 11 | 12 |
| | | L | 5.45 | 5.52 | | |
| | 110 | T | 3.18 | 3.17 | | |
| | | L | 5.52 | 5.61 | | |
| | 100 | T | 3.28 | 3.17 | | |
| | | L | 5.62 | 5.87 | | |
| NaCl | 111 | L | 4.10 | 4.40 | 13 | 10 |
| | 100 | T | 2.44 | 2.42 | | |

[a] The discrepancies for tin are discussed by Prasad and Wooster.[14]
[b] References:
1. Prasad, S. C., and W. A. Wooster, *Acta Crystallogr.* **9**, 169 (1956).
2. Simmons, G., and F. Birch, *J. Apple. Phys.* **34**, 2736 (1963).
3. Prasad, S. C., and W. A. Wooster, *Acta Crystallogr.* **9**, 38 (1956).
4. Waldorf, D. L., and G. A. Alers, *J. Appl. Phys.* **33**, 3266 (1962).
5. Prasad, S. C., and W. A. Wooster, *Acta Crystallogr.* **8**, 506 (1955).
6. McSkimin, H. J., *J. Acoust. Soc. Am.* **31**, 287 (1959).
7. Prasad, S. C., and W. A. Wooster, *Acta Crystallogr.* **8**, 682 (1955).
8. House, D. G., and E. V. Vernon, *Br. J. Appl. Phys.* **11**, 254 (1960).
9. Lucas, B. W., *Acta Crystallogr., Sect. A* **24**, 336 (1968).
10. Lazarus, D., *Phys. Rev.* **76**, 545 (1949).
11. Pirie, J. D., and T. Smith, *J. Phys. C* **1**, 648 (1968).
12. Miller, R. A., and C. S. Smith, *J. Phys. Chem. Solids* **25**, 1279 (1964).
13. Buyers, W. J. L., and T. Smith, *Phys. Rev.* **150**, 758 (1966).
14. Prasad, S. C., and W. A. Wooster, *Acta Crystallogr.* **9**, 35 (1956).

(such as the bulk modulus) will allow the determination of the absolute values of all the moduli.

Thermal diffuse scattering of x rays has been used to define single-crystal elastic moduli of several materials. Symmetries as low as orthorhombic have been investigated successfully with this technique.[86] Elastic moduli deduced from thermal diffuse scattering are compared with ultrasonic data in Table I. The data demonstrate that it was possible to obtain reliable elastic moduli from thermal diffuse scattering measurements even with the level of x-ray technology of three decades ago. Most of these experiments were conducted with the intent of examining the phonon dispersion curve, and the comparisons with ultrasonic results were made by extrapolating the results to a zero value of **q**. In all these studies, large samples were used with conventional x-ray sources and both photographic and counting detectors. With the development of neutron scattering techniques, where phonon energy could be measured directly, x-ray thermal diffuse scattering no longer provided the best measure of phonon dispersion and the number of such efforts dramatically decreased. The advent of synchrotron x-ray sources should enormously improve the accuracy of diffuse scattering measurements in the nondispersive portion of the spectrum in that it will allow measurement of phonons with smaller wave numbers. The x-ray beam can be very finely collimated without reducing intensity to too low a level. Furthermore, a monochromator can be used to yield a narrow and well-defined energy spectrum. All of these advances will allow more precise measurements of the x-ray intensities very close to the Bragg reflection. We anticipate at least an order of magnitude increase in the resolution of x-ray intensity close to a Bragg reflection.

The most problematic aspect of using thermal diffuse scattering for acoustic characterizations is that photon intensity and not energy is measured. Phonon interactions are encoded on the photons by varying the phonon energy. While few other phenomena contribute to altering the photon energy, many factors can contribute to the intensity of diffusely scattered photons. Thus the improved accuracy of the measurements will result in improved accuracies of the elastic moduli only if the limiting factors have been instrumentation. Lal et al.[87] and Lal[88] suggest that for single-crystal silicon, the diffuse scattering in the region of the Bragg reflection is dominated by scattering from the point defect clusters and not by thermal phonons. Thus, considerable effort must be made to ensure that the diffuse scattering is of thermal origin.

## References

1. Birch, F., *J. Geophys. Res.* **66**, 2199 (1961).
2. Simmons, G., *J. Geophys. Res.* **69**, 1123 (1964).
3. Winkler, K. W., and T. J. Plona, *J. Geophys. Res.* **87**, 776 (1982).
4. Christensen, N. I., *in* "Handbook of Physical Properties of Rocks" (R. S. Carmichael, ed.), Vol. 2, p. 1. CRC Press, Boca Raton, Florida, 1982.
5. Bonner, B. P., and R. N. Schock, *in* "Cindas Data Series on Material Properties" (Y. D. Touloukian, W. R. Judd, and R. F. Roy, eds.), Vol. II-2, p. 221. McGraw-Hill, New York, 1981.
6. Christensen, N., *J. Geophys. Res.* **69**, 407 (1974).
7. Christensen, N., and R. Ramananantoandro, *J. Geophys. Res.* **76**, 4003 (1971).
8. Babuska, V., *J. Geophys. Res.* **77**, 6955 (1972).
9. Manghnani, M., E. Schreiber, and N. Soga, *J. Geophys. Res.* **73**, 824 (1968).
10. Fielitz, K. C., *Z. Geophys.* **37**, 943 (1971).
11. Spencer, J. W., Jr., and A. M. Nur, *J. Geophys. Res.* **81**, 899 (1976).
12. Meissner, R., and M. Fakhimi, *Geophys. J.* **49**, 133 (1977).
13. Kern, H., *Tectonophysics* **44**, 185 (1978).
14. Stewart, R., and L. Peselnick, *J. Geophys. Res.* **83**, 831 (1978).
15. Christensen, N. I., *J. Geophys. Res.* **84**, 6849 (1979).

16. Matsushima, S., *Tectonophysics* **75**, 257 (1981).
17. Nur, A., and G. Simmons, *Earth Planet. Sci. Lett.* **7**, 99 (1969).
18. Nur, A., and G. Simmons, *Earth Planet. Sci. Lett.* **7**, 183 (1969).
19. Takeuchi, S., and G. Simmons, *J. Geophys. Res.* **78**, 3310 (1973).
20. Spencer, J. W., Jr., and A. M. Nur, *J. Geophys. Res.* **81**, 899 (1976).
21. Toksoz, M. N., and D. Johnston, "Seismic Wave Attenuation." Soc. Explor. Ceophysicists, Tulsa, Oklahoma, 1981.
22. Nur, A., *Bull. Seismol. Soc. Am.* **62**, 1217 (1972).
23. Scholz, C. H., L. R. Sykes, and Y. P. Aggarwal, *Science* **181**, 803 (1973).
24. Spetzler, H., and R. Martin, *Nature (London)* **252**, 30 (1974).
25. Seya, K., I. Suzuki, and H. Fujiwara, *J. Phys. Earth* **27**, 409 (1979).
26. Spetzler, H. A., G. A. Sobolev, C. H. Soundergeld, B. G. Salov, I. C. Getting, and A. Koltsov, *J. Geophys. Res.* **86**(B2), 1070 (1981).
27. Liebermann, R. C., A. E. Ringwood, D. J. Mayson, and A. Major, *Proc. Int. Conf. High Pressure, 4th, Kyoto, 1974*, p. 495 (1975).
28. Liebermann, R. C., A. E. Ringwood, and A. Major, *Earth Planet Sci. Lett.* **127**, 127 (19⁻6).
29. Mizutani, H., Y. Hamano, and S. Akimoto, *J. Geophys. Res.* **77**, 3744 (1972).
30. Chung, D. H., and G. Sumino, *Earth Planet. Sci. Lett.* **6**, 134 (1969).
31. Spetzler, H., *J. Geophys. Res.* **75**, 2073 (1970).
32. Wang, C. Y., and M. Meltzer, *J. Geophys. Res.* **78**, 1293 (1973).
33. Fukizawa, A., and H. Kinoshita, *J. Phys. Earth* **30**, 245 (1982).
34. Papadakis, E. P., *J. Acoust. Soc. Am.* **42**, 1045 (1967).
35. McSkimin, H. J., *J. Acoust. Soc. Am.* **22**, 413 (1950).
36. McSkimin, H. J., *IEEE Trans. Sonics Ultrason.* **SU-5**, 25 (1957).
37. McSkimin, H. J., *J. Acoust. Soc. Am.* **33**, 12 (1961).
38. McSkimin, H. J., *J. Acoust. Soc. Am.* **37**, 864 (1965).
39. Davies G. F., and R. J. O'Connell, in "High Pressure Research: Applications in Geophysics" (M. H. Manghnani and S.-i. Akimoto, eds.), p. 533. Academic Press, New York, 1977.
40. Jackson, I., H. Niesler, and D. J. Weidner, *J. Geophys. Res.* **86**, 3736 (1981).
41. Jackson, I., and H. Niesler, in "High-Pressure Research in Geophysics" (S.-i. Akimoto and M. H. Manghnani, eds.), p. 93. Cent. Acad. Publ., Tokyo and Reidel Publ., Dordrecht, Netherlands, 1982.
42. Peselnick, L., *J. Geophys. Res.* **87**, 6799 (1982).
43. Lamb, H., *Proc. Math. Soc.* **13**, 189 (1882).
44. Fraser, D. B., and R. C. LeCraw, *Rev. Sci. Instrum.* **35**, 113 (1964).
45. Spinner, S., and W. E. Tefft, *Am. Soc. Test. Mater. Proc.* **61**, 1221 (1961).
46. Schreiber, E., O. L. Anderson, and N. Soga, "Elastic Constants and Their Measurements." McGraw-Hill, New York, 1973.
47. Demarest, H. H., Jr., *J. Acoust. Soc. Am.* **49**, 768 (1971).
48. Ohno, I., *J. Phys. Earth* **24**, 355 (1976).
49. Birch, F., *J. Geophys. Res.* **80**, 756 (1975).
50. Sumino, Y., I. Ohno, T. Goto, and M. Kumazawa, *J. Phys. Earth* **24**, 263 (1976).
51. Soga, N., and O. L. Anderson, *J. Geophys. Res.* **72**, 1733 (1967).
52. Sumino, Y., O. Nishizawa, T. Goto, I. Ohno, and M. Ozima, *J. Phys. Earth* **25**, 377 (1977).
53. Sumino, Y., *J. Phys. Earth* **27**, 209 (1979).
54. Sumino, Y., M. Kumazawa, O. Nishizawa, and W. Pluschkell, *J. Phys. Earth* **28**, 475 (1980).
55. Sumino, Y., O. L. Anderson, and I. Suzuki, *Phys. Chem. Miner.* **9**, 38 (1983).
56. Goto, T., I. Ohno, and Y. Sumino, *J. Phys. Earth* **24**, 149 (1976).

57. Babuska, V., J. Fiala, M. Kumazawa, J. Ohno, and Y. Sumino, *Phys. Earth Plant. Inter.* **16**, 157 (1978).
58. Suzuki, I., O. L. Anderson, and Y. Sumino, *Phys. Chem. Miner.* **10**, 38 (1983).
59. Fleury, P., *in* "Physical Acoustics VI" (W. P. Mason and R. N. Thurston, eds.), p. 1–63. Academic Press, New York, 1970.
60. Weidner, D. J., K. Swyler, and H. R. Carleton, *Geophys. Res. Lett.* **2**, 189 (1975).
61. Gornall, W. S., and B. P. Stoicheff, *Phys. Rev.* **4**, 4518 (1971).
62. Sandercock, J. R., *Proc. Int. Conf. Light Scattering Solids, 2nd, Paris* p. 9 (1971).
63. Vaughan, M. T., and D. J. Bass, *Phys. Chem. Miner.* **10**, 62 (1983).
64. Weidner, D. J., and M. T. Vaughan, *High-Pressure Sci. Technol., AIRAPT Conf., 6th, Boulder, Colo., 1977* **2**, 85 (1979).
65. Fabelinski, I., "Molecular Scattering of Light." P. N. Lebedev Phys. Inst. Acad. Sci. USSR, Moscow, 1968.
66. Weidner, D. J., H. Wang, and J. Ito, *Phys. Earth Planet. Inter.* **17**, P7 (1978).
67. Vacher, R., and L. Boyer, *Phys. Rev.* **6**, 639 (1972).
68. Levien, L., D. J. Weidner, and C. T. Prewitt, *Phys. Chem. Miner.* **4**, 105 (1979).
69. Leitner, B., D. J. Weidner, and R. C. Liebermann, *Phys. Earth Planet. Inter.* **22**, 111 (1980).
70. Bass, J. D., and D. J. Weidner, *J. Geophys. Res.* **89**, 4359 (1984).
71. Vaughan, M. T., and D. J. Weidner, *Phys. Chem. Miner.* **3**, 133 (1978).
72. Bass, D. J., D. J. Weidner, N. Hamaya, M. Ozima, and S. Akimoto, *Phys. Chem. Miner.* **10**, 261 (1984).
73. Weidner D. J., and N. Hamaya, *Phys. Earth Planet. Inter.* **33**, 275 (1983).
74. Weidner, D. J., and H. R. Carleton, *J. Geophys. Res.* **82**, 1334 (1977).
75. Weidner, D. J., J. D. Bass, A. E. Ringwood, and W. Sinclair, *J. Geophys. Res.* **87**, 4740 (1982).
76. Weidner, D. J., H. Sawamoto, S. Sasaki, and M. Kumazawa, *J. Geophys. Res.* **89**, 7852 (1984).
77. Sawamoto, H., D. J. Weidner, S. Sasaki, and M. Kumazawa, *Science* **224**, 749 (1984).
78. Whitfield, C. H., E. M. Brody, and W. A. Bassett, *Rev. Sci. Instrum.* **47**, 942 (1976).
79. Bassett, W. A., and E. M. Brody, *in* "High Pressure Research: Applications in Geophysics" (M. H. Manghnani and S.-i. Akimoto, eds.), p. 519. Academic Press, New York, 1977.
80. Bassett, W. A., H. Shimizu, and E. M. Brody, *in* "High Pressure Research in Geophysics" (S.-i. Akimoto and M. H. Manghnani, eds.), p. 115. Cent. Acad. Publ., Tokyo and Reidel Publ., Dordrecht, Netherlands, 1982.
81. Liu, H.-P., R. N. Schock, and D. L. Anderson, *Geophys. J. R. Astron. Soc.* **42**, 217 (1976).
82. Kuppers, H., and H. Siegert, *Acta Crystallogr., Sect. A* **26**, 401 (1970).
83. Ramachandran, G. N., and W. A. Wooster, *Acta Crystallogr.* **4**, 335 (1951).
84. Wooster, W. A., "Diffuse X-Ray Reflections from Crystals." Oxford Univ. Press (Clarendon), London and New York, 1962.
85. Lucas, B. W., *Acta Crystallogr., Sect. A* **24**, 336 (1968).
86. Garg, A., and R. C. Srivastava, *Acta Crystallogr., Sect. A* **36**, 873 (1980).
87. Lal, K., B. P. Singh, and A. R. Verma, *Acta Crystallogr., Sect. A* **35**, 28 (1979).
88. Lal, K., *Proc. Indian Natl. Sci. Acad., Part A* **7**, 20 (1981).

# 2. LABORATORY MEASUREMENT OF INTERNAL FRICTION IN ROCKS AND MINERALS AT SEISMIC FREQUENCIES

Louis Peselnick
Hsi-Ping Liu

U.S. Geological Survey
Menlo Park, California 94025

## 1. Introduction

Observation of seismic attenuation and other dissipative effects can provide information on the earth's interior. Several examples illustrate this point. (1) Gorshkov (1956) suggested the existence of a magma chamber at a depth of 50–60 km beneath Klyuchevskoi Volcano in the Kamchatka volcanic belt. The suggestion was based on observations that S waves from earthquakes in the Japanese arc failed to arrive at a seismic station at an epicentral distance of 25.6°, whereas S waves were clearly recorded at nearer (22.2°) and farther (26.1°) seismic stations. The arrival of P waves at all three stations and the absence of S waves at 25.6° suggest that the S waves were severely attenuated by the magma chamber. (2) Anderson and Hart (1978) derived seismic attenuation models as a function of the earth's radius from the decay of near-vertical ScS multiple phases, the spectral amplitude decay with distance of surface waves, and measurements of free-oscillation spectral peak half-widths. Their preferred model includes a high-attenuation zone at both the top (quality factor $Q_\alpha \cong 200$ for compressional waves, $Q_\beta \cong 90$ for shear waves) and bottom ($Q_\alpha \cong 270$, $Q_\beta \cong 100$) of the mantle. Possible mechanisms suggested for such values include partial melting (Anderson and Sammis, 1970) and glide of dislocations in mineral grains (Anderson and Minster, 1981). (3) Sipkin and Jordan (1980) determined regional variations of the decay of ScS multiple phases and attributed these variations to temperature differences in the mantle. (4) Theoretically, linear anelasticity implies a dispersion in the elastic response (Liu et al., 1976). Assuming a linear anelastic reponse, Anderson and Minster (1979) and Smith and Dahlen (1981) calculated a lengthening of the theoretical Chandler wobble period on the basis of elastic moduli derived from data on the earth's free oscillation.

Using the observed Chandler wobble period (453.2 days) and quality factor ($Q = 50$–400), these authors placed constraints on the frequency dependence of mantle anelasticity. (5) The amplitude of crustal seismic reflections below a "bright spot" in a seismic section commonly are highly attenuated. This effect is attributed to the higher attenuation coefficient of the pocket of gas-saturated sand whose top boundary is defined by the bright spot (Dobrin, 1976).

One objective of laboratory experiments on internal friction in rocks and minerals is to conduct measurements as a function of frequency in the seismic band ($10^{-4}$–100 Hz) under varying physical conditions (confining pressure, deviatoric stress, temperature, mineralogy and texture, pore fluid saturation, pore pressure, crack density, etc.) to help in the interpretation of field data. The linear dimensions of the rock samples should be large in comparison with the mineral grain dimensions; otherwise, the measured physical quantity is difficult to interpret in terms of the bulk properties of the rock. However, because the wavelength of seismic waves is much longer than the laboratory sample dimensions, laboratory internal friction measurements may not be indicative of the bulk seismic attenuation properties of the Earth, which may be controlled by such larger inhomogeneities as those present in an earthquake fault zone or in a water–steam geothermal field. Elastic scattering is another factor that contributes to the variation of seismic wave amplitude with distance but that cannot be interpreted on the basis of laboratory internal friction measurements. Therefore, the laboratory-measured rock internal friction constitutes only a part of the observed attenuation.

Another objective of internal friction measurements under controlled physical conditions is to isolate and determine the physical mechanisms of internal friction. Nevertheless, even a relatively "homogeneous" rock constitutes a complex physical system. Thus, the physical mechanisms of internal friction in rocks are currently not well understood: loss mechanisms have been ascribed to grain boundary sites, crystalline defects, diffusion of volatiles on the surfaces of microcracks, grain thermoelastic relaxation, and other stress relaxation mechanisms. Precise descriptions of rock samples and of the physical conditions of measurements are, therefore, prerequisite in identifying the mechanisms of internal friction. Single-crystal minerals are much simpler physical systems than rock specimens, and the loss mechanisms are more easily identified in an experiment. Even so, few measurements of mineral internal friction under elevated pressure and temperature conditions relevant to the earth's interior are presently available.

This chapter summarizes the various models and mechanisms of internal friction and describes experimental methods for measuring internal friction in rocks and minerals. We emphasize the seismic frequency range and analyze the subresonance technique that we have investigated.

## 2. Characterization of Nonelastic Behavior of Solids

2.1. Physical and Mathematical Preliminaries

The various types of nonelastic behavior of solids, e.g., plasticity, anelasticity, and viscoelasticity, were characterized by Nowick and Berry (1972). Some basic concepts and commonly used definitions are summarized here.

All nonelastic behavior implies the conversion of some elastic strain energy to heat energy. For solids subjected to cyclic stress, the term "internal friction" is used to describe collectively all mechanisms by which vibrational energy is converted into heat. The specific damping capacity $b$ and the quality parameter $Q$ are two often used definitions of internal friction:

$$b = \Delta W/W \qquad Q^{-1} = (1/2\pi)(\Delta W/W) \qquad (1)$$

where $W$ is the maximum strain energy stored in the sample and $\Delta W$ the energy dissipated per stress cycle. Some of the earliest measurements of $\Delta W$ were by Föppl (1936), who calculated the amount of heat generated by measuring the temperature rise in the sample under cyclic strain. The strain amplitudes used by Föppl were large enough to cause plastic flow, resulting in relatively high temperatures in the steel samples. Such methods are not sufficiently accurate for application to the small strains of seismic interest.

Less direct methods of defining internal friction rely on some characteristic response in the particular experimental method used. Experimental arrangements used to define and measure internal friction include the phase lag of strain behind the stress of a sample under quasi-static cyclic loading, the width of the resonance peak of a sample subjected to forced vibrations, the decrease in amplitude of successively reflected acoustic pulses over a given sample length, and the decay of successive amplitudes of a freely oscillating mechanical system.

With regard to anelastic behavior, the strain response to each level of applied stress is linear, time dependent, yields no permanent set, and has a unique equilibrium value. Anelastic behavior is important for the study of seismic waves at small strain amplitude ($< 10^{-8}$). For anelastic behavior and small internal friction, the relations between the variously defined internal friction parameters are summarized in Eq. (2) (Nowick and Berry, 1972; O'Connell and Budiansky, 1978), in which the error is estimated to be less than 5% for $\phi < 0.1$:

$$Q^{-1} = \tan \phi \cong \phi = \delta/\pi = \alpha_s \lambda/\pi = Q_H^{-1} \qquad (\phi \ll 1) \qquad (2)$$

where $\phi$ (commonly called the internal friction) is the phase lag of strain behind stress in the quasi-static cyclic loading experiment. The logarithmic decrement $\delta$ is obtained from the decay of free oscillations of a mechanical system. The half-power loss parameter $Q_H$ is obtained from the resonant frequency response of a mechanical system in forced vibration. The spatial attenuation coefficient $\alpha_s$ for the wavelength $\lambda$ is obtained from pulse propagation experiments. Each loss parameter in Eq. (2) is associated with an appropriate mode of oscillation determined by the experimental arrangement (e.g., shear, dilatational, Young's modulus mode). For anisotropic solids, the loss parameters may also be a function of direction. Such distinctions must be considered in comparing loss parameters. Additional discussion of the loss parameters in Eq. (2) is given in Section 3.

## 2.2. Models of Internal Friction Relevant to Seismic Waves in Rocks

The internal friction observed in dry monomineralic rocks is much greater than that in the corresponding single-crystal forms (Peselnick and Zietz, 1959; Gordon and Davis, 1968). Application of confining pressure to rock samples generally results in a decrease of internal friction (Birch and Bancroft, 1938; Katahara et al., 1982; Jackson et al., 1984). Experimental data suggest that cracks are associated with mechanisms of internal friction. Observations, beginning with those of Birch and Bancroft (1938), also suggest that $Q$ in many rocks is independent of frequency. This suggestion prompted the development of several frictional models of attenuation for which $\Delta W/W$ is independent of frequency.

Förtsch (1956) derived a nonlinear mathematical model based on Coulomb (sliding) friction to obtain a frequency-independent $Q$. A discussion of this and other models and mechanisms of internal friction was given by White (1965).

Walsh (1966) derived expressions for the longitudinal and shear attenuation resulting from sliding at crack surfaces in terms of crack parameters, the coefficient of sliding friction, and the intrinsic elastic properties of an isotropic rock. An important conclusion of Walsh's nonlinear model in agreement with observations is that internal frictional losses resulting from sliding are very much greater than intrinsic losses in the rock material.

Mavko (1979) considered a sliding frictional model of irregularly shaped nonelliptic cracks. His results show that $Q^{-1}$ increases with strain amplitude but that for small strains ($< 10^{-6}$) frictional attenuation becomes unimportant compared to linear loss mechanisms.

Savage and Hasegawa (1967) presented evidence for a linear internal friction mechanism. The attenuation in metals of both sinusoidal and nonsinusoidal disturbances was found to agree with the principle of superposition. Specifically, the Fourier components of nonsinusoidal disturbances were found to attenuate at the same rate as those of the corresponding sinusoidal

## 2. INTERNAL FRICTION AT SEISMIC FREQUENCIES

disturbances. The same result is suggested by observations in the Pierre Shale and Westerly Granite.

Liu et al. (1976) constructed a linear model of seismic wave attenuation from a spectrum of standard anelastic solids. The value of $Q$ in their model is constant to within ±1.25% over a frequency range of $3 \times 10^{-4}$ to 10 Hz. Although many physical attenuation mechanisms can be represented by the standard linear-solid model, the specific mechanisms operating in rocks still remain unidentified. Kjartansson (1979) presented a mathematical creep function and derived a corresponding linear attenuation model for which $Q$ is exactly constant at all frequencies.

The use of both frictional and viscous elements in models of internal friction is inadequate in the sense that the physical basis of friction and the viscous behavior of solids at small stress amplitudes remain to be identified.

The addition of pore fluids to rocks increases internal friction. Tittmann et al. (1980) observed a strong dependence of internal friction on volatile content for vacuum-dried rocks. Spencer (1981) observed large attenuation peaks and a corresponding dispersion in Young's modulus for water-saturated rocks. Winkler and Nur (1982) found that the addition of water to dry rocks increased $Q^{-1}$ by a factor of 2 or more. Tittmann et al. (1980) presented a qualitative model of seismic wave attenuation based on an interaction between the adsorbed layer of volatiles and the solid surface in terms of the thermally activated motions in the adsorbed film. Spencer (1981) explained his results in terms of electrical interaction between water molecules and the mineral surface. A number of viscous fluid flow models in rocks are discussed by Mavko et al. (1979). The loss results from the relative motion between the solid and pore fluids and from relative motion within the fluid. White (1986) identified internal friction peaks in the laboratory measurement of fluid-saturated porous rocks resulting from fluid motion near the sample surface. White cautioned that results from such laboratory measurements may not be applicable to wave propagation in an extended porous medium.

### 2.3. Mechanisms of Internal Friction

2.3.1 Thermoelastic Mechanisms. In principle, thermal conduction results in a damping of stress waves because heat flow in regions of stress-induced temperature gradients represents and irreversible extraction of elastic energy from the wave. Several thermoelastic loss mechanisms in solids were reviewed by Zener (1948) and Nowick and Berry (1972). Two examples are the heat flow under inhomogeneous stress in the transverse vibration of a thin beam and the intercrystalline heat flow resulting from stress waves in a polycrystalline solid composed of elastically anisotropic grains. Zener demonstrated that these mechanisms are relevant to internal friction in some metals.

Savage (1966) applied Zener's (1948) thermoelastic mechanism to derive equations for the internal friction in solids containing cracks. The values of $Q$ for longitudinal waves ($Q_\alpha$) and shear waves ($Q_\beta$) were calculated from a distribution of cracks in terms of the parameters measured in static testing. Savage's theory gives the correct order of magnitude of $Q$ for both shear and compression; for granite, $Q_\alpha = 200$ and $Q_\beta = 350$. His theory also predicts a temperature dependence of $Q^{-1}$ proportional to $T$; however, laboratory measurements in rocks by Birch and Bancroft (1938) and Volarovich and Gurvich (1957) showed that $Q$ is relatively insensitive to temperature, whereas Kissel (1972) observed peaks in $Q^{-1}$ near room temperature for several rocks. The temperature dependence of $Q$ in rocks is apparently complex and depends on other factors in addition to thermoelastic loss in cracks.

Kjartansson and Denliger (1977) considered the thermoelastic mechanism of loss for pore fluids in rocks. They predict a strongly temperature-dependent attenuation for water-saturated rocks and losses much larger than those for dry rocks.

2.3.2 Internal Friction Resulting from Crystal Imperfections. Imperfections in the structure of single crystals can result in internal friction (Nowick and Berry, 1972). Naturally occurring types of crystal imperfections that have been investigated in rock-forming minerals and glasses include point defects (vacancies, interstitial atoms, and substitutional atoms) and dislocations.

An illustration of internal friction resulting from an interstitial point defect is the Snoek peak (Snoek, 1941) in carbon containing $\alpha$-iron. The lattice is distorted locally by the interstitial C atom. An applied stress results in a tendency for the C atom to migrate to a site of lower free energy. When this migration occurs, the difference in free energy between the two sites is converted first into kinetic energy of the C atom and then, after equilibration, into thermal vibrations of the lattice. Such point defect mechanisms may also be important in silicates and other rocks at seismic frequencies. An internal friction peak in soda–silica glass (maximum $Q^{-1} \cong 0.01$, $f \cong 0.16$ Hz, $T \cong -43\,°\mathrm{C}$) resulting from sodium ion diffusion was reported by Fitzgerald et al. (1952).

2.3.3. Grain Boundary Relaxation. Several experimental observations in metals indicate that relative motion or slip can occur at grain boundaries at elevated temperatures or low strain rates (Zener, 1948). The work of Ke (1947) has commonly been considered an experimental verification of the grain boundary viscous-slip model of Zener (1941). Ke observed a complete relaxational peak and shear modulus defect in polycrystalline aluminium at

300° to 400°C, using a torsion pendulum apparatus. There is some controversy regarding the physical mechanism of this effect; observations by Woirgard and Gueguen (1978) led them to conclude that the effect may not be grain boundary relaxation but instead due to dislocation motion inside the crystals.

2.3.4. Dislocating Damping. Line imperfections or dislocations are responsible for several internal friction peaks in solids previously subjected to large strains. An example is the well-studied Bordoni peak originally observed in face-centered-cubic metals, which display typical relaxation features. Internal friction peaks in highly deformed MgO, LiF, KCl, and PbS are also believed to result from dislocation motions (Nowick and Berry, 1972).

Woirgard and Gueguen (1978) presented significant internal friction measurements with respect to upper-mantle geophysical applications, namely the measurement of $Q$ on peridotite and a single crystal of enstatite at temperatures as high as 1100°C and frequencies from 2 to 8 Hz. Their results showed a large internal friction peak for deformed peridotite that decreased by more than a factor of 2 after annealing at 1100°C. Their measurements on undeformed synthetic fosterite, however, did not show any internal friction peak. From these and other experimental details and because annealing of olivine reduces the dislocation density, Woirgard and Guegen suggested that the observed internal friction peak in deformed peridotite results from a dislocation mechanism.

2.3.5. Phase Transformations. At elevated temperature and pressure, melting of one or more of the mineralogic components in a rock can occur. Vaisnys (1968) considered the propagation of stress waves in a system containing both a solid and a fluid phase in equilibrium at some particular $P$ and $T$. Because of the finite reaction rate associated with melting or crystallization, energy dissipation of the stress wave results when the frequency of the sound wave is of the same order of magnitude as the reaction rate. A frequency-dependent loss $Q^{-1} \cong (\omega/k)/[1 + (\omega/k)^2]$ is predicted, where $k$ is a rate constant determined by the local stress at the phase interface. Experimental data, however, are few. Spetzler and Anderson (1968), using bar resonance techniques at kilohertz frequencies, measured the longitudinal and shear velocities and attenuations in $NaCl-H_2O$ systems containing 1 and 2% NaCl. The velocities and $Q$ values were observed to drop sharply at the onset of partial melting. Berckhemer et al. (1982) measured $Q$ in torsion as a function of frequency ($10^{-3}$–30 Hz) and temperature on forsterite and dunite near or within the temperature regime of partial melting. Their results were summarized by the equation $Q = C\omega^{-0.25}\exp(-A/RT)$, where $C = 5 \times 10^5$ and $A = 48$ kcal/mol for dunite, and $C = 5 \times 10^3$ and $A = 38$ kcal/mol for fosterite. A strong modulus dispersion was noted at higher temperatures (> 1200°C), but no internal friction peaks were observed over their frequency range. The frequency dependence observed by Berckhemer *et al.* disagrees with that predicted theoretically by Vaisnys (1968).

Partial melting and related problems have also been considered in terms of loss models. For example, Walsh (1969) considered a model of a partially molten rock in which thin films of melt are situated along grain boundaries. He calculated the complex moduli of this two-phase system by replacing the rigidity of the liquid phase by $i\omega\eta$, where $\eta$ is a viscous coefficient. Expressions for shear and compressional waves show frequency-dependent internal friction. Additional theoretical contributions, using various models of fluids in solids, were made by Stoll and Bryan (1970), White (1975), O'Connell and Budiansky (1977), and Mavko (1980). The reader is referred to their papers for details.

## 3. Experimental Methods and Associated Problems

Measurements of internal friction in rocks and minerals have been made from infrasonic to ultrasonic frequencies by using creep, subresonance ($10^{-3}$–400 Hz), torsion and flexural pendulum (0.2–10 Hz), resonance (kilohertz range), and pulsed-ultrasonic (megahertz range) methods. High-temperature measurements (> 1000°C) were made by Berckhemer *et al.* (1982) and by Woirgard and Gueguen (1978). Measurements at 0.4 GPa confining pressure, using torsional vibrations of rods at kilohertz frequencies, were made by Birch and Bancroft (1938). Tittmann *et al.* (1976) and Katahara *et al.* (1982) made similar measurements under confining pressure and with samples subjected to vacuum ($10^{-5}$ torr) to remove adsorbed volatile materials. Jackson *et al.* (1984) made subresonance torsional measurements under 167 MPa confining pressure. In this chapter we are concerned with the experimental methods of measuring internal friction in rocks and minerals at predominantly seismic frequencies. We emphasize the subresonance method and direct our attention to those factors that affect the accuracy of internal friction measurements in rocks.

### 3.1. Subresonance Methods

3.1.1. *Principle of Subresonance Methods.* The measurement consists of a determination of the phase angle between the force applied to a specimen and its displacement. The term "subresonance" denotes that the applied frequency is sufficiently small that inertial effects can be neglected. We consider a vertical circular rod clamped at one end ($x = 0$) and loaded at the other end ($x = L$) by a uniformly distributed normal compressive stress $\sigma = \sigma_0 + \sigma_1 \exp(i\omega t)$. The displacement inside the rod is given by

$$u(x, t) = \sigma_0 x/M(0) + [\sigma_1 L \sin(kx)/M(\omega) \sin(kL)] \exp[i(\omega t - \phi(\omega)] \quad (3)$$

where $M^*(\omega) = M(\omega) \exp[i\phi(\omega)]$ is the complex Young's modulus of the anelastic material and $k = \omega[\rho/M^*(\omega)]^{1/2}$. For $kL \ll 1$,

$$u(x, t) = \sigma_0 x/M(0) + [\sigma_1 x/M(\omega)] \exp[i(\omega t - \phi(\omega)] \quad (4)$$

accurate to $O[\omega^2 \rho L^2/M(\omega)]$. Equation (4) shows that the displacement $u(x, t)$ lags behind the stress $\sigma_1 \exp(i\omega t)$ by the phase angle $\phi(\omega)$.

For a vertical circular rod or tube fixed at one end and driven by a torque at the other end, Eq. (4) holds, except that $M^*(\omega)$ is then the complex shear modulus. Subresonance methods are simple in principle but difficult experimentally because of the generally small magnitude of $\phi(\omega)$ in rocks and minerals at seismic frequencies.

3.1.2 *Analysis of Error from Hysteresis Loop Data.* Figure 1 shows the experimental arrangement of Liu and Peselnick (1983) for internal friction measurements under uniaxial compression at 25°C, frequencies of 0.01–1.0 Hz, and strain amplitude of $10^{-8}$–$10^{-7}$. A single column composed of a hardened steel anvil A, a stress sensor S, a rock sample R, a hardened steel

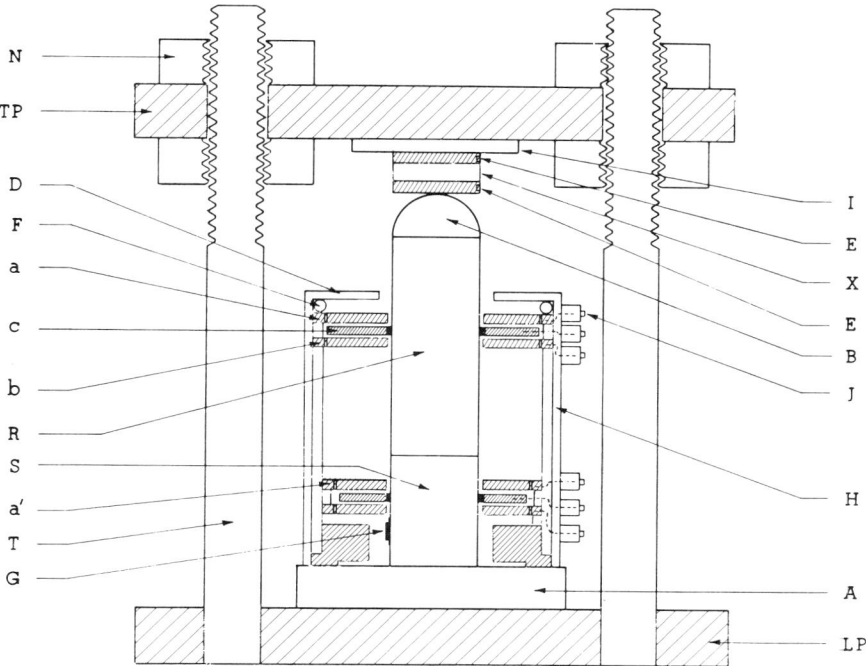

FIG. 1. Sketch of apparatus for measurements of internal friction from hysteresis loop data. See text for explanation of symbols.

hemisphere B, a piezoelectric transducer X, transducer electrodes E, and an insulator I is placed between the platens (TP and LP) of a massive die set. A small compressive stress is applied to the column by tightening the nuts N on the four posts T. This compressive stress maintains alignment and contact of the sample column during the sinusoidal cyclic loading. The sample R is 10 cm long and 3.81 cm in diameter; the stress sensor is 5 cm long and 3.81 cm in diameter. The stress sensor is optical grade fused quartz and has negligible loss at the frequencies used. A set of three annular electrodes a, b, and c form the upper capacitive displacement transducer. The inner electrode c is press-fitted onto the sample; this electrode is insulated from the sample by an annular glass laminate. The outer electrodes a and b are attached to the housing H, which is supported by the steel anvil A. A similar set of three electrodes a', b', and c' make up the lower displacement transducer. The sinusoidal cyclic load is applied to the sample column by driving the piezoelectric transducer with a dc-biased sinusoidal voltage.

Figure 2 is a block diagram of the apparatus and electronics network used to record and process the data. The strains in the sample column appear as vertical displacements of the electrodes c ad c' relative to the stationary outer electrodes (a, b) and (a', b'), respectively. The corresponding proportional changes in capacitance appear as voltages $V_A$ and $V_B$. The attenuator ATT is used to adjust the amplitude, but not the phase, of the voltage $V_A$. The three signals $V_A$, $V_B$, and $V_B - V_A$ are connected to a minicomputer via analog-to-digital converters. The $X$-$Y$ recorder is used to make initial adjustment to

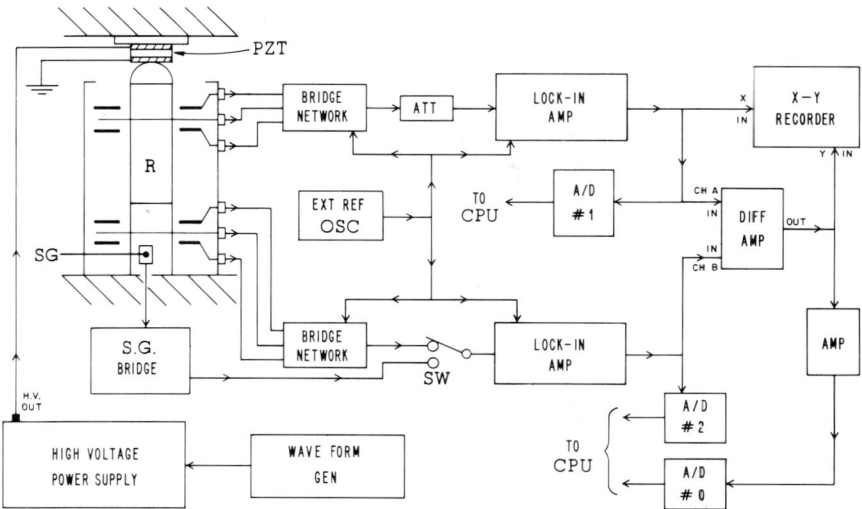

FIG. 2. Block diagram of circuitry for recording and processing hysteresis loop data. See text for explanation of symbols.

the apparatus before a run and to monitor drift or signal changes introduced by external disturbances during a run. The technique of McKavanagh and Stacey (1974) is used to increase the recording sensitivity. With $V_A$ and $V_B - V_A$ as inputs to the $X$-$Y$ recorder, the attenuator ATT is adjusted so that the major axis of the hysteresis loop parallels the $X$ axis. This operation permits amplification of the signal $V_B - V_A$ by a factor of 100.

The quantity $X$ defined below is calculated from the experimental data:

$$X = \left[\oint (V_B - V_A)\, dV_A\right] \bigg/ (\pi V_B^0 V_A^0) \qquad (5)$$

where the expression in square brackets is equivalent to $\oint V_B\, dV_A$ and equals the area enclosed by the hysteresis loop, and $V_A^0$ and $V_B^0$ are the amplitudes of the sinusoidally varying voltages $V_A$ and $V_B$. If

$$V_A = V_A^0 \cos(\omega t - \delta^A) \qquad V_B = V_B^0 \cos(\omega t - \delta^B)$$

then $X = \sin(\delta^A - \delta^B)$, and for small $\delta^A - \delta^B$

$$X \cong \delta^A - \delta^B$$

Provided no loss mechanisms operate at the column interfaces, the experimentally determined quantity $X$ is related to the loss angle of the sample ($\phi^E$) and the loss angle of the stress sensor ($\phi^S$) by

$$X = [A_R/(A_R + A_S)] \sin(\phi^R - \phi^S) \qquad (6)$$

where $A_R$ and $A_S$ are given by

$$A_R = \int_{L_c} \varepsilon_0^R(r_1, z)\, dz \qquad A_S = \int_{L_S} \varepsilon_0^S(r_1, z)\, dz$$

where $L_c$ is the distance from the sample/stress-sensor interface to the electrode c, $L_S$ is the length of the stress sensor, and $\varepsilon_0^R(r_1, z)$ and $\varepsilon_0^S(r_1, z)$ are the strains at the outer diameter of the sample and at the stress sensor, respectively. When $\phi^S \ll \phi^R \ll 1$,

$$\phi^R = [(A_R + A_S)/A_R] X \qquad (7)$$

The factor $[(A_R + A_S)/A_R]$ arises because part of the total elastic energy is stored in the stress sensor. The strain amplitude is determined either directly, by a semiconductor strain gage attached to the sample, or indirectly, by a strain gage attached to the stress sensor.

3.1.3. *Additional Subresonance Techniques.* Table I lists internal friction measurements made by hysteresis loop methods. Figure 3 illustrates the apparatus for torsion measurements used by Berckhemer et al. (1982). Woirgard et al. (1977) directly determined the phase angle between the

TABLE I. Internal Friction Experiments at Seismic Frequencies

| Mode of deformation | Displacement detector | Strain ($10^{-6}$) | Frequency (Hz) | Temperature | Confining pressure | Reference[a] |
|---|---|---|---|---|---|---|
| Uniaxial compression | Strain gage | 10–1000 | 0.0001–10 | Room | Atmospheric | 1 |
| Uniaxial compression | Capacitive bridge | 10 | 0.003–0.1 | Room | Atmospheric | 2 |
| Torsion | Capacitive bridge | 1–30 | 0.001–1.0 | Room | Atmospheric | 3 |
| Torsion | Capacitive bridge | 1 | 0.001–0.5 | Room | Atmospheric | 4 |
| Torsion | Capacitive bridge | 10–50 | 0.003–30 | 1500°C | Atmospheric | 5 |
| Torsion | Capacitive bridge | <1 | 0.003–1.0 | Room | 167 MPa | 6 |

[a] References:
1. Gordon and Davis (1968).
2. McKavanagh and Stacy (1974).
3. Brennan and Stacey (1977).
4. Brennan (1981).
5. Berckhemer et al. (1982).
6. Jackson et al. (1984).

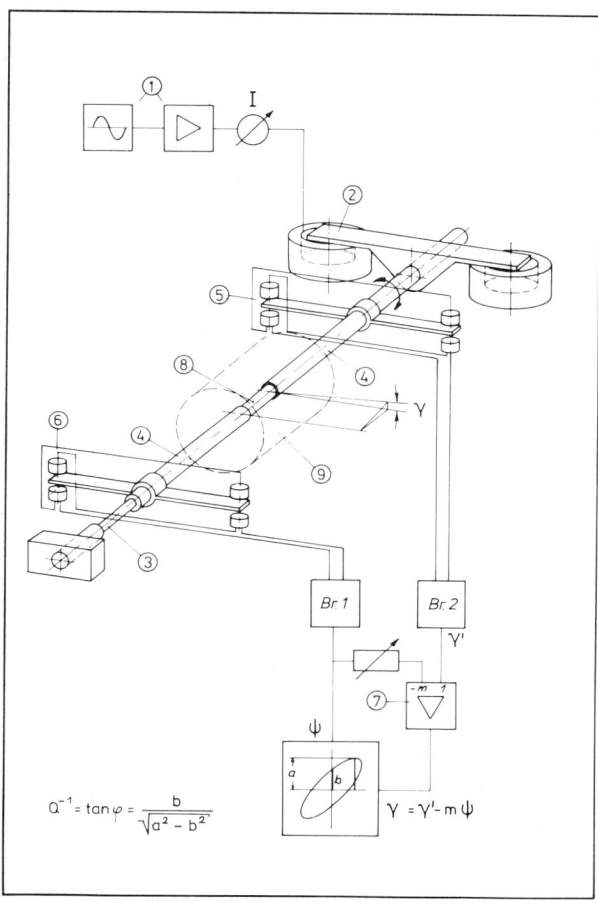

FIG. 3. Sketch of apparatus for measurement of complex shear modulus at high temperature. 1, Driving sinusoidal oscillator; 2, electromagnetic transducer; 3, elastic element; 4, torsion bars; 5, second set of torsion transducers; 6, torsion transducer; 7, differential amplifier; 8, rock specimen; 9, platinum–rhodium furnace; Br-1 and Br-2, bridges for recording stress–strain ellipses. [From Berckhemer et al. (1982). Copyright by Elsevier Scientific Publishing Co.]

torsion angle (measured optically by a mirror and detected by a photodiode) and the driving force (excitation current of the Helmholtz coil) of a torsion pendulum under forced oscillation by shaping the photodiode and the excitation current signals into square waves and measuring the time lag in their zero crossings; Fig. 4 illustrates their apparatus. The typical sample is a flat bar, 50 by 4 by 0.8 mm. The strain amplitude ranges from $8 \times 10^{-7}$ to $3 \times 10^{-5}$. Experiments are performed under vacuum ($10^{-6}$ torr) between room temperature and 800°C over the frequency range $10^{-5}$–10 Hz.

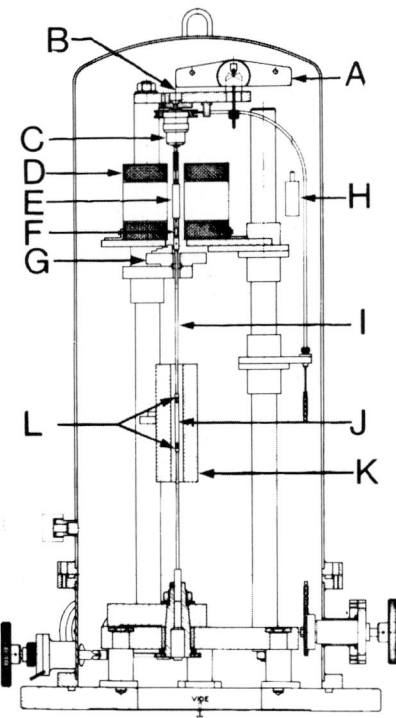

FIG. 4. Sketch of torsion pendulum for measurement of internal friction in flat bars at elevated temperature, seismic frequencies, and under vacuum. A, Scale beam; B, suspension thread; C, mandrel; D, Helmholtz coils; E, permanent magnet; F, spherical mirror; G, mandrel; H, counterweight; I, extension rod; J, specimen; K, furnace; L, molybdenum grips. (From Woirgard et al., 1977.)

Spencer (1981) measured the phase angle difference between an in-line piezoelectric force transducer and a capacitive displacement transducer clamped to one end of a cylindrical sample. The signals were recorded digitally and stacked to reduce the signal-to-noise ratio before Fourier analyzing the averaged signals. The phase difference between the fundamental components was taken to be a measure of the sample's internal friction. Typical sample dimensions were 38.1 mm in diameter and 140 mm long. Experiments were performed at $\sim 10^{-7}$ strain amplitude at room temperature and under varying conditions of fluid saturation.

Jackson et al. (1984) measured the phase angle between the torsional deformation of a rock cylinder and an elastic standard of high-$Q$ steel. The rock cylinder, in series with the elastic standard, is subjected to a low-frequency sinusoidal torque generated by a coil-and-magnet assembly. The torsion is measured by capacitive displacement transducers mounted on lever arms at a distance from the torsional axis. The entire assembly is enclosed in a compound pressure vessel capable of a confining pressure of 700 MPa and includes independent control of the rock pore pressure.

3.1.4. Discussion of Subresonance Methods. Observations of both cusped and elliptical hystersis loops for a given rock type at microstrain levels have resulted in some controversy regarding the linearity of anelastic behavior in rocks. Differences in internal friction values have also been reported for a given rock type. Such discrepancies are due in part to the fact that rocks are complex physical systems, so that variations between samples and in experimental conditions result in a scatter of the data.

Systematic errors in measuring techniques can also contribute to differences in observations among experimenters. Referring to Fig. 5 for illustration, systematic errors that may be present in the subresonance methods include the following. (1) Energy dissipation at interfaces or any loss mechanism in the sample/stress-sensor column results in a phase shift of the upper electrode relative to the displacement of the lower electrode. Surface adhesion at the sample/stress-sensor and anvil/stress-sensor interfaces can also

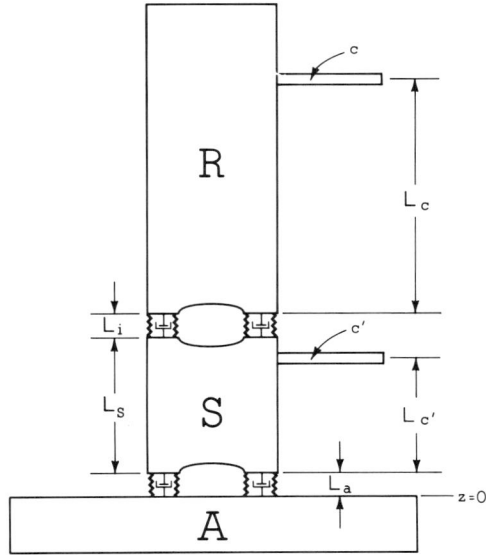

FIG. 5. Sketch of the model of losses for discussion of systematic errors in subresonance methods. Interface elastic stiffness and loss mechanisms are modeled by a distribution of springs and dashpots. Representation of the loss mechanisms by dashpots does not imply that anelastic processes associated with surface adhesion are necessarily linear. Symbols $L_i$, $L_a$, $L_s$, $L_{c'}$, and $L_c$ represent linear dimensions; c and c' are the upper and lower capacitance electrodes, respectively.

introduce erroneous phase shifts (Liu and Peselnick, 1983). This uncertainty can be reduced by using optically smooth (polished) concave interface surfaces to prevent rocking of the sample. (2) Nonsinusoidally applied force introduces systematic errors in internal friction measurements (Liu, 1980). (3) The measured phase angle in the hysteresis loop area method does not equal the internal friction in the sample because a fraction of the total elastic energy is stored in nonsample members of the apparatus [see Eq. (7)]. Such corrections would decrease the observed values of $Q^{-1}$ by a factor dependent on the lengths and elastic constants of the samples and sensors [Eq. (7)].

Such possibilities for systematic error make it imperative to conduct calibration tests. A measure of the apparatus loss for all methods is usually obtained by conducting a run with a sample having negligible internal friction. A revealing test for the hysteresis loop area method is to substitute a single column of a relatively high loss material for the entire sample/stress-sensor column. In this case, $\phi^R = \phi^S$ [see Eq. (6)], and the measured quantity $X$ should be zero, independent of the $Q$ of the material. Woirgard et al. (1977) used the Snoek peak in Fe containing 100 ppm interstitial C to check their $Q$ apparatus. This Snoek peak occurs at $f = 0.1$ Hz (at 13°C), and the magnitude of the peak ($\Delta Q$) is $\cong 118$. These values of $f$ and $\Delta Q$ are in the range of seismic frequencies and observed loss in rocks. The Snoek peak depends on the type and concentration of impurity, the annealing history of the sample, and the instability of the interstitial phase at elevated temperatures.

An alternative internal friction standard in the seismic frequency range would be useful. The potential internal friction peak resulting from the $\alpha$–$\beta$ transformation in single-crystal quartz would be a convenient standard because large crystals of synthetic quartz are easily obtainable, single-crystal quartz is physically and chemically stable, the transition involves minor atomic movements rather than depending on a concentration of impurity atoms, and the transition occurs at a well-defined temperature (573°C) at atmospheric pressure.

### 3.2. Creep Experiments

Formally, linear elasticity can be described by Boltzmann's aftereffect equation (Nowick and Berry, 1972), which can be written for a pure mode of deformation as

$$\varepsilon(t) = \int_{-\infty}^{t} \dot{\sigma}(\tau)\phi(t - \tau)\, d\tau \tag{8}$$

Equation (8) states that the strain $\varepsilon(t)$ at time $t$ is caused linearly by the total history of stress $\sigma(t)$ up to the time $t$ and thus incorporates both the superposition principle and the causality principle. The creep function $\phi(t)$ is determined by the mechanisms of anelasticity.

It can be shown that the complex modulus $M(\omega)$ for sinusoidal loading at angular frequency $\omega$ is related to the Fourier transform of the creep function $F(\omega)$ by

$$M(\omega) = [i\omega F(\omega)]^{-1} \qquad (9)$$

where

$$F(\omega) = \int_0^\infty \phi(t) \exp(-i\omega t)\, dt. \qquad (10)$$

When $\sigma(t) = \sigma_0 H(t)$, where $H(t)$ is the unit step function, then $\dot\sigma(t)$ equals a constant times a delta function and the strain response is given by $\varepsilon(t) = \sigma_0 \phi(t)$.

In the creep experiments, a step load is applied to the sample and the resulting strain response is taken to be the creep function. Internal friction at angular frequency $\omega$ is obtained from the Fourier transform of the creep function by using Eq. (9) and the relation $\tan \delta = \mathrm{Im}[M(\omega)]/\mathrm{Re}[M(\omega)]$

Lomnitz (1956) employed an optical lever magnification system to measure torsional creep in a granodiorite and a gabbro. This early experiment did not have the sensitivity required for measurements at seismic strain levels the maximum strain measured was $\sim 9 \times 10^{-4}$.

A more recent experiment on mantle peridotite samples was conducted by Berckhemer et al. (1979). A step increase of less than 2 MPa with a rise time of 50 ms was applied to a sample under uniaxial compression by a pneumatic system; the axial displacement was measured with an inductive transducer system. The samples were typically 9 mm in diameter and 5–30 mm long. Maximum strain amplitude in the experiments was $6 \times 10^{-5}$ and the maximum temperature attained was 1300°C.

The main difficulty in conducting creep experiments at low strain levels is thermal drift in the apparatus. Problems in data reduction at low strain amplitudes also arise because of the presence of noise in the data, which contributes to systematic errors in the computation of the Fourier transform $F(\omega)$ in Eq. (10).

3.3. Torsion and Flexural Pendulums: Free Decay Methods

The amplitude decay of the free oscillations of a torsion pendulum was used in one of the earliest methods for determining internal friction in solids (Föppl, 1936). Figure 6 shows a simplified sketch of a normal and an inverted torsion pendulum. The idealized apparatus consists of an inertial element I and the sample S, which provides a restoring torque proportional to the angle

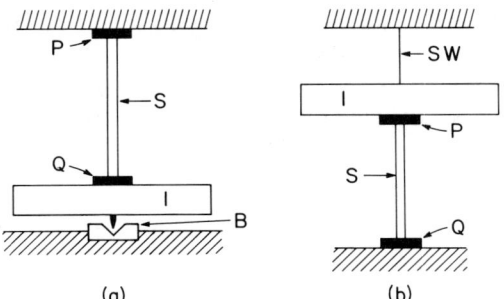

FIG. 6. Simplified sketches of a normal (a) and an inverted (b) torsion pendulum. S, Sample; I, inertial element; P and Q, upper and lower sample clamps; B, bearing (if used); SW, suspension wire. Lined areas represent the apparatus frame.

of twist $\theta$. In the inverted pendulum (Fig. 6b), a fine suspension wire (SW) with negligible restoring torque supports the weight of the inertial element. The tension in the wire is adjusted to eliminate or change the axial tension in the sample. Swartz (1961) discussed methods of clamping, tension adjustment, damping of nontorsional modes, and other experimental details.

For an isotropic homogeneous sample of circular cross section, the shear strain increases linearly with the radius. The equation for free torsional oscillations $\theta(t)$ is $I\ddot{\theta} + R\dot{\theta} + K\theta = 0$, where $K$ is the torque constant and $R$ the internal friction coefficient; $R$ is assumed to be independent of $\theta$ and its time derivatives $\dot{\theta}$ and $\ddot{\theta}$. The solution for $(r/2I)^2 \ll K/I$ is

$$\theta \cong \theta_0 \cos(\omega_0 t)[\exp(-Rt/2I)] \tag{11}$$

$$\omega_0^2 = K/I = (2\pi f_0)^2 \tag{12}$$

The decay term $\exp(-Rt/2I)$ is generally written $\exp(-\delta f_0 t)$, where $\delta$ is the logarithmic decrement. For $\delta > 0.01$, the ratio of $(R/2I)^2$ to $K/I$ is $< 10^{-5}$, and an approximate solution is permissible (in terms of $Q$, $Q = \pi/\delta$). For a solid circular rod of diameter $d$ and length $L$, $K = \pi d^4 G/32L$, where $G$ is the shear modulus. The value of $G$ can be calculated from measurements of $d$, $L$, $I$, and $f_0$. The logarithmic decrement $\delta$ is determined by measuring the time $\Delta t$ required for the amplitude to decay from $\theta_0$ to $\theta_0/e$, giving $\delta = 1/(f_0 \Delta t)$.

The torsion pendulum method has been used in metallurgic studies of relaxation mechanisms, such as the Snoek peak (Otabe, 1980) and the viscous grain boundary relaxation of Ke (1947). In these studies, fine wires are used for the sample element. The experimental procedure consists of varying the temperature and observing the frequency and the amplitude decay. Modulus dispersion and peaks in $Q^{-1}$ are obtained as a function of temperature rather than of frequency. Woirgard et al. (1977) pointed out that variation in the temperature can introduce changes in the structure of sample material, so that the description of the frequency dependence of internal friction in terms of temperature variation may be incorrect.

Only a few applications of the torsion pendulum method to rocks have been made, principally because the grain sizes of rocks are orders of magnitude larger than those of metals. For example, a granite rod with a diameter of 10 mm and average linear grain dimensions of 4 mm would contain fewer than three grains across its diameter. Measurements of the rigidity and internal friction of this sample would not be duplicated in larger samples because of anisotropy and the influence of the grain boundaries. Some fine-grained homogeneous rocks, however, are suitable for torsion pendulum measurements. Peselnick and Outerbridge (1961) used rods of Solenhofen limestone (4.8 mm in diameter by 18 cm long; grain size ~ 9 µm) in a torsion pendulum.

The data of Peselnick and Outerbridge (1961) indicate that density differences between rock samples (air-dried Solenhofen limestone) can significantly affect the results. It is, therefore, important to consider sample variation when comparing data. The determination of the frequency dependence should be made on the same sample. For dry Solenhofen limestone, $Q^{-1}$ varies $<30\%$ from 4 Hz to 18 kHz.

Woirgard et al. (1971) developed an inverted pendulum for determining the internal friction of specimens shaped like thin rectangular plates (~ 2.5 mm thick). They reported observations on the decay of free oscillations in the flexural mode of metallic samples at $10^{-6}$ torr, 20 to 800°C, and frequencies of 0.2–10 Hz. The thinness of the sample would restrict measurements on rocks and minerals to fine-grained rocks and single crystals.

Sources of error in all types of freely oscillating pendulums are (1) losses in the supporting members, which can deform in response to the torsion pendulum oscillations, (2) losses from other modes of vibration in the sample, and (3) frictional losses, such as air damping or losses in bearings (if used). These sources of error at atmospheric pressure can generally be reduced to values much smaller than the internal friction of the rocks. Substitution of a high-$Q$ material for the sample is commonly used to estimate the apparatus loss.

3.4. Bar Resonance Methods

Observations of the resonant frequency, bandwidth, and amplitude decay of torsional, longitudinal, and flexural oscillations of uniform bars have been used to determine the elastic constants and internal friction of solids. The modes of vibration are functions of the bar geometry and boundary conditions. For torsional and longitudinal oscillations, solid rods of circular cross section are generally used. For wavelengths large relative to the diameter of the rod, the longitudinal and shear (torsional) velocities are independent of the wavelength: $V_L^2 = E/\rho$ and $V_s^2 = G/\rho$, where $E$ is Young's modulus, $G$ the shear modulus, and $\rho$ the density of the solid (assumed to be elastically isotropic). Thin beams of rectangular cross section are generally used for excitation of flexural modes of oscillation. For wavelengths large relative to the lateral dimensions of the beam, the flexural velocity is given by $V_f = 2\pi(E/\rho)^{1/2} K/\lambda$, where $K$ is the radius of gyration of a cross section about the neutral axis and $\lambda$ the wavelength. Thus, the flexural modes are not harmonically related (see Kolsky, 1953, for details).

3.4.1. *Resonance Decay in Rods and Beams.* By analogy with the torsion pendulum decay method, we can define a logarithmic decrement for energy dissipation in a solid rod excited in one of its normal modes. When the driving force is removed, the amplitude $A_n(x)$ will decay at every point along the bar (except at the nodes). The logarithmic decrement $\delta$ can then be defined by $\delta = \ln(A_n/A_{n+1})$, where $A_n$ is the amplitude corresponding to the $n$th vibration at a fixed point on the bar after removal of the driving force. For a linear elastic solid the energy is proportional to the square of the amplitude, and so

$$Q^{-1} = (1/2\pi)(\Delta W/W) \cong (1/2\pi)(A_n^2 - A_{n+1}^2)/A_n^2 \qquad (13)$$

For small damping, $A_n \cong A_{n+1}$, and Eq. (13) reduces to the relation between $Q$ and the logarithmic decrement $\delta$ given in Eq. (2), namely

$$Q^{-1} \cong (1/2\pi)(A_n^2 - A_{n+1}^2)/A_n^2 \cong (1/\pi)\ln(A_n/A_{n+1}) = \delta/\pi \qquad (14)$$

A significant advance in the design of the flexural analog of the torsion pendulum for geophysical applications was made by Tittmann and Curnow (1976). They used free decay of flexural oscillations of an inertially loaded sample to determine $Q$ at near-seismic frequencies ($\sim 50$ Hz), small strain amplitudes ($\sim 10^{-7}$), and zero static stress on the samples. In addition, the sample thickness of 0.4 cm illustrated in their work makes this instrument applicable to many rocks of medium grain size. Figure 7 shows a simplified and idealized sketch of their apparatus. The apparatus is suspended by taut wires (TW) in the vertical ($Z$) direction. The inertial elements $I_1$ and $I_2$, the stiff crossbars B, and the sample R have the form of a capital H lying in the horizontal ($XY$) plane; $X$, $Y$, and $Z$ are orthogonal directions. The sample R vibrates in flexure, whereas the inertial elements rotate in the horizontal plane. The arrangement of the supporting wires TW and the rigid bar B results in negligible static stress on the sample.

3.4.2. *Bandwidth Methods.* The sharpness of resonance of a linear oscillating system has been used as an indirect measure of internal friction (Nowick and Berry, 1972). The two frequencies ($f_1, f_2$) on either side of the resonance frequency ($f_0$) at which the square of the amplitude decreases by

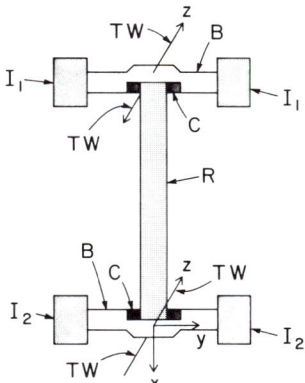

FIG. 7. Simplified sketch of flexural pendulum of Tittmann and Curnow (1976). See text for explanation of symbols.

0.5 of its maximum value defines the full width at half-power of the resonance peak. For small damping, $Q_H$ is defined by $(f_2 - f_1)/f_0 = 1/Q_H$.

Data on the pressure dependence of internal friction for torsional modes of oscillation at kilohertz frequencies have been obtained for rocks by such "resonance bandwidth" methods. Birch and Bancroft (1938) were the first to use this method on rocks as a function of pressure (0.1 and 0.4 GPa). Copper-jacketed cylindrical samples ($\sim 20$ cm long, $\leq 2$ cm in diameter) were driven in the torsional mode by using a magnetic armature cemented to one end of the sample. The motion of a second armature cemented to the other end was detected by the voltage induced in a nearby coil. Torsional vibrations of a circular rod interact with the pressure medium only through viscous forces at the surface of the rod. The viscous damping due to the $N_2$ gas pressure medium was presumed to be negligible relative to the internal friction in the rock samples. The $Q$ values obtained for several rocks at 20 MPa ranged from 100 to 400; all higher values of $Q$ were observed at the higher pressure of 400 GPa. There appeared to be no change in $Q$ with frequency (i.e., with the order of harmonic vibration of the rod).

The torsional resonance bandwidth method was refined by Tittmann *et al.* (1977). Measurements could be made to 200 GPa at room temperature or to 70 GPa at 400 °C. Cylindrical samples (12.7 cm long, 2 cm in diameter) could be outgassed under vacuum ($10^{-5}$ torr) and encapsulated in seamless copper tubing. The operating frequency could be decreased from 10 to $\sim 1$ kHz by mass end-loading.

Katahara *et al.* (1982), adapting many of the techniques of Tittmann *et al.* (1977), increased the pressure range to 500 GPa by using composite piezoelectric torsional transducers in place of the larger magnetic transducers used previously by Tittmann *et al.* and Birch and Bancroft (1938).

### 3.5. Ultrasonic Methods

The attenuation of a plane stress wave in a solid can also be used as a measure of internal friction. For small-amplitude plane sinusoidal progressive waves in an infinitely extended medium, an exponential decrease in the stress amplitude $A$ with distance $x$ is generally observed:

$$A(x) = A_0 \exp(-\alpha_s x) \tag{15}$$

where $A_0$ is the amplitude at $x = 0$ and the quantity $\alpha_s$ is the spatial amplitude attenuation coefficient. [See Eq. (2) for the relation between $\alpha_s$ and other measures of internal friction.] It is necessary to distinguish between shear and compressional waves in Eq. (15).

The earliest ultrasonic methods (for rocks) used the amplitude decay of multiply reflected pulses to determine $\alpha_s$ (Peselnick and Zietz, 1959). Two shear (or compressional) piezoelectric transducers are bonded to two flat surfaces on the rock. A sinusoidal voltage pulse applied to one transducer results in a shear (or compressional) stress pulse and, possibly, multiply reflected pulses, which are detected by the second transducer. Using Eq. (15) for plane stress waves, the coefficient $\alpha_s$ is obtained from observations of $A(x)$ versus $x$. A "pulse transmission" method was used by Toksöz et al. (1979) to determine $\alpha_s$. The amplitude–frequency response of the transmitted signal in the rock sample is compared with the response in a geometrically identical reference sample having low attenuation. The attenuation coefficient for the rock can be calculated from such spectral amplitude ratios by assuming that the ratio of sample to reference geometric factors $(G_1/G_2)$ is independent of frequency (see Toksöz et al., 1979, for details). The principal disadvantage of ultrasonic methods is that the frequencies used are very much greater than seismic frequencies. Mechanisms of attenuation operative at high frequencies may be absent at lower frequencies.

## 4. Conclusions

The disagreement between the various internal friction data results from both sample differences and systematic errors. Factors contributing to sample differences—e.g., porosity, volatile content, crack distribution, and sample size—are common to all methods, and their effects require careful evaluation. For example, measurements of the frequency dependence of $Q$ should be made on the same sample and under the same physical conditions. Systematic errors, however, depend on the method used. For example, in resonance experiments the nodal positions of a granular material such as a medium- or coarse-grained rock are not well defined, and friction at "quasi-nodal" supports can result in systematic error. Distinguishing between instrument losses from the intrinsic internal friction in the sample is difficult. With regard to the various experimental methods for measuring internal friction in rocks and minerals, subresonance methods have several advantages. The frequencies are in the seismic range (e.g., 0.001-20 Hz), and they can be changed by small increments. Small strain amplitudes are applied to the sample. The three sample dimensions can be made large compared to the grain size. The systematic errors can be determined. Such features are important for the application of internal friction measurements to geophysical problems.

## Acknowledgments

We thank G. M. Mavko and J. C. Savage for reviewing the manuscript and George Havach for the technical editing.

## References

Anderson, D. L., and Hart, R. S. (1978). Attenuation models of the earth. *Phys. Earth Planet. Inter.* **16**, 289-306.
Anderson, D. L., and Minster, J. B. (1979). The frequency dependence of $Q$ in the earth and implications for mantle rheology and Chandler wobble. *Geophys. J. R. Astron. Soc.* **58**, 431-440.
Anderson, D. L., and Minster, J. B. (1981). The physics of creep and attenuation in the mantle. *In* "Anelasticity in the Earth" (F. D. Stacey, M. S. Paterson, and A. Nicolas, eds.), Geodynamics Series, Vol. 4, pp. 5-11. Am. Geophys. Union, Washington, D.C.
Anderson, D. L., and Sammis, C. G. (1970). Partial melting in the upper mantle. *Phys. Earth Planet. Inter.* **3**, 41-50.
Berckhemer, H., Auer, F., and Drisler, J. (1979). High-temperature anelasticity and elasticity of mantle peridotite. *Phys. Earth Planet. Inter.* **20**, 48-59.
Berckhemer, H., Kampfmann, W., Aulbach, E., and Schmeling, H. (1982). Shear modulus and $Q$ of forsterite and dunite near partial melting from forced-oscillation experiments. *Phys. Earth Planet. Inter.* **29**, 30-41.
Birch, F., and Bancroft, D. (1938). The effect of pressure on the rigidity of rocks. *J. Geol.* **45**, 59-87.
Brennan, B. J. (1981). Linear viscoelastic behavior in rocks. *In* "Anelasticity in the Earth" (F. D. Stacey, M. S. Paterson, and A. Nicolas, eds.), Geodynamics Series, Vol. 4, pp. 13-22. Am. Geophys. Union, Washington, D.C.
Brennan, B. J., and Stacey, F. D. (1977). Frequency dependence of elasticity of rock—test of seismic velocity dispersion. *Nature (London)* **286**, 220-222.
Dobrin, M. B. (1976). "Introduction to Geophysical Prospecting," 3rd ed., pp. 346-349. McGraw-Hill, New York.
Fitzgerald, J. V., Laing, K. M., and Bachman, G. S. (1952). Temperature variation of the elastic moduli of glass. *Trans. Soc. Glass Technol.* **36**, 90-104.
Föppl, O. (1936). The practical importance of the damping capacity of metals. *J. Iron Steel Inst.* **134**, 393-455.

Förtsch, O. (1956). Die Ursachen der Absorption elastischer Wellen. *Ann. Geofis. Rome* **9**, 469-524.

Gordon, R. B., and Davis, L. A. (1968). Velocity and attenuation of seismic waves in imperfectly elastic rock. *J. Geophys. Res.* **73**, 3917-3935.

Gorshkov, G. S. (1956). On the deep magmatic zone of Klyuchevskoi Volcano. *Dokl. Akad. Nauk SSSR* **106**, 703-705.

Jackson, I., Paterson, M. S., Niesler, H., and Waterford, R. M. (1984). Rock anelasticity measurements at high pressure, low strain amplitude and seismic frequency. *Geophys. Res. Lett.* **11**, 1235-1238.

Katahara, K. W., Manghnani, M. H., Devnani, M., and Tittmann, B. R. (1982). Pressure dependence of $Q$ in selected rocks. *In* "High Pressure Research in Geophysics" (S.-i. Akimoto and M. H. Manghnani, eds.), Cent. Acadm. Publ., Tokyo and Reidel Publ., Dordrecht, Netherlands.

Ke, T.-S. (1947). Experimental evidence of the viscous behavior of grain boundaries in metals. *Phys. Rev.* **71**, 533-546.

Kissell, F. N. (1972). Effect of temperature variation on internal friction in rocks. *J. Geophys. Res.* **77**, 1420-1423.

Kjartansson, E. (1979). Constant $Q$-wave propagation and attenuation. *J. Geophys. Res.* **84**, 4737-4743.

Kjartansson, E., and Denliger, R. (1977). Seismic wave attenuation due to thermal relaxation in porous media. *Geophysics* **42**, 1516. (Abstr.)

Kolsky, H. (1953). "Stress Waves in Solids." Oxford Univ. Press, London and New York.

Liu, H.-P. (1980). Driving-stress waveform and the determination of rock internal friction by the stress-strain curve method. *Geophys. J. R. Astron. Soc.* **63**, 567-572.

Liu, H.-P., and Peselnick, L. (1983). Investigation of internal friction in fused quartz, steel, plexiglass and Westerly granite from 0.01 to 1.00 Hz at $10^{-8}$-$10^{-7}$ strain amplitude. *J. Geophys. Res.* **88**, 2367-2379.

Liu, H.-P., Anderson, D. L., and Kanamori, H. (1976). Velocity dispersion due to anelasticity; implications for seismology and mantle composition. *Geophys. J. R. Astron. Soc.* **47**, 41-58.

Lomnitz, C. (1956). Creep measurements in igneous rocks. *J. Geol.* **64**, 473-479.

McKavanagh, B., and Stacey, F. D. (1974). Mechanical hysteresis in rocks at low strain amplitudes and seismic frequencies. *Phys. Earth Planet. Inter.* **8**, 246-250.

Mavko, G. M. (1979). Frictional attenuation: an inherent amplitude dependence. *J. Geophys. Res.* **84**, 4769-4775.

Mavko, G. M. (1980). Velocity and attenuation in partially molten rocks. *J. Geophys. Res.* **85**, 5173-5185.

Mavko, G. M., Kjartansson, E., and Winkler, K. (1979). Seismic wave attenuation in rocks. *Rev. Geophys. Space Phys.* **17**, 1155-1164.

Nowick, A. S., and Berry, B. S. (1972). "Anelastic Relaxation in Crystalline Solids." Academic Press, New York.

O'Connell, R. J., and Budiansky, B. (1977). Viscoelastic properties of fluid-saturated cracked solids. *J. Geophys. Res.* **82**, 5719-5735.

O'Connell, R. J., and Budiansky, B. (1978). Measures of dissipation in viscoelastic media. *Geophys. Res. Lett.* **5**, 5-8.

Otabe, S. (1980). Snoek peak figures of impure iron in various strain amplitude ranges. *J. Appl. Phys.* **51**, 1011-1013.

Peselnick, L., and Outerbridge, W. F. (1961). Internal friction in shear and shear modulus of Solenhofen limestone over a frequency range of $10^7$ cycles per second. *J. Geophys. Res.* **66**, 581-588.

Peselnick, L., and Zietz, I. (1959). Internal friction of fine-grained limestones at ultrasonic frequencies. *Geophysics* **24**, 285-296.
Savage, J. C. (1966). Thermoelastic attenuation of elastic waves by cracks. *J. Geophys. Res.* **71**, 3929-3938.
Savage, J. C., and Hasegawa, H. S. (1967). Evidence for a linear attenuation mechanism. *Geophysics* **32**, 1003-1014.
Sipkin, S. A., and Jordan, T. H. (1980). Regional variation of $Q_{ScS}$. *Bull. Seismol. Soc. Am.* **70**, 1071-1102.
Smith, M. L., and Dahlen, F. A. (1981). The period and $Q$ of the Chandler wobble. *Geophys. J. R. Astron. Soc.* **64**, 223-281.
Snoek, J. L. (1941). Effect of small quantities of carbon and nitrogen on the elastic and plastic properties of iron. *Physica (Amsterdam)* **8**, 711-733.
Spencer, J. W. (1981). Stress relaxations at low frequencies in fluid-saturated rocks: attenuation and modulus dispersion. *J. Geophys. Res.* **86**, 1803-1812.
Spetzler, H., and Anderson, D. L. (1968). The effect of temperature and partial melting on velocity and attenuation in a simple binary system. *J. Geophys. Res* **73**, 6051-6060.
Stoll, R. D., and Bryan, G. M. (1970). Wave attenuation in saturated sediments. *J. Acoust. Soc. Am.* **47**, 1440-1447.
Swartz, J. C. (1961). Apparatus for measuring internal friction and modulus changes of metals at low frequencies. *Rev. Sci. Instrum.* **32**, 335-338.
Tittmann, B. R., and Curnow, J. M. (1976). Apparatus for measuring internal friction $Q$ factors in brittle materials. *Rev. Sci. Instrum.* **47**, 1516-1518.
Tittmann, B. R., Ahlberg, L., and Curnow, J. M. (1976). Internal friction and velocity measurements. *Geochim. Cosmochim. Acta, Suppl.* No. 7, 3123-3132.
Tittmann, B. R., Ahlberg, L., Nadler, H., Curnow, J. M., Smith, T., and Cohen, E. R. (1977). Internal friction quality-factor $Q$ under confining pressure. *Geochim. Cosmochim. Acta, Suppl.* No. 8, 1209-1224.
Tittmann, B. R., Clark, V. A., Richardson, J. M., and Spencer, T. W. (1980). Possible mechanism for seismic attenuation in rocks containing small amounts of volatiles. *J. Geophys. Res.* **85**, 5199-5208.
Toksöz, M. N., Johnston, D. H., and Timur, A. (1979). Attenuation of seismic waves in dry and saturated rocks: I. Laboratory measurements. *Geophysics* **44**, 681-690.
Vaisnys, J. R. (1968). Propagation of acoustic waves through a system undergoing phase transformations. *J. Geophys. Res.* **73**, 7675-7683.
Volarovich, M. P., and Gurvich, A. S. (1957). Investigation of dynamic moduli of elasticity for rocks in relation to temperature. *Bull. Acad. Sci. USSR, Geophys. Ser.* No. 4, 1-9.
Walsh, J. B. (1966). Seismic wave attenuation in rock due to friction. *J. Geophys. Res.* **71**, 2591-2599.
Walsh, J. B. (1969). New analysis of attenuation in partially melted rock. *J. Geophys. Res.* **74**, 4333-4337.
White, J. E. (1965). "Seismic Waves." McGraw-Hill, New York.
White, J. E. (1975). Computed seismic speeds and attenuation in rocks with partial gas saturation. *Geophysics* **40**, 224-232.
White, J. E. (1968). Biot-Gardner theory of extensional waves in porous rods. *Geophysics* **51**, 742-746.
Winkler, K., and Nur, A. (1982). Seismic attenuation: effects of pore fluids and frictional sliding. *Geophysics* **47**, 1-15.
Woirgard, J., and Gueguen, Y. (1978). Elastic modulus and internal friction in enstatite forsterite and peridotite at seismic frequencies and high temperatures. *Phys. Earth Planet. Inter.* **17**, 140-146.

Woirgard, J., Amirault, J.-P., Chaumet, H., and de Fouquet, J. (1971). Appareil de mesure du module d'élasticitite et du frottement interieur en flexion, a basse frequence, sous vide entre 20 et 800°C. *Rev. Phys. Appl.* **6**, 355–359.

Woirgard, J., Sarrazin, Y., and Chaumet, H. (1977). Apparatus for the measurement of internal friction as a function of frequency between $10^{-5}$ and 10 Hz. *Rev. Sci. Instrum.* **48**, 1322–1325.

Zener, C. (1941). Theory of elasticity of polycrystals with viscous grain boundaries. *Phys. Rev.* **60**, 906–917.

Zener, C. (1948). "Elasticity and Anelasticity of Metals." Univ. of Chicago Press, Chicago, Illinois.

# 3. MEASUREMENT OF ROCK DEFORMATION AT HIGH TEMPERATURES

## D. L. Kohlstedt
## P. N. Chopra

Department of Materials Science and Engineering
Cornell University
Ithaca, New York 14853

## 1. Introduction

High-temperature plastic deformation of rocks and minerals is investigated in laboratory experiments in order to place constraints on the conditions and mechanisms of flow in the earth and to determine constitutive equations (flow laws) necessary for modeling geologic processes. The high-temperature flow properties of olivine and olivine-rich rocks, for example, bear directly on understanding solid-state convective flow in the earth's upper mantle, bending of oceanic lithosphere in subduction zones, and flexure of the lithosphere during loading or unloading as seamounts are formed by volcanic activity or ice sheets are removed by melting. Likewise, the nature of plastic deformation of quartz- and feldspar-bearing rock controls important phenomena such as ductile faulting at depth in the earth's continental crust.

One unique feature of laboratory studies of plastic flow in rocks is that most experiments are carried out not only at high temperatures but also at high confining pressures. In most cases, hydrostatic pressure is applied to suppress fracturing, which occurs because the thermal expansion and elastic deformation are markedly anisotropic for most rock-forming minerals. In a few cases, hydrostatic pressure has also been used to simulate geologic phenomena such as a phase transition which occurs at depth in the earth.

This chapter focuses on the experimental apparatuses and the experimental tests used to study high-temperature flow of rocks and minerals. For summaries of the results of laboratory studies of plastic deformation of rocks and minerals and for extensive biliographies in this area, the reader is referred to review papers by Carter (1976), Tullis (1979), and Kirby (1983).

## 2. Deformation Apparatus

Three distinctly different types of apparatus—one-atmosphere, gas-medium, and solid-medium systems—are used to investigate the high-temperature deformation behavior of rocks and minerals. Details of the design and operation as well as the advantages and limitations of each type of apparatus are discussed in the following paragraphs. All three types of equipment are required to study the wide range of problems which are of interest in the solid earth sciences. However, because of the importance of high-pressure experimentation in rock mechanics and because of the background of the authors, emphasis is given to the gas-medium and one-atmosphere apparatuses.

### 2.1. One-Atmosphere Apparatuses

#### 2.1.1. Creep Experiments.
High-temperature compressive creep experiments at a total pressure of 1 atmosphere, which involve the least complicated of the three types of experimental apparatus, have been used for the past decade to study flow of olivine and quartz single crystals. There are several advantages to performing deformation experiments without a confining pressure. High temperatures ($\sim 1700°C$) can be reached relatively easily; maximum operating temperatures are determined by reactions between the sample and the pistons and/or furnace as well as the strength of the piston material. Samples can be deformed at low stresses ($< 0.1$ MPa), and long run times are practical. In addition, the effects of chemical environment—for example, oxygen partial pressure—can readily be studied. The contribution of individual slip systems to the deformation process can often be studied independently by properly orienting the crystals with respect to the axis of the applied stress. The major limitation of deformation experiments at 1 atmosphere is that they are largely restricted to single-crystal samples; the anisotropy in thermal expansion and elastic deformation of minerals is large enough that coarse-grained polycrystalline samples fracture easily on heating or loading. Based on models for thermal cracking (Evans, 1978), grains in olivine aggregates, for example, must be smaller than approximately 10 µm to prevent microcracking during heating and cooling of unconfined samples. Karato *et al.* (1982) have circumvented this problem by dynamically recrystallizing single crystals of olivine by large strain deformation. The flow law obtained on these special polycrystalline samples is in good agreement with that determined in high-pressure creep experiments (Chopra and Paterson, 1984).

The designs of 1-atmosphere creep rigs used for studying flow of minerals are similar to those used in a number of materials testing laboratories. The

### 3. MEASUREMENT OF ROCK DEFORMATION AT HIGH TEMPERATURES

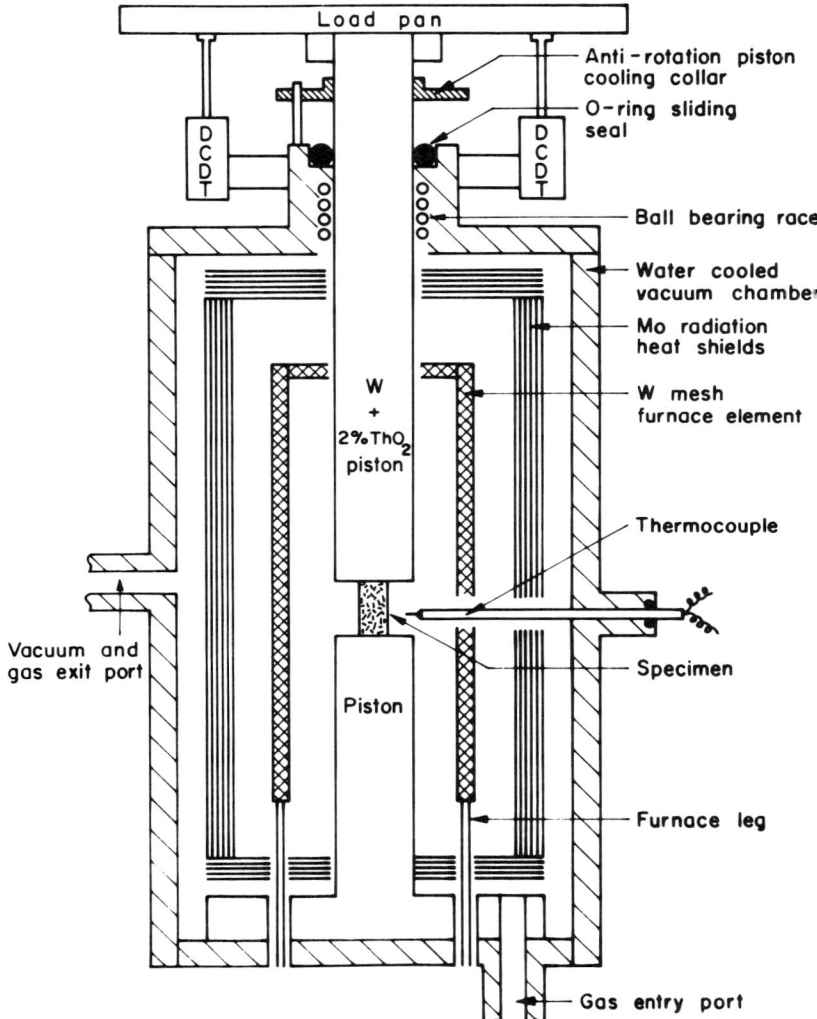

FIG. 1. Deformation apparatus used for one-atmosphere creep experiments. (After Cooper and Kohlstedt, 1984.)

apparatus illustrated in Fig. 1 was constructed at Cornell University around a high-temperature furnace housed in a double-walled, water-cooled chamber of stainless steel. The tungsten mesh heating element, which permits experiments at temperatures in excess of 2000°C, must be operated in vacuum, inert gas, or reducing atmospheres to avoid oxidation. For experiments under more oxidizing conditions, an alumina muffle tube is used to isolate the sample and pistons from the furnace element. The latter can thus be kept in a relatively reducing environment while the former is exposed to more oxidizing conditions.

The sample is positioned at the center of the hot zone on a piston which is rigidly supported on the bottom of the test vessel. The upper piston is brought into contact with the sample though a ball-bearing race in the top cover of the chamber. Thoriated tungsten, alumina, silicon carbide, and graphite have all been used in our laboratory as high-temperature pistons. The specific material selected depends on the temperature and stress levels required as well as potential chemical reactions with the sample. An O-ring seal prevents uncontrolled escape of the buffering gas. The friction between this seal and the piston supports a load of less than 0.1 kg. A uniaxial stress is applied to the sample by placing lead weights on the load pan. As the sample shortens plastically and its cross-sectional area increases, lead shot is added to the load pan to keep the stress approximately constant. The amount of lead shot required is calculated by assuming that the sample shortens homogeneously. A guide pin passing through the collar which is attached to the upper piston prevents the piston from rotating. A pair of direct-current displacement transducers (DCDTs) monitor the position of the weight pan relative to the body of the test chamber and thus the length of the sample. The summed output from the DCDTs is recorded either on a digital data acquisition system or a conventional strip-chart recorder.

To control the concentrations of point defects as well as to remain within the stability field, experiments on minerals which contain transition-metal ions must be carried out under controlled partial pressures of oxygen. The two most commonly used gas mixtures, $H_2$-$CO_2$ and $CO$-$CO_2$, provide a wide range of oxygen partial pressures. Thermodynamic data are available for calculating the oxygen partial pressure for a given mixing ratio and temperature (Dienes *et al.*, 1974). In addition, solid electrolyte (usually CaO-stabilized $ZrO_2$) sensors enable continuous monitoring of the oxygen partial pressure (Sato, 1971). Because the creep strength of many minerals is sensitive not only to the partial pressure of oxygen but also to that of water, $H_2$-$CO_2$ mixtures may not be a good choice for the buffer gases. While the partial pressure of oxygen increases systematically with an increase in the $CO_2 : H_2$ ratio, the partial pressure of water goes through a maximum. Thus in an attempt to separate the effects of water and oxygen partial pressures on the creep behavior of olivine, Poumellec and Jaoul (1984) have used $H_2$-$H_2O$ and $CO$-$CO_2$ gas buffers.

2.1.2. *Load Relaxation Testing.* Load relaxation tests permit determination of stress-strain rate relations over a wide range of strain rate, often six or more orders of magnitude, in a single test. On the one hand, with digital data acquisition, strain rates greater than $10^{-3}$ sec$^{-1}$ can be explored. This

## 3. MEASUREMENT OF ROCK DEFORMATION AT HIGH TEMPERATURES 61

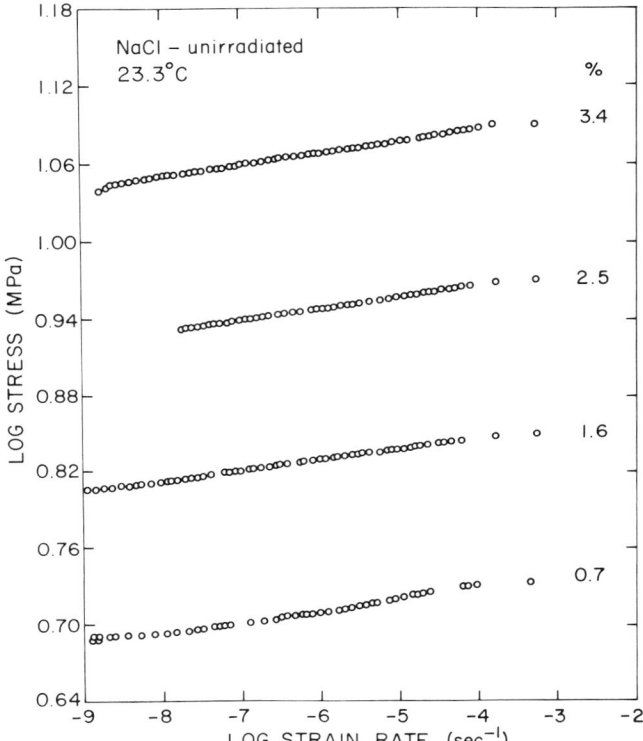

FIG. 2. Log $\sigma$ versus log $\dot\varepsilon$ for four successive load relaxation experiments on one NaCl crystal. The number to the right of each set of data is the strain level prior to the relaxation run. (After Lerner and Kohlstedt, 1981.)

point is emphasized in Fig. 2, in which data from four load relaxation runs on one NaCl crystal are plotted as log stress versus log strain rate (Lerner and Kohlstedt, 1981). On the other hand, with careful control of the temperature of both the sample and the testing apparatus, reliable data can be obtained at strain rates as low as $10^{-9}$–$10^{-10}$ sec$^{-1}$. These rates begin to approach those thought representative of in many geologic settings, $10^{-12}$–$10^{-14}$ sec$^{-1}$, thus reducing the extrapolation necessary for applying laboratory results to problems concerning deformation in the earth. The relationship between stress–strain rate data obtained under creep conditions and those measured during a load relaxation test is not well established. In the former case, results are usually analyzed in terms of flow laws for steady-state deformation of the form

$$\dot\varepsilon = A\sigma^n/d^m \exp(-Q/RT) \qquad (\ )$$

where $\dot{\varepsilon}$ is the strain rate, $\sigma$ the stress, $d$ the grain size, $Q$ the activation energy for creep, $A$ a materials parameter, $n$ the stress exponent, and $m$ the grain size exponent, with $RT$ having the usual meaning. Implicit in this analysis is the assumption that a steady state is reached in which for a constant stress (strain rate), a constant strain rate (stress) condition is attained as the corresponding steady-state dislocation structure develops. In the case of a load relaxation test, the stress and strain rate decrease continuously with increasing time. As a result, at high temperatures the average dislocation structure changes continuously during the test, while at low temperatures the dislocation structure remains essentially constant (Hart and Solomon, 1973; Lerner and Kohlstedt, 1982). A direct comparison of steady-state creep and load relaxation results might be possible for fine-grained materials if deformation occurs by lattice and grain boundary diffusion processes (without substantial dislocation contribution). Whether a direct comparison may be made in the case in which the primary deformation mechanisms are dislocation glide and climb will depend at least in part on the rate at which the microstructure recovers with decreasing stress. Because of the potential of this technique for making deformation measurements at very low strain rates, the testing procedures are discussed in some detail.

Load relaxation experiments are performed in our laboratory on a screw-drive testing machine as illustrated in Fig. 3. In each test a sample is deformed in compression, beyond its yield point, to a predetermined plastic strain. The cross-head motion is then stopped and the load is recorded as a function of time, $P(t)$. During the loading stage of a test, elastic strain energy is stored in the specimen and load train; during the load relaxation stage, this elastic strain is progressively converted to continuous inelastic deformation of the

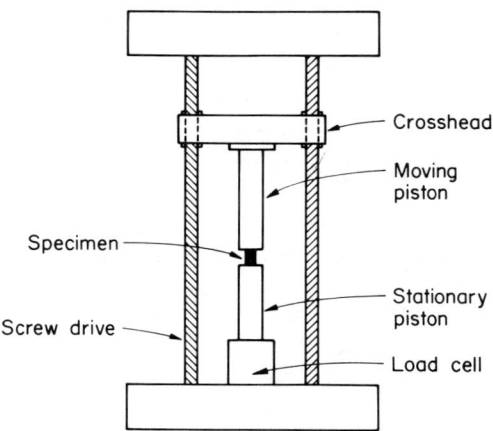

FIG. 3. Load frame used for one-atmosphere load relaxation tests.

sample. With sufficiently stiff compression rods, the sample undergoes only a very small amount of plastic strain (0.1–0.2%) during a relaxation run, and several consecutive runs can often be performed on a single sample at 1–2% strain intervals up to 10–20% total strain.

Good constancy of temperature is necessary to obtain reliable measurements at strain rates as low as $10^{-9}$ sec$^{-1}$ because stresses caused by thermal expansion or contraction of the testing machine will affect the stress state of the specimen. Accordingly, the deformation rig is housed in an insulated wooden box. The box itself is placed in a thermally insulated testing room. To minimize temperature fluctuations in the box, a temperature control unit is situated in the room (outside the box). This unit includes an air conditioner, a space heater, and an on–off temperature controller. While the air conditioner runs continuously, the heater is turned on or off by the temperature controller (via a relay and transformer) whenever the temperature in the room deviates by more than 0.1°C from the set point. The insulated box surrounding the testing machine smooths out the approximately sinusoidal variation of temperature with time set up by the temperature control unit. A set of three small fans circulate the air in the room to maintain a uniform temperature. This system keeps the temperature in the box at the deformation rig within less than ±0.1°C of the set point.

In the experimental procedure used with this apparatus, a sample is placed in the compression rig and the box is sealed 24 hours before an experiment is started. This waiting period allows the system to reach thermal equilibrium. In calibration experiments, a stiff sample was loaded below its yield point shortly after the box was sealed. The temperature reached equilibrium (better than ±0.1°C) in about 12 hours. However, the load required approximately 16 hours to stabilize, as illustrated in Fig. 4. This fact can easily be understood by noting that the drive screws of the testing machine are 100 times longer than the sample. Thus the load cell is a substantially more sensitive detector of thermal fluctuations than the thermocouple.

Two compression loading systems are used. First, in direct compression the sample is mounted between two pistons (Fig. 3). The lower piston is fixed; the upper piston is directly connected to the moving crosshead. To compress the sample the upper piston is driven down toward the lower piston. Second, in indirect compression the sample is mounted in a compression cage, Fig. 5. To put the sample under a compressive load, the primary pistons are pulled in tension. This arrangement minimizes the possibility of buckling of the loading column. Load assemblies made out of TZM (99.4% Mo, 0.5% Ti, 0.08% Zr, 0.015% C), pure Mo, and pure W have been successfully used at elevated temperatures.

A front-loading high-temperature furnace chamber is mounted between the two drive screws of the testing machine. This stainless steel chamber is

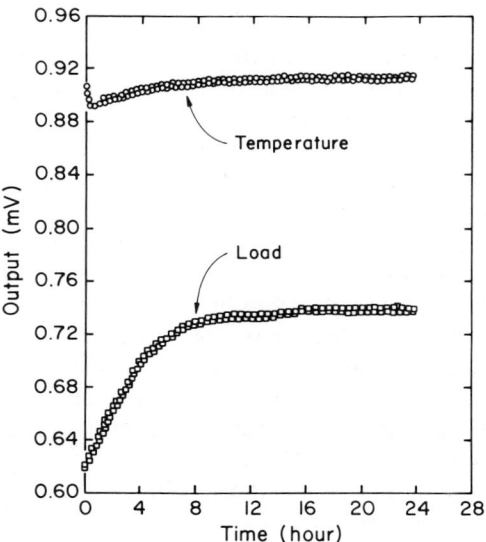

Fig. 4. Temperature and load in millivolts as functions of time during the first 24 hours after the box which houses the load relaxation testing machine was sealed. The calibrations for the load cell and thermocouple are 23.0 kg/mV and 25°C/mV, respectively.

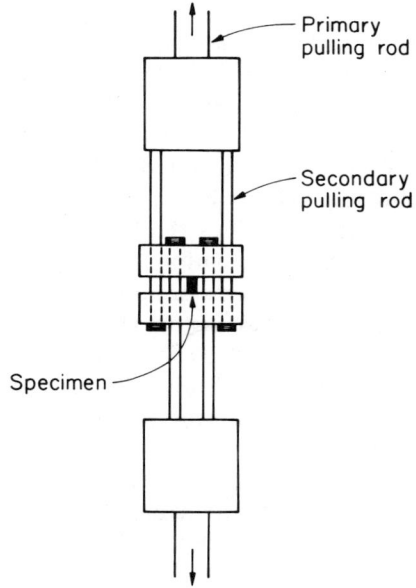

Fig. 5. Fixture used to convert pulling motion of testing machine into compressive motion at the sample.

of double-wall construction to permit it to be water-cooled. The hollow upper and lower stainless steel pull rods are also water-cooled. The temperature of the cooling water is maintained constant to ±0.1°C to minimize thermal expansion and contraction of the loading system. The pistons are sealed to the vessel by means of stainless steel bellows which allow about 3.5 cm of movement. The furnace element is a resistance-heated mesh made of tungsten. It is enclosed in a cylindrical heat shield assembly made out of concentric layers of molybdenum sheets.

To collect a sufficient amount of data to permit accurate calculation of the stress and strain rate in the initial, high strain rate portion of a load relaxation test, a digital data acquisition system was constructed. A "logarithmic" clock interface controls the rate at which the digital voltmeter reading is transmitted to magnetic tape. The rate at which data are collected automatically decreases by a factor of 2 after a preset number of readings are taken and continues to decrease by factors of 2 at predetermined intervals for the remainder of the experiment. Because the initial deformation rate in a load relaxation test is quite high, 10 readings are recorded per second at the start of a run. As the rate of relaxation slows down, the rate of data collection decreases to one reading per minute near the end of a run.

Data from a load relaxation test are recorded as load versus time, $P(t)$. Since stress as a function of strain rate is required, a series of calculations must be used to reduce $P(t)$ to $\sigma(\dot{\varepsilon})$. The procedure for obtaining the stress and the strain rate is detailed below (see also Lerner et al., 1979).

The stress in the plastically deforming specimen as a function of time can be calculated from the relation $\sigma(t) = P(t)/A(t)$, where $A(t)$ is the instantaneous cross-sectional area. It is assumed that the deformation is homogeneous, that no volume change occurs in the specimen throughout the test, and that no barreling of the specimen develops. Hence

$$V_0 = A_0 L_0 = A(t)L(t) \qquad (2)$$

where $A_0$ is the initial cross-sectional area, $L_0$ the initial length, $L(t)$ the instantaneous plastic length, and $V_0$ the initial volume. $A(t)$ can be written as

$$A(t) = A_0 L_0 / L(t) \qquad (3)$$

and $\sigma(t)$ as

$$\sigma(t) = \frac{P(t)L(t)}{A_0 L_0} \qquad (4)$$

The plastic length of the sample can be calculated for both the loading region and the relaxation region from the following equation:

$$L(t) = L_0 - X(t) + P(t)/K \quad (5a)$$

$$= L_0 - \dot{X}t + P(t)/K \quad (5b)$$

where $X$ is the crosshead displacement, $K$ the stiffness constant for the machine plus specimen, and $\dot{X}$ the velocity of the crosshead. Thus

$$\sigma(t) = [P(t)/A_0 L_0][L_0 - \dot{X}t + P(t)/K] \quad (6)$$

In the relaxation region $\dot{X} = 0$ so

$$\sigma(t) = [P(t)/A_0 L_0][L_1 + P(t)/K] \quad (7)$$

where $L_1 = L_0 - X_t$ and $X_t$, the total crosshead displacement, is calculated from $\dot{X}$ and the total loading time.

The strain rate, defined as $\dot{\varepsilon} \equiv d\varepsilon/dt$, can also be calculated in terms of $P(t)$. Now

$$\dot{\varepsilon} = \frac{dL}{L}\frac{1}{dt} = \frac{dL}{dt}\frac{1}{L} = \frac{\dot{L}}{L} \quad (8)$$

and by differentiating Eq. (5b)

$$\dot{L}(t) = -\dot{X} + \dot{P}(t)/K \quad (9)$$

Hence,

$$\dot{\varepsilon}(t) = \frac{-\dot{X} + \dot{P}(t)/K}{L_0 - X(t) + P(t)/K} \quad (10a)$$

In the relaxation region where $\dot{X} = 0$ and $L_1 = L_0 - X(t)$,

$$\dot{\varepsilon}(t) = \frac{\dot{P}(t)/K}{L_1 + P(t)/K} \quad (10b)$$

$\dot{P}(t)$ is computed numerically from the $P(t)$ data, using a nonlinear curve-fitting technique.

To obtain $\dot{P}$ as a function of $t$, experimental load–time data must be differentiated. The technique used is based on a suggestion made by Hart and Solomon (1973) in which each small segment of the data is fitted in the vicinity of a cental point $(\sigma_0, \dot{\varepsilon}_0)$ to an exponential of the form

$$\dot{\varepsilon} = \dot{\varepsilon}_0 \exp\left[n_0\left(\frac{\sigma - \sigma_0}{\sigma_0}\right)\right] \quad (11)$$

where $n_0$ is a constant and $\sigma = \sigma_0$ at $t = 0$. Since in the load relaxation test

$$\dot{\varepsilon} = -\dot{\sigma}/C \quad (12)$$

where $C$ is the combined elastic modulus of the machine and the specimen, Eq. (11) can be rewritten as

$$\dot{\sigma} = -\dot{\sigma}_0 \exp\left[n_0\left(\frac{\sigma - \sigma_0}{\sigma_0}\right)\right] \quad (13)$$

where $\dot{\sigma}_0 = \dot{\varepsilon}_0 C$. Integration of $\dot{\sigma}$ from $t = 0$ to $t = t$ yields

$$\sigma(t) = \sigma_0\left[1 - \left(\frac{1}{n_0}\right)\ln\left(1 + n_0 C \frac{\varepsilon_0}{\sigma_0} t\right)\right] \quad (14)$$

which has the general form

$$\sigma(t) = A_1 + A_2 \ln(1 + A_3 t) \quad (15)$$

where $A_1$, $A_2$, and $A_3$ are constants. The $P(t)$ data obtained in the load relaxation test can be easily transformed into $\sigma(t)$ data because the cross-sectional area can be calculated for every $t$. A nonlinear curve-fitting technique is used for fitting $\sigma$ to Eq. (15).

The stiffness constant $K$ is calculated from the loading part of the load relaxation test. The slope of the loading region combines the elastic stiffness of the machine plus the loading train, $K_m$, with that of the specimen, $K_s$,

$$1/K = 1/K_m + 1/K_s \quad (16)$$

Tests run with a stiff sample demonstrate that $K_m$ is a function of load. The observed dependence of $K_m$ on $P$ is plotted in Fig. 6. The maximum value of $K_m$ is approximately 1000 kg/mm. This value is, for most tests, at least

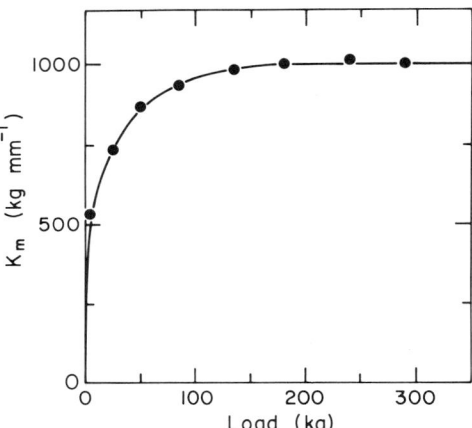

FIG. 6. Elastic stiffness of the testing machine plus load train as a function of applied load.

10 times smaller than $K_s$. The value of $K_s$ can be calculated from the Young's modulus $E$ of the material tested from the relation

$$K_s = EA/L \tag{17}$$

As an example, for a typical NaCl sample, $7 \times 7 \times 14 \text{ mm}^3$, $K_s \cong 18,000$ kg/mm. Thus in most cases $K_s \gg K_m$, so that from Eq. (16), $K \cong K_m$. Nonetheless, $K$ is determined individually for every relaxation run. Because $\sigma$ and $\varepsilon$ calculated from Eqs. (7) and (10b) are the plastic stress and the plastic strain, the elastic part of the $\sigma$–$\varepsilon$ curve should have an infinite slope when the correct $K$ is used. The value of $K$ is adjusted until this criterion is fulfilled.

## 2.2. Gas-Medium Apparatuses

Probably the most mechanically complex types of apparatus currently available for studies of the flow behavior of rocks and minerals at high pressures are those employing a gas confining medium. Complexities arise principally from difficulties associated with the containment of the high-pressure gas and from problems of introducing electrical connections into the vessel for an internal furnace and load cell. In spite of these difficulties, such machines are gaining increasing use in the study of rock and mineral ductility because they allow accurate measurement of flow strength under well-characterized and controlled pressures and temperatures.

The first internally heated gas-medium deformation apparatus used for studies of geological materials was that of Griggs et al. (1960). This machine had a maximum operating temperature of ~800°C at a pressure of 500 MPa and used carbon dioxide as the confining medium. Heard and Carter (1968) subsequently built a more refined apparatus around a water-cooled pressure vessel which was capable of pressures up to 1 GPa with argon and temperatures up to ~1000°C. This machine included the first semi-internal load cell, a device capable of determining the differential stress applied to the specimens of ±10 MPa.

Concurrently, Paterson (1970, 1977) developed another apparatus using argon as the confining medium. The apparatus, which was initially capable of pressures up to 1 GPa and temperatures up to 1000°C, has undergone further development and is now capable of producing specimen temperatures of 1400°C at 300 MPa (Chopra and Paterson, 1984). The internal load cell in this apparatus permits measurement of specimen loads as low as 5 kg (Schmid, 1976), which corresponds to a maximum uncertainty in differential stress on a typical 10-mm-diameter specimen of ±0.2 MPa.

The current status of gas-medium apparatuses and recent developments in techniques are outlined below. This discussion is based on the authors' experiences at Cornell with gas-medium deformation equipment built around a water-cooled pressure vessel designed by W. F. Brace of Massachusetts Institute of Technology, and at the Australian National University with equipment designed by M. S. Paterson of the ANU.

2.2.1. *Pressure Vessel.* The basic elements of the Cornell vessel and some of its ancillary equipment are illustrated schematically in Fig. 7. The pressure vessel is 41 cm in length and has a bore 5 cm in diameter with an outer to inner diameter ratio of 4 : 1. It is sealed at either end by plugs which are held in position by hollow threaded nuts. The upper plug forms the end of the specimen assembly and includes six beryllium–copper electrical

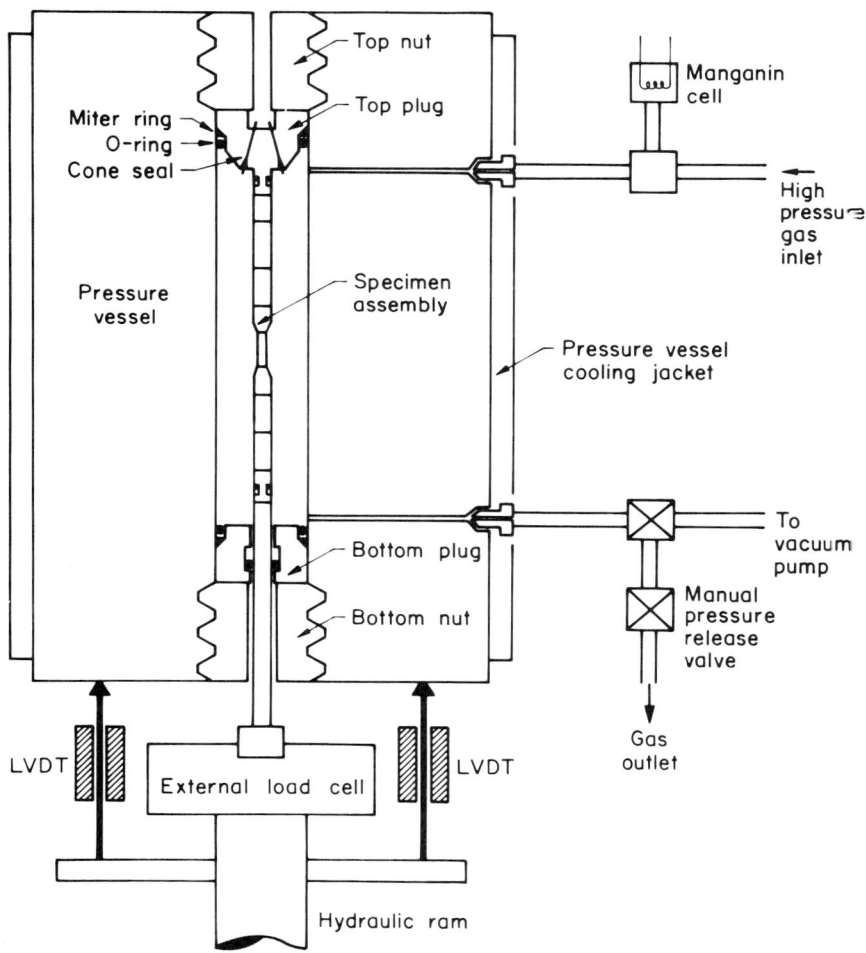

FIG. 7. Gas-medium high-pressure deformation apparatus.

feed-throughs. These Bridgman-type cone seals are electrically insulated from the vessel by pyrophyllite and are used to connect the internal furnace windings to their respective power circuits and to provide electrical connections for a furnace thermocouple. The lower plug, which is hollow, has in common with the upper plug a static O-ring seal on its outer surface to contain the argon gas confining medium within the bore of the pressure vessel. In addition, this plug has an O-ring plus miter ring assembly on its inner cylindrical surface which provides a dynamic seal against the lower piston, allowing the latter to move freely during deformation experiments. The piston, is moved up and down by a hydraulically driven servo-controlled ram, which also provides the force necessary to counter that resulting from the confining pressure acting along the piston. An external load cell interposed between the ram and the piston allows measurement of the cumulative forces applied to the load train.

High-pressure argon is delivered to the pressure vessel, from a gas pumping system with high-pressure tubing and fittings, through a port in the vessel wall. A similar port is used as a gas outlet and also facilitates flushing with dry argon and vacuum pumping of the vessel prior to the experiments, thereby limiting water condensation and corrosion of the bore (Paterson, 1970).

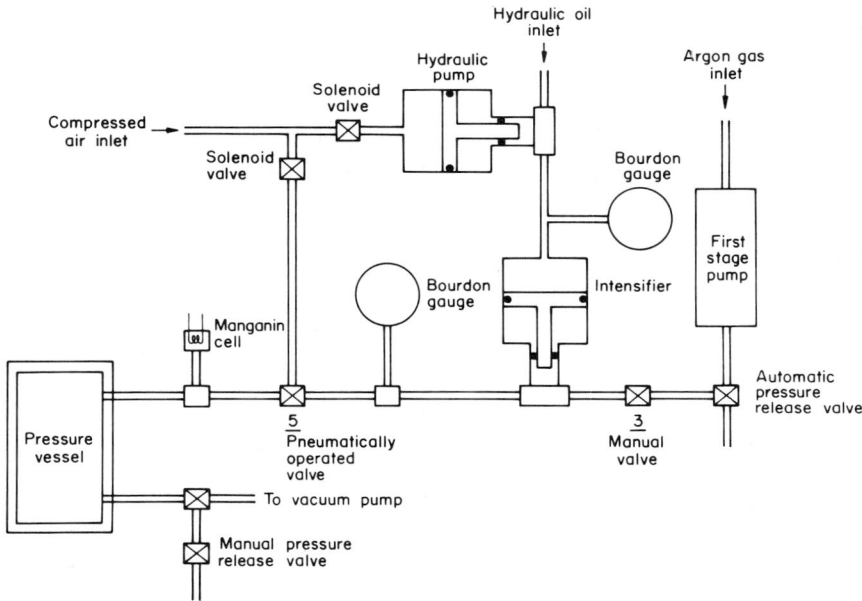

Fig. 8. Schematic diagram of gas pumping system used with pressure vessel shown in Fig. 7.

2.2.2. Pumping System. The gas pumping system used with the Cornell apparatus is illustrated schematically in Fig. 8. The system consists of a double-ended gas pump, driven by compressed air, which can boost the argon pressure in the vessel from the reservoir bottle pressure of 10–15 MPa to a maximum of ~150 MPa. Higher pressures are reached with a 13:1 hydraulically driven intensifier, which has a maximum rated output of 1 GPa. Hydraulic pressure is generated by an oil pump driven by compressed air. Pressure is monitored in the hydraulic line with a Bourdon-type gauge which incorporates two movable electrical contacts. A similar high-pressure gauge is used in the gas lines together with a manganin resistance pressure gauge.

The vessel is brought to high pressure in two stages. First, the argon pressure in the vessel (and simultaneously in the intensifier) is raised to 150 MPa with the air-driven gas pump. Second, after isolation of this first-stage pump, the intensifier is activated to increase the pressure to the required confining pressure. If the experiment is to be carried out at high temperature, a major part of the final increase in pressure is obtained as the constant volume of gas in the vessel is heated. For long-duration experiments, the intensifier can be restroked.

2.2.3. Specimen Assemblies and Jacketing. To study the ductility of rocks in a gas-medium deformation apparatus, a means must be devised to exclude the gas from the specimens. When this condition is met, the gas pressure acts to inhibit dilatant behavior and fracture within the specimens. Such specimens are said to be effectively confined.

Possibly the most reliable specimen assembly used in gas-medium apparatuses, illustrated in Fig. 9, is that developed by Paterson *et al.* (1982). Long thin-walled metal jackets are used to cover both the alumina pistons and the specimens and thereby exclude the high-pressure gas. Pressure seals are made with polyurethane O-rings at the ends of the jacket, which are kept at low temperatures distant from the furnace windings to prevent their decomposition.

The metal jackets are fabricated by the method outlined by Paterson *et al.* (1982) from weld-drawn tube stock. The choice of jacket material for an experiment depends principally on the temperature to be used. For experiments at temperatures below 1000°C, copper jackets (melting point 1083°C) are normally preferred because of their low flow strength and considerable ductility. The latter property is particularly useful when the jacket is required to collapse around prismatic specimens. Jackets of iron (melting point 1535°C) are currently used for experiments at temperatures above 1000°C, although nickel or other ductile metals could also be used if the presence of iron in proximity to the specimen was undesirable.

Dense polycrystalline alumina is commonly used as the piston material because of its moderately low thermal conductivity and high compressive

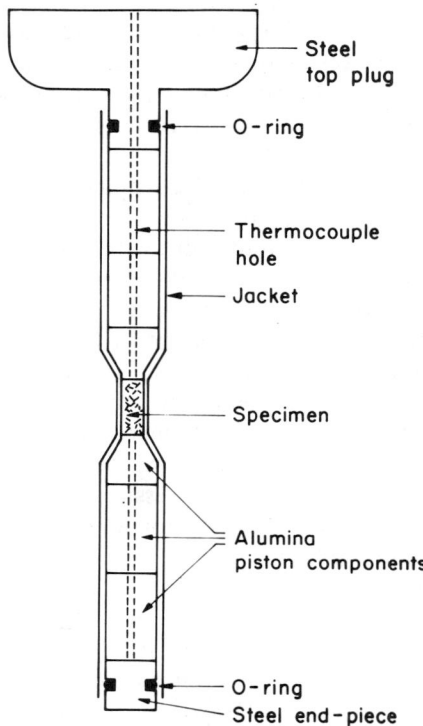

FIG. 9. Piston and jacketing assembly developed by Paterson *et al.* (1982) for gas-medium experiments.

strength under the experimental conditions. The former property is an important factor in preventing the specimen assembly O-rings from decomposing and thus losing their sealing ability at temperatures above ~200°C. As indicated in Fig. 9, both the upper and lower pistons consist of a small stack of alumina components. These components usually have a small axial hole, which allows a movable thermocouple to be positioned immediately above the specimen region in the experiments and provides a vent to atmosphere, thereby reducing the tendency for fluid pressures to build up in the specimens. In recent experiments, the alumina piston pieces at both ends of the deformation column have been replaced by partially stabilized zirconia; because the thermal conductivity of zirconia is approximately one-tenth that of alumina, this modification substantially reduces the temperature at the O-rings.

At the end of a high-pressure experiment the specimen and alumina components are separated by peeling off the thin-walled metal jacket with pliers. Interposing thin foils of gold, platinum, copper, or iron between the specimen and the alumina piston components is often helpful in separating them following experiments at moderate to high temperatures and can also be useful in restricting undesirable chemical interactions (e.g., alumina contamination of silicate specimens). However, care must be taken to avoid eutectic melting at contacts between the foil and the jacket material (e g., gold–copper at ~980°C).

2.2.4. Internal Furnace. The design and construction of internal furnaces for use at high temperature and pressure represents one of the more difficult aspects of experimentation in a gas-medium apparatus, since the nature of the apparatus itself imposes rigid boundary conditions on the permissible temperature distributions. High temperatures in the specimen region must be accompanied by low temperatures at the upper and lower pressure seals of both the vessel and the specimen assembly to avoid decomposing the O-rings. Low temperatures must also be maintained at the wall of the pressure vessel. A successful furnace design therefore must not only result in well-characterized and repeatable temperatures in the specimen region with little or no thermal gradient, but also produce large thermal gradients outside the specimen region in the vertical and radial directions. For example, in the Cornell apparatus temperature gradients outside the specimen region of up to 300°C/cm are needed in order to utilize specimen temperatures of 1300°C.

The aim of furnace design is to produce highly efficient furnaces requiring only small amounts of power to attain the desired specimen temperatures. Such a goal can be achieved by minimizing the cumulative heat losses from the specimen region and furnace windings resulting from thermal conduction, radiation, and convection. Of these three modes of heat transfer, by far the most difficult to restrict in the furnaces is convection in the gas. The high-pressure argon gas confining medium has a relatively high density and hence a substantially higher heat capacity than argon at atmospheric pressure. Thermal convection therefore is a very efficient mechanism of heat transfer (Bett *et al.*, 1971). Experience suggests that the main criteria for efficient furnace design involve measures to restrict convection by bulk overturn of the gas through the furnace, rather than heat loss by convection in small-scale cells or by conduction and radiation.

One method adopted for furnace design and construction is to fill the center of the furnace between the specimen assembly and the windings with loosely packed boron nitride powder. The presence of this powder severely restricts convection along the bore of the furnace and does not necessitate the expensive and time-consuming precision grinding of the furnace cores adopted by Paterson (1977). Boron nitride is used in preference to other refractory ceramics principally because of its self-lubricating and nonabrasive properties, important concerns in view of the position of the dynamic O-ring seal around the lower piston, which is below the furnace. Contamination of the valves and pumps in the argon gas pumping system, which would be deleterious to their continued operation, is avoided by maintaining at all times a positive pressure differential in the gas delivery line relative to the pressure vessel and by jettisoning all the gas after an experiment through the separate outlet port.

Radial temperature gradients in the furnaces are reduced through the use of porous zirconia or alumina ceramics around the furnace cores. As a final precaution against undue heating of the pressure vessel wall, interlock switches included in the furnace power circuits turn off the windings if a flow meter in the water line connected to the pressure vessel cooling jacket indicates that insufficient water is available.

Specimen temperatures are controlled in the way described by Paterson (1970). Power is applied independently to two separate windings, which are positioned one above the other and approximately symmetrically about the specimen. A near-uniform specimen temperature can be achieved by apportioning to the two windings different amounts of power, previously determined in a temperature calibration with a hollow dummy specimen of alumina.

2.2.5. Load Cells. Differential loads applied to the specimens can be measured with a load cell external to the pressure vessel (Fig. 7). The force applied to this load cell as a result of the advance of the hydraulic ram during a typical deformation test under confining pressure is the sum of three components: the force acting along the piston due to the confining pressure, the friction at the dynamic O-ring seal, and the load supported by the specimen. To reliably separate this last component from the measured load, the other components must be both well known and relatively constant. These conditions are met for the component arising from the confining pressure, since the servo control system (described below) keeps the pressure constant to within ±0.1% at 500 MPa and the piston diameter is known. The frictional component is much more difficult to evaluate, since it varies with both confining pressure and piston displacement for a given test and from test to test. These uncertainties introduce errors of at least ±100 kgf in specimen load, which corresponds to ±20 MPa in stress for the usual specimen dimensions. In view of these shortcomings, an internal load cell is essential for experiments carried out at stresses below ~50 MPa.

2.2.6. Instrumentation. The gas pressure in the pressure vessel is monitored with a manganin resistance pressure gauge. This gauge consists of a coil of manganin wire suspended in a small chamber connected to the high-pressure gas inlet line (Fig. 7) and a nearby coil at atmospheric pressure which compensates for ambient temperature changes. These two coils form

### 3. MEASUREMENT OF ROCK DEFORMATION AT HIGH TEMPERATURES 75

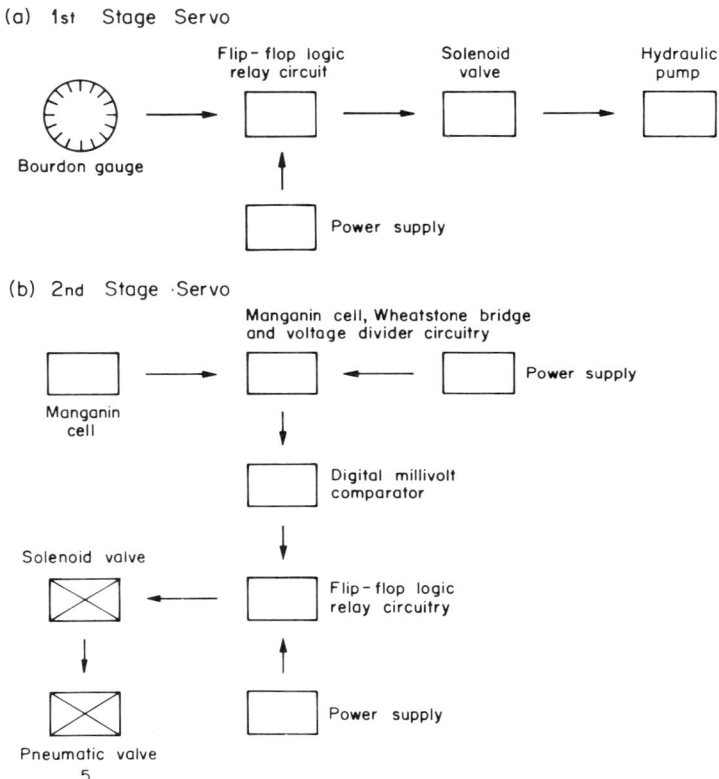

FIG. 10. Flowchart for the pressure servo-control system.

two arms of a Wheatstone bridge, and the amount of imbalance of the bridge is proportional to the confining pressure.

Gas pressure in the vessel is controlled by a servo-control system which consists of two independent servos connected in tandem (see Figs. 8 and 10). The first-stage servo regulates the argon gas pressure delivered by the air-driven hydraulic pump–intensifier system. Electrical contacts in the pressure gauge in the hydraulic line are used to dictate the function of a flip-flop relay circuit which controls a solenoid valve in the compressed air supply line of the hydraulic pump. This servo maintains an argon gas pressure between valves 3 and 5 of 1/2–1 MPa greater than the desired pressure in the pressure vessel. The purposes of this servo are fourfold. First, the positive pressure in the supply line prevents boron nitride powder in the pressure vessel from entering and contaminating the pumps and valves. Second, this positive pressure eliminates gas leakage from the pressure vessel into the line through valve 5. Third, there is no flow of gas into the pressure line from the vessel prior to the activation of the pumps and only a short time delay between the valve opening and the inflow of gas to the vessel. Fourth, and most important, this servo permits the establishment of a small and well-controlled overpressure relative to the vessel, a condition which has proved essential in the operation of the whole system since the pneumatically operated valve 5 is limited in the speed at which it can open and subsequently close. The latter limitation results in positive pressure spikes if the overpressure is ~2 MPa or more.

The second-stage servo controls the actual argon pressure in the pressure vessel. The analog output of the manganin cell Wheatstone bridge is directed to a digital millivolt comparator (Fig. 10b). This device controls the status of a flip-flop logic relay circuit, which in turn determines the mode of a solenoid valve in the air line connected to the pneumatic pressure valve. The second-stage servo operates in the following manner. When the gas pressure in the vessel, as determined by the manganin cell, drops below a lower limit set on the millivolt comparator, one of the comparator's relay circuits is momentarily closed; this process reverses the flip-flop logic relays, thereby opening the solenoid valve and consequently the pneumatic valve. When sufficient gas has flowed into the vessel to raise the pressure to the upper limit set on the millivolt comparator, the pneumatic valve is closed by a similar chain of events.

With this servo-control system, the confining pressure can be maintained to within ±0.3 MPa at 500 MPa. No pressure spikes, either positive or negative, occur outside the preset pressure limits on the comparator. Gas in the high-pressure line and the intensifier restores the pressure in the vessel before the hydraulic pump is activated, and therefore the pneumatic valve is closed before the pressure transients occur in the argon supply. Further improvements could be achieved by controlling the first-stage servo from a gauge in the argon delivery line rather than on the hydraulic side of the 13 : 1 intensifier and by using a millivolt comparator or similar device of higher sensitivity.

The primary source of specimen and furnace temperature data in the experiments is a movable metal (platinum or Inconel 600) sheathed Pt-Pt/Rh thermocouple situated in the bore of the upper alumina piston (see Fig. 9 and the preceding discussion on furnace design). This thermocouple is connected to a digital temperature display and to a temperature control system. An additional thermocouple, which can be connected to two of the electrically insulated cone seals in the top plug, can be positioned in the furnace when information on radial temperature distribution is required.

The hydraulic ram (Fig. 7) is controlled by a servo-control system which operates a two-stage flow control servovalve connected to an electrically operated hydraulic pump. The control electronics permit constant strain rate, constant load, stepping, and cyclic testing.

The displacement of the lower piston, and hence the length of the specimen during deformation tests, is measured with two displacement transducers (see Fig. 7) connected in series. These transducers are connected directly to the servo–hydraulic control system and through it to a chart recorder and/or digital data acquisition system.

2.2.7 Temperature Calibration. The furnaces described by Paterson (1977) and Paterson *et al.* (1982) are capable of temperatures of at least 1450°C. They are constructed from close-fitting, precision-ground dense ceramic components and low-density zirconia or alumina insulation. The heating elements consist of two windings of molybdenum or tungsten, which are powered separately and are positioned one above the other in the furnaces. Calibrations of the temperature distribution along the axis of the internal furnaces are periodically performed by using a dummy specimen of dense polycrystalline alumina with an axial hole (see Fig. 9 above and Fig. 1 of Chopra and Paterson, 1981). The longitudinal temperature distributions within both the specimen region and the lower and upper pistons are determined by translating a thermocouple along the axial hole. For the data obtained in such a calibration to be useful in evaluating temperature distributions in other experiments with the same furnace, both the gas pressure and the specimen assembly must be similar since both influence the extent and efficiency of the thermal convection.

Examples of data obtained in temperature calibration experiments with long jackets of copper, nickel, or iron are shown in Fig. 11 together with a schematic of the specimen assembly drawn to the same scale. As indicated by the two results shown for experiment 4321, the temperature gradient across the specimen region can be adjusted by varying the relative amounts of power (determined by the $R$ setting) fed to the two furnace windings. The effect of the differences in thermal conductivity between jacket materials on the temperature distribution within the furnace is also illustrated in Fig. 11 by experiments 4316 (copper), 4318 (nickel), and 4331 (iron) at ~600°C. The high thermal conductivity of copper, compared with that of nickel or iron, results in a smaller temperature gradient and higher temperatures above the specimen region. It is also noteworthy that even though roughly 80% of the total power fed to the furnace is dissipated by the lower winding, the center of the measured profiles is invariably situated above the specimen region. This observation emphasizes the influence of thermal convection on the operation of these furnaces.

2.2.8. Jacket Load Calibrations. The thin-walled metal jackets used to isolate specimens from the argon gas confining medium are of two types (Paterson *et al.*, (1982)): (1) short cylindrical tubes which can be sealed close

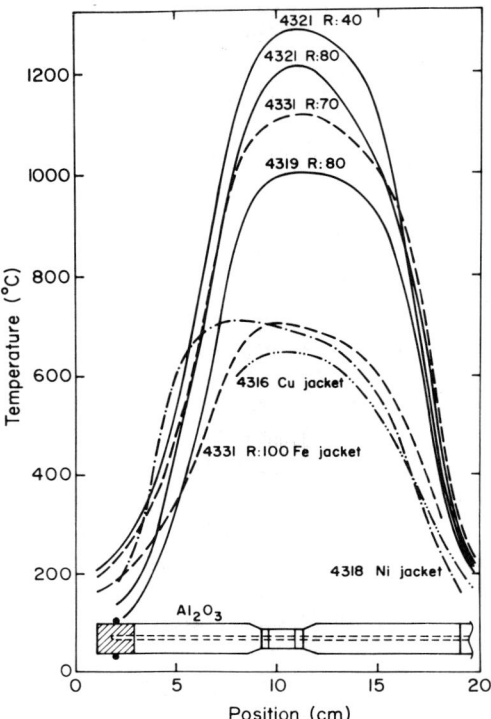

FIG. 11. Temperature profiles for assemblies jacketed with Fe, Ni, and Cu. The center of the specimen assembly is equidistant from the upper and lower furnace windings in each case. The $R$ setting determines the relative amounts of power in the two windings.

to the specimen by push-fitted sealing rings or (2) long contoured tubes covering both the specimen and the alumina pistons which can be sealed far from the specimen with O-rings. The choice of jacket material for an experiment is dictated by considerations of its melting temperature, its strength under the conditions to be used, and the desired chemical environment of the specimen. The jacket materials in general use in the ANU laboratory are copper, nickel, and iron, though in special circumstances gold and platinum have also been used. Whatever the choice of jacket material, some information is required on the contribution of the deforming jacket to the overall load which is measured. Ideally, of course, the strength of the jacket should be both low and relatively constant throughout a given deformation test.

Calibrations of the jacket strength have been carried out by deforming specimens of such materials in the gas-medium apparatus at various temperatures and strain rates. The results for copper, which are the most extensive, are summarized in Table I from the unpublished calibration of J. McDonald

TABLE I. Copper Jacket Flow Stress (MPa) at 5% Strain

| Strain rate (s$^{-1}$) | Flow stress (MPa) at | | | | | |
|---|---|---|---|---|---|---|
| | 500°C | 600°C | 700°C | 800°C | 900°C | 1000°C |
| $10^{-2}$ | 93.9 | 59.2 | 37.1 | 27.0 | 18.5 | 13.6 |
| $10^{-3}$ | 75.9 | 46.1 | 27.8 | 19.2 | 12.7 | 8.7 |
| $10^{-4}$ | 61.4 | 36.0 | 20.1 | 13.1 | 8.6 | 5.6 |
| $10^{-5}$ | 49.6 | 28.1 | 15.7 | 9.5 | 5.9 | 2.6 |
| $10^{-6}$ | 40.5 | 21.9 | 11.8 | 6.9 | 4.0 | 2.4 |

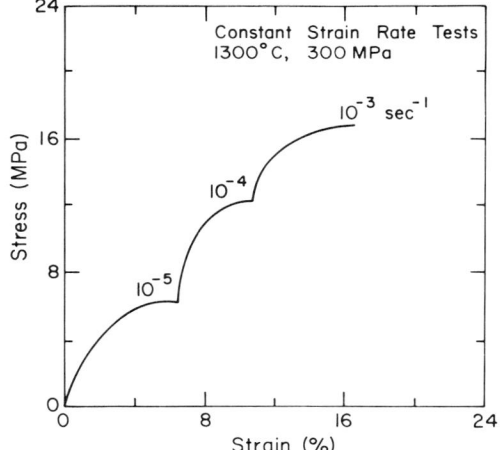

FIG. 12. Stress versus strain curve for mild steel at three strain rates at a temperature of 1300°C and a confining pressure of 300 MPa.

and S. M. Schmid. Some results for iron (P. N. Chopra, 1978 unpublished data) are also shown in Fig. 12. If a power law equation, Eq. (1), is a valid representation of the latter results, it would indicate a stress exponent of ~5.

2.2.9. *Apparatus Distortion Calibrations.* A number of apparatus distortion calibrations using two displacement transducers were performed with the ANU apparatus (P. N. Chopra, 1979 unpublished data). In each case, a specimen of dense polycrystalline alumina was put into a specimen assembly, installed in the pressure vessel, and run up to the temperatures and pressures of interest. The assembly was then gradually loaded up to a maximum of 1 metric ton and subsequently unloaded while observing the amount of elastic distortion of the load train with the displacement transducers. Some typical results are shown in Fig. 13 for three different

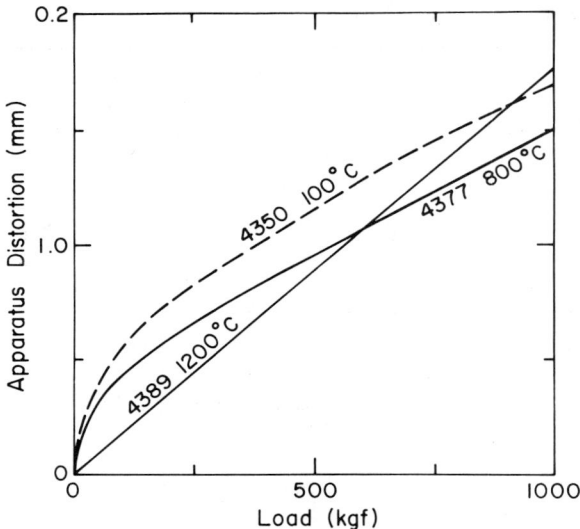

Fig. 13. Apparatus distortion data from three calibration runs at different temperatures.

temperatures in the load range 0–1000 kgf. The following observations can be made. (1) At the lower temperatures there is a pronounced, reproducible nonlinearity in the elastic distortion of the apparatus and specimen assembly at loads up to 500 kgf. (2) At higher loads and higher temperatures, the elastic distortion of the apparatus is proportional to the load applied. (3) There is no detectable hysteresis during loading and unloading. (4) A definite trend can be discerned in which the degree of nonlinearity of the apparatus distortion decreases with increasing temperature.

The pronounced nonlinearity in the elastic response of the apparatus to loading occurs because of the interaction between the various components at their interfaces. For example, at an interface one side might contact on a slight asperity, such as a grinding mark. Initially, the increasing load will be borne largely at this point, resulting in high stress and considerable elastic straining. As the load increases, the asperity will be rapidly flattened, its area of contact increasing. Each increment in stress will produce a smaller increment in strain until the entire interface comes together intimately and a linear elastic response ensues to higher loads.

In view of the observed temperature sensitivity of the nonlinear apparatus distortion, its source must lie relatively close to the hot zone of the internal furnace. This conclusion suggests that the interfaces between the ground alumina components of the specimen assemblies are probably responsible for the initial (~100 μm) nonlinear distortion.

2.2.10. Estimates of Errors. Specimen temperatures are monitored with a Pt/Pt-13% Rh thermocouple located in the bore of the alumina piston above the specimen region. Three styles of thermocouple are used. At temperatures up to 1200°C, commercially available thermocouples with Inconel 600 sheathing, MgO insulation, and closed, ungrounded junctions are normally satisfactory. At higher temperatures, "homemade" thermocouples consisting of two-bore alumina tubing of 1.5 mm outside diameter and fine wire can be used; however, they are extremely fragile and sometimes stick in the piston bore at high temperatures, presumably as a result of sintering. Alternatively, relatively expensive commercially produced platinum-sheathed thermocouples may be used.

While Pt/Pt-Rh thermocouples are stable in oxidizing atmospheres, their use in reducing environments, such as that believed to prevail at the bottom of the vent hole in the upper piston (Chopra and Paterson, 1981), is not recommended, particularly if the couple is in contact with insulation or is exposed to surface contact with other materials (Kinzie, 1973). The principal contaminants likely in experiments are silicon and iron. Trace silicon dioxide, which is likely to be present in the MgO insulation used in the sheathed thermocouples, is a potentially serious contaminant if the sheathing develops a hole and the bimetallic junction is exposed to reducing conditions. Silicon from the silicon dioxide or from any fluids emanating from the specimen may diffuse into the junction. Such contamination causes embrittlement, lowering of the melting point, and erratic thermocouple output. Contamination by silicon is, of course, likely to be much more serious with thermocouples in which the junction is completely exposed. Diffusion of elemental iron into the thermocouple wires also affects the output. For example, Kinzie (1973) reported a drift of 1.4°C after 240 hours at 1380°C in air, resulting from diffusion of iron comprising only 0.04 wt. % of the metal oxide insulator. Drift is reportedly enhanced both by reducing conditions and higher iron contents and hence could be significant with thermocouples with either an exposed junction or an iron alloy sheath.

The quoted tolerance of the commercial sheathed thermocouples is ±0.25%, which represents ±3°C at 1200°C. This tolerance is based on operation in an oxidizing environment and hence should be regarded as a lower limit in view of the foregoing discussion. Further error may be introduced in analog-to-digital conversion in the digital temperature display. Perhaps the largest single source of error in determining the temperature of the specimen arises, however, from the need to extrapolate from the temperature recorded at the bottom of the vent hole in the piston, through the upper spacer, to the specimen. This extrapolation is made on the basis of comparisons with temperature calibrations of the same furnace with a similar type of specimen assembly and may be in error by ±5°C. In summary, then, the overall uncertainty in the temperature of deforming specimens is probably ±10°C at 1200°C.

The internal load cell in the ANU apparatus consists of a thin-walled steel cylinder onto which four electric resistance strain gauges are bonded to form the arms of a Wheatstone bridge (Paterson, 1970). It was calibrated by P. N. Chopra (1977 unpublished data) at confining pressures from 0.1 to 300 MPa in terms of the measured shortening of a helical spring assembly mounted on spherical seats. The spring constant for this assembly was previously determined with a standard testing machine at atmospheric pressure. The load indicated by the internal load cell for a given spring shortening was found to be 2.6% lower on average than that determined with the standard testing machine and was not noticeably sensitive to confining pressure.

A calibration of the linearly variable differential transducer (LVDT) on the apparatus against a cathetometer fitted with a telescopic sight and integral vernier by P. N. Chopra and P. Percival (1977 unpublished data) established the errors shown in Table II. Further errors in the length of the specimen determined during a deformation test are introduced by uncertainties in the magnitude of the apparatus distortion from test to test. Although there appears to be little variation in apparatus distortion calibrations with the same assembly, insufficient calibrations have been performed with different assemblies to enable a reliable estimate of the possible extent of variability.

The calculations of the stress, strain, and strain rate in the deforming specimens assume that the deformation takes place at constant volume and is axisymmetric and cylindrical. In practice, however, there are deviations from this ideality which introduce errors. Friction between the ends of the specimen and the platinum foil which covers the alumina spacers locally restricts deformation. As a result, for the purpose of strain calculation, the specimen should be considered effectively shorter. In most experiments, the end effects are probably significant up to 0.5 mm into the specimens (this estimate is arrived at from observations of final specimen shapes), which

TABLE II. Displacement Calibration of Linearly Variable Differential Transducer

| Full scale displacement range (mm) | Error (%) |
|---|---|
| 5 | ±0.5 |
| 10 | ±1.0 |
| 20 | −3.7 |

corresponds to an underestimate of specimen strain of up to 0.5% at 10% strain. This factor is generally not corrected for in published results.

Bulging occurs as a result of a concentration of deformation in part of the specimen due to the presence of a longitudinal temperature gradient. For example, the worst bulging in the deformed specimens of Chopra and Paterson (1981) was that observed in run 4396, in which the variation in specimen diameter after 15% strain amounted to 12%. As a result, the stress estimate made by assuming homogeneous deformation is 10% higher than that which actually prevailed at the unbulged end and 12% lower than that at the other. In an analogous fashion, the strain and the strain rate varied along the specimen.

Buckling of the specimens of Chopra and Paterson (1981) during deformation became a serious problem following the introduction of the long O-ring seal assemblies. Despite scrupulous attention to the "squareness" of assembly components and specimens, the tendency to buckle remained apparently haphazard. The worst case of buckling occurred in run 4402, where the bottom of a specimen 7 mm in diameter and 20 mm long was offset by 2.5 mm, with respect to the top, after 14% strain. Such a degree of buckling introduces serious errors into stress estimates because the specimen effectively develops an elliptical cross section. In addition, and probably more important, this buckling results in the internal load cell of the apparatus being subjected to a bending moment, whose effect on the output is unknown. Some "steady-state" data can still be obtained from such experiments, however, because the attainment of steady-state deformation is a prerequisite for the buckling (in the work hardening region, the specimen tends to be self-centering because more deformation on one side of the specimen produces hardening and a reduction in the strain rate, enabling the other side to catch up).

## 2.3. Solid-Medium Apparatuses

Solid-medium deformation apparatuses permit high-temperature experiments at pressures significantly higher than are possible in gas-medium systems. Deformation tests are typically run at a confining pressure of 1.5 GPa. Recent modifications (H. W. Green, 1983 personal communication) have extended the maximum pressure range to 3 GPa, a pressure which corresponds to a depth of approximately 100 km in the earth. Two examples illustrate the importance of the high-pressure capability of a solid-medium apparatus. First, to study the change in flow strength at the olivine-spinel phase boundary, Vaughan and Coe (1981) deformed synthetic polycrystalline $Mg_2GeO_4$, which is an analog of the naturally occurring mineral $(Mg, Fe)_2SiO_4$. In the magnesium–silicate system, olivine transforms to spinel at a pressure of about 15 GPa near 1600°C; in magnesium-germanate system, this transformation can be induced at 1.5 GPa near 1200°C and is thus amenable to study in the laboratory. Second, to investigate the effect of water on the flow strength of rocks, high confining pressures appear to be important. Tullis *et al.* (1979), for example, demonstrated that crustal rocks become weaker with increasing confining pressures for temperatures above about 900°C. They suggested that this weakening results from increased solubility of water in the crystal structure with increased pressure.

A schematic drawing illustrating the principal components of a sample assembly used in solid-medium rigs is presented in Fig. 14. Samples are usually jacketed in thin-walled metal tubing to prevent direct contact with the solid materials used to transmit the confining pressure. The jacketed sample is surrounded by several concentric layers including insulation and a furnace. First, a sleeve of a ductile, insulating material such as NaCl or talc is in immediate contact with the jacketed sample. Next, a thin-walled graphite tube is placed for resistance heating. Finally, one or two layers of solid materials such as NaCl or pyrophyllite are used for electrical and thermal insulation. If NaCl is used, it is usually necessary to support the furnace tube with an additional tube of a ceramic material. A thermocouple is brought into contact with the sample jacket near the center.

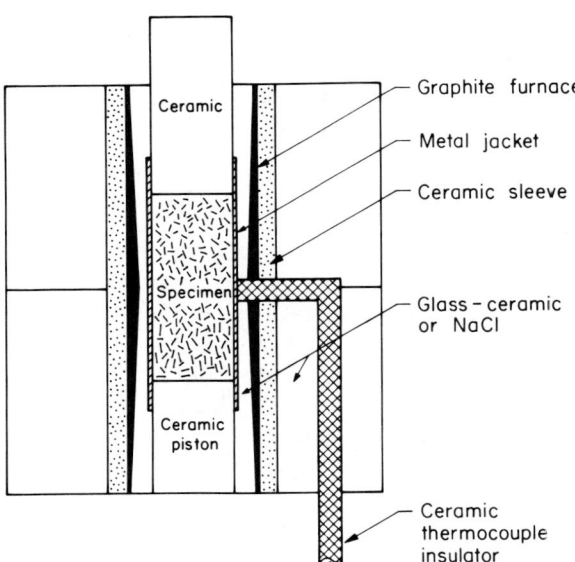

FIG. 14. Solid-medium high-pressure deformation assembly. (After Tullis and Tullis, 1986.)

Such a sample assembly fits snugly into a hardened steel anvil, the bore of which often contains a tungsten carbine sleeve. The system is pressurized by uniaxially compressing the entire sample assembly. A nonhydrostatic stress is applied to the sample by further advancing a hardened steel or tungsten carbide piston against the ceramic piston which contacts the sample.

While the solid-medium approach permits experimentation at pressures significantly higher than those practically attained in gas-medium systems, two major difficulties arise with this design. First, severe temperature gradients can exist between the center and ends of a sample. In more recent designs, however, the temperature drop along a sample has been reduced to generally less than 35°C at an operating temperature of 1000°C with the introduction of tapered or stepped furnace tubes which have smaller cross-sectional areas near the ends of the sample than at the middle. Thus, the resistivity of the furnace is higher and more heat is deposited near the ends. Radial temperature gradients can also be significant. For example, temperature differences greater than 10% have been measured between the central axis and outside wall of hollow specimens (Kirby and Kronenberg, 1984). Second, due to the finite shear strength of the confining medium, the stress state in the sample under nominally hydrostatic conditions may contain significant nonhydrostatic components. As a result, the trend in recent years has been to replace relatively strong confining materials such as AlSiMag 222 and pyrophyllite with highly ductile materials such as NaCl and glass ceramics. In addition, because the stress applied to the sample is measured outside the pressure vessel, friction between the piston and the confining medium itself, as well as the finite strength of the confining medium, will introduce some uncertainties into the estimated value of the stress. Calibration experiments indicate that the stress calculated from the load on the deformation piston may overestimate the stress on the sample by as much as 100 MPa. However, ongoing refinements are resulting in greatly reduced uncertainties in both temperature and stress.

While the accuracy of the rheological data measured in solid-medium apparatuses is at least to some extent compromised by constraints implicit in the design, it must be borne in mind that of all the types of apparatus presently available for high-temperature, high-pressure rock mechanics studies, these machines come closest to reproducing the actual pressure-temperature conditions of the deeper crust and upper mantle of the earth.

## Acknowledgments

Support from the National Science Foundation through grants EAR-8115692 and EAR-8318944 during the development of the one-atmosphere and gas-medium apparatuses at Cornell is gratefully acknowledged.

## References

Bett, K. E., G. Saville, and M. Brown, Internal insulation of high-pressure vessels. *Eng. Solids Pressure, Pap. Int. Conf. High Pressure, 3rd, Aviemore, Scot. 1970*, pp. 38–42 (1971).

Carter, N. L., Steady state flow of rocks. *Rev. Geophys. Space Phys.* **14**, 301–360 (1976).

Chopra, P. N., and M. S. Paterson, The experimental deformation of dunite. *Tectonophysics* **78**, 453–473 (1981).

Chopra, P.N., and M. S. Paterson, The role of water in the deformation of dunite. *J. Geophys. Res.* **89**, 7861–7876 (1984).

Cooper, R. F., and D. L. Kohlstedt, Solution-precipitation enhanced diffusional creep of partially molten olivine-basalt aggregates during hot-pressing. *Tectonophysics* **107**, 207–233 (1984).

Dienes, P., R. H. Nafziger, G. C. Ulmer, and E. Woermann, Temperature–oxygen fugacity tables for selected gas mixtures in the system C-H-O at one atmosphere total pressure. *Bull. Earth Miner. Sci. Exp. St., Pa. State Univ.* No. 88 (1974).

Evans, A. G., Microfracture from thermal expansion anisotropy—I. Single phase systems. *Acta Metall.* **26**, 1845–1853 (1978).

Griggs, D. T., F. J. Turner, and H. C. Heard, Deformation of rocks at 500 to 800°C. *Mem. Geol. Soc. Am.* **79**, 39–104 (1960).

Hart, E. W., and H. D. Solomon, Load relaxation studies of polycrystalline high-purity aluminum. *Acta Metall.* **21**, 295–307 (1973).

Heard, H. C., and N. L. Carter, Experimentally induced "natural" intragranular flow in quartz and quartzite. *Am. J. Sci.* **266**, 1–42 (1968).

Karato, S., M. Toriumi, and T. Fujii, Dynamic recrystallization and high temperature rheology of olivine. *In* "High Pressure Research in Geophysics" (S.-I. Akimoto and M. H. Manghnani, eds.), pp. 171–189. Cent. Acad. Publ., Tokyo and Reidel, Dordrecht, Netherlands, 1982.

Kinzie, P. A., "Thermocouple Temperature Measurement." Wiley, New York, 1973.

Kirby, S. H., Rheology of the lithosphere. *Rev. Geophys. Space Phys.* **21**, 1458–1487 (1983).

Kirby, S. H., and A. K. Kronenberg, Deformation of clinopyroxenite: Evidence for a transition in flow mechanisms and semi-brittle behavior. *J. Geophys. Res.* **89**, 3177–3192 (1984).

Lerner, I., and D. L. Kohlstedt, Effect of $\gamma$ radiation on plastic flow of NaCl. *J. Am. Ceram. Soc.* **64**, 105–108 (1981).

Lerner, I., and D. L. Kohlstedt, Load relaxation studies of AgCl. *Acta Metall.* **30**, 225–233 (1982).

Lerner, I., S.-W. Chiang, and D. L. Kohlstedt, Load relaxation studies of four alkali halides. *Acta Metall.* **27**, 1187–1196 (1979).

Paterson, M. S., A high pressure, high temperature apparatus for rock deformation. *Int. J. Rock Mech. Min. Sci.* **7**, 517–526 (1970).

Paterson, M. S., Experience with an internally heated gas-medium apparatus to 500 MPa. *Proc. Int. Conf. High Pressure Eng., 2nd, Brighton, Engl., 1975* pp. 209–213 (1977).

Paterson, M. S., P. N. Chopra, and G. R. Horwood, The jacketing of specimens in high-temperature, high-pressure rock-deformation experiments. *High Temp. High Pressures* **14**, 315–318 (1982).

Poumellec, B., and O. Jaoul, Influence of $PO_2$ and $PH_2O$ on the high-temperature plasticity of olivine. *In* "Deformation of Ceramic Materials, II" (R. E. Tressler and R. C. Bradt, eds.), pp. 281–306. New York, Plenum, 1984.

Sato, M., Electrochemical measurements and control of oxygen fugacity and other gaseous fugacities with solid electrolyte sensors. *In* "Research Techniques for High Pressure and High Temperature" (G. C. Ulmer, ed.), pp. 43–99. Springer-Verlag, Berlin and New York, 1971.

Schmid, S. M., Rheological evidence for changes in the deformation mechanism of Solenhofen limestone towards low stresses. *Tectonophysics* **31**, T21-T28 (1976).

Tullis, J. A., High-temperature deformation of rocks and minerals. *Rev. Geophys. Space Phys.* **17**, 1137-1154 (1979).

Tullis, J. A., G. L. Shelton, and R. A. Yund, Pressure dependence of rock strength: Implications for hydrolytic weakening. *Bull. Mineral.* **102**, 101-109 (1979).

Tullis, T. E., and J. Tullis, Experimental rock formation techniques. *In* "Mineral and Rock Deformation: Laboratory Studies," The Paterson Volume (B. E. Hobbs and H. C. Heard, eds.), pp. 297-324. Amer. Geophysical Union, Washington, D.C., 1986.

Vaughan, P. J., and R. S. Coe, Creep mechanism in $Mg_2GeO_4$; Effects of a phase transition. *J. Geophys. Res.* **86**, 389-404 (1981).

# 4. DIFFUSION MEASUREMENTS: EXPERIMENTAL METHODS

F. J. Ryerson

Earth Sciences Department
Lawrence Livermore National Laboratory
Livermore, California 94550

## 1. Introduction

For many decades experimental geochemists, petrologists, and mineralogists have focused their studies on the properties of geological systems at equilibrium. In doing so, data have been obtained which define the starting and ending points of geologic processes. These processes may take place on scales ranging from the submicroscopic to the global and occasionally beyond. As these equilibrium end points have become more firmly established, recent years have witnessed an ever increasing number of investigations specifically aimed at understanding the dynamic aspects of geochemical processes, i.e., the phenomena of geochemical transport and kinetics. Paramount in these phenomena is the role of diffusion.

Chemical transport by diffusion through crystals, melts, and aqueous solutions and along grain boundaries plays an important role in many geologic processes. Experimental quantification of diffusion in geologic materials may in some cases enhance our understanding of a particular process or in others simply allow us to better constrain the temporal and/or spatial range over which a particular process may be important.

The spatial and temporal scales of the processes under consideration may be extremely variable. On a microscopic scale interdiffusion data are important in understanding the rates of exsolution and homogenization of exsolved lamallae in important rock-forming minerals such as alkali feldspars and diopside–pigeonite [1, 2, respectively]. On an even smaller scale, the attainment of ordered states in feldspars is a function of the interdiffusion of Al and Si [3]

On a somewhat larger scale, Nagy and Parmentier, [4] using the available data for lattice and grain boundary diffusion data in feldspars, have shown that oxygen transport near intrusive contacts must take place by fluid flow through an interconnected grain boundary phase for distances greater than 1 m. Grain boundary diffusion alone is too slow to explain the observed amounts of isotopic exchange.

Diffusion data can be used to constrain processes which act on a much larger scale. Hofmann and Hart [5] discussed the attainment of both local and regional isotopic equilibria within the upper mantle in light of analytical data on oceanic and mid-ocean ridge basalts, ultramafic xenoliths, and diffusion data from the appropriate minerals and magmas. Their model calculations indicate that isotopic disequilibrium can be maintained on a centimeter scale for periods as long as $10^9$ years in a fluid-free mantle. However, if the grain boundaries are coated by basaltic liquids, i.e., in a partially molten mantle, equilibrium can be attained on a similar scale in only $10^5$-$10^6$ years. The first conclusion is consisted with isotopic inhomogeneities observed in many mantle-derived xenoliths while the second conclusion indicates that isotopic variations between oceanic island and mid-ocean ridge basalts cannot be due to small-scale isotopic heterogeneities within the same source region.

In another application, quantitative data for oxygen self-diffusion in minerals found within Ca, Al-rich inclusions (CAIs) in carbonaceous chondrites, i.e., melilite, diopside, spinel, olivine, etc., may constrain processes governing the distribution of presolar $^{16}O$ excesses in these materials. Clayton et al. [6] have determined the oxygen isotopic composition of mineral separates from a number of CAIs and observed a systematic departure of their isotopic compositions from the terrestrial fractionation line (on a $^{17}O$ vs. $^{18}O$ plot). Melilite falls closest to the terrestrial line while spinel falls farthest away. Diopside has intermediate compositions. The trend produced by these analyses has a slope of unity, consistent with variable additions of $^{16}O$ of presolar origin to these phases. One explanation of the heterogeneous and systematic isotopic distribution within these inclusions invokes a high-temperature origin, with the minerals having an initially large (40 per mil) and homogeneous anomaly. Subsequently, the inclusion may have partially equilibrated with either isotopically normal solar nebular gas or matrix material. Minerals in which oxygen diffused rapidly would more closely approach the terrestrial fractionation line than minerals in which oxygen diffused slowly. Hence, if this model is correct it is expected that the self-diffusion coefficient of oxygen for melilite should be greater than that for diopside, which in turn should be greater than that for spinel. Conversely, if eventual determination of the diffusion coefficients does not confirm this ordering of $^{16}O$ excesses, this model can be rejected.

Another important application concerns the fact that diffusion cannot occur in perfect crystals. Diffusion must take place through a process involving crystalline defects. It follows that the dependence of diffusion coefficients on external parameters may be an excellent means of characterizing the defect chemistry of the diffusive media. Defect chemistry in turn influences a number of other properties of geologic materials, i.e., electrical conductivity and anelastic deformation. Hence, diffusion data may help us to understand these phenomena as well.

Clearly, the data obtained in the experimental determination of diffusion coefficients may play an important role in many areas of geochemistry and geophysics. The relatively small number of publications on this subject (see [7] for a review) reflects a number of experimental difficulties associated with the acquisition of suitable starting materials (large high-quality crystals), but reflects even more the difficulties associated with the measurement of very low diffusion coefficients. For most crystalline materials diffusion coefficients of less than $10^{-12}$ cm$^2$ s$^{-1}$ are observed (see references below). Such diffusivities require either extremely long run times or the ability to reliably measure submicrometer diffusion gradients.

Many of the problems associated with the measurement of near-surface concentration gradients for obtaining diffusion rates are also encountered in a number of areas of materials science, i.e., ion implantation in semiconductors, characterization of thin films, etc. A number of near-surface analysis techniques, including secondary ion mass spectrometry (SIMS), ion backscattering spectroscopy, and nuclear reaction analysis, have been applied to these problems (see [8, 9] for reviews). These techniques are also amenable to problems involving geologic materials and, in recent years, have been applied to the determination of diffusion coefficients [10–15]. The capabilities of these techniques are sure to extend our ability to measure small diffusion coefficients ($10^{-19}$ cm$^2$ s$^{-1}$) and to extend the temperature range of these measurements to those necessary for geologic applications.

In this chapter we present a review of the experimental techniques used in determining diffusion data. The focus will be on the limitations and implementation of these techniques rather than on any synthesis of the data obtained.

## 2. Theory

As the focus of this chapter is experimental technique, theoretical aspects of diffusion will be disussed in general terms. The discussion is necessary, however, since different types of diffusive behavior require different experimental techniques. The reader is directed to texts by Manning [16] and Shewmon [17] as well as the references herein for more detailed discussions.

Diffusive transport can be divided into three categories: volume, grain boundary, and surface diffusion. The subject here is volume diffusion—

diffusive transport that takes place through a crystalline lattice or homogeneous melt or glass, rather than at some structural discontinuity. Volume diffusion may be categorized in terms of whether or not it takes place in a chemical potential gradient. Self-diffusion takes place when no chemical gradient exists. Experimentally, it can be observed only by isotopic labeling of the species of interest. In tracer diffusion an isotopically labeled species not normally present in the material (e.g., $^{63}$Ni tracer diffusion in pure forsterite) is introduced. Hence, a chemical gradient exists for the tracer, but since the tracer concentration is so low, the chemical gradients in the other species are negligible. For natural materials there is very little difference between self-diffusion and tracer diffusion due to natural impurity levels. In the case where the concentration of the tracer becomes large enough that significant gradients exist for the other species in the material, the behavior is described as chemical diffusion. In chemical diffusion the flux of one component is coupled to that of another. For instance, the diffusion of Ca in plagioclase depends not only on the mobilities of the Ca ion and the Na ion which it replaces but also on the mobilities of Si and Al, which must move in order to maintain charge balance. Since chemical gradients are produced in studies of chemical diffusion, the electron microprobe is an ideal tool for measuring the compositional paths.

The dependence of diffusion $D$ on temperature $T$ is given by the Arrhenius relation,

$$D = D_0 \exp(-E/RT)$$

where $D_0$ is the preexponential term or frequency factor, $E$ the activation energy, and $R$ the universal gas constant. The significance of $D_0$ and $E$ is based on diffusion in crystals, which takes place by defect mechanisms. The frequency factor is related to crystal structure, jump frequency and distance, and defect structure, while the activation energy is related to defect formation energy and the energy required to form an activated complex. Although in most instances diffusion in glasses and melts displays Arrhenius behavior, the theoretical validity of these concepts when applied to amorphous materials is questionable [18].

## 3. Solutions to Fick's Second Law

The initial task in determining a diffusion coefficient is that of designing an experimental configuration (initial boundary conditions) for which either (1) a change in bulk composition (chemical or isotopic) or (2) a compositional gradient (chemical or isotopic) can easily be analyzed to derive a diffusivity. The diffusion coefficient can then be calculated through inversion of these data by an appropriate solution to Fick's second law,

$$\frac{\partial c}{\partial t} = D\frac{\partial^2 c}{\partial x^2}$$

where $D$ is the diffusion coefficient, $c$ the concentration, $t$ the time, and $x$ the distance. Crank [19] gives solutions to this equation for a wide variety of initial boundary conditions; only those for the most commonly utilized configurations are presented here.

Assuming that the boundary conditions can be described, diffusion coefficients for a particular sample (typically a powder of known size distribution) can be determined from the bulk gain or loss of some component (chemical or isotopic) from its surrounding medium. The exchange is expressed as a fractional approach to equilibrium, $M_t/M_\infty$, where $M_t$ is the amount of tracer species present in the material at time $t$ and $M_\infty$ is the amount of solute in the material at equilibrium. The actual expressions describing the fractional approach to equilibrium are dependent on the sample geometry, surface area, and boundary conditions [19].

The major advantage of the exchange technique is its applicability in measuring small diffusivities ($D \leq 10^{-12}$ cm$^2$ s$^{-1}$) which could not be easily examined with radiotracer or electron microprobe techniques. The major disadvantage is this technique's susceptibility to mass transport phenomena other than diffusion. For instance, in aqueous exchange media the sample may experience dissolution followed by reprecipitation of tracer-enriched material. Tracer may also migrate along cracks or, in the case of melts, be incorporated by convective mixing. Unfortunately, there is not sufficiently detailed information (i.e., no information on compositional gradients to compare with solution chemistry) available in any single experiment to allow these competing effects to be analyzed.

Hofmann [18] suggests several methods which can be used to ensure that diffusion is the process being measured in fractional exchange experiments: (1) cross-checking with other techniques where available, (2) varying the size and geometry of sample material, (3) time series ($D$ should remain constant with time), and (4) "zero-time" experiments. The zero-time experiment consists of terminating the run as soon as final run conditions are achieved. Analysis then allows evaluation of the amount of exchange that has occurred simply due to run-up and quench.

Experiments in which concentration profiles are measured are typically designed so that the sample can be treated as a one-dimensional semi-infinite medium. The character of the profile, i.e., the solution to Fick's law is dependent on the initial configuration of the tracer and includes thin-source, semi-infinite source, diffusion couple, and thick-source experiments (Fig. 1).

| | Sample configuration | Boundary condition | Solution to Fick's 2nd law | Diffusion profile |
|---|---|---|---|---|
| Semi-infinite sources | x = 0 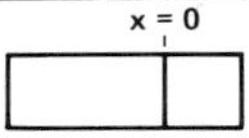 | $C(x, 0) = 0, x > 0$<br>$C(x, 0) = C_0, x \leq 0$<br>$C(0, t) = C_0, t \geq 0$ | $C(x, t) = C_0 \, \text{erfc}(Y)$ | 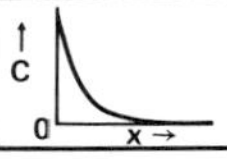 |
| | x = 0 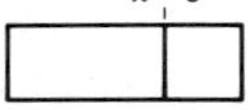 | $C(x, 0) = C_1, x > 0$<br>$C(x, 0) = C_0, x \leq 0$<br>$C(0, t) = C_0, t \geq 0$ | $\dfrac{C(x, t) - C_0}{C_1 - C_0} = \text{erf}(Y)$ | 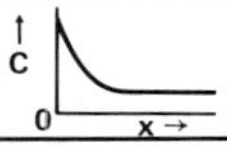 |
| | x = 0 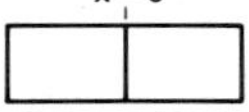 | $C(x, 0) = 0, x > 0$<br>$C(x, 0) = C_0, x \leq 0$ | $C(x, t) = \tfrac{1}{2} C_0 \, \text{erfc}(Y)$ | 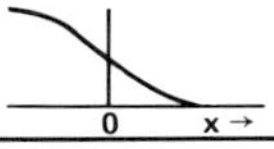 |
| Thick source | 2h, 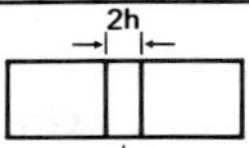 x = 0 | $C(x, 0) = 0, -h > x > h$<br>$C(x, 0) = C_0, -h \leq x \leq h$ | $C(x, t) = \tfrac{1}{2} C_0 [\text{erf}(y' - y) + \text{erf}(y' + y)]$<br>$y' = \dfrac{h}{2(Dt)^{1/2}} \quad y = \dfrac{x}{2(Dt)^{1/2}}$ | 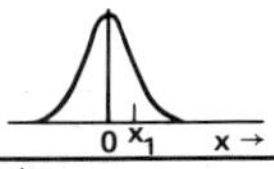 |
| Thin source | 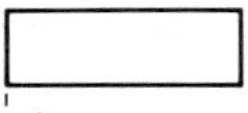 x = 0 | $C(x, 0) = C_0, x = 0$<br>$C(x, 0) = 0, x > 0$ | $C(x, t) = C_0 \exp(-Y^2)$ | 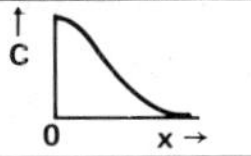 |
| $Y = X/2(Dt)^{1/2}$ | | | | |

FIG. 1. Solutions to Fick's second law for typical experimental configurations.

A major advantage of this technique is the ability to compare the analyzed diffusion profile to that predicted from the solution to Fick's law for the appropriate boundary conditions. Although time series and zero-time experiments are still recommended, the comparison above should quickly reveal transport behavior other than diffusion.

## 4. Experimental Methods

### 4.1. Surface Preparation

Ideally, a diffusion experiment would be conducted such that within a certain region of a material the tracer isotope atoms are distributed among the various sites in the same manner as the nontracer atoms. The concentration of defects would be the equilibrium concentration in the sample for the imposed external conditions; it would not be time dependent. Problems with interfaces would also be avoided. Unfortunately, with a few notable exceptions [20, 21] these initial configurations are rarely approached.

Standard conditions require that the sample plus tracer is in a geometrical configuration which allows both simple analysis of postrun tracer distribution and solutions to Fick's second law (Fig. 2). More often than not, this requires the preparation of a flat planar surface on which either a tracer can be deposited (for a thin- or thick-source configuration), a couple joined, or contact made with the tracer-rich gas, melt, or solution (semi-infinite source configuration).

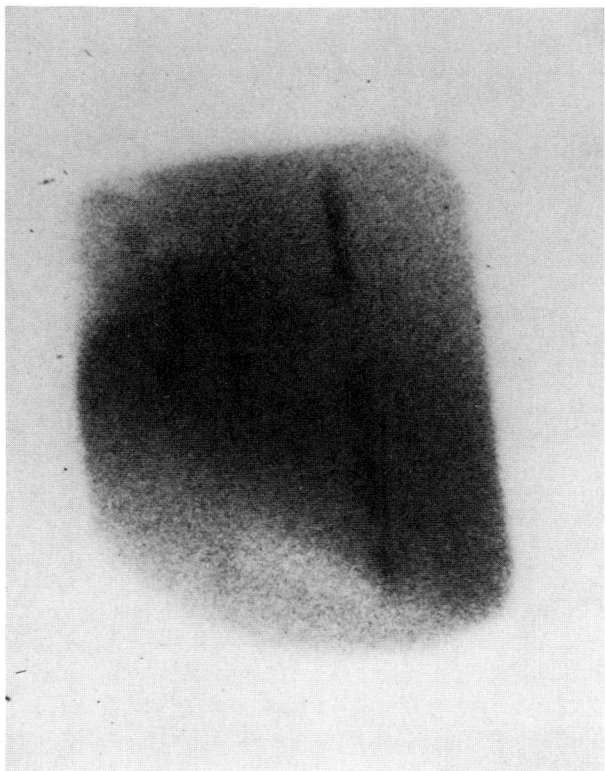

FIG. 2. Autoradiograph of an MgO crystal $^{18}$O annealed subsequent to deliberate surface damage. The vertical zone of high track density corresponds to the zone of high dislocation density induced by the damage. (From Holt and Condit [23]).

Mechanical polishing of crystalline material produces a surface damage layer due to a combination of microcracking and increased dislocation density. These defects can affect diffusion measurements by providing rapid diffusion paths. Hence, the postrun tracer distribution may reflect not only bulk diffusion but also pipe and/or grain boundary diffusion. Enhanced exchange of oxygen due to increased dislocation density in MgO has been revealed through a combination of deliberate surface damage, oxygen exchange, proton activation, and autoradiography (Fig. 2) [22]. Surface damage was induced by running a ballpoint pen over the surface of an MgO crystal. The sample was then annealed in $^{18}$O at 1630°C for 6 h. Following the anneal, the sample surface was analyzed by a proton activation and autoradiographic technique (see below) [23]. The autoradiograph indicates an enrichment of $^{18}$O in the areas of surface damage. Subsequent etching of

TABLE I. Diffusion of Oxygen in $Al_2O_3$

| $D_0$ (cm$^2$ sec$^{-1}$) | $E$ (kJ) | Remarks | Reference |
|---|---|---|---|
| 562 | 665 | Chemical polish $+/-$ ion mill, gaseous exchange | [26] |
| $6.4 \times 10^5$ | 787 | $^{18}$O oxidation of Al, ion probe, prerun anneal 1652°C, in vacuum | [73] |
| 270 | 615 | Preanneal in air at temperature and timer, proton activation | [27] |
| $1.9 \times 10^3$ | 636 | Crushed single crystal gaseous exchange | [24] |
| 56 | 636 | Crushed single crystal, BET surface area measurement, gaseous exchange | [24][a] |
| $1.12 \times 10^3$ | 649 | Diamond-polished $Al_2O_3$, gaseous exchange | [25] |

[a] Data corrected for BET surface area analysis by Oishi et al. [26].

the sample surface in an $AlCl_3$ solution corroborated the increased dislocation density in the regions of enhanced $^{18}$O exchange.

Numerous studies of $^{18}$O diffusion in $Al_2O_3$ have been conducted by a variety of both surface preparation and analytical techniques. Comparison of the results of these investigations illustrates the effects of surface damage on diffusion measurements (Table I and Fig. 3). The earliest data were obtained with the gaseous exchange technique, in which crushed single crystals and small spherical samples were annealed in $^{18}$O followed by bulk mass spectrometric analysis of the oxygen isotope composition of the materials [24]. A number of samples were annealed in air at 1900°C prior to the $^{18}$O exchange, but most samples received no further treatment. The results were in agreement for all samples at temperatures at or above 1600°C. Below this temperature all of the annealed samples were also in agreement with the high-temperature results (only the results from high-temperature and annealed samples are plotted in Fig. 3), but some yielded much higher diffusivities. The higher values were attributed to extrinsic and/or structure-sensitive diffusion.

Oishi et al. [25] used the same isotopic exchange and analysis technique to measure $^{18}$O diffusion in single-crystal $Al_2O_3$. However, in this study the sample surfaces were prepared by mechanically polishing the $Al_2O_3$ surfaces. The sample thicknesses were reduced from 400–300 μm to 200 μm while progressively decreasing the grit diameter from 15 to 1 μm. Prior to exchange, the samples were annealed at run temperature in normal oxygen, but for only 30 minutes. These runs yield the highest known values for single-crystal $Al_2O_3$ (Fig. 3).

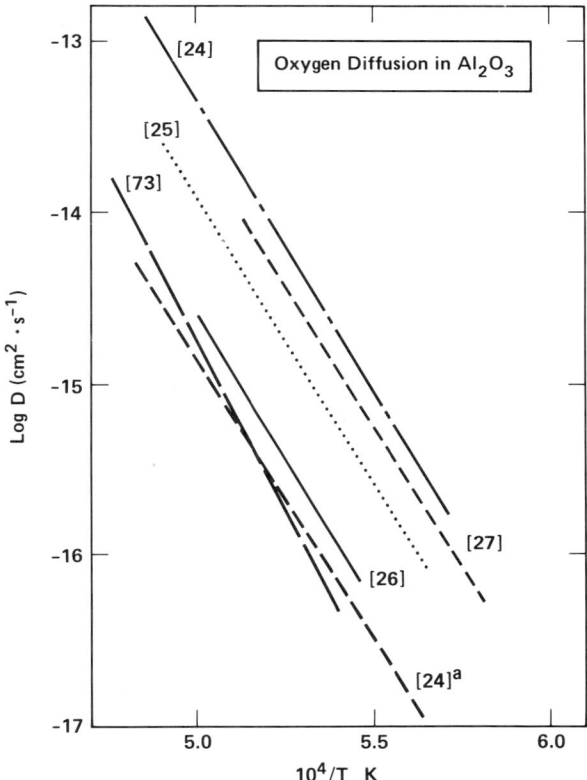

FIG. 3. Oxygen diffusion in $Al_2O_3$. See Table I for references.

In a subsequent investigation, Oishi *et al.* [26] further refined their surface preparation by removing an additional 10 μm of the sample surface by either Ar ion milling (6.0 kV, 30° grazing angle) or chemical etching in $n\text{-}H_3PO_4$ or 1 : 1 $n\text{-}H_3PO_4 : H_2SO_4$. These results yielded diffusion coefficients over an order of magnitude lower than those of Oishi *et al.* [25]. Quantitatively, the difference in the resulting Arrhenius equation is seen in the preexponential term; the activation energies for the results of Oishi and Kingery [24] Oishi *et al.* [25], and Oishi *et al.* [26] are all virtually identical (Table I). The decreased diffusivities are consistent with, and have been interpreted by Oish *et al.* [26] as the result of, elimination of the region of the crystal in which a high dislocation density provides rapid nonlattice diffusional paths. It should be noted that the enhanced surface penetration in these experiments could have been more easily recognizable had an actual gradient in $^{18}O$ been measured as opposed to the fractional exchange measurement.

It should also be noted that Oishi et al. [26] redetermined the surface area of the samples of Oishi and Kingery [24] by the Brunauer-Emmet-Teller (BET) gas absorption method. When corrected for increased surface area (again the correction is only apparent in the preexponential term), the results for the crushed samples are in good agreement with those of the ion-milled and chemically etched materials. If the BET method provides an accurate measure of the exchange surface, then this agreement indicates that normal dislocation density surfaces can be produced in crushed samples provided sufficient long or high-temperature annealing takes place prior to exchange.

Reddy and Cooper [27] have systematically investigated the effects of variations in initial dislocation and annealing on the diffusivities of $^{18}$O in alumina. They obtained $Al_2O_3$ single crystals grown by different techniques (Schmidt-Viechnicki, Czochralski, and Verneuil) in which the dislocation density varied by two orders of magnitude ($10^7$, $10^8$, and $10^9$ m$^{-2}$, respectively). Annealed samples were prepared by heating in air or normal oxygen for times and temperatures identical to those of the $^{18}$O exchange experiments. Depending on the temperature, anneal and exchange times varied between 25 and 100 hours. The runs were analyzed by combined proton activation and alpha spectroscopy (see below). The diffusivities from the annealed samples could all be fit to the same Arrhenius equation (Table I) regardless of initial dislocation density.

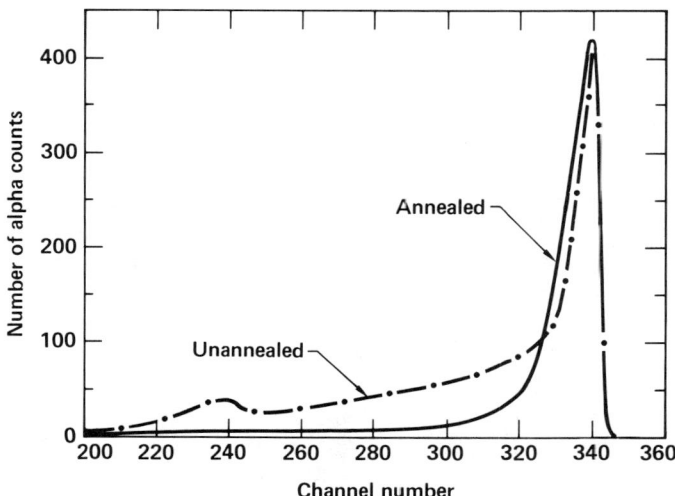

FIG. 4. Non-resonant $\alpha$ spectra from $^{18}$O(p, $\alpha$)$^{15}$N reaction induced in annealed and unannealed $^{18}$O-diffused $Al_2O_3$. Depth increases with decreasing channel number. The high $\alpha$ intensity at depth in the unannealed sample is a result of non-Fickian diffusion due to increased dislocation density. (After Reddy and Cooper [27].)

Reddy and Cooper's [27] nonannealed samples cannot be directly compared to the results for annealed samples as they do not demonstrate Fickian behavior, i.e., $D$ is not constant (Fig. 4). Comparison of the alpha spectra for annealed and unannealed samples exchanged under similar conditions reveals the presence of $^{18}O$ at a much greater depth in the unannealed sample; in fact, over a small range the $^{18}O$ concentration actually increases with depth. These data again illustrate the effect of dislocation-enhanced diffusion.

The results of Reddy and Cooper [27] also argue strongly for the use of in-depth profiling analysis techniques as opposed to bulk exchange. The non-Fickian behavior observed in unannealed specimens could not have been resolved by bulk exchange techniques. Only spatially sensitive techniques can truly substantiate Fickian behavior.

## 4.2. Tracer Emplacement

### 4.2.1. Extended Sources.
Once the initial configuration of the experiment has been defined and the sample prepared for the diffusion anneal, some tracer of the diffusion process must be emplaced. The tracer may be a radioisotope, a stable isotope, or, in the case of chemical diffusion, simply a perturbation in the bulk concentration of one or more of the components. The choice depends on the element of interest (whether a radioisotope is available and is convenient and safe to use), the diffusion type of interest (self-diffusion vs. tracer diffusion vs. chemical diffusion), and the type of analytical techniques available for measuring either the diffusion profile or the extent of exchange. The geometric configuration of the tracer emplacement should also be consistent with selected solutions to Fick's laws. This is not critical, however, as the final results should be tested against a number of possible solutions for the best fit.

The simplest means of tracer emplacement is the use of an infinite exchange medium or limited well-stirred source surrounding the sample. This procedure has been used for both fractional exchange experiments [28, 29] and experiments where a diffusion profile is actually analyzed [12,15].

The exchange medium may be an aqueous solution, a gas, or a melt which may act as source or sink of an isotopic tracer or, in the case of chemical diffusion, a perturbation in the concentration of one or more components. For each case it is extremely important that the exchange medium be in chemical equilibria with the sample. If chemical equilibrium is not obtained prior to the diffusion anneal, transport of tracer material may take place by mechanisms other than diffusion. In the case of aqueous solutions and melts, precipitation or dissolution may occur, both redistributing tracer material and resetting initial boundaries. Disequilibrium may also produce chemical changes in the sample. For instance, for samples containing multivalent cations, the $fO_2$ imposed by the exchange medium must be identical to the intrinsic $fO_2$ of the sample at the same pressure and temperature. If not, the oxidation state of the multivalent cation and consequently the defect chemistry of the sample will readjust with time during the diffusion anneal. Similarly, samples should not be annealed under conditions in which new phases precipitate or exsolution occurs.

Aqueous exchange media were initially used in fractional exchange experiments for elements and minerals important in geochronology [28, 30-32] and solid-state mineral kinetics [33]. Exchange temperatures ranged from 400 to 900°C and measured diffusivities from $10^{-9}$ to $10^{-16}$ cm$^2$ s$^{-1}$. Much of this data has been reviewed by Mussett [34] and Giletti [28]. A radiotracer or isotopically enriched (or depleted) solution is commonly used, and the exchange is analyzed by scintillation counting or mass spectrometric analysis, respectively, of the sample or solution.

An excellent example of a successful application of this technique is given by Foland [35] for alkali diffusion in orthoclase. In this study the diffusivities were determined by isotopic exchange between an aqueous chloride solution and a homogeneous single-phase orthoclase ($Or_{94}$). Prior to the isotopic exchange experiments the equilibrium partitioning of alkalis between the crystal and the solution was determined as a function of temperature in order to obtain proper solution compositions for the subsequent anneals. Grain size and run time were also varied in order to substantiate the predominance of diffusive transport, yielding self-consistent results.

The use of aqueous exchange media is, of course, amenable to techniques in which diffusion profiles are measured [10, 11]. The constraints of chemical equilibrium must also be observed here, but the ability to inspect the character of the profile makes this application much more reliable.

The use of gaseous exchange media is completely analogous to that of aqueous solutions (although dissolution/deprecipitation is not nearly such a problem). The most common applications are for measurements of oxygen diffusion in which the sample is exchanged with an $^{18}$O-enriched gas. Analysis is accomplished by either fractional exchange or the analysis of a gradient [12, 14, 15, 25, 27, 36-45].

Another method in which the infinite reservoir technique can be used to measure oxygen diffusion is through the oxidation of a multivalent cation in the sample. For instance, Wendlandt [41] measured the weight change with time in a number of magmatic liquids as the oxygen fugacity of the ambient atmosphere was changed. It is assumed that the mechanism by which the ferric/ferrous ratio of the liquid reequilibrates with the ambient atmosphere is through diffusion of oxygen. In a similar application, Komatsu et al. [29] measured oxygen diffusion in stabilized $ZrO_2$ by monitoring the progressive weight gain during oxygen exchange with an $^{18}$O-enriched gas. Dunn [42] exchanged magmatic liquids with a solid reservoir, graphite, at elevated pressures and measured the change of oxidation state of iron as a function of time to calculate the amount of exchange. Again, it is assumed that oxygen diffusion is the manner in which the sample equilibrates. These studies are somewhat vulnerable inasmuch as no gradient is measured.

Diffusion data obtained with melts as reservoir media have usually been obtained as the by-product of experimental reversals of trace element partitioning coefficients [43]. More recently experiments have been specifically designed for the purpose of obtaining diffusion coefficients in both oriented minerals and melts [44, 45]. For diffusion in minerals an oriented crystal is placed in a melt which has been presaturated in that phase for the proper run conditions. This minimizes the driving force for dissolution. The melt is also doped with a tracer, which in these experiments is an increased concentration of some trace element, Sr, a rare earth element (REE), Pb, etc. Subsequent to annealing, a microprobe traverse is made perpendicular to the mineral-melt interface and the diffusion profile then inverted to obtain a diffusivity. Profiles as short as 10–20 μm can be analyzed in this fashion. The procedure can also be reversed so that the mineral dissolves into the reservoir, thereby allowing the diffusivity of the tracer to be determined in the melt. In the absence of convection, this procedure can yield excellent results (Fig. 5) provided that the amount of dissolution is small. For small amounts of dissolution the interface is practically static and the geometry one dimensional.

The use of a melt as a reservoir medium as described is obviously limited in sensitivity and spatial resolution by the nature of the analysis technique, the electron probe. The sensitivity of the electron microprobe limits the applicability to chemical diffusion (since the investigators above used this technique for trace element-rich accessory phases, the sensitivity does not at all reduce the applicability of their results). However, there is no *a priori* reason why it could not be used in conjunction with other techniques. For instance, $\beta$-emitting radiotracer- or stable isotope-enriched melts could allow the use of autoradiography or secondary ion mass spectrometry, thereby increasing its sensitivity and more closely approximating self-diffusion behavior. Further, if the crystal can be removed from the quenched melt, additional depth profiling techniques can be used which increase the spatial resolution (see below). As an example, zircon can be easily removed from glass by HF dissolution without causing any apparent damage to the zircon surface (E. B. Watson and T. M. Harrison, personal communication).

4.2.2. Thick vs. Thin Sources. As shown in an earlier section, the mathematics describing thin- and thick-source configurations are distinctly different. Application of a thin source is often more desirable due to the simplicity of the resulting profiles and data reduction. In practice, however, it is often difficult to distinguish which configuration has been obtained prior

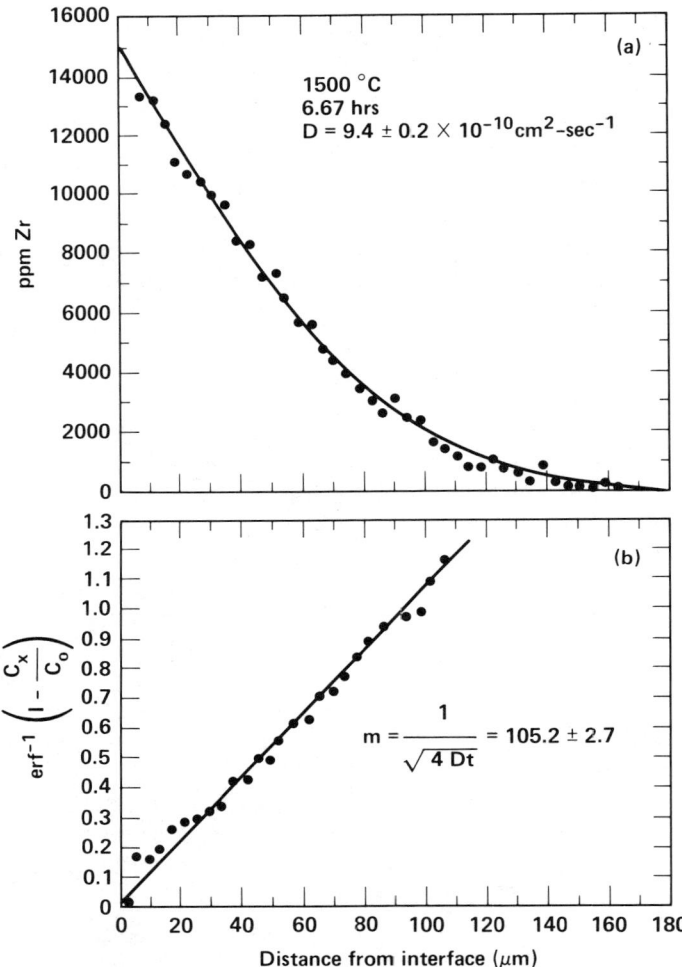

FIG. 5. (a) Zr diffusion profile in obsidian determined by electron microprobe. (b) Inversion of the diffusion profile through the inverse error function to obtain $D$ by least-squares analysis. Sample configuration was a semi-infinite source with constant surface concentration. (After Harrison and Watson [45].)

to analysis of the diffusion profile. The difficulty arises from the deposition of a finite amount of tracer on the prepared sample surface. If the amount of tracer is small and readily dissolves in the surface of the sample, a thin-source configuration may be approximated. However, if the tracer is not readily dissolved in the sample a thick-source or possibly a semi-infinite source configuration with constant surface concentration may result.

## 4. DIFFUSION MEASUREMENTS: EXPERIMENTAL METHODS

FIG. 6. Beta track autoradiographs of (a) $^{151}$Sm$_2$Cl$_3$ deposited on an AG surface by evaporation from solution and (b) $^{63}$NiCl$_2$ evaporated from a heated filament. (Courtesy of K. B. Schwartz.)

Deposition of radiotracers or stable isotopes on the surface of diffusion samples is the typical method for producing thin-source configurations [46–62]. The tracer can be deposited on the sample surface by evaporation from solution, by evaporation of a tracer-enriched salt from a heated filament (Fig. 6), or by sputtering [13]. A thin-source configuration may or may not result.

Sneeringer [63] and Sneeringer et al. [64] deposited $^{85}$Sr on the surface of diopside crystals by drying droplets of a dilute HCl solution. In this instance $^{85}$Sr represented only a few percent of the actual strontium applied; i.e., it was not "carrier-free". The sample was then briefly annealed at 800°C in order to bond and dissolve some of the tracer diopside. It was demonstrated that the resulting profiles were not consistent with a thin-source solution, but more closely approximated that of a semi-infinite medium (extended source) with constant surface concentration. For experiments in which stable $^{83}$Sr was deposited, results calculated for both thin-film and semi-infinite source solutions varied by only a factor of 3. The correlations obtained from regression of linearized data for thin-film solutions were generally better that those obtained by treating the data with a semi-infinite source solution. This may be due to the decreased amount of strontium deposited for the stable isotope experiments.

Thin-source behavior is most often obtained for experiments with melts and glasses [54–57, 62–70]. An excellent example of thin-source behavior for $^{45}$Ca diffusion in melts from Watson [67] is shown in Fig. 7. This is most likely due to the high solubility of most elements in silicate melts. As a result, the tracer does not crystallize as a distinct phase on the sample surface. As an additional precaution, many workers follow the application of the tracer solution with an anneal of short duration at substantially lower temperatures [56, 57, 62]. The sample is then washed or possibly lightly etched with acids to remove the remaining surface material. The result is a thin source of enriched material at the surface, but not on the surface.

When a tracer solution is deposited on the surface of a sample, the distribution of the precipitated salt is rarely homogeneous (Fig. 6a). Although it has been shown that an uneven source distribution will not affect the results of serial sectioning analysis [72], it will certainly complicate the results from

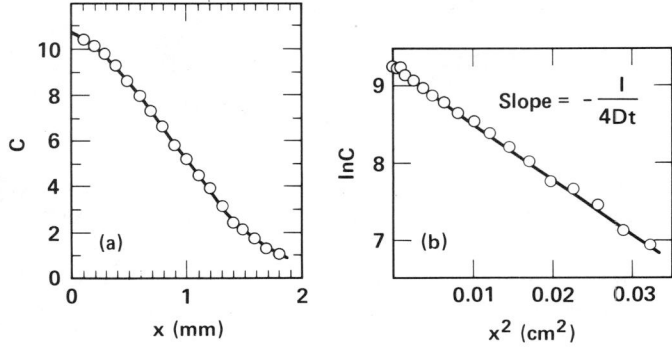

FIG. 7. (a) $^{45}$Ca diffusion profile in a silicate melt; (b) inversion of the profile to obtain $D$. Sample configuration was a thin source. (After Watson [67].)

other analytical techniques (some segments of a sample surface could be tracer-free and no diffusion gradient would be observed in such regions). In this regard, evaporation of the salt onto the sample from a heated filament produces a much more uniform tracer distribution. This is illustrated in Fig. 6, which shows autoradiographs of polished YAG crystal surfaces on which (1) $^{63}$NiCl$_2$ had been deposited from a heated filament and (2) $^{151}$Sm$_2$Cl$_3$ had been precipitated from solution.

Jaoul et al. [13] were able to fit their $^{30}$Si diffusion data in forsterite to a thin-film solution. In this application the tracer was applied as a 10-nm layer of $^{30}$Si-enriched forsterite. Geometrically, this configuration more closely approximates an extended source at the end of a semi-infinite medium. In contrast, Cygan and Lasaga [72] measured the diffusion of $^{25}$Mg in silicate garnets by decomposing $^{25}$MgC$_2$O$_4 \cdot$2H$_2$O precipitated from oxalic acid to produce a surface layer of polycrystalline $^{25}$MgO. These results were in excellent agreement with the semi-infinite source with constant surface composition.

Extended sources can be produced by a number of other methods including epitaxial growth. An example is provided by a study of oxygen diffusion in Al$_2$O$_3$ by Reed and Wuensch [73]. A thick source of Al$^{18}$O$_3$ on Al$_2$O$_3$ was produced by oxidizing a vapor-deposited film of Al metal with $^{18}$O gas. The resulting profiles were in good agreement with an extended source solution to Fick's second law.

*In situ* irradiation has been used to produce extended sources in the interiors of samples. Varshneya et al. [20] produced $^{42}$K in a sample of K$_2$O–SrO–SiO$_2$ glass by neutron irradiation. During irradiation the sample was encapsulated in a cadmium cylinder which masked all of the sample except for a central portion that was surrounded by an Al ring. As the Cd is virtually opaque to neutrons, only the central portion encased in Al is neutron-irradiated. This produces a distribution of tracer which is approximately Gaussian in shape

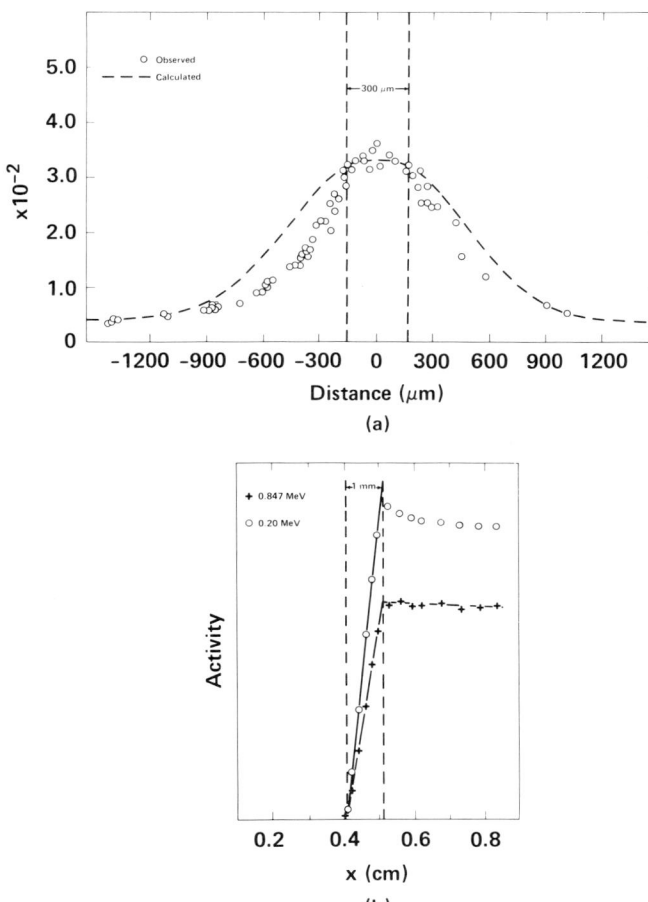

FIG. 8. (a) Initial distribution of $^{41}$K produced by neutron irradiation. The region not shielded by Cd during irradiation was 300 μm wide. The dashed curve is the distribution calculated from the irradiation geometry (after Varshneya et al. [22]). (b) Initial distribution (residual activity) for high-energy ($^{60}$Co) gamma radiation and low-energy x-rays (Pt) produced by deuteron irradiation. The lower-energy curve shows the effect of sample absorption. (After Hofmann and Brown [21].)

(Fig. 8a) and rather broad due to diffusion of neutrons in the sample and neutron penetration of the Cd. Comparison of zero-time and annealed samples yields diffusion coefficients which are in agreement with those obtained by more conventional methods. The initial distribution of activated sample limits use of this technique to values of $Dt$ greater than $10^{-6}$ cm$^2$. Hence, its applicability is limited mostly to glasses and melts.

Hofmann and Brown [21] have used a collimated beam of fast deuterons (1 mm wide) to produce a thick source in extended medium configuration in basaltic glass samples. This produces a much sharper interface between irradiated and nonirradiated material than is obtained with neutron irradiation. A residual activity profile for a deuteron-irradiated sample displays a well-defined 1 mm wide radiotracer-enriched zone with uniform activity (Fig. 8b). Sippel [74] has used 2-MeV deuteron irradiation to produce $^{24}$Na sources in a number of geologic materials. In this application a polished surface (perpendicular to the diffusion direction) was bombarded, producing an irradiated zone extending 20 μm into the sample (details of the $^{24}$Na distribution were not presented). The profiles observed on annealing were fit by a thin-source solution. Some deviation existed between the thin-source solution and the observed results and was attributed to the finite thickness of this initial tracer zone.

Another method of producing thin-source configurations which has not received a great deal of attention is ion implantation. A notable exception is a study of Sr diffusion in orthoclase and microline by Misra and Venkatasubramanian [75]. Strontium-90 was implanted at 30–40 keV; the median range of the Sr ions was 20 nm but was not verified experimentally. Typical diffusion profiles were 4 mm deep and fit a thin-source solution to Fick's second law. Zinner et al. [76] implanted a variety of ions (C, Cr, Na, Si, H, He) in labradorite and ilmenite at energies between 0.6 and 2.0 keV. The distribution of implanted ions was approximately Gaussian, but, unfortunately, no absolute depth scale was given for the profiles. The redistribution of implanted ions during short low-temperature anneals (3 h at less than 1000°C) could not be explained by simple diffusive mechanisms. One possibility suggested to explain the non-Fickian redistribution of implanted ions is radiation damage in the crystals due to implantation. Such a phenomenon is common in ion-implanted semiconductors [9]. Similar deviations were not observed by Misra and Venkatasubramanian [76]. This may be due to the much longer run times, allowing the radiation damage to be annealed. Thus the fraction of the total diffusion profile due to the initial non-Fickian transport becomes negligible.

## 5. Analytical Methods

### 5.1. Serial Sectioning

Serial sectioning is performed by repeated removal of sample volume perpendicular to the diffusion direction in a "one-dimensional" sample configuration (thin-source, thick-source, couples, or semi-infinite source configurations). The segment of material removed (through dissolution or grinding), $x$, is monitored at each step, and the concentrations of the species of interest, $C$, are measured for each segment. The measurement of concentration can be made either on the actual segment removed [49] or by analysis of the remaining material, i.e., the residual method [77]. In almost all cases (see [78] for an exception) the concentration is monitored by recording the activity of a radiotracer.

The ultimate applicability of the serial sectioning method is determined by the thickness of the segment of material removed. If the concentration is measured in the segment removed, then the concentration is that in a finite segment and spatial resolution is sacrificed (Fig. 9). This source of error can be avoided by using the residual activity technique, in which the total length of material removed and the activity of the remaining sample are measured (Fig. 10). Inversion of profiles obtained in this manner requires that the solutions to Fick's second law be integrated from $x$ to $\infty$. As examples, the solution for a thin-source configuration becomes

$$A_{\text{resid}} = A_0 \operatorname{erfc} x/(4Dt)^{1/2}$$

while that for a diffusion couples becomes

$$A_{\text{resid}} = A_0(Dt)^{1/2} 2 \operatorname{ierfc}(x/(4Dt)^{1/2}$$

where $A_{\text{resid}}$ is the residual activity, $A_0$ the initial activity, $x$ the sample length removed, and

$$\operatorname{ierfc} x = \int_x^\infty \operatorname{erfc} n \, dn = \frac{1}{\sqrt{\pi}} e^{-x^2} - x \operatorname{erfc} x$$

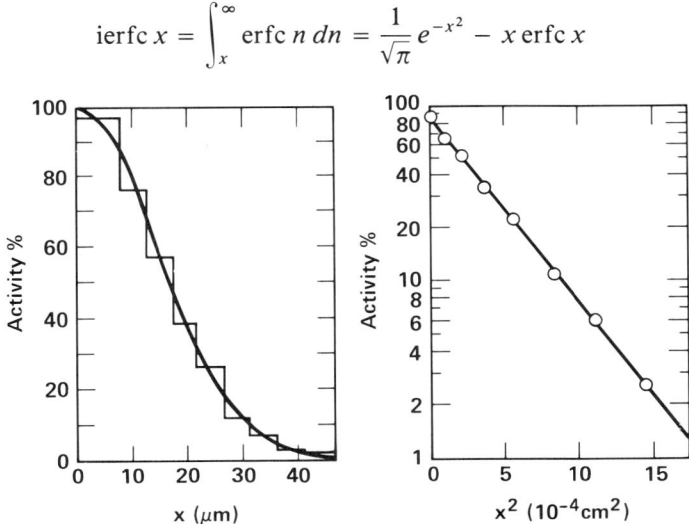

FIG. 9. (a) $^{28}$Mg diffusion profile in MgO determined by serial sectioning. The activity in the removed segment was analyzed, yielding a step function. (b) Inversion of the profile to obtain $D$. (After Linder and Parfitt [47].)

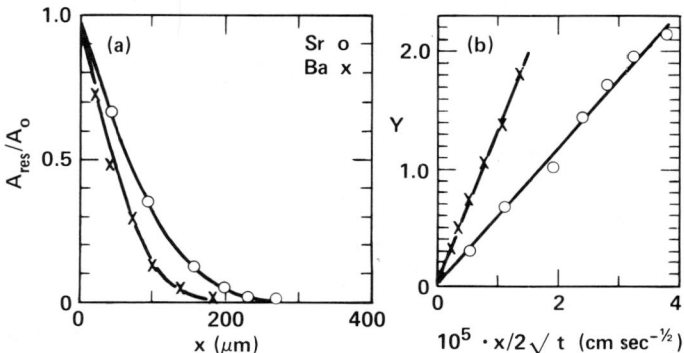

FIG. 10. (a) Residual activity profiles obtained for the diffusion of Sr and Ba in obsidian. (b) Inversion of the data through the inverse error function complement to obtain $D$. The sample configuration was a thin source. (After Margaritz and Hofmann [56].)

Additional solutions are given in Frischat and Oel [77] and Frischat [79]. Nevertheless, the lower limit of diffusivities that can be measured by this technique is still dependent on the size of the segments which can be either mechanically or chemically removed. This distance is typically greater than 0.5 μm; the most accurate measurements are obtained with either bench micrometers or comparators or weight loss from samples with known density and fixed geometry.

Due to the relatively large sampling intervals required, the serial sectioning technique has been used mostly for simple oxide phases (e.g., Mg self diffusion in MgO [47], Co self-diffusion in $Co_{1-x}O$ [80], Cr tracer diffusion in MgO [81], cation diffusion in simple oxides [58–61]; see Freer [82] for a bibliography) and glasses and quenched melts of geologic interest (see [18] for a review). In both instances the diffusivities are relatively high ($>10^{-13}$ cm$^2$ s$^{-1}$), as are the temperatures for which the data are applicable. The nature of the technique has limited its usefulness for measuring the low diffusion rates typical of most silicate minerals. Very few investigations of diffusion in rock-forming silicates have been undertaken with the serial sectioning approach. Sippel [74] has measured Na self-diffusion for a number of minerals and an obsidian in the range $10^{-9}$–$10^{-11}$ cm$^2$ s$^{-1}$. Strontium diffusion in orthoclase and microcline has been determined by serial sectioning (Misra and Venkatasubramanian [75]; $D \approx 10^{-13}$ cm$^2$ s$^{-1}$), and Sneeringer [63] and Sneeringer *et al.* [64] were able to obtain measurements of Sr diffusion in synthetic diopside for values of $D$ as low as $10^{-15}$ cm$^2$ s$^{-1}$ ($Dt = 10^{-9}$ cm$^2$) with typical errors of 10–20%. In Sneeringer's [63] experiments the sample surface area was measured by using a microscope with a grid and sample removed was calculated from weight loss and density.

The lowest diffusivities obtained by a serial sectioning technique are those reported by Jambon [62] for the diffusion of cerium in dehydrated obsidian at 875°C. The diffusivity, $2.5 \times 10^{-16}$ cm$^2$ s$^{-1}$ m($Dt = 2 \times 10^{-10}$ cm$^2$) was measured by etching the obsidian with HF and determining the weight loss in order to calculate the volume removed. The entire profile in this experiment was less that 0.5 μm deep. This approach was aided by the isotropic and amorphous nature of the obsidian, which precludes preferential etching along crystallographic axes and the development of etch pits. These problems should be expected for crystalline materials. The nature of the dehydrated obsidian also affords the opportunity to heal microcracks and surface imperfections with a short (15 minute) high-temperature anneal (1110°C) prior to tracer deposition. This eliminated many of the diffusion "short circuits" which can obscure such short profiles. This procedure is not useful for most crystalline silicates.

In addition to measurements with radiotracers a type of serial sectioning method has been used to measure the chemical diffusion of $H_2O$ in obsidian [78]. Platinum capillaries filled with dehydrated obsidian and open at the ends were heated in $H_2O$ (semi-infinite source, constant surface concentration). The $H_2O$ profiles were determined by sectioning the capillary and measuring the $H_2O$ content in each segment by weight loss on ignition.

The most common pitfall in serial sectioning is the transport of radioactive tracer by mechanisms other than solid diffusion. These processes include volatile transport and surface diffusion of tracer to the sides and the back of the diffusion sample. This can be particularly problematic when measuring activity by the residual methods, resulting in a relatively constant activity "tail" in the residual profile.

A number of precautions can be taken to avoid these problems. Many tracers may be volatile as the salts in which they are deposited. A low-temperature anneal followed by grinding the sample surface (except for the deposition surface) may serve to implant the tracer and remove any residual salt transported by surface diffusion [56, 57]. Surface-transported material may also be removed by grinding subsequent to the diffusion anneal; Weber et al. [81] have ground the edge and back of MgO crystals to remove a surface layer as deep as 15 $(Dt)^{1/2}$ in order to eliminate surface transported $^{51}Cr$. Another precaution when using the residual method is simply that of saving the grinding paper used to remove each segement. If the residual activity becomes constant, indicating surface transport, the activity in the grinding paper can be counted and the sectioned profile reconstructed. In some cases where the oxide of the tracer is volatile at high temperatures, a "sandwich" configuration has been used in which identical crystals are placed on both sides of the tracer film [83–85]. Finally, and especially important when dealing with melts, a time series is necessary to evaluate the contribution of convective transport [55].

## 5.2. Autoradiography

Autoradiographic analysis of diffusion profiles makes use of the sensitivity of photographic emulsions and other spatially sensitive detectors to particles emitted during either the decay of various radiotracers or the fission of high atomic number (high $Z$) elements during neutron irradiation. In analyzing diffusion profiles, the experimental charge is sectioned parallel to the diffusion direction, polished, and placed in contact with a track detector. The majority of investigations of geologic materials have used $\beta$-emitting radiotracers, $^{45}Ca$, $^{61}Ni$, $^{151}Sm$, $^{14}C$, etc. [56, 65, 67–70], although Th and U diffusion has been measured by mapping fission tracks emitted from neutron-irradiated samples [86]. Ideally, the track density detected is proportional to the concentration of tracer material present within a region of the sample (limitations are discussed below). The track density can be recorded in a number of ways. A microdensitometer can measure the transmittance of a photographic plate (complement of track density) to obtain a profile. Alternatively, the track density can be determined optically or with a scanning electron microscope (SEM) [87], or, in the case of silver halide emulsions, the concentration of silver measured in a microprobe traverse of the developed emulsion can be related to track density [88].

The major factor governing the accuracy of the $\beta$-track method, as well as the lower limit of diffusivities for which it may be used, is broadening due to $\beta$-particle ranges greater than zero. Subsequent to emission, the $\beta$ particle travels through some segment of the sample before encountering the detector. Hence, the point at which some particles are detected will not correspond to the point from which they originated. Similar broadening is common to many instrumental techniques, and a number of formalisms have been derived for extracting the true diffusion profile from the observed gradient [89, 90]. The broadening in the $\beta$-track method is dependent on the $\beta$-particle absorption spectrum in the study material. The shape of the absorption spectrum (frequency vs. range) is approximately Gaussian, and the ultimate range is determined by the particle energy and the density and chemistry (predominantly an atomic number effect) of the material [91]. Range decreases with density and atomic number and increases with particle energy.

Mysen and Seitz [92] have outlined the $\beta$-track mapping techniques for trace element partitioning experiments and calculated the total range of electrons in many common minerals. The data appear to be in error, however, underestimating the ranges by as much as two orders of magnitude. Brady and McCallister [2] attempted measurements of $^{45}Ca$ diffusion in diopside by using a $^{45}Ca$ tracer (0.25-MeV $\beta$-emitter) in a thin-source configuration. Analysis of zero-time experiments indicated the presence of tracks at depths greater than expected. The Mysen and Seitz [92] range for

0.25-MeV electrons in diopside is approximately $3.12 \times 10^{-4}$ g cm$^{-'2}$ (from linear interpolation of their 0.2- and 0.3-MeV data, their Table 4). For a diopside density of 3.22 g cm$^{-3}$ this yields a total range of approximately 1 μm. McCallister and Brady [2] obtained an approximately Gaussian absorption curve for $^{45}$Ca betas in diopside with a half-width at half-maximum of ~25–30 μm and track density above background at distances in excess of 100 μm. Friedlander *et al.* [91] give the range of 0.25-MeV electrons in aluminium as $5.5 \times 10^{-2}$ g cm$^{-2}$ (their Fig. 4-10, p. 107). The average atomic number of diopside is 20.7 compared to 26.9815 for aluminium, so longer rather than shorter ranges should be expected for diopside. The procedure of Brady and McCallister [2] is recommended for the use of β emitters for the measurement of diffusion in minerals. The β-particle ranges observed in these zero-time results can be used in conjunction with the expected diffusivities to yield model profiles. These in turn can guide the selection of subsequent experimental parameters.

Another problem in using β-emitting radiotracers is encounted when the radiotracer of interest decays to another β-emitting radiotracer. For instance, the mobility of lead is of great interest in geochronology. Lead-210 ($t_{1/2}$ = 22 years) is a low-energy (0.015-MeV) β-emitting radiotracer that could be used in experiments. However, the first daughter in the $^{210}$Pb decay chain is $^{210}$Bi, which also decays by β emission (1.16 MeV, $t_{1/2}$ = 5 days). Consequently, $^{210}$Pb and $^{210}$Bi in the tracer very quickly reach isotopic equilibrium, and equal activities of both tracers will be applied to the sample at the start of the experiment. This results in a composite profile of both $^{210}$Pb and $^{210}$Bi β particles which cannot easily be deconvoluted. One way of solving the problem is to let the initial $^{210}$Bi decay after the experiment (initial meaning that which was originally present in the tracer and transported as Bi). This will not eliminate the $^{210}$Bi tracks, but the $^{210}$Bi tracks will orginate from $^{210}$Bi which was transported as $^{210}$Pb. A similar approach could be used for $^{32}$Si, which decays through β-emitting $^{32}$P.

Nonlinear detector response must also be addressed when using β-track autoradiography. At some track density the emulsion becomes saturated, and the tracks are therefore undercounted. Watson [67] investigated this problem for detection of $^{45}$Ca tracks in Ilford K-5 emulsions and found saturation effects occurring for a transmittance less than 50% of the value in the absence of tracks.

5.3. Electron Microprobe

The application of the electron microprobe (EMPA) to geochemical analysis is well known, and the technique is not discussed in detail here. The reader is referred to Heinrich [93] for a more detailed description of this technique and its limitations. The application to analysis of diffusion profiles is straightforward; analytical traverses are made parallel to the diffusion direction (normal to the tracer–sample interface), yielding a plot of concentration versus distance. Since EPMA is not specific to isotopes, its applicability is limited to measurements of chemical diffusion. For most geologically important materials, the spatial resolution of EPMA is 1–2 μm for accelerating voltages of 15–20 kV.

Some of the earliest applications of EPMA were in the analysis of chemical diffusion of transition metal ions in MgO [83–85]; a number of different couple configurations were analyzed in these experiments. Later applications in materials science included the analysis of multicomponent diffusion in simple oxide glasses and melts [94].

Geological applications of EPMA were initially confined to the measurement of Mg-Fe interdiffusion in olivine [95–97] and chemical diffusion in olivine [98]. These studies were facilitated in part by the high-temperature stability of olivine, which yields relatively high diffusion coefficients—$D_{Ni}$ (1200°C) $\approx 10^{-12}$ cm$^2$ s$^{-1}$ [98], $D_O$ (1200°C) $\cong 10^{-15}$ cm$^2$ s$^{-1}$ [13]. However, Clark and Long [98] measured diffusivities of Ni as low as $4 \times 10^{-14}$ cm$^2$ s$^{-1}$ ($Dt = 4 \times 10^{-8}$ cm$^2$). The total profile lengths were as small as 10 μm and represent a practical lower limit of applicability.

More recent applications include the determination of alkali interdiffusion in magmatic liquids [99] and the chemical diffusion of Zr in magmatic liquids [47]. Chemical diffusion of trace elements (Sr, Pb, REE) in accessory phases is also being determined with the electron probe [46, 100].

One precaution that should be observed in using EPMA for analyzing thick-source or semi-infinite source configurations is the correction for secondary fluorescence near a phase boundary [101]. An illustration is given by Harrison and Watson [45]. Analysis of a "blank couple" formed by zircon crystal (semi-infinite source) tightly bound to a slab of polished obsidian in which Zr diffusion was to be measured yielded Zr counts above background as far as 30 μm from the boundary. This fluorescence gradient should be subtracted from the observed diffusion profile.

### 5.4. In-Depth Analysis

5.4.1. Nuclear Reaction Techniques. For the light elements ($Z \leq 17$) there are few sufficiently long-lived radioactive isotopes to act as tracers for diffusion studies. Nuclear reactions induced by bombardment with protons and deuterons [102] and, to a lesser extent, $^3$He and $^4$He [103, 104] can be used to great advantage in determining the diffusive transport of the low-$Z$ elements. Nuclear reactions can be used in three major applications: (1) nonresonance reaction depth profiling, (2) resonance reaction depth

## 4. DIFFUSION MEASUREMENTS: EXPERIMENTAL METHODS

profiling, and (3) as an activation technique which may be coupled with the more conventional procedures of serial sectioning and autoradiography.

The development of nuclear reactions for microanalytical applications can be credited most notably to the work of Amsel and co-workers [102, 105-110]. More recent applications of these techniques have been made at Case Western Reserve and the State University of New York at Albany in the United States [15, 27, 39, 111] and at Orsay [12, 14]. In most applications, depth profiling by nuclear reaction analysis makes use of the progressive energy loss of bombarding and emitted particles as they move through the sample. A list of nuclear reactions applicable to low-$Z$ element depth profiling is given in Table II [101].

The most widely applied nuclear reaction for nonresonant reaction depth profiling is $^{18}O(p, \alpha)^{15}N$ [12, 14, 15, 27, 39, 40, 109, 110]. This reaction may also be the most important for geologic applications and, therefore, serves as a good example for illustrating this technique.

TABLE II. Nuclear Reactions for Light Isotopes

| Isotope | Isotope | Isotope |
|---|---|---|
| | $(p, \alpha)$ reactions | |
| $^7Li$ | $^6Li$ | $^9Be$ |
| $^{11}B$ | $^8O$ | $^{31}P$ |
| $^{19}F$ | $^{37}Cl$ | $^{27}Al$ |
| $^{15}N$ | $^{23}Na$ | $^{17}O$ |
| | | $^{10}B$ |
| | $(d, \alpha)$ reactions | |
| $^{10}B$ | $^{11}B$ | $^{32}S$ |
| $^6Li$ | $^{15}N$ | $^{18}O$ |
| $^7Li$ | $^9Be$ | $^{30}Si$ |
| $^{11}N_{(0)}$ | $^{25}Mg$ | $^{16}O$ |
| $^{19}F$ | $^{23}Na$ | $^{26}Mg$ |
| $^{17}O$ | $^{27}Al$ | $^{24}Mg$ |
| $^{14}N_{(1)}$ | $^{29}Si$ | $^{28}Si$ |
| $^{31}P$ | $^{13}C$ | $^{12}C$ |
| | $(d, p)$ reactions | |
| $^{10}B$ | $^{17}O$ | $^{26}Mg$ |
| $^{25}Mg$ | $^{27}Al$ | $^{12}C$ |
| $^{14}N_{(p)}$ | $^{24}Mg$ | $^{16}O$ |
| $^{29}Si$ | $^6Li$ | $^{18}O$ |
| $^{32}S$ | $^{23}Na$ | $^{14}N_{(p)}$ |
| $^{29}Si$ | $^9Be$ | $^{11}B$ |
| $^{13}C$ | $^{19}F$ | $^{15}N$ |
| $^{31}P$ | $^{30}Si$ | $^7Li$ |

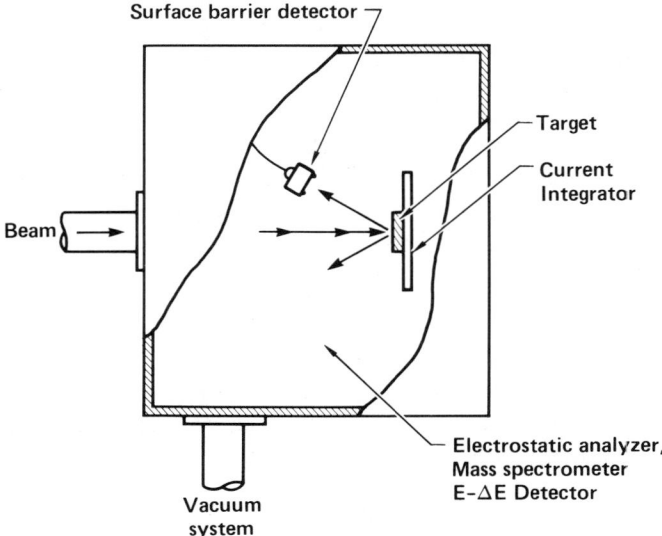

FIG. 11. Typical experimental setup for ion backscattering or nuclear reaction analysis.

The experimental setup for nuclear reaction analysis is shown in Fig. 11. The sample material is placed with the target area of a particle accelerator and is bombarded with a monoenergetic beam of protons, which induce the reaction $^{18}\text{O}(p, \alpha)^{15}\text{N}$ within a shallow depth beneath the surface. For crystalline material the sample should be oriented such that the beam is not parallel to any of the major crystallographic axes in order to prevent channeling effects [112]. The $\alpha$ spectrum is recorded by energy dispersive analysis, using a solid-state surface barrier detector located in a backward direction to the incident beam at an angle $\theta$. A Mylar foil is insered in the $\alpha$ beam to absorb the backscattered protons (use of these elastically backscattered particles for depth profiling of heavy elements in low-$Z$ matrices is discussed in the next section). Alternatively, an $E$-$\Delta E$ detector can be used to discriminate $\alpha$ particles from backscattered protons.

The energy chosen for the bombarding particles is dependent on the shape of the cross-section curve for the reaction of interest. For the $^{18}\text{O}(p, \alpha)^{15}\text{N}$ reaction, proton energies between 650 and 800 keV fall in the region of smoothly varying, high yield (Fig. 12).

Robin et al. [111] have outlined the energy–depth relationships for the $^{18}\text{O}(p, \alpha)^{15}\text{N}$ reaction, as well as the limitations of the method. As a proton of initial energy $E_p(0)$ enters the sample it progressively loses energy through interactions with the solid (Fig. 13a). At depth $x$ the initial proton energy is reduced to $E_p(x)$. Alpha particles are produced at depth $x$ with an energy

4. DIFFUSION MEASUREMENTS: EXPERIMENTAL METHODS

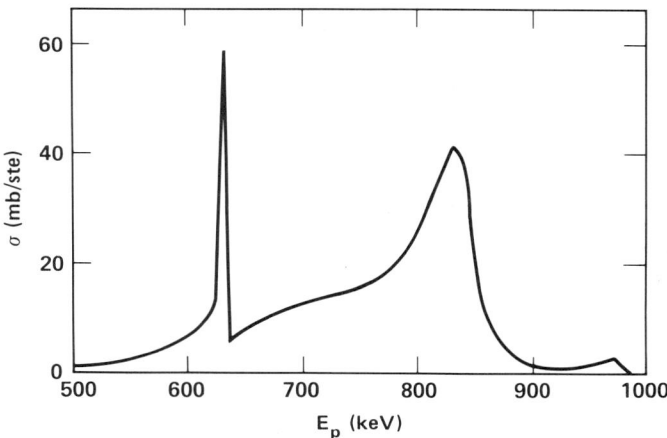

FIG. 12. Absolute cross section of $^{18}$O(p, α)$^{15}$N reaction as a function of proton energy. Note the resonances at approximately 650 and 850 keV and the smoothly varying yield between 650 and 800 keV.

$E(x, x)$ whose variation with $E_p(x)$ is approximately linear. The α particles also lose energy as the leave the sample; the energy of an α particle at depth $x_1$, generated at depth $x$, is $E(x, x_1)$. The differential energy loss, $dE_z/dx$ ($z$ refers to the particle in question) is dependent on the composition of the

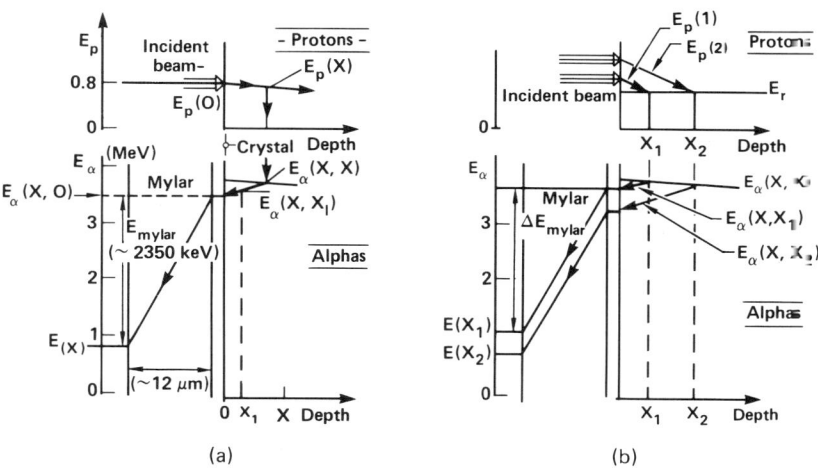

FIG. 13. Schematic energy–depth relations for (a) nonresonance and (b) nuclear reaction resonance (p, α) depth profiling. In (a) the energy spectrum $E(x)$ is analyzed to yield a profile, while in (b) the α yield for a given proton energy is indicative of the target concentration at depth $x$. Hence $I_{E(x_1)}$ is related to $E_p(1)$ and $I_{E(x_2)}$ is related to $E_p(2)$, where $I$ is intensity.

material and either is known experimentally or can be calculated by the additive rule. The α-particle energy is further reduced by interaction with the Mylar foil, and the particle arrives at the detector with energy $E(x)$. The α spectra [intensity vs. $E(x)$] can then be used to deduce the $^{18}$O vs. depth relation in the sample.

In practice, the actual α spectrum is the convolution of the idealized profile and a spreading function $P(E_i, E_j)$, which is the probability that an α particle with energy $E_i$ will be recorded as having energy $E_j$. The spreading function comprises the following distortions [112]: (a) energy spread of the incident proton beam, (b) proton and α-particle straggling in the sample, (c) proton and α-particle straggling in the Mylar foil, (d) geometric spreading, (e) electronic resolution of the processing circuit, and (f) proton pulse pileup. The major factors in the spreading function are (c) and (e); both are Gaussian-like, resulting in an ~40-keV standard deviation in $P(E_i, E_j)$ for the conditions used by Robin et al. [111]. The authors concluded that the spatial resolution of the technique is 0.01 μm and that measurements of diffusivities as low as $5 \times 10^{-17}$ cm$^2$s$^{-1}$ can be made. These limits can be extended by increasing either the irradiation time or the number of detectors. Detectors capable of resolving backscattered protons from α particles (i.e., high-resolution magnetic spectrometer) could also be used to great advantage, as the major cause of α-particle straggling, the Mylar foil, could be eliminated. It is also worth noting that Robin et al. [111] concluded that the major systematic error in the technique is due to the uncertainty in the calculation of stopping powers ($dE_z/dx$) from the additive rule. The uncertainty is reflected only in the preexponential term and should not affect the determination of activation energies. Experimental measurements of $dE_z/dx$ for the diffusive media could reduce this uncertainty.

The yield curve for the reaction $^{18}$O(p, α)$^{15}$N displays resonances at 629 and 840 keV (Fig. 12). As discussed by Amsel et al. [102], these resonances can also be used for depth profiling as shown schematically in Fig. 15b. As a proton of initial energy $E_0$ travels through the sample, it loses energy and eventually reaches the resonance energy $E_r$ at some depth $x_0$. The yield is, therefore, proportional to the concentration of the target isotope at $x_0$, $C(x_0)$. The yield curve for a diffused sample as a function of incident particle energy $N(E_0)$ is, therefore, an image of the concentration profile $C(x)$.

In practice, the experimentally obtained excitation function differs from the ideal due the same distortions which induce beam spreading in the single-spectrum technique, plus additional spreading due to the finite width of the resonance. The experimentally obtained spectrum is the convolution of the idealized spectrum and the probability function describing the resonance width and straggling effects. Since this method makes use of the variation in total intensity of reaction product as a function of beam energy and not

## 4. DIFFUSION MEASUREMENTS: EXPERIMENTAL METHODS

the shape of the intensity profile to obtain the concentration profile, reactions of the type (p, $\gamma$) and (d, $\gamma$) can also be used for depth profiling. For instance, the reaction $^{27}$Al(p, $\gamma$)$^{28}$Si has a resonance at 992 keV with a $\Gamma$ (full width at half-maximum) of only 100 eV. Using this reaction, Amsel et al. [102] demonstrated 6-nm resolution in $Al_2O_3$.

Reddy and Cooper [27] used the nonresonance depth profiling technique for the $^{18}$O(p, $\alpha$)$^{15}$N reaction to analyze $^{18}$O-diffused $Al_2O_3$ sample prepared by Reed and Wuensch [73]. Reed and Wuensch [73] had previously analyzed these by SIMS depth profiling. The results of Reddy and Cooper [27] are in excellent agreement with those obtained by SIMS. Rajan et al. [113] used the 840-keV resonance in the $^{18}$O(p, $\alpha$)$^{15}$N reaction to analyze a number of the $^{18}$O-diffused forsterite samples prepared by Reddy et al. [15]. The results of the resonance analysis agree within a factor of 2 with the data of Reddy et al. [15] obtained by the nonresonance reaction technique. Hence, in the few examples where the various in-depth techniques can be compared, the agreement is excellent.

Nuclear reaction analysis can be combined with the more conventional techniques of serial sectioning and autoradiography to analyze diffusion profiles. In the combination with serial sectioning, the bombarding particles are used to analyze the near-surface concentration of tracer isotope between the removal of sections of the sample. This technique makes use of the fact that the most energetic product particles originate near the sample surface. Hence, if irradiation conditions can be held constant for each irradiation run, then the intensity for the most energetic particles should reflect the surface concentration of tracer isotope. This intensity can be plotted against weight loss or distance to obtain a diffusion profile. This technique has been used for a number of studies involving the diffusion of oxygen. Choudhury et al. [108] and Hadari et al. [114] used the reactions $^{18}$O(p, $\alpha$)$^{15}$N and $^{18}$O(p, $\gamma$)$^{19}$F to study oxygen diffusion in quartz and $UO_2$, respectively. Cox and Roy [103] oxidized Zr metal in $^{17}$O and used serial sectioning coupled with the $^{17}$O($^3$He, $\alpha$)$^{16}$O reaction to measure diffusion profiles.

The resolution of combined irradiation and serial sectioning should be determined by the serial sectioning step of the analysis and, hence, cannot compare with that of single-spectrum and resonance profiling. However, the maximum diffusivities that can be measured by the single-spectrum and resonance techniques is limited by the maximum particle accelerator energies. Combined serial sectioning has an unlimited maximum range.

Post diffusion anneal irradiation may also produce radioactive isotopes that are positron- or $\beta$-emitting; the distribution of these elements can then be determined by autoradiography, yielding a diffusion coefficient. A specific example is a technique developed for the activation of $^{18}$O [22, 23, 115]. A gas enriched in oxygen-18 (normal concentration 0.2%) is used as a tracer in a gas–solid semi-infinite source configuration. The exchange surface may them be bombarded with 3-MeV protons to promote the reaction $^{18}O(p, n)^{18}F$. This reaction produces fluorine-18, a positron emitter, with a half-life of 109 min. This is adequate time to obtain autoradiographs, mapping the distribution of $^{18}O$-generated $^{18}F$. The energy of the incident protons is only a little above that required to produce the nuclear reaction. Therefore, as the protons pass through the surface their energy is attenuated below the reaction threshold. Consequently, a layer of oxygen no more than a couple of micrometers deep is activated. This has the advantage that no subsurface activation is created which would contribute to diffuse radiation darkening of the film and smearing of the autoradiographic image. Distance resolutions of 2–3 μm are possible.

Silicon presents problems similar to those of oxygen. Silicon-31 has a half-life of 2.6 h, too short for use in long diffusion anneals. Silicon-32, with a half-life of 280 years, is hard to obtain and has a low specific activity. The stable isotope, $^{30}Si$ (normal abundance 3.1%), can be obtained in ~95% enrichment. Ghoshtagore [116] measured self-diffusion in silicon, using this isotope followed by neutron activation whereby the $^{30}Si(n, \gamma)^{31}Si$ reaction gave a $^{31}Si$ distribution corresponding to the $^{30}Si$ tracer penetration. Serial sectioning was used to determine this distribution. Schaeffer [117] has reviewed applications of $^{30}Si$ to self-diffusion investigations and pointed out that neutron activation has several disadvantages: neutrons are not selective in what they activate (sodium is prevalent in mineral materials and is easily activated), and the activation is relatively homogeneous throughout the activated specimen (unlike ion bombardment activation). A partial solution to these problems might be to use a $^{30}Si(d, p)^{31}Si$ reaction. We are not aware that this has been attempted.

5.4.2. *Backscattering Techniques.* Practical application of depth profiling with ion backscattering is quite similar to that used in nuclear reaction analysis (Fig. 11). The diffused sample is placed in a beam of monoenergetic ions of hydrogen, helium, or some other light element. The energy spectrum of the backscattered ion is then recorded with one or a combination of surface barrier, electrostatic, or magnetic detectors. In contrast to nuclear reaction analysis, backscattered ion spectroscopy can use (depending on the specific application) lower incident ion energies and, because of the higher backscatter cross sections, lower incident ion currents (see [18] for a review).

The conversion of energy spectra to depth profiles is quite similar to that for nonresonance nuclear reaction depth profiling. Ions are accelerated at an energy $E_0$ and collide with the surface of the diffused sample at $x_0$ (ideally, the incident sample surface is perpendicular to the diffusion profile, but it may need to be altered if channeling along crystallographic axes occurs). The energy spectrum of the backscattered particles is collected by a detector at

## 4. DIFFUSION MEASUREMENTS: EXPERIMENTAL METHODS

some angle $\theta$ to the incident beam. The particles scattered from the surface of the sample ($x = 0$) have an energy $E_1$ (surface energy)

$$E_1 = K_m E_0$$

where $K_m$ is the kinematic recoil factor,

$$K_m = \frac{m \cos \theta + M^2 - m^2 \sin^2 \theta}{m + M}$$

where $M$ and $m$ are the masses of the target and analyzing particle, respectively. Values of $K_m$ are less than unity and increase with the mass of the target atom. Hence, the energy of the backscattered ions is less than that of the incident ions, and, for a given depth within the sample, ions scattered from heavy atoms have energies greater than those scattered from light atoms. As the incident ion penetrates into the sample it progressively loses energy until at some energy $E_2$ it undergoes a scattering collision and is backscattered with an initial energy $E_3$,

$$E_3 = E_2 K_m$$

The backscattered ion again loses energy on its outward path and arrives at the surface with an energy $E_4$. Therefore, the energy of a particular ion corresponds to a depth within the sample. Also, for a given counting geometry and incident current, the backscattered ion intensity is directly proportional to the concentration of target atoms. Hence, the energy spectrum can easily be related to the depth profile.

Backscattering spectroscopy has been put to great use in the semiconductor industry to determine the thicknesses of surface films and the depth of implants. Sensitivities as low as $5 \times 10^9$ atoms/cm$^2$ and energy resolutions as low as 0.5 keV have been obtained [8]. The energy resolution $\Delta E$ can be related to depth resolution $\Delta X$ by the material stopping power $S$,

$$\Delta X = \Delta E / S$$

To date, the technique has received little application in the determination of diffusion profiles in geologic materials. One limitation of the technique for geologic samples concerns the mass resolution at atomic number. For masses less than 40, isotopic species can be distinguished. For heavier elements mass differences greater than 10 are necessary for resolution. For instance, E. B. Watson and T. M. Harrison (1983, personal communication) attempted depth profiling of lead in zircon with $\alpha$-particle backscattering but were unable to resolve the lead signal from that produced by the hafnium within the sample.

Sneeringer et al. [64] have successfully used Rutherford backscattering (RBS) to determine strontium depth profiles in synthetic diopside. This

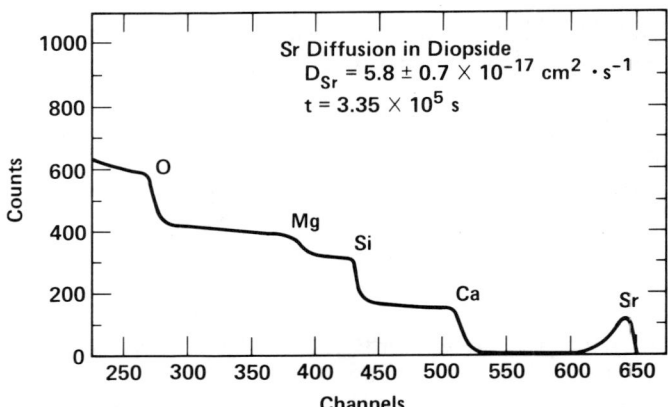

FIG. 14. Analysis of an Sr diffusion profile in diopside by Rutherford backscattering. The labels indicate the surface energies of oxygen, magnesium, silicon, calcium, and strontium. The "flat" curves for O, Mg, Si, and Ca indicate homogeneous distribution at depth. The decrease in Sr intensity at lower channel number (lower energy, greater depth) indicates a decrease in concentration. (After Sneeringer et al. [64].)

situation, a single heavy element in a light-element matrix, is ideal for the application of ion backscattering spectroscopy, allowing mass interferences to be minimized. The RBS spectrum from synthetic diopside diffused with strontium at 1100°C illustrates the technique (Fig. 14). The surface energies of the constituent atoms increase with atomic number for O, Mg, Si, Ca, and Sr. The signal intensity for the matrix atoms does not decrease at energies below their surface energy (in fact, the intensity increases slightly due to the additions of ions backscattered from heavier target atoms at greater depth). At energies below the strontium surface energy the signal intensity decreases, indicative of a decrease in strontium concentration with depth. In this example the gradient is approximately 150 nm deep.

5.4.3. *Secondary Ion Mass Spectrometry.* In secondary ion mass spectrometry or ion microprobe analysis, the surface of a sample is eroded by sputtering with an energetic primary ion beam. The primary ions are typically oxygen, argon, nitrogen, and cesium. The secondary ions produced during sputtering are then mass analyzed (quadrupole or magnetic mass spectrometry) and detected. As erosion proceeds, successively deeper regions in the sample are removed and analyzed. This process is excellently suited for in-depth analysis and has been used to great advantage in the analysis of dopants in electric devices (see [9] for a review) and, to a lesser extent, in analyzing diffusion profiles in crystals and glass or quenched melts [10–13, 63, 64, 72, 118–124].

In an in-depth profiling mode, SIMS analysis is capable of analyzing profiles as short as 30 nm [125]. The relative depth resolution in this mode,

$\Delta Z/Z$, where $\Delta Z$ is the broadening of a compositional discontinuity located at depth $Z$, is about 5% for most applications [9, 125, 126] and is limited by the mean escape depth of secondary ions produced by the sputtering process itself [127]. In addition, SIMS has very low limits of sensitivity ($10^{13}$ atoms/cm$^3$) and, unlike nuclear reaction and ion backscattering techniques, is applicable to the entire mass range. Multiple tracers in the same sample can also be measured without difficulty. The attributes make it an extremely valuable tool in measuring the low diffusivities typical of rock-forming minerals.

The factors which influence depth profiles measured by secondary ion mass spectrometry can be divided into those affecting (1) the measurement of depth and (2) the measurement of elemental composition. These factors, along with a summary of principles and applications, have been reviewed by Zinner [9] and are summarized in Table III. Depth measurement is largely influenced by a broadening of the true concentrations and/or an uncertainty in the depth from which a particular secondary ion signal is generated. Measurements of elemental concentrations are influenced when the detected signal over a given time increment is not truly indicative of the material eroded during that increment.

In general, many of the factors producing deviations from the true concentration profiles can be minimized through careful attention to instrumental

TABLE III. Factors Influencing Depth Profiles Measured by Secondary Ion Mass Spectrometry[a]

| Factors affecting measurement of depth | Factors affecting measurement of elemental concentrations |
|---|---|
| Time constancy of primary beam | Chemical effect |
| Constancy of erosion rate | Matrix effect |
| Preferential sputtering effects | Constancy of erosion rate |
| Uniformity of the primary beam, crater effect, edge effect, halo effect | Preferential sputtering effects |
| Microroughness of the crater bottom, faceting, cone formation | Chemical composition of the primary beam |
| Atomic mixing | Redeposition of sputtered material |
| Primary beam heating induced diffusion | Memory effect |
| Primary beam radiation enhanced diffusion | Recontamination by residual gas |
| Primary beam charging effects | Interferences |
| Lattice dilation | Noise, detection limits |
| Escape depth of sputtered ions | |
| Sample consumption | |

[a] After Zinner [9].

conditions. In measuring self-diffusion in geologic materials, the nature of the experiment, i.e., chemically homogeneous phases and isotopic tracers, also minimizes the effects of many additional factors. As examples, current instruments can achieve primary beam stabilities of 1% relative, thereby minimizing effects associated with variable erosion rates due to primary beam instability. For self-diffusion experiments, an isotope of a matrix element (one for which no gradient exists) can be measured in order to track variations in secondary ion beam intensity. Primary beam charging effects can be controlled by deposition of metal films or placement of conducting grids on the surface of insulating samples or, in some cases (positive primary beam), by use of an electron flood gun. Microroughness of the sputter crater can be minimized by rastering with a small primary beam or through use of a static defocused beam. Edge and halo effects are limited through use of a raster pattern which is large with respect to the analyzed area. Edge effects and, to some extent, the effect of redeposition of sputtered material are further limited by placement of a physical aperture within the virtual image plane of the secondary ion optics [12, 65]; or by electronic gating of the detection system such that only ions emitted from the central portion of the imaged field are counted [73]. Molecular interferences can be eliminated through a combination of high mass resolution and energy filtering (the energy distribution of atomic ions displays a more pronounced skewedness toward high energies than do molecular ions) by use of a sample voltage offset in combination with mechanical slits. High mass resolution and energy filtering to overcome molecular interferences raise the minimum sensitivity limit for which SIMS is useful [128].

Of particular interest in measuring elemental concentrations are chemical and matrix effects and the effects of preferential sputtering. The chemical effect is extremely important in depth profiling of metals with nitrogen or argon beams. Here the presence of oxygen, or another reactive gas on the sample surface, increases the yield of positive secondary ions [129, 130]. Electropositive elements have a similar effect on negative secondary ion yields. Bombardment with primary oxygen and cesium beams minimizes this problem (a small initial transient is still observed while a steady state between primary ion implantation and sputtering is obtained). Nevertheless, this should not be a problem in the analysis of oxide phases.

The matrix effect refers to the composition-dependent ion yield of elements in multielement samples. However, since only relative intensities are required for diffusion measurements, this effect too is eliminated.

Zinner [131] has demonstrated the effects of preferential sputtering on elemental depth profiling in a homogeneous feldspar crystal. Ideally, secondary ion yields should remain constant with depth. This is the case, except for a short initial transient. The transient results from depletion of elements with high sputter rates from the sample surface. The transient persists until a steady state is achieved in which the high sputter rate material is replenished from below [128, 131].

Another effect which is of particular interest when measuring the diffusivities of oxygen is the mixing or dilution of the $^{18}O$ tracer and matrix $^{16}O$ with $^{16}O$ from the primary beam [11]. In order to assess this effect, Giletti et al. [11] analyzed an anorthite which had been exchanged in an $^{18}O$-enriched solution with $N^-$ and $O^-$ primary beams. High $^{18}O/^{16}O$ ratios were obtained with the $N^-$, corroborating the dilution. They concluded that dilution takes place in two modes: (1) an initial transient in which oxygen from the primary beam dilutes that in the secondary, which is followed by (2) a steady-state dilution through primary beam implantation. Since only $^{18}O$ and $^{16}O$ are analyzed (along with selected matrix elements), a possible, though somewhat expensive, solution to this dilution problem is an $^{17}O$ primary beam.

Many of the effects noted above produce an initial transient deviation from the true composition. Also, the concentration gradients may be quite steep at low penetrations. Both factors make the true initial concentration difficult to estimate. As discussed for electron microprobe analysis, this requires using the gradient at depth coupled with the appropriate solution to Fick's second law to estimate the true surface concentration. This technique has the advantage of avoiding the data for perturbed initial transients and focusing on data for the steady-state regime.

A final problem is "knock-on", in which tracer atoms are implanted farther into the sample by collisions with ions from the primary beam. This has the effect of both broadening and deepening the profile. The effect can be minimized by use of a primary beam with low energy and high mass/charge ratio [76], but it will always be present to some extent. When possible, the significance of this effect can be evaluated by use of a zero-time experiment in which the entire experimental assembly is brought to run conditions and then quenched. The sample is analyzed by the normal procedure. The resulting "profile" can then be used as a baseline for comparison with the actual diffusion anneals.

Unfortunately, there are relatively few studies in which diffusion profiles analyzed by SIMS have undergone analysis by another depth profiling technique. However, in cases where comparisons can be made, the agreement with other methods is good. Sneeringer [63] has analyzed strontium diffusion profiles in diopside by serial sectioning, Rutherford backscattering, and SIMS techniques. These results agree within a factor of 2 for profiles as short as 70 nm. Similar agreement was demonstrated between resonance and nonresonance nuclear reaction depth profiling and SIMS for the analysis of oxygen diffusion profiles in forsterite [12]. These studies show that, when technique-specific instrumental effects are properly evaluated, the agreement between instrumental depth profiling techniques can be excellent.

In addition to the depth profiling mode, SIMS may be used in a step-scanning mode in a manner similar to that used for the electron microprobe [123, 124]. The spatial resolution in this mode can be comparable to that obtained with the electron probe. This allows SIMS analysis to be used in analyzing diffusion gradients over a larger penetration range than any other technique.

## 6. Summary

Investigations of phase equilibria are required to demonstrate the attainment of equilibrium. In studies of diffusion it must be demonstrated that the phenomenon being observed is truly diffusion and not some other means of chemical transport. Simple demonstration of Arrhenius behavior does not constitute such proof, as many physical processed may display this relation.

Time series and zero-time experiments provide important data in establishing the measurement of diffusive behavior. The zero-time experiment isolates the contribution of transport phenomena other than diffusion. This type of experiment should be performed early in a study since it will alert the experimenter to any major flaws in experimental design. For constant external conditions, the measured diffusivity remains constant with time if diffusion is the only process involved. Typically, experiments of shorter duration yield greater apparent diffusivities, which decrease and become constant with time. The attainment of constant diffusivities at one set of conditions yields a value of $Dt$ which may be used to guide the selection of run times at other conditions. It should be noted that the foregoing applies only to concentration independent diffusion. Consideration of concentration dependent diffusion is beyond the scope of this chapter. However, this process is also amenable to the experimental techniques described here. Examples of solutions to concentration dependent diffusion problems are given in Shewmon [17] and Crank [19].

The most detailed information obtainable for demonstrating diffusive behavior is the direct determination of a diffusion gradient. The ability to compare observed and predicted profiles is the single strongest argument for use of direct observation techniques versus the fractional exchange technique. It also makes the determination of variations in diffusivity as a function of crystallographic orientation much simpler.

Advantages and disadvantages of the various direct techniques and the applicable diffusion ranges in terms of $Dt$ [experimentally observable penetration distances are on the order of $2(Dt)^{1/2}$] are given in Table IV and

TABLE IV. Summary of Analytical Techniques for Direct Measurement of Diffusion Profiles

| Method | Advantages | Disadvantages |
|---|---|---|
| Autoradiography | Fast, inexpensive, nondestructive. Enables visual inspection of tracer distribution. | Single tracer technique, poor spatial resolution. Production of emitting daughters. Many elements without suitable tracers. |
| Serial sectioning | Multiple tracers. Inexpensive. | Time-consuming, destructive. Subject to sectioning error. Many elements without suitable tracers. |
| Electron microprobe | Fast, nondestructive. Available. | Chemical diffusion only. Low $Z$ not possible. |
| SIMS | Superior depth resolution. Multiple tracers, high sensitivity, full mass range, high mass resolution, large range in $Dt$. | Instrumental effects. Molecular interferences. Destructive, expensive. |
| Nuclear reactions | Superior depth resolution. Fast, high sensitivity, nondestructive. | Single tracer. Limited to low $Z$. Competing reactions. |
| Ion backscattering | Superior depth resolution. High sensitivity. Multiple tracers (?). | Low mass resolution. |

Fig. 15, respectively. The choice of technique is dependent on (1) the type of diffusion to be measured, self-, tracer, or chemical diffusion, (2) the element or elements (in the case of multiple tracers), (3) the concentration of the tracer in the sample, sensitivity, and (4) the predicted penetration range.

If chemical diffusion is the process of interest, the electron microprobe is the technique of choice. The technique is limited to profiles longer than 5 μm (Fig. 15) and is also limited solely to measurements of chemical diffusion.

The remaining techniques are largely applicable to studies of tracer and self-diffusion. The element of interest is a major determinant of analytical technique. Serial sectioning and autoradiography require the availability of suitable radiotracers. Such tracers are unavailable for many low-$Z$ elements, limiting the applicability of these techniques. Further, autoradiography requires either positron- or electron-emitting radiotracers. Autoradiography is also limited to the use of one tracer at a time. Multiple tracers can be used in serial sectioning analysis. SIMS is also amenable to the use of multiple tracers. The difficulty here involves the finite measurement time for each

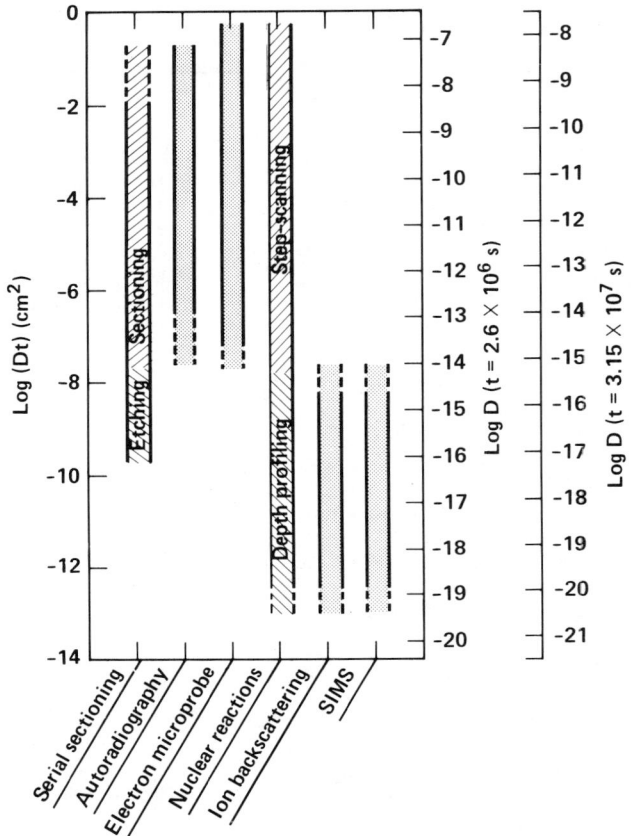

Fig. 15. Ranges of applicability ($Dt$) for the direct analysis technique. Diffusivities corresponding to run durations of 30 days and 1 year are given on the right.

tracer. If the time required to make statistically significant measurements on all the tracers is longer than the time required to sputter through the profile, there will obviously be a problem. In such cases the number of tracers must be reduced. SIMS is the only technique applicable over the entire periodic table. Nuclear reaction analysis is limited to low-$Z$ elements by the energy limitations of available accelerators and the increasing number of competing reactions as incident ion energies increase. Ion backscattering is also applicable over a large mass range, but exploitation of this capability and the use of multiple tracers are complicated by poor mass resolution.

The type of diffusion and element of interest narrow the choice of analytical technique. Penetration range and availability dictate the final choice. If penetrations are large ($Dt > 10^{-7}$ cm$^2$) and the appropriate tracers available, then either serial sectioning or autoradiography can be used. Both are straightforward and inexpensive to implement. For small penetrations, SIMS, ion backscattering, or nuclear reaction analysis must be employed. Again, the choice depends on the availability of the element of interest, although SIMS has the largest range of applicability for both element of interest and penetration.

There are many ways of conducting and analyzing diffusion experiments. The development of state-of-the-art technology such as SIMS and the application of analytical techniques previously employed in other areas of materials science to geological materials are sure to extend the number and range of geological diffusion measurements to lower and more relevant ranges. In this pursuit, the geoscientist has much to gain from collaborative efforts with workers in nuclear physics and chemistry, semiconductors, and materials science.

## Acknowledgments

The preparation of this review was partially supported by the Department of Energy's Office of Basic Energy Sciences. The author is grateful to K. B. Schwartz for the use of his unpublished data. The author would also like to express his gratitude to all of the other investigators and organizations who allowed their illustrations to be reproduced here. Thanks are also due Ralph Condit and Randall Cygan for their reviews and Donna Scacutto for typing the manuscript.

## References

1. J. B. Brady and R. A. Yund, *Am. Mineral.* **68**, 106-111 (1983).
2. J. B. Brady and R. H. McCallister, *Am. Mineral.* **68**, 95-105 (1983).
3. R. A. Yund, *in* "Reviews in Mineralogy: Feldspar Mineralogy" (P. Ribbe, ed.), 2nd ed., p. 362. Mineral. Soc. Am., Washington, D.C.
4. K. Nagy and E. M. Parmentier, *Trans. Am. Geophys. Union* **62**, 428 (1981).
5. A. W. Hofmann and S. R. Hart, *Earth Planet. Sci. Lett.* **38**, 44-62 (1978).
6. R. N. Clayton, N. Onuma, L. Grossman, and T. K. Mayeda, *Earth Planet. Sci. Lett.* **34**, 209-224 (1979).
7. R. Freer, *Contrib. Mineral. Petrol.* **76**, 440-454 (1981).
8. W. K. Chu, J. W. Mayer, M. A. Nicolet, T. M. Buck, G. Amsel, and F. Eisen, *Thin Solid Films* **19**, 423-463 (1973).
9. E. Zinner, *Scanning* **3**, 57-78 (1980).
10. A. W. Hofmann, B. J. Giletti, J. R. Hinthorne, C. A. Andersen, and D. A. Comaford, *Earth Planet. Sci. Lett.* **24**, 48-52 (1974).
11. B. J. Giletti, M. P. Semet, and R. A. Yund, *Geochim. Cosmochim. Acta* **42**, 45-58 (1978).
12. O. Jaoul, C. Froidevaux, W. B. Durham, and M. Michaut, *Earth Planet. Sci. Lett.* **47**, 391-397 (1980).
13. O. Jaoul, M. Poumellec, C. Froidevaux, and A. Havette, *in* "Anelasticity in the Earth" (F. D. Stacey, M. S. Paterson, and A. Nicolas, eds.), pp. 95-100. Am. Geophys. Union, Washington, D.C., 1981.
14. O. Jaoul, B. Houlier, and F. Abel, *J. Geophys. Res.* **88**, 613-624 (1983).

15. K. P. R. Reddy, S. M. Oh, L. D. Major, Jr., and A. R. Cooper, *J. Geophys. Res.* **85**, 322–326 (1980).
16. J. R. Manning, "Diffusion Kinetics in Atomic Crystals." Van Nostrand, Princeton, New Jersey, 1968.
17. P. G. Shewmon, "Diffusion in Solids," p. 203. McGraw-Hill, New York, 1963.
18. A. W. Hofmann, "Diffusion in Silicate Melts: A Critical Review in Physics of Magmatic Processes" (R. B. Hargraves, ed.), pp. 385–418. Princeton Univ. Press, Princeton, New Jersey, 1980.
19. J. Crank, "The Mathematics of Diffusion," 2nd ed., p. 414. Oxford Univ. Press, London and New York, 1975.
20. A. K. Varshneya, A. R. Cooper, R. B. Diegle, and S. A. Chin, *J. Am. Ceram. Soc.* **56**, 245–247 (1973).
21. A. W. Hofmann and L. Brown, *Year Book Carnegie Inst. Wash.* **75**, 259–262 (1976).
22. R. H. Condit and J. B. Holt, *J. Electrochem. Soc.* **111**, 1192–1194 (1964).
23. J. B. Holt and R. H. Condit, "Materials Science Research," Vol. 3. Plenum, New York, 1966.
24. Y. Oishi and W. D. Kingery, *J. Chem. Phys.* **33**, 480–486 (1960).
25. Y. Oishi, K. Ando, and Y. Kubota, *J. Chem. Phys.* **73**, 1410–1412 (1980).
26. Y. Oishi, K. Ando, N. Suga, and W. D. Kingery, *J. Am. Ceram. Soc.* **66**, C130–C131 (1983).
27. K. P. R. Reddy, and A. R. Cooper, *J. Am. Ceram. Soc.* **65**, 634–638 (1982).
28. B. J. Giletti, *in* "Geochemical Transport and Kinetics" (A. W. Hofmann, B. J. Giletti, H. S. Yoder, Jr., and R. A. Yund, eds.), *Carnegie Inst. Wash. Publ.* No. 634, 61–76 (1974).
29. W. Komatsu, Y. Ikuma, M. Kato, and K. Uematsu, *J. Am. Ceram. Soc.* **65**, C211–C212 (1982).
30. A. W. Hofmann and B. J. Giletti, *Ecol. Geol. Helv.* **63**, 141–150 (1970).
31. T. H. Lin and R. A. Yund, *Contrib. Mineral. Petrol.* **34**, 177–184 (1972).
32. K. A. Foland, *Geochim. Cosmochim. Acta* **38**, 151–166 (1974).
33. R. A. Yund and T. F. Anderson, *Geochim. Cosmochim. Acta* **42**, 235–239 (1978).
34. A. E. Mussett, *Geophys. J. R. Astron. Soc.* **18**, 257–303 (1969).
35. K. A. Foland, *in* "Geochemical Transport and Kinetics" (A. W. Hofmann, B. J. Giletti, H. S. Yoder, Jr., and R. A. Yund, eds.), *Carnegie Inst. Wash. Publ.* No. 634, 77–98 (1974).
36. K. Muehlenbachs and I. Kushiro, *Year Book Carnegie Inst. Wash.* **73**, 232–236 (1974).
37. K. Muehlenbachs and H. A. Schaeffer, *Can. Mineral.* **15**, 179–184 (1977).
38. T. Dunn, *Geochim. Cosmochim. Acta* **46**, 2293–2299 (1982).
39. K. P. R. Reddy and A. R. Cooper, *J. Am. Ceram. Soc.* **66**, 664–666 (1983).
40. H. Yinnon and A. R. Cooper, *Phys. Chem. Glasses* **21**, 204–211 (1980).
41. R. Wendlandt, *Trans. Am. Geophys. Union* **61**, 1142 (1980).
42. T. Dunn, *Trans. Am. Geophys. Union* **63**, 1141 (1982).
43. W. J. Harrison and B. J. Wood, *Contrib. Mineral. Petrol.* **72**, 145–155 (1980).
44. E. B. Watson and T. H. Green, *Earth Planet. Sci. Lett.* **56**, 405–421 (1981).
45. T. M. Harrison and E. B. Watson, *Contrib. Mineral. Petrol.* **84**, 66–72 (1983).
46. R. Lindner, *J. Chem. Phys.* **23**, 410–411 (1955).
47. R. Lindner and G. D. Parfitt, *J. Chem. Phys.* **26**, 182–185 (1957).
48. J. Rungis and A. J. Mortlock, *Philos. Mag.* **14**, 821–827 (1966).
49. B. C. Harding, *Philos. Mag.* **16**, 1039–1048 (1967).
50. W. K. Chen, N. L. Peterson, and W. T. Reeves, *Phys. Rev.* **186**, 887–891 (1969).
51. M. L. Volpe, N. L. Peterson, and J. Reddy, *Phys. Rev. B* **3**, 1417–1421 (1971).

52. B. C. Harding and D. M. Price, *Philos. Mag.* **26**, 253–260 (1972).
53. W. K. Chen and N. L. Peterson, *J. Phys. Chem. Solids* **36**, 1097–1103 (1975).
54. A. Jambon and J. P. Carron, *Geochim. Cosmochim. Acta* **40**, 897–904 (1976).
55. A. W. Hofmann and M. Margaritz, *J. Geophys. Res.* **82**, 5432–5440 (1977).
56. M. Margaritz and A. W. Hofmann, *Geochim. Cosmochim. Acta* **42**, 595–605 (1978).
57. M. Margaritz and A. W. Hofmann, *Geochim. Cosmochim. Acta* **42**, 847–858 (1978).
58. W. K. Chen and N. L. Peterson, *J. Phys. Chem. Solids* **41**, 335–339 (1980).
59. W. K. Chen and N. L. Peterson, *J. Phys. Chem. Solids* **41**, 647–652 (1980).
60. N. L. Peterson, W. K. Chen, and D. Wolf, *J. Phys. Chem. Solids* **41**, 709–719 (1980).
61. N. L. Peterson and W. K. Chen, *J. Phys. Chem. Solids* **43**, 29–38 (1982).
62. A. Jambon, *J. Geophys. Res.* **87**, 10797–10810 (1983).
63. M. A. Sneeringer, Strontium and samarium diffusion in diopside. Ph.D. Thesis, MIT, Cambridge, Massachusetts, 1981.
64. M. A. Sneeringer, S. R. Hart, and N. Shimizu, *Geochim. Cosmochim. Acta* **48**, 1589–1603 (1984).
65. G. A. Medford, *J. Earth Sci.* **10**, 394–402 (1973).
66. A. Jambon and M. Sennet, *Earth Planet. Sci. Lett.* **37**, 445–450 (1978).
67. E. B. Watson, *Geochim. Cosmochim. Acta* **43**, 313–322 (1979).
68. E. B. Watson, *Science* **205**, 1259–1260 (1979).
69. E. B. Watson, *Earth Planet. Sci. Lett.* **53**, 291–301 (1981).
70. E. B. Watson, *Earth Planet. Sci. Lett.* **61**, 346–358 (1982).
71. D. S. Tannhauser, *J. Appl. Phys.* **27**, 662 (1956).
72. R. T. Cygan and A. Lasaga, *Am. J. Sci.* **285**, 328–350 (1985).
73. D. J. Reed and B. J. Wuensch, *J. Am. Ceram. Soc.* **63**, 88–92 (1980).
74. R. F. Sippel, *Geochem. Cosmochim. Acta* **27**, 107–120 (1963).
75. N. K. Misra and V. S. Venkatasubramanian, *Geochim. Cosmochim. Acta* **41**, 837–858 (1977).
76. E. Zinner, R. M. Walker, J. Chaumont, and J. C. Dran, *Geochim. Cosmochim. Acta, Suppl.* No. 7, 953–984 (1976).
77. G. H. Frischat and H. J. Oel, *Z. Angew. Phys.* **20**, 195–201 (1966).
78. A. Jambon, *Trans. Am. Geophys. Union* **69**, 409 (1979).
79. G. H. Frischat, "Ionic Diffusion in Oxide Glasses." Transtech. Publ., Bay Village, Ohio, 1975.
80. S. F. Rahman and M. F. Berard, *J. Am. Ceram. Soc.* **60**, 67–71 (1977).
81. G. W. Weber, W. R. Bitler, and V. S. Stubican, *J. Am. Ceram. Soc.* **60**, 61–64 (1977).
82. R. Freer, *J. Mater. Sci.* **15**, 803–824 (1980).
83. B. J. Wuensch and T. Vasilos, *J. Chem. Phys.* **36**, 2917–2922 (1962).
84. B. J. Wuensch and T. Vasilos, *J. Chem. Phys.* **42**, 4113–4115 (1965).
85. B. J. Wuensch and T. Vasilos, *J. Chem. Phys.* **54**, 1123–1129 (1971).
86. M. G. Seitz, *Year Book Carnegie Inst. Wash.* **72**, 586–588 (1973).
87. T. M. Benjamin, N. T. Arndt, and J. R. Holloway, *Year Book Carnegie Inst. Wash.* **76**, 658–659 (1977).
88. J. R. Holloway and M. J. Drake, *Geochim. Cosmochim. Acta* **41**, 1395–1397 (1977).
89. C. C. Lo and D. E. Schuele, *J. Appl. Phys.* **46**, 5004–5009 (1975).
90. P. M. Hall and J. M. Morabito, *Surf. Sci.* **54**, 79–90 (1976).
91. G. Friedlander, J. W. Kennedy, and J. M. Miller, "Nuclear and Radiochemistry," 2nd ed. Wiley, New York, 1964.
92. B. O. Mysen and M. G. Seitz, *J. Geophys. Res.* **80**, 2627–2635 (1974).
93. K. F. J. Heinrich, "Electron Beam X-Ray Microanalysis." Van Nostrand-Reinhold, New York, 1981.

94. A. K. Varshneya and A. R. Cooper, *J. Am. Ceram. Soc.* **55**, 312 (1972).
95. D. J. Misener, *Year Book Carnegie Inst. Wash.* **71**, 516-520 (1972).
96. D. J. Misener, *Year Book Carnegie Inst. Wash.* **73**, 117-129 (1974).
97. D. K. Buening and P. R. Buseck, *J. Geophys. Res.* **78**, 6852-6862 (1973).
98. A. M. Clark and J. V. P. Long, in "Thomas Graham Memorial Symposium on Diffusion Processes," pp. 511-521. Gordon & Breach, London, 1971.
99. H. D. Smith, An experimental study of diffusion of Na, K, and Rb in magmatic silicate liquids. Ph.D. Thesis, Univ. of Oregon, Eugene, 1974.
100. E. B. Watson, T. M. Harrison, and F. J. Ryerson, *Geochim. Cosmochim. Acta* **49**, 1813-1824 (1985).
101. S. J. B. Reed and J. V. P. Long, in "X-Ray Optics and X-Ray Microanalysis" (H. H. Pattee, V. E. Coslett, and A. Engstrom, eds.), p. 317. Academic Press, New York, 1963.
102. G. Amsel, J. P. Nadai, E. D'Artemare, D. David, E. Girard, and J. Moulin, *Nucl. Instrum. Methods* **92**, 481-498 (1971).
103. R. W. Ollerhead, E. Almquist, and Knehner, *J. Appl. Phys.* **37**, 2440 (1966).
104. B. Cox and C. Roy, *Electrochem. Technol.* **4**, 122-127 (1966).
105. G. Amsel and D. Samuel, *Anal. Chem.* **39**, 1689-1698 (1967).
106. G. Amsel, G. Beranger, B. de Gelas, and P. Lacombe, *J. Appl. Phys.* **39**, 2246-2255 (1968).
107. G. Amsel, D. David, G. Beranger, and P. Boiset, *Rev. Phys. Appl.* **3**, 373-386 (1968).
108. G. Amsel, D. David, G. Beranger, P. Boisot, B. de Gelas, and P. Lacombe, *J. Nucl. Mater.* **29**, 144-153 (1969).
109. A. Choudhury, D. W. Palmer, G. Amsel, H. Curien, and P. Baruch, *Solid State Commun.* **3**, 119-122 (1965).
110. D. W. Palmer, *Nucl. Instrum. Methods* **38**, 187-191 (1965).
111. R. Robin, A. R. Cooper, and A. H. Heuer, *J. Appl. Phys.* **44**, 3770-3777 (1973).
112. A. L'Hoir, D. Schmaus, J. Cawley, and O. Jaoul, *Nucl. Instrum. Methods* **191**, 357-366 (1981).
113. R. S. Rajan, C. L. Melcher, S. Faragalla, M. H. Mendenhall, and T. A. Tombrello, *Lunar Planet. Sci.* **XIV**, 625 (1983).
114. Z. Hadari, M. Kroupp, and V. Wolfson, *J. Appl. Phys.* **42**, 534-535 (1971).
115. R. Condit, H. C. Weed, and A. W. Piwinskii, "Point Defects in Minerals," Monogr. No. 31. Am. Geophys. Union, Washington, D.C., 1985.
116. R. N. Ghoshtagore, *Phys. Rev. Lett.* **16**, 890-892 (1966).
117. H. A. Schaeffer, *Phys. Status Solidi* **22**, 281-291 (1974).
118. J. N. Coles and J. V. P. Long, *Philos. Mag.* **29**, 457-471 (1974).
119. A. Jambon and M. Semet, *Earth Planet. Sci. Lett.* **37**, 445-450 (1978).
120. H. G. Sockel, D. Hallwig, and R. Schachtner, *Mater. Sci. Eng.* **42**, 59-64 (1980).
121. J. R. Delaney and J. L. Karsten, *Earth Planet. Sci. Lett.* **52**, 191-202 (1981).
122. R. K. Lowry, S. J. B. Reed, J. Nolan, P. Henderson, and J. V. P. Long, *Earth Planet. Sci. Lett.* **53**, 36-40 (1981).
123. A. Ross, *Lunar Planet. Sci.* **14**, 650-651 (1983).
124. N. Shimizu and I. Kushiro, *Trans. Am. Geophys. Union* **64**, 347 (1983).
125. R. E. Pawel, J. P. Pemsler, and C. A. Evans, Jr., *J. Electrochem. Soc.* **119**, 24-29 (1972).
126. H. W. Werner, *Vacuum* **24**, 493-504 (1974).
127. C. A. Evans, Jr., *J. Vac. Sci. Technol.* **12**, 144-155 (1975).
128. N. Shimizu and S. R. Hart, *Annu. Rev. Earth Planet. Sci.* **10**, 483-523 (1981).
129. G. Slodzian, and Hennequin, *C. R. Hebd. Seances Acad. Sci., Ser. B* **263**, 1246-1249 (1966).
130. G. Slodzian, *Ann. Phys. (Paris)* **9**, 591-648 (1964).
131. E. Zinner, *Proc. Annu. Conf. Microbeam Anal. Soc.* **13**, 32A-32D (1978).

# 5. ROCK FRACTURE AND FRICTIONAL SLIDING

## Hartmut Spetzler

Department of Geological Sciences and
Cooperative Institute for Research in Environmental Sciences
University of Colorado
Boulder, Colorado 80309

## Symbols in Order of Appearance in the Chapter

| | |
|---|---|
| $K_i$ | Stress intensity factor for mode $i$ |
| $\sigma_{ij}$ | Stress component |
| $c$ | Crack length |
| $K_{IC}$ | Fracture toughness |
| $\nu$ | Poisson ratio |
| $P$ | Load |
| $d$ | Sample thickness; see Fig. 3 |
| $d_n$ | See Fig. 3 |
| $W$ | Sample width; see Figs. 3 and 7 |
| $W_m$ | see Fig. 3 |
| $\xi$ | Stress intensity correction factor for thick specimens |
| $\alpha$ | $2d/W$ |
| $\lambda$ | Compliance of double torsion specimen |
| $\Delta$ | Deflection of double torsion specimen |
| $B$ | Slope of compliance vs. crack length curve |
| $\lambda_0$ | Compliance at zero crack length |
| $G$ | Shear modulus |
| $t$ | Time |
| $y$ | Displacement |
| $dy/dt$ | Displacement rate |
| $v$ | Crack tip velocity |
| $t_0$ | Specimen thickness; see Fig. 7 |
| $W$ | Specimen width; see Fig. 7 |
| $W_m$ | Specimen width between grooves; see Fig. 7 |
| $b$ | Specimen thickness; see Fig. 12 |
| $h$ | Specimen width; see Fig. 9 |
| $M$ | Applied moment; see Fig. 10 |
| $I$ | Moment of inertia of one arm; see Fig. 10 |
| $E$ | Young's modulus |
| $h$ | Specimen half-width; see Fig. 11 |
| $L$ | See Fig. 12 |
| $l$ | See Fig. 12 |

$c'_0$      $(c_0/d)$; see Fig. 12 and Eqs. (12) and (13)
$q_i$      Volume flow per unit time; see Eq. (14)
$k_{ij}$      Permeability tensor
$\mu$      Viscosity of fluid
$dP/dx_j$      Pressure gradient

## 1. Introduction

In this chapter various aspects of experimental rock fracture are discussed. No attempt has been made to be complete nor has the subject been treated historically. New and novel ideas have received special attention, not because they are necessarily more important than the more conventional approaches, but because they are not as readily available to the traditional rock-mechanician and because they make the arduous task of writing more palatable. Much duplication with the existing literature is thus avoided. References to rock mechanics books, containing nearly up-to-date references, are given throughout the chapter.

An understanding of the propagation of single cracks is paramount to eventually being able to predict the large-scale failure of rocks. The study of single cracks is therefore treated first, followed by measurements that can be made within a pressure vessel. Optical holography and new strain gauge technology are introduced there. The section on acoustic emissions includes up-to-date developments in transducers. Potential and often ignored problems that plague the interpretation of frictional sliding are pointed out in the section on frictional sliding. The application of radioactive tracers in permeability and gas conduit studies is introduced in the last section.

## 2. Single-Crack Propagation

Brittle failure in rocks occurs by the interaction of individual microcracks, which grow in response to the stress field, the temperature, and the chemical environment at their tips. It is paramount to understand the mechanisms that control single-crack propagation if we ever expect to reliably predict failure of rocks under engineering or geological conditions. The techniques for the study of single-crack propagation were developed initially for ductile materials like metals.[1] They were modified for brittle amorphous materials like glasses[2] and more recently for ceramics and rock.[3,4]

Before describing the experimental techniques that are involved in single crack propagation we must define the fracture parameters that can be measured. There are three modes of fracture. They are illustrated in Fig. 1. Mode I is by far the most important mode of propagation in brittle materials. In isotropic materials cracks have a tendency to propagate in a direction

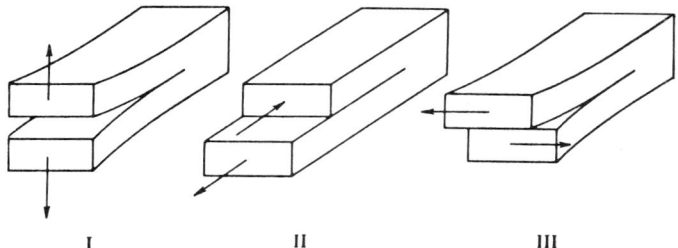

FIG. 1. The three modes of fracture: I, opening mode; II, sliding mode; III, tearing mode. (With permission from Cambridge Univ. Press; see reference 7.)

normal to the maximum tensile stress. Mode II and mode III propagation occur in general only in highly ductile materials such as polymers and highly plastic metals. Shear fractures also occur in geologic situations where the large confining pressures suppress large-scale tensile ruptures. On a small scale, however, microcrack growth may indeed occur under mode I loading.[5,6] Figure 2[7] together with Eq. (1) gives the definition for the

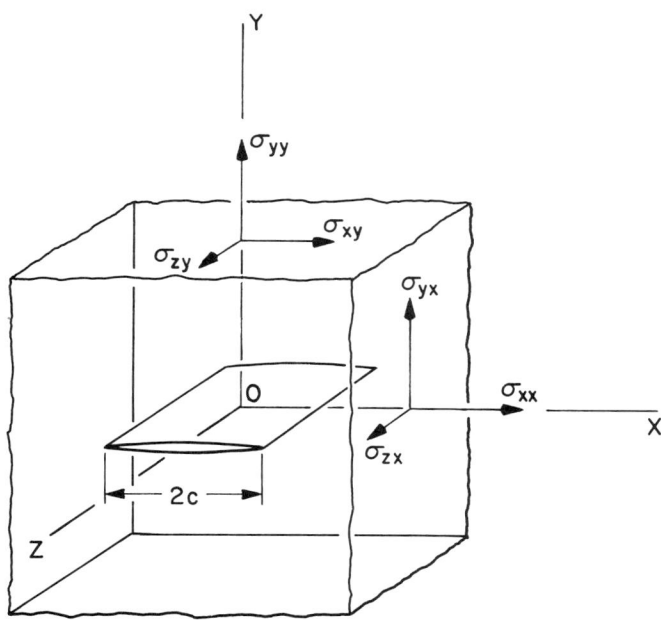

FIG. 2. Uniform loading configurations for plane cracks with straight fronts: internal crack in infinite plate (all modes operating). (With permission from Cambridge Univ. Press; see reference 7.)

stress-intensity factors for all three modes for homogeneous loading in the infinite plate approximation.

$$K_\mathrm{I} = (\sigma_{yy})_\mathrm{L}(\pi c)^{1/2} \tag{1}$$

$$K_\mathrm{II} = (\sigma_{xy})_\mathrm{L}(\pi c)^{1/2}$$

$$K_\mathrm{III} = (\sigma_{zy})_\mathrm{L}(\pi c)^{1/2}$$

Note that the stress-intensity factors depend linearly on the remotely applied stress $(\sigma_{ij})_\mathrm{L}$ and on the crack length $c$ to the 1/2 power. The form is the same for all three modes.

The fracture toughness $K_\mathrm{IC}$ is a material property applicable under mode I loading. Crack growth occurs subcritically for values of $K_\mathrm{I} < K_\mathrm{IC}$ and unstably for values of $K_\mathrm{I} \geq K_\mathrm{IC}$. Several techniques have been developed to measure crack growth parameters and fracture toughness.

## 3. Double Torsion Technique

A double torsion (DT) specimen and associated loading arrangement are shown in Fig. 3. Thin plates, similar in geometry to microscope slides, are subjected to torsion which results in crack growth under mode I loading.

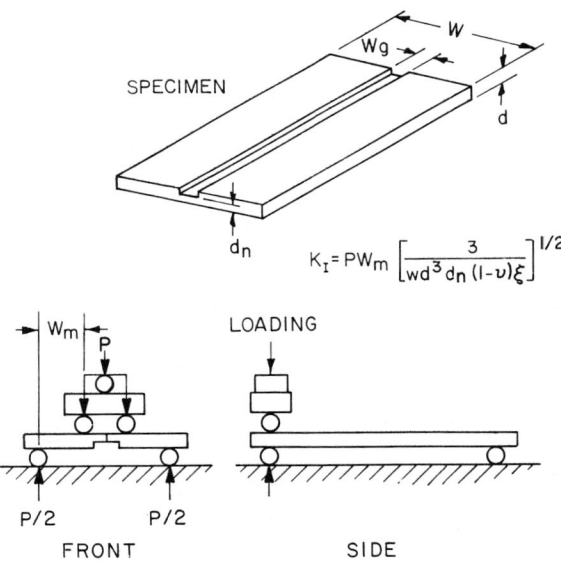

FIG. 3. Double torsion specimen with loading arrangement. P, Applied load. Geometric parameters are defined in the figure, others in the text through Eqs. (2) and (3). (With permission from ASTM; see reference 9.)

In general, a side groove guides the crack while it is propagating. Fuller[8] and Pletka et al.[9] give evaluations and detailed descriptions of the double torsion technique. The specimen geometry is such that the stress-intensity factor is independent of crack length over most of the sample length; i.e., a DT specimen is a "constant $K$" specimen. From the change in torsional compliance with crack extension, the relationship between $K_I$ and the specimen dimensions is

$$K_I = PW_m[3/Wd^3 d_n(1 - \nu)\xi]^{1/2} \qquad (2)$$

where $P$ is the load, $\nu$ is Poisson's ratio, and the other terms are defined in Fig. 3. The $\xi$ is a geometric correction factor for specimen thickness. It is given to within 0.1% by

$$\xi = 1 - 0.6302\alpha + 1.20\alpha e^{-\pi/\alpha} \qquad (3)$$

where $\alpha$ is the thickness ratio, $\alpha = 2d/W$. The independence of $K_I$ on crack length makes it possible to use opaque specimens. It is not necessary to observe the crack tip, which greatly facilitates the adaption of this technique to hostile environments such as high temperature and corrosive chemicals. Williams and Evans[10] and Evans[11] have shown that the compliance $\lambda$ of the DT specimens depends linearly on the crack length $c$, i.e.,

$$\lambda = \Delta/P = (Bc + \lambda_0) \qquad (4)$$

where $\Delta$ is the deflection of the plate, $B$ the slope of the compliance versus crack length curve, and $\lambda_0$ the intercept, i.e., the compliance at zero crack length. The slope $B$ may also be determined analytically as

$$B = 3W_m^2/Wd^3 G \qquad (5)$$

where $G$ is the shear modulus.

In practice, there are three ways of obtaining the crack velocity without visual observations. In all cases the specimen is precracked; that is, a crack is initiated either by increasing the load incrementally or applying a constant displacement rate until crack initiation is noted by a sudden decrease in the load.

In constant load experiments the deflection of the sample is measured as the crack propagates. The crack tip velocity $v$ can be obtained directly from the deflection rate through the compliance equation, Eq. (4). The constant load technique is especially useful at very low crack propagation rates and at very high temperatures, where extraneous relaxations of the apparatus can otherwise become a problem.

Evans and Wiederhorn[12] showed that a constant displacement rate $dy/dt$ could be achieved at a load plateau such that

$$v = \frac{dy/dt}{PB} \qquad (6)$$

Thus when equilibrium crack propagation has been achieved the constant displacement rate and constant load experiments are equivalent. They are only different in the manner in which equilibrium is reached. Servo-controlled equipment is almost necessary if both of these techniques are to be used with the same apparatus. Constant load and constant displacement rate testing devices correspond to soft and stiff machines, respectively.

The load relaxation method is generally the preferred method for obtaining $K_I$-$v$ data. Williams and Evans[10] also showed that for a fixed grip (constant displacement) experiment, the crack tip velocity depends on the instantaneous load and on the corresponding load relaxation rate ($dP/dt$)

$$v = \frac{-\Delta}{BP^2}\left(\frac{dP}{dt}\right) \approx -\frac{(P_{i,f})(c_{i,f})}{P^2}\left(\frac{dP}{dt}\right) \qquad (7)$$

where $P_i$ is the initial load, $P_f$ the final load, $c_i$ the initial crack length, and $c_f$ the final crack length. The load decreases as the crack propagates. The crack tip velocity can then be calculated from a load versus time record (Fig. 4) and initial or final crack length according to Eq. (7). Data with a range of several orders of magnitude in velocity can thus be obtained in a single experiment.

In general, the crack tip velocity is not a single-valued function of the stress-intensity factors. It also depends on the chemical environment of the crack tip. Corrosive agents such as water molecules enhance the breaking of

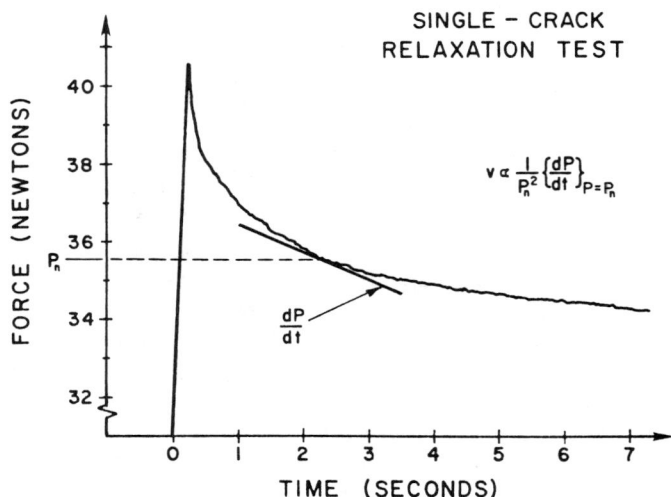

FIG. 4. Data from a single-crack relaxation test performed on a double torsion specimen. The crack tip velocity is directly proportional to the rate at which the load decreases.

## 5. ROCK FRACTURE AND FRICTIONAL SLIDING

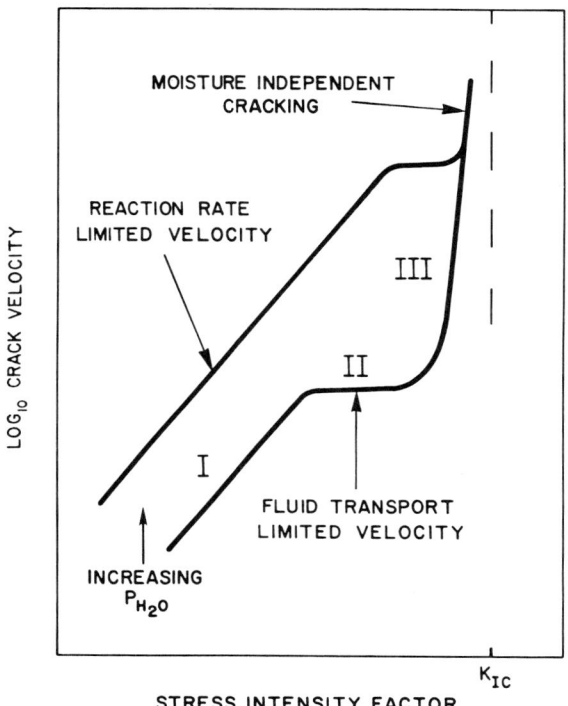

FIG. 5. Single-crack propagation is a sensitive function of the chemical environment and stress. Three regions are identified. In region I the rate of crack propagations is directly proportional to the moisture content and exponentially dependent on the stress intensity. In region II the crack growth is independent of stress but depends on the rate at which moisture can be transported to the crack tip. In region III the rate of crack growth is again exponentially dependent on stress, but independent of moisture. $K_{IC}$, fracture toughness, a material property.

atomic bonds at the crack tip. The higher the concentration of moisture at the crack tip, the greater is the crack tip velocity at constant stress-intensity factor. Figure 5 illustrates the form of $K_I$-$v$ data found for glass. In region I crack propagation is controlled by the moisture at the crack tip. In region II the crack tip is outrunning the moisture and the velocity is limited by the rate at which moisture can be transported to the crack tip. Propagation in region III is very rapid and mostly independent of moisture. At $K_{IC}$, the crack velocity is unstable and propagates close to elastic wave speed. The double torsion technique has yielded consistent results for glasses. Data from the work of Wiederhorn[13] spanning all three regions are shown in Fig. 5. Reliable data for rocks are sparse.

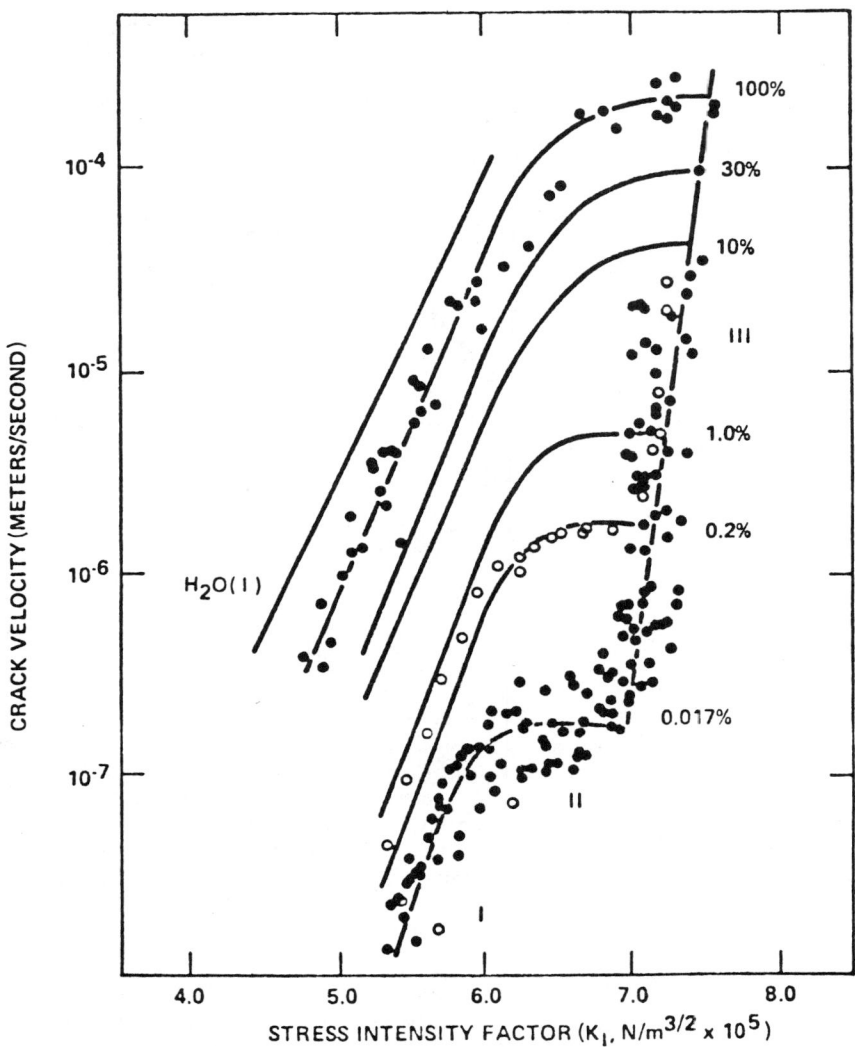

FIG. 6. Crack velocity vs. stress intensity data for soda lime glass. Data are shown for all three regions illustrated in Fig. 5. (With permission from Plenum Publishing Corp.; see reference 3.)

## 4. Double Cantilever Beam Technique

The double cantilever beam (DCB) technique has been used in fracture mechanics testing.[14,15] A DCB specimen is shown in Fig. 7 and a typical experimental setup in Fig. 8. The stress-intensity factor for this arrangement is given by

## 5. ROCK FRACTURE AND FRICTIONAL SLIDING

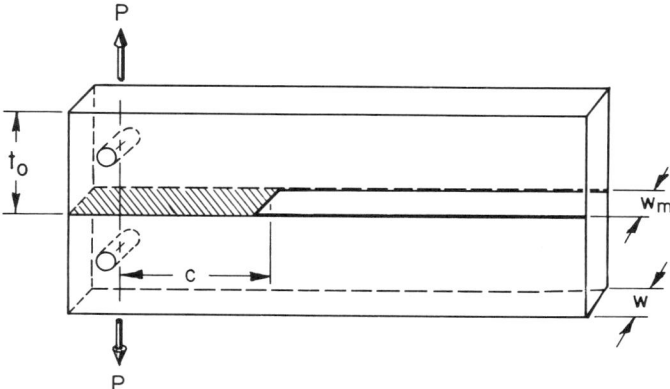

Fig. 7. Double cantilever beam specimen. (With permission from ASTM; see reference 14.)

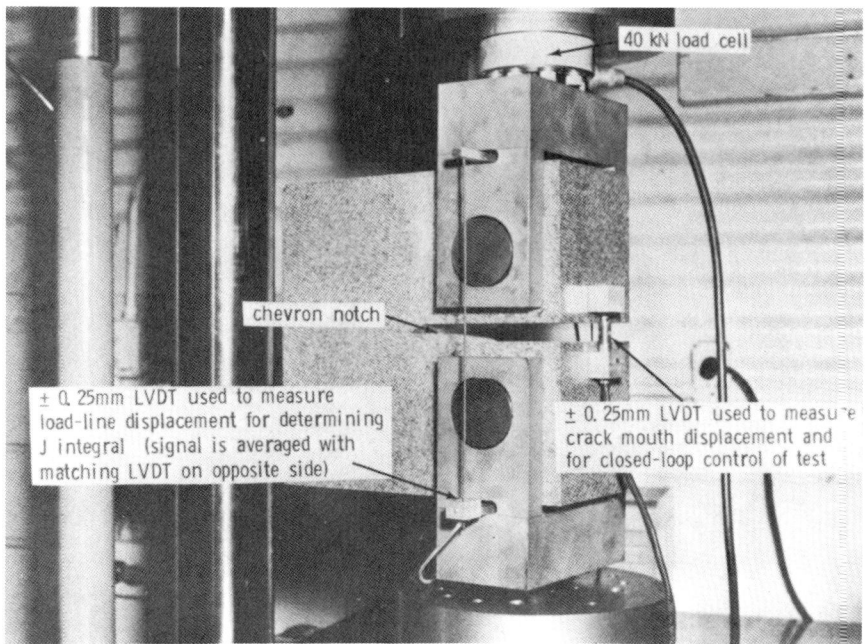

Fig. 8. Experimental setup for a compact double cantilever beam specimen. (With permission from ASTM; see reference 15.)

$$K_I = [12F(c)/WW_m t_0]^{1/2} P \tag{8}$$

where the dimensional terms are given in Fig. 7. $P$ is the load, and $F(c) = c^2 + 1.32ct_0 + 0.542t_0^2$. The specimens are usually grooved on both sides to provide guidance for the crack. A precrack of minimum length $2t_0$[16] is established before $K_{IC}$ testing commences. It is often convenient to arrange the test so that the crack propagation is horizontal. In such a case the torque on the specimen may not be negligible and it may be necessary to provide a support on the end opposite the loading pins to ensure that the initial load $P$ is zero.

Variations of the DCB technique are the tapered double cantilever beam (TDCB) technique[17] and the constant moment[18] (CM) configuration. Specimens for these techniques are shown in Figs. 9 and 10, respectively. Equations (9) and (10) give the $K_I$ vs. geometry and loading relationships for the TDCB and CM techniques, respectively.

$$K_I = 2P\left(\frac{m}{WW_m}\right)^{1/2} \quad m = \frac{1}{h} + 3\frac{c^2}{h^3} \tag{9}$$

$$K_I = \frac{M}{(IW)^{1/2}} \tag{10}$$

where $M$ is the applied moment and $I$ the moment of inertia of one arm.

The constant moment and TDCB specimens are constant $K$ specimens (like the DT specimens) provided the latter is shaped so that $m$ is constant.

Another variation on the DCB method is the loading of the specimen with a wedge.[19] This arrangement is shown in Fig. 11. It is inherently a stiff

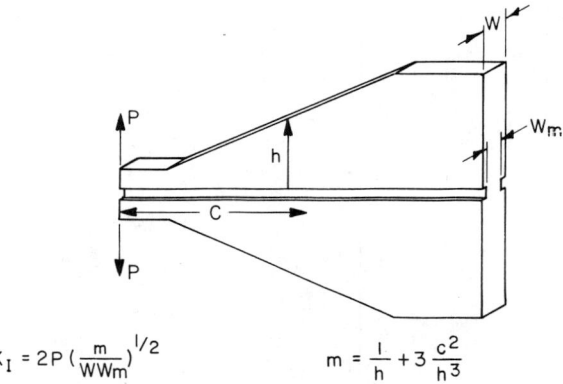

FIG. 9. Tapered double cantilever beam specimen. Constant $K$ conditions are obtained by shaping the specimen to give constant $m$. (With permission from Plenum Publishing Corp.; see reference 25.)

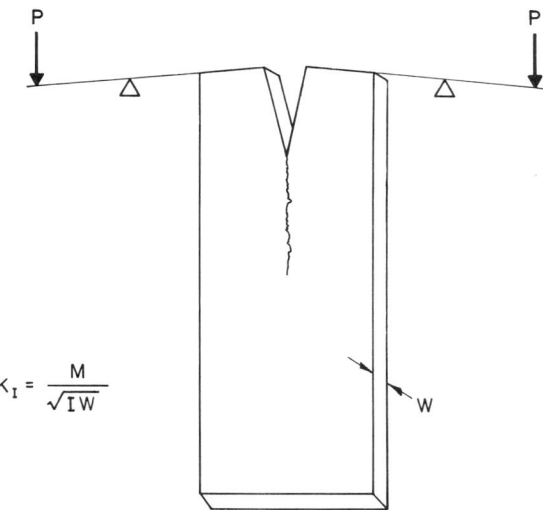

FIG. 10. Constant moment specimen. $M$, applied moment; $I$, moment of inertia of one arm. (With permission from Plenum Publishing Corp.; see reference 25.)

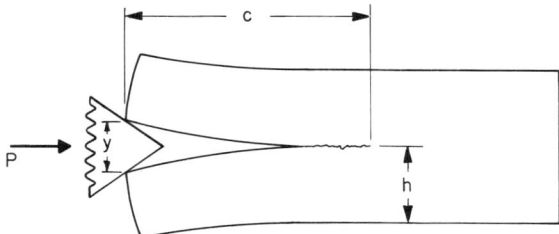

FIG. 11. Wedge-loaded double cantilever beam specimen. (With permission from Plenum Publishing Corp.; see reference 25.)

loading system and can rather easily lead to crack arrest. With this loading arrangement

$$K_{\mathrm{I}} = \frac{\sqrt{3}}{2} \frac{Eyh^{3/2}}{c^2(1 + 0.64h/c)^2} \tag{11}$$

where $E$ is the Young's modulus and the other parameters are defined in Fig. 11. The analysis that leads to Eq. (11) is based on the work of Kanninen. [20] The effect of axial loading has so far been ignored and is not included in Eq. (11). Its importance has recently been recognized by Swanson[21] and Peck et al.[22] In a given experimental arrangement, as the wedge angle and therefore the axial force are increased, the propagation of the crack in its own plane becomes more likely.

## 5. Notched Bending Beam Technique

Variations of the bending beam configuration are the four- or three-point bend (FPB)[23] and the single-edged notched beam (SENB)[24,25] arrangements. A specimen of the SENB method is shown in Fig. 12. The stress-intensity factor in terms of geometry and loading is

$$K_{IC} = \frac{3P_{\max}(L - l)}{2bd^2} c_0^{1/2} Y(c_0') \tag{12}$$

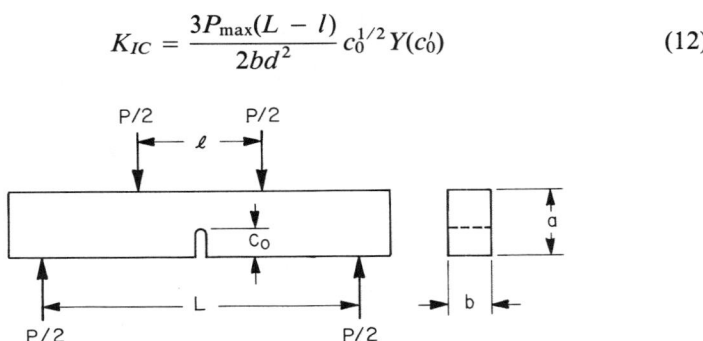

FIG. 12. Schematic of test specimen geometry for single-edge notched beam tests. (With permission from ASTM; see reference 24.)

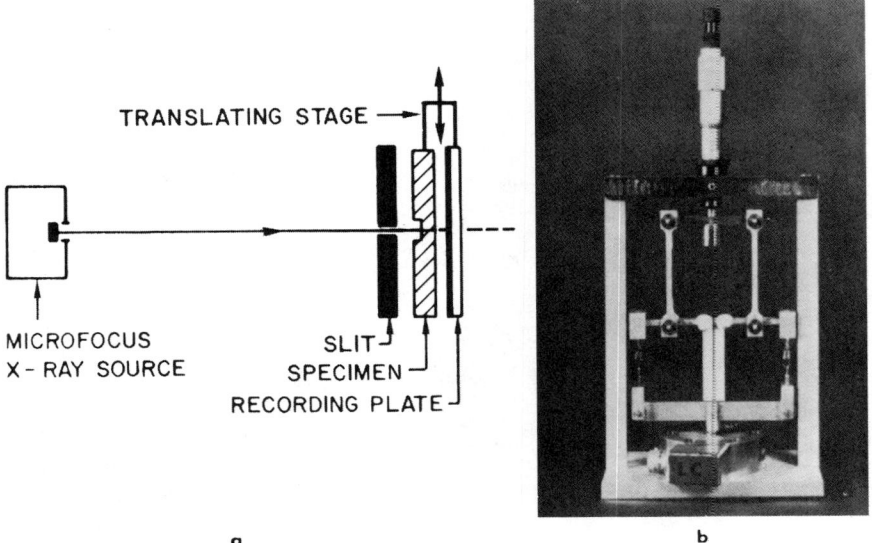

FIG. 13. (a) Schematic representation of the principle of X-ray microradiography and (b) loading fixture with built-in load cell (LC) and constant moment DCB test arrangement. (With permission from ASTM; see reference 28.)

where

$$Y(c_0') = [3.86 - 6.15c_0' + 21.7(c_0')^2]^{1/2} \quad \text{and} \quad c_0' = c_0/d \quad (13)$$

The SENB technique is very convenient for $K_{IC}$ determinations, but because of the $K$ dependence on crack length it is difficult to obtain reliable $K$ vs. $v$ data.

Fracture toughness determinations based on controlled surface flaws have been adapted for the characterization of ceramics[26, 27] but have not been used extensively for rocks. Because of the inherent anisotropy and variation of grain size in rocks, it is unlikely that these techniques will soon be adapted for rocks. Wu *et al.*[28] used X-rays in conjunction with the DCB arrangement to image the region of the crack tip while the specimen was under stress. Their experimental arrangement is shown in Fig. 13. A collimated X-ray beam passes through the specimen and produces an image on film. Cracks, being filled with air only, attenuate the X-rays less than the intact rock and are therefore imaged as highly exposed areas. Figure 14, from Wu *et al.*, shows X-ray microradiographs of $Al_2O_3$.

Wu *et al.*[28] also introduced a technique whereby cracks can be viewed *in situ* in a scanning electron microscope (SEM) while the specimen is under

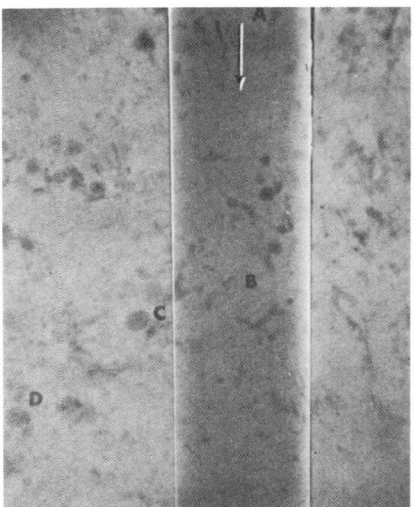 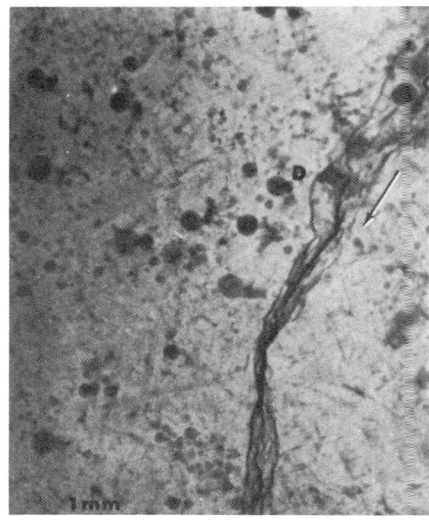

FIG. 14. (a) Composite micrograph of a grooved specimen before propagation of a rock. A and B are in the groove. The specimen has large grains (50–2000 μm) and preexisting microcracks. (b) Micrograph showing the area left (note C and D) of the groove after a crack propagated from A to B and then left the groove near C. Note that there is little or no effect of the spherical pores (dark circular features) on crack propagation in contrast to the microcracks (dark elongated features). With permission from ASTM; see reference 28.)

FIG. 15. (a) *In situ* SEM specimen stage and (b) detail of specimen loading arrangement. Note the tapered specimen. (With permission from ASTM; see reference 28.)

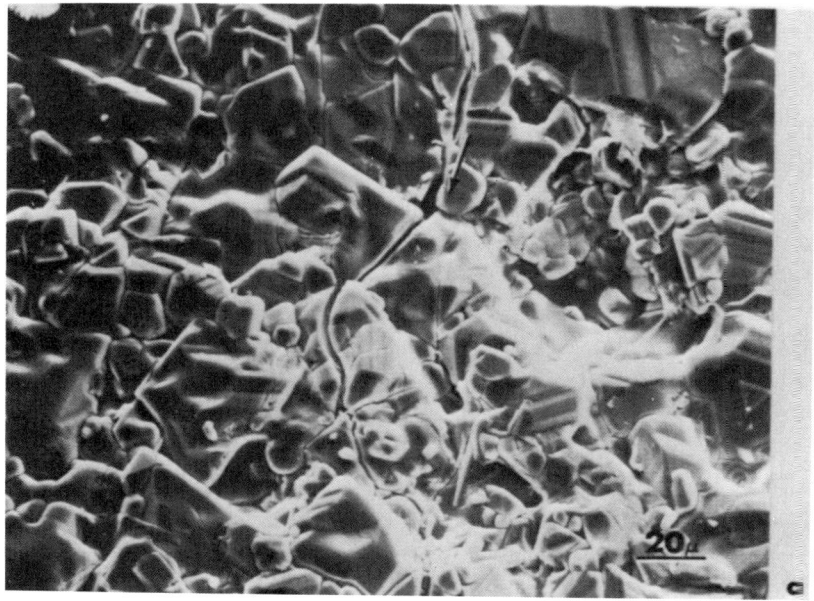

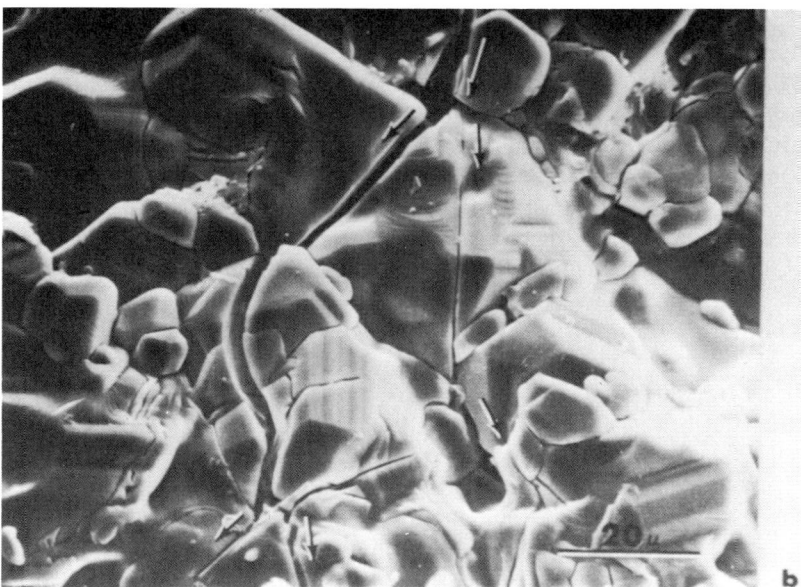

Fig. 16. Crack branching seen in Lucalox; (b) is a higher-magnification micrograph. (With permission from ASTM; see reference 28.)

stress (see Fig. 15). The tapered DCB arrangement was used. A mechanical feed-through normally used for positioning is modified to force a tungsten carbide wedge into the machined notch. (See Fig. 9 for the TDCB method.) While only surface phenomena can be seen, they can be resolved to a fraction of a micrometer. The big advantage of viewing the cracks *in situ* rather than in a recovered sample is that it is possible to observe the progress of crack growth and to see the cracks while they are open. The linking of cracks and the role that preexisting cracks play become readily apparent. An example of crack branching in $Al_2O_3$ is shown in Fig. 16.

## 6. *In Situ* Measurements

In this section we will examine the *in situ* measurements that can be made during rock deformation experiments. These range from externally imposed variables such as temperature, confining pressure, and differential stress to physical properties of the rock such as its elastic and anelastic moduli, shape, electrical and thermal conductivity, acoustic emissions, and permeability.

In general, the measurement and control of the externally imposed variables can be accomplished with commercially available equipment. When using thermocouples under confining pressure, care must be taken to correct for the pressure effect on their calibration.[29]

Sample deformation can be measured in a number of different ways. In confined experiments, where the sample is in a pressure vessel, the axial shortening of the sample can be measured by measuring the advance of the piston. A simple mechanical dial gauge or, if an electrical output is desired, a linear variable differential transformer can be used. A careful calibration is necessary, taking the distortion of the entire apparatus into consideration. This is readily accomplished if a stiff (i.e., much stiffer than the rock sample) dummy sample of known elastic moduli is compressed over the entire anticipated force range.

The deformation perpendicular to the axial direction, the tangential strain, is usually measured within the pressure chamber. Notable exceptions are the indirect measurements of the volume change in the pressure chamber.[30-32] In the first technique one measures the volume of the confining medium, which must be added or subtracted from the chamber in order to keep the pressure constant; a calibrated piston is advanced or retracted. In the second,[32] the volume change is measured by measuring the level change of the liquid with an ultrasonic interferometer.

Commercially available solid-state or resistance strain gauges are most commonly used. Such gauges come with known gauge factors and temperature corrections. When used under confining pressure, they must be calibrated against materials with known properties. Solid-state gauges have the highest sensitivity, i.e., the largest gauge factors, but are limited by breakage to a small range of strain (typically 0.2%). Metal foil strain gauges can be used up to about 2% strain and are by far the most common. The bonding of strain gauges is slowly emerging from the realm of magic into that of art. Especially if the gauges are to be used at high temperatures, the bonding problems become severe and the useful range of the gauges is limited to about 1.5%. Commercially available gauges can be used to 300°C. Bonner and Heard[33] have developed a technique that has been successful to 800°C. A strain gauge without the conventional plastic backing material was attached to the metal jacket by spraying porous ceramic over the gauge. The strain measurements were very reproducible and, in spite of the very small useful range ($<1$%), quite adequate for the anelasticity measurements for which they were designed. The preparation of the gauges was quite elaborate and consequently expensive. A different, as yet untried technique that should be useful to very high temperatures is suggested in Fig. 17. Tubes or rods of $Al_2O_3$ are glued on the jacket as shown. Two loops of strain gauge wire are threaded and tied through holes in the ceramic pieces. This will further ensure that the ceramic pieces do not twist during an experiment. Approximately 30 windings of 0.12-mm-diameter strain gauge wire such as Constantan™ or Karma™ on a 20-mm-diameter sample will produce a standard 120Ω gauge. The wire should be wound under constant tension and the ends secured by threading and typing them to the ceramic rods through holes in the rocks. Transverse changes in the specimen dimensions will be translated into strains in the wire. With a wire diameter about one-half of the jacket thickness, there will be no appreciable added constraint on the sample in the transverse direction. As the temperature is raised the glue that was originally used to attach the ceramic pieces will fail and the tension on the wire will hold the gauge on the rock. The strain gauge can be calibrated using materials with well-known thermal expansion coefficients and elastic moduli. Other lateral

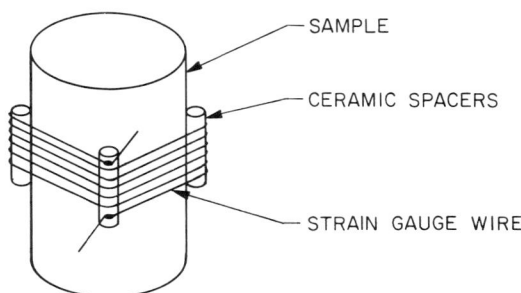

FIG. 17. Tangential strain gauge for use at high temperatures.

deformation gauges that do not require bonding of transducers to the sample were developed by Schuler[34] and Holcomb and McNamee.[35]

In recent years optical holographic interferometry has been adapted to measure deformation of rock samples.[36-39] Since this technique is not in wide use, but offers some unique advantages over other methods, it will be described in some detail.

When viewing a hologram one sees a three-dimensional image. It is equivalent to looking through a window at an object. The image is generally recorded on a photographic emulsion on a flat glass plate and becomes visible when the developed emulsion is illuminated with a laser beam. The image appears behind the glass plate and the glass plate becomes the window through which the three-dimensional viewing can be done. It is not possible to distinguish visually between a good holographic image and the original object, when it is illuminated by laser light.

The optical record of the image is an interference pattern formed by combining a coherent reference beam with the light that is scattered from the object, as shown in Fig. 18. Two or more images can be recorded on one emulsion. Let us assume that two images of the same object are recorded on one plate and the object has been strained between the two exposures. After developing the hologram and viewing it, the two very similar images can be seen. Since the images were formed with coherent laser light, the light from them will interfere and the observer sees the object with superimposed interference fringes, which are a measure of the distortion that occurred between the two exposures. It is also possible to make one exposure, develop the plate, and superimpose the image over the real object. Any subsequent distortion of the object will result in fringes that are visible in real time. This method is referred to as stored beam holography. The developing and repositioning

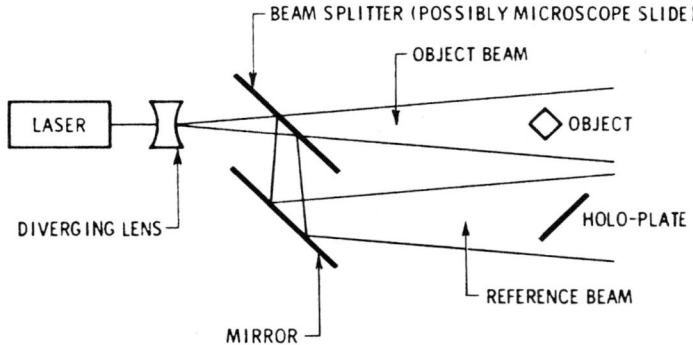

FIG. 18. Simple arrangement for making holograms, including provisions for an object and a reference beam. (With permission from *Pure and Applied Geophysics*; see reference 36.)

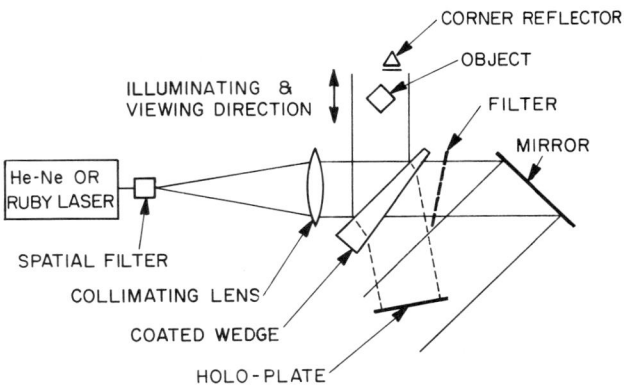

FIG. 19. Holography system as used in the author's laboratory. Illuminating the object with a parallel beam and ensuring that the illuminating and viewing directions are coincident make the interpretation of fringes very simple. (With permission from *Pure and Applied Geophysics*; see reference 36.)

of the photographic plate must be done with utmost care to minimize the number of fringes due to shrinking emulsion and positioning errors. With stored beam holography the sample distortion can be recorded continuously on film or videotape. A new hologram must be made when the fringe density becomes too great to be resolvable.

To make holographic interferometry quantitative, Heflinger et al.[40] developed a technique whereby the illumination and viewing directions are coincident and the sample is illuminated with a parallel beam. In our laboratory we have adapted this experimental technique, using the arrangement shown in Fig. 19. Small rigid body translations do not result in fringes, and rotation results in straight fringes regardless of the shape of the body (for details see Heflinger et al.[40] and Meyer and Spetzler.[41] These straight fringes are parallel to the axis of rotation. Their spacing is a measure of the angle of rotation.

The interpretation of the fringe patterns obtained by using the arrangement of Fig. 19 is very simple. The pattern corresponds to a topographic map with a contour interval equal to one-half the wavelength of the illuminating laser light. The value of the wavelength must be taken in the medium in which the change in optical path length occurred. In the case of measuring the distortion of a sample while it is under confining pressure it is necessary to know the index of refraction of the pressure medium. We have measured the index of our pressure medium (Dow Corning 200 fluid) as a function of pressure.[42] The data are shown in Fig. 20. For a He–Ne laser with a wavelength of 638 nm (in vacuum) the contour intervals for holograms taken of

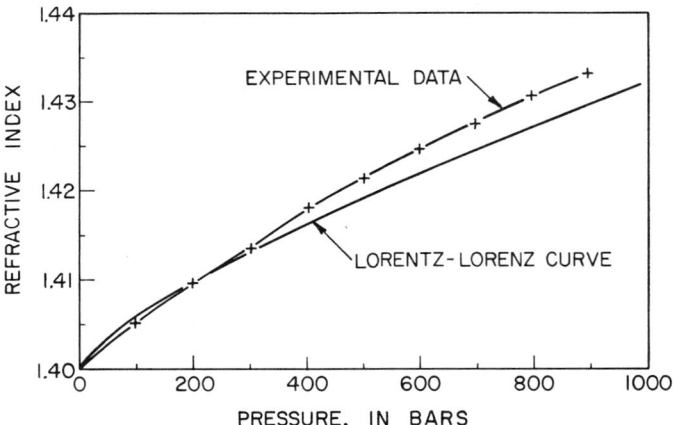

Fig. 20. Refractive index $n$ vs. pressure for the pressure fluid (Dow Corning 200 fluid). The manufacturer's compression data ($\rho$ = density) were used to calculate the index in accordance with the Lorentz–Lorenz law $K\rho = (n^2 - 1)/(n^2 + 2)$, where $K$ is a constant. Maximum error in holographic strain measurements introduced by use of the Lorentz–Lorenz extrapolation is less than 0.5%. (With permission from Plenum Publishing Corp.; see reference 42.)

a sample in our pressure vessel under 100 MPa confining pressure is approximately 210 nm.

The possibilities for extending the usefulness of holography seem endless. Any diffusely reflecting surface, i.e., a nonmirror finish, can serve as a reference surface without the need for special preparation. With $Q$-switched lasers the exposure time can be a fraction of a nanosecond, which makes it possible to capture phenomena of very short duration. With mirrors the sample may be viewed from most directions. In many cases, motions that do not in themselves involve any differential motion in the viewing direction may be used to generate displacements with a component in that direction. An example of how the axial strain of a sample was measured is illustrated in Fig. 21. Note that the inherent sensitivity due to the laser light wavelength can be increased or decreased by choosing an appropriate gauge geometry. The major benefit that is derived from using holography is that the entire surface deformation in the viewing direction is obtained and not just a spot measurement. The photo insert in Fig. 21 is an example in which the tilt of the sample is obtained in addition to the axial strain.

In certain cases it is convenient to use optical holography to check on and modify design criteria of equipment. An example of this is shown in Fig. 22a–c, where finite-element calculations and deformation measurements by optical holography were used in the design of an optical window[43] for a high-pressure vessel. The window allows us to perform holographic deformation

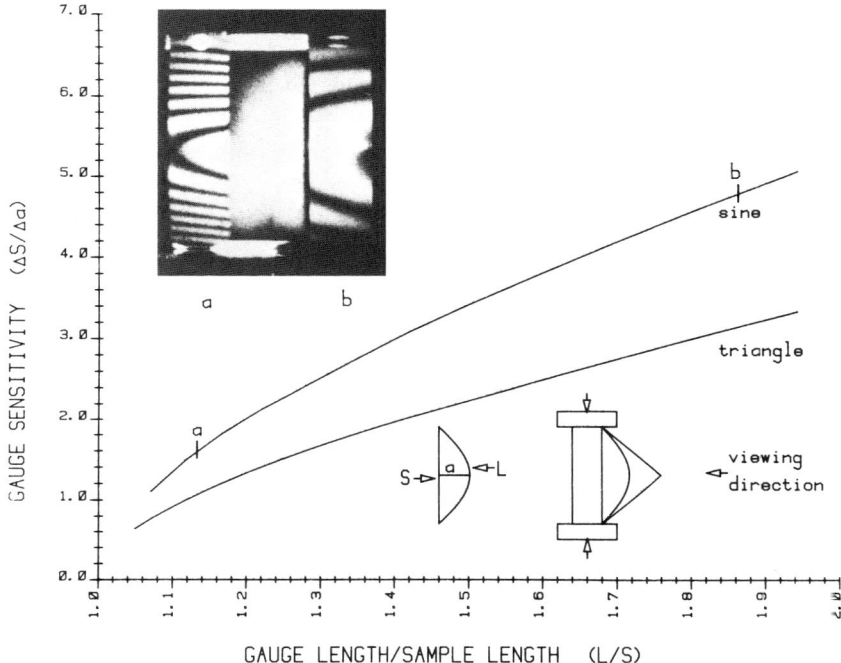

FIG. 21. Gauge sensitivity vs. gauge length to sample length ratio. Photo insert shows the response of two sinusoidal gauges to a nominal sample shortening of 3 μm. Sample length is 44 mm and gauge length/sample length ratios for a and b are 1.13 and 1.86, respectively. Nonparallelism of fringes is the result of a tilt or less than 0.2 μm across the sample. (With permission from Plenum Publishing Corp.; see reference 42.)

measurements under confining pressure. In this case the entire inside (high-pressure side) surface of the window was painted white with diffusely reflecting paint and a white cross was painted on the outside (atmospheric pressure) surface. With the window installed, the pressure was increased and the window deformation measured by interpreting the fringes on doubly exposed holograms (Fig. 22b).

A bulge in rocks[6, 38, 39, 44] that precedes failure as shown in Fig. 23 is another example of a subtle deformation that would be difficult to detect and measure with more conventional techniques. Liu and Livanos[45] used slit diffraction to detect a precursor bulge on an unconfined sample. Their experimental setup is shown in Fig. 24. A diffraction pattern is formed between a sharp edge and the sample. The pattern is recorded on film, and as the sample deforms the width of the slit changes nonuniformly and shortly before failure reveals a precursory bulge.

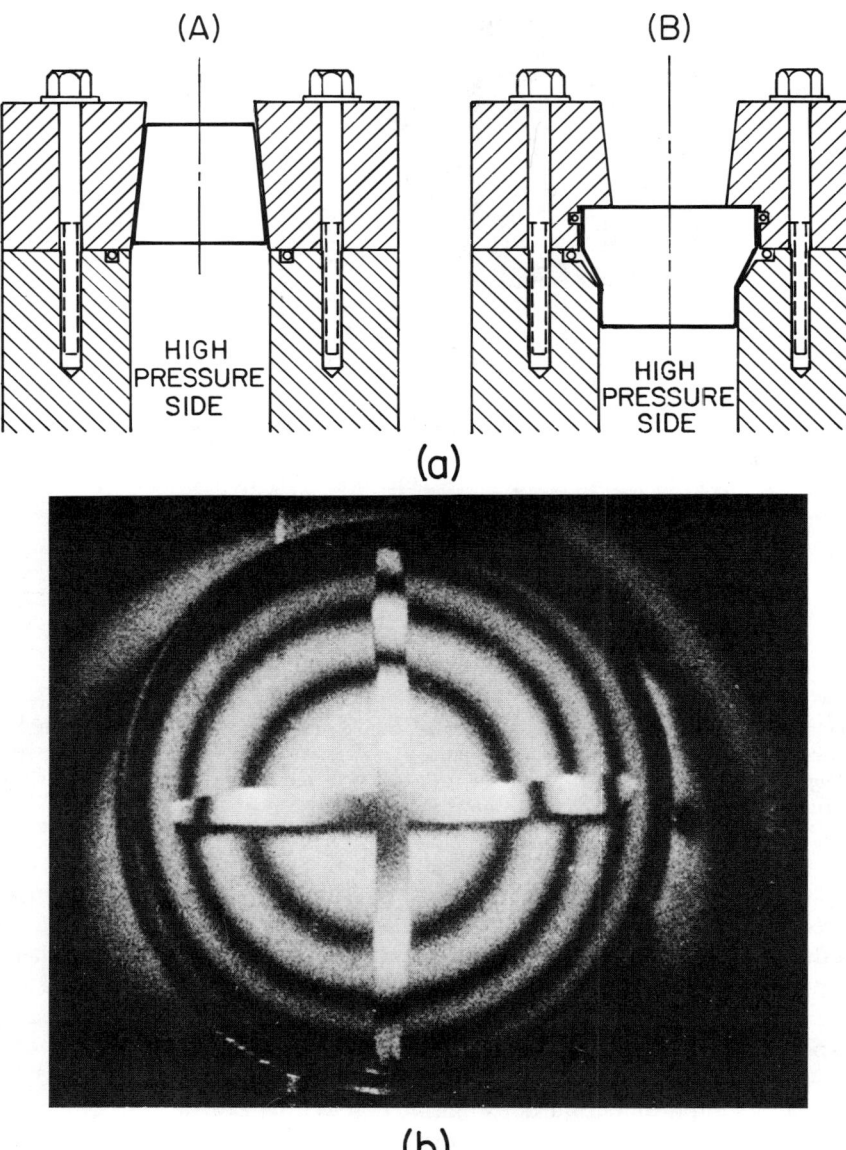

FIG. 22. (a) Design of optical windows (A) and (B) installed in high-pressure chambers. (b) Double exposed hologram showing fringes produced by a load of 6.9 MPa applied to inner surface of window (A). (c) Displacement of the surface of window (A), calculated by finite-element analysis with a load difference of 6.9 MPa. Open circles represent the holographic results. (With permission from *Review of Scientific Instuments*; see reference 43.)

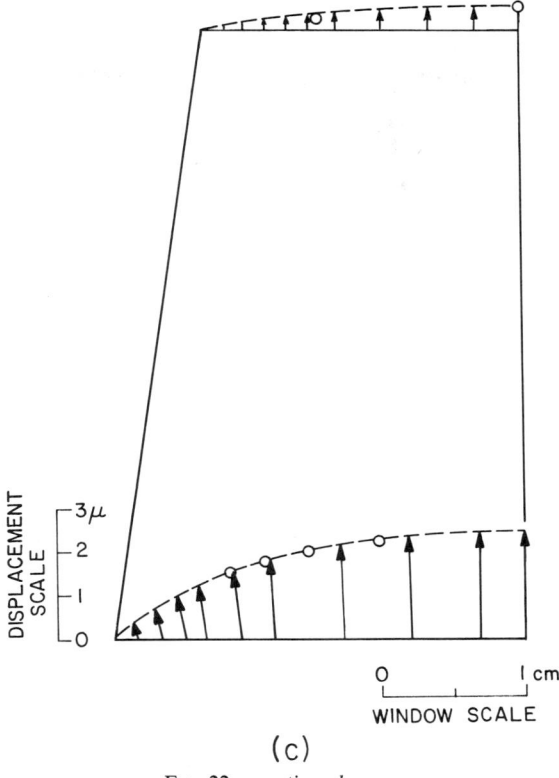

(c)

Fig. 22—*continued*

## 7. Acoustic Emissions

By acoustic emissions (AE) we mean the elastic waves generated when rapid localized failure occurs in a stressed material. The stresses may be externally applied or they may be internal residual stresses which are the result of the thermal and stress history of the sample. The recording and evaluation of acoustic emissions are useful in nondestructive testing of engineering materials and in understanding the failure mechanisms of engineering as well as geological materials.

There are a multitude of techniques for recording AE. These range from simply recording their approximate number above some threshold to obtaining many displacement vs. time records, similar to seismograms, for an individual AE event. The former gives an indication of the total AE activity and can be very useful in a statistical sense for failure prediction. It is

Fig. 23. Bulge on a Westerly granite sample ($\sim 18 \times 18 \times 40$ mm) outlining the intense deformation zone which precedes failure and delineates the eventual fracture plane. During low stain rate experiments ($\varepsilon < 10^{-7}$/s) the intense deformation zone first becomes apparent at about 60% of the axial strain at failure. This hologram was made through an optical window while the sample was under a confining pressure of 50 MPa. The axial strain was 96% of that at failure. (With permission from Academic Press; see reference 44.)

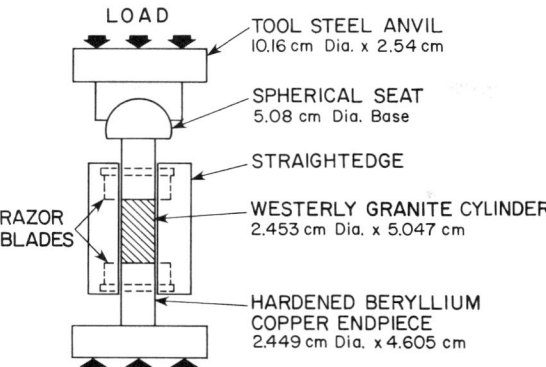

FIG. 24. Uniaxial compression test arrangement using slit diffraction method to map the rock sample surface deformation. (With permission from American Geophysical Union; see reference 45.)

furthermore useful even at very high AE rates. The recording of entire AE events is appealing because of the vast amount of information that is contained in such records. In ideal cases the seismograms yield the location of the AE event, its fault plane solution, its radiated energy, and the power spectrum of the radiated energy.

The device that detects the elastic wave energy and sends a corresponding electrical signal is referred to as a transducer. The most common transducers used in AE work are made of piezoelectric materials. In response to a change in shape these materials become electrically charged and vice versa. Thin disks are cut from the piezoelectric material to make transducers, the thickness being determined by the desired resonance frequency. The disk's diameter is typically 5 to 10 times its thickness. The book "Fundamentals of Ultrasonics"[46] gives many practical hints for the selection, bonding, and damping of piezoelectric transducers.

Figure 25 shows a simple schematic for recording AE. In this case three transducers are used to allow for discrimination against electrical noise and false AE signals that originate outside the sample. A typical AE in rock is shown in Fig. 26. When counting such signals one has to decide where to set an amplitude threshold as well as a time duration (dead time) before a new event will be counted. In the case of large events the amplitude may still be above the threshold after the dead time and the event will be recorded as more than one event. The AE that occur outside the sample can be recognized by their delay between transducers A and C (see Fig. 25). Electrical noise will arrive at the transducers virtually simultaneously and can thus be recognized. All three transducers must be checked, however, since a simultaneous arrival at any two of them could result from an event appropriately located within

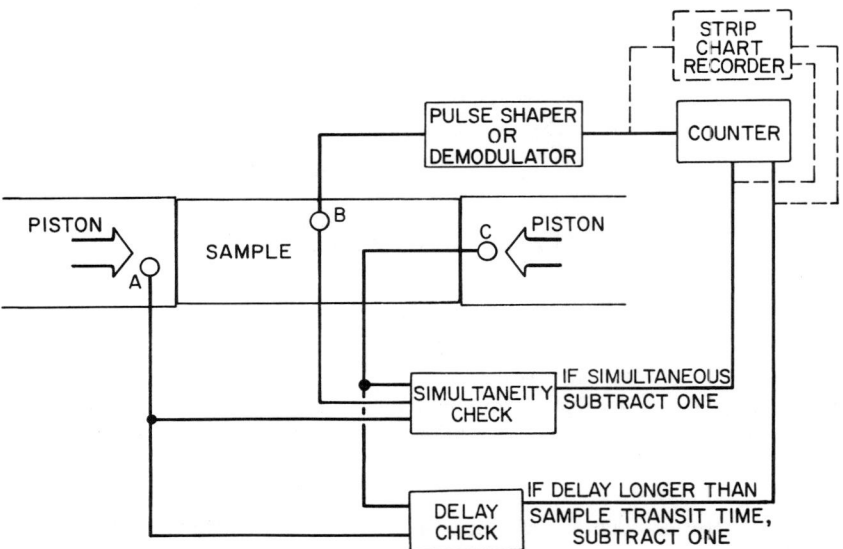

Fig. 25. A simple system for recording acoustic emissions incorporating both simultaneity and delay checks. The simultaneity check discriminates against electrical noise and the delay check against events that occur outside the sample. The dashed lines show optional analog recording. A, B, and C are piezoelectric transducers.

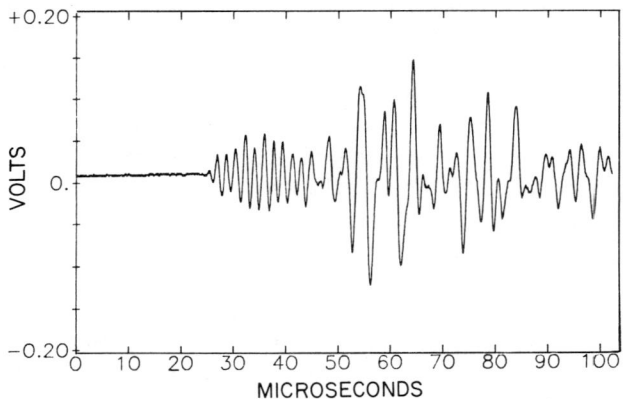

Fig. 26. Typical acoustic emission events from a large sample (79 × 70 × 70 cm) showing both the compressional and shear waves.

the sample. If the number of AE events is of secondary importance but a measure of the energy that was radiated is desired, the dashed circuit in Fig. 25 may be more desirable. It may, of course, be used in addition to the counting circuit. In the demodulator box the signal is amplified, demodulated, and integrated. This can be done simply by charging a capacitor and

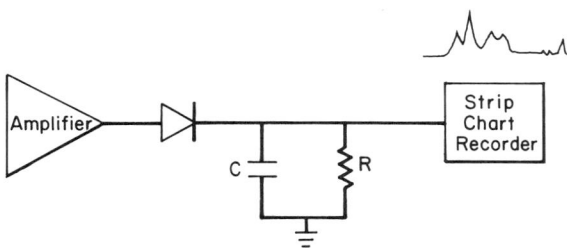

Fig. 27. Demodulator circuit for analog recording (see Fig. 25).

recording the output on a strip chart recorder. Figure 27 shows an appropriate circuit. The time constant $RC$ must be chosen so that multiple events do not saturate the system. Signals from the delay and simultaneity checks can be recorded on a second pen to ensure recognition and discrimination of false events. This analog recording has the advantage over digital recording that it does not tie up expensive digital equipment and that the progress of the experiment is readily visible at any time. The logic described here can also be applied to purely digital recording.

When more than AE counts and some sense of their energy is desired, the instrumentation and its calibration and the interpretation of the data become much more critical. In order to locate AE events the location of the transducers and the velocity within the test specimen must be known. A minimum of four transducers must be used to be able to determine the three spatial coordinates and the time of the event. In practice it is best to use as many transducers as feasible, since some redundancy in the location determinations is desirable and not all transducers will yield usable signals for all events. A state-of-the-art system for recording AE events is described by Sondergeld and Estey[47] and shown schematically in Fig. 28. This system incorporates an effective noise discriminator[48] that accepts only acoustic signals which are in a predetermined frequency range and cross a minimum amplitude threshold for a specified number of cycles, typically 6 to 10. A typical sample and transducer arrangement is shown in Fig. 29.[49]

Unlike the case in seismology, where the size of the transducer (the seismometer) is a very small fraction of a wavelength, when piezoelectric transducers are used for AE recordings, the diameter of the transducer may actually be several wavelengths. This introduces considerable errors if the transducers are considered as single points located at the center of their contact with the sample. The transducers have an effective radius for sensing an incoming signal. The more oblique the incidence of the signal, the larger is the effect of the finite size of the transducer. This effect is shown in Fig. 30[50] for a transducer with an effective radius of 3 mm. The effective size of

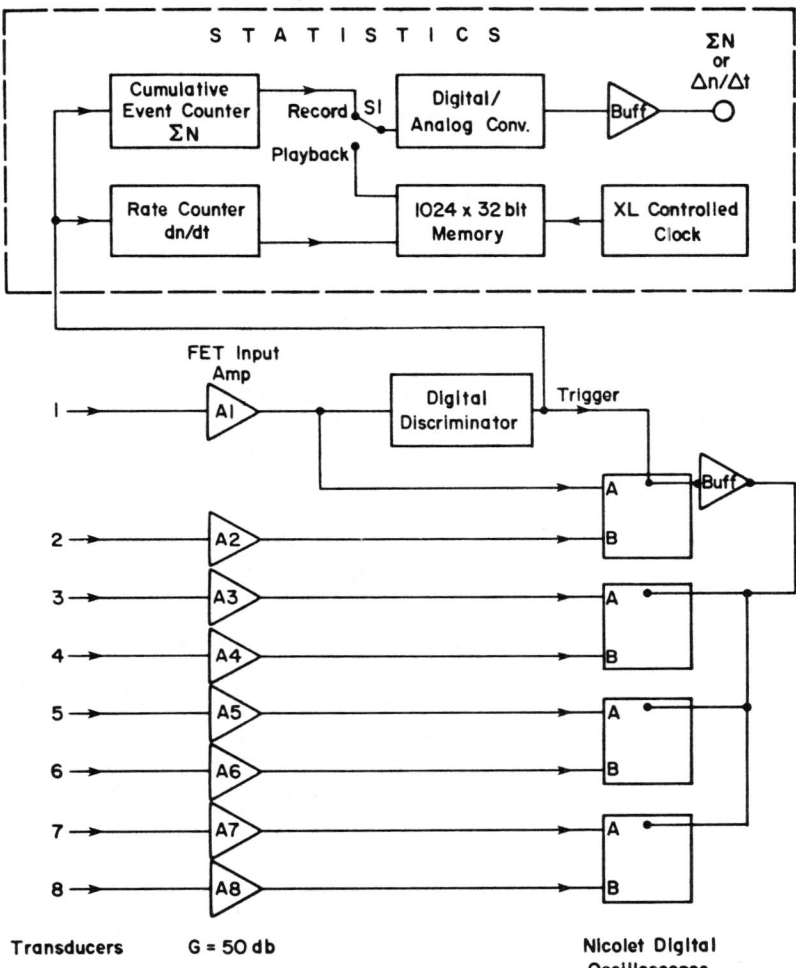

FIG. 28. Block diagram of the acoustic emission monitoring system. Signals from piezoelectric transducers (1–8) are amplified by 50 dB with the FET input amplifiers. Master transducers (1) is filtered digitally by the discriminator and used to trigger four Nicolet digital oscilloscopes. The four oscilloscopes all trigger within 10 ns of the main trigger and, after capturing the transient, can record the waveforms on floppy disks built into the system. Waveforms are analyzed after the experiment. (From Roecken,[49] p. 36.)

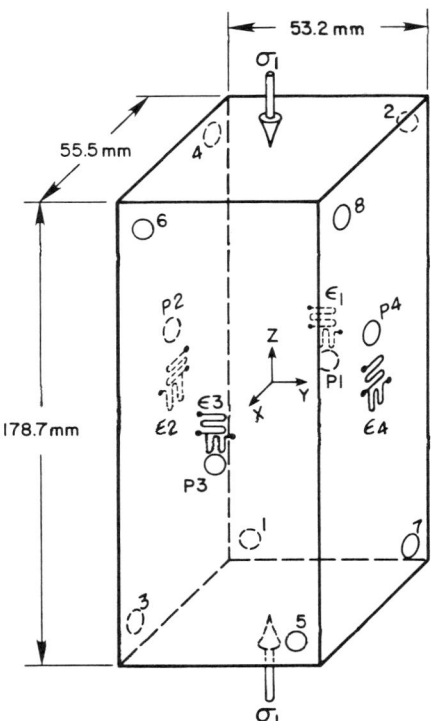

FIG. 29. Typical sample with transducers and strain gauge locations. The receiving transducers have numbers 1 to 8. The strain gauge locations are indicated. The source transducers or pulsers are indicated at locations P1, P2, P3, and P4. The origin of the coordinate system used for the locations of the hypocenters is in the center of the sample. (From Roecken,[49] p. 31.)

the transducer must depend on the physical size of the real transducer as well as on the wavelength of the incoming signal. In the results reported by Roecken *et al.*[50] the effective transducer sizes were between 50 and 70% of their physical sizes.

During deformation experiments the elastic wave velocity often becomes anisotropic. To obtain accurate locations it becomes necessary to incorporate a velocity model in the location determination. This velocity model must be continuously updated to reflect the velocity changes, which may be as large as a factor of 2. An example of the changes that are involved when Westerly granite is slowly stressed to failure is shown in Fig. 31.[39]

To find the location of an AE one may choose to follow the procedure outlined by Sondergeld and Estey[47] with some modifications. This was done by Roecken.[49] First a trial hypocenter (location of an AE event) and an origin

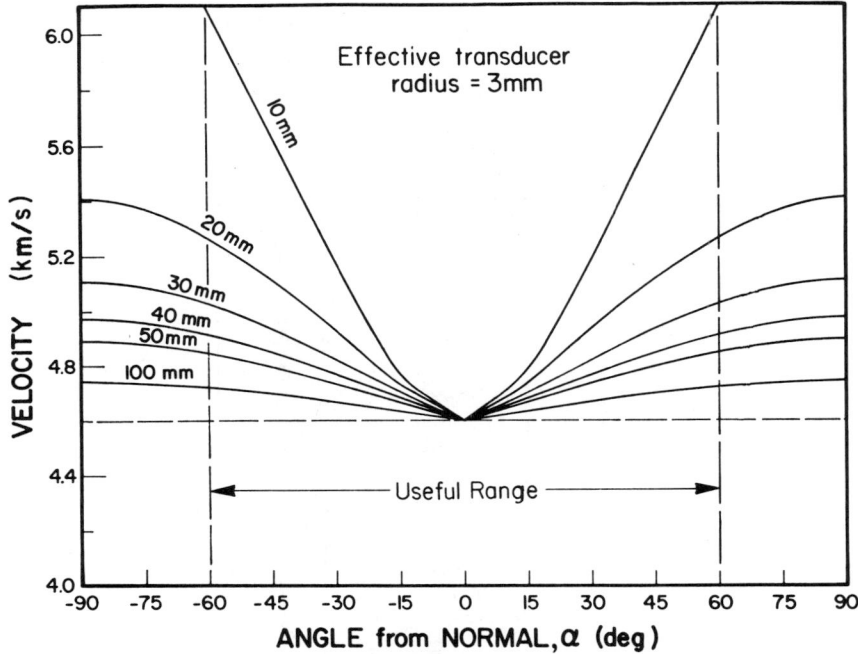

FIG. 30. Apparent velocity dependence on the angle of incidence on the receiver. The parameter that changes from curve to curve is the distance between the source and the center of the receiver. The greatest apparent velocity anomaly can be seen for a distance of 10 mm. The other apparent velocities are calculated for distances of 20–100 mm. (From Roecken,[49] p. 74.)

time are selected and errors are calculated for these values. By iterations the errors are reduced and a preliminary hypocenter is found. With the preliminary location, the directions and distances to the transducers can be calculated and the travel times corrected for the effective transducer sizes and the velocity anisotropy in the sample. Further iteration in the location of the AE event including these corrections will further reduce errors and increase the precision of the hypocenter locations. An example of the average location errors at various stages of deformation is shown in Fig. 32. The data are from Roecken et al.;[50] the velocity model and transducer locations are given in Figs. 33 and 29, respectively. The accuracy with which hypocenters can be located also depends on their locations relative to the transducers. Highest accuracy is achieved when the hypocenter is located within a volume circumscribed by the transducers. Figure 34[49] shows this effect.

As described above, the technology now exists for obtaining accurate locations for AE events. But there is potentially much more information

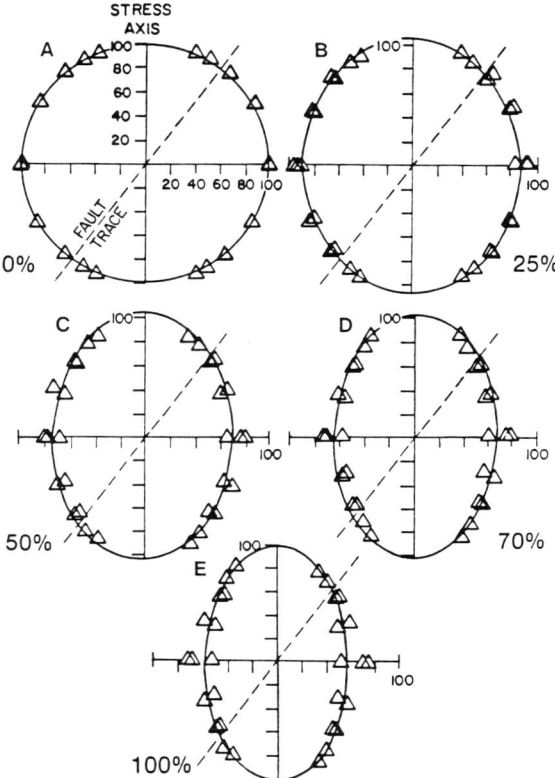

Fig. 31. Normalized velocity for a sample of Westerly granite as a function of angle from the stress axis at 0, 25, 50, 70, and ~100% final tangential strain. At 25% the velocities have decreased in the transverse direction, but little change is seen in other directions. By 50% all observed velocities have decreased, some as much as 30%. The ratio of major to minor axes continually increases as tangential strain increases. At 25% it is 1.13 and by failure it is 1.75. The confining pressure was 50 MPa. (With permission from American Geophysical Union; see reference 39.)

available from recorded waveforms. Focal mechanisms may be determined if the direction of the first motion is clear. The polarity response of the transducers may be found by checking their response, for example, to the drop of a ball bearing or to the breaking of the synthetic lead of a mechanical pencil, the former sending a first arrival that is compressional and the latter a mostly dilatational one. With data obtained with the system shown in Fig. 28, Sondergeld and Estey[51] plotted first arrivals on focal spheres to obtain focal mechanisms for AE events in Westerly granite. While the response of transducers to first arrivals is easily determined for normal or near-normal

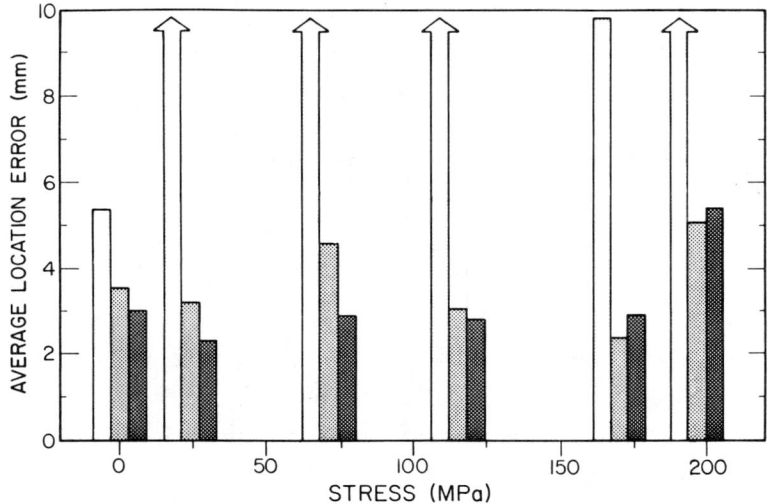

FIG. 32. Average location errors for the source transducers with various corrections. The leftmost bars are based on a constant isotropic velocity. The center bars are based on the stress-dependent anisotropic velocity model shown in Fig. 33. The righmost bars are based on the anisotropic velocity model with the inclusion of transducer size effects shown in Fig. 30.

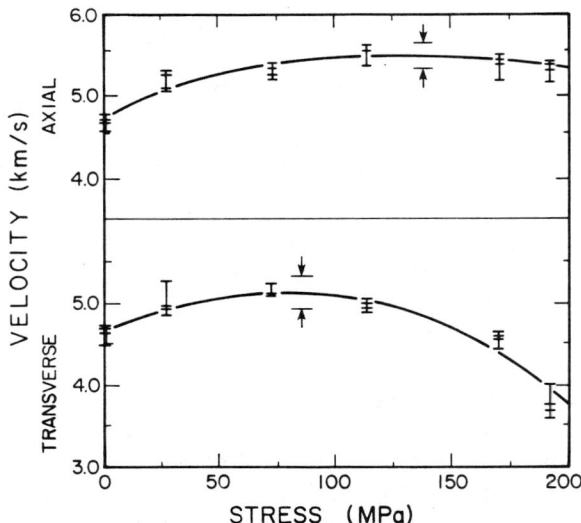

FIG. 33. Axial and transverse velocity models for an experiment by Roecken.[50] These models were used to calculate the errors shown in Fig. 32.

# 5. ROCK FRACTURE AND FRICTIONAL SLIDING

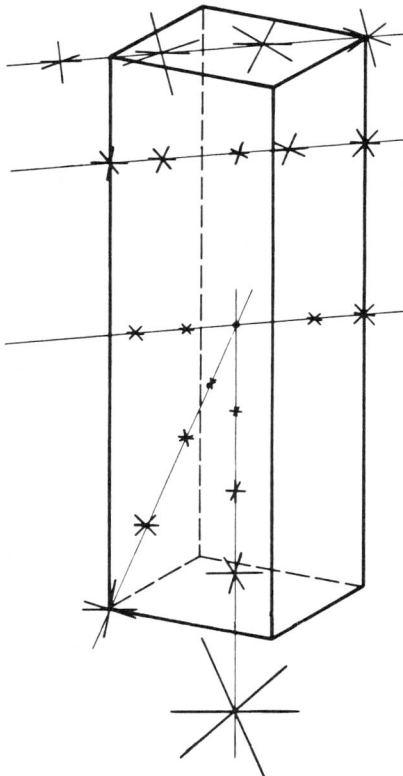

FIG. 34. Location errors and their dependence on source location along six different profiles through the samples. The location errors are calculated from synthetic data for the locations where the centers of the error crosses are plotted. The size of the error crosses is drawn in scale to the rock sample. (From Roecken,[49] p. 130.)

incidence, when the arrival becomes oblique the transducer response becomes more complicated. Roecken, in his studies[49,50] of the effective size of the transducers, also noted that for angles of about 60° off the normal, the first arrival could not be detected anymore and a later arrival would show a polarity reversal leading to incorrect arrival times and erroneous focal mechanism determinations. The same problem is also reflected in the velocity determinations shown in Fig. 30. As a guideline, for hypocenter and focal mechanism determinations one should choose the location and the number of transducers so that signals that make an angle greater than 60° with the normal of any particular transducer can be ignored in the analysis.

From the waveforms shown by Sondergeld and Estey[47,51] it is clear not only that focal mechanism determinations are possible, but also that power spectra can potentially be wrung from the records. Here the transducer problem that plagued hypocenter and focal mechanism determinations becomes even more severe but may also be overcome. The convenience of piezoelectric transducers suggests their use again. They are usually categorized as compressional or shear transducers and as having a specific resonance frequency. These specifications refer to their response for plane waves with normal incidence. When these conditions do not hold the mode of the transducers is no longer pure shear or compressional and other resonances are excited. Uncalibrated, they can only be used for relative changes in spectra for events that occur at the same locations. Various attempts have been made to calibrate piezoelectric transducers,[52] usually for normal incidence. Ideally, transducers would have a flat frequency response and be as sensitive as a piezoelectric transducer while being much smaller than a wavelength— good luck.

While the above dream has not been realized entirely, approximations to it do exist and can at least be used in the calibration of piezoelectric transducers. One such device is based on optical interferometry. It was developed by Palmer and Green[53] and used and evaluated by Kline.[54] The device is

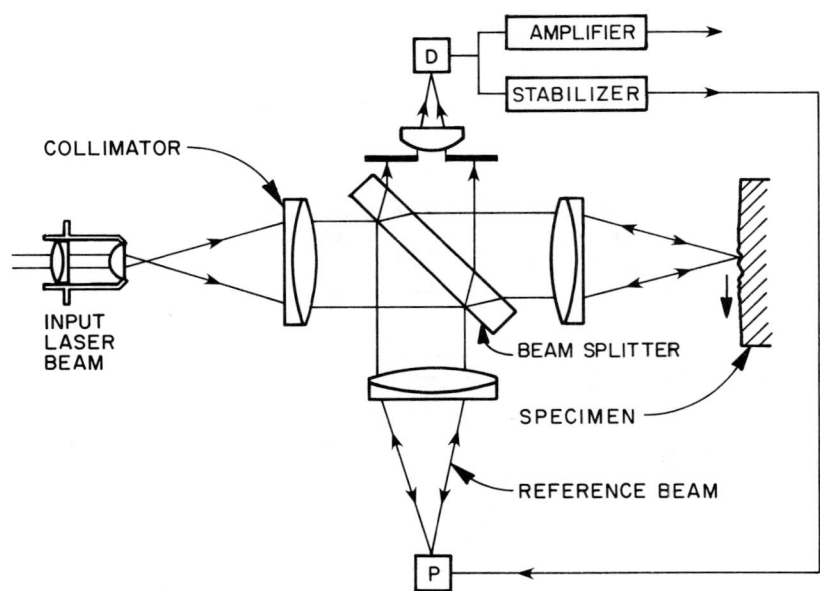

FIG. 35. Schematic of the optical interferometer AE transducer developed by Palmer and Green.[53] Vibration of the sample surface results in variation of the optical path length of the laser beam incident on the sample, while the path length of the reference beam remains constant. (With permission from R. A. Kline.[54])

5. ROCK FRACTURE AND FRICTIONAL SLIDING 165

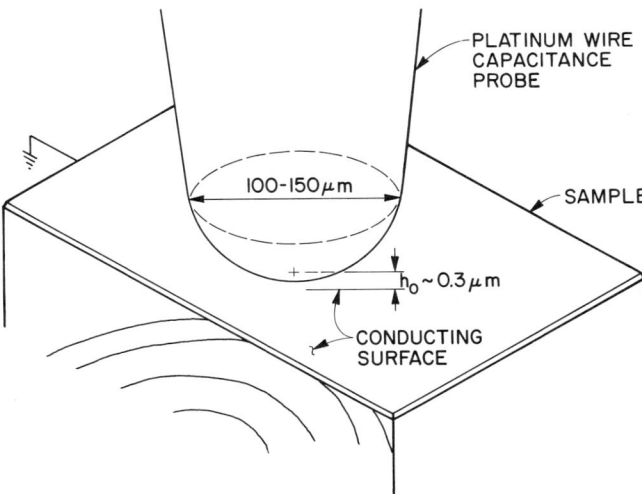

FIG. 36. Capacitance AE transducer probe positioned above the grounded, conducting sample surface. Incoming waves from an AE event change the gap and hence the capacitance between the probe and the sample surface.

shown schematically in Fig. 35. A He–Ne laser is used as the light source in a modified Michelson interferometer. The object beam returns from the sample and the reference beam from a piezoelectrically driven reference mirror which compensates for vibrations within the experimental setup. The advantages of an optical system are its inherent calibration, since the wavelength of the laser light is precisely known, its flat frequency response, and the fact that no contact with the sample is required. The components are somewhat cumbersome and not readily mountable on the sample, which requires a stability for positioning on the order of one wavelength between the sample and the rest of the interferometer. For more detail on the optical interferometer the reader is referred to the original articles.[53, 54]

Capacitance microphones, for example,[55] and electromagnetic sensors[56] offer other means of obtaining AE signals that can be interpreted in terms of their power spectra. The sensing areas have been on the same order as those of piezoelectric transducers and have thus yielded complicated signals for nonnormal incidence. A new device based on the capacitive pickup of the RCA Video-Disc[57, 58] has been developed.[59, 60] The main advantage of this device is its small sensing surface, as shown in Fig. 36, and its portability. Figure 37 is a photograph of the present version of the capacitive transducer (CAP). The physical design is such that the signal from the AE event reaches the pickup capacitor approximately 20 μs before the signal that traveled through the structure. Thus 20 μs of undistorted signal is available for

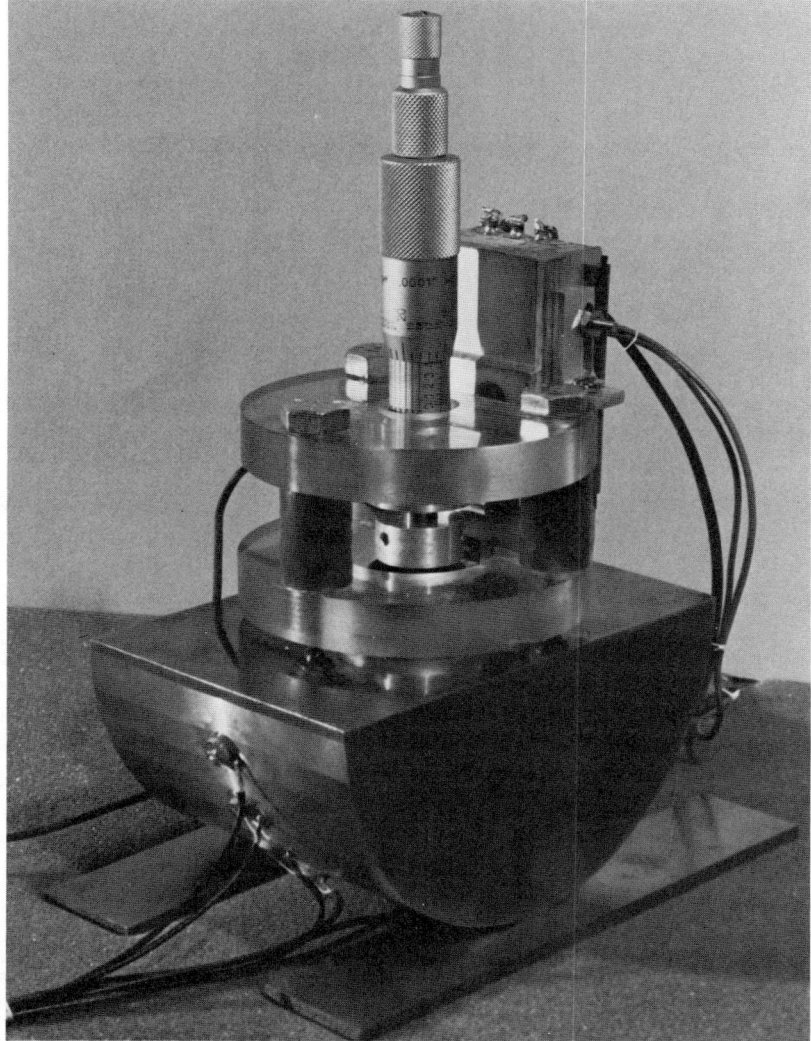

Fig. 37. Photograph of the capacitance transducer on a semicylindrical sample used for piezoelectric transducer calibration.[61] The micrometer head provides for coarse positioning of the capacitance probe. The transducer height including micrometer head is 14.4 cm. The diameter of the horizontal supports is 8.2 cm.

5. ROCK FRACTURE AND FRICTIONAL SLIDING   167

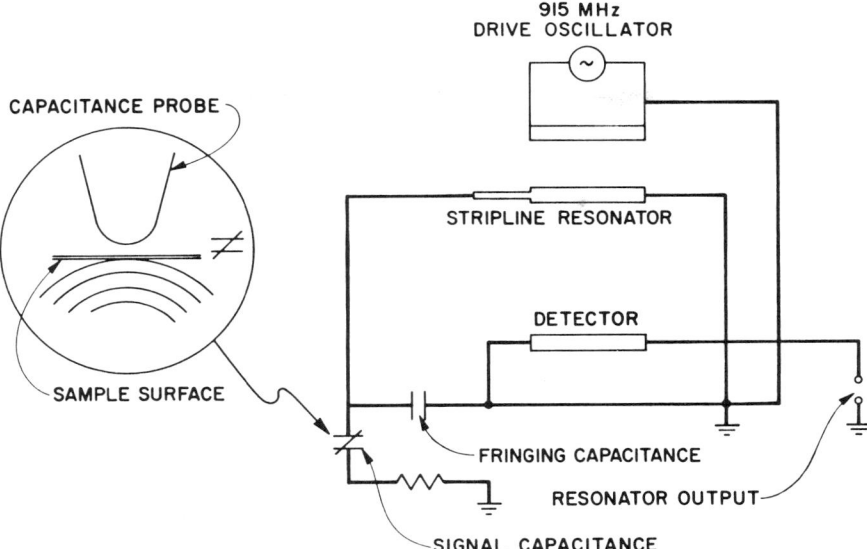

FIG. 38. Capacitance pickup circuitry designed by RCA[57,58] using stripline (transmission line) circuit techniques. The resonator center frequency (910 MHz) changes as a result of the changing signal capacitance. The 915-MHz drive oscillator injects a 4-V peak-to-peak signal. The detector senses the changes of that signal induced in the resonator.

analysis. The schematic of the resonance circuit is shown in Fig. 38 and the principle of operation illustrated in Fig. 39. It is important that the average distance between the stylus and the sample be maintained such that the condition illustrated in Fig. 39 is maintained. This requires extremely close proximity, which is accomplished by using a small modified voice coil from a commercial headphone in a low-frequency ($<20$ Hz) feedback circuit. The output from the resonance circuit (Fig. 39) is kept at a steady value of about 2 V by controlling the current through the voice coil. The stylus is attached to the voice coil.

Surface displacements of a fraction of an angstrom (tens of picometers) are measurable above the noise.[57,60] A comparison between a piezoelectric transducer and the CAP was made with the arrangement shown in Fig. 40. The results for a ball bearing drop and the dynamic propagation of a single crack are given in Fig. 41. It is clear how the signal from the piezoelectric transducer is dominated by its resonances. Piezoelectric transducers are now being calibrated with the help of the CAP.[61] These calibrations will be used to obtain power spectra and moment tensor representations of AE events.[62,63]

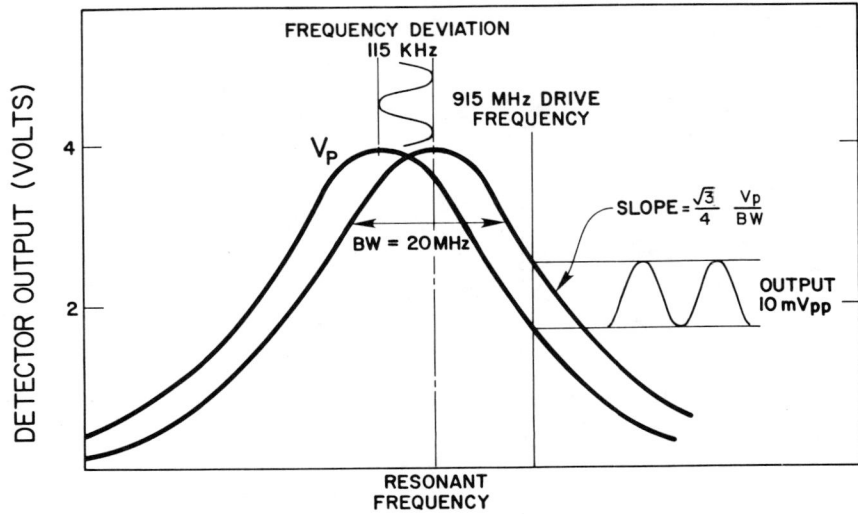

FIG. 39. Capacitance pickup resonator center frequency variation with changing signal capacitance. The magnitude of the output signal depends on the slope of the resonance curve at the 915-MHz drive frequency. For a bell-shaped resonance curve, the slope is a function of the peak voltage (Vp) and the bandwidth (BW).

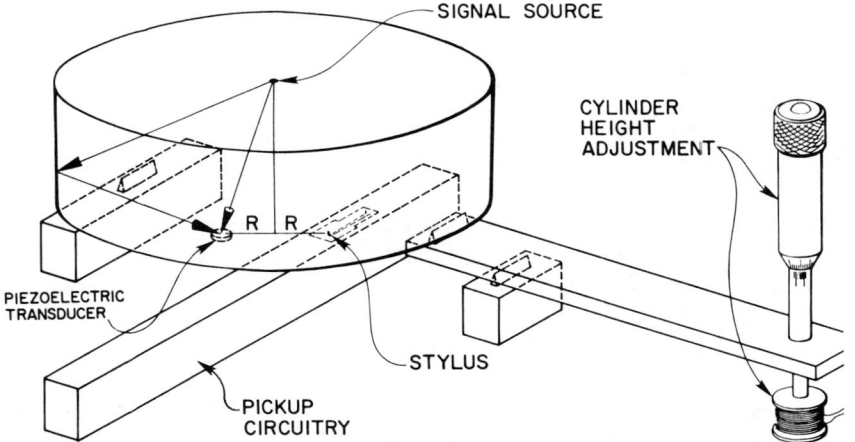

FIG. 40. Apparatus used for comparison of piezoelectric and capacitance transducer responses at an early stage of capacitance transducer development. Both sensors are positioned equidistant from the axis of the cylindrical medium. Signals from a source at the center of the upper cylinder surface are nominally identical on arrival at each receiver. The levers and height adjustment are for optimum positioning of the medium surface relative to the capacitance pickup styles.

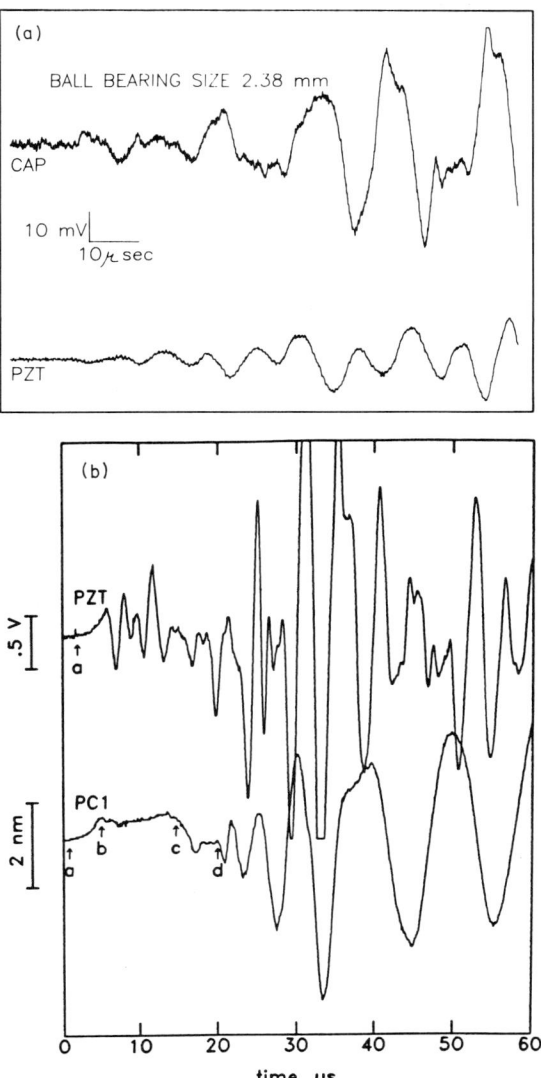

FIG. 41. (a) Results of dropping a 2.38-mm-diameter ball bearing from a height of 2 cm to generate a signal in the medium shown in Fig. 40. PZT, Piezoelectric transducer output; CAP, capacitance transducer output. The PZT signal is dominated by transducer resonances. (b) Seismic waveforms from a single thermal fracture in a thin glass plate, observed at a distance of 150 mm and at an angle of 90° to the propagation direction of the crack. The PZT signal shows the first arrival at a. Later phases are not recognizable. The signal from the capacitance transducer shows the acceleration phase (a to b), the propagation phase (b to c), and the stopping phase starting at c. A dispersed wave plate arrives at d.

## 8. Frictional Sliding

Stable and unstable sliding between rock surfaces and between rock surfaces and gouge may be responsible for failures on a scale covering several orders of magnitude, from small man-made structures to large earthquakes. The variables that determine stability, stable sliding, or stick–slip behavior are many. M. S. Paterson in his recent book "Experimental Rock Deformation—The Brittle Field"[64] devotes a chapter to friction and sliding phenomena. "Fundamentals of Rock Mechanics"[65] by Jaegar and Cook also has a chapter on friction. The author recommends both books highly. References to many earlier works may be found there. In this section we will only discuss some apparatuses that are suitable for friction measurements.

Friction is defined as the ratio of the shear stress to the normal stress at which sliding starts for the static case and which is necessary to maintain sliding without acceleration in the dynamic case. In a friction apparatus it must therefore be possible to measure the normal load, the shear load, and the displacement as a function of time.

The principles of various friction measurements are shown in Fig. 42. Those in Fig. 42a and b are suitable for static friction measurements on saw cuts and previously induced shear fractures under triaxial conditions. Rummel et al.[30] and Stesky[66] among other,[64,65] made friction measurements on saw cuts and induced fractures, respectively. Both sets of experiments were performed in a gas high-pressure environment and over a range of temperatures. Stesky[66] also measured acoustic emissions at temperatures up to 700°C. This experimental configuration is shown in Fig. 43.

Once there has been a slip on the fault, the distribution of forces becomes complicated. This is illustrated in Fig. 44. If sliding is to occur on the saw cut or fault and the two sample halves are to remain relatively undeformed, there must be motion on some interfaces that are perpendicular to the

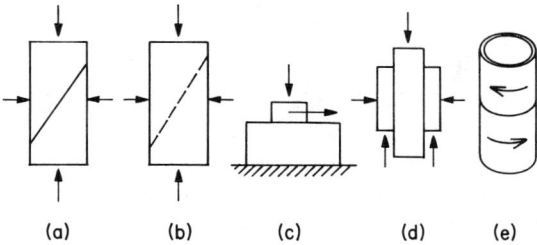

FIG. 42. Common types of friction tests: (a) sliding on saw cut in triaxial test; (b) sliding on previously induced shear fracture in triaxial test; (c) conventional shear test; (d) double shear test; (e) shear test on thin-walled hollow cylinders. (With permission from Springer-Verlag; see reference 64.)

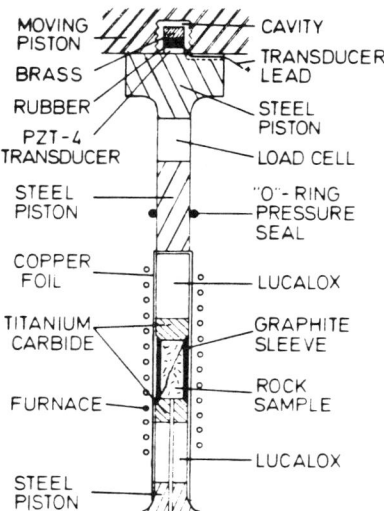

FIG. 43. Experimental arrangement used by Stesky[66] for frictional sliding experiments at high temperature and confining pressure. Note the transducer (on the steel piston) for acoustic emission studies. (With permission from *Pure and Applied Geophysics*; see reference 66.)

compression axes. As soon as sliding has commenced, the cross section over which the force is applied and that over which sliding takes place become variables. Scholz et al.[67] have avoided some of these difficulties by applying the force to the sample through rollers. This arrangement is shown in Fig. 45. It was also used in the author's laboratory to study the uniformity or lack thereof of strain accumulation before stick–slip and as a result of stick–slip. Using holography, it was found that prior to stick–slip the saw cut did not appear anomalous; i.e., the fringes as well as their spacing and curvature were continuous across the saw cut. At this resolution, the surface deformation in the direction perpendicular to the sample did not reveal any nonuniformity. The change in surface deformation that accumulates during stick–slip events is very nonuniform, revealing evidence of nonuniform slip and locking of the fault. Repeated force applications show the same uniform deformation before stick–slip and the nonuniform deformation spanning the stick–slip events.

The other experimental arrangements shown in Fig. 42c, d, and e do not share the difficulties of those of Fig. 42a and b that were illustrated in Fig. 44. They are, however, difficult to adapt to work under confining pressure. The arrangements in c and d can easily be adapted to large specimens and are amenable to static, dynamic, and cycling tests. During cycling

172   HARTMUT SPETZLER

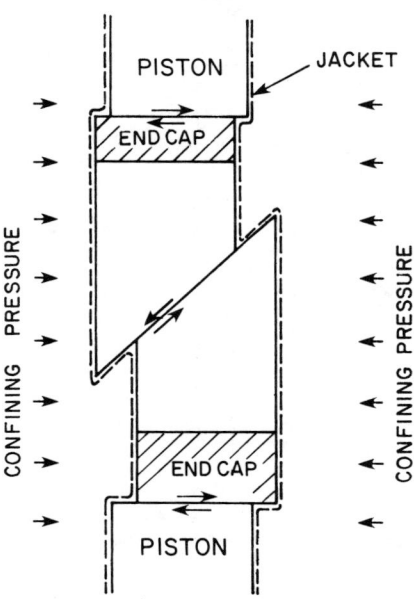

FIG. 44. Complicated distribution of forces and geometry once sliding has commenced in simple triaxial friction tests (Fig. 42a and b).

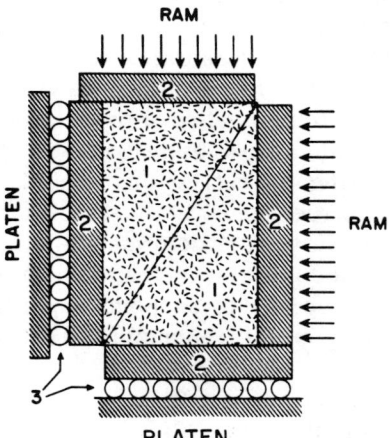

FIG. 45. Schematic diagram of loading configuration used by Scholz et al.:[67] (1) specimen; (2) steel end caps; (3) roller bearings. (With permission from American Geophysical Union; see reference 67.)

experiments, as gouge is generated from the large blocks, their surfaces become nonplanar and the geometry changes.

Most of the problems mentioned above are avoided if the arrangement in Fig. 42e is used. The cylinders must be thin-walled so that the differences in linear speed as a function of radius between the inside and the outside of the cylinders becomes negligible. Continuous dynamic friction and many multiple cycle tests can easily be performed with or without fault gouge.

## 9. Permeability

The permeability of a substance is a measure of its ability to transmit a fluid. Its mathematical definition is analogous to those of electrical conductivity (Ohm's law) and of thermal conductivity. Darcy' law states

$$q_i = \frac{k_{ij}}{\mu} \frac{\partial P}{\partial x_j} \tag{14}$$

$$q = -\frac{k}{\mu} \frac{\partial P}{\partial x} \tag{15}$$

where $q_i$ is the volume flow per unit time, $\mu$ the viscosity of the fluid, $\partial P/\partial x$ the pressure gradient, and $k_{ij}$ the tensor form of the permeability. In most cases the permeability is quoted according to Eq. (15), that is, as a scalar quantity. A convenient unit for the permeability is the darcy. One darcy $(d) = 0.907 \times 10^{-12}$ m$^2$.

A knowledge of permeability values of rocks is important in many engineering applications, such as in petroleum, hydrological, and mining engineering. Underground storage and retrieval of natural gas, safe storage or disposal of toxic and nuclear wastes, and underground gasification of coal and gas are examples of such applications. Before embarking on any rock permeability measurements, be they in the laboratory or *in situ*, the reader is encouraged to read a paper by Brace,[68] where the available data are analyzed. The range of permeabilities at a single site may vary over six orders of magnitude while still not showing a recognizable trend with depth. Similarly, large ranges in values for laboratory measurements cast some doubt on the usefulness of absolute permeability values for any specific rocks. Relative changes in permeability values as functions of externally applied variables may indeed be quite useful. In the following we will examine some techniques for studying the permeability of rocks.

For permeability values above about a microdarcy measurements are made under steady-state conditions; i.e., the fluid flow is measured under a constant pressure gradient.[69,70] To measure smaller values, Brace *et al.*[71]

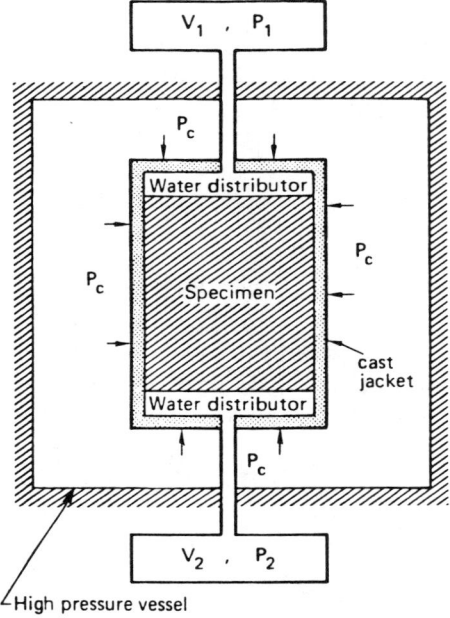

Fig. 46. Schematic diagram of the permeability measurement apparatus. $V_1$ and $V_2$, volumes of upstream and downstream reservoirs, respectively; $P_1$ and $P_2$, pressures in these reservoirs; $P_c$, confining pressure. (With permission from Lawrence Livermore Laboratory Report; see reference 74.)

developed the transient method, which was refined by Lin[72] and Heard et al.[73] to allow the determination of values as low as $10^{-12}$ d. A schematic for the low-permeability measurement technique is shown in Fig. 46 and a schematic for the appropriate apparatus in Fig. 47. These figures are from Lin,[72] who used water for the permeating fluid. Darcy's law holds for fluids of varying viscosity,[71] including gases, as long as the viscosity of the fluid is taken into consideration. The sample is initially fully saturated by applying pore pressure to both the upstream and downstream reservoirs. A small increase of pressure in the upstream reservoir results in a pressure front that migrates into the sample, thus reducing the pressure difference between the two reservoirs. The decrease of the pressure is a function of the sample dimensions, the reservoir sizes, the viscosity of the fluid, and of course the permeability of the sample. Lin[74] developed a computer code for generating pressure vs. time curves for constant values of viscosity. Such curves can be generated for any sample, fluid, and reservoir arrangement. Figure 48 shows such a set of curves and some experimental data. For details of the instrumentation the reader is referred to the original papers.[71–74]

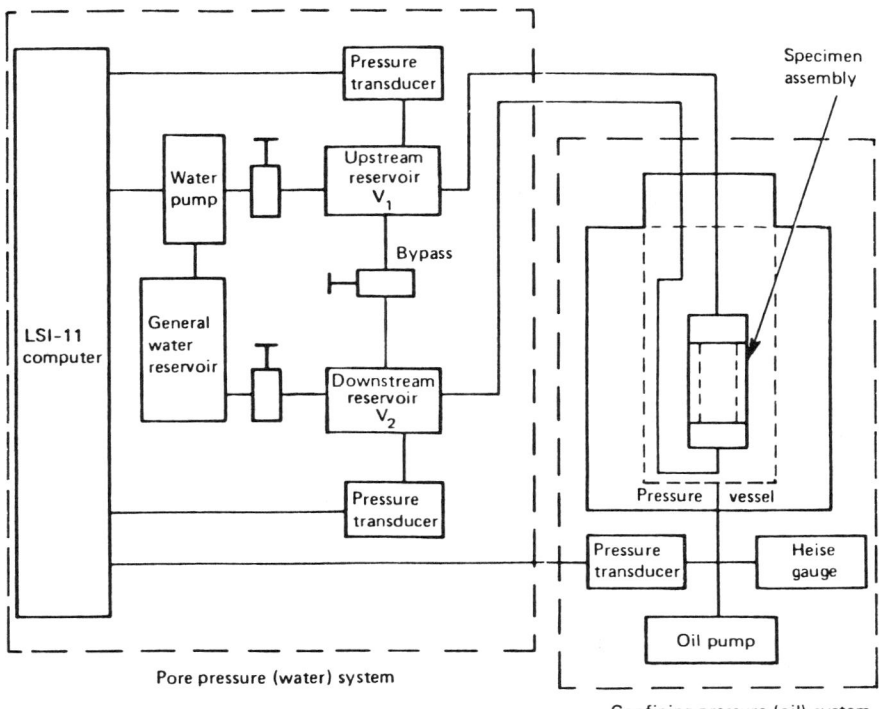

FIG. 47. Simplified diagram showing connections among the three main parts of the permeability apparatus: specimen assembly, confining pressure system, and pore pressure system. (With permission from Lawrence Livermore Laboratory Report; see reference 74.)

In addition to the techniques mentioned above for measuring bulk rock properties, it is often of interest to know where and in what quantities the permeating medium resided within the rock and via what paths it flowed through the specimen. This is especially interesting when the rock is under stress and at elevated temperature. The use of radioactive tracers in conjunction with holography makes this possible. The experimental arrangement shown in Fig. 49, similar to that in Fig. 47, has provisions for a superimposed axial stress in addition to confining and pore pressures. A small reservoir containing a radioactive tracer gas is connected into the upstream part of the pore pressure system. When conventional permeability measurements are being made the trace gas reservoir is closed. When knowledge of the gas distribution is desired, the tracer gas is introduced into the sample and allowed to come to equilibrium. The sample is then removed from the pressure vessel and the gas distribution determined.

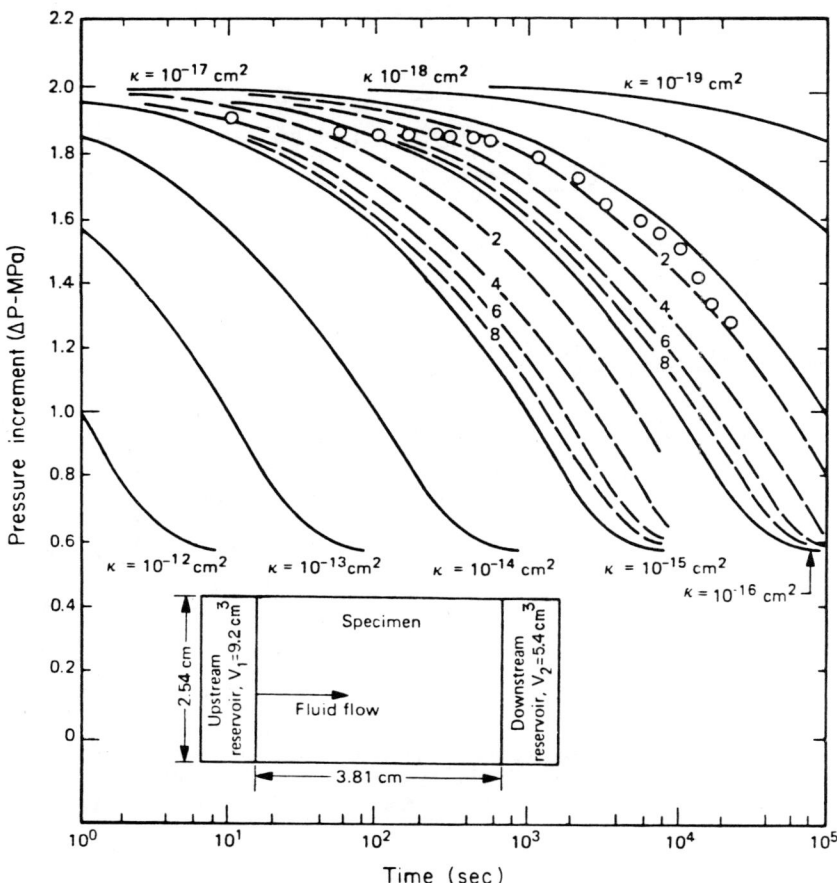

FIG. 48. Comparison of corrected observation ($O$) with calculated pressure decay curves (solid and dashed lines) for specimen 1. Permeability ($\kappa$) is determined to be 1.52–2.0 × $10^{-17}$ cm$^2$. (Insert) Configuration of model study. $V_1$ and $V_2$, volumes of the upstream and downstream reservoirs, respectively; fluid flows from $V_1$ to $V_2$. (With permission from Lawrence Livermore Laboratory Report; see reference 74.)

The ideal tracer gas is chemically inert and has a half-life that is very long in comparison to the duration of the experiment. It decays into a radioactive daughter that is a solid and has a half-life on the order of the duration of the experiment, hours to at most days. While the tracer gas is in the rock its decay product, the radioactive solid, is deposited in the cracks and pores that are occupied by gas. As the sample is removed from the high-pressure, high-temperature environment within the pressure vessel, the gas will at least partially escape. The rest may be driven off by heating the sample. The

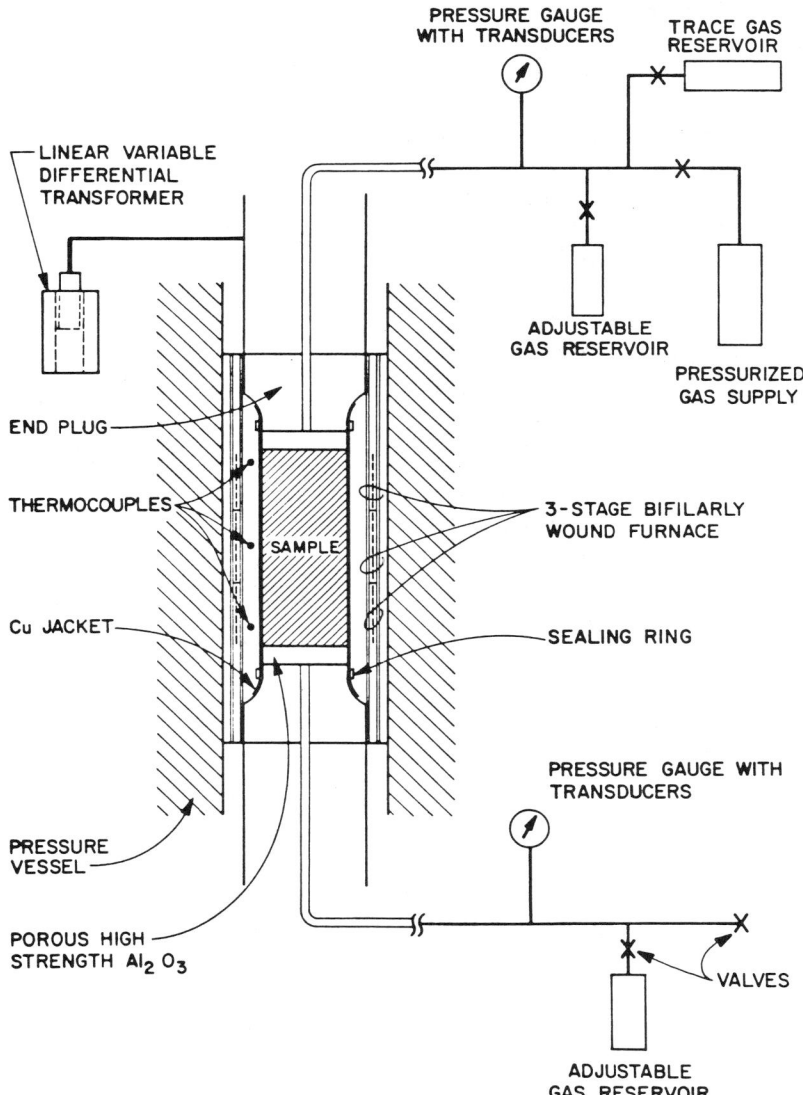

FIG. 49. Experimental arrangement for permeability and gas conduit measurements. A three-stage bifilarly wound furnace ensures good temperature distribution and low electrical interference from the heater.

radioactive decay product, a solid, will remain in the sample in the same proportions in which the gas had occupied the rock.

There are several means of measuring the radioactivity within the sample, each yielding unique information. If there is sufficient gamma ray activity, it is possible to obtain the bulk distribution of the spaces that were occupied by the gas. Gamma rays have a range of several centimeters in rock and can thus escape easily from the interior of typical laboratory samples. One possible arrangement for detecting the former gas distribution is shown in Fig. 50. The sample is inserted into a perforated lead shield, which in turn is wrapped in film with a radiation enhancement backing. The gamma radiation reaches the film from small solid angles, resulting in exposures of the film that are proportional to the activity in those solid angles. If alpha or beta radiation is present, a copper jacket of appropriate thickness may be placed around the sample to shield against that radiation. The exposure on the film will indicate the region or regions where the gas permeated the sample and can be correlated with the bulging of the sample as observed by holography; see Fig. 51.

More detailed information can be obtained on the microscopic scale by sectioning the sample and using autoradiography to record the images. A

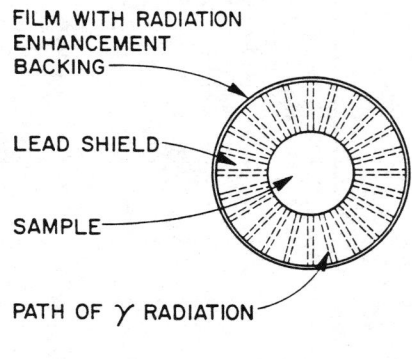

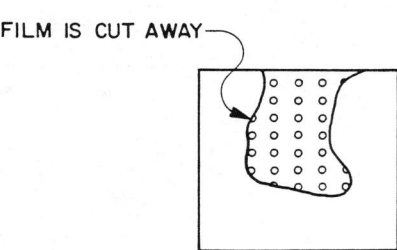

Fig. 50. Arrangement for determining gas distribution. Radial holes in a cylindrical lead shield allow $\gamma$-radiation to reach the film only from a small part of the sample. The exposed film gives an indication of the distribution of the radioactive tracer in the sample.

possible procedure for this is indicated in Fig. 51. After the sample has been removed from the pressure vessel—or, if the experiment was performed in a vessel with an optical window, while the sample is still in place—the bulge is recorded by holography. A cutting plan is made for the sample and autoradiographs are produced by placing the appropriate film in contact with the cut faces of the sample. Film sensitive to beta or alpha radiation should be used. The resolution of the film is typically a fraction of a micrometer. The image on the film will show the location where the gas was and the image intensities will be proportional to the quantity of the gas that was in the pores and cracks. Comparisons of the autoradiographs with scanning electron photomicrographs can yield important data on crack volumes. Since the integrated intensity for a single crack on the autoradiographs is proportional to the volume of the crack as it was when the gas was in it, the crack aspect ratio (length/width) may be calculated from the SEM and autoradiography data.

In the following we will examine several candidates for tracer gases. In searching through the nuclear chart, it seems that $Ar^{42}$ has nearly ideal properties. It has a half-life of 33 years and decays into $K^{42}$, which has a half-life of 12.4 hours. The $Ar^{42}$ decays directly to the ground state of $K^{42}$ with a beta particle with a maximum energy of 0.6 MeV. Of the $K^{42}$ nuclei, 82% go directly to the ground state of $Ca^{42}$ with a beta of maximum energy 3.52-MeV and 18% decay to an excited state of $Ca^{42}$, which then emits a prompt 1.5 MeV $\gamma$ ray. While the $Ar^{42}$ is in a rock sample, it may be kept at high temperature and pressure for several half-lives (or a large fraction of one half-life) of $K^{42}$ to allow $K^{42}$ to come to secular equilibrium (or a reasonable fraction thereof). Since $Ar^{42}$ has no $\gamma$-radiation, a whole-body count of the 1.57-MeV $\gamma$ from the $K^{42}$ will be a measure of the total porosity that the rock sample had when it was at high temperature and pressure. Argon-42 may be produced by double neutron capture, $Ar^{40}(n, \gamma)Ar^{41}(n, \gamma)Ar^{42}$,[75] or by triton capture, $Ar^{40}(t, p)Ar^{42}$.[76] Because of the small neutron cross sections of $A^{40}$ and $Ar^{41}$ (both less than 1 barn) and because of the short half-life of $A^{41}$ ($\sim 1.3$ hours), a large neutron flux is needed to produce $Ar^{42}$ by double neutron capture.

Another possibility where an inert gas has an intermediate radioactive solid daughter exists in the decay chain of radium. Radon-222 can be milked continuously from radium, such that its short half-life of 3.82 days is not a detriment. As $Rn^{222}$ decays, $P_0^{210}$ grows in. It has a half-life of 138.4 days and is primarily an alpha emitter and thus very useful for autoradiography.

Should neither $Ar^{42}$ nor $Rn^{222}$ prove to be practical because of difficulties in obtaining them, it may be necessary to use radioactive tracer gases that do not have a radioactive solid daughter. In that case the whole-sample

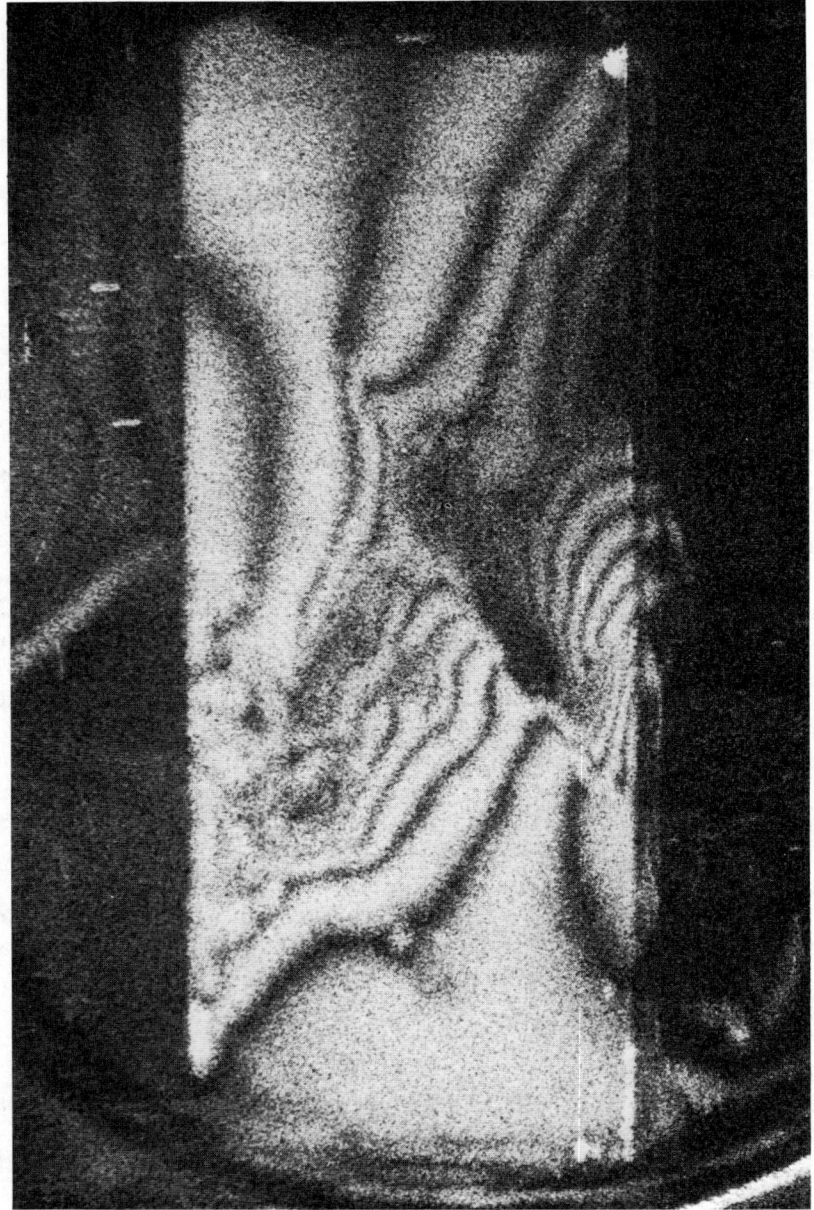

FIG. 51. (a) Doubly exposed hologram clearly showing the surface deformation associated with the development of the failure zone. (b) Cutting plan made for scanning electron microscopy and autoradiography studies.

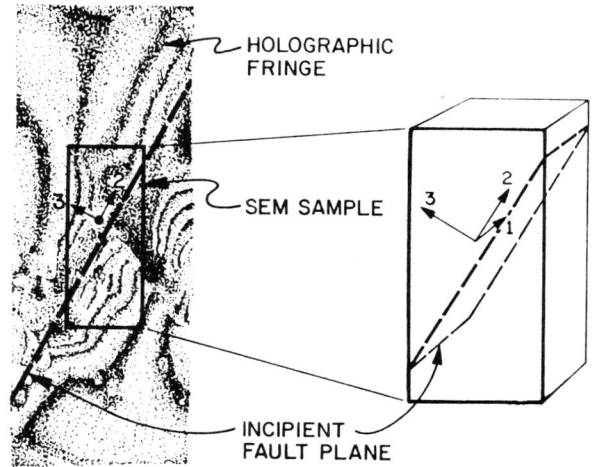

Fig. 51—*continued*

autoradiography (Fig. 49) can still be done quantitatively. It must be done within a pressure vessel while the sample is under stress and the cracks are open. The microautoradiography must then rely on the gas that was trapped within the sample. It thus becomes a qualitative rather than a quantitative method. Several gases, some commercially available, are attractive in this case.

Xenon-133 is commercially used in hospitals for lung scans. It has a half-life of ~5 days, is a $\beta$ emitter (~0.4 MeV), and has an abundant ~80 keV X-ray that results from an excited state of $Cs^{133}$ into which it decays. The range of 80-keV X-rays is somewhat less than 20 mm in rock, which makes $Xe^{133}$ still useful although somewhat less desirable because radiation from different parts of the sample would contribute with significantly different efficiencies.

Krypton-85 has a half-life of about 11 years, which avoids the supply problem with $Xe^{133}$. It decays to the ground state of $Rb^{85}$ with a probability in excess of 99%, emitting a $\beta$ particle with a maximum energy of ~0.7 MeV.

## References

1. A. S. Tetelman and A. J. McEvily, Jr., "Fracture of Structural Materials." Wiley, New York, 1967.
2. S. W. Freiman, "Fracture Mechanics of Glass: Science and Technology," Vol. 5, 21–78. Academic Press, New York, 1980.
3. S. M. Wiederhorn, *in* "Fracture Mechanics of Ceramics" (R. C. Bradt, D. P. H. Hasselman, and F. F. Lange, eds.), Vol. 2, pp. 613–646. Plenum, New York, 1974.
4. O. L. Anderson and P. C. Grew, *Rev. Geophys. Space Phys.* **B15**, 7 (1977).

5. A. R. Ingraffea, F. E. Heuze, H. Y. Ko, and K. Gerstle, *Proc. U.S. Symp. Rock Mech., 18th* (F. D. Wang and G. B. Clark, eds.), 2A4-1, p. 7. Colo. Sch. Mines Press, Keystone, Colorado, 1977.
6. H. A. Spetzler, G. A. Sobolev, C. H. Sondergeld, B. G. Salov, I. C. Getting, and A. Koltsov, *J. Geophys. Res.* **86**, 1070 (1981).
7. B. R. Lawn and T. R. Wilshaw, "Fracture of Brittle Solids," p. 59. Cambridge Univ. Press, London and New York, 1975.
8. E. R. Fuller, *in* "Fracture Mechanics Applied to Brittle Materials" (S. W. Freiman, ed.), ASTM STP 678, Phi- p. 3. ASTM, Philadelphia, Pennsylvania, 1979.
9. B. J. Pletka, E. R. Fuller, Jr., and B. G. Koepke, *in* "Fracture Mechanics Applied to Brittle Materials" (S. W. Freiman, ed.), ASTM STP 678, p. 19. ASTM, Philadelphia, Pennsylvania, 1979.
10. D. P. Williams and A. G. Evans, *J. Test. Eval.* **1**, 264 (1973).
11. A. G. Evans, *J. Mater. Sci.* **7**, 1137 (1972).
12. A. G. Evans and S. M. Wiederhorn, *J. Mater. Sci.* **9**, 270 (1974).
13. S. M. Wiederhorn, *J. Am. Ceram. Soc.* **50**, 407 (1967).
14. F. P. Champomier, *in* "Fracture Mechanics Applied to Brittle Materials" (S. W. Freiman, ed.), ASTM STP 678, p. 60. ASTM, Philadelphia, Pennsylvania, 1979.
15. R. A. Schmidt and T. J. Lutz, *in* "Fracture Mechanics Applied to Brittle Materials" (S. W. Freiman, ed.), ASTM STP 678, p. 166. ASTM, Philadelphia, Pennsylvania, 1979.
16. S. M. Wiederhorn, A. M. Shorb, and R. L. Moses, *J. Appl. Phys.* **39**, 1569 (1968).
17. S. Mostovoy, P. B. Crosley, and E. J. Ripling, *J. Mater.* **2**, 661 (1967).
18. S. W. Freiman, D. R. Mulville, and P. W. Mark, *Rep. NRL Prog. Feb.*, p. 36 (1972).
19. R. G. Hoagland, A. R. Rosenfield, and G. T. Hahn, *Metall. Trans.* **3**, 123 (1972).
20. M. F. Kanninen, *Int. J. Fract. Mech.* **9**, 83 (1973).
21. P. Swanson, Ph.D. Thesis, Univ. of Colorado, Boulder, 1984.
22. L. Peck, C. C. Barton, and R. B. Gordon, *J. Geophys. Res.* **90**, 11533 (1985).
23. W. F. Brown and J. E. Srawley, *ASTM Spec. Tech. Publ.* No. 410 (1966).
24. M. Srinivasan and S. C. Seshadri, *in* "Fracture Mechanics for Ceramics, Rocks, and Concrete" (S. W. Freiman and E. R. Fuller, Jr., eds.), ASTM STP 745, p. 46. ASTM, Baltimore, Maryland, 1981.
25. A. G. Evans, *in* "Fracture Mechanics of Ceramics" (R. C. Bradt, D. P. H. Hasselman, and F. F. Lange, eds.), Vol. 1, p. 17. Plenum, New York, 1974.
26. J. J. Petrovic and M. G. Mendiratta, *in* "Fracture Mechanics Applied to Brittle Materials" (S. W. Freiman, ed.), ASTM STP 678, p. 83. ASTM, Philadelphia, Pennsylvania, 1979.
27. A. G. Evans, *in* "Fracture Mechanics Applied to Brittle Materials" (S. W. Freiman, ed.), ASTM STP 678, p. 112. ASTM, Philadelphia, Pennsylvania, 1979.
28. C. C. Wu, R. W. Rice, and P. F. Becher, *in* "Fracture Mechanics for Ceramics, Rocks, and Concrete" (S. W. Freiman and E. J. Fuller, eds.), ASTM STP 745, p. 127. ASTM, Baltimore, Maryland, 1981.
29. I. C. Getting and G. C. Kennedy, *Appl. Phys.* **41**, 4552–4562 (1970).
30. F. Rummel, H. J. Alheid, and C. Frohn, *Pure Appl. Geophys.* **116**, 743 (1978).
31. H. J. Alheid, Ph.D. Thesis, Ruhr Univ., Bochum, F.R.G., 1981.
32. H. A. Spetzler and M. D. Meyer, *Rev. Sci. Instrum.* **45**, 911 (1974).
33. B. P. Bonner and H. C. Heard, personal communication, 1984.
34. K. W. Schuler, *Exp. Mech.* **18**, 477 (1978).
35. D. Holcomb and M. J. McNamee, *Sandia Lab. [Tech. Rep.] SAND* **SAND84-10651** (1984).
36. H. Spetzler, C. H. Scholz, and Chi-Ping J. Lu, *Pure Appl. Geophys.* **112/113**, 571 (1974).
37. H. Spetzler and R. J. Martin, III, *Nature (London)* **252**, 30 (1974).
38. K. Kurita, P. L. Swanson, I. C. Getting, and H. Spetzler, *Geophys. Res. Lett.* **10**, 75 (1983).

39. L. Granryd, I. C. Getting, and H. Spetzler, *Geophys. Res. Lett.* **10**, 71 (1983).
40. L. O. Heflinger, R. F. Wuerker, and H. Spetzler, *Rev. Sci. Instrum.* **44**, 5 (1973).
41. M. D. Meyer and H. Spetzler, *Exp. Mech.* **16**, 454 (1976).
42. H. Spetzler, I. C. Getting, and R. J. Martin, III, *in* "High Pressure Science and Technology" (K. D. Timmerhaus and M. S. Barber, eds.), Vol. 1, p. 883. Plenum, New York, 1979.
43. N. Soga, D. Holcomb, and H. Spetzler, *Rev. Sci. Instrum.* **47**, 1453 (1976).
44. H. Spetzler, N. Soga, H. Mizutani, and R. J. Martin, III, *in* "High Pressure Research: Applications to Geophysics" (M. H. Manghnani and S.-i. Akimoto, eds.), p. 625. Academic Press, New York, 1977.
45. H. P. Liu and A. C. R. Livanos, *J. Geophys. Res.* **18**, 3495 (1976).
46. J. Blitz, "Fundamentals of Ultrasonics." Plenum, New York, 1967.
47. C. H. Sondergeld and L. H. Estey, *J. Geophys. Res.* **86**, 2915 (1981).
48. C. H. Sondergeld, *Rev. Sci. Instrum.* **51**, 1342 (1980).
49. D. Roecken, M.S. Thesis, Univ. Of Colorado, Boulder, 1982.
50. I. C. Getting, C. Roecken, and H. Spetzler, *J. Nondestructive Eval.* (in press).
51. C. H. Sondergeld and L. H. Estey, *Pure Appl. Geophys.* **120**, 151 (1982).
52. W. Sachse and N. N. Hsu, *in* "Physical Acoustics" (W. P. Mason, ed.), Vol. 14, pp. 277–406. Academic Press, New York, 1979.
53. C. H. Palmer and R. E. Green, Jr., *Proc. Sagamore Army Mater. Res. Conf.: Nondestr. Eval. Mater., 23rd, Raquette Lake* (J. J. Burke and V. Weiss, eds.), p. 347. Plenum, New York, 1976.
54. R. A. Kline, Ph.D. Thesis, Johns Hopkins Univ., Baltimore, Maryland, 1978.
55. N. Hsu, J. Simmons, and S. Hardy, *Mater. Eval. (Res. Suppl.)* **35**, 100 (1977).
56. B. Maxfeld and R. Cochran, *Mater. Eval.* **31**, 17 (1973).
57. J. K. Clemens, *RCA Rev.* **39**, 33 (1978).
58. R. C. Palmer, E. J. Denlinger, and H. Kawamoto, *RCA Rev.* **43**, 211 (1982).
59. F. M. Boler and H. A. Spetzler, *EOS, Trans. Am. Geophys. Union* **63**, 1112 (1982). Abstr.
60. F. M. Boler, H. A. Spetzler, and I. C. Getting, *Rev. Sci. Instrum.* **55**, 1293 (1984).
61. F. M. Boler, L. H. Estey, and H. A. Spetzler, *EOS, Trans. Am. Geophys, Union* **64**, 862 (1983).
62. F. Boler, Ph.D. Thesis, Univ. of Colorado, Boulder, 1985.
63. L. H. Estey, Ph.D. Thesis, Univ. of Colorado, Boulder, in progress 1986.
64. M. D. Paterson, "Experimental Rock Deformation—The Brittle Field." Springer-Verlag, Berlin and New York, 1978.
65. J. C. Jaeger and N. G. W. Cook, "Fundamentals of Rock Mechanics." Wiley, New York, 1977.
66. R. M. Stesky, *Pure Appl. Geophys.* **113**, 31 (1975).
67. C. Scholz, P. Molnar, and T. Johnson, *J. Geophys. Res.* **77**, 6392 (1972).
68. W. F. Brace, *Int. J. Rock Mech. Min. Sci. Geomech.* **17**, 241 (1980). Abstr.
69. R. F. Scott, "Principles of Soil Mechanics." Addison-Wesley, Reading, Massachusetts, 1963.
70. E. L. Ohle, *Econ. Geol.* **46**, 667 (1951).
71. W. F. Brace, J. B. Walsh, and W. T. Frangos, *J. Geophys. Res.* **73**, 2225 (1968).
72. W. Lin, *Lawrence Livermore Lab. Rep. UCRL* **UCRL-52604** (1978).
73. H. C. Heard, D. Trimmer, A. Duba, and B. Bonner, *Lawrence Livermore Lab. Rep. UCRL* **UCRL-82609** (1979).
74. W. Lin, *Lawrence Livermore Lab. Rep. UCRL* **UCRL-52304** (1977).
75. S. Katcoff, *Phys. Rev.* **87**, 886 (1952).
76. N. Jarmie and M. G. Silbert, *Phys. Rev.* **123**, 909 (1961).

# 6. SHOCK WAVE TECHNIQUES FOR GEOPHYSICS AND PLANETARY PHYSICS

Thomas J. Ahrens

Seismological Laboratory
California Institute of Technology
Pasadena, California 91125

## 1. Introduction

Shock wave techniques have a special place in the study of the earth's interior and the interiors of both the terrestrial and major plants because virtually the entire pressure and temperature ranges existing within these objects can be achieved in the laboratory. Although shock wave methods have historically seen most applications in the measurement of density at high pressure, other properties of earth and planetary materials whose measurements are discussed in this chapter include sound speed and temperature. Review articles by Grady (1977), Yakushev (1978), Davison and Graham (1979), Murri et al. (1974), and Al'tschuler (1965) summarize experimental techniques for measuring dynamic yielding, absorption spectra, index of refraction, electrical conductivity at radio and microwave frequencies, and viscosity. These are among the many physical properties of minerals and fluids which can and have been measured under shock loading conditions. Other properties studied under shock having less application to the study of planetary interiors include piezoelectricity, ferroelectricity, shock-induced polarization, and shock-induced demagnetization. An important application of shock and related properties is found in the accretion mechanics of terrestrial planets and the solid satellites of the terrestrial and major planets from asteroid-sized protoplanetesimals (Gehrels, 1978). Another application of both shock compression and isentropic release experiments on rocks and minerals (Ahrens and O'Keefe, 1972, 1977) is in the mechanics of the continued bombardment and hence cratering on planetary objects through geologic time (Roddy et al., 1977). Finally, recovery and characterization of shock-compressed materials have provided important insights into the nature of shock deformation mechanisms and, in some cases, provided physical data on the nature of either shock-induced phase changes or phase changes which occur on isentropic release from the high-pressure shock state (e.g., melting) (Stöffler, 1972, 1974).

Three pressure units are commonly in use in shock wave research: kilobar (kbar), gigapascal (GPa), and megabar (Mbar). These are equal to $10^9$, $10^{10}$, and $10^{12}$ dyne/cm$^2$, respectively.

The shock pressure range of primary interest in this review is $\sim 100$ to $\sim 4000$ kbar. The former overrides many strength-related effects in minerals and the latter is the pressure at the earth's center.

### 1.1. Shock Wave Generating Systems

Two general techniques are used to generate dynamic high pressures in materials: the explosive in contact and flyer plate impact methods (Fig. 1). Initial shock wave research on solid materials employed explosive in contact techniques in a plane geometry as indicated in Fig. 2. The pressure profile sketched in Fig. 1 for the shock wave propagating from high explosive

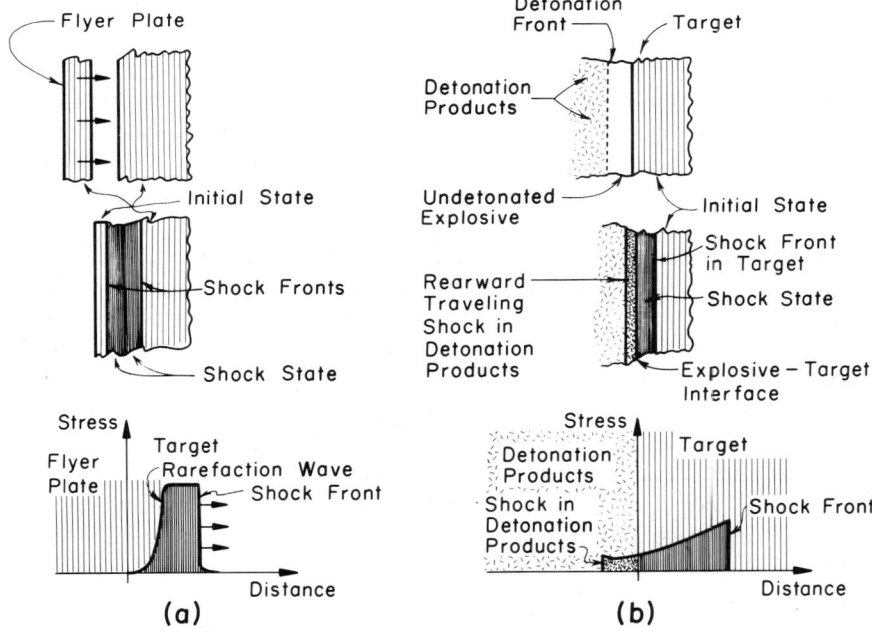

FIG. 1. Generation of shock waves by flyer plate impact and by explosive detonation. (a) Impact-induced steady flat-topped shock wave and following rarefaction wave. (b) Detonation wave in explosive propagating into the target as a decaying shock wave. The decrease with distance (and time, time constant $\tau_d$) of the pressure in the target results from the expansion of the detonation products.

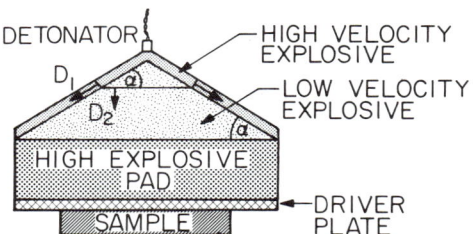

FIG. 2. Use of plane wave generators to induce shock wave in sample via explosive in contact with a plane. Point detonation of an explosive (lens) configuration (10–30 cm in diameter) constructed of explosives with fast ($D_1$) and slow ($D_2$) detonation velocities produces a planar detonation in an underlying explosive pad (e.g., TNT) if $D_2 = D_1 \sin \alpha$. The resulting shock wave propagates through the base plate into the sample. In aluminum, shock pressures of $\sim 25$ GPa (0.25 Mbar) result if TNT is used. (After Ahrens, 1980. Copyright by the AAAS.)

indicates that the pressure vs. distance profile demonstrates a slightly decaying amplitude (with respect to time or distance), whereas flyer plate impact yields a flat-topped shock wave in the sample. In the explosive in contact method, as well as explosively driven oblique shock (Fig. 3), the shock wave is induced in the sample via the propagation from a detonating high explosive. In the case of the oblique shock, because the characteristic thickness of the explosive is less than the shock propagation path, the shock amplitude decays sharply. This, in principle, allows several shock states to be determined in a single experiment. In addition to chemical explosives, Ragan *et al.* (1977) have described the use of a plate of nearly pure $^{235}$U as

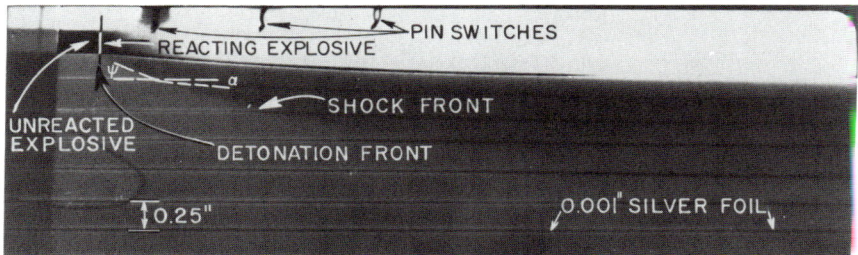

FIG. 3. Oblique shock, flash x-ray method for obtaining Hugoniot data. High-explosive slab is detonated from left to right, with detonation velocity $D$ measured by closure of pin switches shorted by the electrically conducting detonation products. The explosive induces an oblique decaying shock in slabs of sample material, here sandstone. At a given depth in the sample, the angle $\psi$ of the shock front visible in the x-ray photograph is related to the shock velocity by $\sin \psi = U/D$. The particle velocity (see Section 1.2) associated with a point at the shock front is obtained from the bending angle $\alpha$ of 0.025-mm- or 0.001-in.-thick silver foils placed between 6-mm-thick slabs of specimen material. At the intersection of a foil with the shock front, the particle velocity $u$ was obtained from $(U - u)/u = \tan(\psi - \alpha)/\tan \psi$. (After Ahrens and Gregson, 1964.)

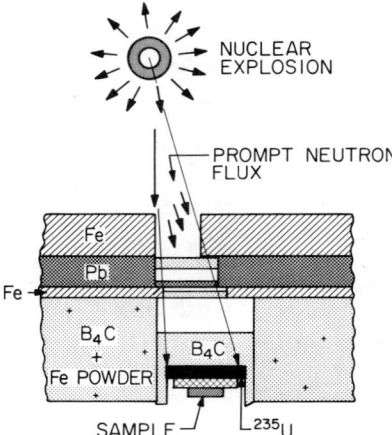

FIG. 4. Experimental geometry for using a nuclear explosion to drive shock into a sample. Prompt neutrons from a nuclear explosion nearly uniformly irradiate a $^{235}$U plate, causing internal fission-induced heating. The resulting expansion (explosion) of the $^{235}$U plate drives an intense shock into the base and sample. Pressures of 2 TPa (20 Mbar) have been induced in molybdenum. (After Ragan, 1978.)

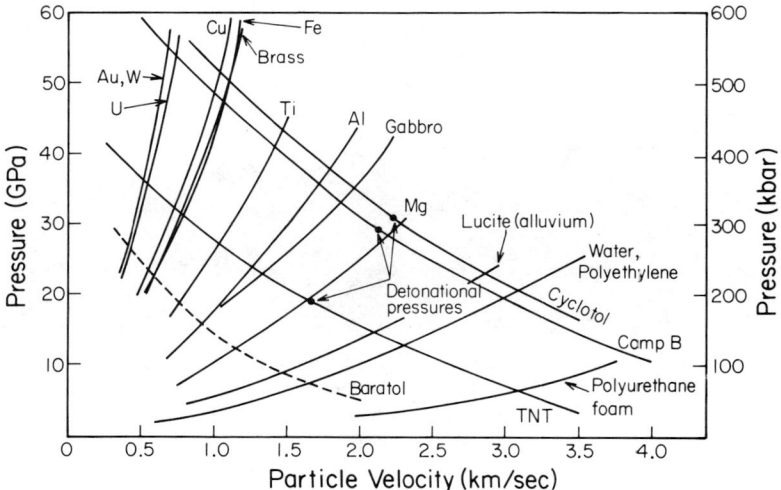

FIG. 5. Shock pressure vs. particle velocity for engineering materials, geological materials, and explosive detonation products. Intersection of detonation product curves with nonreactive media predicts shock pressure and particle velocity at an explosive sample interface. (After Jones, 1972.)

a neutron-activated explosive (Fig. 4). Unlike the chemical explosives, whose intrinsic detonation pressures vary from ~2 to 40 GPa (20–400 kbar) (Fig. 5), the $^{235}$U plate acts like a superexplosive when it is placed in the vicinity of a nuclear explosion. It derives its energy from the neutron-induced fission of the $^{235}$U atoms. This (subcritical) process raises the pressures in the $^{235}$U to values in the range of ~10 TPa (~$10^2$ Mbar).

Acceleration of flyer plates to various speeds to produce impacts and hence flat-topped shock pressure pulses (Fig. 1) in materials can be accomplished by using plane flow explosive products to achieve speeds of ~4.5 km/s (Fig. 6)

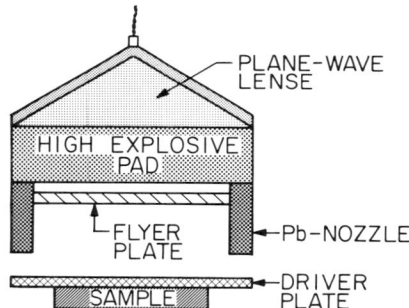

FIG. 6. High-explosive system used to accelerate metal flyer plate via planar expansive flow of detonation products. Typically the plane wave detonated explosive pad accelerates the metal flyer plate to ~4.5 km/s to impact the sample assemblies. With an iron flyer plate, pressures up to 140 GPa (1.4 Mbar) are achieved in copper base plates. (After Ahrens, 1980. Copyright by the AAAS.)

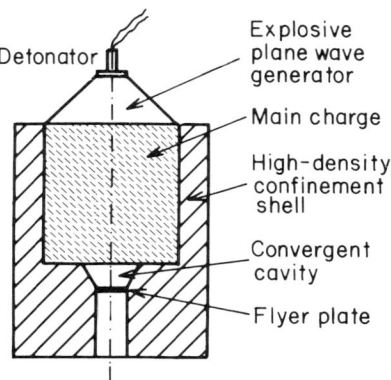

FIG. 7. Augmented explosive acceleration plane wave system similar to that of Fig. 6. A convergent cavity is used to channel detonation product gases so that they act on the flyer plate for a longer time. The sketched system is capable of launching flyer plates to speeds of ~6.8 km/s. (After Tan Bing-Shen and Jing Fu-Qian, 1982.)

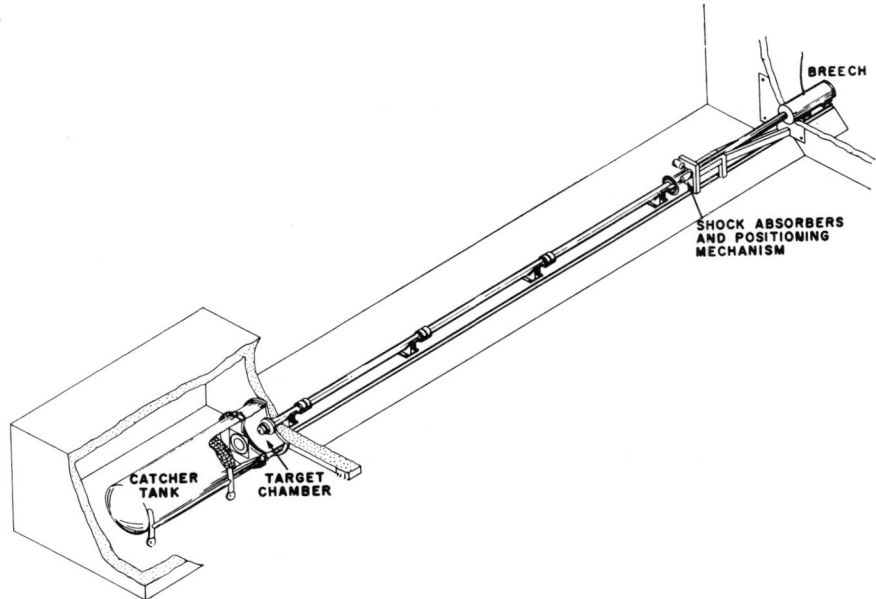

FIG. 8. Sketch of one-stage light-gas gun 10 cm in diameter and 14 m long. This gun, which operates with 28 liters of He compressed to 413 bars, can launch ~1-kg projectiles to speeds of ~1 km/s or 0.5-kg projectiles to speeds of ~1.5 km/s. (After Fowles et al., 1970.)

and by using nozzle shaping to achieve speeds of 6.8 km/s (Fig. 7). One- and two-stage light gas guns achieve speeds up to 1.5 and 8 km/s, respectively (Figs. 8 and 9).

### 1.2. Shock Wave Relations

Explosives in contact and the impact of flyer plates both induce nearly steady waves in materials. For steady waves a shock velocity $U$ with respect to the laboratory, independent of time, can be defined and conservation of mass, momentum, and energy across a shock front can be expressed as

$$\rho_1 = \rho_0(U - u_0)/(U - u_1) \tag{1}$$

$$P_1 - P_0 = \rho_0(u_1 - u_0)(U - u_0) \tag{2}$$

$$E_1 - E_0 = (P_1 + P_0)(1/\rho_0 - 1/\rho_1)/2 = \tfrac{1}{2}(u_1 - u_0)^2 \tag{3}$$

where $\rho$, $u$, $P$, and $E$ are density, particle velocity, shock pressure, and internal energy and, as indicated in Fig. 9, the subscripts 0 and 1 refer to the state in front of and behind the shock front, respectively. It should be understood that in this section pressure is used in place of stress in the indicated

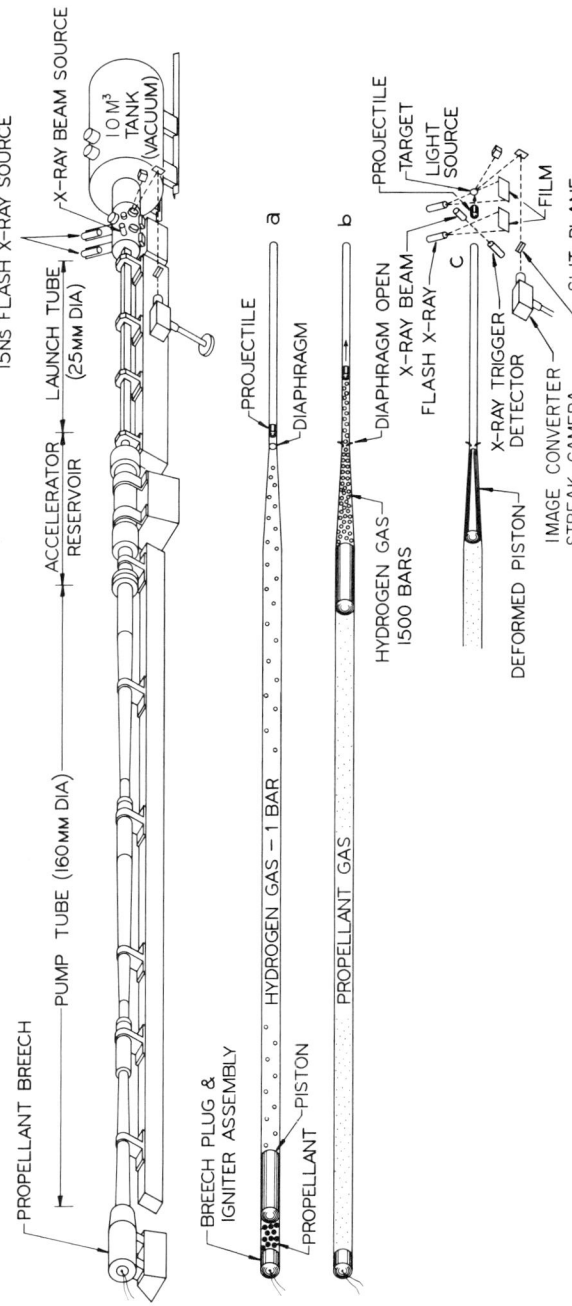

FIG. 9. Diagrammatic view of the Caltech two-stage light-gas gun used for shock wave research on earth materials. The total length of the apparatus is 33 m, total mass approximately 35 tons. (a) When the chemical propellant ignites, a 20-kg plastic piston compresses hydrogen in the pump tube. (b) As the projectile enters the high-pressure reservoir section, the diaphragm ruptures and the projectile begins to accelerate down the launch tube. (c) As a result of the deformation of the plastic piston in the high-pressure reservoir, gas pressure is maintained on the base of the projectile as it is accelerated, until it clears the launch tube. After leaving the launch tube, the projectile, which usually has a tantalum plate in its nose, intersects a continuous x-ray beam and triggers two 15-n flash x-ray sources. The resulting x-ray shadowgraphs permit the projectile velocity to be measured to within 0.2%. When the projectile hits the sample, the streak camera is activated, recording the shock wave velocity through the sample. Projectiles of 15 g mass are accelerated to speeds of ~7 km/s with this apparatus. (After Ahrens, 1980. Copyright by the AAAS.)

191

wave propagation direction. Actually stress, in the wave propagation direction, is what is specified by Eq.(2). A detailed derivation of Eqs. (1), (2), and (3) is given in Duvall and Fowles (1963). Equation (3) also indicates that the material achieves an increase in internal energy (per unit mass) which is exactly equal to the kinetic energy per unit mass.

In the simplest case when a single shock state is achieved via a shock front, the Rankine-Hugoniot equations involve six variables ($U$, $u_1$, $\rho_0$, $\rho_1$, $E_1 - E_0$, and $P_1$); thus, measuring three, usually $U$, $u_1$, and $\rho_0$, determines the shock state, $\rho_1$, $E_1 - E_0$, and $P_1$. The key assumpion underpinning the validity of Eqs. (1)–(3) is that the shock wave is steady so that the rise time $\tau_s$ (Fig. 10) is short compared to the characteristic decay time $\tau_d$ (see Fig. 1). Upon driving a shock of pressure $P_1$ into a material, a final shock state is achieved which is described by Eqs. (1)–(3). This shock state is shown in relation to other thermodynamic paths in Fig. 11, The pressure-volume plane. Here $V_0 = 1/\rho_0$ and $V = 1/\rho$. In the case of the isotherm and

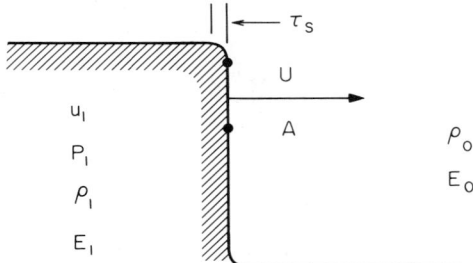

FIG. 10. Profile of a steady shock wave, rise time $\tau_s$, imparting a particle velocity $u_1$, pressure $P_1$, density $\rho_1$, and internal energy density $E_1$, propagating with velocity $U$ into material that is at rest at density $\rho_0$ and internal energy density $E_0$.

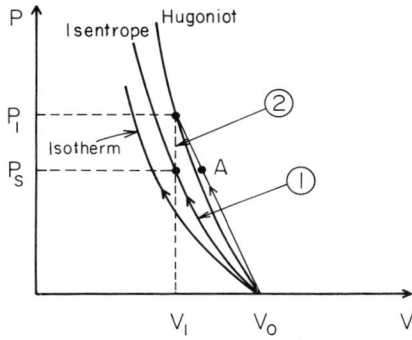

FIG. 11. Pressure-volume compression curves. For isentrope and isotherm, the thermodynamic path coincides with the locus of states, whereas for shock, the thermodynamic path is a straight line to point $P_1$, $V_1$ on the Hugoniot curve, which is the locus of shock states.

isentrope, it is possible to follow, as a thermodynamic path, the actual isothermal or isentropic curve to achieve a state on the isotherm or isentrope. A shock or Hugoniot state is different, however. The Hugoniot state $P_1$, $V_1$ is achieved via a thermodynamic path given by the *straight line* called a Rayleigh line (Fig. 11). Thus successive states along the Hugoniot curve *cannot* be achieved, one from another, by a shock process. The Hugoniot curve itself then just represents the locus of final shock states.

To demonstrate that the Rayleigh line actually represents the thermodynamic path to which material is subjected on being shocked from state $P = 0$, $V = V_0$ to $P = P_1$, $V = V_1$, it is essential to the assumptions underlying Eqs. (1)–(3) that the shock wave sketched in Fig. 10 is *steady*. Thus, the Rankine–Hugoniot equations [Eqs. (1)–(3)] not only describe the conservation of mass, momentum, and energy from state 0 to state 1, but also describe conservation of these quantities from state 0 to an *arbitrary* intermediate state such as state A (Figs. 10 and 11). If the pressure and specific volume of state A, which can lie at any point along the Rayleigh line, are given by $P$ and $V$, the pressure at A can be written as

$$P = U^2/V_0 - (U^2/V_0^2)V \tag{4}$$

or

$$U = V_0[P/(V_0 - V)]^{1/2} \tag{4a}$$

where Eq. (4) is obtained by eliminating $u$ between Eqs. (1) and (2). Equation (4) is recognized as the equaton of a line of slope $-U^2/V_0^2$ and its intercept is at a value of $V = 0$ of $U^2/V_0$. Since state A can represent any state between $P = 0$ and $P = P_1$, Eq. (4) represents a series of thermodynamic paths which the material follows on being shocked from state 0 to state 1. Thus, although the Hugoniot represents a series of thermodynamically defined states, these states are always achieved by a Rayleigh line thermodynamic path and not from another state on the curve. When centered at ambient conditions, this Hugoniot curve is called a principal Hugoniot. The isentrope centered at ambient conditions is similarly designated as a principal isentrope. Some principal Hugoniots for earth materials are shown in Fig. 12.

## 2. Impedance Match Solutions

Hugoniot curves, such as those depicted in Fig. 12, may be transformed from the pressure–volume plane to the pressure–particle velocity plane (Fig. 13) using

$$u = [(P_1 - P_0)(V_0 - V_1)]^{1/2} \tag{5a}$$

$$U = V_0[(P_1 - P_0)/(V_0 - V_1)]^{1/2} \tag{5b}$$

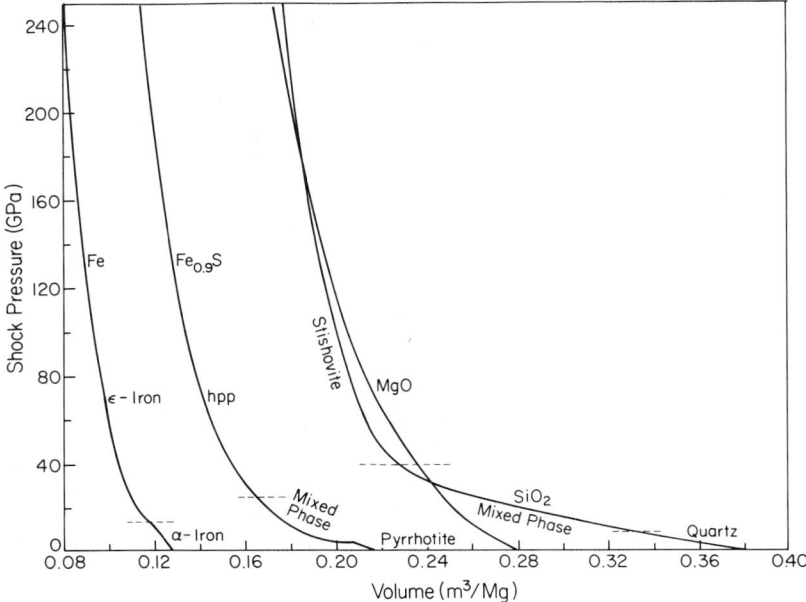

FIG. 12. Pressure–volume Hugoniots for four earth materials. Of these, only MgO does not undergo a shock-induced phase transition over the pressure range shown. In the case of $SiO_2$ (quartz) the dashed line indicates the onset and completion of the shock-induced phase change to the rutile-structured phase (stishovite). The dashed lines shown for $Fe_{0.9}S$ and $\gamma$-iron indicate completion pressure of shock-induced phase change.

We assume that in Eq. (5), all velocities are measured with respect to the same coordinate system (at rest in the laboratory) and the particle velocities are in the same orientation (normal to the shock front). When a plane shock wave propagates from one material into another the pressure (stress) and particle velocity across the interface are continuous. Therefore, the pressure–particle velocity plane representation proves a convenient framework from which to describe the plane impact of a gun- or explosive-accelerated flyer plate with a sample target. Also of importance (and discussed below) is the interaction of plane shock waves with a free surface or higher- or lower-impedance media.

2.1. Plane Impact of a Flyer Plate

The physical state of the sample before and after impact is sketched in Fig. 14a. Positive velocity, indicating mass motion to the right (in the laboratory), is plotted toward the positive, $u$, axis. Hence, in the initial state 0, the target B is at $u = 0$ and $P = 0$, whereas the initial state in the flyer plate 0' is

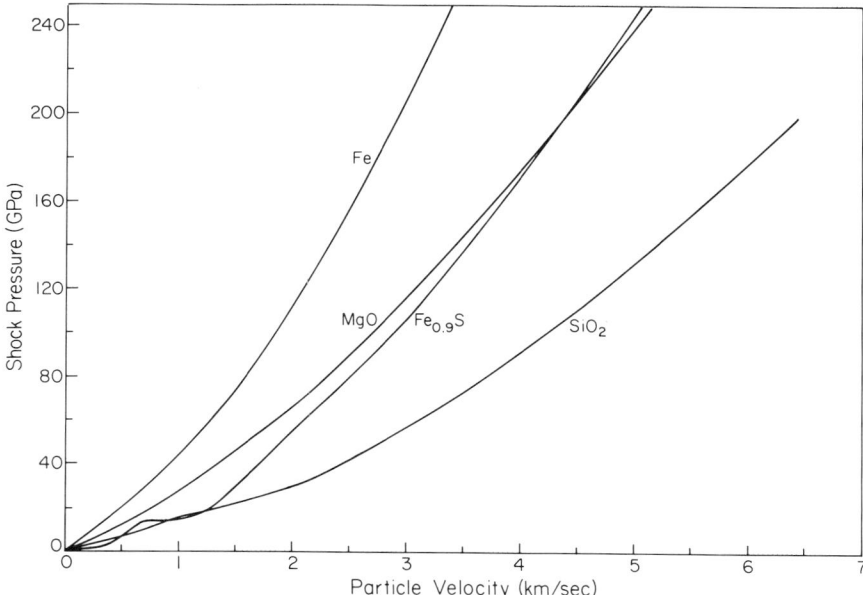

FIG. 13. Pressure–particle velocity Hugoniot for four earth materials.

$u = u_{fp}$ and $P = 0$. Upon interaction of flyer plate A with target B, a shock wave propagates forward in the sample and rearward in the flyer plate. Because the pressure and particle velocity are continuous at the flyer–sample interface, the pressure and particle velocity behind the shock wave propagating forward in the sample equal those behind the shock wave propagating rearward in the flyer plate. Note that the particle velocity of the flyer plate is *slowed down* from $u_{fp}$ to $u_1$ by the shock wave in the flyer plate. Since each material is shocked to pressure $P_1$ along its Hugoniot curve, the shock state achieved is indicated in Fig. 14b. The particle velocity of the target moves from $u = 0$ to $u = u_1$, whereas the state in the flyer plate moves from $u = u_{fp}$ to $u = u_1$. The state $P_1$, $u_1$ is thus determined from the intersection of the rightward-facing Hugoniot of the target material and the leftward-facing Hugoniot of the flyer plate materials. Figure 14 may be used to demonstrate the usual situation in which the Hugoniot state achieved in the target is unknown and the shock velocity in B is measured along with the initial density of the sample. In general, the Hugoniot of the flyer plate is known. The Hugoniot state is determined from the intersection of the Rayleigh line of slope $\rho_0 U$ with the Hugoniot of A as indicated in Fig. 14b.

As further discussed in several review articles on shock compression (Davison and Graham, 1979; McQueen *et al.*, 1970; Al'tschuler, 1965),

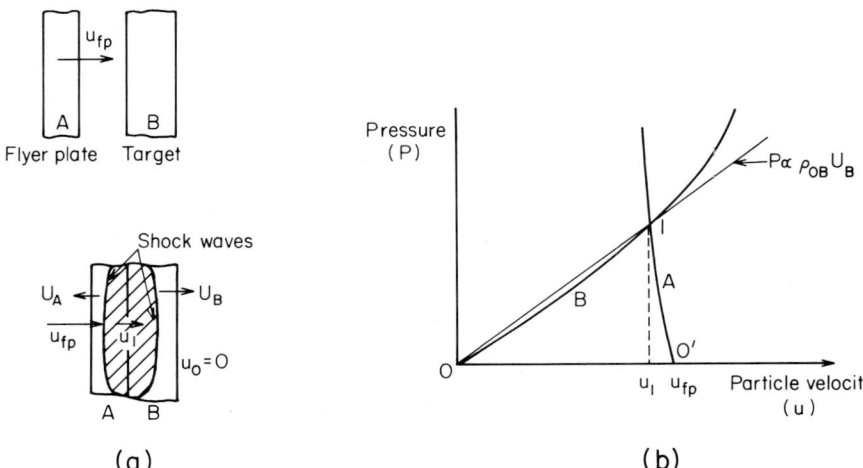

Fig. 14. Diagrammatic sketch of impedance match method for obtaining Hugoniot states. On impact of flyer plate A onto sample B shock waves propagate forward (a) in the sample and rearward in the target. Because the pressure and particle velocity are continuous at the flyer–target interface, the state achieved in the sample may be obtained from knowledge of the flyer plate velocity $u_{fp}$, the initial sample density $\rho_{0B}$, and the sample shock velocity $U_B$. Equation (2) states that the Hugoniot state lies along the line through the origin of slope $\rho_{0B} U_B$. On constructing this line the shock state $P_1$ and $u$ lies at the intersection of the line $P = \rho_{0B} U_B u$ with the known Hugoniot of the flyer plate. The latter is oriented so that the effect of the shock is to *decrease* the particle velocity from $u_{fp}$ to $u_1$.

Hugoniot data for many condensed media may be described over varying ranges of pressure and density in terms of a linear relation of shock and particle velocity such as

$$U = C_0 + Su \qquad (6)$$

In the absence of pronounced dynamic yielding effects or phase transitions, $C_0$ is the zero-pressure isentropic bulk sound speed, and $S$ is a dimensionless parameter which is related (Ruoff, 1967) to the pressure derivative of the isentropic bulk modulus ($dK_{0s}/dP$) by

$$dK_{0s}/dP = 4S - 1 \qquad (7)$$

Also

$$C_0 = \sqrt{K_{0s}/\rho_0} \qquad (8)$$

If the Hugoniot of the flyer plate (A) and the target (B) are known and expressed in the form of Eq. (5), the particle velocity $u_1$ and pressure $P_1$ of the shock state produced on impact may be calculated from the solution of the equation equating the shock pressures in the flyer and driver plate:

$$\rho_{0A}(u_{fp} - u_1)(C_{0A} + S_A(u_{fp} - u_1)) = \rho_{0B} u_1(C_{0B} + S_B u_1) \tag{9}$$

is

$$u_1 = (-b - \sqrt{b^2 - 4ac})/2a \tag{10}$$

where

$$a = S_A \rho_{0A} - \rho_{0B} S_B \tag{11}$$

$$b = -C_{0A}\rho_{0A} - 2S_A\rho_{0A}u_{fp} - \rho_{0B}C_{0B} \tag{12}$$

and

$$c = u_{fp}(C_{0A}\rho_{0A} + S_A\rho_{0A}u_{fp}) \tag{13}$$

In the usual situation the Hugoniot of the flyer plate (A) is known and given by an expression of the form of Eq. (6), but the Hugoniot of the target is not. From the impedance match condition that the pressure and particle velocity at the flyer plate–target interface are equal, it follows that on measuring the density $\rho_{0B}$ and shock velocity $U_1$ in the target, that the pressure equality in the flyer plate and target can be written as

$$\rho_{0A}(u_{fp} - u_1)[C_{0A} + S_A(u_{fp} - u_1)] = \rho_{0B} u_1 U_1 \tag{14}$$

which has a solution

$$u_1 = u_{fp} + a' - [a'^2 + (\rho_{0B}/\rho_{0A})U_1 u_{fp}/S_A]^{1/2} \tag{15}$$

where

$$a' = (C_{0A} + U_1\rho_{0B}/\rho_{0A})/2S_A \tag{16}$$

2.2. Reflection from a Free Surface

On reflection of a righward-traveling shock wave at a free surface, a leftward-propagating rarefaction wave releases the pressure in the shock state along (assumedly) an isentrope to zero pressure. The mathematics describing the mapping of the pressure–particle velocity unloading path to the pressure–volume plane is discussed in Section 5. If the material remains in the same phase and the shock process is nearly reversible (i.e., not in a porous medium which undergoes permanent compaction), the resulting free-surface velocity is

$$u_{fs} \approx 2u_1 \tag{17}$$

Equation (17) would be an equality if, on unloading, the entire internal energy budget of the material were converted to kinetic energy. In the case of a truly elastic response, the internal energy density of the shock state specified by Eq. (3) exactly equals the kinetic energy.

In general, when a solid returns to its initial phase on unloading from high pressure, or when the postshock temperature is sufficiently low that appreciable vaporization does not occur, $u_{fs}$ exceeds $2u_1$ by only a few percent (Walsh and Christian, 1955). A detailed treatment of the degree to which the "free-surface approximation" [Eq. (17)] is valid is given in Walsh and Christian (1955). An approximation which is often made in constructing Hugoniots and release isentropes in the pressure–particle velocity plane, such as those shown in Figs. 14–16, is that the release isentrope (and shock compression Hugoniot) from a previous shock state can be approximated by the pressure–particle velocity curve corresponding to the principal Hugoniot. This approximation is often made for construction in the pressure–particle velocity plane as outlined in the cases below.

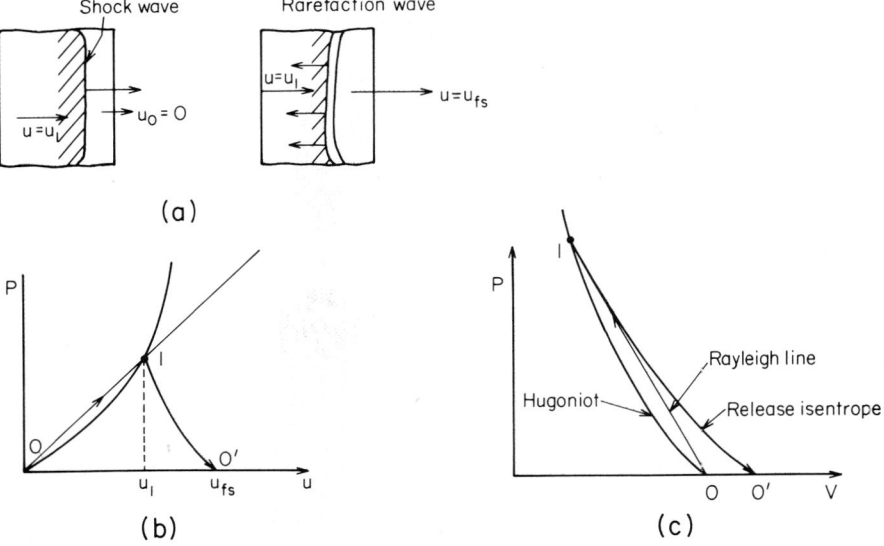

FIG. 15. Internal reflection of shock wave from free surface. (a) Reflection of shock wave from free surface causes a reflected rarefaction wave. As indicated in (b), this increases the velocity of the shocked material from $u_1$ to $u_{fs}$. The path upon shocking is Rayleigh line 0–1, whereas unloading occurs along release isentrope curve 1–0. (c) Release isentrope path in $P$–$V$ plane is indicated.

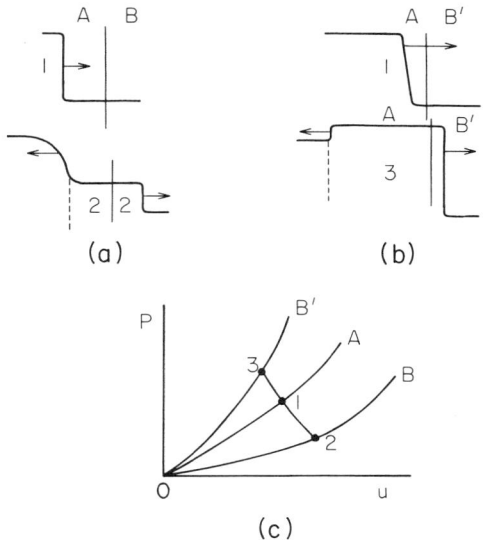

FIG. 16. (a) On reflection of a shock wave bringing material A to state 1 against an interface with lower shock impedance material (B), the reflected wave (rarefaction) propagates back into material A, bringing it to state 2, and a shock, bringing material B to state 2, propagates forward. (b) Upon reflection of a shock bringing material A to state 1 against an interface with higher shock impedance material (B′), the reflected shock propagates back into material A, bringing it to state 3, and a shock bringing material B′ to state 3 propagates forward. (c) Pressure–particle velocity plane representation of relative Hugoniots of A, B, and B′ and reflected shock state (3) and release isentropic state (2).

### 2.3. Reflection from a Lower- or Higher-Impedance Boundary

Understanding such interaction is important both in predicting the amplitudes of shock waves transmitted across interfaces (in the case where the equations of state of all materials are known) and in determining release isentropes or reflected Hugoniots (when measurement of the equation of state is needed). Consider first a shock wave in material A being transmitted to a lower-impedance medium, B. As indicated in Fig. 16a, after interaction at the interface, a lower-amplitude shock is transmitted into B and a reflected wave (rarefaction) propagates backward in A. The pressure $P_2$ and particle velocity $u_2$ associated with *both* the shock wave transmitted to material B and that associated with the backward-propagating rarefaction wave are determined in the pressure–particle velocity plane from the intersection of the release isentrope of material A, centered at state 1, and the Hugoniot of material B, centered at state 0. Here we use the continuity of pressure and particle velocity at the interface of materials A and B. In the case of shock wave interaction with a higher-impedance medium as indicated in Fig. 16b, a shock is transmitted into B′ as state 3 and a reflected higher-pressure shock propagates backward into material A. The pressure and particle velocity achieved at shock state 3 are determined from the intersection of the reflected Hugoniot of material A, centered at state 1, and the principal Hugoniot of material B′, centered at state 0.

An important application of the impedance match method is demonstrated by the pressure–particle velocity curves of Fig. 5 for various explosives. Using the above method, the detonation pressure (Chapman–Jouget states) for various explosives is inferred from the intersection of the explosive Hugoniot with the explosive product release isentropes and reflected shock compression Hugoniots (Zel'dovich and Kompaneets, 1960). The amplitudes of explosively induced shock waves which can be propagated into nonreacting materials are calculable using results such as those of Fig. 5.

## 3. Shock-Induced Dynamic Yielding and Phase Transitions

Both dynamic yielding and phase transitions give rise to multiple shock wave profiles as depicted in Figs. 17 and 18. Virtually all nonporous minerals and rocks in which dynamic compaction has been studied demonstrate dynamic yielding, and most minerals demonstrate shock-induced phase changes. In several interesting cases a separate phase transition wave shock front is formed, for example, in Fe (Bancroft et al., 1956), FeS (Ahrens, 1979), and $Mg_2SiO_4$ (Watt and Ahrens, 1983). The general conditions required to produce multiple wave structures when phase transitions occur are discussed by McQueen et al. (1970).

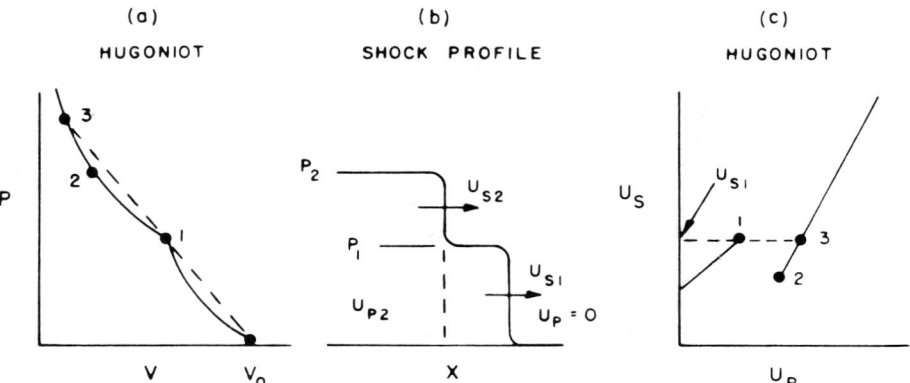

FIG. 17. Type of Hugoniot necessary to produce a two-wave shock structure and resulting wave profile. This type of Hugoniot will in general give a $U - u_p$ locus as shown, with a flat region of constant shock velocity. Point 2 will not be observed with techniques that measure only the first arrival of the shock wave. (After McQueen et al., 1970.)

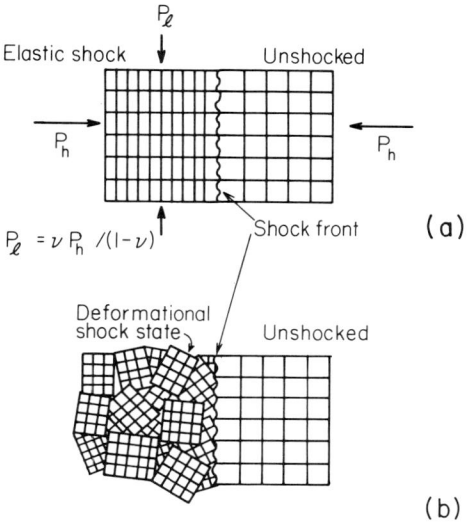

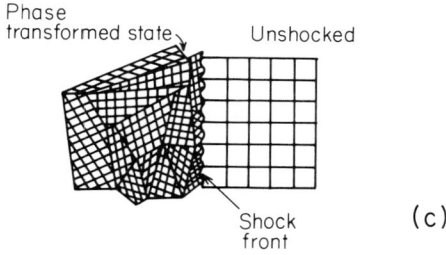

FIG. 18. Diagrammatic sketches of atomic lattice rearrangements as a result of dynamic compression which give rise to (a) elastic shock, (b) deformational shock, and (c) shock-induced phase change. In the case of an elastic shock in an isotropic medium, the lateral stress is a factor $\nu/(1 - \nu)$ less than the stress in the shock propagation direction. In cases (b) and (c) stresses are assumed equal in all directions if the shock stress amplitude is much greater than the material strength.

The condition that gives rise to multiple shock fronts (i.e., allows a shock wave to bifurcate as indicated in Fig. 17b) will occur when the second wave propagation velocity (with respect to the laboratory) is given by Eq. (5b). However, now we have three subscripts: 0, which as before indicates the initial state; 1, which corresponds to an *intermediate* shock state; and 2, which corresponds to the final shock state. The second shock wave propagates slower than the first shock wave into material already traveling at particle velocity $u_1$. The condition for the formation of two shock waves, one from state $P = P_0$, $V = V_0$, $u = u_0$ to state $P = P_1$, $V = V_1$, $u = u_1$ and the second from state $P = P_1$, $V = V_1$, $u = u_1$ to state $P = P_2$, $V = V_2$, $u = u_2$, is then

$$u_1 + V_1[(P_2 - P_1)/(V_1 - V_2)]^{1/2} < V_0[(P_1 - P_0)/(V_0 - V_1)]^{1/2} \quad (18)$$

or using Eq. (5b)

$$V_1[(P_2 - P_1)/(V_1 - V_2)]^{1/2} < V_1[(P_1 - P_0)/(V_0 - V_1)]^{1/2} \quad (19)$$

Figure 17 indicates that if the Rayleigh line (0-2) from the initial to the final shock state intersects the Hugoniot at an intermediate shock state, two shock waves will form, one from 0-1 and one from 1-2. Thus two shocks form for final shock states between 1 and 3. For states at stresses higher than state 3, only one shock forms.

In the case of most nonporous minerals at sufficiently low shock stresses, two shock fronts form. The first wave is the elastic shock, a finite-amplitude nearly elastic wave as indicated in Fig. 18. The amplitude of this shock is often called the Hugoniot elastic limit $P_{HEL}$. This would correspond to state 1 of Fig. 17a. The Hugoniot elastic limit is defined as *the maximum stress sustainable by a solid in one-dimensional shock compression without irreversible deformation taking place at the shock front*. In the case of a polycrystalline and/or isotropic material at shock stresses $P_h$ at or below $P_{HEL}$, the lateral compressive stress in a plane perpendicular to the shock front is given by

$$P_\ell = \nu P_h/(1 - \nu) \quad (20)$$

where $\nu$ is Poisson's ration ($0 < \nu < 0.5$).

The maximum shear stress $\tau_{max}$ is then

$$\tau_{max} = \tfrac{1}{2}[(1 - 2\nu)/(1 - \nu)]P_h \quad (21)$$

Values of the Hugoniot elastic limit for nonporous minerals vary from $\sim 2$ kbar for halite to $\sim 200$ kbar for diamond. If the material in the shocked state at stresses above $P_{HEL}$ can withstand a shear stress $\tau$, the Hugoniot state will be offset above the hydrostatic Hugoniot (which assumes fluidlike or hydrodynamic rheology) by an amount $4\tau/3$ (see, e.g., Fowles, 1960). Figure 19 indicates that immediately above the Hugoniot elastic limit the strength effect can offset the actual Hugoniot above the theoretical (hydrostatic) Hugoniot by an appreciable amount which may be specified as $4\tau/3$. With increasingly higher shock stress (because the stress sustainable in the material is bounded by the strength of the material and the increasing shock temperature), the Hugoniot curve approaches the hydrostatic Hugoniot. Thus, whatever the strength of the material actually is, at sufficiently high shock pressure it becomes small compared to $P_h$ and over much of the range of geophysical interest ($\sim 100$ kbar to $\sim 4$ Mbar) the shock stress turns out to be nearly equal to the mean hydrostatic stress.

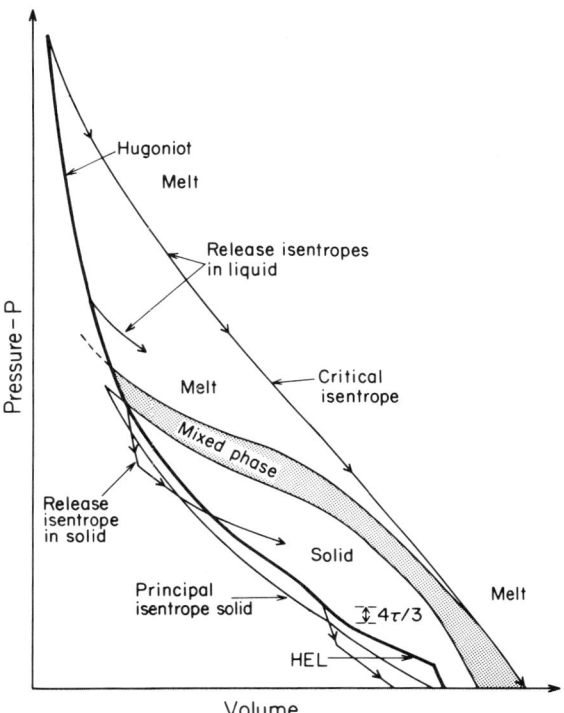

FIG. 19. Hugoniot curve relative to principal isentrope of solid and release isentropes. Above the Hugoniot elastic limit (HEL) the Hugoniot curve may be offset in pressure above the principal isentrope by an amount $4\tau/3$, where $\tau$ is the maximum shear strength sustainable by the solid in the shocked state. On unloading, the release curve may be steep, indicating elastic-like behavior followed by deformational unloading with decreasing pressure. Elastic followed by deformational unloading will occur on unloading from shock pressures up to those at which the Hugoniot crosses the fusion curve. Above this pressure unloading occurs in the liquid (melt) field. The critical isentrope crosses the Hugoniot at the point at which complete melt is retained on release to zero pressure.

## 4. Shock Wave Velocity Measurements

Both optical and electronic techniques are used to measure shock propagation times through samples and hence shock velocity. These are often used in conjunction with particle velocity and shock pressure profile measurements and radiative measurements of shock temperatures.

### 4.1. Optical Method

Two methods which continue to be used for measuring shock velocities through samples and buffer materials are the flash-gap method and the

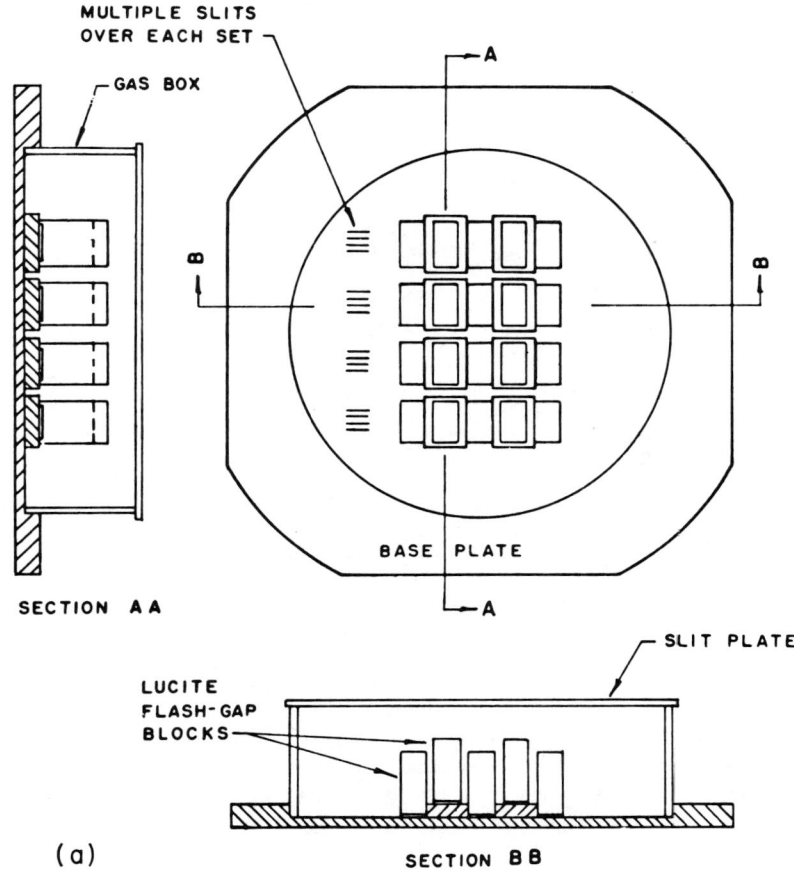

Fig. 20. Diagram of flash-gap shock transit-time experimental assembly and resulting film streak camera record. (a) Two columns of four samples each (indicated by crosshatching in the section views) are placed on the base plate as shown. Two of these samples are identical in composition to the base plate and are used to determine the pressure of the standard. Plastic flash-gap blocks are placed on the base plate and on top of these slugs. These blocks have a 0.01-cm groove in the bottom to provide the space for the gas that becomes luminous when strongly shocked. The plastic provides not only a surface for multiple-shock reflections in the gas but also a surface that extinguishes the light, thus providing a short burst of light that records as a line when viewed through the narrow slits. (b) Enlargement of a photographic record. Time increases downward; thus, the upper set of traces indicates the shock arrival at the top of the 2024 Al base plate. The shock arrival at the top of the sample is indicated by the lower set of traces. A smooth curve is fit through the reference traces; thus, wave tilt and curvature can be accounted for in measuring transit times. The letters beside each group of offsets correspond to different samples: D, bronzitite; F, diabase; K, granite; H, dunite; J, eclogite; and A, albitite. Al indicates travel time through 2024 aluminum standard samples. (After McQueen et al., 1967. Copyright by the American Geophysical Union.)

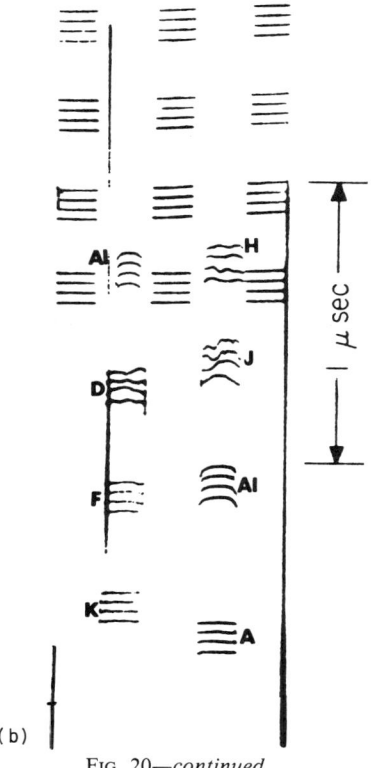

FIG. 20—*continued*

reflected light method. The flash-gap method, one of the earliest shock wave techniques (Fig. 20), offers the advantage of simple design and the ability, in the case of explosive generation of shock waves, to obtain data for many samples in a single experiment. The method employs a series of Lucite blocks which are set ~0.01 mm above the surface at which the shock wave arrival is to be detected. The 0.01-mm-thick space or "flash gap" is filled with argon or xenon to a pressure slightly in excess of an atmosphere. As illustrated in Fig. 20, the usual configuration has blocks on either side of a sample to record shock entrance into the sample and on the upper surface of the sample to detect the completion of propagation of the shock through the sample. On shock arrival and impact of the sample or driver plate against the gap, the argon or xenon gas trapped between the Lucite blocks is suddenly shock-heated to temperatures of ~30,000–50,000 K. The radiance from this highly shocked gas is easily recorded with a streak camera. A summary of the operation of both rotating mirror and electronic streak cameras is given in

Zukas *et al.* (1982). The duration of the light induced by the flash gap can be varied from 5 to 50 ns by varying the thickness of the flash gap and will be affected by the strength of the shock inducing the flash. As demonstrated in Fig. 20, the flash is generally short with respect to the travel time through the sample. The sharp decrease of light intensity when the gap closes is thought to occur because Lucite adjacent to the hot gases rapidly becomes opaque. The advantage of the flash-gap technique, aside from its simplicity, is its inherent reproducibility. This is also demonstrated in Fig. 20 by the redundant flashes for the 2024 Al test sample. Like the pin contactor electrical method described below, the flash-gap method is usually sensitive to the initial shock wave and hence is useful in measuring the velocity of the final shock state only in the case of simple shock. By placing the Lucite block several millimeters above the free surface and placing a thin shim 0.01 mm away from the Lucite block, the method may also be easily adapted to

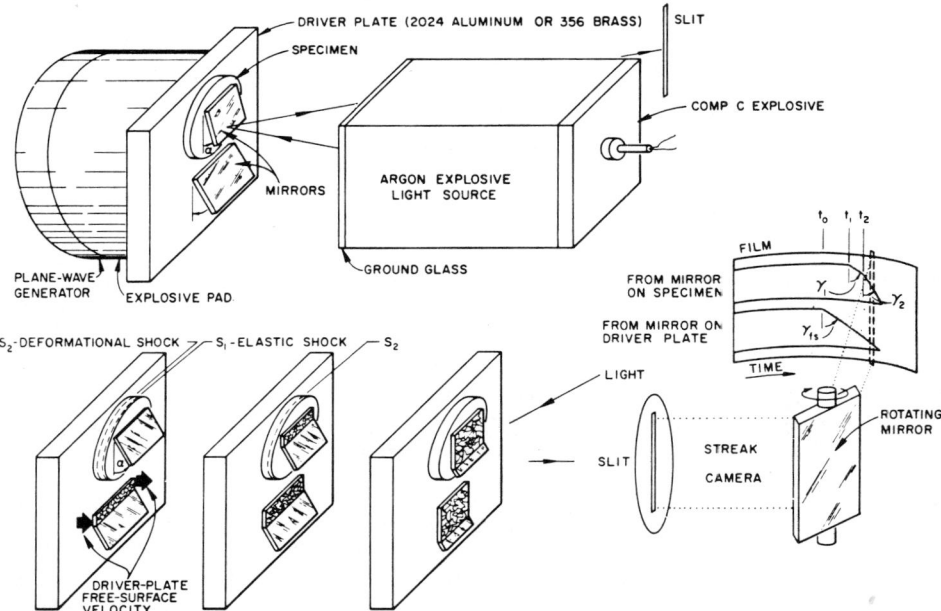

FIG. 21. Diagrammatic view of explosive in contact, inclined mirror Hugoniot experiment. Two shock fronts, $S_1$ and $S_2$, form in the specimen. These shocks successively impact the specimen inclined mirror at times $t_1$ and $t_2$; the resultant specimen free-surface velocities, $u_{fs1}$ and $u_{fs2}$, are calculated with geometric factors, initial mirror angle $\alpha$, and film cutoff angles $\gamma_1$ and $\gamma_2$. The driver plate free-surface velocity (and hence particle velocity at the driver plate–specimen interface) is obtained from driver plate mirror cutoff angle $\gamma_{fs}$. (After Ahrens and Rosenberg, 1968.)

measure the transit time of a shock-induced free-surface motion to the Lucite block and hence provide a measurement of the free-surface velocity.

A second optical technique often employed to measure shock properties of rocks and minerals is the use of reflected light, which is also recorded with a streak camera (Ahrens et al., 1968). The image of a bright light source reflected by the polished driver plate, sample surface, or a mirror in contact with these is recorded as a function of time by the camera. The change of light intensity due either to a roughening of the free surface when the shock wave arrives or a tilting of the free surface may be used as a sensitive shock wave detector. Alternatively, when a specularly reflecting glass mirror is placed in close contact with a lapped surface and the lapped surface is driven into the specular reflecting mirror, the arrival of a shock wave can be detected on a nanosecond time scale as indicated in Fig. 21. When using explosive sources for shock wave generation, the use of an explosively driven light source is convenient. For gun-launched impactors the use of a synchronous electronic xenon light source (Vassiliou and Ahrens, 1982) is convenient, as demonstrated by the streak record obtained from a gun apparatus (Fig. 22).

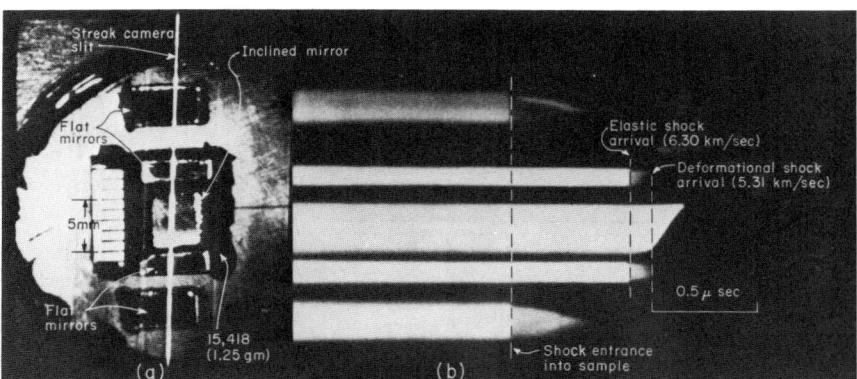

FIG. 22. Streak camera photograph of Hugoniot experiment carried out on lunar sample 15,418. (a) Still photograph of specimen viewed through streak camera; slit image is swept across film and mirror reflectivity is destroyed by shock wave. (b) Resulting streak photograph showing streak cutoffs of mirror reflectivities. Shock pressures of 65 ± 10 and 282 ± 6 kbar were determined for the elastic and deformational shock wave from this record. (After Ahrens et al., 1973. Reprinted with permission from *Geochim. Cosmochim. Acta* **3**, Copyright 1973, Pergamon Press, Ltd.)

4.2. Electrical Methods

One of the simplest methods for measuring shock velocity is with electrical contactor pins (Bancroft et al., 1956). These are basically switches which are closed by the particle velocity induced by the shock wave, or the shock pressure, which induces electrical conductivity in a thin insulating layer. The method has the advantage of intrinsic simplicity (Fig. 23). Very fast responses of less than 1 ns may be obtained by preparing extremely uniform and thin mechanically stable dielectric films as insulators, as, for example, described by Mitchell and Nellis (1981). These allow shock wave measurements in millimeter-sized samples with nanosecond time resolution (Fig. 24). Piezo-electric and ferroelectric crystals can also be employed as shock wave profile and arrival detectors (Graham and Asay, 1978). Recording of electric signals is often carried out with delay lines to delay the signal generated on entrance of a shock wave into a sample such that the pulses produced on entrance and exit of the shock wave through the sample may be displayed on the same oscilloscope. Writing rates as fast as 50 ns/cm with 300-MHz bandwidth oscilloscopes are used with delay lines. However, digital transient recorders will undoubtedly supersede delay lines in the future. Although most shock wave measurements with electrical contractors have been carried out on metallic or conducting mineral targets, measurements have been successfully carried out on cryogenic liquids of cosmochemical interest such as $CH_4$ and $D_2$ (Nellis *et al.*, 1981, 1983). The application of pin techniques to study shock waves in minerals has been more limited because these virtually all display prominent elastic shock precursors, which, as in the case of optical flash gaps, can lead to ambiguity as to which wave front is being detected at lower shock pressures.

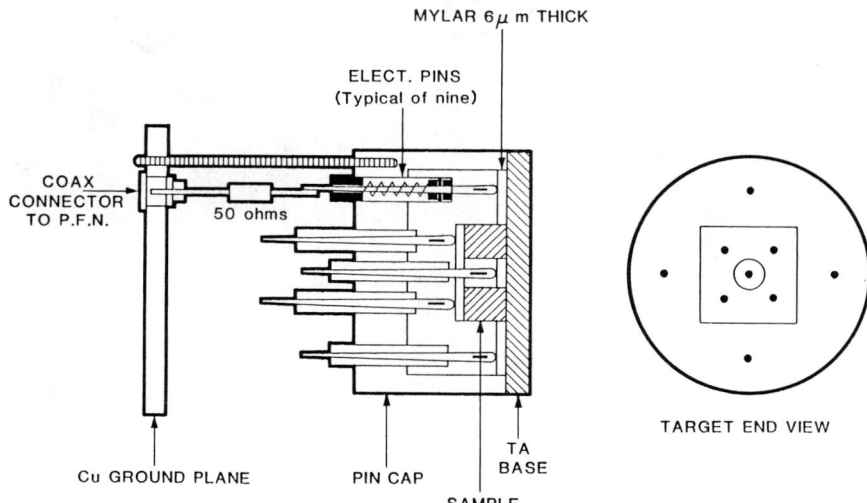

FIG. 23. Electrical pin-contactor equation-of-state experiment. Five pins detect shock arrival at the Ta base plate–sample interface and four pins detect shock arrival at the upper sample surface. (After Brown *et al.*, 1984.)

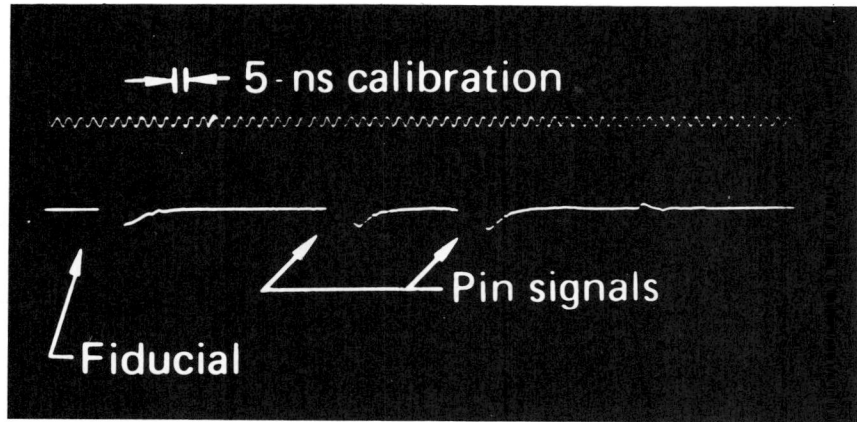

Fig. 24. Electrical contactor pin signals from experiment similar to that sketched in Fig. 23. Fiducial signals are used to cross-calibrate time of signals between different oscilloscopes. To record pin signals which occur ~200 ns apart on an oscilloscope sweep of 100 ns duration, the first pin signal is passed through a fixed 200-ns delay line. (After Mitchell and Nellis, 1981.)

## 5. Release Isentrope Experiments

Release isentropes are the pressure–density (or volume)–energy paths followed by shocked material on release to ambient pressure from the high-pressure shock state. The term "release adiabats" is also used in some cases. This, of course, implies that no heat flow with respect to a control volume occurs during the unloading portion of the dynamic experiment, which for a laboratory-sized sample implies times of $10^{-6}$ to $10^{-5}$ s. Thermodynamic constraints related to maintaining the more restrictive constant entropy (isentropic) flow during unloading are discussed by Jeanloz and Ahrens (1979), and constraints on maintaining constant entropy during passage through a two-phase regime are discusssed by Cowperthwaite and Ahrens (1967). Since on pressure release from the shock state an initially condensed material may become partially or completely melted or partially or completely volatilized, different properties of the shock state are demonstrated by the release isentropes (Fig. 25). At low stresses, when unloading from the solid regime occurs, the release isentropes can indicate the stress differences and shear modulus retained by the shock state when one observes the amplitude of the initial longitudinal unloading wave of velocity

$$C_1 = \sqrt{(K_s + 4\mu/3)/\rho} \tag{22}$$

where $K_s$ and $\mu$ are isentropic bulk modulus and shear modulus, respectively. This initial release is followed by unloading along a deformational isentrope

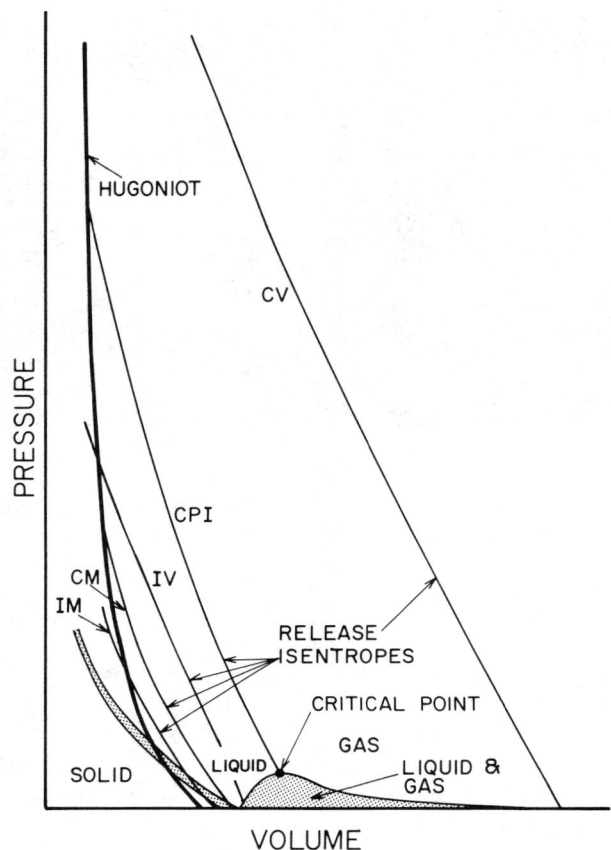

Fig. 25. Diagrammatic sketch of critical isentropes, which are defined as isentropes passing through point on Hugoniot at onset or completion of phase change on release to ambient pressure. IM, CM, IV, and CV indicate isentropes resulting in incipient melting, complete melting, incipient vaporizaton, and complete vaporization, respectively. CPI indicates isentrope passing through the liquid–vapour (gas) critical point (discussed by Zel'dovich and Raizer, 1967).

(Fowles, 1961). At the onset of the regime where the Hugoniot crosses the fusion curve of material, the velocity of the head of the rarefaction wave propagates at the compressed-fluid sound speed

$$C_b = \sqrt{K_s/\rho} \qquad (23)$$

Also, the initial unloading wave speed can be measured. This provides constraints on whether the material in the high-pressure state is solid or fluid and allows an explicit measurement of the Gruneisen parameter (see Section 6).

Two general methods have been used to measure release isentropes: (1) the buffer method and (2) release wave profile analysis.

## 5.1. Buffer Method

The simplest method for measuring release isentropes of materials is to carry out a series of buffer experiments in which a shock wave of a certain amplitude is allowed to interact with a series of lower-impedance materials. In general, separate experiments (e.g., with buffers A and B) are required for describing points along the release isentrope of a material (Fig. 26). Since the

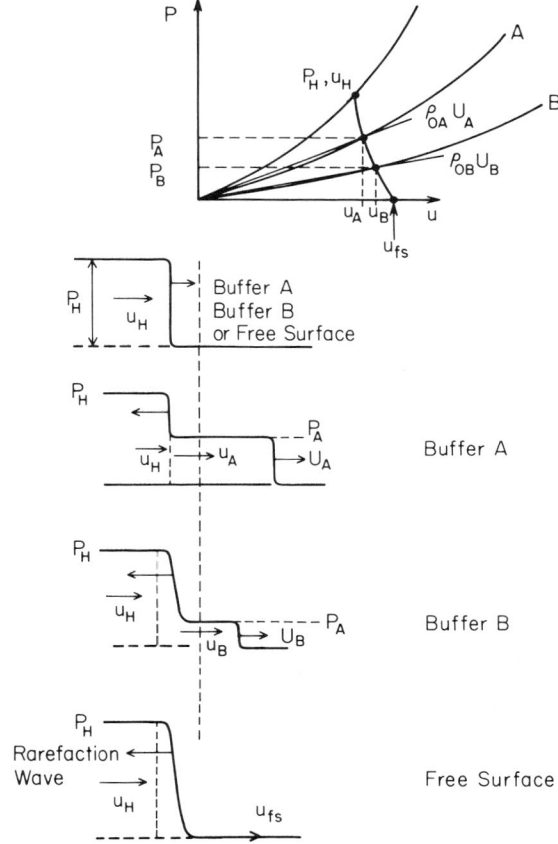

FIG. 26. Pressure–particle velocity diagram and sketches of wave profiles on interaction of shock wave of amplitude $P_H$ with two different impedance buffers A and B and free surface. Pressure–particle velocity states achieved in buffers A and B and free-surface velocity $u_{fs}$ map out release isentrope in the $P$–$u$ plane.

Hugoniot curves for the buffers are known. A simple measurement of shock velocity determines the Hugoniot shock state in the buffer and hence the target state along the release isentrope in the pressure–particle velocity plane. The buffer materials which can be used for measuring release isentrope states in minerals include relatively low shock impedance solids such as plastic (e.g., Lexan, polyethylene), various plastic, graphite, and ceramic foam materials, organic fluids (e.g., ethanol), and compressed gases (Ahrens *et al.*, 1968; Podurets *et al.*, 1976; Vizgirda and Ahrens, 1982).

To obtain the pressure–volume or pressure–density path corresponding to the pressure–particle velocity trajectory, it is necessary to assume that the

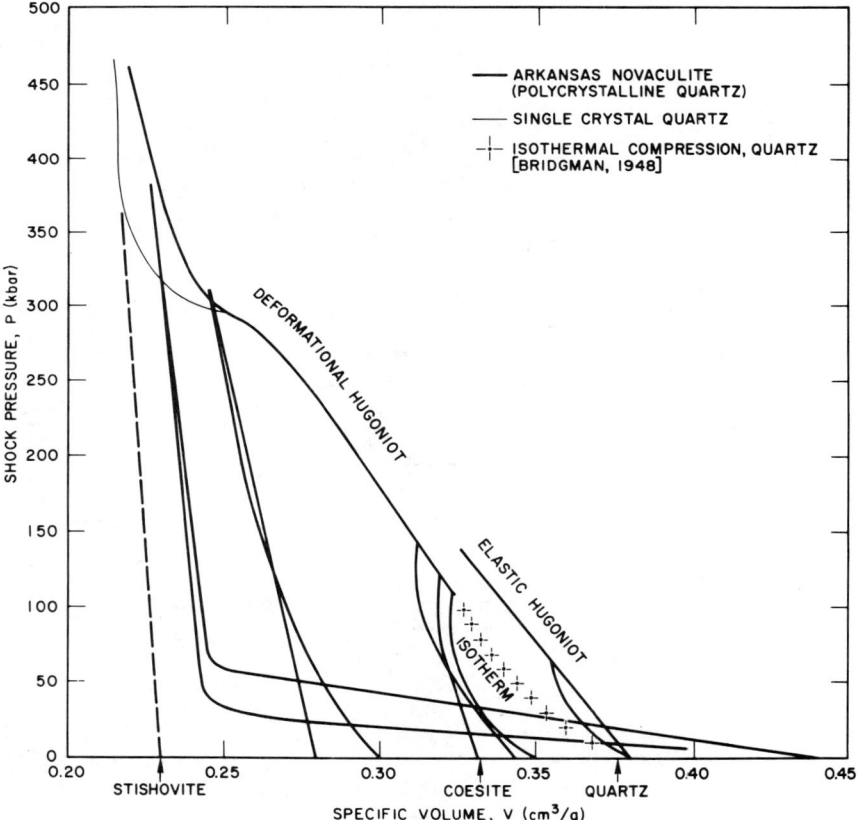

FIG. 27. *P–V* release isentropes for quartz. The Hugoniot is from Fig. 12. Release isentropes are transformations of curves measured by the method outlined in Fig. 26. Specific volumes of quartz, fused quartz, coesite, and stishovite phases of $SiO_2$ are indicated. (After Ahrens and Rosenberg, 1968.)

release isentrope is truly isentropic and that the pressure is a single-valued function of density. Assuming that pressure–particle velocity states are measured from the Hugoniot ($P_H$, $u_H$) state down to the zero-pressure, free-surface velocity, the specific volume along the release isentrope is given by the Riemann integral formula (Lyzenga and Ahrens, 1978).

$$V = V_H + \int_{u_H}^{u} \left(\frac{\partial u}{\partial p}\right)_s du \qquad (24)$$

For example, release isentropes obtained in this way for quartz shocked into a mixed-phase quartz–stishovite regime are shown in Fig. 27.

## 5.2. Stress and Particle Velocity Profile Methods

By measuring either the particle velocity or the shock stress profile during loading and unloading of geological materials at two or more positions in the sample it is possible to obtain both the loading and unloading paths in the pressure–particle velocity plane. Again, using the assumption of isentropicity, pressure–particle velocity data may be inverted to obtain pressure–specific volume or pressure–density paths. Two types of gauges are used for such measurements: particle velocity and shock pressure gauges. The two gauge types also may be used in combination. Figure 28 shown the stress wave and particle velocity profiles expected on shocking and releasing a geological material and how they are related to the sound speed $C$ in the high-pressure shock state and at ambient pressure $C_0$ (see also Section 5.3). Release of pressure occurs both from a rarefaction wave at the target free surface and from the free surface of the rear of the projectile.

Although several methods of particle velocity profile measurements are in use, the most common method was first introduced by Zaitsev *et al.* (1960) for measuring wave profiles in detonating explosives. The method utilizes a series of loops of wire or metallic films which are placed in slices of the rock or mineral in the expected plane of the shock (Figs. 29 and 30). Also in the plane of the shock but perpendicular to the loop is a strong magnetic field (e.g., $\sim 10^3$ to $10^4$ gauss), which is produced, usually via an electromagnet, in a steady or pulsed mode. The particle velocity is then determined by the voltage generated by each of several loops as they move through the magnetic field. The voltage may be written as

$$v(t) = 10^{-2} Blu(t) \qquad (25)$$

where $v$ is in volts, $B$ in gauss, $l$ in centimeters, and $u$ in centimeters per second. The analysis of particle velocity profile data is discussed below. The major drawback in obtaining just particle velocity profiles is the requirement that all the components and experimental assembly except for the magnetic

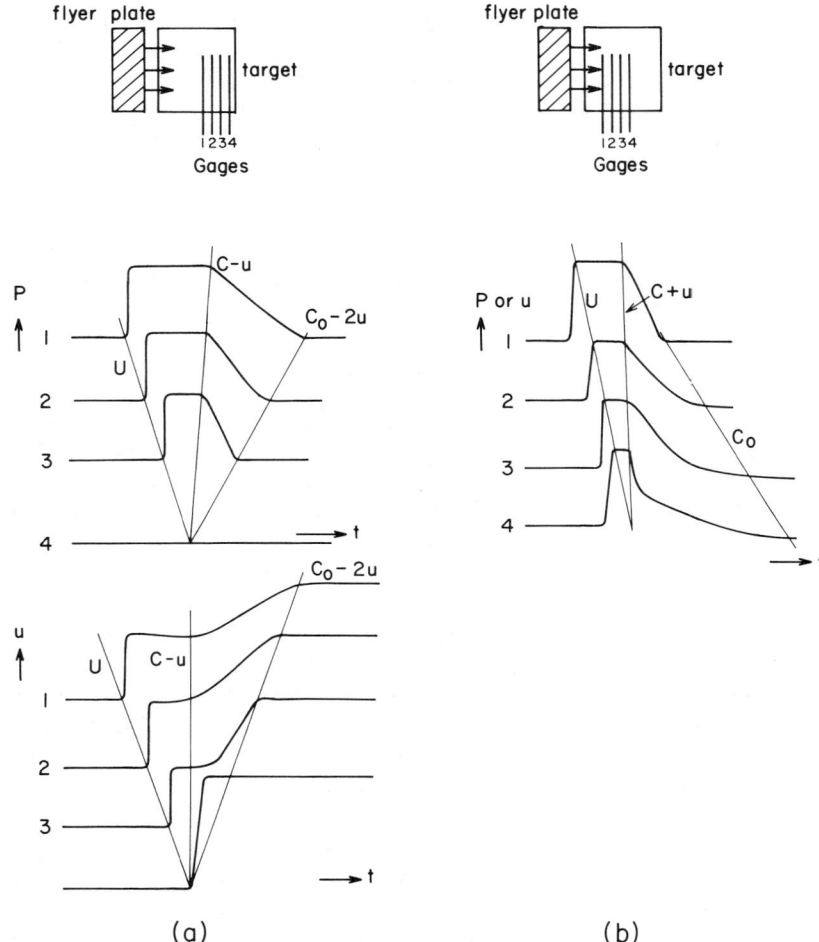

FIG. 28. Gauge configurations and loading and unloading wave profiles for carrying out release isentrope experiments. (a) Gauge configuration and pressure and particle velocity wave profile on pressure release from target free surface. (b) Gauge configuration and pressure or particle velocity profile on pressure release from rear surface of flyer plate. Wave velocities $U$, $C - u$, $C_0 - 2u$, $u + C$, and $C_0$ are indicated by solid narrow lines.

loops and velocity detectors must be nonmetallic (Boslough and Ahrens, 1984, 1985). Any metallic components will induce eddy currents from their motion in the magnetic field and defeat the operation of the magnetic velocity-detecting loops. In practice, the requirement of nonconducting samples and projectiles limits projectile velocities to speeds of ~3 km/s or shock pressures to ~350 kbar in silicate rocks and minerals.

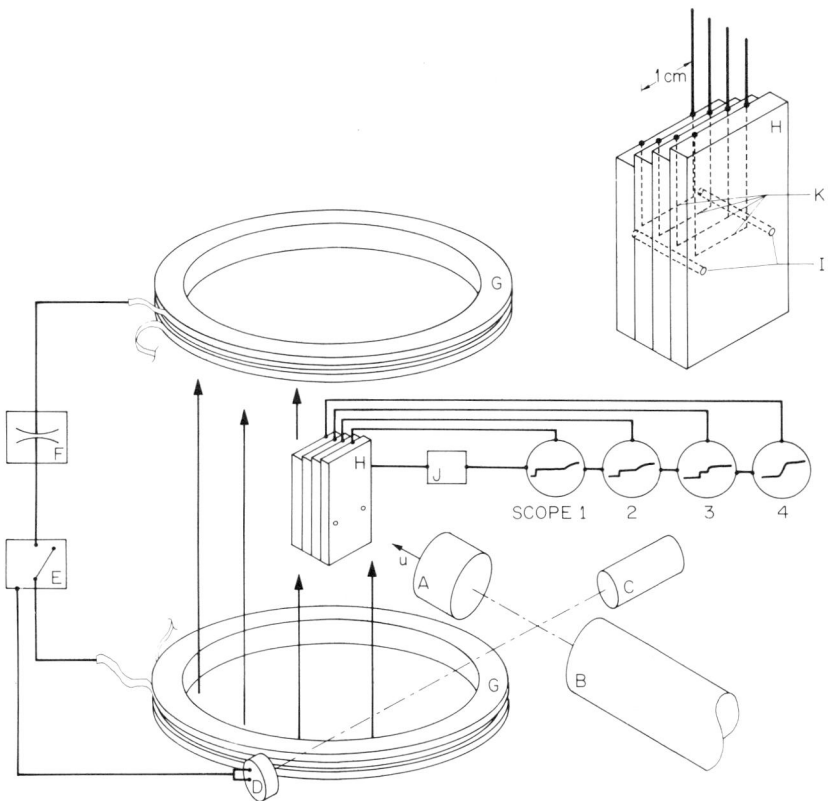

FIG. 29. Schematic drawing of particle velocity experiment using a one-stage gun where unloading results from rarefaction wave from sample free surface. Major components are indicated: (a) polycarbonate projectile, (b) 40-mm-bore gun barrel, (c) timing laser, (d) photodetector, (e) high-power switch (ignitron), (f) capacitor bank, (g) Helmholtz coils, (h) rock target, (i) self-shorting trigger pins, (j) fiducial pulse generator, (k) copper foil particle velocity gauge elements.

Shock pressure may also be directly measured by using the pressure effect of the increase of electrical resistivity of metals. This adaptation of a method first used to measure high hydrostatic pressure was carried out as early as 1964 by Fuller and Price (1964) and Bernstein and Keough (1964). The two most common piezoresistive materials utilized for shock pressure gauges are manganin (84% Cu, 12% Mn, and 4% Ni) and elemental ytterbium (usually vapor deposited on an insulating substrate). Manganin is used as a resistive gauge material because it has a low thermal coefficient of resistivity, whereas Yb is used as a gauge material because, although chemically reactive, its

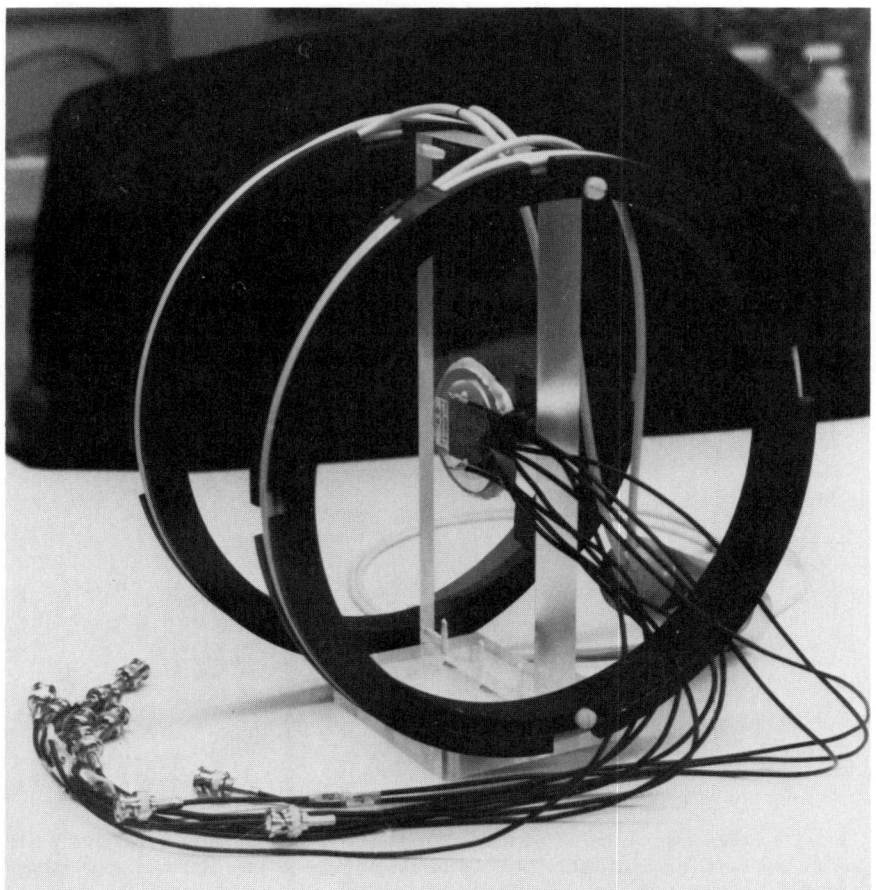

Fig. 30. Helmholtz coil assembly with rock target and particle velocity gauge foils in place.

resistivity is very stress-sensitive. A typical gauge configuration is shown in Fig. 31. Manganin gauges have been used successfully in quartzose rocks to pressures of 400 kbar (Grady, 1977), whereas Yb has been used in the stress range below 10 kbar (Gupta, 1983). For both metals, the change in resistance with pressure may be expressed as

$$\Delta R/R_0 = KP \tag{26}$$

where $\Delta R$ is the change in resistance and $R_0$ the initial resistance of the gauge, usually measured by imposing a constant current through a gauge as sketched in Fig. 29. The voltage change across the gauge is proportional to $\Delta R$.

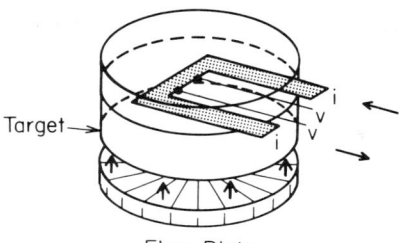

Flyer Plate

FIG. 31. Geometric configuration of four-terminal piezoresistive dynamic pressure gauge. Usually a pulsed high current $i$ ($\sim 10^3$ A) is driven through the outer foil or wire gauge lead and a voltage $v$ is detected between the inner voltage leads. A compilation of gauge and insulating materials is given in Graham and Asay (1978).

Thus $K$ is the gauge constant where $P$ is the shock pressure. Unfortunately, although considerable care has gone into gauge design and construction, both manganin and ytterbium suffer considerable dependence of the gauge constant or strain history (Gupta, 1983). Thus, for manganin $K \sim 0.002$, whereas the value of $K$ for Yb varies from 0.04 to $\sim 0.07$ (kbar)$^{-1}$ in the range 2–10 kbar. Because of the requirements that manganin and Yb gauges be mounted on a medium which remains insulating and the deficiencies in understanding the behavior of these materials under shock, they have found relatively limited application in absolute pressure–density measurements.

### 5.3. Wave Profile Analysis

When particle velocity or shock pressure vs. time is measured at two adjacent positions $h = h_a$ and $h = h_b$ as depicted in Fig. 32, an apparent velocity $(\partial h/\partial t)_{u_p} = C_{u_p}(u_p)$ or $(\partial h/\partial t)_p = C_p(P)$ corresponding to the wave speed of particle velocity and stress, respectively, may be defined (Fowles and Williams, 1970; Grady, 1973). Here $h$ is the distance coordinate in the wave propagation direction in the *uncompressed medium* (initial configuration). Since the gauges (particle velocity or pressure) move with the medium, these initial coordinates are called the Lagrangian coordinates. Therefore the Lagrangian wave speed as shown in Fig. 32 for two adjacent gauges located at $h = h_a$ and $h = h_b$ reflects the speed of propagation of a value of particle velocity or pressure $(\Delta h/\Delta t)_{u_p}$ or $(\Delta h/\Delta t)_p$ as a function of particle velocity or pressure. Thus

$$C_p \text{ or } C_{u_p} = (h_b - h_a)/(t_{b'_1} - t_{a'_1}) \tag{27}$$

In this and the following relations [Eqs. (28)–(31)] we do not specify whether the shocked material is acting like a fluid, with sound speed $C_b$ [Eq. (23)], or behaving elastically, with sound speed $C_1$ [Eq. (22)].

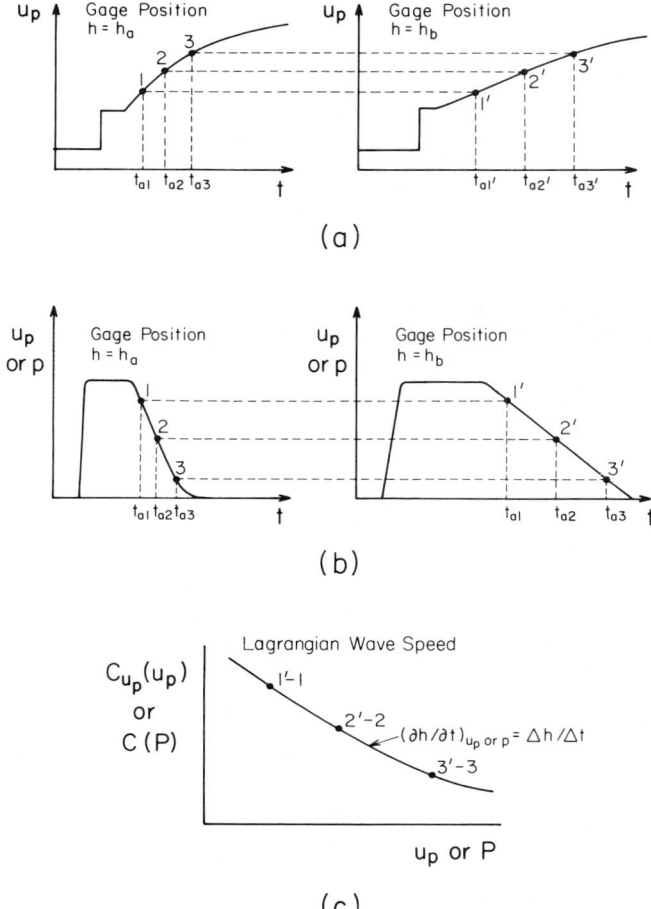

FIG. 32. Wave profile analysis from particle velocity or pressure vs. time data. (a) Wave profiles as measured at two adjacent particle velocity gauges; unloading occurs from rarefaction wave from target free surface as in Fig. 28a. (b) Wave profiles as measured at two adjacent particle velocity or pressure gauges; unloading occurs from rarefaction wave originating from rear surface of flyer plate. (c) Lagrangian wave speed as obtained from a series of pressure or particle velocity gauges.

When pressure profiles for simple waves as depicted in Fig. 32 are measured the mean particle velocity between two gauges as a function of time is obtained from (Grady, 1977; Seaman, 1974).

$$u(t) = u_0 + V_0 \int_{P_0}^{P(t)} \frac{dP}{C_p(P)} \qquad (28)$$

# 6. SHOCK WAVE TECHNIQUES

and the corresponding specific volume is given by

$$V(t) = V_0 - V_0 \int_{u_{p_0}}^{u_p(t)} \frac{du_p}{C_p} \tag{29}$$

If, on the other hand, measurements of particle velocity profiles are carried out, the pressure is calculated from

$$P(t) = P_0 + \rho_0 \int_{u_{0p}}^{u_p} C_{u_p} \, du_p \tag{30}$$

and the specific volume is calculated from

$$V(t) = V - V_0 \int_{u_{0p}}^{u_p(t)} \frac{du_p}{C_{u_p}} \tag{31}$$

Here, as usual, the subscript 0 corresponds to the initial value of the variable. Equation (31) is similar to Eq. (24). Seaman (1974) has considered how best to fit both pressure and particle velocity profile data when both are available. Examples of actual records obtained during release isentrope measurement on anorthosite are shown in Fig. 33 and the resulting release isentropes are shown in Fig. 34.

## 5.4. Laser Velocity Interferometer

A very useful technique for measuring wave profiles inside a transparent medium or for following the motion of the free surface induced by shock and release wave is the technique of velocity interferometry for any reflector

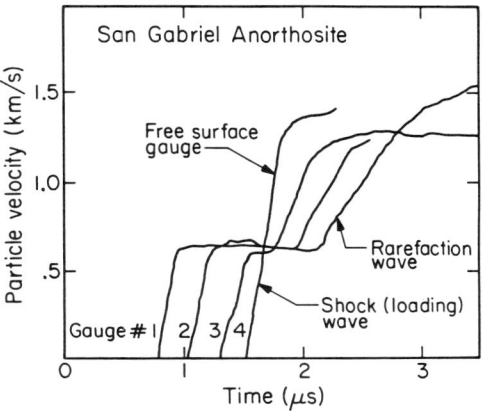

FIG. 33. Digitized particle velocity gauge records from experiment in which anorthosite was shocked to 10 Gpa.

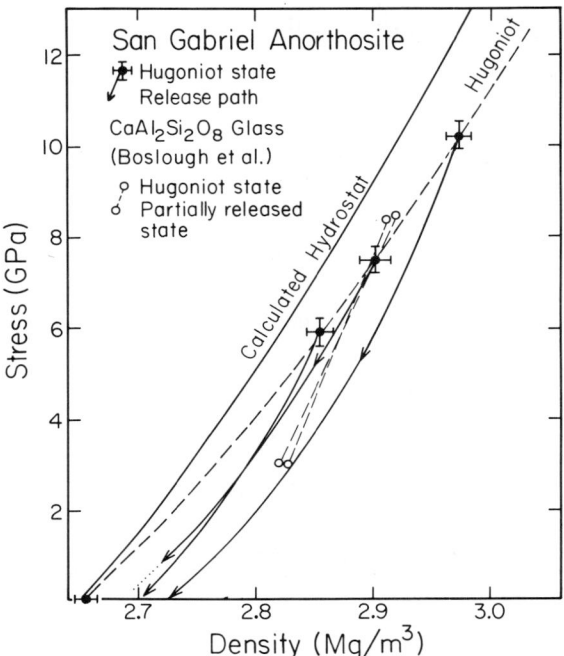

FIG. 34. Pressure–volume release isentrope curves for anorthosite obtained from particle velocity records like those of Fig. 33. (After Boslough and Ahrens, 1984. Copyright by the American Geophysical Union.)

(VISAR) (Barker and Hollenback, 1970). The technique makes use of a wide-angle Michelson velocity interferometer, which allows monitoring of the time-varying interference from a laser beam that is coherently but not necessarily specularly reflected. Thus heavily shocked mineral surfaces or light-reflecting buffer materials (in contact with geological materials) may be used to monitor both loading and unloading profiles. The geometry of the instrument (Fig. 35) is designed such that the light path in the delay leg appears to have the same optical path length (right) as that of the undelayed leg (left). This is accomplished by placing $\sim 10^2$ cm of material with a relatively high index of refraction (usually Schlieren-grade fused silica as used for étalons) in the delay leg. The velocity $u$ on the surface reflecting the laser beam is given as a function of time by (Barker, 1968; Barker and Hollenbach, 1970, 1972)

$$u(t - \tau/2) = \lambda F(t)/2\tau(1 + \Delta v/v_0) \qquad (32)$$

where $\tau$ is the delay time for the right-hand leg. (The other term in the

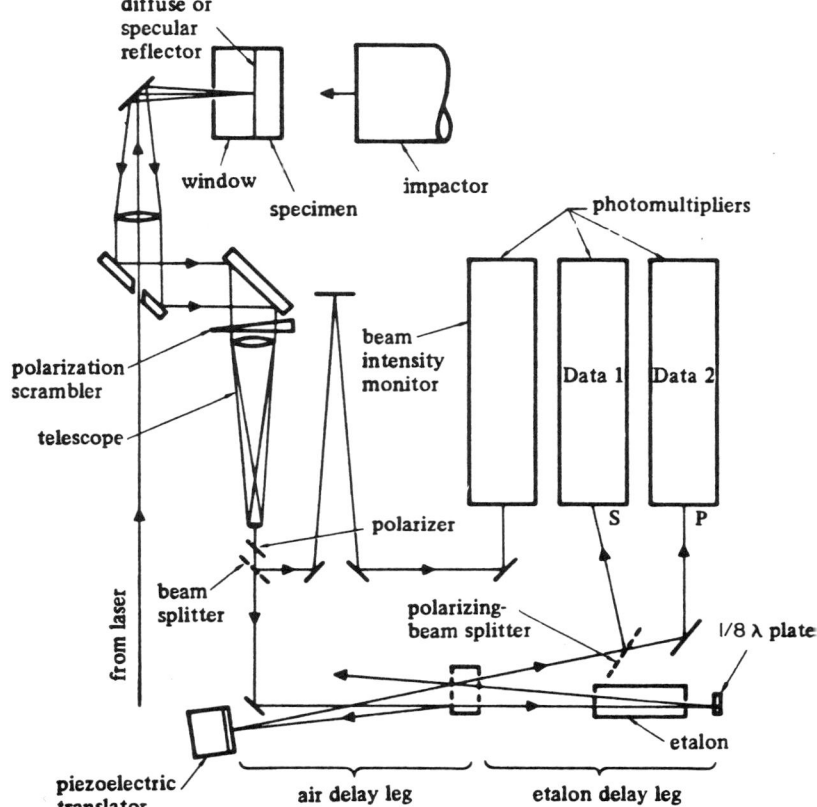

FIG. 35. Schematic diagram of the VISAR detector system. By utilizing air and étalon delay legs of the same optical length but with different delay times, this system can monitor the velocity of a diffusely reflecting surface. (After Graham and Asay, 1978.)

denominator is explained below.) Assuming that *all* the path distance between the left- and right-hand legs of the interferometer is due to the higher-index delay medium, then

$$\tau = (2h/c)(n - 1/n) \qquad (33)$$

where $h$ is the length of the delay in the medium of index of refraction $n$, and $c$ and $\lambda$ are the speed of light and the laser wavelength in vacuum. The fringe order as a function of time, $F(t)$, detected by the pair of photomultiplier tubes which record signals 90° out of phase (filtering using a 1/4 wave plate and inducing polarization at 45° to the horizontal in the delay leg) is obtained from the expressions

$$A_p(t) = \tfrac{1}{2}A_{\max}\{1 + \sin[2\pi F(t) + \delta_p]\} \quad (34)$$

$$A_s(t) = \tfrac{1}{2}A_{\max}\{1 + \sin[2\pi F(t) + \delta_s]\}$$

These equations represent the amplitude of the P and S polarizations, respectively. Here $A_{\max}$ is the amplitude of the signal determined from the beam intensity monitor (Fig. 35), and phase lags $\delta_p$ and $\delta_s$ are inferred from the value of $A_p(t)$ or $A_s(t)$ when $u = 0$.

When the particle velocity profile is recorded through a range of compressed transparent window materials, e.g., polymethyl methacrylate, fused quartz, sapphire, or lithium fluoride, a correction term $(1 + \Delta v/v_0)$ must be used in Eq. (32). Strictly speaking, Eq. (32) gives the correction term in the case in which a steady wave is present in the window material of unshocked index of refraction $v_0$ and it is assumed that the index of refraction changes by an amount $\Delta v$ as it would in the geometry of the experiment shown in Fig. 36. Details on correcting the velocity interferometer for geometries such as indicated in Fig. 36 are discussed by Barker and Hollenbach (1974).

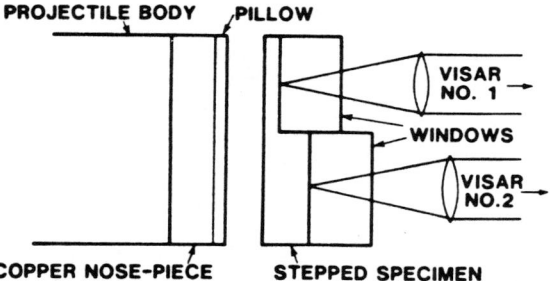

FIG. 36. Schematic of dual-VISAR experiment to obtain wave profiles at two propagation distances. (After Barker, 1984. Copyright by North-Holland Publishing Company.)

## 6. Measurement of Sound Speed Behind the Shock Front

Manganin stress gauges, particle velocity gauges, and velocity interferometers described above are all capable of measuring the sound speed behind the shock front in the high-pressure shock state. In the case of fluid-like unloading behavior, the measurement of isentropic wave velocity through the high-pressure shock state taken with knowledge of the Hugoniot curve provides a critical measurement of the Gruneisen parameter. Knowledge of this thermodynamic quantity, defined as

$$\gamma = V\left(\frac{dP}{dE}\right)_V = \frac{\alpha K_S}{C_p \rho} = \frac{\alpha K_T}{C_V \rho} \quad (35)$$

is a critical requirement for calculating the pressure–density isentrope or isotherm, such as depicted in Fig. 11, from the Hugoniot curve. Here $\alpha$ is the thermal expansion coefficient and the subscripts $T$ and $S$ indicate constant temperature or entropy for the bulk modulus $K$. Also, $C_p$ and $C_v$ are specific heat at constant pressure and constant volume, respectively. Both experiments and theoretical considerations suggest that the Gruneisen parameter can be a function of volume or density alone (and not temperature) for metals and many minerals. This dependence is also used in Section 7 and is applied to calculate shock temperatures and the temperature on isentropic decompression.

For the case depicted in Fig. 11, the pressure along the isentrope $P_s$ at the volume $V_1$ corresponding to a Hugoniot state $(P_1, V_1)$ is given by

$$\frac{P_1}{2}(V_{00} - V_1) = -\int_{V_0}^{V_1} P\, dV + \frac{V_1}{\gamma}(P_1 - P_s) + E_{TR} \tag{36}$$

where the left-hand side is the Rankine–Hugoniot energy, and the first and second terms on the right represent the gain in the internal energy along the paths 1 and 2 of Fig. 11. Here $V_{00}$ is the specific volume of the initial material and $V_0$ the specific volume of the shock-induced high-pressure phase, or the intrinsic volume of the sample if the initial state is distended. Also $E_{TR}$ is the energy of transition to the high-pressure phase at STP. In the case of no phase change, $E_{TR} = 0$. For zero initial porosity $V_{00} = V_0$. The unknown parameter in Eq. (36) is $P_s$, which is implicit in the first integral term on the right-hand side and explicit in the second term. The second term is obtained by using the definition of the Gruneisen parameter [Eq. (35)] to calculate the change in energy associated with the pressure difference $(P_1 - P_s)$ at constant volume.

On unloading from a high-pressure state the sound speed

$$C_s = V(-\partial P/\partial V)_s^{1/2} \tag{37}$$

associated with the intersection of the release isentrope and the Hugoniot (Fig. 37) may be related to the Gruneisen parameter at the Hugoniot state $P_1$, $V_1$ by

$$\frac{P_1}{2}(V_0 - V_1) - \tfrac{1}{2}\left[P_1 + \left(\frac{\partial P}{\partial V}\right)_H \Delta V\right][V_0 - (V_1 + \Delta V)] \tag{38}$$

$$= P_1\, \Delta V + \frac{V_1'}{\gamma}\left[-\left(\frac{\partial P}{\partial V}\right)_H \Delta V - \left(-\frac{\partial P}{\partial V}\right)_s \Delta V\right]$$

Here the terms on the left-hand side represent the Rankine–Hugoniot energy difference between $P_1'$ and $P_1$, the pressures along the Hugoniot at $V_1'$ and $V_1$, located infinitesimal specific volumes apart (by $\Delta V$) (represented by path 4 in

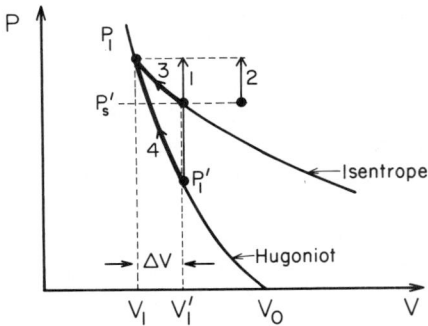

FIG. 37. Pressure–volume paths used to relate slope of Hugoniot $(\partial P/\partial V)_H$ to isentropic sound speed $C_s$ in Eq. (37).

Fig. 37). This energy is set equal to the energy difference between $P'_s$ and $P_1$ along the isentropic path 3 (first term on right-hand side) plus the energy difference associated with the pressure difference between $P'_s$ and $P'_1$. This is represented by the second term on the right-hand side. The latter is the energy equivalent of path 2 minus path 1. Using Eqs. (35) and (37) in Eq. (38) and taking into account that $\Delta V$ is infinitesimal, it follows that

$$C_s = V_1 \left\{ \left(\frac{dP}{dV}\right)_H \left[(V_0 - V_1)\frac{\gamma}{2V_1} - 1\right] + P_1 \frac{\gamma}{2V_1} \right\} = C_b \qquad (39)$$

where $(dP/dV)_H$ is the slope of the Hugoniot curve at $P_1$. Thus if the Hugoniot and bulk sound speed $C_s$ are measured, the Gruneisen parameter may be determined.

The sound (elastic wave) speed in the high-pressure shock state is an important geophysical property which can help determine whether a solid or a fluid phase exists at the shocked state sound speed in the shock state. Before the wave profile methods of Section 5 were developed, simpler methods for measuring the sound speed in the shocked state were described by Al'tschuler et al. (1960) and Fowles (1960). The simplest geometry which these papers describe is shown in Fig. 38. Here the flyer plate and sample are like materials. On impact of the flyer plate of thickness $f$, which can, in practice, be either explosively or gun-launched with the sample, shock waves propagate in both the flyer plate and sample. On reflection of the shock wave at the rear surface of the flyer plate, the resulting rarefaction wave propagates forward and will catch up with the shock front propagating into the sample, since in general the rarefaction velocity $C_i$, in the compressed state, exceeds the shock velocity. The point at which the rarefaction wave originating at the rear of the flyer, or driver plate, overtakes the shock front is measured. Here $i = \ell$ or b, where $\ell$ indicates longitudinal and b indicates bulk sound velocity in the high-pressure shock state [Eqs. (22)–(23)], respectively.

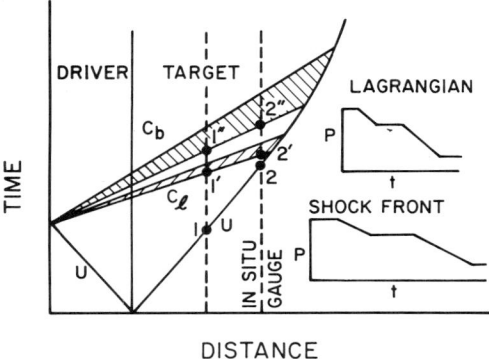

FIG. 38. Schematic distance–time diagram of the shock and rarefaction process for ideal elastic–plastic flow. $U$, shock wave; $C_l$ and $C_b$, Langrangian longitudinal and bulk wave velocities. The cross hatched areas represent the region bounded by the lead and tail characteristics. The $P$ vs. $t$ insert labeled "Lagrangian" represents what an *in situ* pressure gauge record might look like as it moves along in the flow and the corresponding pressure vs. time at the shock front is indicated below. As shown, the two *in situ* gauges would record the arrival of the shock at 1 and 2, the elastic unloading wave at 1' and 2', and the deformational unloading wave at 1" and 2". (After McQueen *et al.*, 1982.)

At this point it is useful to define the velocity of a sound ($\ell$ or b) wave propagating in a moving medium, which may also be compressed, The velocity with respect to stations moving with the medium is termed Lagrangian, $C^L$. The position of a station (for the purpose of calculating the velocity) is taken to be specified by its initial position. Sound velocity with respect to distances, measured with respect to the laboratory, is termed *Eulerian*, $C^e$.

As indicated in Fig. 38, $C_i$ is the Langrangian wave speed of the head on the rarefaction wave propagating forward into the shock state. Thus, measuring the time intervals 1–1', 2–2', and 2'–2" at two different gauge positions between the arrivals of the heads of the longitudinal rarefaction wave and bulk rarefaction wave determines the rarefaction wave velocities $C_l$ and $C_b$. However, determining with high precision the onset of the rarefaction arrivals with particle velocity or shock pressure gauges is not simple because these devices have a response which is proportional to pressure or particle velocity.

The thickness of the target at the point at which the rarefaction wave catches up to the shock front and begins to rapidly attenuate the pressure of the shock front is readily definable in the Lagrangian time vs. distance diagram of Fig. 38. In the Langrangian (material) coordinates, this distance $d$ may be calculated from equal time paths for the direct shock $d/U$ and the initially backward-propagating shock and subsequent forward-reflecting rarefaction wave propagating at velocity $C_i^L$ from

$$\frac{d}{U} = \frac{f}{U} + \frac{f}{C_i^L} + \frac{d}{C_i^L} \tag{40}$$

or

$$\frac{d}{U} = \frac{f}{U} + \frac{U-u}{U}\left[\frac{f+d}{C_i^e}\right] \tag{41}$$

which corresponds to the Eulerian (laboratory) coordinates. Also,

$$C_i^e = (\rho_0/\rho)C_i^L \tag{42}$$

where $\rho_0$ and $\rho$ are the initial and high-pressure densities.

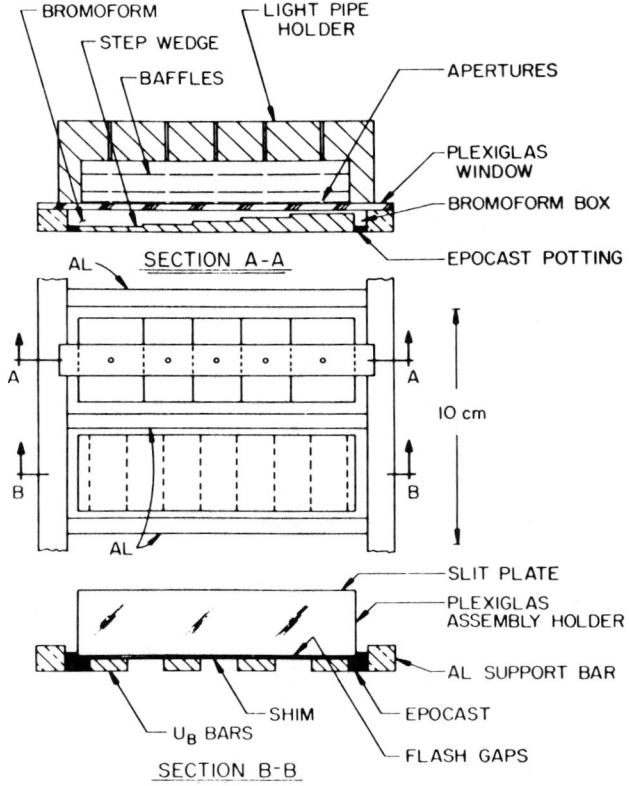

FIG. 39. High-explosive assembly for measuring overtaking wave speed with an optical light pipe detector viewing an optical analyzer (bromoform in this example). The detector and analyzer use photomultipliers and oscilloscopes. Section AA shows target of varying thickness. Section BB shows flash-gap system for measuring impact velocity from the difference in time between shock arrival through $u_B$ bar and direct impact on flash gap with a streak camera (after McQueen et al., 1982). Since the difference in time of the shock driven through the metal bar ($u_B$) and the direct impact is measured, the impact velocity is determined.

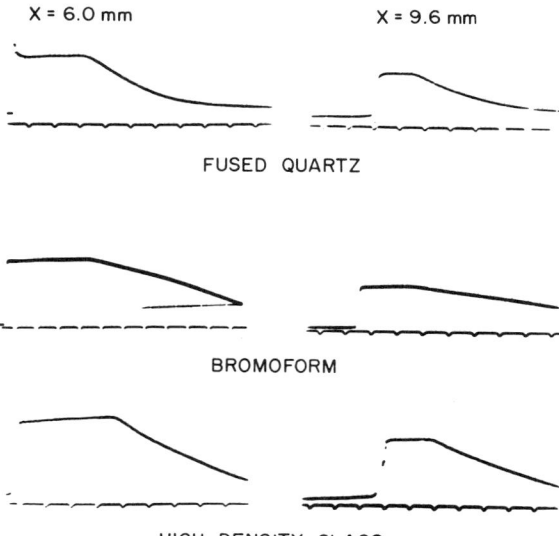

FIG. 40. Optical signals recorded via photo multiplier and oscilloscope for measuring release wave velocity in 347 stainless steel with various optical analyzer materials. (After McQueen *et al.*, 1982.)

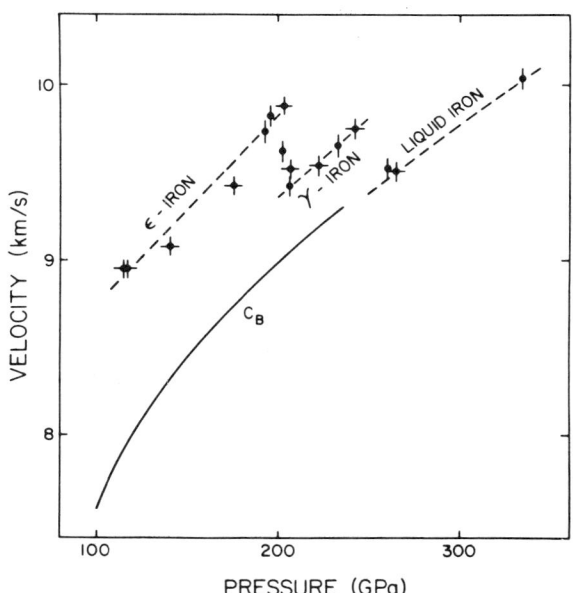

FIG. 41. Elastic wave velocities as a function of pressure along the Hugoniot of iron. The solid curve is the calculated bulk sound velocity. (From Brown and McQueen, 1982.)

McQueen *et al.* (1982) demonstrated that by placing a high-impedance transparent material (called an analyzer) over the sample at a series of thicknesses less than $d$ in the target, the arrival of rarefaction waves could be very readily detected by the change in light radiance caused by the onset of a decrease in shock amplitude when the rarefaction wave caught up to the shock front (Figs. 39 and 40). Materials which have been found useful as analyzers include bromoform, $Br_3HC$, which has an STP density of 2.89 mg/m$^3$, and some high-density glasses (4.2 and 5.3 mg/m$^3$), as well as crystalline and fused quartz. In the range ~50–200 GPa these materials achieve shock temperatures on the order of $10^3$ to $10^4$ K and hence have their peak blackbody radiation near the optical range of the spectrum. Since shock temperatures are proportional to shock amplitude in this pressure range, the peak wavelengths of the radiation intensity in the optical range are proportional to $T^4$. The radiance of the shock front vs. time as detected with a photomultiplier is shown in Fig. 40. This system is an extremely sensitive indicator of the pressure at the shock front. It has been used to detect small changes in the overtaking velocity which occur when phase changes such as melting take place (Fig. 41). The sound velocity behind the shock front along the Hugoniot on crossing from the $\varepsilon$-iron to $\gamma$-iron to the liquid field was reported by Brown and McQueen (1982) (Fig. 41).

## 7. Shock and Postshock Temperatures

### 7.1. Theory

For many condensed media of geophysical interest such as metals and minerals, the Mie–Gruneisen equation of state, based on a finite-difference formulation of the Gruneisen parameter [Eq. (35)], can be used to describe shock and postshock temperatures. The temperature along the isentrope is given by

$$T_s = T_i \exp\left[-\int_{V_a}^{V_b}\left(\frac{\gamma}{V}\right)dV\right] \quad (43)$$

where $T_i$ is the initial temperature. For the principal isentrope $T_i = T_0$, room temperature, $V_a = V_0$, initial volume, and $V_b = V$, compressed volume. For the calculation of postshock temperatures $T_i = T_H$, the Hugoniot temperature, $V_a = V_H$, the volume of the shock state, and $V_b = V'_{00}$, the postshock volume corresponding to the postshock temperature. For shock compression to a volume $V$, $P_s$ is first obtained by using Eq. (36); then $T_s$, the isentropic compression temperature at volume $V$, may be calculated by using Eq. (43).

Finally, using Eq. (35), the shock temperature $T_H$ is given by

$$\frac{V}{\gamma}(P_H - P_s) = \int_{T_s}^{T_H} C_V dT \qquad (44)$$

In the case of molecular fluids such as water, a formulation based on the near constancy of $C_p$ at constant pressure is used (Rice and Walsh, 1957; Bakanova et al., 1976).

It is useful to carry out both postshock and shock temperature measurements as they provide complementary information on the thermal equation of state.

Postshock temperatures are very sensitive to the models which specify $\gamma$ and its volume dependence, in the case of the Gruneisen equation of state

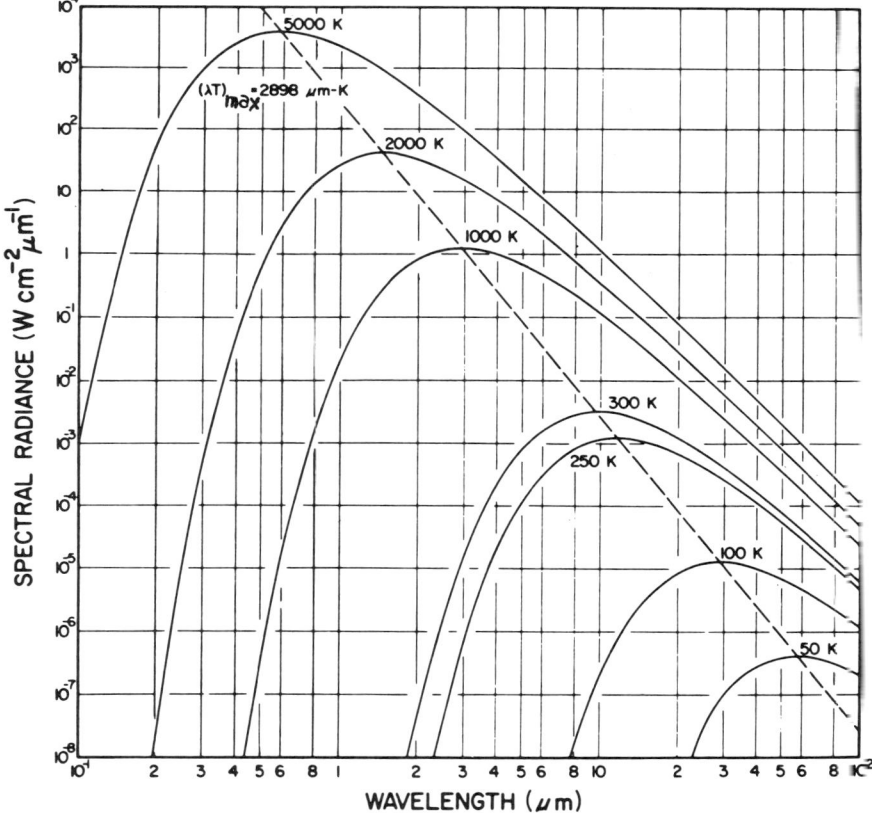

FIG. 42. The Planck distribution law spectral radiance of blackbody radiation as a function of temperature and wavelength. (After Touloukian and DeWitt, 1972. Copyright by Plenum Press.)

(Raikes and Ahrens, 1979a, 1979b). In contrast, the absolute values of shock temperatures are sensitive to the phase transition energy $E_{TR}$ of Eq. (36), whereas the slope of the $T_H$ vs. pressure curve is sensitive to the specific heat (Lyzenga *et al.*, 1983).

### 7.2. Shock Temperature Determination

Although some measurements of shock temperatures in the metals have been carried out using thermistors and the thermoelectric effect (Bloomquist and Duvall, 1979; Rosenberg and Partom, 1984), most determinations of shock temperatures have been carried out radiatively by analysis of radiations from transparent media, many of the these being minerals. As a strong shock wave propagates through a transparent material, the temperature of the material in the shock-compressed state is calculated by measuring

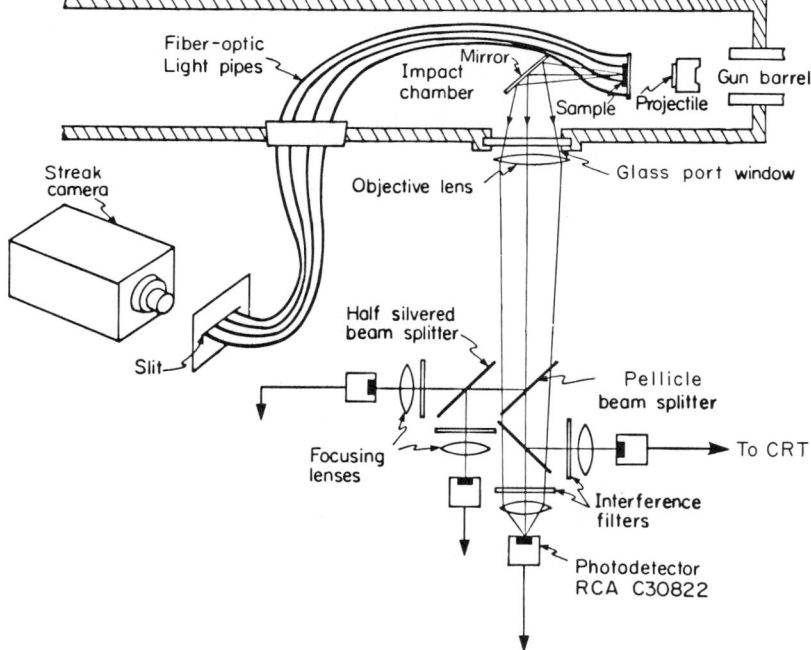

FIG. 43. Experimental configuration for carrying out shock temperature measurements with a high-speed, wide-bandwidth optical pyrometer. The ends of the fiber-optic light pipes are shocked either on arrival of the shock wave at the sample–driver interface or at the sample free surface. Since the radiance induced by this shock arrival is recorded by the streak camera, a Hugoniot state is obtained in each experiment in which the shock temperature is determined. (After Boslough and Ahrens, 1984. Copyright by the American Geophysical Union.)

the radiative spectrum of the shock-compressed material as transmitted through the transparent unshocked material assuming thermal radiation and a graybody spectrum. The dependence of the radiative power $N_\lambda$ or wavelength $\lambda$ for a black, or gray, body is shown in Fig. 42 and is given by

$$N_\lambda = \varepsilon C_1 \lambda^{-5} (\exp C_2/\lambda T - 1)^{-1} \qquad (45)$$

where $\varepsilon$ is emissivity, $C_1 = 1.191 \times 10^{-16}$ W m$^2$/steradian, and $C_2 = 1.439 \times 10^{-2}$ m K. The figure demonstrates that a system which is sensitive to radiation from the near infrared ($\sim 1$ μm) into the visible ($\sim 0.6$ μm = 600 nm) will record peak radiances for blackbodies ($\varepsilon = 1$) between $\sim 2000$ and 5000 K. This is generally the temperature range of the mantle and core of the earth and hence is of geophysical interest, although in general Hugoniot temperatures for mantle silicates are less than or approximately

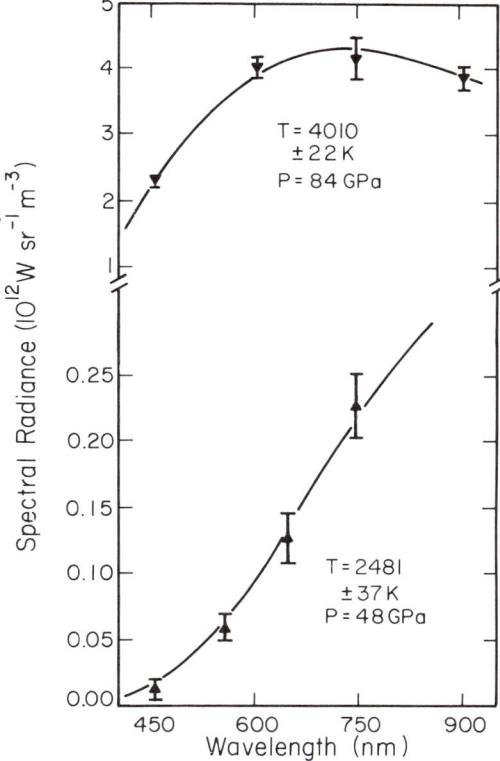

FIG. 44. Spectral radiance vs. wavelength for CaAl$_2$Si$_2$O$_8$ glass shocked to 48 and 84 GPa. Best-fitting Planck blackbody curves are shown in relation to the radiance data. (After Boslough and Ahrens, 1984. Copyright by the American Geophysical Union.)

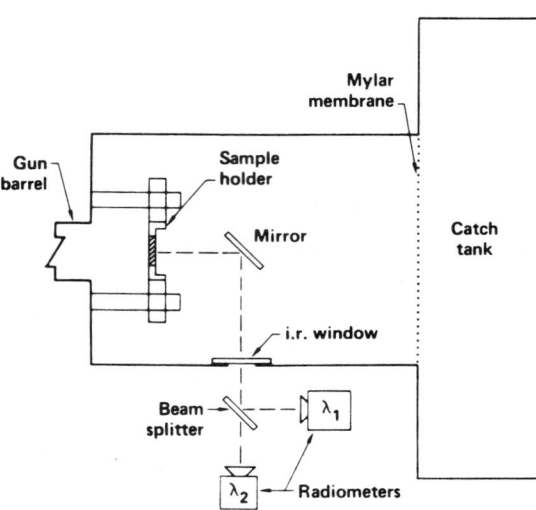

FIG. 45. Experiment configuration for using infrared radiometers for postshock temperature measurements. Typically one radiometer will have an InSb (2–5.5 μm&) and the other an HgCdTe (5–11 μm) detector, both operating at 77 K. (After Von Holle and McWilliams, 1983.)

FIG. 46. Photograph of HgCdTe infrared radiometer for submicrosecond postshock temperature measurement. (After Von Holle and McWilliams, 1983.)

equal to those existing in the earth at comparable pressures for the upper mantle and greater for the lower mantle. A number of radiative sensing systems utilizing interference filters and photomultipliers or photodiodes have been used to record shock temperatures (Kormer, 1965; Lyzenga and Ahrens, 1979; Boslough and Ahrens, 1986). A system of four wideband beam splitters and interference filters in the range 450–900 nm is shown in Fig. 43. Sensitivity to radiation at relatively low shock temperatures is achieved with this system because of the wide aperture (0.03 steradian), large bandwidth per channel ($\sim 40$ nm)), and large photodiode detector area ($\sim 0.2$ cm$^2$). Some typical shock temperature data for $CaAl_2Si_2O_8$ glass are shown in Fig. 44.

## 7.3. Postshock Temperatures

Although there have been relatively few postshock temperature measurements of minerals, the considerable data obtained on metals provide unexpectedly strong constraints on the thermomechanical properties of metals (Taylor, 1964; King et al., 1968; Raikes and Ahrens, 1979a). Although originally postshock temperature measurements were feasible only with photomultipliers used to detect radiation emitted from shocked metal surfaces, advances in high-speed infrared-sensitive detectors, InSb and HgCdTe (Von Holle and McWilliams, 1983), hold much promise for applications to minerals over a wide range of conditions. Initial experiments on several minerals in earlier versions of the Von Holle and McWilliams apparatus (Fig. 45 and 46) were reported by Raikes and Ahrens (1979a).

## Acknowledgments

I thank G. Abrahamson (Stanford Research Institute), W. Von Holle and W. Nells (Lawrence Livermore National Laboratory), and R. G. McQueen (Los Alamos National Laboratory) for copies of figures. I thank S. Rigden, J. Tyburczy, B. Svendsen, G. Miller, and P. Kasiraj for critical comments on this chapter. This work was supported under grants from the National Science Foundation and National Aeronautics and Space Administration. Contribution No. 4088, Division of Geological and Planetary Sciences, California Institute of Technology, Pasadena.

## References

T. J. Ahrens, *J. Geophys. Res.* **84**, 985 (1979).
T. J. Ahrens, *Science* **207**, 1035 (1980).
T. J. Ahrens and V. G. Gregson, Jr., *J. Geophys. Res.* **26**, 4839 (1964).
T. J. Ahrens and J. D. O'Keefe, *Moon* **4**, 214 (1972).
T. J. Ahrens and J. D. O'Keefe, in "Impact and Explosion Cratering" (D. J. Roddy, R. O Pepin, and R. B. Merrill, eds.), p. 639. Pergamon, New York, 1977.
T. J. Ahrens and J. T. Rosenberg, in "Shock Metamorphism of Natural Materials" (B. M. French and N. M. Short, eds.), p. 59. Mono Book, Baltimore, Maryland, 1968.

T. J. Ahrens, W. H. Gust, and E. B. Royce, *J. Appl. Phys.* **39**, 4610 (1968).
T. J. Ahrens, J. D. O'Keefe, and R. V. Gibbons, *Geochim. Cosmochim. Acta, Suppl.* No. 4, 2575 (1973).
L. V. Al'tschuler, *Sov. Phys. Usp. (Engl. Transl.)* **8**, 52 (1965).
L. V. Al'tschuler, S. B. Kormer, M. I. Brazhnik, L. A. Vladimirov, M. P. Speranskaya, and A. I. Funtikov, *Sov. Phys. JETP (Engl. Transl.)* **11**, 766 (1960).
A. A. Bakanova, V. N. Zubarev, Y. N. Sutulov, and R. F. Trunin, *Sov. Phys. JETP (Engl. Transl.)* **41**, 544 (1976).
D. Bancroft, E. L. Peterson, and S. Minshall, *J. Appl. Phys.* **27**, 291 (1956).
L. M. Barker, *in* "Behavior of Dense Media under High Dynamic Pressures," IUTAM Symp., p. 483. Gordon & Breach, New York, 1968.
L. M. Barker, *in* "Shock Waves in Condensed Matter—1983" (J. R. Assay, R. A. Graham, and G. K. Straub, eds.), p. 217. Elsevier, Amsterdam, 1984.
L. M. Barker and R. E. Hollenbach, *J. Appl. Phys.* **41**, 4208 (1970).
L. M. Barker and R. E. Hollenbach, *J. Appl. Phys.* **43**, 4669 (1972).
L. M. Barker and R. E. Hollenbach, *J. Appl. Phys.* **45**, 4872 (1974).
P. Bernstein and D. D. Keough, *J. Appl. Phys.* **35**, 1471 (1964).
D. D. Bloomquist, G. E. Duvall, and J. J. Dick, *J. Appl. Phys.* **50**, 4838 (1979).
M. B. Boslough and T. J. Ahrens, *in* "Shock Waves in Condensed Matter—1983" (J. R. Asay, R. A. Graham, and G. K. Straub, eds.), p. 525. Elsevier, Amsterdam, 1984.
M. B. Boslough and T. J. Ahrens, *J. Geophys. Res.* **90**, 7814 (1985).
M. B. Boslough and T. J. Ahrens, submitted (1986).
J. M. Brown and R. G. McQueen, *in* "High Pressure Research in Geophysics" (S.-i. Akimoto and M. H. Manghnani, eds.), p. 611. Cent. Acad. Publ., Tokyo and Reidel, Dordrecht, Netherlands, 1982.
J. M. Brown, T. J. Ahrens, and D. L. Shampine, *J. Geophys. Res.* **84**, 6041 (1984).
M. Cowperthwaite and T. J. Ahrens, *Am. J. Phys.* **35**, 951 (1967).
L. Davison and R. A. Graham, *Phys. Rep.* **55**, 255 (1979).
G. E. Duvall and G. R. Fowles, *in* "High Pressure Physics and Chemistry" (R. S. Bradley, ed.), Vol. 2, p. 209. Academic Press, New York, 1963.
G. R. Fowles, *J. Appl. Phys.* **31**, 655 (1960).
G. R. Fowles, *J. Appl. Phys.* **32**, 1475 (1961).
G. R. Fowles and R. F. Williams, *J. Appl. Phys.* **41**, 360 (1970).
G. R. Fowles, G. E. Duvall, J. Asay, P. Bellamy, F. Feistmann, D. Grady, J. Michaels, and R. Mitchell, *Rev. Sci. Instrum.* **41**, 984 (1970).
P. J. A. Fuller and J. H. Price, *Br. J. Appl. Phys.* **15**, 751 (1964).
T. Gehrels, "Protostars and Planets," p. 756. Univ. of Arizona Press, Tucson, 1978.
D. E. Grady, *J. Geophys. Res.* **78**, 1299 (1973).
D. E. Grady, *in* "High Pressure Research: Applications to Geophysics" (M. H. Manghnani and S.-i. Akimoto, eds.), p. 389. Academic Press, New York, 1977.
R. A. Graham and J. R. Asay, *High Temp. High Pressures* **10**, 355 (1978).
Y. M. Gupta, *J. Appl. Phys.* **54**, 6094 (1983).
R. Jeanloz and T. J. Ahrens, *J. Geophys. Res.* **84**, 7545 (1979).
O. E. Jones, *in* "Behavior and Utilization of Explosives in Engineering Design" (R. L. Henderson, ed.), p. 125. Univ. of New Mexico Press, Albuquerque, 1972.
P. J. King, D. F. Cotgrove, and P. M. B. Slate, *in* "Behaviour of Dense Media under High Dynamic Pressures" (J. Berger, ed.), p. 513. Gordon & Breach, New York, 1968.
S. B. Kormer, *Sov. Phys. Usp. (Engl. Transl.)* **21**, 689 (1965).
G. A. Lyzenga and T. J. Ahrens, *J. Appl. Phys.* **49**, 201 (1978).
G. A. Lyzenga and T. J. Ahrens, *Rev. Sci. Instrum.* **50**, 1421 (1979).

G. A. Lyzenga, T. J. Ahrens, and A. C. Mitchell, *J. Geophys. Res.* **88**, 2431 (1983).
R. G. McQueen, S. P. Marsh, and J. N. Fritz, *J. Geophys. Res.* **72**, 4999 (1967).
R. G. McQueen, S. P. Marsh, J. W. Taylor, J. N. Fritz, and W. J. Carter, in "High Velocity Impact Phenomena" (R. Kinslow, ed.), p. 294. Academic Press, New York, 1970.
R. G. McQueen, J. W. Hopson, and J. N. Fritz, *Rev. Sci. Instrum.* **53**, 245 (1982).
A. C. Mitchell and W. J. Nellis, *Rev. Sci. Instrum.* **52**, 347 (1981).
W. J. Murri, D. R. Curran, C. F. Petersen, and R. C. Crewdson, *Adv. High Pressure Res.* **4**, 1 (1974).
W. J. Nellis, F. H. Ree, M. van Thiel, and A. C. Mitchell, *J. Chem. Phys.* **75**, 3055 (1981).
W. J. Nellis, M. Ross, A. C. Mitchell, M. van Thiel, D. A. Young, F. H. Ree, and R. J. Trainer, *Phys. Rev. A* **27**, 608 (1983).
M. A. Podurets, G. V. Simakov, and R. F. Trunin, *Izv. Earth Phys.* **7**, 419 (1976).
C. E. Ragan, III in "Behavior of Dense Media under High Dynamic Pressures" (R. Chéret, ed.), p. 477. Ed. Commis. Energie At., Saclay, France, 1978.
C. E. Ragan, III, M. G. Silbert, and B. C. Diven, *J. Appl. Phys.* **48**, 2860 (1977).
S. A. Raikes and T. J. Ahrens, *Geophys. J. R. Astron. Soc.* **58**, 717 (1979a).
S. A. Raikes and T. J. Ahrens, in "High Pressure Science and Technology" (K. D. Timmerhaus and M. S. Barber, eds.), p. 889. Plenum, New York, 1979b.
M. H. Rice and T. M. Walsh, *J. Chem. Phys.* **26**, 824 (1957).
D. J. Roddy, R. O. Pepin, and R. B. Merrill, "Impact and Explosion Cratering," p. 1301. Pergamon, Oxford, 1977.
Z. Rosenberg and Y. Partom, in "Shock Waves in Condensed Matter—1983" (J. R. Asay, R. A. Graham, and G. K. Straub, eds.), p. 251. Elsevier, Amsterdam, 1984.
A. L. Ruoff, *J. Appl. Phys.* **38**, 4976 (1967).
L. Seaman, *J. Appl. Phys.* **45**, 4303 (1974).
D. Stöffler, *Fortschr. Mineral.* **49**, 50 (1972).
D. Stöffler, *Fortschr. Mineral.* **51**, 256 (1974).
Tan Bing-Shen and Jing Fu-Qian, *Proc. Detonation Symp., 7th, Nav. Surf. Weapons Cent., Silver Springs, Md.* (1982).
J. W. Taylor, *J. Appl. Phys.* **34**, 2727 (1964).
Y. S. Touloukian and D. P. DeWitt, "Thermophysical Properties of Matter," Vol. 8. Plenum, New York, 1972.
M. S. Vassiliou and T. J. Ahrens, *Rev. Sci. Instrum.* **53**, 108 (1982).
J. Vizgirda and T. J. Ahrens, *J. Geophys. Res.* **87**, 4747 (1982).
W. G. Von Holle and R. A. McWilliams, *Rev. Sci. Instrum.* **54**, 1218 (1983).
J. M. Walsh and R. H. Christian, *Phys. Rev.* **97**, 1544 (1955).
J. P. Watt and T. J. Ahrens, *J. Geophys. Res.* **88**, 9500 (1983).
V. V. Yakushev, *Fiz. Goreniya Vzryva* **14**, 3 (1978).
V. M. Zaitzev, P. F. Pokhil, and K. K. Shvedov, *Dokl. Akad. Nauk. SSSR* **132**, 1339 (1960).
Y. B. Zel'dovich and A. S. Kompaneets, "Theory of Detonation." Academic Press, New York, 1960.
Y. B. Zel'dovich and Y. P. Raizer, "Physics of Shock Waves and High-Temperature Hydrodynamic Phenomena," Vol. 2. Academic Press, New York, 1967.
J. A. Zukas, T. Nicholas, H. F. Swift, L. B. Grezczuk, and D. R. Curran, "Impact Dynamics." Wiley, New York, 1982.

# 7. THE MULTIANVIL PRESS

E. K. Graham

Department of Geosciences and the Materials Research Laboratory
The Pennsylvania State University
University Park, Pennsylvania 16802

## 1. Introduction

In contrast to the generation of very high static pressure within a very small working volume, as exemplified by the diamond anvil cell, multianvil press designs have sought to achieve larger working volumes within a more moderate pressure range. Although, at the time of this writing, multianvil high-pressure methods are not being employed extensively in the United States, many foreign laboratories, notably in Japan and the Soviet Union, are using multianvil devices in a variety of ways. In particular, multianvil units recently have been used in various aspects of new materials synthesis and engineering and in the measurement of material physical properties at high pressure and temperature.

Multianvil high-pressure devices incorporate the principle of "massive support" through the use of four or more coupled or independent anvil systems. Such units are capable of generating pressures of up to 10 GPa in sample volumes of several cubic centimeters. Conventional systems employ either four or six anvils. In the case of the former, the anvil units are designed with triangular faces to generate pressure within a tetrahedral sample cell. Six-anvil devices have square-faced anvils which are arrayed in such a manner that pressure is applied to a cubic-shaped sample cell. Other configurations are possible, but design and application complexities have discouraged their development. One successful alternative design, however, involves the use of multiple anvil sliding systems (MASS), which incorporate arrangements that allow mutual support to maintain anvil strength while large volume reduction generates high pressure in the sample cell. Pressures of up to 20 GPa have been attained in MASS units. Another multianvil design which has been used to generate pressure in excess of 30 GPa is the split-sphere arrangement. In all cases, of course, the ultimate pressure attainable depends on the strength characteristics of the anvils and the support provided by the anvil–gasket configuration.

Multianvil research relevant to the geosciences has involved both materials synthesis and phase equilibria, as well as the measurement of various physical properties at high pressure and temperature. Of course, much of the general interest in high-pressure research in the recent past has centered on the synthesis of special materials. In particular, the preparation of synthetic diamonds and other ultrahard materials, such as cubic boron nitride, has fostered interest in high-pressure research in industry, as well as in government and university laboratories. In this regard, the relatively large sample volume capability of multianvil devices has been an attractive characteristic. Large tetrahedral and cubic anvil presses have been constructed which are capable of generating a maximum of 7 or 8 GPa quasi-hydrostatic pressure at over 1300°C on a sample volume of $0.25 \text{ cm}^3$. Such units also have provided the opportunity to study solid-state phase equilibria, melting relations, and reaction kinetics in the high-pressure regime, in addition to special materials synthesis. Obviously, in the case of the geosciences, such research efforts have been directed toward fundamental earth-forming materials; in particular, silicates and oxides. Cubic- and tetrahedral-anvil systems, as well as MASS devices, have been used for many years, especially in Japan, to synthesize and characterize the phase relations of mineral systems relevant to the earth's upper mantle. More recently, multianvil units, particularly cubic systems, have been employed in the measurement of various mineral physical properties at high pressure and temperature. These efforts have been characterized and motivated by the design and use of more sophisticated liquid–solid hybrid sample cells, which provide a near-hydrostatic pressure environment to over 8 GPa. This moderately high pressure capability, coupled with a relatively large specimen working volume (compared to the diamond-anvil cell, for example), provides the means for carrying out certain types of precise physical property experiments which otherwise could not be performed because of pressure or space limitations. For example, cubic-anvil sample cells have been designed to provide hydrostatic pressure up to 5 GPa within a working volume of over $2 \text{ cm}^3$. Such a volume is sufficient to allow the measurement of elastic constants by precision ultrasonic techniques.

## 2. Design and Construction of Multianvil Presses

The generation of high pressure on a specimen of interest with a multianvil system actually involves a two-phase process. First, the force of the rams or anvils of the multianvil press is transmitted onto the walls of a cell–sample assembly. Second, the resulting pressure is transmitted through the high-pressure cell assembly which contains the specimen and the instrumentation required for the specific experiment under consideration. In this section, the salient features of the design and construction of the most commonly used multianvil systems (tetrahedral-anvil, cubic-anvil, split-sphere, and MASS devices) will be described. For a more complete discussion, the reader should refer to more comprehensive descriptions which are available in the literature.[1-7] In the next section, a discussion of the design and characteristics of various cell–sample assemblies will be presented.

The first successful design and construction of a tetrahedral-anvil press was carried out by Hall[8] at Brigham Young University in 1958. Since that time, a number of other units of various capacities and modifications have been built.[3, 9-11] In general, all tetrahedral-anvil devices are characterized by the arrangement shown in Fig. 1. Force is applied to a tetrahedron pressure cell by four anvils driven by external rams. Each anvil has a triangular face which directly compresses the tetrahedron pressure cell. Three slanting faces are cut at an angle to the triangular contact face such that the four anvils pack efficiently around the pressure cell. For optimal results, in terms of anvil support and generated pressure, the slanting faces are cut at an angle of 35° relative to the load-bearing triangular face. The tetrahedron pressure cell is made somewhat larger than the volume afforded by the anvils on complete closure. As a result, the pressure cell material flows into the gaps

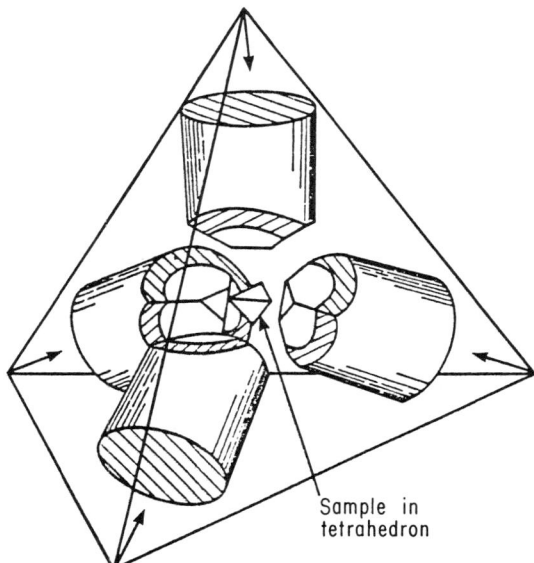

FIG. 1. General pressure cell–anvil arrangement of a tetrahedral-anvil press. The sample is contained within the tetrahedron pressure cell.

between the anvils as compression proceeds. This characteristic of the method is the basis for the generation of high internal pressure within the cell–sample assembly volume. The extrusion of the cell material provides support for the anvils as well as a gasket to retain the pressure within the tetrahedron. Clearly, proper choice of the pressure cell material is very important to achieving optimal pressure generation.

In the original tetrahedral press designed by Hall,[8] four individual rams held together with steel tie rods were used to apply the load to the tetrahedron pressure cell. However, maintaining alignment and symmetric compression in such a unit proved to be difficult. In multianvil presses, in general, precise alignment of the load-bearing rams is essential to avoid premature anvil failure. In order to ameliorate this problem, Hall developed a "guide-pin system" in subsequent units which provided continuous adequate alignment during operation, in addition to individual or synchronous load application to the rams. Another design which minimizes alignment problems, and which is less expensive to construct and operate, is the wedge-action press developed at the National Bureau of Standards.[9] In this tetrahedral unit, three of the anvils are situated within a cone wedge support. The fourth and upper anvil is driven down in opposition to the lower three by a single ram. A symmetric load is applied to the tetrahedron pressure cell by the reaction of the lower three anvils against the cone wedge support. Friction between the cone wedge and lower anvils is minimized by placing Teflon sheets between the sliding surfaces. The economy of construction and operation of the wedge-action apparatus is countered by size limitations and experimental access constraints.

A considerably larger tetrahedral device has been designed and constructed by Barogenics Incorporated.[10] This unit generates an 8000-ton load through anvils with triangular faces 6.5 cm on edge (see Fig. 2). In this design, the four individual ram–anvil assemblies are held together by large pin rods which are inserted into interlocking hinges. Therefore, the high loads which are generated are distributed over the entire length of the pin–hinge intersection. This serves to reduce the occurrence of alignment problems initiated during operation of the press. The unit shown in Fig. 2, which weighs 8 tons, has been used[12] to generate a maximum of 7 GPa quasi-hydrostatic pressure on a specimen volume of 0.23 cm$^3$ at temperatures up to 1300°C.

The cubic-anvil press conceptually is very similar to the tetrahedral design. However, as the name implies, the cubic configuration uses six anvils with square faces to apply pressure to a pressure cell assembly which is in the shape of a cube (see Fig. 3). As in the case of the tetrahedral apparatus, there are several different designs for the ram–anvil linkage systems. The largest units[4, 13] generally employ six independent rams, which may be operated individually or synchronously. Other systems use a single ram with wedge or linkage supports for alignment and to drive the anvils in unison.[14–18] The

7. THE MULTIANVIL PRESS

FIG. 2. Barogenics tetrahedral press at the U.S. Steel Research Laboratory, Monroeville, Pennsylvania. This unit is now at the Materials Research Laboratory of the Pennsylvania State University. (Photograph provided by the courtesy of Dr. T. G. Nilan of the United State Steel Corp.)

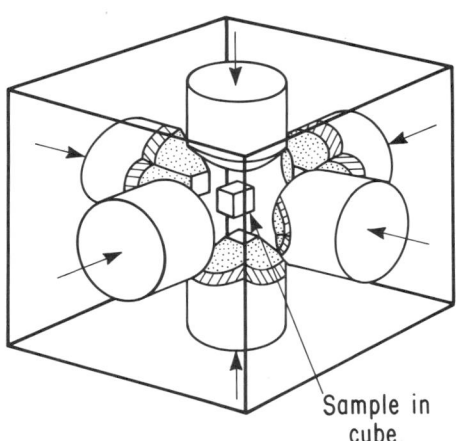

FIG. 3. Pressure cell and anvil–ram arrangement of a cubic-anvil press system. The sample and experimental instrumentation are contained within the indicated cube high-pressure cell.

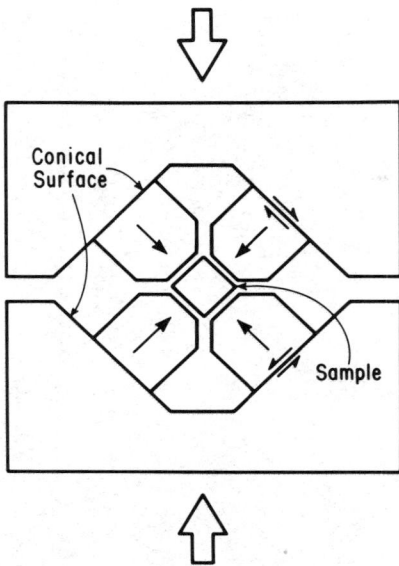

Fig. 4. Principle of the NBS wedge-type cubic-anvil system. The upper and lower cone supports each drive three anvils which are situated 120° apart. The system may be driven by a single hydraulic ram.

single-ram designs are more common because of their simplicity and economy of operation compared to independent-ram devices. However, the latter are preferable for larger-volume research efforts and commercial applications.

A recent version of the wedge-type cubic-anvil apparatus has been described by Wakatsuki and Ichinose.[19] It is based on a design originally developed at the National Bureau of Standards[14] which employs two opposing wedge cones to transmit the force provided by a single ram to the six anvils. A schematic diagram of the NBS cone-wedge principle is shown in Fig. 4. The three anvils in the upper cone-wedge are offset 120° relative to those in the lower cone support. As a result, the six anvils are arranged and close in a cubic sense. In the modification of the NBS design described by Owen,[15] a pressure of 6 GPa can be obtained at a temperature of 1500°C. However, as pointed out by Wakatsuki and Ichinose,[19] the basic NBS design is characterized by problems with pressure reproducibility, maintenance, and ease of operation. In order to ameliorate these difficulties, they have incorporated several new features into the NBS arrangement. Instead of a continuous cone-wedge support, each anvil is supported by a separate inclined wedge, which is machined with a V-shaped groove. The groove defines the interface between the inclined wedge and the anvil and provides lateral alignment. A Teflon sheet on the anvil–wedge interface allows vertical slip and adjustment. Therefore, misalignment from cubic-anvil closure will tend to be self-correcting. In addition, a small guiding wedge is provided at the end of the anvil support shoe to ensure synchronized motion. The apparatus has anvils with square faces 16 mm on edge and is actuated by a single 600-ton hydraulic press. It has been used extensively by Wakatsuki and Ichinose[1] to study diamond nucleation from graphite and other materials synthesis at pressures to 7 GPa at 1500° to 1700°C.

As in the case of the tetrahedral-anvil apparatus, a much larger version of the cubic-anvil press has been designed and constructed by Barogenics Incorporated.[4,10] Like its tetrahedral counterpart, described previously, the individual ram–anvil assemblies (in this case, six) are held together by large pin rods inserted through interlocking hinges. Each of the hydraulic rams, which may be run independently or synchronously, develops a load of 2000 tons. The anvils are ground with square faces 35 mm on edge. This cubic-anvil apparatus has been used in conjunction with a liquid–solid hybrid pressure cell system to generate hydrostatic pressure up to 6 GPa within a usable working volume of 2.33 cm$^3$ with high reliability.[20,21] The actual pressure capability of the Barogenics cubic-anvil press is in excess of 9 GPa. Its pressure-generating efficiency and uniformity have been studied in detail by Samara et al.[4]

Another cubic-anvil design, originally proposed by von Platen,[22] avoids the need for individual or wedge-support ram systems to drive the six anvils. The anvils are actually the segments of a sphere which are separated by gasket-spacers and contained by a deformable jacket. The inner tips of the sphere segments are ground into flat anvil faces which load a cubic sample block. The entire assembly is immersed in a fluid which is compressed to moderated pressure. The load pressure exerted on the sample block is considerably greater than the outer fluid pressure because of the magnification provided by the differential areas of the outer sphere segment surface relative to the inside anvil face. A schematic diagram of this system, referred to as a "split sphere," is shown in Fig. 5. In the case of von Platen's[22] apparatus, an outer fluid pressure of 0.6 GPa with a load magnification factor of 20 provided a potential 12.0-GPa sample block pressure. However, because of the reaction of the gasket-spacers, the actual load transmitted to the specimen was probably considerably less.

The principle of the split sphere has been developed and used extensively by Kawai and associates to generate pressures in excess of 70 GPa.[5,23-27] The more recent designs have utilized a two-stage approach, whereby six outer hardened steel sphere segment anvils are arranged to drive an inner system of eight tungsten carbide anvils which contact and load the cell-sample assembly (see Section 3). The latest versions[27] have also incorporated

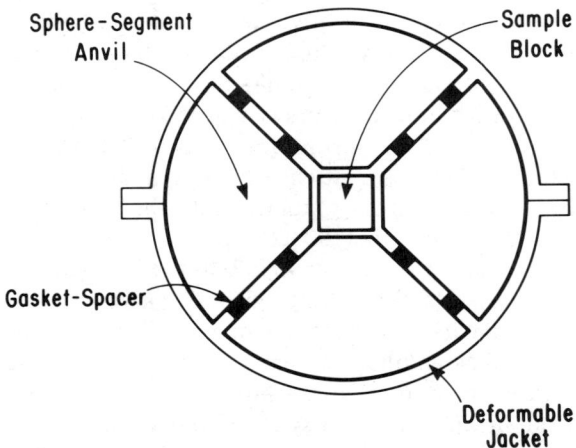

Fig. 5. Schematic representation of the basic split-sphere high-pressure system. When the assembly is placed in a pressurized external fluid, the sphere-segment anvils are forced inward on the sample block.

a third stage involving two innermost opposed anvils of sintered diamond. This multiple-stage split-sphere arrangement has generated pressures in excess of 100 GPa.

A unique version of the multianvil press is the multiple anvil sliding system. The idea of using sliding anvils to generate very high pressure on a relatively large volume was suggested by Epain *et al.*[6] and developed by Kumazawa and co-workers.[7,28-30] In general, the MASS method involves a configuration of several anvils which provide massive support to each other while an enclosed volume is decreased by a sliding rearrangement of the system. The volume reduction acts to produce the increase in pressure. Two basic MASS mechanisms have been described by Kumazawa.[7] In two dimensions (see Fig. 6, a and b) these may be described in terms of a rotation (type R), in which the anvils (in the case illustrated, four) move tangentially around the enclosed pressure zone, and a radial motion (type I, irrotation), which involves inward and outward movement of the four anvils relative to the pressure zone. There are numerous possible configurations or modifications of the basic two-dimensional MASS mechanisms. Two example systems are shown in Fig. 6, c and d.

Kumazawa and co-workers[7,28] have described, in addition, a number of different three-dimensional MASS mechanisms. In particular, their MASS 318-90 design[30] (see Fig. 7) was developed to generate pressures of up to 50 GPa in a volume of 7.5 mm. It consists of two truncated cubes (N or normal anvils), six rectangular prisms (W or wedge anvils), and 12 rectangular

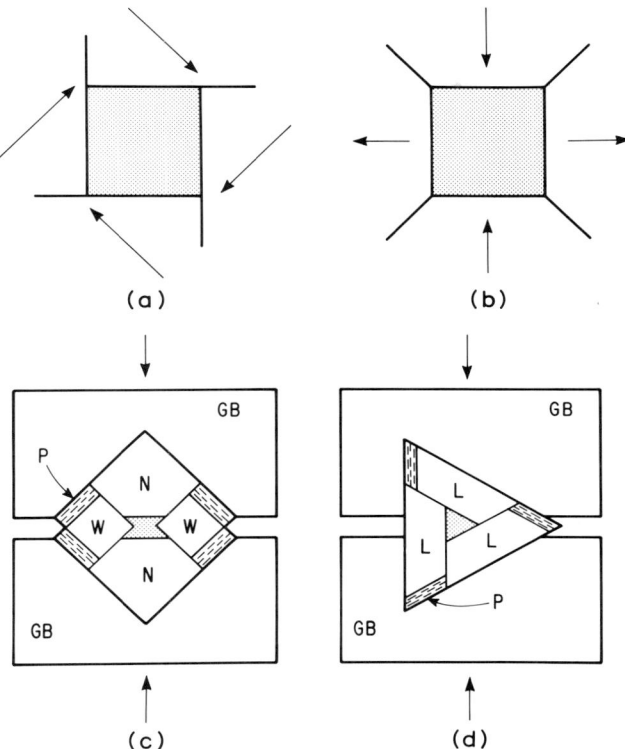

FIG. 6. The two basic MASS mechanisms in two-dimensions: (a) rotation or R type and (b) irrotation or I type. Schematic diagrams of the guide block–anvil arrangement for two representative two-dimensional MASS mechanisms: (c) 2I-n type and (d) 2R-n type. Abbreviations: GB, guide block; N, normal anvil; W, wedge anvil; L, lateral anvil; P, compressible pad. The stippled areas represent the zone of pressurization.

compressible pads which act to absorb and support the lateral motion of the wedge anvils during pressurization of the unit. The anvils are assembled to form a cube. Pressure is exerted on a triangular bipyramid sample cell situated in the central part of the assembly at the truncated ends of the N anvils. A cubic-anvil press is used to drive the MASS assembly. In this sense, the MASS mechanism represents a secondary stage of pressure intensification from a cubic-anvil primary stage (see Section 3). The MASS 3I8–90 system was used successfully[31–33] to study the decomposition of aluminium and silicate spinels to pressures of 33 GPa at a temperature of 1000°C.

The ultimate pressure generation capability of all multianvil press devices depends primarily on the level of applied load on the anvils, the choice of

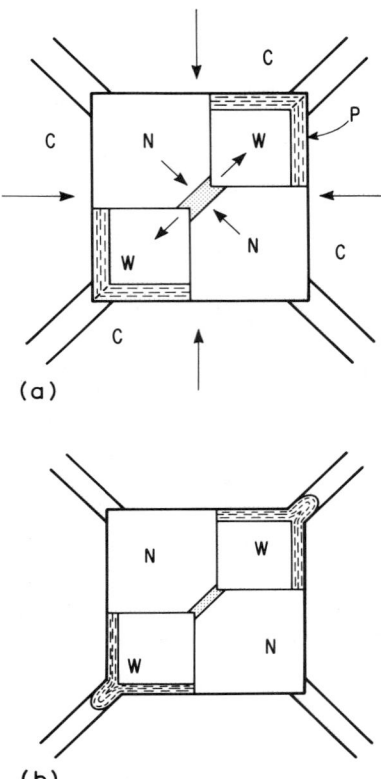

FIG. 7. Principle of operation of the MASS 3I8-90 design actuated by a cubic-anvil press: (a) initial compression of the anvil system and (b) after considerable pressurization. Abbreviations: C, anvil of cubic press; all others as in Fig. 6. The stippled areas represent the compressed sample cell volume. (After K. Masaki, et al.[32])

anvil material, the design of the anvil system configuration, and the choice and use of gasket materials.

Clearly, the compressive strength of the anvil material is a major consideration in designs requiring optimal pressure generation. However, other factors, such as size, operating temperature, cost, and machinability, are often also of some concern. The most commonly used materials for moderate and very high pressure generation are various alloy steels and cemented tungsten carbide. Alloy steels (nickel, chromium, molybdenum alloys) have the tensile strength and ductility properties which are appropriate for moderate pressure range (1-2 GPa) containing vessels. However, steels do not have a sufficient compressive strength to be used in very high pressure multianvil systems.

The most widely used material for pistons, anvils and supporting blocks, which must sustain high compressive stress, is cemented tungsten carbide. Although it is relatively expensive, it can be prepared in large sizes, and it can be machine-ground into precision-shaped components. Primary synthesis involves mixing tungsten and carbon powders with 3–30% cobalt. The mixture is then hot-pressed into the desired form. The hardness (which is related to the tensile and compressive strength of the material) is a function of the amount of the cobalt binder (lower cobalt percentages tend to increase the hardness). Cemented tungsten carbide can have a compressive strength up to 5 GPa.

The most recent innovation in the preparation of very high compressive strength anvils has involved the use of sintered or polycrystalline diamond. This material has considerably greater strength and rigidity than tungsten carbide or single-crystal diamond. The latter tends to have weaker cleavage planes along which failure occurs; therefore, precise alignment is very critical for ultrahigh-pressure operation. In addition, of course, size is very limited. In contrast, polycrystalline diamond sintered from fine powders is considerably tougher (having no continuous cleavage) and can be formed into relatively large pieces.[34,35]

Bundy[26] used cemented tungsten carbide anvils with sintered diamond tips in a Drickamer-type press to generate pressures in excess of 40 GPa.[36] The superior performance of the sintered diamond-tipped Drickamer (supported Bridgman) anvils, compared to cemented tungsten carbide, was demonstrated clearly (see also reference 2). The use of sintered diamond for ultrahigh-pressure anvils has been developed further by Endo and Ito.[27] In an early design,[26] these investigators used a tungsten carbide sphere and a sintered diamond flat plate as opposed anvils. They demonstrated that with this arrangement the higher rigidity of sintered diamond (compared to tungsten carbide) provides a significantly higher generated pressure for a given external load. Later designs have incorporated a pair of opposed anvils made of sintered diamond which are set into an octahedral or cubic high-pressure cell of pyrophyllite. In the case of the cubic assembly, pressure is generated by placing the unit into a cubic-anvil press. The octahedral cell assembly is used as the final stage in a 6–8–2 multianvil system (see Section 7.3). The authors[27] indicate that pressures of over 100 GPa can be achieved with their sintered diamond assembly.

Ultimate pressure generation in a multianvil system also is a function of the anvil geometry. Opposed-anvil and multianvil system designs incorporate Bridgman's[37] principle of "massive support." The principle generally is applied to the case of two opposed truncated-cone anvils without external support. It indicates that the compressive yield stress which can be attained by the truncated anvils is greater than the compressive yield stress of the anvil material because of the extra support provided by the anvil mass lateral to the pressure-generating face. The resulting "strengthening factor" (enhanced compressive yield stress divided by material compressive yield stress) varies from 1.0 for a truncated cone semiangle of 0° (cylindrical indenter) to about 3.0 for a flat plate (cone semiangle of 90°). The strengthening factor as a function of cone semiangle for several anvil materials has been reviewed by Lees.[3] Clearly, anvils with larger cone semiangles can generate higher levels of pressure.

Application of the massive support principle and strengthening factors to tetrahedral and cubic multianvil systems is constrained by the anvil geometry requirements. According to the relationship between strengthening factor and truncated cone semiangle (see references 2 and 3), a tetrahedral-anvil press should have a mean strengthening factor of about 2.1 (for maximum and minimum cone semiangles of 71° and 55° as demanded by the anvil system geometry). Therefore, with anvils of cemented tungsten carbide, a tetrahedral press should be capable of use to about 10.5 GPa. In contrast, a cubic-anvil press, with a mean strengthening factor of about 1.8 (for maximum and minimum cone semiangles of 55° and 45°), should be able to generate up to 9.0 GPa. These values may be compared to the material compressive strength of cemented tungsten carbide of 5.0 GPa.

The foregoing assessment of the ultimate strength characteristics of multianvil presses did not consider the influence of gaskets, which provide additional support across the anvil faces and thereby reduce stress gradients that can initiate failure. In general, the gasket material is also used for the basic sample cell assembly which is compressed in the multianvil unit. The sample cell gasket is cut somewhat oversized so that material flows out between the anvils as compression proceeds. The selection of an appropriate sample cell gasket material is very important for maximum pressure generation. It must deform sufficiently to provide low internal stress gradients (quasi-hydrostatic pressure) in the region of the specimen, and it must remain rigid enough as it flows between the anvils to provide adequate lateral support. In some cases the gasket material must be able to withstand high temperatures or satisfy other experimental requirements.

The most commonly used sample cell gasket material is pyrophyllite. Pyrophyllite is a naturally occurring hydrous aluminum silicate mineral. It tends to be reasonably homogeneous and it may be obtained from several commercial sources. Pyrophyllite is a good electrical and thermal insulator, but its porosity and hydrous properties limit some applications (heat and compression treatments mitigate these problems to some extent). With regard to pressure generation efficiency and ease of machining, pyrophyllite is superior to most other gasket materials.[38] In addition to pyrophyllite, talc, boron nitride, and mixtures of lithium hydride and boron, and magnesium oxide and epoxy resin, have been used successfully. Special mixtures of the latter have been found[3] to be about 25% more efficient than pyrophyllite when used under ambient temperature conditions.

In practice, tetrahedral- and cubic-anvil presses are not often operated in excess of 6–8 GPa. The necessity for achieving optimal pressure generation in a given experiment must be considered in relation to normal anvil life under repeat loading. Clearly, the probability of anvil failure is greater at high loads. Moreover, it is more critical to maintain proper anvil alignment to prevent fracture at very high pressure. Lees[3] has provided an analysis of the operating characteristics of tetrahedral presses in which a discussion of fracture in tungsten carbide anvils is presented. In general, anvil fracture is generated and aggravated by thermal or mechanical shock. Most often, this occurs on decompression as a result of pressure cell–sample assembly "blowout" as the rams are being retracted. Some anvils may last (with only minor fractures) up to 100 loading cycles of about 6 GPa; others may last only 20 or 30 runs. Presumably, individual anvil life is a function of microstructural characteristics from fabrication and the extent and uniformity of support afforded by the pressure cell gasket.[3] It seems reasonable to expect that cubic-anvil systems would behave in a similar manner.

## 3. Pressure Cell–Sample Assemblies

The primary function of the multianvil press, as described in the preceding section, is to apply (via the anvil–ram system) a high load to the walls of a high-pressure cell–sample assembly. Proper design of the pressure cell–sample system is critical to the successful completion of a high-pressure experiment. The assembly must provide adequate gasket support to the loading anvils, transmit pressure to the specimen in a uniform manner, and allow space and access for the sample and experimental instrumentation. Numerous designs for pressure cell–sample assemblies have been used with various levels of success for multianvil press experiments. Only a few representative examples are presented in this section.

The bulk of a pressure cell–sample assembly consists of material intended to provide gasket anvil support and transmit pressure to the interior location of the specimen. As discussed previously, pyrophyllite is probably the most widely used material for this purpose. Talc and boron nitride also have been used frequently. More recently, pressure cells have been fabricated from semisintered $MgO^{39}$ and mixtures of epoxy resin and $MgO^{39}$ or boron.[40,41] In proximity to the specimen, NaCl is often used because its low shear strength provides a more uniform distribution of pressure. For high-temperature experiments, the sample is generally situated within a graphite or platinum foil furnace assembly. Above 10 GPa and at very high temperature (where graphite transforms to diamond), Ohtani et al.[39] successfully used lanthanum chromite, $LaCrO_3$, as a heater material. Titanium diboride also serves as a suitable electrode and furnace material at very high pressure and temperature. In many experiments the specimen must be packed within boron nitride or platinum to avoid reaction at high temperature with the heater or pressure cell assembly materials.

Clearly, the shape of the pressure cell–sample assembly must conform to the anvil configuration of the press unit within which it is to be used. On this basis, there are four general kinds of pressure cell designs. Tetrahedral and cubic-anvil presses require pressure cell–sample assemblies in the shape of a tetrahedron and a cube, respectively. Multianvil press units incorporating a multiple-stage pressure generation system usually use an octahedron pressure cell, and MASS arrangements require sample cells which must be designed especially for each individual internal sliding anvil configuration. In the following discussion, examples of each of the foregoing general pressure cell–sample assemblies will be described.

The tetrahedron pressure cell is generally machined about 10–25% longer on edge than the anvil faces in order to provide adequate volume for compression and ample gasket material. The initial size depends on the tetrahedron material and the desired range of pressure. Larger tetrahedron sizes allow greater pressure to be achieved, but with less load efficiency. The distribution of pressure within a tetrahedron pressure cell–sample assembly has been studied[3] by placing wire mesh or pressure-sensitive monitoring materials within the unit. Approximate homogeneous (quasi-hydrostatic) conditions are approached within only a few percent of the total volume of the cell. For this reason, the actual sample volume is restricted to a small fraction of the central region.

Figure 8 illustrates a particularly simple version of a tetrahedron pressure cell–sample assembly with an internal heater. The bulk of the pressure cell is machined from pyrophyllite. The sample of interest is formed into a thin wire, which is placed within an AgCl sleeve. Because of the low shear strength of the latter, it provides a more uniform pressure environment around the specimen. Indium and NaCl are suitable alternatives for low-temperature experiments. Above about 400°C these materials should be replaced by boron nitride. The furnace assembly consists of an outer sleeve of graphite. Electrical contact between the heater sleeve and the anvils is provided by copper or nickle electrode strips as shown in Fig. 8. This kind of arrangement can operate to temperatures up to 2000°C. Pyrophyllite has a low enough thermal conductivity to provide a high internal pressure cell temperature without excessively heating the anvils. In addition, although pyrophyllite melts at about 1500°C at ambient pressure, at 10 GPa it remains solid to 2500°C.

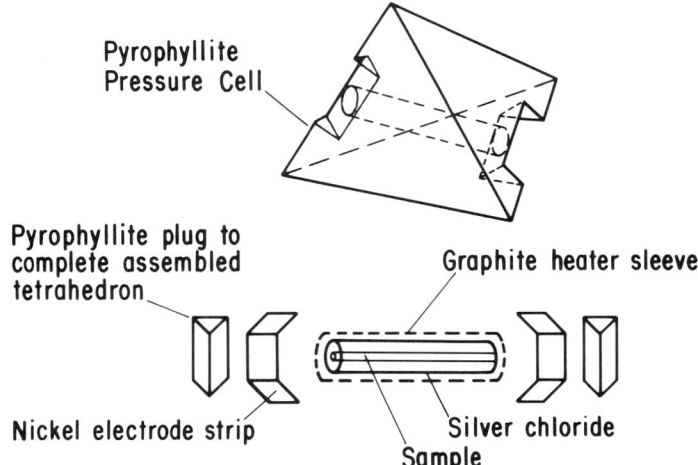

FIG. 8. Tetrahedron pressure cell–sample assembly with internal heater. (After Bradley.[1])

The edge-to-edge heater–specimen assembly in the design shown in Fig. 8 provides higher temperatures as a result of the length of the furnace tube. Other designs of slightly reduced temperature generation use a face-to-vertex or face-to-face heater arrangement. All of these designs generally are effective for very high temperature synthesis work. The major disadvantage of the long furnace tube is interaction with the gasket fractions of the pressure cell, particularly in the case of the edge-to-edge assembly. This, of course, enhances the possibility of failure during an experiment. Moreover, unless the specimen is cut shorter and confined to the center of the heater tube, it experiences large pressure gradients and nonhydrostatic stress. In order to compensate for the foregoing difficulties, tetrahedron pressure cell–sample assemblies have been designed[3,12,42] with more centrally located furnace–specimen arrangements.

The tetrahedron pressure cell–sample assembly designed by Nilan,[12] for use with the 8000-ton load Barogenics tetrahedral press described in Section 2 minimizes nonhydrostatic stress and limits the high-temperature region to the immediate environment of the specimen. A schematic drawing of the assembly is shown in Fig. 9. The bulk of the unit is the 7.0 cm on edge pyrophyllite tetrahedron. The disk specimen (0.32 cm thick and 0.95 cm diameter) of volume 0.23 cm$^3$ is placed in the center of the tetrahedron and encapsulated in boron nitride. Titanium diboride heater elements are situated outside the boron nitride specimen capsule. The electrodes which connect the furnace assembly to the anvils are also titanium diboride. An alternative used in earlier designs incorporated graphite cloth heaters with graphite

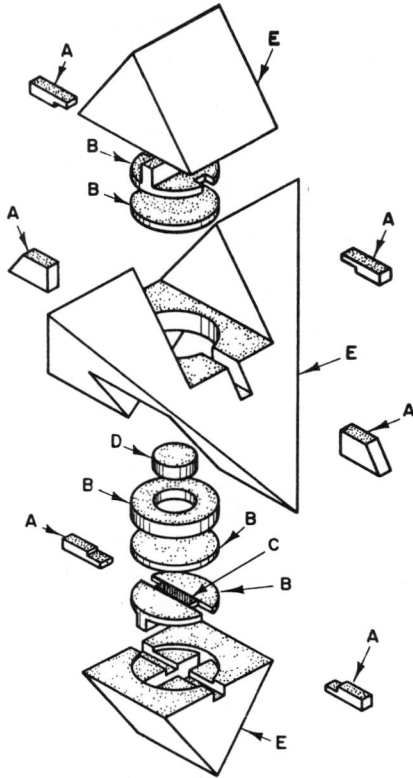

FIG. 9. Tetrahedron pressure cell–sample arrangement designed by Nilan[12] for operation with the 8000-ton load Barogenics tetrahedral press. Letter designations: A, titanium diboride; B, boron nitride; C, titanium diboride heating element; D, specimen; E, pyrophyllite.

electrodes. The furnace assembly is capable of generating about 1300°C at 7.0 GPa pressure. The cooling rate after the current is cut off is about 50°C sec$^{-1}$. Nilan[12] used this tetrahedron pressure cell–sample assembly to study the phase equilibria of low-carbon steels and the morphology and kinetics of austenite decomposition at high pressure and temperature.

Other than consideration of the obvious geometric differences, the design of cubic-anvil pressure cell–sample assemblies is very similar to the tetrahedral arrangements discussed previously. However, as a result of the cubic symmetry, cube sample cells have some definite advantages. In particular, the internal pressure distribution tends to be more uniform and a larger central quasi-hydrostatic region is provided than in a tetrahedral assembly. In addition, cubic arrangements are more conveniently used as a basis for multiple-stage pressure generation. The operating characteristics of pyrophyllite cubic pressure cell–sample assemblies have been discussed extensively by Samara et al.[4] Of particular interest is an analysis of the use and benefits of preformed gaskets, which greatly reduce the amount of internal pressure cell–sample deformation and provide self-alignment and increased support for the anvils. The latter results in long anvil life and fewer "blowouts" during operation. Samara et al.[4] also described the effects of several other pressure cell design variables, such as the performance of "intensifier" edge plates, the influence of heating elements and specimen shape on pressure gradients and calibration, and load cycling.

Simple cubic pressure cell–sample assemblies for synthesis or phase equilibrium experiments can be designed in the manner of the tetrahedron arrangement shown in Fig. 8. Again, generally pyrophyllite is chosen for the bulk of the pressure cell, and a graphite cylindrical sleeve (with a suitable electrode arrangement for electrical contact through a pair of opposite anvils) serves as a heater. Ordinarily, a face-to-face furnace–sample assembly is preferred. Again, depending on the nature of the experiment, the specimen may be encapsulated in some material (boron nitride, NaCl, or platinum, for example) to provide a more hydrostatic pressure field and to avoid chemical reaction.

A more sophisticated cubic pressure cell is illustrated in Fig. 10. This assembly was designed and used by Yagi et al.[43] to make X-ray diffraction measurements under hydrostatic pressure conditions. In this example, the outer housing of the pressure cell (edge length, 8 mm) is made of a 2 : 1 mixture of amorphous boron and epoxy resin. The specimen is placed within a cylindrical Teflon capsule, which is inserted into the central part of the pressure cell. The Teflon capsule is filled with a pressure-transmitting fluid to provide the hydrostatic environment around the sample. Yagi et al.[43] found a 1 : 1 (by volume) mixture of ethanol and methanol to be a satisfactory pressure fluid up to at least 7 GPa. For the X-ray diffraction measurements of interest in this example, the powdered specimen (precompressed into the form of a small slab as shown in Fig. 10) was placed adjacent to a slab of polycrystalline NaCl, which served as an internal pressure standard. The specimen and NaCl were supported and positioned within the Teflon capsule by inserting them into the slot of a cylindrical epoxy resin "sample chamber" (see Fig. 10). Yagi et al.[43] used this pressure cell assembly to determine the pressure dependence of the lattice parameters and unit cell volume of fayalite ($Fe_2SiO_4$) olivine.

The foregoing pressure cell–sample assembly has, of course, the advantage of providing a pressure environment for the specimen which is almost ideally hydrostatic (neglecting slight possible viscosity effects in the fluid at elevated pressure). However, as shown, the design has no facility for operation at high

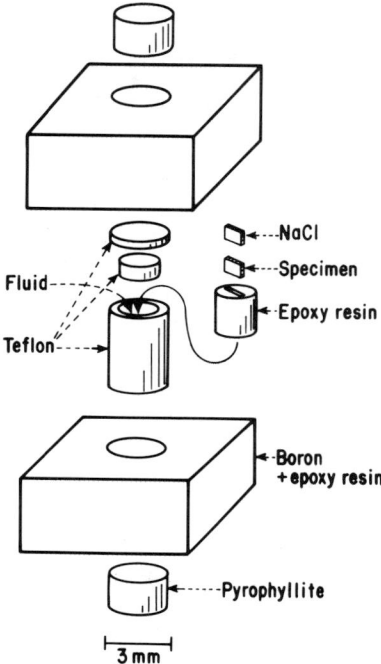

FIG. 10. Cubic pressure cell used by Yagi et al.[43] for X-ray diffraction measurements under hydrostatic pressures to 7 GPa. The X-ray beam enters the cell through one of the edge gaskets (between adjacent anvils).

temperature. To carry out X-ray diffraction measurements at simultaneous conditions of high pressure and temperature, Akimoto and co-workers[40,41] developed a cubic pressure cell with an internal heater assembly. The basic design is very similar to that shown in Fig. 10, except that the Teflon cell–sample chamber assembly is replaced by a boron nitride cylinder with graphite or stainless steel disk furnace elements. The powdered specimen in this case is mixed with the NaCl pressure reference and placed in a slot within the boron nitride insert cylinder. This arrangement was operated successfully[40,41] to temperatures of almost 1300°C and pressures up to 10 GPa. The primary disadvantage of this assembly design, compared to the Teflon capsule, is the nonhydrostatic pressure distribution in the region of the specimen and NaCl pressure standard. This has been demonstrated[44] to produce some systematic error in the pressure–volume relation as perceived by the X-ray diffraction measurements.

Another variation of a liquid–solid hybrid system for the generation of hydrostatic pressure has been designed by Barnett and Bosco[20] and Zeto *et al.*[21] for use with the large Barogenics cubic-anvil press described in Section 2. The system is essentially an improvement of an earlier technique[45,46] used to produce pressures up to 6 GPa in viscous fluids encapsulated in pyrophyllite pressure cells loaded by a tetrahedral-anvil press. The basic elements of the cubic pressure cell-sample assembly are shown in Fig. 11. Again, the block portion of the pressure cell is machined from pyrophyllite. The basic cube unit measures 5.3 cm on edge; however, with the addition of the preformed gaskets, the pressure cell block is 7.3 cm on a side. Thin plates of stainless steel and pyrophyllite are placed on each of the cube faces to "intensify" the internal pressure generation for a given load. As shown in Fig. 11, a hole is machined through the center of the pyrophyllite block to accommodate the stainless steel sample chamber within a cylindrical pyrophyllite sleeve.

The critical component of the assembly for the generation of hydrostatic pressure is the steel specimen capsule or chamber.[21] It is machined from 304

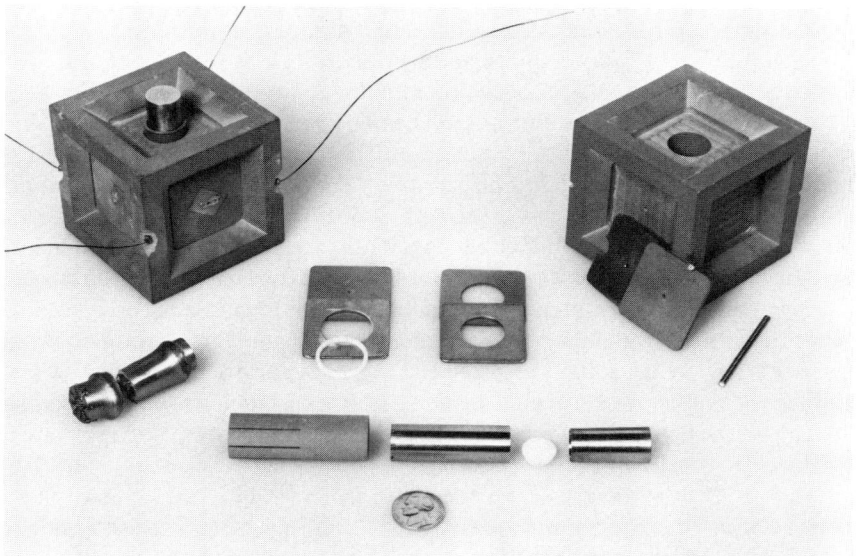

FIG. 11. Liquid–solid hybrid pressure cell–sample assembly designed[20,21] for use with the Barogenics 2000-ton cubic-anvil press. The upper level of the photograph shows (left to right) an assembled pressure cell and sample chamber prior to compression, a pair of lower and upper "intensifier" faceplates, and the basic cube pyrophyllite pressure cell (including preformed edge gaskets) with a pair of side faceplates. The lower part of the photograph includes (right to left) the stainless steel specimen chamber (cap, Teflon wiring base plug, bottom section), a pyrophyllite sleeve insert (accommodates wires from the specimen chamber base), and a stainless steel capsule (cut into two parts) after compression.

stainless steel and has two primary parts. The bottom section provides the housing for the specimen and internal instrumentation. Holes and a Teflon plug in the base allow access and support for 10 electrical leads. The capsule is contained by a large cap which fits within the bottom section along a 1° taper. A thin indium plate on the surfaces of contact provides an initial seal for the internal fluid, as well as a means for adjusting the capsule volume by varying the plating thickness. The latter is necessary to minimize capsule deformation under compression when different specimen and instrumentation volumes are used. Selection of an appropriate internal fluid for the capsule is also very important. The viscosity must remain sufficiently low throughout the pressure–temperature range of interest in the experiment. Although other liquids (for example, petroleum ether or mixtures of methanol and ethanol) have been used successfully to pressures in excess of 6 GPa,[20,43,47] in the present case a 1 : 1 mixture of $n$-pentane and isopentane was found to provide satisfactory results. Barnett and Bosco[48] reported measurements of the viscosity of this liquid to 5.4 GPa, where it was found to have a value of about $10^6$ poise. This corresponds to pressure equalization in the capsule by viscous flow in times on the order of seconds at 5 GPa and minutes at 6 GPa.

The liquid–solid hybrid hydrostatic pressure cell system has been used extensively[20,21,48–52] and reliably for numerous experiments into the 5–6-GPa pressure range. The stainless steel capsule provides an internal working volume at 6 GPa hydrostatic pressure of 2.33 cm$^3$ described by a 1.08-cm diameter and 2.54-cm length. The capability for access of 10 electrical leads allows several experiments to be performed during a single run. Zeto et al.[21] have reported that "blowout" or the loss of an electrical lead occurred in less than 10% of the experiments carried out in their laboratory. In one instance, they performed 25 pressure cycles in a single experiment over the period of a month without cell failure. Experiments also have been conducted[21] at temperatures up to 500°C at 4.0 GPa by incorporating a nichrome-coil furnace within the pressure cell capsule. The primary limitation of the experiments with the liquid–solid pressure cell is the possibility of loss of a specimen by blowout in runs in excess of 5 GPa.

Large cubic-anvil presses have been used by several investigators to drive secondary anvil systems onto smaller internal pressure cell assemblies. Examples of these configurations have been described in Section 2 in reference to the driving mechanisms for sintered-diamond opposed anvil pressure cells[26,27] and MASS assemblies. Such systems, which employ the multiple-stage or "cascade" principle, can generate very high pressures on the innermost stage (which ordinarily contains the specimen) by virtue of the support and strengthening provided by the external stage anvils.

Kawai and Endo[24] devised a multiple-stage system which involves eight truncated tungsten carbide "cubes" as the intermediate stage. These anvil

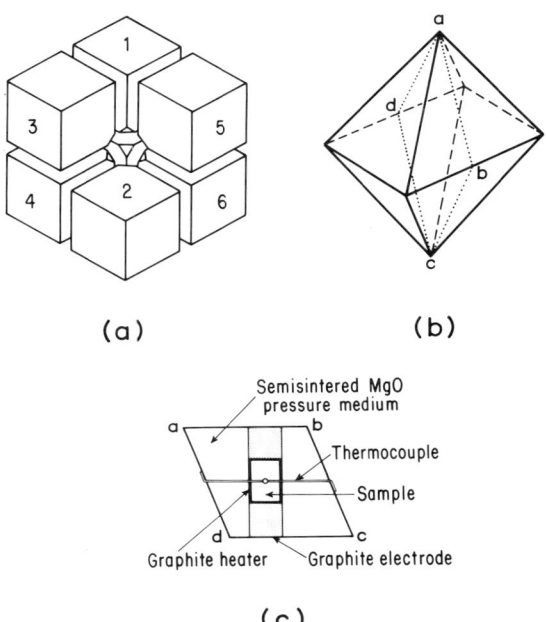

FIG. 12. The eight-cube anvil arrangement and octahedron inner pressure cell of the 6-8 type multiple-stage system. (a) Assembly of truncated anvil "cubes." The front anvil has been removed to expose the inner octahedron pressure cell cavity. Gasket spacers are placed between adjacent cubes to prevent extrusion of the pressure cell and provide lateral support to the anvils. (b) An octahedron pressure cell illustrating the profile schematic shown in (c). (c) The inner specimen–furnace assembly of a typical 6-8 type octahedron high-pressure cell. (Fig. 12c after Ohtani et al.[39])

elements are arranged in the form of a large cube assembly (see Fig. 12) which loads an interior octahedral pressure cell on the truncated faces. The entire assembly may be driven by a cubic-anvil press or six-section split-sphere unit (for example, see Fig. 5). In consideration of the number of anvil elements in each stage, this kind of two-stage multianvil system is referred to as a 6-8 type. A typical octahedron high-pressure cell is shown in Fig. 12. The particular design[39] illustrated incorporates a graphite electrode heater assembly within a sintered-MgO octahedral cell. It has been used by Ohtani et al.[39] to 10 GPa at 2000°C. A similar design, with a $LaCrO_3$–TiC electrode heater,[39] was used to pressures up to 20 GPa in a 6-8 type multianvil system. Ohtani et al.[39] used the foregoing assemblies to characterize the high-pressure melting behavior of several silicate minerals. Kawai and Nishiyama[25,53] measured the electrical resistance of several oxides to pressures in excess of 25 GPa with a similar 6-8 type system. In their assembly, two of the eight inner-stage cubes were made of tungsten carbide and provided electrical continuity between the sample and outer-stage anvils. The other six inner-stage cubes were made of sintered alumina ($Al_2O_3$). More recently, the 6-8 type system and octahedron high-pressure cell have been used in conjunction with very large uniaxial split-sphere presses developed by Kawai et al.[54-56] For example, Ito and Yamada[55] have investigated the stability relations of silicate spinels at pressures up to 27 GPa and temperatures from 900° to 1400°C with such a system.

The basic 6-8 type arrangement was used by Endo and Ito[27] to drive an additional internal third stage. The innermost stage features a pair of opposed sintered-diamond anvils situation within an octahedron pressure cell (see Section 2). This multiple-stage system, designated a 6-8-2 type, is shown in Fig. 13. It was used by Endo and Ito[27] to measure the electrical resistance of several oxides and other compounds to pressures in excess of 77 GPa. An alternative version of the multiple-stage sintered-diamond anvil arrangement designed by Endo and Ito[27] utilizes a cubic pressure cell. This double-stage

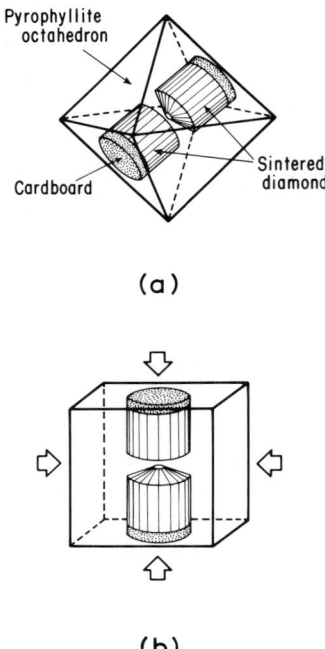

FIG. 13. Inner-stage opposed sintered-diamond anvil arrangements used by Endo and Ito:[27] (a) 6-8-2 triple-stage type in an octahedral pressure cell and (b) 6-2 double-stage type within a cube cell.

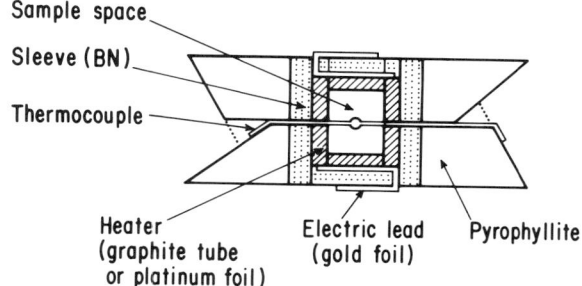

FIG. 14. Internal high-pressure cell and heater assembly designed for use with a MASS 3I8 apparatus. (After Sawamoto et al.[57])

system (6–2 type) is also shown in Fig. 13. Experience in the usage of both of these arrangements[27] has indicated that the 6-8-2 type is superior to the cubic assembly in providing stronger lateral support to the diamond anvils. Therefore, higher pressure levels (up to 100 GPa) may be generated in the triple-stage version.

The internal high-pressure cells for MASS devices must be designed to conform to each particular anvil arrangement. A specific example is illustrated in Fig. 14. It was designed to carry out phase equilibrium studies at high pressure and temperature within a MASS 3I8-90 type unit (refer to Section 2 and Fig. 7 for a discussion of the specific anvil arrangement).[30] The basic volume-filling elements of the cell are machined from pyrophyllite. The sample is placed inside a graphite tube or platinum foil furnace assembly, which is encapsulated within a boron nitride sleeve and cap arrangement. Electrical contact to the heater is made through gold foil leads to the N-anvils (see Fig. 7), and the thermocouple leads are connected directly to the W-anvils. The high-pressure cell will accommodate a sample of 1–3 mg within an overall volume of about 20 mm³. It may be used in a MASS 3I8 apparatus to pressures up to 40 GPa at 1400°C.[31, 57] However, it is estimated[31] that the value of the pressure at high temperature may be in error by as much as 5 GPa as a result of the unknown effects of thermal expansion and pressure cell deformation.

## 4. Pressure Calibration and Accuracy

It is a rather difficult problem to determine the actual pressure which a specimen experiences in a multianvil device. In the case of a solid-medium high-pressure cell, the anvil load is transmitted through the cell assembly in a complicated manner which depends on the nature and configuration of the individual parts. As a result, the internal stress field is very difficult to assess. This fundamental problem also persists for liquid–solid hybrid pressure cell systems because, again, the anvil load is dispersed through the gaskets and the outer solid portion of the cell. Therefore, the determination of pressure in multianvil systems usually is accomplished by placing a calibrated standard which can be monitored externally in the immediate vicinity of the sample.

Primary pressure standards, or methods of direct pressure measurement, are few and restricted to a relatively low range. For example, the measurement of pressure in fluid systems may be carried out by direct comparison to the height of a column of mercury. Although accurate, this method may only be used to a few hundredths of a gigapascal. Another primary pressure standard, which may be used up to 2.6 GPa, is the dead weight or free piston gauge. In these devices, fluid pressure is balanced by a piston loaded with weights. In the version developed by the National Bureau of Standards and Harwood Engineering Company,[58] which employs the "controlled-clearance principle," the indicated accuracy is ±0.0025 GPa at 2.6 GPa. Unfortunately, free piston gauges can only be used for measuring fluid pressure, and they are cumbersome. Moreover, relative to the pressures generated by multianvil systems, they are restricted to a low range. As a result of these primary standard deficiencies, multianvil systems invariably rely on secondary pressure standards.

Secondary pressure standards require calibration by either a primary standard or some other means. In the case of the latter, the usual approaches involve either direct evaluation from observed anvil load or extrapolation based on a theoretical equation of state. Neither of these methods is as reliable as a primary standard. The former is subject to systematic error arising from frictional effects in the press, nonuniform stress distribution through the internal pressure cell, and hysteresis effects associated with the apparatus and standard itself. Equation of state model standards are limited by the functional form and convergence properties of the equation of state selected to characterize the compression. Because of these limitations, the selection of appropriate secondary standards for the measurement of very high pressures has been a matter of continuing controversy among workers in the field.

For convenience, secondary pressure standards may be described as "fixed-point" or "continuous." Fixed-point standards are defined by abrupt changes in the physical properties of an appropriate material which result from a pressure-induced polymorphic phase transformation. The use of various phase transitions as a means of calibrating pressure stems from the early work of Bridgman,[59,60] who generally used volume and electrical resistance as the diagnostic physical properties. Pressure at intermediate points can usually be inferred from observed anvil load pressure by interpolation and extrapolation from the fixed-point calibrations. Useful fixed points should be distinguished by sharpness of the phase transformation, ease of measurement, and reproducibility.

Fixed points in the pressure range 0–3 GPa are the most accurately defined because they may be referred to a primary standard. Frequently used examples in this range include the pressure-induced freezing point of mercury at various temperatures[61–63] and the bismuth I–II and II–III solid–solid transitions.[49,50,64] The values for these transitions are given in Table I. In the case of bismuth, the more recent values of Zeto and Vanfleet[50] are listed. They were obtained in a liquid–solid hybrid hydrostatic system,[21,48] using the relative resistance change of a seasoned manganin wire coil. The earlier data

TABLE I. Common Fixed-Point Secondary Pressure Standards

| Material | Phase transition | Pressure (GPa) | Reference |
|---|---|---|---|
| Mercury | Freezing point at 0°C | 0.7569 ± 0.0001 | 61 |
| Mercury | Freezing point at 20°C | 1.154 ± 0.002 | 62, 63 |
| Cesium I-II | Solid-solid (25°C) | 2.26 ± 0.06 | 64 |
| Bismuth I-II | Solid-solid (25°C) | 2.5368 ± 0.0028 | 50 |
| Bismuth II-III | Solid-solid (25°C) | 2.6861 ± 0.0042 | 50 |
| Thallium II-III | Solid-solid (25°C) | 3.6569 ± 0.0153 | 50 |
| Cesium II-III | Solid-solid (25°C) | 4.17 ± 0.10 | 64 |
| Barium I-II | Solid-solid (25°C) | 5.6273 ± 0.0521 | 50 |
| | | 5.85 ± 0.05 | 65 |
| | | 5.50 ± 0.05 | 66 |
| Bismuth III-V[a] | Solid-solid (25°C) | 8.9 ± 0.2 | 67 |
| | | 7.4 | 36 |
| Iron ($\alpha$-$\varepsilon$) | Solid-solid (25°C) | 11.2 | 36 |
| Barium II-III | Solid-solid (25°C) | 12.0 | 36 |
| Silicon | Solid-solid (25°C) | 12.5 ± 0.5[b] | 71 |
| Lead I-II | Solid-solid (25°C) | 13.0 | 36 |
| ZnSe | Solid-solid (25°C) | 13.7 ± 0.3[b] | 71 |
| ZnS | Solid-solid (25°C) | 15.0 ± 0.5[b] | 71 |
| Fe20Co ($\alpha$-$\varepsilon$) | Solid-solid (25°C) | 19.0 | 36 |
| CdS | Solid-solid (25°C) | 19.0–20.0 | 36 |
| GaP (metallic) | Solid-solid (25°C) | 22.0 ± 1.0[b] | 71 |
| | | 23.0–24.0 | 36 |
| Fe40Co ($\alpha$-$\varepsilon$) | Solid-solid (25°C) | 28.5–29.5 | 36 |
| NaCl (B1-B2) | Solid-solid (25°C) | 29.0–30.0 | 36 |
| EuO (B1-B2) | Solid-solid (25°C) | 40 | 36 |

[a] Nomenclature established by Bridgman.[67]

[b] Uncertainties based on experimental reproducibility and the estimated uncertainty in Decker's[72] reference equation of state.

of Kennedy and La Mori[64] were measured in a piston–cylinder apparatus and required corrections for frictional effects and bore distortion. Although the hydrostatic system values are slightly lower than the piston–cylinder results, the two data sets are consistent in terms of the stated uncertainties.

Within the range of pressure 3.0–10 GPa the use of fixed-point secondary standards is somewhat less reliable because of the lack of an opportunity to calibrate against a primary standard. However, reasonable accuracy is provided by several independent methods of measurement and calculation of fixed-point pressures. Below 5 GPa, there are piston–cylinder data[64] for the cesium I-II, cesium II-III, and thallium II-III phase transitions (see Table I). In the case of the latter, Zero and Vanfleet[50] have provided a hydrostatic manganin coil measurement, which is, again, somewhat lower than the piston–cylinder result, but within the stated error estimate. Zeto and Vanfleet[50] also extended their work to include the barium I-II point above 5 GPa. Their value (see Table I) is 0.250 GPa lower than the result obtained by Vereshchangin et al.,[65] who used a rotating free piston technique. The reason for this significant discrepancy is not clear. However, it does emphasize the growing problem of systematic experimental error as pressure increases. An additional value for the barium I-II transition by Haygarth et al.,[66] obtained with a piston–cylinder apparatus, is even lower (see Table I). A value for the bismuth III-V transition above 8 GPa has been reported by Bridgman;[67] but, again, considerable systematic error is likely.

Above 10 GPa pressure calibration from secondary standard fixed points is increasingly equivocal. A number of values based on electrical discontinuities in various metals (e.g., lead, iron, calcium, barium) have been reported by Drickamer and co-workers.[68,69] Their determinations were based originally on extrapolation of an electrical resistance scale for platinum "tied" to early lower-pressure fixed points. Following a downward revision of the latter,[69] Drickamer[70] adjusted the higher-pressure fixed points accordingly. More recently, Bundy[36] has extended the fixed-point pressure scale up to approximately 40 GPa, using a modified Drickamer opposed-anvil apparatus with sintered-diamond tips. Calibration was based on load pressure extrapolation from fixed points on the 1970 revised pressure scale of Drickamer.[70] Another development in the use of fixed-point pressure calibration has issued from diamond-anvil cell research. Piermarini and Block[71] have used the ruby R-line fluorescence method of "continuous" pressure calibration to redetermine several earlier electrical resistance phase transition fixed points. Their work, in addition to that of Bundy,[36] has made necessary another downward revision of many of the fixed points above 10 GPa. Some of the more pertinent results are listed in Table I.

The use of fixed points for pressure calibration is also complicated somewhat by the systematic response of various phase transitions on compression and decompression. Both solid-medium systems and hydrostatic pressure cells invariably are characterized by an initiation pressure of transformation hysteresis. In the specific case of the the bismuth I-II transition in a hydrostatic system,[52] the interval between the initiation of the phase change on pressure increase and the reverse transformation on system decompression is about 0.072 GPa. The origin of the hysteresis of initiation in hydrostatic pressure systems has been attributed by Zero and Vanfleet[52] to the strain energy and chemical kinetics of nucleation of the specimen. In solid-medium systems, the interval of hysteresis can be as much as several tenths of a gigapascal due to deformation of the pressure medium and gasket friction.[51] Obviously, these effects result in discrepancies and imprecision in the use of phase transitions as fixed-point standards for pressure calibration. However, uncertainty in this regard can be minimized, as demonstrated by the bismuth I-II study of Zeto and Vanfleet,[52] by identification of the fixed-point calibration with the equilibrium pressure of the transition, as delineated by the center of the region of indifference. The latter was defined by Bridgman[37] as the range of pressure over which both phases of the transformation are present. For the bismuth I-II transition Zeto and Vanfleet[52] observed a region of indifference of 0.003 GPa. Their determination of the equilibrium pressure[50] yielded 2.5368 ± 0.0028 GPa.

Secondary pressure standards which provide a continuous evaluation of pressure during an experiment have a clear advantage over discrete fixed points. However, all continuous pressure scales must be calibrated with respect to either a primary standard, fixed points, or an assumed reference equation. Often, extrapolation beyond the range of the calibration standard is necessary, attaching additional significance to the functional form of the reference equation. In this regard, although continuous pressure scales can be defined with high precision, inaccuracy arising from intangible systematic errors can remain a problem. In addition, generally continuous secondary pressure scales are limited to use in hydrostatic fluid pressure cells.

For many years the electrical resistance of manganin wire coils has provided one of the most accurate and convenient means of monitoring hydrostatic pressure up to 2.5 GPa.[1,2] Within this pressure range the manganin coil resistance can be calibrated with a free piston gauge primary standard. Bridgman[72] demonstrated many years ago that the resistance of manganin wire is linear with pressure to within 0.1% up to 1.2 GPa and to within 2% at 2.5 GPa. More recently, Zeto and Vanfleet[50] have extended the use of manganin coil gauges up to 6.0 GPa. Their results indicate that a two-point quadratic calibration curve is satisfactory for pressures up to at least 3.7 GPa. Above this range the lack of a primary standard calibration point precludes a quantitative assessment of accuracy. However, using the manganin coil quadratic representation, Zeto and Vanfleet[50] determined a value of 5.627 ± 0.052 GPa for the barium I–II fixed point, which is about 0.25 GPa less than the previously accepted value.[59,65] The use of manganin wire coil pressure gauges requires some preparation or "seasoning" in terms of initial heat and pressure cycling. A properly prepared manganin gauge yields very reproducible pressures and has negligible hysteresis. Above ambient temperature manganin resistance has a significant temperature coefficient. Therefore, if possible, manganin gauges should be placed some distance from the high-temperature region of an experiment. In solid-medium pressure cells nonhydrostatic stresses generate effects which preclude the use of manganin resistance coils as a continuous secondary pressure scale.

In liquid–solid hybrid pressure cells used in multianvil systems, and especially in diamond-anvil high-pressure cells, it is very common practice to use the known volume behavior of an internal standard to monitor pressure. This is especially the case of X-ray diffraction studies at high pressure and temperature. Jamieson et al.[73] have suggested the following four attributes for a good high-pressure internal standard: (1) a reasonably large compression and precisely measurable property to monitor pressure over the range of interest; (2) availability of accurate experimental data to high pressure relative to the range of interest to reduce the need for equivocal extrapolations; (3) material availability in the required form and level of purity; and (4) chemical inertness relative to the experiment to be performed. Clearly, few potential internal standard materials would be capable of satisfying the foregoing set of criteria for a very extended range of experiments. Particular internal standard substances are more suitable for a specific type or range of experiments.

In the case of X-ray diffraction studies up to approximately 10 GPa, NaCl has been a common internal standard. It has a simple cubic structure which yields several well-defined diffraction lines for monitoring volume compression from lattice spacings. Pressure is established by defining the NaCl volume compression in terms of a suitable equation of state. In this regard, the equation of Decker[74–76] has been used extensively. The 1971 version of Decker's equation[76] is based on the Mie–Grüneisen equation of state[77] with a Born–Mayer type[78] formulation of the lattice potential energy. The latter is characterized by first and second nearest-neighbor interactions, van der Waals potential terms for dipole–dipole and dipole–quadrupole interactions, and two arbitrary parameters evaluated from experimental data. Updated experimental values of the bulk modulus and lattice parameter were incorporated in the 1971 version to evaluate the arbitrary constants. The accuracy of the Decker NaCl pressure scale obviously is dependent on the extent to which the functional form chosen actually represents the compression of

NaCl, as well as the accuracy of the experimental data used to evaluate the arbitrary parameters. In this regard, there have been several efforts to assess the reliability of NaCl equations of state and compressibility data.[78-81] Although some discrepancies have been noted,[80,81] the NaCl secondary pressure scale is generally reliable and certainly provides a very practical and convenient means of evaluating pressure in many experimental arrangements.

Although the NaCl pressure gauge has been used successfully for static compression experiments at ambient temperature and moderate pressure, several alternative materials, such as KCl, NaF, and cesium halides, also have been suggested as continuous secondary scales.[76,82-84] However, of special interest in this regard, because of the restricted pressure–temperature range of NaCl (which undergoes a solid–solid phase transition from the B1 to B2 structure at about 29 GPa[36]) and the chemical activity of halides in many experiments, is the lattice compression of metals, several of which have equations of state defined into the 100 GPa-plus range.[2] Two of the most promising are platinum and gold. The latter has been advocated by Jamieson et al.[73] for use as a pressure reference in very high pressure and temperature X-ray diffraction studies carried out in diamond-anvil systems. Gold is particularly appropriate for use at high temperatures (e.g., $>500°C$) because it generally remains chemically inert, and it has a simple cubic X-ray diffraction pattern which may be defined precisely in terms of volume over an extended pressure–temperature range.[85] Although the NaCl, Au, and related pressure scales are particularly suited to diamond-anvil X-ray static compression measurements, they also may be used in multianvil systems with hydrostatic pressure cells.[43] It has been demonstrated,[44,86] however, that nonhydrostatic stress produces systematic inaccuracy in the NaCl pressure scale.

The NaCl pressure scale based on Decker's equation of state[76] also has been used to calibrate the ruby R-line fluorescence scale developed at the National Bureau of Standards by Forman et al.[87,88] This unique secondary scale is based on the shift of the $R_1$-fluorescence line of ruby with pressure. The precision of the ruby $R_1$-line scale is better than 1/2% up to 10 GPa. Moreover, because only a few small ruby particles are required within the high-pressure cell, it is extremely space efficient. As a result, the ruby $R_1$-line scale has been used extensively in diamond-anvil research. Mao et al.[89] have extended the scale to over 100 GPa, using a calibration based on the isothermal equation of state of four metals (Cu, Mo, Ag, and Pd) derived from shock wave experimental data. Unfortunately, the use of the ruby $R_1$-line fluorescence secondary pressure scale in multianvil systems is very limited because of the necessity for transparent windows to provide light access and egress.

## 5. Conclusions: Experiments with Multianvil Systems

Multianvil press systems provide the means for carrying out a variety of high pressure–temperature experiments within a range of conditions which are not sufficiently covered by the use of alternative devices. Although conventional piston-cylinder units are more convenient and economical to use below 4 ot 5 GPa, multianvil presses generally provide a more hydrostatic pressure field in the region of the specimen, as well as larger volume. Moreover, multianvil systems can be operated up to 8 or 9 GPa with conventional pressure cell–sample assemblies and over 40 GPa with MASS or multiple-stage pressure cell systems. Diamond-anvil cell units, of course, afford the opportunity to extend high-pressure experiments into the 150-GPa range, but provide for very small specimen volumes. In summary, the most useful application of multianvil presses probably involves experiments in the pressure range 4–9 GPa, where a large specimen volume is desirable. However, specialized and sophisticated pressure cell–sample systems provide for a variety of other unique applications.

The earliest uses of multianvil presses centered on materials synthesis and phase equilibrium studies. An example in this regard is the 1965 study of Akimoto *et al.*[42] of the olivine-spinel transition in $Fe_2SiO_4$ and $Ni_2SiO_4$. In this work a tetrahedral-anvil press was used with a pressure cell assembly which provided a temperature of 1500°C at pressures up to 7 GPa. With the development of larger multianvil units and more sophisticated pressure cells, phase equilibrium experiments have been conducted with higher precision and accuracy,[55,56] as well as increased pressure and temperature. In addition, specially designed pressure cell–sample systems have provided the opportunity for accurate melting experiments up to 20 GPa[39] and studies of the reaction kinetics and mechanisms of phase transformations.[12,90]

Numerous measurements of various material physical properties, including volume compression, electrical conductivity, and thermal expansion, have been carried out in multianvil presses. For example, Kawai and Nishiyama[25,53] have used electrical conductivity response to study the insulator–metallic transition in MgO, FeO, and $SiO_2$ to pressures in excess of 25 GPa. Static compression observations have been made with multianvil units for several years by standard X-ray diffraction techniques.[43,91] More recently, energy dispersive X-ray methods have been applied to the study of phase transformation kinetics with a cubic-anvil press.[92,93] This technique is also applicable to measurements of volume compression at high pressure using lattice parameter data. Although the accuracy of the earlier volume compression experiments was limited by the use of solid-medium pressure cell–sample assemblies,[44] more recent designs utilizing liquid–solid hybrid systems[43,48] have solved this problem by providing a hydrostatic pressure field.

In addition to materials synthesis, phase equilibrium studies, and physical property measurements in the moderate pressure range, the design of multianvil press systems provides the opportunity for other more specialized experiments. In particular, Shimada and co-workers[94,95] have adapted a cubic-anvil press for the triaxial testing of rocks at very high confining pressure. Prior work in the fracture and plastic deformation of rocks was generally limited to a confining pressure of 1 or 2 GPa. In the cubic-anvil apparatus, experiments (at ambient temperature) have been carried out at confining pressures up to 3.7 GPa.[94] The six independently moving rams of the cubic-anvil system allow the application of a uniaxial load on a specimen while the high confining pressure is maintained. The latter is applied to the cylindrical rock specimen through a silver chloride sleeve in a pyrophyllite pressure cell by the four horizontal anvils. The axial stress is applied through the upper and lower anvils such that strain rates of about $10^{-5}$ to $10^{-6}$ per second are achieved. With some modification of the pressure cell–sample assembly, it is likely that this technique could be extended to include the effects of high temperature.

Multianvil high-pressure systems should continue to provide the most suitable alternative for many synthesis and phase equilibrium studies in the 4–9 GPa range requiring a relatively large specimen volume. In addition, advances in the design of liquid–solid hybrid pressure cell–sample assemblies have provided the opportunity to make accurate and precise physical property measurements up to 6 or 7 GPa under hydrostatic conditions. Although such a pressure range is modest compared to diamond-anvil cell capabilities, the very much larger high-pressure working volume allows for more options in regard to specimen size and experimental instrumentation. For example, possible applications would include the precise measurement of thermoelastic constants with ultrasonic methods and the measurement of tensor transport properties at high pressure and temperature. In the future, it is likely that the pressure–temperature–volume range of multianvil devices can be extended, perhaps significantly. The design of multiple-stage anvil systems and the development of higher-strength anvil materials (e.g., sintered diamond, boron nitride, boron carbide) should be the most important factors in this regard. Although the cost of large multianvil devices is high, they provide a range of basic research, engineering, and commercial applications which cannot be duplicated by other methods generating high-pressure.

### References

1. C. C. Bradley, "High Pressure Methods in Solid State Research." Plenum, New York, 1969.
2. I. L. Spain, in "High Pressure Technology" (I. L. Spain and J. Paauwe, eds.), Vol. I, p. 395. Dekker, New York, 1977.

3. J. Lees, in "Advances in High Pressure Research" (R. S. Bradley, ed.), Vol. 1, p. 1. Academic Press, New York, 1966.
4. G. A. Samara, A. Henius, and A. A. Giardini, *J. Basic Eng.* **86**, 729 (1964).
5. N. Kawai, in "Accurate Characterization of the High Pressure Environment" (E. C. Lloyd, ed.), p. 45. *NBS Spec. Publ.* No. 326 (1971).
6. R. Epain, C. Susse, and B. Vodar, *C. R. Hebd. Seances Acad. Sci., Ser. A* **265**, 323 (1967).
7. M. Kumazawa, *High Temp.—High Pressures* **3**, 243 (1971).
8. H. T. Hall, *Rev. Sci. Instrum.* **29**, 267 (1958).
9. E. C. Lloyd, U. O. Hutton, and D. D. Johnson, *J. Res. Natl. Bur. Stand., Sect. C* **63**, 59 (1959).
10. A. Zeitlin, *Sci. Am.* **212**, 38 (1965).
11. H. T. Hall, *Rev. Sci. Instrum.* **33**, 1278 (1962).
12. T. G. Nilan, *Trans. AIME* **239**, 898 (1967).
13. L. F. Vereschagin, in "Progress in Very High Pressure Research" (F. P. Bundy, W. R. Hubbard, and H. M. Strong, eds.), p. 290. Wiley, New York, 1960.
14. J. C. Houck and U. O. Hutton, in "High Pressure Measurement" (A. A. Giardini and E. C. Lloyd, eds.), p. 221, Butterworth, London, 1963.
15. N. B. Owen, *J. Sci. Instrum.* **43**, 765 (1966).
16. J. Osugi, K. Shimizu, K. Inoue, and K. Yasunami, *Rev. Phys. Chem. Jpn.* **34**, 1 (1964).
17. M. Wakasuki, K. Ichinose, and T. Aoki, *Jpn. J. Appl. Phys.* **10**, 357 (1971).
18. S. Saito, A. Sawaoka, E. Tani, T. Mashimo, and Y. Ozaki, *Proc. Int. Conf. High Pressure, 4th, Kyoto, 1974* p. 786 (1975).
19. M. Wakatsuki and K. Ichinose, in "High Pressure Research in Geophysics" (S. Akimoto and M. H. Manghnani, eds.), *Adv. Earth Planet. Sci.* No. 12, p. 13 (1982).
20. J. D. Barnett, and C. D. Bosco, *Rev. Sci. Instrum.* **38**, 957 (1967).
21. R. J. Zeto, E. Hryckowian, and H. B. Vanfleet, *Rev. Sci. Instrum.* **43**, 132 (1972).
22. B. von Platen, in "Modern Very High Pressure Techniques" (R. H. Wentorf, ed.), p. 9. Butterworth, London, 1962.
23. N. Kawai, *Proc. Jpn. Acad.* **42**, 385 (1966).
24. N. Kawai and S. Endo, *Rev. Sci. Instrum.* **41**, 1178 (1970).
25. N. Kawai and A. Nishiyama, *Proc. Int. Conf. High Pressure, 4th, Kyoto, 1974* p. 324 (1975).
26. K. Ito and S. Endo, *Jpn. J. Appl. Phys.* **16**, 1279 (1977).
27. S. Endo and K. Ito, in "High-Pressure Research in Geophysics" (S. Akimoto and M. Manghnani, eds.), *Adv. Earth Planet. Sci.* No. 12, p. 3 (1982).
28. M. Kumazawa, K. Masaki, H. Sawamoto, and M. Kato, *High Temp.—High Pressures* **4**, 293 (1972).
29. M. Kumazawa, *High Temp.—High Pressures* **5**, 599 (1973).
30. K. Masaki, H. Sawamoto, E. Ohtani, M. Kumazawa, M. Machida, S. Mizukusa, and N. Nakayama, *Rev. Sci. Instrum.* **46**, 84 (1975).
31. E. Ohtani, H. Sawamoto, K. Masaki, and M. Kumazawa, *Proc. Int. Conf. High Pressure, 4th Kyoto, 1974* p. 185 (1975).
32. K. Masaki, H. Sawamoto, and M. Kumazawa, *Proc. Int. Conf. High Pressure, 4th, Kyoto, 1974* p. 832 (1975).
33. M. Kumazawa, H. Sawamoto, E. Ohtani, and K. Masaki, *Nature (London)* **247**, 356 (1974).
34. H. T. Hall, *Science* **169**, 868 (1970).
35. L. F. Vereschangin, E. N. Yakovlev, T. D. Varfolomeeva, V. N. Seslarev, and L. E. Sterenberg, *High Temp.—High Pressures* **3**, 239 (1971).
36. F. P. Bundy, *Rev. Sci. Instrum.* **46**, 1318 (1975).
37. P. W. Bridgman, "The Physics of High Pressure." Bell, London, 1952.

38. J. H. King, *J. Sci. Instrum.* **42**, 374 (1965).
39. E. Ohtani, M. Kumazawa, T. Kato, and T. Irifune, in "High Pressure Research in Geophysics" (S. Akimoto and M. Manghnani, eds.), *Adv. Earth Planet. Sci.* No. 12, p. 259 (1982).
40. S. Akimoto and Y. Sato, in "Physics and Chemistry of the Earth" (L. H. Ahrens, J. B. Dawson, A. R. Duncan, and A. J. Erlank, eds.), Vol. 9, p. 837. Pergamon, Oxford, 1975.
41. T. Yagi and S. Akimoto, *Tectonophysics* **35**, 259 (1975).
42. S. Akimoto, H. Fujisawa, and T. Katsura, *J. Geophys. Res.* **70**, 1969 (1965).
43. T. Yagi, Y. Ida, Y. Sato, and S. Akimoto, *Phys. Earth Planet. Inter.* **10**, 348 (1975).
44. Y. Sato, S. Akimoto, and K. Inoue, *High Temp.—High Pressures* **5**, 289 (1973).
45. R. H. Curtin, D. L. Decker, and H. B. Vanfleet, *Phys. Rev.* **139**, A1552 (1965).
46. D. I. R. Norris, *Br. J. Appl. Phys.* **16**, 709 (1965).
47. G. J. Piermarini, S. Block, and J. D. Barnett, *J. Appl. Phys.* **44**, 5377 (1973).
48. J. D. Barnett and C. D. Bosco, *J. Appl. Phys.* **40**, 3144 (1969).
49. R. J. Zeto, H. B. Vanfleet, E. Hryckowian, and C. D. Bosco, in "Accurate Characterization of the High Pressure Environment" (E. C. Lloyd, ed.), p. 45. *NBS Spec. Publ.* No. 326 (1971).
50. R. J. Zeto and H. B. Vanfleet, *J. Appl. Phys.* **40**, 2227 (1969).
51. H. B. Vanfleet and R. J. Zeto, *J. Appl. Phys.* **42**, 4955 (1971).
52. R. J. Zeto and H. B. Vanfleet, *J. Appl. Phys.* **42**, 1001 (1971).
53. N. Kawai and A. Nishiyama, *Proc. Jpn. Acad.* **50**, 72 (1974).
54. N. Kawai, M. Togaya, and A. Onodera, *Proc. Jpn. Acad.* **49**, 623 (1973).
55. E. Ito and H. Yamada, in "High-Pressure Research in Geophysics" (S. Akimoto and M. Manghnani, eds.), *Adv. Earth Planet. Sci.* No. 12, p. 405 (1982).
56. E. Takahashi, H. Yamada, and E. Ito, *Geophys. Res. Lett.* **9**, 805 (1982).
57. H. Sawamoto, E. Ohtani, and M. Kumazawa, *Proc. Int. Conf. High Pressure, 4th, Kyoto, 1974* p. 194 (1975).
58. D. P. Johnson and P. L. M. Heydemann, *Rev. Sci. Instrum.* **38**, 1294 (1967).
59. P. W. Bridgman, *Proc. Am. Acad. Arts Sci.* **74**, 425 (1942).
60. P. W. Bridgman, *Proc. Am. Acad. Arts Sci.* **81**, 167 (1952).
61. R. S. Dadson and R. G. P. Greig, *Br. J. Appl. Phys.* **16**, 1711 (1965).
62. S. E. Babb, in "High Pressure Measurement" (A. A. Giardini and E. C. Lloyd, eds.), p. 115. Butterworth, London, 1963.
63. S. E. Babb, in "Technique of Inorganic Chemistry," Vol. 6, p. 83. Wiley, New York, 1966.
64. G. C. Kennedy and P. N. La Mori, *J. Geophys. Res.* **67**, 851 (1962).
65. L. F. Vereshchagin, E. V. Zubova, I. P. Buimova, and K. P. Burdina, *Sov. Phys—Dokl (Engl. Transl.)* **11**, 585 (1966).
66. J. C. Haygarth, I. C. Getting, and G. C. Kennedy, *J. Appl. Phys.* **38**, 4557 (1967).
67. P. W. Bridgman, *Proc. Am. Acad. Arts Sci.* **76**, 55 (1948).
68. A. S. Balchan and H. G. Drickamer, *Rev. Sci. Instrum.* **32**, 308 (1961).
69. R. N. Jeffrey, J. D. Barnett, H. B. Vanfleet, and H. T. Hall, *J. Appl. Phys.* **37**, 3172 (1966).
70. H. G. Drickamer, *Rev. Sci. Instrum.* **41**, 1667 (1970).
71. G. J. Piermarini and S. Block, *Rev. Sci. Instrum.* **46**, 973 (1975).
72. P. W. Bridgman, *Proc. Am. Acad. Arts Sci.* **47**, 321 (1912).
73. J. C. Jamieson, J. N. Fritz, and M. H. Manghnani, in "High-Pressure Research in Geophysics" (S. Akimoto and M. Manghnani, eds.), *Adv. Earth Planet. Sci.* No. 12, p. 27 (1982).
74. D. L. Decker, *J. Appl. Phys.* **36**, 157 (1965).
75. D. L. Decker, *J. Appl. Phys.* **37**, 5012 (1966).
76. D. L. Decker, *J. Appl. Phys.* **42**, 3239 (1971).

77. E. Grüneisen, in "Handbuch der Physik" (H. Geiger and K. Scheel, eds.), Vol. 10, Chap. d, Springer-Verlag, Berlin and New York, 1926.
78. M. Born and K. Huang, "Dynamical Theory of Crystal Lattices," Chaps. 1-3. Oxford Univ. Press, London, 1954.
79. F. Birch, *J. Geophys. Res.* **83**, 1257 (1978).
80. D. L. Decker and T. G. Worlton, *J. Appl. Phys.* **43**, 4799 (1972).
81. A. L. Ruoff and L. C. Chhabildas, *J. Appl. Phys.* **47**, 4867 (1976).
82. M. Spieglan and J. C. Jamieson, *High Temp.—High Pressures* **6**, 479 (1974).
83. T. Yagi, *Year Book—Carnegie Inst. Washington* **76**, 528 (1977).
84. G. R. Barsch and Z. P. Chang, in "Accurate Characterization of the High Pressure Environment" (E. C. Lloyd, ed.), *NBS Spec. Publ.* No. 326, p. 173 (1971).
85. M. H. Manghnani, E. F. Skelton, L. C. Ming, J. C. Jamieson, S. Qadri, D. Schiferl, and J. Balogh, in "Physics of Solids under High Pressure" (J. S. Schilling and R. N. Shelton, eds.), p. 47. North-Holland Publ., Amsterdam, 1981.
86. A. K. Singh and G. C. Kennedy, *J. Appl. Phys.* **45**, 4686 (1974).
87. R. A. Forman, G. J. Piermarini, J. D. Barnett, and S. Block, *Science* **176**, 284 (1972).
88. G. J. Piermarini, S. Block, J. D. Barnett, and R. A. Forman, *J. Appl. Phys.* **46**, 2774 (1975).
89. H. K. Mao, P. M. Bell, J. W. Shaner, and D. J. Steinberg, *J. Appl. Phys.* **49**, 3276 (1978).
90. N. Hamaya and S. Akimoto, in "High-Pressure Research in Geophysics" (S. Akimoto and M. Manghnani, eds.), *Adv. Earth Planet. Sci.* No. 12, p. 373 (1982).
91. S. Mizukami, A. Ohtani, N. Kawai, and E. Ito, *Phys. Earth Planet. Inter.* **10**, 177 (1975).
92. S. Akimoto, N. Hamaya, and T. Yagi, in "High Pressure Science and Technology" (B. Vodar and P. Marteau, eds.), p. 194. Pergamon, Oxford, 1980.
93. T. Yagi and S. Akimoto, *J. Geophys. Res.* **85**, 6991 (1980).
94. M. Shimada, *Tectonophysics* **72**, 343 (1981).
95. M. Shimada and H. Yukutake, in "High-Pressure Research in Geophysics" (S. Akimoto and M. Manghnani, eds.), *Adv. Earth Planet. Sci.* No. 12, p. 193 (1982).

# 8. THERMAL CONDUCTIVITY OF ROCKS AND MINERALS*

## K. Horai
Meteorological College
Kashiwa-Shi, Chiba-Ken
Japan 277

## T. Shankland
Geophysics Group
Los Alamos National Laboratory
Los Alamos, New Mexico 87545

## 1. Thermal Conductivity

Conduction of heat in rock ordinarily occurs through the lattice vibrations of crystals composing the rock-forming minerals; at high temperatures transfer of heat by radiation through the crystal becomes important. In this section we review methods of thermal conductivity measurement at various conditions under which the lattice vibration is the principal mode of thermal conduction. Measurement of the radiative component of thermal conductivity requires special techniques that are discussed in Section 2.

### 1.1. Techniques at Zero Pressure

Thermal conductivity measurements at zero pressure are essential to the study of terrestrial heat flow. To determine heat flow from underground temperature profiles, the thermal conductivity representative of rock samples obtained along the temperature profile must be measured at pressures at or only slightly above ordinary (atmospheric) pressure of 1.03 bars (0.103 MPa). Techniques suitable for this purpose will be described first.

1.1.1. Divided-Bar Method. The divided-bar method is a standard technique for thermal conductivity measurement. The basis of this measure is the continuity of a steady linear flow of heat through a bar. A rock sample

---

* This work was supported by the U. S. Department of Energy.

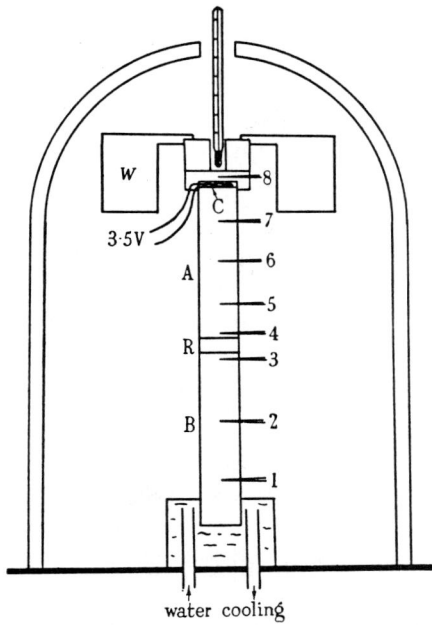

FIG. 1. Divided-bar apparatus for thermal conductivity measurement.[1]

is cut into a flat circular cylinder and sandwiched between metal cylindrical bars of the same diameter (Fig. 1).[1] The top of the upper bar is heated and the bottom of the lower bar is cooled so that heat flows vertically downward from the upper bar to the lower one through the sample. When a steady state is reached, heat flow is constant and is given by

$$Q = -S_m k_m (\text{grad } T)_m \qquad (1)$$

where $S_m$ is the cross-sectional area of the bar, $k_m$ the thermal conductivity of the bar, and $(\text{grad } T)_m$ the linear thermal gradient in the bar along the axial direction. Thermally conductive metal such as brass is most commonly used for the bar. The diameter of the bar is usually a few centimeters.

Use of a heating wire wound on a mica flake and encased in a metal container attached to the top of the bar is one method for generating a constant heat flow.[1,2] In this case, however, since there is no stabilization of the bar's temperature at the top, it varies from one measurement to another depending on the thermal resistance of the sample. A better method is to keep the bar's ends constant high and low temperatures by circulating thermostatically controlled fluids.[3] The temperature difference between the temperature baths is usually a few tens of degrees Celsius.

## 8. THERMAL CONDUCTIVITY OF ROCKS AND MINERALS

To measure temperatures along the bar, thermocouples are held in double-hole porcelain tubes that are inserted into holes drilled from the bar's wall to its center along a radius. Each hole must be thin enough (less than 2 mm in diameter) to minimize disturbances to the uniform flow of heat in the bar. A difference in temperature $\Delta T_m$ measured between two adjacent holes separated by distance $l$ along the bar's axis gives $\Delta T_m/l$, a measure of (grad $T)_m$. Similarly, $\Delta T$ measured by thermocouples immediately above and below the sample of thickness $d$ can give an estimate of thermal gradient in the sample (grad $T)_s$. Using the sample cross-sectional area $S_s$ equal to $S_m$ of the metal bar and the sample conductivity $k_s$, we have the heat flow through the sample

$$Q = -S_s K_s(\text{grad } T)_s \qquad (2)$$

Equation (2) is equated to (1) for continuous heat flow across the sample interfaces.

Eliminating $S_m = S_s$ from Eqs. (1) and (2) yields

$$k_s = k_m \frac{(\text{grad } T)_m}{(\text{grad } T)_s} = k_m \frac{(\Delta T_m/l)}{(\Delta T/d)} \qquad (3)$$

which gives the unknown thermal conductivity $k_s$ of the sample in terms of the metal's thermal conductivity $k_m$.

For relationship (3) to hold, heat flow should be kept constant along the length of the bar by minimizing lateral heat loss on the sides. The bar-sample assembly can be shielded by a guard ring, a metal tube concentric with the bar with its upper and lower ends connected thermally to the bar's ends so that the longitudinal distribution of temperature is about the same as that of the bar.[3] Thus, heat exchange between the guard ring and the bar (Fig. 2) and the radiative heat loss from the side of the bar are nearly null. More commonly, the bar-sample assembly is wrapped by a thermally insulating polyester foam to prevent conductive heat loss.[1] Close contact of the insulating foam with the bar also serves to suppress heat loss by advection of air around the bar.

It is equally important that interfaces between the bars and the sample achieve very good thermal contact. End surfaces of the sample must be ground flat and smooth to fit the smooth end surfaces of the bars. A heat transfer compound (typically glycerine or a silicone grease) applied to the interface improves the bar-sample thermal contact. In addition, a compressive load is commonly applied to the bar-sample interface to further enhance thermal contract. A mechanical load on the top of the upper bar can serve this purpose;[4] or, more typically, a hydraulic pressure device applies uniaxial pressure—usually less than 0.1 bar—across the bar-sample assembly.[1]

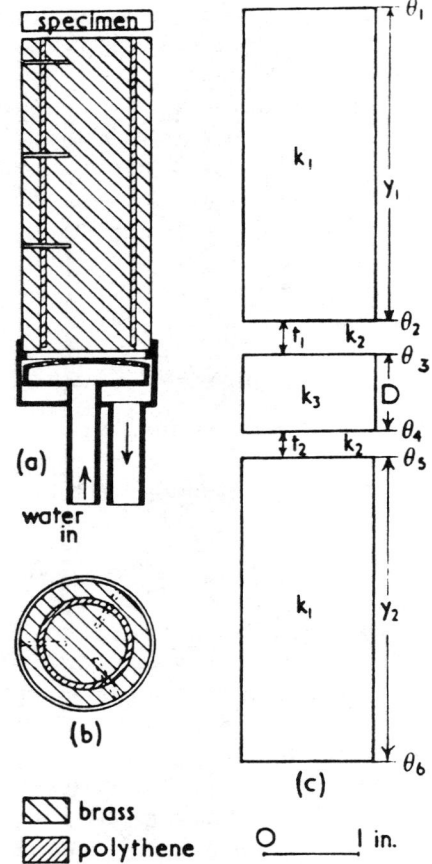

FIG. 2. Use of a guard ring in the divided-bar apparatus.[3]

The amount of thermal resistance at the bar–sample interface can be evaluated if a set of samples with different thicknesses is available.[1] The temperature difference $\Delta T$ between the thermocouple junctions immediately above and below the sample is a sum of the temperature difference in the bars $\Delta T_B$, at the interfaces $\Delta T_F$, and across the sample $\Delta T_s$. Each of these can be assumed to be proportional to $(\text{grad } T)_m$:

$$\Delta T_B = C_B (\text{grad } T)_m \qquad \Delta T_F = C_F (\text{grad } T)_m$$

$$\Delta T_s = d(\text{grad } T)_s = (k_m/k_s)(\text{grad } T)_m \, d$$

Hence, the expression

$$\Delta T/(\text{grad } T)_m = C_B + C_F + (k_m/k_s) \, d \qquad (4)$$

allows one to estimate $C_B + C_F$ from the intercept of measured $\Delta T/$ (grad $T$)$_m$ plotted against various sample thicknesses $d$. Here $C_B$ is the thermal resistance corresponding to the length of the bar from the position of the thermocouple to the bar's end surfaces and $C_F$ is the interface's thermal resistance.

For a carefully conducted experiment, thermal gradients measured in the upper and lower bars should show reasonable agreement, corresponding to a uniform, continuous flow of heat through the bars and the sample. However, for constant heat flow the thermal gradient in the upper bar is actually expected to be a little lower than that in the lower bar because the conductivity of brass increases with temperature between 0° and 100°C. The ratio of measured thermal gradients between the lower and upper bars is about 1.15 if measurements are made between 0° and 30°C (Table I). Comparison of thermal gradient values is an effective way to establish the validity of the measurements.

Equation (3) gives the sample thermal conductivity $k_s$ relative to the standard value of brass having conductivity $k_m$ (Table I). It is often desirable to evaluate the accuracy of the result by measuring the thermal conductivity of standard substances. The most common standard substances are fused and crystalline quartz (Table II). Fused quartz is isotropic, but crystalline $\alpha$-quartz is anisotropic; its thermal conductivity is axisymmetric with respect to the optic axis (or crystallographic c-axis). Crystalline quartz samples are therefore cut so that the direction of heat flow is either parallel or perpendicular to the symmetry axis. Measurements of these samples by the divided-bar apparatus should agree with those listed in Table II. Alternatively, $k_m$ of brass can be determined from values of $k_s$ for quartz; in this case, the experimental value of $k_m$ should agree with that given in Table I.

In porous rock samples, water content strongly influences thermal conductivity. Accordingly, restoration of interstitial water is necessary to simulate *in situ* conditions of crustal rocks beneath the ground water level. Shelf-dried rock samples stored in the laboratory are placed in a vacuum oven, heated to over 100°C for several hours to remove moisture, then cooled and thrust

TABLE I. Thermal Conductivity of Brass[5] (Cu + Zn $\geq$ 99.5%)

| Temperature $T$ (K) | Thermal conductivity $k$ (W cm$^{-1}$ K$^{-1}$) |
|---|---|
| 273 | 1.34 |
| 300 | 1.39 |
| 350 | 1.47 |
| 373 | 1.51 |

TABLE II. Thermal Conductivity of Crystalline and Fused Quartz[6]

| Temperature T (K) | Thermal conductivity | | |
|---|---|---|---|
| | Crystalline | | Fused |
| | $k_\parallel{}^a$ | $k_\perp{}^b$ | |
| | (W cm$^{-1}$ K$^{-1}$) | | |
| 273 | 0.116 | 0.0648 | 0.0133 |
| 300 | 0.104 | 0.0621 | 0.0138 |
| 350 | 0.088 | 0.0530 | 0.0145 |
| 400 | 0.076 | 0.0470 | 0.0151 |

[a] Parallel to crystallographic c-axis.
[b] Normal to crystallographic c-axis.

into a basin of distilled water while still under vacuum. During the thermal conductivity measurement, water evaporation is prevented by encircling the sample with a waterproof wrapping. The simplest wrapping is transparent tape, but rubber is more secure.[7]

1.1.1.1. MEASUREMENT OF SOFT SEDIMENT SAMPLES. The divided-bar method can also be used to measure thermal conductivity of soft sediment samples.[8,9] A ring having the same outer diameter as the bar is placed in the sample position in the divided-bar apparatus in order to hold the sample material (Fig. 3). The ring must be filled to its upper edge to ensure thermal contact of the sample and the upper bar. To prevent the sample's interstitial water from evaporating, the ring is sealed with a waterproof sealant.

Equation (3) is valid if it allows for the effective cross section of the sample. For a ring made of thermally insulating ebonite or synthetic resin, it suffices to multiply the right-hand side of Eq. (3) by $S_m/S_s'$ where $S_s'$ is the cross-sectional area of the sample whose radius is reduced from that of the bar by the thickness of the ring wall.

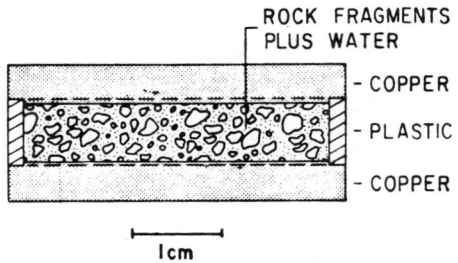

FIG. 3. Thermal conductivity cell for deformable samples in a divided-bar apparatus.[4]

1.1.1.2. HIGH-TEMPERATURE MEASUREMENTS. When the divided-bar method is applied to high-temperature measurements, bars are made of a high-temperature material such as nickel whose melting point at 1 atm pressure is over 2000°C.[10] Iron cylinders wound with a coil of nichrome wire are used for heating the bars. The bars are surrounded by copper tube to shield against radiative heat loss, and the whole assembly is installed in an electric furnace to raise the ambient temperature. The ambient atmosphere is made reducing to suppress oxidation of materials.

Measurements of various mantle substances up to 600°C are possible with this apparatus. Crystalline and fused quartz can be used as reference materials to above 600°C. For measurement near the Curie temperature of nickel, effects of the nickel phase transformation (particularly a break in thermal conductivity as a function of temperature) must be taken into account.

1.1.2. Thermal Stack. The thermal stack is similar in its principle of measurement to the divided-bar method but is usually more suitable for samples of larger diameter. There are several variations of the method.

1.1.2.1. MEASUREMENT OF SOLID ROCK. A standard apparatus is shown in Fig. 4.[11] The sample is in the shape of a circular disk, about 6 mm thick and 38.1 mm in diameter with its flat surfaces finished smooth and parallel to each other. The main part of the apparatus consists of a stack of the rock sample, thin (2 mm thick) copper plates containing thermocouple junctions, and plates of reference material (Pyrex). On top of the stack is a heater with ceramic and glass plates on its top and bottom faces that serve as thermal buffers. All plates are circular disks having the same diameter as the rock sample and with their axes aligned and placed between the platens of a hydraulic press. The disks' interfaces are thinly coated with high-temperature silicone grease, and the stack is compressed by a uniaxial stress of 35–150 bars to reduce thermal resistance between disks.

The heater in the stack is electrically powered, and the stack's lower end is cooled by circulating cold water. The stack is shielded by a heavy steel cylinder on which is wound a coil of heating wire. Heating currents are adjusted to keep the temperature drops across the Pyrex reference plates about 7°C and the temperature of the shielding cylinder about equal to the sample's mean temperature.

A notable feature of this method is the incorporation of a standard substance of known thermal conductivity such as Pyrex in the system of linear flow of heat in the stack. When the temperature drop across the thermally conductive copper plate is neglected, differential thermoelectric potentials of the thermocouple junctions across the sample and the Pyrex plate are proportional, respectively, to the temperature differences across the sample $\Delta T_s$ and across the Pyrex $\Delta T_r$. With the stack's lateral heat loss suppressed

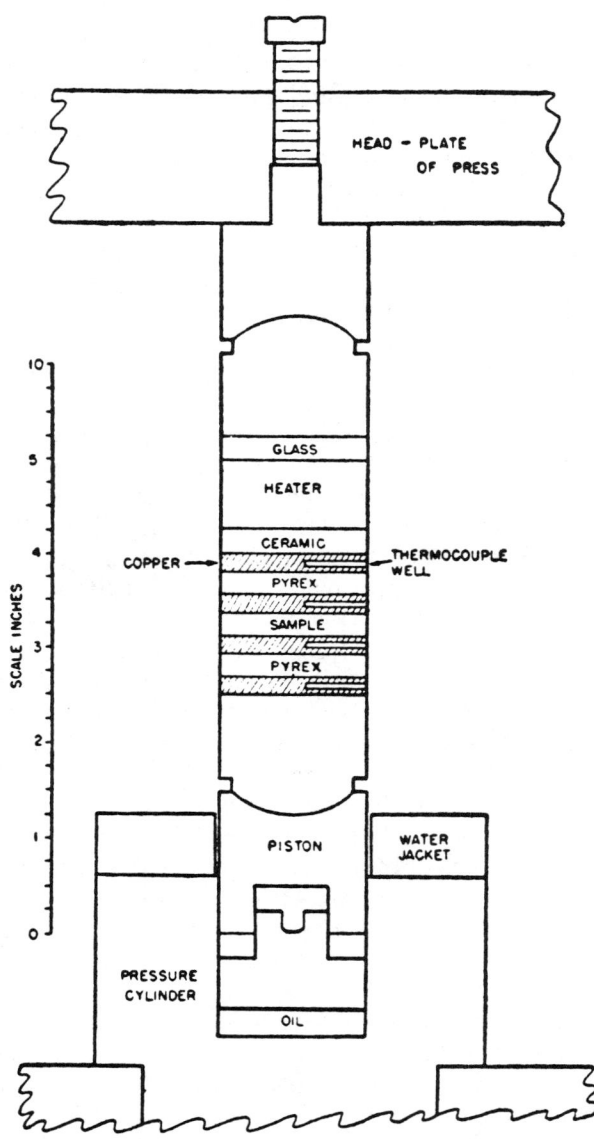

Fig. 4. Thermal stack for relative conductivity measurement.[11] Three differential thermocouples, not shown, give differences of temperature across the two disks of Pyrex glass and the sample.

by equalizing the shielding cylinder's temperature to the sample's mean temperature, the temperature differences are related to the ratio of the thermal conductivities of the sample $k_s$ and the Pyrex $k_r$ as

$$\frac{k_s}{k_r} = \frac{d_s/d_r}{\Delta T_s/\Delta T_r} \tag{5}$$

where $d_s$ and $d_r$ are the thicknesses of the sample and the Pyrex plate.

Thus, $k_s$ is determined in terms of Pyrex thermal conductivity $k_r = 2.96$ mcal/cm sec °C at 30°C. Other standard materials such as fused and crystalline quartz or obsidian are also used as reference materials.

1.1.2.2. MEASUREMENT OF STANDARD SUBSTANCES. Figure 5 illustrates a thermal stack used to measure thermal conductivity of standard materials.[6] The fundamental elements of the apparatus are a flat circular metal plate containing an electric heater, a pair of water-cooled cold plates, and several thin metal plates containing thermocouple junctions for measuring temperature. The standard samples, either fused or crystalline quartz cut into circular disks with flat faces finished smooth and parallel to each other, are placed between the plates. The samples must be of the same thickness and

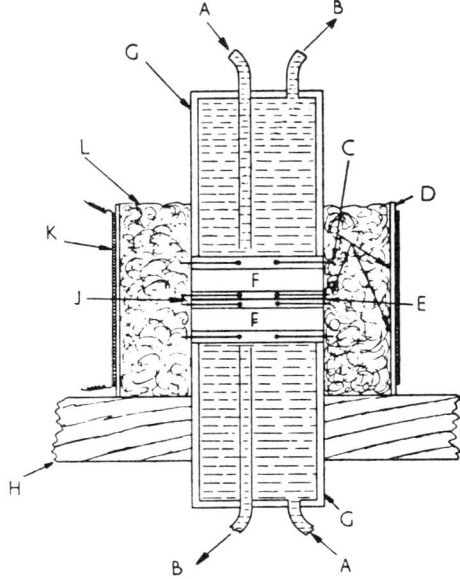

FIG. 5. Thermal stack apparatus for measuring conductivities of standard materials.[6] Thermocouple and heater leads not shown. A, water inflow; B, water outflow; C, thermocouples; D, metal tube; E, electrical heater; F, test disks; G, cold plates; H, wooden shelf; J, hot plate; K, cylindrical guard heater; L, lagging.

the temperature of the cold plates the same so that the flow of heat will be symmetrical with respect to the heating plate; the stack is surrounded by thermally insulating foam or glass wool to reduce lateral heat loss. Interfaces are coated with thin films of glycerine, and a vertical load of 0.2 bar is applied.

Precise potentiometric measurements of current and voltage give the hot plate's heat generation $Q$, for which the relation

$$Q/2 = k_s(\Delta T_s/d)S_s \qquad (6)$$

holds under the condition of steady heat flow. Here the temperature difference $\Delta T_s$ between the metal plates on either side of the sample divided by the sample thickness $d$ is an estimation of thermal gradient in the sample, and $S_s$ is the sample's cross-sectional area.

Because $k_s$ can be determined without recourse to a reference material, the method is suitable for studies of standard substances. Accurate measurement of the heat input $Q$ to the stack and thermal insulation of the system from lateral heat losses are essential.

1.1.2.3. MEASUREMENT AT ELEVATED TEMPERATURES. The thermal stack method can be successfully applied at higher temperatures; Fig. 6 illustrates an apparatus used in these measurements.[12] A circular disk-shaped rock sample S, 38.1 mm in diameter and 6.35 mm thick, is placed on the base plate P and is separated from the isolantite guard ring G by lightly touching points of three silica glass pegs that are used to adjust the sample's position on the base plate. On the sample rests a heater H containing heating nichrome wire wound on mica flake, and on the guard ring is mounted a copper cylinder "dome" D that is fixed to the base plate by metal screws; the screws are thermally insulated from the base plate by Pyrex bushings and mica washers. The base plate, the heater, and the dome are made of annealed copper with their contact surfaces lapped flat and plated with chromium or gold.

The power output $Q$ of the heater again is found by precise measurement of the current and the potential drop across the heating element. The high-resistance nichrome heating wire is connected to low-resistance copper leads so that the power in the heating element is virtually confined within the heater. The heating current is adjusted to maintain the heater's temperature about 5°C above that of the base plate. A heating element in the dome is also adjusted to keep the dome isothermal to the heater, thus nullifying any thermal exchange, either convective or radiative, between the heater and the dome. Under the condition of steady temperature for the heater $T_h$ and the base plate $T_p$, the sample's thermal conductivity is given by

$$Q = k_s[(T_h - T_p)/d]S_s \qquad (7)$$

## 8. THERMAL CONDUCTIVITY OF ROCKS AND MINERALS

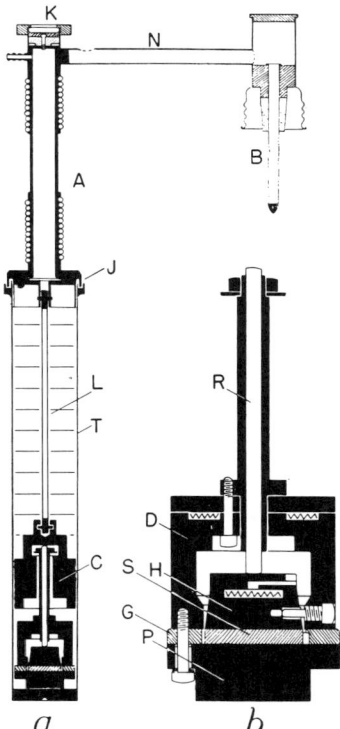

FIG. 6. Thermal conductivity apparatus for high-temperature measurement.[12] (b) Enlarged drawing of the lower part of (a).

The assembly of the sample, heater, base plate, and dome is hung loosely from the steel cylindrical weight C of 1.36 kg, which in turn is suspended by the thin steel rod L from the bottom of the upper tube A. The assembly including the weight is then enclosed by the lower steel tube T, 7.62 cm in diameter and 50.8 cm long. As the tube is lifted into place and its upper edge soldered to the bottom of the upper tube at joint J, the bottom of the tube coming in contact with the base plate releases the tension of the steel rod, and the compressive load of the weight is exerted through the Pyrex rod R on the heater, which then presses the sample against the base plate.

The sample temperature can be varied from 0° to 400°C by immersing the lower 30.5 cm of the tube in baths of thermostatically controlled liquids. Baths are filled with motor oil for temperatures below 200°C, a mixture of sodium and potassium nitrates for temperatures up to 400°C, and ice for measurements near 0°C. The thermal liquids are contained in steel cylinders of large capacity, each wrapped with heating nichrome ribbons wound on asbestos sheets and with a removable fan to control the temperature of the well-stirred liquid. The heavy weight's large heat capacity is effective in stabilizing the sample temperature.

No contact material is used in this experiment. The effect of thermal resistance at the interface between the heater and the sample and between the sample and the base plate can be eliminated by changing the species of gas around the sample. The steel tube is first evacuated and then filled with either helium or nitrogen at 1.3 bars pressure. Under uniaxial compressive stress of 0.1 bar, the average width of the interfacial gap is of the order of 0.003 mm. If the apparent thermal conductivities of the sample are $k'_s$ and $k''_s$ when the gap is filled with helium and nitrogen gases, the sample's true thermal conductivity $k_s$ is given by

$$1/k_s = [(1/k'_s) - (1/k''_s)r]/(1 - r) \qquad (8)$$

where $r = k_{N_2}/k_{He}$ is the ratio of the thermal conductivities of nitrogen and helium gases at the appropriate temperature. Between 0° and 400°C the factor $r$ is approximately 1/6.

1.1.3. *Angstrom Method and Its Modifications.* In the divided-bar and thermal stack methods, a steady-state temperature distribution is employed to obtain thermal conductivity. However, time-varying temperatures are also useful for determining thermal properties. In the Angstrom method, one end of a metal bar is subjected to a periodic sinusoidal variation of temperature, and the measurement of amplitude decay and phase lag of the temperature wave traveling down the bar is used to determine thermal diffusivity. The bar is supposed to be thin enough so that it is isothermal in cross section and long enough so that the other end of the bar is virtually free from the source alternation. The bar is allowed a radiative heat loss from its side surfaces into surrounding space, the temperature of which is taken as the zero of the experiment.

After the transient component subsides, the stationary variation of temperature in the bar is given by

$$T(x,t) = Ae^{-qx}\cos(\omega t - q'x + \varepsilon) \qquad (9)$$

where

$$q = \{[v + (v^2 + \omega^2)^{1/2}]/2\kappa\}^{1/2}$$

and

$$q' = \{[-v + (v^2 + \omega^2)^{1/2}]/2\kappa\}^{1/2}$$

for the alternation period $2\pi/\omega$. Suppose the temperature is measured at two points along the bar with amplitudes $a_1$ and $a_2$ and phases $\phi_1$ and $\phi_2$, respectively, at $x = x_1$ and $x = x_2$. Using Eq. (2) gives

$$a_1/a_2 = e^{q(x_2 - x_1)} \qquad \phi_2 - \phi_1 = q'(x_2 - x_1) \tag{10}$$

so that the thermal diffusivity $\kappa = k/\rho c$ is

$$\kappa = (x_2 - x_1)^2 \omega / 2(\phi_1 - \phi_2)(\log a_1/a_2) \tag{11}$$

Here $\rho$ is density and $c$ is the heat capacity per unit mass.

The original Angstrom method is not suitable for use with rocks and minerals since they are not readily shaped into a bar. However, the idea of determining thermal diffusivity from the attenuation of a temperature wave is applicable to samples of rocks and minerals because the temperature wave decays rapidly owing to their low thermal diffusivity, which is many times less than that of metals. The sample shape can be either linear (see below), cylindrical (Section 1.2.3), or spherical (Section 1.1.3.2).

1.1.3.1. MODIFIED ANGSTROM METHOD. An adaptation of the original Angstrom method for a bar of small length (the modified Angstrom Method) is useful for measuring $\kappa$ of earth materials. The sample size can be less than 1 cm so that the method is suitable for precious specimens such as minerals of gem quality or lunar samples. Figure 7 illustrates the sample configuration of an apparatus used for the modified Angstrom method.[13] The sample is a rectangular prism, 3-5 mm long and 10 mm$^2$ in cross section, which is silver-pasted to the nickel pedestal. The nichrome heating wire is wound on the stem of a pedestal that has been wrapped by a sheet of mica for insulation.

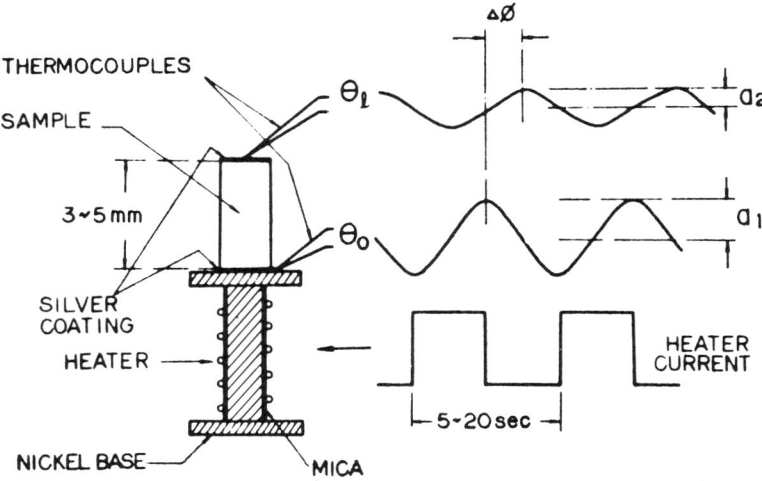

FIG. 7. Modified Angstrom method for measurements of thermal diffusivity.[13] Amplitude ratio $a_2/a_1$ and phase shift $\Delta\phi$ of temperatures $\theta_1$ and $\theta_0$ at both ends of the sample are measured to determine diffusivity. (Copyright 1968 by the American Geophysical Union.)

The heating current is switched on and off every 5–20 sec to generate a periodic temperature wave, and its higher harmonic components decay rapidly as they propagate through the relatively conductive pedestal. At the base of the sample, the temporal variation of temperature is nearly a pure sinusoidal wave with less than 2% distortion. The thermal diffusivity and the radiation constant $v$, which when multiplied by the sample's surface temperature yields the lateral radiative heat loss, are determined by measuring the amplitude decay $a_2/a_1$ and the phase lag $\Delta\phi$ of the sinusoidal temperature wave that is transmitted across the sample of length $l$ from its base to the top:

$$\kappa = \pi/\alpha\beta\tau \tag{12a}$$

$$v = \pi(\alpha^2 - \beta^2)/\alpha\beta\tau \tag{12b}$$

where $\alpha = \ln(2a_1/a_2)/l$, $\beta = \Delta\phi/l$, and $\tau$ is the period of the sinusoidal temperature wave.

For a sample in the shape of an elongated prism, consideration of radiative heat loss from the side surfaces of the sample is sufficient.[14] However, if samples are in the shape of a flattened rectangular parallelepiped or flat disk, the effect of radiative heat loss from end surfaces must be considered.[15] Mainly because only a small sample size is needed, the method is suitable for measurements at elevated temperatures. Measurements at temperatures up to 830°C are easily made by putting the apparatus in an electric furnace filled with argon gas.[13]

1.1.3.2. METHOD EMPLOYED BY K. YAMAGAWA (SPHERICAL ANGSTROM METHOD). It is appropriate to mention here that the propagation of a sinusoidal temperature wave through material for a determination of the thermal diffusivity can also be applied to a sample of spherical shape. One such measurement was conducted nearly 100 years ago.[16] The sample used for the study was a sphere of marble with density 2.71 g/cm$^3$ and radius 10.46 cm. Along a radius of the spherical sample a hole 6 mm in diameter was cut; into this hole a thermocouple encased in a fine glass tube 4.2 mm in diameter was inserted to measure temperature at the center of the sphere.

The sample was alternately immersed in baths of boiling and ice water, with a time interval of 40–50 min. Thus, the sphere's surface was subjected to a change of temperature varying as a periodic square wave. The amplitude decay and the phase lag of the Fourier components as the wave traveled from the sphere's surface to the center were used to determine the thermal conductivity of the sample.

The temperature in a sphere of radius $R$ with surface temperature alternating between $T_0/2$ and $-T_0/2$ and with period $\tau$ is given by

$$T(r, t) = \frac{1}{r} \sum_{n=0}^{\infty} C_{2n+1} \exp\{(-\sqrt{(2n+1)\omega/2\kappa}\, r)$$

$$\sin[(2n+1)\omega t - \sqrt{(2n+1)\omega/2\kappa}\, r + D_{2n+1}]$$

$$-\exp(\sqrt{(2n+1)\omega/2\kappa}\, r)$$

$$\sin[(2n+1)\omega t + \sqrt{(2n+1)\omega/2\kappa}\, r + D_{2n+1}]\}$$

where

$$\omega = 2\pi/\tau$$

$$C_{2n+1} = 2T_0 R/(2n+1)\pi[\exp(-2\sqrt{(2n+1)\omega/2\kappa}\, R)$$
$$+ \exp(2\sqrt{(2n+1)\omega/2\kappa}\, R) - 2\cos(2\sqrt{(2n+1)\omega/2\kappa}\, R)]^{1/2}$$

$$D_{2n+1} = \tan^{-1}[\{\exp(2\sqrt{(2n+1)\omega/2\kappa}\, R) + 1\}/$$
$$\exp(2\sqrt{(2n+1)\omega/2\kappa}\, R) - 1\}\tan(\sqrt{(2n+1)\omega/2\kappa}\, R)]$$

From the measured temperature at $r = 0$ expanded in Fourier series,

$$T(0, t) = \alpha_1 \sin(\omega t + \beta_1) + \alpha_3 \sin(3\omega t + \beta_3) + \cdots$$

the values of

$$X_{2n+1} = (\tau/2)\alpha_{2n+1} \cos \beta_{2n+1} \quad \text{and} \quad Y_{2n+1} = (\tau/2)\alpha_{2n+1} \sin \beta_{2n+1}$$

were read graphically with the aid of a planimeter. Then,

$$\alpha_{2n+1} = (2/\tau)\sqrt{X_{2n+1}^2 + Y_{2n+1}^2} \quad \text{and} \quad \tan \beta_{2n+1} = Y_{2n+1}/X_{2n+1}$$

were compared with the theoretical $C_{2n+1}$'s and $D_{2n+1}$'s. Yamagawa thought that the first Fourier component was most reliable and derived the thermal diffusivity from data on $\alpha_1$ and $\beta_1$.

1.1.4. Use of Linear Heat Sources.

1.1.4.1. NEEDLE PROBE METHOD. This is a rapid method of determining thermal conductivity of soft, deformable material such as soil, wet clay, or sand. Because of its simplicity the method is widely used in the measurement of oceanic soft sediments.

Figure 8 is a schematic diagram of the apparatus.[17] The essential part is a stainless steel hypodermic needle, 6.4 cm long and 0.76 mm in diameter, that contains a single loop of heating wire and a temperature sensor (thermistor) held in place by electrically insulating but thermally conductive epoxy.

In the measurement, the needle is inserted as a probe into the sample material and a constant current is switched into the heater. The temperature $T$ at the center of the needle is recorded as a function of time $t$. The sample's

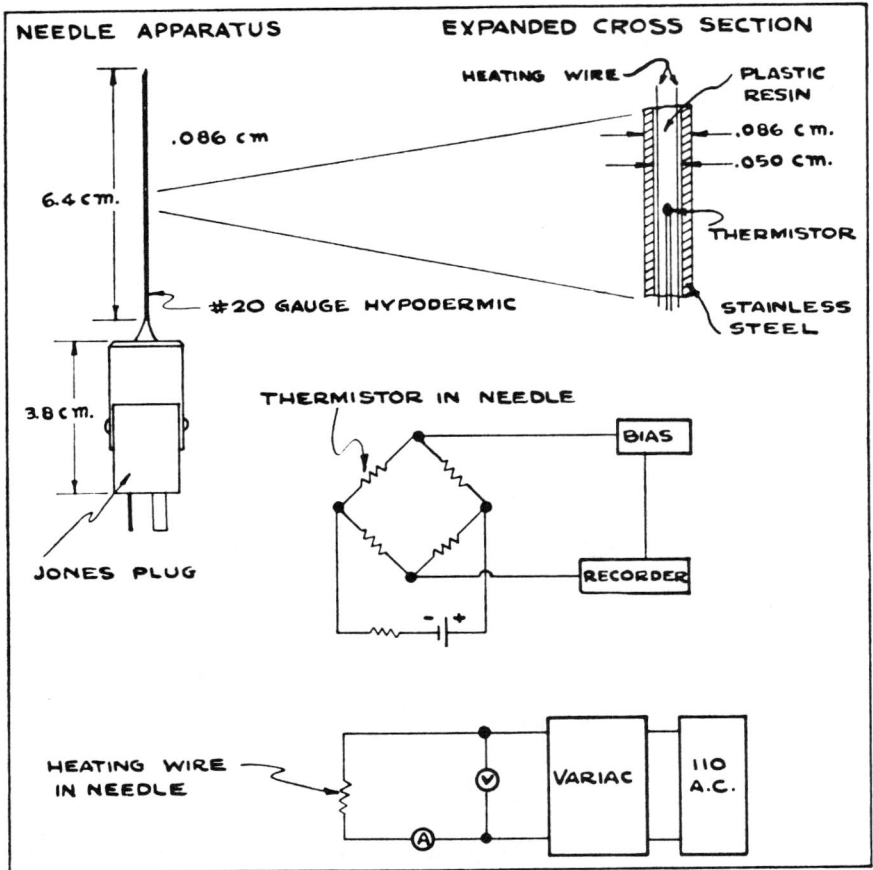

FIG. 8. Needle probe apparatus for thermal conductivity measurement.[17] (Copyright 1959 by the American Geophysical Union.)

thermal conductivity $k$ is then determined by

$$k = (q/2\pi)(\ln t)/T \tag{13}$$

where $q$ is the rate of heat emission per unit length of the needle.

Equation (13) was derived from the theory of thermal conduction for an infinitely long linear heat source embedded in a homogeneous isotropic medium of infinite extent. It is assumed that the needle of radius $a$ has an infinite thermal conductivity so that its temperature is isothermal and equal to that of the heater. Also, the needle's thermal contact with the surrounding medium is assumed to be perfect. The needle's length $l$ must be long compared with its radius, and the distribution of the heating wire in the needle must be uniform throughout the length of the needle to yield constant heat emission. The thermistor must be positioned at the needle's center to record a temperature that is least disturbed by end effects. The linear relationship between $\ln t$ and $T$ must hold as an asymptote when $\kappa t/a^2 > 20$ and $2\pi a^2 k/C_l \kappa > 1$ in order to use Eq. (13) to determine thermal conductivity.[18] Here $C_l$ is the needle's heat capacity per unit length. For measurements on oceanic sediment having a typical thermal diffusivity of $2 \times 10^{-2}$ cm$^2$ sec$^{-1}$ and with a needle probe of 1 mm diameter, the first of the above two conditions indicates that a plot of $T$ against $\ln t$ becomes linear within 10 sec after the start of heating. The second condition is easily met unless the sample's specific heat is unusually low.

The measurement procedure, apparently simple and straightforward, requires some precautions to achieve high reliability; a drift of baseline temperature during the measurement is particularly harmful. It is possible to remove the drift component of measured temperature by adding an empirical term proportional to time $t$ to the equation when analyzing the data by least-squares criteria.

1.1.4.2. METHODS WITH LINE HEAT SOURCES AND DIFFERENTIAL LINE HEAT SOURCES. The needle probe is one example of the line heat source method. The line heat source method is also extensively used for measurement of particulate material such as lunar fines in vacuum.[19] In this case, the heating element is a wire stretched straight and embedded in the sample of particulate or powdered material. The heater is energized by passing a constant dc current through the wire, and the temperature increase is measured as a function of time by a temperature sensor placed in the vicinity of the heater. The temperature increment is given by

$$\Delta T(t) = -\frac{q}{4\pi k} E_i(-r^2/4\kappa t) \qquad (14)$$

where $q$ is the constant rate of heat emission per unit length of the wire, $k$ and $\kappa$ are the thermal conductivity and diffusivity of the sample, $r$ is the distance of the temperature sensor from the heating wire, and $E_i$ is the exponential integral. Equation (13) for the needle probe method is an asymptotic expansion of Eq. (14) for small values of $r^2/\kappa t$.

In the differential line heat source method, the heater–sample configuration is the same as that of the line heat source method. However, the method of processing the output from the temperature sensor is different.[20] The instrumentation contains an additional amplifier and a differentiating circuit that records the time derivative of the thermocouple voltage from the temperature sensor.

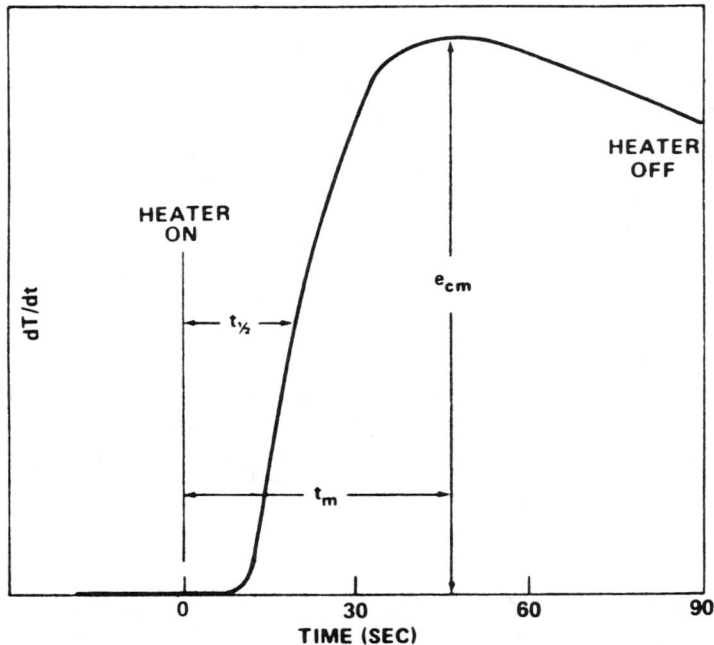

FIG. 9. Output record of differential line heat source apparatus.[19]

Differentiating Eq. (14) with respect to time, one obtains

$$dT/dt = (q/4\pi kt) \exp(-r^2/4\kappa t) \tag{15}$$

which has a maximum at $t_m = r^2/4\kappa$. Therefore, the thermal conductivity is obtained as

$$k = q/4\pi e t_m (dT/dt)_m \tag{16}$$

where $e$ is the base of natural logarithms and $(dT/dt)_m$ the maximum value of $dT/dt$. In order to determine the value of $(dT/dt)_m$, the maximum differential voltage $e_{cm}$ read on the recording chart (Fig. 9) must be corrected for the thermoelectric coefficient of the thermocouple, the amplification factor of the microvolt amplifiers, and the time constant of the differentiating circuit. It was found that $t_{1/2}$, the time necessary to reach one-half of $e_{cm}$, can be determined more precisely than $t_m$ (Fig. 9). Therefore, the relation $t_{1/2} = 0.37337 t_m$ can be used instead of $t_m$. A comparison of both methods showed[20] that measurement by the differential line heat source method can be completed in a much shorter period of time, as the heater can be turned off soon after the maximum $dT/dt$ is observed.

## 1.2. Techniques at High Pressure

Knowledge of the thermal conductivity of rocks and minerals under high pressure is needed for understanding thermal structure and thermal evolution of the earth's interior. Pressure ranges up to 10 kbar are sufficient for studying the outer lithosphere. However, to cover conditions in the whole mantle, pressures greater than the order of 1 Mbar would be necessary. The *in situ* pressure may contain triaxial stress components in the shallowest part of earth's crust, but in most of the deeper interior it is dominantly hydrostatic.

### 1.2.1. Application of the Thermal Stack at High Pressure.

The effect of uniaxial compressive load on the thermal conductivity of a solid rock sample can be judged by increasing the loading pressure on the thermal stack apparatus. An example of such measurements[7] is that of a sample of granite from Casco, Maine, with total porosity of 0.7%; a sample was placed in an apparatus modified from that shown in Fig. 4. For a reference material a circular disk of silica glass was used, and the apparatus was calibrated by two standard materials: crystalline quartz, cut to conduct in the direction perpendicular to the optic axis, and fused quartz (Table II). The stack was jacketed by a carefully machined styrofoam insulator to reduce lateral heat loss.

Measurements were made with the sample either completely dry or completely saturated with water. Loss of interstitial water was prevented by sealing the wet sample's lateral surface with a rubber jacket. The uniaxial compressive load was raised to 930 bars, which is high enough to close microcracks oriented normal to the direction of applied stress. Crack closure was judged by observing the thermal conductivity of the water-saturated sample as it converged toward that of the dry sample in this pressure range. A small discrepancy of the thermal conductivities between the dry and wet samples could be attributed to microcracks oriented parallel to the stress direction and to the spherical pores that remain open under stress of this magnitude. Microcrack porosity estimated from the conductivity data was 0.4%, and the remaining porosity (0.3%) was believed to be in microspherical pores and cracks parallel to the stress direction.

### 1.2.2. Bridgman Method.

P. W. Bridgman, a pioneer of experimental high-pressure physics, studied the thermal conductivity of organic and inorganic liquids at pressures up to 12 kbar.[21] The apparatus used for that experiment can be converted to the study of rocks. Figure 10 is a schematic sample configuration.[22] The rock sample is in the form of hollow cylinder 2.5 cm long and having 1.27 and 1.02 cm outer and inner radii; on both the inside and the outside are closely fitting copper cylinders. The inner one contains a heater, an insulated wire carrying an electric current stretched along the cylinder's axis. Heat emitted is conducted radially through the sample from the inner copper cylinder to the outer one and is carried away

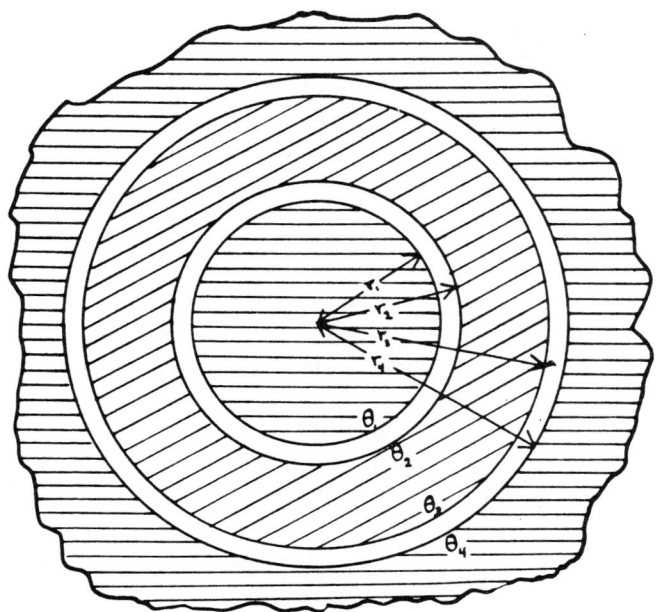

FIG. 10. Sample configuration for high-pressure conductivity apparatus.[22] Horizontal shading represents copper, diagonal shading the rock under measurement, and the unshaded part the pressure-transmitting liquid.

by liquid in a temperature bath through the metallic wall of the pressure vessel, which is in thermal contact with the outer copper cylinder.

The pressure vessel containing the thermal conductivity apparatus (the cylinder assembly) is filled with pressure-transmitting fluid, an electrically insulating liquid such as petroleum ether (for measurements to 30°C), kerosene (to 75°C), or Dow-Corning 200 silicone oil (to 200°C). Pressure is raised by means of an external intensifier. Temperatures are measured by thermocouples. Under steady-state conditions,

$$\Delta T = \frac{q}{2\pi} \left[ \frac{1}{k_1} \log\left(\frac{r_2 \, r_4}{r_1 \, r_3}\right) + \frac{1}{k_s} \log \frac{r_3}{r_2} \right] \tag{17}$$

where $q$ is the rate of heat emission per unit time per unit length of the heating wire, $\Delta T$ the difference between temperatures measured at the surfaces of the inner and outer copper cylinders, $k_1$ the thermal conductivity of the pressure-transmitting fluid, $k_s$ the sample's thermal conductivity, and $r_1$, $r_4$, and $r_3$, $r_2$ are, respectively, the copper cylinders' and the sample's outer and inner radii (Fig. 10), which can be determined by precise measurement of the dimensions. It should be noted that the ratios of the radii of the copper

## 8. THERMAL CONDUCTIVITY OF ROCKS AND MINERALS

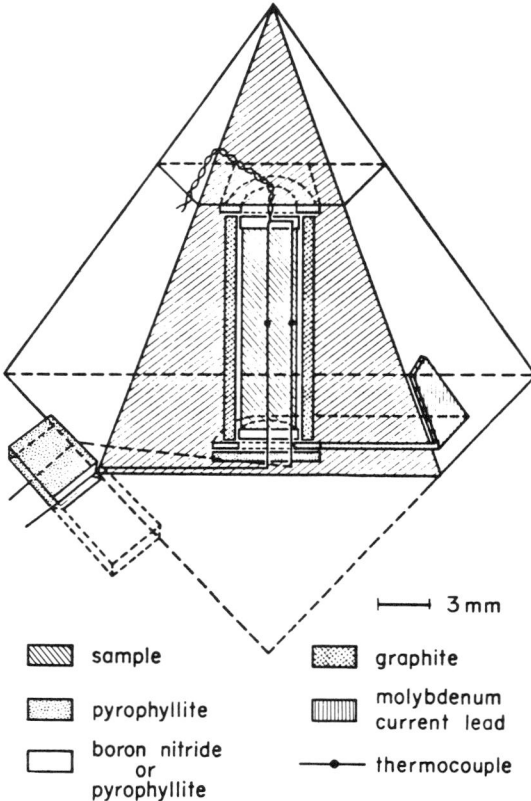

FIG. 11. Cylindrical sample assembly encased in pyrophyllite tetrahedron for high temperature and pressure conductivity measurement.[23] (Copyright 1968 by the American Geophysical Union.)

cylinders, $r_4/r_1$, and the sample, $r_3/r_2$, are invariant despite their deformation under hydrostatic pressure. Therefore, $k_s$ can be determined without making a geometric correction. The liquid's thermal conductivity $k_l$ is determined by a separate experiment under pressure.

1.2.3. Cylindrical Angstrom Method. The measurement principle of the modified Angstrom method can be adapted for determining the thermal diffusivity of a cylindrical sample under high pressure. The experimental configuration is shown schematically in Fig. 11.[23] Powders, e.g., synthetic olivine ($Fe_2SiO_4$ or $Mg_2SiO_4$ with grain size 1–5 μm), are packed in a graphite tube, 10–12 mm long and 3.5–3.8 mm in diameter, that serves as a heater as well as a sample container. The sample is placed in a 25- or 30-mm-edge tungsten carbide anvil encased in a 30- or 36-mm-edge pyrophyllite tetrahedron to raise the pressure to 30–50 kbar in a tetrahedral anvil high-pressure apparatus.

Sample temperature is controlled from 300 to 1400 K by passing current through the graphite heater. Superimposed on it is a secondary current that is switched on and off at a period of 1–3 sec to generate a cyclic temperature wave at angular frequency $\omega$. As the higher harmonic components rapidly decay, its waveform in the sample becomes nearly sinusoidal at a depth of 0.3 mm from the sample–heater boundary, where a chromel–alumel thermocouple junction is located as an input detector. Another thermocouple junction is at the sample's center to detect the output signal. The sample $\kappa$ is determined from either the amplitude decay $A$ or the phase lag $\Delta\phi$ of the sinusoidal temperature wave that propagates through the cylindrical sample (radius $R$) from the surface toward the center,

$$A = \{(\text{bei } l)^2 + (\text{ber } l)^2\}^{1/2}$$
$$\Delta\phi = \tan^{-1}(\text{bei } l/\text{ber } l) \qquad (18)$$
$$l = \sqrt{\omega/\kappa}\, R$$

where $\omega$ is the angular frequency of the periodic temperature wave, and bei and ber are Thomson's functions in the theory of Bessel functions. Generally, determination of $\kappa$ from the amplitude decay is more accurate than that from the phase lag.

## 2. Radiative Thermal Conductivity

Thermal radiation contributes significantly to heat transfer in earth materials when (a) temperature is high enough so that there is significant energy in the blackbody emission spectrum and (b) the blackbody spectrum has its peak in or near a region of transparency. In silicates there are strong lattice absorption bands at wavelengths greater than about 5000 nm (5 μm) so that, in practice, temperatures must at least exceed 500°C. We discuss the physical problem of heat transfer by thermal diffusion of photons in analogy to the thermal diffusion of phonons that prevails in lattice conductivity $k_L$ discussed above. As in the original treatment by Rosseland[24] for stellar interiors, one can define an effective conductivity $k_R$ due to radiation provided that the mean free path $l_\nu$ for light of frequency $\nu$ is much less than the dimensions of the sample material. Although this condition is not always achieved in the laboratory (where radiation can complicate conductivity measurements in ways that are difficult to compensate for), there are many situations in the earth where $k_R$ can be used meaningfully.

Radiative heat loss has long concerned the glass industry; theory and experiments were reviewed by Gardon.[25] As introduced to the geophysical literature by Clark,[26] radiative thermal conductivity is given by

$$k_R = \frac{4\pi}{3} \int_0^\infty l_\nu \frac{\partial I_{b\nu}(T)}{\partial T} d\nu \qquad (19)$$

where $T$ is absolute temperature and $I_{b\nu}(T)$ the spectral intensity of blackbody radiation given by the Planck formula

$$I_{b\nu}(T) = 2h\nu^3 n_\nu^2(T)/c^2(e^{h\nu/k_B T} - 1) \qquad (20)$$

Here $h$ is Plancks's constant, $n_\nu$ the real part of the dielectric constant at frequency $\nu$, $c$ the velocity of light in vacuum, and $k_B$ the Boltzmann constant. In a semitransparent material each element of volume absorbs a fraction of the radiation passing through it and reradiates an equal amount; there is a net transfer of energy down a thermal gradient because more heat radiates into the volume from the hot than from the cold side.[27, 28]

When $l_\nu(T)$ is much less than the boundaries of a system, then the total conductivity $k = k_L + k_R$ is measured naturally. However, there are situations in which $l_\nu$ is comparable to available sample dimensions, and these require that it be measured directly in order to calculate $k_R$ from Eq. (19), as described below.

### 2.1. Measurement Methods

The mean free path is the reciprocal of opacity

$$\varepsilon_\nu = l_\nu^{-1} = \alpha_\nu + \sigma_\nu(1 - \overline{\cos \theta}) \qquad (21)$$

where $\alpha_\nu$ and $\sigma_\nu$ are the absorption and scattering coefficients and $\overline{\cos \theta}$ gives the mean scattering direction. In many earth materials scattering occurs at grain boundaries so that $\sigma_\nu^{-1}$ is of the order of the grain size and $\overline{\cos \theta} \simeq 0.98$.[29, 30] This weak contribution arises from the strong forward bias of scattering that occurs with weak contrasts in refractive indices and therefore weak reflectivities at grain boundaries.

The usual method for evaluating $k_R$ is to directly obtain the extinction coefficient $\varepsilon_\nu(T) \simeq \alpha_\nu(T)$ in an experiment to measure optical transmittance $t$ from the formula for light transmitted through a flat sample of thickness $d$,

$$t = \frac{(1 - R)^2 e^{-\alpha d}}{1 - R^2 e^{-\alpha d}} \qquad (22)$$

$R$ is the specular reflection coefficient of a light beam normally incident on a polished surface. Figure 12 depicts an apparatus for measuring $t(\lambda, T)$, the ratio of light intensity $I$ at wavelength $\lambda$ passing through the sample to reference intensity $I_0$ along the same path without the sample. The $R$ can be

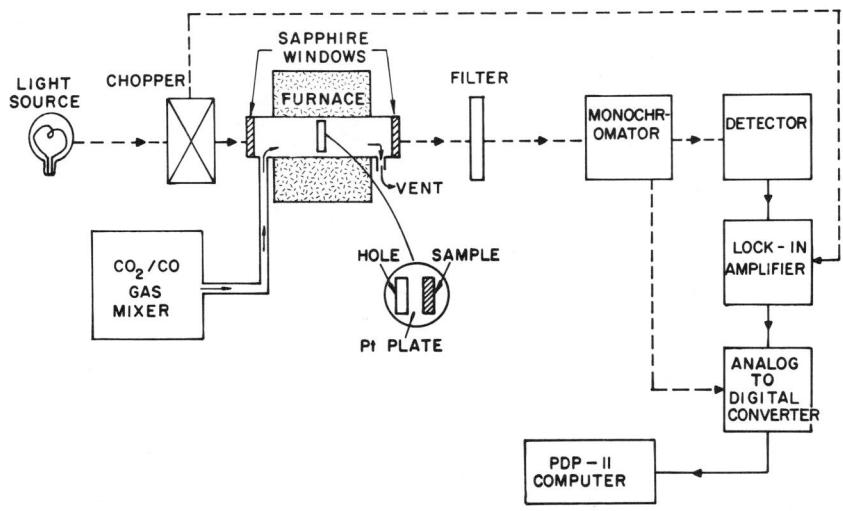

FIG. 12. Schematic diagram of apparatus[33] used to measure absorption spectra of olivine at high temperature and under controlled $O_2$ partial pressure. (Copyright 1979 by the American Geophysical Union.)

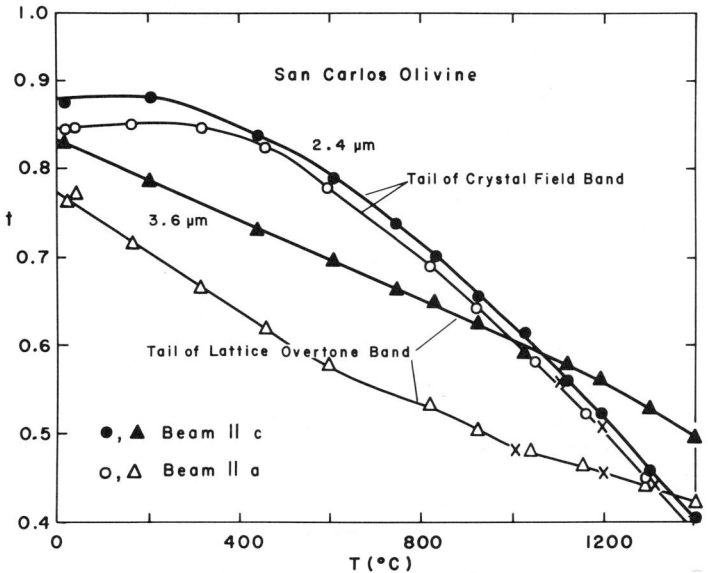

FIG. 13. Transmittance of olivine at 2.4 and 3.6 μm as a function of temperature.[33] Values with the beam parallel to the $a$ and $c$ axes are given. Measurement reversibility measured for the $c$-axis orientation between 1000°C and 1400°C is indicated by the crosses. (Copyright 1979 by the American Geophysical Union.)

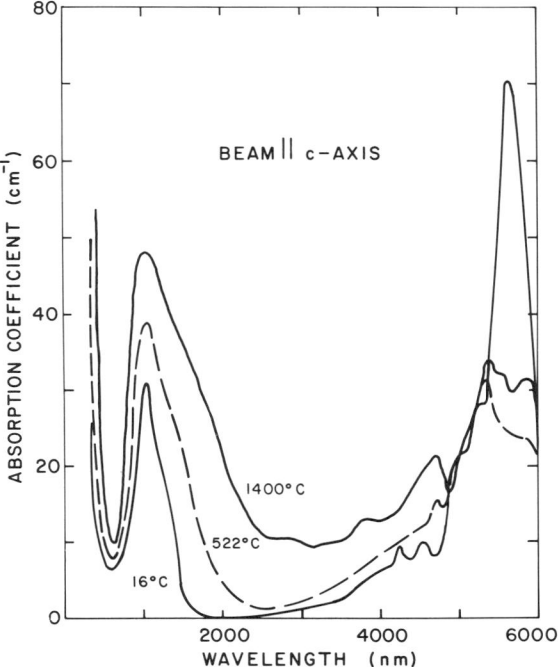

FIG. 14. Absorption spectra in olivine at several temperatures with beam along the $c$-axis.[33] (Copyright 1979 by the American Geophysical Union.)

calculated from the Fresnel formula

$$R(\lambda, T) = \left[\frac{n(\lambda, T) - 1}{n(\lambda, T) + 1}\right]^2 \tag{23}$$

Athough relative values of $t$ can readily be obtained, calculations of $\alpha$ require that $t$ be known with some accuracy. Hence, it is best to first precisely measure $t(\lambda_r, 300\text{ K})$ at a reference wavelength $\lambda_r$ with the sample outside the furnace and free of light obstructions. It is then possible to normalize subsequent high-temperature values $t(\lambda_r, T)$ to the precise value of $t(\lambda_r, 300\text{ K})$. Finally, spectral scans of $t(\lambda, T)$ can be normalized to the $t(\lambda_r, T)$. Figure 13 shows examples for the orthorhombic mineral olivine of $t(\lambda_r, T)$ for two reference wavelengths and two crystal directions; Fig. 14 shows the resulting normalized absorption spectra for one beam direction. As can be seen from Eqs. (19) and (21), $k_R$ depends strongly on $\alpha$ in its smallest (most transparent) regime so normalization is very important. In the single-beam apparatus of Fig. 1, it is necessary to scan twice over a wavelength range to obtain $I$ and then $I_0$.[31-33] Although with a double-beam apparatus[34] the division $I/I_0$

can be performed electronically, it is still necessary to make a baseline scan without a sample present in order to correct for the fact that the $I$ and $I_0$ beams are not optically identical.

The light chopper ahead of the furnace in Fig. 12 is essential for distinguishing the signal beam from the blackbody radiation emitted by the sample. It is also essential to have the monochromator follow the furnace to prevent broadband light and heat from the furnace from saturating the detector and causing it to become nonlinear. If the samples are not stable in air, as may be the case when they contain transition metal ions, then it is necessary to control oxygen partial pressure in the furnace; otherwise, the sample can change color and have a drastically altered absorption spectrum.[34] It is ordinarily not sufficient to use an "inert" atmosphere such as argon because even at high purity it can have oxygen pressures of $10^{-6}$ atm, well outside the stability of transparent iron-bearing minerals such as olivine.[35]

In the apparatus of Fig. 12, the detectors were a photomultiplier with S-1

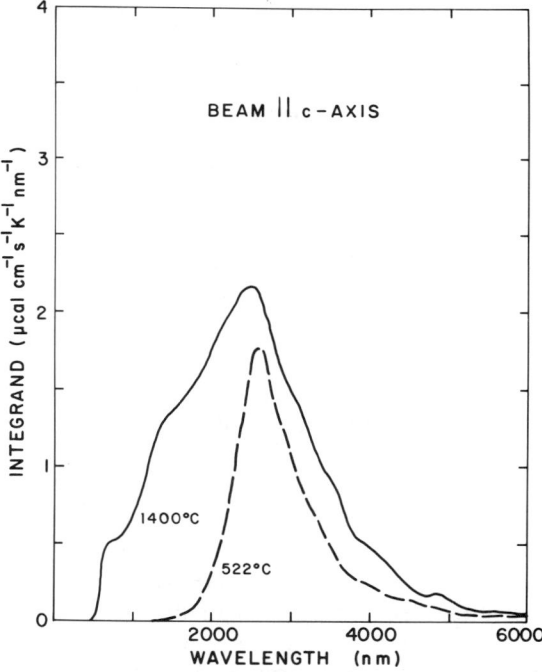

FIG. 15. Contribution to radiative heat conductivity per unit wavelength, illustrating an infrared "window" at several temperatures for beam parallel to the $c$-axis.[33] (Copyright 1979 by the American Geophysical Union.)

photocathode for the visible to near infrared (NIR) (1100 nm) and a cooled indium antimonide photovoltaic cell for the NIR to 5500 nm. Single-crystal sapphire, preferably oriented with its c-axis parallel to the furnace axis, is a reasonable material for furnace windows to stand high temperatures over the passband of the detectors. It is transparent in the 5-μm range of silica lattice overtone bands. A workable container for melted specimens can be made by sandwiching them (in their glassy phase) between two sapphire plates held apart by ceramic cement. There is negligible diffusion between the silica melts and the sapphire during the time scale of the experiments.[36]

## 2.2. Methods of Calculation

It is possible to put Eq. (19) into a form that is more useful for calculation:

$$k_R = \frac{8\pi k^4 T^3}{3c^2 h^3} \int_0^\infty l_x \left[ \frac{e^x x^4 n_x^2}{(e^x - 1)^2} + \frac{2x^3 n_x T}{e^x - 1} \frac{\partial n_x}{\partial T} \right] dx \quad (24)$$

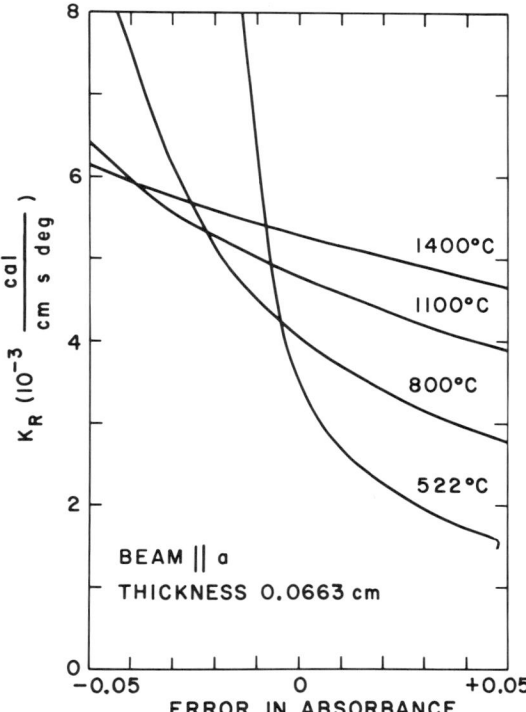

FIG. 16. Effect on $k_R$ of different choices of baseline absorbance.[33] (Copyright 1979 by the American Geophysical Union.)

where $x = h\nu/k_B T$. Figure 15 shows the result for the absorption data of Fig. 14; the area under the curve gives the value of $k_R$ at the temperature of measurement.

Effects of uncertainties in $n(\lambda, T)$ on calculated $k_R$ have been evaluated for olivine by Shankland et al.,[33] who estimated that this effect was of the order of $\pm 10\%$. As mentioned above, the greatest uncertainty in $k_R$ comes when $\alpha(\lambda, T)$ is very small, as occurs in transparent materials at low temperature. Figure 16 illustrates the effect of small errors in absorbance for an olivine specimen.

We note that Eq. (24) should yield a relatively high value for $k_R$. It treats

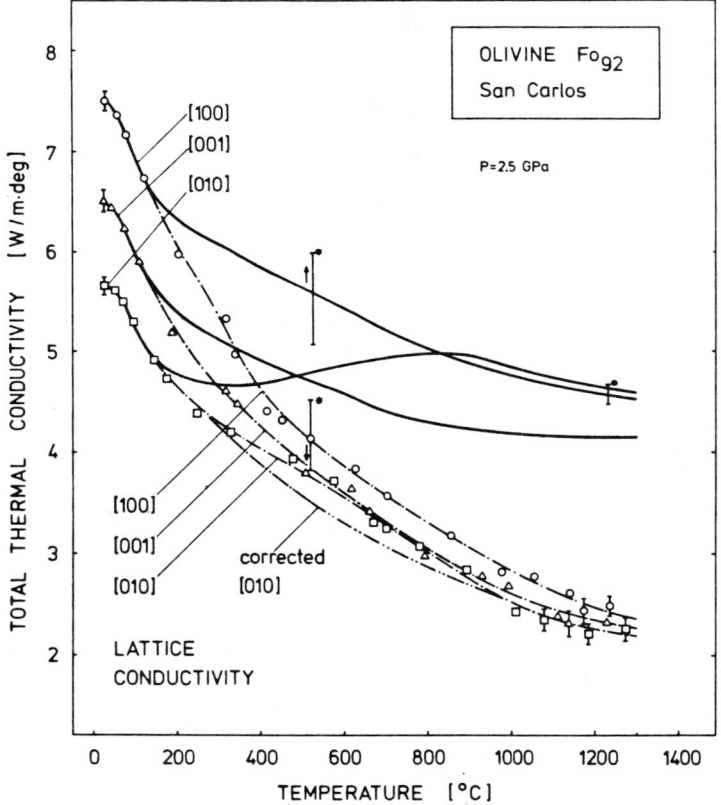

FIG. 17. Thermal conductivity vs. temperature as calculated for large olivine crystals or systems of oriented crystals.[39] Lattice thermal conductivities (dot-dashed lines) are determined from experiments on San Carlos samples using literature optical absorption data. Radiative thermal conductivity was added to lattice conductivity to give total conductivity (solid lines). The error bars of the solid curves are related to the radiative conductivity.

the material as a large single crystal of pure material. Another difficulty is treating scattering, which is difficult to evaluate in laboratory specimens because it requires measurements of intensity as a function of angular distance from the center of the light beam.

For the most part, minerals have too much optical structure to be regarded as "graybodies" whose extinction coefficient is independent of wavelength. However, when scattering overwhelms absorption, as in extremely fine-grained or vesicular material,[37] it is possible to approximate $l_\nu$ as $l$, which is independent of wavelength. Neglecting dispersion and thermal dependences of $n$ in Eq. (19) produces the graybody equation

$$k_R = (16/3)n^2ST^3/\langle\varepsilon(T)\rangle \tag{25}$$

where $S$ is the Stefan–Boltzmann constant and $\langle\varepsilon(T)\rangle$ the thermally weighted opacity from Eq. (19). However, the strong temperature increase of $\varepsilon(\lambda, T)$ with temperature in minerals with transition metal ions[31] means that the $T^3$ dependence is hard to realize. On the other hand, a material like obsidian has a virtually temperature-independent spectrum, and its radiative transfer increases very rapidly from initially low values.[38]

There are a large number of measurements in the literature where $k$ has been observed to rise steeply at the onset of radiative transfer. This is particularly true for measurements in high-pressure cells, where samples are necessarily small. Schärmeli[39] has numerically treated the problem of evaluating radiative corrections using optical absorption measurements in order to obtain $k$, $k_L$, and $k_R$ at 2.5 GPa pressure. His results for $k$ and $k_L$ of olivine are shown in Fig. 17.

### 2.3. Method of J. F. Schatz

Schatz and Simmons[40,41] described a modification of the Angstrom method that allows simultaneous determinations of both lattice and radiative thermal conductivities at high temperature. When $l_\nu \lesssim$ the sample length, part of the signal in an oscillatory heating experiment can be attributed to a radiative component that passes more rapidly across the sample than does the lattice component.

In this method a measure of $\langle\varepsilon(T)\rangle$ is obtained by using an optical detector to measure the phase shift of a temperature wave propagating through the sample. The lattice thermal conductivity $k_L$ of the sample can be derived from the corresponding thermal diffusivity $\kappa_L$, which is also derived from analysis of the temperature wave.

Figure 18 shows a schematic diagram of the experimental setup. A disk-shaped sample is held vertically at the center of the furnace tube, which in turn is placed in a silicon carbide furnace to maintain the sample at high

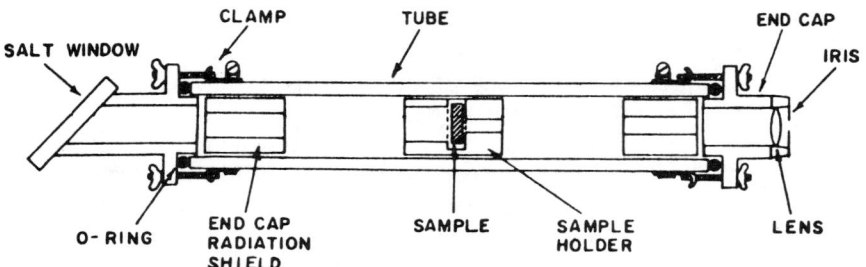

Fig. 18. Furnace tube containing a sample for obtaining both lattice vibrational and radiative components of thermal conductivity using remote heat input and an optical sensor.[40]

temperature. The furnace tube is filled by dry 95% $N_2$–5% He gas with its pressure reduced to 1–5 torr to retard oxidation of the sample.

One side of the sample is heated periodically at angular frequency $\omega$ by a carbon dioxide gas laser beam that is transmitted through the optical window of the vacuum furnace. The laser beam of 10.6 μm wavelength has a diameter of 2 cm and is operated in the power range 10–20 W. It is turned on and off with period 10–30 sec to generate a temperature wave in the sample. The variation of the sample temperature is detected by a lead sulfide infrared detector from the other side of the sample. Because samples such as silicate minerals are partially transparent, the infrared detector not only "sees" the nearest surface of the sample but also "sees into" the sample's interior. The total radiation from the back surface of the sample is the integrated sum of infrared emission that is radiated from depth $x$ within the sample and that is attenuated exponentially on its way to the sample surface

$$R_\lambda(t) = \int_0^L \alpha_\lambda I_{b\lambda}(x, t) e^{-\varepsilon_\lambda(L-x)} \, dx \qquad (26)$$

where $\alpha_\lambda$, $I_{b\lambda}$, and $\varepsilon_\lambda$ are, respectively, wavelength-dependent absorption coefficient, blackbody emission power, and extinction coefficient, and $L$ is sample thickness. The total radiation received by the thermal detector is

$$R(t) = \int_0^\infty S_\lambda R_\lambda(t) \, d\lambda = (\text{const}) \int_0^L T^4 e^{-\varepsilon(L-x)} \, dx \qquad (27)$$

where $S_\lambda$ is the spectral sensitivity of the detector and $T$ is sample temperature; $T$ consists of a constant $T_0$ and a variable component $T(x, t)$ that can be kept small compared to $T_0$,

$$T^4 = T_0^4 + 4T_0^3 T(x, t) + \cdots \qquad (28)$$

The component $T(x, t)$, a sinusoidal temperature wave with its amplitude decaying with distance $x$, is obtained by solving the thermal conduction equation. The solution is similar to that of the modified Angstrom method, but it satisfies the boundary conditions on both surfaces of the sample, where radiation is an important factor in maintaining the heat balance. It is

$$T(x, t) = Ue^{-\beta x + i(\omega t + \delta)} + Ve^{\beta x + i(\omega t + \gamma)} \qquad (29)$$

where $U$, $V$, $\delta$, $\gamma$, and $\beta$ are functions of $\varepsilon$, $k_L$, and $\omega$.
The integration (27) is performed with (26) and (28) to yield

$$R(t) = R_0 e^{i\omega t} e^{i\phi} \qquad (30)$$

Phase measurements of $R(t)$ at two or more distinct values of angular frequency $\omega$ can be used to obtain $k_L$ and $\bar{\varepsilon}$, because it can be shown that the phase lag $\phi$ of the output signal depends only on $k_L$ and $\bar{\varepsilon}$.

At each freqency $\omega$, Schatz took an average of at least five waveforms to determine the phase lag $\phi$ and its statistical error. Instead of solving the equation for $k_L$ and $\bar{\varepsilon}$, the range of these parameters that predicts a theoretical $\phi$ within the confidence limits of the measured $\phi$ was sought by computer. Independent information on the sample's refractive index, density, and specific heat is necessary to calculate $k_R$ and the total thermal conductivity $k$ from $k_L$ and $\bar{\varepsilon}$.

This analysis is difficult, particularly if the detector sensitivity does not span the transparent "window" region of the specimen, but results agree to within 20% with the results obtained from optical absorption for olivine.[33]

## Acknowledgments

This work was supported by the Division of Basic Energy Sciences of the Department of Energy through contract W-7405-ENG-36 with the University of California at the Los Alamos National Laboratory.

## References

1. A. E. Benfield, *Proc. R. Soc. London, Ser. A* **173**, 428 (1939).
2. S. Uyeda, T. Yukutake, and I. Tanaoka, *Tokyo Daigaku Jishin Kenkyusho Iho* **36**, 251 (1958).
3. A. E. Beck, *J. Sci. Instrum.* **34**, 186 (1957).
4. J. H. Sass, A. H. Lachenbruch, R. J. Munroe, G. W. Green, and T. H. Moses, *J. Geophys. Res.* **76**, 6376 (1971); J. H. Sass, A. H. Lachenbruch, and R. J. Munroe, *J. Geophys. Res.* **76**, 3391 (1971).
5. Y. S. Touloukian, R. W. Powell, C. Y. Ho, and P. G. Klemens, "Thermophysical Properties of Matter," Vol. 1, p. 589. IFI/Plenum, New York, 1970.
6. E. H. Ratcliffe, *Br. J. Appl. Phys.* **10**, 22 (1959).
7. J. B. Walsh and E. R. Decker, *J. Geophys. Res.* **71**, 3053 (1966).
8. K. Horai and S. Uyeda, *Tokyo Daigaku Jishin Kenkyusho Iho* **38**, 99 (1960).
9. J. H. Sass, A. H. Lachenbruch, and R. J. Munroe, *J. Geophys. Res.* **76**, 3391 (1971).
10. K. Kawada, *Tokyo Daigaku Jishin Kenkyusho Iho* **42**, 631 (1964).
11. F. Birch, *Bull. Geol. Soc. Am.* **61**, 567 (1950).

12. F. Birch and H. Clark, *Am. J. Sci.* **238**, 529 (1940).
13. H. Kanamori, N. Fujii, and N. Mizutani, *J. Geophys. Res.* **73**, 595 (1968).
14. H. Kanamori, H. Mizutani, and N. Fujii, *J. Phys. Earth.* **17**, 43 (1969).
15. K. Horai, *J. Geophys. Res.* **86**, 7163 (1981).
16. K. Yamagawa, *J. Coll. Sci. Imp. Univ. Tokyo* **2**, 263 (1889).
17. R. P. von Herzen and A. E. Maxwell, *J. Geophys. Res.* **64**, 1557 (1959).
18. J. C. Jaeger, *J. Geophys. Res.* **39**, 708 (1958).
19. R. W. Scott, J. A. Fountain, and E. West, *Rev. Sci. Instrum.* **44**, 1058 (1973).
20. R. B. Merrill, *NASA Tech. Note* **NASA TN D-5063** (1969).
21. P. W. Bridgman, "The Physics of High Pressure," p. 307. Bell, London, 1949.
22. P. W. Bridgman, *Am. J. Sci.* **7**, 81 (1924).
23. H. Fujisawa, N. Fujii, H. Mizutani, H. Kanamori, and S. Akimoto, *J. Geophys. Res.* **73**, 4727 (1968).
24. S. Rosseland, *in* "Handbuch der Astrophysik" (G. Eberhard, A. Kohlschutter, and H. Luddendorff, eds.), Vol. 3/1, pp. 452–455. Springer-Verlag, Berlin, 1930.
25. R. Gardon, *J. Am. Ceram. Soc.* **44**, 305 (1961).
26. S. P. Clark, *Trans. Am. Geophys. Union* **38**, 931 (1957).
27. H. C. Hottel and A. F. Serofim, "Radiative Transfer." McGraw-Hill, New York, 1967.
28. R. Siegel and J. R. Howell, "Thermal Radiation Heat Transfer." McGraw-Hill, New York, 1972.
29. U. Nitsan, *EOS Trans. Am. Geophys. Union* **57**, 1005 (1976).
30. G. D. Pitt and D. C. Tozer, *Phys. Earth Planet. Int.* **2**, 189 (1970).
31. J. R. Aronson, L. H. Bellotti, S. W. Eckroad, A. G. Emalie, R. K. McConnell, and P. C. von Thuna, *J. Geophys. Res.* **75**, 3443 (1970).
32. T. A. Weaver, The opacities of transparent materials as a function of temperature and wavelength and their geophysical implications. Ph.D. Thesis, Dep. Geophys. Sci., Univ. of Chicago, Chicago, Illinois, 1973.
33. T. J. Shankland, U. Nitsan, and A. G. Duba, *J. Geophys. Res.* **84**, 1603 (1979).
34. Y. Fukao, H. Mizutani, and S. Uyeda, *Phys. Earth Planet. Int.* **1**, 57 (1968).
35. U. Nitsan, *J. Geophys. Res.* **79**, 706 (1974).
36. C. W. Gable and T. J. Shankland, *J. Geophys. Res.* **89**, 7106 (1984).
37. G. H. Schärmeli, *Proc. AIRAPT Conf., 6th* (K. D. Timmerhauf and M. S. Barber, eds.), Vol. 2, p. 60. Plenum, New York, 1979.
38. J. Stein, T. J. Shankland, and U. Nitsan, *J. Geophys. Res.* **86**, 3684 (1981).
39. G. H. Schärmeli, *in* "High-Pressure Researches in Geoscience" (W. Schreyer, ed.), pp. 349–373. Schweizerbart, Stuttgart, 1982.
40. J. F. Schatz and G. Simmons, *J. Appl. Phys.* **43**, 2586 (1972).
41. J. F. Schatz and G. Simmons, *J. Geophys. Res.* **77**, 6966 (1972).

# 9. EXPERIMENTAL METHODS IN ROCK MAGNETISM AND PALEOMAGNETISM

## M. Fuller

Department of Geological Sciences
University of California
Santa Barbara, California 93106

## 1. Introduction

The 30 or so years of modern rock magnetism and paleomagnetism have coincided with a period of remarkable development in scientific instrumentation. Workers in rock magnetism and paleomagnetism have been able to take advantage of these developments, so that a typical modern laboratory is a far cry from those in which much of the classical work was done. No longer does one squint at a lamp and scale system which invariably drifts at high sensitivity; instead, one measures the weak remanent magnetization of rocks by using SQUID magnetometers with response times of a second. Moreover, on-line computers give real-time plots of the results. The improved techniques not only make paleomagnetism more convenient, but also permit a new scale of paleomagnetic endeavor. Present studies routinely involve larger numbers of samples and more thorough analysis than was feasible 20 years ago. Rock magnetism has also been able to take advantage of the new techniques, so that the individual fine particles can now be measured and we no longer have to rely on measurements of assemblages.

One of the earliest reviews of instrumentation of rock magnetism and paleomagnetism is in Nagata's classical text "Rock Magnetism" (Nagata, 1961). Other more recent texts, such as Irving (1964), Stacey and Banerjee (1974), Merrill and McElhinny (1983), and O'Reilly (1984), have not been much concerned with instrumentation. In fact, the principal reviews all stem from the Newcastle University group. The first such review was entitled "Methods in Paleomagnetism" and was edited by Collinson, Creer, and Runcorn. It was the Proceedings of a NATO Advanced Study Institute held at Newcastle in 1967. Two particularly useful reviews have subsequently come from Collinson. The first was published in *Reviews of Geophysics and Space Physics* (Collinson, 1975). The second is a recently published book entitled "Methods in Rock Magnetism and Paleomagnetism" (Collinson, 1983). This review is indeed so comprehensive that it has strongly influenced the writing of the present chapter. There seems little point in repeating details given in Collinson's book, so a rather more general discussion has been given of areas which are covered extensively by Collinson, while areas not emphasized have been developed in this chapter. For example, the SQUID magnetometers are not covered in much detail by him and so are discussed at greater length here. Again, Collinson does not consider phase-sensitive detectors, analog-to-digital (A/D) converters, multiplexers, and interfacing magnetometers to computers. Accordingly, a section is devoted to those matters here. Even in the black box era in which we live, some understanding of such matters seems appropriate. The relative emphasis in the various sections in this chapter has therefore been influenced by the Collinson book. However, this is intended to serve as a comprehensive review of the instrumental techniques of rock magnetism and paleomagnetism, at least to the extent of introducing the various possibilities.

In describing the experimental methods of rock magnetism and paleomagnetism, the question of an ideal order of coverage arises because of the overlap of techniques in the two areas. In this chapter, the methods of paleomagnetism are described first and followed by those of rock magnetism. Thus the collection and orientation of samples for paleomagnetism are considered first. After that the various magnetometers and techniques of analysis of paleomagnetism follow. The methods of rock magnetism are then described within the framework of a scheme of identification and characterization of the magnetic phases in rocks. Finally, various special techniques are described, such as those used in the observation of the effect of stress on magnetization.

Over the years a number of techniques have been developed in our laboratory, not all of which have been published. Several of these are described here. They have involved the work of many people and credit is assigned as faithfully as memory permits. In the 1960s, a robust vibrating sample magnetometer was built and applied to various observations in rock magnetism and paleomagnetism with Professor Kobayashi. Later at Pittsburgh applications were developed for one of the first SQUID rock magnetometers used in paleomagnetism and rock magnetism. The instrument was designed and built by Dr. W. S. Goree, then of Develco Co. Professor V. S. Schmidt played an important role in the early days of the use of that instrument. However, both at the University of Pittsburgh and later at the University of California at Santa Barbara, the key person in our group who has been responsible for instrument design and development has been J. R. Dunn. M. Stein has also made innovative contributions to a number of instruments during our time at Santa Barbara.

It is hoped that this chapter will prove a useful introduction to the experimental methods of rock magnetism and paleomagnetism. Established workers in the field will perhaps find some new approaches to old problems, but essentially the chapter is written as an introduction for the general reader and for those beginning work in the subject.

## 2. Fundamental Concepts in Rock Magnetism and Paleomagnetism

One suspects that, to an outsider, the physical basis of rock magnetism and paleomagnetism is reasonably obscure. The magnetization vector **M**, with which the subject is primarily concerned, is little discussed in elementary physics texts, remanent magnetism gets a few sentences in historical inventories, and the distinction between magnetic moment and intensity of magnetization is rarely mentioned. Moreover, the results have appeared in rival sets of units. It therefore seems appropriate to include a brief review of the rudimentary magnetism and electromagnetism which will be utilized. The sophisticated reader, to whom this is all second nature, can safely skip the section.

### 2.1. The Magnetic Vectors **B**, **H**, and **M**

The magnetization vector **M** is but one of three magnetic vectors **B**, **H**, and **M**. The **H** field is the magnetizing field due to electric current sources, while the **B** field is the magnetic flux density, or magnetic induction, produced in a medium by the **H** field. Magnetostatics can be developed in direct analogy with electrostatic fields. The magnetic poles take the part of the electrostatic positive and negative charges and a magnetic scalar potential ($\phi_m$) is used in the same way as the scalar potential of electrostatics ($\phi$). The problem with this approach is that there is no evidence for the existence of such magnetic poles. It is therefore more satisfactory to develop a theory of magnetic fields in terms of current sources, since they do give rise to magnetic fields. A magnetic vector potential **A** is then introduced such that

$$\mathbf{E} = -\nabla\phi - \partial\mathbf{A}/\partial t$$

and since

$$\nabla\times\mathbf{E} = -\partial\mathbf{B}/\partial t$$

$$\mathbf{B} = \nabla\times\mathbf{A}$$

This is the approach taken in SI units, the system of units in which modern physics is taught. However, much of the literature of paleomagnetism is in the older CGSEMU system. Confusion over units is a sufficiently serious cause of misunderstanding in geomagnetism that both systems are developed here in an attempt to clarify the matter.

2.1.1. *Magnetizing H Fields of Electrical Currents.* Let us begin by considering the magnetic fields due to electric current sources. The magnetic field around a wire along which a current is flowing was investigated experimentally by Oersted and later by Biot and Savart. It was analysed by Laplace. The expression is

$$d\mathbf{H} = \mathbf{I}\,d\mathbf{l}\sin\theta/4\pi r^2 \text{ A m}^{-1}$$

where $\mathbf{I}$ is the current, $d\mathbf{l}$ the length of wire, and $r$ the distance from the wire. In the CGSEMU system the expression is

$$d\mathbf{H} = \mathbf{I}\,d\mathbf{l}\sin\theta/r^2 \text{ oe}$$

The $\mathbf{H}$ field has units of ampere-turns per meter in the SI system and oersteds in the CGSEMU system. The expressions differ in the two systems because the SI system is rationalized, which introduces a factor of $1/4\pi$ in this expression. One can, of course, write these expressions in terms of the vector potential. However, for purposes of clarifying the units, the present form is preferred.

The magnetic field of a current loop is readily derived from that due to the infinitesimal current element by integrating around the circumference of the loop. The value of $\sin\theta$ is 1, since we are interested in the axial field at the center of the loop. Hence the final expression is

$$\mathbf{H} = \mathbf{I}/2r \text{ A m}^{-1}$$

$$\mathbf{H} = 2\pi\mathbf{I}/r \text{ oe}$$

It is then clear why the unit for magnetic field in the SI system is amperes per meter. The rationale behind the CGSEMU unit, the oersted, will be discussed below.

2.1.2. *Relationship between H and B Fields.* As a result of an $\mathbf{H}$ field, a medium acquires a $\mathbf{B}$ field or magnetic flux density. This flux density is related to the magnetizing field through the permeability of the medium ($\mu$). In free space,

$$\mathbf{B} = \mu_0\mathbf{H}$$

The permeability describes the ease with which a medium acquires magnetic flux density $\mathbf{B}$ in the presence of a magnetizing $\mathbf{H}$ field. The units of $\mathbf{B}$ are the tesla, or webers per square meter, in SI and the gauss in the CGSEMU system.

To clarify the units of $\mu_0$, note that **B** has the dimensions of flux ($\phi$) per unit area (square meter) and **H** has dimensions of current times inverse length, so that

$$[\mu_0] = [\phi\ \mathrm{m}^{-2}][\mathrm{A\ m}^{-1}]^{-1}$$

The magnetic flux $\phi$ induced by an electric current flowing in a circuit is defined in terms of the inductance of the circuit $L$, the flux around the circuit per unit current, which gives dimensionally

$$[L] = [\phi \mathrm{A}^{-1}]$$

so that

$$[\mu_0] = \left[\frac{L\ \mathrm{A\ m}^{-2}}{\mathrm{A\ m}^{-1}}\right]$$
$$= [L\ \mathrm{m}^{-1}]$$

Hence the dimensions of $\mu_0$ are inductance times inverse length, giving units of henry/meter in the SI system.

The permeability of free space is set to unity in the CGSEMU system. It therefore follows that **B** and **H** have the same dimensions in this system. Moreover, the permeability of air is sufficiently close to 1 that the two are essentially indistinguishable in air. This is the root of much of the confusion in units in electromagnetism because **B** and **H** tend to be used interchangeably in CGSEMU. The confusion is best avoided by maintaining a strict distinction between the magnetizing **H** field and the magnetic flux density or **B** field it generates. As a consequence, some of the classical units used in CGSEMU are found to be unsatisfactory. Yet these units have a long and honorable history of use and will continue to be encountered, so they cannot be ignored.

2.1.3. *Magnetic Pole Approach to Magnetostatics.* Following the development in terms of magnetic poles of the CGSEMU system, the force between two unit magnetic poles is defined to be 1 dyne at a separation of 1 cm.

$$\mathbf{F} = mm/r^2\ \text{dynes}$$

The oersted is then defined as the field in which a unit pole experiences a force of 1 dyne.

$$\mathbf{H} = \mathbf{F}/m_+\ \text{oe}$$

It is here that one encounters a fundamental conflict between the CGSEMU and SI systems because the SI system treats the response of the magnet in terms of the **B** field.

As we noted above, a magnetic scalar potential is defined by analogy with electrostatic theory. The **H** field can then be obtained from the magnetic scalar potential by taking its negative gradient.

$$H_x = -\partial \phi_m/\partial x$$

The **H** field in a particular direction is obtained by taking the partial derivative in the appropriate direction.

The magnetic scalar potential can be used to calculate the magnetizing **H** field of a dipole. This is equivalent to the **H** field of a bar magnet at a distance from the magnet which is large compared with its dimensions. It is the dipole approximation to the field of a magnet. One first calculates the superposed potentials of the **H** fields of the two poles. Then one differentiates to get the radial and tangential components of the **H** field.

$$H_r = 2\mathbf{M} \cos \theta/r^3$$

$$H_\theta = \mathbf{M} \sin \theta/r^3$$

In these expressions, the magnetic moment **M** is introduced. The magnetic moment in the CGSEMU system is the product of the pole strength $m$ and the length of the magnet.

To help visualize the **H** field around the dipole, lines of force are frequently drawn. In Fig. 1, they are illustrated with the familiar iron filings experiment. They are to be thought of as having a tension along them and repelling each other. By convention, they are drawn from north, or positive, poles to south, or negative, poles. These lines of force were first introduced by Michael Faraday and are extremely helpful in visualizing both **H** and **B** fields.

The alignment of a compass is the fundamental response of a magnet to a magnetic field (Fig. 2). To understand why the needle aligns with the **H** field in terms of the pole approach, note that each pole experiences a force which tends to accelerate it. The forces on the two poles are equal in magnitude and

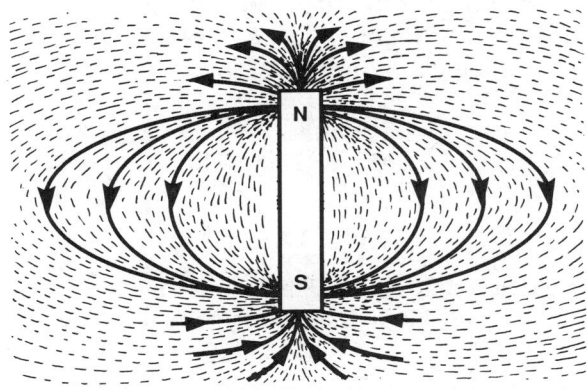

FIG. 1. Lines of force around a bar magnet.

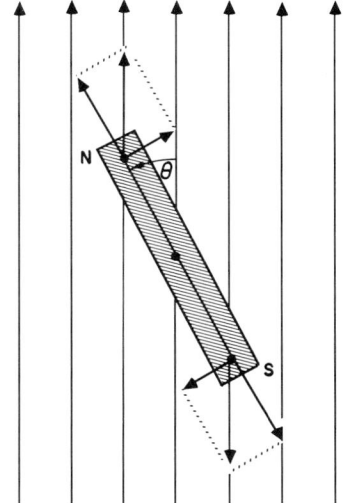

FIG. 2. Alignment of the compass needle.

opposite in sign. The net effect is that a compass needle experiences a rotational torque of $MH \sin \theta$, as illustrated in Fig. 2. This torque aligns the needle parallel to the **H** field lines.

A magnet, by virtue of its degree of alignment to **H**-field lines, has potential energy in that magnetic field. This energy is equal to the work done in rotating the magnet from the position of zero potential energy to the orientation of interest. Conventionally the zero potential energy position is taken to be perpendicular to the field lines. The work done $dw$ in rotating through an angle $d\theta$ is the product of the torque and the angle through which it turns, so that

$$dw = MH \sin \theta \, d\theta$$

$$E = \int_{\pi/2}^{\theta} MH \sin \theta \, dw$$

$$= -MH \cos \theta$$

Thus the magnetic potential energy is $-\mathbf{MH}$ when the magnet is parallel to the field and **MH** when it antiparallel.

Although magnets experience rotational torques in homogeneous **H** fields, it is evident from everyday experience that magnets also experience accelerating forces in **H** fields. These accelerating forces are experienced when the **H** field is inhomogeneous. They arise because the two poles of the magnet experience forces of different magnitude in the inhomogeneous field. The forces on the two poles are of opposite sign, but the magnitudes are different so that there is a net force on the magnet. It is for this reason that magnetic balances, separators, and a wide variety of other magnetic devices work.

2.1.4. *Equivalence of Dipole and Current Loop as Sources of* **H** *Fields.* The axial **H** field of a current loop was shown to be a function of the radius of the loop and the current flowing in the loop.

$$\mathbf{H} = I/2r \text{ A m}^{-1}$$

$$\mathbf{H} = 2\pi I/r \text{ oe}$$

The axial **H** field of the dipole was shown to be a function of **M**, the magnetic moment

$$\mathbf{H} = 2\mathbf{M}/r^3 \text{ oe}$$

To this must be introduced the same factor of $1/4\pi$ to convert to the SI expression due to the rationalization of these units. Hence in SI the dipole **H** field is

$$\mathbf{H} = \mathbf{M}/2\pi r^3$$

It is then evident that in either system the two **H** fields are equivalent if the dipole moment is replaced by the product of the current and the area of the coil for the loop.

$$\mathbf{M}_L = \pi r^2 \mathbf{I}$$

Hence, magnetic dipole sources can always be replaced by current loops and the **H** fields generated cannot be distinguished. In fact, Ampere suggested long ago that microscopic current loops are the fundamental sources of magnetism.

The analogy between a current loop and a dipole can be extended to the equivalence of the torque which each experiences in a magnetic field. The same approach can be used to show that the accelerating force experienced by a dipole, or the equivalent current loop, in an inhomogeneous magnetic field is also the same.

2.1.5. *Magnetic Induction—the Faraday Law.* Electric currents give rise to magnetic fields, and magnetic fields, when they change, give rise to electric fields. The relationship is defined by the Faraday law, which states that the electric motive force (EMF) induced in an electric circuit is proportional to the negative rate of change of flux linked to the circuit. Note that the flux linkage may change due to either a change in **B** or in the area enclosed by the circuit.

$$\mathcal{E} = -d\mathbf{B}/dt$$

From the form of the Faraday law, the magnetic flux is seen to have dimensions of volt seconds. In the SI system the unit is the weber—the flux

9. ROCK MAGNETISM AND PALEOMAGNETISM METHODS

which when cut in 1 second gives rise to an EMF of 1 volt. Magnetic flux density, or **B**, thus has units of webers per square meter. The CGSEMU system has the maxwell as the unit of flux.

2.1.6. The Three Magnetic Vectors **B**, **H**, and **M** in Materials. Magnetic materials exhibit a magnetization **M** in the presence of a magnetizing field **H**. Note that this magnetization vector **M** is to be distinguished from the magnetic moment. The magnetization is defined as the magnetic moment per unit volume. To use the same symbol for each is to invite confusion. However, to change either involves the loss of familiar expressions. As a compromise, $\mathbf{M}_0$ will be used in this chapter where confusion might otherwise arise. Thus we write

$$\mathbf{M} = \mathbf{M}_0/\text{vol}$$

as a definition of magnetization. The SI unit is Amperes per meter and the CGSEMU the gauss.

The ease with which magnetization is acquired is determined by the susceptibility $k$, and we write

$$\mathbf{M} = k\mathbf{H}$$

In the SI units $k$ is dimensionless; **M** and **H** are measured in the same units of Amperes per meter. Thus in SI the relationship between the three vectors is

$$\mathbf{B} = \mu_0(\mathbf{H} + \mathbf{M})$$

There is then a magnetic flux density due to the magnetization. The total flux density consists of the part due to the **H** field and the part due to the magnetizable material. A detailed analysis of this relationship is given in Halliday and Resnick (1960). The expression can be rearranged to give

$$\mu = \mu_0(1 + \mathbf{M}/\mathbf{H})$$
$$= \mu_0(1 + k)$$
$$= \mu_0 \mu_r$$

The factor $(1 + k)$ is called the relative permeability. Like $k$, it is dimensionless. The product $\mu_0 \mu_r$ is termed the absolute permeability and has the same dimensions as $\mu_0$. The dimensions of $\mu_0$ are, as discussed above, henry/meter. Its absolute value is fixed by the experimentally determinable force between two wires carrying current. Thus in SI, **H** and **M** have the same dimensions and **B** is related to them via $\mu_0$.

The relationship between **B**, **H**, and **M** in the CGSEMU system is necessarily different from that in SI because **B** and **H** are dimensionally the same, as the result of setting $\mu_0$ to unity in CGSEMU system. The relationship between the three vectors is generally explained by considering the relationship in pill- and needle-shaped cavities in a magnetic material (Chapman and

TABLE I. Units in Magnetism[a]

| Property | SI | CGSEMU |
|---|---|---|
| Magnetic field, $H$ | A m$^{-1}$ | $= 1.25 \times 10^{-2}$ oe $= 4\pi \times 10^{-3}$ oe |
| Magnetic flux density, $B$ | tesla | $= 10^4$ gauss |
| Magnetic moment, $M_{(0)}$ | A m$^2$ | $= 10^3$ gauss cm$^3$ |
| Magnetization, $M$ | | |
| (mass) | A m$^2$ kg$^{-1}$ | $=$ gauss cm$^3$ g$^{-1}$ |
| (vol) | A m$^{-1}$ | $= 10^{-3}$ gauss |
| Susceptibility, | | |
| k (vol) | — | $= 0.0796$ gauss oe$^{-1}$ |
| | | $= 1/4\pi$ gauss oe$^{-1}$ |
| $\chi$ (mass) | m$^3$ kg$^{-1}$ | $= 79.6$ gauss cm$^3$ oe$^{-1}$ g$^{-1}$ |
| | | $= 1/4\pi \times 10^{-3}$ gauss cm$^3$ oe$^{-1}$ g$^{-1}$ |

[a] Note that although the name gauss appears in the CGSEMU system for the magnetic flux density $B$ and for units related to the magnetization $M$, this usage obscures a difference between these units. Since in the CGSEMU system

$$B = \mu_0 H + 4\pi M$$

the $B$ gauss is related to the $M$ gauss such that 1 $B$ gauss = $4\pi$ $M$ gauss. In an attempt to clarify this, it was suggested by Collinson et al. (1967) that the name $J$. gauss be used for the magnetization-related Gauss. The $J$ comes from the usual CGSEMU symbol for magnetization. Unfortunately, this suggestion has not been widely used. Note also that the ease of the conversion of gauss to tesla, compared with oersted to Amperes per meter, has led to the demise of the use of the $H$ field in SI by paleomagnetists. Thus the geomagnetic field and the fields used in AF demagnetization, or in high-field DC experiments, are usually described in tesla, millitesla, or microtesla. The geomagnetic field becomes not 0.5 oe, but 50 microtesla, and AF demagnetization fields of hundreds of oersteds become tens of milliteslas. A gamma is then a nanotesla. All this may offend the purist who wishes to use $H$ fields, but purists will probably fall by the wayside as usual, and I suspect we will talk about the $B$ field and not the $H$ field. In a similar way the conversion listed for magnetic moment and derived quantities, such as magnetization per unit volume and per unit mass, is preferred to the more cumbersome

$$\text{weber m} = 1/4\pi \times 10^{-10} \text{ gauss cm}^3$$

Bartels, 1940). The total flux density consists of two parts, the effect of the $H$ field and of the magnetized material. The result is

$$\mathbf{B} = \mu_0 \mathbf{H} + 4\pi \mathbf{M}$$

$$\mu = \mu_0 + 4\pi \mathbf{M}/\mathbf{H}$$

$$= \mu_0 + 4\pi k$$

Conversions for commonly used units are given in Table I.

## 2.2. Physics of Magnetism

The origin of magnetism lies in the orbital motion and spin of the electron. The orbital motion of the electrically charged electron about the nucleus constitutes an elementary current loop with a magnetic moment of magnitude $0.927 \times 10^{-23}$ A m² ($0.927 \times 10^{-20}$ gauss cm³). This is the Bohr magneton ($\mu_B$), the elementary magnetic moment. The moment due to the spin of the electron is the same, both being determined by the quantum of angular momentum. An atom contains many electrons orbiting the nucleus, so an immediate distinction arises. Either the spin and orbital contributions of the various electrons are self-compensating, giving zero sum, or there may be only partial self-cancellation, so that the atom has a net magnetic moment.

2.2.1. Types of Magnetic Order. Diamagnetic atoms have zero net moment in the absence of a field. However, when a magnetic field is introduced the individual electron orbits respond to the change of flux of magnetic field in accordance with the Faraday law and give rise to a moment opposed to the applied field. Hence, in the presence of a positive **H** field, they exhibit a negative magnetization

$$\mathbf{M} = -k\mathbf{H}$$

Thus susceptibility is negative. It is also small, being of the order of $10^{-5}$ in SI ($10^{-6}$ gauss oe$^{-1}$). When the field is removed a diamagnetic material reverts to its zero net moment state. Quartz is an example of a diamagnetic mineral.

Unlike diamagnets, other elements and compounds have a net atomic moment because of imbalance of the various electron contributions. This imbalance arises due to the particular way in which the electron shells are filled to give the various atoms. This is discussed in elementary chemistry texts. Among the various atoms which do have net moments, two fundamentally different types of magnetic behavior are found.

In paramagnetic materials the individual atoms do not interact magnetically and their elementary moments are not preferentially aligned in the absence of an external field. However, paramagnets have positive susceptibility due to the alignment of the moments of individual atoms or molecules by an applied $H$ field. This alignment is opposed by the randomizing effect of thermal energy. The classical theory of paramagnetism describes the magnetization acquired in the presence of a field in terms of the Langevin function $L$ operating on the ratio of the magnetostatic energy aligning the moments to the randomizing thermal energy, e.g.,

$$M = N\mu L(a)$$

where

$$a = \mu H/kT$$

or

$$M = N\mu \left( \coth \frac{\mu H}{kT} - \frac{1}{\mu H/kT} \right)$$

for $a \ll 1$, $L(a) = a/3$

$$M = \frac{N\mu^2 H}{3kT}$$

where $\mu$ is the moment of the atom or molecule, $k$ the Boltzmann constant, and $T$ the absolute temperature in degrees Kelvin. It is evident that the susceptibility will have an inverse dependence on $T$. The quantum mechanical treatment yields analogous results with the Brillouin function taking the place of the Langevin function. This inverse temperature dependence of the susceptibility is the diagnostic characteristic of paramagnetism.

In contrast to diamagnetic and paramagnetic materials, ferromagnetic materials when placed in a magnetic field retain a memory of this field after the field has been removed. The behavior of an assemblage of fine particles is illustrated in Fig. 3. As the magnetic field increases, the magnetization increases to a saturation value $M_s$. On reduction and removal of the field the magnetization decreases to give the remanent magnetization $M_r$. Application of a negative field reduces the magnetization to zero. The fundamental explanation of this phenomenon can be grasped by noting two effects. The first is that, in these materials, the moments of individual atoms preferentially align parallel to each other. This is due to the exchange energy, the fundamental cause of ferromagnetism. The second effect is that there is a preferred direction of magnetization with respect to the lattice or to the shape of the grain. For convenience, let the easy axis be parallel to the long axis of the grain. These effects determine the sequence illustrated in Fig. 3, which gives a hysteresis, or a magnetic memory, of the field in the following way.

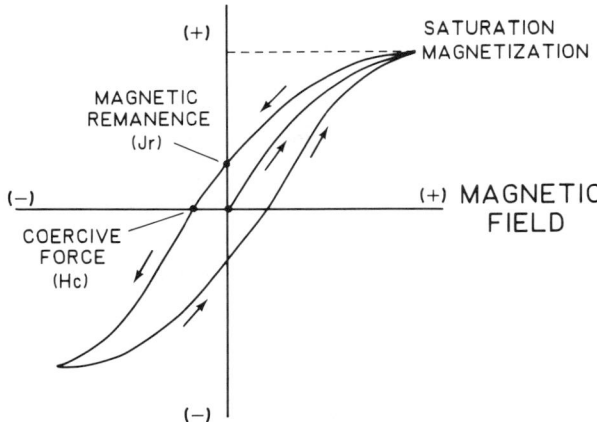

FIG. 3. Hysteresis loop.

In the saturation $H$ field all of the spins are parallel to the field. When the field is removed, the direction of magnetization of the individual grains reverts to the nearest easy direction, giving a nonzero net magnetization for the assemblage. At high temperatures first the anisotropy energy and then the interaction energy are overcome by thermal energy. The Curie point is the temperature at which the material loses its magnetic ordering due to the exchange force and reverts to paramagnetic behavior.

2.2.2. *Magnetic Phases in Rocks.* In lunar samples and meteorites, ferromagnetic Fe and various Fe-Ni compounds occur. Although terrestrial rocks do not contain ferromagnetic materials, they do contain iron oxides, which are ferrimagnetic. For the purposes of our discussion, we distinguish between ferromagnetic and ferrimagnetic states, noting that they have very different elementary orders (Fig. 4). Yet their magnetic behavior is very similar. For example, they both exhibit remanence and become paramagnetic at high temperatures. Because the ferrimagnetic minerals are opaque and frequently occur as very fine grains in rocks, they tend to be poorly studied by petrologists, being unceremoniously lumped into the category of opaques.

Oxide minerals of the $FeO-Fe_2O_3-TiO_2$ ternary system (Fig. 5). This is the dominant system of magnetic minerals. There are other magnetic minerals of interest, but the iron titanium minerals discussed here are by far the most important.

$Fe_3O_4$—magnetite (Fig. 6). Magnetite is the most important magnetic mineral to paleomagnetists and rock magnetists. It is an inverse spinel. The A and B sites form two sublattices with opposed magnetic moments. There are eight formula units in the unit cell, so the net moment should be $4\mu_B$.

The observed moment is somewhat in excess ($0.07\mu_B$), which may be due to an orbital contribution or to a departure of the structure from true inverse. The Curie point is 578°C and the saturation magnetization 476 gauss.

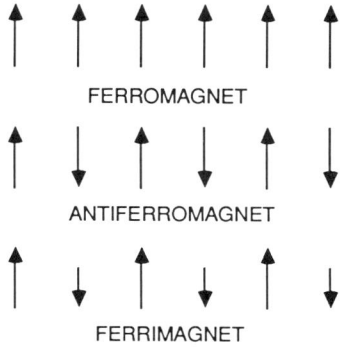

Fig. 4. Magnetic order.

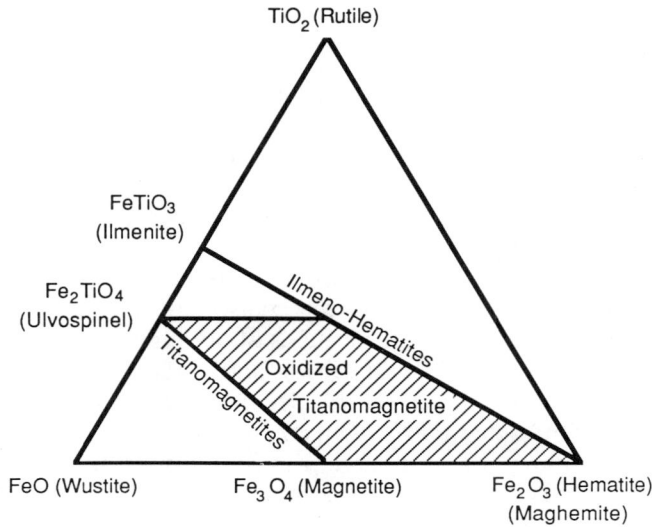

FIG. 5. Magnetic oxides of the FeO-Fe$_2$O$_3$-TiO$_2$ ternary system.

Fe$_2$TiO$_4$—ulvospinel. Ulvospinel is the other end member of the titanomagnetite series. It is antiferromagnetic with an ordering temperature below room temperature at $-153°$C. Ulvospinel shows a weak ferromagnetism below its ordering temperature. The explanation may lie in the differential quenching of the orbital moment in the A and B sites.

Fe$_3$O$_4$-Fe$_2$TiO$_4$ solid solution—the titanomagnetite solid solution series—$\beta$ series. Magnetite and ulvospinel form a completely miscible solid solution series with an inverse spinel structure at temperatures above approximately 700°C. The series is usually represented by

$$(1-x)\text{Fe}_3\text{O}_4 \cdot x\text{Fe}_2\text{TiO}_4 \qquad v \leq x \leq 1$$

The titanium substitution is as

$$2\text{Fe}^{3+} \rightleftharpoons \text{Fe}^{2+} + \text{Ti}^{4+}$$

Different structural formulas have been proposed. In the Akimoto model Ti$^{4+}$ always replaces Fe$^{3+}$ in the octahedral or B sites and Fe$^{2+}$ replaces Fe$^{3+}$ on the tetrahedral or A sites. Néel, Chevallier, and others have assumed that the Ti$^{4+}$ enters the octrahedral sites and the Fe$^{2+}$ first replaces Fe$^{3+}$ on the B sites and, only after that, the Fe$^{3+}$ on the tetrahedral sites (Nagata, 1961). The variation with $x$ of the cell size and Curie point is given in Fig. 7.

$\alpha$-Fe$_2$O$_3$—hematite. The structure of hematite is illustrated in Fig. 8a. It is essentially an antiferromagnet. However, due to spin canting, there is a weak ferromagnetism. There is also a possibility of defect ferromagnetism

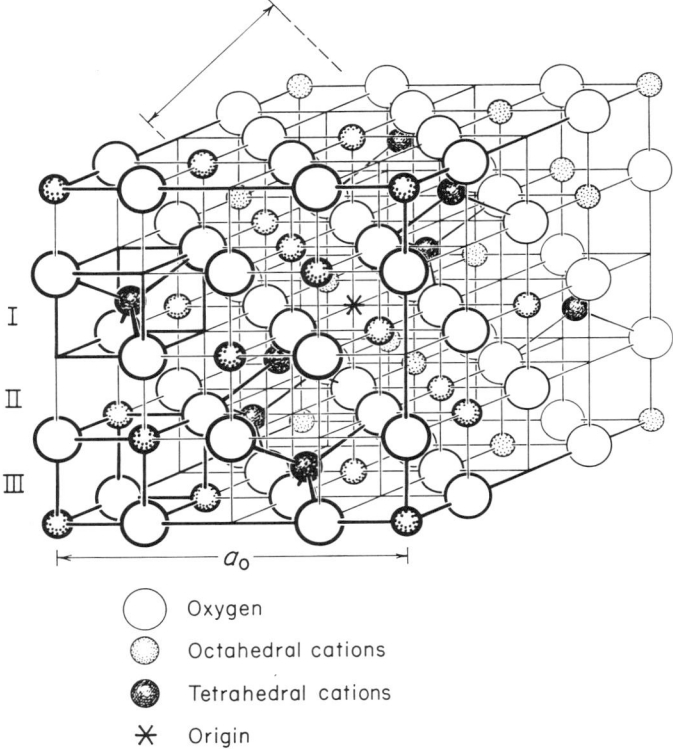

FIG. 6. Structure of magnetite. (From Lindsley, 1976.)

due to local sources within the structure. The magnetic alignment switches at the Morin transition as illustrated in Fig. 8b. It has a Curie point of 696°C and a saturation magnetization of approximately 2 gauss.

Ilmenite—$FeTiO_3$. The structure of ilmenite is similar to that of hematite except that the nonmagnetic $Ti^{4+}$ ion substitutes for alternate basal layers of the structure (Fig. 9). Ilmenite is an antiferromagnet with an ordering temperature of $-233°C$.

Hemoilmenite series—the rhombohedral series—$\alpha$ series. There is a solid solution between the two end members with miscibility above 1000°C. It can be expressed as

$$Fe^{3+}_{2-2x}Fe^{2+}Ti_xO_3.$$

The variations of cell parameters with $x$ are shown in Fig. 10.

Maghemite—$\gamma$-$Fe_2O_3$. Despite its chemical formula, maghemite is cubic and not, like hematite, rhombohedral. It has an inverse spinel structure with

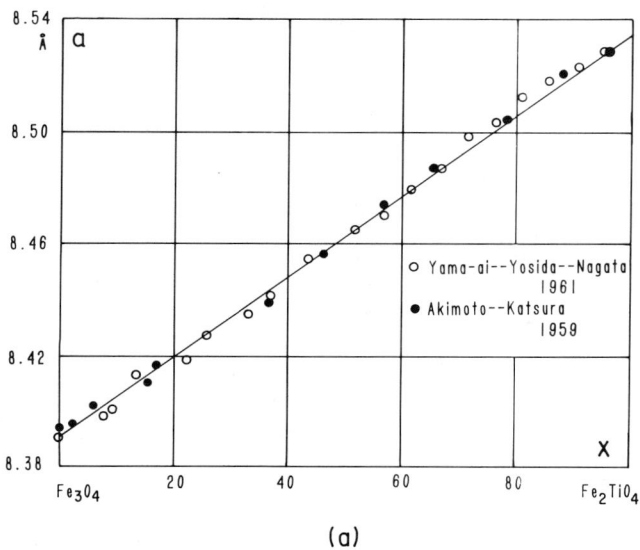

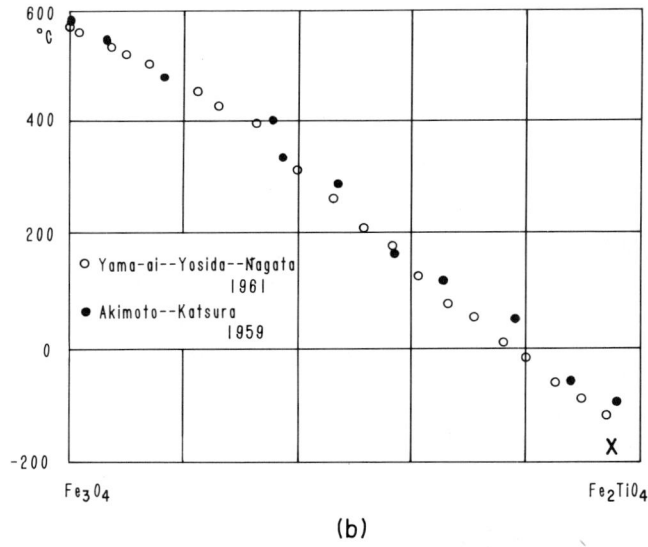

Fig. 7. Variation of (a) cell size and (b) Curie point with composition in the titanomagnetites. (From Nagata, 1961.)

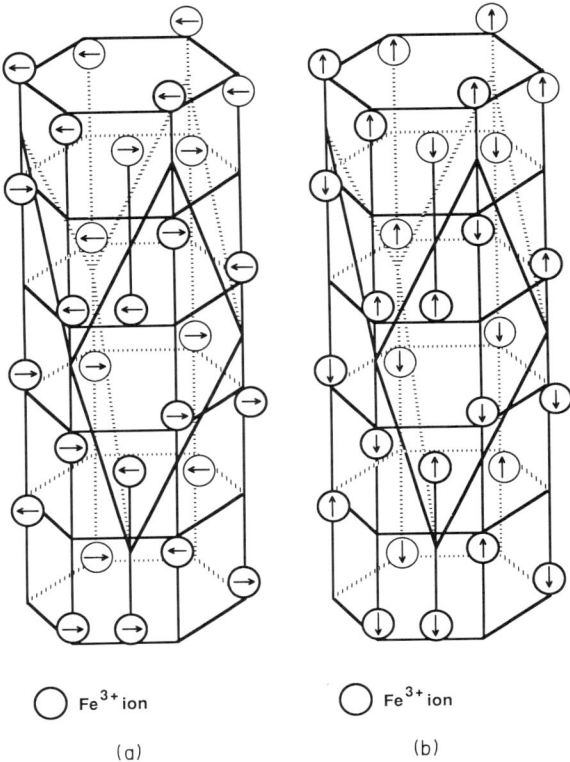

FIG. 8. Structure of hematite (a) above and (b) below the Morin transition. (From Nagata, 1961.)

one-ninth of the iron positions vacant so that it should be written

$$Fe^{3+}[Fe^{3+}_{1.67}\square_{0.33}]O_4$$

These vacancies are preferentially on the octahedral or B sites. The average magnetic moment is 1.18 $\mu_B$ per iron atom. Maghemite is metastable, inverting to hematite irreversably on heating. Temperatures for the inversion are reported between 275° and as much as 800°C. Maghemite can be stabilized by a number of cations. However, it must be noted that there is a good deal of confusion over the structure of maghemite and its magnetic properties.

Maghemite-magnetite solid solution series—$\gamma$ series. Compositions intermediate between $Fe_3O_4$ and $Fe_2O_3$ are found and oxidation may take place by the addition of oxygen or removal of metal. In the former mechanism oxygen atoms are adsorbed on the surface, reduced by locally mobile electrons, and bound to the existing structure. This causes a cation concentration gradient since the surface will be richer in $Fe^{3+}$ than $Fe^{2+}$ or $Ti^{4+}$.

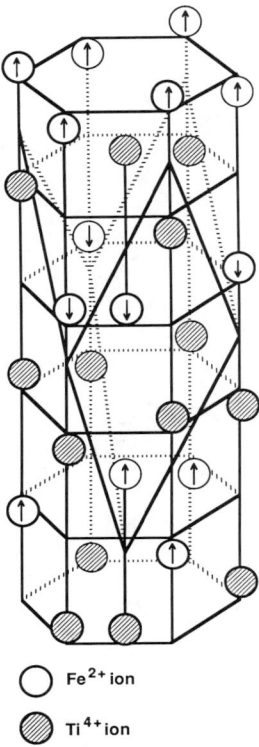

Fig. 9. Structure of ilmenite. (From Nagata, 1961.)

This gradient will drive diffusion to give a homogeneous grain. The removal of iron cations is preceded by their conversion by mobile electrons, giving Fe in atomic form, which is then no longer bound to the structure. Again a cation concentration gradient will drive diffusion to give a homogeneous grain. The oxidation parameter $Z$, which varies from zero for magnetite to one for maghemite, describes the oxidation.

Titanomaghemites. Spinels intermediate in composition between the $\alpha$ and $\beta$ joins are found. They are formed by oxidation of the $Fe_3O_4$–$Fe_2TiO_4$ at low temperatures. Presumably the oxidation process is similar to that discussed for the maghemites except that the additional oxygen framework now incorporates the Fe from the interior. For each oxygen added two $Fe^{2+}$ are oxidized to $Fe^{3+}$. The variation of Curie point, cell size, and saturation magnetization with oxidation is shown in Fig. 11.

Iron oxyhydroxides. There are a number of minerals of the hydrous ferric oxides family which are of interest magnetically.

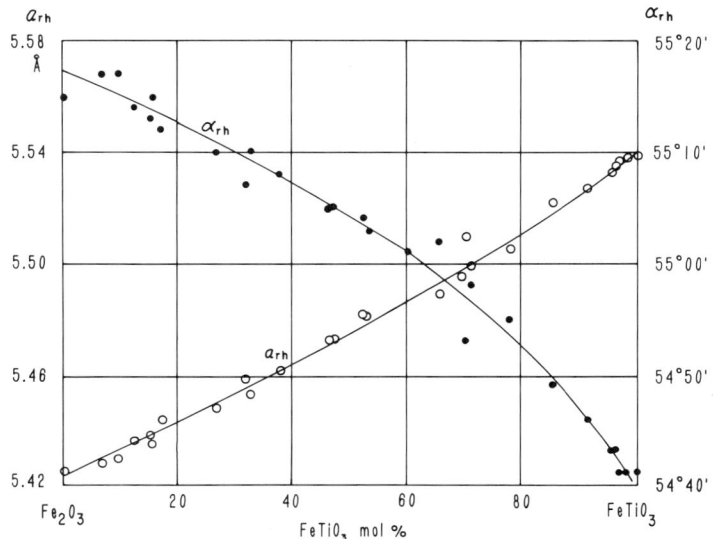

FIG. 10. Variation of cell parameters with composition in the hemoilmenites. (From Nagata, 1961.)

Goethite: $\alpha$-FeOOH. Goethite has a structure similar to that of hematite, to which it inverts between 200°C and 400°C. It is an antiferromagnet at room temperature, with a Néel point of approximately 120°C.

Lepidocrocite: $\alpha$-FeOOH. Lepidocrocite has a structure similar to maghemite, to which it inverts between 200° and 250°C.

Akaganite: $\alpha$-FeOOH. Akaganite has a tetragonal structure. It is antiferromagnetic, with a Néel point below room temperature. It dehydrates at about 200°C to form hematite.

Sulfides. The principal sulfides of interest are the troilite pyrrhotite series: $FeS-Fe_{1-x}S$.

Pyrrhotite. The minerals grouped as pyrrhotite are variable in their Fe deficiency and have magnetic properties dependent on the composition. For $0 < x < 0.09$ they are antiferromagnetic. For $0.09 < x < 0.14$ they are ferrimagnetic with an easy basal plane and a strong saturation magnetization per unit volume of 83 gauss. The Curie point is 325°C.

Troilite. Troilite is antiferromagnetic with a Néel point of 320°C. It has a hexagonal structure with alternating layers of Fe and S.

Greigite: $Fe_3S_4$. Greigite has the same crystal structure as magnetite and is strongly magnetic. However, its magnetic properties and indeed its stability field remain problematic. Skinner et al. (1964) report that it inverts on heating to between 238° and 282°C to pyrrhotite + sulfur.

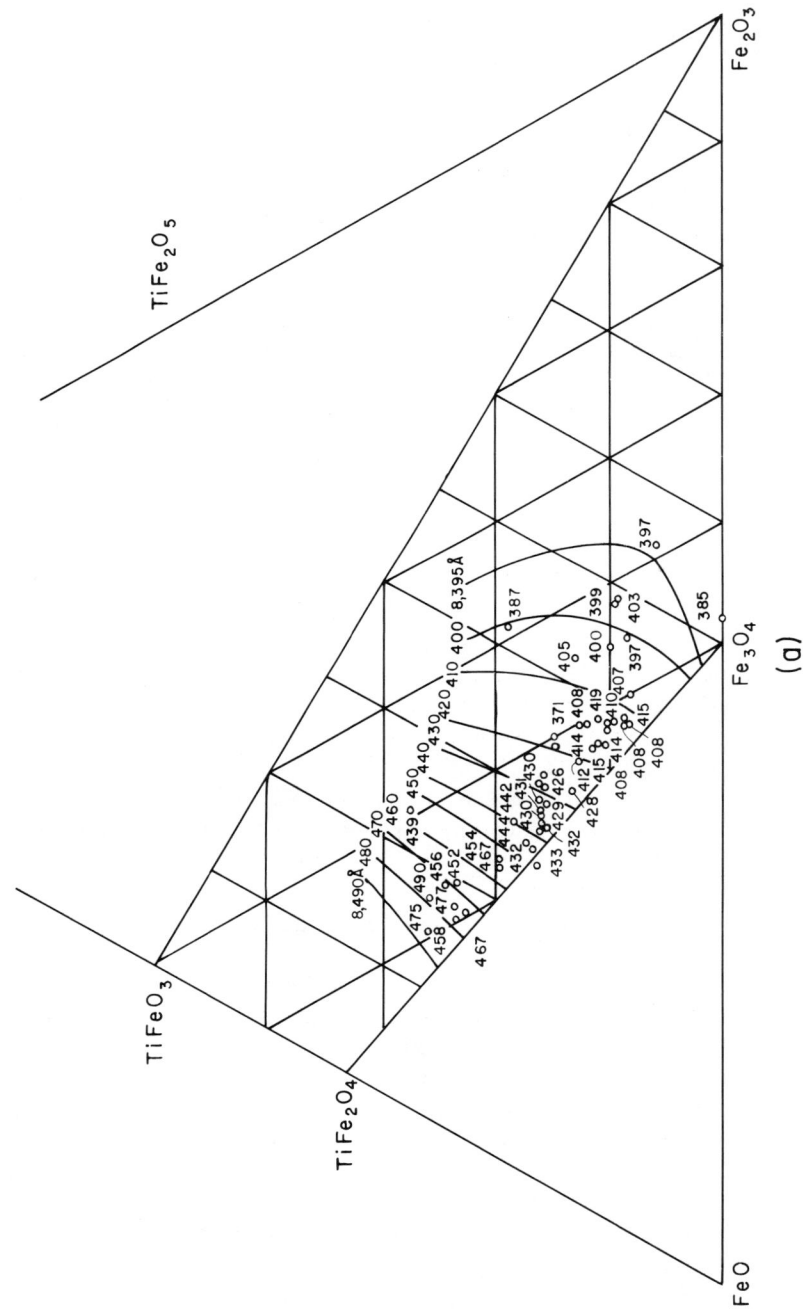

Fig. 11. Variation of (a) cell parameters, (b) saturation magnetization, and (c) Curie point in the titanomaghemites. (From Nagata, 1961.)

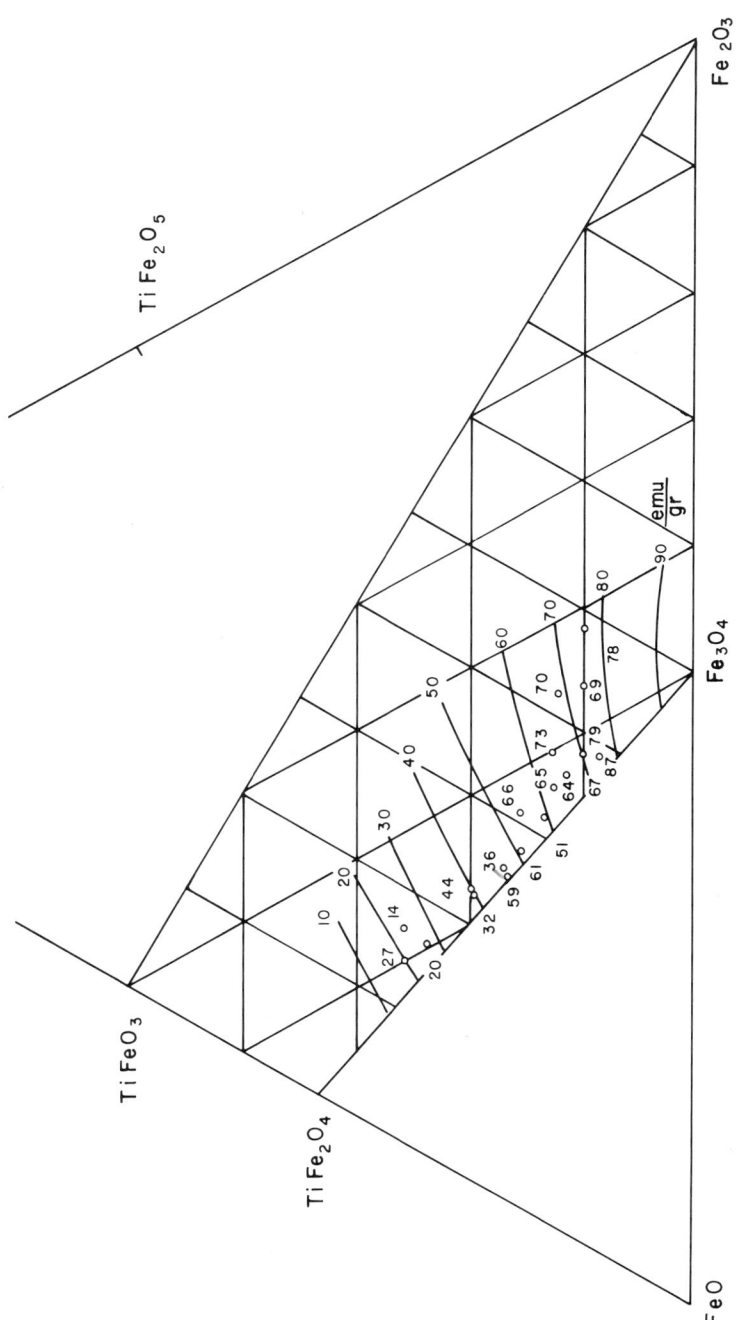

Fig. 11 —continued

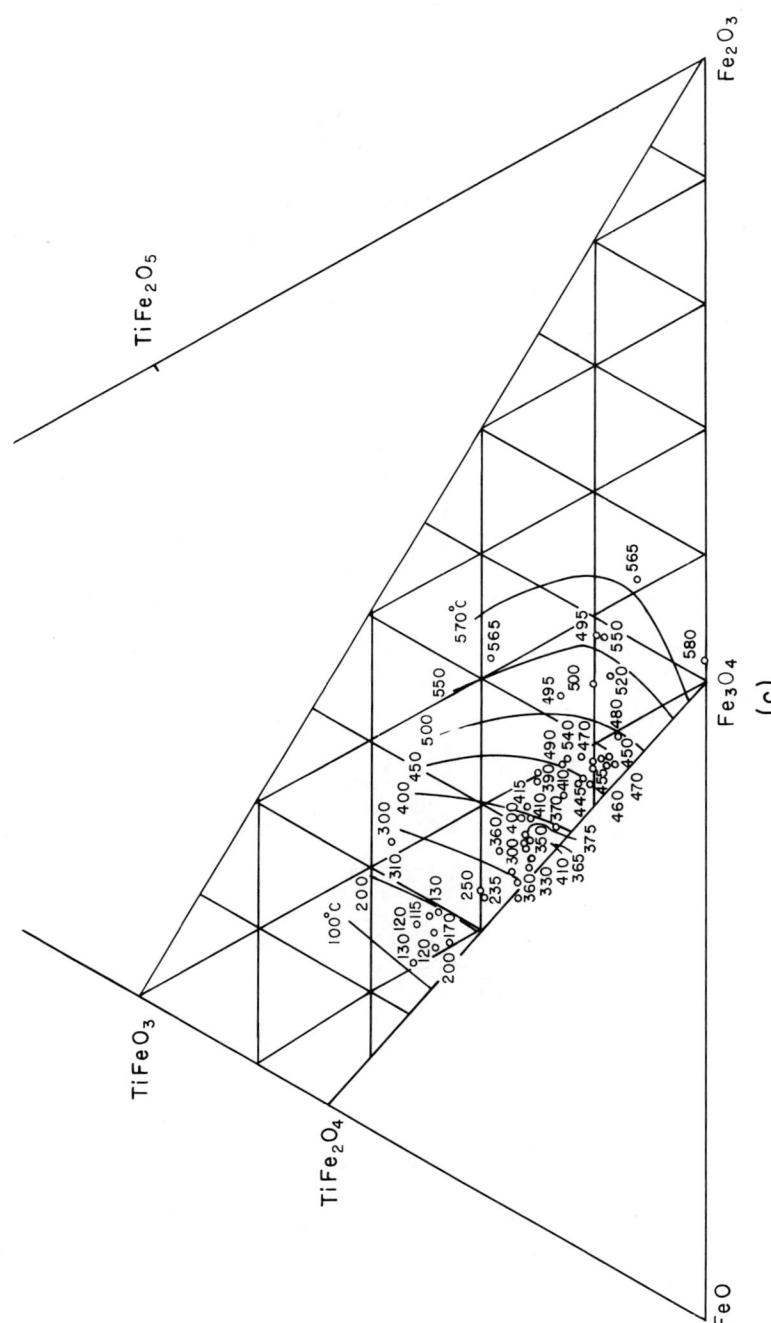

Fig. 11—continued

## 9. ROCK MAGNETISM AND PALEOMAGNETISM METHODS

Minerals that have been described as antiferromagnets are not expected to exhibit remanent magnetization. However, in antiferromagnets it is common to find defect ferromagnetism, which does indeed exhibit behavior like ferromagnetism or ferrimagnetism. It is often not clear whether this is an intrinsic feature of the lattice of the antiferromagnet, such as the spin canting in hematite, or is due to lattice defects. These lattice defects may amount to small regions of a magnetic phase in the antiferromagnet, or they may be true defects in the parent lattice not related to any known magnetic mineral phase. Such structures have not been fully elucidated so we note that certain antiferromagnets may exhibit natural remanent magnetization for one or the other of those reasons.

2.2.3. *Behavior of Magnetic Phases in Rocks.* Magnetic material in rocks exhibits a great range of hysteresis loops. An important variable which determines magnetic behavior is the grain size. Whereas an assemblage of very fine grains of magnetite might exhibit a loop as in Fig. 3, large grains have magnetically softer characteristics; that is, they are magnetized and demagnetized by smaller fields, giving much thinner hysteresis loops (Fig. 12). Small grains are magnetized homogeneously; large grains are subdivided by walls into domains of mutually opposed magnetization. The domains reduce the magnetostatic self-energy of the grain. In those grains changes in magnetization can be brought about by wall movement (Fig. 13). This is a lower-energy process than magnetization rotation, so multidomain grains are magnetized and demagnetized by weaker fields than single-domain grains.

In the hysteresis loops illustrated, three important states were noted. There is the state of saturation, at which all spins are aligned parallel with the applied field. There is the state of remanent magnetization, at which a

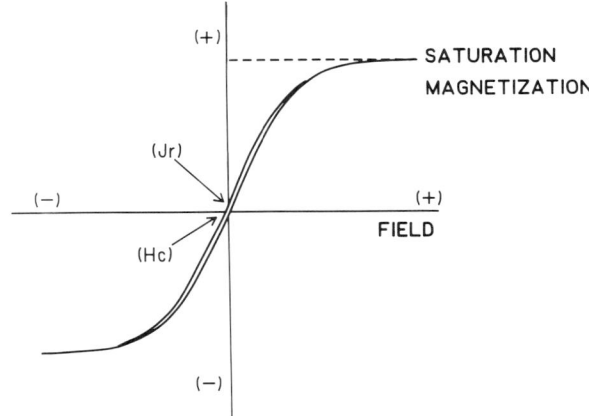

FIG. 12. Multidomain hysteresis loop.

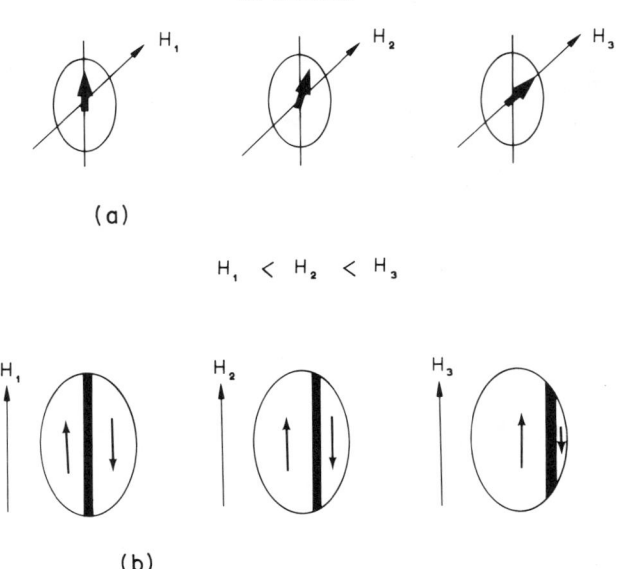

FIG. 13. Magnetization change by (a) rotation and (b) wall motion.

memory of the field is retained, although the field has been reduced to zero. Finally, there is the coercive force field, the back field which reduces the magnetization to zero. For single-domain grains, the remanent magnetization is a large fraction of saturation magnetization and the coercive force tends to be of the order of $10^2$ oe. In multidomain materials, which can change their state of magnetization by the movement of walls, coercive force is lower because wall motion is a low-energy process. Remanent magnetization tends to be a small fraction of saturation magnetization in multidomain material. In connection with the paleomagnetic record, the single-domain grains are more desirable than the large multidomain grains, whose magnetization is easily reset. It has long been something of a puzzle that the grain size of the magnetic particles in rocks is far too large for them to be single-domain according to standard theory (Kittel, 1949), yet rocks frequently exhibit magnetic behavior which has single-domain-like aspects. It has become clear that some of this behavior is due to particles which are large enough to be multidomain but small enough that they do not nucleate a wall in the state of saturation remanence. Thus pseudo-single-domain behavior, as it has been termed, may be largely controlled by wall nucleation phenomena (Halgedahl and Fuller, 1983).

If a ferromagnetic material is of a very fine grain size, say $10^2$ Å, it remains in thermal equilibrium with its environment and fails to exhibit hysteresis. It will be in thermal equilibrium with a magnetic field, but when that field is switched off the thermal energy will be sufficient to randomize the magnetization and give zero net remanent moment. The relaxation of the magnetization of the assemblage may be described by the following equation:

$$-dM/dt = M/\tau$$

where $\tau$ is a characteristic relaxation time. To establish the nature of the decrease in magnetization with time, we rearrange, integrate, and obtain the usual exponential expression

$$\int \frac{dM}{M} = -\int_0^t dt$$

$$\ln \frac{M(t)}{M(0)} = -\frac{t}{\tau}$$

$$M(t) = M(0)e^{-t/\tau}$$

If $\tau$ is very large compared with $t$, no relaxation takes place. However, if $\tau$ is smaller, the magnetization will decrease. The relaxation time is related to the height of the energy barrier which must be overcome for the magnetization to reverse from one easy direction to another and to the thermal energy available for passage over the barrier. The actual expression for $\tau$ is

$$1/\tau = f_0 \exp(-K_u V/kT)$$

where $f_0$ is a frequency factor that depends on the nature of the interaction whereby the thermal energy affects the spin alignment, $K_u$ a measure of the energy aligning the magnetization with respect to the lattice, $V$ the volume, $k$ the Boltzmann constant, $1.38 \times 10^{-16}$ erg deg$^{-1}$, and $T$ the temperature. The exponent therefore reflects the balance between the magnetic energy of alignment and thermal energy tending to disorder.

A convenient boundary between stable single-domain behavior and the superparamagnetic condition is when $K_u V \cong 25kT$ or $\tau \approx 10^2$ seconds. The term superparamagnetism (Bean, 1955) is used because the magnetic behavior is indeed like paramagnetism, but the magnetic moments involved are the moments of the whole grain, not of an individual atom or molecule. The idea of superparamagnetism is of particular importance in rock magnetism. Particles pass through this state if they grow as authigenic minerals at low temperature. Fine particles pass through the same state as they cool from high temperature in, for example, an igneous rock. Hence the remanent magnetization acquired by both of these types of paleomagnetic carriers depends on the passage from the superparamagnetic state to the stable single domain.

2.2.4. Natural Remanent Magnetization. Since the geomagnetic field is a weak field, one must ask how grains, which have coercive forces many orders of magnitude larger, manage to become magnetized in that field. By now a large number of mechanisms of magnetization have been investigated. One of the simplest accounts for the magnetization of many sediments.

Due to the geologic cycle of weathering and erosion, individual particles of magnetic minerals will eventually settle through water and be deposited as sediments. As the small grains settle through the water, they acquire a statistically important preferential alignment with the ambient field. When they reach the bottom of the lake or sea, they become part of the accumulating sediment pile and give to it a net remanent magnetization parallel to the field. In the waterlogged sediments, the grains are initially free to rotate, so the magnetic couple **M** × **B** in the earth's field will continue to align them. In this way a sediment can acquire, at the time of its deposition or soon after, a net magnetization in the direction of the geomagnetic field, This is achieved without switching of the magnetization in the individual grains, which would have required a much stronger field.

Although sediments can acquire magnetization in the way suggested, this does not explain how individual magnetic grains became magnetized in an igneous rock. The natural remanent magnetization (NRM) which igneous rocks acquire as they cool from high temperature is thermoremanent magnetization (TRM). An explanation of TRM was provided by the French theoretician Néel for single-domain particles (Néel, 1949).

The first important aspect of Néel's explanation is the observation that, with increasing temperature, the hysteresis loops of materials shrink in the manner illustrated in Fig. 14. This reveals that the coercive force required to switch the magnetization at high temperatures is smaller that at room temperature. The second aspect is the role of thermal energy in controlling the relaxation time of the magnetization of individual grains. As noted above, the magnetization of a material is constrained to be in particular orientations with respect to the lattice and it is energetically favorable for the magnetization to be parallel to an external field. If a dispersion of single-domain grains is taken out of an applied field, the magnetization of each individual grain returns to the nearest easy direction, leaving a net remanent moment which remains constant indefinitely. However, if the particles are fine enough or at a high enough temperature to be superparamagnetic, they continue to relax to zero remanent moment at a rate in accordance with their relaxation time $\tau$.

The relaxation time $\tau$ is for zero field. However, in the presence of a field, there is a splitting of the energy levels parallel and antiparallel to the applied field. The effect of this is to make the energy barrier to be passed in switching from parallel to antiparallel slightly higher than for the passage in the opposite sense (Fig. 15). Hence, if a large number of grains switch their magnetization in response to thermal activation, at any one instant there will

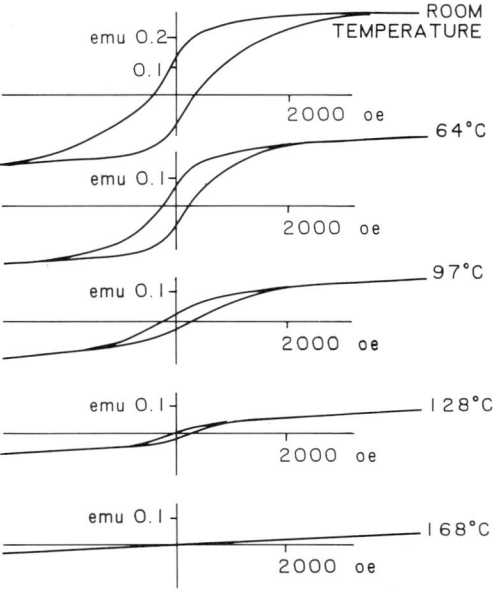

FIG. 14. Hysteresis loops of Al-substituted titanomagnetites as a function of temperature (After Ozdemir, 1979.)

## TRM AQUISITION
### (SD)

| TEMP. T | T ABOVE $T_C$ | T BETWEEN $T_C$ & $T_B$ | T BELOW $T_B$ | ROOM TEMP. |
|---|---|---|---|---|
| MAG. CURVE | 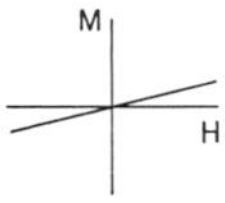 M/H | 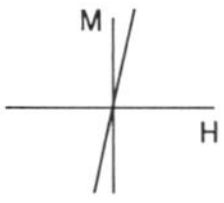 M/H | 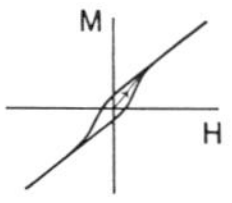 M/H | 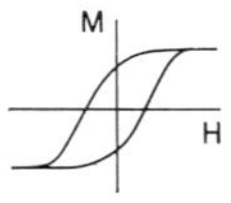 M/H |
| MAG. BEHAVIOR | PARA-MAGNETISM | SUPER PARAMAG. | STABLE SINGLE DOMAIN | |
| $H \neq 0$ | $M \neq 0$ k, SMALL | $M \neq 0$ k, LARGE | $M \neq 0$ k, MEDIUM | M INCREASES WITH FALLING T |
| $H \to 0$ | $M = 0$ | $M \cong 0$ | $M \neq 0$ | |
| MAG. RELAXATION | | $M(t) = M(o)e^{-t/\tau}$ $\tau$ SHORT ($10^{-11}$ SEC) $\tau_{(+)\to(-)} > \tau_{(-)\to(+)}$ NET M ∥ H | $\frac{1}{\tau} \propto e^{\frac{-Kuv}{kT}}$ $\tau$ LONG ($10^{12}$ y) TRM BLOCKED | TRM INCREASES WITH M |

FIG. 15. Schematic outline of single-domain thermoremanent magnetization.

be more in the parallel than in the antiparallel state. Thus, while the material is still at high temperature and able to switch magnetization direction from one easy direction to another at high frequency, there will be statistical bias in favor of the parallel state. As the rock continues to cool, the magnetization of the grains eventually can no longer switch because the relaxation time is too long. The statistical bias in favor of the field direction is then recorded as a thermoremanent magnetization of the rock. It is important to notice that it is only the magnetization of the grain which switches direction; the grain does not rotate, being firmly held in solid rock. The magnetization is acquired below the Curie point of magnetite, which is 580°C, well below the solidification temperature of the majority of igneous rocks. The Néel model is analogous to the quantum mechanical model of paramagnetism for $J = 1/2$ and gives

$$M(TRM) = NM_s \tanh[M_s(\tau_b)vH/kT_b]$$

Models for multidomain TRM are less well developed, although Néel (1955) has given an analysis in terms of the temperature variation of the critical energy terms. This was presented in the form of a computer model of TRM for a two-domain particle by Schmidt (1973).

The approach used in the single-domain TRM model can be extended to explain magnetization as a small particle grows through a superparamagnetic range of grain size to the stable single domain. Note that in the expression

TABLE II. Mechanisms of Remanent Magnetization

| Type | Mechanism |
|---|---|
| ARM—anhysteretic | Generated by decrease of alternating field in presence of DC bias field. Useful in magnetic characterization. |
| CRM—chemical | Acquired by magnetic phases formed in the presence of a magnetic field. Increase in grain size plays similar role to decrease in temperature in TRM process. |
| DRM—depositional (detrital) | Acquired by sediments as individual magnetic grains are oriented by $\mathbf{M} \cdot \mathbf{H}$ in the earth's field. |
| IRM—isothermal | Acquired by isothermal exposure to magnetic field. |
| NRM—natural | Remanence carried by rock sample in natural state. |
| PRM—pressure (Piezo-) | Magnetization brought about by changes in stress in the presence of a field. |
| SRM—shock | Magnetization brought about by passage of shock waves through material in the presence of a field. |
| TRM—thermal | Probably most fundamentally important mechanism. Acquired during field cooling. |
| VRM—viscous | Magnetization acquired due to time-dependent effects—the magnetization in a particular field increases with time due to relaxation phenomena. |

for the relaxation time for the single-domain particle, volume as well as temperature occurs in the exponent $K_u V/kT$. Hence an increase in grain size has the same effect as a decrease in temperature. These ideas were developed into models of chemical remanent magnetization by Kobayshi (1961).

It is not the purpose of this chapter to develop the theory of rock magnetism further than is necessary to understand the requirements for instrumentation. The remaining important mechanisms of magnetization are therefore given in Table II. The reader is referred to standard texts, such as Nagata (1961), Stacey and Banerjee (1974), and O'Reilly (1984), for further details.

## 3. Experimental Methods of Paleomagnetism

A paleomagnetic survey involves a number of conveniently defined steps. First, the samples must be collected and oriented at the site. Next, the NRM must be measured, which requires sensitive magnetometers to determine the weak remanent moments of the samples. Some degree of demagnetization, usually either alternating field (AF) or thermal, will almost always be necessary to eliminate magnetic contamination. Finally, the results must be presented in a meaningful manner and subjected to suitable statistical analysis.

### 3.1. Field Techniques; Collection and Orientations of Samples

Two techniques of collection have been used. Either samples are collected in the field as hand samples, from which the standard cylindrical samples are drilled on return to the laboratory, or they are drilled at the outcrop with a portable drill.

3.1.1. Collection and Orientation of Hand Samples. The collection of hand samples has a degree of historical precedence and will be described first. It is straightforward, and not too much time need be spent describing the obvious. The simplest method of orientation consists of using a Brunton compass to mark a dip and strike on a suitably smooth surface. In favorable circumstances this method is sufficient. However, frequently rocks do not have suitably flat surfaces and some improvement of technique is required, if accuracy to within ±2° is to be maintained.

Some form of tripod (Fig. 16) can be used to provide a smooth surface related to the rock's orientation via the points of contact of the legs of the tripod. The position of these points must be unambiguously marked on the rock. Indeed, a template can be used to create small holes, so that the tripod sits in a uniquely recoverable orientation. One can then determine the strike and dip of the surface on which the Brunton rests and mark it on the rock.

FIG. 16. Tripod for orientation of hand samples. The platform on which the Brunton compass rests can be rotated about two axes. The first is perpendicular to the base of the tripod and is used to bring the second axis into the horizontal. The platform itself is then made horizontal by rotation about the second axis.

## 9. ROCK MAGNETISM AND PALEOMAGNETISM METHODS

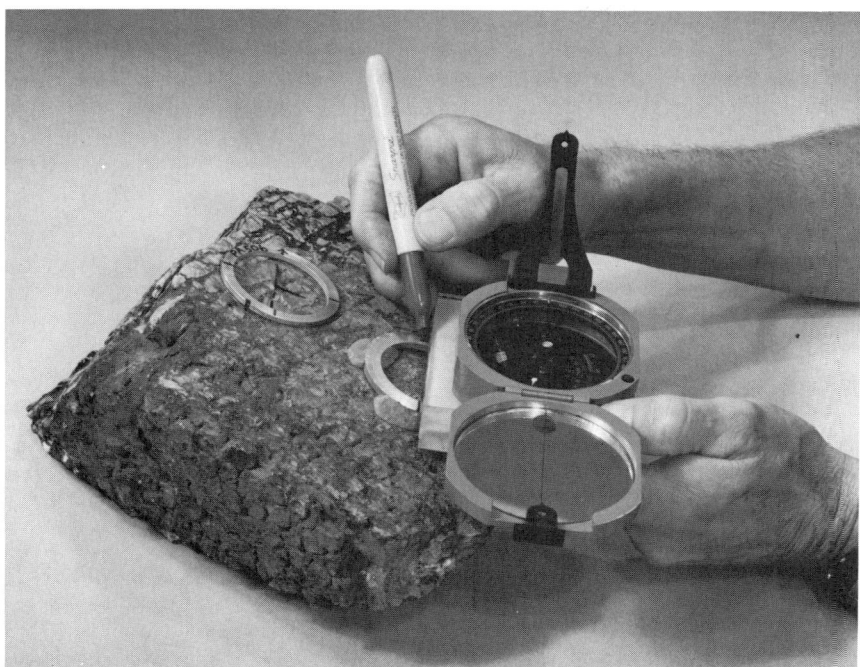

FIG. 17. Ring method for hand sample orientation.

Another approach is to glue to the rock a brass ring on which a Brunton compass can be seated (see Fig. 17). This method has been successfully used by J. R. Dunn (unpublished observations) and has the advantage of extreme simplicity. The dip and strike directions of the surface defined by the plane of the ring are then marked on the rock.

If the rocks are so strongly magnetized that they distort the geomagnetic field, then a method which does not involve using the magnetic compass near the outcrop is required. One such device shown in Fig. 18 is a modified astrocompass (Bidgood and Harland, 1959). The device has a baseplate in the form of a tripod. This is placed on the rock in the manner discussed above. The dip and strike of the base of the baseplate is obtained by rotation of the tilt table into the horizontal while noting the readings on the two dials. Azimuth is obtained with the sighting device on the top of the compass.

A second approach to avoid the effects of very strongly magnetized samples on a magnetic compass is to use a sun compass. This consists of a vertical needle whose shadow can be observed on a graduated scale around it (Fig. 19). Thus any form of tilt table can be used to obtain the orientation of the dip and strike of the plane define in the usual way by the baseplate.

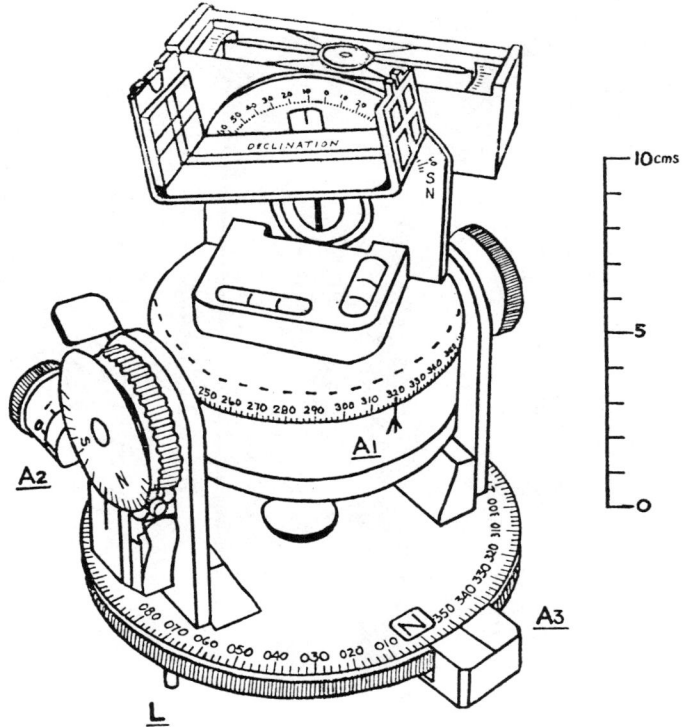

Fig. 18. Astrocompass modified for hand sample orientation. The L refers to one of the three legs. The A3 is the scale for rotation about the vertical axis to bring the A2 rotation axis into the horizontal. The A2 scale is the dip scale. The A1 rotation axis is perpendicular to the level plate and permits sighting on a distant object or reading magnetic bearings with the trough compass. The sighting arm can be elevated for convenience or as a part of surveying procedure. (After Bidgood and Harland, 1959.)

However, to obtain the azimuth once the table is horizontal, one uses knowledge of the time and hence the position of the sun to fix the observed azimuth of a reference line in terms of the azimuth of the shadow.

Following Creer and Sanver (1967), we see that two angles are required for the calculation of the sun's position relative to the horizontal and to geographic north at the site. Both of these angles are tabulated in the Air Almanac. The first is the sun's declination, the angle between the sun's direction and the horizontal plane. This is D in Fig. 20A and B. The second angle is the local hour angle, the angle between the meridians containing the site and the sun. This is H in Fig. 20A. The remaining symbols in Fig. 20 are O, the location of the site, S the intersection of the sun line on the surface of the earth, P the geographic north pole, and L the latitude of the site.

# 9. ROCK MAGNETISM AND PALEOMAGNETISM METHODS

FIG. 19. Sun compass.

Application of spherical trigonometry permits the determination of the sun's azimuth, $\gamma$ in Fig. 20C.

The great disadvantage of making hand sample collections is the large mass of material carried back to the laboratory. A second disadvantage is that on return to the laboratory the samples still have to be oriented and drilled. These are time-consuming endeavors, which can introduce addition errors. It is possible that with the increasing use of SQUID magnetometers and gradiometers irregularly shaped samples could be measured. Yet other aspects of the analysis would make handling irregularly shaped samples inconvenient. In the face of these difficulties, most people drill in the field and reserve the use of hand samples for special cases, when the rock is hard to drill or transporting the water for the drills becomes a major problem.

3.1.2. Drilling Samples in the Field. A number of different gasoline-driven portable drills have been developed. The earlier models were derived from a McCulloch chain saw. The drill was a little heavy, but had plenty of

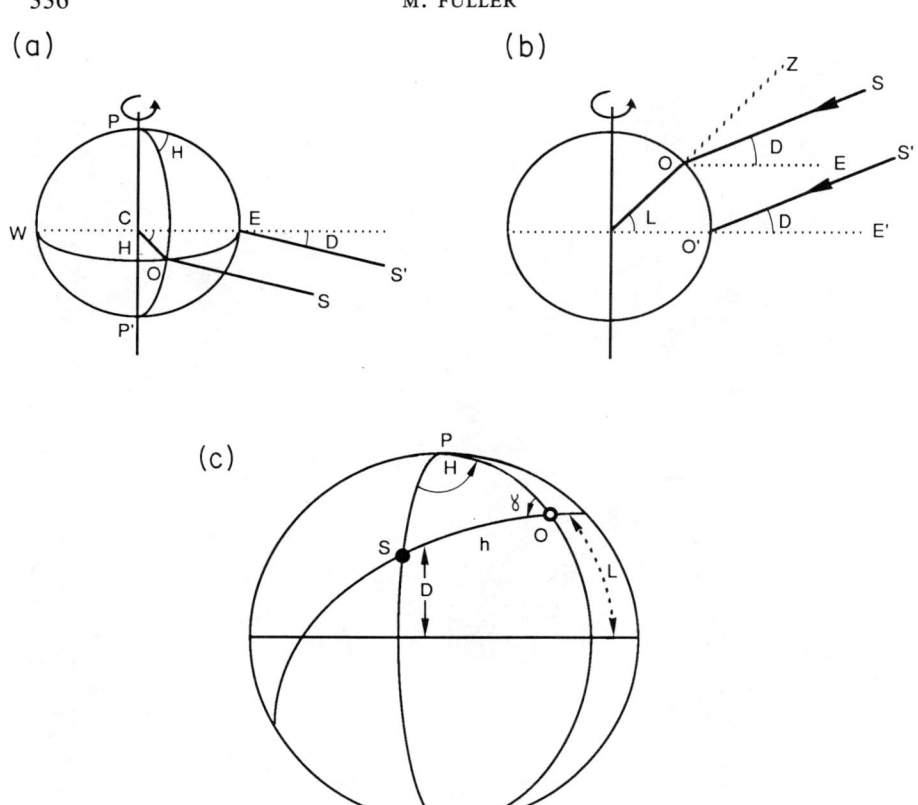

FIG. 20. Sun compass calculation of azimuth. (A) Sun's local hour angle, H, the listed Greenwich hour angle plus easterly longitude. POP' denotes the site meridian and PEP' the meridian plane containing the sun. (B) Sun's declination, the angle between the equatorial plane and the sun. (C) Stereoplot illustrating calculation of azimuth. Apply the cosine rule to POS to get $h$: $\cos H = \sin L \sin D + \cos L \cos D \cos h$. Apply the sine rule to get $\sin \gamma = -\cos D \sin H / \sin h$. The quadrant is determined by the signs of $H$, $L$, and $D$. (After Creer and Sanver, 1967.)

power. A number of commercial devices are now available based on the various lighter chain saws. These tend to be somewhat underpowered, but are light and compact (Fig. 21). All of these motors have to be modified to take a chuck capable of accepting the drill bits used for drilling the rocks (Fig. 22).

Drilling, whether carried out in the field or in the laboratory, makes use of water-cooled, diamond-impregnated drill bits. In drilling many rocks, standard drill bits whose diamonds have diameters some tenths of a millimeter are suitable. The use of soluble oil reduces wear on drill bits and time spent drilling. However, in drilling poorly indurated sedimentary rocks, the

# 9. ROCK MAGNETISM AND PALEOMAGNETISM METHODS

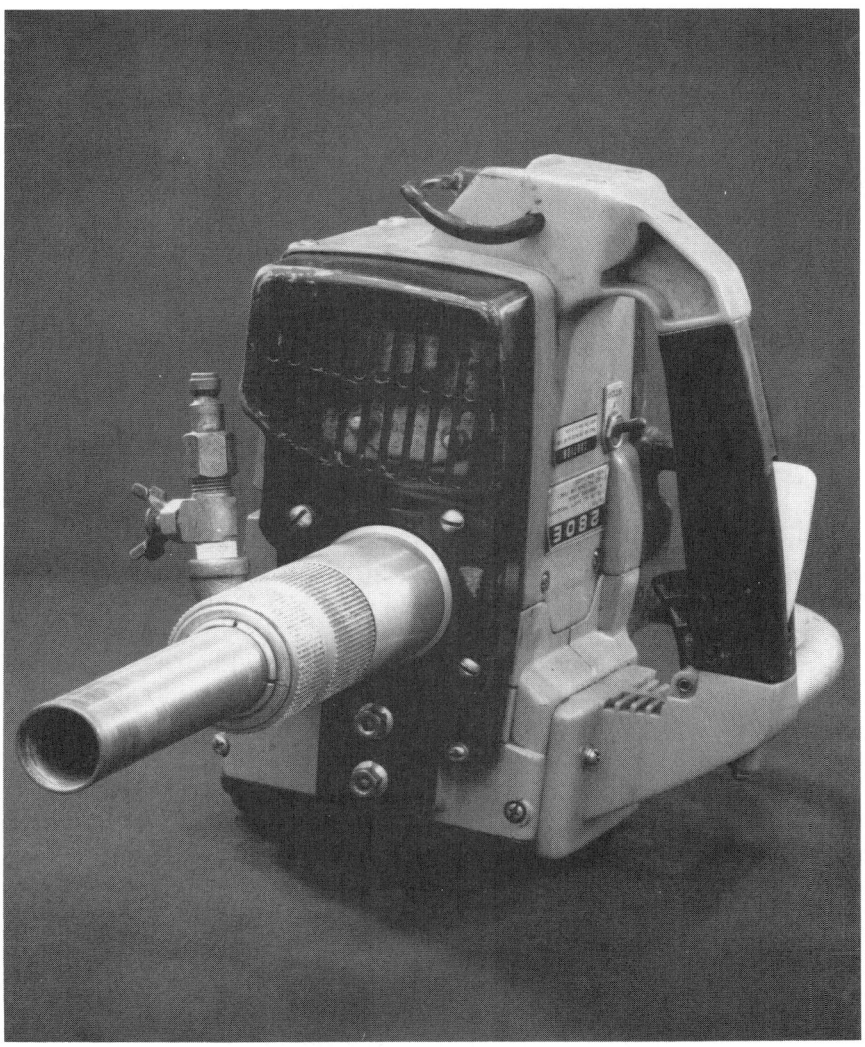

Fig. 21. Chain saw modified as rock drill.

lubricant serves little purpose and tends to bind the bit in the hole. In such material, it is better to drill with a plentiful water supply and use a modified bit, either with coarser diamonds or with a cut to allow the water to wash away fragments more easily. There remains the problem of drilling highly siliceous rocks such as cherts. Since these rocks are often badly fractured as

Fig. 22. Drill bit, chuck, and water attachment for rock drill.

well as extremely hard, it is often better to bring hand samples home and drill under the more favorable conditions of the laboratory.

3.1.3. Orientation of Samples Drilled in the Field. For samples drilled in the field, a small orienting platform mounted on a cylindrical tube fits into the annulus cut by the drill (Fig. 23). The tube is split so that a mark can be made on the rock cylinder while it is in place. The device is first rotated in the annulus and a level used so that the axis about which the platform can be tilted is oriented horizontally. This direction is then determined by a compass mounted on the platform, which is rotated to the horizontal. The inclination of the cylinder axis can now be measured either with a scale mounted on the device, as illustrated, or independently with a Brunton or an inclinometer. The strike and dip of the surface perpendiclar to the cylinder axis are recorded in geographic coordinates. Finally, the rock is scored along the split in the cylinder and broken out with a small brass screwdriver.

As noted above, the need may arise for a sun compass because the geomagnetic field can be distorted by outcrops of particularly strongly magnetic rocks. Such a sun compass can be of varying degrees of complexity, ranging from the poor man's version described by Verosub (1977) to devices available from commercial outfits as a part of complete systems for field collection.

3.1.4. Drill-Induced Remanent Magnetization. Drilling is not without its difficulties, whether it is carried out in the field or in the laboratory. One problem is the possibility of magnetic contamination. The question of contamination has been raised many times (Kuster, 1969; Burmester, 1977; Jackson and Van der Voo, 1985). Unfortunately, it has never been resolved in a satisfactory manner. In part this is because different rocks behave in different ways, making generalization difficult. Several years ago some experiments were carried out in our laboratory by R. E. Dodson (unpublished observations). The principal result was that in fields of 20 oe (2 mT) magnetization was picked up both by ocean basalt rocks dominated by fine grain carriers and by those with large multidomain particles. Demagnetization

9. ROCK MAGNETISM AND PALEOMAGNETISM METHODS 339

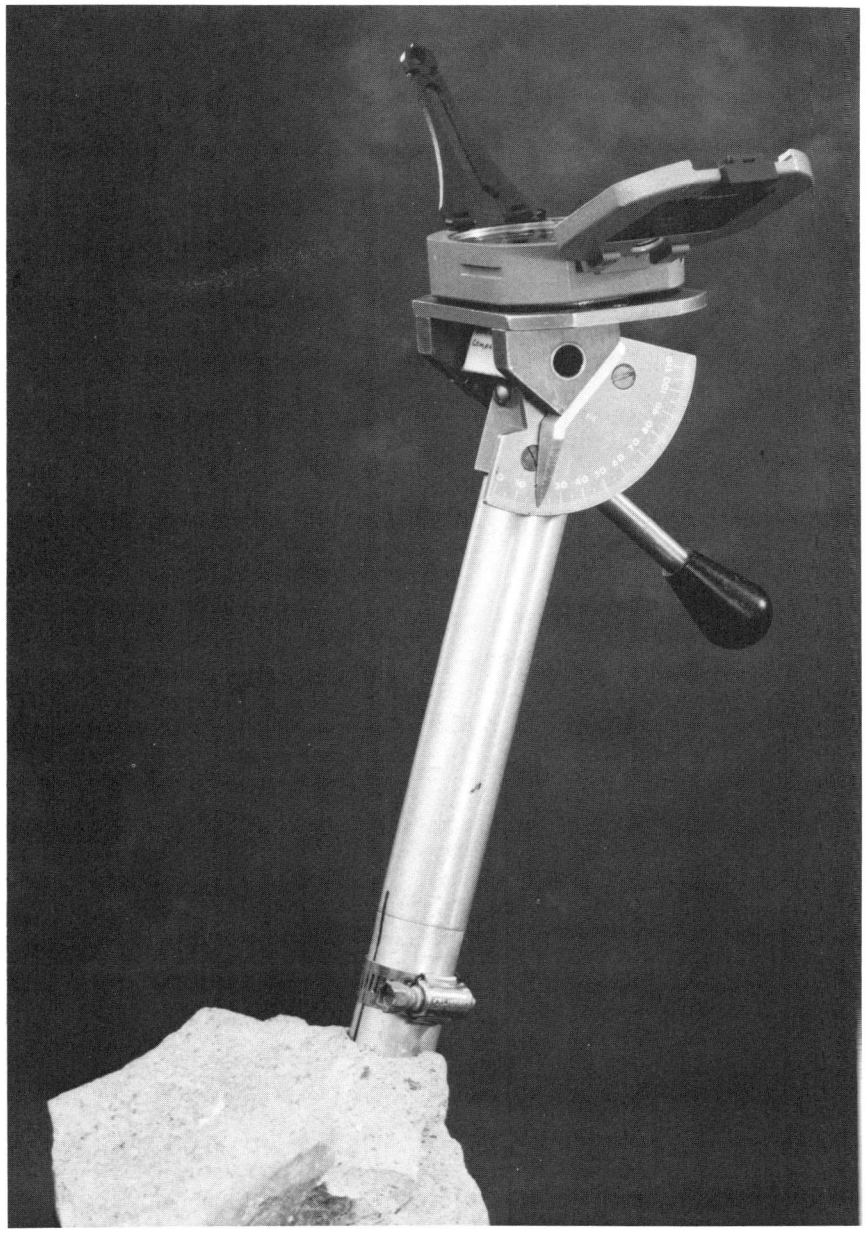

FIG. 23. Orientation platform with Brunton compass.

340      M. FULLER

in alternating fields of as high as 400 oe (40 mT) did not totally remove the contamination. Such results are consistent with other reports and reveal that the drilling-induced remanence is probably a stress, or shock-promoted, magnetization.

Drilling-induced magnetization has proved to be particularly troublesome in secondary drilling of sedimentary cores recovered from boreholes (Sallomy and Briden, 1975; S. Halgedahl, personal communication). This can be mitigated by drilling pairs of cores from opposite sides of the drill core, whereupon the drill moments are in opposite directions. By analyzing the data from the pair of samples, one can then get considerable reduction of the effect. This approach takes advantage of the fact that the drill magnetization appears to be largely induced in the direction of the projection of the local field along the drilling direction.

A comprehensive study of the drill magnetization for a variety of rock types would be a useful contribution. It could, for example, tell whether it is worthwhile to attempt to cancel the geomagnetic field at the location where we drill.

3.1.5. *Special Collection Techniques.* The discussion of sample collection has so far focused on the collection of standard samples for paleomagnetism. There are, however, a number of situations for which special techniques are required. Archeomagnetic samples frequently come from partially consolidated fire-hearth material. Such samples must be very accurately oriented because they are used for studies of secular variation, which involves observation of the small departures of the geomagnetic field from its average value. A method due to Professor Thellier involves cutting

FIG. 24. Collection technique for archeomagnetic samples. (Right) Former assembled around sample; (left) exploded view after Plaster of Paris has been poured and set.

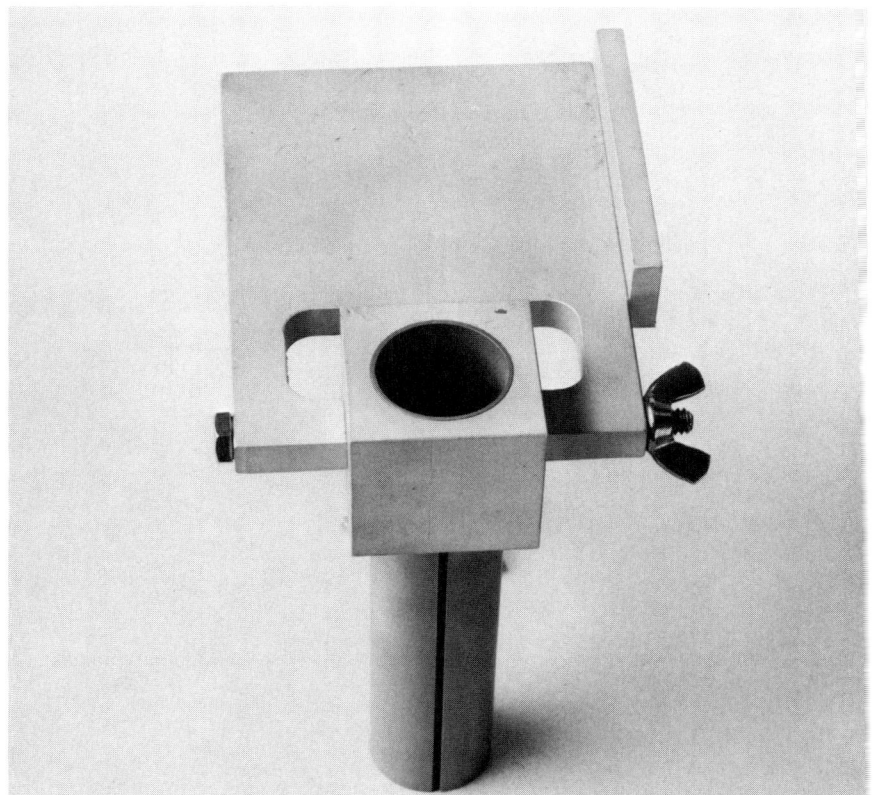

Fig. 25. Soft sediment corer: orientation platform with sharpened cutting surface.

around the region to be collected so that a brass mold can be placed around the sample and plaster of Paris used to form a sample with square cross section (Fig. 24). The mold can be used to obtain an accurate orientation of the sample, which is preserved for eventual measurements of cubes whose sides are parallel to the original mold.

In collections from unconsolidated sediments another special situation is encountered. A good solution to this problem is to use a small sample corer which can be forced into the sediment to recover a sample, whose orientation can be related to the corer (Fig. 25). The sample can be extruded into a sample holder for measurement. There is virtue in using a quartz holder so that the sample can later be thermally demagnetized if necessary (Kirschvink, private communication).

The collection of long cores for paleomagnetic purposes has followed standard coring techniques such as the use of the Livingstone corer (Livingstone,

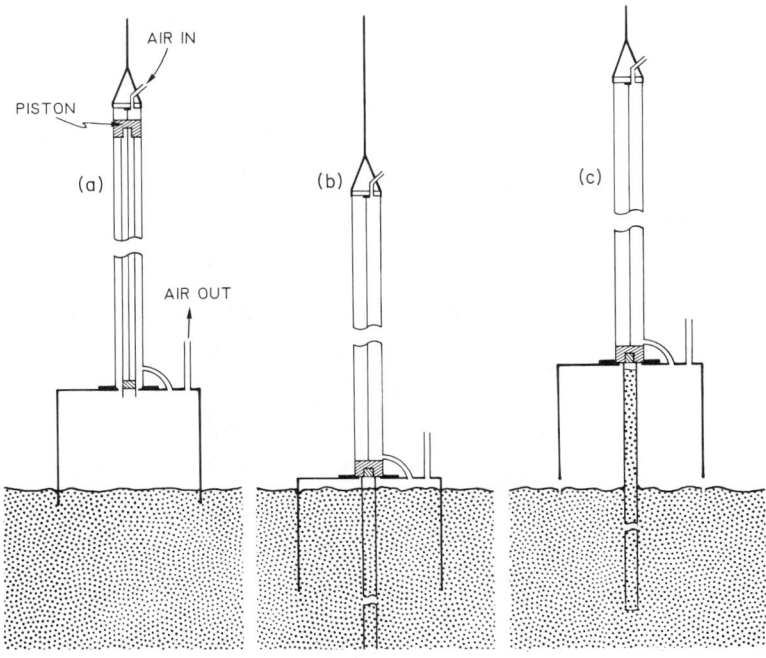

FIG. 26. MacKereth corer (after Collinson, 1983). (A) Corer on impact at lake bottom; (B) drum emplaced and corer driven into sediments; (C) ascent of corer.

1955), which is a modified piston corer. However, one ingenious device, the MacKereth corer (MacKereth, 1958, 1969), has been developed. The device was designed for operation in shallow lakes with depths of up to about 100 m and makes use of compressed air both to drive the corer into sediment and to recover the core. Figure 26 shows the system, which can be transported on relatively small inflatable rafts or boats. It is lowered over the side until the drum penetrates the sediments. Water is then pumped out of the drum, using pressure lines from the boat. The hydrostatic load of the 100 m or so of water drives the drum securely into the sediment. The corer is then driven down into the sediment by compressed air. Finally, the compressed air is allowed to fill the drum, creating the buoyancy necessary to recover the whole device. The core is then recovered and extruded into a suitable holder. The return of the corer to the surface should be brought about with minimum necessary vertical velocity to avoid disturbing the core. Moreover, spectacular though pictures of the cores breaching the surface can be, it should be remembered that this is a potentially dangerous device, which has already caused one tragic accident.

## 3.2. Measurement of Natural Remanent Magnetization

The measurement of remanent magnetization is the central measurement of paleomagnetism and indeed of much of rock magnetism. The classical work was done with the astatic magnetometer. This instrument is now largely of historical interest only, but it remains a useful device and probably is the only really inexpensive way to measure NRM. A brief description is therefore given. From about the early 1960s to the late 1970s, spinner magnetometers were the dominant instruments in paleomagnetism laboratories and a number of commercial instruments became available. Spinners have the great advantage over astatic magnetometers that they can be used in the magnetically noisy environment of a modern laboratory. They utilize phase-sensitive detectors which were developed in the 1960s. However, they suffer from the usual problem of long integration times at high sensitivity, which ultimately limits measurements of this type. Nevertheless, the spinner is probably still the most commonly used magnetometer. During the late 1970s the SQUID magnetometers arrived. Alone, they would probably soon have dominated paleomagnetic measurements because of their high sensitivity, fast response, and the nature of the measurement. However, at about the same time as the SQUIDs became available, interfacing small inexpensive microcomputers to the magnetometers became common, so that the combination of SQUIDs and microcomputers gave a new level of measuring capability to paleomagnetism. Most major laboratories are now equipped with SQUID magnetometers interfaced to microcomputers. These are sophisticated commercial systems which for the most part are operated in a black box mode. The various magnetometers are now discussed.

3.2.1. *Astatic Magnetometers.* An astatic magnetometer consists of a pair of astaticized magnets mounted on a lightweight rigid frame which is suspended from a torsion fiber (Fig. 27). If the magnets are perfectly astaticized the system does not respond to a homogeneous $B$ field. However, the system does respond to a field with a gradient, when the resulting torques on the two magnets differ. In application of the device as a rock magnetometer, the sample is introduced in such a way that its field at one magnet is large compared with that at the other. The instrument is essentially operated as a gradiometer in the near-field mode. Collinson (1983) relates the long history of use of the astatic magnetometer for measurements of the remanent magnetization of rocks and its development to a new level of sophistication by Blackett (1954) in connection with his studies of the magnetism of massive rotating bodies.

Assuming that the field due to the sample does not affect the upper magnet, the torque of the system is just that due to the field of the sample on the bottom magnet. Hence if $B$ is the field due to the sample, and $M$ the

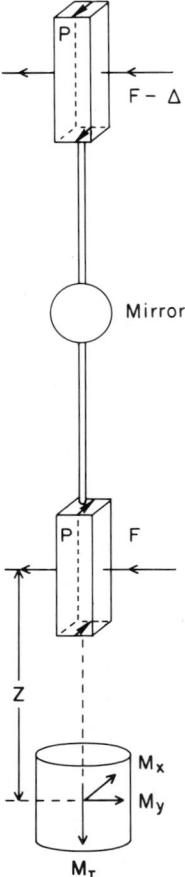

Fig. 27. Astatic magnetometer: magnet system.

magnetic moment of the bottom magnet, and $k$ the torsion constant, the sample will produce a deflection $\theta$

$$MB = k\theta$$

To maximize the deflection of the system for a given sample, one needs to increase $M$ and decrease $k$. The other critical relation for the operation of the astatic magnetometer is the period of oscillation $T$, which is

$$T = 2\pi\sqrt{cI/k}$$

where $I$ is the moment of inertia of the individual magnets and $c$ a constant for each particular astatic system given its total moment of inertia.

# 9. ROCK MAGNETISM AND PALEOMAGNETISM METHODS

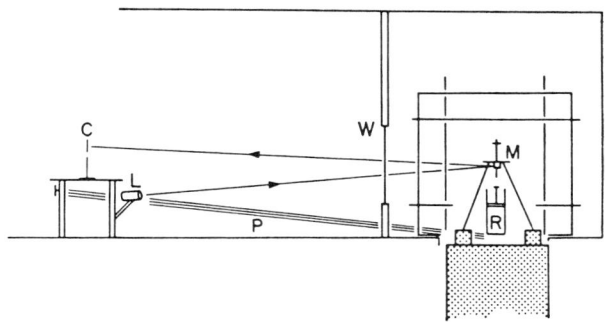

FIG. 28. Astatic magnetometer: arrangement for remote operation. The operator is seated at the table to the left, reads the scale C, and controls the sample platform R with the pulleys P to introduce the sample beneath the magnet system M. The magnetometer is isolated in a chamber and the light beam passes through the window W. (After Collinson, 1983.)

Combining these two results to eliminate $k$, we get

$$\theta/B = (1/4\pi^2)T^2M/cI$$

This makes clear the need to maximize $M/I$ and minimize $c$. Collinson (1983) describes the details of the magnet systems and procedures of astaticization. An instrument is illustrated in Fig. 28. It should, however, be noted that astatic magnetometers do not have to be operated by peering at lamp and scale arrangements. Spot followers can be used to give automatic readout by negative feedback (Petherbridge et al., 1972). Nevertheless, the requirement of magnetically noise-free and mechanically quiet environments severely limits the use of astatic magnetometers, despite the fact that in such environments their sensitivity compares favorably with all other magnetometers but the most recent SQUID magnetometers.

3.2.2. Spinner Magnetometers. In spinner magnetometers a stationary sensor continuously measures the $B$ field of a rotating specimen. In principle, the sensor can be revolved about the specimen, but this has not proved so convenient an arrangement. The sensor can be a pickup coil, in which case the changes in flux cutting the coil during the rotation of the specimen give by the Faraday–Lenz law an induced EMF which can be detected and amplified. It can be a flux gate which directly measure the $B$ field. A thin-film sensor was developed by Chiron and De La Pierre (1979). The device detected the rotation of magnetization of the thin film caused by the changing $B$ field of the spinning sample.

A crucial aspect of all spinners is signal conditioning, and two approaches to this problem have developed. The standard approach for many instruments was the use of a phase-sensitive detector. These devices are so central to many of the instruments used in paleomagnetism and rock magnetism that a brief description is given of their principles in Section 3.2.4. The second approach is to obtain a record of the signal by sampling as many times as is feasible per cycle, so that a Fourier analysis can be carried out to obtain the magnitude and those of the fundamental frequency. Either method gives the magnitude and direction of the components of magnetization in the plane perpendicular to the rotation axis.

The voltage $V$ induced in the pickup coil by the rotation of a specimen is a function of the following variables:

$$V \propto M_\perp, \omega, C_p$$

where $M_\perp$ is the moment of the component of magnetization in the plane perpendicular to the rotation axis, $\omega$ the frequency of rotation in cycles per second, and $C_p$ represents pickup coil parameters such as turns, radius, and length.

Clearly one has some flexibility in obtaining favorable values of the various coil parameters and in $\omega$. Considerable effort was expended on optimizing coil design for spinner magnetometers; for example, coil assemblies were produced which wrap around the sample, closing with a clamshell-like operation during measurement and being opened to insert and extract the samples. In principle, sensitivity is improved by increasing the rotation rate of the sample, so efforts were made to utilize turbine-driven systems (Gough, 1964) as the rotation rates exceeded those readily obtained with direct drives. However, modern coil instruments tend to use relatively low rotation speeds, have nominally optimized pickup coils, and rely on phase-sensitive detectors or waveform analyzers to get the necessary sensitivity.

The signal obtained from the flux gate sensor instruments is independent of frequency of rotation since one measures the change in $B$ field at the sensor rather than an induced EMF. These instruments (Fig. 29) have evolved along parallel lines to the coil instruments, with attention being focused on sensor pickup arrays to achieve cancellation of unwanted signals. Developments in flux gate sensors have permitted considerable improvement in sensitivity.

At present a number of commercial instruments are available, and over the nearly 50 years since Johnson and McNish (1938) first described a practical spinner magnetometer for paleomagnetic purposes a number of important steps can be traced in the development of spinners. In the early 1960s the use of modern phase-sensitive detectors produced a major increase in the reliability and sensitivity of the instruments.

The Digico magnetometer uses the second approach to signal enhancement by sampling the waveform 128 times per cycle of rotation. The data are therefore taken roughly every 3° of rotation. The outputs are stored in a computer and the digital records of the waveform analyzed by the fast Fourier transform technique to give amplitude and phase of the fundamental.

# 9. ROCK MAGNETISM AND PALEOMAGNETISM METHODS

Fig. 29. Schonstedt spinner magnetometer.

A convenient aspect of this instrument is that the sample spins until the output satisfies a prescribed statistical criterion, so one does not waste time spinning unnecessarily.

Modern versions of the Schonstedt spinner have on-line computer facilities which permit optimization of measuring time. The UGF-JR Institute of Applied Geophysics at Prague also produces an excellent spinner magnetometer.

Kono *et al.* (1981) developed an ingenious spinner which permits determination of the total vector without replacing the sample in different orientations. This is achieved by rotating the sample simultaneously about two axes, but at different velocities. The output contains signals from the moments perpendicular to both axes of rotation and hence has sufficient data to determine the moment of the sample. The magnetometer is not comparable in sensitivity to the best commercial devices, but it is suitable for rapid measurement of more strongly magnetized samples.

3.2.3. SQUID Magnetometers. The advent of magnetometers with superconducting quantum interference device (SQUID) sensors has brought about a major breakthrough in paleomagnetic measurements. SQUID magnetometers permit rapid determinations of remanent magnetism, orders of magnitude more sensitive than previous measurement. There are by now numerous descriptions of SQUIDs and their operation (Jaklevic et al., 1965; Zimmerman et al., 1970; Mercereau, 1970; Nisenhoff, 1970; Josephson, 1974; Clarke, 1974). In addition, there are excellent descriptions of both SQUIDs and SQUID magnetometers in recent review articles on biomagnetic instrumentation (Romani et al., 1982). Descriptions in the literature of paleomagnetism are limited (Fuller et al., 1986).

3.2.3.1. SQUID PRINCIPLES. The development of the SQUIDs followed theoretical and experimental work on superconductivity, which culminated in the late 1950s and early 1960s in the Bardeen–Cooper–Schrieffer (BCS) theory of superconductivity (Bardeen et al., 1957) and in the prediction (Josephson, 1962) and observation (Anderson and Rowell, 1962) of electron pair tunneling.

The phenomenon of superconductivity was discovered in 1911 by Kamerlingh Onnes shortly after he succeeded in liquefying helium. He found that the resistance of a sample of mercury dropped to an immeasurably low value just above 4 K. Subsequent to this discovery many other superconducting metals were discovered; two of the most useful for instrument applications are lead (transition temperature 7.2 K) and niobium (transition temperature 9.2 K).

In the superconducting state, metals are able to transport a dc current with zero resistance. To begin to interpret this, assume that when a metal is cooled below its transition temperature, a fraction of the electrons condense into the superconducting state. The colder the metal, the larger the fraction of condensed electrons becomes. This model is commonly known as the two-fluid model. When a DC field is impressed on a superconductor the current is carried exclusively by the superelectrons, which are able to move through the lattice without scattering. When an AC field is impressed some energy is imparted to the normal electrons. Hence, the resistance is not zero in this case.

Another important characteristic of superconductors is that they spontaneously exclude magnetic flux—the Meissner effect. When a superconducting body is cooled below its transition temperature in the presence of a magnetic field, currents are spontaneously generated in the body to exclude any magnetic field from the interior. We know today that the Meissner effect is generally not perfect; much of the flux penetrating a metallic body when it becomes superconducting is trapped in it. The flux becomes pinned to local impurity sites in the metal, and more energy is required to drive the flux from the pinning site than is gained by removing it from the superconductor volume. Superconducting shields therefore tend to trap the ambient field on cooling instead of excluding it (Meissner effect). Note, however, that because of the Meissner effect substantial field modification occurs on cooling through the transition temperature.

The response to applied magnetic fields defines two types of superconductors, types 1 and 2. Type 1 superconductors are the mechanically soft elements such as lead, tin, and niobium, which have transition temperatures below 9 K. They exhibit perfect flux shielding in fields below the critical field $H_c$, which is generally less than 1000 gauss (0.1 T) for most type 1 superconductors. Type 2 superconductors are mechanically harder materials and are for the most part alloys and compounds. They have higher critical fields of up to $10^5$ gauss and critical temperatures of up to 21.5 K. Perfect flux shielding is only exhibited by these materials in fields up to about $10^2$ gauss (10 mT); in higher fields the flux starts to enter the material. This field value is the lower critical field $H_{c1}$. The material is still superconducting and the flux continues to penetrate to the higher critical field $H_{c2}$, at which point superconductivity is destroyed. In low-field applications such as the rock magnetometer, to be described later, one uses type 1 superconductors to provide magnetic shielding. In contrast, in high-field applications such as superconducting magnets, one uses type 2 superconductors. Most SQUID sensors are constructed with type 2 materials, particularly work-hardened niobium and niobium–titanium.

From a phenomenological viewpoint, we noted that superconductivity can be understood by assuming that below the transition temperature a fraction of the electrons in a metal condense into a single quantum macrostate, which can be described by a single wave function. The idea of such a macrostate was initially proposed by Fritz London and was based on his concept of long-range order in momentum space. Subsequently, Ginzburg and London further developed the concept by introducing an order parameter into the theory to characterize the degree of superconductivity.

The microscopic theory of superconductivity was developed by Bardeen *et al.* (1957) and was based on an electron pairing concept. In explaining superconductivity, BCS theory postulates the existence of a weak attractive force between electrons in the superconductor. This is the long-range order, whose importance had been earlier appreciated by London. The idea of correlated motion can be used to explain superconductivity, or the absence of normal electrical resistance, in a simple qualitative way. Normal electrical resistance is the result of scattering of the conduction electrons by the lattice. If the motion of all of the electrons is correlated, then scattering of one electron would involve scattering of the whole assembly of electrons taking part in the correlated motion. Such scattering has a very low probability. Therefore when a supercurrent flows, it is not significantly affected by the normal scattering that constitutes electrical resistance. London had recognized the importance of the long-range order, but had not appreciated that it is the electron pair (rather than the single electron) that enters into the correlated motion. This pair coupling is central to BCS theory. The coupling gives rise to a lower-energy state separated from the excited states by an energy gap.

The physical basis of the coupling is through the intermediary of the lattice; loosely speaking, one electron is attracted to the wake of the other. Such coupling is very weak, as is evident from the low temperature at which it is broken by thermal energy. The electron pairs are known as Cooper pairs.

Flux quantization in a superconducting ring was proposed by London (1950) and observed by Deaver and Fairbank (1961) and Doll and Nabauer (1961). It plays an important role in SQUID magnetometers. When a superconducting ring is cooled through its transition temperature in the presence of a magnetic field, flux will be excluded from the material of the ring due to the Meissner effect and flux will be trapped in the center of the ring. This trapped flux can only take on certain values which are multiples of the flux quantum $\phi_0 = h/2e$, where $h$ is Planck's constant, $6.624 \times 10^{-34}$ joule sec, and $e$ the charge of the electron, $1.602 \times 10^{-19}$ coulomb. Persistent currents will flow in the ring as it cools through its transition temperature and becomes superconducting, if the flux does not have the correct value. The flux quantum has a numerical value of $2.07 \times 10^{-15}$ weber, or $2.07 \times 10^{-7}$ maxwell. Thus the persistent currents in superconducting rings are induced by extremely low levels of magnetic flux.

The phenomenon of flux quantization did not achieve much practical importance until the ideas of Josephson resulted in the development of practical devices for detecting magnetic fields. Josephson (1962) pointed out that a supercurrent should be able to pass across a thin dielectric barrier separating two superconductors. The essential requirement is that the quantum mechanical wave functions for the Cooper pairs in the two superconductors extend beyond the surface of the superconductors and coherently link up across the barrier.

A typical Josephson junction consisting of two superconductors separated by a thin dielectric barrier is shown in Fig. 30. Above the critical temperature

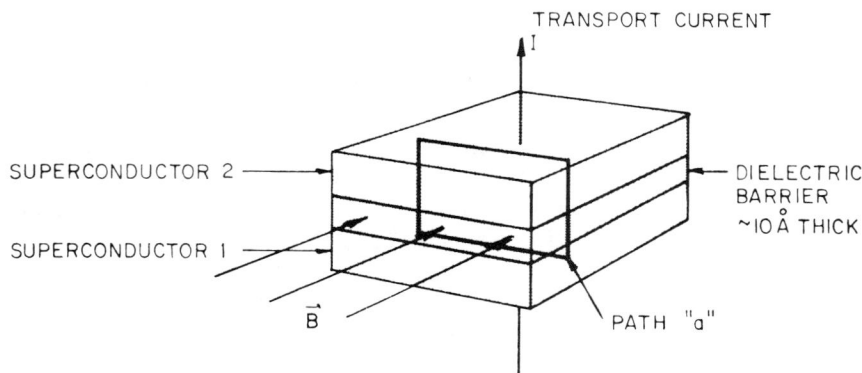

Fig. 30. Josephson junction.

of the superconductors, the device has a resistance of a few ohms. Below the transition temperature, this resistance vanishes and the tunneling of the Cooper pairs gives a zero-voltage current across the device.

To understand the current, we return to the concept of the correlated motion of Cooper pairs with the same quantum mechanical phase angle in a superconductor on which BCS theory rests. In the Josephson junction, two superconductors are brought so close to each other that the phases of the pairs in the two superconductors are coupled by tunneling of pairs across the junction. Josephson predicted that for certain phase differences between the two superconductors, the pairs would be preferentially transferred in one direction across the junction. This is because motion in the one direction brings pairs from the first superconductor to the second with the correct phase to join the correlated motion. Motion in the opposite direction would not bring this about, so a pair moving in this direction would not be able to join the correlated motion in the first superconductor. Thus, the current across the junction is dependent on the phase difference of the pairs in the two superconductors.

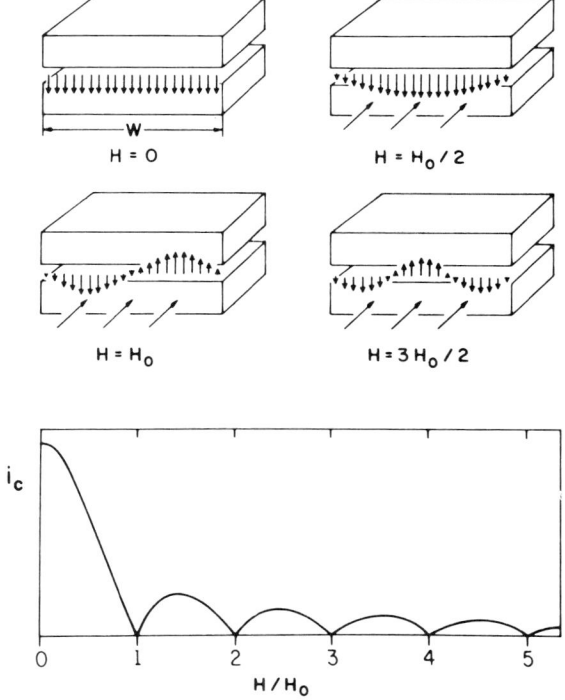

FIG. 31. Field dependence of current across Josephson junction.

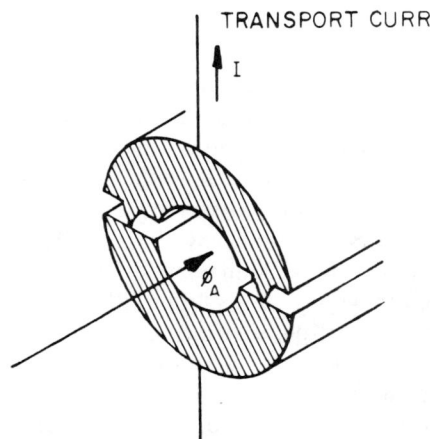

Fig. 32. DC SQUID.

The phase angle of the Cooper pairs is dependent on the magnetic vector potential $A$. Thus, given that a certain current flows when the $B$ field is zero, the effect of the field is to vary the phase angle across the junction, as shown in the upper part of Fig. 31. This modulates the current across the junction and gives the characteristic periodic $B$-field dependence of the current, which makes possible the measurement of magnetic fields with these devices. It is therefore in principle a magnetometer in which the supercurrent is the measure of the field. However, the intrinsic sensitivity of the device is small because the field required to produce one flux quantum is relatively large due to the small area of the junction. Much higher sensitivity can be obtained by using a double junction.

Direct use of Josephson junctions was made in the DC SQUID developed by Clarke (1974). It consists of a superconducting ring with two Josephson junctions arranged as illustrated schematically in Fig. 32. The device is biased by a DC current $I$. In the absence of a magnetic field the maximum current through the device is simply twice the current through each of the junctions. However, when a field is applied to the device perpendicular to the plane of the ring, the accompanying magnetic vector potential is parallel to the current in one arm of the ring and opposite in the other. This means that the phase shifts through the individual junctions are opposite and the two currents interfere where they meet at P. The phases of the two currents are equal when the magnetic field gives a flux between the ring which is a multiple of $\phi_0$. It is this interference of the currents in the two arms of the ring which gave rise to the term superconducting quantum *interference* device or SQUID. The expression for the current as a function of field has the same form as

9. ROCK MAGNETISM AND PALEOMAGNETISM METHODS 353

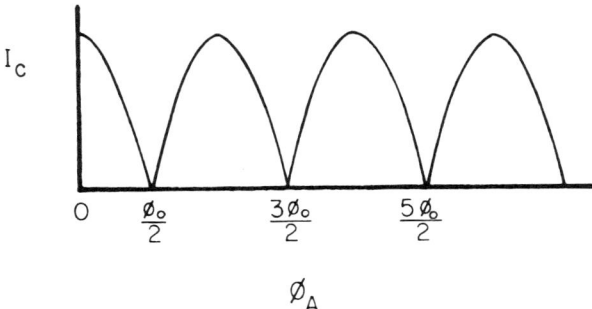

FIG. 33. Field dependence of current for SQUID.

double-slit Fraunhofer diffraction (Fig. 33). In this case the Josephson junctions are coupled to a superconducting ring whose area is large compared with that of the Josephson junction. This gives the enhanced sensitivity. Although the DC-driven SQUID may eventually prove of higher sensitivity than the radio frequency (RF) driven SQUIDs, it is principally the latter which have been used so far in magnetometers for geological applications.

The RF SQUID sensor consists of a superconducting ring or loop of inductance $L$ in series with a weak link. The early designs of the weak link took many different forms, ranging from a piece of wire with a blob of solder on it to a cylinder with saw cuts. The factors which govern the topology of the loops are their inductance, shielding, mechanical stability, and flux coupling efficiency. The Dayhem bridge and the point contact have been the most commonly used SQUIDs in the magnetometers to be discussed. Neither of these two devices is a true Josephson junction. However, they do have the essential characteristic of giving an output which is a periodic function of applied $B$ fields.

Figure 34 illustrates the Dayhem bridge. A superconducting thin film is laid down on a quartz substrate and cuts are made as shown. The cuts give a constriction, through which all of the current must flow. This then is the point at which the device goes normal. The RF drive field is applied to the device via an RF coil. The output of the device is detected inductively with a pickup coil. This type of SQUID was used in many of the earliest magnetometers built for paleomagnetism laboratories. It was favored at that time over the point contact SQUID because of difficulties encountered with mechanical stability of the point contacts.

In its simplest form, the point contact has the geometry illustrated in Fig. 35A. The point contact serves as the weak link in the superconducting ring. The contact consists of a niobium point driven into a niobium surface. The simple point contact gave rise to the "two-hole" point contact, from which

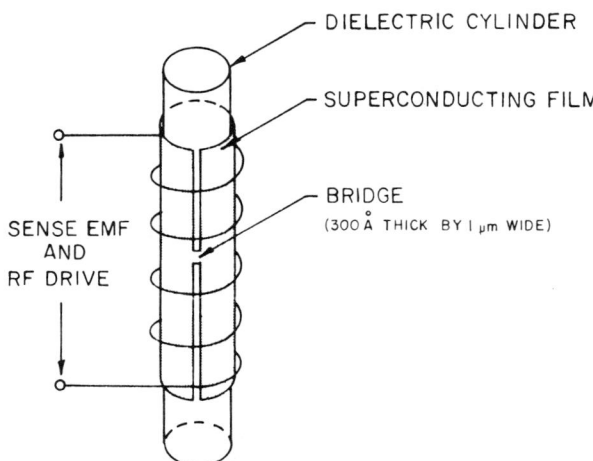

FIG. 34. Dayhem bridge.

in turn came the toroidal point contact. The various geometries are illustrated in Fig. 35B and C. The configuration of the toroidal SQUID can be visualized by regarding it as a two-hole SQUID in which the holes have been brought back on themselves to form the toroidal hole. As we shall see, the toroidal contact is now the most popular of the RF-driven SQUIDs.

A typical electronics system used with a SQUID sensor is illustrated in Fig. 36 (see also Forgacs and Warnick, 1967). The sensor is excited by a sinusoidally varying RF magnetic field of such magnitude that the critical current of the sensor is exceeded in each cycle. The frequency of the exciting field is usually in the 20–30-MHz range. It is applied via a small coil embedded in the cavity of the toroid (Fig. 35C). To increase the input impedance of the device the RF coil is frequently resonated with a small capacitor across it. The impedance matching is necessary because the small voltage produced across the RF coil must be amplified by a room temperature FET amplifier whose optimum performance is achieved with an input impedance in the 1–5-kilohm range. The real part of the SQUID impedance looking into the RF coil is of the order of 1 ohm when the SQUID is operating. The required impedance matching is achieved with a $Q$ of about 30 in the resonant circuit.

When the SQUID is excited at a proper flux level, its critical current is exceeded twice during each RF cycle. This allows flux to enter into the SQUID loop, which in turn produces a back EMF in the RF coil. The exact way in which the flux enters into the loop depends on the detailed characteristics of the weak link, specifically on the exact relationship between the circulating weak link current and the superconducting wave function phase. A simple qualitative model of the flux entry will, however, account for most

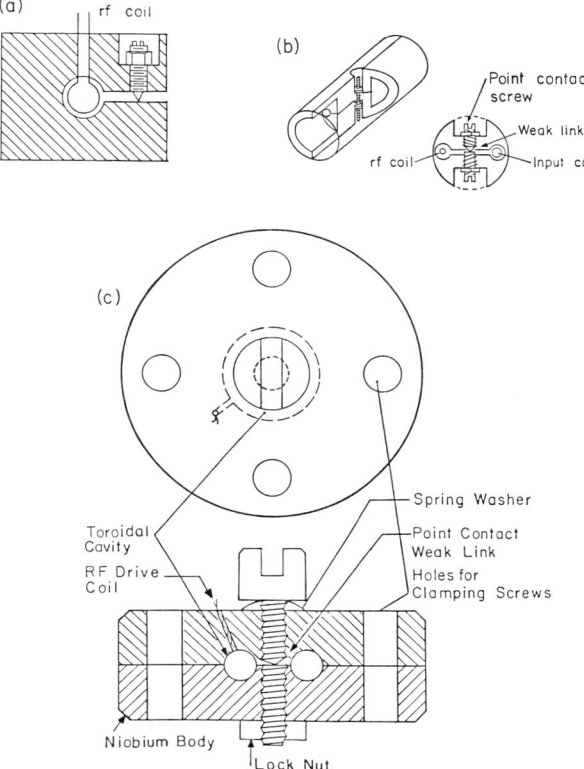

Fig. 35. Contact SQUIDs: (A) point contact; (B) two-hole point contact; and (C) toroidal SQUID.

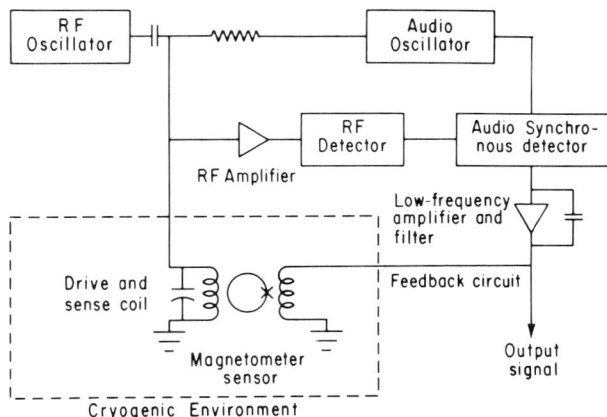

Fig. 36. Electronics for SQUID sensor.

of the observed effects (Silver and Zimmerman, 1967). This model assumes that the SQUID is completely self-shielding until the weak link critical current is exceeded. When this happens a flux quantum enters the SQUID loop. If the exciting flux changes and the weak link current are reversed and the critical current is again exceeded, the flux quantum pops out of the loop. Each time a flux quantum enters or exits the SQUID loop, it excites a voltage spike across the RF coil. The frequency spectrum of the spike produces voltage components at the resonant frequency of the tank circuit which, depending on their phase, are either positive or negative.

The phase of the voltage spikes induced in the RF coil with reference to the drive phase is determined by the dc magnetic flux threading the SQUID loop. Hence, if this flux changes, the phase of the spikes changes. To geophysicists familiar with the operation of flux gate magnetometers it may be helpful to recognize that the SQUID operation is closely analogous to the operation of flux gates. The effect is illustrated in Fig. 37. Note that in the absence of flux threading the loop, the phase of the voltage spikes is given by the solid line in Fig. 37a. However, the presence of the dc flux makes the point in the RF cycle at which the critical current is exceeded different from that in the flux-free situation. This leads to the desired result; i.e., the magnitude of the RF voltage across the tuned circuit driving the SQUID is a periodic function of the DC flux threading the SQUID loop. Specifically

$$v(t) \propto \cos 2\pi\phi_s/\phi_0$$

where $\phi_s$ represents the DC flux through the SQUID loop.

The simplest way to obtain an indication of the flux threading the SQUID loop is to monitor the magnitude of the RF voltage across the SQUID drive coil. Such a scheme has two basic problems. First, it is essentially a DC measurement and so is more liable to drift than are AC techniques available for detection of comparable voltage levels. Second, the output voltage is periodic with respect to the sensor flux, which greatly hampers measurements of high accuracy and wide dynamic range because the flux sensitivity varies periodically and is only rarely near the maximum value at

$$\phi_s = \left(\frac{n}{2} + \frac{1}{4}\right)\phi_0 \qquad n = 0, \pm 1$$

The first of the two problems can be overcome by applying a small low-frequency (50 kHz) magnetic flux to the SQUID loop and measuring the amplitude of the resulting tank voltage modulation envelope $E_m$. For values of flux less than $\phi_0$, $E_m$ is roughly proportional to the slope $v(t)$

$$E_m \propto \sin 2\pi\phi_s/\phi_0$$

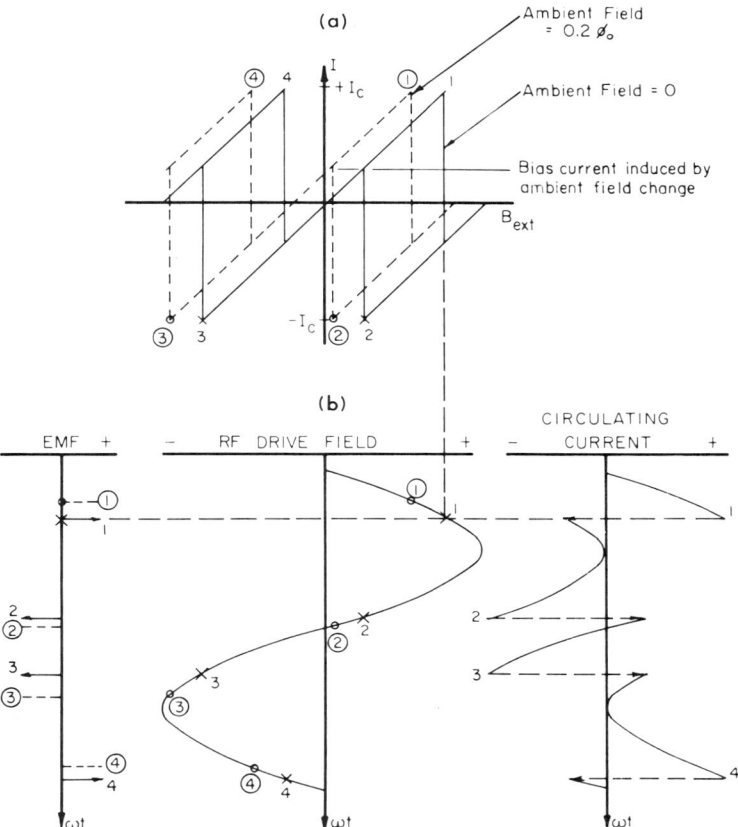

FIG. 37. Detection of flux changes in SQUID.

Therefore $E_m$ is also periodic in $\phi_s$ and can be used as a measure of this quantity. However, $E_m$ is the amplitude of an AC signal and is therefore immune to thermal and other drift effects that affect a DC signal. It can also be detected with a phase-sensitive detector, greatly increasing the signal-to-noise ratio.

To eliminate the problem of the nonlinearity of the SQUID output voltage, the SQUID is used in a null detector mode by employing negative feedback to lock the magnetometer at its maximum flux sensitivity position. The electronics used to achieve this are shown in Fig. 36. In such a system, flux changes are sensed and cancelled by application of reversed flux. This flux is generated by applying current to the RF coil.

To increase the dynamic range of the magnetometer, one modifies the feedback loop circuit. Many magnetometers have a number of sensitivity scales for which the full scale value will be 1, 10, and 100$\phi_0$. On the 1$\phi_0$ scale the sensitivity of the instrument depends on the resolution with which the feedback current can be determined. This gives sensitivities better than 1 part in $10^3$ of a $\phi_0$. The instrument resets when $\phi_0$ is reached. On lower sensitivity scales the instrument will reset at the 10 or 100$\phi_0$ flux level. The resetting process consists of reducing the feedback current on the SQUID to zero. The SQUID then sees the total flux from the pickup coils. This is sufficient to exceed the critical current of the SQUID, which will then go normal and admit the flux quanta. In the earlier systems, stability of this process was considered of prime importance and so the reset circuits had relatively slow time constants of the order of milliseconds. Recently, considerable improvements in dynamic range have been achieved by making the time constants of the resetting circuit of the order of microseconds. At the limit of the dynamic range, one counts resets at the maximum possible frequency. This is the measure of the changes in flux threading the SQUID loop.

The physical size of the superconducting ring in the SQUID is constrained by its inductance $L_s$, the critical current $I_{max}$, and the operating temperature as follows. The output signal from a SQUID is a function of the amount that the critical current $i_c$ changes with the application of magnetic flux to the SQUID ring. This variable is a maximum when

$$i_c L_s \sim \phi_0$$

where $\phi_0$ is the flux quantum. Further, the energy associated with a quantum of magnetic flux $\phi_0$ being switched into and out of the ring must be larger than the thermal energy, i.e.,

$$\phi_0^2/2L_s \geq kT$$

where $k$ is Boltzmann's constant ($1.38 \times 10^{-23}$ J K$^{-1}$) and $T$ the absolute temperature. These constraints set the critical current in the range of several microamperes and the ring (SQUID loop) inductance in the range of $10^{-9}$ henry or smaller.

Loops with inductance of $10^{-9}$ henry are 1-2 mm in diameter. One of the most significant design problems with SQUID instruments is how to couple a magnetic signal to this very small sensing element. Three general solutions are used. (1) Insert the sample directly into the SQUID. This provides optimum flux coupling but restricts the measurement to small samples at helium temperatures (Fig. 38a). (2) Place the sample as near the SQUID as possible and measure the flux coupled to the SQUID (Fig. 38b). This technique provides poorer coupling and the signal is a strong function of sample position. (3) Couple the flux from a sample to the SQUID with a superconducting flux transformer (Fig. 38c).

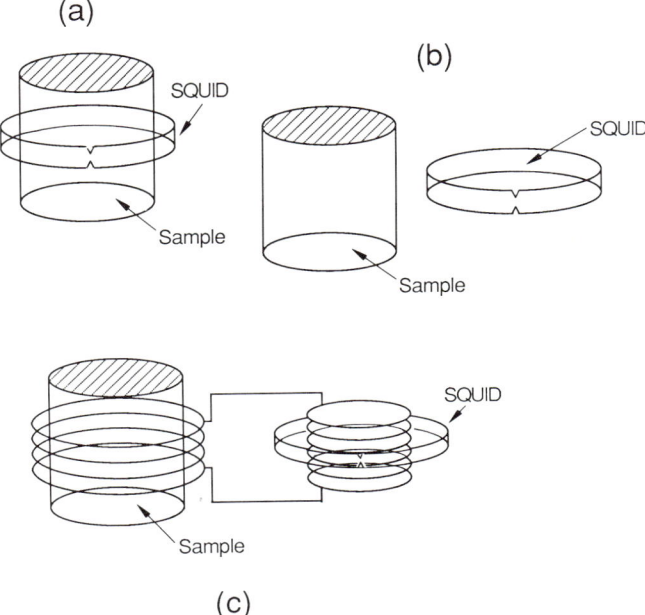

FIG. 38. Coupling of SQUIDs to magnetic fields: (a) insertion of sample into SQUID; (b) sample beside SQUID; and (c) transformer coupling.

The flux transformer is most often used with SQUID systems because of the flexibility it provides. Pickup coils can be built with a configuration to match the particular measurement requirement. Figure 39 shows a typical magnetometer pickup coil circuit, with its transformer coupling to the SQUID. The output of the two coils as a sample is passed through the magnetometer is as shown. The entire pickup coil–transformer circuit is usually superconducting, so its response is to net flux change $\phi$ and not the time rate of change ($\dot{\phi}$) as with a resistive coil. The superconducting circuit is a noiseless $B$ field amplifier.

A magnetic shield is an essential component of the magnetometers discussed in this chapter if their full sensitivity is to be realized. Ferromagnetic shields can attenuate external fields by factors of up to $10^4$, but superconducting shields can easily provide attenuation factors of $10^8$ and larger. The shielding is independent of frequency from DC to gigahertz. A completely closed superconducting shell will trap whatever field is present when the shell goes superconducting. External fields will be shielded unless the initial field of the superconductor is exceeded. If the shell has an opening, the field can leak inside; however, by proper design these fringing fields can be made very small.

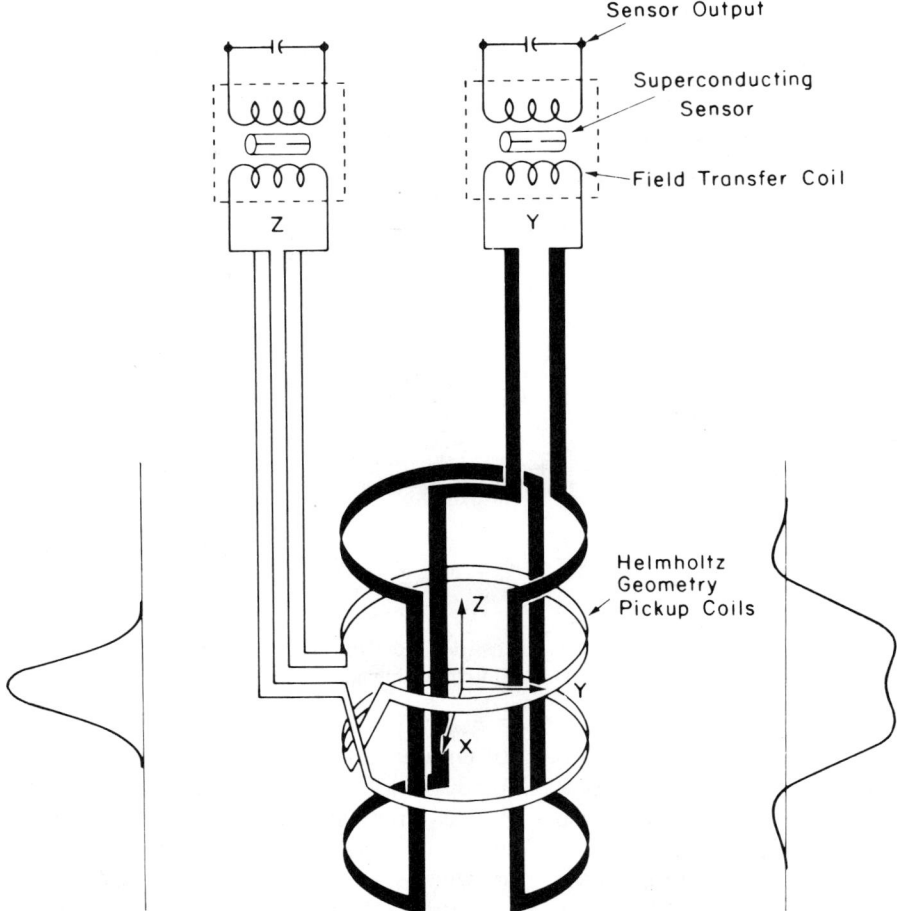

FIG. 39. Magnetometer pickup coil configuration and signal for passage of sample through coil array.

The principle of operation of the shield is now illustrated by considering a superconducting ring which is cooled below its critical temperature in zero field. If a uniform axial field is subsequently applied, a current will flow. Since the resistance is zero, this current will be whatever value is required to cancel the applied field. The field produced by the current will be non-uniform, but when its value is integrated over the area of the ring the flux will exactly cancel the total applied flux.

Figure 40 shows the field around a superconducting cylinder treated in the same manner as the ring. The field induced by the current is much more

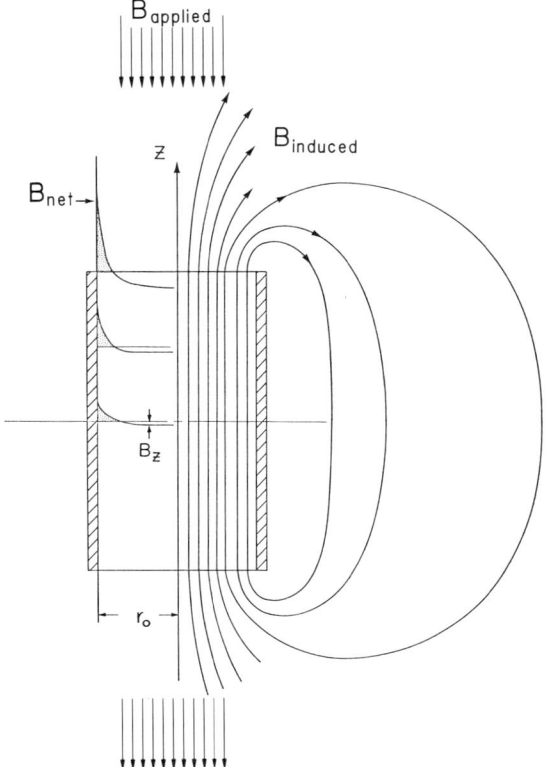

FIG. 40. Superconducting shield.

uniform, but the same qualitative effects are present. The difference between applied and induced fields is shown on the left side of the figure, and we see the remaining axial field, which has leaked or fringed into the shield. On the axis the residual field is in the same direction as the applied field, but close to the wall of the cylinder it is opposed to the applied field. Near the end of the cylinder, the induced field is much less radially uniform than it is near the center.

3.2.3.2. CRYOGENICS. The low temperatures at which available superconductors operate require that the SQUIDs and associated flux transformers be maintained at temperatures in the vicinity of 10 K. Eventually such temperatures may be attainable without the use of a cryogen, but at present the operation of SQUID magnetometers necessitates the use of liquid helium.

The very low heat of vaporization of liquid helium (a heat load of only 28 mW will evaporate 1 liter of liquid helium a day) requires that liquid helium dewars have high thermal efficiency. The instrument system inserted into the liquid helium container must have low internal heat production with a minimal amount of heat conducted down electrical leads to the instrument system from the outside. The efficiency of the dewar is determined by the heat leaking down the access into the helium reservoir, or the neck tube losses, and the heat conducted and radiated through the vacuum space. The neck tube losses are comprised of radiation, solid conduction down the tube itself, conduction and convection in the helium gas column, and conduction down shield tubes and electrical leads. The heat load through the vacuum space comprises radiation between the various thermal layers and conduction which can exist if reflecting layers placed within the vacuum space have contact with each other. There can also be a heat leak due to residual gas, especially helium gas in the vacuum space. Cryopumping by the liquid helium reservoir will maintain an extremely high vacuum as long as no helium gas enters the vacuum space.

While liquid helium has a low heat of vaporization, gaseous helium has a high specific heat, and since the gaseous helium leaves the liquid surface at about 4.2 K, there is a large potential cooling source available in warming this cold gas to room temperature. In fact, this sensible heat is about 75 times larger than the heat of vaporization of the liquid (Long and Loveday, 1968, p. 284). This large heat capacity can be used to intercept various sources of heat leaking into the reservoir, as will be described in the following sections.

Further improvements in performance can be achieved by adding thermally conducting shields within the multiple reflecting layers and providing good heat exchange between these shields and the helium boil-off gas. The combination of high vacuum, multiple reflecting layers, and vapor-cooled shields is termed superinsulation. The reflecting layers are usually 0.006 mm thick aluminized Mylar sheets separated by a spacer such as 0.05-mm fiberglass cloth. The vapor-cooled shields are copper or aluminium sheets 0.1 mm thick that completely surround the helium reservoir within the reflecting layers. Heat exchange is provided by soldering or epoxy bonding these shields directly to the dewar neck tube. A dewar of this general design with two vapor-cooled shields can exhibit overall thermal conductance of 1–5 $\mu$W cm$^2$ of dewar room temperature surface area. For a 5-liter dewar the *total* heat load reaching the liquid helium can be about 20 mW giving a loss rate of 0.8 liter per day. About 50% of this loss is due to conduction, convection, and radiation down the dewar neck tube.

The optimum SQUID system would incorporate active cooling that could maintain the system at its operating temperature (liquid helium range) without the use of liquid cryogens. Helium liquefiers are commercially available that will easily provide enough cooling, but they often cost more than the SQUID system ($50,000 or more), are large, and are very magnetic.

The mechanical motion produces vibration and fluctuating magnetic signals that can cause magnetic noise many orders of magnitude above the SQUID noise level.

SQUID systems, such as rock magnetometers, that have the pickup coils inside a superconducting magnetic shield have been operated in a hybrid fashion, where a small cryocooler is used to cool a thermal shield surrounding the liquid helium reservoir to the 15 K range, thereby greatly reducing the liquid loss rate. Such a hybrid cryostat is described by Testard and Locatell. (1982). A rock magnetometer system with a cryocooler recently introduced by 2-G Enterprises achieves 250 days of continuous operation on a single fil of the 100-liter helium reservoir.

3.2.3.3. INSTRUMENT CONFIGURATIONS AND SAMPLE HANDLING. Two basic configurations have been adopted in the rock magnetometers: a straight-through access system operated with the access either horizontal or vertical and a vertical single-ended access system. The instruments utilize the same RF-driven SQUID or DC SQUID and electronics; they differ only in that their configurations are modified to suit the particular applications for which they are developed. The output is in analog and digital format for recording and processing with standard computer interfacing.

Three types of cryogenic assemblies have been developed. The simplest system has a 3-mm inside diameter access as shown in Fig. 41a. The probe assembly is immersed directly in liquid helium, which is contained in a standard superinsulated dewar. An advantage of this system is that the sensors and other parts of the magnetometer are immediately accessible. A disadvantage is that since the shield is immersed in liquid helium, it cannot be thermally switched to trap desired fields without taking the probe out of the dewar or boiling off the helium.

This special vertical system was made to measure very small samples and has a sample access diameter of 3 mm with a magnetic moment sensitivity of $2 \times 10^{-10}$ gauss cm$^3$ ($2 \times 10^{13}$ amp m$^2$). This brings within the range of measurement individual pseudo-single-domain particles. The sample access region is evacuated so that the samples can be measured at room temperature. Sample cooling occurs by radiation to the pickup coil support, which is at helium temperature. This cooling rate extends up into the insulated region of the access tube. The approximate sample temperature has been monitored by using the Morin transition in hematite, and cooling rates of 0.5 K/min appear normal. The 3-mm system has an axial and a transverse coil, so that the three orthogonal components of magnetization can be measured by inserting the sample and then rotating it 90°. Sample handling can be tricky. This is partly due to the size of the samples, which at a few micrometers are at the limit of visibility. In addition, the actual sample holder insertion to the sense region presents problems because there is so little clearance. The sample

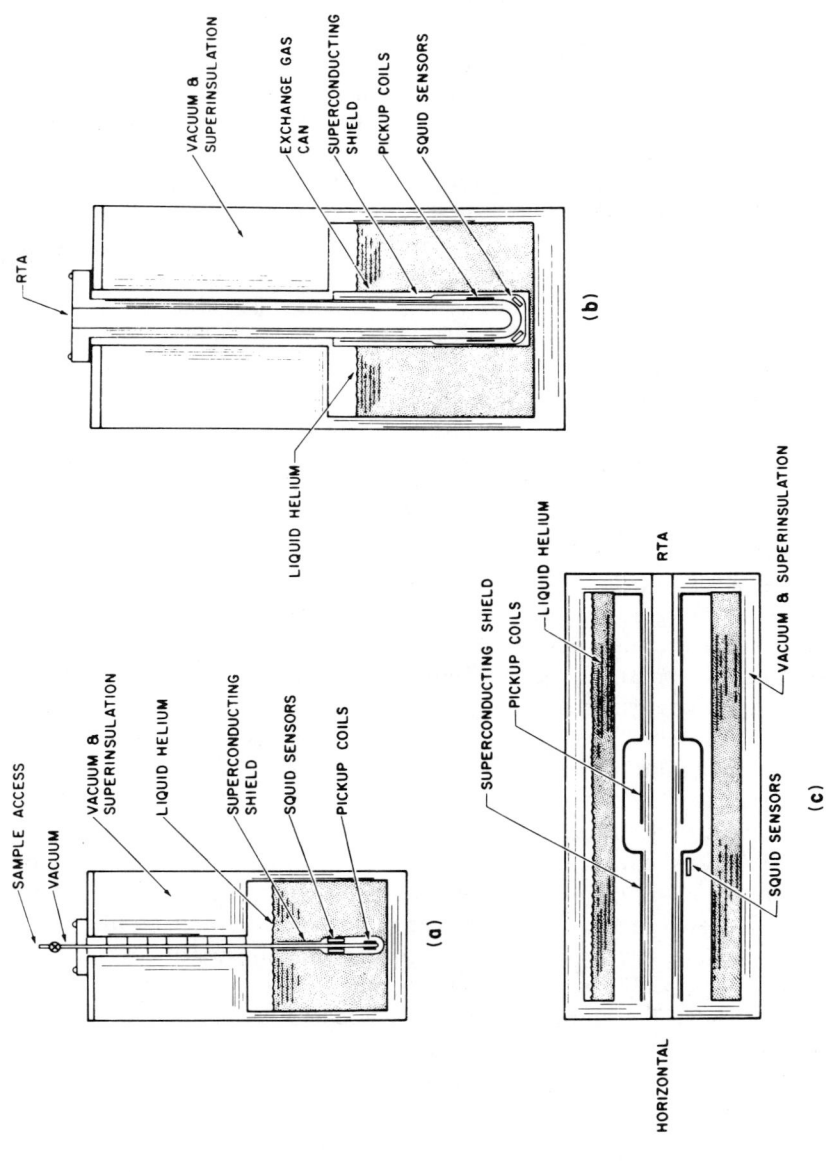

FIG. 41. Cryogenic magnetometer designs: (a) direct immersion vertical system; (b) vacuum-isolated vertical system; and (c) horizontal system.

is glued to a quartz rod, which is attached to the end of a long brass rod. The rod extends through the whole assembly and can be rotated prescribed amounts using the compass card at the top. Since the system must be evacuated to reduce cooling of the sample and sample holder in the sense region, care must be taken in loading samples. The sample assembly is first lowered until the sample which is withdrawn into the outer tube is just above the vacuum valve. The top part of the system can then be pumped down. When a pressure of a few micrometers of mercury is reached, the stopcock is opened and the sample assembly inserted to the measuring position. Finally, the sample is brought out of the protective outer tube and can be measured. This system has proved its value in single-particle measurements, but its operation is time consuming. Wu *et al.* (1974) constructed an AF demagnetization system for it which could be used without bringing the sample out of the vacuum. It was also possible to obtain magnetization acquisition curves and carry out DC demagnetization by placing an electromagnet at the top of the system.

The early rock magnetometers developed at Superconducting Technology Inc. used a modification of the immersion type. In these systems, the shield and sensors are placed in a partially evacuated region, as shown in Fig. 41b. A pressure of a few micrometers of helium exchange gas provides a weak, but controllable, thermal link to the reservoir. This design overcomes the difficulty of switching the shield, since the shield can be heated above its critical temperature while the probe is still immersed in liquid helium. The probe assembly is housed in a standard superinsulated dewar. Rock magnetometers of this design are also available from CTF Systems and Cryogenic Consultants Ltd. Sample handling with this instrument is relatively straightforward; the sample is measured in a room temperature access hole. The sample must be transported down into the sense region and accurately placed and aligned. If the instrument has only a single axial sensor, then three insertions are required for the measurement of the total vector unless a sophisticated rotation device is used. A simpler rotation system is required if there is a single transverse coil and a vertical coil, so that a total determination can be made with a single insertion and one rotation. Systems can be built in which a single SQUID serves two pickup coils. The sample passes through the axial coil first, giving the axial component of magnetization. Then it enters a single transverse coil sense region. Rotation through 90° then completes the determination of the vector. The sample handling for these vertical systems invites mechanization via stepping motors, and a number of laboratories have such automatic measuring devices.

The third cryogenic design is that used in the horizontal access magnetometer and illustrated in Fig. 41c. The system also permits shield switching and makes particularly efficient use of the vapor cooling principle. It is well suited to the refrigerator approach to minimize helium loss. The major advantages of this design are (1) proximity of the shield to the sample entry, (2) low neck tube loss, (3) simplicity and versatility of straight-through sample access, and (4) greatly improved thermal stability of the superconducting components, resulting in reduced noise. A very different design for a horizontal access magnetometer has been developed by ter Brake *et al.* (1984), in which the superconducting elements of the detection system are rigidly mounted to the bottom plate of the helium reservoir.

The horizontal open-ended system has a sample access hole of 6.4 cm. The system was designed in 1972 and has been in almost continuous use since then. For sample handling this system requires a horizontal translation device, which must permit accurate placement and alignment (Fig. 42). Since out system has three pickup coils and SQUIDs a single insertion suffices to determine the total vector.

In using the horizontal system to measure the remanent magnetism of long cores, a means of moving the core through the sense region must be developed. The core, in its core liner, was mounted on shoes which travel along the plastic trackway (Fig. 43a). The mechanism used to pull the core through the magnetometer also trips a microswitch, controlling the time of measurement. The data reduction scheme is illustrated in Fig. 43b for a single component measurement (Dodson *et al.*, 1979). The cores are AF demagnetized by passing through axial and transverse coils carrying the required AC fields. Figure 43c shows results for determination of the total vector, and Fig. 43d presents combined results for a group of cores from Lake Michigan.

The problems of sample handling have been ameliorated by the reduction in vibration sensitivity of the new instruments; whereas in the past it was important to isolate the sample handling device from the magnetometer, this is no longer necessary. The open access system makes possible a wide variety of applications which are less readily achieved with the vertical systems. For example, with our horizontal system we have developed methods of continuous thermal demagnetization and techniques for monitoring the effect on magnetization of stress.

In addition to the commercially developed instruments, a number of laboratories have produced their own instruments. At both the University of Boulder at Colorado and at the University of Southern California at Los Angeles vertical systems were built. It is, however, probably true that for most paleomagnetic and rock magnetism laboratories, lack of familiarity with low-temperature dewar techniques makes competition with the commercial groups difficult.

3.2.3.4. GRADIOMETERS. Gradiometer circuits are a straightforward extension of the magnetometers designed to measure fields in geophysical and submarine detection applications, using a multicoil continuous superconducting circuit to detect the difference in field (or field gradient) between two

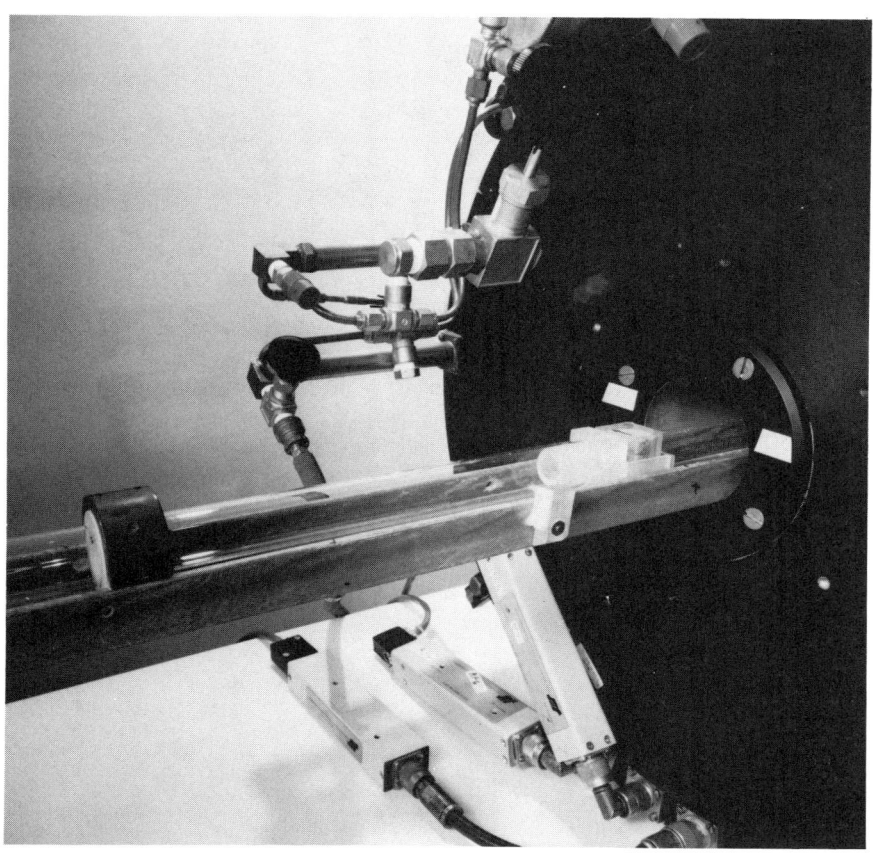

Fig. 42. Standard sample holder for horizontal system.

regions of space. Figure 44a shows a gradiometer for measuring the first derivative of the field in an axial direction. Off-axis gradients can be measured with coils configured as shown in Fig. 44b. The complete gradient tensor consisting of nine components can be measured with multiple pickup coil SQUID assemblies Only five assemblies are needed since

$$\nabla \cdot \mathbf{B} = 0 = \frac{\partial B_x}{\partial x} + \frac{\partial B_y}{\partial y} + \frac{\& B_z}{\partial z}$$

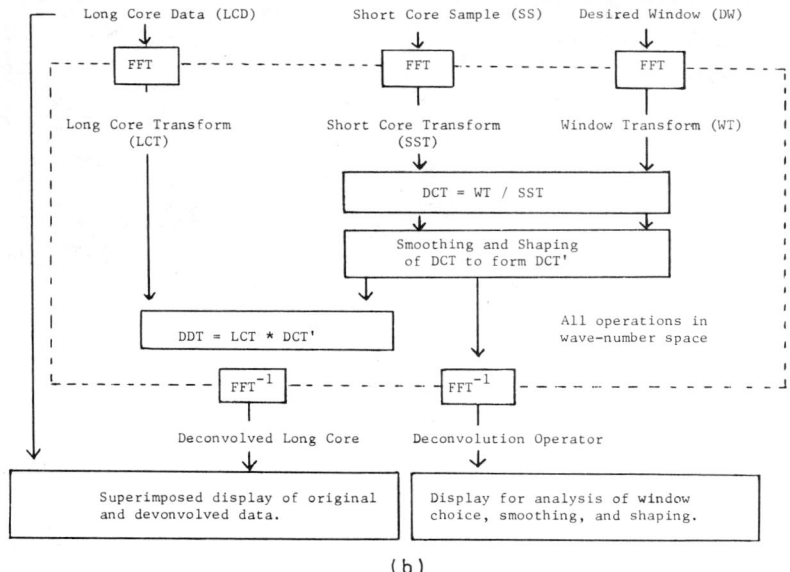

FIG. 43. Long core measurement. (a) Core holder system. (b) Data reduction scheme.

9. ROCK MAGNETISM AND PALEOMAGNETISM METHODS

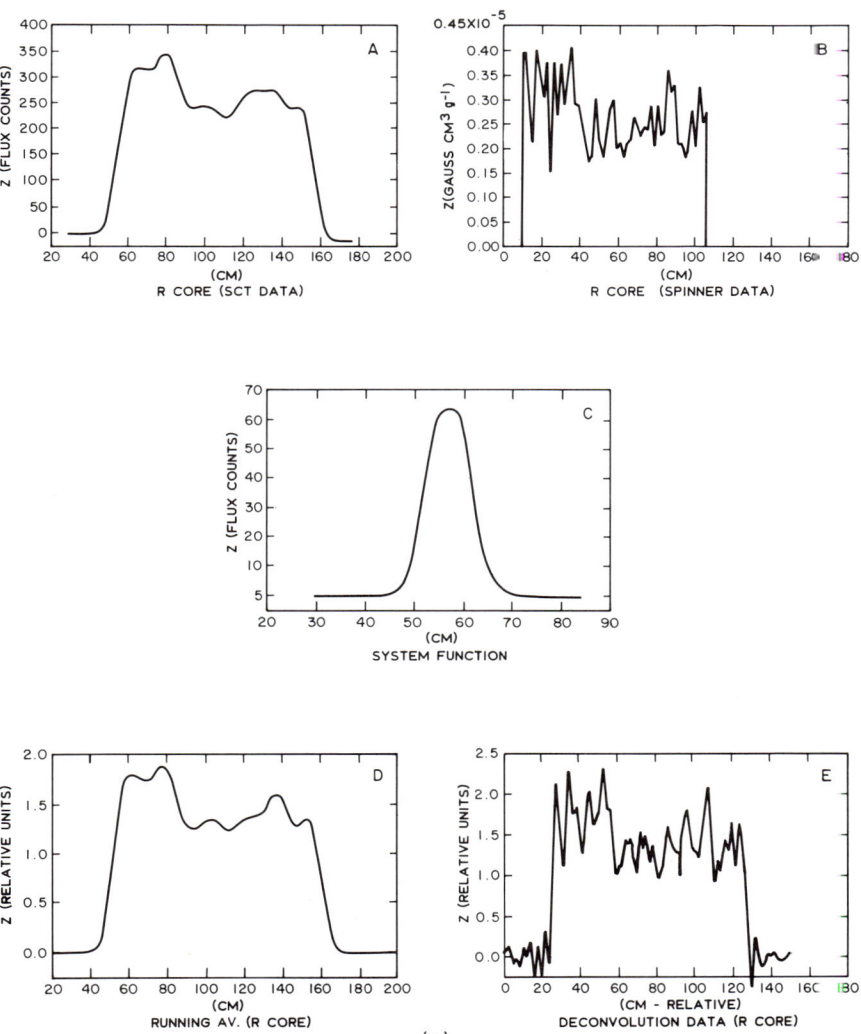

FIG. 43. (c) Demonstration of method: A, raw long core data; B, raw data when the core has been measured as individual samples with a spinner; C, is the response of the SCT magnetometer to a single sample, the system function; D, convolution of the system function with the individual sample raw data; E, deconvolution of the long core data with the system function.

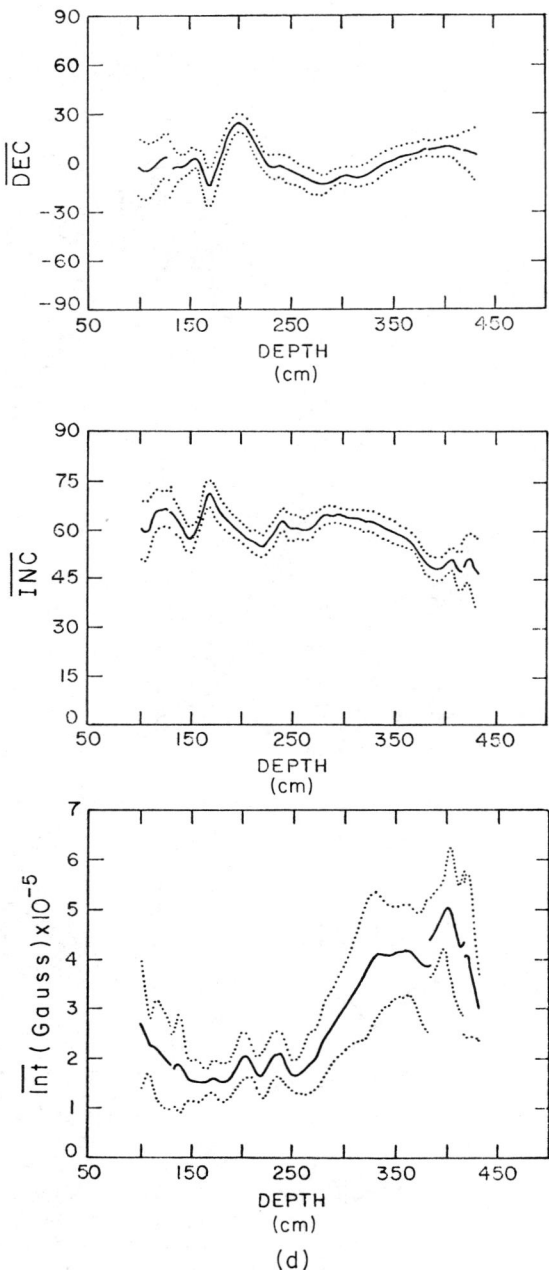

Fig. 43. (d) Combination of results from several cores from Lake Michigan.

(a)

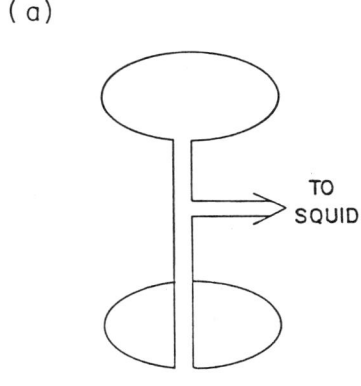

(b)

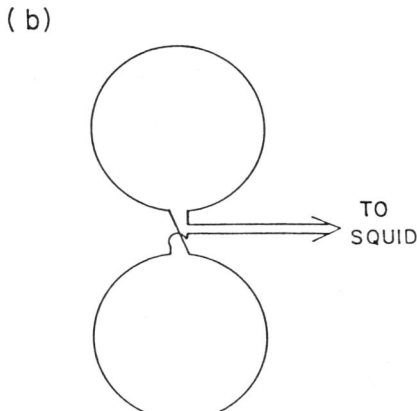

FIG. 44. Coil configurations for gradiometers: (a) first derivative of axial component and (b) first derivative of off-axis component.

and the gradient tensor is symmetric so

$$\frac{\partial B_x}{\partial y} = -\frac{\partial B_y}{\partial x}$$

$$\frac{\partial B_y}{\partial z} = -\frac{\partial B_z}{\partial y}$$

$$\frac{\partial B_z}{\partial x} = -\frac{\partial B_x}{\partial z}$$

Higher-order gradients can also be measured with superconducting circuits. The second derivative of the axial field $\partial^2 B_z/\partial z^2$ is obtained with a circuit which connects the output (induced current) or two first-derivative gradiometers in series opposition. The resulting net current is proportional to the *difference* in the gradient signal between the two circuits, i.e., the derivative of the gradient. Higher-order axial and off-axis gradients can be measured with similarly connected superconducting pickup coil structures.

The gradiometer circuits measure the gradient of the induction field averaged over the baseline or pickup coil separation. Often gradiometers are actually used to measure the magnetic field from a sample placed close to one of the pickup coils. The remaining coil is then used to cancel magnetic noise from sources more distant than the sample. The very large noise immunity achieved with gradiometer circuits results from the rapid fall-off of the magnetic field from localized magnetic sources. This is referred to as near-field mode of operation.

The DC magnetic field from a dipole source $M$ is

$$H_r = 2\mathbf{M}\cos\theta/4\pi r^3$$

$$H_\theta = \mathbf{M}\sin\theta/4\pi r^3$$

where $r$ is the distance from the dipole source to the observation point and $\theta$ the polar angle. The gradient of these field components is the derivative with respect to $r$ and varies as $1/r^4$. The second-order gradient varies as $1/r^5$, etc. This very rapid decay with distance means that remote field sources will produce very little signal at a first- or second-derivative gradiometer. A signal source located very near one of the pickup coils will produce flux that mostly links this one coil, and the circuit essentially measures the magnetic *field* of the sample (Vrba *et al.*, 1982).

The degree to which the signal from distant sources is rejected by a gradiometer circuit depends on the accuracy with which the coils are constructed and aligned. This noise rejection is termed the common mode rejection or balance of the gradiometer pickup coils and is measured by determining the signal that a first-order gradiometer would detect if placed in a time-varying but perfectly uniform magnetic field. For example, in the gradiometer circuit shown in Fig. 44a, if the upper pickup coil had a larger area than the lower coil, a signal would be detected even if the gradient were zero. Another source of imbalance is tilt of one coil relative to the other. This couples off-axis field changes as net signals.

Since the gradient subtraction is done within the closed superconducting circuit the process is passive and is only dependent on the mechanical accuracy and stability of the pickup coil structure. Typically, the pickup coils are made of niobium–titanium wire bonded to quartz or silicon substrates.

The substrate is machined and ground to tolerances of the order of 0.01 mm. The coil planes can be aligned for better than $0.01°$, giving an intrinsic balance of the order of $10^{-3}/m$, where the balance is defined as the error signal in units of gradient divided by the uniform field change. A simple way to measure the balance of a gradiometer circuit is to rotate the entire circuit through a 360° revolution in the earth's field in a site remote from large magnetic objects. The measured peak-to-peak signal divided by twice the earth's field component along the gradiometer axis is the balance.

The balance can be adjusted mechanically and electronically to the order of $10^{-8}/m$. Mechanical adjustment consists of placing small pieces of superconducting material (balance disks) near one of the pickup coils to distort the field and couple more or less flux to one coil relative to the other. These superconducting balance disks may be bonded to the gradiometer substrate, which requires repeated warming and cooling of the gradiometer to achieve a high balance, or they may be attached to rods that extend from the top of the gradiometer probe to the pickup coils. The disks are then moved with micrometer adjustments at the probe top.

Electronic balancing is also very effective in improving the common mode rejection. In this case, the error signal profile is measured with respect to the ambient magnetic field by simultaneously sensing the field and the gradient. This balance scale factor can then be used to provide a compensation signal that is fed back into the gradiometer or its output. Mechanical adjustment is normally used to achieve a balance of $10^{-5}/m$ and electronic feedback is used for further improvement (Vrba et al., 1982).

Gradiometers are available from CTF Systems, Cryogenic Consultants, 2-G Enterprises, and S.H.E. Corporation in a wide variety of configurations. Specific biological applications are for magnetocardiagrams and magneto-encephalograms, as well as testing samples for the presence of magnetic inclusions. Noise levels are determined by the nature of the ambient magnetic noise and subtleties in dewar design. In an unshielded environment, noise levels of $2 \times 10^{-9}\,T\,m^{-1}$ can be achieved. Gradiometers may eventually become the workhorses of paleomagnetism and rock magnetism for remanence measurements and weak field susceptibility measurements. Their great advantage over standard rock magnetometers is that, when measured, the sample is external to the magnetometer. Sample handling and the use of auxiliary equipment are therefore much easier than with the instruments which have limited room temperature access holes. (Sugiura et al., 1985).

3.2.4. Electronics, Computer Interfacing and Computers. A major aspect of the new paleomagnetism is a reflection of the development of electronics and computers in the past decades. In the 1960s and 1970s the growing availability of phase-sensitive detectors provided the principal means of signal enhancement for the spinner magnetometers. During the 1970s there was increased use of digital data presentation, so that for a brief period one wrote down outputs from digital panel meters. These results were later fed to the campus mainframe for processing. This inefficient procedure soon changed, as it became feasible to use the campus mainframe via a terminal and telephone modem. Finally, in the late 1970s, with the availability of such microcomputers as the Altair, one could have a dedicated microcomputer for a cryogenic or spinner magnetometer. These early microcomputers were less convenient than the present IBM PCs and Apples, but they permitted the development of on-line data analysis, which made a substantial difference to the way in which paleomagnetism was done. The next stage will presumably be increased automation of the measurement procedure. Indeed, this has already been begun in several laboratories, so one does not need to sit in front of the equipment during measurements; samples can be automatically loaded and demagnetized.

3.2.4.1. SIGNAL ENHANCEMENT. From the time of the earliest spinner magnetometers some form of phase determination was required, because it is the phase of the signal generated by the rotating sample which gives the direction of its magnetization. A simple method of obtaining the necessary reference voltage is to mount a small magnet in the rotating shaft of the spinner so that a second pickup coil can be used to detect this voltage. Then, knowing the orientation of the reference magnet and the phase difference between the reference and signal voltages, one can determine the magnetization direction in the sample. Another possibility is to use a modulated light source to provide the reference voltage. The standard method of determining the phase difference between the signal and reference voltages is to use a phase-sensitive detector. Thus there was an initial requirement for phase determination. However, the phase-sensitive detector also provides signal enhancement.

Phase-sensitive detectors, or lock-in amplifiers, exploit the correlation known to exist between the signal and reference voltages (Meade, 1982). Thus, the signal and reference must be at the same frequency when they come from two magnets, mounted on the same rotating shaft. In contrast, at least some of the noise will be uncorrelated with the reference voltage. The critical parts of a lock-in amplifier are the mixer, the low-pass filter, and the amplifier.

The mixer carries out the multiplication on which the phase-sensitive detection depends. Representing the signal as

$$V = V_p \sin wt + \theta$$

where $w = 2vf$, with $f$ frequency, $t$ time, and $\theta$ and phase angle, we write

$$V_1 V_2 = V_{p1} V_{p2} (\sin w_1 t + \theta_1)(\sin w_2 t + \theta_2)$$

so that elementary trigonometry gives

$$V_1 V_2 = V_{p1} V_{p2} \tfrac{1}{2} \{\cos[(w_1 - w_2)t + \theta_1 - \theta_2]$$
$$- \cos[(w_1 + w_2)t + \theta_1 + \theta_2]\}$$

The first term within the brackets is a frequency difference term and the second a frequency sum term. Letting $w_1$ equal $w_2$ gives

$$V_1 V_2 = V_{p1} V_{p2} \tfrac{1}{2} [\cos(\theta_1 - \theta_2) - \cos 2wt + \theta_1 + \theta_2)]$$

The first term is a DC term, which is a function of the phase difference we seek. The second is a high-frequency term, which can be discriminated against by a low-pass filter. The output is

$$V_1 V_2 = V_{p1} V_{p2} \tfrac{1}{2} \cos(\theta_1 - \theta_2)$$

This has precisely the information we require, namely the phase difference between the reference and signal voltages.

Having seen the mathematical background, we now proceed to the method of achieving the result electronically. This is described in more detail in such standard texts as Malmstead *et al.* (1973). A block diagram of a phase-sensivitive detector is given in Fig. 45a. The heart of the instrument is the synchronous demodulator or multiplier. However, before the voltages are fed to it, they may be preamplified. The reference voltage is also squared, which facilitates the operation of the demodulator. Squaring is achieved with a comparator, a circuit element which has two output states of equal fixed positive or negative voltages. When the input voltage reaches a prescribed level, the device switches state. If the input signal is noisy, there can be false state switching activated by noise. To avoid this a Schmitt trigger is used. Once the first positive-going crossing has taken place, the switching voltage is modified to take it out of the range of the noise. The two voltages enter the demodulator, as illustrated in Fig. 45b. The demodulator is frequently a four-quadrant multiplier as discussed in Malmstead *et al.* (1973). One can think of the device as a switch activated by the reference voltage. The switch is between the input and the inverse of the input as illustrated in Fig. 45c. Note that the signal input has indeed been inverted at the lower position of the switch. The resulting output is then a rectified voltage whose magnitude is dependent on the difference in phase of the signal and reference. The dependence can be seen clearly in Fig. 45d. Of course, there are numerous different ways of achieving the demodulation, but the final output is a DC voltage proportional to the phase difference between the two voltages. For several years in the 1960s and 1970s, the Princeton applied research (PAR) spinner was one of the most popular instruments because it incorporated state-of-the-art phase-sensitive detectors.

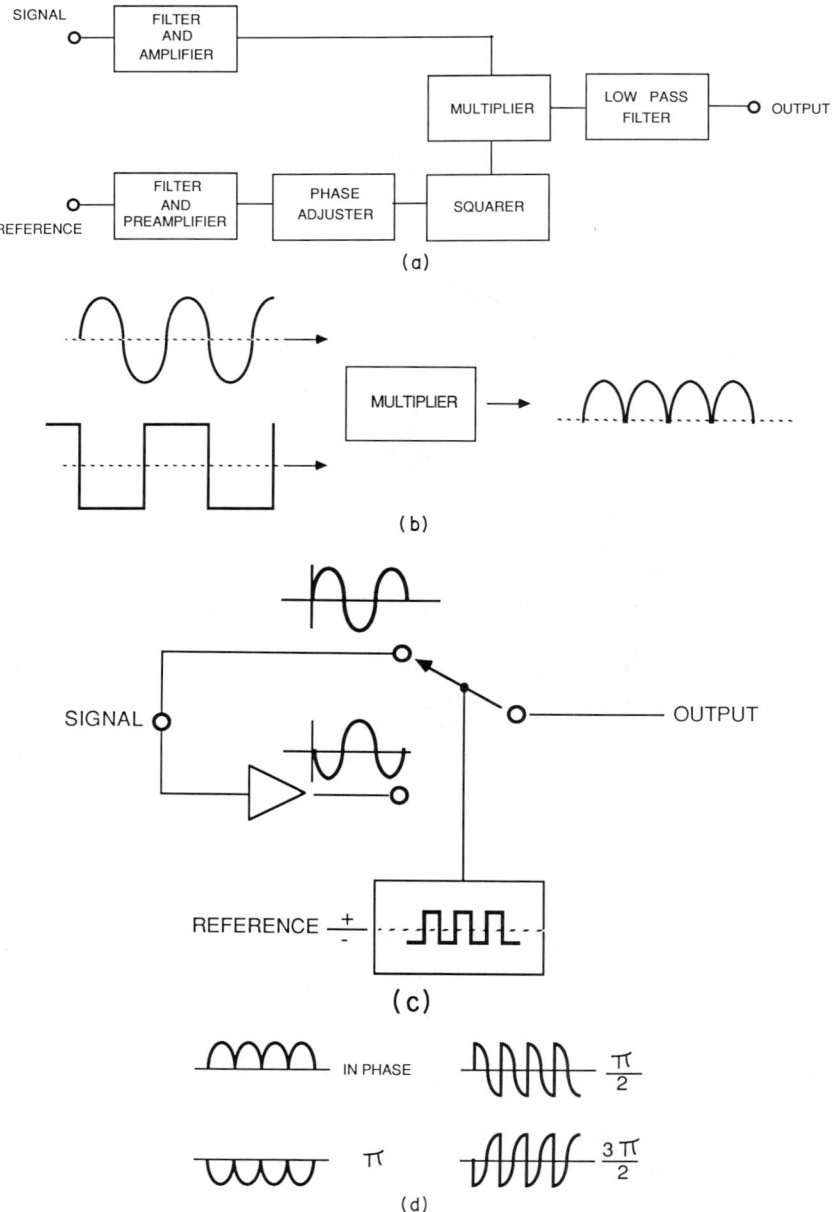

FIG. 45. Phase-sensitive detector: (a) block diagram; (b) voltages entering and leaving multiplier; (c) multiplier as a switch; and (d) dependence of output of multiplier on phase difference between signal and reference voltages.

A phase-sensitive detector is not the only method of signal enhancement used in spinners. Another approach is to use a shaft encoder to sample the output voltage during rotation of the sample. A rudimentary version of this was used by Kobayashi and Fuller (1967) in an application of a vibration magnetometer to measure remanent magnetization. As the sample rotated within the pickup coil array, the carriage activated a microswitch and the output voltage was determined. The data were analyzed by a Fourier transform method. Such methods are now much improved and form the basis of operation of the digital versions of the Schonstedt magnetometer.

It seems very likely that in the near future signal enhancement will be increasingly carried out by software in a computer, rather than by the electronic devices we have discussed. However, they will be useful devices for many years to come.

3.2.4.2. COMPUTER INTERFACING. As part of the microcomputer revolution it has become much easier to achieve interfacing between computers and devices. Routinely one hooks up printers and plotters to microcomputers through "industry standard connectors." The printer may not function immediately because one finds the industry standards are not so standard as one hoped, but the problem is usually solved with off-the-shelf equipment. In rock magnetism and paleomagnetism one seeks to interface an analog voltage or a number of analog voltages in a particular sequence to a computer. There are now practical guides to interfacing which make simple solutions to these problems accessible to all (Leibson, 1985).

To interface a spinner or a cryogenic magnetometer one must sample and digitize the two or three voltages which carry the information concerning the magnetization vector, with possible auxiliary channels to carry information about temperature or pressure or some other aspect of the conditions of measurement. The approach is to multiplex the various analog signals first, so that a single A/D converter can service the instrument.

A multiplexer can be visualized as a rotary switch which brings successively on line to the A/D each of the various voltages to be sampled. The voltages applied to the multiplexer from the computer determine the voltages to be sampled. Critical factors to be considered in choice of multiplers are power requirements and switching times.

The job of converting the analog voltages, brought on-line by the multiplexer, into digital form is done by the A/D converter. A wide variety of A/D converters are available, from the fast but complex flash converters to the simple but slower integrating converters. To illustrate a method of A/D conversion, let us consider a popular type which involves the use of D/A converters. Figure 46a illustrates a simple D/A circuit. As long as the switches are all open there is no current through the resistor circuit and the output is zero. If one of the switches is closed, a current flows through the

(a)

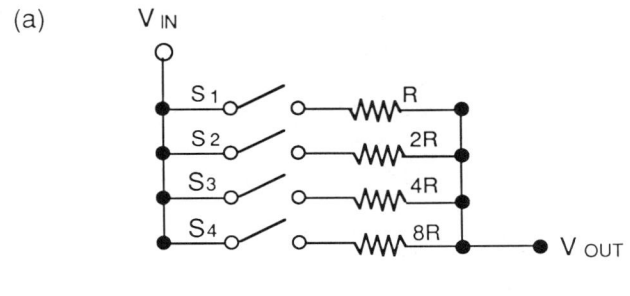

(b)

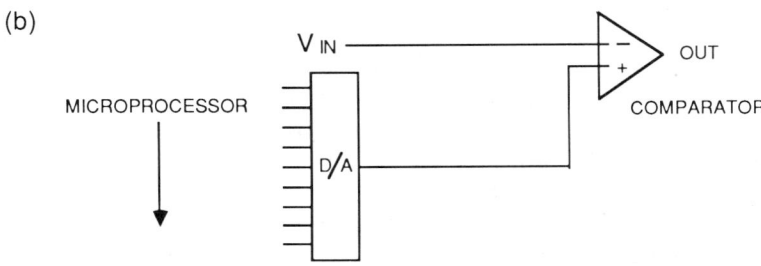

FIG. 46. (a) Digital-to-analog converter circuit and (b) analog-to-digital converter circuit. (After Leibson, 1983.)

resistance network and the output will rise to $V$, $V/2$, $V/4$, or $V/8$ depending on which switch is closed. This involves the use of an operational amplifier to apply negative feedback at the output point so that it appears as a ground throughout. When more than one switch is closed at a time, the currents through the resistors add and we get 16 different voltage levels for the 16 combinations of switch closings. This provides a means of converting a 4-bit binary number into the required 16 different voltage levels. Although this circuit illustrates the principal of D/A conversion, one would not be well advised to market this particular device. Given a practical D/A, it can readily be used to act as an element in an A/D. Figure 46b illustrates a simple version of such an A/D. A routine from the microprocessor begins by generating a zero output from the D/A. The output is increased incrementally until the input voltage is matched at the comparator. This involves counting the increments by which the D/A output was increased. Knowing the magnitude of the increment, one has the voltage. Again, marketable versions of such devices involve more sophisticated approaches and utilize optimized successive approximations to the voltage. There are a number of important considerations in selection of an A/D. One is the resolution required, which is determined by the number of bits in the output of the A/D. A second is the input voltage range. To make full use of the converter one must use the input voltage range for which it is designed. Conversion speed may also be critical in certain applications.

Parallel interfaces are commonly used with both D/As and A/Ds. Zero wire handshakes can be used to drive D/As. An 8-bit latch stores the state of the microprocessor's data bus when given a write pulse and valid address. The voltages then appear on the output lines, from the latch to the device. Conversely, the same zero wire handshake can be used to read the D/A. In this case, an input buffer replaces the latch. A read pulse to the appropriate address will now transfer the states of the lines in the buffer to the microprocessor bus. The most common interfaces for A/Ds are two-wire handshakes. The two-wire handshake not only is able to inform the microprocessor when valid data are available, but also permits a beginning and end of data conversion to be transmitted. At this point the reader is referred to such handbooks as Leibson (1983) for more detailed discussions. The only purpose of the present discussion is to give some familiarity with the rudiments of interfacing. This amount of knowledge is useful in choosing between the various data gathering boards which are available to be inserted into such microcomputers as the IBM PC or Apple. Such boards are available with a wide variety of numbers of inputs, input voltages, resolutions, and speeds.

3.2.5. Controlled Magnetic Field Environments. The analysis of paleomagnetic samples requires magnetic field control over volumes, which vary from that of a single sample to that of a whole laboratory. These requirements may be for high fields, for example, in hysteresis measurements, or for zero-field environments for thermal demagnetization. A thorough discussion of such matters is given in Collinson (1984). Traditionally, there have been two approaches to the low-field environment problem. The first is to build a coil set in the Helmholtz or the Fanselau configuration and then, by use of the appropriate currents, to cancel the geomagnetic or local laboratory field. The second is to use magnetic shielding, whereby high-permeability magnetic material distors the ambient field in such a way that a reduced field region is produced. A third method, which has recently been used, is superconducting shielding. However, this method is not practical for shielding large regions. Its use in connection with cryogenic magnetometers has already been discussed.

Rather than considering the details of the two traditional methods, their comparative merits will be discussed here and the reader is again referred to Collinson (1983) for a more comprehensive treatment. First, let us consider the case in which we wish to cancel the geomagnetic field, but we are not concerned with any fluctuation in that field. Even a large set of Helmholtz coils gives a relatively small volume of field cancellation to a few tens of gammas. For example a 6-ft-diameter coil set will produce field cancellation of this type over little more than the volume of a few samples. Moreover, to bring about this field reduction from the ambient geomagnetic field will involve a very large local field gradient. However, the construction of such coils and the power requirements are not formidable. The cost of construction of such a system need not be more than a few hundred dollars or at most about $1000. In contrast, if shielding is undertaken the volume of the reduced field region is essentially the region enclosed by the shield, gradients within the region are small, and the construction difficulties and cost increase substantially. Thus to shield a facility which can house a couple of magnetometers, AF and thermal demagnetization equipment, and some storage space with soft steel will cost about $30,000. In a two-layer steel room, recently constructed at our laboratory by Lodestar Magnetics, the internal field value is reduced to between 100 and 200 gammas. The field gradients are also small, of the order of a few gammas per centimeter. The details of constructing such a shield are described in Scott and Frohlich (1985).

It should be recognized that both of the techniques discussed above only give environments which are magnetically protected in a DC sense. The coil array has a fixed current, preset to cancel an observed field at some initial time. Similarly, the shielded room provides DC field cancellation against the field at the time of construction, and much of the success of such rooms lies in the care with which the steel is treated as the room is constructed. If, after construction, the external field changes, this change will generate a disturbance within the room. Both techniques can of course be protected against changing fields. The coil array can be provided with a flux gate sensor, which monitors the field changes and, using a feedback loop to the power supply coils, compensates for the changes. This active system involves additional equipment and circuitry and raises the price of the array to the range of some tens of thousands of dollars. To protect the shielded room against AC fields requires use of material whose skin depth is sufficiently small to make construction feasible. The principle of this shielding is simply eddy current shielding. The time-varying fields set up eddy currents in the highly conducting shield material, according to the Faraday–Lenz law, such that entry of the field into the material is opposed. Consequently, the field does not reach the enclosed space. This does not, however, provide protection against DC or slowly varying magnetic fields. To combine the effects of the eddy current shielding and the magnetic shielding of the high-permeability steel, one uses $\mu$-metal (Cohen, 1970). This, however, raises the price of a room of useful size to the order of hundreds of thousands of dollars. Patton and Fitch (1962) were early users of $\mu$-metal, which permitted measurements of ARM acquisition in low fields. More recently biomagnetists have taken advantage of $\mu$-metal rooms and reviews of techniques have appeared in their literature (Erné, 1983).

## 9. ROCK MAGNETISM AND PALEOMAGNETISM METHODS

FIG. 47. Shielded room.

A possible escape from the very high cost of $\mu$-metal rooms may eventually emerge from the use of flexible woven $\mu$-metal and other like materials. At present, it appears that the combination of coil compensation techniques in conjunction with high-permeability steel rooms offers a practical solution (Fig. 47). For example, within a room in which the field is reduced to about 100 gammas, a coil array can give a low-field region large enough for a multiple-sample thermal demagnetization furnace. Field cancellation to about 1 gamma is practicable. Moreover, this does not involve strong gradients. However, it must be remembered that this does not provide protection against variation in the field outside the room. The opening of a steel door within 10 or 20 ft of the furnace will be seen as a disturbance of several gammas.

### 3.3. Data Analysis

A major part of the data analysis of paleomagnetism is statistical. One does not collect a single sample, measure its inclination, and assign a paleolatitude for the locality on the basis of the measurement. One makes a large number of measurements and obtains an estimate of the mean and an estimate of the variance. Then one can place a confidence interval on the estimate of the true mean. To do this for directional data requires an analog of Gaussian statistics. This was provided by Fisher, who developed a statistical distribution to describe the populations of unit vectors on the unit sphere. This statistic is repeatedly used in paleomagnetism, e.g., to combine individual measurements of a single sample (but see Briden and Arthur, 1981), to combine measurements of samples from a site, and to combine results from different sites.

A second important part of paleomagnetic analysis consists of the various coordinate transformations required to return the orientation of the sample to its initial configuration, in which it was drilled, and to make structural corrections. These are handled as matrix operations in various computer programs. They can also be done by hand on stereonets. Both methods are described below.

Finally, there is the problem of presentation of directional data on a two-dimensional piece of paper. To solve this, we use the classical projection methods of cartography and crystallography. The use of the projections is a prerequisite for the discussion of paleomagnetic data, so it will be described first.

3.3.1. Projections. Projections play a major role in paleomagnetism because we need to represent the directions of vectors on the unit sphere on two-dimensional paper. The two most commonly used projections are the equal angle and equal area projections, with their corresponding Wulff and Schmidt nets.

Figure 48A illustrates the relationship between the directions of vectors on the unit sphere and the stereographic projection. The plane of projection is the equatorial plane of the unit sphere. The location of the vector on the stereographic projection is obtained by drawing a line from the projection point (P) to the end of the vector (C). The point at which the line PC cuts the projection plane (C') locates the vector in this projection. With the compass rose in the orientation shown, the north–south and east–west lines becomes radii in the stereographic projection. Vertically down is at the center and horizontal is on the primitive. To plot directions on the upper hemisphere of the unit sphere (D), one first projects these points over to the equivalent point on the lower hemisphere (D'), as illustrated, and then follows the same procedure as before to get D".

The stereographic projection distorts area, so that for applications in which the density of points is of interest, it is useful to use a projection for which equal areas on the unit sphere are preserved as equal areas. The equal area projection, as its name indicates, does this. The principle of the equal area projection is illustrated in Fig. 48b. To represent the unit vector $B$, one

9. ROCK MAGNETISM AND PALEOMAGNETISM METHODS

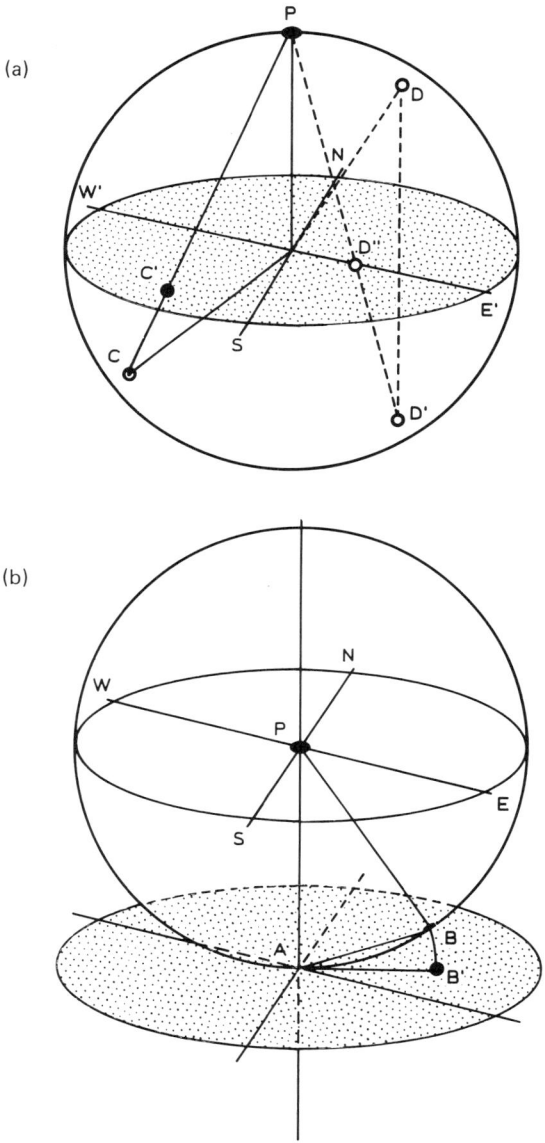

FIG. 48. Projections used in the presentation of paleomagnetic data: (A) stereographic and (B) equal area.

projects from the center of the unit sphere as shown. One then lays off a radius vector from the south pole of the unit sphere (P) to the end of the unit vector (B). This is then rotated down onto the projection plane (B'), which is tangential to the sphere at the south pole. This defines the position of the pole on the projection plane. The final result is a projection which preserves areas on the projection plane, but distorts angles.

3.3.2. Fisher Statistics. The tricky part of the statistics of paleomagnetism, which has given rise to a new branch of statistics, is the need to describe populations of directions. Gauss faced the same problem in applying his normal distribution to the analysis of astronomical data, but as the errors were small, he was able to analyze the directions as points on a flat surface— the tangent plane—rather than on the celestial sphere. Langevin (1905) introduced the appropriate azimuthally symmetrical distribution in his treatment of paramagnetism, and Arnold (1941) demonstrated that this distribution was indeed analogous to the Gauss normal distribution on a line. Meanwhile, Von Mises (1918) had developed an analogous distribution for directions in a circle. However, it was Fisher, after discussions with Hospers and others at the Geophysics Department at Cambridge, who eventually provided the appropriate statistical analysis in his famous paper (Fisher, 1953). As a starting point for a more detailed treatment than will be given here, the reader is referred to the text by Mardia (1972). This text is a little easier going than the Fisher paper, which is probably one of the most frequently referenced and least read papers in the field. Watson (1983) provides another important source, as does a recent series of papers by McFadden and co-workers (McFadden, 1980a, b, 1982a, b; McFadden and Lowes, 1981).

Fisher assumed that the unit vectors are distributed about the true mean according to an $\exp(\kappa \cos \theta)$ dependence. The distribution is azimuthally symmetric (Fig. 49a). To describe the variance of the population, he used the precision parameter $\kappa$, such that the larger $\kappa$ is the more tightly the distribution is peaked (Fig. 49b).

Consider the directions as unit vectors defining points on the unit sphere. This gives a probability density function for the points per unit area of

$$P_A \, dA = c e^{\kappa \cos \theta} \sin \theta \, d\theta \, d\theta$$

The constant $c$ is the normalization constant equal to $\kappa/4\pi \sinh \kappa$ so that the expression integrates to one for the sphere.

As the distribution is azimuthally symmetric, the probability density as a function of $\theta$ is

$$P_\theta \, d\theta = (\kappa/2 \sinh \kappa) c^{\kappa \cos \theta} \sin \theta \, d\theta$$

By far the most common estimate $\kappa$ of $k$ is that given by Fisher (1953) as the best estimate of $\kappa$,

$$k = (N - 1)/(N - R)$$

However, as pointed out by McFadden (1980b), it is by no means the only one. Of the others, at least the maximum likelihood estimate is worthy of mention. This approach gives

$$\coth k - 1/k = R/N$$

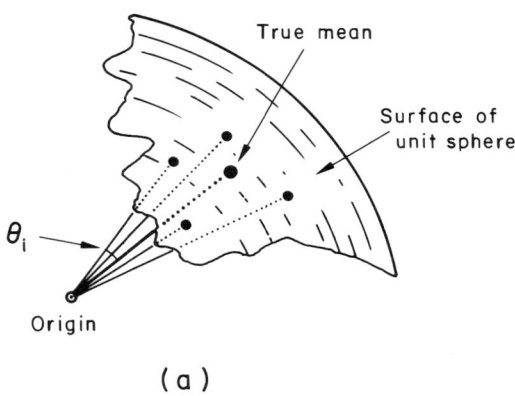

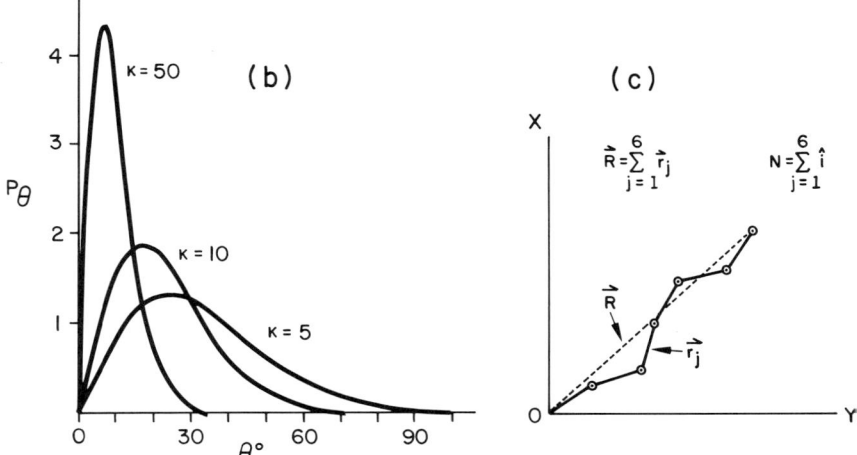

Fig. 49. Fisher statistics: (a) the basis; (b) populations with different $k$ values (after Irving, 1964); (c) an estimate of $k$.

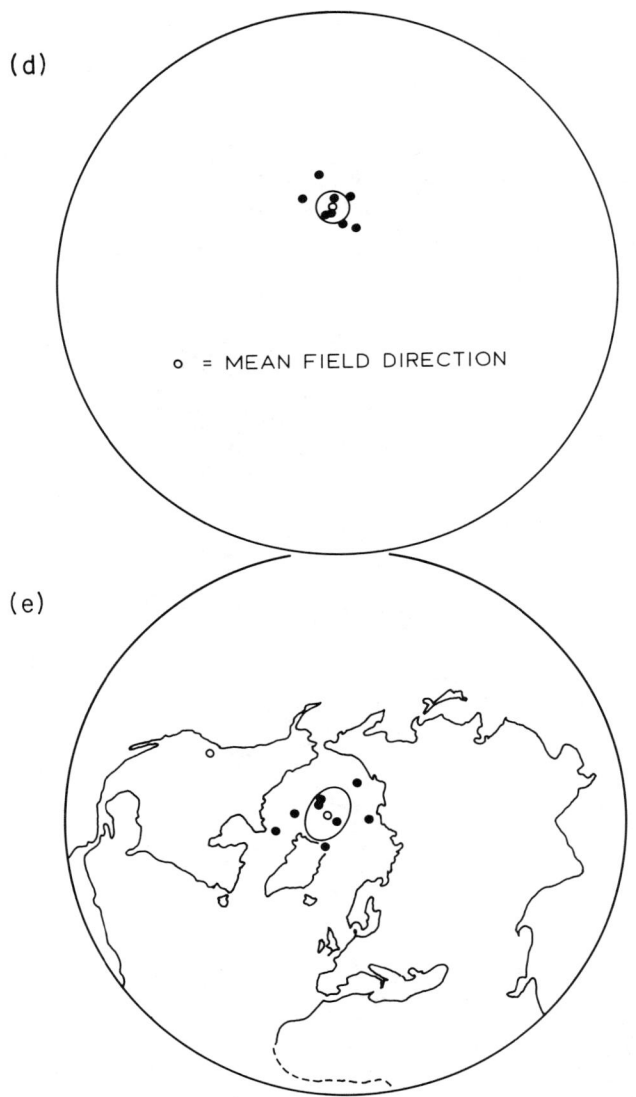

FIG. 49. (d) Use of confidence ellipse (radius $\alpha$) for field data and (e) VHPs.

so that when $R/N$ is near unity we get

$$k = N/(N - R)$$

The estimate (Fig. 49c) draws attention to the similarity between the Langevin function of paramagnetism and the Fisher statistics; $k$ is seen to be analogous to the ratio of the magnetic aligning energy to the thermal randomizing energy in paramagnetic theory.

To the experimentalist, an important question is when particular estimates of $\kappa$ should be used. McFadden (1980b) notes that the maximum likelihood estimate should be used when $X^2$ testing for goodness of fit, while the Fisher best estimate should be used to test inferences from data sets. This is then analogous to usage in Gaussian normal statistics.

Although paleomagnetists usually show scant concern about whether their data sets are Fisher distributed, there are straightforward tests which can be made to check the matter. Such a test was carried out by Watson and Irving (1957) on a large number of samples cut from a single block of rock. The directions should be azimuthally symmetric, which can be tested by comparing the observed and expected values in particular azimuthal ranges. The Fisherian distribution also predicts the number of directions, which fall into particular annuli corresponding to particular values of $\theta$. McFadden (1980b) questions the choice of estimate of $k$ used by Watson and Irving (1957), but does conclude, as they did, that the hypothesis that the directions are Fisher distributed cannot be rejected.

The combination of individual estimates of a direction of magnetization is the most common use of Fisher statistics. An estimate of the mean is obtained and with it a determination of how far from the true mean our estimate is likely to lie. To do this we first calculate the unit vector sum $R$ of the $N$ directions $(I_j, D_j)$:

$$R = (X, Y, Z) \qquad |R| = (X^2 + Y^2 + Z^2)^{1/2}$$

where

$$X = \sum_{j=1}^{N} \cos I_j \cos D_j \qquad Y = \sum_{j=1}^{N} \cos I_j \sin D_j \qquad Z = \sum_{j=1}^{N} \sin I_j$$

Conveniently, $R$ is the only quantity required for inference by Fisher's spherical statistics. Obviously, the direction of $R$ corresponds to the calculated mean direction. If $R$ is small (limit, $R = 0$), then the individual vectors are highly dispersed, and we would suspect that the estimate of the true mean direction is of little interest. On the other hand, when $R$ is large (limit, $R = N$), one can assume that $R$ is an accurate estimate of the true mean and that the time mean may be of interest.

To assign confidence intervals for the estimate of the mean, the Fisher analog of the confidence intervals ascribed to normal distributions is used. This permits us to comment on the estimate of the mean in terms of the sample of the population. In particular, it allows a circle to be defined about the estimated mean direction on the unit sphere, within which the true mean has a certain probability of being found. The derivation of this confidence interval is a somewhat involved statistical discussion (Fisher, 1953). The result is

$$\cos \alpha_{1-P} = 1 - \frac{N - R}{R}\left[\left(\frac{1}{P}\right)^{1/(N-1)} - 1\right]$$

where $P$ is normally taken as 0.05. An approximation for the circle of 95% confidence is

$$\alpha_{95} = 140/\sqrt{KN}$$

This then defines the radius of a circle on the unit sphere about the estimated mean direction, within which there is a 95% probability of the true mean being found. Figure 49 illustrates the use of $\alpha$ and $k$ in the description of a population of directions of magnetization and of a population of individual estimates of the virtual geomagnetic pole.

Other statistical desciptions have been used, but Fisher's statistics predominate. Some workers have favored direct contouring of the unit directions. Some have advocated the use of the mode as an alternative to the mean (Van Alstine, 1980). However, the only statistic other than Fisher that has been utilized extensively is the Bingham statistic (Bingham, 1974). This assumes that the directions are distributed as $e^{k \cos^2 \theta}$. It is designed to describe populations of unit vectors which are distributed about the two ends of an axis, rather than about a single direction. A very promising moment of inertia approach has been suggested by Kirschvink (1980). This has the advantage of being a less model-dependent statistic. Confidence intervals could be assigned using the method of Hext (1963).

3.3.3. Transformation of Coordinates. The magnetometers give directions of magnetization in terms of the specimen coordinates $(x, y, z)$ because it is in terms of the specimen geometry that the measurement is made. We generally need to transform to the coordinate system of the earth's surface, from which the sample was drilled $(X, Y, Z)$. Sometimes it will also be necessary to rotate the result again to give it in the coordinate of the ancient surface of the earth $(X', Y', Z')$, which can be obtained from the bedding plane of a sedimentary rock. This is called a structural or tectonic correction. Accurate determination of structural corrections is not always easy because of lack of outcrop and the nature of the rock. In particular, it is difficult to make structural corrections accurately if folds are steeply plunging because it is hard to get sufficient estimates of the bedding on the fold to determine its plunge. Finally, we may wish to express a result in terms of geomagnetic pole coordinates $(X'', Y'', Z'')$.

In commonly used systems (Schmidt, 1974), the transformation or rotation always refers to a rotation of the coordinate system, while the vector remains stationary. The rotation is achieved with standard matrix algebra,

$$\begin{pmatrix} x' \\ y' \\ z' \end{pmatrix} = \begin{pmatrix} A_{11} & A_{12} & A_{13} \\ A_{21} & A_{22} & A_{23} \\ A_{31} & A_{32} & A_{33} \end{pmatrix} \begin{pmatrix} x \\ y \\ z \end{pmatrix}$$

The following are examples of rotation operators.

1. Rotate counterclockwise about the $x$ axis (as viewed from $+x$ looking toward $-x$) through an angle $\phi$

$$\begin{pmatrix} 1 & 0 & 0 \\ 0 & \cos\phi & \sin\phi \\ 0 & -\sin\phi & \cos\phi \end{pmatrix}$$

2. Rotate counterclockwise about the $y$ axis through an angle $\phi$

$$\begin{pmatrix} \cos\phi & 0 & -\sin\phi \\ 0 & 1 & 0 \\ \sin\phi & 0 & \cos\phi \end{pmatrix}$$

3. Rotate counterclockwise about the $z$ axis through an angle $\phi$

$$\begin{pmatrix} \cos\phi & \sin\phi & 0 \\ -\sin\phi & \cos\phi & 0 \\ 0 & 0 & 1 \end{pmatrix}$$

The rotation to bring $(x, y, z)$ specimen coordinates into $(x, y, z)$ field coordinates is now given and illustrated in Fig. 50.

$$\begin{pmatrix} X \\ Y \\ Z \end{pmatrix} = (AB) \begin{pmatrix} x \\ y \\ z \end{pmatrix}$$

The operator $B$ must be applied first and followed by $A$.

$$B = \begin{pmatrix} \cos\phi & 0 & -\sin\phi \\ 0 & 1 & 0 \\ \sin\phi & 0 & \cos\phi \end{pmatrix} \quad \begin{array}{l} \phi = \text{sample dip angle} \\ \text{(case 2 above)} \end{array}$$

$$A = \begin{pmatrix} \cos\phi & \sin\phi & 0 \\ -\sin\phi & \cos\phi & 0 \\ 0 & 0 & 1 \end{pmatrix} \quad \begin{array}{l} \phi = 90 - \text{sample strike} \\ \text{(case 3 above)} \end{array}$$

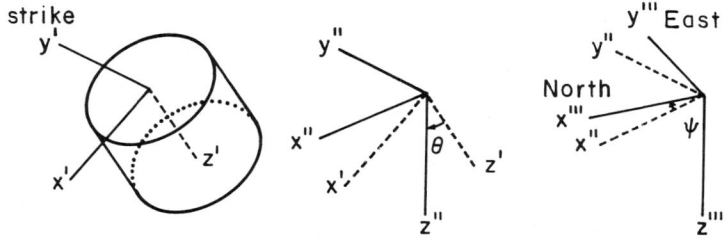

FIG. 50. Rotation from cylinder to field coordinates. (After Schmidt, 1974.)

where

$x$ is oriented down dip
$y$ is oriented along strike to the viewer's left when looking up dip (toward the $-x$ direction)
$z$ is oriented downward along the core axis

and

$X$ is oriented toward the north
$Y$ is oriented toward the east
$Z$ is oriented vertically downward

The $B$ rotation is counterclockwise about $+y$ to account for the dip of the sample. The $A$ rotation is counterclockwise about $+Z$ to bring about the change in azimuth. These two rotations are sufficient to change from specimen to field coordinates.

The next required correction is that for bedding dip. This involves rotating the bedding plane about the strike direction through an angle equal to the bedding dip. The remanent vector is rotated along with the bedding plane because it is fixed with respect to the bedding plane. The sequence of rotations is

1. Rotate counterclockwise by $\phi =$ bedding strike $- 90$ about the $z$ axis to bring the bedding strike into the $y'$ axis. This is equivalent to case 3 above.
2. Rotate about $y'$ by $\phi = -$ bedding dip to bring the bedding plane into the horizontal. This is equivalent to case 2 above.
3. Rotate about $z''$ by $\phi = 90 -$ bedding strike, which returns the strike to its original orientation by a second application of case 3 above.

For those who prefer to do these operations manually, or at least to visualize them using a stereonet, they are illustrated in Fig. 51. These and other transformations, such as the more complicated plunging fold correction, are by now routinely applied in all paleomagnetic studies by the various data reduction programs.

Paleomagnetic results are frequently presented in terms of the virtual geomagnetic pole (VGP). This is the pole (usually the magnetic south pole) of the dipole field which accounts for the observed declination and inclination at a site. The VGP can be determined by spherical trigonometry as shown in Fig. 52. However, this approach requires multiple testing, to assign the appropriate quadrant of the unit sphere. It is therefore more convenient to use matrix operators, as one does in the other coordinate transformations described above.

$$\begin{pmatrix} X \\ Y \\ Z \end{pmatrix} = (ABC) \begin{pmatrix} x \\ y \\ z \end{pmatrix}$$

To visualize these transformations, the reader may find it easiest to consider the application, in the reverse order, of the inverse of each of the operators, so as to obtain field directions from a given dipole configuration. Note that the $C$ operator is nonorthogonal and modifies the vector to take account of the relationship between inclination and polar angle. The operators follow in the order of application.

$$C = \begin{pmatrix} -1 & 0 & 0 \\ 0 & 1 & 0 \\ 0 & 0 & \frac{1}{2} \end{pmatrix}$$

$$B = \begin{pmatrix} \cos\phi & 0 & \sin\phi \\ 0 & 1 & 0 \\ -\sin\phi & 0 & \cos\phi \end{pmatrix}$$

with $\phi = \pi/2 -$ site latitude, and

$$A = \begin{pmatrix} \cos\phi & -\sin\phi & 0 \\ \sin\phi & \cos\phi & 0 \\ 0 & 0 & 1 \end{pmatrix}$$

with $\phi =$ site longitude. The result is now finally in VGP coordinates.

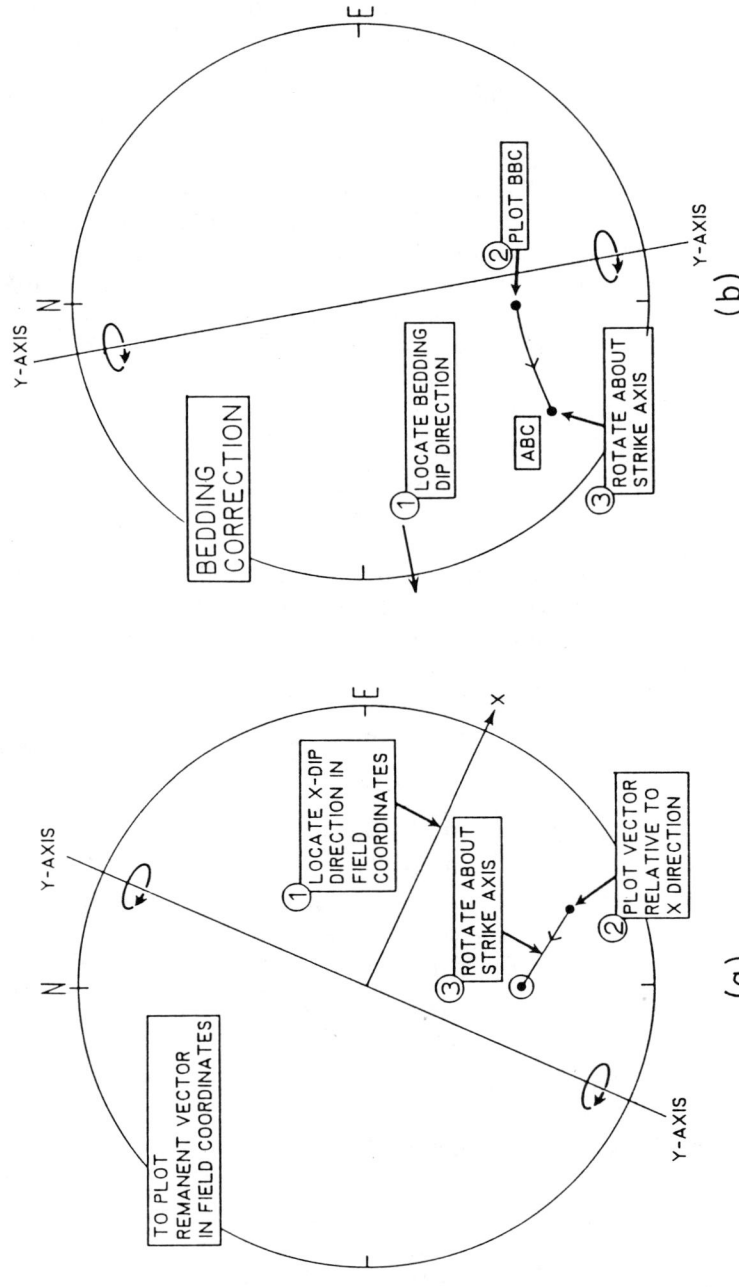

Fig. 51. Rotations performed on equal area net: (a) cylinder to field coordinates and (b) tectonic correction.

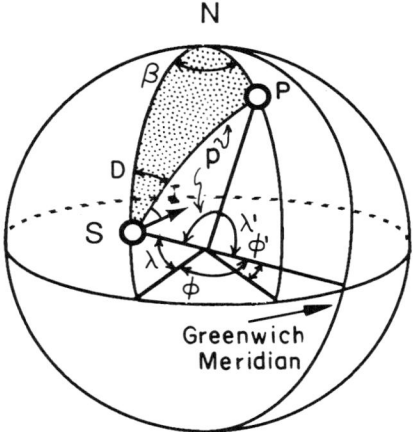

FIG. 52. Calculation of VGP. Apply cosine law to SNP to find $90 - \lambda' \cos(90 - \lambda') = \cos p \cos(90 - \lambda) + \sin p \sin(90 - \lambda) \cos D$. Apply sine law to get $\beta$: $\sin \beta = \sin p \sin D/\cos \lambda'$. The quadrant depends on the signs of $D$, $p$, and hence $\beta$ and $\lambda'$.

### 3.4. Signal-to-Noise Discrimination in Paleomagnetism—Practical Guide to Stability Tests and Demagnetization Techniques

The need for signal-to-noise discrimination in paleomagnetism arises because all or some of the NRM of a paleomagnetic sample may have been acquired long after the formation of the rock. To isolate the primary magnetization some treatment is required. Field tests have been developed to place the age of the magnetization in terms of a geologic event, e.g., folding. A number of terms have originated to describe the various magnetization components. Commonly a distinction will be made between primary magnetization, acquired at the time of formation of the rock, and subsequent or secondary magnetization. Characteristic magnetization is also sometimes used with a meaning similar to primary. Laboratory tests have now been devised to distinguish between primary and secondary magnetizations. These have developed into standard procedures in paleomagnetic studies and are somewhat euphemistically called cleaning. Here, one takes advantage of some distinction between the secondary and primary magnetizations to destroy the secondary preferentially, leaving the primary magnetization. For example, if the noise is blocked at a lower temperature than the signal, thermal demagnetization is used. One arranges to heat the sample and eliminate the noise, while leaving untouched the primary magnetization. The practical details will be discussed below but the principle is reviewed here. Recall that we can write magnetization as a typical relaxation phenomenon described by

$$M(t) = M(0)e^{-t/\tau}$$

where the relaxation time $\tau$ is obtained via Néel theory as

$$1/\tau = f_0 e^{-K_u V/kT}$$

Hence, if the sample is heated, the relaxation time will clearly decrease. As we noted before, for time constants of the order of experimental times, we require $\tau$ to reach about $10^2$ seconds. Now, if it happens that this condition is reached by 300°C for the noise and the signal is blocked at a much higher temperature, we have a technique for signal-to-noise enhancement. In this case, thermal demagnetization would be a useful technique.

One does not have to use thermal demagnetization on all occasions. There are numerous other techniques, of which the most popular is alternating-field demagnetization. This relies on the signal being preferentially carried by phases with higher coercive forces than those carrying the noise. Increasingly sophisticated analyses of the demagnetization data make it possible to separate primary and secondary magnetizations with some degree of confidence.

3.4.1. Thermal Demagnetization. The principle of thermal demagnetization has been discussed above; one takes advantage of the difference in blocking temperature of the signal and the noise to enhance the signal. There are two approaches to the experiment. One can heat the sample and cool it a minimal field, so that the magnetization which was unblocked is not reset on cooling. Thus the lower-temperature magnetization components are demagnetized, leaving untouched the phases with higher blocking temperatures. This technique has the advantage that several samples can be heated simultaneously. It has the disadvantage that it is hard to ensure that the cooling does not produce some remagnetization. The second approach is to demagnetize at high temperature and to measure at that temperature. The advantage of this method is that one is free from the problem of remagnetization because the sample is never cooled. Moreover, it is maintained in an exceptionally low field region—the measuring region with the magnetometer. The chief problem is that the experiment can only be carried out with one sample at a time. However, even this has some side benefit since one can conveniently carry out on-line analysis of the results. The method also encourages one to get much more detailed thermal demagnetization curves than are practical with the stepwise method.

The stepwise method can be carried out in regions where the field is cancelled with Helmholtz coils (Fig. 53a) or in $\mu$-metal shields (Fig. 53b). The coil arrays cancel the field initially over a limited region to a few tens of

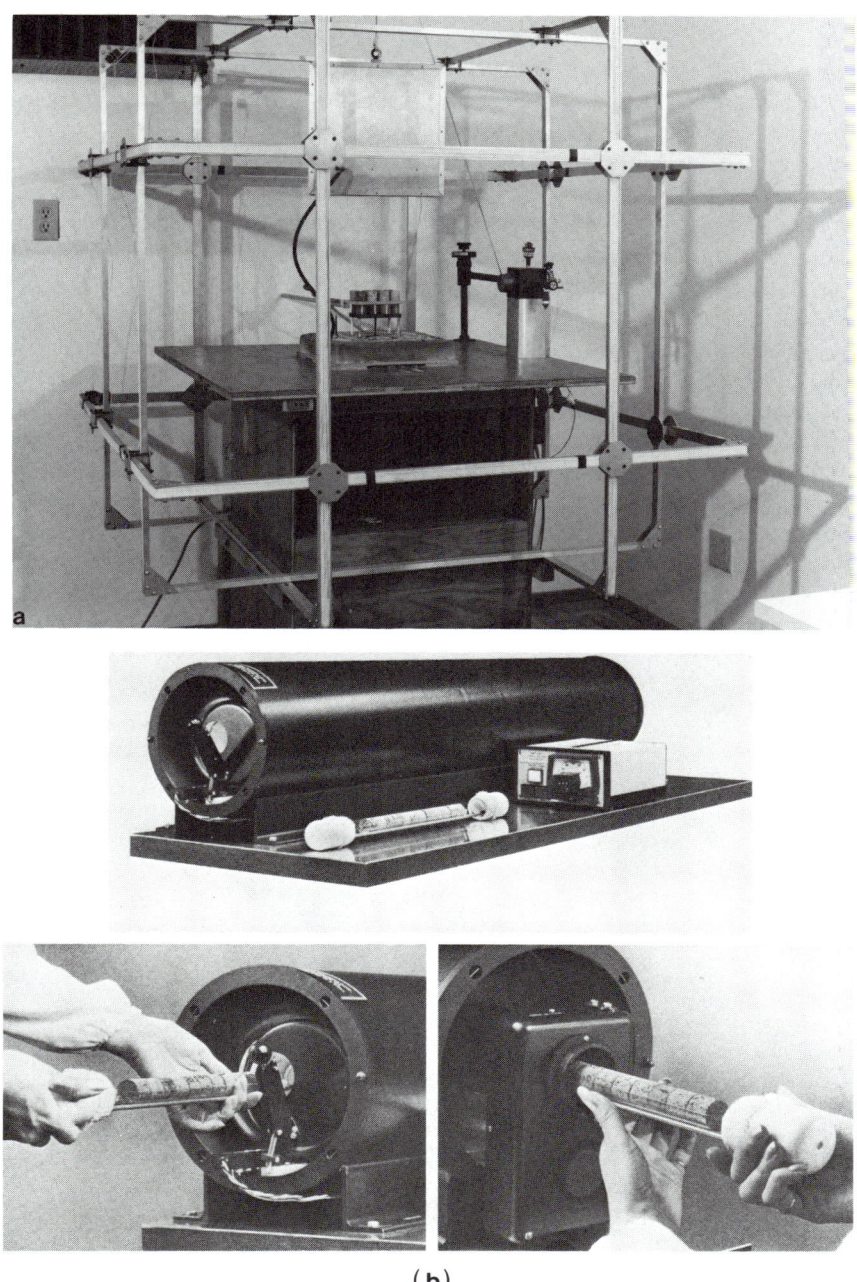

FIG. 53. Thermal demagnetization by stepwise heating method: (a) field cancellation by coils in shielded room and (b) field cancellation by metal shields (Schonstedt system).

gammas, but unless they have field-sensing devices with feedback loops they will usually be at least an order of magnitude worse than the initial setting by the end of the experiment. Hence this method in its simplest form will involve cooling in fields of at least hundreds of gammas. The $\mu$-metal shields do considerably better than this. There is little reason for them to give rise to fields worse than a few tens of gammas during the heating and cooling process. In our tube furnace, the sample is heated in a furnace region and then pushed through into a cooling region in which the field is less than 10 gammas. The temperature is monitored with thermocouples in the sample and in the furnace.

For high-temperature measurements, nonmagnetic furnaces have been constructed beneath astatic magnetometers and beneath SQUID gradiometers (Sugiura *et al.*, 1985). The sample could be rotated within the furnace to permit total determination of the vector. Spinner magnetometers were also modified to provide high-temperature measurements (Schmidt and Clarke, 1985). We attempted to use laser heating of samples inside the cryogenic magnetometer with limited success. Recently a technique has been developed in our laboratory, whereby the sample is heated outside the magnetometer and moved into the sense region in a well-lagged sample holder (Dunn and Fuller, 1984). It has been demonstrated that important cooling does not take place and so the

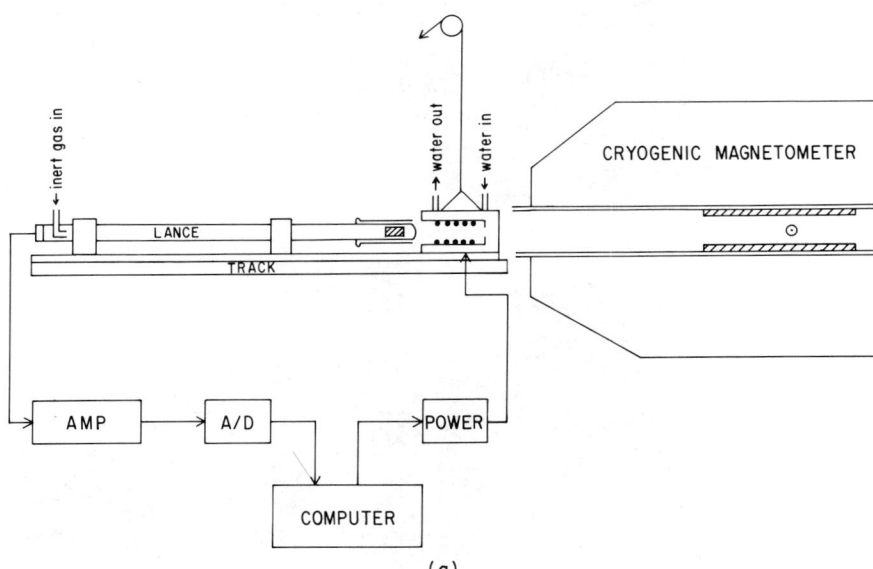

FIG. 54. Thermal demagnetization by Dunn method with measuremments at high temperature: (a) experimental configuration.

9. ROCK MAGNETISM AND PALEOMAGNETISM METHODS

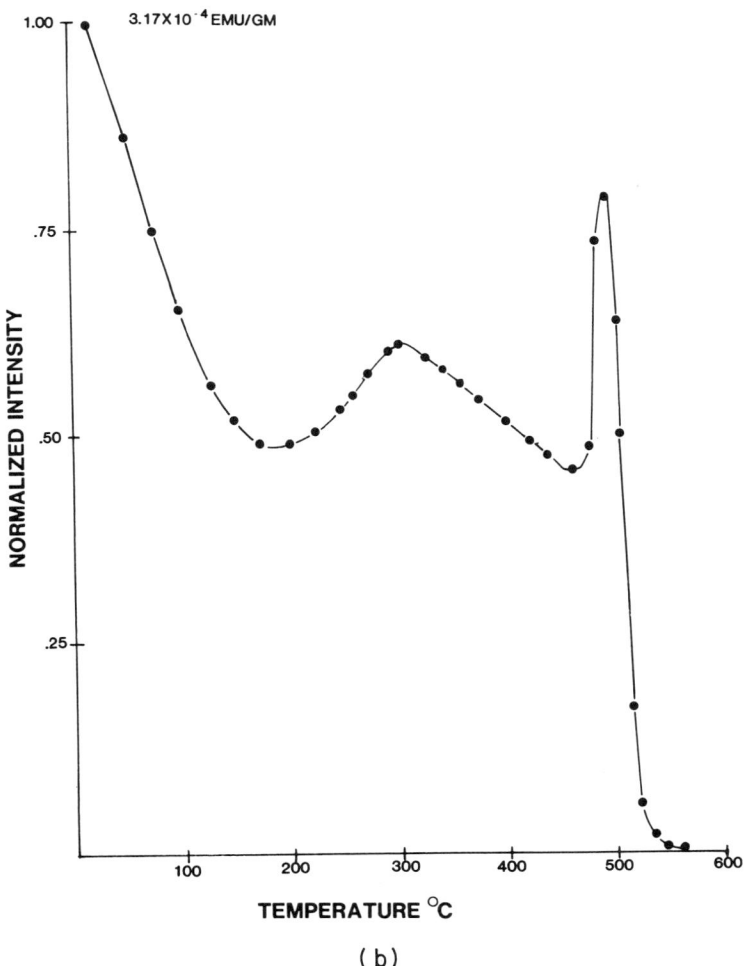

FIG. 54. (b) Results.

technique provides a means of measurement at high temperature without the difficulty of placing a furnace within the cryogenic magnetometer. Figure 54a illustrates the experimental arrangement. Results of such an analysis are given in Fig. 54b. Note that it is possible to take many more readings than are feasible with the stepwise system. The method has made possible recovery of useful data from samples which could not be analyzed satisfactorily by stepwise thermal demagnetization with our equipment. Two notes of caution are important. First, care must be taken if one wishes to analyze multicomponent magnetizations blocked at different temperatures. The determined direction of the component unblocked at low temperatures will be affected by the change of intensity of the blocked high-temperature component due to the change in saturation magnetization with temperature. One can correct for this effect by adjusting the value of the saturation magnetization to the appropriate value for the temperature. Second, at high temperature the induced magnetization becomes large compared with the blocked remanent magnetization. It is therefore critically important that the ambient field in the sense region be as small as possible. With the new generation of 2G magnetometers, it appears to be possible to trap fields as low as 1 gamma. Despite the limitations of the method, it has proved extremely useful. One application is to select temperatures for stepwise thermal demagnetization. Another is for detailed analysis of samples of particular interest.

3.4.2. *Alternating Field Demagnetization.* This is the most commonly used technique of demagnetization. It derives, I suspect, from the watchmaker's technique for demagnetization of parts of mechanical watches. It consists of exposing the sample to an alternating field, which is slowly ramped down to zero. The process is carried out in a region from which DC magnetic fields have been eliminated as far as possible. There are two main variants of the method as applied to rock samples. Either the sample is rotated with respect to the alternating field, or it is successively demagnetized along the three axes $x$, $y$, and $z$. It was noted early in the use of the technique that anomalous magnetization can be produced by the demagnetization process. Recently several analysis of rotational remanent magnetization (RRM) have appeared. We will note certain precautions which can be taken to minimize these effects. First, we analyze the process of AF demagnetization.

Consider the artificial case of a sample whose distribution of microscopic coercivities is as illustrated in Fig. 55a. Its state of magnetization is shown in Fig. 55b. Positive magnetization is carried by phases with microscopic coercivities of less than 100 oe and the phases with higher coercivities are negatively magnetized. The sample is now exposed to a succession of DC fields of alternating polarity to simulate AF demagnetization. The maximum field is 100 oe, which is negative. This aligns all of the carriers with coercivities less than 100 oe parallel to it. This field is then reduced to 75 oe and the sign switched. Carriers with coercivities between 100 and 75 oe remain in the direction of the negative field. Those with lower coercivities switch to the negative configuration. This field is then reduced to 50 oe and the polarity switched, whereupon the 75–50-oe particles are left positive. This process is repeated to give the configuration seen in Fig. 55c. There is then no net contribution from the carriers with coercivities less than 100 oe, while the negative moment carried by the harder carriers is unaffected. In this way

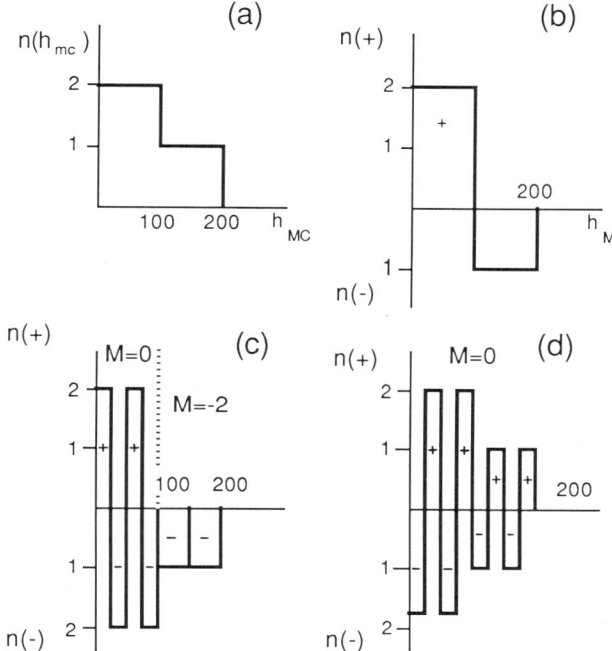

FIG. 55. Alternating field demagnetization principles: (a) distribution of microscopic coercivities; (b) state of magnetization; (c) partial demagnetization; and (d) complete demagnetization.

partial demagnetization is achieved. Had the maximum applied field exceeded the maximum coercivity in the sample, it would have been completely demagnetized (Fig. 55d).

The process of magnetization by rotation of the sample with respect to the AF is similar in principle. However, instead of attempting to get perfect cancellation of the magnetization via equal contributions of opposite sign, one attempts to leave the remagnetized phases magnetized with equal magnitudes in all directions and hence again zero net moment.

To make the discussion of AF demagnetization more realistic, the succession of DC fields must be replaced by a smoothly decreasing AC field and the distribution of microscopic coercivities in the sample made more like those found in nature. Nevertheless, the principle remains the same; one takes advantage of differences in the microscopic coercivities of the signal and noise to eliminate noise preferentially.

The equipment required to do this is relatively simple (Fig. 56). It consists of a power supply and coil capable of giving the necessary fields. In addition, it is desirable to tune the circuit. A means of smoothly decreasing the field

Fig. 56. Alternating field demagnetization equipment: Schonstedt system with remote control for power supply for use in shielded room.

is also required. Design of coils capable of giving fields up to 0.2 T (2000 oe) are given in Collinson (1983) and Kono (1982). Commercial devices are marketed by Schonstedt.

In the equipment at the University of California at Santa Barbara, a Behlman variable-frequency power supply is used. It is important to have a good power supply so that the waveform of the AC in the coil is as near a perfect sinusoid as possible. The reason for this will be discussed in the next section, which deals with the things that can go wrong. The power supply must be able to deliver the needed current through the prescribed coil. The circuit is tuned for two reasons: (1) the current through the coil is maximized and (2) the harmonics present are minimized.

3.4.2.1. PROBLEMS WITH AF DEMAGNETIZATION. There are a number of things that can go wrong with AF demagnetization. Unfortunately, their analysis is extremely difficult because nearly all of them manifest themselves as the result of a complex interaction of equipment and sample. For example, some samples can be exposed to very sloppy AF demagnetization techniques and give very nice results. Others will give poor results under any treatment.

It is therefore hard to assess the equipment unless one specifies a particular sample to be demagnetized. Nevertheless, a number of effects can be recognized and will now be considered.

The chief problem is that the process may generate spurious magnetization rather than simply demagnetize the sample. The term anhysteretic remanent magnetization (ARM) describes magnetization acquired by a sample exposed to a decreasing AF in the presence of a biasing DC field. To visualize the process, consider the loop shown in Fig. 57, in which the actual DC bias is much exaggerated compared with typical ratio of DC bias to AC field. The maximum positive value of the field is larger by $2H_{dc}$ that the negative value. (Whether we consider single-domain particles or movement of sections of walls, the discussion is still applicable). The magnetic regions which are aligned parallel to the positive field are all those whose microscopic coercivity is exceeded by the positive field. When the field reaches its maximum negative value some of the regions will not reverse because the maximum $-$/ve field is less than the $+$/ve field. As each cycle is carried out there will always be an accumulation of regions left magnetized in the $+$/ve sense which constitutes ARM. The properties of this ARM have been investigated in some detail and it is found to be somewhat analogous to weak-field TRM; it follows, for example, the same AF demagnetization characteristics, it is linear in DC field, and there is an additivity law of partial ARMs. Such magnetization will be picked up by our samples during AF demagnetization unless precautions are taken against the sample seeing the DC bias field. It is for this reason that we have $\mu$-metal shields around our AF demagnetization equipment.

An ARM magnetization can be acquired if the sample sees an AC field which has asymmetric waveforms of particular types. If there are odd

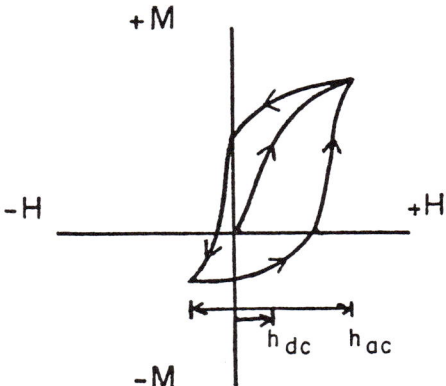

Fig. 57. Anhysteretic magnetization.

harmonics present there is distortion, but the peak heights are the same in each half-cycle. On the other hand, even harmonics with nonzero phase lags from the fundamental give uneven peaks. This then gives ARM. For this reason, we attempt to reduce harmonics by tuning the coil.

If, instead of shielding the sample, one tumbles it, one can also reduce the ARM due to DC bias. In this case, one sets the magnetization by an essentially ARM process, but one assumes that the sample is oriented sufficiently randomly during the process that no net moment is acquired. One can also tumble the sample in a $\mu$-metal shield to get the best of both worlds.

Unfortunately, a direct effect of tumbling the sample is to induce a rotational remanent magnetization, as was recognized by Doell and Cox (1967), Wilson and Lomax (1972), and Stephenson (1980). The form of the magnetization is to induce a moment antiparallel to the sample's rotation vector. For this reason, one can eliminate the effect by arranging for the rotation vector to be reversed to give equal amounts of time with $+w$ and $-w$ (R. L. Wilson, personal communication). A number of analyses of the effect have appeared, of which the most successful appears to be that of Stephenson (1980) for the single-domain case. We still need a multidomain model.

3.4.3. Other Methods of Demagnetization. In addition to AF and thermal demagnetization, there are other methods which have been used for demagnetization. None of these methods has the general applicability of thermal and AF, but in special cases they may be useful.

3.4.3.1. CHEMICAL DEMAGNETIZATION. This method relies on the preferential destruction of the carrier of a particular component of magnetization. There are a number of devices for pumping a chemical fluid into a rock under pressure (Burek, 1969). The simplest technique is to place the rock in the leaching solution. If the permeability of the rock is low, it is sometimes advantageous to make cuts into the cylinder to increase surface area. A variety of solutions have been used. Hydrochloric acid was favored by Burek. The process of high-pressure treatment according to Burek produces bleaching without disintegration.

3.4.3.2. LOW-TEMPERATURE DEMAGNETIZATION. It was shown in the 1960s that the behavior of magnetite cycled across its low-temperature crystalline anisotropy minimum and of hematite across the Morin transition tended to eliminate multidomain magnetization and leave untouched single-domain magnetization. The process of low-temperature cleaning was therefore attempted by a number of workers with varying degrees of success (Ozima *et al.*, 1964).

3.4.3.3. GENERAL COMMENT. Presumably, almost any method of getting energy into the magnetic lattice will bring about demagnetization in the absence of a field and will give magnetization in the presence of a sufficiently strong field. Certainly shock will; probably, exposure to neutrons will. Nevertheless, for a practical demagnetization method AF, with its ability to eliminate soft magnetization, and thermal, with its ability to eliminate viscous and low blocking temperature TRM, are the most important.

3.4.3.4. MICROSCOPIC TECHNIQUES. Some years ago Wu *et al.* (1974) attempted to separate individual multidomain grains and study their demagnetization behavior to contrast them with individual feldspar crystals which contained fine magnetite. In this way one can investigate individual magnetic phases in the rock. More recently Larson (1981) has tried a similar technique, using progressive removal of magnetic phases from disks cut from standard cylinders.

3.4.4. Analysis of Demagnetization Curves. Quite a few techniques have now been developed for the analysis of demagnetization curves. They have been used primarily for AF demagnetization data, but in principle there is no reason why they cannot be used for other data. The analyses have as an overall objective the separation of primary from secondary magnetization. With the microcomputer revolution, most laboratories have on-line analysis, which can guide one during the demagnetization process. By judicious use of a text editor or D-Base system, one can also carry out the same type of analysis for data collected over a time interval, such as happens in stepwise thermal demagnetization. In addition, there are methods which are more suitable for the analysis of data sets for a site or from several sites.

3.4.4.1. VECTOR DIFFERENCES. A starting point for discussion of analysis of demagnetization data is the relationship between the initial NRM, the vector removed, and the remaining vector. Remember that subtraction of vectors is defined by adding the negative

$$\mathbf{A} - \mathbf{B} = \mathbf{A} + (-\mathbf{B})$$

In other words, $\mathbf{A} - \mathbf{B}$ is the vector which must be added to $\mathbf{B}$ to give $\mathbf{A}$. Hence it runs from the tip of $\mathbf{B}$ to the tip of $\mathbf{A}$, when $\mathbf{A}$ and $\mathbf{B}$ are drawn as in Fig. 58. The three vectors are coplanar; in fact, in the figures we have just used a two-dimensional representation. The vector subtraction illustrated so far is for a single demagnetization step.

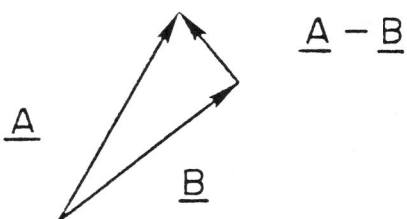

FIG. 58. Difference vector obtained by vector subtraction.

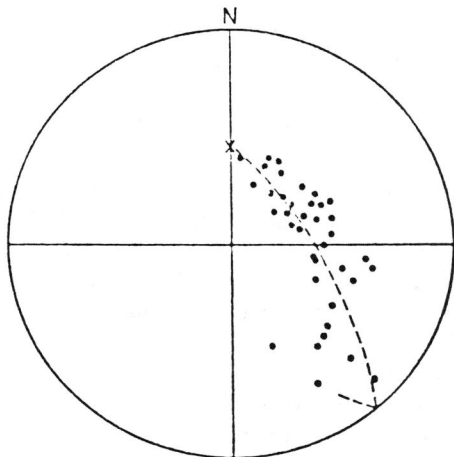

Fig. 59. Planar distribution of NRM vectors (Nagata, 1961).

NRM results often fall along a great circle distribution on the stereoplot, which means that the vectors lie in a single plane. This is a manifestation of a two-component magnetization. Frequently, one of the directions will be the present field and the other a stable primary direction. This case is illustrated in Fig. 59.

By looking at the vector difference throughout demagnetization, we can see that in the early stages of AF demagnetization a vector parallel to the present field is destroyed by the AF demagnetization (Fig. 60). For small range of AF field, an intermediate vector is taken out, and eventually the difference vector is parallel to the remaining vector. This is a particularly simple and straightforward case of demagnetization, but it does illustrate that in a two-component system when the difference vector moves into the same direction as the remaining vector one is demagnetizing a single component of magnetization. This analysis can be used to orient borehole cores, when they have soft or viscous components in the present field direction (Fuller, 1969).

Hoffman and Day (1978) took this type of analysis further ans showed how to separate three components of magnetization (Fig 61). The particular point of interest is that they were able to separate the intermediate direction, even if it was never seen as a separate difference vector. The idea is evident from the figure. Note the effect of increasing overlap of the microscopic coercivities carrying the three components of magnetization. In the final case, D, one is taking advantage of the orientation of the difference vectors when C and B are being demagnetized and when B and A are being demagnetized to obtain the direction of B. Hence it is the planar distribution of the difference vectors which is the key.

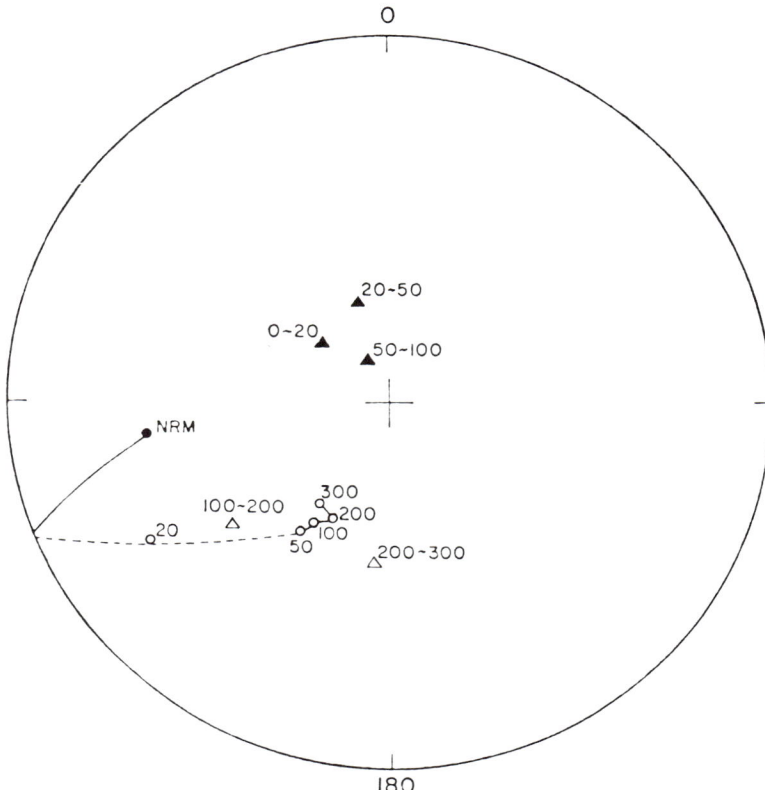

FIG. 60. Vector differences obtained during demagnetization of sample with two components of magnetization, one close to the present field direction. Circles, remanence vectors; triangles, difference vectors; open symbols, upper hemisphere; and filled symbols, lower hemisphere.

One difficulty with using difference vectors is that they are inherently rather poorly determined compared with the remanence vectors before and after demagnetization. The difference vector is often a small quantity obtained by subtraction of a large vector from another large vector. Hence the errors in the difference vector are proportionately larger than in the vectors before and after demagnetization. An extreme example of this arises when one does a repeat demagnetization at some value. A possible solution to this problem is to fit the experimental data with analytical functions, so exact difference vectors can be obtained between different calculated values (Dunn, unpublished work).

3.4.4.2. REMAGNETIZATION CIRCLES. Having recognized that the planar distribution of vectors during a demagnetization sequence is indeed reflecting

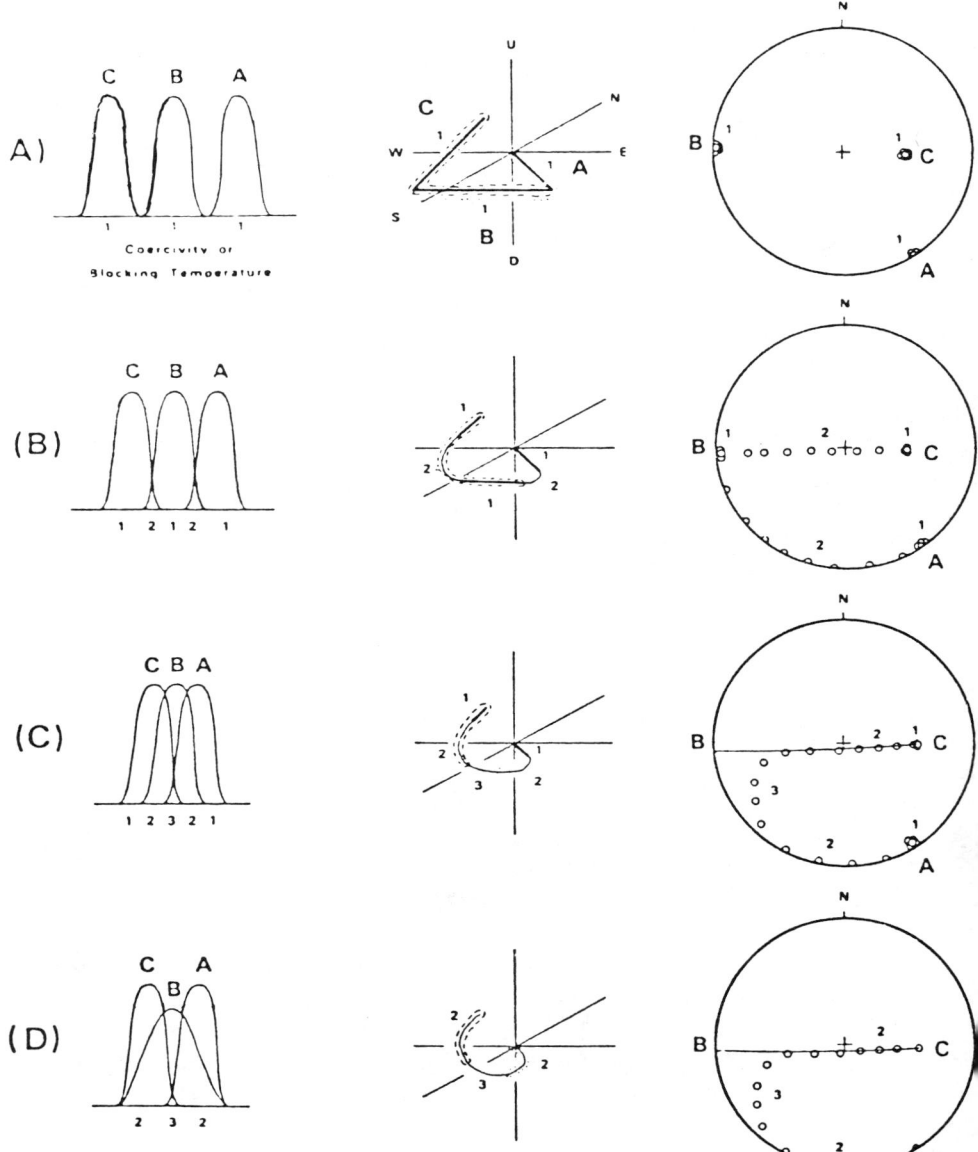

FIG. 61. Analysis of demagnetization with difference vectors. For each example, the distribution of microscopic coercivities or blocking temperatures, a three-dimensional figure showing the changing direction of magnetization and a stereoplot are given. (A) Results for three components of NRM with no overlap of distribution functions; (B)–(D) results for increasing overlap. [After Kirschvink (1980) and Hoffman and Day (1978).]

## 9. ROCK MAGNETISM AND PALEOMAGNETISM METHODS

demagnetization of two components of magnetization as discussed above, one can use these planar distribution to find either the primary or the secondary vector, in some situations. Halls (1976, 1978) used the technique particularly successfully to establish a secondary direction of magnetization associated with impact remagnetization. One can also use the technique to project demagnetization trajectories onto the primary direction. The trick is to get intersecting great circles. To recover a secondary direction, there must have been a variety of primary directions in the sample at the time the secondary magnetization was acquired. This can come about if the rocks are folded before the secondary magnetization. We then plot the results in the before bedding correction (BBC) configuration (Fig. 62). The various demagnetization paths project back into a single region and this will be the direction of the secondary magnetization acquired, e.g. in Halls' example the impact magnetization direction. Conversely, if we wish to obtain the primary direction, we plot in the after bedding correction (ABC) configuration (Fig. 63). If there is indeed a single primary direction in the collection, it should then become apparent because all great circles will converge.

The discussion so far has been entirely qualitative. However, obtaining best-fitting great circles to data is a problem that was discussed by Watson (1960). Halls also gives a great circle fitting program. These approaches define best-fitting great circles with confidence intervals on them. There then remains the problem of describing the errors associated with direction obtained by the intersections. Analyses of this problem have been given by McFadden (1977), Halls (1977), Bailey and and Halls (1984), and Schmidt (1985).

3.4.4.3. ZIJDERVELD DIAGRAMS. The oldest method of analysis of AF demagnetization data was due to Zijderveld (1967), who built some of the first AF demagnetization systems. It has the great virtue of simplicity and

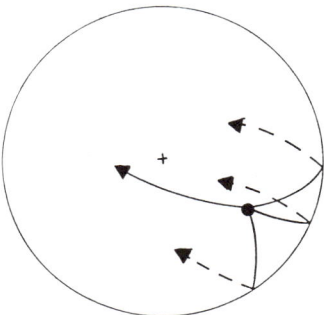

FIG. 62. Recovery of secondary magnetization direction with demagnetization great circles. Results are plotted before bedding correction (BBC); on demagnetization the vectors systematically move away from the secondary direction if it is softer than the prmary.

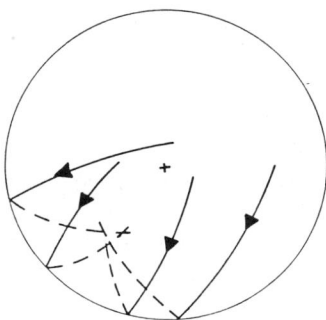

FIG. 63. Recovery of primary magnetization with demagnetization circles. Results are plotted after bedding correction (ABC); the great circles converge on the primary direction if it is harder than the secondary.

yet gives much useful information. The idea is simply to plot the values of the $x$, $y$, and $z$ components of magnetization throughout the AF or thermal demagnetization as in the upper right part of Fig. 64. In the illustrated plots, the vertical component $Z$ is plotted against the horizontal component $H$ in one diagram and $X$ against $Y$ in the other. This method has an advantage in that it gives declination and inclination directly, but since both $X$ and $Y$ are involved in $H$ their interpretation is not quite as direct as the use of $X$ against $Y$ and $Y$ against $Z$. A number of very simple interpretations are immediately apparent. Thus, convergence to the origin indicates demagnetization of a single vector. Conversely, if the results do not track to the origin, more than one magnetization is still in the rock. One can of course plot these Zijderveld diagrams in whatever sample coordinates one likes.

3.4.4.4. STABILITY INDEX. Symons and Stupavsky (1974) describe what they term a rational stability index. They therefore define a measure of directional change with incremental increase in AF demagnetization field. This is linearly dependent on the rate of change of direction with demagnetization field. When this index falls to a minimum one has defined the stable direction. One can be misled by this index, but if it is used intelligently it may have some value.

3.4.4.5. CONCLUDING COMMENT. The availability of on-line computers provides plots such as those shown in Fig. 64, while demagnetization is being carried out. The computers coupled to instruments which measure sample magnetization very rapidly have brought about an increased emphasis on analysis of demagnetization data. Numerous systems have been proposed and, although it is by no means clear that the optimum system is yet available, it is worth reviewing some of the systems.

A number of schemes begin with the Zijderveld plot and use some form of line fitting to obtain line segments from the data. Such segments represent

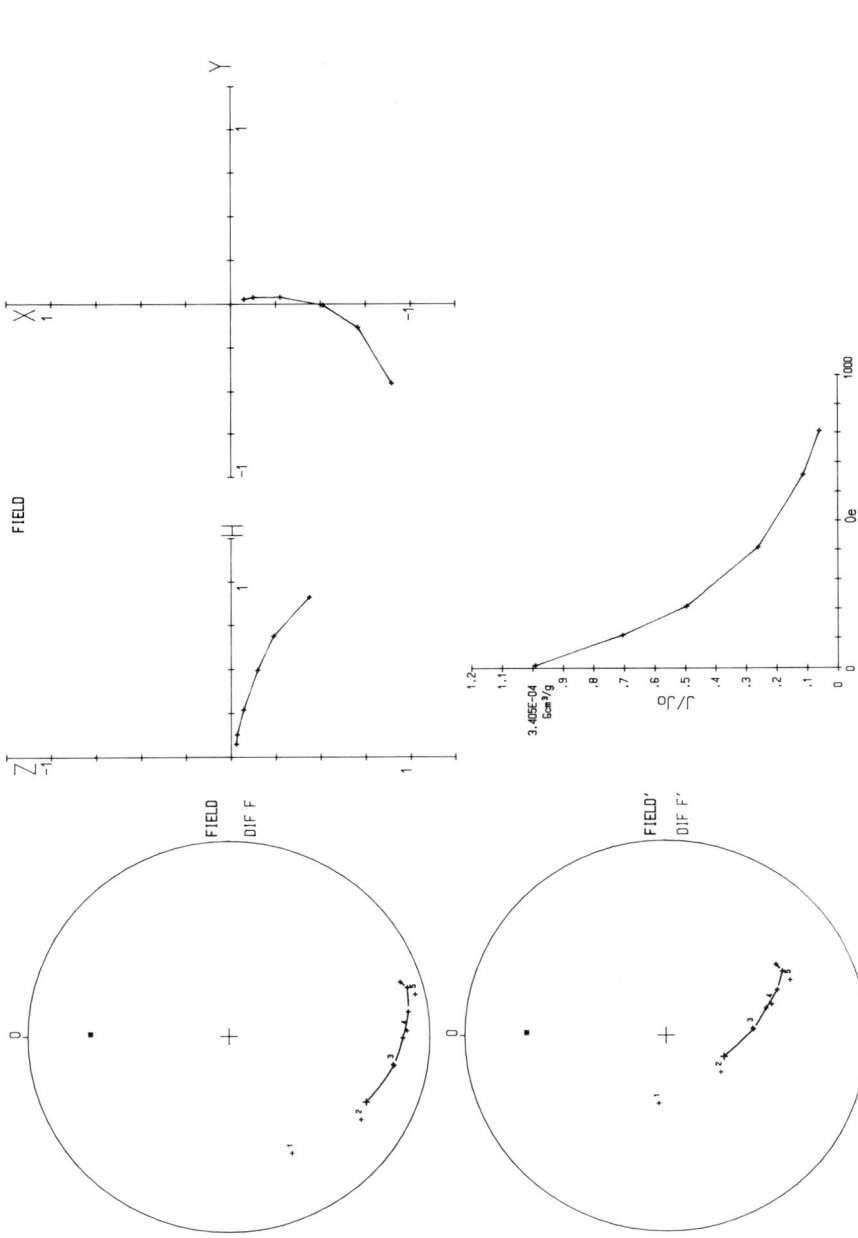

FIG. 64. On line plot of AF demagnetization. Top left: directions of magnetization joined by line, difference vectors numbered, in field coordinates before tectonic correction. Bottom left: same in field[1] coordinates after tectonic correction. Top centre and right: Zijderveld plots. Bottom right: normalized intensity plot.

individual components of magnetization. For exmple in the illustrated Zijderveld plot (Fig. 64), there is an identifiable high-field component, but at the lowest fields a second component is also being demagnetized. Such statements can be made qualitatively or some form of line fitting program can be used to make quantitative statements about the degree of fit. One of the most sophisticated, due to Kent (1985), calculates goodness of fit criteria for all possible line segments obtained with three or more consecutive points. An interactive version of such a system has been developed by Perroud (1985). In this version, the Zijderveld diagram is brought up on a monitor and straight lines fitted by eye. Such a technique has the great virtue of ease and speed. There are some questions about the degree to which an arbitrary choice of segments to be fitted may affect the final fit. Nevertheless, what the technique lacks in statistical rigor may well be compensated for by what it saves in computer bills.

It may turn out that analyses of single-sample demagnetization data are not best handled through the Zijderveld diagram even though it is most useful for a quick look. Given that there are sufficient data, a moment of inertia analysis of the type developed by Kirschvink (1980) seems appropriate. Such an analysis would also involve tests for planar distributions. Certainly something of this type is becoming mandatory for the description of complicated paleomagnetic data from sites at which several directions of magnetization are recorded. It seems likely that in the near future paleomagnetic studies not only will give a primary direction, but also will routinely discuss all secondary directions uncovered and, where possible, interpret them.

3.4.5. *Field Tests of Stability of NRM*. In addition to laboratory experiments which seek to distinguish between stable and unstable NRM, there are tests which permit an assessment of the geological age of the magnetization. Principal examples are the fold test, the conglomerate test, and the baked contact tests. Of these, the fold test is the most useful and universally used.

3.4.5.1. FOLD TEST. The fold test was first suggested by Graham (1949) and was used in Irving's early work in the Torridonian SST (Irving, 1957). The test is illustrated in Fig. 65. In this example, the magnetization, which is represented by the arrow in the folded bed, is evidently rotated out of

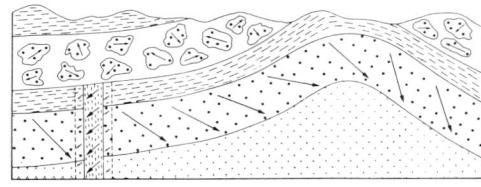

FIG. 65. Field tests of timing of magnetization, fold, conglomerate, and baked contact test.

a single coherent direction by the folding. This magnetization therefore was acquired before the folding. Conversely, if the magnetization is coherent in the folded configuration it was acquired after folding and fails the fold test. The interpretation stable, or passes fold test, implies that the magnetization is at least older than the folding. Unstable, or fails fold test, implies magnetization during or subsequent to folding. One can use Fisher statistics to establish properties of the mean and variance before and after folding corrections (McFadden and Jones, 1981). A recent development has been the recognition of "synfolding" magnetization, that is, magnetization acquired during folding (e.g., Kodamar, 1986).

3.4.5.2. CONGLOMERATE TEST. This test is not quite as direct as the fold test but it does give some indication of the stability of the remanence carried by material which has subsequently been incorporated into a conglomerate (Fig. 65). If it is randomly oriented, it survived the process of transport and deposition in the conglomerate.

3.4.5.3. BAKED CONTACT TEST. This test takes advantage of the baked contact zone around a minor instrusion. The intrusive rock is hot enough and has a sufficient supply of heat to remagnetize some of the country rock. If this happens the magnetization of the country rock will vary systematically with distance from the intrusions (Fig. 65). The pattern is then consistent with the magnetization having been acquired at the time of the intrusion.

3.5. Paleointensity Determination

The geomagnetic field is a vector quantity, and although more is heard about the paleodirection of the field, there has been a steady effort to obtain its paleointensity as well. The work has been primarily with lavas and archeomagnetic artifacts which acquire TRM in their formation. The fundamental assumption is that in the weak field range of the earth's field, TRM is linear with field. Hence if one gives such a sample a TRM in the laboratory and does not change the sample in any other way, the following relationship should apply:

$$H(\text{ancient})/H(\text{laboratory}) = \text{NRM}/\text{TRM}$$

Unfortunately, giving the sample a TRM in the laboratory frequently changes it irreversibly, so one cannot recover the intensity of the ancient field in this simple way. Indeed, even if one had recovered the appropriate ancient field, one would not know that one had. Moreover, the NRM of the sample may have changed since the acquisition of a primary magnetization, during its initial cooling. An ideal method would therefore not only give a paleofield intensity, but also demonstrate that the NRM was indeed a TRM and that the sample had not been altered in the process of the intensity determination.

The Thellier–Thellier method of intensity determination comes about as close to such an ideal experiment as one can expect on this earth (Thellier, 1937, 1938, 1941; Thellier and Thellier, 1959). It arose out of work carried out in Europe and Japan prior to World War II. Following Nagata (1974), I like to call this method the KTT method, thereby acknowledging the contribution of Koenigsberger (1938). It is a tribute to the experimental skills of these early workers that, despite numerous attempts at improvements and shortcuts, the original method remains the most widely accepted one to this day.

3.5.1. *The Koenigsberger–Thellier–Thellier Method.* The KTT method takes advantage of a property of TRM in fine particles which was discovered by these early workers in Europe and Japan. The property is sometimes referred to as the law of additivity of partial TRMs; the total TRM acquired in a single field cooling from the Curie point to room temperature is indeed the sum of the partial TRMs acquired when field cooling is carried out incrementally as illustrated in Fig. 66. Thus

$$M(\text{TRM})_{T(\text{RT})}^{T(C)} = \sum_{T(L_i) = T(\text{RT})}^{T(U_i) = T(C)} M(\text{TRM})_{T(l_i)}^{T(U_i)}$$

This result indicates that the TRM in these fine particles is blocked in discrete temperature intervals and that the partial thermoremanent magnetization (pTRM) blocked in a temperature range $T(U_i) - T(L_i)$ is unaffected by heating to the lower temperature of the $i$th interval $T(L_i)$ and totally demagnetized by heating to the upper temperature of the $i$th interval $T(U_i)$. It is also assumed that the magnetization blocked in one temperature interval

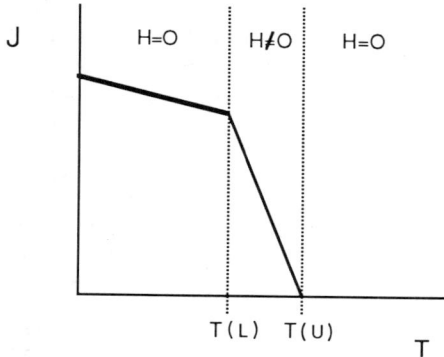

Fig. 66. Acquisition of partial thermoremanent magnetization. The field $H$ is applied during cooling from $T(U)$ to $T(L)$ and magnetization is blocked. Below $T(L)$ the magnetization increases due only to the increase of saturation magnetization during cooling.

does not interact with that blocked in any other range. It will be evident that these assumptions are more realistic for ensembles of single-domain particles than for multidomain material, and indeed Thellier was particularly careful to point out the assumptions and implicit limitations of the method.

The KTT method consists of comparing the pTRM acquired incrementally throughout the temperature range from the Curie point to room temperature with the NRM demagnetized in the same temperature increments. This is illustrated in Fig. 67. The observations are all made at room temperature. A double heating method is used in which the pTRM is first acquired parallel to the NRM and then antiparallel. The various required quantities can then be obtained by using a sum and difference technique as follows.

$$M(+) = M_{T(1)}^{T(2)} H(\text{LAB}) + M_{T(2)}^{T(C)} H(\text{ANCIENT})$$

and

$$M(-) = -M_{T(1)}^{T(2)} H(\text{LAB}) + M_{T(2)}^{T(C)} H(\text{ANCIENT})$$

so that

$$M(+) + M(-) = 2 M_{T(2)}^{T(C)} H(\text{ANCIENT})$$

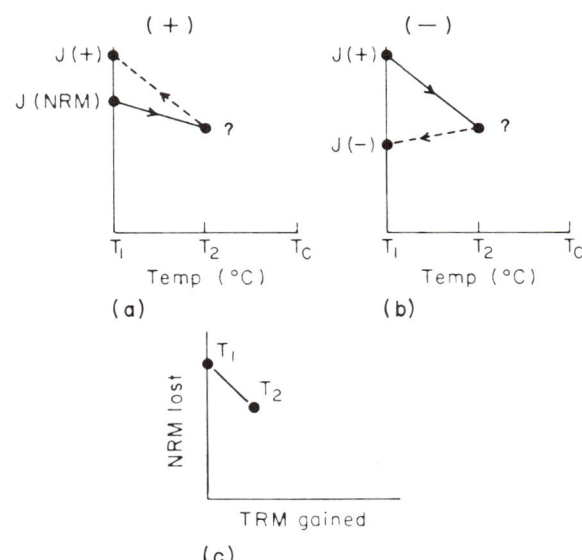

FIG. 67. Koenigsberger–Thellier–Thellier method of intensity determination. Only the first heating cycle is shown. (a) +/ve field heating cycle with $H$ parallel to the NRM; (b) −/ve field heating cycle with $H$ antiparallel to the NRM; and (c) plot of NRM lost against TRM acquired in known field.

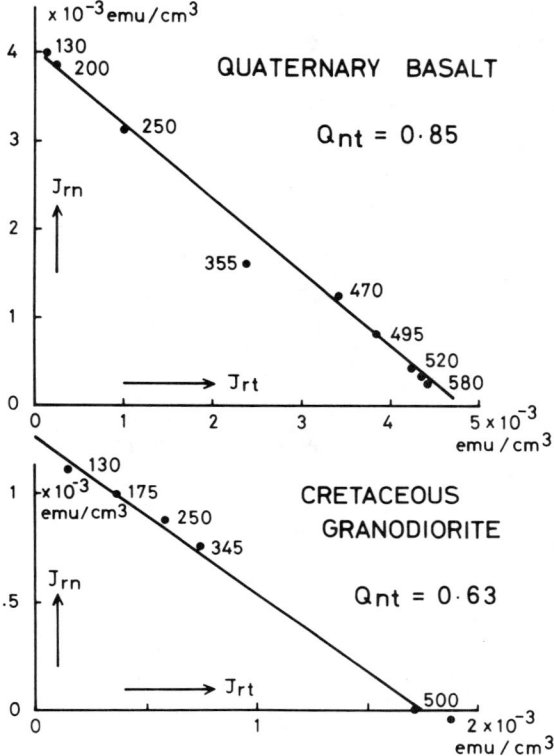

FIG. 68. Plot of the results of KTT intensity determinations. [From Nagata (1974); after Koenigsberger (1938).]

and

$$M(+) - M(-) = 2M_{T(1)}^{T(2)} H(\text{LAB})$$

Hence, knowing the initial NRM value and those of $M(+)$ after the positive heating cycle and $M(-)$ after the negative heating cycle, one has the pTRM gained and the NRM lost in the temperature interval from $T(1)$ up to $T(2)$. One can then enter the first point on the eventual plot of pTRM gained against NRM lost.

The procedure is then repeated throughout the temperature range to the Curie point and the plot completed (Fig. 68). By this method one now has a number of determinations of the ancient field from the single sample. If the NRM is in fact a TRM and was acquired in a low field, there will be a linear relationship between the NRM lost in each increment and the pTRM acquired. From the slope of the curve, one can therefore obtain the ratio of the laboratory and ancient fields. The linearity of the plot also suggests that magnetic phases are neither created nor destroyed during the experiment.

There is by now a formidable literature on the KTT method, but a short paper by Thellier (1977) in a special issue of *Physics of Earth and Planetary Interiors* devoted to intensity determinations is particularly informative. A second paper by Levi (1977) provides experimental testing of the limits of the method in coarse-grained material. As mentioned earlier, there have been a number of attempts at shortcuts and improvements on the KTT method. One which is commonly used replaces the first field cooling with a thermal demagnetization (Nagata *et al.*, 1963). Another less commonly used is the single heating version (Kono and Ueno, 1977).

The beauty of the KTT method is that it tests for a TRM origin of the NRM and for irreversible changes in the sample during the heating process. Its simplicity lies in its room temperature measurements of remanence. While it may seem churlish to criticize such a successful method, there are some problems, which should be recognized. For example, weak field TRM in single-domain material is a weak function of cooling rate (Dodson and McClelland-Brown, 1980; Halgedahl *et al.*, 1980). While this may not be a serious problem for archaeomagnetic samples, for which the method was developed, the cooling rates of intrusions may indeed pose serious problems for the method. The blocking temperature is a function of inducing field, so that for an optimum experiment the laboratory field should be the same as the ancient field. Walton (1983) has pointed out that if a magnetic phase is being destroyed by a thermally activated process, one can still get a linear plot of NRM lost to pTRM gained and hence the method can give a false value of the field. A third heating reveals the problem.

At the risk of losing much of the virtue of the KTT method, one can make an "improvement" whereby observations are made at high temperature (Day *et al.*, 1977). This could be particularly valuable in cases where the KTT method breaks down, indicating nonlinearity. One such case is when there are interactions within certain temperature ranges. We have attempted such experiments with limited success (Dunn *et al.*, 1981). The idea here is that over a certain temperature interval one replaces precisely the same NRM by a pTRM. The criterion is for identical thermal demagnetization in that range. One obtains the field required for this by successive approximation. Another high-temperature method has been developed by Walton (1983), but it must be admitted these are tricky experiments and that what they may gain in additional information is probably outweighed by the complexity compared with the KTT method.

Shaw (1974) adopted a different approach from the KTT method in seeking to establish that the NRM was indeed a TRM and that no irreversible

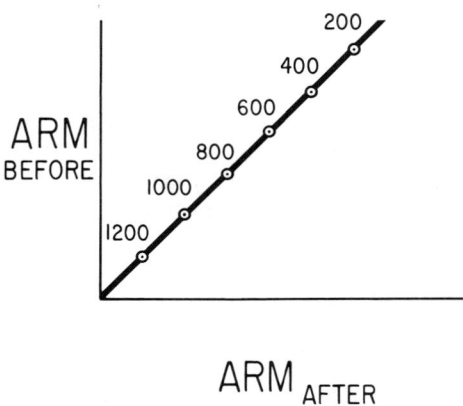

Fig. 69. Test for sample degradation in Shaw determination. Idealized case of identical AF demagnetization characteristics of ARM before and after TRM is given.

changes had taken place during the intensity determination. In his method anhysteretic remanent magnetization is used and comparisons of alternating field demagnetization behavior are made. The experiment is as follows. First, the NRM is AF demagnetized. It is then given an ARM and this is demagnetized. The sample is next given a TRM, which is again AF demagnetized. Finally, the sample is given a second ARM, which is AF demagnetized. By comparing the two AF demagnetization curves of the ARM, one tests whether the sample changed during TRM acquisition (Fig. 69). By comparing the AF demagnetization of the NRM and TRM one tests whether the NRM was indeed a TRM. An idealized Shaw analysis is given in Fig. 70. Shaw's

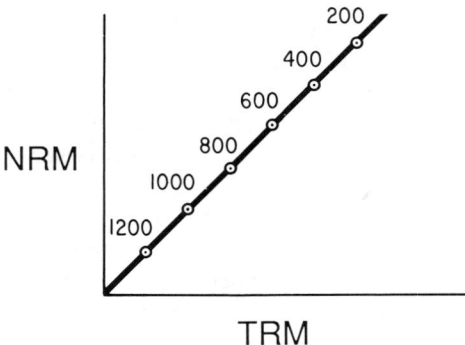

Fig. 70. Shaw intensity determination method. Idealized case of identical AF demagnetization characteristics of NRM and TRM.

method is particularly useful if the blocking temperature of the TRM is very narrow, for in that case the KTT method is hard to use. Shaw's method is then an example of a single heating method. Rigotti (1978a, b) suggested that it is better to use the acquisition of ARM rather than the demagnetization of ARM as the monitor of heating effects on the sample. Both of these methods can in principle be modified to take account of effects of heating that are detected by the degradation tests (Fuller et al., 1979).

Unlike the two methods described so far which involve giving the sample a TRM, normalization methods have been developed that do not involve TRM. Such methods suffer from the difficulty of carrying out a successful calibration experiment, but in some circumstances they may be justified. The simplest such method is saturation isothermal remanent magnetization [IRM(s)] normalization, developed to aid in the interpretation of lunar paleointensities by Fuller (1974) and improved later (Cisowski et al., 1983). The difficulty with lunar intensity determinations is that heating lunar samples invariably brings about sample degradation. In addition, in the case of lunar paleointensities, a result accurate to about a factor of 5 would be of great interest. In this situation, the simplest solution seemed to be IRM(s) normalization. The problem, of course, lies in the calibration experiment, which remains to be satisfactorily completed. Nevertheless, the method did reveal that samples magnetized in the strongest fields have a limited range of ages between 3.9 and 3.6 AE. An ARM normalization experiment developed by Stephenson et al. (1974) was also extensively applied to the lunar samples and again succeeded in isolating a range of ages for the most strongly magnetized rocks.

The discussion of paleointensity determinations has been confined so far to samples thought to carry TRM. Attempts to recover intensity information from rocks carrying other types of NRM have been much less satisfactory. The most pressing need has been for a method which will work with the sedimentary rocks which have been used to recover recent records of secular variation. A number of normalization methods have been proposed, of which the most extensively used is the ARM normalization of Levi and Banerjee (1976). Despite the general indication of relative intensity which comes from such approaches, we are a long way from a satisfactory method for recovering intensity even from lake sediments, which are likely to have the simplest NRM. If the NRM of sediments is acquired during the dewatering process during sediment accumulation, some form of reworking of the sediments may eventually give a method, but there seems to be little progress in this direction. In sediments in which the NRM is some combination of a depositional or postdepositional remanence with later chemical remanent magnetization (CRM) carried by authigenic phases, recovery of intensity may be well nigh impossible.

# 4. Rock Magnetism

Rock magnetism has for its charge the description of the magnetic phases in rocks and the determination and understanding of their magnetic behavior. It provides the physical basis for paleomagnetism—interpreting, for example, the mechanisms of natural remanent magnetization. In its more general role, it involves other endeavors less directly related to paleomagnetism, such as the determination of anisotropy of susceptibility for use as a fabric element and the interpretation of the effects of stress on magnetization. In this discussion, the treatment will follow a scheme of identification and characterization of magnetic phases. In this way the major instruments will be described in terms of their principal role. Special instrumentation for susceptibility anisotropy determination and stress effects will be descibed subsequently.

## 4.1. Identification of Magnetic Phases in Rocks

The classic method of identification of magnetic materials is by determination of their Curie points, the temperature at which the ferromagnetic order is overcome by thermal energy. The observations are made with a number of instruments loosely known as thermomagnetic balances. They use the force experienced by a magnetic material in a $B$ field with a gradient to measure the saturation magnetization $M_s$ of the material. Thus the Curie point is determined as the point at which this force disappears when $M_s$ is lost.

Thermomagnetic analysis permits observation of $M_s$ over a wide range of temperatures and can be used to detect the diagnostic $1/T$ dependence of paramagnetism, or to distinguish between different types of ferrimagnets, as well as to determine Curie points. In addition to balances, vibrating sample magnetometers (VSMs) and high-field SQUID susceptometers can be used.

Another approach to the identification of magnetic phases in rocks is to use the anisotropy transitions, at which the crystalline anisotropy is minimized, giving anomalies in remanence, susceptibility, and coercivity. These can be detected with a variety of instruments.

4.1.1. Curie Point Determination. The principle on which magnetic balances work is to measure the force which a magnetic sample experiences in a $B$-field gradient. This principle is utilized in numerous systems which derive from classical methods, such as the Gouy or Faraday methods. The instruments can be divided into horizontal and vertical systems. The most common devices for measuring Curie points are vertical systems. The sample is heated in a furnace and placed between the pole pieces of an electromagnet,

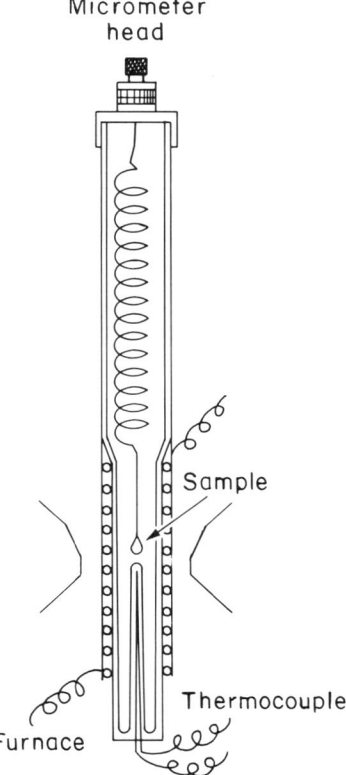

FIG. 71. Thermomagnetic balance with quartz spring. Note shape of pole pieces to give required field gradient.

giving a vertical gradient of the field. The force on the sample is downward and is measured with a balance (Fig. 71).

Assuming that the field in the $y$ and $z$ directions is small compared with that in the $x$ direction, the increment of force is

$$dF_z = k\, dv\, B_y \frac{\partial B_y}{\partial z}$$

where $k$ is the susceptibility of the material and $v$ the volume. If the field is strong enough to saturate the sample, the force is a linear function of the saturation magnetization. The design of the pole pieces is a compromise between maximizing the gradient and field for sensitivity and having a region of constant gradient for stability of sample position (Collinson, 1983).

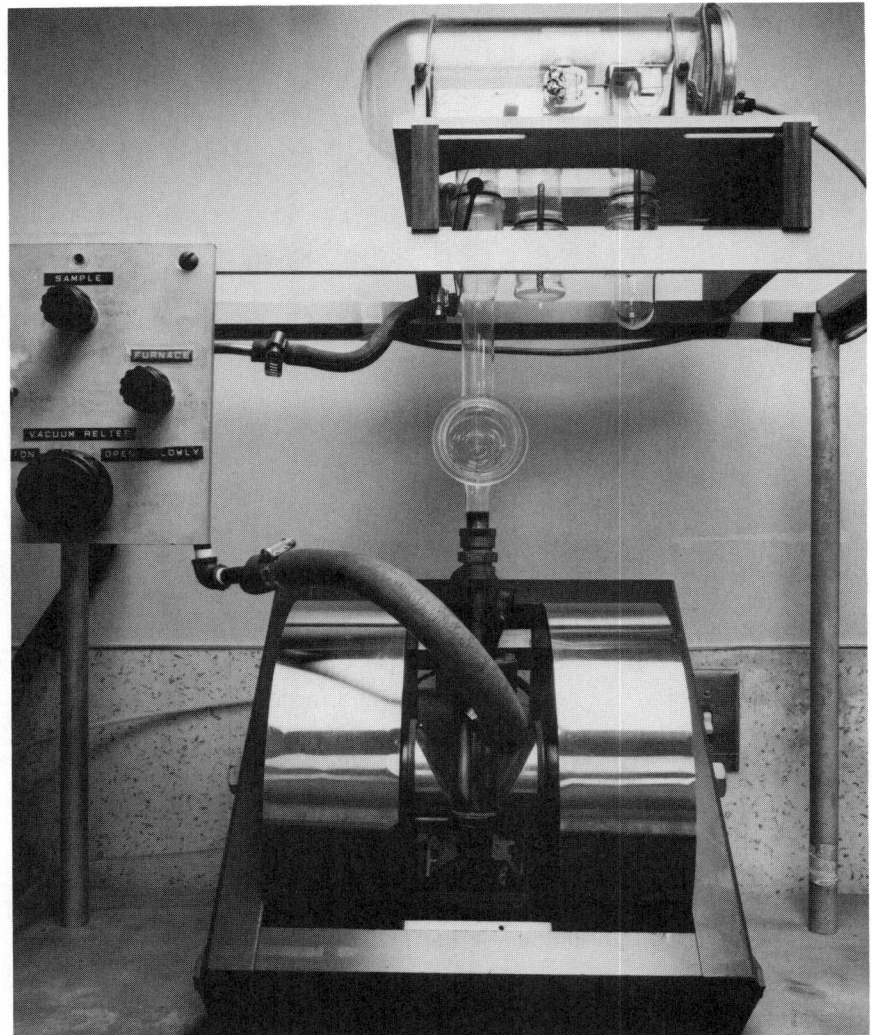

Fig. 72. Thermomagnetic balance.

Figure 72 illustrates a balance used at the laboratory at the University of California at Santa Barbara. It consists of a standard electromagnet capable of giving 700 mT (7000 oe). The balance itself is a commercially available Cahn microbalance. The sample is placed in a quartz bucket, which is suspended on a quartz rod assembly. The rod chain is interrupted at the window for ease of loading, but this remains a delicate operation. The furnace is an evacuated metal assembly built by Dr. Chris Haile when he was a student at UC Santa Barbara. The furnace can reach temperatures of about 1000°K, which is in excess of the common Curie points determined in paleomagnetic laboratories. The sample region can be evacuated to approximately 1 μtorr. The thermocouple which measures the temperature of the sample is inserted from below and adjusted to be as close as possible to the sample. One of the more difficult features of the experiment is the accurate determination of the temperature of the sample. Some improvement can be achieved by placing the thermocouple in a comparable quartz container. Additional thermocouples can also be used to establish thermal gradients in the furnace.

Figure 73 illustrates the horizontal translation balance developed by Weiss and Foex (1911), which is a very sensitive device. The specimen is mounted on a beam which places it in the gradient of the pole piece, so that it is in a horizontal gradient of the magnetic field. The beam is constrained to move horizontally. The movement of the beam can be used as a measure of the change of the force on the sample due to the change in saturation magnetization.

Thermomagnetic balances tend to be rather delicate instruments and so are not well suited to routine use in laboratories, where not everyone is as careful as is required to operate them. Among the various instruments which have been tried in their place are vibrating sample magnetometers (see Section 4.2.1) and AC susceptibility bridges (see Section 4.3.2). In a novel technique differential thermal analysis (DTA) has been used to detect the thermal anomaly associated with the Curie point (Vollstadt, 1968). All of these methods have the advantage that one does not have to prepare a magnetic separate for the determination. The DTA method does, however, appear likely to suffer from sensitivity problems (Collinson, 1983). The AC bridge method described by Petersen (1967) appears to be a viable approach, usable

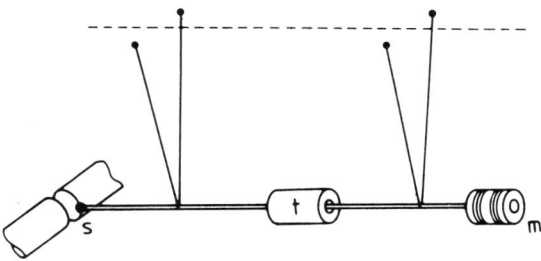

FIG. 73. Horizontal thermomagnetic balance, showing transducer (t) for position and magnet (m) for restoring force. (After Collinson, 1983.)

with the majority of samples studied in paleomagnetism. As will be described below, the VSM too provides a useful technique. One instrument whose potential for these measurements does not appear to have been developed is the SQUID magnetometer.

The obvious difficulty with the use of the SQUIDs is that the sensor and pickup coils must be maintained at a temperature in the vicinity of 10 K while the samples must be at about 1000 K. It was noted by a distinguished geophysicist visiting our laboratory that if one uses a cryogenic magnetometer to measure Curie points, one does not know thermodynamics. However, the situation is not as bleak as it may appear. As was noted in the discussion of thermal demagnetization, one can take advantage of the excellent thermal insulation required to maintain the low heat leak into the cryogenic region of the magnetometer. Second, the fast response times of the instrument make measurements possible without undue disturbance to the thermal equilibrium. One should therefore be able to develop techniques such that the high sensitivity of the instrument can be used to determine the Curie points of the standard samples of paleomagnetism. In principle, one can of course make a high-field measurement, but in general it is more practicable to use an intermediate field of about 10 µT ($10^{-1}$ oe). One can then use standard rock magnetometers (Section 3.7.3) provided there is a means of trapping a field of this order of magnitude. The use of this range of field has the advantage that one can make use of the Hopkinson rise to gain resolution in the determination of the Curie point.

Probably the most practical way to use the SQUID magnetometers for Curie point determination is to utilize a gradiometer. A gradiometer with attached coil has been used successfully by biomagnetists to detect extremely low magnetic induced moments (Romani et al., 1982). With the addition of a furnace of the type already developed for astatic magnetometers (Collinson, 1983), very sensitive devices should be achieved relatively easily. This device would have sufficient sensitivity that standard paleomagnetic samples could be routinely subjected to Curie point determination.

4.1.2. Thermomagnetic Analysis. It is convenient to distinguish measurements in which the primary concern is to obtain a Curie point from measurements in which a more complete determination of the variation of magnetization with temperature is carried out. In general, rock magnetists and paleomagnetists have not been strongly concerned with such measurements. However, in both biomagnetic and lunar sample studies such determinations were critical, as indeed they are for distinguishing between the various types of ferrimagnetic behavior discussed by Néel (1955). Two instruments are particularly well suited to the observations. They are the VSM and the high-field SQUID susceptometer. The VSM is described in Section 4.2.1. The high-field susceptometer is described here.

4.1.2.1. HIGH-FIELD SQUID SUSCEPTOMETERS. The susceptometer systems are of similar design to the standard vertical rock magnetometers. The instrument at UC Santa Barbara has a 7-mm room temperature access and a superconducting magnet capable of giving 2 T (20 koe). A superconducting shield is mounted inside the magnet coil to trap the high field and provide the stability required for the SQUID to make high-sensitivity field measurements in the background of the strong DC field. If one wishes to detect a field due to the sample, which is, say, 1 part in $10^9$ of the magnetizing $H$ field, this field must be stable to 1 part in $10^9$.

The operation of superconducting magnets requires some care. In this system the power supply generates the particular field required in the superconducting coil. This field is then trapped in a superconducting shield around the sample region. Care must be taken to match the current in the coils, when the field is to be changed, to avoid discharging the coils. The shield is then warmed to set it normal and the new field trapped. This method is time-consuming (Fig. 74a). However, in low-temperature thermomagnetic analysis it does not cause any difficulty because a single field will be used through the measurement while the temperature is brought from 4.2 K to room temperature.

The temperature regulation system uses helium transfer gas, which passes over a heating coil at the base of the access hole. This permits convenient variation of temperature from 4.2 K to a temperature approaching room temperature. Other more recent designs permit temperatures in excess of room temperature to be achieved, but this tends to be at the price of helium boil-off, so that unless one can develop a system whereby the sample is heated externally, the instrument is probably most conveniently operated for low-temperature measurements.

Figure 74b illustrates the variation of high-field susceptibility of a paramagnetic sample. Figure 74c gives the observed dependence of susceptibility on inverse temperature. These observations are made at low temperature.

Susceptibility systems are available for S.H.E. Inc. The newer systems have applied fields of 4 T (40 koe) and temperature cycling up to 400 K, and the measurement is greatly simplified with computer-controlled sample movement and field and temperature change.

4.1.3. Detection of Magnetocrystalline Anisotropy Transitions. In addition to their distinctive Curie points and Néel points, ferromagnets and ferrimagnets exhibit magnetic anisotropy transitions. Magnetic anisotropy refers to preferred directions of magnetization within a grain. In such a direction, the energy associated with the magnetized state is minimized. One form of anisotropy is magnetocrystalline anisotropy, which is defined with respect to the crystal lattice. Thus magnetite is most easily magnetized along the body diagonal (111) directions at room temperature. However, at low

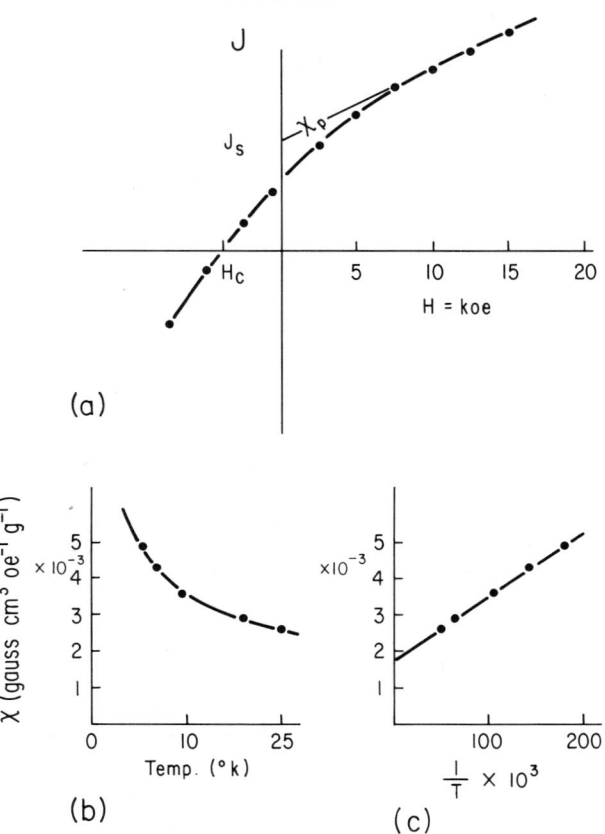

FIG. 74. High-field susceptometer: (a) part of hysteresis loop; (b) and (c) paramagnetic susceptibility plotted against temperature and against inverse temperature.

temperature the easy directions become the (100) cube edge directions, in association with a crystalline transition from cubic to orthorhombic. A simple identification technique for magnetite was developed by making use of the behavior of magnetic remanence across this transition (Nagata *et al.*, 1964; Fuller and Kobayashi, 1964). The procedure is to magnetize the sample to saturation at liquid nitrogen temperature and to observe the warming curve of this saturation remanent magnetization. This can be carried out either in the standard rock magnetometer, with suitable thermal lagging of the sample, or in the high-field susceptometer with zero field. As the anisotropy transition is approached, the remanent magnetization decreases sharply to give a minimum at the transition temperature. Above the transition, a memory of the low-temperaturature magnetization is acquired

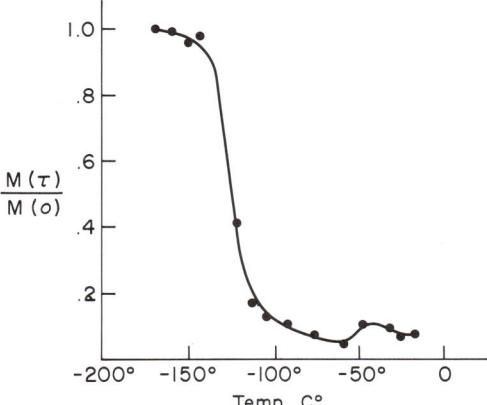

FIG. 75. Idenitification of multidomain magnetite by demagnetization at low-temperature anisotropy transition.

(Kobayashi and Fuller, 1968). An example of identification of magnetite from a stingray (Dunn, Fuller, and Zoeger, unpublished observations) is illustrated in Fig. 75. This technique is only suitable for magnetite which is relatively coarse-grained; the transition in remanence depends on the rearrangement of the domain pattern at low temperature and is not seen in single-domain magnetite. More sophisticated techniques are required for the determination of its presence in single-domain material, but the transition is reflected in changes in other magnetic properties, such as coercive force, which can be measured as a function of temperature. An important advantage of using these anisotropy transitions for identification is that the sample need not be heated.

The various techniques discussed in this section are summarized in a simplified flow diagram (Fig. 76). The diagram illustrates the use of the various techniques to identify the state of magnetic order and, in the case of ferromagnets and ferrimagnets, to identify the phase.

4.2. Magnetic Characterization

After identification of a particular ferromagnetic or ferrimagnetic material in a sample, the next stage in description is to establish its magnetic behavior—to characterize it. The principal means of characterization is to measure the hysteresis loop, for this gives the coercive force and the ratio of saturation remanence to saturation magnetization, the fundamental parameters used to describe the behavior of a magnetic material. They indicate, for example, whether the sample is single-domain or multidomain.

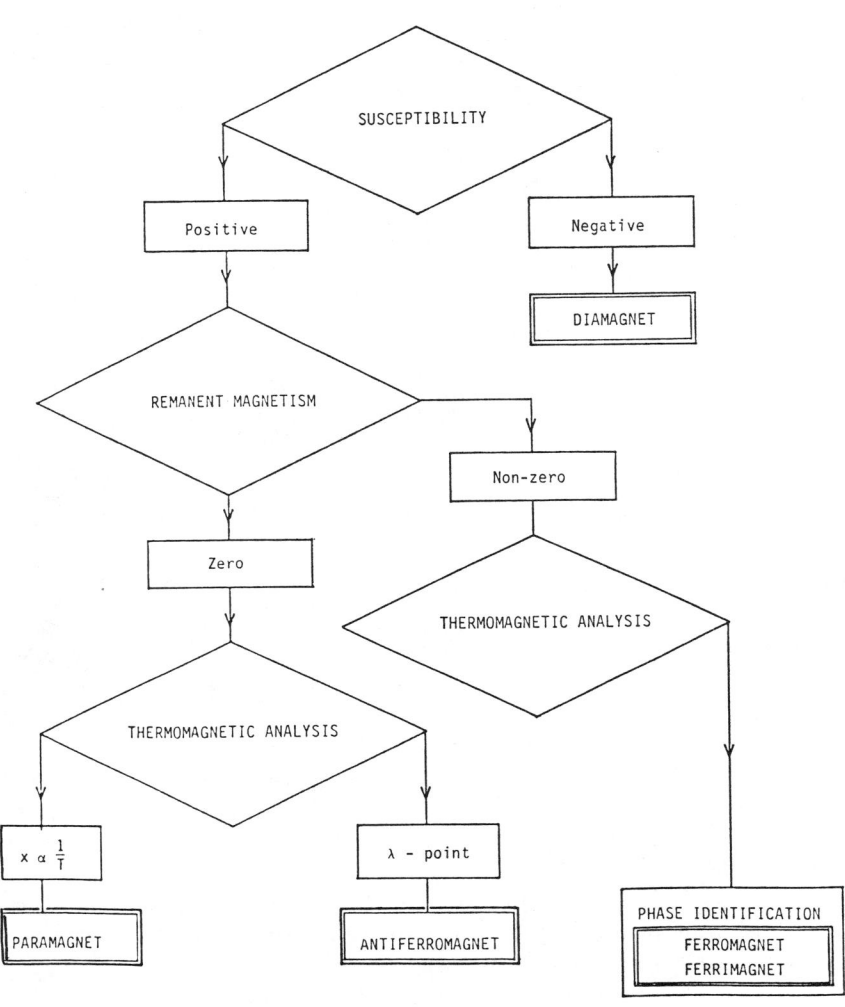

Fig. 76. Flow diagram for identification of magnetic phases.

In some instances they may give an indication of the internal stress state or grain shape. Thus the hysteresis observation establishes the structure-dependent magnetic properties, while the Curie point determination identifies the substance.

Hysteresis loops were initially made in a stepwise manner. The sample was first measured in zero field. The field was then increased and the sample remeasured. The process was then repeated with as many observations as a suitably small incremental increase and decrease of the field demanded.

The measurement can be carried out with a magnetic balance or a ballistic magnetometer (Collinson, 1983). A high-field SQUID susceptometer can also be used. All of these observations are extremely time-consuming and a continuous method of observation is preferable. In such an observation, the field is changed continuously and the magnetization measured in the changing field. Two methods of making the observation are available, the VSM and the AC loop plotter. The most important instrument for rock magnetists has been the VSM, which has always been the workhorse of rock magnetism. It is an extremely versatile instrument. It can be used not only for hysteresis measurements, but also for thermomagnetic analysis at high or low temperature, for initial susceptibility, and indeed for remanent magnetization. The AC loop plotter has not enjoyed the same popularity in rock magnetism. Nevertheless, it is a powerful device and is described below. SQUIDs cannot be used for the continuous observation of hysteresis loops because the changing field drives the sensors out of lock.

4.2.1. Vibration Sample Magnetometer. The magnetization of an object may be measured by vibrating it with respect to an appropriate pickup coil array. In principle, either the sample or coils may be vibrated to induce an EMF in the detection-coil circuit. Successful magnetometers were developed using the vibrating-coil technique (Smith, 1956; Dwight *et al.*, 1958). If it is impractical to vibrate the sample, this method may have to be used However, an extremely uniform magnetic field is required for measurement at high sensitivity. Even the small nonuniformity in the earth's magnetic field found in most laboratories due to nearby instruments can be a source of unacceptable noise. As a consequence of this difficulty, the vibrating-sample technique has generally been preferred to the vibrating-coil method. The theory and construction of such instruments have been described by Foner (1959), Krause (1963), Kobayashi and Fuller (1967), Pacyna (1982), Zelinka (1979), and Zelinka *et al.* (1984).

Let us consider a magnetic dipole moment which experiences a simple harmonic oscillation between $A(0, 0, 0)$ and $B(0, 0, dZ)$, where $dZ$ is small. The time-dependent variation in the field is equivalent to that of the quadrupole which is obtained by alternately reversing the moment of the

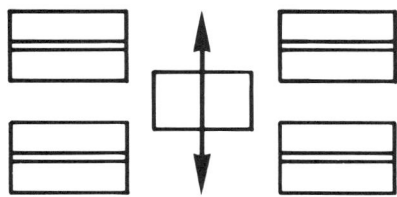

FIG. 77. Optimized coil array for vibration magnetometer. (After Zelinka *et al.*, 1984.)

dipole at positions $A$ and $B$. The amplitude of the magnetic potential of this quadrupole, a distance $r$ away from this point, is given by Stratton (1941):

$$U_{zz} = \frac{1}{4\pi} m_z \, dz \frac{\partial^2}{\partial z^2}\left(\frac{1}{r}\right)$$

$$U_{xz} = \frac{1}{4\pi} m_x \, dz \frac{\partial^2}{\partial x \, \partial z}\left(\frac{1}{r}\right)$$

$$U_{yz} = \frac{1}{4\pi} m_y \, dz \frac{\partial z}{\partial y \, \partial z}\left(\frac{1}{r}\right)$$

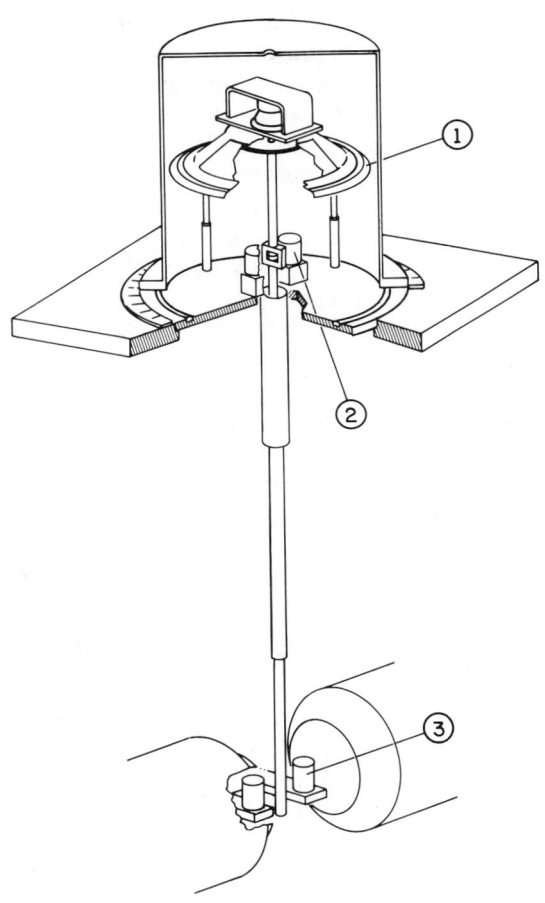

FIG. 78. Loudspeaker drive vibration magnetometer: 1, loudspeaker; 2, reference coils; 3, signal coils. (After Foner, 1959.)

The flux pattern of the variations in the field with time is then obtained as $H = -\nabla u$. The sense coil array advocated by Zelinka et al. (1984) is illustrated in Fig. 77. An optimization procedure gave, for a sample of diameter 8 mm and length 10 mm with a vibration amplitude of 2.5 mm, a coil length of 6 mm, diameter of 12 mm winding thickness of 1 mm, 1200 turns, and distance between coil axes of 14 mm. The advantage of the four-coil array is that it is an astatic arrangement and hence only minimally affected by homogeneous field. It is, however, clear that the signal is very sensitive to sample position. Model calculations showed the sensitivity to be to the inverse fifth power, so the vibration must be accurately maintained along the midline of the system.

A loudspeaker drive was used by Foner to obtain a vibration of 90 Hz over 1.5 mm (Fig. 78). However, this system was designed to carry specimens substantially smaller than those used in paleomagnetism. A sturdier motor driven vibrating head was, therefore, used in the VSM instrument described here. A 3 : 1 belt drive is used to obtain 90 c/sec from an 1800-rpm synchronous motor. A mechanical converter, commercially sold as part of a miniature drill, provides variable amplitude of vertical vibration from 0.2 to 5 mm and is strong enough to carry several grams of rock. The vibration assembly is mounted on a turntable driven by a rubber wheel at variable speeds from 1 to 1/6 turn/min. The specimen may therefore be turned about an axis parallel to the vibration direction at a designated speed (Fig. 79).

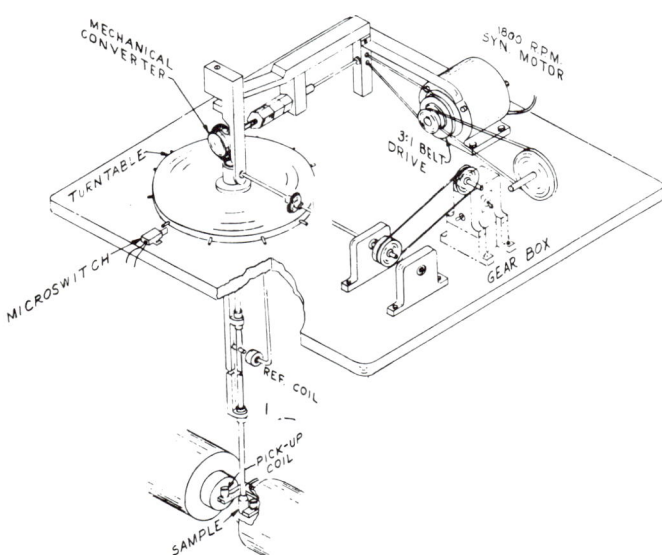

FIG. 79. Vibration magnetometer with mechanical drive.

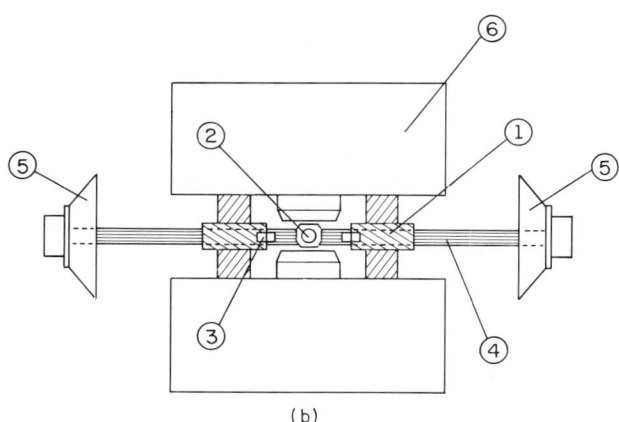

(b)

Fig. 80. Stein double loudspeaker drive vibration magnetometer. (a) Configuration. (b) Schematic plan view: 1, coil assembly; 2, sample holder; 3, pickup coils; 4, sample support; 5, loudspeakers; 6, electromagnet.

The signal from the pickup coils is amplified first by a wideband transistor amplifier and then by a tuned amplifier. It is rectified in a phase-sensitive detector by using a reference signal obtained from a pickup coil beside a small magnet mounted in the vibrating head. The output of the system is fed to the $Y$ axis of an $X$-$Y$ recorder.

A convenient VSM has recently been developed in our laboratory (M. Stein, unpublished work). The system consists of a double loudspeaker drive, with the two speakers driven 180° out of phase by a hi-fi amplifier. The device is illustrated in Fig. 80. Note that the vibration is in the horizontal plane, which makes sample handling convenient. This device is cheaply produced and has intermediate sensitivity. Attempts are under way to produce a high temperature version of the device using an induction heater as the means of heating the sample.

The instrument described by Zelinka et al. (1984) has a mechanical drive system (Fig. 81). This was preferred to the loudspeaker drive because loudspeakers generate magnetic noise, which becomes a factor in high-sensitivity measurements. In this instrument special care has been taken to ensure vertical vibration of the sample. The uppermost section of the drive shaft has a square cross section and the bushing consists of vertical plates which can be adjusted to give an accurately vertical motion. The length of the drive shaft has also been minimized in a further effort to ensure true vertical displacement. The reference voltage in this instrument is obtained with an optical system.

The magnetic fields for VSMs are invariably produced by electromagnets. The requirements are usually for fields of the order of 1 T (10 koe). The field must have some form of ramping control. Moreover, the AC ripple is a source of noise in the measurement, so a superior power supply for the magnet is an important aspect of the instrument.

For measurements involving only intermediate sensitivity, say of order $10^{-3}$ A m$^2$ (1 gauss cm$^3$), one can operate the VSM with a continuously changing field and make measurements rapidly. However, for high-sensitivity measurements it is best to set the field and measure the magnetization over an integrating time interval of some minutes. Thus the measurement is no longer continuous at the highest sensitivities. However, the instrument can be operated under the control of a microprocessor, so the operator does not have to be present throughout the measurement. Using this technique with a curve fitting program (Hejda, 1985), sensitivities of order $10^{-9}$ Wb m kg$^{-1}$ are quoted by Zelinka et al. (1984). This is a little hard to translate into an equivalent moment sensitivity since it depends on the sample used. However, assuming that the standard samples have a mass of about 5 g and noting that Wb m kg$^{-1}$ = $(1/4\pi)10^7$ A m$^2$ kg$^{-1}$ (or gauss cm$^3$ g$^{-1}$), this sensititivity appears to represent a moment sensitivity of order $10^{-3}$ gauss cm$^3$

Fig. 81. Zelinka vibration magnetometer.

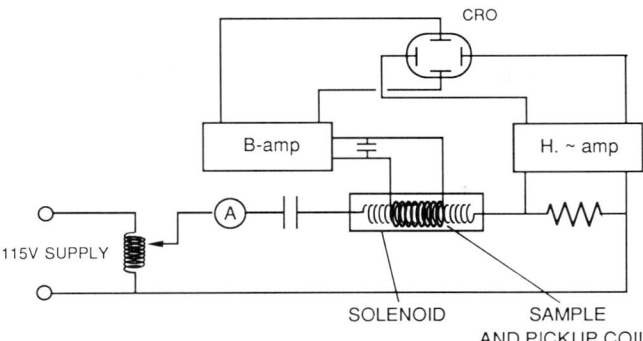

Fig. 82. AC loop plotter block diagram from Scherb (1948).

or $10^{-6}$ A m$^2$. These sensitivities surpass those of the old vibration magnetometers (Kobayashi and Fuller, 1967).

4.2.2. AC Loop Plotter. The second method of obtaining continuous magnetization curve plots is to make use of an oscilloscope to present the loops. The standard method is to apply a voltage to a coil or an electromagnet to the abscissa and apply the output of a pickup coil to the ordinate. As the supply passes through the AC cycle the sample is exposed to a range of $H$ fields. This gives rise to a magnetization in the sample, which is detected by the sense coils. One of the earliest of these devices was developed by Scherb (1948).

In Scherb's instrument a solenoid is used to magnetize the sample as illustrated in Fig. 82. The solenoid gave fields of order $10^5$ A m$^{-1}$ ($10^3$ oe). In more recent devices, electromagnets are used to increase the available fields. The pickup coils are placed within the solenoid with their position relative to the samples optimized for sensitivity.

A loop plotter was described by Likhite *et al.* (1965). Numerous investigations of hysteresis loops of rocks at low temperature as well as room temperature have been made with this instrument (Radhkrishnamurty and Deutsch, 1974).

4.2.3. Discussion of Magnetic Characterization. The estimation of grain size can be attempted using any of the properties that reflect the different behavior in the single-domain and multidomain states (Day *et al.*, 1976a). One of the simplest such indicators is the ratio of saturation remanent magnetization to saturation magnetization, which is obtained from the hysteresis loops. The magnetic hardness is also an indication of domain state and is reflected in DC magnetization and demagnetization curves. Figure 83 illustrates the behavior of a sample of whale dura. The material is evidently magnetically hard; a field of nearly 50 mT (500 oe) was required to reach a

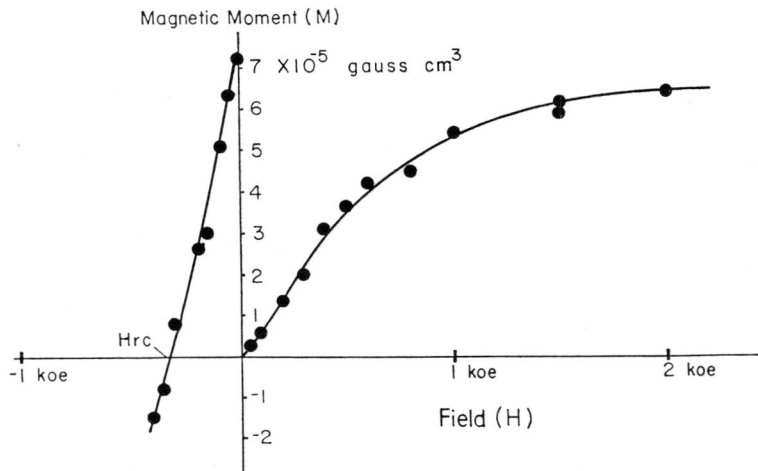

FIG. 83. Magnetic characterization by DC acquisition and AF demagnetization.

half-saturation value and 20 mT (2 koe) to reach saturation remanence. The remanent coercivity, the back field to reduce the remanent magnetization to zero, is roughly 30 mT (300 oe). The determination of these curves is experimentally simple; it requires only the measurement of remanent magnetization, which is readily carried out with rock magnetometers. The necessary magnetizing fields can be generated with coils or electromagnets. AF demagnetization provides yet another means of establishing the magnetic hardness of the material (Collinson et al., 1967). The AF demagnetization equipment is universally available in paleomagnetic laboratories.

The combined use of DC magnetization curves and AF demagnetization permits the detection of interactions between magnetic particles (Cisowski, 1981). The test involves comparison of the DC magnetization curve and the AF demagnetization curve as in Fig. 84. If there are no interactions the curves are symmetrical (as in Fig. 84a), and they intersect at the remanent coercivity field value. In contrast, if interactions are important the curves are no longer symmetric (Fig. 84b). Figure 84b is for chiton teeth, in which the fine particles of magnetite are known to be so close to each other that interactions will be strong (Kirschvink and Lowenstam, 1972). This test also distinguishes between multidomain and interacting single-domain material. Figure 84c shows the curves for a rock with multidomain magnetite. Note that in comparison with the interacting single-domain material, the multidomain sample acquires magnetization more readily in the low field and saturates at lower fields.

The problem of magnetic granulometry of lake sediments has attracted a good deal of attention because it has applications to limnology and it is

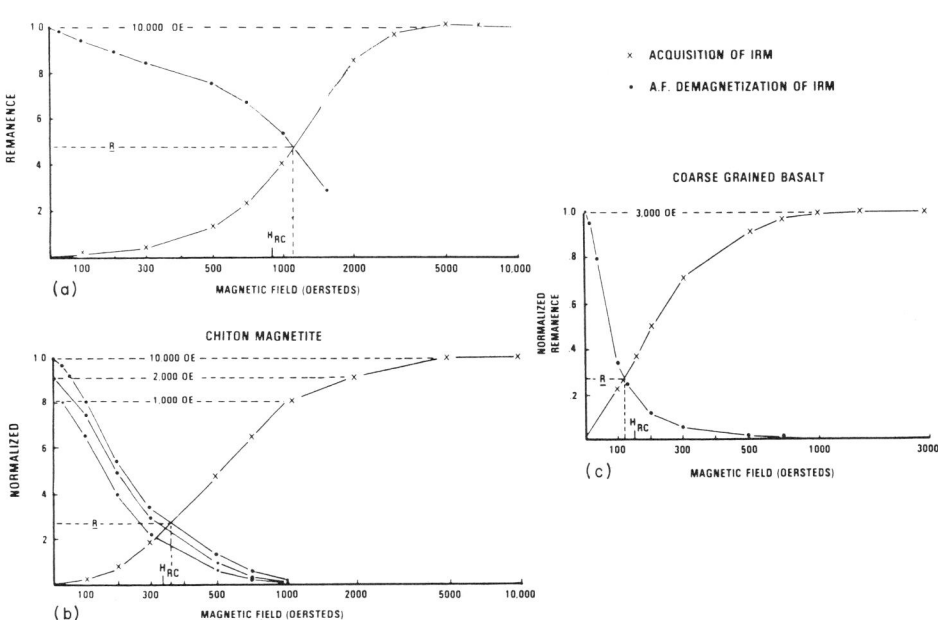

FIG. 84. Cisowski interaction test: (a) no interactions present; (b) interactions present; and (c) multidomain response. (After Cisowski, 1981.)

essential to an understanding of the magnetization of these sediments. The techniques can be applied immediately to biomagnetic analysis; indeed, it is possible that some of the magnetite in lake sediments has a biological origin. A promising method of granulometry has been suggested by King *et al.* (1982). They have chosen two parameters for their scheme. The acquisition of anhysteretic remanence is one. Anhysteretic remanence is acquired when a magnetic material is exposed to an AF alternating field which is allowed to decrease in amplitude in the presence of a biasing DC field. The ARM is particularly sensitive to the presence of single-domain particles. The other parameter is weak field susceptibility, which is sensitive to multidomain grains. Figure 85a shows the results of such an analysis for certain assemblages, and Fig. 85b presents a simple interpretational model.

The use of these granulometry techniques permits the determination of grain size via its effect on domain state and hence on magnetic behavior. All of these methods assume that the material is in a grain size range which is at least large enough to be stable single domain. There remains the extremely fine grain size range, which is too small to exhibit stable single-domain behavior and is termed superparamagnetic.

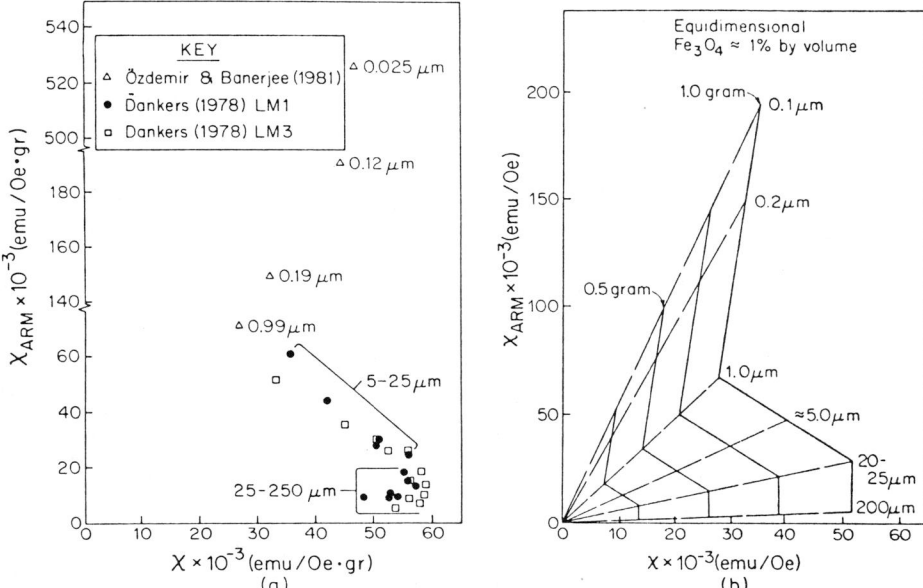

FIG. 85. Granulometry of magnetic phases in lake sediments: (a) results and (b) model. (After King *et al.*, 1982.)

Standard methods of detecting the presence of superparamagnetic material have been developed, making use of the inability of superparamagnets to exhibit remanent magnetization, although they do have strong susceptibility. We noted that the phenomenon of superparamagnetism is necessarily a function of temperature as well as grain size. The most direct way to demonstrate the presence of a superparamagnet is therefore to study the relaxation time $\tau$ of magnetization as a function of temperature. If the material is in the superparamagnetic state, there must be some lower temperature at which the particles will achieve stable single-domain behavior. The relaxation time will sharply increase at this temperature. Relaxation times can be determined conveniently with the VSM or SQUID rock magnetometers—the sample is magnetized in a field, placed in the magnetometer, and the decay of remanence observed. The process is then repeated at progressively lower temperatures, so that the relaxation time can be observed as a function of temperature. A quick and dirty, but still effective, way of doing the experiment is to measure the saturation remanent magnetization at different temperatures. When the grain size is stable single domain the saturation remanence will be large, but when it becomes superparamagnetic the remanence will decrease to zero. Another way is to measure

9. ROCK MAGNETISM AND PALEOMAGNETISM METHODS 437

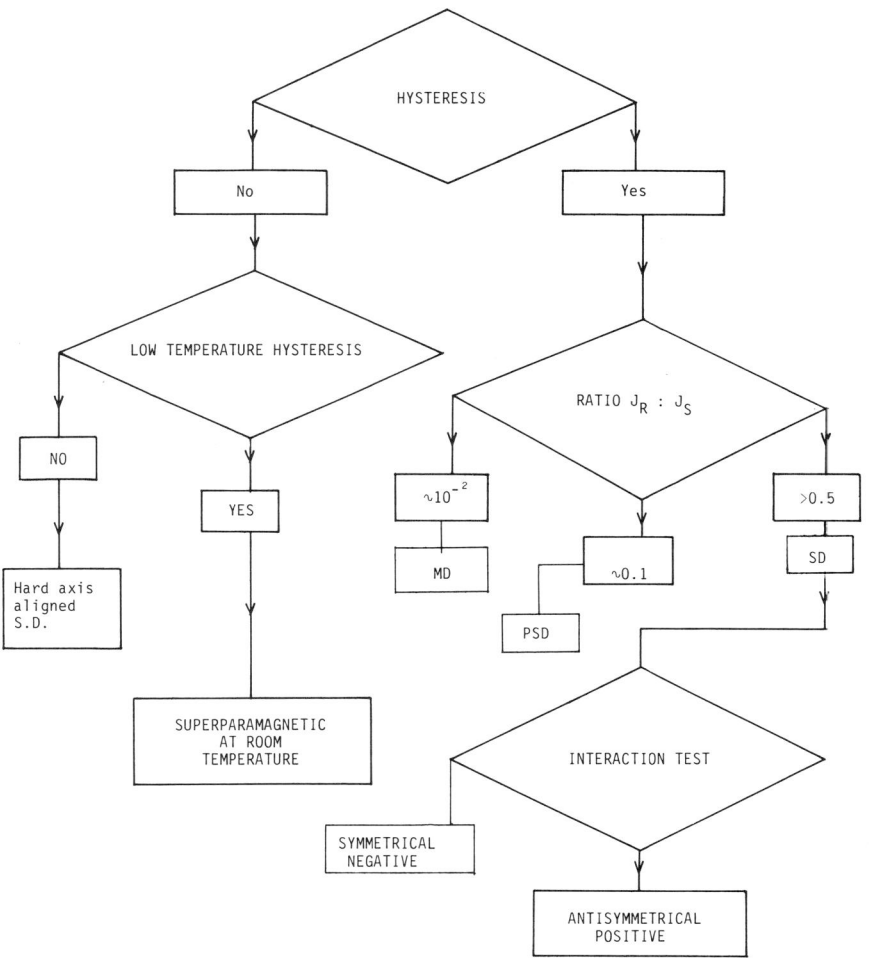

FIG. 86. Flow diagram for characterization of magnetic materials.

susceptibility. As the material changes from single domain to superparamagnetic, there will be a large associated increase in susceptibility. The observations can also be made with SQUID rock magnetometers by trapping a weak field in the superconducting shield.

A scheme for distinguishing the magnetic behavior of magnetite in superparamagnetic, single-domain, pseudo-single-domain, and multidomain states is summarized in Fig. 86. As discussed in this section, these parameters can be used to establish granulometry schemes. The choice of the parameters used will be controlled by the availability of equipment to measure them and the degree to which they uniquely determine domain state.

### 4.3. Initial Susceptibility

Susceptibility describes the ease with which magnetic materials are magnetized when they are exposed to $H$ fields

$$M = kH$$

As noted in Section 2, in the SI system susceptibility is dimensionless as $M$ and $H$ have the same dimensions. In the CGSEMU system of units, susceptibility has units of gauss cubic centimetres per oersted per unit volume or per unit mass. Initial susceptibility, or weak field susceptibility, is used to describe the susceptibility of materials in fields which are small compared with their coercive force.

Initial susceptibility is of interest for a number of reasons, some of which are of a practical nature, while others are related to the basic understanding of magnetization processes. Since the geomagnetic field is small compared with the coercive force of most naturally occurring magnetic materials, the initial susceptibility is of immediate interest in geomagnetism. For example, a useful number which describes the ratio of NRM to induced magnetization in the geomagnetic field is the Koenigsberger ratio $Q_n$. It is defined as follows:

$$Q_n = \text{NRM}/kH$$

In either system of units, it is dimensionless. The Koenigsberger ratio for many oceanic basalts is large compared to 1, reflecting the dominance of the remanent over induced magnetization in these rocks. In general, a high $Q_n$ value is a reflection of the fine grain size of the magnetic carriers in the rocks.

The temperature dependence of initial susceptibility is of interest as an important aspect of the acquisition of thermoremanent magnetization. It is also of some practical importance; the increase in initial susceptibility immediately below the Curie point, known as the Hopkinson rise, facilitates the determination of Curie points by an initial susceptibility method.

Initial susceptibility is of interest to geologists as a means of stratigraphic correlation. It has the added advantage that it can be measured down boreholes without the recovery of cores. It is also of interest as a method of determining the amount of magnetic material present in a rock, which can be indicative of changing source environment or diagenetic change in sedimentary rocks.

4.3.1. DC Measurements of Initial Susceptibility. Measurements of initial susceptibility can be made by either DC or AC methods. For example, an astatic magnetometer can be used to obtain a DC measure of susceptibility by exposing the system to a homogeneous $H$ field. The astatic system pair does not respond significantly to the inducing field, so the induced moment of the sample can be measured. However, the system also responds to the remanent moment of the sample. A simple method of discrimination between the two is to complete a scheme of measurements which permits pairs of the form

$$M_{+x} = \text{NRM}_x + kH$$

$$M_{-x} = -\text{NRM}_x + kH$$

The sums and differences of such measurements separate remanent and induced moments. The sensitivity of such measurements is comparable to that of the measurement of remanent magnetization with the same magnetometer.

The most sensitive DC measurement of susceptibility is made with a SQUID magnetometer, with a field trapped in the superconducting shield. Such measurements have been described by Schmidt and Ellwood (1983). They are subject to the same difficulty as measurements with astatic magnetometers; a means of separating induced and remanent moments must be developed. The trapping of fields in these instruments is not a very convenient process. Perhaps the best method is to use a gradiometer with a field coil attached (Sugiura et al., 1985).

4.3.2. AC Measurement of Initial Susceptibility. The most convenient methods of measuring susceptibility are the AC methods. One measures the change in inductance of an air-cored coil brought about by the introduction of the rock sample. As noted in Section 2, the inductance of an electrical circuit is the flux linked to the circuit when unit current flows in it. We also noted that the flux density is related to the magnetizing field of an electric circuit as

$$B = \mu H$$

Moreover, the permeability $\mu$ is equal to the product of the permeability of free space and the relative permeability $\mu_r$:

$$\mu = \mu_0 \mu_r = \mu_0(1 + k)$$

Hence the flux density produced by a circuit can be altered by changing the permeability (or susceptibility) of the region in the vicinity of the coil. The inductance $L$ of a coil is

$$L = \mu N^2 A / l$$

where $\mu$ is the permeability of the medium, $N$ the number of turns, $A$ the area, and $l$ the length of the coil. As Collinson (1983) shows nicely, this gives a relationship between the difference in inductance of the coil, with and without the sample in it, and the difference in susceptibility of the medium ($K_m$) and the sample ($K_s$).

$$\Delta L = c(K_s - k_m)$$

where $c$ is a constant involving coil form parameters and the permeability of free space. To measure weak field susceptibility, we therefore need to measure the small differences in inductance of air-cored coils brought about insertion of the sample.

The standard methods of measuring the inductance of coils are bridge methods. These methods derive from the old Wheatstone bridge method of measuring resistance, with which every schoolboy used to be familiar. The unknown resistance ($R_u$) is placed in one arm of the bridge (Fig. 87A). The resistance $R_v$ is variable and is adjusted until no current flows through the detector. In this condition, the potential at A and C must be the same; hence

$$I_2 R_2 = (I_1 - I_2) R_u$$
$$I_2 R_1 = (I_1 - I_2) R_v$$
$$R_u = \frac{R_v R_2}{R_1}$$

and so one obtains the value of the unknown resistance in terms of the known resistances. To measure the inductance of coils one uses analogous techniques, but there are differences because one measures the complex impedance of the coil and because AC detection techniques can be used.

Three networks which have been used to make susceptibility measurements are shown in Fig. 87B.

The first suffers from asymmetry. This aspect was improved by Michelson (1952), who used two air-cored coils in an effort to reduce thermal drift of the apparatus. The third network has particular advantages due to the tightly coupled ratio arms, which are the two windings of 1 : 1 transformer (Hague, 1952). At balance:

$$\frac{Z_1}{Z_2} = \frac{L_3 + M}{L_4 + M}$$
$$= \frac{L_3 + (L_3 L_4)^{1/2}}{L_4 + (L_3 L_4)^{1/2}} \approx 1$$

## 9. ROCK MAGNETISM AND PALEOMAGNETISM METHODS

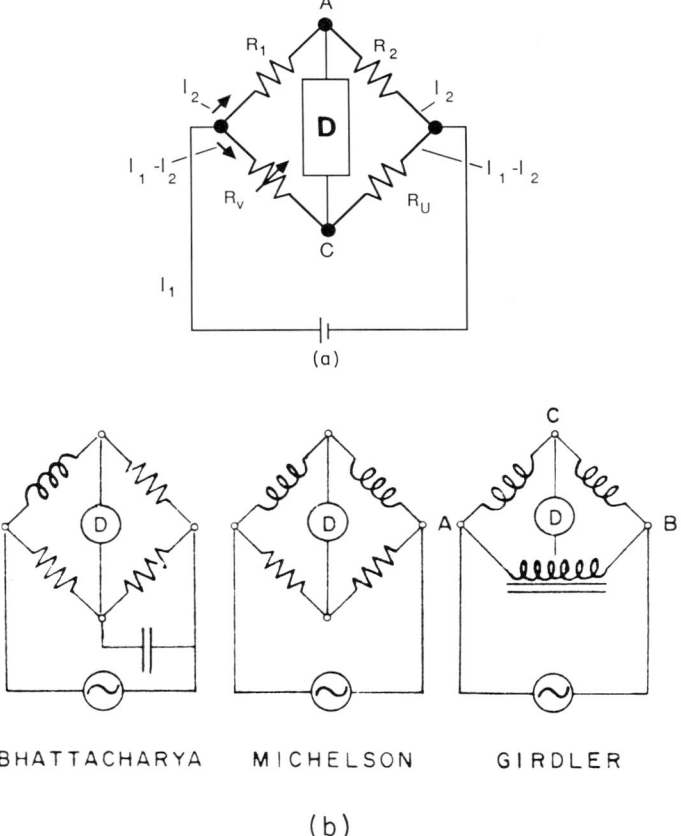

FIG. 87. Principle of susceptibility determination by bridge methods. (A) Wheatstone bridge method for resistance. (B) Bridge circuits for susceptibility measurement: Bhattacharya (1950) bridge, Michelson (1952) Maxwell bridge, and Girdler transformer bridge.

The potential differences between AD and BD may be written as follows for a bifilar winding:

$$V_{AD} = jwL_3 i_1 - jwMi_1$$

$$V_{BD} = jwL_4 i_1 - jwMi_1$$

$$V_{DD} \approx V_{BD} \approx 0$$

Hence, at balance, A, B, and D may all be held at earth potential by grounding the center point of the transformer. This helps greatly in eliminating stray capacitance to earth. Moreover, since the mutual and self-inductances are additive for currents entering from the detector, the ratio arms act as high-impedance arms. The detector current is, therefore, determined solely by $Z_1$ and $Z_2$.

In both Michelson's and Girdler's networks, the movement of a ferrite slug along the axis of the second coil was used to null the detector current. This method has the following disadvantages: (1) it involves making mechanical adjustments to the bridge, which directly increases the demands on stability, (2) the selection of the balance point is difficult, (3) because of (1) and (2) the experiment time is long, and (4) because of the nonlinear dependence of $\Delta L/L$ on the slug movement, the initial position of the slug determines the displacement necessary to null a given detector current. Use of the bridge output as the measure of susceptibility eliminates all of these problems, provided that the output is indeed linear with susceptibility. This can be tested experimentally. By rotating the sample one can facilitate the detection of the anisotropy signal (Graham, 1967) by using low frequency phase sensitive detection.

The bridge requires a signal generator which can give an output of about 1 W with low distortion and good frequency stability. A convenient frequency is 1000 Hz, a compromise between higher frequencies, which make bridge design difficult, and lower frequencies, which give too small a reactance. A standard phase-sensitive detector with a low-impedance input preamplifier is suitable for the detector. In our laboratory we use a PAR phase-sensitive detector.

One might expect that the experimental limit would be due to the sensitivity of the detector. However, it appears to be the thermal drift that is the practical limiting factor. Even when the bridge is not in use it will drift if care is not taken to maintain the mechanical stability of any shielding used. When the bridge is being used the principal problem appears to be the change in temperature in the test coil brought about by insertion of the sample. This can be reduced by isolating the measuring access from the coil by inserting a vacuum flask, or by using a double-ended access system which is maintained at room temperature by circulating air.

A commercial susceptibility bridge has been marketed as the Kappabridge KLY-2. The instrument is an inductance bridge following the design of Jelinek (1973). A sensitivity of $10^{-8}$ SI units or $10^{-7}$ gauss oe$^{-1}$ in CGSEMU is quoted.

A second AC method of determining susceptibility is used in the Bartington magnetic susceptibility meter. The sample is used to change the resonant frequency of a circuit including the test coil. The change in inductance of the coil can then be measured by the change in frequency. The quoted sensitivities are comparable with those of the Kappabridge.

4.3.3. *Susceptibility Anisotropy.* The anisotropy of susceptibility has proved to be of some interest to geologists as a fabric element. The susceptibility of a rock sample varies with direction, reflecting preferred alignments of inherently anisotropic magnetic mineral particles. The individual grains may be anisotropic due to shape anisotropy or intrinsic crystalline anisotropy (Uyeda et al., 1963). These fabrics give intimations of processes the rock has experienced (Owens and Bamford, 1976; Wood et al., 1976).

In anisotropic material, susceptibility is a second-rank tensor property. Mathematically, this means that it obeys certain transformation laws. Practically, it means that susceptibility is specified by an array of nine numbers:

$$\begin{pmatrix} k_{11} & k_{12} & k_{13} \\ k_{21} & k_{22} & k_{23} \\ k_{31} & k_{32} & k_{33} \end{pmatrix}$$

where $k_{ij}$ refers to the directions $x, y, z$, with $j$ the direction of the applied field and $i$ that of the measured moment. Symmetry dictates that three are redundant because off-axis coefficients such as $k_{xz}$ are equal to those with field and observation reversed $k_{zx}$. The six numbers may either be the six coefficients

$$\begin{pmatrix} k_{11} & & \\ k_{21} & k_{22} & \\ k_{31} & k_{32} & k_{33} \end{pmatrix}$$

or the principal susceptibilities $k_{11}$, $k_{22}$, and $k_{33}$ accompanied by their associated directions. The tensor takes a particularly simple form when it is referred to its principal axes:

$$\begin{pmatrix} k_{11} & & \\ & k_{22} & \\ & & k_{33} \end{pmatrix}$$

If the field is applied parallel to one of the principal axes the magnetization is also parallel to the field, i.e.,

$$M_1 = k_{11} H l_1 \text{ etc.}$$

This is analogous to the relationship between stress and strain in the directions of principal stresses. In describing susceptibility anisotropy, this form is very convenient.

In general, the relationship between field and magnetization is of course more complicated. If a field $H$ is applied with directional cosines $l_1 l_2 l_3$

$$M_1 = (l_1 l_2 l_3) \begin{pmatrix} k_{11} & k_{12} & k_{13} \\ k_{21} & k_{22} & k_{23} \\ k_{31} & k_{32} & k_{33} \end{pmatrix} \begin{pmatrix} H_1 \\ H_2 \\ H_3 \end{pmatrix}$$

or the susceptibility in the direction of the applied field is

$$k_1 = l_1^2 k_{11} + l_2^2 k_{22} + l_3^2 k_{33} + 2l_1 l_2 k_{12}$$
$$+ 2l_2 l_3 k_{23} + 2l_3 l_1 k_{31}$$

To obtain the transformation to the principal axes, we eliminate all off-axis contributions such as $k_{12}$. This diagonalization of the matrix gives the principal susceptibility coordinates. The transformation of axes is an eigenvalue problem; the principal susceptibilities are the eigenvalues of the susceptibility matrix. To approach the problem analytically, one notes that when the field is applied along one of the principal directions, the magnetic moment is simply proportional to the field. We therefore write

$$\begin{pmatrix} M_1 \\ M_2 \\ M_3 \end{pmatrix} = \begin{pmatrix} k_{11} & k_{12} & k_{13} \\ k_{21} & k_{22} & k_{23} \\ k_{31} & k_{32} & k_{33} \end{pmatrix} \begin{pmatrix} H_1 \\ H_2 \\ H_3 \end{pmatrix} = k \begin{pmatrix} H_1 \\ H_2 \\ H_3 \end{pmatrix}$$

Since

$$\begin{pmatrix} H_1 \\ H_2 \\ H_3 \end{pmatrix} = H \begin{pmatrix} l_1 \\ l_2 \\ l_3 \end{pmatrix}$$

we obtain for $k$, i.e., $M/H$, the following system of equations:

$$k_{11} l_1 + k_{12} l_2 + k_{13} l_3 = k l_1$$
$$k_{21} l_1 + k_{22} l_2 + k_{23} l_3 = k l_2$$
$$k_{31} l_1 + k_{32} l_2 + k_{33} l_3 = k l_3$$

which gives

$$(k_{11} - k) l_1 + k_{12} l_2 + k_{13} l_3 = 0$$
$$k_{21} l_1 + (k_{22} - k) l_2 + k_{23} l_3 = 0$$
$$k_{31} l_1 + k_{32} l_2 + (k_{33} - k) l_3 = 0$$

This system of equations will have a nonzero solution only if the determinant of the coefficients is zero. The cubic equation obtained by expanding the determinant

$$\begin{pmatrix} (k_{11} - k) & k_{12} & k_{13} \\ k_{21} & (k_{22} - k) & k_{23} \\ k_{31} & k_{32} & (k_{33} - k) \end{pmatrix} = 0$$

has three roots, the eigenvalues, which define the three directions, the eigenvectors, in which the magnetization will be parallel to the field.

## 9. ROCK MAGNETISM AND PALEOMAGNETISM METHODS

An alternative approach to the determination of the eigenvectors and eigenvalues comes from an iterative technique of postmultiplication, which seems a bit like magic initially, but can be understood by thinking about its implications in terms of the representation quadric. The technique consists of postmultiplying the susceptibility tensor obtained from the least-squares analysis by a unit column vector, i.e.,

$$\begin{pmatrix} k_{11} & k_{12} & k_{13} \\ k_{21} & k_{22} & k_{23} \\ k_{31} & k_{32} & k_{33} \end{pmatrix} \begin{pmatrix} 1 \\ 0 \\ 0 \end{pmatrix}$$

The resulting column matrix is then used to postmultiply the original susceptibility tensor again. This process is repeated and one finds that it converges rapidly on the maximum eigenvector. The reason is readily seen from the representation quadric. As illustrated in Fig. 88, the direction of magnetization when the field is applied in the direction of the arbitrary unit vector is perpendicular to the representation quadric surface, where the unit vector intersects the surface. The second multiplication is then equivalent to application of the field parallel to the first direction of magnetization. This will converge on the minimum axis of the quadric, which is parallel to the maximum susceptibility. To find the direction of minimum susceptibility, one carries out the same procedure on the magnitude ellipse (Fig. 89). The third direction is then immediately available from the orthogonality condition. The eigenvalues in the three directions are obtained from the original tensor by multiplying by the appropriate direction cosines.

Two geometric figures discussed in the previous paragraph are commonly used to represent the susceptibility tensor of a sample. One is called the representation quadric or ellipsoid. The length of the radius vector of this

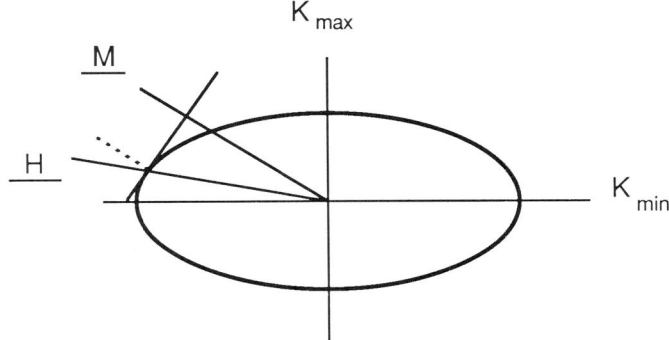

FIG. 88. Representation quadric for susceptibility.

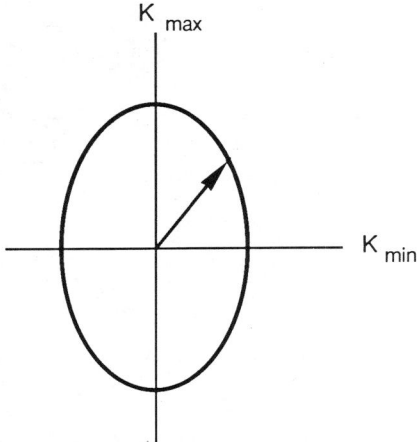

FIG. 89. Magnitude ellipsoid for susceptibility.

body is equal to the inverse square root of the susceptibility in that direction, as can be seen for the principal susceptibilities from the form of its equation

$$\frac{x^2}{(1/\sqrt{k_a})^2} + \frac{x^2}{(1/\sqrt{k_b})^2} + \frac{z^2}{(1/\sqrt{k_c})^2} = 1$$

The direction of magnetization $M$ is parallel to the normal to the tangent plane at the point at which the radius vector parallel to $H$ meets the surface (see Fig. 88).

The second geometric body used is the magnitude ellipsoid. This is the second-degree surface familiar to geologists and geophysicists from its use in stress and strain ellipsoids. It has the form

$$\frac{x^2}{k_a^2} + \frac{y^2}{k_b^2} + \frac{z^2}{k_c^2} = 1$$

It is this second body, the magnitude ellipsoid, which is commonly used to describe susceptibility anisotropy (Fig. 89).

There are two different approaches to the measurement of susceptibility anisotropy. The first is to measure the susceptibility in various directions and from these measurements obtain the six independent coefficients to specify the susceptibility tensor. The second is to measure the difference in susceptibility. Thus one obtains an independent determination of the deviatoric part of the susceptibility tensor. The approach is to measure the difference in three orthogonal planes within the sample. Given a determination of one of the susceptibilities, one can then obtain the six coefficients again. The simplest method of operation of the AC bridge is an example of the first method. The bridge can also be rebalanced after the sample has been inserted and the difference in susceptibility within a plane obtained by rotating the sample. The spinner and torque methods are examples of determination of susceptibility differences within specified planes. To complete the determination of the susceptibility tensor one requires one determination of the susceptibility. Both types of measurements use redundant data to obtain a least-squares set of estimates.

Susceptibility anisotropy is determined in various field strengths, and it is important to recognize the effect of field strength on the observed anisotropy. Different minerals respond to different field strengths. Thus, paramagnetic contributions will not saturate, while ferromagnetic ones will. A means of separating the two is therefore available. In intermediate field strengths the situation is complicated by rotational hysteresis losses (Day *et al.*, 1970). It should also be noted that weak field determinations, such as those made with the bridge, may be affected by the state of remanence (Kobayashi and Smith, 1965).

4.3.3.1. AC Bridge Methods. In its simplest form, the AC bridge method of determination of susceptibility anisotropy consists of measuring the susceptibility of a sample in a number of different directions in order to specify the six coefficients of the susceptibility tensor. Initially, a scheme based on measurements with the following direction cosines was used:

$$A_1 \quad 1\ 0\ 0 \qquad A_4 \quad \frac{1}{\sqrt{2}}\ \frac{1}{\sqrt{2}}\ 0 \qquad A_7 \quad -\frac{1}{\sqrt{2}}\ \frac{1}{\sqrt{2}}\ 0$$

$$A_2 \quad 0\ 1\ 0 \qquad A_5 \quad \frac{1}{\sqrt{2}}\ 0\ \frac{1}{\sqrt{2}} \qquad A_8 \quad -\frac{1}{\sqrt{2}}\ 0\ \frac{1}{\sqrt{2}}$$

$$A_3 \quad 0\ 0\ 1 \qquad A_6 \quad 0\ \frac{1}{\sqrt{2}}\ \frac{1}{\sqrt{2}} \qquad A_9 \quad 0\ -\frac{1}{\sqrt{2}}\ \frac{1}{\sqrt{2}}$$

This design oversamples directions in the planes normal to the cube faces at the expense of body diagonal directions. To measure the normals to the faces of an icosahedron would be better, but is not so convenient. The initial design gives three more measurements than needed for the determination of the six coefficients, so a least-squares reduction can be carried out on the overspecified data set. In matrix notation this is

$$\mathbf{A} = \theta \mathbf{k}$$

where **A** is the column matrix of the measured susceptibilities and $\theta$ the design matrix of directions of measurement having rows of the form

$$j_1H_1, j_2H_2, j_3H_3, j_2H_3 + j_3H_2, j_1H_3 + j_3H_1, j_1H_2 + j_2H_1$$

for example,

$$\theta_1 = 1 \quad 0 \quad 0 \quad 0 \quad 0 \quad 0$$

and

$$\theta_9 = 0 \quad \tfrac{1}{2} \quad \tfrac{1}{2} \quad -1 \quad 0 \quad 0$$

Standard matrix algebra then gives for the least-squares reduction from the overspecified data

$$\mathbf{k} = (\theta_t\theta)^{-1}\theta_t\mathbf{A}$$

We now have the necessary specification of the best-fitting susceptibility

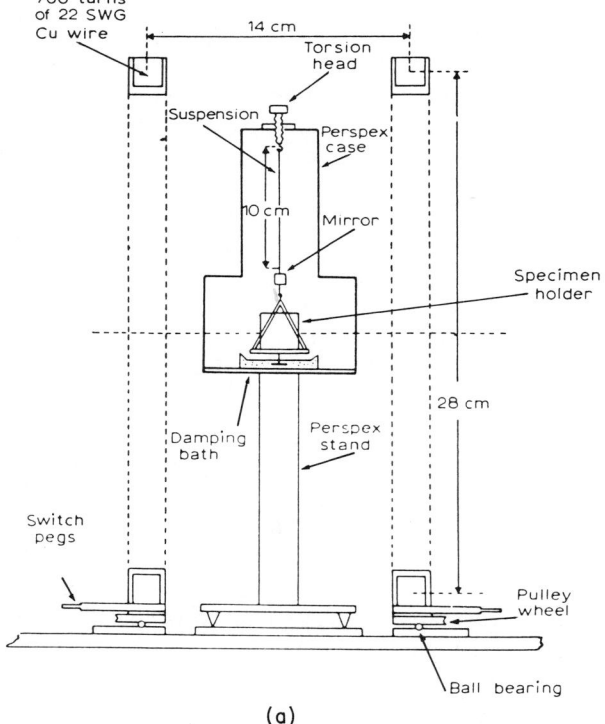

FIG. 90. Torquemeter measurement of susceptibility anisotropy: (a) instrument.

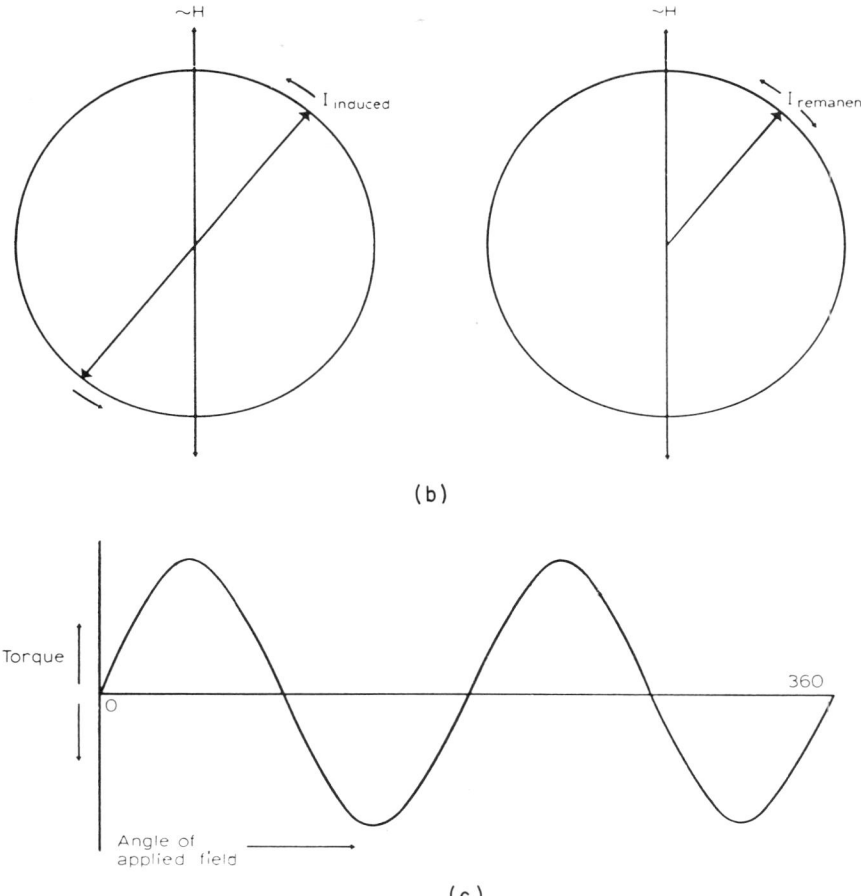

FIG. 90. (b) Torque curve.

ellipsoid to the observed data in the least-squares sense. Diagonalization gives the principal susceptibilities.

4.3.3.2. SPINNER AND TORQUE MEASUREMENTS OF SUSCEPTIBILITY ANISOTROPY. To make torque measurements of anisotropy, the sample is suspended vertically and a horizontal field applied (Fig. 90a). In general, the magnetization will not be parallel to the applied $H$ field. The sample will therefore experience a torque aligning the induced moment with the $B$ field (Fig. 90b). However, there will be a similar torque due to the remanent moment of the sample which will also be in an energetically favorable configuration when it is parallel to the $B$ field. To avoid the effect due to remanence, an alternating field is used. This alternating field gives torques of opposite sense in each half-cycle on the remanent moment. It is of sufficiently high frequency that the torsion system does not respond. Meanwhile, the torque due to the induced moment is in a constant sense throughout each field cycle. The torsion system does respond to it.

If the applied field is rotated with respect to the sample, there will be four occasions in each cycle when it is parallel to the induced moment. These will be when it is parallel to the maximum and minimum axes of the susceptibility in the plane. At these points the torque will be zero. When the applied field is 45° from the principal axes, the torque will be a maximum, so a record for the torque as a function of an angle of the applied field will be as in Fig. 90.

To calculate the susceptibility anisotropy from the variations in the magnitude of the torque requires the derivation of the relationship between susceptibility differences in the plane and the torque. In a field $H$ applied to $k_{max}$ at an angle $\theta$, the induced magnetization parallel to the principal axes will be

$$M_1 = Hk_1 \cos \theta$$

$$M_2 = Hk_2 \sin \theta$$

The torque will then be

$$\tau = B(Hk_1 \sin \theta \cos \theta - Hk_2 \cos \theta \sin \theta)$$

$$= BH \frac{\sin 2\theta}{2} (k_1 - k_2)$$

In the simplest form of the experiment, the torque is balanced by the torsion fiber and measured with a lamp and scale. Given a torsion fiber constant $G$, a path length $r$, and a deflection of $d$ on a scale, e.g., of $d/2r$ radians, the torque is equal to

$$\frac{Gd}{2r} = BH \frac{\sin 2\theta}{2} (k_1 - k_2)$$

so the difference in susceptibility is

$$k_1 - k_2 = Gd/rBH \sin 2\theta$$

Details of the design of the various instruments used for these experiments can be found in Collinson (1983) and in *Methods in Palaeomagnetism* (1967).

The spinner magnetometer affords a convenient and rapid means of determining susceptibility anisotropy, although it is not as sensitive as the torque method. A field is applied perpendicular to the spin axis and the variation in the induced moment measured as the sample spins. As the sample rotates, the magnetization will be a maximum when the maximum susceptibility axis is parallel to the field and a minimum when the minimum susceptibility is parallel to the field. This therefore gives a sin $2\theta$ curve, as opposed to the sin $\theta$ of the dipole moment determination for which spinners are usually used. To use the same electronics, the sample is spun at half the frequency. The method was described by Noltimier (1976), and commercial spinner magnetometers, such as the Schonstedt instruments, have susceptibility anisotropy capability.

To analyze the data, consider the general expression for the susceptibility applied to the case of variation in the plane perpendicular to spin

$$A = l_i l_j K_{ij}$$

Assume that the directional cosines of the field are $\cos \theta$, 0, $-\sin \theta$. Then

$$A = k_{11} \cos^2 \theta + k_{33} \sin^2 \theta - 2k_{31} \sin \theta \cos \theta$$

$$= \frac{k_{11} + k_{31}}{2} + \frac{k_{11} - k_{31}}{2} \cos 2\theta - k_{31} \sin 2\theta$$

This can be written as

$$A = \text{constant} + c \cos(2\theta - \delta)$$

with

$$c \cos \delta = (k_{11} - k_{33})/2$$

$$c \sin \delta = -k_{31}$$

Hence the amplitude of the fluctuation in output, $P$, is $2C$ and the phase is such that the maximum value occurs when $\theta = \delta/2$. The results from the first spin can then be expressed in terms of the susceptibility matrix elements in sample coordinates as

$$P_1 \cos \delta_1 = k_{11} - k_{33}$$

and

$$P_1 \sin \delta_1 = -2k_{31}$$

Spins about the other two orthogonal axes give similar results. With the addition of one measurement of bulk susceptibility, a set of equations is obtained from which the elements of the susceptibility matrix can be calculated. The diagonalization then follows as in the analysis of the bridge data.

4.3.3.3. STATISTICAL ANALYSIS OF ANISOTROPY DATA. The earliest analysis of the statistical aspects of the anisotropy data was by Hext (1963), working in conjunction with Girdler (1961). The essence of the method is to use the calculated tensor elements to get a model value of **A***

$$\mathbf{A}^* = \theta\mathbf{k}$$

This then permits the determination of residuals **E**

$$\mathbf{E} = \mathbf{A} - \mathbf{A}^*$$

These errors provide the basic data for establishing the quality of the measurement. Hext (1963) used them to determine confidence ellipses on the principal directions. A similar but more extensive analysis was given by Jelinek (1978), who described the calculation of a mean tensor from measurements of a number of specimens and derived confidence intervals about the mean principal axes from the variance.

Frequently, a simpler technique is used. Fisher statistics are applied to the principal directions, treating them as unit vectors. One problem with this approach is that, if the maximum-to-intermediate ratio is very different from the intermediate-to-minimum ratio, then the distributions of the unit vectors representing the three principal axes are likely to be non-Fisherian. For example, if the maximum and intermediate values are very similar and markedly larger than the minimum, the minimum is likely to be well determined and probably the distribution of estimates will be Fisherian, but the maximum and intermediate values are likely to be poorly determined within the maximum–intermediate plane. This will give the distribution of estimates a planar aspect. These problems are obviated by using the estimation of a mean tensor.

The presentation of susceptibility anisotropy data has taken a number of forms. Sometimes, the ratios of maximum to intermediate susceptibility and maximum to minimum values are given. Sometimes, the differences between principal values are used. The Flinn diagram of structural geologists is particularly convenient. In it, the ratio of maximum to intermediate susceptibility is plotted against the ratio of intermediate to minimum susceptibility. The upper left of such diagrams represents strongly prolate ellipsoids and the lower right strongly oblate ones (Fig. 91).

### 4.4. Measurement of the Effects of Stress on Magnetization

The study of stress effects on magnetization has a long experimental history, reaching back well into the past century (Nagaoka, 1889). It has been of interest to paleomagnetists and rock magnetists for two reasons. First, paleomagnetists have long been concerned that NRM may be affected by the stress history of a rock. This was the motivation behind the work of Graham *et al.* (1957). Second, there has also long been a hope that a magnetic precursor might be used as method of earthquake prediction. It was therefore

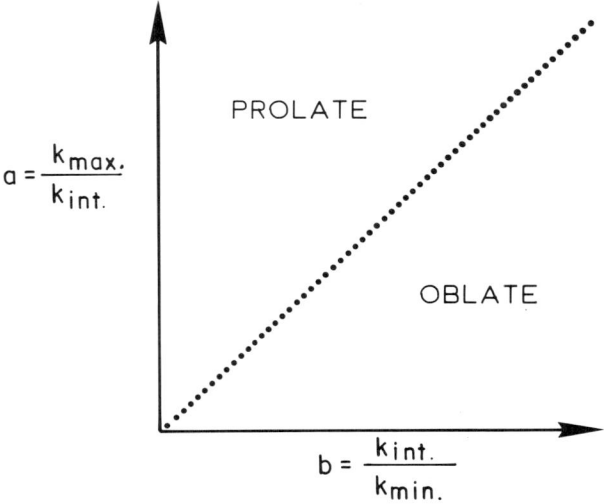

FIG. 91. Flinn diagram in which ellipsoid is represented by a point in Kmax/Kint Kint/Kmin span (Flinn, 1962).

of importance to establish the nature of the effect of stress on rocks. Despite periods of optimism, it is fair to say that, even if such a precursor is present, it is an extremely difficult experiment to demonstrate it. Hence, its use as a prediction technique is not likely to be realized in the near future. In addition to these motivations for studying stress effects, it should not be forgotten that the stress effects are another manifestation of the magnetic behavior of rocks and that they may yield clues to help in our general understanding of rock magnetism.

The experimental studies can be divided into a number of different areas. For example, there have been a variety of studies of the effect of stress on susceptibility. There have been documentations of the acquisition of remanent magnetization by the application of stress in the presence of a magnetizing field (Nagata, 1970). Stress demagnetization has also been investigated (Ohnaka, 1969). Many of the earlier experiments were not very concerned about the nature of the stress to which the sample was exposed and simple uniaxial presses were used. Increasingly complicated equipment has been introduced more recently, so that hydrostatic as well as uniaxial stress can be applied in an attempt to simulate more accurately the conditions under which rocks are stressed in the earth's crust. In a similar spirit, attempts to carry out the experiments at elevated temperature are also under way. An important distinction to be made is the degree to which stress effects are reversible or irreversible.

4.4.1. Stress Effects on Susceptibility and Remanence. The general effect of stress on susceptibility is to give an induced anisotropy, which is lost on removal of the field. To measure this susceptibility anisotropy, one can modify the various methods of susceptibility to incorporate a device to apply stress. Probably one of the simplest techniques is to use a small nonmagnetic plastic sample holder with which one can apply uniaxial pressure a few hundred bars (Kean *et al.*, 1976). The device can be rotated within the access region of the measuring coil of an AC bridge and the anisotropy measured in the usual manner. The amount of stress applied is measured by the turn of the screw. An independent measurement is required to calibrate the device. This can be done by replacing the sample with a load cell. Other methods which involve the use of a load cell in the equipment are more difficult to use in the bridge, either because it is hard to apply the stress other than along the coil axis or because the device has too high a susceptibility. One possibility is to use a press such as that described by Revol *et al.* (1977), which is illustrated in Fig. 92, to measure susceptibility changes parallel to stress and use this value to calibrate the plastic device (Y. Hamano and M. Fuller, unpublished observations).

By measuring the induced moment of the sample with an external sensor, rather than placing the stress equipment inside the susceptibility bridge or magnetometer, the constraints on the stress equipment are reduced and one can build more sophisticated equipment. This route has been followed by Martin *et al.* (1978) to study the effect of uniaxial stress in the presence of hydrostatic pressure. The equipment is illustrated in Fig. 93 and can be used for studies of the effect of remanent magnetization or susceptibility. The magnetization is measured by a flux gate magnetometer. A difficulty with such techniques is to obtain sufficient sensitivity to measure the necessary

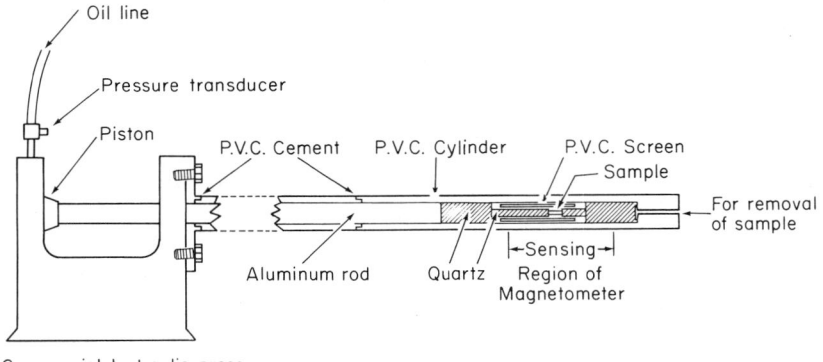

FIG. 92. Uniaxial press for measuring susceptibility under compression.

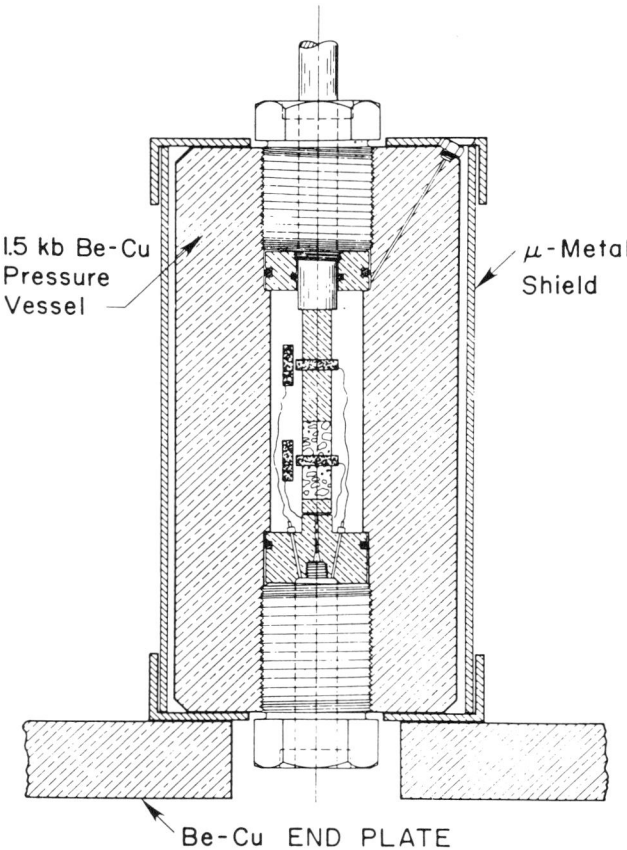

Fig. 93. Measurement of magnetic effects of stress with flux gate magnetometer. (After Martin et al., 1978.)

small changes in magnetization. This may eventually be overcome by using a SQUID gradiometer to measure the necessary magnetic fields. However, with the increased sensitivity the constraints on the equipment will again increase because one must avoid measuring changes in magnetization of the stress device. We have constructed nonmagnetic presses to operate in a horizontal SCT magnetometer, but the need to keep the material sufficiently nonmagnetic makes the equipment difficult to construct. One such device is illustrated in Figure 94, from Pike et al. (1984).

In addition to experiments in which one attempts to measure stress effects on magnetization while the stress is being applied, a much easier type of experiment permits the measurement of irreversible effects of the application

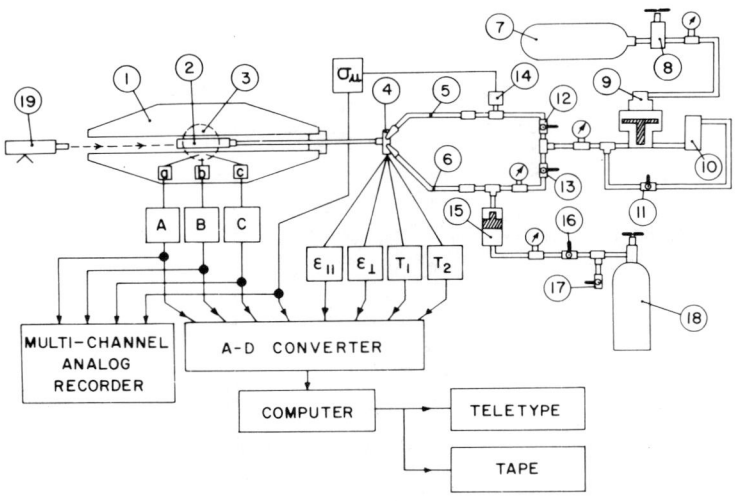

FIG. 94. Three-axis pressure cells for use in horizontal access magnetometer. (After Pike *et al.*, 1984.)

of stress. In this case, one can apply the stress without restrictions due to the requirement of measurement of magnetization. Subsequently, the magnetic properties can be measured. In this way, Kapicka (1983) was able to show an irreversible part of the susceptibility anisotropy induced by stress. Recently M. Lanham (unpublished observations) has demonstrated changes in remanence associated with longitudinal crack development in unconfined compression tests. Again, this work can be carried out without observations during stress.

## 4.5. Domain Observations

A critical aspect of understanding the magnetic behavior of the fine particles which occur in rocks is to establish their domain state, for this determines their magnetic characteristics. Initially, the problem was approached indirectly through the interpretation of hysteresis parameters and AF demagnetization characteristics. However, such properties are not uniquely interpretable in terms of domain state, so controversy arose over the size for the single-domain/multidomain transition and over the number of domains in particles of a given size. Soffel (1963, 1965) established domain studies of the magnetic materials in rocks, and the work of accumulating the necessary data began. More recently, this work has been extended to observations at high temperatures (Appel and Soffel, 1985; Metcalf and Fuller, 1985) and used to explain aspects of pseudo-single-domain behavior as nucleation-controlled behavior (Halgedahl and Fuller, 1980, 1983). The observations in these studies were by the Bitter pattern method, which is described below. However, with the increasing interest in understanding the fundamental behavior of the magnetic particles in rocks, we can expect increasing utilization of other methods of domain observations. The various methods are discussed here and assessed in terms of their possible applications to problems in rock magnetism. For a more general discussion the text by Craik and Tebble (1965) is recommended.

### 4.5.1. Bitter Patterns.
The simplest and best known method of domain observation is the Bitter pattern method. Bitter (1931) and von Hamos and Thiessen (1931) independently proposed that if a fine magnetic powder were spread across the surface of the magnetic material of interest, it might reveal inhomogeneities of magnetization and hence demonstrate the presence of magnetic domains. The technique was improved by Elmore and McKeehan (1936), who applied colloids to carefully polished surfaces of magnetic materials. These techniques revealed the maze patterns, convoluted closely spaced patterns. Elmore (1937) later showed that the maze patterns were indeed an artifact of the sample preparation and could be removed by electrolytic polishing so that the body domains could be seen. Williams *et al.* (1949) describe a wealth of observations made by using the Bitter method on single crystals of silicon–iron, which demonstrated the nature of closure domains, patterns on surfaces with oblique magnetization, and the spin configuration in Bloch walls.

As noted above, Soffel (1963) was the first to apply these techniques in rock magnetism. Initially, he followed earlier workers in using electrolytic polishing to remove the maze patterns. However, a major advance was made by Soffel and Petersen (1971) in introducing the ion bombardment method of preparing the surface after mechanical polishing. With this technique, the stressed region due to the mechanical polishing which produces the maze pattern is removed by ionic bombardment. This procedure is not always necessary, but it was critical in making the titanomagnetites available for domain observations. These high-titanium titanomagnetites are particularly important in domain studies because their low Curie points make the

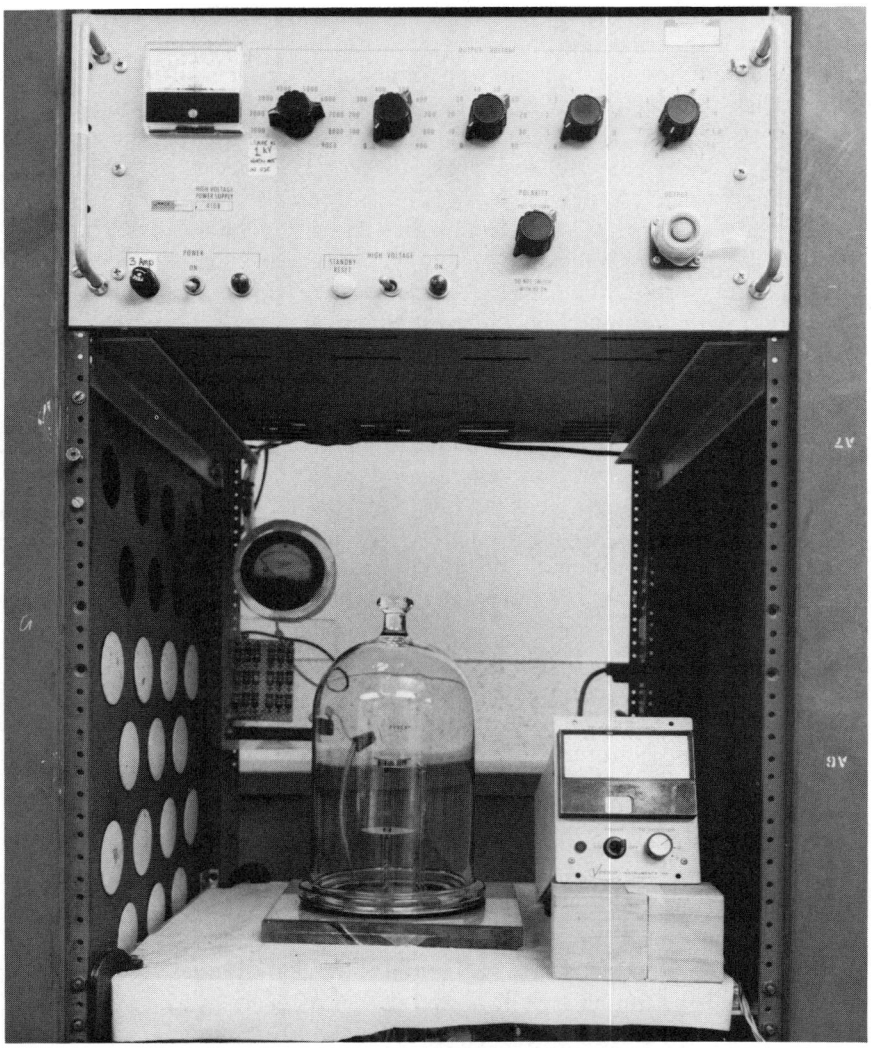

Fig. 95. Ionic polisher. The sample is placed inside the bell jar, in the center of the negative electrode. The power supply is above and the vacuum gauge to the right.

observation of thermal demagnetization and the acquisition of TRM possible with the Bitter method.

To prepare a sample for Bitter pattern work, it is first mechanically polished. The standard procedure for preparing polished sections for reflected light is followed. The samples are polished with a succession of commercial powders, whose grain size is progressively decreased. This can be done by hand or with standard automatic devices. The sample is then placed in the ion bombarder (Fig. 95). It consists of a chamber which can be evacuated and back-filled to a pressure of few millitorr with helium. The sample is placed in the target electrode and a voltage of 4 kV applied. The ions are accelerated toward the target electrode and strike the polished surface, thereby etching the surface and removing the stressed region. The success of this polishing technique tends to be something of a hit-or-miss proposition. A current of a few milliamperes is recommended and it is important to keep the sample cool. This can be done by interrupting the applied voltage to give a duty cycle of 50%. The sample can also be water-cooled. E. Appel (private communication) suggests that oblique incidence gives better results.

After preparation is complete, the colloid is placed on the sample, a coverslip is applied, and it is ready for observation. Several commercial colloids are available. Those we have used are supplied by Ferrofluids. The observation relies on the attraction of the magnetic particles in the colloid to the high gradients immediately above the domain walls (Fig. 96). The walls are then decorated with the fine magnetic particles in the colloid.

Although the Bitter method is simple and convenient, it has a number of disadvantages stemming from the fact that the observation is of the surface pattern. Hence, one does not always know whether the domains observed are indeed body domains, or a surface feature. Similarly, one does not know whether the visible surface of the particle is a true indication of the size of the particle, or whether one is, figuratively speaking, looking at the tip of an iceberg. Both these problems can be somewhat ameliorated if one takes advantage of the surface relief produced by the ionic bombardment.

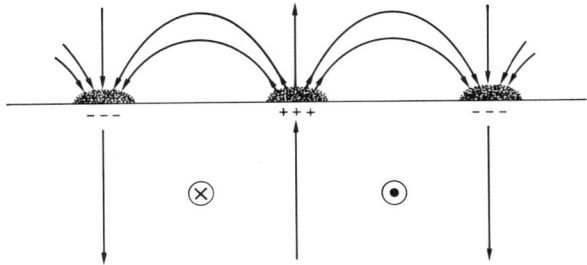

Fig. 96. Decoration of domain walls by colloid in the Bitter pattern technique.

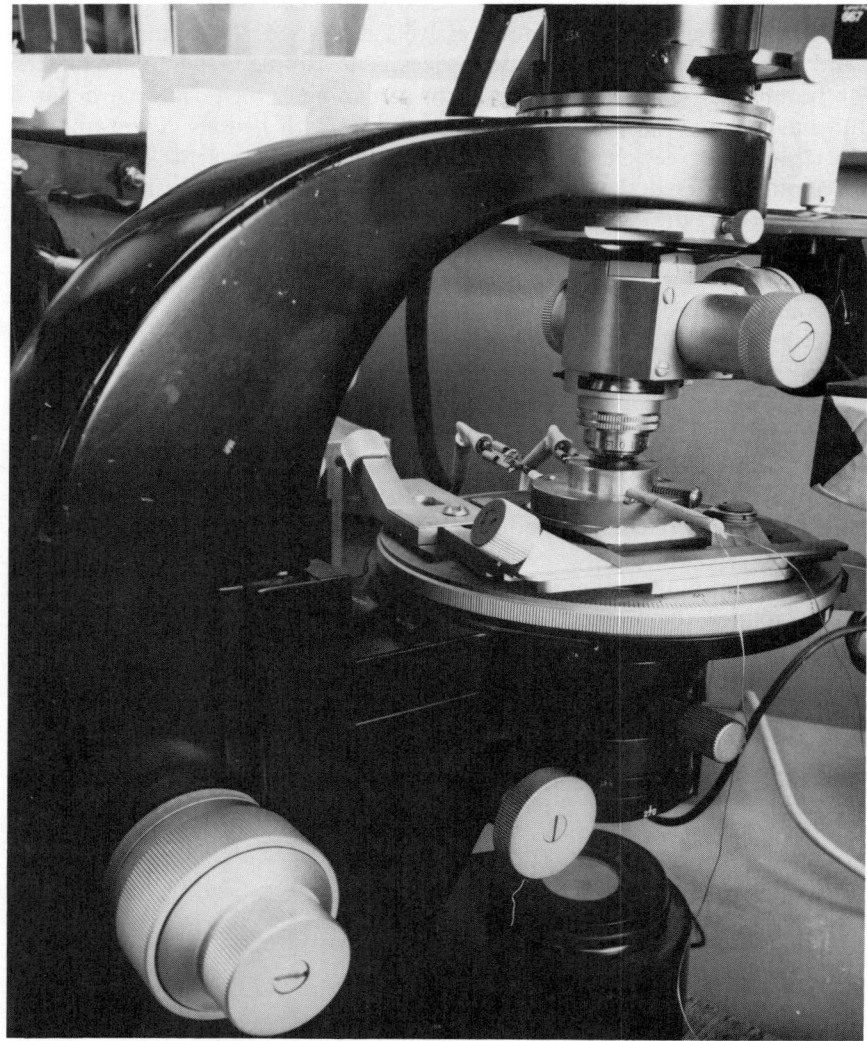

Fig. 97. Observation of domains by Bitter patterns at elevated temperature. The sample is placed in the brass heating stage beneath the microscope. The power leads can be seen entering from the far side of the stage. Temperature is measured with the thermocouple whose leads emerge on the near side of the stage.

The Bitter pattern technique can be extended to modest temperatures with commercial colloids, such as the colloid available from Ferrofluids, but above 200°C most bases evaporate. The observations made possible by these high-temperature colloids are particularly important in rock magnetism because they permit observations of the acquisition of TRM and of the process of thermal demagnetization. These observations are carried out with the titanomagnetites, which have relatively low Curie points of about 150°C. Such observations have been made by Appel and Soffel (1985) and Metcalf and Fuller (1986). Figure 97 illustrates the heating stage with a sample ready for observation.

As Soffel (1963) showed, one can observe the domain pattern changes during hysteresis or the application of stress with the Bitter technique. Such observations have led to recognition of the importance of nucleation energy in controlling the behavior of fine particles of magnetite during both hysteresis (Halgedahl and Fuller, 1983) and stress cycling (Boyd *et al.*, 1984).

The resolution of the Bitter pattern method can be improved by a replica method. The pattern is obtained in the usual manner except that a special colloid is used which, when allowed to dry, forms an acetate peel. This peel can be examined with a scanning electron microscope (SEM) to gain the additional resolution.

4.5.2. Transmission Electron Microscopy (TEM). When an electron passes through a magnetic field, it experiences a Lorentz force. This force is in the direction perpendicular to the velocity vector and the $B$ field. Thus, when electrons pass through a magnetic material they are defected. This is the basis of the TEM method of domain observation. Suppose that two regions of opposite polarity adjoin each other. Then the deflections of the electron beams in the two regions will be opposite. In the out-of-focus mode, the overlap of the beams gives white lines, representing domain walls between domains, which give convergent beams (Fig. 98). Dark lines reveal walls where beams are divergent. Numerous studies with transmission microscopy established important aspects of domain wall behavior in the 1950s and 1960s, after Fuller and Hale (1960) established the out-of-focus imaging of domain walls and gave estimates for their thickness. The interactions of domain walls with inclusions and microstructure were illustrated (Grundy and Tebble, 1963). The only application to rock magnetic studies is the paper

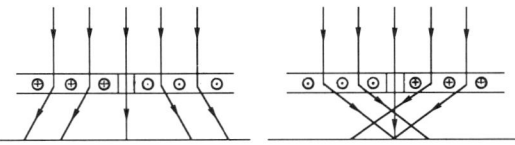

FIG. 98. Principle of contrast in TEM mode of domain observations. (After Wade, 1962.)

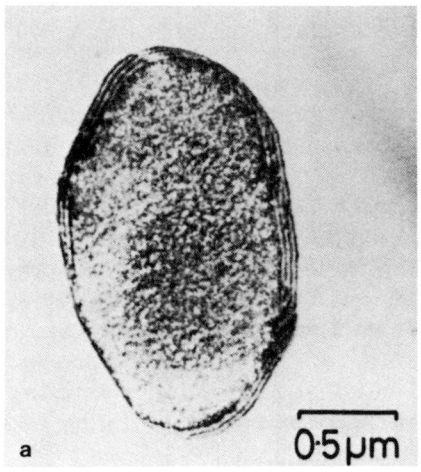 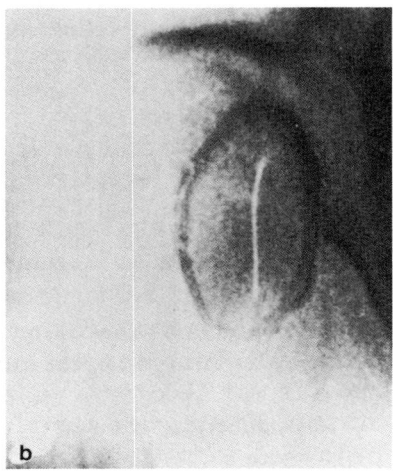

Fig. 99. TEM studies of domain patterns in fine magnetite particles: (a) in focus and (b) out of focus for domain configuration. (After Smith, 1980.)

by Smith (1980). This shows domain walls in small magnetite particles as illustrated in Fig. 99. Like the Bitter pattern studies, it reveals fewer walls than predicted by the classical theory of Kittel (1949).

Despite the obvious importance of the transmission or Lorentz microscopy method, it suffers from certain disadvantages in applications to rock magnetism. First, the preparation of samples is a tricky procedure involving thinning of samples to the appropriate thickness. Second, the fields of the microscope make weak field applications difficult. Nevertheless, it is time these techniques were more generally used in rock magnetism to settle the questions of domain structure of the finest particles in which domains can be observed and to clarify the mode of reversal of such fine particles.

4.5.3. Scanning Electron Microscopy. Just as electrons experience a Lorentz force when they pass through a magnetized region, so when they are reflected from a magnetized surface their paths are modulated by the fields from the magnetic material. The basis of the relection method of domain observation was used on a far grander scale, when the backscattered electrons from the moon were used to map lunar magnetic surface fields (Anderson et al., 1976). The principle of electron mirror microscopy for domain observations is that inhomogeneities in the field in front of the sample give contrast-forming defelections (Mayer, 1957). Unfortunately, the method suffers from the severe limitation that the deflections during passage to and from the surface are mutually cancelling. This led to the use of the radial component of the velocity. Developments of the method such as that by

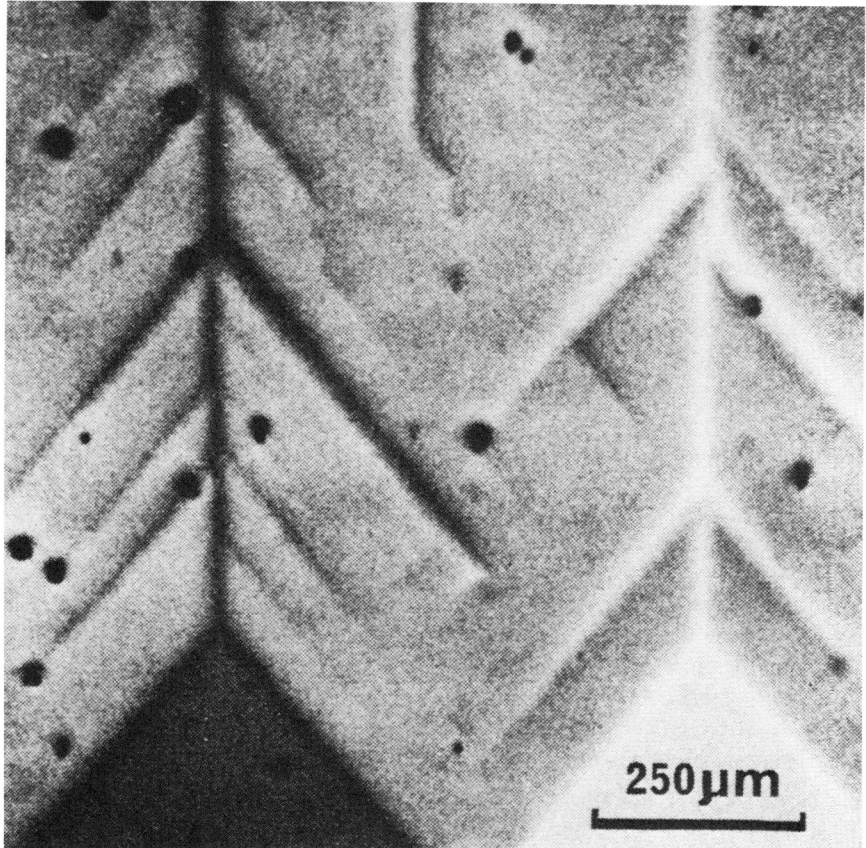

FIG. 100. SEM imaging of domain walls. (After Yamamoto, 1976.)

Yamamoto (1976) show that the major earlier problems have been largely overcome and excellent patterns have been achieved (Fig. 100). An important feature of these developments is the recognition that domain contrast is maximized for a 60° takeoff angle for the reflected beam.

The potential of the reflection method of domain observation is very great. The preparation requirements are far less daunting than for transmission methods, so applications are likely to be easier. The technique was used by Brecher and Cutrera (1983) to study the magnetic phases in meteorites.

4.5.4. *Faraday Effect.* The presence of domains can be demonstrated by making use of the rotation of the plane of polarization of light as it propagates through a magnetized region. Just as the Lorentz force gives contrast between regions magnetized in opposite directions, so does the rotation of the plane of polarization. This method has been used to make important observations in transparent ferrites. However, it seems unlikely to make such contributions in rock magnetism because the important magnetic materials are all opaque.

4.5.5. *Kerr Effect.* The reflection microscopy technique has its analogous optical method based on the Kerr effect. The magnetic field in front of the sample rotates the plane of polarization of light. Unfortunately, the rotation is very small, so the contrast is small. If this method could be developed to give the necessary detactable rotation contrast, it would be the obvious technique for rock magnetic studies, just as reflected light is the standard method of observing the relevant materials petrologically. However, the requisite techniques do not appear to be available at present.

4.5.6. *Other Methods.* In addition to the various methods described so far, which may be regarded as standard techniques, there are techniques which have not yet reached the same level of utilization. For example, Lang and Polcarova (1965) demonstrated a method of X-ray topography for displaying dislocations in single crystals. The X-ray contrast comes from the imperfections or irregularities in the lattice. These workers noted that their studies were complicated by the ferromagnetism of the materials. The 90° Bloch walls cover the whole field with a stripe pattern (Polcarova and Lang, 1962). These results were followed up by Planinsek (1968), who showed that indeed domain walls and dislocations gave contrast, so the potential to study the interactions between the two was there. This method is likely to be too specialized for general use in rock magnetism laboratories. However, it is clearly a powerful technique which could give important results.

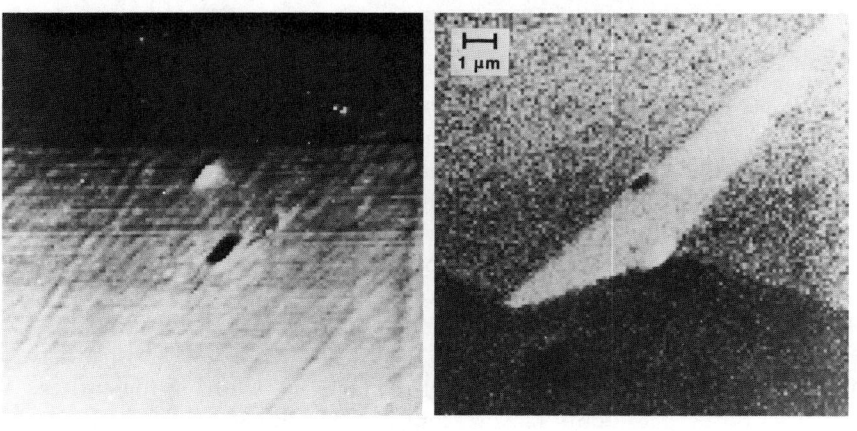

FIG. 101. Spin polarization imaging (from Unguris *et al.*, 1985). Note the imaging of both magnetization direction and defects.

A combination of scanning electron microscopy and determination of the spin of secondary electrons has been shown to provide a domain imaging technique (Fig. 101). The promise of the method is great because it requires little in the way of special sample preparation. The spin is detected by a Mott analyzer. The instrument is described by Unguris *et al.* (1985). With such a device it should be possible to settle the long-standing arguments about domain state in fine magnetite.

## 5. Concluding Comments

Rock magnetism and paleomagnetism have generated a wealth of experimental techniques, which have been touched on in this chapter. As noted at the outset, these subjects have taken part in the general and remarkable advance in experimental techniques since World War II. It was the development in electronics during that conflict which marked the first stage of the major advance. Two decades later, with the advent of the transistor, the tedium of building amplifiers, in which one wired in individual circuit elements and valves (or tubes), was replaced by the availability of the requisite operation amplifiers. This was eventually followed by the stage in which whole phase-sensitive detectors are on a single chip. The two critical developments that then followed were (1) the availability of cheap microcomputers and microprocessors and (2) the advent of the SQUID magnetometers. With the recent production of magnetometers having hold times of 1 to 2 years, one no longer has to be involved with cryogenics to use SQUID magnetometers; it is practical to have the fill carried out and the magnetometer sit in a laboratory available for use with zero maintenance. However, our laboratory remains, as I suspect many others do, a curious mixture of the sealing wax and string, with which an earlier generation of physicists would have been familiar, and devices which would have caused them some amazement.

The advent of the new magnetometers and computers is permitting techniques of measurement and data analysis that promise to rid us of some of the most subjective data selection, which has plagued the subject of paleomagnetism for so long. Nevertheless, we are still frequently not able to interpret the various components of magnetization in a sample in terms of a particular event in the history of the rock responsible for the magnetization. With the developments of new techniques of analysis this may one day be possible. Rock magnetism is faced with the development of techniques for measuring individual particles. Such measurements are in the range of sensitivity of the SQUIDs, but systematic studies remain to be done. An area of considerable interest at present is the preparation of synthetic samples with restricted grain size distributions, so that adequate tests of models of TRM and other aspects of magnetic behavior can be achieved. Domain observations are another area of considerable topical interest as a means of constraining the present models. Important developments may well come from some new technique, such as the combination of electron spin resonance with scanning electron microscopy being developed at the National Bureau of Standards.

## Acknowledgments

I wish to thank my colleagues who have worked with me in our laboratory. In particular, Bob Dunn has played a crucial role in all of the developments, so that the ones which have proved useful nearly always do so due to his insight. Bill Goree and Bill Goodman introduced me to and tutored me in the mysteries of the SQUID magnetometers, for which I am most grateful. I also wish to acknowledge with gratitude the support from the NSF, NASA, the Universities of Pittsburgh and California at Santa Barbara, and the various private companies which have provided the support that has made the laboratory possible. Finally, I wish to thank Rick Lopez for his photography, Dave Crouch for his drafting help, and Ellie Dzuro for transforming my illegible drafts into a finished manuscript.

## References

K. A. Anderson, R. P. Lin, J. E. McCoy, R. E. McGuire, C. T. Russell, P. J. Coleman, and L. B. Johnson, *Lunar Sci.* **7**, 16-18 (1976). Abstr.
P. W. Anderson and J. M. Rowell, *Phys. Rev. Lett.* **10**, 251-253 (1962).
E. Appel and H. C. Soffel, *J. Geophys.* **56**, 121-132 (1985).
K. J. Arnold, Ph.D. Thesis, Cambridge, Massachusetts, 1941.
R. C. Bailey and H. C. Halls, *J. Geophys.* **54**, 174-182 (1984).
J. Bardeen, L. N. Cooper, and J. R. Schrieffer, *Phys. Rev.* **108**, 1175 (1957).
C. P. Bean, *J. Appl. Phys.* **26**, 1381 (1955).
P. K. Bhattacharya, Ph.D. Thesis, California Inst. Technol., Pasadena, 1950.
D. E. T. Bidgood and W. B. Harland, *Bull. Geol. Soc. Am.* **70** 641 (1959).
C. Bingham, *Ann. Stat.* **2**, 1201-1225 (1974).
F. Bitter, *Phys. Rev.* **38** 1903 (1931).
P. M. S. Blackett, *Philos. Trans. R. Soc. London, Ser. A* **245**, 309 (1952),
J. R. Boyd, M. Fuller, and S. Halgedahl, *Geophys. Res. Lett.* **1**, 193-196 (1984).
A. Brecher and M. Cutrera, *J. Geomagn. Geoelectr.* **28**, 31-45 (1976).
J. C. Briden and G. R. Arthur, *Can. J. Earth Sci.* **18**, 527-538 (1981).
P. J. Burek, *J. Geophys. Res.* **74**, 6710 (1969).
R. F. Burmester, *Trans. Am. Geophys. Union* **50**, 134 (1977).
S. E. Chapman and J. Bartels, "Geomagnetism." Oxford Univ. Press, London, 1940.
G. Chiron and G. De La Pierre, *IEEE Trans. Magn.* **MAG-15**, 1815-1817 (1979).
S. M. Cisowski, *Phys. Earth Planet. Int.* **26**, 56 (1981).
S. M. Cisowski, D. W. Collinson, S. K. Runcorn, A. Stephenson, and M. Fuller, *J. Geophys. Res.* **88**, A691-A704 (1983).
J. Clarke, *Science* **184**, 1235 (1974).
J. Clarke, W. M. Goban, and M. B. Ketchen, *IEEE Trans. Magn.* **MAG-11** 724 (1974).
D. Cohen, *Rev. Sci. Instrum.* **5**, 53-58 (1970).
D. W. Collinson, *Rev. Geophys. Space Phys.* **43**, 659 (1975).

## 9. ROCK MAGNETISM AND PALEOMAGNETISM METHODS

D. W. Collinson, "Methods in Rock Magnetism and Paleomagnetism." Chapman & Hall, London, 1983.
D. W. Collinson, K. M. Creer, and S. K. Runcorn, eds., "Methods in Paleomagnetism." Elsevier, Amsterdam, 1967.
D. J. Craik and R. S. Tebble, "Ferromagnetism and Ferromagnetic Domains." Wiley (Interscience), New York, 1965.
K. M. Creer and M. Sanver, in "Methods in Palaeomagnetism" (D. W. Collinson, K. M. Creer, and S. K. Runcorn, eds.), Elsevier, Amsterdam, 1967.
R. Day, W. O'Reilly, and S. K. Banerjee, J. Geophys. Res. **75**, 375-386 (1970).
R. Day, M. Fuller, and V. A. Schmidt, J. Geophys. Res. **81**, 873 (1976).
R. Day, J. R. Dunn, and M. Fuller, Phys. Earth Planet. Inter. **13**, 301-304 (1977).
B. Deaver and W. M. Fairbank. Phys. Rev. Lett. **7**, 43 (1961).
M. H. Dodson and E. McClelland-Brown, J. Geophys. Res. **85**, 2625-2637 (1980).
R. E. Dodson, M. Fuller, and W. Pilant, Geophys. Res. Lett. **1**, 185 (1974).
R. R. Doell and A. Cox, in "Methods in Palaeomagnetism" (D. W. Collinson, K. M. Creer, and S. K. Runcorn, eds.), pp. 241-253. Elsevier, Amsterdam, 1967.
R. Doll and N. Nabauer, Phys. Rev. Lett. **7**, 51 (1961).
J. R. Dunn, D. A. Clauter, and M. Fuller, Proc. Lunar Planet. Sci. Conf. **12B**, 1747-1758 (1981).
J. R. Dunn and M. Fuller, EOS Trans. Am. Geophys. Union **65**, 863 (1984).
K. Dwight, N. Menyuk, and D. O. Smith, J. Apple. Phys. **29**, 491 (1958).
W. C. Elmore, Phys. Rev. **51**, 982 (1937).
W. C. Elmore and L. W. McKeehan, Trans. Am. Inst. Min. Met. Eng. **120**, 236 (1936).
S. N. Erné, in "Biomagnetism" (S. J. Williamson, G. L. Romani, L. Kaufman, and I. Modena, eds.), pp. 569-577. Plenum, New York, 1983.
R. A. Fisher, Proc. R. Soc. London, Ser. A **217**, 295 (1953).
D. Flinn, Geol. Soc. London Quart. Jour. **118**, 385-433 (1962).
S. Foner, Rev. Sci. Instrum. **30**, 548-557 (1959).
R. L. Forgacs and A. Warnick, Rev. Sci. Instrum. **38**, 214 (1967).
H. W. Fuller and M. E. Hale, J. Appl. Phys. **31**, 238 (1960).
M. Fuller, in "Methods in Palaeomagnetism" (D. W. Collinson, K. M. Creer, and S. K. Runcorn, eds.), pp. 403-408. Elsevier, Amsterdam, 1967.
M. Fuller, Geophysics **34**, 772-774 (1969).
M. Fuller, Rev. Geophys. Space Phys. **12**, 23-70 (1974).
M. Fuller, W. Goree, and W. Goodman, in "Magnetite Mineralization and Magnetoreception in Organisms—A New Biomagnetism" (J. L. Kirschwink, D. S. Jones, and B. J. McFadden, eds.), pp. 103-151. Plenum, New York, 1986.
M. Fuller and K. Kobayashi, J. Geophys. Res. **69**, 2111 (1964).
M. Fuller, E. Meshkov, S. Cisowski, and C. Hale, Proc. Lunar Sci. Conf. **10**, 2211-2233 (1979).
R. W. Girdler, Geophys. J. R. Astron. Soc. **5**, 34-44 (1961).
D. I. Gough, J. Geophys. Res. **69**, 2455 (1964).
J. Graham, J. Geophys. Res. **54**, 131-167 (1949).
J. Graham, in "Methods in Paleomagnetism" (D. W. Collinson, K. M. Creer, and S. K. Runcorn, eds.), pp. 409-424. Elsevier, Amsterdam, 1967.
J. Graham, A. F. Buddington, and J. Balsley, J. Geophys. Res. **62**, 465-474 (1957).
P. J. Grundy and R. S. Tebble, Proc. Phys. Soc. **81**, 971-972 (1963).
B. Hague, "Alternating Current Bridge Methods." Pitman, London, 1952.
S. Halgedahl and M. Fuller, J. Geophys. Res. **88**, 6505 (1983).
S. Halgedahl, R. Day, and M. Fuller, J. Geophys. Res. **85**, 3690-3698 (1980).
D. Halliday and R. Resnick, "Physics for Students of Science and Engineering." Wiley, New York, 1960.

H. C. Halls, *Geophys. J. R. Astron. Soc.* **45**, 297-304 (1976).
H. C. Halls, *Geophys. J. R. Astron. Soc.* **48**, 551-552 (1977).
H. C. Halls, *Phys. Earth Planet. Inter.* **16**, 1 (1978).
P. Hejda, *Czech. J. Phys.* **B35**, 442-458 (1985).
G. Hext, *Biometrika* **50**, 353-373 (1963).
K. A. Hoffman and R. Day, *Earth Planet. Sci. Lett.* **40**, 433 (1978).
E. Irving, *Phil. Trans. R. Sci. London* **3250**, 100-160 (1957).
E. Irving, "Paleomagnetism and Its Application to Geological and Geophysical Problems." Wiley, New York, 1964.
M. Jackson and R. Van der Voo, *Geophys. J. R. Astron. Soc.* **81**, 75 (1985).
R. C. Jaklevic, J. Lamke, J. E. Mercereau, and A. H. Silver, *Phys. Rev.* **A140**, 1628 (1965).
V. Jelinek, *Stud. Geophys. Geod.* **17**, 36 (1973).
E. A. Johnson and A. G. McNish, *Terr. Magn. Atmos. Electr.* **43**, 393 (1938).
B. D. Josephson, *Phys. Lett.* **1**, 251-253 (1962).
B. D. Josephson, *Science* **184**, 527 (1974).
A. Kapicka, *J. Geophys.* **53**, 144-148 (1983).
W. A. Kean, R. Day, M. Fuller, and V. A. Schmidt, *J. Geophys. Res.* **81**, 861-872 (1976).
J. T. Kent, *I.A.G.A. Gen. Assem., 5th, Prague, Abstr.* **1**, 176 (1985).
J. King, S. K. Banerjee, J. Marvin, and O. Ozdemir, *Earth Planet. Sci. Lett.* **59**, 404 (1982).
J. L. Kirschvink, *Geophys. J. R. Astron. Soc.* **62**, 699-718 (1980).
J. L. Kirschvink and H. A. Lowenstam, *Earth Planet. Sci. Lett.* **44**, 193-204 (1972).
C. Kittel, *Rev. Mod. Phys.* **21**, 541-583 (1949).
K. Kobayashi, *J. Geomagn. Geoelectr.* **12**, 148 (1961).
K. Kobayashi and M. Fuller, *in* "Methods in Palaeomagnetism" (D. W. Collinson, K. M. Creer, and S. K. Runcorn, eds.), pp. 450-456. Elsevier, Amsterdam, 1967.
K. Kobayashi and M. Fuller, *Philos. Mag.* **18**, 601 (1968).
K. Kobayashi and R. W. Smith, *J. Geomagn. Geoelectr.* **17**, 325 (1965).
K. P. Kodama, EOS, *Trans. Am. Geophys. Union* **67**, 368 (1986).
J. G. Koenigsberger, *Terr. Magn. Atmos. Electr.* **43**, 119-127 (1938).
M. Kono, *J. Geophys. Res.* **87**, B1142-B1148 (1982).
M. Kono and N. Ueno, *Phys. Earth Planet. Inter.* **13**, , 305-314 (1977).
M. Kono, Y. Hamano, T. Nishitani, and T. Tosha, *Geophys. J. R. Astron. Soc.* **67**, 217 (1981).
B. R. Krause, *Can. J. Phys.* **41**, 750 (1963).
G. Kuster, *Trans. Am. Geophys. Union* **50**, 134 (1969). Abstr.
A. R. Lang and M. Polcarova, *Philos. Mag.* **15**, 297-311 (1965).
P. Langevin, *Ann Chim. Phys.* **5**, 70-127 (1905).
E. E. Larson, *Geology* **9**, 350 (1981).
S. Leibson, "The Handbook of Microcomputer Interfacing." TAB Books, Blue Ridge Summit, PA. 1983.
S. Levi, *Phys. Earth Planet. Inter.* **13**, 245-259 (1977).
S. Levi and S. K. Banerjee, *Earth Planet. Sci. Lett.* **29**, 219-226 (1976).
S. D. Likhite, C. Radhakrishnamurty, and P. W. Sahasrabudhe, *Rev. Sci. Instrum.* **36**, 1558-1564 (1965).
D. H. Lindsley, *in* "Oxide Minerals" (D. Rumble, ed.), Southern Printing Co., Blacksburg, Virginia, 1976.
D. A. Livingstone, *Ecology* **36**, 137 (1955).
F. London, "Superfluids," Vol. 1, p. 152. Wiley, New York, 1950.
H. M. Long and P. E. Loveday, *in* "Technology of Liquid Helium" (R. H. Kropschot, B. W. Birmingham, and D. B. Mann, eds.), Chap. 6. *NBS Monogr. (U.S.)* No. 111 (1968).
P. L. McFadden, *Geophys. J. R. Astron. Soc.* **48**, 549-550 (1977).

P. L. McFadden, *Geophys. J. R. Astron. Soc.* **60**, 391-396 (1980a).
P. L. McFadden, *Geophys. J. R. Astron. Soc.* **60**, 397-407 (1980b).
P. L. McFadden, *Geophys. J. R. Astron. Soc.* **71**, 519-543 (1982a).
P. L. McFadden, *Earth Planet. Sci. Lett.* **61**, 397-395 (1982b).
P. L. McFadden and D. I. Jones, *Geophys. J. R. Astron. Soc.* **67**, 53-58 (1981).
P. L. McFadden and F. J. Lowes, *Geophys. J. R. Astron. Soc.* **67**, 19-33 (1981).
F. J. H. Mackereth, *Limnol. Oceanogr.* **3**, 181 (1958).
F. J. H. Mackereth, *Limnol. Oceanogr.* **14**, 145 (1969).
H. V. Malmstead, C. G. Enke, and S. R. Crouch, "Electronic Measurements for Scientists." Benjamin, New York, 1973.
K. V. Mardia, "The Statistics of Directional Data." Academic Press, New York, 1972.
R. J. Martin, R. E. Habermann, and M. Wyss, *J. Geophys. Res.* **83**, 3485-3496 (1978).
L. Mayer, *J. Appl. Phys.* **28**, 9, 975 (1957).
M. L. Meade, *J. Phys. E.* **15**, 395-403 (1982).
J. E. Mercereau, *Rev. Phys. Appl.* **5**, 13 (1970).
R. T. Merrill and M. W. McElhinny, "The Earth's Magnetic Field; Its History, Origin and Planetary Perspective." Academic Press, New York, 1983.
M. Metcalf and M. Fuller, *Nature* **321**, 6073, 847-849 (1986).
P. E. Michelson, *Carnegie Inst. Wash. Publ. Dep. Terr. Magn. Year Book* **112** (1952).
H. Nagaoka, *Philos. Mag.* **5**, 117-132 (1889).
T. Nagata, "Rock Magnetism." Maruzen, Tokyo, 1961.
T. Nagata, *Tectonophysics* **9**, 167-195 (1970).
T. Nagata, *Proc. Nagata Conf., Pittsburgh* pp. 4-29 (1974).
T. Nagata, Y. Arai, and K. Momose, *J. Geophys. Res.* **68**, 5277-5281 (1963).
T. Nagata, K. Kobayashi, and M. Fuller, *J. Geophys. Res.* **69**, 2111 (1964).
L. Néel, *Ann. Geophys.* **5**, 99 (1949).
L. Néel, *Adv. Phys.* **4**, 191 (1955).
M. Nisenhoff, *Rev. Phys. Appl.* **5**, 21-24 (1970).
H. Noltimier, in "Methods in Paleomagnetism" (D. W. Collinson, K. M. Creer, and S. K. Runcorn, eds.), pp. 400-402. Elsevier, Amsterdam, 1967.
M. Ohnaka, *J. Geomagn. Geoelectr.* **21**, 495-505 (1969).
W. O'Reilly, "Rock and Mineral Magnetism." Blackie, Chapman & Hall, London, 1984.
W. H. Owens and D. Bamford, *Philos. Trans. R. Soc. London, Ser. A* **283**, 27-42 (1976).
O. Ozdemir, Ph.D. Thesis, Univ. of Newcastle upon Tyne, 1979.
M. Ozima, M. Ozima, and T. Nagata, *J. Geomagn. Geoelectr.* **16**, 37 (1964).
A. W. Pacyna, *J. Phys. E.* **15**, 663-669 (1982).
B. J. Patton and J. L. Fitch, *J. Geophys. Res.* **67**, 1117 (1962).
H. Perroud, *I.A.G.A. Gen. Assem., 5th, Prague, Abstr.* **1**, 178 (1985).
N. Petersen, in "Methods in Paleomagnetism" (D. W. Collinson, K. M. Creer, and S. K. Runcorn, eds.), pp. 445-446. Elsevier, Amsterdam, 1967.
J. Petheridge, A. de Sa, and K. M. Creer, *J. Phys. E* **5**, 579 (1972).
S. J. Pike, T. L. Henyey, J. Revol, and M. Fuller, *J. Geomagn. Geoelectr.* **33**, 449-466 (1984).
F. Planinsek, Ph.D. Thesis, Univ. of Pittsburgh, Pittsburgh, Pennsylvania, 1968.
M. Polcarova and A. R. Lang, *Appl. Phys. Lett.* **1**, 13 (1962).
C. Radhkrishnamurty and E. Deutsch, *J. Geophys. Res.* **40**, 453-465 (1974).
J. Revol, R. Day, and M. Fuller, *Earth Planet. Sci. Lett.* **37**, 296-306 (1977).
P. Rigotti, *Earth Planet. Sci. Lett.* **39**, 133-141 (1978a).
P. Rigotti, *Earth Planet. Sci. Lett.* **39**, 417-426 (1978b).
G. L. Romani, S. J. Williamson, and L. Kaufman, *Rev. Sci. Instrum.* **53**, 1815, (1982).
J. T. Sallomy and J. C. Briden, *Earth Planet. Sci. Lett.* **24**, 369-376 (1975).

M. V. Scherb, *Rev. Sci. Instrum.* **19**, 411–419 (1948).
P. W. Schmidt, *I.A.G.A. Gen. Assem., 5th, Prague, Abstr.* **1**, 177 (1985).
P. W. Schmidt and H. C. Clarke, *Geophys. J. R. Astron. Soc.* (in press).
V. A. Schmidt, *J. Geomagn. Geoelectr.* **26**, 475 (1973).
V. A. Schmidt and B. Ellwood, *EOS Trans. Am. Geophys. Union* **64**, 682 (1983).
G. Scott and C. Frohlich, in "Magnetite Biomineralization and Magnetoreception in Organisms" (J. L. Kirschvink, D. S. Jones, and B. J. MacFadden, eds.), pp. 197–220. Plenum, New York, 1985.
J. Shaw, *Geophys. J. R. Astron. Soc.* **39**, 133–141 (1974).
A. H. Silver and J. E. Zimmerman, *Phys. Rev.* **157**, 317 (1967).
B. J. Skinner, R. C. Erd, and F. S. Grimaldi, *Ann. Mines* **49**, 543–559 (1964).
D. Smith, *Rev. Sci. Instrum.* **27**, 261 (1956).
P. P. K. Smith, *Conf. Ser.—Inst. Phys.* No. 52, 125–128 (1980).
H. Soffel, *Z. Geophys.* **29**, 21–34 (1963).
H. Soffel, *Z. Geophys.* **6**, 345–361 (1965).
H. Soffel and N. Petersen, *Earth Planet. Sci. Lett.* **11**, 312 (1971).
F. D. Stacey and S. K. Banerjee, "The Physical Principles of Rock Magnetism." Elsevier, Amsterdam, 1974.
A. Stephenson, *Nature (London)* **284**, 48 (1980).
A. Stephenson, D. W. Collinson, and S. K. Runcorn, *Proc. Lunar Sci. Conf.* **5**, 2859–2871 (1974).
R. W. Stephenson, *Geophys. J. R. Astron. Soc.* **47**, 363–373 (1976).
J. A. Stratton, "Electromagnetic Theory." McGraw-Hill, New York, 1941.
N. Sugiura, J. D. Redman, H. Hyodo, and D. W. Strangway, *Phys. Earth Planet. Int.* **41**, 101–107 (1985).
D.T.A. Symons and M. Stupavsky, *J. Geophys. Res.* **79**, 1718 (1974).
H. J. M. ter Brake, J. A. Ulfman, and J. Flokstra, *J. Phys. E* **17**, 1024–1030 (1984).
D. A. Testard and M. Locatelli, *Proc. ICEC9*, G1-8 (1982).
E. Thellier, *C. R. Hebd. Seances Acad. Sci.* **204**, 184–186 (1937).
E. Thellier, *Ann. Inst. Phys. Globe Univ. Paris Bur. Cent. Magn. Terr.* **16**, 157–302 (1938).
E. Thellier, *C. R. Hebd. Seances Acad. Sci.* **212**, 281–283 (1941).
E. Thellier, *Phys. Earth Planet. Inter.* **13**, 241–244 (1977).
E. Thellier and O. Thellier, *Ann. Geophys.* **15**, 285–376 (1959).
J. Unguris, G. Hembrei, R. Celotta, and D. Pierce, *J. Microsc. (Oxford)* **139**, RP1-2 (1985).
S. Uyeda, M. D. Fuller, J. C. Belshe, and R. W. Girdler, *J. Geophys. Res.* **68**, 279 (1963).
D. R. Van Alstine, *Geophys. J. R. Astron. Soc.* **61**, 101–113 (1980).
K. L. Verosub, *Geology* **5**, 319 (1977).
H Vollstadt, *Geophys. J. R. Astron. Soc.* **16**, 71 (1968).
L. von Hamos and P. A. Thiessen, *Z. Phys.* **71**, 42 (1931).
R. Von Mises, *Phys. Z.* **19**, 490–500 (1918).
J. Vrba, A. A. Fife, M. B. Burbank, H. Wenberg, and F. A. Brickett, *Can. J. Phys.* **60**, 1 (1982).
R. H. Wade, *Proc. Philos. Soc.* **79**, 1237–1244 (1962).
D. Walton, *Nature (London)* **295**, 512–515 (1982).
D. Walton, in "Geomagnetism of Baked Clays and Recent Sediments" (K. M. Creer, P. Tucholka, and C. E. Barton, eds.), pp. 88–97. Elsevier, Amsterdam, 1983.
G. S. Watson, *Biometrika* **47**, 87 (1960).
G. S. Watson, "Statistics on Spheres." Wiley (Interscience), New York, 1983.
G. S. Watson and E. Irving, *Mon. Not. R. Astron. Soc. Geophys. Suppl.* **7**, 289–300 (1957).
P. Weiss and G. Föex, *J. Phys.* **5**, 274–287 (1911).
H. J. Williams, R. M. Bozorth, and W. Shockley, *Phys. Rev.* **75**, 155–178 (1949).

R. L. Wilson and R. Lomax, *Geophys. J. R. Astron. Soc.* **30**, 295-304 (1972).
D. S. Wood, G. Oertel, J. Singh, and H. F. Bennett, *Philos. Trans. R. Soc. London, Ser. A* **283**, 27-42 (1976).
Y.-M. Wu, M. Fuller, and V. A. Schmidt, *Earth Planet. Sci. Lett.* **23**, 275 (1974).
T. Yamamoto, *JEOL News* **14**(2), 11-18 (1976).
T. Zelinka, *Stud. Geophys. Geod.* **23**, 299-300 (1979).
T. Zelinka, P. Hejda, and V. Kropacek, *TESLA Electron.* **2**, 35-43 (1984).
J. A. Zijderveld, *in* "Methods of Paleomagnetism" (D. W. Collinson, K. M. Creer, and S. K. Runcorn, eds.), pp. 254-286, 1967.
J. E. Zimmerman, P. Thiene, and J. T. Harding, *J. Appl. Phys.* **41**, 1572 (1970).

# INDEX

## A

α particle energy spectrum, 115–116
Acoustic emissions
  focal mechanism, 161–164
  location, 157
  moment tensor, 167
  power spectrum, 167
  transducer, 155, 164–165
  waveform, 161
Acousto-optical measurements, 23
Arrhenius relation, 92
Attenuation, *see also* Internal friction
  amplitude coefficient, 52
  logarithmic decrement, 50
  $Q$, 12–13, 33–34, 50
  Snoek peak, 36, 48
  specific damping capacity, 33

## B

$\beta$-emitting radiotracers, 110–111
BET gas absorption, 98
Boltzmann's aftereffect equation, 46
Brillouin function, 314
Brillouin spectroscopy
  diamond anvil high-pressure cell, 22
  Fabry-Perot interferometer, 15–19
  goniometer, 20
  photon–phonon interaction, 14
  spectral intensity, 21–22

## C

Causality principle, 47
Compressional wave velocities, 2
Confining materials, 85
Crack propagation
  chemical environment, 136–137
  double cantilever beam, 138–140
  double torsion, 134–138
  *In situ* measurements, 146–152
  load relaxation, 136
  notched bending beam, 142–146
  scanning electron microscope
    observations, 146–150
  stress intensity factor, 134–135, 138–142
  subcritical crack growth, 134
  velocity, 135–138
Cryogenics, 361–363
Curie point
  definition, 315, 330
  measurement, 418–423

## D

Dayhem bridge, 353–354
Demagnetization
  alternating field, 398–402
  analysis of curves, 403–410
  chemical, 402
  low temperature, 402
  stability index, 408
  thermal, 394–398
  Zijderveld diagrams, 407–408
Diamond anvils
  Brillouin scattering, 22
  sintered, 247
Diffusion *see also* Self-diffusion
  alkali in orthoclase, 100
  $^{45}Ca$ in melts, 103–104
  cerium in obsidian, 109
  $^{51}Cr$ in MgO, 108–109
  exchange
    isotopic, 100
    medium, 99–101
    technique, 93
  Fick's second law, 92–94, 107
  $H_2O$ in obsidian, 109
  $^{42}K$ in $K_2O$-$SrO$-$SiO_2$
  measurement
    surface preparation, 94–99
    tracer emplacement, 99–106
  $^{25}Mg$ in silicate garnets, 104
  Ni in olivine, 112
  profile
    autoradiography, 110–111
    electron microprobe, 111–112
    ion backscattering, 118–120
    nuclear reactions, 112–118

secondary ion mass spectrometry, 120–124
serial sectioning, 106–109
$^{30}$Si in forsterite, 104
$^{85}$Sr in diopside, 119–120
Sr in orthoclase and microcline thick vs thin sources, 101–106
tracer, 92
volume, 92
Zr in obsidian, 102

## E

Earthquake prediction, dilatancy diffusion model, 5
Elastic Moduli
anisotropy, 4
complex, 47
dispersion, 37
measurement
Brillouin spectroscopy, 13–23
thermal diffuse scattering of x rays, 23–28
ultrasonics, 2–13
pore fluids, effect on, 5
pressure derivatives, 10
elevated temperature and pressure, 4–5

## F

Fission tracks, 110
Flux transformer, 359
Fracture
modes, 132–133
precursory bulge, 151
toughness, 134, 143
Fresnel formula, 293
Frictional sliding
cycling tests, 171, 173
fault gouge, 173
measurement, 170–171
stick-slip, 171
Furnace, gas pressure apparatus, 73–74

## G

Gray body equation, 299
Gruneisen parameter, 222–224

## H

Heat flow, 272–273
High-temperature flow, see Plastic deformation
Holographic interferometry, 148–152

## I

Internal friction, see also Attenuation
bar resonance decay, 49–51
creep experiments, 46–49
crystal imperfections, 36
dislocation damping, 37
errors in measurement, 45–46
grain boundary relaxation, 36–37
hysteresis loop data, 39–41
pendulum free decay, 47–49
phase transformations, 37–38
pore fluids, effect on, 35
pressure dependence, 51
resonance bandwidth, 50–51
sliding at crack surfaces, 34
standard linear solid model, 35
subresonance measurement, 38–46
thermoelastic mechanisms, 35–36
torsion measurement, 41–45
ultrasonic measurement, 52
Ion implantation, 106

## J

Josephson junction, 350–352

## K

Kinematic recoil factor, 119

## L

Lengevin function, 313
Linear variable differential transducer, 82
Load cell, 74, 82
LVDT, see Linear variable differential transducer

## M

Magnetic
dipole, 309–310
domain
Bitter patterns, 457–461
Faraday effect, 463–464
Kerr effect, 464
multidomain minerals, 326
scanning electron microscopy, 462–463
transmission electron microscopy, 461–462
flux density, 305–307

hysteresis
  saturation, 325
  remanent magnetization, 325
induction, Faraday law, 310
order
  diamagnetic, 313
  ferromagnetic, 314
  paramagnetic, 313, 330
permeability, 306, 311
phases in rock, 315-325
potential
  scalar, 307
  vector, 305
shield, 359
Magnetization, 305-311
Magnetizing field, 305
Magnetometer
  astatic, 343-345
  computer interface, 377-379
  controlled magnetic field environment, 379-381
  signal enhancement, 374-377
  spinner, 345-347
  superconducting
    gradiometer, 366-373
    principles of operation, 348-361
    sample handling, 363-366
    SQUID, see Superconducting quantum interference device
    superconducting quantum interference device, 352-354
  vibration sample, 427-433
Magnetostatics
  compass, 308
  magnetic pole strength, 308
  potential energy, 309
Massive support principle, 247-248
Microcracks, 132
Mie-Gruneisen equation of state, 228, 264
Morin transition, hematite, 363
Multianvil press
  calibration, 259-265
  cubic anvil press, 240-243
  design and construction, 238-249
  internal heater, 249-252
  multiple anvil sliding system press, 244-246
  pressure cell-sample asembly, 249-259
  split sphere press, 243-244
  tetrahedral anvil press, 239-240

## N

Neutron scattering, 28

## O

Opacity, 21
Optical window, 150-152
Oxygen partial pressure, 60

## P

Paleomagnetism
  data analysis
    field tests of stability, 410-411
    Fisher statistics, 384-388
    projections, 382-384
    signal-to-noise discrimination, 393-411
    transformation of coordinates, 388-393
  paleointensity
    Koenigsberger-Thellier-Thellier method, 412-417
    Shaw analysis, 415-416
  remanent magnetization, measurement, 343-417
  sampling
    collection, 331-342
    drilling, 335-340
    orientation, 331-335, 338
    sediments, unconsolidated, 341-342
Partial melting, 37-38
Permeability
  Darcy's law, 173
  radioactive tracers, 175-181
  steady-state techniques, 173
  transient technique, 174
Phonon dispersion, 28
Plastic deformation
  gas-medium apparatus, 68-83
  load relaxation, 60-68
  solid-medium apparatus, 83-85
  unconfined creep, 58-62
Pressure seals
  Bridgeman-type cone seals, 70
  Porophyllite gaskets, 248-249
Pressure standards
  barium transitions, 262-264
  bismuth transitions, 261-263
  cesium transitions, 262
  fixed point, 261-262
  Hg, freezing point, 261
  manganin wire coil, 74, 215-217, 263-264
  ruby R-line fluorescence, 262, 265
  thallium transitions, 262
Pressure vessel 69-70

## R

Radiative thermal conductivity
  calculation, 297–299
  measurement, 293–297
  method of J. F. Schatz, 299–301
Remanent magnetization, natural
  mechanisms, 330
  Néel model, 328–330
  sediments, 328
  thermoremanent magnetization, 328–331
Rock magnetism
  ac loop plotter, 433
  magnetic characterization, 425–427
  magnetic phases, identification, 418–422
  magnetocrystalline anisotropy transitions, 423–425
  stress effects, 452–456
  susceptibility
    anisotropy, 442–452
    initial, 438–442
  thermomagnetic analysis, 422–423
Rutherford backscattering, 119–120

## S

Self-diffusion, *see also* Diffusion
  Co in $Co_{1-x}O$, 108
  $^{28}Mg$ in MgO, 107–108
  Na in minerals, 108
  $^{18}O$ in $Al_2O_3$, 96–99, 104, 117
  $^{18}O$ in anorthite, 123
  $^{18}O$ in olivine, 112, 117, 123
  $^{18}O$ in quartz, 117
  $^{18}O$ in $UO_2$, 117
  $^{18}O$ in $ZrO_2$, 100
  oxygen, 90
  silicon isotopes, 118
Shear wave velocities, 3
Shock waves
  dynamic yielding, 200–203
  generating systems, 186–190
  governing equations, 190–193
  Hugoniot
    elastic limit, 202
    Rankine–Hugoniot equations, 192–193
  isentrope, release, 209–222
  light gas guns, 190–191
  multiple shock fronts, 201
  particle velocity gauge, 213–214
  phase transitions, 200–203
  plane impact of a flyer plate, 194–197
  Rayleigh line, 193, 195, 202
  reflection
    free surface, 197–199
    impedance boundary, 199–200
  temperatures, shock and postshock, 228–233
  velocity measurement
    electrical, 207–208
    optical, 203–207
Stopping power, 119
Strain gauges, 146–147
Superconductivity, BCS theory, 349–352
Superparamagnetic condition, 327
Superposition principle, 47
Susceptometer, 423

## T

Temperature calibration, 77
Thermal conductivity
  high pressure, 289–292
  high temperature, 277, 280
  measurement
    Angstrom method, 282–285, 291–292
    Bridgman method, 289–291
    divided bar method, 271–277
    linear source methods, 285–288
    thermal stack method, 277–282, 289
  porous rock, 275–276
  soft sediment, 276
  solid rock, 277
  standard substances, 279–280
Thermal resistance, 274–275
Thermocouple, Pt/Pt-Rh, 81
Thermomagnetic balance, 421–422
Tungsten carbide anvils, cemented, 247

## U

Ultrasonic wave transmission
  buffer rod, 3, 5
  echo methods
    pulse superposition, 7
    pulse comparison, 7
  free vibrations, 12–13
  phase shift, transducer-bond, 8–11
  pulse transmission, 2–6
  transducers, 3

## V

Velocity interferometer, 219–222

## W

Water weakening, 84

# CONTENTS OF VOLUME 24, PART B

10. Seismic Instrumentation
    TA-LIANG TENG

11. Marine Acoustic Techniques
    F. N. SPIESS

12. Surface Measurements of the Earth's Gravity Field
    JAMES H. WHITCOMB

13. Satellite Measurement of the Earth's Gravity Field
    WILLIAM M. KAULA

14. Experimental Methods in Continental Heat Flow
    DAVID D. BLACKWELL AND ROBERT E. SPAFFORD

15. Measurement of the Oceanic Heat Flow
    R. P. VON HERZEN

16. Electrical Methods in Geophysical Prospecting
    STANLEY H. WARD

17. Measurement of *In Situ* Stress
    BEZALEL C. HAIMSON

18. Continuous Measurement of Crustal Deformation
    DUNCAN CARR AGNEW

19. Geophysical Well Logging
    JAY TITTMAN

    INDEX

RAYMOND H. FOGLER LIBRARY
DATE DUE